Jill Smith

Webster's Vest Pocket Dictionary

A Merriam-Webster®

G. & C. Merriam Company, *Publishers*
Springfield, Massachusetts, U.S.A.

Copyright © 1981 by G. & C. Merriam Co.

Philippines Copyright 1981 by G. & C. Merriam Co.

Library of Congress Cataloging in Publication Data

Main entry under title:

Webster's vest pocket dictionary

   1. English language—Dictionaries.
PE1628.W567   423   80–29018
ISBN 0-87779-190-2

Made in the United States of America

           1 2 3 4 5 6 IB 82 81

Preface

WEBSTER'S VEST POCKET DICTIONARY is a new and extremely concise reference to those words which form the very core of the English vocabulary. It shares many details of presentation with older and more comprehensive members of the Merriam-Webster family of dictionaries, such as Webster's New Collegiate Dictionary, but it also incorporates several features uniquely its own. A few points require special mention.

Main entries follow one another in alphabetical order. Centered periods within the entries show points at which a hyphen may be put at the end of a line. Homographs of closely related origin are run into a single main entry, second and succeeding homographs being represented by a swung dash: ~. Homographs of distinctly different origin (as **¹fare** and **²fare**) are given separate entries with preceding raised numerals.

Variant spellings that are quite common appear at the main entry following a comma (as **judg·ment, judge·ment**).

Inflected forms of nouns, verbs, adjectives, and adverbs are shown when they are irregular, when adding the suffix makes a change, or when there might be doubt about their spelling. They are given either in full (as **bet·ter . . .; best** at **good**) or cut back to a convenient point of division (as **-ried; -ry·ing** at **hur·ry**).

Common variants of inflected forms are also shown even if they are regular (as **seed or seeds** at **seed**). When the inflected forms of a verb involve no irregularity except the doubling of a final consonant, the double consonant is shown instead of full or cutback inflected forms (as **lug . . . vb -gg-**).

Several other kinds of entries are also found in this dictionary. A variant or inflected form whose alphabetical place is distant from the main entry is entered at its own place with a cross-reference in small capital letters to the main entry (as **hung** past of HANG). A run-in entry is a term related to a main entry that appears within a definition (as **jet engine** at **jet-propelled**). It is set off by parentheses. An undefined run-on entry appears after all definitions of a main entry set off by a dash (as **—like·ness** at **¹like**). Its meaning can be inferred from the meaning of the main entry where it appears and that of another main entry, often a suffix, elsewhere. A run-on phrase is a group of two or more words involving as a major element the main entry where it appears and having a special meaning of its own (as **by way of** at **way** or **come to** at **come**). It always has a definition. Lists of undefined words whose meanings can be inferred from the meaning of a prefix and that of a word entered in the dictionary will be found at the following places: *anti-, bi-, co-, counter-, extra-, hyper-, in-, inter-, mini-, multi-, non-, over-, post-, pre-, re-, self-, sub-, super-, un-,* and *vice-.*

Information about the *pronunciation* of every entry in the dictionary is either given explicitly or implied. A full list of the symbols used is shown on the next page. Pronunciations are placed within slant lines (as \'dab∂l\ at **dab·ble**).

Every main entry has an italic label (as *vb, n,* or *prefix*) indicating its grammatical function. All abbreviations used in these labels and all other abbreviations used in the dictionary are listed, along with a number of other common abbreviations, in a special section immediately following the dictionary proper. This section is followed in turn by a brief Handbook of Style discussing and illustrating the chief points of English punctuation, italicization, capitalization, and the formation of plurals.

Pronunciation Symbols

ə	banana, collide, abut; raised \ə\ in \əl\, \ən\ as in battle, cotton, in \lə, mə, rə\ as in French table, prisme, titre	ȯi	toy, sawing
		p	pepper, lip
		r	rarity
'ə, ˌə	humbug, abut	s	source, less
ər	operation, further	sh	shy, mission
a	map, patch	t	tie, attack
ā	day, fate	th	thin, ether
ä	bother, cot, father	th	then, either
à	father as pronounced by those who do not rhyme it with *bother*	ü	boot, few \'fyü\
		u̇	put, pure \'pyu̇r\
		ue̵	German füllen
au̇	now, out	ue̵	French rue, German fühlen
b	baby, rib	v	vivid, give
ch	chin, catch	w	we, away
d	did, adder	y	yard, cue \'kyü\; raised \y\ indicates that a preceding \l\, \n\, or \w\ is modified by the placing of the tongue tip against the lower front teeth, as in French digne \dēnʸ\
e	set, red	
ē	beat, nosebleed, easy	
f	fifty, cuff	
g	go, big	
h	hat, ahead	
hw	whale	
i	tip, banish	
ī	site, buy	z	zone, raise
j	job, edge	zh	vision, pleasure
k	kin, cook	\	slant line used in pairs to mark the beginning and end of a transcription
ḵ	German ich, Buch	
l	lily, cool	
m	murmur, dim	'	mark at the beginning of a syllable that has primary (strongest) stress: \'penmənˌship\
n	nine, own; raised \n\ indicates that a preceding vowel or diphthong is pronounced through both nose and mouth, as in French bon \bōn\	
		ˌ	mark at the beginning of a syllable that has secondary (next-strongest) stress: \'penmənˌship\
ŋ	sing, singer, finger, ink	
ō	bone, hollow	( )	indicate that what is symbolized between is present in some utterances but not in others: *factory* \'fakt(ə)rē\
ȯ	saw, cork	
œ	French bœuf, German Hölle	
œ̄	French feu, German Höhle	

A

¹a \'ā\ *n, pl* **a's** *or* **as** \'āz\ : 1st letter of the alphabet

²a \ə, (')ā\ *indefinite article* : one or some—used to indicate an unspecified or unidentified individual

aard·vark \'ärd,värk\ *n* : ant-eating African mammal

aback \ə'bak\ *adv* : by surprise

aba·cus \'abəkəs\ *n, pl* **aba·ci** \'abə,sī, -,kē\ *or* **aba·cus·es** : calculating instrument using rows of beads

abaft \ə'baft\ *adv* : toward or at the stern

ab·a·lone \,abə'lōnē\ *n* : large edible shellfish

¹aban·don \ə'bandən\ *vb* : give up without intent to reclaim —**abandon·ment** *n*

²abandon *n* : thorough yielding to impulses

aban·doned \ə'bandənd\ *adj* : morally unrestrained

abase \ə'bās\ *vb* **abased; abas·ing** : lower in dignity —**abase·ment** *n*

abash \ə'bash\ *vb* : embarass —**abashment** *n*

abate \ə'bāt\ *vb* **abat·ed; abat·ing** : decrease or lessen

abate·ment \ə'bātmənt\ *n* : tax reduction

ab·at·toir \'abə,twär\ *n* : slaughterhouse

ab·bess \'abəs\ *n* : head of a convent

ab·bey \'abē\ *n, pl* **-beys** : monastery or convent

ab·bot \'abət\ *n* : head of a monastery

ab·bre·vi·ate \ə'brēvē,āt\ *vb* **-at·ed; -at·ing** : shorten —**ab·bre·vi·a·tion** \ə,brēvē'āshən\ *n*

ab·di·cate \'abdi,kāt\ *vb* **-cat·ed; -cat·ing** : renounce —**ab·di·ca·tion** \,abdi'kāshən\ *n*

ab·do·men \'abdəmən, ab'dōmən\ *n* **1** : body area between chest and pelvis **2** : hindmost part of an insect —**ab·dom·i·nal** \ab'dämən³l\ *adj* —**ab·dom·i·nal·ly** *adv*

ab·duct \ab'dəkt\ *vb* : kidnap —**ab·duc·tion** \-'dəkshən\ *n* —**ab·duc·tor** \-tər\ *n*

abed \ə'bed\ *adv or adj* : in bed

ab·er·ra·tion \,abə'rāshən\ *n* : deviation or distortion —**ab·er·rant** \a'berənt\ *adj*

abet \ə'bet\ *vb* **-tt-** : incite or encourage —**abet·tor, abet·ter** \-ər\ *n*

abey·ance \ə'bāəns\ *n* : state of inactivity

ab·hor \əb'hòr, ab-\ *vb* **-rr-** : hate —**ab·hor·rence** \-əns\ *n* —**ab·hor·rent** \-ənt\ *adj*

abide \ə'bīd\ *vb* **abode** \-'bōd\ *or* **abid·ed; abid·ing** **1** : remain, last, or endure **2** : endure

ab·ject \'ab,jekt, ab-\ *adj* : low in spirit or hope —**ab·jec·tion** \ab'jekshən\ *n* —**ab·ject·ly** *adv* —**ab·ject·ness** *n*

ab·jure \ab'jùr\ *vb* **1** : renounce **2** : abstain from —**ab·ju·ra·tion** \,abjə'rāshən\ *n*

ablaze \ə'blāz\ *adj or adv* : on fire

able \'ābəl\ *adj* **abler** \-b(ə)lər\; **ablest** \-b(ə)ləst\ **1** : having sufficient power, skill, or resources **2** : skilled or efficient —**abil·i·ty** \ə'bilətē\ *n* —**ably** \'āblē\ *adv*

-able, -ible \əbəl\ *adj suffix* **1** : capable of, fit for, or worthy of **2** : tending, given, or liable to

ab·lu·tion \ə'blüshən, a'blü-\ *n* : washing of one's body

ab·ne·gate \'abni,gāt\ *vb* **-gat·ed; -gat·ing** **1** : renounce **2** : relinquish —**ab·ne·ga·tion** \,abni'gāshən\ *n*

ab·nor·mal \ab'nòrməl\ *adj* : deviating from the normal or average —**ab·nor·mal·i·ty** \,abnər'malətē, -(,)nòr-\ *n* —**ab·nor·mal·ly** *adv*

aboard \ə'bòrd\ *adv* : on, onto, or within a car, ship, or aircraft ~ *prep* : on or within

abode \ə'bōd\ *n* : residence

abol·ish \ə'bälish\ *vb* : do away with —**ab·o·li·tion** \,abə'lishən\ *n*

abom·i·na·ble \ə'bäm(ə)nəbəl\ *adj* : thoroughly unpleasant or revolting

abom·i·nate \ə'bämə,nāt\ *vb* **-nat·ed; -nat·ing** : hate —**abom·i·na·tion** \ə,bämə'nāshən\ *n*

ab·orig·i·nal \ˌabə'rij(ə)nəl\ adj 1 : original 2 : primitive

ab·orig·i·ne \-'rijəněn\ n : original inhabitant

abort \ə'bȯrt\ vb : terminate prematurely —**abor·tive** \-'bȯrtiv\ adj

abor·tion \ə'bȯrshən\ n : removal or induced expulsion of a fetus

abound \ə'baůnd\ vb : be plentiful

about \ə'baůt\ adv : around ~ prep 1 : on every side of 2 : on the verge of 3 : having as a subject

above \ə'bəv\ adv : in or to a higher place ~ prep 1 : in or to a higher place than 2 : more than

above·board adv or adj : without deception

abrade \ə'brād\ vb abrad·ed; abrad·ing : wear away by rubbing —**abra·sion** \-'brāzhən\ n

abra·sive \ə'brāsiv\ adj 1 : tending to abrade 2 : causing irritation ~ n : substance for grinding, smoothing, or polishing —**abra·sive·ly** adv —**abra·sive·ness** n

abreast \ə'brest\ adv or adj 1 : side by side 2 : up to a standard or level

abridge \ə'brij\ vb abridged; abridg·ing : shorten or condense —**abridg·ment, abridge·ment** n

abroad \ə'brȯd\ adv or adj 1 : over a wide area 2 : outside one's country

ab·ro·gate \'abrəgāt\ vb -gat·ed; -gat·ing : annul or revoke —**ab·ro·ga·tion** \ˌabrə'gāshən\ n

abrupt \ə'brəpt\ adj 1 : sudden 2 : so quick as to seem rude —**abrupt·ly** adv

ab·scess \'ab,ses\ n : collection of pus surrounded by inflamed tissue —**ab·scessed** \-,sest\ adj

ab·scond \ab'skänd\ vb : run away and hide

ab·sent \'absənt\ adj : not present ~ **ab·sent** \ab'sent\ vb : keep oneself away —**ab·sence** \'absəns\ n —**ab·sen·tee** \ˌabsən'tē\ n

ab·sent-mind·ed \ˌabsənt'mīndəd\ adj : unaware of one's surroundings or action —**ab·sent·mind·ed·ly** adv —**ab·sent·mind·ed·ness** n

ab·so·lute \'absəˌlüt, ˌabsə'-\ adj 1 : pure 2 : free from restriction 3 : definite —**ab·so·lute·ly** adv

ab·so·lu·tion \ˌabsə'lüshən\ n : remission of sins

ab·solve \əb'zälv, -'sälv\ vb -solved; -solv·ing : set free of the consequences of guilt

ab·sorb \əb'sȯrb, -'zȯrb\ vb 1 : suck up or take in as a sponge does 2 : engage (one's attention) —**ab·sor·ben·cy** \-'sȯrbənsē, -'zȯr-\ n —**ab·sor·bent**

\-bənt\ adj or n —**ab·sorb·ing** adj —**ab·sorb·ing·ly** adv

ab·sorp·tion \əb'sȯrpshən, -'zȯrp-\ n : process of absorbing —**ab·sorp·tive** \-tiv\ adj

ab·stain \əb'stān\ vb : refrain from doing something —**ab·stain·er** n —**ab·sten·tion** \-'stenchən\ n —**ab·sti·nence** \'abstənəns\ n

ab·ste·mi·ous \ab'stēmēəs\ adj : sparing in use of food or drink —**ab·ste·mi·ous·ly** adv

ab·stract \ab'strakt, 'ab,-\ adj 1 : expressing a quality apart from an object 2 : not representing something specific ~ \'ab,-\ n : summary ~ \ab'-, 'ab,-\ vb 1 : remove or separate 2 : make an abstract of —**ab·stract·ly** adv —**ab·stract·ness** \-'strak(t)nəs, -,strak(t)-\ n

ab·strac·tion \ab'strakshən\ n : act of abstracting 2 : abstract idea or work of art

ab·struse \əb'strüs, ab-\ adj : hard to understand —**ab·struse·ly** adv —**ab·struse·ness** n

ab·surd \əb'sərd, -'zərd\ adj : ridiculous or unreasonable —**ab·sur·di·ty** \-ətē\ n —**ab·surd·ly** adv

abun·dant \ə'bəndənt\ adj : more than enough —**abun·dance** \-dəns\ n —**abun·dant·ly** adv

abuse \ə'byüz\ vb abused; abus·ing 1 : attack with words 2 : misuse 3 : mistreat ~ \-'byüs\ n 1 : corrupt practice 2 : improper use 3 : mistreatment 4 : coarse and insulting speech —**abu·sive** \-'byüsiv\ adj —**abu·sive·ly** adv —**abu·sive·ness** n

abut \ə'bət\ vb -tt- : touch along a border

abut·ment \ə'bətmənt\ n : structure that supports weight or withstands lateral pressure

abys·mal \ə'bizməl\ adj : immeasurably deep —**abys·mal·ly** adv

abyss \ə'bis\ n : bottomless pit

-ac \ˌak\ n suffix : one affected with

aca·cia \ə'kāshə\ n : leguminous tree or shrub

ac·a·dem·ic \ˌakə'demik\ adj 1 : relating to schools or colleges 2 : theoretical —**ac·a·dem·i·cal·ly** \-ik(ə)lē\ adv

acad·e·my \ə'kadəmē\ n, pl -mies 1 : private high school 2 : society of scholars or artists

acan·thus \ə'kanthəs\ n 1 : prickly Mediterranean herb 2 : ornament representing acanthus leaves

ac·cede \ak'sēd\ vb -ced·ed; -ced·ing 1 : become a party to an agreement 2

: express approval **3** : enter upon an office

ac·cel·er·ate \ik'selə₁rāt, ak-\ vb **-at·ed; -at·ing 1** : bring about earlier **2** : speed up —**ac·cel·er·a·tion** \₁selə'rāshən\ n

ac·cel·er·a·tor \ik'selə₁rātər, ak-\ n : foot-operated pedal for controlling the speed of a motor vehicle

ac·cent \'ak₁sent\ n **1** : distinctive manner of pronunciation **2** : prominence given to one syllable of a word **3** : mark (as ˊ, ˋ, ˆ) over a vowel in writing or printing to indicate pronunciation ~ \'ak-, ak'-\ vb : emphasize —**ac·cen·tu·al** \ak'sench(ə)wəl\ adj

ac·cen·tu·ate \ak'senchə₁wāt\ vb **-at·ed; -at·ing** : stress or show off by a contrast —**ac·cen·tu·a·tion** \₁senchə'wāshən\ n

ac·cept \ik'sept, ak-\ vb **1** : receive willingly **2** : agree to —**ac·cept·abil·i·ty** \ik₁septə'bilətē, ak-\ n —**ac·cept·able** \'septəbəl\ adj —**ac·cep·tance** \-'septəns\ n

ac·cess \'ak₁ses\ n : capability or way of approaching —**ac·ces·si·bil·i·ty** \ik₁sesə'bilətē, ak-\ n —**ac·ces·si·ble** \-'sesəbəl\ adj

ac·ces·sion \ik'seshən, ak-\ n **1** : something added **2** : act of taking office

ac·ces·so·ry \ik'ses(ə)rē, ak-\ n, pl **-ries 1** : nonessential addition **2** : one guilty of aiding a criminal —**accessory** adj

ac·ci·dent \'aksədənt\ n **1** : event occurring by chance or unintentionally **2** : chance —**ac·ci·den·tal** \₁aksə'dent[ə]l\ adj —**ac·ci·den·tal·ly** \-'dentlē, -ᵊlē\ adv

ac·claim \ə'klām\ vb or n : praise

ac·cla·ma·tion \₁aklə'māshən\ n **1** : eager applause **2** : unanimous vote

ac·cli·mate \'aklə₁māt, ə'klīmət\ vb **-mat·ed; -mat·ing** : accustom to a new climate or situation —**ac·cli·ma·tion** \₁aklə'māshən, ₁ak₁lī-\ n

ac·cli·ma·tize \ə'klīmə₁tīz\ vb **-tized; -tiz·ing** : acclimate —**ac·cli·ma·ti·za·tion** \-₁klīmətə'zāshən\ n

ac·co·lade \'akə₁lād\ n : award

ac·com·mo·date \ə'kämə₁dāt\ vb **-dat·ed; -dat·ing 1** : adapt **2** : provide with something needed **3** : hold without crowding

ac·com·mo·da·tion \ə₁kämə'dāshən\ n **1** : quarters —usu. pl. **2** : act of accommodating

ac·com·pa·ny \ə'kəmp(ə)nē\ vb **-nied; -ny·ing 1** : go or occur with **2** : play supporting music —**ac·com·pa·ni**-

ment \-mənt\ n —**ac·com·pa·nist** \-(ə)nəst\ n

ac·com·plice \ə'kämpləs, -'kəm-\ n : associate in crime

ac·com·plish \ə'kämplish, -'kəm-\ vb : do, fulfill, or bring about —**ac·com·plished** adj —**ac·com·plish·er** n —**ac·com·plish·ment** n

ac·cord \ə'kȯrd\ vb **1** : grant **2** : agree ~ n : agreement —**ac·cor·dance** \-'kȯrd°ns\ n —**ac·cor·dant** \-°nt\ adj

ac·cord·ing·ly \ə'kȯrdiŋlē\ adv : consequently

according to prep **1** : in conformity with **2** : as stated by

ac·cor·di·on \ə'kȯrdēən\ n : keyboard instrument with a bellows and reeds ~ adj : folding like an accordion bellows

ac·cost \ə'kȯst\ vb : approach and speak to

ac·count \ə'kaunt\ n **1** : statement of business transactions **2** : credit arrangement with a vendor **3** : report **4** : worth **5** : sum deposited in a bank ~ vb : give an explanation

ac·count·able \ə'kauntəbəl\ adj : responsible —**ac·count·abil·i·ty** \-₁kauntə'bilətē\ n

ac·coun·tant \ə'kaunt°nt\ n : one skilled in accounting —**ac·coun·tan·cy** \-°nsē\ n

ac·count·ing \ə'kautiŋ\ n : financial record keeping

ac·cou·tre, ac·cou·ter \ə'kütər\ vb **-tred** or **-tered; -tring** or **-ter·ing** \-'kütəriŋ, -'kütriŋ\ : equip

ac·cred·it \ə'kredət\ vb **1** : approve officially **2** : attribute

ac·crue \ə'krü\ vb **-crued; -cru·ing** : be added by periodic growth —**ac·cru·al** \-əl\ n

ac·cu·mu·late \ə'kyümyə₁lāt\ vb **-lat·ed; -lat·ing** : collect or pile up —**ac·cu·mu·la·tion** \-₁kyümyə'lāshən\ n —**ac·cu·mu·la·tor** \-'kyümyə₁lātər\ n

ac·cu·rate \'akyərət\ adj : free from error —**ac·cu·ra·cy** \-rəsē\ n —**ac·cu·rate·ly** adv —**ac·cu·rate·ness** n

ac·cursed \ə'kərst, -'kərsəd\, **ac·curst** \ə'kərst\ adj **1** : being under a curse **2** : damnable

ac·cuse \ə'kyüz\ vb **-cused; -cus·ing** : charge with an offense —**ac·cu·sa·tion** \₁akyə'zāshən\ n —**ac·cus·er** n

ac·cused \ə'kyüzd\ n, pl **-cused** : defendant in a criminal cause

ac·cus·tom \ə'kəstəm\ vb : cause to treat something as usual or accept-

4

able esp. through repeated experience

ace \'ās\ *n* : one that excels

ac·e·tate \'asə,tāt\ : fast-drying fabric or plastic derived from acetic acid

ace·tic acid \ə,sētik-\ *n* : acid like that found in vinegar

acet·y·lene \ə'set²lən, -²l,ēn\ *n* : colorless gas used as a fuel in welding

ache \'āk\ *vb* ached; ach·ing 1 : suffer a dull persistent pain 2 : yearn —**ache** *n*

achieve \ə'chēv\ *vb* achieved; achiev·ing : gain by work or effort —**achieve·ment** *n* —**achiev·er** *n*

ac·id \'asəd\ *adj* 1 : sour or biting to the taste 2 : of or relating to an acid ~ *n* 1 : sour substance 2 : usu. water-soluble chemical compound —**acid·ic** \ə'sidik\ *adj* —**acid·i·fy** \-'sidə,fī\ *vb* —**acid·i·ty** \-ətē\ *n*

ac·knowl·edge \ik'nälij, ak-\ *vb* -edged; -edg·ing 1 : admit as true 2 : admit the authority of 3 : express thanks for —**ac·knowl·edg·ment** *n*

ac·me \'akmē\ *n* : highest point

ac·ne \'aknē\ *n* : skin disorder marked esp. by pimples

ac·o·lyte \'akə,līt\ *n* : one who assists the clergyman in a service

acorn \ā,kȯrn, -kərn\ *n* : nut of the oak

acous·tic \ə'küstik\ *adj* : relating to hearing or sound —**acous·ti·cal** \-stikəl\ *adj* —**acous·ti·cal·ly** \-k(ə)lē\ *adv*

acous·tics \ə'küstiks\ *n sing or pl* 1 : science of sound 2 : qualities in a room that affect how sound is heard

ac·quaint \ə'kwānt\ *vb* 1 : inform 2 : make familiar

ac·quain·tance \ə'kwānt²ns\ *n* 1 : personal knowledge 2 : person with whom one is acquainted —**ac·quain·tance·ship** *n*

ac·qui·esce \,akwē'es\ *vb* -esced; -esc·ing : consent —**ac·qui·es·cence** \-'es²ns\ *n* —**ac·qui·es·cent** \-²nt\ *adj* —**ac·qui·es·cent·ly** *adv*

ac·quire \ə'kwī(ə)r\ *vb* -quired; -quir·ing : gain

ac·qui·si·tion \,akwə'zishən\ *n* : a gaining or something gained —**ac·qui·si·tive** \ə'kwizətiv\ *adj*

ac·quit \ə'kwit\ *vb* -tt- 1 : pronounce not guilty 2 : conduct (oneself) usu. well —**ac·quit·tal** \-²l\ *n*

acre \'ākər\ *n* 1 *pl* : lands 2 : 4840 square yards

acre·age \'āk(ə)rij\ *n* : area in acres

ac·rid \'akrəd\ *adj* : sharp and biting —**acrid·i·ty** \ə'kridətē, ə-\ *n* —**ac·rid·ness** *n*

ac·ri·mo·ny \'akrə,mōnē\ *n, pl* -nies : harshness of language or feeling —**ac·ri·mo·ni·ous** \,akrə'mōnēəs\ *adj*

ac·ro·bat \'akrə,bat\ *n* : performer of tumbling feats —**ac·ro·bat·ic** \,akrə'batik\ *adj*

across \ə'krȯs\ *adv* : to or on the opposite side ~ *prep* 1 : to or on the opposite side of 2 : on so as to cross

acryl·ic \ə'krilik\ *n* : plastic used for molded parts or in paints

act \'akt\ *n* 1 : thing done 2 : law 3 : main division of a play ~ *vb* 1 : perform in a play 2 : conduct oneself 3 : operate 4 : produce an effect

ac·tion \'akshən\ *n* 1 : legal proceeding 2 : manner or method of performing 3 : activity 4 : thing done over a period of time or in stages 5 : combat 6 : events of a literary plot 7 : operating mechanism

ac·ti·vate \'aktə,vāt\ *vb* -vat·ed; -vat·ing : make active or reactive —**ac·ti·va·tion** \,aktə'vāshən\ *n*

ac·tive \'aktiv\ *adj* 1 : causing action or change 2 : lively, vigorous, or energetic 3 : now in operation —**active** *n* —**ac·tive·ly** *adv*

ac·tiv·i·ty \ak'tivitē\ *n, pl* -ties 1 : quality or state of being active 2 : what one is actively doing

ac·tor \'aktər\ *n* : one that acts —**actress** \-trəs\ *n*

ac·tu·al \'akch(əw)əl\ *adj* : really existing —**ac·tu·al·i·ty** \,akchə'walətē\ *n* —**ac·tu·al·iza·tion** \,akch(əw)ələ'zāshən\ *n* —**ac·tu·al·ize** \'akch(əw)ə,līz\ *vb* —**ac·tu·al·ly** *adv*

ac·tu·ary \'akchə,werē\ *n, pl* -ar·ies : one who calculates insurance risks and premiums —**ac·tu·ar·i·al** \,akchə'werēəl\ *adj*

ac·tu·ate \'akchə,wāt\ *vb* -at·ed; -at·ing : put into action —**ac·tu·a·tor** \-,wātər\ *n*

acu·men \ə'kyümən\ *n* : mental keenness

acu·punc·ture \'akyü,pəŋkchər\ *n* : treatment by puncturing the body with needles —**acu·punc·tur·ist** \,akyü'pəŋkchərəst\ *n*

acute \ə'kyüt\ *adj* acut·er; acut·est 1 : sharp 2 : containing less than 90 degrees 3 : mentally alert 4 : severe —**acute·ly** *adv* —**acute·ness** *n*

ad \'ad\ *n* : advertisement

ad·age \'adij\ *n* : old familiar saying

ad·a·mant \'adəmant, -,mant\ *adj* : insistent —**ad·a·mant·ly** *adv*

adapt \ə'dapt\ *vb* : adjust to be suitable for a new use or condition

—adapt·abil·i·ty \ə‚daptə'bilətē\ *n*
—adapt·able \'adaptəbəl\ *adj*

ad·ap·ta·tion \‚ad‚ap'tāshən, -əp-\ *n* **—adapt·er** *n*
—adap·tive \ə'daptiv\ *adj*

add \'ad\ *vb* **1** : join to something else so as to increase in amount **2** : find a sum **—ad·di·tion** \ə'dishən\ *n*

ad·der \'adər\ *n* **1** : poisonous European snake **2** : No. American snake

ad·dict \'ad‚(,)ikt\ *n* : one who is psychologically or physiologically dependent (as on a drug) ~ \ə'dikt\ *vb* : cause to become an addict **—ad·dic·tion** \ə'dikshən\ *n* **—ad·dic·tive** \-'diktiv\ *adj*

ad·di·tion·al \ə'dish(ə)nəl\ *adj* : existing as a result of adding **—ad·di·tion·al·ly** *adv*

ad·di·tive \'adətiv\ *adj* : substance added to another

ad·dle \'ad⁰l\ *vb* **-dled; -dling** : confuse

ad·dress \ə'dres\ *vb* **1** : direct one's remarks to **2** : mark an address on ~ \ə'dres, 'ad‚res\ *n* **1** : formal speech **2** : place where a person may be reached or mail may be delivered

ad·duce \ə'd(y)üs\ *vb* **-duced; -duc·ing** : offer as proof

ad·e·noid \'ad⁰n‚òid, -ə‚nòid\ *n* : enlarged tissue near the opening of the nose into the throat —usu. pl. **—ad·e·noi·dal** \-əl\ *adj*

adept \ə'dept\ *adj* : highly skilled **—adept·ly** *adv* **—adept·ness** *n*

ad·e·quate \'adikwət\ *adj* : good or plentiful enough **—ad·e·qua·cy** \-kwəsē\ *n* **—ad·e·quate·ly** *adv*

ad·here \ad'hiər, əd-\ *vb* **-hered; -her·ing** **1** : remain loyal **2** : stick fast **—ad·her·ence** \-'hirəns\ *n* **—ad·her·ent** \-ənt\ *adj or n*

ad·he·sion \ad'hēzhən, əd-\ *n* : act or state of adhering

ad·he·sive \-'hēsiv, -ziv\ *adj* : tending to adhere ~ *n* : adhesive substance

adieu \ə'd(y)ü\ *n, pl* **adieus** *or* **adieux** \ə'd(y)üz\ : farewell

ad·ja·cent \ə'jās⁰nt\ *adj* : situated near or next

ad·jec·tive \'ajiktiv\ *n* : word that serves as a modifier of a noun **—ad·jec·ti·val** \‚ajik'tīvəl\ *adj* **—ad·jec·ti·val·ly** *adv*

ad·join \ə'jóin\ *vb* : be next to

ad·journ \ə'jərn\ *vb* : end a meeting **—ad·journ·ment** *n*

ad·judge \ə'jəj\ *vb* **-judged; -judg·ing** **1** : think or pronounce to be **2** : award by judicial decision

ad·ju·di·cate \ə'jüdi‚kāt\ *vb* **-cat·ed; -cat·ing** : settle judicially **—ad·ju·di·ca·tion** \-‚jüdi'kāshən\ *n*

ad·junct \'aj‚əŋkt\ *n* : something joined or added but not essential

ad·just \ə'jəst\ *vb* : fix, adapt, or set right **—ad·just·able** *adj* **—ad·just·er, ad·jus·tor** \ə'jəstər\ *n* **—ad·just·ment** \ə'jəs(t)mənt\ *n*

ad·ju·tant \'ajətənt\ *n* : one who helps esp. a commanding officer

ad-lib \'ad'lib\ *vb* **-bb-** : speak without preparation **—ad-lib** *n or adj*

ad·min·is·ter \ad'minəstər\ *vb* **1** : manage **2** : give out esp. in doses **—ad·min·is·tra·ble** \-strəbəl\ *adj* **—ad·min·is·trant** \-strənt\ *n*

ad·min·is·tra·tion \ad‚minə'strāshən, (,)ad-\ *n* **1** : process of managing **2** : persons responsible for managing **—ad·min·is·tra·tive** \ad'minə‚strātiv\ *adj* **—ad·min·is·tra·tive·ly** *adv*

ad·min·is·tra·tor \ad'minə‚strātər\ *n* : one that manages

ad·mi·ra·ble \'adm(ə)rəbəl\ *adj* : worthy of admiration **—ad·mi·ra·bly** \-blē\ *adv*

ad·mi·ral \'adm(ə)rəl\ *n* : commissioned officer in the navy ranking next below a fleet admiral

ad·mire \ad'mīr\ *vb* **-mired; -mir·ing** : have high regard for **—ad·mi·ra·tion** \‚admə'rāshən\ *n* **—ad·mir·er** *n* **—ad·mir·ing·ly** *adv*

ad·mis·si·ble \ad'misəbəl\ *adj* : that can be permitted **—ad·mis·si·bil·i·ty** \-‚misə'bilətē\ *n* **—ad·mis·si·bly** \-'misəblē\ *adv*

ad·mis·sion \ad'mishən\ *n* **1** : acknowledgment of a fact **2** : act of admitting **3** : admittance or a fee paid for this

ad·mit \ad'mit\ *vb* **-tt-** **1** : allow to enter **2** : permit **3** : recognize as genuine **—ad·mit·ted·ly** *adv*

ad·mit·tance \ad'mit⁰ns\ *n* : permission to enter

ad·mix·ture \ad'mikschər\ *n* **1** : mixture **2** : thing added in mixing

ad·mon·ish \ad'mänish\ *vb* : rebuke **—ad·mo·ni·tion** \‚admə'nishən\ *n* **—ad·mon·i·to·ry** \ad'mänə‚tōrē\ *adj*

ado \ə'dü\ *n* **1** : fuss **2** : trouble

ado·be \ə'dōbē\ *n* : sun-dried building brick **—adobe** *adj*

ad·o·les·cence \‚ad⁰l'es⁰ns\ *n* : period of growth between childhood and maturity **—ad·o·les·cent** \-⁰nt\ *adj or n*

adopt \ə'däpt\ *vb* **1** : take (a child of other parents) as one's own child **2** : take up and practice as one's own **—adop·tion** \-'däpshən\ *n*

adore \ə'dōr\ *vb* **adored; ador·ing** **1** : worship **2** : be extremely fond of

—**ador·a·ble** *adj* —**ador·a·bly** *adv*
—**ad·o·ra·tion** \,adə'rāshən\ *n*

adorn \ə'dórn\ *vb* : decorate with ornaments —**adorn·ment** *n*

adrift \ə'drift\ *adv or adj* 1 : afloat without motive power or moorings 2 : without guidance or purpose

adroit \ə'dróit\ *adj* : dexterous or shrewd —**adroit·ly** *adv* —**adroit·ness** *n*

adult \ə'dəlt, 'ad,əlt\ *adj* : fully developed and mature ~ *n* : grown-up person —**adult·hood** *n*

adul·ter·ate \ə'dəltə,rāt\ *vb* -**at·ed**; -**at·ing** : make impure by mixture —**adul·ter·a·tion** \-,dəltə'rāshən\ *n*

adul·tery \ə'dəlt(ə)rē\ *n, pl* -**ter·ies** : sexual unfaithfulness of a married person —**adul·ter·er** \-tərər\ *n* —**adul·ter·ess** \-t(ə)rəs\ *n* —**adul·ter·ous** \-t(ə)rəs\ *adj*

ad·vance \əd'vans\ *vb* -**vanced**; -**vanc·ing** 1 : bring or move forward 2 : promote 3 : lend ~ *n* 1 : forward movement 2 : improvement 3 : offer ~ *adj* : being ahead of time —**ad·vance·ment** *n*

ad·van·tage \əd'vantij\ *n* 1 : superiority of position 2 : benefit or gain —**ad·van·ta·geous** \,ad,van'tājəs, -vən-\ *adj* —**ad·van·ta·geous·ly** *adv*

Ad·vent \'ad,vent\ *n* : period before Christmas

ad·ven·ti·tious \,advən'tishəs\ *adj* : accidental —**ad·ven·ti·tious·ly** *adv* —**ad·ven·ti·tious·ness** *n*

ad·ven·ture \əd'venchər\ *n* 1 : risky undertaking 2 : exciting experience —**ad·ven·tur·er** \-'vench(ə)rər\ *n* —**ad·ven·ture·some** \-'venchərsəm\ *adj* —**ad·ven·tur·ous** \-'vench(ə)rəs\ *adj*

ad·verb \'ad,vərb\ *n* : word that modifies a verb, an adjective, or another adverb —**ad·ver·bi·al** \ad'vərbēəl\ *adj* —**ad·ver·bi·al·ly** *adv*

ad·ver·sary \'advər(,)serē\ *n, pl* -**sar·ies** : enemy or rival —**adversary** *adj*

ad·verse \ad'vərs, 'ad-,\ *adj* : opposing or unfavorable —**ad·verse·ly** *adv*

ad·ver·si·ty \əd'vərsətē\ *n, pl* -**ties** : hard times

ad·vert \əd'vərt\ *vb* : refer

ad·ver·tise \'advər,tīz\ *vb* -**tised**; -**tis·ing** : call public attention to —**ad·ver·tise·ment** \,advər'tīzmənt, əd'vərtəzmənt\ *n* —**ad·ver·tis·er** *n*

ad·ver·tis·ing \'advər,tīziŋ\ *n* : business of preparing advertisements

ad·vice \əd'vīs\ *n* : recommendation with regard to a course of action

ad·vis·able \əd'vīzəbəl\ *adj* : wise or

prudent —**ad·vis·abil·i·ty** \-,vīz-ə'bilətē\ *n*

ad·vise \əd'vīz\ *vb* -**vised**; -**vis·ing** : give advice to —**ad·vis·er** *or* **ad·vi·sor** \-'vīzər\ *n*

ad·vise·ment \əd'vīzmənt\ *n* : careful consideration

ad·vi·so·ry \əd'vīz(ə)rē\ *adj* : having power to advise

ad·vo·cate \'advəkət, -,kāt\ *n* : one who argues or pleads for a cause or proposal ~ \-,kāt\ *vb* -**cat·ed**; -**cat·ing** : recommend —**ad·vo·ca·cy** \-və-kə-sē\ *n*

adz, adze \'adz\ *n* : tool for shaping wood

ae·gis \'ējəs\ *n* : protection or sponsorship

ae·on \'ēən, 'ē,än\ *n* : indefinitely long time

aer·ate \'a(ə)r,āt\ *vb* -**at·ed**; -**at·ing** : supply or impregnate with air —**aer·a·tion** \,a(ə)r'āshən\ *n* —**aer·a·tor** \'a(ə)r,ātər\ *n*

ae·ri·al \'arēəl, ā'irēəl\ *adj* : inhabiting, occurring in, or done in the air ~ *n* : antenna

ae·rie \'a(ə)rē, 'i(ə)rē\ *n* : eagle's nest

aer·o·bic \,a(ə)r'rōbik\ *adj* : using or needing oxygen

aero·dy·nam·ics \,arōdī'namiks\ *n* : science of the motion of gases —**aero·dy·nam·ic** \-ik\, **aero·dy·nam·i·cal** \-ikəl\ *adj* —**aero·dy·nam·i·cal·ly** \-ik(ə)lē\ *adv*

aero·nau·tics \,arə'nótiks\ *n* : science dealing with aircraft —**aero·nau·ti·cal** \-ikəl\, **aero·nau·tic** \-ik\ *adj* —**aero·nau·ti·cal·ly** \-ik(ə)lē\ *adv*

aero·sol \'arə,säl, -,sól\ *n* 1 : liquid or solid particles suspended in a gas 2 : substance sprayed as an aerosol

aero·space \'arō,spās\ *n* : earth's atmosphere and the space beyond —**aerospace** *adj*

aes·thet·ic \es'thetik\ *adj* : relating to beauty —**aes·thet·i·cal·ly** \-ik(ə)lē\ *adv*

aes·thet·ics \-'thetiks\ *n* : branch of philosophy dealing with beauty

afar \ə'fär\ *adv* : from, at, or to a great distance —**afar** *n*

af·fa·ble \'afəbəl\ *adj* : easy to talk to —**af·fa·bil·i·ty** \,afə'bilətē\ *n* —**af·fa·bly** \'afəblē\ *adv*

af·fair \ə'faər\ *n* : something that relates to or involves one

¹**af·fect** \ə'fekt, a-\ *vb* : assume for effect —**af·fec·ta·tion** \,af,ek'tāshən\ *n*

²**affect** *vb* : produce an effect on

af·fect·ed \ə'fektəd, a-\ *adj* 1 : pretending to some trait **2** : artificially assumed to impress —**af·fect·ed·ly** adv

af·fect·ing \ə'fektiŋ, a-\ adj : arousing pity or sorrow —**af·fect·ing·ly** adv

af·fec·tion \ə'fekshən\ n : kind or loving feeling —**af·fec·tion·ate** \-sh(ə)nət\ adj —**af·fec·tion·ate·ly** adv

af·fi·da·vit \ˌafə'dāvət\ n : sworn statement

af·fil·i·ate \ə'filē,āt\ vb -at·ed; -at·ing : become a member or branch —**af·fil·i·ate** \-ēət\ n —**af·fil·i·a·tion** \ˌ-filē'āshən\ n

af·fin·i·ty \ə'finətē\ n, pl -ties : close attraction or relationship

af·firm \ə'fərm\ vb : assert positively —**af·fir·ma·tion** \ˌafər'māshən\ n

af·fir·ma·tive \ə'fərmətiv\ adj : asserting the truth or existence of something ~ n : statement of affirmation or agreement

af·fix \ə'fiks\ vb : attach

af·flict \ə'flikt\ vb : cause pain and distress to —**af·flic·tion** \-'flikshən\ n

af·flu·ence \'a,flüən(t)s; a'flü-, ə-\ n : wealth —**af·flu·ent** \-ənt\ adj

af·ford \ə'fōrd\ vb **1** : manage to bear the cost of **2** : provide

af·fray \ə'frā\ n : fight

af·front \ə'frənt\ vb or n : insult

af·ghan \'af,gan, -gən\ n : crocheted or knitted blanket

afire \ə'fī(ə)r\ adj or adv : being on fire

aflame \ə'flām\ adj or adv : flaming

afloat \ə'flōt\ adj or adv : floating

afoot \ə'füt\ adv or adj **1** : on foot **2** : in progress

afore·said \ə'fōr,sed\ adj : said or named before

afraid \ə'frād, South also ə'fre(ə)d\ adj : filled with fear

afresh \ə'fresh\ adv : anew

aft \'aft\ adv : to or toward the stern or tail

af·ter \'aftər\ adv **1** : at a later time **2** : at the back ~ prep **1** : behind in place or time **2** : intent on gaining ~ conj : following the time when ~ adj **1** : later **2** : located toward the back

af·ter·life \'aftər,līf\ n : existence after death

af·ter·math \-,math\ n : results

af·ter·noon \ˌaftər'nün\ n : time between noon and evening

af·ter·thought n : later thought

af·ter·ward \'aftə(r)wərd\, **af·ter·wards** \-wərdz\ adv : at a later time

again \ə'gen, -'gin\ adv **1** : once more **2** : on the other hand **3** : in addition

against \ə'genst\ prep **1** : directly op-

posite to **2** : in opposition to **3** : so as to touch or strike

agape \ə'gāp, -'gap\ adj or adv : having the mouth open in astonishment

ag·ate \'agət\ n : quartz with bands or masses of various colors

age \'āj\ n **1** : length of time of life or existence **2** : particular time in life (as majority or the latter part) **3** : quality of being old **4** : long time **5** : period in history ~ vb **1** : become old or mature

-age n suffix **1** : aggregate **2** : action or process of **3** : result of **4** : rate of **5** : place of **6** : state or rank **7** : fee

aged adj **1** \'ājəd\ : old **2** \'ājd\ : allowed to mature

age·less \'ājləs\ adj : eternal

agen·cy \'ājənsē\ n, pl -cies **1** : one through which something is accomplished **2** : office or function of an agent **3** : government administrative division

agen·da \ə'jendə\ n : list of things to be done

agent \'ājənt\ n **1** : means **2** : person acting or doing business for another

ag·gran·dize \ə'gran,dīz, 'agrən-\ vb -dized; -diz·ing : make great or greater —**ag·gran·dize·ment** \ə'grandəzmənt, -,dīz-; ,agrən'dīz-\ n

ag·gra·vate \'agrə,vāt\ vb -vat·ed; -vat·ing **1** : make more severe **2** : irritate —**ag·gra·va·tion** \ˌagrə'vāshən\ n

ag·gre·gate \'agrigət\ adj : formed into a mass ~ \-i,gāt\ vb -gat·ed; -gat·ing : collect into a mass ~ \-gət\ n **1** : mass **2** : whole amount

ag·gres·sion \ə'greshən\ n **1** : unprovoked attack **2** : hostile behavior —**ag·gres·sor** \-'gresər\ n

ag·gres·sive \ə'gresiv\ adj **1** : easily provoked to fight **2** : hard working and enterprising —**ag·gres·sive·ly** adv —**ag·gres·sive·ness** n

ag·grieve \ə'grēv\ vb -grieved; -griev·ing **1** : cause grief to **2** : inflict injury on

aghast \ə'gast\ adj : struck with amazement or horror

ag·ile \'ajəl\ adj : able to move quickly and easily —**agil·i·ty** \ə'jilətē\ n

ag·i·tate \'ajə,tāt\ vb -tat·ed; -tat·ing **1** : shake or stir back and forth **2** : excite or trouble the mind of **3** : try to arouse public feeling —**ag·i·ta·tion** \ˌajə'tāshən\ n —**ag·i·ta·tor** \'ajə,tātər\ n

ag·nos·tic \ag'nästik, əg-\ n : one who doubts the existence of God

ago \ə'gō\ *adj or adv* : earlier than the present

agog \ə'gäg\ *adj* : full of excitement

ag·o·nize \'agə,nīz\ *vb* **-nized; -niz·ing** : suffer mental agony —**ag·o·niz·ing·ly** *adv*

ag·o·ny \'agənē\ *n, pl* **-nies** : extreme pain or mental distress

agrar·i·an \ə'grerēən\ *adj* : relating to land ownership or farming interests —**agrarian** *n* —**agrar·i·an·ism** *n*

agree \ə'grē\ *vb* **agreed; agree·ing** 1 : be of the same opinion 2 : express willingness 3 : get along together 4 : be similar 5 : be appropriate, suitable, or healthful

agree·able \-əbəl\ *adj* 1 : pleasing 2 : willing to give approval —**agree·able·ness** *n* —**agree·ably** *adv*

agree·ment \-mənt\ *n* 1 : harmony of opinion or purpose 2 : mutual understanding or arrangement

ag·ri·cul·ture \'agri,kəlchər\ *n* : farming —**ag·ri·cul·tur·al** \,agri'kəlch(ə)rəl\ *adj* —**ag·ri·cul·tur·ist** \-rəst\, **ag·ri·cul·tur·al·ist** \-(ə)rələst\ *n*

aground \ə'graünd\ *adv or adj* : on or onto the bottom or shore

ague \'āgyü\ *n* 1 : fever with recurrent chills and sweating 2 : malaria

ahead \ə'hed\ *adv or adj* 1 : in or toward the front 2 : into or for the future 3 : in a more advantageous position

ahead of *prep* 1 : in front or advance of 2 : in excess of

ahoy \ə'hói\ *interj* —used in hailing

aid \'ād\ *vb* : provide help or support ~ *n* : help

aide \'ād\ *n* : helper

ail \'āl\ *vb* 1 : trouble 2 : be ill

ai·le·ron \'ālə,rän\ *n* : movable part of an airplane wing

ail·ment \'ālmənt\ *n* : bodily disorder

aim \'ām\ *vb* 1 : point or direct (as a weapon) 2 : direct one's efforts ~ *n* 1 : an aiming or the direction of aiming 2 : something meant to be achieved —**aim·less** *adj* —**aim·less·ly** *adv* —**aim·less·ness** *n*

air \'aər\ *n* 1 : mixture of gases surrounding the earth 2 : compressed air 3 : travel by or use of aircraft 4 : medium of transmission of radio waves 5 : outward appearance 6 : artificial manner ~ *vb* 1 : expose to the air 2 : broadcast —**air·borne** \-,bórn\ *adj*

air-condition *vb* : equip with an apparatus (**air conditioner**) for filtering and cooling the air

air·craft *n, pl* **aircraft** : craft that flies

Aire·dale terrier \'aər,dāl-\ *n* : large terrier with a hard wiry coat

air·field *n* : airport or its landing field

air force *n* : military organization for conducting warfare by air

air·lift *n* : a transporting of esp. emergency supplies by aircraft —**airlift** *vb*

air·line *n* : air transportation system —**air·lin·er** *n*

air·mail *n* : system of transporting mail by airplane —**airmail** *vb*

air·man \-mən\ *n* 1 : enlisted man in the air force in one of the 3 ranks below sergeant 2 : enlisted man in the air force ranking below airman first class and above airman basic 3 : aviator

airman basic *n* : enlisted man of the lowest rank in the air force

airman first class *n* : enlisted man in the air force ranking below sergeant and above airman

air·plane *n* : fixed-wing aircraft heavier than air

air·port *n* : place for landing aircraft and receiving passengers

air·ship *n* : propelled lighter-than-air aircraft

air·strip *n* : airfield runway

air·tight *adj* : tightly sealed to prevent flow of air

air·waves \-,wāvz\ *n pl* : medium of transmission of radio waves

airy \'a(ə)rē\ *adj* **air·i·er; -est** 1 : delicate 2 : breezy

aisle \'īl\ *n* : passage between sections of seats

ajar \ə'jär\ *adj or adv* : partly open

akim·bo \ə'kimbō\ *adj or adv* : having the hand on the hip and the elbow turned outward

akin \ə'kin\ *adj* 1 : related by blood 2 : similar in kind

-al \əl\ *adj suffix* : of, relating to, or characterized by

al·a·bas·ter \'alə,bastər\ *n* : white or translucent mineral

alac·ri·ty \ə'lakrətē\ *n* : cheerful readiness

alarm \ə'lärm\ *n* 1 : warning signal 2 : fear at sudden danger ~ *vb* 1 : warn 2 : frighten

al·ba·tross \'albə,tròs, -,träs\ *n, pl* **-tross** or **-tross·es** : large seabird

al·be·it \ól'bēət, al-\ *conj* : even though

al·bi·no \al'bīnō\ *n, pl* **-nos** : person or animal with abnormally white skin —**al·bi·nism** \'albə,nizəm\ *n*

al·bum \'albəm\ *n* 1 : book for displaying a collection (as of photographs) 2 : phonograph record

al·bu·men \al'byümən\ n 1 : white of an egg 2 : albumin

al·bu·min \-mən\ n : protein found in blood, milk, egg white, and tissues

al·che·my \'alkəmē\ n : medieval chemistry —**al·chem·ic** \al'kemik\, **al·chem·i·cal** \-ikəl\ adj —**al·che·mist** \'alkəməst\ n

al·co·hol \'alkə,hol\ n 1 : intoxicating element in liquor 2 : liquor —**al·co·hol·ic** adj

al·co·hol·ic \,alkə'holik, -'häl-\ n : person affected with alcoholism

al·co·hol·ism \'alkə,hol,izəm\ n : addiction to alcoholic beverages

al·cove \'al,kōv\ n : recess in a room or wall

al·der·man \'oldərmən\ n : city official

ale \'āl\ n : beerlike beverage —**ale·house** n

alert \ə'lərt\ adj 1 : watchful 2 : quick to perceive and act ~ n : warning signal ~ vb : warn —**alert·ly** adv —**alert·ness** n

ale·wife n : fish of the herring family

al·fal·fa \al'falfə\ n : cloverlike forage plant

al·ga \'algə\ n, pl **-gae** \'al(,)jē\ : any of a group of lower plants that includes seaweed —**al·gal** \-gəl\ adj

al·ge·bra \'aljəbrə\ n : branch of mathematics using symbols —**al·ge·bra·ic** \,aljə'brāik\ adj —**al·ge·bra·i·cal·ly** \-'brāik(ə)lē\ adv

alias \'āleəs, 'ālyəs\ adv : otherwise called ~ n : assumed name

al·i·bi \'alə,bī\ n 1 : defense of having been elsewhere when a crime was committed 2 : justification ~ vb **-bied; -bi·ing** : offer an excuse

alien \'ālēən, 'ālyən\ adj : foreign ~ n : foreign-born resident

alien·ate \'ālēə,nāt, 'ālyə-\ vb **-at·ed; -at·ing** : cause to be no longer friendly —**alien·ation** \,ālēə'nāshən, ,ālyə-\ n

alight \ə'līt\ vb : dismount

align \ə'līn\ vb : bring into line —**align·ment** n

alike \ə'līk\ adj : identical or very similar ~ adv : equally

al·i·men·ta·ry \,alə'ment(ə)rē\ adj : relating to or functioning in nutrition

al·i·mo·ny \'alə,mōnē\ n, pl **-nies** : money paid to a separated or divorced spouse

alive \ə'līv\ adj 1 : having life 2 : lively or animated

al·ka·li \'alkə,lī\ n, pl **-lies** or **-lis** : strong chemical base —**al·ka·line** \-kələn, -,līn\ adj —**al·ka·lin·i·ty** \,alkə'linətē\ n

all \'ol\ adj 1 : the whole of 2 : greatest possible 3 : every one of ~ adv 1 : wholly 2 : so much 3 : for each side ~ pron 1 : every one 2 : every bit 3 : everything

Al·lah \'alə, ä'lä\ n : supreme being of the Muslims

all-around adj : versatile

al·lay \ə'lā\ vb : relieve or dispel

al·lege \ə'lej\ vb **-leged; -leg·ing** : state as a fact without proof —**al·le·ga·tion** \,alə'gāshən\ n —**al·leg·ed·ly** \ə'lejədlē\ adv

al·le·giance \ə'lējəns\ n : loyalty

al·le·go·ry \'alə,gōrē\ n, pl **-ries** : story in which figures and actions are symbols of general truths —**al·le·gor·i·cal** \alə'gorikəl\ adj

al·le·lu·ia \,alə'lüyə\ interj : hallelujah

al·ler·gen \'alərjən\ n : something that causes allergy —**al·ler·gen·ic** \,alər'jenik\ adj

al·ler·gy \'alərjē\ n, pl **-gies** : abnormal reaction to a substance —**al·ler·gic** \ə'lərjik\ adj —**al·ler·gist** \'alərjəst\ adj

al·le·vi·ate \ə'lēvē,āt\ vb **-at·ed; -at·ing** : relieve or improve —**al·le·vi·a·tion** \ə,lēvē'āshən\ n

al·ley \'alē\ n, pl **-leys** 1 : narrow passage between buildings 2 : place for bowling

al·li·ance \ə'līəns\ n : association

al·lied \ə'līd, 'al,īd\ adj : joined

al·li·ga·tor \'alə,gātər\ n : large aquatic reptile related to the crocodiles

al·lit·er·a·tion \ə,litə'rāshən\ n : repetition of initial sounds of words —**al·lit·er·a·tive** \-'litə,rātiv\ adj

al·lo·cate \'alə,kāt\ vb **-cat·ed; -cat·ing** : assign —**al·lo·ca·tion** \,alə'kāshən\ n

al·lot \ə'lät\ vb **-tt-** : distribute as a share —**al·lot·ment** n

al·low \ə'laú\ vb 1 : permit 2 : agree to the truth of —**al·low·able** adj

al·low·ance \-əns\ n 1 : allotted share 2 : money given regularly for expenses

al·loy \'al,oi, ə'loi\ n : metals fused together —**alloy** vb

all right adv or adj 1 : satisfactorily 2 : yes 3 : certainly

all·spice \'olspīs\ n : berry of a West Indian tree made into a spice

al·lude \ə'lüd\ vb **-lud·ed; -lud·ing** : refer indirectly —**al·lu·sion** \-'lüzhən\ n —**al·lu·sive** \-'lüsiv\ adj —**al·lu·sive·ly** adv —**al·lu·sive·ness** n

al·lure \ə'lür\ vb **-lured; -luring** : attract —**allure** n —**al·lure·ment** n

al·ly \ə'lī, 'al,ī\ vb **-lied; -ly·ing** : unite

in alliance \~ \al,ī, ə'lī\ *n, pl* -lies : member of an alliance

al·ly \(ə)lē\ *adv suffix* : -ly

al·ma·nac \'ȯlmə,nak, 'al-\ *n* : annual information book

al·mighty \ȯl'mītē\ *adj* : having absolute power

al·mond \'ämənd, 'am-; 'älmənd\ *n* : tree with nutlike fruit kernels

al·most \'ȯl,mōst, ȯl-\ *adv* : only a little less than

alms \'ämz, 'älmz\ *n, pl* alms : charitable gift

aloft \ə'lȯft\ *adv* : high in the air

alo·ha \ə'lōə, ä'lōhä\ *interj* —used to express greeting or farewell

alone \ə'lōn\ *adj* 1 : separated from others 2 : not including anyone or anything else —alone *adv*

along \ə'lȯŋ\ *prep* 1 : on or near in a lengthwise direction 2 : at a point on or during ~ *adv* 1 : forward 2 : as a companion 3 : all the time

along·side *adv* : along or by the side ~ *prep* : side by side with

alongside of *prep* : alongside

aloof \ə'lüf\ *adj* : indifferent and reserved —aloof·ness *n*

aloud \ə'laȯd\ *adv* : so that the voice can be heard

al·paca \al'pakə\ *n* 1 : So. American mammal related to the llama 2 : alpaca wool or cloth made of this

al·pha·bet \'alfə,bet, -bət\ *n* : ordered set of letters of a language —al·pha·bet·ic \,alfə'betik\, al·pha·bet·i·cal \-ikəl\ *adj* —al·pha·bet·i·cal·ly \-k(ə)lē\ *adv*

al·pha·bet·ize \'alfəbə,tīz\ *vb* -ized; -iz·ing : arrange in alphabetic order —al·pha·bet·iz·er *n*

al·ready \ȯl'redē\ *adv* : by a given time

al·so \'ȯlsō\ *adv* : in addition

al·tar \'ȯltər\ *n* : structure for rituals

al·ter \'ȯltər\ *vb* : make different —al·ter·a·tion \,ȯltər'āshən\ *n*

al·ter·ca·tion \,ȯltər'kāshən\ *n* : dispute

al·ter·nate \'ȯltərnət, 'al-\ *adj* 1 : arranged or succeeding by turns 2 : every other ~ \-,nāt\ *vb* -nat·ed; -nat·ing : occur or cause to occur by turns ~ \-nət\ *n* : replacement —al·ter·nate·ly *adv* —al·ter·na·tion \,ȯltər'nāshən, ,al-\ *n*

alternating current *n* : electric current that regularly reverses direction

al·ter·na·tive \ȯl'tərnətiv, al-\ *adj* : offering a choice —alternative *n*

al·ter·na·tor \'ȯltər,nātər, 'al-\ *n* : alternating-current generator

al·though \ȯl'thō\ *conj* : even though

al·tim·e·ter \al'timətər, 'altə,mētər\ *n* : instrument for measuring altitudes

al·ti·tude \'altə,t(y)üd\ *n* 1 : distance up from the ground 2 : angular distance above the horizon

al·to \'al,tō\ *n, pl* -tos : contralto

al·to·geth·er \,ȯltə'gethər\ *adv* 1 : wholly 2 : on the whole

al·tru·ism \'altrü,izəm\ *n* : concern for others —al·tru·ist \-əst\ *n* —al·tru·is·tic \altrü'istik\ *adj* —al·tru·is·ti·cal·ly \-tik(ə)lē\ *adv*

al·um \'aləm\ *n* : crystalline compound containing aluminum

alu·mi·num \ə'lümənəm\ *n* : silver-white malleable ductile light metallic element

alum·na \ə'ləmnə\ *n, pl* -nae \-(,)nē\ : woman graduate

alum·nus \ə'ləmnəs\ *n, pl* -ni \-,nī\ : graduate

al·ways \'ȯlwēz, -wəz, -(,)wāz\ *adv* 1 : at all times 2 : forever 3 : without exception

am *pres 1st sing of* BE

amal·gam \ə'malgəm\ *n* 1 : mercury alloy 2 : mixture

amal·gam·ate \ə'malgə,māt\ *vb* -at·ed; -at·ing : unite —amal·ga·ma·tion \-,malgə'māshən\ *n*

am·a·ryl·lis \,amə'riləs\ *n* : bulbous herb with clusters of colored flowers like lilies

amass \ə'mas\ *vb* : gather

am·a·teur \'amə,tər, -,ətər, -ə,t(y)úr, -ə,chúr, -əchər\ *n* 1 : person who does something for pleasure rather than for pay 2 : person who is not expert —amateur *adj* —am·a·teur·ish \,amə'tərish, -'t(y)úr-\ *adj* —am·a·teur·ism \'amə,tər,izəm, -,ətə,riz-, -ə,t(y)úr,iz-, -,chúr,iz-, -chə,riz-\ *n*

am·a·to·ry \'amə,tōrē\ *adj* : of or expressing sexual love

amaze \ə'māz\ *vb* amazed; amazing : overwhelm with wonder —amaze·ment *n* —amaz·ing·ly *adv*

am·a·zon \'amə,zän, -əzən\ *n* : tall strong woman —am·a·zo·ni·an \,amə'zōnēən\ *adj*

am·bas·sa·dor \am'basədər\ *n* : country's representative in a foreign land —am·bas·sa·do·ri·al \-,basə'dōrēəl\ *adj* —am·bas·sa·dor·ship *n*

am·ber \'ambər\ *n* : yellowish fossil resin or its color

am·ber·gris \'ambər,gris, -,grēs\ *n* : waxy substance from certain whales used in making perfumes

am·bi·dex·trous \,ambi'dekstrəs\ *adj* : equally skilled with both hands —am·bi·dex·trous·ly *adv*

am·big·u·ous \am¹bigyəwəs\ *adj* : having more than one interpretation —**am·bi·gu·i·ty** \¸ambə¹gyüətē\ *n*

am·bi·tion \am¹bishən\ *n* : eager desire for success or power

am·bi·tious \-əs\ *adj* : characterized by ambition —**am·bi·tious·ly** *adv*

am·biv·a·lence \am¹bivələns\ *n* : simultaneous attraction and repulsion —**am·biv·a·lent** \-lənt\ *adj*

am·ble \¹ambəl\ *vb* **-bled; -bling** : go at a leisurely gait —**amble** *n*

am·bu·lance \¹ambyələns\ *n* : vehicle equipped for carrying injured or sick persons

am·bu·la·to·ry \¹ambyələ¸tōrē\ *adj* 1 : relating to or adapted to walking 2 : able to walk about

am·bush \¹am¸bush\ *n* : trap by which a surprise attack is made from a place of hiding —**ambush** *vb*

ame·lio·rate \ə¹mēlyə¸rāt\ *vb* **-rat·ed; -rat·ing** : make or grow better —**ame·lio·ra·tion** \-¸mēlyə¹rāshən\ *n*

amen \(¹)ā¹men, (¹)ä-\ *interj* —used esp. at the end of prayers

ame·na·ble \ə¹mēnəbəl, -¹mena-\ *adj* : ready to yield or be influenced

amend \ə¹mend\ *vb* 1 : improve 2 : alter in writing

amend·ment \ə¹men(d)mənt\ *n* : change made in a formal document (as a law)

amends \ə¹men(d)z\ *n sing or pl* : compensation for injury or loss

ame·ni·ty \ə¹menətē, -¹mēnət-\ *n, pl* **-ties** 1 : agreeableness 2 : something serving to comfort or convenience 3 *pl* : social conventions

am·e·thyst \¹amathəst\ *n* : blue-purple gemstone

ami·a·ble \¹āmēəbəl\ *adj* : easy to get along with —**ami·a·bil·i·ty** \¸āmēə¹bilətē\ *n* —**ami·a·bly** \¹āmēəblē\ *adv*

am·i·ca·ble \¹amikəbəl\ *adj* : friendly —**am·i·ca·bly** \-blē\ *adv*

amid \ə¹mid\, **amidst** \-¹midst\ *prep* : in or into the middle of

amino acid \ə¸mēnō-\ *n* : any of numerous nitrogen-containing acids some of which are components of proteins

amiss \ə¹mis\ *adv* : in the wrong way ~ *adj* : wrong

am·me·ter \¹am¸ētər\ *n* : instrument for measuring amperes

am·mo·nia \ə¹mōnyə\ *n* 1 : colorless gaseous compound of nitrogen and hydrogen 2 : solution of ammonia in water

am·mu·ni·tion \¸amyə¹nishən\ *n* 1

: projectiles fired from guns 2 : explosive items used in war

am·ne·sia \am¹nēzhə\ *n* : sudden loss of memory —**am·ne·si·ac** \-z(h)ē¸ak\, **am·ne·sic** \-zik, -sik\ *adj* or *n*

am·nes·ty \¹amnəstē\ *n, pl* **-ties** : a pardon for a group —**amnesty** *vb*

amoe·ba \ə¹mēbə\ *n, pl* **-bas** *or* **-bae** \-(¸)bē\ : tiny one-celled animal that occurs esp. in water —**amoe·bic** \-bik\ *adj*

amok \ə¹mək, -¹mäk\ *adv* : in an uncontrolled often murderous way

among \ə¹məŋ\ *prep* 1 : in or through 2 : in the number or class of 3 : in shares to each of

am·o·rous \¹am(ə)rəs\ *adj* 1 : inclined to love 2 : being in love —**am·o·rous·ly** *adv* —**am·o·rous·ness** *n*

amor·phous \ə¹mórfəs\ *adj* : shapeless

amor·tize \¹amər¸tīz, ə¹mór-\ *vb* **-tized; -tiz·ing** : get rid of (as a debt) gradually with periodic payments —**amor·ti·za·tion** \¸amərt-ə¹zāshən, ə¸mórt-\ *n*

amount \ə¹maunt\ *vb* 1 : reach as a total 2 : be equivalent ~ *n* : total number or quantity

amour \ə¹mur, ä-, a-\ *n* : love affair

am·pere \¹am¸piər\ *n* : unit of electric current

am·per·sand \¹ampər¸sand\ *n* : character & used for the word *and*

am·phib·i·ous \am¹fibēəs\ *adj* 1 : able to live both on land and in water 2 : adapted for both land and water —**am·phib·i·an** \-ən\ *n*

am·phi·the·ater \¹amfə¸thēətər\ *n* : oval or circular structure with rising tiers of seats around an arena

am·ple \¹ampəl\ *adj* **-pler** \-plər\; **-plest** \-pləst\ 1 : large 2 : sufficient —**am·ply** \-plē\ *adv*

am·pli·fy \¹amplə¸fī\ *vb* **-fied; -fy·ing** : make louder, stronger, or more thorough —**am·pli·fi·ca·tion** \¸ampləfə¹kāshən\ *n* —**am·pli·fi·er** \¹amplə¸fī(ə)r\ *n*

am·pli·tude \-¹t(y)üd\ *n* 1 : fullness 2 : extent of a vibratory movement

am·pu·tate \¹ampyə¸tāt\ *vb* **-tat·ed; -tat·ing** : cut off (a body part) —**am·pu·ta·tion** \¸ampyə¹tāshən\ *n* —**am·pu·tee** \¸ampyə¹tē\ *n*

amuck \ə¹mək\ *var of* AMOK

am·u·let \¹amyələt\ *n* : ornament worn as a charm against evil

amuse \ə¹myüz\ *vb* **amused; amusing** 1 : engage the attention of in an interesting and pleasant way 2 : make laugh —**amuse·ment** *n*

an \ən, (')an\ *indefinite article* : a —used before words beginning with a vowel sound

-an \ən\, **-ian** \(ē)ən\, **-ean** \(ē)ən, 'ēan\ *n suffix* 1 : one that belongs to 2 : one skilled in — *adj suffix* 1 : of or belonging to 2 : characteristic of or resembling

anach·ro·nism \ə'nakrə₁nizəm\ *n* : one that is chronologically out of place —**anach·ro·nis·tic** \ə₁nakrə'nistik\ *adj*

an·a·con·da \₁anə'kändə\ *n* : large So. American snake

ana·gram \'anə₁gram\ *n* : word or phrase made by transposing the letters of another word or phrase

anal \'ānᵊl\ *adj* : relating to the anus

an·al·ge·sic \₁anᵊl'jēzik, -sik\ *n* : pain reliever

anal·o·gy \ə'naləjē\ *n, pl* **-gies** 1 : similarity between unlike things 2 : example of something similar —**an·a·log·i·cal** \₁anᵊl'äjikəl\ *adj* —**an·a·log·i·cal·ly** \-ik(ə)lē\ *adv* —**anal·o·gous** \ə'naləgəs\ *adj*

anal·y·sis \ə'naləsəs\ *n, pl* **-y·ses** \-₁sēz\ 1 : examination of a thing to determine its parts 2 : psychoanalysis —**an·a·lyst** \'anᵊl'əst\ *n* —**an·a·lyt·ic** \₁anᵊl'itik\, **an·a·lyt·i·cal** \-ikəl\ *adj*

an·a·lyze \'anᵊl₁īz\ *vb* **-lyzed; -lyzing** : make an analysis of

an·ar·chism \'anər₁kizəm\ *n* : theory that all government is undesirable —**an·ar·chist** \-kəst\ *n* —**an·ar·chis·tic** \₁anər'kistik\ *adj*

an·ar·chy \'anərkē\ *n* : lack of orderly government —**an·ar·chic** \a'närkik\ *adj*

anath·e·ma \ə'nathəmə\ *n* 1 : solemn curse 2 : person or thing accursed or intensely disliked

anat·o·my \ə'natəmē\ *n, pl* **-mies** : science dealing with the structure of organisms —**an·a·tom·ic** \₁anə'tämik\, **an·a·tom·i·cal** \-ikəl\ *adj* —**ana·tom·i·cal·ly** *adv* —**anat·o·mist** \ə'natəməst\ *n*

-ance \əns\ *n suffix* 1 : action or process 2 : quality or state 3 : amount or degree

an·ces·tor \'an₁sestər\ *n* : one from whom an individual is descended —**an·ces·tress** \-trəs\ *n*

an·ces·try \-trē\ *n* 1 : line of descent 2 : ancestors —**an·ces·tral** \an'sestrəl\ *adj*

¹an·chor \'aŋkər\ *n* : heavy device that catches in the sea bottom to hold a ship in place ∼ *vb* : hold or become

held in place by or as if by an anchor —**an·chor·age** \-k(ə)rij\ *n*

an·chor·man \'aŋkər₁man\ *n* : news broadcast coordinator

an·cho·vy \'an₁chōvē, an'chō-\ *n, pl* **-vies** *or* **-vy** : small herringlike fish

an·cient \'ānshənt\ *adj* 1 : having existed for many years 2 : belonging to times long past —**ancient** *n*

-ancy \ansē\ *n suffix* : quality or state

and \ən(d), (')an(d)\ *conj* —used to indicate connection or addition

and·iron \'an₁dī(ə)rn\ *n* : one of 2 metal supports for wood in a fireplace

an·ec·dote \'anik₁dōt\ *n* : brief story —**an·ec·dot·al** \₁anik'dōtᵊl\ *adj*

ane·mia \ə'nēmēə\ *n* : blood deficiency —**ane·mic** \ə'nēmik\ *adj*

anem·o·ne \ə'nemənē\ *n* : small herb with showy usu. white flowers

an·es·the·sia \₁anəs'thēzhə\ *n* : loss of bodily sensation

an·es·thet·ic \₁anəs'thetik\ *n* : agent (as ether) that produces anesthesia —**anesthetic** *adj* —**anes·the·tist** \ə'nesthətəst\ *n* —**anes·the·tize** \-₁tīz\ *vb*

anew \ə'n(y)ü\ *adv* : over again

an·gel \'ānjəl\ *n* : spiritual being superior to humans —**an·gel·ic** \an'jelik\, **an·gel·i·cal** \-ikəl\ *adj* —**an·gel·i·cal·ly** *adv*

an·ger \'aŋgər\ *n* : strong feeling of displeasure ∼ *vb* : make angry

an·gi·na \an'jīnə\ *n* : painful disorder of heart muscles —**an·gi·nal** \an'jīnᵊl\ *adj*

¹an·gle \'aŋgəl\ *n* 1 : figure formed by the meeting of 2 lines in a point 2 : sharp corner 3 : point of view ∼ *vb* **-gled; -gling** : turn or direct at an angle

²angle *vb* **an·gled; an·gling** : fish with a hook and line —**an·gler** \-glər\ *n* —**an·gle·worm** *n* —**an·gling** *n*

an·go·ra \aŋ'gōrə, an-\ *n* : yarn or cloth made from the hair of an Angora goat or rabbit

an·gry \'aŋgrē\ *adj* **-gri·er; -est** : feeling or showing anger —**an·gri·ly** \-grəlē\ *adv*

an·guish \'aŋgwish\ *n* : extreme pain or distress of mind

an·gu·lar \'aŋgyələr\ *adj* 1 : having many or sharp angles 2 : thin and bony —**an·gu·lar·i·ty** \₁aŋgyə'larətē\ *n*

an·i·line \'anᵊlən\ *n* : oily poisonous liquid used esp. in making dyes

an·i·mal \'anəməl\ *n* 1 : living being capable of feeling and voluntary motion **2** : lower animal as distinguished from man

an-i-mate \'anəmət\ *adj* : having life ~ \-ˌmāt\ *vb* **-mat-ed; -mat-ing 1** : give life or vigor to **2** : make appear to move —**an-i-mat-ed** *adj*

an-i-ma-tion \ˌanəˈmāshən\ *n* **1** : liveliness **2** : animated cartoon

an-i-mos-i-ty \ˌanəˈmäsətē\ *n, pl* **-ties** : resentment

an-i-mus \'anəməs\ *n* : deep-seated hostility

an-ise \'anəs\ *n* : an herb related to the carrot with aromatic seeds (**aniseed** \-ˌs(s)ēd\) used in flavoring

an-kle \'aŋkəl\ *n* : joint or region between the foot and the leg —**an-kle-bone** *n*

an-nals \'an⁰lz\ *n pl* : chronological record of history —**an-nal-ist** \-⁰ləst\ *n*

an-neal \ə'nēl\ *vb* : make less brittle by heating and then cooling

an-nex \ə'neks, 'anˌeks\ *vb* : assume political control over (a territory) ~ \'anˌeks, -iks\ *n* : added building —**an-nex-a-tion** \ˌanˌekˈsāshən\ *n*

an-ni-hi-late \ə'nīəˌlāt\ *vb* **-lat-ed; -lat-ing** : destroy —**an-ni-hi-la-tion** \-ˌnīəˈlāshən\ *n*

an-ni-ver-sa-ry \ˌanəˈvərs(ə)rē\ *n, pl* **-ries** : annual return of the date of a notable event or its celebration

an-no-tate \'anəˌtāt\ *vb* **-tat-ed; -tat-ing** : furnish with notes —**an-no-ta-tion** \ˌanəˈtāshən\ *n* —**an-no-ta-tor** \'anəˌtātər\ *n*

an-nounce \ə'naůns\ *vb* **-nounced; -nounc-ing** : make known publicly —**an-nounce-ment** *n* —**an-nounc-er** *n*

an-noy \ə'nói\ *vb* : disturb or irritate —**an-noy-ance** \-əns\ *n* —**an-noy-ing-ly** \-'nóiiŋlē\ *adv*

an-nu-al \'anyə(wə)l\ *adj* **1** : occurring once a year **2** : living only one year —**annual** *n* —**an-nu-al-ly** *adv*

an-nu-ity \ə'n(y)üətē\ *n, pl* **-ities** : amount payable annually or the right to such a payment

an-nul \ə'nəl\ *vb* **-ll-** : make legally void —**an-nul-ment** *n*

an-ode \'anˌōd\ *n* **1** : positive electrode **2** : negative battery terminal —**an-od-ic** \aˌnädik\ *adj* —**an-od-al** \-'nōd⁰l\ *adj* —**an-od-i-cal-ly** \-ik(ə)lē\, **an-od-al-ly** \-⁰lē\ *adv*

anoint \ə'nóint\ *vb* : apply oil to as a rite —**anoint-ment** *n*

anom-a-ly \ə'näməlē\ *n, pl* **-lies** : something abnormal or unusual —**anom-a-lous** \ə'näməl əs\ *adj*

anon-y-mous \ə'nänəməs\ *adj* : of un-

known origin —**an-o-nym-i-ty** \ˌanə'nimətē\ *n* —**anon-y-mous-ly** *adv*

an-oth-er \ə'nəthər\ *adj* **1** : any or some other **2** : one more ~ *pron* **1** : one more **2** : one different

an-swer \'ansər\ *n* **1** : something spoken or written in return to a question **2** : solution of a problem ~ *vb* **1** : reply to **2** : be responsible **3** : be adequate —**an-swer-er** *n*

an-swer-able \'ans(ə)rəbəl\ *adj* : subject to taking blame or responsibility

ant \'ant\ *n* : small social insect —**ant-hill** *n*

-ant \ənt\ *n suffix* **1** : one that performs or causes an action **2** : thing that is acted upon ~ *adj suffix* **1** : performing an action or being in a condition **2** : causing an action or process

an-tag-o-nism \an'tagəˌnizəm\ *n* : active opposition or hostility —**an-tag-o-nist** \-ənəst\ *n* —**an-tag-o-nis-tic** \-ˌtagə'nistik\ *adj*

an-tag-o-nize \an'tagəˌnīz\ *vb* **-nized; -niz-ing** : cause to be hostile

ant-arc-tic \ant'ärktik, -'ärtik\ *adj* : relating to the region near the south pole

antarctic circle *n* : circle parallel to the equator approximately 23°27' from the south pole

an-te-bel-lum \ˌanti'beləm\ *adj* : existing before the U.S. Civil War

an-te-ced-ent \ˌantə'sēd⁰nt\ *n* : one that comes before —**antecedent** *adj*

an-te-lope \'ant⁰lˌōp\ *n, pl* **-lope** or **-lopes** : deerlike mammal related to the ox

an-ten-na \an'tenə\ *n, pl* **-nae** \-(ˌ)ē\ *or* **-nas 1** : one of the long slender paired sensory organs on the head of an arthropod **2** *pl* **-nas** : metallic device for sending or receiving radio waves

an-te-ri-or \an'tirēər\ *adj* : located before in place or time

an-them \'anthəm\ *n* : song or hymn of praise or gladness

an-ther \'anthər\ *n* : part of a seed plant that contains pollen

an-thol-o-gy \an'thäləjē\ *n, pl* **-gies** : literary collection

an-thra-cite \'anthrəˌsīt\ *n* : hard coal

an-thro-poid \'anthrəˌpóid\ *adj* : like humans ~ *n* : large ape

an-thro-pol-o-gy \ˌanthrə'päləjē\ *n* : science dealing with humans —**an-thro-po-log-i-cal** \-pə'läjikəl\ *adj* —**an-thro-pol-o-gist** \-'päləjəst\ *n*

anti- \ˌanti, -ē; ˌanˌtī\, **ant-, anth-** *prefix* **1** : opposite in kind, position, or action **2** : opposing or hostile toward **3** : defending against **4** : curing or treating

antiabortion	antidemocratic
antiacademic	antidiscrimina-
antiadministra-	tion
tion	antidrug
antiaggression	antidumping
antiaggressive	antieavesdrop-
antiaircraft	ping
antialien	antiestablishment
antianarchic	antievolution
antianarchist	antievolutionary
antiannexation	antifanatic
antiapartheid	antifascism
antiaristocrat	antifascist
antiaristocratic	antifatigue
antiart	antifemale
antiatheism	antifeminine
antiatheist	antifeminism
antiauthoritarian	antifeminist
antibacterial	antifertility
antibigotry	antiforeign
antiblack	antiforeigner
anti-Bolshevik	antifraud
anti-Bolshevism	antifungus
anti-Bolshevist	antigambling
antibourgeois	antiglare
antiboxing	antigonorrheal
antiboycott	antigovernment
antibureaucratic	antigraft
antiburglar	antiguerrilla
antiburglary	antigun
antibusiness	antihijack
anticancer	antihomosexual
anticapitalism	antihuman
anticapitalist	antihumanism
anticapitalistic	antihumanistic
anti-Catholic	antihumanity
anticensorship	antihunting
anti-Christian	anti-imperialism
anti-Christianity	anti-imperialist
antichurch	anti-inflation
anticigarette	anti-inflationary
anticlerical	anti-institutional
anticollision	anti-integration
anticolonial	anti-intellectual
anticommunism	anti-intellectual-
anticommunist	ism
anticonservation	antijamming
anticonservation-	anti-Japanese
ist	anti-Jewish
anticonsumer	antilabor
anticonventional	antiliberal
anticorrosion	antiliberalism
anticorrosive	antilitter
anticorruption	antilittering
anticrime	antiloitering
anticruelty	antilynching
anticultural	antimale
antidandruff	antimanagement

antimaterialism	antisexual
antimaterialist	antishoplifting
antimaterialis-	antislavery
tic	antismoking
antimicrobial	antismuggling
antimilitarism	antismut
antimilitarist	antispending
antimilitaristic	antistrike
antimilitary	antistudent
antimiscegena-	antisubmarine
tion	antisubversion
antimonopolist	antisubversive
antimonopoly	antisuicide
antimosquito	antisyphilis
antinoise	antitank
antiobesity	antitax
antiobsceness	antitechnologi-
antipapal	cal
antipersonnel	antitechnology
antipolice	antiterrorism
antipollution	antiterrorist
antipornograph-	antitheft
ic	antitobacco
antipornography	antitotalitarian
antipoverty	antitoxin
antiprofiteering	antitraditional
antiprogressive	antitrust
antiprostitution	antituberculo-
antirabies	sis
antiracing	antitumor
antiracketeer-	antityphoid
ing	antiulcer
antiradical	antiunemploy-
antirape	ment
antirealism	antiunion
antirealistic	antiuniversity
antirecession	antiurban
antireform	antivandalism
antireligious	antiviolence
antirepublican	antiviral
antirevolution-	antivivisection
ary	antiwar
antiriot	antiweed
antirobbery	anti-West
antiromantic	anti-Western
antirust	antiwhite
antisegregation	antiwiretap-
antisex	ping
antisexist	antiwoman

an·ti·bi·ot·ic \ˌantibīˈätik, -bē-\ *n* : substance that inhibits harmful microorganisms —**antibiotic** *adj*

an·ti·body \ˈanti͵bädē\ *n* : bodily substance that counteracts the effects of a foreign substance or organism

an·tic \ˈantik\ *n* : playful act ~ *adj* : playful

an·tic·i·pate \anˈtisə͵pāt\ *vb* -**pat·ed;** -**pat·ing 1** : be prepared for **2** : look forward to —**an·tic·i·pa·tion** \-͵tisə-

\'pāshən\ *n* —**an·tic·i·pa·to·ry** \-'tisəpə̩tōrē\ *adj*

an·ti·cli·max \ˌanti'klīˌmaks\ *n* : something strikingly less important than what has preceded it —**an·ti·cli·mac·tic** \-klī'maktik\ *adj*

an·ti·dote \'antiˌdōt\ *n* : remedy for poison

an·ti·freeze \'antiˌfrēz\ *n* : substance to prevent a liquid from freezing

an·ti·mo·ny \'antəˌmōnē\ *n* : brittle white metallic chemical element

an·tip·a·thy \an'tipəthē\ *n*, *pl* **-thies** : strong dislike

an·ti·quar·i·an \ˌantə'kwerēən\ *adj* : relating to antiquities or old books —**antiquarian** —**an·ti·quar·i·an·ism** *n*

an·ti·quary \'antəˌkwerē\ *n*, *pl* **-quar·ies** : one who collects or studies antiquities

an·ti·quat·ed \'antəˌkwātəd\ *adj* : out-of-date

an·tique \an'tēk\ *adj* : very old or out-of-date —**antique** *n*

an·tiq·ui·ty \an'tikwətē\ *n*, *pl* **-ties** 1 : ancient times 2 *pl* : relics of ancient times

an·ti·sep·tic \ˌantə'septik\ *adj* : killing or checking the growth of germs —**antiseptic** *n* —**an·ti·sep·ti·cal·ly** \-tik(ə)lē\ *adv*

an·tith·e·sis \an'tithəsəs\ *n*, *pl* **-e·ses** \-ˌsēz\ : direct opposite

ant·ler \'antlər\ *n* : solid branched horn of a deer —**ant·lered** \-lərd\ *adj*

ant·onym \'antəˌnim\ *n* : word of opposite meaning

anus \'ānəs\ *n* : the rear opening of the alimentary canal

an·vil \'anvəl\ *n* : heavy iron block on which metal is shaped

anx·i·ety \aŋ'zīətē\ *n*, *pl* **-eties** : uneasiness usu. over an expected misfortune

anx·ious \'aŋkshəs\ *adj* 1 : uneasy 2 : earnestly wishing —**anx·ious·ly** *adv*

any \'enē\ *adj* 1 : one chosen at random 2 : of whatever number or quantity ~ *pron* 1 : any one or ones 2 : any amount ~ *adv* : to any extent or degree

any·body \-ˌbädē, -ˌbəd-\ *pron* : anyone

any·how \-ˌhau̇\ *adv* 1 : in any way 2 : nevertheless

any·more \ˌenē'mōr\ *adv* : at the present time

any·one \-(ˌ)wən\ *pron* : any person

any·place *adv* : anywhere

any·thing *pron* : any thing whatever

any·time *adv* : at any time whatever

any·way *adv* : anyhow

any·where *adv* : in or to any place

aor·ta \ā'ortə\ *n*, *pl* **-tas** or **-tae** \-ē\ : main artery from the heart —**aor·tic** \-'ortik\ *adj*

apart \ə'pärt\ *adv* 1 : separately in place or time 2 : aside 3 : to pieces

apart·heid \ə'pär̩tāt, -ˌtīt\ *n* : racial segregation

apart·ment \ə'pärtmənt\ *n* : set of usu. rented rooms

ap·a·thy \'apəthē\ *n* : lack of emotion or interest —**ap·a·thet·ic** \ˌapə'thetik\ *adj* —**ap·a·thet·i·cal·ly** \-ik(ə)lē\ *adv*

ape \'āp\ *n* : large tailless primate ~ *vb* **aped; ap·ing** : imitate

ap·er·ture \'apə(r)ˌchu̇r, -chər\ *n* : opening

apex \'āˌpeks\ *n*, *pl* **apex·es** or **api·ces** \'āpəˌsēz, 'apə-\ : highest point

aphid \'āfəd, 'afəd\ *n* : small insect that sucks plant juices

aph·o·rism \'afəˌrizəm\ *n* : short saying stating a general truth —**aph·o·ris·tic** \ˌafə'ristik\ *adj*

aph·ro·dis·i·ac \ˌafrə'dizē̩ak\ *n* : substance that excites sexual desire

api·a·rist \'āpēərəst\ *n* : beekeeper —**api·ary** \-ˌerē\ *n*

apiece \ə'pēs\ *adv* : for each one

aplomb \ə'pläm, -'pləm\ *n* : complete calmness or self-assurance

apoc·a·lypse \ə'päkəˌlips\ *n* : writing prophesying a cataclysm in which evil forces are destroyed —**apoc·a·lyp·tic** \-ˌpäkə'liptik\, **apoc·a·lyp·ti·cal** \-tikəl\ *adj*

apoc·ry·pha \ə'päkrəfə\ *n* : writings of dubious authenticity —**apoc·ry·phal** \-fəl\ *adj*

apol·o·get·ic \ə̩pälə'jetik\ *adj* : expressing apology —**apol·o·get·i·cal·ly** \-ik(ə)lē\ *adv*

apol·o·gize \ə'päləˌjīz\ *vb* **-gized; -giz·ing** : make an apology —**apol·o·gist** \-jəst\ *n*

apol·o·gy \ə'päləjē\ *n*, *pl* **-gies** 1 : formal justification 2 : expression of regret for a wrong

ap·o·plexy \'apəˌpleksē\ *n* : sudden loss of consciousness caused by rupture or obstruction of an artery of the brain —**ap·o·plec·tic** \ˌapə'plektik\ *adj*

apos·ta·sy \ə'pästəsē\ *n*, *pl* **-sies** : abandonment of a former loyalty —**apos·tate** \ə'päsˌtāt, -tət\ *adj* or *n*

apos·tle \ə'päsəl\ *n* : disciple or advocate —**apos·tle·ship** *n* —**ap·os·tol·ic** \ˌapə'stälik\ *adj*

apos·tro·phe \ə'pästrə(ˌ)fē\ *n* : punctuation mark ' to indicate the possessive case or the omission of a letter or figure

apoth·e·cary \ə'päthə,kerē\ *n, pl* **-car·ies** : druggist

ap·pall \ə'pol\ *vb* : fill with horror or dismay

ap·pa·ra·tus \,apə'ratəs, -'rāt-\ *n, pl* **-tus·es** *or* **-tus** 1 : equipment 2 : complex machine or device

ap·par·el \ə'parəl\ *n* : clothing

ap·par·ent \ə'parənt\ *adj* 1 : visible 2 : obvious 3 : seeming —**ap·par·ent·ly** *adv*

ap·pa·ri·tion \,apə'rishən\ *n* : ghost

ap·peal \ə'pēl\ *vb* 1 : try to have a court case reheard 2 : ask earnestly 3 : have an attraction —**appeal** *n*

ap·pear \ə'piər\ *vb* 1 : become visible or evident 2 : come into the presence of someone 3 : seem

ap·pear·ance \ə'pirəns\ *n* 1 : act of appearing 2 : outward aspect

ap·pease \ə'pēz\ *vb* **-peased; -peas·ing** : pacify with concessions —**ap·pease·ment** *n*

ap·pel·late \ə'pelət\ *adj* : having power to review decisions

ap·pend \ə'pend\ *vb* : attach

ap·pend·age \ə'pendij\ *n* : something attached

ap·pen·dec·to·my \,apən'dektəmē\ *n, pl* **-mies** : surgical removal of the appendix

ap·pen·di·ci·tis \ə,pendə'sītəs\ *n* : inflammation of the appendix

ap·pen·dix \ə'pendiks\ *n, pl* **-dix·es** *or* **-di·ces** \-də,sēz\ 1 : supplementary matter 2 : narrow closed tube extending from lower right intestine

ap·pe·tite \'apə,tīt\ *n* 1 : natural desire esp. for food 2 : preference

ap·pe·tiz·er \-,tīzər\ *n* : food or drink to stimulate the appetite

ap·pe·tiz·ing \-zin\ *adj* : tempting to the appetite —**ap·pe·tiz·ing·ly** *adv*

ap·plaud \ə'plod\ *vb* : show approval esp. by clapping

ap·plause \ə'ploz\ *n* : a clapping in approval

ap·ple \'apəl\ *n* : rounded fruit with firm white flesh

ap·ple·jack \-,jak\ *n* : brandy made from cider

ap·pli·ance \ə'plīəns\ *n* : household appliance or device

ap·pli·ca·ble \'aplikəbəl, ə'plikə-\ *adj* : capable of being applied —**ap·pli·ca·bil·i·ty** \,aplikə'bilətē, ə,plikə-\ *n*

ap·pli·cant \'aplikənt\ *n* : one who applies —**ap·pli·can·cy** \-kənsē\ *n*

ap·pli·ca·tion \,aplə'kāshən\ *n* 1 : act

of applying or thing applied 2 : constant attention 3 : request

ap·pli·ca·tor \'aplə,kātər\ *n* : device for applying a substance

ap·pli·qué \,aplə'kā\ *n* : cut-out fabric decoration —**appliqué** *vb*

ap·ply \ə'plī\ *vb* **-plied; -ply·ing** 1 : place in contact 2 : put to practical use 3 : devote (one's) attention or efforts to something 4 : submit a request 5 : have reference or a connection

ap·point \ə'point\ *vb* 1 : set or assign officially 2 : equip or furnish —**ap·point·ee** \ə,poin'tē, ,a-\ *n*

ap·point·ment \ə'pointmənt\ *n* 1 : act of appointing 2 : nonelective political job 3 : arrangement for a meeting

ap·por·tion \ə'pōrshən\ *vb* : distribute proportionately —**ap·por·tion·ment** *n*

ap·po·site \'apəzət\ *adj* : suitable —**ap·po·site·ly** *adv* —**ap·po·site·ness** *n*

ap·praise \ə'prāz\ *vb* **-praised; -prais·ing** : set value on —**ap·prais·al** \-'prāzəl\ *n* —**ap·prais·er** *n*

ap·pre·cia·ble \ə'prēshəbəl\ *adj* : considerable —**ap·pre·cia·bly** \-blē\ *adv*

ap·pre·ci·ate \ə'prēshē,āt\ *vb* **-ated; -at·ing** 1 : value justly 2 : be grateful for 3 : increase in value —**ap·pre·ci·a·tion** \-,prēshē'āshən\ *n*

ap·pre·cia·tive \ə'prēshətiv, -shē,āt-\ *adj* : showing appreciation

ap·pre·hend \,apri'hend\ *vb* 1 : arrest 2 : look forward to in dread 3 : understand —**ap·pre·hen·sion** \-'henchən\ *n*

ap·pre·hen·sive \-'hensiv\ *adj* : fearful —**ap·pre·hen·sive·ly** *adv* —**ap·pre·hen·sive·ness** *n*

ap·pren·tice \ə'prentəs\ *n* : person learning a craft ~ *vb* **-ticed; -tic·ing** : employ or work as an apprentice —**ap·pren·tice·ship** *n*

ap·prise \ə'prīz\ *vb* **-prised; -pris·ing** : inform

ap·proach \ə'prōch\ *vb* 1 : move nearer or be close to 2 : make initial advances or efforts toward —**approach** *n* —**ap·proach·able** *adj*

ap·pro·ba·tion \,aprə'bāshən\ *n* : approval

ap·pro·pri·ate \ə'prōprē,āt\ *vb* **-at·ed; -at·ing** 1 : take possession of 2 : set apart for a particular use ~ \-'prēət\ *adj* : suitable —**ap·pro·pri·ate·ly** *adv* —**ap·pro·pri·ate·ness** *n* —**ap·pro·pri·a·tion** \ə,prōprē'āshən\ *n*

ap·prov·al \ə'prüvəl\ *n* : act of approving

ap·prove \ə'prüv\ *vb* **-proved; -prov·ing** : accept as satisfactory

ap·prox·i·mate \ə'präksəmət\ *adj* : nearly correct or exact ~ \-,māt\ *vb* **-mat·ed; -mat·ing** : come near —**ap·prox·i·mate·ly** *adv* —**ap·prox·i·ma·tion** \-,präksə'māshən\ *n*

ap·pur·te·nance \ə'pərt(ə)nəns\ *n* : accessory —**ap·pur·te·nant** \-'pərtnənt, -ənənt\ *adj*

apri·cot \'aprə,kät, 'āprə-\ *n* : peach-like fruit

April \'āprəl\ *n* : 4th month of the year having 30 days

apron \'āprən, -pərn\ *n* : protective garment

ap·ro·pos \,aprə'pō, 'aprə,pō\ *adv* : suitably ~ *adj* : being to the point

apropos of *prep* : with regard to

apt \'apt\ *adj* **1** : suitable **2** : likely **3** : quick to learn —**apt·ly** *adv* —**apt·ness** \'ap(t)nəs\ *n*

ap·ti·tude \'aptə,t(y)üd\ *n* **1** : capacity for learning **2** : natural ability

aqua \'akwə, 'äk-\ *n, pl* **aquae** \'ak(,)wē, 'äk,wī\ *or* **aquas** \-z\ : light greenish blue color

aquar·i·um \ə'kwareəm\ *n, pl* **-i·ums** *or* **-ia** \-ēə\ : container in which aquatic animals and plants are kept (as in the home)

aquat·ic \ə'kwätik, -'kwat-\ *adj* : of or relating to water —**aquatic** *n*

aq·ue·duct \'akwə,dəkt\ *n* : conduit for carrying running water

aq·ui·line \'akwə,līn, -lən\ *adj* : hooked like an eagle's beak

-ar \ər\ *adj suffix* **1** : of, relating to, or being **2** : resembling

ar·a·besque \,arə'besk\ *n* : intricate design

ar·a·ble \'arəbəl\ *adj* : fit for crops

ar·bi·ter \'ärbətər\ *n* : final authority

ar·bi·trary \'ärbə,trerē\ *adj* **1** : selected at random **2** : autocratic —**ar·bi·trari·ly** \,ärbə'trerəlē\ *adv* —**ar·bi·trari·ness** \'ärbə,trerēnəs\ *n*

ar·bi·trate \'ärbə,trāt\ *vb* **-trat·ed; -trat·ing** : settle a dispute as arbitrator —**ar·bi·tra·tion** \,ärbə'trāshən\ *n*

ar·bi·tra·tor \'ärbə,trātər\ *n* : one chosen to settle a dispute

ar·bor \'ärbər\ *n* : shelter under branches or vines

ar·bo·re·al \är'bōrēəl\ *adj* : living in trees

arc \'ärk\ *n* **1** : part of a circle **2** : bright streak of an electrical discharge ~ *vb* : form an arc

ar·cade \är'kād\ *n* : arched passageway between shops

ar·cane \är'kān\ *adj* : mysterious or secret

¹arch \'ärch\ *n* **1** : curved structure

spanning an opening ~ *vb* : cover with or form into an arch

²arch *adj* **1** : chief —usu. in combination **2** : mischievous —**arch·ly** *adv* —**arch·ness** *n*

ar·chae·ol·o·gy, ar·che·ol·o·gy \,ärkē'äləjē\ *n* : study of past human life —**ar·chae·log·i·cal** \-kēə'läjikəl\ *adj* —**ar·chae·ol·o·gist** \-kē'äləjəst\ *n*

ar·cha·ic \är'kāik\ *adj* : belonging to an earlier time —**ar·cha·i·cal·ly** \-ik(ə)lē\ *adv*

arch·an·gel \'ärk,ānjəl\ *n* : angel of high rank

arch·bish·op \ärch'bishəp\ *n* : chief bishop —**arch·bish·op·ric** \-ə(,)prik\ *n*

arch·di·o·cese \-'dī-əsəs, -ə,sēz, -,sēs\ *n* : diocese of an archbishop

ar·chery \'ärch(ə)rē\ *n* : shooting with bow and arrows —**ar·cher** \'ärchər\ *n*

ar·che·type \'ärki,tīp\ *n* : original pattern or model

ar·chi·pel·a·go \,ärkə'pelə,gō, ,ärchə-\ *n, pl* **-goes** *or* **-gos** : group of islands

ar·chi·tect \'ärkə,tekt\ *n* : building designer

ar·chi·tec·ture \'ärkə,tekchər\ *n* **1** : building design **2** : style of building —**ar·chi·tec·tur·al** \,ärkə'tekchərəl, -'tekshrəl\ *adj* —**ar·chi·tec·tur·al·ly** *adv*

ar·chives \'är,kīvz\ *n pl* : public records or their storage place —**ar·chi·vist** \'ärkəvəst, -,kī-\ *n*

arch·way *n* : passageway under an arch

arc lamp *n* : lamp that produces light when a current arcs between electrodes

arc·tic \'är(k)tik\ *adj* **1** : relating to the region near the north pole **2** : frigid

arctic circle *n* : circle parallel to the equator approximately 23°27′ from the north pole

-ard \ərd\ *n suffix* : one that is

ar·dent \'ärd²nt\ *adj* **1** : characterized by warmth of feeling —**ar·dent·ly** *adv*

ar·dor \'ärdər\ *n* : warmth of feeling

ar·du·ous \'ärj(ə)wəs\ *adj* : difficult —**ar·du·ous·ly** *adv* —**ar·du·ous·ness** *n*

are *pres 2d sing or pres pl of* BE

ar·ea \'areə\ *n* **1** : space for something **2** : amount of surface included **3** : region **4** : range covered by a thing or concept

area code *n* : 3-digit area-identifying telephone number

are·na \ə'rēnə\ *n* **1** : enclosed exhibition area **2** : sphere of activity

ar·gon \'är₁gän\ *n* : colorless odorless gaseous chemical element

ar·got \'ärgət, -₁gō\ *n* : special language (as of the underworld)

argu·able \'ärgyəwəbəl\ *adj* : open to dispute

ar·gue \'ärgyü\ *vb* **-gued; -guing 1** : give reasons for or against something **2** : disagree in words

ar·gu·ment \'ärgyəmənt\ *n* **1** : reasons given to persuade **2** : dispute with words

ar·gu·men·ta·tive \₁ärgyə'mentətiv\ *adj* : inclined to argue

ar·gyle \'är₁gīl\ *n* : colorful diamond pattern in knitting

aria \'ärēə\ *n* : opera solo

ar·id \'arəd\ *adj* : dry and barren —**arid·i·ty** \ə'ridətē\ *n*

arise \ə'rīz\ *vb* **arose** \-'rōz\; **aris·en** \-'riz³n\; **aris·ing** \-'rīziŋ\ **1** : get up **2** : originate

ar·is·toc·ra·cy \₁arə'stäkrəsē\ *n*, *pl* **-cies** : upper class —**aris·to·crat** \ə'ristə₁krat\ *n* —**aris·to·crat·ic** \ə₁ristə'kratik\ *adj*

arith·me·tic \ə'rithmə₁tik\ *n* : mathematics that deals with numbers —**ar·ith·met·ic** \₁arith'metik\, **ar·ith·met·i·cal** \-ikəl\ *adj*

ark \'ärk\ *n* : big boat

¹arm \'ärm\ *n* **1** : upper limb **2** : branch —**armed** \'ärmd\ *adj* —**arm·less** *adj*

²arm *vb* : furnish with weapons ~ *n* **1** : weapon **2** : branch of the military forces **3** *pl* : family's heraldic designs

ar·ma·da \är'mädə, -'mäd-\ *n* : naval fleet

ar·ma·dil·lo \₁ärmə'dilō\ *n*, *pl* **-los** : burrowing mammal covered with bony plates

ar·ma·ment \'ärməmənt\ *n* : military arms and equipment

ar·ma·ture \'ärmə₁chur, -chər\ *n* : part in an electric generator or motor in which the current is induced

armed forces *n pl* : military

ar·mi·stice \'ärməstəs\ *n* : truce

ar·mor \'ärmər\ *n* : protective covering —**ar·mored** \-mərd\ *adj*

ar·mory \'ärm(ə)rē\ *n*, *pl* **-mor·ies** : factory or storehouse for arms

arm·pit *n* : hollow under the junction of the arm and shoulder

ar·my \'ärmē\ *n*, *pl* **-mies 1** : body of men organized for war esp. on land **2** : great number

aro·ma \ə'rōmə\ *n* : usu. pleasing odor —**ar·o·mat·ic** \₁arə'matik\ *adj*

around \ə'raund\ *adv* **1** : in or along a circuit **2** : on all sides **3** : near **4** : in

an opposite direction ~ *prep* **1** : surrounding **2** : along the circuit of **3** : to or on the other side of **4** : near

arouse \ə'rauz\ *vb* **aroused; arousing 1** : awaken from sleep **2** : stir up —**arous·al** \-'rauzəl\ *n*

ar·raign \ə'rān\ *vb* **1** : call before a court to answer to an indictment **2** : accuse —**ar·raign·ment** *n*

ar·range \ə'rānj\ *vb* **-ranged; -rang·ing 1** : put in order **2** : settle or agree on **3** : adapt (a musical composition) for voices or instruments —**ar·range·ment** *n* —**ar·rang·er** *n*

ar·ray \ə'rā\ *vb* **1** : arrange in order **2** : dress esp. splendidly ~ *n* **1** : arrangement **2** : rich clothing **3** : imposing group

ar·rears \ə'rirz\ *n pl* : state of being behind in paying debts

ar·rest \ə'rest\ *vb* **1** : stop **2** : take into legal custody —**arrest** *n*

ar·rive \ə'rīv\ *vb* **-rived; -riv·ing 1** : reach a destination, point, or stage **2** : come near in time —**ar·riv·al** \-əl\ *n*

ar·ro·gant \'aragənt\ *adj* : showing an offensive sense of superiority —**ar·ro·gance** \-gəns\ *n* —**ar·ro·gant·ly** *adv*

ar·ro·gate \-₁gāt\ *vb* **-gat·ed; -gat·ing** : to claim without justification

ar·row \'arō\ *n* : slender missile shot from a bow —**ar·row·head** *n*

ar·royo \ə'rȯiə, -ȯ\ *n*, *pl* **-royos 1** : watercourse **2** : gully

ar·se·nal \'ärsnəl, -³nəl\ *n* **1** : place where arms are made or stored **2** : store

ar·se·nic \'ärsnik, -³nik\ *n* : solid gray-ish poisonous chemical element —**ar·sen·i·cal** \är'senikəl\ *adj or n* —**ar·se·ni·ous** \är'sēnēəs\ *adj*

ar·son \'ärs³n\ *n* : malicious burning of property

art \'ärt\ *n* **1** : skill **2** : branch of learning **3** : creation of things of beauty or works so produced **4** : ingenuity

art·ful \-fəl\ *adj* **1** : ingenious **2** : crafty —**art·ful·ly** *adv* —**art·ful·ness** *n*

ar·te·rio·scle·ro·sis \är₁tirēōsklə'rōsəs\ *n* : hardening of the arteries —**ar·te·rio·scle·rot·ic** \-'rätik\ *adj or n*

ar·tery \'ärtərē\ *n*, *pl* **-ter·ies 1** : tubular vessel carrying blood from the heart **2** : thoroughfare —**ar·te·ri·al** \är'tirēəl\ *adj*

ar·thri·tis \är'thrītəs\ *n*, *pl* **-ti·des** \-'thrītə₁dēz\ : inflammation of the joints —**ar·thrit·ic** \-'thritik\ *adj or n*

ar·thro·pod \'ärthrə₁päd\ *n* : invertebrate animal (as an insect or spider) with segmented body and jointed limbs —**arthropod** adj

ar·ti·choke \'ärtə‚chōk\ n : tall thistle-like herb

ar·ti·cle \'ärtikəl\ n 1 : distinct part of a written document 2 : nonfictional published piece of writing 3 : word (as *an, the*) used to limit a noun 4 : item or piece

ar·tic·u·late \är'tikyələt\ adj : able to speak effectively ~ \-‚lāt\ vb -**lat·ed**; -**lat·ing** 1 : utter distinctly 2 : unite by joints —**ar·tic·u·late·ly** adv —**ar·tic·u·late·ness** n —**ar·tic·u·la·tion** \-‚tikyə'lāshən\ n

ar·ti·fact \'ärtə‚fakt\ n : object of human workmanship

ar·ti·fi·cial \‚ärtə'fishəl\ adj 1 : man-made 2 : not genuine —**ar·ti·fi·ci·al·i·ty** \-‚fishē'alətē\ n —**ar·ti·fi·cial·ly** adv —**ar·ti·fi·cial·ness** n

ar·ti·fice \'ärtəfəs\ n 1 : trick or trickery 2 : ingenious device or ingenuity

ar·til·lery \är'til(ə)rē\ n, pl -**ler·ies** : large caliber firearms

ar·ti·san \'ärtəzən, -sən\ n : skilled craftsman

art·ist \'ätəst\ n : one who creates art —**ar·tis·tic** \är'tistik\ adj —**ar·tis·ti·cal·ly** \-ik(ə)lē\ adv —**ar·tis·try** \'ärtəstrē\ n

art·less \'ärtləs\ adj : sincere or natural —**art·less·ly** adv —**art·less·ness** n

arty \'ärtē\ adj art-i-er, -est : pretentiously artistic —**art·i·ly** \'ärtəlē\ adv —**art·i·ness** n

-**ary** \‚erē\ adj suffix : of, relating to, or connected with

as \əz, (‚)az\ adv 1 : to the same degree 2 : for example — conj 1 : in the same way or degree as 2 : while 3 : because 4 : though ~ pron —used after *same* or *such* ~ prep : in the capacity of

as·bes·tos \as'bestəs, az-\ n : fibrous incombustible mineral

as·cend \ə'send\ vb : move upward —**as·cen·sion** \-'senchən\ n

as·cen·dan·cy \ə'sendənsē\ n : domination

as·cen·dant \ə'sendənt\ n : dominant position ~ adj 1 : moving upward 2 : dominant

as·cent \ə'sent\ n 1 : act of moving upward 2 : degree of upward slope

as·cer·tain \asər'tān\ vb : determine —**as·cer·tain·able** adj

as·cet·ic \ə'setik\ adj : self-denying —**ascetic** n —**as·cet·i·cism** \-'setə‚sizəm\ n

as·cribe \ə'skrīb\ vb -**cribed**; -**crib·ing**

: attribute —**as·crib·able** adj —**as·crip·tion** \-'skripshən\ n

asep·tic \ā'septik\ adj : free of disease germs

¹ash \'ash\ n : tree related to the olives

²ash n : matter left when something is burned —**ash·tray** n

ashamed \ə'shāmd\ adj : feeling shame —**asham·ed·ly** \-'shāmədlē\ adv

ash·en \'ashən\ adj : deadly pale

ashore \ə'shōr\ adv : on or to the shore

aside \ə'sīd\ adv 1 : toward the side 2 : out of the way

aside from prep 1 : besides 2 : except for

as·i·nine \'asə‚nīn\ adj : foolish —**as·i·nin·i·ty** \‚asə'ninətē\ n

ask \'ask\ vb **asked** \'as(k)t\; **ask·ing** 1 : call on for an answer or help 2 : utter (a question or request) 3 : invite

askance \ə'skans\ adv 1 : with a side glance 2 : with mistrust

askew \ə'skyü\ adv or adj : out of line

asleep \ə'slēp\ adv or adj 1 : sleeping 2 : numbed 3 : inactive

as long as conj 1 : on condition that 2 : because

as of prep : from the time of

as·par·a·gus \ə'sparəgəs\ n : tall herb related to the lilies or its edible stalks

as·pect \'as‚pekt\ n 1 : way something looks to the eye or mind 2 : phase

as·pen \'aspən\ n : poplar

as·per·i·ty \a'sperətē, ə-\ n, pl -**ties** 1 : roughness 2 : harshness

as·per·sion \ə'spərzhən\ n : remark that hurts someone's reputation

as·phalt \'as‚fólt\, **as·phal·tum** \as'fóltəm\ n : tarlike substance used in paving and in paints —**as·phal·tic** \as'fóltik\ adj

as·phyx·ia \as'fiksēə\ n : lack of oxygen causing unconsciousness

as·phyx·i·ate \-sē‚āt\ vb -**at·ed**; -**at·ing** : suffocate —**as·phyx·i·a·tion** \-‚fiksē'āshən\ n

as·pi·ra·tion \aspə'rāshən\ n : strong desire to achieve a goal

as·pire \ə'spī(ə)r\ vb -**pired**; -**pir·ing** : have an ambition —**as·pi·rant** \'asp(ə)rənt, ə'spīrənt\ n

as·pi·rin \'asp(ə)rən\ n, pl **aspirin** or **aspirins** : pain reliever

ass \'as\ n 1 : long-eared animal related to the horse 2 : stupid person

as·sail \ə'sāl\ vb : attack violently —**as·sail·able** adj —**as·sail·ant** n

as·sas·si·nate \ə'sas(ə)n‚āt\ vb -**nat·ed**; -**nat·ing** : murder esp. for political reasons —**as·sas·sin** \-'sas°n\ n —**as·sas·si·na·tion** \-‚sas°n'āshən\ n

as·sault \ə'sólt\ n or vb : attack

as·say \'as,ā, a'sā\ n : analysis (as of an ore) to determine quality or properties —**as·say** \a'sā, 'as,ā\ vb

as·sem·ble \a'sembal\ vb -bled; -bling -b(a)liŋ\ 1 : collect into one place 2 : fit together the parts

as·sem·bly \-blē\ n, pl -blies 1 : meeting 2 cap : legislative body 3 : a fitting together of parts

as·sem·bly·man \-man\ n : member of a legislative assembly —**as·sem·bly·wom·an** n

as·sent \a'sent\ vb or n : consent

as·sert \a'sart\ vb 1 : declare 2 : defend —**as·ser·tion** \-'sarshan\ n —**as·ser·tive** \-'sartiv\ adj —**as·ser·tive·ness** n

as·sess \a'ses\ vb 1 : impose (as a tax) 2 : evaluate for taxation —**as·sess·ment** n —**as·ses·sor** \-ar\ n

as·set \'as,et\ n 1 pl : individually owned property 2 : advantage or resource

as·sid·u·ous \a'sij(a)was\ adj : diligent —**as·si·du·i·ty** \,asa'd(y)üatē\ n —**as·sid·u·ous·ly** adv —**as·sid·u·ous·ness** n

as·sign \a'sīn\ vb 1 : transfer to another 2 : appoint to a duty 3 : designate as a task 4 : attribute —**as·sign·able** adj —**as·sign·ment** \-mant\ n

as·sim·i·late \a'sima,lāt\ vb -lat·ed; -lat·ing 1 : absorb as nourishment 2 : understand —**as·sim·i·la·tion** \-,simə'lāshən\ n

as·sist \a'sist\ vb : help —**assist** n —**as·sis·tance** \-'sistans\ n —**as·sis·tant** \-tant\ n

as·so·ci·ate \a'sōs(h)ē,āt\ vb -at·ed; -at·ing 1 : join in companionship or partnership 2 : connect in thought —**as·so·ci·ate** \-s(h)ēat, -,shāt\ n —**as·so·ci·a·tion** \-,sōs(h)ē'āshən\ n

as soon as conj : when

as·sort·ed \a'sórtad\ adj : consisting of various kinds

as·sort·ment \-mant\ n : assorted collection

as·suage \a'swāj\ vb -suaged; -suag·ing : ease or satisfy

as·sume \a'süm\ vb -sumed; -sum·ing 1 : take upon oneself 2 : pretend to have 3 : take as granted

as·sump·tion \a'sampshan\ n : something assumed

as·sure \a'shúr\ vb -sured; -sur·ing 1 : give confidence or conviction to 2 : guarantee —**as·sur·ance** \-ans\ n

as·ter \'astar\ n : herb with daisylike flowers

as·ter·isk \'asta,risk\ n : a character * used as a reference mark or as an indication of omission of words

astern \a'starn\ adv or adj 1 : behind 2 : at or toward the stern

as·ter·oid \'asta,róid\ n : one of thousands of small planets between Mars and Jupiter —**as·ter·oi·dal** \,asta'róid°l\ adj

asth·ma \'azma\ n : disorder with a cough and difficulty in breathing —**asth·mat·ic** \az'matik\ adj or n

astig·ma·tism \a'stigma,tizam\ n : visual defect —**as·tig·mat·ic** \,as-tig'matik\ adj

as to prep 1 : concerning 2 : according to

as·ton·ish \a'stänish\ vb : amaze —**as·ton·ish·ing·ly** adv —**as·ton·ish·ment** n

as·tound \a'staúnd\ vb : fill with confused wonder —**as·tound·ing·ly** adv

astrad·dle \a'strad°l\ adv or prep : so as to straddle

as·tral \'astral\ adj : relating to the stars

astray \a'strā\ adv or adj : off the right way

astride \a'strīd\ adv : with legs apart or one on each side ~ prep : with one leg on each side of

as·trin·gent \a'strinjant\ adj : causing shrinking or puckering of tissues —**as·trin·gen·cy** \-jansē\ n —**astringent** n

as·trol·o·gy \a'strälajē\ n : prediction of events by the stars —**as·trol·o·ger** \-ajar\ n —**as·tro·log·i·cal** \,astra'läjikal\ adj

as·tro·naut \'astra,nót\ n : space traveler

as·tro·nau·tics \astra'nótiks\ n : construction and operation of spacecraft —**as·tro·nau·tic** \-ik\, **as·tro·nau·ti·cal** \-ikal\ adj —**as·tro·nau·ti·cal·ly** adv

as·tro·nom·i·cal \,astrə'nämikəl\, **as·tro·nom·ic** \-ik\ adj 1 : relating to astronomy 2 : extremely large

as·tron·o·my \a'stränamē\ n, pl -mies : study of the celestial bodies —**as·tron·o·mer** \-amar\ n

as·tute \a'st(y)üt, a-\ adj : shrewd —**as·tute·ly** adv —**as·tute·ness** n

asun·der \a'sandar\ adv or adj 1 : into separate pieces 2 : separated

asy·lum \a'sīlam\ n 1 : refuge 2 : institution for care esp. of the insane

asym·met·ric \,āsa'metrik\, **asym·met·ri·cal** \-trikal\ adj : not symmetrical —**asym·me·try** \(')ā'simatrē\ n

at \at, 'at\ prep 1 —used to indicate a point in time or space 2 —used to indicate a goal 3 —used to indicate condition, means, cause, or manner

at all \ət'ȯl, ə'tȯl, at'ȯl\ *adv* **1** : without restriction or under any circumstances

ate *past of* EAT

-ate \ət, (,)āt\ *n suffix* **1** : office or rank **2** : group of persons holding an office or rank ~ *adj suffix* **1** : brought into or being in a state **2** : marked by having

athe·ist \'āthēəst\ *n* : one who denies the existence of God —**athe·ism** \-,izəm\ *n* —**athe·is·tic** \,āthē'istik\ *adj*

ath·ero·scle·ro·sis \,athərōsklə'rōsəs\ *n* : arteriosclerosis with deposition of fatty substances in the arteries —**ath·ero·scle·rot·ic** \-'rätik\ *adj*

ath·lete \'ath,lēt\ *n* : one trained to compete in athletics

ath·let·ics \ath'letiks\ *n sing or pl* : exercises and games requiring physical skill —**ath·let·ic** \-ik\ *adj*

-a·tion \'āshən\ *n suffix* : action or process

-a·tive \,ātiv, ətiv\ *adj suffix* **1** : of, relating to, or connected with **2** : tending to

at·las \'atləs\ *n* : book of maps

at·mo·sphere \'atmə,sfiər\ *n* **1** : mass of air surrounding the earth **2** : surrounding influence —**at·mo·spher·ic** \,atmə'sfiərik, -'sfer-\ *adj* —**at·mo·spher·i·cal·ly** \-ik(ə)lē\ *adv*

atoll \'a,tȯl, -,täl, 'ā-\ *n* : ring-shaped coral island

at·om \'atəm\ *n* **1** : tiny bit **2** : smallest particle of a chemical element that can exist alone or in combination

atom bomb *n* : bomb utilizing the energy released by splitting the atom

atom·ic \ə'tämik\ *adj* : relating to atoms, atom bombs, or atomic energy

atomic energy *n* : energy that can be liberated by changes in the nucleus of an atom

at·om·iz·er \'atə,mīzər\ *n* : device for reducing a liquid to a very fine spray

atone \ə'tōn\ *vb* **atoned**; **aton·ing** : make amends —**atone·ment** *n*

atop \ə'täp\ *prep* : on top of

atro·cious \ə'trōshəs\ *adj* : appalling or abominable —**atro·cious·ly** *adv* —**atro·cious·ness** *n*

atroc·i·ty \ə'träsətē\ *n, pl* **-ties** : savage act

at·ro·phy \'atrəfē\ *n, pl* **-phies** : wasting away of a bodily part or tissue —**at·ro·phy** *vb*

at·ro·pine \'atrə,pēn\ *n* : poisonous drug used esp. to relieve spasms

at·tach \ə'tach\ *vb* **1** : seize legally **2** : bind by personalities **3** : join —**at·tach·ment** *n*

at·ta·ché \,atə'shā, ,atə ta-, ə,ta-\ *n* : technical expert on a diplomatic staff

at·tack \ə'tak\ *vb* **1** : try to hurt or destroy with violence or words **2** : set to work on ~ *n* **1** : act of attacking **2** : fit of sickness

at·tain \ə'tān\ *vb* **1** : achieve or accomplish **2** : reach —**at·tain·abil·i·ty** \ə,tānə'bilətē\ *n* —**at·tain·able** *adj* —**at·tain·ment** *n*

at·tempt \ə'tempt\ *vb* : make an effort toward —**attempt** *n*

at·tend \ə'tend\ *vb* **1** : handle or provide for the care of something **2** : accompany **3** : be present at **4** : pay attention —**at·ten·dance** \ə'tendəns\ *n* —**at·ten·dant** \-dənt\ *adj or n*

at·ten·tion \ə'tenchən\ *n* **1** : concentration of the mind on something **2** : notice or awareness —**at·ten·tive** \-'tentiv\ *adj* —**at·ten·tive·ly** *adv* —**at·ten·tive·ness** *n*

at·ten·u·ate \ə'tenyə,wāt\ *vb* **-at·ed**; **-at·ing** **1** : make or become thin **2** : weaken —**at·ten·u·a·tion** \-,tenyə'wāshən\ *n*

at·test \ə'test\ *vb* : certify or bear witness —**at·tes·ta·tion** \,a,tes'tāshən\ *n*

at·tic \'atik\ *n* : space just below the roof

at·tire \ə'tī(ə)r\ *vb* **-tired**; **-tir·ing** : dress —**attire** *n*

at·ti·tude \'atə,t(y)üd\ *n* **1** : posture or relative position **2** : feeling, opinion, or mood

at·tor·ney \ə'tərnē\ *n, pl* **-neys** : legal agent

at·tract \ə'trakt\ *vb* **1** : draw to oneself **2** : have emotional or aesthetic appeal for —**at·trac·tion** \-'trakshən\ *n* —**at·trac·tive** \-'traktiv\ *adj* —**at·trac·tive·ly** *adv* —**at·trac·tive·ness** *n*

at·tri·bute \'atrə,byüt\ *n* : inherent characteristic ~ \ə'tribyət\ *vb* **-trib·ut·ed**; **-ut·ing** **1** : regard as having a specific cause or origin **2** : regard as a characteristic —**at·trib·ut·able** *adj* —**at·tri·bu·tion** \,atrə'byüshən\ *n*

at·tune \ə't(y)ün\ *vb* : bring into harmony

au·burn \'ȯbərn\ *adj* : reddish brown

auc·tion \'ȯkshən\ *n* : public sale of property to the highest bidder —**auction** *vb* —**auc·tion·eer** \,ȯkshə'niər\ *n*

au·dac·i·ty \ȯ'dasətē\ *n* : boldness or insolence —**au·da·cious** \ȯ'dāshəs\ *adj*

au·di·ble \'ȯdəbəl\ adj : capable of being heard —**au·di·bly** \'ȯdəblē\ adv

au·di·ence \'ȯdēəns\ n 1 : formal interview 2 : group of listeners or spectators

au·dio \'ȯdē,ō\ adj : relating to sound or its reproduction ~ n : television sound

au·dio·vi·su·al \,ȯdēō'vizh(ə)wəl\ adj : relating to both hearing and sight

au·dit \'ȯdət\ vb : examine financial accounts —**audit** n —**au·di·tor** \'ȯdətər\ n

au·di·tion \ȯ'dishən\ n : tryout performance —**au·di·tion** vb

au·di·to·ri·um \,ȯdə'tōrēəm\ n : room or building used for public gatherings

au·di·to·ry \'ȯdə,tōrē\ adj : relating to hearing

au·ger \'ȯgər\ n : boring tool

aug·ment \ȯg'ment\ vb : enlarge or increase —**aug·men·ta·tion** \,ȯgmən'tāshən\ n

au·gur \'ȯgər\ n : prophet ~ vb : predict —**au·gu·ry** \'ȯg(y)ərē\ n

au·gust \ȯ'gəst\ adj : majestic

Au·gust \'ȯgəst\ n : 8th month of the year having 31 days

auk \'ȯk\ n : stocky diving seabird

aunt \'ant, 'änt\ n 1 : sister of one's father or mother 2 : wife of one's uncle

au·ra \'ȯrə\ n 1 : distinctive atmosphere 2 : luminous radiation

au·ral \'ȯrəl\ adj : relating to the ear or to hearing

au·ri·cle \'ȯrikəl\ n 1 : external ear 2 : chamber of the heart that receives blood from the veins

au·ro·ra bo·re·al·is \ə,rōrə,bōrē'aləs\ n : display of light in the night sky of northern latitudes that is held to be of electrical origin

aus·pic·es \'ȯspəsəz, -,sēz\ n pl : patronage and protection

aus·pi·cious \ȯ'spishəs\ adj : favorable

aus·tere \ȯ'stiər\ adj : severe —**aus·tere·ly** adv —**aus·ter·i·ty** \ȯ'sterətē\ n

au·then·tic \ə'thentik, ȯ-\ adj : genuine —**au·then·ti·cal·ly** \-ik(ə)lē\ adv —**au·then·tic·i·ty** \,ȯ,then'tisətē\ n

au·then·ti·cate \ə'thenti,kāt, ȯ-\ vb -**cat·ed; -cat·ing** : prove genuine —**au·then·ti·ca·tion** \-,thenti'kāshən\ n

au·thor \'ȯthər\ n 1 : writer 2 : creator —**au·thor·ess** \-th(ə)rəs\ n —**au·thor·ship** n

au·thor·i·tar·i·an \ə,thȯra'terēən, ə-,

-,thȯr-\ adj : marked by blind obedience to authority

au·thor·i·ta·tive \ə'thȯrə,tātiv, ȯ-, -'thȯr-\ adj : being an authority —**au·thor·i·ta·tive·ly** adv

au·thor·i·ty \ə'thȯrətē, ȯ-, -'thȯr-\ n, pl -**ties** 1 : expert 2 : right, responsibility, or power to influence 3 pl : persons in official positions

au·tho·rize \'ȯthə,rīz\ vb -**rized; -riz·ing** : permit or give official approval for —**au·tho·ri·za·tion** \,ȯth(ə)rə'zāshən\ n

au·to \'ȯtō\ n, pl **autos** : automobile

au·to·bi·og·ra·phy \,ȯtə(,)bī'ägrəfē, -bē-\ n : writer's own life story —**au·to·bi·og·ra·pher** \-fər\ n —**au·to·bi·o·graph·i·cal** \-,bīə'grafikəl\ adj

au·toc·ra·cy \ȯ'täkrəsē\ n, pl -**cies** : government by one person having unlimited power —**au·to·crat** \'ȯtə,krat\ n —**au·to·crat·ic** \,ȯtə'kratik\ adj —**au·to·crat·i·cal·ly** \-ik(ə)lē\ adv

au·to·graph \'ȯtə,graf\ n : signature ~ vb : write one's name on

au·to·mate \'ȯtə,māt\ vb -**mat·ed; -mat·ing** : make automatic —**au·to·ma·tion** \,ȯtə'māshən\ n

au·to·mat·ic \,ȯtə'matik\ adj 1 : involuntary 2 : designed to function without human intervention ~ n : automatic device (as a firearm) —**au·to·mat·i·cal·ly** \-ik(ə)lē\ adv

au·tom·a·ton \ȯ'tämətən, -ə',tän\ n, pl -**atons** or **-a·ta** \-ətə, -ə',tä\ : robot

au·to·mo·bile \,ȯtəmō'bēl, -'mō,bēl\ n : 4-wheeled passenger vehicle with its own power source —**au·to·mo·bil·ist** \-'bēləst, -,bē-\ n

au·to·mo·tive \,ȯtə'mōtiv\ adj : relating to automobiles

au·ton·o·mous \ȯ'tänəməs\ adj : self-governing —**au·ton·o·mous·ly** adv —**au·ton·o·my** \-mē\ n

au·top·sy \'ȯ,täpsē, 'ȯtəp-\ n, pl -**sies** : medical examination of a corpse

au·tumn \'ȯtəm\ n : season between summer and winter —**au·tum·nal** \ȯ'təmnəl\ adj

aux·il·ia·ry \ȯg'zilyərē, -'zil(ə)rē\ adj 1 : being a supplement or reserve 2 : accompanying a main verb form to express person, number, mood, or tense —**auxiliary** n

avail \ə'vāl\ vb : be of use or make use ~ n : use

avail·able \ə'vāləbəl\ adj 1 : usable 2 : accessible —**avail·abil·i·ty** \-,vālə'bilətē\ n

av·a·lanche \'avə,lanch\ n : mass of sliding or falling snow or rock

av·a·rice \'av(ə)rəs\ n : greed — **av·a·ri·cious** \ˌavə'rishəs\ adj

avenge \ə'venj\ vb **avenged; aveng·ing** : take vengeance for — **aveng·er** n

av·e·nue \'avəˌn(y)ü\ n 1 : way of approach 2 : broad street

av·er·age \'av(ə)rij\ adj 1 : being about midway between extremes 2 : ordinary ~ vb 1 : be usually 2 : find the mean of ~ n : mean

averse \ə'vərs\ adj : feeling dislike or reluctance — **aver·sion** \-'vərzhən\ n

avert \ə'vərt\ vb : turn away

avi·ary \'āvēˌerē\ n, pl **-ar·ies** : place where birds are kept

avi·a·tion \ˌāvē'āshən, ˌavē-\ n : operation or manufacture of airplanes — **avi·a·tor** \'āvēˌātər, 'avē-\ n

av·id \'avəd\ adj 1 : greedy 2 : enthusiastic — **avid·i·ty** \ə'vidətē, a-\ n — **av·id·ly** adv

av·o·ca·do \ˌavə'kädō, ˌäv-\ n, pl **-dos** : tropical fruit

av·o·ca·tion \ˌavə'kāshən\ n : hobby

avoid \ə'vȯid\ vb 1 : keep away from 2 : prevent the occurrence of 3 : refrain from — **avoid·able** adj — **avoid·ance** \-ᵊns\ n

av·oir·du·pois \ˌavərdə'pȯiz\ n : system of weight, based on the pound of 16 ounces

avow \ə'vau̇\ vb : declare openly — **avow·al** \-'vau̇(ə)l\ n

await \ə'wāt\ vb : wait for

awake \ə'wāk\ vb **awoke** \-'wōk\ or **awaked; awaked** or **awoke** or **awok·en** \-'wōkən\; **awak·ing** : wake up — **awake** adj

awak·en \ə'wākən\ vb **-ened; -en·ing** : wake up

award \ə'wȯrd\ vb : give (something

won or deserved) ~ n 1 : judgment 2 : prize

aware \ə'waər\ adj : having realization or consciousness — **aware·ness** n

awash \ə'wȯsh, -'wȧsh\ adv or adj : flooded

away \ə'wā\ adv 1 : from this or that place or time 2 : out of the way 3 : in another direction 4 : from one's possession ~ adj 1 : absent 2 : distant

awe \'ȯ\ n 1 : respectful fear or wonder ~ vb : awed; aw·ing : fill with awe — **awe·some** \-səm\ adj — **awe·struck** adj

aw·ful \'ȯfəl\ adj 1 : inspiring awe 2 : extremely disagreeable 3 : very great — **aw·ful·ly** adv

awhile \ə'hwīl\ adv : for a while

awk·ward \'ȯkwərd\ adj 1 : clumsy 2 : embarrassing — **awk·ward·ly** adv — **awk·ward·ness** n

awl \'ȯl\ n : hole-making tool

aw·ning \'ȯniŋ\ n : window cover

awry \ə'rī\ adv or adj : wrong

ax, axe \'aks\ n : chopping tool

ax·i·om \'aksēəm\ n : generally accepted truth — **ax·i·om·at·ic** \ˌaksēə'matik\ adj

ax·is \'aksəs\ n, pl **ax·es** \-ˌsēz\ : center of rotation — **ax·i·al** \-sēəl\ adj — **ax·i·al·ly** adv

ax·le \'aksəl\ n : shaft on which a wheel revolves

aye \'ī\ n : yes ~ n : a vote of yes

aza·lea \ə'zālyə\ n : rhododendron with funnel-shaped blossoms

az·i·muth \'az(ə)məth\ n 1 : arc measured along the horizon 2 : horizontal direction — **az·i·muth·al** \ˌazə'məthəl\ adj

azure \'azhər\ n : blue of the sky — **azure** adj

B

b \'bē\ n, pl **b's** or **bs** \'bēz\ : 2d letter of the alphabet

bab·ble \'babəl\ vb **-bled; -bling** 1 : utter meaningless sounds 2 : talk foolishly or too much — **babble** n — **bab·bler** n

babe \'bāb\ n : baby

ba·bel \'bābəl, 'bab-\ n : noisy confusion

ba·boon \ba'bün\ n : large Asian or African ape with a doglike muzzle

ba·by \'bābē\ n, pl **-bies** : very young child ~ vb **-bied; -by·ing** : pamper — **baby** adj — **ba·by·hood** n — **ba·by·ish** adj

ba·by-sit vb **-sat; -sit·ting** : care for children while parents are away — **ba·by-sit·ter** n

bac·ca·lau·re·ate \ˌbakə'lȯrēət\ n : bachelor's degree

bac·cha·na·lia \ˌbakə'nālyə\ n, pl **-lia** : drunken orgy — **bac·cha·na·lian** \-yən\ adj or n

bach·e·lor \'bach(ə)lər\ n 1 : holder of lowest 4-year college degree 2 : unmarried man — **bach·e·lor·hood** n

ba·cil·lus \bə'siləs\ n, pl **-li** \-ˌlī\ : rod-shaped bacterium — **bac·il·lary** \'basəˌlerē\ adj

back \'bak\ n 1 : part of a human or

animal body nearest the spine **2** : part opposite the front **3** : player farthest from the opponent's goal ~ *adv* **1** : to or at the back **2** : ago **3** : to or in a former place or state **4** : in reply ~ *adj* **1** : located at the back **2** : not paid on time **3** : moving or working backward ~ *vb* **1** : support **2** : go or cause to go back **3** : form the back of —**back-ache** *n* —**back-er** *n* —**back-ing** *n* —**back-less** *adj* —**back-rest** *n*

back-bite *vb* **-bit; -bit-ten; -bit-ing** : say spiteful things about someone absent —**back-bit-er** *n*

back-bone *n* **1** : bony column in the back that encloses the spinal cord **2** : firm character

back-drop *n* : painted cloth hung across the rear of a stage

back-fire *n* : explosion in the intake or exhaust passages of an internal-combustion engine —**back-fire** *vb*

back-gam-mon \'bak,gamən\ *n* : board game

back-ground *n* **1** : scenery behind something **2** : sum of a person's experience or training

back-hand *n* : stroke (as in tennis) made with the back of the hand turned forward —**backhand** *adj or vb* —**back-hand-ed** *adj*

back-lash *n* : adverse reaction —**back-lash-er** *n*

back-log *n* **1** : reserve of unfilled orders **2** : accumulation of things to be done —**backlog** *vb*

back-pack *n* : camping pack carried on the back ~ *vb* : hike with a backpack —**back-pack-er** *n*

back-slide *vb* **-slid; -slid** *or* **-slid-den** \-,slidⁿn\; **-slid-ing** : lapse in morals or religious practice —**back-slid-er** *n*

back-stage *adv or adj* : in or to an area behind a stage

back-up *n* : substitute

back-ward \'bakwərd\, **back-wards** *adv* **1** : toward the back **2** : with the back foremost **3** : in a reverse direction **4** : toward an earlier or worse state ~ *adj* **1** : directed, turned, or done backward **2** : retarded in development —**back-ward-ness** *n*

back-woods *n pl* : remote or isolated place

ba-con \'bākən\ *n* : salted and smoked meat from a pig

bac-te-ri-um \bak'tirēəm\ *n, pl* **-ria** \-ēə\ : microscopic plant —**bac-te-ri-al** \-ēəl\ *adj* —**bac-te-ri-o-log-ic** \-,tirēə'läjik\, **bac-te-ri-o-log-i-cal** \-əl\ *adj* —**bac-te-ri-ol-o-gist**

\-ē'äləjəst\ *n* —**bac-te-ri-ol-o-gy** \-jē\ *n*

bad \'bad\ *adj* **worse** \'wərs\; **worst** \'wərst\ **1** : not good **2** : naughty **3** : faulty **4** : spoiled —**bad** *n or adv* —**bad-ly** *adv* —**bad-ness** *n*

bade *past of* BID

badge \'baj\ *n* : symbol of status

bad-ger \'bajər\ *n* : burrowing mammal with long claws on the forefeet ~ *vb* **-gered; -ger-ing** : harass

bad-min-ton \'bad,mintⁿn\ *n* : tennis-like game played with a shuttlecock

baf-fle \'bafəl\ *vb* **-fled; -fling** : perplex ~ *n* : device to alter flow (as of liquid or sound)

bag \'bag\ *n* : flexible usu. closable container ~ *vb* **-gg-** **1** : bulge out **2** : put in a bag **3** : catch in hunting

bag-a-telle \,bagə'tel\ *n* : trifle

ba-gel \'bāgəl\ *n* : hard doughnut-shaped roll

bag-gage \'bagij\ *n* : traveler's bags and belongings

bag-gy \'bagē\ *adj* **-gi-er; -est** : puffed out like a bag —**bag-gi-ly** *adv* —**bag-gi-ness** *n*

bag-pipe *n* : musical instrument with a bag, a tube with valves, and sounding pipes —often *pl.*

1bail \'bāl\ *n* **1** : security given to guarantee a prisoner's appearance in court **2** : release secured by bail ~ *vb* : bring about the release of by giving bail —**bail-able** *adj* —**bails-man** \'bālzmən\ *n*

2bail *n* : container for scooping water out of a boat —**bail** *vb*

bai-liff \'bāləf\ *n* **1** : a British sheriff's aide **2** : minor officer of a U.S. court

bai-li-wick \'bāli,wik\ *n* : one's special field or domain

bait \'bāt\ *vb* **1** : harass with dogs usu. for sport **2** : furnish (a hook or trap) with bait ~ *n* : lure esp. for catching animals

bake \'bāk\ *vb* **baked; bak-ing** : cook in dry heat esp. in an oven ~ *n* : party featuring baked food —**bak-er** *n* —**bak-ery** \'bāk(ə)rē\ *n* —**bake-shop** *n*

bal-ance \'baləns\ *n* **1** : weighing device **2** : counter-acting weight, force, or influence **3** : equilibrium **4** : that which remains ~ *vb* **-anced; -anc-ing** **1** : compute the balance **2** : equalize **3** : bring into harmony or proportion —**bal-anced** *adj*

bal-co-ny \'balkənē\ *n, pl* **-nies** : platform projecting from a wall

bald \'bold\ *adj* **1** : lacking a natural or

usual covering (as of hair) **2** : plain —**bald·ing** adj —**bald·ly** adv

bal·der·dash \'bȯldər,dash\ n : nonsense

bale \'bāl\ n : large bundle ~ vb **baled**; **bal·ing** : pack in a bale —**bal·er** n

bale·ful \'bālfəl\ adj **1** : deadly **2** : ominous

balk \'bȯk\ n : hindrance ~ vb **1** : thwart **2** : stop short and refuse to go on —**balky** adj

¹ball \'bȯl\ n **1** : rounded mass **2** : game played with a ball ~ vb : form into a ball

²ball n : large formal dance —**ball·room** n

bal·lad \'baləd\ n **1** : narrative poem **2** : slow romantic song —**bal·lad·eer** \,balə'di(ə)r\ n

bal·last \'baləst\ n : heavy material to steady a ship or balloon ~ vb : provide with ballast

bal·le·ri·na \,balə'rēnə\ n : female ballet dancer

bal·let \'ba,lā; ba'lā\ n : theatrical dancing

bal·lis·tics \bə'listiks\ n sing or pl : science of projectile motion —**ballistic** adj

bal·loon \bə'lün\ n : inflated bag ~ vb **1** : travel in a balloon **2** : swell out —**bal·loon·ist** n

bal·lot \'balət\ n **1** : paper used to cast a vote **2** : system of voting ~ vb : vote

bal·ly·hoo \'balē,hü\ n : publicity —**ballyhoo** vb

balm \'bäm, 'bälm\ n **1** : fragrant healing or soothing preparation **2** : spicy fragrant herb

balmy \'bämē, 'bälmē\ adj **balm·i·er**; **-est** : gently soothing —**balm·i·ness** n

ba·lo·ney \bə'lōnē\ n : nonsense

bal·sa \'bȯlsə\ n : very light wood of a tropical tree

bal·sam \-səm\ n **1** : aromatic resinous plant substance **2** : balsam-yielding plant

bal·us·ter \'baləstər\ n : upright support of a rail

bal·us·trade \-,strād\ n : row of balusters topped by a rail

bam·boo \bam'bü\ n : tall tropical grass with strong hollow stems

bam·boo·zle \bam'büzəl\ vb **-zled**; **-zling** : deceive

ban \'ban\ vb **-nn-** : prohibit ~ n : legal prohibition

ba·nal \bə'näl, -'nal; 'bān⁹l\ adj : ordinary and uninteresting —**ba·nal·i·ty** \bə'nal·at·ē\ n

ba·nana \bə'nanə\ n : elongated fruit

of a treelike tropical plant or the plant itself

¹band \'band\ n **1** : something that constrains or restrains **2** : strip that brings or holds together **3** : range of radio wavelengths ~ vb **1** : enclose with a band **2** : unite for a common end —**band·ed** adj —**band·er** n

²band n **1** : group **2** : musicians playing together

ban·dage \'bandij\ n : material used esp. in dressing wounds ~ vb : dress or cover with a bandage

ban·dan·na, ban·dana \ban'danə\ n : large colored figured handkerchief

ban·dit \'bandət\ n : outlaw or robber —**ban·dit·ry** \-dətrē\ n

band·stand n : stage for band concerts

band·wag·on n : candidate, side, or movement gaining support

¹han·dy \'bandē\ vb **-died**; **-dy·ing** : exchange in rapid succession

²bandy adj : curved outward

bane \'bān\ n **1** : poison **2** : cause of woe —**bane·ful** adj

¹bang \'baŋ\ vb : strike, thrust, or move usu. with a loud noise ~ n **1** : blow **2** : sudden loud noise ~ adv : directly

²bang n : fringe of short hair over the forehead —usu. pl. ~ vb : cut in bangs

ban·gle \'baŋgəl\ n : bracelet

ban·ish \'banish\ vb **1** : force by authority to leave a country **2** : expel —**ban·ish·ment** n

ban·is·ter \-əstər\ n : upright support of a staircase handrail or the handrail itself

ban·jo \-,jō\ n, pl **-jos** : stringed instrument with a drumlike body —**ban·jo·ist** n

¹bank \'baŋk\ n **1** : piled-up mass **2** : rising ground along a body of water **3** : sideways slope along a curve ~ vb **1** : form a bank **2** : cover (as a fire) to keep inactive **3** : incline (an airplane) laterally

²bank n : tier of objects

³bank n **1** : money institution **2** : reserve supply ~ vb : conduct business in a bank —**bank·book** n —**bank·er** n —**bank·ing** n

bank·rupt \-(,)rəpt\ n : one required by law to forfeit assets to pay off debts ~ adj **1** : legally a bankrupt **2** : lacking something essential —**bankrupt** vb —**bank·rupt·cy** \-(,)rəp(t)sē\ n

ban·ner \'banər\ n : flag — adj : excellent

banns \'banz\ n pl : announcement in church of a proposed marriage

ban·quet \'baŋkwət\ *n* : ceremonial dinner —**banquet** *vb*

ban·shee \'banshē\ *n* : wailing female spirit that foretells death

ban·tam \'bantəm\ *n* : miniature domestic fowl

ban·ter \-ər\ *n* : good-natured joking —**banter** *vb*

ban·yan \'banyən\ *n* : large tree that grows new trunks from the limbs

bap·tism \'bap,tizəm\ *n* : Christian rite signifying spiritual cleansing —**bap·tis·mal** \bap'tizməl\ *adj*

bap·tize \bap'tīz, 'bap,tīz\ *vb* -**tized**; -**tiz·ing** : administer baptism to

bar \'bär\ *n* **1** : long narrow object used esp. as a lever, fastening, or support **2** : barrier **3** : body of practicing lawyers **4** : wide stripe **5** : food counter **6** : place where liquor is served **7** : vertical line across the musical staff ~ *vb* -**rr-** **1** : obstruct with a bar **2** : shut out **3** : prohibit ~ *prep* : excluding —**barred** *adj* —**bar·room** *n* —**bar·tend·er** *n*

barb \'bärb\ *n* : sharp projection pointing backward —**barbed** *adj*

bar·bar·i·an \bär'berēən\ *adj* **1** : relating to people considered backward **2** : not refined —**barbarian** *n*

bar·bar·ic \-'barik\ *adj* : barbarian

bar·ba·rous \'bärb(ə)rəs\ *adj* **1** : lacking refinement **2** : mercilessly cruel —**bar·ba·rism** \-bə,rizəm\ *n* —**bar·bar·i·ty** \bär'barətē\ *n* —**bar·ba·rous·ly** *adv*

bar·be·cue \'bärbi,kyü\ *n* : gathering at which barbecued food is served ~ *vb* -**cued**; -**cu·ing** : cook over hot coals or on a spit often with a highly seasoned sauce

bar·ber \'bärbər\ *n* : one who cuts hair

bar·bi·tu·rate \bär'bichərət\ *n* : chemical used as a sedative or hypnotic

bard \'bärd\ *n* : poet

bare \'baər\ *adj* **bar·er**; **bar·est** **1** : naked **2** : not concealed **3** : empty **4** : leaving nothing to spare **5** : plain ~ *vb* **bared**; **bar·ing** : make or lay bare —**bare·foot**, **bare·foot·ed** *adv* or *adj* —**bare·hand·ed** *adv* or *adj* —**bare·head·ed** *adv* or *adj* —**bare·ly** *adv* —**bare·ness** *n*

bare·backed, **bare·backed** *adv* or *adj* : without a saddle

bare·faced *adj* : open and esp. brazen

bar·gain \'bärgən\ *n* **1** : agreement **2** : something bought for less than its value ~ *vb* **1** : negotiate **2** : barter

barge \'bärj\ *n* : broad flat-bottomed boat ~ *vb* **barged**; **barg·ing** : move rudely or clumsily —**barge·man** *n*

bari·tone \'barə,tōn\ *n* : male voice between bass and tenor

bar·i·um \'barēəm\ *n* : silver-white metallic chemical element

¹bark \'bärk\ *vb* **1** : make the sound of a dog **2** : speak in a loud curt tone ~ *n* : sound of a barking dog

²bark *n* : tough corky outer covering of a woody stem or root ~ *vb* : remove bark or skin from

³bark *n* : 3-masted ship

bark·er \'bärkər\ *n* : one who calls out to attract people to a sideshow

bar·ley \-lē\ *n* : cereal grass or its seeds

barn \'bärn\ *n* : building for keeping hay or livestock —**barn·yard** *n*

bar·na·cle \'bärnikəl\ *n* : marine crustacean

barn·storm *vb* : tour through rural districts giving performances

ba·rom·e·ter \bə'rämətər\ *n* : instrument for measuring atmospheric pressure —**baro·met·ric** \,barə'metrik\, **baro·met·ri·cal** \-əl\ *adj*

bar·on \'barən\ *n* : British peer —**bar·on·age** \-ij\ *n* —**ba·ro·ni·al** \bə'rōnēəl\ *adj* —**bar·ony** \'barənē\ *n*

bar·on·ess \-ənəs\ *n* **1** : baron's wife **2** : woman holding a baronial title

bar·on·et \-ənət\ *n* : man holding a rank between a baron and a knight —**bar·on·et·cy** \-sē\ *n*

ba·roque \bə'rōk, -'räk\ *adj* : elaborately ornamented

bar·racks \'barəks\ *n sing or pl* : soldiers' housing

bar·ra·cu·da \,barə'küdə\ *n*, *pl* -**da** *or* -**das** : large predatory sea fish

bar·rage \bə'räzh, -'räj\ *n* : heavy artillery fire

bar·rel \'barəl\ *n* **1** : closed cylindrical container **2** : amount held by a barrel **3** : cylindrical part ~ *vb* -**reled** *or* -**relled**; -**rel·ing** *or* -**rel·ling** : pack in a barrel —**bar·reled** *adj*

bar·ren \'barən\ *adj* **1** : unproductive of life **2** : uninteresting —**bar·ren·ness** \-ənnəs\ *n*

bar·rette \bä'ret, bə-\ *n* : clasp for a woman's hair

bar·ri·cade \,barə,kād, ,barə'-\ *n* : barrier —**barricade** *vb*

bar·ri·er \'barēər\ *n* : something that separates or obstructs

bar·ring \'bariŋ\ *prep* : omitting

bar·ris·ter \'barəstər\ *n* : British trial lawyer

bar·row \'barō\ *n* : wheelbarrow

bar·ter \'bärtər\ *vb* : trade by exchange of goods —**barter** *n*

ba·salt \bə'sȯlt, 'bā,-\ *n* : dark fine-grained igneous rock —**ba·sal·tic** \bə'soltik\ adj

¹base \'bās\ n, pl **bas·es 1** : bottom **2** : fundamental part **3** : beginning point **4** : supply source of a force **5** : compound that reacts with an acid to form a salt ~ vb **based; bas·ing** : establish —**base·less** adj

²base adj **bas·er; bas·est 1** : inferior **2** : contemptible —**base·ly** adv —**base·ness** n

base·ball n : game played with a bat and ball by 2 teams

base·ment \-mənt\ n : part of a building below ground level

bash \'bash\ vb : strike violently ~ n : heavy blow

bash·ful \-fəl\ adj : self-conscious —**bash·ful·ness** n

ba·sic \'bāsik\ adj **1** : relating to or forming the base or essence **2** : relating to a chemical base —**ba·si·cal·ly** adv —**ba·sic·i·ty** \bā'sisətē\ n

ba·sil \'bazəl, 'bās-\ n : aromatic mint

ba·sil·i·ca \bə'silikə\ n : church or cathedral of high rank

ba·sin \'bās⁰n\ n **1** : large bowl or pan **2** : depression containing a pond or lake **3** : region drained by a river

ba·sis \'bāsəs\ n, pl **ba·ses** \-ˌsēz\ **1** : something that supports **2** : fundamental principle

bask \'bask\ vb : enjoy pleasant warmth

bas·ket \-ət\ n : woven container —**bas·ket·ful** n

bas·ket·ball n : game played with a ball on a court by 2 teams

bas-re·lief \ˌbäri'lēf\ n : flat sculpture with slightly raised design

¹bass \'bas\ n, pl **bass** or **bass·es** : spiny-finned sport and food fish

²bass \'bās\ n **1** : deep tone **2** : lowest male voice

bas·set hound \'basət-\ n : short-legged dog with long ears

bas·si·net \ˌbasə'net\ n : baby's bed

bas·soon \bə'sün, ba-\ n : low-pitched wind instrument

bas·tard \'bastərd\ n **1** : illegitimate child **2** : offensive person ~ adj **1** : illegitimate **2** : inferior —**bas·tard·ize** vb —**bas·tardy** n

¹baste \'bāst\ vb **bast·ed; bast·ing** : sew temporarily with long stitches

²baste vb **bast·ed; bast·ing** : moisten with liquid at intervals while cooking

bas·tion \'baschən\ n : fortified position —**bas·tioned** adj

¹bat \'bat\ n **1** : stick or club **2** : sharp blow ~ vb **-tt-** : hit with a bat

²bat n : small flying mammal

³bat vb **-tt-** : wink or blink

batch \'bach\ n : quantity used or produced at one time

bate \'bāt\ vb **bat·ed; bat·ing** : moderate or reduce

bath \'bath, 'bäth\ n, pl **baths** \'bathz, 'baths, 'bäthz, 'bäths\ **1** : a washing of the body **2** : water for washing the body **3** : liquid in which something is immersed **4** : bathroom —**bath·tub** n

bathe \'bāth\ vb **bathed; bath·ing 1** : wash in liquid **2** : flow against so as to wet **3** : shine light over **4** : take a bath or a swim —**bath·er** n

bath·robe n : robe worn around the house

bath·room n : room with a bathtub or shower and usu. a washbowl and toilet

ba·tiste \bə'tēst\ n : fine sheer fabric

ba·ton \bə'tän\ n : musical conductor's stick

bat·tal·ion \bə'talyən\ n : military unit composed of a headquarters and two or more companies

bat·ten \'bat⁰n\ n : strip of wood used to seal or reinforce ~ vb : furnish or fasten with battens

¹bat·ter \-ər\ vb : beat or damage with repeated blows

²batter n : mixture of flour and liquid

³batter n : player who bats

bat·tery \'bat(ə)rē\ n, pl **-ter·ies 1** : illegal beating of a person **2** : group of artillery guns **3** : group of electric cells

bat·ting \-iŋ\ n : layers of cotton or wool for stuffing

bat·tle \-⁰l\ n : military fighting ~ vb **-tled; -tling** : engage in battle —**bat·tle·field** n

bat·tle-ax n : long-handled ax formerly used as a weapon

bat·tle·ment \-mənt\ n : parapet on top of a wall

bat·tle·ship n : heavily armed warship

bat·ty \-ē\ adj **-ti·er; -est** : crazy

bau·ble \'böbəl\ n : trinket

bawdy \'bódē\ adj **bawd·i·er; -est** : obscene or lewd —**bawd·i·ly** adv —**bawd·i·ness** n

bawl \'böl\ vb : cry loudly ~ n : long loud cry

¹bay \'bā\ adj : reddish brown ~ n : bay-colored animal

²bay n : European laurel

³bay n **1** : compartment **2** : area projecting out from a building and containing a window (**bay window**)

⁴bay vb : bark with deep long tones ~ n **1** : position of one unable to escape danger **2** : baying of dogs

⁵bay n : body of water smaller than a gulf that is nearly surrounded by land

bay-ber-ry \-₁berē\ n : shrub bearing small waxy berries

bay-o-net \'bāənət, ₁bāə'net\ n : dagger that fits on the end of a rifle ~ vb **-net-ed; -net-ing** : stab with a bayonet

bay-ou \'bīō, -ü\ n : creek flowing through marshy land

ba-zaar \bə'zär\ n 1 : market 2 : fair for charity

ba-zoo-ka \-'zükə\ n : weapon that shoots armor-piercing rockets

BB n : small shot pellet

be \(')bē\ vb **was** \(')wəz, 'wäz\, **were** \(')wər\; **been** \(')bin\; **be-ing** \'bēiŋ\; **am** \əm, 'am\, **is** \(')iz, əz\, **are** \ər, (')är\ **1** : equal 2 : exist 3 : occupy a certain place 4 : occur ~ verbal auxiliary —used to show continuous action or to form the passive voice

beach \'bēch\ n : shore of a sea, lake, or river ~ vb : drive ashore

beach-comb-er \-₁kōmər\ n : one who searches the shore for useful objects

beach-head n : shore area held by an attacking force

bea-con \'bēkən\ n : guiding or warning light or signal —**beacon** vb

bead \'bēd\ n : small round body esp. strung on a thread ~ vb : form into a bead —**bead-ing** n —**beady** adj

bea-gle \'bēgəl\ n : small short-legged hound

beak \'bēk\ n : bill of a bird —**beaked** adj

bea-ker \'bēkər\ n 1 : large drinking cup 2 : laboratory vessel

beam \'bēm\ n 1 : large long piece of timber or metal 2 : ray of light 3 : directed radio signals for the guidance of pilots ~ vb 1 : send out light 2 : smile 3 : aim a radio broadcast

bean \'bēn\ n : edible plant seed borne in pods

¹bear \'baər\ n, pl **bears** 1 or **bear** : large heavy mammal with shaggy hair 2 : gruff or sullen person —**bear-ish** adj

²bear vb **bore** \'bōr\; **borne** \'bōrn\; **bear-ing** 1 : carry 2 : give birth to or produce 3 : endure 4 : press —**bear-able** adj —**bear-er** n

beard \'biərd\ n 1 : facial hair on a man 2 : tuft like a beard ~ vb : confront boldly —**beard-ed** adj —**beard-less** adj

bear-ing n 1 : way of carrying oneself 2 : supporting object or purpose 3

: significance 4 : machine part in which another part turns 5 : direction with respect to compass points

beast \'bēst\ n 1 : animal 2 : brutal person —**beast-li-ness** n —**beast-ly** adj

beat \'bēt\ vb **beat; beat-en** \'bēt⁲n\ or **beat; beat-ing** 1 : strike repeatedly 2 : defeat 3 : act or arrive before 4 : throb ~ n 1 : single stroke or pulsation 2 : rhythmic stress in poetry or music —adj : exhausted —**beat-er** n

be-atif-ic \₁bēə'tifik\ adj : blissful

be-at-i-fy \bē'atə₁fī\ vb **-fied; -fy-ing** : make happy or blessed —**be-at-i-fi-ca-tion** \-₁atəfə'kāshən\ n

be-at-i-tude \-'atə₁t(y)üd\ n : saying in the Sermon on the Mount (Matthew 5:3-12) beginning "Blessed are"

beau \'bō\ n, pl **beaux** \'bōz\ or **beaus** : suitor

beau-ty \'byütē\ n, pl **-ties** : qualities that please the senses or mind —**beau-te-ous** \-ēəs\ adj —**beau-te-ous-ly** adv —**beau-ti-fi-ca-tion** \₁byütəfə'kāshən\ n —**beau-ti-fi-er** \'byütə₁fīər\ n —**beau-ti-ful** \-ifəl\ adj —**beau-ti-ful-ly** adv —**beau-ti-fy** \-ə₁fī\ vb

bea-ver \'bēvər\ n : large fur-bearing rodent

be-cause \bi'kóz, -'kəz\ conj : for the reason that

because of prep : by reason of

beck \'bek\ n : summons

beck-on \-ən\ vb : summon esp. by a nod or gesture

be-come \bi'kəm\ vb **-came** \-'kām\; **-come; -com-ing** 1 : come to be 2 : be suitable —**be-com-ing** adj —**be-com-ing-ly** adv

bed \'bed\ n 1 : piece of furniture to sleep on 2 : flat or level surface ~ vb **-dd-** : put or go to bed —**bed-spread** n

bed-bug n : wingless bloodsucking insect

bed-clothes n pl : bedding

bed-ding n 1 : sheets and blankets for a bed 2 : soft material (as hay) for an animal's bed

be-deck \bi'dek\ vb : adorn

be-dev-il \-'devəl\ vb : harass

bed-lam \'bedləm\ n : uproar and confusion

be-drag-gled \bi'dragəld\ adj : dirty and disordered

bed-rid-den \'bed₁rid³n\ adj : kept in bed by illness

bed-rock n : solid subsurface rock —**bedrock** adj

bee \'bē\ *n* **1** : 4-winged honey-producing insect **2** : neighborly work session —**bee·hive** *n* —**bee·keep·er** *n* —**bees·wax** *n*

beech \'bēch\ *n, pl* **beech·es** *or* **beech** : tree with smooth gray bark and edible nuts (**beech·nuts**) —**beech·en** \-ən\ *adj*

beef \'bēf\ *n, pl* **beefs** \'bēfs\ *or* **beeves** \'bēvz\ : flesh of a steer, cow, or bull ~ *vb* : strengthen —used with *up* —**beef·steak** *n*

bee·line *n* : straight course

been *past part of* BE

beer \'bir\ *n* : alcoholic drink brewed from malt and hops —**beery** *adj*

beet \'bēt\ *n* : garden root vegetable

bee·tle \'bētəl\ *n* : 4-winged insect

be·fall \bi'fol\ *vb* -**fell**; -**fall·en** : happen to

be·fit \bi'fit\ *vb* : be suitable to

be·fore \bi'fōr\ *adv* **1** : in front **2** : earlier ~ *prep* **1** : in front of **2** : earlier than ~ *conj* : earlier than

be·fore·hand *adv or adj* : in advance

be·friend \bi'frend\ *vb* : act as friend to

be·fud·dle \-'fədəl\ *vb* : confuse

beg \'beg\ *vb* -**gg**- : ask earnestly

be·get \bi'get\ *vb* -**got**; -**got·ten** *or* -**got**; -**get·ting** : produce (offspring) as a father

beg·gar \'begər\ *n* : one that begs ~ *vb* : make poor —**beg·gar·ly** *adj* —**beg·gary** *n*

be·gin \bi'gin\ *vb* -**gan** \-'gan\; -**gun** \-'gən\; -**gin·ning** **1** : start **2** : come into being —**be·gin·ner** *n*

be·gone \bi'gon\ *vb* : go away

be·go·nia \-'gōnyə\ *n* : tropical herb with waxy flowers

be·grudge \-'grəj\ *vb* **1** : concede reluctantly **2** : envy

be·guile \-'gīl\ *vb* -**guiled**; -**guil·ing** **1** : deceive **2** : amuse

be·half \-'haf, -'häf\ *n* : benefit

be·have \-'hāv\ *vb* -**haved**; -**hav·ing** : act in a certain way

be·hav·ior \-'hāvyər\ *n* : way of behaving —**be·hav·ior·al** \-'əl\ *adj*

be·head \-'hed\ *vb* : cut off the head of

be·hest \-'hest\ *n* : command

be·hind \bi'hīnd\ *adv* : at the back ~ *prep* **1** : in back of **2** : less than **3** : supporting

be·hold \-'hōld\ *vb* -**held**; -**hold·ing** : see —**be·hold·er** *n*

be·hold·en \-'hōldən\ *adj* : indebted

be·hoove \-'hüv\, **be·hove** \-'hōv\ *vb* -**hooved** *or* -**hoved**; -**hoov·ing** *or* -**hov·ing** : be necessary for

beige \'bāzh\ *n* : yellowish brown —**beige** *adj*

be·ing \'bēiŋ\ *n* **1** : existence **2** : living thing

be·la·bor \bi'lābər\ *vb* **1** : beat **2** : carry on to absurd lengths

be·lat·ed \-'lātəd\ *adj* : delayed

belch \'belch\ *vb* **1** : expel stomach gas orally **2** : emit forcefully —**belch** *n*

be·lea·guer \bi'lēgər\ *vb* **1** : besiege **2** : harass

bel·fry \'belfrē\ *n, pl* -**fries** : bell tower

be·lie \bi'lī\ *vb* -**lied**; -**ly·ing** **1** : misrepresent **2** : prove false

be·lief \-'lēf\ *n* **1** : trust **2** : something believed

be·lieve \-'lēv\ *vb* -**lieved**; -**liev·ing** **1** : trust in **2** : accept as true **3** : hold as an opinion —**be·liev·able** *adj* —**be·liev·ably** *adv* —**be·liev·er** *n*

be·lit·tle \bi'litᵊl\ *vb* -**lit·tled**; -**lit·tling** : make seem unimportant or worthless

bell \'bel\ *n* : hollow metallic device that rings when struck ~ *vb* : provide with a bell

bel·la·don·na \,belə'dänə\ *n* : poisonous nightshade yielding a drug used esp. to relieve intestinal spasms

belle \'bel\ *n* : beautiful woman

bel·li·cose \'beli,kōs\ *adj* : pugnacious —**bel·li·cos·i·ty** \,beli'käsətē\ *n*

bel·lig·er·ent \bə'lij(ə)rənt\ *adj* **1** : waging war **2** : truculent —**bel·lig·er·ence** \-rəns\ *n* —**bel·lig·er·en·cy** \-rənsē\ *n* —**belligerent** *n*

bel·low \'belō\ *vb* : make a loud deep roar or shout —**bellow** *n*

bel·lows \-ōz, -əz\ *n sing or pl* : device with sides that can be compressed to expel air

bell·weth·er \-'wethər, -,weth-\ *n* : leader

bel·ly \'belē\ *n, pl* -**lies** : abdomen ~ *vb* -**lied**; -**ly·ing** : bulge

be·long \bi'lon\ *vb* **1** : be suitable **2** : be owned **3** : be a part of

be·long·ings \-inz\ *n pl* : possessions

be·loved \bi'ləv(ə)d\ *adj* : dearly loved —**beloved** *n*

be·low \-'lō\ *adv* : in or to a lower place ~ *prep* : lower than

belt \'belt\ *n* **1** : strip (as of leather) worn about the waist **2** : endless band passing around pulleys or cylinders and used to impart motion **3** : distinct region ~ *vb* **1** : put a belt around **2** : thrash

be·moan \bi'mōn\ *vb* : lament

be·muse \-'myüz\ *vb* : confuse

bench \'bench\ *n* **1** : long seat **2** : judge's seat **3** : court

bend \'bend\ *vb* **bent** \'bent\; **bend·ing** **1** : curve or cause a change of shape in **2** : turn in a certain direction ~ *n* **1** : act of bending **2** : curve

be·neath \bi'nēth\ *adv or prep* : below

bene·dic·tion \,benə'dikshən\ *n* : closing blessing

bene·fac·tor \'benə,faktər\ *n* : one who gives esp. charitable aid —**bene·fac·tion** \,benə'fakshən\ *n* —**ben·e·fac·tress** \,benə,faktrəs\ *n*

be·nef·i·cence \bə'nefəsəns\ *n* : quality of doing good —**be·nef·i·cent** \-sənt\ *adj*

ben·e·fi·cial \,benə'fishəl\ *adj* : being of benefit —**ben·e·fi·cial·ly** *adv*

ben·e·fi·cia·ry \-'fishē,erē, -'fish(ə)rē\ *n, pl* **-ries** : one who receives benefits

ben·e·fit \'benə,fit\ *n* **1** : something that does good : help **3** : fund-raising event —**benefit** *vb*

be·nev·o·lence \bə'nev(ə)ləns\ *n* **1** : charitable nature **2** : act of kindness —**be·nev·o·lent** \-lənt\ *adj*

be·night·ed \bi'nītəd\ *adj* : ignorant

be·nign \bi'nīn\ *adj* **1** : gentle or kindly **2** : not malignant —**be·nig·ni·ty** \-'nignətē\ *n*

be·nig·nant \-'nignənt\ *adj* : benign

bent \'bent\ *n* : aptitude or interest

be·numb \bi'nəm\ *vb* : make numb esp. by cold

ben·zene, ben·zine \'ben,zēn\ *n* : colorless flammable liquid

be·queath \bi'kwēth, -'kwēth\ *vb* **1** : give by will **2** : hand down

be·quest \bi'kwest\ *n* : something bequeathed

be·rate \-'rāt\ *vb* : scold harshly

be·reaved \-'rēvd\ *adj* : suffering the death of a loved one ~ *n, pl* **bereaved** : one who is bereaved —**be·reave·ment** *n*

be·reft \-'reft\ *adj* : deprived of or lacking something

be·ret \bə'rā\ *n* : round soft visorless cap

beri·beri \,berē'berē\ *n* : thiamine-deficiency disease

ber·ry \'berē\ *n, pl* **-ries** : small pulpy fruit

ber·serk \bə(r)'sərk, -'zərk\ *adj* : crazed —**berserk** *adv*

berth \'bərth\ *n* **1** : place where a ship lies at anchor **2** : place to sit or sleep esp. on a ship **3** : job ~ *vb* : to bring or come into a berth

ber·yl \'berəl\ *n* : light-colored silicate mineral

be·seech \bi'sēch\ *vb* **-sought** \-'sȯt\ or **-seeched; -seech·ing** : entreat

be·set \-'set\ *vb* **1** : harass **2** : hem in

be·side \-'sīd\ *prep* **1** : by the side of **2** : besides

be·sides \-'sīdz\ *adv* **1** : in addition **2** : moreover ~ *prep* **1** : other than **2** : in addition to

be·siege \-'sēj\ *vb* : lay siege to —**be·sieg·er** *n*

be·smirch \-'smərch\ *vb* : soil

be·sot \-'sät\ *vb* **-tt-** : become drunk

be·speak \bi-\ *vb* **-spoke; -spo·ken; -speak·ing** : indicate

best \'best\ *adj, superlative of* GOOD **1** : excelling all others **2** : most productive **3** : largest ~ *adv, superlative of* WELL **1** : in the best way **2** : most ~ *n* : one that is best ~ *vb* : outdo

bes·tial \'beschəl\ *adj* **1** : relating to beasts **2** : brutish —**bes·ti·al·i·ty** \,beschē'alətē\ *n*

be·stir \bi-\ *vb* : rouse to action

best man *n* : chief male attendant at a wedding

be·stow \bi'stō\ *vb* : give —**be·stow·al** \-əl\ *n*

bet \'bet\ *n* **1** : agreement that one whose guess about a result proves wrong will give something to one whose guess proves right **2** : money risked on a bet ~ *vb* **bet; bet·ting 1** : risk (as money) on an outcome **2** : make a bet with

be·tide \bi'tīd\ *vb* : happen to

be·to·ken \bi'tōkən\ *vb* : give an indication of

be·tray \bi'trā\ *vb* **1** : seduce **2** : deliver to an enemy by treachery **3** : prove unfaithful to **4** : reveal unintentionally —**be·tray·al** *n* —**be·tray·er** *n*

be·troth \-'träth, -'trȯth, -'trōth, or with th \ *vb* : promise to marry —**be·troth·al** *n* —**be·trothed** *n*

bet·ter \'betər\ *adj, comparative of* GOOD **1** : more than half **2** : improved in health **3** : of higher quality ~ *adv, comparative of* WELL **1** : in a superior manner **2** : more ~ *n* **1** : one that is better **2** : advantage ~ *vb* **1** : improve **2** : surpass —**bet·ter·ment** \-mənt\ *n*

bet·tor, bet·ter \'betər\ *n* : one who bets

be·tween \bi'twēn\ *prep* **1** —used to show two things considered together **2** : in the space separating **3** —used to indicate a comparison or choice ~ *adv* : in an intervening space or interval

bev·el \'bevəl\ *n* : slant on an edge ~ *vb* **-eled** or **-elled; -el·ing** or **-el·ling 1** : cut or shape to a bevel **2** : incline

bev·er·age \'bev(ə)rij\ *n* : drink

bevy \'bevē\ *n, pl* **bev·ies** : large group

be·wail \bi'wāl\ vb : lament

be·ware \-'waər\ vb : be cautious

be·wil·der \-'wildər\ vb : confuse —be·wil·der·ment n

be·witch \-'wich\ vb 1 : affect by witchcraft 2 : charm —be·witch·ment n

be·yond \bē'änd\ adv 1 : farther 2 : besides ~ prep 1 : on or to the farther side of 2 : out of the reach of 3 : besides

bi- \(')bī-, ,bī\ prefix 1 : two 2 : coming or occurring every two 3 : twice, doubly, or on both sides

bicolored	bimetal
biconcave	bimetallic
biconcavity	binational
biconvex	binationalism
biconvexity	biparental
bicultural	bipolar
bidirectional	biracial
biethnic	biracially
bifunctional	bitonal

bi·an·nu·al \(')bī-\ adj : occurring twice a year —bi·an·nu·al·ly adv

bi·as \'bīəs\ n 1 : line diagonal to the grain of a fabric 2 : prejudice ~ vb -ased or -assed; -as·ing or -as·sing : prejudice

bib \'bib\ n : protective cover tied under a child's chin

Bi·ble \'bībəl\ n 1 : sacred scriptures of Christians 2 : sacred scriptures of Judaism or of some other religion —bib·li·cal \'biblikəl\ adj

bib·li·og·ra·phy \,biblē'ägrəfē\ n, pl -phies : list of writings on a subject or of an author —bib·li·og·ra·pher \-fər\ n —bib·li·o·graph·ic \-lēə'grafik\, bib·li·o·graph·i·cal \-əl\ adj

bi·cam·er·al \'bī'kam(ə)rəl\ adj : having 2 legislative branches

bi·car·bon·ate \-'kärbə,nāt, nət\ n : acid carbonate

bi·cen·ten·ni·al \,bīsen'tenēəl\ n : 200th anniversary —bicentennial adj

bi·ceps \'bī,seps\ n : large muscle of the upper arm

bick·er \'bikər\ vb or n : squabble

bi·cus·pid \bī'kəspəd\ n : double-pointed tooth

bi·cy·cle \'bī,sikəl\ n : 2-wheeled vehicle moved by pedaling ~ vb -cled; -cling : ride a bicycle —bi·cy·cler \-(ə)lər\, bi·cy·clist \-ləst\ n

bid \'bid\ vb bade \'bad, 'bād\ or bid; bid·den \'bid°n\ or bid; bid·ding 1 : order 2 : invite 3 : express 4 : make a bid ~ n 1 : act of bidding 2 : buy-

er's proposed price —bid·da·ble \-əbəl\ adj —bid·der n

bide \'bīd\ vb bode \'bōd\ or bid·ed; bided; bid·ing 1 : wait 2 : dwell

bi·en·ni·al \bī'enēəl\ adj 1 : occurring once in 2 years 2 : lasting 2 years —biennial n —bi·en·ni·al·ly adv

bier \'bir\ n : stand for a coffin

bifocals \bī'fōkəlz\ n pl : eyeglasses that correct for near and distant vision

big \'big\ adj -gg- : large in size, amount, or scope —big·ness n

big·a·my \'bigəmē\ n : marrying one person while still married to another —big·a·mist \-məst\ n —big·a·mous \-məs\ adj

big·horn n, pl -horn or -horns : wild mountain sheep

bight \'bīt\ n 1 : loop of a rope 2 : bay

big·ot \'bigət\ n : one who is intolerant of others —big·ot·ed \-ətəd\ adj —big·ot·ry \-ətrē\ n

big·wig n : important person

bike \'bīk\ n : bicycle or motorcycle

bi·ki·ni \bə'kēnē\ n : woman's brief 2-piece bathing suit

bi·lat·er·al \bī'-\ adj : involving 2 sides —bi·lat·er·al·ly adv

bile \'bīl\ n 1 : greenish liver secretion that aids digestion 2 : bad temper

bi·lin·gual \bī'lingwəl\ adj : using 2 languages

bil·ious \'bilyəs\ adj : irritable —bil·ious·ness n

bilk \'bilk\ vb : cheat

¹bill \'bil\ n 1 : jaws of a bird together with their horny covering ~ vb : caress fondly —billed adj

²bill n 1 : draft of a law 2 : list of things to be paid for 3 : printed advertisement 4 : piece of paper money ~ vb : submit a bill or account to

bill·board n : surface for displaying advertising bills

bil·let \'bilət\ n : soldiers' quarters ~ vb : lodge in a billet

bill·fold n : wallet

bil·liards \'bilyərdz\ n : game of driving balls into one another or into pockets on a table

bil·lion \-yən\ n, pl billions or billion : 1000 millions —billion adj —bil·lionth \-yənth\ adj or n

bil·low \'bilō\ n 1 : great wave 2 : rolling mass ~ vb : swell out —bil·lowy \'biləwē\ adj

billy goat n : male goat

bin \'bin\ n : storage box

bi·na·ry \'bīnərē\ adj : consisting of 2 things —binary n

bind \'bīnd\ vb bound \'baůnd\; binding 1 : tie 2 : obligate 3 : unite into a mass 4 : bandage —**bind·er** n —**bind·ing** n

binge \'binj\ n : spree

bin·go \'biŋgō\ n, pl **-gos** : game of covering numbers on a card

bin·oc·u·lar \bī'näkyələr, bə-\ adj : of or relating to both eyes ~ n : binocular optical instrument —usu. pl. **bin·oc·u·lar·ly** adv

bio·chem·is·try \ˌbīō-\ n : chemistry dealing with organisms —**bio·chem·i·cal** adj or n —**bio·chem·ist** n

bio·de·grad·able \ˌbīō-\ adj : able to be reduced to harmless products by organisms —**bio·de·grad·abil·i·ty** n —**bio·deg·ra·da·tion** n —**bio·de·grade** vb

bi·og·ra·phy \bī'ägrəfē, bē-\ n, pl **-phies** : written history of a person's life —**bi·og·ra·pher** \-fər\ n —**bio·graph·ic** \ˌbīə'grafik\, **bio·graph·i·cal** \-ikəl\ adj

bi·ol·o·gy \bī'äləjē\ n : science of living beings and life processes —**bio·log·ic** \ˌbīə'läjik\, **bio·log·i·cal** \-əl\ adj —**bi·ol·o·gist** \bī'äləjəst\ n

bio·phys·ics \ˌbīō-\ n : application of physics to biological problems —**bio·phys·i·cal** adj —**bio·phys·i·cist** n

bi·op·sy \'bī,äpsē\ n, pl **-sies** : removal of live bodily tissue for examination

bi·par·ti·san \bī'pärtəzən\ adj : involving members of 2 parties

bi·ped \'bī,ped\ n : 2-footed animal

birch \'bərch\ n : deciduous tree with close-grained wood —**birch**, **birch·en** \-ən\ adj

bird \'bərd\ n : warm-blooded egg-laying vertebrate with wings and feathers —**bird·bath** n —**bird·house** n —**bird·seed** n

bird's-eye \'bərd,zī\ adj 1 : seen from above 2 : cursory

birth \'bərth\ n 1 : act or fact of being born or of producing young 2 : origin —**birth·day** n —**birth·place** n —**birth·rate** n

birth·mark n : unusual blemish on the skin at birth

birth·right n : something one is entitled to by birth

bis·cuit \'biskət\ n : a bread made with leavening other than yeast

bi·sect \'bī,sekt\ vb : divide into 2 parts —**bi·sec·tion** \'bī-\ n —**bi·sec·tor** \-tər\ n

bish·op \'bishəp\ n 1 : a clergyman higher than a priest or minister 2 : a chess piece

bish·op·ric \-rik\ n 1 : diocese 2 : office of bishop

bis·muth \'bizməth\ n : heavy brittle metallic element

bi·son \'bīsᵊn, 'bīz-\ n, pl **-son** : large shaggy wild ox of central U.S.

bis·tro \'bēstrō, 'bis-\ n, pl **-tros** : small restaurant or bar

¹**bit** \'bit\ n 1 : part of a bridle that goes in a horse's mouth 2 : drilling tool —**bit·stock** n

²**bit** n 1 : small piece or quantity 2 : small degree

bitch \'bich\ n : female dog ~ vb : complain

bite \'bīt\ vb **bit** \'bit\; **bit·ten** \'bitᵊn\; **bit·ing** \'bītiŋ\ 1 : to grip or cut with teeth or jaws 2 : dig in or grab and hold 3 : sting 4 : take bait ~ n 1 : act of biting 2 : bit of food 3 : wound made by biting —**bit·ing** adj

bit·ter \'bitər\ adj 1 : having an acrid lingering taste 2 : intense or severe 3 : extremely harsh or resentful —**bit·ter·ly** adv —**bit·ter·ness** n

bit·tern \-ərn\ n : small heron

bi·tu·men \bə't(y)ümən, bī-\ n : mixture of hydrocarbons (as asphalt or tar)

bi·tu·mi·nous \-mənəs\ adj 1 : resembling or containing bitumen 2 : being coal that yields bituminous matter when heated

bi·valve \'bī-\ n : animal (as a clam) with a shell of 2 parts —**bivalve** adj

biv·ouac \'biv(ə),wak\ n : temporary camp ~ vb **-ouacked**; **-ouack·ing** : camp

bi·zarre \bə'zär\ adj : very strange —**bi·zarre·ly** adv

blab \'blab\ vb **-bb-** : talk too much

black \'blak\ adj 1 : of the color black 2 : Negro 3 : soiled 4 : lacking light 5 : wicked or evil 6 : gloomy ~ n 1 : black pigment or dye 2 : something black 3 : color of least lightness 4 : person of a dark-skinned race ~ vb : blacken —**black·ing** n —**black·ish** adj —**black·ly** adv —**black·ness** n

black-and-blue adj : darkly discolored from bruising

black·ball n : negative vote —**black·ball** vb

black·ber·ry \-ˌberē\ n : black or purple fruit of a bramble

black·bird n : bird of which the male is largely or wholly black

black·board n : dark surface for writing on with chalk

black·en \-ən\ vb 1 : make or become black 2 : defame

black·guard \'blagərd, -ˌärd\ n : scoundrel

black·head *n* : small oily mass plugging the outlet of a skin gland

black·jack *n* **1** : flexible leather-covered club **2** : card game ~ *vb* : hit with a blackjack

black·list *n* : list of persons to be punished —**blacklist** *vb*

black·mail *n* **1** : extortion by threat of exposure **2** : something extorted by blackmail —**blackmail** *vb* —**black·mail·er** *n*

black·out *n* **1** : darkness due to electrical failure **2** : brief fainting spell —**black out** *vb*

black·smith *n* : one who forges iron

black·top *n* : bituminous material for surfacing roads —**blacktop** *vb*

blad·der \'bladər\ *n* : sac into which urine passes from the kidneys

blade \'blād\ *n* **1** : leaf esp. of grass **2** : something resembling the flat part of a leaf **3** : cutting part of an instrument or tool

blame \'blām\ *vb* **blamed; blam·ing 1** : find fault with **2** : hold responsible or responsible for —**blam·able** *adj* —**blame** *n* —**blame·less** *adj* —**blame·less·ly** *adv* —**blame·wor·thi·ness** *n* —**blame·worthy** *adj*

blanch \'blanch\ *vb* : make or become white or pale

bland \'bland\ *adj* **1** : smooth in manner **2** : soothing **3** : tasteless —**bland·ly** *adv* —**bland·ness** *n*

blan·dish·ment \-ishmənt\ *n* : flattering or coaxing speech or act

blank \'blaŋk\ *adj* **1** : showing or causing a dazed look **2** : lacking expression **3** : empty **4** : free from writing **5** : downright ~ *n* **1** : an empty space **2** : form with spaces to write in **3** : unfinished form (as of a key) **4** : cartridge with no bullet ~ *vb* : cover or close up —**blank·ly** *adv* —**blank·ness** *n*

blan·ket \-ət\ *n* **1** : heavy covering for a bed **2** : covering layer ~ *vb* : cover ~ *adj* : applying to a group

blare \'blaər\ *vb* **blared; blar·ing** : make a loud harsh sound —**blare** *n*

blar·ney \'blärnē\ *n* : skillful flattery

bla·sé \blä'zā\ *adj* : indifferent to pleasure or excitement

blas·pheme \blas'fēm\ *vb* **-phemed; -phem·ing** : speak blasphemy

blas·phe·my \'blasfəmē\ *n*, *pl* **-mies** : irreverence toward God or anything sacred —**blas·phe·mous** *adj*

blast \'blast\ *n* **1** : violent gust of wind **2** : explosion ~ *vb* **1** : shrivel up **2** : shatter by or as if by explosive

—**blast off** *vb* : take off esp. in a rocket

bla·tant \'blāt³nt\ *adj* : offensively showy —**bla·tan·cy** \-³nsē\ *n*

¹blaze \'blāz\ *n* **1** : fire **2** : intense direct light **3** : strong display ~ *vb* **blazed; blaz·ing** : burn or shine brightly

²blaze *n* **1** : white mark on an animal's face **2** : mark made on a tree ~ *vb* **blazed; blaz·ing** : mark with blazes

blaz·er \-ər\ *n* : sports jacket

bleach \'blēch\ *vb* : whiten —**bleach** *n*

bleach·ers \-ərz\ *n sing or pl* : uncovered stand for spectators

bleak \'blēk\ *adj* **1** : desolately barren **2** : lacking cheering qualities —**bleak·ish** *adj* —**bleak·ly** *adv* —**bleak·ness** *n*

blear \'bliər\ *adj* : dim with water or tears —**blear-eyed** *adj*

bleary \'bli(ə)rē\ *adj* : dull or dimmed esp. from fatigue

bleat \'blēt\ *n* : cry of a sheep or goat or a sound like it —**bleat** *vb*

bleed \'blēd\ *vb* **bled** \'bled\; **bleed·ing 1** : lose or shed blood **2** : feel distress **3** : flow from a wound **4** : draw fluid from **5** : extort money from —**bleed·er** *n*

blem·ish \'blemish\ *vb* : spoil by a flaw ~ *n* : noticeable flaw

¹blench \'blench\ *vb* : flinch

²blench *vb* : grow or make pale

blend \'blend\ *vb* **1** : mix thoroughly **2** : combine into an integrated whole ~ *n* : product of blending —**blend·er** *n*

bless \'bles\ *vb* **blessed** \'blest\; **bless·ing 1** : consecrate by religious rite **2** : invoke divine care for **3** : make happy —**bless·ed** \'blesəd\, **blest** *adj* —**bless·ed·ness** *n* —**bless·ing** *n*

blew *past of* BLOW

blight \'blīt\ *n* **1** : plant disorder marked by withering or an organism causing it **2** : harmful influence ~ *vb* : affect with or suffer from blight

blimp \'blimp\ *n* : small airship holding form by pressure of contained gas

blind \'blīnd\ *adj* **1** : lacking or quite deficient in ability to see **2** : not intelligently controlled **3** : having no way out ~ *vb* **1** : to make blind **2** : dazzle ~ *n* **1** : something to conceal or darken **2** : place of concealment —**blind·ly** *adv* —**blind·ness** *n*

blind·fold *vb* : cover the eyes of —**blindfold** *n*

blink \'bliŋk\ *vb* **1** : wink **2** : shine intermittently ~ *n* : wink

blink·er \'\ *n* : a blinking light

bliss \'blis\ *n* 1 : complete happiness 2 : heaven or paradise —**bliss·ful** *adj* —**bliss·ful·ly** *adv*

blis·ter \'blistər\ *n* 1 : raised area of skin containing watery fluid 2 : raised or swollen spot ~ *vb* : develop or cause blisters

blithe \'blīth, 'blīth\ *adj* **blith·er; blith·est** : cheerful —**blithe·ly** *adv* —**blithe·some** \-səm\ *adj*

blitz \'blits\ *n* 1 : series of air raids 2 : fast intensive campaign —**blitz** *vb*

bliz·zard \'blizərd\ *n* : severe windy snowstorm

bloat \'blōt\ *vb* : swell

blob \'bläb\ *n* : small lump or drop

bloc \'bläk\ *n* : group working together

block \'bläk\ *n* 1 : solid piece 2 : frame enclosing a pulley 3 : quantity considered together 4 : large building divided into separate units 5 : a city square or the distance along one of its sides 6 : obstruction 7 : interruption of a bodily or mental function ~ *vb* : obstruct or hinder

block·ade \bä'kād\ *n* : the shutting off of a place usu. by troops or ships ~ *vb* **-ad·ed; -ad·ing** : impose a blockade upon

block·head *n* : stupid person

blond, blonde \'bländ\ *adj* 1 : fair in complexion 2 : of a light color —**blond, blonde** *n*

blood \'bləd\ *n* 1 : red liquid that circulates in the heart, arteries, and veins of animals 2 : lifeblood 3 : lineage —**blood·ed** *adj* —**blood·less** *adj* —**blood·stain** *n* —**blood·stained** *adj* —**blood·suck·er** *n* —**blood·suck·ing** *n* —**bloody** *adj*

blood·cur·dling *adj* : terrifying

blood·hound *n* : large hound with a keen sense of smell

blood·mo·bile \-mō͵bēl\ *n* : truck for collecting blood from donors

blood·shed *n* : slaughter

blood·shot *adj* : inflamed to redness

blood·stream *n* : blood in a circulatory system

blood·thirsty *adj* : eager to shed blood —**blood·thirst·i·ly** *adv* —**blood·thirst·i·ness** *n*

bloom \'blüm\ *n* 1 : flower 2 : period of flowering 3 : fresh or healthy look ~ *vb* : yield flowers —**bloomy** *adj*

bloo·mers \'blümərz\ *n pl* : woman's underwear of short loose trousers

bloop·er \'blüpər\ *n* : public blunder

blos·som \'bläsəm\ *n or vb* : flower

blot \'blät\ *n* 1 : stain 2 : blemish ~ *vb*

-tt- 1 : spot 2 : dry with absorbent paper —**blot·ter** *n*

blotch \'bläch\ *n* : large spot —**blotch** *vb* —**blotchy** *adj*

blouse \'blaůs, 'blaůz\ *n* : loose garment reaching from the neck to the waist

¹blow \'blō\ *vb* **blew** \'blü\; **blown** \'blōn\; **blow·ing** 1 : move forcibly 2 : send forth a current of air 3 : sound 4 : shape by blowing 5 : explode ~ *n* 1 : gale 2 : a blowing from the mouth —**blow·er** *n* —**blowy** *adj*

²blow *n* 1 : forcible stroke 2 *pl* : fighting 3 : calamity

³blow *vb* **blew; blown; blow·ing** : flower

blow·out *n* : bursting of a tire

blow·torch *n* : small torch that uses a blast of air

¹blub·ber \'bləbər\ *n* : fat of whales

²blubber *vb* : cry noisily

blud·geon \'bləjən\ *n* : short club ~ *vb* : hit with a bludgeon

blue \'blü\ *adj* **blu·er; blu·est** 1 : of the color blue 2 : melancholy ~ *n* : color of the clear sky —**blu·ish** \-ish\ *adj*

blue·bell *n* : plant with blue bell-shaped flowers

blue·ber·ry \-͵berē, -b(ə)rē\ *n* : edible blue or blackish berry

blue·bird *n* : small bluish songbird

blue·fish *n* : bluish marine food fish

blue jay *n* : American crested jay

blue·print *n* 1 : photographic print in white on blue of a mechanical drawing 2 : plan of action —**blueprint** *vb*

blues \'blüz\ *n pl* 1 : depression 2 : music in a usu. melancholy style of American Negro origin

¹bluff \'bləf\ *adj* 1 : rising steeply with a broad flat front 2 : frank ~ *n* : cliff

²bluff *vb* : deceive by pretense ~ *n* : act of bluffing —**bluff·er** \-ər\ *n*

blu·ing, blue·ing \'blüiŋ\ *n* : dye used in laundering to keep fabrics white

blun·der \'bləndər\ *vb* 1 : move clumsily 2 : make a stupid mistake ~ *n* : bad mistake

blun·der·buss \-͵bəs\ *n* : obsolete short-barreled firearm

blunt \'blənt\ *adj* 1 : not sharp 2 : tactless ~ *vb* : make dull —**blunt·ly** *adv* —**blunt·ness** *n*

blur \'blər\ *n* 1 : smear 2 : something vaguely seen ~ *vb* **-rr-** : make or become indistinct —**blur·ry** \-ē\ *adj*

blurb \'blərb\ *n* : short publicity notice

blurt \'blərt\ *vb* : utter suddenly

blush \'bləsh\ *n* : reddening of the face —**blush** *vb* —**blush·ful** *adj*

blus·ter \'bləstər\ *vb* 1 : blow violently

2 : to talk or act with boasts or threats —**blus·ter** n —**blus·tery** adj

boa \'bōə\ n **1** : a large snake (as the **boa con·stric·tor** \·ˌbōəkən'striktər\) that crushes its prey **2** : fluffy scarf

boar \'bōr\ n : male swine

board \'bōrd\ n **1** : long thin piece of sawed lumber **2** : flat thin sheet esp. for games **3** : daily meals furnished for pay **4** : official body ~ vb **1** : go aboard **2** : cover with boards **3** : supply meals to —**board·er** n

board·walk \·ˌwȯk\ n : wooden walk along a beach

boast \'bōst\ vb : praise oneself or one's possessions —**boast** n —**boast·er** n —**boast·ful** adj —**boast·ful·ly** adv

boat \'bōt\ n : vessel for traveling on water —**boat** vb —**boat·man** \-mən\ n

boat·swain \'bōs³n\ n : ship's officer in charge of the hull

¹bob \'bäb\ vb **-bb-** **1** : move up and down **2** : appear suddenly

²bob n **1** : float **2** : woman's short haircut ~ vb : cut hair in a bob

bob·bin \'bäbən\ n : spindle for holding thread

bob·ble \'bäbəl\ vb **-bled; -bling** : fumble —**bobble** n

bob·cat n : small American lynx

bob·o·link \'bäbəˌliŋk\ n : American songbird

bob·sled \-ˌsled\ n : racing sled —**bobsled** vb

bob·white \(')bäb'hwīt\ n : quail

bock \'bäk\ n : dark beer

¹bode \'bōd\ vb **bod·ed; bod·ing** : indicate by signs

²bode past of BIDE

bod·ice \'bädəs\ n : close-fitting top of dress

bodi·ly \'bäd³lē\ adj : relating to the body ~ adv **1** : in the flesh **2** : as a whole

body \'bädē\ n, pl **bod·ies** **1** : the physical whole of an organism **2** : human being **3** : main part **4** : mass of matter **5** : group —**bod·ied** adj —**bodi·less** \-iləs, -ē´ləs\ adj —**body·guard** n

bog \'bäg, 'bȯg\ n : swamp ~ vb **-gg-** : sink in or as if in a bog —**bog·gy** adj

bo·gey \'bu̇gē, 'bō-\ n, pl **-geys** : someone or something frightening

bog·gle \'bägəl\ vb **-gled; -gling** : overwhelm with amazement

bo·gus \'bōgəs\ adj : fake

bo·he·mi·an \bō'hēmēən\ n : one living unconventionally —**bohemian** adj

¹boil \'bȯil\ n : inflamed swelling

²boil vb **1** : heat to a temperature (**boiling point**) at which vapor forms **2**

: cook in boiling liquid **3** : be agitated —**boil** n

boil·er \'bȯilər\ n : tank holding hot water or steam

bois·ter·ous \'bȯistərəs\ adj : noisily turbulent —**bois·ter·ous·ly** adv

bold \'bōld\ adj **1** : courageous **2** : insolent **3** : daring —**bold·ly** adv —**bold·ness** \'bōl(d)nəs\ n

bo·le·ro \bə'le(ə)rō\ n, pl **-ros** : Spanish dance **2** : short open jacket

boll \'bōl\ n : seed pod

boll weevil n : a small grayish weevil that infests the cotton plant

bo·lo·gna \bə'lōnē\ n : large smoked sausage

bol·ster \'bōlstər\ n : long pillow ~ vb **-stered; -ster·ing** : support

¹bolt \'bōlt\ n **1** : flash of lightning **2** : sliding bar used to fasten a door **3** : roll of cloth **4** : threaded pin used with a nut ~ vb **1** : move suddenly **2** : fasten with a bolt **3** : swallow hastily

²bolt vb : sift

bomb \'bäm\ n : explosive device ~ vb : attack with bombs —**bomb·proof** adj

bom·bard \bäm'bärd, bəm-\ vb : attack with or as if with artillery —**bom·bard·ment** n

bom·bar·dier \ˌbämb(r)'di(ə)r\ n : one who releases the bombs from a bomber

bom·bast \'bäm₂bast\ n : pretentious language —**bom·bas·tic** \bäm'bastik\ adj

bomb·er n **1** : one that bombs **2** : airplane for dropping bombs

bomb·shell n **1** : bomb **2** : great surprise

bona fide \'bōnə₂fīd, 'bän-; ˌbōnə'fīdē\ adj **1** : made in good faith **2** : genuine

bo·nan·za \bə'nanzə\ n : something yielding a rich return

bon·bon \'bän₂bän\ n : piece of candy

bond \'bänd\ n **1** pl : fetters **2** : uniting force **3** : obligation made binding by money **4** : interest-bearing certificate ~ vb **1** : insure **2** : cause to adhere —**bond·hold·er** n

bond·age \'bändij\ n : slavery —**bond·man** \-mən\ n —**bond·wom·an** n

¹bonds·man \'bän(d)zmən\ n : slave

²bondsman n : surety

bone \'bōn\ n : skeletal material ~ vb **boned; bon·ing 1** : to free from bones —**bone·less** adj —**bony, bon·ey** \'bōnē\ adj

bon·er \'bōnər\ n : blunder

bon·fire \'bän₂fī(ə)r\ n : outdoor fire

bo·ni·to \bə'nētō\ *n, pl* **-tos** *or* **-to** : medium-sized tuna

bon·net \'bänət\ *n* : hat for a woman or infant

bo·nus \'bōnəs\ *n* : extra payment

boo \'bü\ *n, pl* **boos** : shout of disapproval —**boo** *vb*

boo·by \'bübē\ *n, pl* **-bies** : dunce

book \'bůk\ *n* **1** : paper sheets bound into a volume **2** : long literary work or a subdivision of one ~ *vb* : reserve —**book·case** *n* —**book·let** \-lət\ *n* —**book·mark** *n* —**book·sell·er** *n* —**book·shelf** *n*

book·end *n* : support to hold up a row of books

book·ie \-ē\ *n* : bookmaker

book·ish \-ish\ *adj* : fond of books and reading

book·keep·er *n* : one who keeps business accounts —**book·keep·ing** *n*

book·mak·er *n* : one who makes bets —**book·mak·ing** *n*

book·worm *n* : one devoted to reading

1boom \'büm\ *n* **1** : long spar to extend the bottom of a sail **2** : beam projecting from the pole of a derrick

2boom *vb* **1** : make a deep hollow sound **2** : grow rapidly esp. in value ~ *n* **1** : booming sound **2** : rapid growth

boo·mer·ang \'bümə,raŋ\ *n* : angular club that returns to the thrower

1boon \'bün\ *n* : benefit

2boon *adj* : congenial

boon·docks \'bün,däks\ *n pl* : rural area

boor \'bůr\ *n* : rude person —**boor·ish** *adj*

boost \'büst\ *vb* **1** : raise **2** : promote —**boost** *n* —**boost·er** *n*

boot \'büt\ *n* **1** : covering for the foot and leg **2** : kick ~ *vb* : kick

boo·tee, boo·tie \'bütē\ *n* : infant's knitted sock

booth \'büth\ *n, pl* **booths** \'büthz, 'büths\ : small enclosed stall or seating area

boot·leg \'büt,leg\ *vb* : make or sell liquor illegally —**boot·leg** *adj or n* —**boot·leg·ger** *n*

boo·ty \'bütē\ *n, pl* **-ties** : plunder

booze \'büz\ *vb* **boozed; booz·ing** : drink liquor to excess ~ *n* : liquor —**booz·er** *n* —**boozy** *adj*

bo·rax \'bōr,aks\ *n* : crystalline compound of boron

bor·der \'bōrdər\ *n* **1** : edge **2** : boundary ~ *vb* **1** : put a border on **2** : be close

1bore \'bōr\ *vb* **bored; bor·ing 1** : pierce **2** : make by piercing ~ *n*

: cylindrical hole or its diameter —**bor·er** *n*

2bore *past of* BEAR

3bore *n* : one that is dull ~ *vb* **bored; bor·ing** : tire with dullness —**bore·dom** \'bōrdəm\ *n*

born \'bōrn\ *adj* **1** : brought into life **2** : being such by birth

borne *past part of* BEAR

bo·ron \'bōr,än\ *n* : dark-colored chemical element

bor·ough \'bərō\ *n* : incorporated town or village

bor·row \'bärō\ *vb* **1** : take as a loan **2** : take into use

bo·som \'buzəm, 'bü-\ *n* : breast ~ *adj* : intimate —**bo·somed** *adj*

boss \'bòs\ *n* : employer or supervisor ~ *vb* : supervise —**bossy** *adj*

bot·a·ny \'bät(ᵊ)nē\ *n* : plant biology —**bo·tan·ic** \bə'tanik\, **bo·tan·i·cal** \-əl\, *adj* —**bot·a·nist** \'bät(ᵊ)nəst\ *n* —**bot·a·nize** \-ᵊn,īz\ *vb*

botch \'bäch\ *vb* : do clumsily —**botch** *n*

both \'bōth\ *adj or pron* : the one and the other ~ *conj* —used to show each of two is included

both·er \'bäthər\ *vb* **1** : annoy or worry **2** : take the trouble —**bother** *n* —**both·er·some** \-səm\ *adj*

bot·tle \'bätᵊl\ *n* : container with a narrow neck and no handles ~ *vb* **bot·tled; bot·tling** : put into a bottle

bot·tle·neck *n* : place or cause of congestion

bot·tom \'bätəm\ *n* **1** : supporting surface **2** : lowest part or place —**bottom** *adj* —**bot·tomed** *adj* —**bot·tom·less** *adj*

bot·u·lism \'bächə,lizəm\ *n* : acute food poisoning

bou·doir \'büd,wär, 'büd-\ *n* : woman's private room

bough \'bau̇\ *n* : large tree branch

bought *past of* BUY

bouil·lon \'bü,yän; 'bůl,yän, -yən\ *n* : clear soup

boul·der \'bōldər\ *n* : large rounded rock —**boul·dered** *adj*

bou·le·vard \'bůlə,värd, 'bü-\ *n* : broad thoroughfare

bounce \'bau̇ns\ *vb* **bounced; bounc·ing 1** : spring back **2** : make bounce —**bounce** *n*

1bound \'bau̇nd\ *adj* : intending to go

2bound *n* : limit or boundary ~ *vb* : be a boundary of —**bound·less** *adj* —**bound·less·ness** *n*

3bound *adj* **1** : obliged **2** : having a binding **3** : determined **4** : incapable of failing

⁴bound n : leap ~ vb : move by springing

bound·ary \'baund(ə)rē\ n, pl **-aries** : line marking extent or separation

boun·ty \'bauntē\ n, pl **-ties** 1 : generosity 2 : reward —**boun·te·ous** \-ēəs\ adj —**boun·te·ous·ly** adv —**boun·ti·ful** \-ifəl\ adj —**boun·ti·ful·ly** adv

bou·quet \bō'kā, bü-\ n 1 : bunch of flowers 2 : fragrance

bour·bon \'bərbən\ n : corn whiskey

bour·geoi·sie \,bürzh,wä'zē\ n : middle class of society —**bour·geois** \'bürzh,wä, bürzh'wä\ n or adj

bout \'baut\ n 1 : contest 2 : outbreak

bou·tique \bü'tēk\ n : specialty shop

bo·vine \'bō,vīn, -,vēn\ adj : relating to cattle —**bovine** n

¹bow \'bau\ vb 1 : submit 2 : bend the head or body ~ n : act of bowing

²bow \'bō\ n 1 : bend or arch 2 : weapon for shooting arrows 3 : knot with loops 4 : rod with stretched horsehairs for playing a stringed instrument ~ vb : curve or bend —**bow·man** \-mən\ n —**bow·string** n

³bow \'bau\ n : forward part of a ship —**bow** adj

bow·els \'bau(ə)ls\ n pl 1 : intestines 2 : inmost parts

bow·er \'bau(ə)r\ n : arbor

¹bowl \'bōl\ n : concave vessel or part —**bowl·ful** \-,ful\ n

²bowl n : round ball for bowling ~ vb : roll a ball in bowling —**bowl·er** n

bowl·ing n : game in which balls are rolled to knock down pins

¹box \'bäks\ n, pl box or box·es : evergreen shrub —**box·wood** \-,wud\ n

²box n 1 : container usu. with 4 sides and a cover 2 : small compartment ~ vb : put in a box

³box n : slap ~ vb 1 : slap 2 : fight with the fists —**box·er** n —**box·ing** n

box·car n : roofed freight car

box office n : theater ticket office

boy \'boi\ n : male child —**boy·hood** n —**boy·ish** adj —**boy·ish·ly** adv —**boy·ish·ness** n

boy·cott \-,kät\ vb : refrain from dealing with —**boycott** n

brace \'brās\ n 1 : crank for turning a bit 2 : something that resists weight or supports ~ vb **braced; brac·ing** 1 : make taut or steady 2 : invigorate 3 : strengthen

brace·let \'brāslət\ n : ornamental band for the wrist or arm

brack·et \'brakət\ n 1 : projecting support 2 : punctuation mark [or] 3 : class ~ vb 1 : furnish or fasten with

brack·ets 2 : place within brackets 3 : group

brack·ish \-ish\ adj : salty

brad \'brad\ n : nail with a small head

brag \'brag\ vb **-gg-** : boast —**brag** n

brag·gart \'bragərt\ n : boaster

braid \'brād\ vb : interweave ~ n : something braided

braille \'brāl\ n : system of writing for the blind using raised dots

brain \'brān\ n 1 : organ of thought and nervous coordination enclosed in the skull 2 : intelligence ~ vb : smash the skull of —**brained** adj —**brain·less** adj —**brainy** adj

braise \'brāz\ vb **braised; brais·ing** : cook (meat) slowly in a covered dish

brake \'brāk\ n : device for slowing up ~ vb **braked; brak·ing** : slow or stop by a brake

bram·ble \'brambəl\ n : prickly shrub

bran \'bran\ n : broken grain husks

branch \'branch\ n 1 : division of a plant stem 2 : part ~ vb 1 : develop branches 2 : diverge —**branched** adj

brand \'brand\ n 1 : identifying mark made by burning 2 : stigma 3 : distinctive kind (as of goods from one firm) ~ vb : mark with a brand

bran·dish \'brandish\ vb : wave

brand-new adj : unused

bran·dy \'brandē\ n, pl **-dies** : liquor distilled from wine

brash \'brash\ adj 1 : impulsive 2 : aggressively self-assertive

brass \'bras\ n 1 : alloy of copper and zinc 2 : brazen self-assurance —**brassy** adj

bras·siere \brə'zir\ n : woman's undergarment to support the breasts

brat \'brat\ n : ill-behaved child —**brat·ty** adj

bra·va·do \brə'vädō\ n, pl **-does** or **-dos** : false bravery

¹brave \'brāv\ adj **brav·er; brav·est** : showing courage ~ vb **braved; brav·ing** : face with courage —**brave·ly** adv —**brav·ery** \-(ə)rē\ n

²brave n : Indian warrior

bra·vo \'brävō\ n, pl **-vos** : shout of approval

brawl \'brol\ n : noisy quarrel or violent fight —**brawl** vb —**brawl·er** n

brawn \'brón\ n : muscular strength —**brawny** adj

bray \'brā\ n : harsh cry of a donkey —**bray** vb

bra·zen \'brāz³n\ adj 1 : made of brass 2 : bold —**bra·zen·ly** adv —**bra·zen·ness** \-(n)əs\ n

bra·zier \'brāzhər\ n : charcoal grill

breach \\'brēch\ *n* **1** : breaking of a law, obligation, or standard **2** : gap ~ *vb* : make a breach in

bread \\'bred\ *n* : baked food made of flour ~ *vb* : cover with bread crumbs

breadth \\'bredth\ *n* : width

bread·win·ner *n* : wage earner

break \\'brāk\ *vb* **broke** \\'brōk\; **bro·ken** \\'brōkən\; **break·ing** **1** : knock into pieces **2** : transgress **3** : force a way into or out of **4** : exceed **5** : interrupt **6** : fail ~ *n* **1** : act or result of breaking **2** : stroke of good luck —**break·able** *adj or n* —**break·age** \\'brākij\ *n* —**break·er** *n* —**break in** *vb* **1** : enter by force **2** : interrupt **3** : train —**break out** *vb* : develop a rash

break·down *n* : physical or mental failure —**break down** *vb*

break·fast \\'brekfəst\ *n* : first meal of the day —**breakfast** *vb*

breast \\'brest\ *n* **1** : milk-producing gland esp. of a woman **2** : front part of the chest

breast·bone *n* : sternum

breath \\'breth\ *n* **1** : slight breeze **2** : air breathed in or out —**breath·less** *adj* —**breath·less·ly** *adv*

breathe \\'brēth\ *vb* **breathed; breath·ing 1** : draw air into the lungs and expel it **2** : live **3** : utter

breath·tak·ing *adj* : exciting

breech·es \\'brichəz\ *n pl* : trousers ending near the knee

breed \\'brēd\ *vb* **bred** \\'bred\; **breed·ing 1** : give birth to **2** : propagate **3** : raise ~ *n* **1** : kind of plant or animal usu. developed by man **2** : class —**breed·er** *n*

breeze \\'brēz\ *n* : light wind ~ *vb* **breezed; breez·ing** : move fast —**breezy** *adj*

breth·ren \\'breth(ə)rən, -ərn\ *pl of* BROTHER

bre·via·ry \\'brēv(y)ərē, -vē,erē\ *n, pl* **-ries** : prayer book used by Roman Catholic priests

brev·i·ty \\'brevətē\ *n, pl* **-ties** : shortness or conciseness

brew \\'brü\ *vb* : make by fermenting or infusing —**brew** *n* —**brew·er** *n* —**brew·ery** \\'brüərē, 'brü(ə)rē\ *n*

bribe \\'brīb\ *vb* **bribed; brib·ing** : corrupt or influence by gifts ~ *n* : something offered or given in bribing —**brib·ery** \\-(ə)rē\ *n*

bric-a-brac \\'brikə,brak\ *n pl* : small ornamental articles

brick \\'brik\ *n* : building block of baked clay —**brick** *vb* —**brick·lay·er** *n* —**brick·lay·ing** *n*

bride \\'brīd\ *n* : woman just married or about to be married —**brid·al** \\-ᵊl\ *adj*

bride·groom *n* : man just married or about to be married

brides·maid *n* : woman who attends a bride at her wedding

¹bridge \\'brij\ *n* **1** : structure built for passage over a depression or obstacle **2** : upper part of the nose **3** : platform over the deck of a ship **4** : artificial replacement for missing teeth ~ *vb* : build a bridge over —**bridge·able** *adj*

²bridge *n* : card game for 4 players

bri·dle \\'brīdᵊl\ *n* : headgear to control a horse ~ *vb* **-dled; -dling 1** : put a bridle on **2** : restrain **3** : show hostility or scorn

brief \\'brēf\ *adj* : short or concise ~ *n* : concise summary (as of a legal case) ~ *vb* : give final instructions or essential information to —**brief·ly** *adv* —**brief·ness** *n*

brief-case *n* : case for papers

¹bri·er, bri·ar \\'brī(ə)r\ *n* : thorny plant

²brier *n* : heath of southern Europe

¹brig \\'brig\ *n* : 2-masted ship

²brig *n* : jail on a naval ship

bri·gade \\brig'ād\ *n* **1** : a large military unit **2** : a group organized for a special activity

brig·a·dier general \\,brigə,diər-\ *n* : officer ranking next below a major general

brig·and \\'brigənd\ *n* : bandit —**brig·and·age** \\-ij\ *n*

bright \\'brīt\ *adj* **1** : radiating or reflecting light **2** : cheerful **3** : intelligent —**bright·en** \\-ᵊn\ *vb* —**bright·en·er** \\'brītnər, -ᵊnər\ *n* —**bright·ly** *adv* —**bright·ness** *n*

bril·liant \\'brilyənt\ *adj* **1** : very bright **2** : splendid **3** : very intelligent —**bril·liance** \\-yəns\, **bril·lian·cy** \\-yənsē\ *n* —**bril·liant·ly** *adv*

brim \\'brim\ *n* : edge or rim —**brim·less** *adj* —**brimmed** *adj*

brim·ful \\-'fu̇l\ *adj* : full to the brim

brim·stone *n* : sulfur

brin·dled \\'brindᵊld\ *adj* : gray or tawny with dark streaks or flecks

brine \\'brīn\ *n* **1** : salt water **2** : ocean —**brin·i·ness** *n* —**briny** *adj*

bring \\'brin\ *vb* **brought** \\'brȯt\; **bring·ing 1** : cause to come with one **2** : persuade **3** : produce **4** : sell for —**bring·er** *n* —**bring about** *vb* : make happen —**bring up** *vb* **1** : care for and educate **2** : cause to be noticed **3** : vomit

brink \'briŋk\ *n* : edge

bri·quette, bri·quet \brik'et\ *n* : pressed mass (as of charcoal)

brisk \'brisk\ *adj* 1 : lively 2 : invigorating —**brisk·ly** *adv* —**brisk·ness** *n*

bris·ket \'briskət\ *n* : breast or lower chest of a quadruped

bris·tle \'brisəl\ *n* : short stiff hair ~ *vb* **-tled; -tling** 1 : stand erect 2 : show angry defiance 3 : appear as if covered with bristles —**bris·tly** *adj*

brit·tle \'brit'l\ *adj* **-tler, -tlest** : easily broken or snapped

broach \'brōch\ *n* : pointed tool (as for opening casks) ~ *vb* 1 : pierce (as a cask) to open 2 : introduce for discussion

broad \'brod\ *adj* 1 : wide 2 : spacious 3 : clear or open 4 : obvious 5 : liberal in outlook 6 : widely applicable 7 : dealing with essential points —**broad·en** \-ᵊn\ *vb* —**broad·ly** *adv* —**broad·ness** *n*

broad·cast *n* 1 : transmission by radio waves 2 : radio or television program ~ *vb* **-cast; -cast·ing** 1 : scatter or sow in all directions 2 : make widely known 3 : send out on a broadcast —**broad·cast·er** *n*

broad·cloth *n* : fine cloth

broad·loom *adj* : woven on a wide loom esp. in solid color

broad-mind·ed *adj* : free from prejudice —**broad-mind·ed·ly** *adv* —**broad-mind·ed·ness** *n*

broad·side *n* 1 : simultaneous firing of all guns on one side of a ship 2 : verbal attack

bro·cade \brō'kād\ *n* : usu. silk fabric with a raised design

broc·co·li, broc·o·li \'bräk(ə)lē\ *n* : green vegetable akin to cauliflower

bro·chure \brō'shu̇r\ *n* : pamphlet

brogue \'brōg\ *n* : Irish accent

broil \'broi̇l\ *vb* : cook by radiant heat —**broil** *n*

broil·er *n* 1 : utensil for broiling 2 : chicken fit for broiling

¹**broke** \'brōk\ *past of* BREAK

²**broke** *adj* : out of money

bro·ken \'brōkən\ *adj* 1 : imperfectly spoken —**bro·ken·ly** *adv*

bro·ken-heart·ed \-'härtəd\ *adj* : woeful

bro·ker \'brōkər\ *n* : agent who buys and sells for a fee —**bro·ker·age** \-k(ə)rij\ *n*

bro·mide \-ˌmīd\ *n* : compound of bromine 2 : trite remark or notion —**bro·mid·ic** \brō'midik\ *adj*

bro·mine \'brō,mēn\ *n* : deep red liquid corrosive chemical element

bron·chi·tis \brän'kītəs, bräŋ-\ *n* : inflammation of the bronchi

bron·chus \'bräŋkəs\ *n, pl* **-chi** \-ˌkī, -ˌkē\ : division of the windpipe leading to a lung —**bron·chi·al** \-kēəl\ *adj*

bron·co \'bräŋkō\ *n, pl* **-cos** : small half-wild horse

bronze \'bränz\ *vb* **bronzed; bronz·ing** : make bronze in color ~ *n* 1 : alloy of copper and tin 2 : yellowish brown —**bronzy** \-ē\ *adj*

brooch \'brōch, 'brüch\ *n* : ornamental clasp or pin

brood \'brüd\ *n* : family of young ~ *vb* 1 : sit on eggs to hatch them 2 : ponder ~ *adj* : kept for breeding —**brood·er** *n*

¹**brook** \'bru̇k\ *vb* : tolerate

²**brook** *n* : small stream

broom \'brüm, 'bru̇m\ *n* 1 : flowering shrub 2 : implement for sweeping —**broom·stick** *n*

broth \'brȯth\ *n, pl* **broths** \'brȯths, 'brȯthz\ : liquid in which meat has been cooked

broth·el \'bräthəl, 'brȯth-\ *n* : house of prostitutes

broth·er \'brəthər\ *n, pl* **brothers** *also* **breth·ren** \'breth(ə)rən, 'brethərn\ 1 : male sharing one or both parents with another person 2 : kindred human being —**broth·er·hood** *n* —**broth·er·li·ness** *n* —**broth·er·ly** *adj*

broth·er-in-law *n, pl* **brothers-in-law** : brother of one's spouse or husband of one's sister or of one's spouse's sister

brought *past of* BRING

brow \'brȧu̇\ *n* 1 : eyebrow 2 : forehead 3 : edge of a steep place

brow·beat *vb* **-beat; -beat·en** *or* **-beat; -beat·ing** : intimidate

brown \'brȧu̇n\ *adj* 1 : of the color brown 2 : of dark or tanned complexion ~ *n* : a color like that of coffee ~ *vb* : make or become brown

browse \'brȧu̇z\ *vb* **browsed; brows·ing** 1 : graze 2 : look over casually —**brows·er** *n*

bru·in \'brüən\ *n* : bear

bruise \'brüz\ *vb* **bruised; bruis·ing** 1 : make a bruise on 2 : become bruised ~ *n* : surface injury to flesh

brunch \'brənch\ *n* : late breakfast, early lunch, or combination of both

bru·net, bru·nette \brü'net\ *adj* : having dark skin, hair, and eyes —**brunet** *n*

brunt \'brənt\ *n* : main impact

¹**brush** \'brəsh\ *n* 1 : small cut

branches **2** : coarse shrubby vegetation

2brush *n* : bristles set in a handle used esp. for cleaning or painting **2** : light touch ~ *vb* **1** : apply a brush to **2** : remove with or as if with a brush **3** : dispose of in an offhand way **4** : touch lightly —**brush up** *vb* : renew one's skill

3brush *n* : skirmish

brush-off *n* : abrupt dismissal

brusque \'brəsk\ *adj* : curt or blunt in manner —**brusque-ly** *adv*

bru-tal \'brüt³l\ *adj* : like a brute and esp. cruel —**bru-tal-i-ty** \brü'talətē\ *n* —**bru-tal-ize** \'brüt³l,īz\ *vb* —**bru-tal-ly** \-³lē\ *adv*

brute \'brüt\ *adj* **1** : of or typical of beasts **2** : unreasoning **3** : purely physical ~ *n* **1** : beast **2** : brutal person —**brut-ish** \-ish\ *adj*

bub-ble \'bəbəl\ *vb* -bled; -bling : form, rise in, or give off bubbles ~ *n* : globule of gas in or covered with a liquid —**bub-bly** \-(ə)lē\ *adj*

bu-bo \'b(y)übō\ *n, pl* **buboes** : inflammatory swelling of a lymph gland —**bu-bon-ic** \b(y)ü'bänik\ *adj*

buc-ca-neer \,bəkə'niər\ *n* : pirate

buck \'bək\ *n, pl* **buck** or **bucks** : male animal (as a deer) ~ *vb* **1** : jerk forward **2** : oppose

buck-et \'bəkət\ *n* : pail —**buck-et-ful** *n*

buck-le \-əl\ *n* **1** : clasp (as on a belt) for two loose ends **2** : bend or fold ~ *vb* -led; -ling **1** : fasten with a buckle **2** : apply oneself **3** : bend or crumple

buck-ler \-lər\ *n* : shield

buck-shot *n* : coarse lead shot

buck-skin *n* : soft leather (as from the skin of a buck) —**buckskin** *adj*

buck-tooth *n* : large projecting front tooth —**buck-toothed** *adj*

buck-wheat *n* : herb whose seeds are used as a cereal grain or the seeds themselves

bu-col-ic \byü'kälik\ *adj* : rural

bud \'bəd\ *n* **1** : undeveloped plant shoot **2** : partly opened flower ~ *vb* -dd- **1** : form or put forth buds **2** : be or develop like a bud

Bud-dhism \'bü,dizəm, 'bud,iz-\ *n* : religion of eastern and central Asia —**Bud-dhist** \'büdəst, 'büd-\ *n or adj*

bud-dy \'bədē\ *n, pl* -dies : friend

budge \'bəj\ *vb* budged; budg-ing : move from a place

bud-get \'bəjət\ *n* **1** : estimate of income and expenses **2** : plan for coordinating income and expenses —**bud-get** *vb* —**bud-get-ary** \-ə,terē\ *adj*

buff \'bəf\ *n* **1** : dull yellow-orange color **2** : enthusiast ~ *adj* : of the color buff ~ *vb* : polish

buf-fa-lo \'bəfə,lō\ *n, pl* -lo or -loes also -los : wild ox (as a bison)

1buf-fer \'bəfər\ *n* : one that buffs

2buffer *n* : something that lessens shock

1buf-fet \-ət\ *n* : blow or slap ~ *vb* : hit esp. repeatedly

2buf-fet \(,)bə'fā, bü-\ *n* **1** : sideboard **2** : meal at which people serve themselves

buf-foon \(,)bə'fün\ *n* : clown —**buf-foon-ery** \-(ə)rē\ *n*

bug \'bəg\ *n* **1** : small usu. obnoxious crawling creature **2** : 4-winged sucking insect **3** : disease-producing germ **4** : hidden microphone ~ *vb* -gg- **1** : pester **2** : conceal a microphone in

bug-a-boo \'bəgə,bü\ *n, pl* -boos : bogey

bug-bear *n* : source of dread

bug-gy \'bəgē\ *n, pl* -gies : light carriage

bu-gle \'byügəl\ *n* : trumpetlike brass instrument —**bu-gler** \-glər\ *n*

build \'bild\ *vb* built \'bilt\; build-ing **1** : put together **2** : establish **3** : increase ~ *n* : physique —**build-er** *n*

build-ing \'bildiŋ\ *n* **1** : roofed and walled structure **2** : art or business of constructing buildings

bulb \'bəlb\ *n* **1** : large underground plant bud **2** : rounded or pear-shaped object —**bul-bous** \-əs\ *adj*

bulge \'bəlj\ *n* : swelling projecting part ~ *vb* bulged; bulg-ing : swell out

bulk \'bəlk\ *n* **1** : magnitude **2** : indigestible fibrous food residues **3** : large mass **4** : major portion ~ *vb* : have bulk —**bulky** \-ē\ *adj*

bulk-head *n* : ship's partition

1bull \'bul\ *n* **1** : adult male of a bovine or other large animal ~ *adj* : male

2bull *n* : papal letter

bull-dog *n* : compact short-haired dog

bull-doze \-,dōz\ *vb* **1** : move or level with a tractor (**bull-doz-er**) having a broad blade **2** : force

bul-let \'bulət\ *n* : missile to be shot from a gun —**bul-let-proof** *adj*

bul-le-tin \-³n\ *n* **1** : brief public report **2** : periodical

bull-fight *n* : sport of taunting and killing bulls —**bull-fight-er** *n*

bull-finch *n* : English songbird

bull-frog *n* : large deep-voiced frog

bull-head-ed *adj* : stupidly stubborn

bul-lion \'bulyən\ *n* : gold or silver esp. in bars

bull-ock \-ək\ *n* **1** : young bull **2** : steer

bull's–eye n, pl **bull's–eyes** : center of a target

bul·ly \'bülē\ n, pl **-lies** : one who hurts or intimidates others ~ vb **-lied; -ly·ing** : act like a bully toward

bul·rush \'bül₁rəsh\ n : tall coarse rush or sedge

bul·wark \-(₁)wərk, -₁wȯrk; 'bəl(₁)wərk\ n 1 : wall-like defense 2 : strong support or protection

bum \'bəm\ vb **-mm-** 1 : wander as a tramp 2 : seek by begging ~ n : idle worthless person ~ adj : worthless

bum·ble·bee \'bəmbəl₁bē\ n : large hairy bee

bump \'bəmp\ vb : strike or knock forcibly ~ n 1 : sudden blow 2 : small bulge or swelling —**bumpy** adj

¹bum·per \'bəmpər\ adj : unusually large

²bump·er \'bəmpər\ n : shock-absorbing bar at either end of a car

bump·kin \'bəmpkən\ n : awkward country person

bun \'bən\ n : sweet biscuit or roll

bunch \'bənch\ n : group ~ vb : form into a group —**bunchy** adj

bun·dle \'bənd⁰l\ n 1 : several items bunched together 2 : something wrapped ready for carrying 3 : large amount ~ vb **-dled; -dling** : gather into a bundle

bun·ga·low \'bəngə₁lō\ n : one-story house

bun·gle \'bəngəl\ vb **-gled; -gling** : do badly —**bungle** n —**bun·gler** n

bun·ion \'bənyən\ n : inflamed swelling of the first joint of the big toe

¹bunk \'bəŋk\ n : built-in bed that is often one of a tier ~ vb : sleep

²bunk n : nonsense

bun·ker \-ər\ n 1 : storage compartment 2 : protective embankment

bun·kum, bun·combe \'bəŋkəm\ n : nonsense

bun·ny \'bənē\ n, pl **-nies** : rabbit

¹bunt·ing \'bəntiŋ\ n : small finch

²bunting n : flag material

buoy \'büē, 'bȯi\ n : floating marker anchored in water ~ vb 1 : keep afloat 2 : raise the spirits of —**buoy·an·cy** \'bȯiənsē, 'büyən-\ n —**buoy·ant** \-ənt, -yənt\ adj

bur, burr \'bər\ n : rough or prickly covering of a fruit —**bur·ry** adj

bur·den \'bərd⁰n\ n 1 : something carried 2 : something oppressive ~ cargo ~ vb : load or oppress —**bur·den·some** \-səm\ adj

bur·dock \'bər₁däk\ n : tall coarse herb with prickly flower heads

bu·reau \'byürō\ n 1 : chest of drawers

2 : administrative unit 3 : business office

bu·reau·cra·cy \byü'räkrəsē\ n, pl **-cies** 1 : body of government officials 2 : unwieldy administrative system —**bu·reau·crat** \'byürə₁krat\ n —**bu·reau·crat·ic** \₁byürə'kratik\ adj

bur·geon \'bərjən\ vb : grow

bur·glary \'bərglərē\ n, pl **-glar·ies** : forcible entry into a building to steal —**bur·glar** \-glər\ n —**bur·glar·ize** \'bərglə₁rīz\ vb

bur·gle \'bərgəl\ vb **-gled; -gling** : commit burglary on or in

Bur·gun·dy \'bərgəndē\ n, pl **-dies** : kind of table wine

buri·al \'berēəl\ n : act of burying

bur·lap \'bər₁lap\ n : coarse fabric usu. of jute or hemp

bur·lesque \(₁)bər'lesk\ n 1 : witty or derisive imitation 2 : broadly humorous variety show ~ vb **-lesqued; -lesqu·ing** : mock

bur·ly \'bərlē\ adj **-li·er; -est** : strongly and heavily built

burn \'bərn\ vb **burned** \'bərnd, 'bərnt\ or **burnt** \'bərnt\; **burn·ing** 1 : be on fire 2 : feel or look as if on fire 3 : alter or become altered by or as if by fire or heat 4 : cause or make by fire ~ n : injury or effect produced by burning —**burn·er** n

bur·nish \'bərnish\ vb : polish

burp \'bərp\ n or vb : belch

bur·ro \'bərō, 'bȯr-\ n, pl **-os** : small donkey

bur·row \'bərō\ n : hole in the ground made by an animal ~ vb : make a burrow —**bur·row·er** n

bur·sar \'bərsər\ n : treasurer esp. of a college

bur·si·tis \(₁)bər'sītəs\ n : inflammation of a sac (**bur·sa** \'bərsə\) in a joint

burst \'bərst\ vb **burst** or **burst·ed; burst·ing** 1 : fly apart or into pieces 2 : enter or emerge suddenly ~ n : sudden outbreak or effort

bury \'berē\ vb **bur·ied; bury·ing** 1 : deposit in the earth 2 : hide

bus \'bəs\ n, pl **bus·es** or **bus·ses** : large motor-driven passenger vehicle ~ vb : **bused** or **bussed; bus·ing** or **bus·sing** : travel or transport by bus

bus·boy n : waiter's helper

bush \'bush\ n 1 : shrub 2 : rough uncleared country 3 : a thick tuft or mat —**bushy** adj

bush·el \'bushəl\ n : 4 pecks

bush·ing \'bushiŋ\ n : metal lining used as a guide or bearing

busi·ness \'biznəs, -nəz\ *n* **1** : vocation **2** : commercial or industrial enterprise **3** : personal concerns —**busi·ness·man** \-ˌman\ *n* —**busi·ness·wom·an** \-ˌwümən\ *n*

¹bust \'bəst\ *n* **1** : sculpture of the head and upper torso **2** : breasts of a woman

²bust *vb* **1** : burst or break **2** : tame ~ *n* **1** : punch **2** : failure

¹bus·tle \'bəsəl\ *vb* **-tled; -tling** : move or work briskly ~ *n* : energetic activity

²bustle *n* : pad or frame formerly worn under a woman's skirt

busy \'bizē\ *adj* **busi·er; -est 1** : engaged in action **2** : being in use **3** : full of activity ~ *vb* **bus·ied; busy·ing** : make or keep busy —**busi·ly** *adv*

busy·body *n* : meddler

but \(')bət\ *conj* **1** : if not for the fact **2** : that **3** : without the accompanying condition **4** : rather **5** : yet nevertheless ~ *prep* : other than

butch·er \'bu̇chər\ *n* **1** : one who slaughters animals or dresses their flesh **2** : brutal killer —**butcher** *vb* —**butch·ery** \-(ə)rē\ *n*

but·ler \'bətlər\ *n* : chief male household servant

¹butt \'bət\ *vb* : strike with a butt ~ *n* : blow with the head or horns

²butt *n* **1** : target **2** : victim

³butt *vb* : join edge to edge

⁴butt *n* : large end or bottom

⁵butt *n* : large cask

butte \'byüt\ *n* : isolated steep hill

but·ter \'bətər\ *n* : solid edible fat churned from cream ~ *vb* : spread with butter —**but·tery** *adj*

but·ter·cup *n* : yellow-flowered herb

but·ter·fat *n* : natural fat of milk and of butter

but·ter·fly *n* : insect with 4 broad wings

but·ter·milk *n* : liquid remaining after butter is churned

but·ter·nut *n* : edible nut of a tree related to the walnut or this tree

but·ter·scotch \-ˌskäch\ *n* : candy made from sugar, corn syrup, and water

but·tocks \'bətəks\ *n pl* : rear part of the hips

but·ton \'bət⁰n\ *n* : small knob for fastening clothing **2** : buttonlike object ~ *vb* : fasten with buttons

but·ton·hole *n* : hole or slit for a button ~ *vb* : hold in talk

but·tress \'bətrəs\ *n* **1** : projecting structure to support a wall **2** : support —**buttress** *vb*

bux·om \'bəksəm\ *adj* : full-bosomed

buy \'bī\ *vb* **bought** \'bȯt\; **buy·ing** : purchase ~ *n* : bargain —**buy·er** *n*

buzz \'bəz\ *vb* : make a low humming sound ~ *n* : act or sound of buzzing

buz·zard \-ərd\ *n* **1** : heavy slow-flying hawk **2** : American vulture

buzz·er *n* : signaling device that buzzes

by \(')bī, bə\ *prep* **1** : near **2** : through **3** : beyond **4** : throughout **5** : no later than ~ \'bī\ *adv* **1** : near **2** : farther

by·gone \'bīˌgȯn\ *adj* : past —**bygone** *n*

by·law, bye·law *n* : organization's rule

by·line *n* : writer's name on an article

by·pass *n* : alternate route ~ *vb* : go around

by·prod·uct *n* : product in addition to the main product

by·stand·er *n* : spectator

by·way \'bīˌwā\ *n* : side road

by·word *n* : proverb

C

c \'sē\ *n, pl* **c's** *or* **cs** \'sēz\ : 3d letter of the alphabet

cab \'kab\ *n* **1** : light closed horse-drawn carriage **2** : taxicab **3** : compartment for a driver —**cab·by, cab·bie** *n* —**cab·man** \-mən\ *n* —**cab·stand** *n*

ca·bal \kə'bal\ *n* : group of conspirators ~ *vb* **-ll-** : plot

ca·bana \kə'ban(y)ə\ *n* : shelter at a beach or pool

cab·a·ret \ˌkabə'rā\ *n* : nightclub

cab·bage \'kabij\ *n* : vegetable with a dense head of leaves

cab·in \-ən\ *n* **1** : private room on a

ship **2** : small house **3** : airplane compartment

cab·i·net \-(ə)nət\ *n* **1** : display case or cupboard **2** : advisory council of a head of state —**cab·i·net·mak·er** *n* —**cab·i·net·mak·ing** *n* —**cab·i·net·work** *n*

ca·ble \'kābəl\ *n* **1** : strong rope, wire, or chain **2** : cablegram **3** : bundle of electrical wires ~ *vb* **-bled; -bling** : send a cablegram to

ca·ble·gram \-ˌgram\ *n* : message sent by a submarine telegraph cable

ca·boose \kə'büs\ *n* : crew car on a train

ca·cao \kə·kau̇, -ˈkāō\ *n*, *pl* cacaos : So. American tree whose seeds (ca·cao beans) yield cocoa and chocolate

cache \ˈkash\ *n* 1 : hiding place 2 : something hidden ~ *vb* cached; cach·ing : place in a cache

cack·le \ˈkakəl\ *vb* -led; -ling : make a cry or laugh like the sound of a hen —cackle *n* —cack·ler *n*

ca·coph·o·ny \ka·ˈkäfənē\ *n*, *pl* -nies : harsh noise —ca·coph·o·nous \-nəs\ *adj*

cac·tus \ˈkaktəs\ *n*, *pl* cac·ti \-ˌtī\ *or* -tus·es : drought-resistant flowering plant with scales or prickles

cad \ˈkad\ *n* : ungentlemanly person —cad·dish \-ish\ *adj* —cad·dish·ly *adv* —cad·dish·ness *n*

ca·dav·er \kə·ˈdavər\ *n* : dead body —ca·dav·er·ous \-(ə)rəs\ *adj*

cad·die, cad·dy \ˈkadē\ *n*, *pl* -dies : golfer's helper —caddie, caddy *vb*

cad·dy \ˈkadē\ *n*, *pl* -dies : small tea chest

ca·dence \ˈkādⁿs\ *n* : measure of a rhythmical flow —ca·denced \-ⁿst\ *adj*

ca·det \kə·ˈdet\ *n* : student in a military academy

cadge \ˈkaj\ *vb* cadged; cadg·ing : beg —cadg·er *n*

cad·mi·um \ˈkadmēəm\ *n* : grayish metallic chemical element

cad·re \ˈka-ˌrē\ *n* : nucleus of highly trained people

ca·fé \ka·ˈfā, kə-\ *n* : restaurant

caf·e·te·ria \ˌkafə·ˈtirēə\ *n* : self-service restaurant

caf·feine \ka·ˈfēn, ˈkaˌfēn\ *n* : stimulating alkaloid in coffee and tea

cage \ˈkāj\ *n* : box of wire or bars for confining an animal ~ *vb* caged; cag·ing : put or keep in a cage

ca·gey \-ē\ *adj* -gi·er; -est : shrewd —ca·gi·ly *adv* —ca·gi·ness *n*

cais·son \ˈkāˌsän, ˈkāsⁿn\ *n* 1 : ammunition carriage 2 : watertight diving chamber

ca·jole \kə·ˈjōl\ *vb* -joled; -jol·ing : persuade or coax —ca·jol·ery \-(ə)rē\ *n*

cake \ˈkāk\ *n* : food of baked or fried usu. sweet batter ~ *vb* caked; cak·ing 1 : form into a cake 2 : encrust

cal·a·bash \ˈkaləˌbash\ *n* : gourd

cal·a·mine \ˈkaləˌmīn\ *n* : lotion of oxides of zinc and iron

ca·lam·i·ty \kə·ˈlamətē\ *n*, *pl* -ties : disaster —ca·lam·i·tous \-ətəs\ *adj* —ca·lam·i·tous·ly *adv* —ca·lam·i·tous·ness *n*

cal·ci·fy \ˈkalsəˌfī\ *vb* -fied; -fy·ing

: harden —cal·ci·fi·ca·tion \ˌkalsəfə·ˈkāshən\ *n*

cal·ci·um \ˈkalsēəm\ *n* : silver-white soft metallic chemical element

cal·cu·late \ˈkalkyə·ˌlāt\ *vb* -lat·ed; -lat·ing 1 : determine by mathematical processes 2 : judge —cal·cu·la·ble \-ˌləbəl\ *adj* —cal·cu·la·bly \-blē\ *adv* —cal·cu·la·tion \ˌkalkyə·ˈlāshən\ *n* —cal·cu·la·tor \ˈkalkyə·ˌlātər\ *n*

cal·cu·lat·ing *adj* : shrewd

cal·cu·lus \ˈkalkyələs\ *n*, *pl* -li \-ˌlī, -ˌlē\ : higher mathematics dealing with rates of change

cal·dron \ˈkȯldrən\ *n* : large kettle

cal·en·dar \ˈkaləndər\ *n* : list of days, weeks, and months

¹calf \ˈkaf, ˈkȧf\ *n*, *pl* calves \ˈkavz, ˈkȧvz\ : young cow or related mammal —calf·skin *n*

²calf *n*, *pl* calves : back part of the leg below the knee

cal·i·ber, cal·i·bre \ˈkaləbər\ *n* 1 : diameter of a bullet or shell or of a gun bore 2 : degree of mental or moral excellence

cal·i·brate \-ˌbrāt\ *vb* -brat·ed; -brat·ing : determine, correct, or put measuring marks on —cal·i·bra·tion \ˌkalə·ˈbrāshən\ *n* —cal·i·bra·tor \ˈkalə·ˌbrātər\ *n*

cal·i·co \ˈkaliˌkō\ *n*, *pl* -coes *or* -cos : printed cotton fabric —calico *adj*

cal·i·pers, cal·li·pers \ˈkaləpərz\ *n* : measuring instrument with two adjustable legs

ca·liph, ca·lif \ˈkāləf, ˈkal-\ *n* : title of head of Islam —ca·liph·ate \-ˌāt, -ət\ *n*

cal·is·then·ics \ˌkaləs·ˈtheniks\ *n sing or pl* : bending, stretching, and jumping exercises —cal·is·then·ic *adj*

calk \ˈkȯk\ *var of* CAULK

call \ˈkȯl\ *vb* 1 : shout 2 : summon 3 : demand 5 : telephone 5 : make a visit 6 : name —call *n* —call·er *n* —call down *vb* : reprimand —call off *vb* : cancel

call·ing *n* : vocation

cal·li·ope \kə·ˈlīə(ˌ)pē, ˈkalēˌōp\ *n* : musical instrument of steam whistles

cal·lous \ˈkaləs\ *adj* 1 : thickened and hardened 2 : unfeeling ~ *vb* : make callous —cal·los·i·ty \ka·ˈläsətē\ *n* —cal·lous·ly *adv* —cal·lous·ness *n*

cal·low \ˈkalō\ *adj* : inexperienced or innocent —cal·low·ness *n*

cal·lus \ˈkaləs\ *n* : callous area on skin or bark ~ *vb* : form a callus

calm \ˈkäm, ˈkälm\ *n* 1 : period or condition of peacefulness or stillness

~ *adj* : still or tranquil — *vb* : make calm —**calm·ly** *adv* —**calm·ness** *n*

ca·lor·ic \kə'lórik\ *adj* : relating to heat or calories

cal·o·rie \'kalərē\ *n* : unit for measuring heat and energy value of food

ca·lum·ni·ate \kə'ləmnē,āt\ *vb* **-at·ed; -at·ing** : slander —**ca·lum·ni·a·tion** \-,ləmnē'āshən\ *n*

cal·um·ny \'kaləmnē\ *n, pl* **-nies** : false and malicious charge —**ca·lum·ni·ous** \kə'ləmnēəs\ *adj*

calve \'kav, 'kåv\ *vb* **calved; calv·ing** : give birth to a calf

calves *pl of* CALF

ca·lyp·so \kə'lipsō\ *n, pl* **-sos** : satirical song of the West Indies

ca·lyx \'kāliks, 'kal-\ *n, pl* **-lyx·es** *or* **-ly·ces** \-lə,sēz\ : sepals of a flower

cam \'kam\ *n* : bump (as on a shaft) for pushing another part

ca·ma·ra·de·rie \,kăm(ə)'rädərē, ,kam-, -'rad-\ *n* : fellowship

cam·bric \'kāmbrik\ *n* : fine thin linen or cotton fabric

came *past of* COME

cam·el \'kaməl\ *n* : large hoofed mammal of desert areas

ca·mel·lia \kə'mēlyə\ *n* : shrub or tree grown for its showy roselike flowers or the flower itself

cam·eo \'kamē,ō\ *n, pl* **-eos** : gem carved in relief

cam·era \'kam(ə)rə\ *n* **1** : box with a lens for taking pictures **2** : part of a television transmitter to convert an image to signals —**cam·era·man** \-,man, -mən\ *n*

cam·ou·flage \'kamə,fläzh, -,fläj\ *vb* : hide by disguising —**camouflage** *n*

camp \'kamp\ *n* **1** : place to stay temporarily esp. in a tent **2** : group living in a camp ~ *vb* : make or live in a camp —**camp·er** *n* —**camp·ground** *n* —**camp·site** *n*

cam·paign \kam'pān\ *n* : series of military operations or of activities meant to gain a result —**campaign** *vb* —**cam·paign·er** *n*

cam·pa·nile \,kampə'nēlē, -'nē(ə)l\, *n, pl* **-ni·les** *or* **-ni·li** \-'nēlē\ : bell tower

cam·phor \'kam(p)fər\ *n* : gummy volatile fragrant compound from an evergreen tree (**cam·phor tree**)

cam·pus \'kampəs\ *n* : grounds and buildings of a college or school

¹can \'kan, (')kan\ *vb, past* **could** \('kud\; *pres sing & pl* **can 1** : be able to **2** : be permitted to by conscience or feeling **3** : have permission or liberty to

²can \'kan\ *n* : metal container ~ *vb*

-nn- : preserve by sealing in airtight cans or jars —**can·ner** *n* —**can·nery** \-(ə)rē\ *n*

ca·nal \kə'nal\ *n* **1** : tubular passage in the body **2** : channel filled with water —**ca·nal·boat** *n*

can·a·pé \'kanəpē, -,pā\ *n* : appetizer

ca·nard \kə'närd\ *n* : false report

ca·nary \-'ne(ə)rē\ *n, pl* **-nar·ies** : yellow or greenish finch

can·cel \'kansəl\ *vb* **-celed** *or* **-celled; -cel·ing** *or* **-cel·ling 1** : cross out **2** : destroy, neutralize, or match the force or effect of —**cancel** *n* —**can·cel·la·tion** \,kansə'lāshən\ *n*

can·cer \'kansər\ *n* **1** : malignant tumor that tends to spread **2** : slowly destructive evil —**can·cer·ous** \-(ə)rəs\ *adj* —**can·cer·ous·ly** *adv*

can·de·la·bra \,kandə'läbrə, -'lab-\ *n* : candelabrum

can·de·la·brum \-rəm\ *n, pl* **-bra** \-rə\ : ornamental branched candlestick

can·did \'kandəd\ *adj* **1** : frank **2** : unposed —**can·did·ly** *adv* —**can·did·ness** *n*

can·di·date \'kan(d)ə,dāt, -(d)ədət\ *n* : one who seeks an office or membership —**can·di·da·cy** \-(d)ədəsē\ *n*

can·dle \'kand²l\ *n* : tallow or wax molded around a wick and burned to give light —**can·dle·light** *n* —**can·dle·stick** *n*

can·dor \'kandər\ *n* : frankness

can·dy \-dē\ *n, pl* **-dies** : food made from sugar ~ *vb* **-died; -dy·ing** : encrust in sugar

cane \'kān\ *n* **1** : slender plant stem **2** : a tall woody grass or reed **3** : stick for walking or beating ~ *vb* **caned; can·ing 1** : beat with a cane **2** : weave or make with cane —**can·er** *n*

ca·nine \'kā,nīn\ *adj* **1** : relating to dogs **2** : being the pointed tooth next to the incisors ~ *n* **1** : canine tooth **2** : dog

can·is·ter \'kanəstər\ *n* : small storage box

can·ker \'kaŋkər\ *n* : mouth ulcer —**can·ker·ous** \-k(ə)rəs\ *adj*

can·na·bis \'kanəbəs\ *n* : dried hemp spikes

can·ni·bal \-əbəl\ *n* : human or animal that eats its own kind —**can·ni·bal·ism** \-bə,lizəm\ *n* —**can·ni·bal·is·tic** \,kanəbə'listik\ *adj*

can·ni·bal·ize \-bə,līz\ *vb* **-ized; -iz·ing 1** : take usable parts from **2** : practice cannibalism

can·non \-ən\ *n, pl* **-nons** *or* **-non** : artillery piece —**can·non·ball** *n* —**can·non·eer** \,kanə'niər\ *n*

can·non·ade \ˌkanəˈnād\ *n* : heavy artillery fire — *vb* **-ad·ed; -ad·ing** : bombard

can·not \ˈkanˌät; kəˈnät\ : can not — **cannot but** : be bound to

can·ny \ˈkanē\ *adj* **-ni·er; -est** : shrewd — **can·ni·ly** *adv* — **can·ni·ness** *n*

ca·noe \kəˈnü\ *n* : narrow sharp-ended boat propelled by paddles — **canoe** *vb* — **ca·noe·ist** *n*

¹can·on \ˈkanən\ *n* **1** : regulation governing a church **2** : authoritative list **3** : an accepted principle

²canon *n* : clergyman in a cathedral — **can·on·ry** \-rē\ *n*

ca·non·i·cal \kəˈnänikəl\ *adj* **1** : relating to or conforming to a canon **2** : orthodox — **ca·non·i·cal·ly** *adv*

can·on·ize \ˈkanəˌnīz\ *vb* **-ized** \-ˌnīzd\; **-iz·ing** : recognize as a saint — **can·on·iza·tion** \ˌkanənəˈzāshən\ *n*

can·o·py \ˈkanəpē\ *n, pl* **-pies** : overhanging cover — **canopy** *vb*

¹cant \ˈkant\ *n* **1** : slanting surface **2** : slant — *vb* **1** : tip up **2** : lean to one side

²cant *vb* : talk hypocritically ~ *n* **1** : jargon **2** : insincere talk

can't \ˈkant, ˈkänt, ˈkänt\ : can not

can·ta·loupe \ˈkantəlˌōp\ *n* : muskmelon with orange flesh

can·tan·ker·ous \kanˈtaŋk(ə)rəs\ *adj* : hard to deal with — **can·tan·ker·ous·ly** *adv* — **can·tan·ker·ous·ness** *n*

can·ta·ta \kənˈtätə\ *n* : choral work

can·teen \kanˈtēn\ *n* **1** : place of recreation for servicemen **2** : water container

can·ter \ˈkantər\ *n* : slow gallop — **canter** *vb*

can·ti·cle \ˈkantikəl\ *n* : liturgical song

can·ti·le·ver \ˈkantəlˌēvər, -ˌev-\ *n* : beam or structure supported only at one end

can·to \ˈkanˌtō\ *n, pl* **-tos** : major division of a long poem

can·tor \ˈkantər\ *n* : synagogue official who sings liturgical music

can·vas \ˈkanvəs\ *n* **1** : strong cloth orig. used for making tents and sails **2** : set of sails **3** : oil painting

can·vass \-vəs\ *vb* : solicit votes, orders, or opinions from ~ *n* : act of canvassing — **can·vass·er** *n*

can·yon \-yən\ *n* : deep valley with steep sides

cap \ˈkap\ *n* **1** : covering for the head **2** : top or cover like a cap — *vb* **-pp- 1** : provide or protect with a cap **2** : climax — **cap·ful** \-ˌful\ *n*

ca·pa·ble \ˈkāpəbəl\ *adj* : able to do

something — **ca·pa·bil·i·ty** \ˌkāpəˈbilətē\ *n* — **ca·pa·bly** \ˈkāpəblē\ *adv*

ca·pa·cious \kəˈpāshəs\ *adj* : able to contain much

ca·pac·i·tance \-ˈpasətəns\ *n* : ability to store electrical energy

ca·pac·i·tor \-ətər\ *n* : device having capacitance

ca·pac·i·ty \-ətē\ *n, pl* **-ties 1** : ability to contain **2** : volume **3** : ability **4** : role or job — *adj* : equaling maximum capacity

¹cape \ˈkāp\ *n* : point of land jutting out into water

²cape *n* : garment that drapes over the shoulders

¹ca·per \ˈkāpər\ *n* : flower bud of a shrub pickled for use as a relish

²caper *vb* : leap or prance about ~ *n* **1** : frolicsome leap **2** : illegal escapade

cap·il·lary \ˈkapəˌlerē\ *adj* **1** : resembling a hair **2** : having a very small bore ~ *n, pl* **-lar·ies** : tiny thin-walled blood vessel

¹cap·i·tal \-ətᵊl\ *adj* **1** : punishable by death **2** : being in the series A, B, C rather than a, b, c **3** : relating to capital **4** : excellent ~ *n* **1** : capital letter **2** : seat of government **3** : wealth **4** : total face value of a company's stock **5** : capitalists as a group

²capital *n* : top part of a column

cap·i·tal·ism \-ˌizəm\ *n* : economic system of private ownership of capital

cap·i·tal·ist \-əst\ *n* **1** : person with capital invested in business **2** : believer in capitalism — *adj* **1** : owning capital **2** : practicing, advocating, or marked by capitalism — **cap·i·tal·is·tic** \ˌkapətᵊlˈistik\ *adj* — **cap·i·tal·is·ti·cal·ly** \-k(ə)lē\ *adv*

cap·i·tal·ize \-ˌīz\ *vb* **-ized; -iz·ing 1** : write or print with a capital letter **2** : use as capital **3** : supply capital for **4** : turn something to advantage — **cap·i·tal·iza·tion** \ˌkapətᵊlə-ˈzāshən\ *n*

cap·i·tol \ˈkapətᵊl\ *n* : building in which a legislature sits

ca·pit·u·late \kəˈpichəˌlāt\ *vb* **-lat·ed; -lat·ing** : surrender — **ca·pit·u·la·tion** \-ˌpichəˈlāshən\ *n*

ca·pon \ˈkāˌpän, -pən\ *n* : castrated male chicken

ca·price \kəˈprēs\ *n* : whim — **ca·pri·cious** \-ˈprishəs\ *adj*

cap·size \ˈkapˌsīz, kapˈsīz\ *vb* **-sized; -siz·ing** : overturn

cap·stan \ˈkapstən, -ˌstan\ *n* : upright winch

cap·sule \'kapsəl, -sül\ *n* **1** : enveloping cover (as for medicine) **2** : small pressurized compartment for astronauts ∼ *vb* **-suled; -sul·ing** : put in compact form ∼ *adj* **1** : very brief or compact or compact **—cap·su·lar** \-sələr\ *adj* **—cap·su·late** \-sə, lāt, -sələt\ *adj* **—cap·su·lat·ed** \-sə, lātəd\ *adj*

cap·tain \'kaptən\ *n* **1** : commander of a body of troops **2** : officer in charge of a ship **3** : commissioned officer in the navy ranking next below a rear admiral or a commodore **4** : commissioned officer (as in the army) ranking next below a major **5** : leader ∼ *vb* : be captain of **—cap·tain·cy** *n* **—cap·tain·ship** *n*

cap·tion \-shən\ *n* **1** : title **2** : explanation with an illustration **—caption** *vb*

cap·tious \-shəs\ *adj* : tending to find fault **—cap·tious·ly** *adv*

cap·ti·vate \-tə, vāt\ *vb* **-vat·ed; -vat·ing** : attract and charm **—cap·ti·va·tion** \, kaptə'vāshən\ *n* **—cap·ti·va·tor** \'kaptə, vātər\ *n*

cap·tive \-tiv\ *adj* **1** : made prisoner **2** : confined or under control **—captive** *n* **—cap·tiv·i·ty** \kap'tivətē\ *n*

cap·tor \'kaptər\ *n* : one that captures

cap·ture \-chər\ *n* : seizure by force or trickery ∼ *vb* **-tured; -tur·ing** : take captive

1car \'kär\ *n* **1** : vehicle moved on wheels **2** : cage of an elevator

ca·rafe \kə'raf, -'räf\ *n* : decanter

car·a·mel \'karəməl, 'kärməl\ *n* **1** : burnt sugar used for flavoring and coloring **2** : firm chewy candy

1carat *var of* KARAT

2car·at \'karət\ *n* : unit of weight for precious stones

car·a·van \'karə, van\ *n* : travelers journeying together (as in a line)

car·a·way \'karə, wā\ *n* : aromatic herb with seeds used in seasoning

car·bine \'kär, bēn, -, bīn\ *n* : short-barreled rifle

car·bo·hy·drate \, kärbō'hī, drāt, -drət\ *n* : compound of carbon, hydrogen, and oxygen

car·bon \'kärbən\ *n* **1** : chemical element occurring in nature as diamond and graphite **2** : piece of carbon paper or a copy made with it

1car·bon·ate \'kärbə, nāt, -nət\ *n* : salt or ester of a carbon-containing acid

2car·bon·ate \-, nāt\ *vb* **-at·ed; -at·ing** : impregnate with carbon dioxide **—car·bon·a·tion** \, kärbə'nāshən\ *n*

carbon paper *n* : thin paper coated with a pigment for making copies

car·bun·cle \'kär, bəŋkəl\ *n* : painful inflammation of the skin and underlying tissue

car·bu·re·tor \'kärb(y)ə, rātər\ *n* : device for mixing fuel and air

car·cass \-kəs\ *n* : dead body

car·cin·o·gen \kär'sinəjən\ *n* : agent causing cancer **—car·ci·no·gen·ic** \, kärs'nō'jenik\ *adj*

car·ci·no·ma \, kärs'n'ōmə\ *n, pl* **-ma** *or* **-ma·ta** \-mətə\ : malignant tumor **—car·ci·no·ma·tous** \-mətəs\ *adj*

1card \'kärd\ *vb* : comb (fibers) before spinning ∼ *n* : device for carding fibers **—card·er** *n*

2card *n* **1** : playing card **2** *pl* : game played with playing cards **3** : small flat piece of paper

card·board *n* : stiff material like paper

car·di·ac \'kärdē, ak\ *adj* : relating to the heart

car·di·gan \-igən\ *n* : sweater with an opening in the front

1car·di·nal \'kärdnəl, -'nəl\ *n* **1** : official of the Roman Catholic Church **2** : bright red songbird

2cardinal *adj* : of basic importance

cardinal number *n* : number (as 1, 82, 357) used in counting

car·dio·gram \'kärdēə, gram\ *n* : line made by a cardiograph

car·dio·graph \-, graf\ *n* : instrument that graphically registers movements of the heart **—car·dio·graph·ic** \, kärdēə'grafik\ *adj* **—car·di·og·ra·phy** \-'ägrəfē\ *n*

car·di·ol·o·gy \, kärdē'äləjē\ *n* : study of the heart **—car·di·ol·o·gist** \-jəst\ *n*

car·dio·vas·cu·lar \-ō'vaskyələr\ *adj* : relating to the heart and blood vessels

care \'keər\ *n* **1** : anxiety **2** : watchful attention **3** : supervision ∼ *vb* **cared; car·ing 1** : feel anxiety or concern **2** : like **3** : provide care **—care·free** *adj* **—care·ful** \-fəl\ *adj* **—care·ful·ly** *adv* **—care·ful·ness** *n* **—care·less** *adj* **—care·less·ly** *adv* **—care·less·ness** *n*

ca·reen \kə'rēn\ *vb* **1** : lean over **2** : sway from side to side

ca·reer \kə'riər\ *n* : vocation ∼ *vb* : go at top speed

ca·ress \kə'res\ *n* : tender touch ∼ *vb* : touch lovingly or tenderly

car·et \'karət\ *n* : mark ∧ showing where something is to be inserted

care·tak·er *n* : one in charge for another or temporarily

car·go \'kärgō\ *n, pl* **-goes** *or* **-gos** : transported goods

car·i·bou \'karə, bü\ *n, pl* **-bou** *or* **-bous** : large No. American deer

car·i·ca·ture \'karikə,chūr\ *n* : distorted representation for humor or ridicule —**caricature** *vb* —**car·i·ca·tur·ist** \-əst\ *n*

car·ies \'ka(ə)rēz\ *n, pl* **caries** : tooth decay

car·il·lon \'karə,län\ *n* : set of tuned bells

car·mine \'kärmən, -,mīn\ *n* : vivid red

car·nage \'kärnij\ *n* : slaughter

car·nal \'kärnᵊl\ *adj* : sensual —**car·nal·i·ty** \kär'nalətē\ *n* —**car·nal·ly** *adv*

car·na·tion \kär'nāshən\ *n* : showy flower

car·ni·val \'kärnəvəl\ *n* 1 : festival 2 : traveling enterprise offering amusements

car·ni·vore \-,vōr\ *n* : flesh-eating animal —**car·niv·o·rous** \kär'niv(ə)rəs\ *adj* —**car·niv·o·rous·ly** *adv* —**car·niv·o·rous·ness** *n*

car·ol \'karəl\ *n* : song of joy —**carol** *vb*

car·om \-əm\ *n or vb* : rebound

ca·rouse \kə'raúz\ *vb* —**roused; -rous·ing** : drink and be boisterous —**carouse** *n* —**ca·rous·er** *n*

car·ou·sel, car·rou·sel \,karə'sel, 'karə,-\ *n* : merry-go-round

¹carp \'kärp\ *vb* : find fault

²carp *n, pl* **carp** *or* **carps** : freshwater fish

car·pel \'kärpəl\ *n* : modified leaf forming part of the ovary of a flower

car·pen·ter \'kärpəntər\ *n* : one who builds with wood —**carpenter** *vb* —**car·pen·try** \-trē\ *n*

car·pet \-pət\ *n* : fabric floor covering ~ *vb* : cover with a carpet —**car·pet·ing** \-iŋ\ *n*

car·port *n* : open-sided automobile shelter

car·riage \'karij\ *n* 1 : conveyance 2 : manner of holding oneself 3 : wheeled vehicle

car·ri·on \-ēən\ *n* : dead and decaying flesh

car·rot \-ət\ *n* : root vegetable

car·ry \'karē\ *vb* **-ried; -ry·ing** 1 : move while supporting in a specified way 3 : support 4 : keep in stock 5 : reach to a distance 6 : win —**car·ri·er** \-ēər\ *n* —**carry on** *vb* 1 : conduct 2 : behave excitedly —**carry out** *vb* : put into effect

cart \'kärt\ *n* : wheeled vehicle ~ *vb* : carry in a cart —**cart·age** \-ij\ *n* —**cart·er** *n*

car·tel \kär'tel\ *n* : business combination designed to limit competition

car·ti·lage \'kärtᵊlij\ *n* : elastic skeletal tissue —**car·ti·lag·i·nous** \,kärtᵊl'ajənəs\ *adj*

car·tog·ra·phy \kär'tägrəfē\ *n* : making of maps —**car·tog·ra·pher** \-fər\ *n*

car·ton \'kärtᵊn\ *n* : cardboard box

car·toon \kär'tün\ *n* 1 : humorous drawing 2 : comic strip —**cartoon** *vb* —**car·toon·ist** *n*

car·tridge \'kärtrij\ *n* 1 : tube containing powder and a bullet or shot for a firearm 2 : container of material for insertion into an apparatus

carve \'kärv\ *vb* **carved; carv·ing** 1 : cut with care 2 : cut into pieces or slices —**carv·er** *n*

cas·cade \kas'kād\ *n* : small steep waterfall ~ *vb* **-cad·ed; -cad·ing** : fall in a cascade

¹case \'kās\ *n* 1 : particular instance 2 : convincing argument 3 : inflectional form esp. of a noun or pronoun 4 : fact 5 : lawsuit 6 : instance of disease —**in case** : if —**in case of** : in the event of

²case *n* 1 : box 2 : outer covering ~ *vb* **cased; cas·ing** 1 : enclose 2 : inspect

case·ment \-mənt\ *n* : window opening on hinges

cash \'kash\ *n* 1 : ready money 2 : money paid at the time of purchase ~ *vb* : give or get cash for

ca·shew \'kashü, ka'shü\ *n* : tropical American tree or its nut

¹ca·shier \ka'shiər\ *vb* : dismiss in disgrace

²cash·ier *n* : person who handles money

cash·mere \'kazh,miər, 'kash-\ *n* : fine goat's wool or a fabric of this

ca·si·no \kə'sēnō\ *n, pl* **-nos** : place for gambling

cask \'kask\ *n* : barrel-shaped container for liquids

cas·ket \'kaskət\ *n* : coffin

cas·se·role \'kasə,rōl, 'kaz-\ *n* : baking dish or the food cooked in this

cas·sette *or* **ca·sette** \kə'set, ka-\ *n* : case containing two reels of magnetic tape

cas·sock \'kasək\ *n* : long clerical garment

cast \'kast\ *vb* **cast; cast·ing** 1 : throw 2 : deposit (a ballot) 3 : assign parts in a play 4 : mold ~ *n* 1 : throw 2 : appearance 3 : rigid surgical dressing 4 : actors in a play

cas·ta·nets \,kastə'nets\ *n pl* : shells clicked together in the hand

cast·away \'kastə,wā\ *n* : survivor of a shipwreck

caste \'kast\ *n* : social class or rank

cast·er *or* **cas·tor** \ˈkastər\ *n* : small wheel on furniture

cas·ti·gate \ˈkastəˌgāt\ *vb* **-gat·ed; -gat·ing** : chastise severely —**cas·ti·ga·tion** \ˌkastəˈgāshən\ *n* —**cas·ti·ga·tor** \ˈkastəˌgātər\ *n*

cast iron *n* : hard brittle alloy of iron

cas·tle \ˈkasəl\ *n* : fortified building

cast-off *adj* : thrown away —**cast-off** *n*

cas·trate \ˈkasˌtrāt\ *vb* **-trat·ed; -trat·ing** : remove the testes of —**cas·tra·tion** \kaˈstrāshən\ *n*

ca·su·al \ˈkazh(əw)əl\ *adj* **1** : happening by chance **2** : showing little concern **3** : informal —**ca·su·al·ly** \-ē\ *adv* —**ca·su·al·ness** *n*

ca·su·al·ty \-tē\ *n, pl* **-ties 1** : serious or fatal accident : one injured, lost, or destroyed

ca·su·ist·ry \ˈkazhəwəstrē\ *n, pl* **-ries** : adroit and esp. false reasoning —**ca·su·ist** \-wəst\ *n*

cat \ˈkat\ *n* **1** : small domestic mammal **2** : related animal (as a lion) —**cat-like** *adj*

cat·a·clysm \ˈkatəˌklizəm\ *n* : violent change —**cat·a·clys·mic** \ˌkatəˈklizmik\ *adj*

cat·a·comb \ˈkatəˌkōm\ *n* : underground burial place

cat·a·log, cat·a·logue \ˈkatᵊlˌȯg\ *n* **1** : list **2** : book containing a description of items — *vb* **-loged** *or* **-logued; -log·ing** *or* **-logu·ing 1** : make a catalog of **2** : enter in a catalog —**cat·a·log·er, cat·a·logu·er** *n*

ca·tal·pa \kəˈtalpə\ *n* : tree with broad leaves and long pods

ca·tal·y·sis \-əsəs\ *n, pl* **-y·ses** \-ˌsēz\ : increase in the rate of chemical reaction caused by a substance (**cat·a·lyst** \ˈkatᵊləst\) that is itself unchanged —**cat·a·lyt·ic** \ˌkatᵊlˈitik\ *adj*

cat·a·ma·ran \ˌkatəməˈran\ *n* : boat with twin hulls

cat·a·mount \ˈkatəˌmaúnt\ *n* : cougar

cat·a·pult \-ˌpəlt, -ˌpúlt\ *n* : device for hurling or launching —**catapult** *vb*

cat·a·ract \-ˌrakt\ *n* **1** : large waterfall **2** : cloudiness of the lens of the eye

ca·tarrh \kəˈtär\ *n* : inflammation of the nose and throat

ca·tas·tro·phe \kəˈtastrə(ˌ)fē\ *n* **1** : great disaster or misfortune **2** : utter failure —**cat·a·stroph·ic** \ˌkatəˈsträfik\ *adj* —**cat·a·stroph·i·cal·ly** \-ik(ə)lē\ *adv*

cat·bird *n* : American songbird

cat·call *n* : noise of disapproval

catch \ˈkach, ˈkech\ *vb* **caught** \ˈkȯt\; **catch·ing 1** : capture esp. after pur-

suit **2** : trap **3** : detect esp. by surprise **4** : grasp **5** : get entangled **6** : become affected with or by **7** : seize and hold firmly — *n* **1** : act of catching **2** : something caught **3** : something that fastens **4** : hidden difficulty —**catch·er** *n*

catch·ing \-iŋ\ *adj* : infectious

catch-up \ˈkechəp, ˈkach-; ˈkatsəp\ *var of* CATSUP

catch·word *n* : slogan

catchy \-ē\ *adj* **catch·i·er; -est** : likely to catch interest

cat·e·chism \ˈkatəˌkizəm\ *n* : set of questions and answers esp. to teach religious doctrine —**cat·e·chist** \-kist\ *n* —**cat·e·chize** \-ˌkīz\ *vb*

cat·e·gor·i·cal \ˌkatəˈgȯrikəl\ *adj* : absolute —**cat·e·gor·i·cal·ly** \-k(ə)lē\ *adv*

cat·e·go·ry \ˈkatəˌgȯrē\ *n, pl* **-ries** : group or class —**cat·e·go·ri·za·tion** \ˌkatigərəˈzāshən\ *n* —**cat·e·go·rize** \ˈkatigəˌrīz\ *vb*

ca·ter \ˈkātər\ *vb* **1** : provide food for **2** : supply what was wanted —**ca·ter·er** *n*

cat·er·cor·ner \ˌkatēˈkȯrnər, ˌkatə-, ˌkitē-\, **cat·er·cor·nered** *adv or adj* : in a diagonal position

cat·er·pil·lar \ˈkatə(r)ˌpilər\ *n* : butterfly or moth larva

cat·er·waul \ˈkatər₁wȯl\ *vb* : make the harsh cry of a cat —**caterwaul** *n*

cat·fish *n* : big-headed fish with feelers about the mouth

cat·gut *n* : tough cord made usu. from sheep intestines

ca·thar·sis \kəˈthärsəs\ *n, pl* **ca·thar·ses** \-ˌsēz\ : a purging —**ca·thar·tic** \kəˈthärtik\ *adj or n*

ca·the·dral \-ˈthēdrəl\ *n* : principal church of a diocese

cath·e·ter \ˈkathətər\ *n* : tube for insertion into a body cavity

cath·ode \ˈkaˌthōd\ *n* **1** : negative electrode **2** : positive battery terminal —**ca·thod·ic** \kaˈthädik\ *adj*

cath·o·lic \ˈkath(ə)lik\ *adj* **1** : universal **2** *cap* : relating to Roman Catholics

Cath·o·lic *n* : member of the Roman Catholic Church —**Ca·thol·i·cism** \kəˈthäləˌsizəm\ *n*

cat·kin \ˈkatkən\ *n* : long dense flower cluster

cat·nap *n* : short light nap —**catnap** *vb*

cat·nip \-ˌnip\ *n* : aromatic mint relished by cats

cat's-paw *n, pl* **cat's-paws** : person used as a tool

cat·sup \ˈkechəp, ˈkach-; ˈkatsəp\ *n* : spicy tomato sauce

cat·tail \'kat-,tāl\ n : marsh herb with furry brown spikes

cat·tle \'kat³l\ n pl : domestic bovines —**cat·tle·man** \-mən, -,man\ n

cat·ty \'katē\ adj -ti·er; -est : mean or spiteful —**cat·ti·ly** adv —**cat·ti·ness** n

cat·walk n : high narrow walk

Cau·ca·sian \kȯ'kāzhən, -'kazh-\ adj : relating to the white race —**Caucasian** n —**Cau·ca·soid** \'kȯkə,sȯid\ adj or n

cau·cus \'kȯkəs\ n : political meeting —**caucus** vb

caught past of CATCH

cauldron var of CALDRON

cau·li·flow·er \'kȯli,flaü(ə)r, 'käl-\ n : vegetable having a compact head of undeveloped flowers

caulk \'kȯk\ vb : make seams watertight —**caulk·er** n —**caulk·ing** n

caus·al \'kȯzəl\ adj : relating to or being a cause —**cau·sal·i·ty** \kȯ'zalətē\ n —**caus·al·ly** \'kȯzəlē\ adv

cause \'kȯz\ n 1 : something that brings about a result 2 : reason 3 : lawsuit 4 : principle or movement to support ~ vb caused; caus·ing : be the cause of —**cau·sa·tion** \kȯ'zāshən\ n —**caus·ative** \'kȯzətiv\ adj —**cause·less** adj —**caus·er** n

cause·way n : raised road esp. over water

caus·tic \'kȯstik\ adj 1 : corrosive 2 : sharp or biting —**caustic** n

cau·ter·ize \'kȯtə,rīz\ vb -ized; -iz·ing : burn to prevent infection or bleeding —**cau·ter·i·za·tion** \,kȯtərə'zāshən\ n

cau·tion \'kȯshən\ n 1 : warning 2 : care or prudence ~ vb : warn —**cau·tion·ary** \-shə,nerē\ adj

cau·tious \'kȯshəs\ adj : taking caution —**cau·tious·ly** adv —**cau·tious·ness** n

cav·al·cade \,kavəl'kād\ n 1 : procession on horseback 2 : series

cav·a·lier \,-ə'liər\ n : mounted soldier ~ adj : disdainful or arrogant —**cav·a·lier·ly** adv —**cav·a·lier·ness** n

cav·al·ry \'kavəlrē\ n, pl -ries : troops on horseback or in vehicles —**cav·al·ry·man** \-mən, -,man\ n

cave \'kāv\ n : natural underground chamber —**cave in** vb : collapse

cav·ern \'kavərn\ n : large cave —**cav·ern·ous** adj —**cav·ern·ous·ly** adv

cav·i·ar, cav·i·are \'kavē,är, 'kāv-\ n : salted fish roe

cav·il \'kavəl\ vb -iled or -illed; -il·ing or -il·ling : find fault without good reason —**cavil** n —**cav·il·er, cav·il·ler** n

cav·i·ty \'-otē\ n, pl -ties : unfilled place within a mass

ca·vort \kə'vȯrt\ vb : prance or caper

caw \'kȯ\ vb : utter the harsh call of the crow —**caw** n

cay·enne pepper \,kī-,en-, ,kā-\ n : ground dried fruits of a hot pepper

cay·man var of CAIMAN

cease \'sēs\ vb ceased; ceas·ing : stop

cease·less \-ləs\ adj : continuous

ce·dar \'sēdər\ n : cone-bearing tree with fragrant durable wood

cede \'sēd\ vb ced·ed; ced·ing : surrender —**ced·er** n

ceil·ing \'sēliŋ\ n 1 : overhead surface of a room 2 : upper limit

cel·e·brate \'selə,brāt\ vb -brat·ed; -brat·ing 1 : perform with appropriate rites 2 : honor with ceremonies 3 : extol —**cel·e·brant** \-brənt\ n —**cel·e·bra·tion** \,selə'brāshən\ n —**cel·e·bra·tor** \'selə,brātər\ n

cel·e·brat·ed \-əd\ adj : renowned

ce·leb·ri·ty \sə'lebrətē\ n, pl -ties 1 : renown 2 : well-known person

ce·ler·i·ty \sə'lerətē\ n : speed

cel·ery \'sel(ə)rē\ n, pl -er·ies : herb grown for crisp edible stalks

ce·les·ta \sə'lestə\ n : keyboard musical instrument

ce·les·tial \sə'leschəl\ adj 1 : relating to the sky 2 : heavenly

cel·i·ba·cy \'seləbəsē\ n 1 : state of being unmarried 2 : abstention from sexual intercourse —**cel·i·bate** \'seləbət\ n or adj

cell \'sel\ n 1 : small room 2 : tiny mass of protoplasm that forms the fundamental unit of living matter 3 : container holding an electrolyte for generating electricity —**celled** adj

cel·lar \'selər\ n : room or area below ground

cel·lo \'chelō\ n, pl -los : bass member of the violin family —**cel·list** \-ist\ n

cel·lo·phane \'selə,fān\ n : thin transparent cellulose wrapping

cel·lu·lar \-yələr\ adj : relating to or consisting of cells

cel·lu·lose \'selyə,lōs\ n : complex plant carbohydrate

Cel·sius \'selsēəs\ adj : relating to a thermometer scale on which the freezing point of water is 0° and the boiling point is 100°

ce·ment \si'ment\ n 1 : powdery mixture of clay and limestone that hardens when wetted 2 : binding agent ~ vb : unite or cover with cement —**ce·men·ta·tion** \,sē,men'tāshən\ n —**ce·ment·er** n

cem·e·tery \'semə,terē\ n, pl **-ter·ies** : burial ground

cen·ser \'sensər\ n : vessel for burning incense

cen·sor \-sər\ n : one with power to suppress anything objectionable (as in printed matter) ~ vb : be a censor of —**cen·so·ri·al** \sen'sōrēəl\ adj —**cen·sor·ship** \-,ship\ n

cen·so·ri·ous \sen'sōrēəs\ adj : critical —**cen·so·ri·ous·ly** adv —**cen·so·ri·ous·ness** n

cen·sure \'senchər\ n : official reprimand ~ vb **-sured; -sur·ing** : find blameworthy

cen·sus \-səs\ n : periodic population count

cent \'sent\ n : monetary unit equal to 1/100 of a basic unit of value

cen·taur \'sen,tȯr\ n : mythological creature that is half man and half horse

cen·ten·ni·al \sen'tenēəl\ n : 100th anniversary —**centennial** adj

cen·ter \'sentər\ n 1 : middle point 2 : point of origin or greatest concentration 3 : region of concentrated population 4 : player near the middle of his team ~ vb 1 : place, fix, or concentrate at or around a center 2 : have a center —**cen·tered** adj —**cen·ter·piece** n

cen·ti·grade \'sentə,grād, 'sänt-\ adj : Celsius

cen·ti·me·ter \'sentə,mētər, 'sänt-\ n : 1/100 meter

cen·ti·pede \'sentə,pēd\ n : long flat many-legged arthropod

cen·tral \'sentrəl\ adj 1 : constituting or being near a center 2 : essential or principal —**cen·tral·ly** adv

cen·tral·ize \-trə,līz\ vb **-ized; -iz·ing** : bring to a central point or under central control —**cen·tral·iza·tion** \,sentrələ'zāshən\ n —**cen·tral·iz·er** n

cen·tre chiefly Brit var of CENTER

cen·trif·u·gal \sen'trifyəgəl, -'trifigəl\ adj : acting in a direction away from a center or axis —**cen·trif·u·gal·ly** adv

cen·tri·fuge \'sentrə,fyüj\ n : machine that separates substances by spinning

cen·trip·e·tal \sen'tripətəl\ adj : acting in a direction toward a center or axis —**cen·trip·e·tal·ly** adv

cen·tu·ri·on \sen'tu̇(ə)rēən\ n : Roman military officer

cen·tu·ry \'sench(ə)rē\ n, pl **-ries** : 100 years

ce·ram·ic \sə'ramik\ n 1 pl : art or process of shaping and hardening articles from clay 2 : product of ceramics —**ceramic** adj

ce·re·al \'sirēəl\ adj : made of or relating to grain or to the plants that produce it ~ n 1 : grass yielding edible grain 2 : cereal grain used as food

cer·e·bel·lum \serə'beləm\ n, pl **-bel·lums** or **-bel·la** \-'belə\ : part of the brain controlling muscular coordination —**cer·e·bel·lar** \-ər\ adj

cerebral palsy n : disorder caused by brain damage and marked esp. by defective muscle control

cer·e·brate \'serə,brāt\ vb **-brat·ed; -brat·ing** : think —**cer·e·bra·tion** \,serə'brāshən\ n

ce·re·brum \sə'rēbrəm, 'serə-\ n, pl **-brums** or **-bra** \-brə\ : part of the brain that contains the higher nervous centers —**ce·re·bral** \-brəl\ adj —**ce·re·bral·ly** adv

cer·e·mo·ny \'serə,mōnē\ n, pl **-nies** 1 : formal act prescribed by law, ritual, or convention 2 : prescribed procedures —**cer·e·mo·ni·al** \,serə'mōnēəl\ adj or n —**cer·e·mo·ni·ous** \-nēəs\ adj

ce·rise \sə'rēs\ n : moderate red

cer·tain \'sərt^ən\ adj 1 : settled 2 : true 3 : specific but not named 4 : bound 5 : assured ~ pron : certain ones —**cer·tain·ly** adv —**cer·tain·ty** \-tē\ n

cer·tif·i·cate \sər'tifikət\ n : document establishing truth or fulfillment

cer·ti·fy \'sərtə,fī\ vb **-fied; -fy·ing** 1 : verify 2 : endorse —**cer·ti·fi·able** \-,fīəbəl\ adj —**cer·ti·fi·ably** \-blē\ adv —**cer·ti·fi·ca·tion** \,sərtəfə'kāshən\ n —**cer·ti·fi·er** n

cer·ti·tude \'sərtə,t(y)üd\ n : state of being certain

cer·vix \'sərviks\ n, pl **-vi·ces** \-və,sēz\ or **-vix·es** 1 : neck 2 : narrow end of the uterus —**cer·vi·cal** \-vikəl\ adj

ce·sar·e·an \si'zarēən\ n : surgical operation to deliver a baby —**cesarean** adj

ce·si·um \'sēzēəm\ n : silver-white soft ductile chemical element

ces·sa·tion \se'sāshən\ n : a halting

ces·sion \'seshən\ n : a yielding

cess·pool \'ses,pül\ n : underground sewage pit

Cha·blis \'shab,lē; shä'blē\ n, pl **Cha·blis** \-,lēz, -'blēz\ : dry white wine

chafe \'chāf\ vb **chafed; chaf·ing** 1 : fret 2 : make sore by rubbing

chaff \'chaf\ n 1 : debris separated from grain 2 : something worthless 3 : banter ~ vb : tease —**chaffy** adj

chaf·ing dish \'chāfiŋ-\ *n* : utensil for cooking at the table

cha·grin \sha'grin\ *n* : embarrassment or humiliation ~ *vb* : cause to feel chagrin

chain \'chān\ *n* **1** : flexible series of connected links **2** *pl* : fetters **3** : linked series ~ *vb* : bind or connect with a chain

chair \'cheər\ *n* **1** : seat with a back **2** : position of authority or dignity **3** : chairman ~ *vb* : act as chairman of

chair·man \-mən\ *n* : presiding officer —**chair·man·ship** *n* —**chair·wom·an** *n*

chaise longue \'shāz'lòŋ\ *n*, *pl* **chaise longues** \'lòŋ(z)\ : long couchlike chair

cha·let \sha'lā\ *n* : Swiss mountain cottage with overhanging roof

chal·ice \'chaləs\ *n* : eucharistic cup

chalk \'chòk\ *n* **1** : soft limestone **2** : chalky material used as a crayon ~ *vb* : mark with chalk —**chalk up** *vb* **1** : credit **2** : achieve —**chalky** *adj*

chalk·board \-n : blackboard

chal·lenge \'chalənj\ *vb* **-lenged; -leng·ing 1** : dispute **2** : invite or dare to act or compete —**challenge** *n* —**chal·leng·er** *n*

cham·ber \'chāmbər\ *n* **1** : room **2** : enclosed space **3** : legislative meeting place or body **4** *pl* : judge's consultation room —**cham·bered** *adj*

cham·ber·maid *n* : bedroom maid

chamber music *n* : music by a small group for a small audience

cha·me·leon \kə'mēlyən\ *n* : small lizard whose skin changes color

cham·ois \'shamē\ *n*, *pl* **cham·ois** \-ē(z)\ **1** : goatlike antelope **2** : soft leather

¹champ \'champ, 'chämp\ *vb* : chew noisily

²champ \'champ\ *n* : champion

cham·pagne \sham'pān\ *n* : sparkling white wine

cham·pi·on \'champēən\ *n* **1** : advocate or defender **2** : winning contestant ~ *vb* : protect or fight for

cham·pi·on·ship \-,ship\ *n* **1** : title of a champion **2** : contest to pick a champion

chance \'chans\ *n* **1** : unpredictable element of existence **2** : opportunity **3** : probability **4** : risk **5** : raffle ticket ~ *vb* **chanced; chanc·ing 1** : happen **2** : encounter unexpectedly **3** : risk —**chance** *adj*

chan·cel \'chansəl\ *n* : part of a church around the altar

can·cel·lery, chan·cel·lory \'chans(ə)lərē\ *n*, *pl* **-ler·ies** *or* **-lor·**

ies 1 : position of a chancellor **2** : chancellor's office

chan·cel·lor \-s(ə)lər\ *n* **1** : chief or high state official **2** : head of a university —**chan·cel·lor·ship** *n*

chan·cre \'shaŋkər\ *n* : skin ulcer esp. from syphilis

chancy \'chansē\ *adj* **chanc·i·er; -est** : risky

chan·de·lier \,shandə'liər\ *n* : hanging lighting fixture

chan·dler \'chandlər\ *n* : provisions dealer —**chan·dlery** *n*

change \'chānj\ *vb* **changed; chang·ing 1** : make or become different **2** : exchange **3** : give or receive change for ~ *n* **1** : a changing **2** : excess from a payment **3** : money in smaller denominations **4** : coins —**change·able** *adj* —**change·less** *adj* —**chang·er** *n*

chan·nel \'chan²l\ *n* **1** : deeper part of a waterway **2** : means of passage or communication **3** : strait **4** : broadcast frequency ~ *vb* **-neled** *or* **-nelled; -nel·ing** *or* **-nel·ling** : make or direct through a channel

chant \'chant\ *vb* : sing or speak in one tone —**chant** *n* —**chant·er** *n*

chan·tey, chan·ty \'shantē, 'chant-\ *n*, *pl* **-teys** *or* **-ties** : sailors' work song

Cha·nu·kah \'känəkə, 'hän-\ *var of* HANUKKAH

chaos \'kā,äs\ *n* **1** : complete disorder —**cha·ot·ic** \kā'ätik\ *adj* —**cha·ot·i·cal·ly** \-ik(ə)lē\ *adv*

¹chap \'chap\ *n* : fellow

²chap \'chap\ *vb* **-pp-** : dry and crack open usu. from wind and cold

cha·pel \'chapəl\ *n* : private or small place of worship

chap·er·on, chap·er·one \'shapə,rōn\ *n* : older person who accompanies young people at a social gathering ~ *vb* **-oned; -on·ing** : act as chaperon at or for —**chap·er·on·age** \-ij\ *n*

chap·lain \'chaplən\ *n* : clergyman in a military unit or a prison —**chap·lain·cy** \-sē\ *n*

chap·ter \'chaptər\ *n* **1** : main book division **2** : branch of a society

char \'chär\ *vb* **-rr- 1** : burn to charcoal **2** : scorch

char·ac·ter \'kariktər\ *n* **1** : letter or graphic mark **2** : trait or distinctive combination of traits **3** : peculiar person **4** : fictional person —**char·ac·ter·i·za·tion** \,karikt(ə)rə'zāshən\ *n* —**char·ac·ter·ize** \'kariktə,rīz\ *vb*

char·ac·ter·is·tic \,kariktə'ristik\ *adj* : typical ~ *n* : distinguishing quality —**char·ac·ter·is·ti·cal·ly** \-tik(ə)lē\ *adv*

cha·rades \shə'rādz\ *n sing or pl* : pantomime guessing game

char·coal \'chär,kōl\ *n* : porous carbon prepared by partial combustion

chard \'chärd\ *n* : leafy vegetable

charge \'chärj\ *vb* **charged; charg·ing** 1 : give an electric charge to 2 : impose a task or responsibility on 3 : command 4 : accuse 5 : rush forward in assault 6 : assume a debt for 7 : fix as a price ~ *n* 1 : excess or deficiency of electrons in a body 2 : tax 3 : responsibility 4 : accusation 5 : cost 6 : attack —**charge·able** *adj*

charg·er \-ər\ *n* : horse ridden in battle

char·iot \'chärēət\ *n* : ancient 2-wheeled vehicle —**char·i·o·teer** \,chärēə'tir\ *n*

cha·ris·ma \kə'rizmə\ *n, pl* **cha·ris·ma·ta** \kə'rizmətə\ : special ability to lead —**char·is·mat·ic** \,karəz'matik\ *adj*

char·i·ty \'charətē\ *n, pl* **-ties** 1 : love for mankind 2 : generosity or leniency 3 : alms 4 : institution for relief of the needy —**char·i·ta·ble** \-əbəl\ *adj* —**char·i·ta·bly** \-blē\ *adv*

char·la·tan \'shärlətən\ *n* : impostor

charm \'chärm\ *n* 1 : something with magic power 2 : appealing trait 3 : small ornament ~ *vb* : fascinate —**charm·er** *n* —**charm·ing** *adj* —**charm·ing·ly** *adv*

char·nel \'chärnᵊl\ *n* : place for dead bodies —**charnel** *adj*

chart \'chärt\ *n* 1 : map 2 : diagram ~ *vb* 1 : make a chart of 2 : plan

char·ter \-ər\ *n* 1 : document granting rights 2 : constitution ~ *vb* 1 : establish by charter 2 : rent —**char·ter·er** *n*

char·treuse \shär'trüz, -'trüs\ *n* : brilliant yellow green

char·wom·an \'chär,wumən\ *n* : cleaning woman

chary \'cha(ə)rē\ *adj* **chari·er; -est** : cautious —**char·i·ly** \'charəlē\ *adv*

¹chase \'chās\ *vb* **chased; chas·ing** 1 : follow trying to catch 2 : drive away —**chase** *n* —**chas·er** *n*

²chase *vb* **chased; chas·ing** : decorate (metal) by embossing or engraving

chasm \'kazəm\ *n* : gorge

chas·sis \'chasē, 'chas-\ *n, pl* **chas·sis** \-ēz\ : framework

chaste \'chāst\ *adj* **chast·er; chast·est** 1 : abstaining from all or unlawful sexual relations 2 : modest or decent 3 : severely simple —**chaste·ly** *adv* —**chaste·ness** *n* —**chas·ti·ty** \'chastətē\ *n*

chas·tise \chas'tīz\ *vb* **-tised; -tis·ing** 1 : punish 2 : censure —**chas·tise·ment** \-mənt, 'chastəz-\ *n*

chat \'chat\ *n* : informal talk —**chat** *vb* —**chat·ty** \-ē\ *adj*

châ·teau \sha'tō\ *n, pl* **-teaus** \-'tōz\ or **-teaux** \-'tō(z)\ 1 : large country house 2 : French vineyard estate

chat·tel \'chatᵊl\ *n* : item of tangible property other than real estate

chat·ter \'chatər\ *vb* 1 : utter rapidly succeeding sounds 2 : talk fast or too much —**chatter** *n* —**chat·ter·er** *n*

chat·ter·box *n* : incessant talker

chauf·feur \'shōfər, shō'fər\ *n* : hired car driver ~ *vb* : work as a chauffeur for

chau·vin·ism \'shōvə,nizəm\ *n* : excessive patriotism —**chau·vin·ist** \-vənəst\ *n* —**chau·vin·is·tic** \,shōvə'nistik\ *adj*

cheap \'chēp\ *adj* 1 : inexpensive 2 : shoddy —**cheap** *adv* —**cheap·en** \'chēpən\ *vb* —**cheap·ly** *adv* —**cheap·ness** *n*

cheap·skate *n* : stingy person

cheat \'chēt\ *n* 1 : act of deceiving 2 : one that cheats ~ *vb* 1 : deprive through fraud or deceit 2 : violate rules dishonestly —**cheat·er** *n*

check \'chek\ *n* 1 : sudden stoppage 2 : restraint 3 : test or standard for testing 4 : written order to a bank to pay money 5 : ticket showing ownership 6 : slip showing an amount due 7 : pattern in squares or fabric in such a pattern 8 : mark placed beside an item noted ~ *vb* 1 : slow down or stop 2 : restrain 3 : compare or correspond with a source or original 4 : inspect or test for condition 5 : mark with a check 6 : leave or accept for safekeeping or shipment 7 : checker —**check in** *vb* : report one's arrival —**check out** *vb* : settle one's account and leave

check·er \-ər\ *n* : piece in checkers ~ *vb* : mark with different colors or into squares

²checker *n* : one that checks

check·er·board \-ə(r),bōrd\ *n* : board of 64 squares of alternate colors

check·ers \-ərz\ *n* : game for 2 played on a checkerboard

check·mate *vb* : thwart completely —**checkmate** *n*

check·point *n* : place where traffic is checked

check·up *n* : physical examination

ched·dar \'chedər\

cheek \'chēk\ n 1 : fleshy side part of the face 2 : impudence —**cheeked** \'chēkt\ adj —**cheeky** adj

cheep \'chēp\ vb : utter faint shrill sound —**cheep** n

cheer \'chiər\ n 1 : good spirits 2 : food and drink for a feast 3 : shout of applause or encouragement ~ vb 1 : give hope or courage to 2 : make or become glad 3 : urge on or applaud with shouts —**cheer·er** n —**cheer·ful** \-fəl\ adj —**cheer·ful·ly** adv —**cheer·ful·ness** n —**cheer·lead·er** n —**cheer·less** adj —**cheer·less·ly** adv —**cheer·less·ness** n

cheery \'chiə)rē\ adj **cheer·i·er; -est** : cheerful —**cheer·i·ly** adv —**cheer·i·ness** n

cheese \'chēz\ n : curd of milk usu. pressed and cured —**cheesy** adj

cheese·cloth n : light-weight coarse cotton gauze

chee·tah \'chētə\ n : spotted swift-moving African cat

chef \'shef\ n : chief cook

chem·i·cal \'kemikəl\ adj 1 : relating to chemistry 2 : working or produced by chemicals ~ n : substance obtained by chemistry —**chem·i·cal·ly** \-k(ə)lē\ adv

che·mise \shə'mēz\ n 1 : woman's one-piece undergarment 2 : loose dress

chem·ist \'keməst\ n 1 : one trained in chemistry 2 Brit : pharmacist

chem·is·try \-əstrē\ n, pl -tries : science that deals with the composition and properties of substances

che·mo·ther·a·py \ˌkēmō-, ˌkemō-\ n : use of chemicals in treatment of disease —**che·mo·ther·a·peu·tic,** che·mo·ther·a·peu·ti·cal adj

che·nille \shə'nēl\ n : yarn with protruding pile or fabric of such yarn

cheque \'chek\ chiefly Brit var of CHECK 5

cher·ish \'cherish\ vb : hold dear

cher·ry \'cherē\ n, pl -ries : small fleshy fruit of a tree related to the roses or the tree or its wood

cher·ub \-əb\ n, pl -ubs or -u·bim \-(y)ə,bim\ 1 : angel 2 : chubby child —**che·ru·bic** \chə'rübik\ adj

chess \'ches\ n : game for 2 played on a checkerboard —**chess·board** n —**chess·man** n

chest \'chest\ n 1 : boxlike container 2 : part of the body enclosed by the ribs and breastbone —**chest·ed** adj

chest·nut \'ches(ˌ)nət\ n : nut of a tree related to the beech or the tree

chev·i·ot \'shevēət\ n 1 : heavy rough wool fabric 2 : soft-finished cotton fabric

chev·ron \'shevrən\ n : V-shaped insignia

chew \'chü\ vb : crush or grind with the teeth ~ n : something to chew —**chew·able** adj —**chew·er** n —**chewy** adj

chic \'shēk\ n : smart elegance of dress or manner ~ adj 1 : stylish 2 : currently fashionable

chi·ca·nery \shik'ān(ə)rē\ n, pl -ner·ies : trickery

chick·a·dee \-ˌ(ə)dē\ n : small grayish American bird

chick·en \-ən\ n 1 : common domestic fowl or its flesh used as food 2 : coward

chicken pox n : acute contagious virus disease esp. of children

chi·cle \'chikəl\ n : gum from a tropical evergreen tree

chic·o·ry \'chik(ə)rē\ n, pl -ries : herb used in salad or its dried ground root used to adulterate coffee

chide \'chīd\ vb \'chīd\ or chid·ed \'chīdəd\; chid or chid·den \'chid³n\ or chided; chid·ing \'chīdiŋ\ : scold

chief \'chēf\ n : leader ~ adj 1 : highest in rank 2 : most important —**chief·dom** n —**chief·ly** adv

chief·tain \'chēftən\ n : chief —**chief·tain·cy** \-sē\ n

chif·fon \shif'än, 'shif-ˌ\ n : sheer fabric

chig·ger \'chigər\ n : bloodsucking mite

chi·gnon \'shēnˌyän\ n : knot of hair

chil·blain \'chilˌblān\ n : sore or inflamed swelling caused by cold

child \'chīld\ n, pl chil·dren \'childrən\ 1 : unborn or recently born person 2 : son or daughter —**child-bear·ing** n or adj —**child-birth** n —**child·hood** n —**child·ish** adj —**child·ish·ly** adv —**child·ish·ness** n —**child·less** adj —**child·less·ness** n —**child·like** adj

chili, chile, chil·li \'chilē\ n, pl chil·ies or chil·es or chil·lies 1 : hot pepper 2 : spicy stew of ground beef, chilies, and beans

chill \'chil\ vb : make or become cold or chilly ~ adj : moderately cold ~ n 1 : feeling of coldness with shivering 2 : moderate coldness

chilly \-ē\ adj chill·i·er; -est : noticeably cold —**chill·i·ness** n

chime \'chīm\ n : set of tuned bells or their sound —vb : make bell-like sounds —chime in vb : break into or join in a conversation

chi·me·ra \kī'mirə, kə-\ n : imaginary monster —chi·me·ri·cal \-'merikəl\, chi·me·ric \-'ik\ adj

chim·ney \'chimnē\ n, pl -neys 1 : passage for smoke 2 : glass tube around a lamp flame

chimp \'chimp, 'shimp\ n : chimpanzee

chim·pan·zee \,chim,pan'zē, ,shim-; chim'panzē, shim-\ n : manlike ape smaller than a gorilla

chin \'chin\ n : part of the face below the mouth —chin·less adj

chi·na \'chīnə\ n 1 : porcelain ware 2 : domestic pottery

chin·chil·la \chin'chilə\ n : small So. American rodent with soft pearl-gray fur

chink \'chink\ n : small crack —vb : fill chinks of

chintz \'chints\ n : printed cotton cloth

chip \'chip\ n 1 : small thin flat piece cut or broken off 2 : thin crisp morsel of food 3 : counter used in games 4 : flaw where a chip came off —vb -pp- : cut or break chips from —chip in vb : contribute

chip·munk \-,məŋk\ n : small striped ground-dwelling squirrel

chip·per \-ər\ adj : lively and cheerful

chi·rop·o·dy \kə'räpədē, shə-\ n : podiatry —chi·rop·o·dist \-ədəst\ n

chi·ro·prac·tic \'kīrə,praktik\ n : system of healing based esp. on manipulation of body structures —chi·ro·prac·tor \-tər\ n

chirp \'chərp\ n : short sharp sound like that of a bird or cricket —chirp vb

chis·el \'chizəl\ n : sharp-edged metal tool —vb -eled or -elled; -el·ing or -el·ling 1 : work with a chisel 2 : cheat —chis·el·er \-(ə)lər\ n

chit \'chit\ n : signed voucher for a small debt

chit·chat \-,chat\ n : casual conversation

chiv·al·rous \'shivəlrəs\ adj 1 : relating to chivalry 2 : honest, courteous, or generous —chiv·al·rous·ly adv —chiv·al·rous·ness n

chiv·al·ry \-rē\ n, pl -ries 1 : system or practices of knighthood 2 : spirit or character of the ideal knight —chi·val·ric \shə'valrik\ adj

chive \'chīv\ n : herb related to the onion

chlo·ride \'klōr,īd\ n : compound of chlorine

chlo·ri·nate \-ə,nāt\ vb -nat·ed; -nat·ing : treat or combine with chlorine —chlo·ri·na·tion \,klōrə'nāshən\ n —chlo·ri·na·tor \'klōrə,nātər\ n

chlo·rine \-,ēn\ n : chemical element that is a heavy strong-smelling greenish yellow irritating gas

chlo·ro·form \'klōrə,form\ n : etherlike colorless heavy fluid —vb : anesthetize or kill with chloroform

chlo·ro·phyll \-ə,fil\ n : green coloring matter of plants

chock \'chäk\ n : wedge for blocking the movement of a wheel —chock vb

chock-full \'chäk'fül, 'chäk-\ adj : full to the limit

choc·o·late \'chäk(ə)lət, 'chök-\ n 1 : ground roasted cacao beans or a beverage made from them 2 : candy made of or with chocolate 3 : dark brown

choice \'chois\ n 1 : act or power of choosing 2 : one selected 3 : variety offered for selection —adj choic·er; choic·est 1 : worthy of being chosen 2 : selected with care 3 : of high quality

choir \'kwī(ə)r\ n : group of singers esp. in church —choir·boy n —choir·mas·ter n

choke \'chōk\ vb choked; chok·ing 1 : hinder breathing 2 : clog or obstruct —n 1 : a choking or sound of choking 2 : valve for controlling air intake in a gasoline engine

chok·er \-ər, n 1 : tight necklace

chol·er \'kälər, 'kō-\ n : bad temper —cho·ler·ic \'kälərik, kə'ler-\ adj

chol·era \'kälərə\ n : disease marked by severe vomiting and dysentery

cho·les·ter·ol \kə'lestə,rōl, -,rôl\ n : waxy substance in animal tissues

choose \'chüz\ vb chose \'chōz\; cho·sen \'chōz'n\; choos·ing 1 : select after consideration 2 : see fit 3 : decide —choos·er n

choosy, choos·ey \'chüzē\ adj choos·i·er, -est : fussy in making choices

chop \'chäp\ vb -pp- 1 : cut by repeated blows 2 : cut into small pieces —n 1 : sharp downward blow 2 : small cut of meat often with part of a rib

chop·per \-ər\ n 1 : one that chops 2 : helicopter

chop·py \-ē\ adj -pi·er, -est 1 : rough with small waves 2 : jerky or disconnected —chop·pi·ly adv —chop·pi·ness n

chops \\'chäps\\ *n pl* : fleshy covering of the jaws

chop-sticks *n pl* : pair of sticks used in eating in oriental countries

cho-ral \\'kōrəl\\ *adj* : relating to or sung by a choir or chorus or in chorus —**cho-ral-ly** *adv*

cho-rale \\kə'ral, -'räl\\ *n* 1 : hymn tune or harmonization of a traditional melody 2 : chorus or choir

¹chord \\'kȯrd\\ *n* : harmonious tones sounded together

²chord *n* 1 : cordlike anatomical structure 2 : straight line joining 2 points on a curve

chore \\'chȯr\\ *n* 1 *pl* : daily household or farm work 2 : routine or disagreeable task

cho-re-og-ra-phy \\ˌkōrē'ägrəfē\\ *n, pl* -phies : art of dancing or of arranging dances —**cho-reo-graph** \\'kōrēəˌgraf\\ *vb* —**cho-re-og-ra-pher** \\ˌkōrē'ägrəfər\\ *n* —**cho-reo-graph-ic** \\-ēə'grafik\\ *adj*

cho-ris-ter \\'kȯrəstər\\ *n* : choir singer

chor-tle \\'chȯrtᵊl\\ *vb* -tled; -tling : laugh or chuckle —**chortle** *n*

cho-rus \\'kōrəs\\ *n* 1 : group of singers or dancers 2 : part of a song repeated at intervals 3 : composition for a chorus ~ *vb* : sing or utter together

chose *past of* CHOOSE

cho-sen \\'chōzᵊn\\ *adj* : favored

¹chow \\'chaü\\ *n* : food

²chow *n* : thick-coated muscular dog

chow-der \\'chaüdər\\ *n* : thick soup usu. of seafood and milk

chow mein \\-'mān\\ *n* : thick stew of shredded vegetables and meat

chris-ten \\'krisᵊn\\ *vb* 1 : baptize 2 : name —**chris-ten-ing** *n*

Chris-ten-dom \\-dəm\\ *n* : areas where Christianity prevails

Chris-tian \\'krischən\\ *n* : adherent of Christianity ~ *adj* : relating to or professing a belief in Christianity or Jesus Christ —**Chris-tian-ize** \\'krischə,nīz\\ *vb*

Chris-ti-an-i-ty \\ˌkrischē'anətē\\ *n* : religion derived from the teachings of Jesus Christ

Christian name *n* : first name

Christ-mas \\'krisməs\\ *n* : December 25 celebrated as the birthday of Christ

chro-mat-ic \\krō'matik\\ *adj* 1 : relating to color 2 : proceeding by half steps of the musical scale

chrome \\'krōm\\ *n* : chromium or something plated with it

chro-mi-um \\-ēəm\\ *n* : a bluish white metallic element used esp. in alloys

chro-mo-some \\-ə,sōm, -ˌzōm\\ *n* : part

of a cell nucleus that contains the genes —**chro-mo-som-al** \\ˌkrōmə'sōməl, -'zō-\\ *adj*

chron-ic \\'kränik\\ *adj* : frequent or persistent —**chron-i-cal-ly** \\-(ə)lē\\ *adv*

chron-i-cle \\-əl\\ *n* : history ~ *vb* -cled; -cling : record —**chron-i-cler** \\-(ə)lər\\ *n*

chro-nol-o-gy \\krə'näləjē\\ *n, pl* -gies : list of events in order of their occurrence —**chron-o-log-i-cal** \\ˌkränᵊl'äjikəl\\ *adj* —**chron-o-log-i-cal-ly** \\-ik(ə)lē\\ *adv*

chro-nom-e-ter \\krə'nämətər\\ *n* : very accurate timepiece

chrys-a-lis \\'krisələs\\ *n, pl* **chrys-al-i-des** \\kris'alə,dēz\\ *or* **chrys-a-lis-es** : insect pupa enclosed in a shell

chry-san-the-mum \\kris'anthəməm\\ *n* : plant with showy flowers

chub-by \\'chəbē\\ *adj* **-bi-er; -est** : fat —**chub-bi-ness** *n*

¹chuck \\'chək\\ *vb* 1 : tap 2 : toss ~ *n* 1 : light pat under the chin 2 : toss

²chuck *n* 1 : cut of beef 2 : machine part that holds work or another part

chuck-le \\'chəkəl\\ *vb* -led; -ling : laugh quietly —**chuckle** *n*

chug \\'chəg\\ *n* : sound of a laboring engine ~ *vb* -gg- : work or move with chugs

chum \\'chəm\\ *n* : close friend ~ *vb* -mm- : be chums —**chum-my** \\-ē\\ *adj*

chump \\'chəmp\\ *n* : fool

chunk \\'chəŋk\\ *n* 1 : short thick piece 2 : sizable amount

chunky \\-ē\\ *adj* **chunk-i-er; -est** 1 : stocky 2 : containing chunks

church \\'chərch\\ *n* 1 : building esp. for Christian public worship 2 : whole body of Christians 3 : denomination 4 : congregation —**church-go-er** *n* —**church-go-ing** *adj or n*

church-yard *n* : cemetery beside a church

churl \\'chərl\\ *n* : rude ill-bred person —**churl-ish** *adj*

churn \\'chərn\\ *n* : container in which butter is made ~ *vb* 1 : agitate in a churn 2 : shake violently

chute \\'shüt\\ *n* : trough or passage

chut-ney \\'chətnē\\ *n, pl* -neys : sweet and sour relish

chutz-pah, chutz-pa \\'hütspə, 'kút-, -(ˌ)spä\\ *n* : nerve or insolence

ci-ca-da \\sə'kādə\\ *n* : stout-bodied insect with transparent wings

ci-der \\'sīdər\\ *n* : apple juice

ci-gar \\sig'är\\ *n* : roll of leaf tobacco for smoking

cig·a·rette \ˌsigəˈret, ˈsigəˌret\ *n* : cut tobacco rolled in paper for smoking

cinch \ˈsinch\ *n* **1** : strap holding a saddle or pack in place **2** : sure thing —**cinch** *vb*

cin·cho·na \sinˈkōnə\ *n* : So. American tree that yields quinine

cinc·ture \ˈsiŋkchər\ *n* : belt

cin·der \ˈsindər\ *n* **1** *pl* : ashes **2** : piece of partly burned wood or coal

cin·e·ma \ˈsinəmə\ *n* : movies or a movie theater —**cin·e·mat·ic** \ˌsinəˈmatik\ *adj*

cin·na·mon \ˈsinəmən\ *n* : aromatic tree bark used as a spice

ci·pher \ˈsīfər\ *n* **1** : zero **2** : code

cir·ca \ˈsərkə\ *prep* : about

cir·cle \ˈsərkəl\ *n* **1** : closed symmetrical curve **2** : cycle **3** : group with a common tie ~ *vb* -**cled;** -**cling 1** : enclose in a circle **2** : move or revolve around

cir·cuit \ˈkət\ *n* **1** : boundary **2** : regular tour of a territory **3** : complete path of an electric current

cir·cu·itous \ˌsərˈkyüətəs\ *adj* : circular or winding

cir·cuit·ry \ˈsərkətrē\ *n, pl* -**ries** : arrangement of an electric circuit

cir·cu·lar \ˈkyələr\ *adj* **1** : round **2** : moving in a circle ~ *n* : advertising leaflet —**cir·cu·lar·i·ty** \ˌsərkyəˈlaretē\ *n*

cir·cu·late \ˈsərkyəˌlāt\ *vb* -**lat·ed;** -**lat·ing** : move or cause to move in a circle or from place to place or person to person —**cir·cu·la·tion** \ˌsərkyəˈlāshən\ *n* —**cir·cu·la·to·ry** \ˈsərkyələˌtōrē\ *adj*

cir·cum·cise \ˈsərkəmˌsīz\ *vb* -**cised;** -**cis·ing** : cut off the foreskin of —**cir·cum·ci·sion** \ˌsərkəmˈsizhən\ *n*

cir·cum·fer·ence \sərˈkəmf(ə)rəns\ *n* : perimeter of a circle

cir·cum·flex \ˈsərkəmˌfleks\ *n* : phonetic mark (as ˆ)

cir·cum·lo·cu·tion \ˌsərkəmlō-ˈkyüshən\ *n* : excessive use of words

cir·cum·nav·i·gate \ˌsərkəm-\ *vb* : sail completely around —**cir·cum·nav·i·ga·tion** *n*

cir·cum·scribe \ˈsərkəmˌskrīb\ *vb* **1** : draw a line around **2** : limit

cir·cum·spect \ˈsərkəmˌspekt\ *adj* : careful —**cir·cum·spec·tion** \ˌsərkəmˈspekshən\ *n*

cir·cum·stance \ˈsərkəmˌstans\ *n* **1** : fact or event **2** *pl* : surrounding conditions **3** *pl* : financial situation —**cir·cum·stan·tial** \ˌsərkəm-ˈstanchəl\ *adj*

cir·cum·vent \-ˈvent\ *vb* : get around esp. by trickery

cir·cus \ˈsərkəs\ *n* : show with feats of skill, animal acts, and clowns

cir·rho·sis \səˈrōsəs\ *n, pl* -**rho·ses** \-ˌsēz\ : fibrosis esp. of the liver —**cir·rhot·ic** \-ˈrätik\ *adj or n*

cir·rus \ˈsirəs\ *n, pl* -**ri** \-ˌī\ : wispy white cloud

cis·tern \ˈsistərn\ *n* : underground water tank

cit·a·del \ˈsitədˈl, - əˌdel\ *n* : fort

cite \ˈsīt\ *vb* **cit·ed; cit·ing 1** : summon before a court **2** : quote **3** : refer to esp. in commendation —**ci·ta·tion** \sīˈtāshən\ *n*

cit·i·zen \ˈsitəzən\ *n* : member of a country —**cit·i·zen·ry** \-rē\ *n* —**cit·i·zen·ship** *n*

cit·ron \ˈsitrən\ *n* : lemonlike fruit

cit·rus \ˈsitrəs\ *n, pl* -**rus** *or* -**rus·es** : evergreen tree or shrub grown for its fruit (as the orange or lemon)

city \ˈsitē\ *n, pl* **cit·ies** : place larger or more important than a town

civ·ic \ˈsivik\ *adj* : relating to citizenship or civil affairs

civ·ics \-iks\ *n* : study of citizenship

civ·il \ˈsivəl\ *adj* **1** : relating to citizens **2** : polite **3** : relating to or being a lawsuit —**civ·il·ly** \-(l)ē\ *adv*

ci·vil·ian \səˈvilyən\ *n* : person not in a military, police, or fire-fighting force

ci·vil·i·ty \səˈvilətē\ *n, pl* -**ties** : courtesy

civ·i·li·za·tion \ˌsivələˈzāshən\ *n* **1** : high level of cultural development **2** : culture of a time or place

civ·i·lize \ˈsivəˌlīz\ *vb* -**lized;** -**liz·ing** : raise from a primitive stage of cultural development —**civ·i·lized** *adj*

civil liberty *n* : freedom from arbitrary governmental interference —usu. pl.

civil rights *n pl* : nonpolitical rights of a citizen

civil service *n* : government service

civil war *n* : war among citizens of one country

clack \ˈklak\ *vb* : make or cause to clatter —**clack** *n*

clad \ˈklad\ *adj* : covered

claim \ˈklām\ *vb* **1** : demand or take as the rightful owner **2** : maintain ~ *n* **1** : demand of right or ownership **2** : declaration **3** : something claimed —**claim·ant** \-ənt\ *n*

clair·voy·ant \klaərˈvoiənt\ *adj* : able to perceive things beyond the senses —**clair·voy·ance** \-əns\ *n* —**clairvoy·ant** *n*

clam \ˈklam\ *n* : bivalve mollusk

clam·ber \'klambər\ *vb* : climb awkwardly

clam·my \'klamē\ *adj* **-mi·er; -est** : being damp, soft, and usu. cool —**clam·mi·ness** *n*

clam·or \-ər\ *n* **1** : uproar **2** : protest —**clamor** *vb* —**clam·or·ous** *adj*

clamp \'klamp\ *n* : device for holding things together —**clamp** *vb*

clan \'klan\ *n* : group of related families —**clan·nish** *adj* —**clan·nish·ness** *n*

clan·des·tine \klan'destən\ *adj* : secret

clang \'klaŋ\ *n* : loud metallic ringing —**clang** *vb*

clan·gor \-(g)ər\ *n* : jumble of clangs

clank \'klaŋk\ *n* : brief sound of struck metal —**clank** *vb*

clap \'klap\ *vb* **-pp- 1** : strike noisily **2** : applaud ~ *n* **1** : loud crash **2** : noise made by clapping the hands

clap·board \'klabərd; 'kla(p),bōrd\ *n* : narrow tapered board used for siding

clap·per \'klapər\ *n* : tongue of a bell

claque \'klak\ *n* : group hired to applaud at a performance

clar·et \'klarət\ *n* : dry red wine

clar·i·fy \'klarə,fī\ *vb* **-fied; -fy·ing** : make or become clear —**clar·i·fi·ca·tion** \,klarəfə'kāshən\ *n*

clar·i·net \,klarə'net\ *n* : woodwind instrument shaped like a tube —**clar·i·net·ist, clar·i·net·tist** \-əst\ *n*

clar·i·on \'klarēən\ *adj* : loud and clear

clar·i·ty \'klarətē\ *n* : clearness

clash \'klash\ *vb* **1** : make or cause a clash **2** : be in opposition or disharmony ~ *n* **1** : crashing sound **2** : hostile encounter

clasp \'klasp\ *n* **1** : device for holding things together **2** : embrace or grasp ~ *vb* **1** : fasten **2** : embrace or grasp

class \'klas\ *n* **1** : group of the same status or nature **2** : social rank **3** : course of instruction **4** : group of students ~ *vb* : classify —**class·less** *adj* —**class·mate** *n* —**class·room** *n*

clas·sic \'klasik\ *adj* **1** : serving as a standard of excellence : classical ~ *n* : work of enduring excellence and esp. of ancient Greece or Rome —**clas·si·cal** \-ikəl\ *adj* —**clas·si·cal·ly** \-k(ə)lē\ *adv* —**clas·si·cism** \'klasə,sizəm\ *n* —**clas·si·cist** \-səst\ *n*

clas·si·fied \'klasə,fīd\ *adj* : restricted for security reasons

clas·si·fy \-,fī\ *vb* **-fied; -fy·ing** : arrange in or assign to classes —**clas·si·fi·ca·tion** \,klasəfə'kāshən\ *n*

clat·ter \'klatər\ *n* : rattling sound —**clatter** *vb*

clause \'klóz\ *n* **1** : separate part of a document **2** : part of a sentence with a subject and predicate

claus·tro·pho·bia \,klóstrə'fōbēə\ *n* : fear of closed or narrow spaces

clav·i·chord \'klavə,kórd\ *n* : early keyboard instrument

clav·i·cle \-ikəl\ *n* : collarbone

claw \'kló\ *n* : sharp curved nail or process (as on the toe of an animal) ~ *vb* : scratch or dig —**clawed** *adj*

clay \'klā\ *n* : plastic earthy material —**clay·ey** \-ē\ *adj*

clean \'klēn\ *adj* **1** : free from dirt or disease **2** : pure or honorable **3** : thorough ~ *vb* : make or become clean —**clean** *adv* —**clean·er** *n* —**clean·ly** \-lē\ *adv* —**clean·ness** *n*

clean·ly \'klenlē\ *adj* **-li·er, -est** : clean —**clean·li·ness** *n*

cleanse \'klenz\ *vb* **cleansed; cleans·ing** : make clean —**cleans·er** *n*

clear \'klir\ *adj* **1** : bright **2** : free from clouds **3** : transparent **4** : easily heard, seen or understood **5** : free from doubt **6** : free from restriction or obstruction ~ *vb* **1** : make or become clear **2** : go away **3** : free from accusation or blame **4** : explain or settle **5** : net **6** : jump or pass without touching ~ *n* : clear space or part —**clear** *adv* —**clear·ance** \'klirəns\ *n* —**clear·ly** *adv* —**clear·ness** *n*

clear·ing \'kli(ə)riŋ\ *n* : land cleared of wood

cleat \'klēt\ *n* : projection that strengthens or prevents slipping

¹cleave \'klēv\ *vb* **cleaved** \'klēvd\ *or* **clove** \'klōv\; **cleav·ing** : adhere

²cleave *vb* **cleaved** \'klēvd\; **cleav·ing** : split apart —**cleav·age** \'klēvij\ *n*

cleav·er \'klēvər\ *n* : heavy chopping knife

clef \'klef\ *n* : sign on the staff in music to show pitch

cleft \'kleft\ *n* : crack

clem·ent \'klemənt\ *adj* **1** : merciful **2** : temperate or mild —**clem·en·cy** \-ənsē\ *n*

clench \'klench\ *vb* **1** : hold fast **2** : close tightly

cler·gy \'klərjē\ *n* : body of religious officials —**clergy·man** \-jimən\ *n*

cler·ic \'klerik\ *n* : clergyman

cler·i·cal \-ikəl\ *adv* **1** : relating to the clergy **2** : relating to a clerk or office worker

clerk \'klərk, *Brit* 'klärk\ *n* **1** : official responsible for record-keeping **2** : person doing general office work **3**

: salesperson in a store —**clerk** vb
—**clerk·ship** n

clev·er \'klevər\ adj 1 : resourceful 2
: marked by wit or ingenuity —**clev·
er·ly** adv —**clev·er·ness** n

clew var of CLUE

cli·ché \kli'shā\ n : trite phrase —**cli·
chéd** \-'shād\ adj

click \'klik\ n : slight sharp noise ~ vb
: make or cause to make a click

cli·ent \'klīənt\ n 1 : person who engages professional services 2 : customer

cli·en·tele \,klīən'tel, ,klē-\ n : body of
customers

cliff \'klif\ n : high steep face of rock

cli·mate \'klīmət\ n : average weather
conditions over a period of years
—**cli·mat·ic** \klī'matik\ adj

cli·max \'klī,maks\ n : the highest
point ~ vb : come to a climax —**cli·
mac·tic** \klī'maktik\ adj

climb \'klīm\ vb 1 : go up or down by
use of hands and feet 2 : rise ~ n : a
climbing —**climb·er** n

clinch \'klinch\ vb 1 : fasten securely 2
: settle 3 : hold fast or firmly —**clinch**
n —**clinch·er** n

cling \'kliŋ\ vb clung \'kləŋ\; **cling·ing**
1 : adhere firmly 2 : hold on tightly

clin·ic \'klinik\ n : facility for diagno-
sis and treatment of outpatients
—**clin·i·cal** \-əl\ adj

clink \'kliŋk\ vb : make a slight metallic sound —**clink** n

clin·ker \'kliŋkər\ n : fused stony matter esp. in a furnace

¹**clip** \'klip\ vb -pp- : fasten with a clip
~ n : device to hold things together

²**clip** vb -pp- 1 : cut or cut off 2 : hit
~ n 1 : clippers 2 : sharp blow 3 : rapid
pace

clip·per \'klipər\ n 1 pl : implement
for clipping 2 : fast sailing ship

clique \'klēk, 'klik\ n : small exclusive
group of people

cli·to·ris \'klitərəs, kli'tōrəs\ n : small
organ at the anterior part of the
vulva

cloak \'klōk\ n 1 : loose outer garment
2 : something that conceals ~ vb
: cover or hide with a cloak

clob·ber \'kläbər\ vb : hit hard

clock \'kläk\ n : timepiece not carried
on the person ~ vb : record the time
of

clock·wise \-,wīz\ adv or adj : in the
same direction as hands of a clock

clod \'kläd\ n 1 : lump esp. of earth 2
: dull insensitive person

clog \'kläg\ n 1 : restraining weight 2
: thick-soled shoe ~ vb -gg- 1 : im-

pede with a clog 2 : obstruct passage
through 3 : become plugged up

clois·ter \'klóistər\ n 1 : monastic establishment 2 : covered passage ~
vb : shut away from the world

¹**close** \'klōz\ vb closed; clos·ing 1
: shut 2 : cease operation 3 : terminate 4 : bring or come together n
: conclusion or end

²**close** \'klōs\ adj clos·er; clos·est 1
: confining 2 : secretive 3 : strict 4
: stuffy 5 : having little space between items 6 : fitting tightly 7 : near
8 : intimate 9 : accurate 10 : nearly
even —**close** adv —**close·ly** adv —
close·ness n

clos·et \'kläzət, 'klóz-\ n : small compartment for household utensils or
clothing ~ vb : take into a private
room for a talk

clo·sure \'klōzhər\ n 1 : act of closing
2 : something that closes

clot \'klät\ n : dried mass of a liquid —
clot vb

cloth \'klóth\ n, pl cloths \'klóthz,
'klóths\ 1 : fabric 2 : tablecloth

clothe \'klōth\ vb clothed or clad
\'klad\; **cloth·ing** : dress

clothes \'klō(th)z\ n pl : clothing

cloth·ier \'klōthyər, -thēər\ n : maker
or seller of clothing

cloth·ing \'klōthiŋ\ n : covering for the
human body

cloud \'klaúd\ n 1 : visible mass of
particles in the air 2 : something that
darkens, hides, or threatens ~ vb
: darken or hide —**cloud·i·ness** n
—**cloud·less** adj —**cloudy** adj

cloud·burst n : sudden heavy rain

clout \'klaút\ n 1 : blow 2 : influence
~ vb : hit forcefully

¹**clove** \'klōv\ n : section of a bulb

²**clove** past of CLEAVE

³**clove** n : dried flower bud of an East
Indian tree used as a spice

clo·ver \'klōvər\ n : leguminous herb
with usu. 3-parted leaves

clo·ver·leaf n, pl -leafs or -leaves : highway intersection without left-hand
turns or direct crossings

clown \'klaún\ n : funny costumed en-
tertainer esp. in a circus ~ vb : act
like a clown —**clown·ish** adj —**clown·
ish·ly** adv —**clown·ish·ness** n

cloy \'klói\ vb : disgust with excess

club \'kləb\ n 1 : heavy wooden stick 2
: playing card of a suit marked with a
black figure like a clover leaf 3
: group associated with a common purpose ~ vb -bb- : hit with a club

club·foot n : misshapen foot twisted out

of position from birth **—club·foot·ed**
\'·ˌfu̇təd\ adj

cluck \'klək\ n : sound made by a hen
—cluck vb

clue, clew \'klü\ n : piece of evidence
that helps solve a problem ~ vb
clued or **clewed; clue·ing** or **clew·ing**
: provide with a clue

clump \'kləmp\ n 1 : cluster 2 : heavy
tramping sound ~ vb : tread heavily

clum·sy \'kləmzē\ adj **-si·er; -est** 1
: lacking dexterity, nimbleness, or
grace 2 : tactless **—clum·si·ly** adv
—clum·si·ness n

clung past of CLING

clus·ter \'kləstər\ n : group ~ vb
: grow or gather in a cluster

clutch \'kləch\ vb : grasp ~ n 1
: grasping hand or claws 2 : control
or power 3 : coupling for connecting
two working parts in machinery

clut·ter \'klətər\ vb : fill with things
that get in the way **—clutter** n

co- prefix : with, together, joint, or
jointly

coact	coinvent
coactor	coinventor
coauthor	coinvestigator
coauthorship	coleader
cocaptain	comanagement
cochairman	comanager
cochampion	co-officiate
cocomposer	co-organizer
coconspirator	co-own
cocreator	co-owner
codefendant	copartner
codesign	copartnership
codesigner	copresident
codevelop	coprincipal
codeveloper	coprisoner
codirect	coproduce
codirector	coproducer
codiscoverer	coproduction
codrive	copromote
codriver	copromoter
coedit	coproprietor
coeditor	coproprietorship
coexecutor	copublish
coexist	copublisher
coexistence	corecipient
coexistent	coresident
cofeature	cosignatory
cofinance	cosigner
cofound	cosponsor
cofounder	costar
coheir	cowinner
coheiress	co-worker
cohost	cowrite
cohostess	

coach \'kōch\ n 1 : closed 2-door

4-wheeled carriage 2 : railroad passenger car 3 : bus 4 : 2d-class air
travel 5 : one who instructs or trains
performers ~ vb : instruct or direct
as a coach

co·ag·u·late \kō'agyəˌlāt\ vb **-lat·ed;
-lat·ing** : clot **—co·ag·u·lant** \-lənt\ n
—co·ag·u·la·tion \-ˌagyə'lāshən\ n

coal \'kōl\ n 1 : ember 2 : black solid
mineral used as fuel **—coal·field** n

co·alesce \ˌkōə'les\ vb **-alesced; -alesc·
ing** : grow together **—co·ales·cence**
\-'lesəns\ n

co·ali·tion \-'lishən\ n : temporary alliance

coarse \'kōrs\ adj **coars·er; coars·est** 1
: composed of large particles 2
: rough or crude **—coarse·ly** adv
—coars·en \-ᵊn\ vb **—coarse·ness** n

coast \'kōst\ n : seashore ~ vb : move
without effort **—coast·al** \-ᵊl\ adj

coast guard n : military force that
guards or patrols a coast **—coast·
guards·man** \'kōstˌgärdzmən\ n

coast·line n : shape of a coast

coat \'kōt\ n 1 : outer garment for the
upper body 2 : external growth of fur
or feathers 3 : covering layer ~ vb
: cover with a coat **—coat·ed** adj
—coat·ing n

coax \'kōks\ vb : move to action or
achieve by gentle urging or flattery
—coax·er n

cob \'käb\ n : corncob

co·balt \'kōˌbȯlt\ n : shiny silver-white
magnetic metallic chemical element

cob·bler \'käblər\ n 1 : shoemaker 2
: deep-dish fruit pie **—cob·ble**
\'käbəl\ vb

cob·ble·stone n : small round paving
stone

co·bra \'kōbrə\ n : venomous snake

cob·web \'käbˌweb\ n : network
spun by a spider or a similar filament

co·caine \kō'kān, 'kōˌkān\ n : drug
obtained from the leaves of a So.
American shrub (**co·ca** \'kōkə\)

co·chlea \'kōklēə, 'kä-\ n, pl **-chle·as**
or **-chle·ae** \-lē,ē, -ˌī\ : the usu. spiral
part of the inner ear **—coch·le·ar**
\-lēər\ adj

cock \'käk\ n 1 : male fowl 2 : valve or
faucet ~ vb 1 : draw back the hammer of a firearm 2 : tilt to one side
—cock·fight n

cock·ade \kä'kād\ n : badge on a hat

cock·a·too \ˌkäkəˌtü\ n, pl **-toos** : large
Australian parrot

cock·le \'käkəl\ n : edible shellfish

cock·pit \-ˌpit\ n : place for a pilot,
driver, or helmsman

cock·roach \n : nocturnal insect often infesting houses

cock·tail \'käk,tāl\ n 1 : iced drink of liquor and flavorings 2 : appetizer

cocky \-ē\ adj cock·i·er; -est : overconfident —**cock·i·ness** n

co·coa \'kōkō\ n 1 : cacao 2 : powdered chocolate or a drink made from this

co·co·nut \-kə(,)nət\ n : nutlike fruit of a tropical palm (**coconut palm**)

co·coon \kə'kün\ n : case protecting an insect pupa

cod \'käd\ n, pl **cod** : food fish of the No. Atlantic

cod·dle \'käd°l\ vb -dled; -dling : pamper

code \'kōd\ n 1 : system of laws or rules 2 : system of signals

co·deine \'kō,dēn, 'kōdēən\ n : narcotic drug used in cough remedies

cod·ger \'käjər\ n : odd fellow

cod·i·cil \'kädəsəl, -,sil\ n : postscript to a will

cod·i·fy \'kädə,fī, 'kōd-\ vb -fied; -fy·ing : arrange systematically —**cod·i·fi·ca·tion** \,kädəf ə'kāshən, ,kōd-\ n

co·ed \'kō,ed\ n : female student in a coeducational institution —**coed** adj

co·ed·u·ca·tion \,kō-\ n : education of the sexes together —**co·ed·u·ca·tion·al** adj

co·ef·fi·cient \,kōə'fishənt\ n 1 : number that is a multiplier of another 2 : number that serves as a measure of some property

co·erce \kō'ərs\ vb -erced; -erc·ing : force —**co·er·cion** \-'ərzhən, -shən\ n —**co·er·cive** \-'ərsiv\ adj

cof·fee \'kȯfē\ n : drink made from the roasted and ground seeds (**coffee beans**) of a tropical shrub —**cof·fee·house** n —**cof·fee·pot** n

cof·fer \'kȯfər\ n : box for valuables

cof·fin \-fən\ n : box for burial

cog \'käg\ n : tooth on the rim of a gear —**cogged** \'kägd\ adj —**cog·wheel** n

co·gent \'kōjənt\ adj : compelling or convincing —**co·gen·cy** \-jənsē\ n

cog·i·tate \'käjə,tāt\ vb -tat·ed; -tat·ing : think over —**cog·i·ta·tion** \,käjə'tāshən\ n —**cog·i·ta·tive** \'käjə,tātiv\ adj

co·gnac \'kōn,yak\ n : French brandy

cog·nate \'käg,nāt\ adj : related —**cognate** n

cog·ni·tion \käg'nishən\ n : act or process of knowing —**cog·ni·tive** \'kägnətiv\ adj

cog·ni·zance \'kägnəzəns\ n : notice or awareness —**cog·ni·za·ble** \-nəzəbəl, käg'nī-\ adj —**cog·ni·zant** \'kägnəzənt\ adj

co·hab·it \kō'habət\ vb : live together as husband and wife —**co·hab·i·ta·tion** \-,habə'tāshən\ n

co·here \kō'hiər\ vb -hered; -her·ing : stick together

co·her·ent \-'hirənt\ adj 1 : able to stick together 2 : logically consistent —**co·her·ence** \-əns\ n —**co·her·ent·ly** adv

co·he·sion \-'hēzhən\ n : a sticking together —**co·he·sive** \-siv\ adj

co·hort \'kō,hȯrt\ n 1 : group of soldiers 2 : companion

coif·fure \kwä'fyu̇r\ n : hair style

coil \'kȯil\ vb : wind in a spiral ~ n : series of loops (as of rope)

coin \'kȯin\ n : piece of metal used as money ~ vb 1 : make (a coin) by stamping 2 : create —**coin·age** \-ij\ n —**coin·er** n

co·in·cide \,kōən'sīd, 'kōən,sīd\ vb -cid·ed; -cid·ing 1 : be in the same place 2 : happen at the same time 3 : be alike —**co·in·ci·dence** \kō'insədəns\ n —**co·in·ci·dent** \-ənt\ adj —**co·in·ci·den·tal** \-,insə'dent°l\ adj

co·itus \'kōətəs\ n : sexual intercourse —**co·ital** \-ət°l\ adj

coke \'kōk\ n : fuel made by heating soft coal

co·la \'kōlə\ n : carbonated soft drink

col·an·der \'kələndər, 'käl-\ n : perforated utensil for draining food

cold \'kōld\ adj 1 : having a low or below normal temperature 2 : lacking warmth of feeling 3 : suffering from lack of warmth ~ n 1 : low temperature 2 : minor respiratory illness —**cold·ly** adv —**cold·ness** \'kōl(d)nəs\ n —**in cold blood** : with premeditation

cold-blood·ed adj 1 : cruel or merciless 2 : having a body temperature that varies with the temperature of the environment

cole·slaw \'kōl,slȯ\ n : cabbage salad

col·ic \'kälik\ n : sharp abdominal pain —**col·icky** adj

col·i·se·um \,kälə'sēəm\ n : arena

col·lab·o·rate \kə'labə,rāt\ vb -rat·ed; -rat·ing 1 : work jointly with others 2 : help the enemy —**col·lab·o·ra·tion** \-,labə'rāshən\ n —**col·lab·o·ra·tor** \-'labə,rātər\ n

col·lapse \kə'laps\ vb -lapsed; -laps·ing 1 : fall in 2 : break down physically or mentally **3** : fold down ~ n : breakdown —**col·laps·ible** adj

col·lar \'kälər\ n **1** : part of a garment around the neck ~ vb **1** : seize by the collar **2** : grab —**col·lar·less** adj

col·lar·bone n : bone joining the breastbone and the shoulder blade

col·lards \'kälərdz\ n pl : kale

col·late \kə'lāt; 'käl,āt, 'kōl-\ vb -**lat·ed; -lat·ing 1** : compare carefully **2** : assemble in order

col·lat·er·al \kə'lat(ə)rəl\ adj **1** : secondary **2** : descended from the same ancestors but not in the same line **3** : similar ~ n : property used as security for a loan

col·league \'käl,ēg\ n : associate

col·lect \kə'lekt\ vb **1** : bring, come, or gather together **2** : receive payment of ~ adv or adj : to be paid for by the receiver —**col·lect·ible, col·lect·able** adj —**col·lec·tion** \-'lekshən\ n —**col·lec·tor** \-'lektər\ n

col·lec·tive \-tiv\ adj : denoting or shared by a group ~ n : a cooperative unit —**col·lec·tive·ly** adv

col·lege \'kälij\ n : institution of higher learning granting a bachelor's degree —**col·le·gian** \kə'lējən\ n —**col·le·giate** \kə'lējət\ adj

col·lide \kə'līd\ vb -**lid·ed; -lid·ing** : strike together —**col·li·sion** \-'lizhən\ n

col·lie \'kälē\ n : large long-haired dog

col·loid \'käl,ȯid\ n : tiny particles in suspension with a fluid —**col·loi·dal** \kə'lȯid³l\ adj

col·lo·qui·al \kə'lōkwēəl\ adj : used in informal conversation —**col·lo·qui·al·ism** \-ə,lizəm\ n

col·lo·quy \'käləkwē\ n, pl -**quies** : formal conversation or conference

col·lu·sion \kə'lüzhən\ n : secret cooperation for deceit —**col·lu·sive** \-'lüsiv\ adj

co·logne \kə'lōn\ n : perfumed liquid

¹co·lon \'kōlən\ n, pl colons or co·la \-lə\ : lower part of the large intestine —**co·lon·ic** \kō'länik\ adj

²colon n, pl colons or co·la \-lə\ : punctuation mark : used esp. to direct attention to following matter

col·o·nel \'kərn³l\ n : commissioned officer (as in the army) ranking next below a brigadier general

col·on·nade \,kälə'nād\ n : row of supporting columns

col·o·ny \'kälənē\ n, pl -**nies 1** : people who inhabit a new territory or the territory itself **2** : animals of one kind (as bees) living together —**col·o-**

nial \kə'lōnēəl\ adj or n —**col·o·nist** \'kälənəst\ n —**col·o·nize** \-,nīz\ vb

col·or \'kälər\ n **1** : quality of visible things distinct from shape that results from light reflection **2** pl : flag **3** : liveliness ~ vb **1** : give color to **2** : blush —**col·or·fast** adj —**col·or·ful** adj —**col·or·less** adj

col·or-blind adj : unable to distinguish colors —**color blindness** n

col·ored \'kälərd\ adj **1** : having color **2** : of a race other than the white ~ n, pl colored or coloreds : colored person

co·los·sal \kə'läsəl\ adj : very large or great

co·los·sus \-əs\ n, pl -**sus·es** or -**si** \-'läs,ī\ : something of great size or scope

colt \'kōlt\ n : young male horse —**colt·ish** adj

col·umn \'käləm\ n **1** : vertical section of a printed page **2** : special item (as in a newspaper) **3** : pillar **4** : row (as of soldiers) —**co·lum·nar** \kə'ləmnər\ adj —**col·um·nist** \'käləm(n)əst\ n

co·ma \'kōmə\ n : deep prolonged unconsciousness —**co·ma·tose** \-,tōs, 'kämə-\ adj

comb \'kōm\ n **1** : toothed instrument for arranging the hair **2** : crest on a fowl's head —**comb** vb —**combed** \'kōmd\ adj

com·bat \kəm'bat, 'käm,bat\ vb -**bat·ed** or -**bat·ted; -bat·ing** or -**bat·ting** : fight —**com·bat** \'käm,bat\ n —**com·bat·ant** \kəm'batᵊnt, 'kämbətənt\ n —**com·bat·ive** \kəm'bativ\ adj

com·bi·na·tion \,kämbə'nāshən\ n **1** : process or result of combining **2** : code for opening a lock

com·bine \kəm'bīn\ vb -**bined; -bin·ing** : join together ~ \'käm,bīn\ n **1** : association for business or political advantage **2** : harvesting machine

com·bus·ti·ble \kəm'bəstəbəl\ adj : apt to catch fire —**com·bus·ti·bil·i·ty** \-,bəstə'bilətē\ n —**combustible** n

com·bus·tion \-'bəschən\ n : process of burning —**com·bus·tive** \-tiv\ adj

come \(')kəm\ vb came \'käm\; come; com·ing **1** : move toward or arrive at something **2** : reach a state **3** : originate or exist **4** : amount —**come across** vb : meet or find by chance —**come off** vb : succeed —**come to** vb : regain consciousness —**come to pass** vb : happen —**come upon** vb : come across come·back n 1 : retort 2 : return to a former position —come back vb

co·me·di·an \kə'mēdēən\ n 1 : comic actor 2 : funny person —co·me·di·enne \-ˌmēdē'en\ n

com·e·dy \'kämədē\ n, pl -dies : an amusing play

come·ly \'kəmlē\ adj -li·er; -est : good-looking —come·li·ness n

com·et \'kämət\ n : small bright celestial body

com·fort \'kəmfərt\ n 1 : consolation 2 : well-being or something that gives it ∼ vb 1 : give hope to 2 : console —com·fort·able \'kəmf(f)təbəl, 'kəmfərt-\ adj —com·fort·ably \-blē\ adv —com·fort·less adj

com·fort·er \'kəmfə(r)tər\ n 1 : one that comforts 2 : quilt

com·ic \'kämik\ adj 1 : relating to comedy 2 : funny ∼ n 1 : comedian 2 : sequence of cartoons —com·i·cal adj

com·ing \'kəmiŋ\ adj : next

com·ma \'kämə\ n : punctuation mark , used esp. to separate sentence parts

com·mand \kə'mand\ vb 1 : order 2 : control ∼ n 1 : act of commanding 2 : an order given 3 : mastery 4 : troops under a commander —com·man·dant \'kämənˌdant, -ˌdänt\ n

com·man·deer \ˌkämən'diər\ vb : seize by force

com·mand·er \kə'mandər\ n 1 : officer commanding an army or subdivision of an army 2 : commissioned officer in the navy ranking next below a captain

com·mand·ment \-'man(d)mənt\ n : order

command sergeant major n : noncommissioned officer in the army ranking above a first sergeant

com·mem·o·rate \kə'meməˌrāt\ vb -rat·ed; -rat·ing : celebrate or honor —com·mem·o·ra·tion \-ˌmemə'rāshən\ n —com·mem·o·ra·tive \-'mem(ə)rətiv, -'meməˌrāt-\ adj

com·mence \kə'mens\ vb -menced; -menc·ing : start

com·mence·ment \-'mənt\ n 1 : beginning 2 : graduation ceremony

com·mend \kə'mend\ vb 1 : entrust 2 : recommend 3 : praise —com·mend·able \-əbəl\ adj —com·men·da·tion \ˌkämən'dāshən, -ˌen-\ n

com·men·su·rate \kə'mens(ə)rət, -'mench(ə)-\ adj : equal in measure or extent

com·ment \'käm,ent\ n : statement of opinion or remark —comment vb

com·men·tary \-ənˌterē\ n, pl -tar·ies : series of comments

com·men·ta·tor \-ˌtātər\ n : one who discusses news

com·merce \'käm(ˌ)ərs\ n : business

com·mer·cial \kə'mərshəl\ adj : designed for profit or for mass appeal ∼ n : broadcast advertisement —com·mer·cial·ize \-ˌīz\ vb —com·mer·cial·ly \-ē\ adv

com·min·gle \kə'miŋgəl\ vb : mix

com·mis·er·ate \kə'mizəˌrāt\ vb -at·ed; at·ing : sympathize —com·mis·er·a·tion \-ˌmizə'rāshən\ n

com·mis·sary \'käməˌserē\ n, pl -sar·ies : store esp. for military personnel

com·mis·sion \kə'mishən\ n 1 : order granting power or rank 2 : panel to judge, approve, or act 3 : the doing of an act 4 : agent's fee ∼ vb 1 : confer rank or authority to or for 2 : request something be done or made

com·mis·sion·er \-'mish(ə)nər\ n 1 : member of a commission 2 : head of a government department

com·mit \kə'mit\ vb -tt- 1 : turn over to someone for safekeeping or confinement 2 : perform or do 3 : pledge —com·mit·ment n —com·mit·tal \-ᵊl\ n

com·mit·tee \kə'mitē\ n : panel that examines or acts on something

com·mo·di·ous \kə'mōdēəs\ adj : spacious

com·mod·i·ty \-'mädətē\ n, pl -ties : article for sale

com·mo·dore \'kämə,dōr\ n 1 : former commissioned officer in the navy ranking next below a rear admiral 2 : officer commanding a group of merchant ships

com·mon \'kämən\ adj 1 : public 2 : shared by several 3 : widely known, found, or observed 4 : ordinary ∼ n : community land —com·mon·ly adv —in common : shared together

com·mon·place \'kämənˌplās\ n : cliché ∼ adj : ordinary

common sense n : good judgment

com·mon·weal \-ˌwēl\ n : general welfare

com·mon·wealth \-ˌwelth\ n : state

com·mo·tion \kə'mōshən\ n : disturbance

¹com·mune \kə'myün\ vb -muned; -mun·ing : communicate intimately

²com·mune \'käm,yün\ n : community that shares all ownership and duties —com·mu·nal \-ᵊl\ adj

com·mu·ni·cate \kə'myünəˌkāt\ vb -cat·ed; -cat·ing 1 : make known 2

: exchange information or opinions —com·mu·ni·ca·ble \-'myünikəbəl\ adj —com·mu·ni·ca·tion \-,myüni'kāshən\ n —com·mu·ni·ca·tive \-'myüni,kātiv, -kət-\ adj

Com·mu·nion \-'myünyən\ n : Christian sacrament of partaking of bread and wine

com·mu·ni·qué \kə'myünə,kā, -,myünə'kā\ n : official bulletin

com·mu·nism \'kämyə,nizəm\ n 1 : social organization in which goods are held in common 2 cap : political doctrine based on revolutionary Marxian socialism —com·mu·nist \-nəst\ n or adj, often cap —com·mu·nis·tic \,kämyə'nistik\ adj, often cap

com·mu·ni·ty \kə'myünətē\ n, pl -ties : body of people living in the same place under the same laws

com·mute \kə'myüt\ vb -mut·ed; -mut·ing 1 : reduce (a punishment) 2 : travel back and forth regularly ~ n : trip made in commuting —com·mu·ta·tion \,kämyə'tāshən\ n —com·mut·er n

¹com·pact \kəm'pakt, (')käm-\ adj 1 : hard 2 : small or brief ~ vb : pack together ~ \'käm,pakt\ n 1 : cosmetics case 2 : small car —com·pact·ly adv —com·pact·ness n

²com·pact \'käm,pakt\ n : agreement

com·pan·ion \kəm'panyən\ n 1 : close friend 2 : one of a pair —com·pan·ion·able adj —com·pan·ion·ship n

com·pa·ny \'kəmp(ə)nē\ n, pl -nies 1 : business organization 2 : group of performers 3 : guests 4 : infantry unit

com·par·a·tive \kəm'parətiv\ adj 1 : relating to or being an adjective or adverb form that denotes increase 2 : relative —comparative n —com·par·a·tive·ly adv

com·pare \kəm'paər\ vb -pared; -par·ing 1 : represent as similar 2 : check for likenesses or differences ~ n : comparison —com·pa·ra·ble \'kämp(ə)rəbəl\

com·par·i·son \kəm'parəsən\ n 1 : act of comparing 2 : change in the form and meaning of an adjective or adverb to show different levels of quality, quantity, or relation

com·part·ment \kəm'pärtmənt\ n : section or room

com·pass \'kəmpəs, 'käm-\ n 1 : scope 2 : device for drawing circles 3 : device for determining direction

com·pas·sion \kəm'pashən\ n : pity —com·pas·sion·ate \-(ə)nət\ adj

com·pat·i·ble \-'patəbəl\ adj : harmonious —com·pat·i·bil·i·ty \-,patə'bilətē\ n

com·pa·tri·ot \kəm'pātrēət, -trē,ät\ n : fellow countryman

com·pel \kəm'pel\ vb -ll- : cause through necessity

com·pen·di·um \-'pendēəm\ n, pl -diums or -dia \-dēə\ : summary

com·pen·sate \'kämpən,sāt\ vb -sat·ed; -sat·ing 1 : offset or balance 2 : repay —com·pen·sa·tion \,kämpən-'sāshən\ n —com·pen·sa·to·ry \kəm'pensə,tōrē\ adj

com·pete \kəm'pēt\ vb -pet·ed; -pet·ing : strive to win —com·pe·ti·tion \,kämpə'tishən\ n —com·pet·i·tive \kəm'petətiv\ adj —com·pet·i·tor \kəm'petətər\ n

com·pe·tent \'kämpətənt\ adj : capable —com·pe·tence \-əns\ n —com·pe·ten·cy \-ənsē\ n

com·pile \kəm'pīl\ vb -piled; -pil·ing : collect or compose from several sources —com·pi·la·tion \,kämpə'lāshən\ n —com·pil·er \kəm'pīlər\ n

com·pla·cence \kəm'plāsᵊns\ n : self-satisfaction —com·pla·cen·cy \-ᵊnsē\ n —com·pla·cent \-ᵊnt\ adj

com·plain \kəm'plān\ v 1 : express grief, pain, or discontent 2 : make an accusation —com·plain·ant n —com·plain·er n

com·plaint \-'plānt\ n 1 : expression of grief or discontent 2 : ailment 3 : formal accusation

com·ple·ment \'kämpləmənt\ n 1 : something that completes 2 : full number or amount ~ \-,ment\ vb : complete —com·ple·men·ta·ry \,kämplə'ment(ə)rē\ adj

com·plete \kəm'plēt\ adj -plet·er; -est 1 : having no part lacking 2 : finished 3 : total ~ vb -plet·ed; -plet·ing 1 : make whole 2 : finish —com·plete·ly adv —com·plete·ness n —com·ple·tion \-'plēshən\ n

com·plex \käm'pleks, kəm-; 'käm,pleks\ adj 1 : having many parts 2 : intricate ~ \'käm,pleks\ n : psychological problem —com·plex·i·ty \käm'pleksətē, käm-\ n

com·plex·ion \kəm'plekshən\ n : hue or appearance of the skin esp. of the face —com·plex·ioned adj

com·pli·cate \'kämplə,kāt\ vb -cat·ed; -cat·ing : make complex or hard to understand —com·pli·cat·ed \-əd\ adj —com·pli·ca·tion \,kämplə-'kāshən\ n

com·plic·i·ty \kəm'plisətē\ *n, pl* **-ties** : participation in guilt

com·pli·ment \'kämpləmənt\ *n* **1** : flattering remark **2** *pl* : greeting — \-,ment\ *vb* : pay a compliment to

com·pli·men·ta·ry \,kämplə'ment(ə)rē\ *adj* **1** : praising **2** : free

com·ply \kəm'plī\ *vb* **-plied; -ply·ing** : obey — **com·pli·ance** \-əns\ *n* — **com·pli·ant** \-ənt\ *adj*

com·po·nent \kəm'pōnənt, 'käm,pō-\ *n* : part of something larger ~ *adj* : serving as a component

com·port \kəm'pōrt\ *vb* **1** : agree **2** : behave — **com·port·ment** \-mənt\ *n*

com·pose \kəm'pōz\ *vb* **-posed; -pos·ing 1** : create (as by writing) or put together **2** : calm **3** : set type — **com·pos·er** \-ər\ *n* — **com·po·si·tion** \,kämpə'zishən\ *n*

com·pos·ite \käm'päzət, kəm-\ *adj* : made up of diverse parts — **composite** *n*

com·post \'käm,pōst\ *n* : decayed organic fertilizing material

com·po·sure \kəm'pōzhər\ *n* : calmness

com·pote \'käm,pōt\ *n* : fruits cooked in syrup

1com·pound \(')käm'paúnd, kəm-\ *vb* **1** : combine or add **2** : pay (interest) on principal and accrued interest — \'käm,paúnd\ *adj* : made up of 2 or more parts ~ \'käm,paúnd\ *n* : something compounded

2com·pound \'käm,paúnd\ *n* : enclosure

com·pre·hend \,kämpri'hend\ *vb* **1** : understand **2** : include — **com·pre·hen·si·ble** \-'hensəbəl\ *adj* — **com·pre·hen·sion** \-'henchən\ *n* — **com·pre·hen·sive** \-siv\ *adj*

com·press \kəm'pres\ *vb* : squeeze together ~ \'käm,pres\ *n* : pad for pressing on a wound — **com·pres·sion** \-'preshən\ *n* — **com·pres·sor** \-'presər\ *n*

compressed air *n* : air under pressure greater than that of the atmosphere

com·prise \kəm'prīz\ *vb* **-prised; -pris·ing 1** : contain or cover **2** : be made up of

com·pro·mise \'kämprə,mīz\ *vb* **-mised; -mis·ing** : settle differences by mutual concessions — **compromise** *n*

comp·trol·ler \kən'trōlər, 'kämp,trō-\ *n* : financial officer

com·pul·sion \kəm'pəlshən\ *n* **1** : coercion **2** : irresistible impulse — **com·pul·sive** \-siv\ *adj* — **com·pul·so·ry** \-'pəls(ə)rē\ *adj*

com·punc·tion \-'pəŋkshən\ *n* : remorse

com·pute \-'pyüt\ *vb* **-put·ed; -put·ing** : calculate — **com·pu·ta·tion** \,kämpyü'tāshən\ *n*

com·put·er \kəm'pyütər\ *n* : electronic data processing machine

com·rade \'käm,rad, -rəd, -,rad\ *n* : companion — **com·rade·ship** *n*

1con \'kän\ *adv* : against ~ *n* : opposing side or person

2con *vb* **-nn-** : swindle

con·cave \(')kän'kāv\ *adj* : curved like the inside of a sphere — **con·cav·i·ty** \kän'kavətē\ *n*

con·ceal \kən'sēl\ *vb* : hide — **con·ceal·ment** *n*

con·cede \-'sēd\ *vb* **-ced·ed; -ced·ing** : grant

con·ceit \-'sēt\ *n* : excessively high opinion of oneself — **con·ceit·ed** \-əd\ *adj*

con·ceive \-'sēv\ *vb* **-ceived; -ceiv·ing 1** : become pregnant **2** : think of — **con·ceiv·able** \-'sēvəbəl\ *adj* — **con·ceiv·ably** \-blē\ *adv*

con·cen·trate \'känsən,trāt\ *vb* **-trat·ed; -trat·ing 1** : gather together **2** : make stronger **3** : fix one's attention on one thing ~ *n* : something concentrated — **con·cen·tra·tion** \,känsən'trāshən\ *n*

con·cen·tric \kən'sentrik\ *adj* : having a common center

con·cept \'kän,sept\ *n* : thought or idea

con·cep·tion \kən'sepshən\ *n* **1** : act of conceiving **2** : idea

con·cern \kən'sərn\ *vb* **1** : relate to **2** : involve ~ *n* **1** : affair **2** : worry **3** : business — **con·cerned** \-'sərnd\ *adj* — **con·cern·ing** \-'sərniŋ\ *prep*

con·cert \'sərt\ *n* **1** : plan together ~ \'kän(,)sərt\ *n* **1** : agreement or joint action **2** : public performance of music

con·cer·ti·na \,känsər'tēnə\ *n* : accordionlike instrument

con·cer·to \kən'chertō\ *n, pl* **-ti** \-(,)tē\ *or* **-tos** : orchestral work with solo instruments

con·ces·sion \-'seshən\ *n* **1** : act of conceding **2** : something conceded **3** : right to do business on a property

conch \'käŋk, 'känch\ *n, pl* **conchs** \'käŋks\ *or* **conch·es** \'känchəz\ : large spiral-shelled marine mollusk

con·cil·i·ate \kən'silē,āt\ *vb* **-at·ed; -at·ing** : gain the goodwill of — **con·cil·i·a·tion** \-,silē'āshən\ *n* — **con·cil·ia·to·ry** \-'silyə,tōrē, -'silē-\ *adj*

con·cise \kən'sīs\ *adj* : said in few

words —**con·cise·ly** adv —**con·cise·ness** n

con·clave \'kän‚klāv\ n : private meeting

con·clude \kən'klüd\ vb **-clud·ed; -cluding** 1 : end 2 : decide —**con·clu·sion** \-'klüzhən\ n —**con·clu·sive** \-siv\ adj —**con·clu·sive·ly** adv

con·coct \kən'käkt, kän-\ vb : prepare or devise —**con·coc·tion** \-'käkshən\ n

con·com·i·tant \-'kämətənt\ adj : accompanying —**concomitant** n

con·cord \'kän‚kȯrd, 'käŋ-\ n : agreement

con·cor·dance \kən'kȯrdᵊns\ n 1 : agreement 2 : index of words —**con·cor·dant** \-ᵊnt\ adj

con·course \'kän‚kōrs\ n : open space where crowds gather

con·crete \kän'krēt, 'kän‚krēt\ adj 1 : naming something real 2 : actual or substantial 3 : made of concrete ∼ \'kän‚krēt, kän'krēt\ n : hard building material made of cement, sand, gravel, and water

con·cre·tion \kän'krēshən\ n : hard mass

con·cu·bine \'käŋkyu‚bīn\ n : mistress

con·cur \kən'kər\ vb **-rr-** : agree —**con·cur·rence** \-'kərəns\ n

con·cur·rent \-ᵊnt\ adj : happening at the same time

con·cus·sion \kən'kəshən\ n 1 : shock 2 : brain injury from a blow

con·demn \-'dem\ vb 1 : declare to be wrong, guilty, or unfit for use 2 : sentence —**con·dem·na·tion** \‚kän‚dem'nāshən\ n

con·dense \kən'dens\ vb **-densed; -dens·ing** 1 : make or become more compact 2 : change from vapor to liquid —**con·den·sa·tion** \‚kän‚den-'sāshən, kän-\ n —**con·dens·er** n

con·de·scend \‚kändi'send\ vb 1 : lower oneself 2 : act haughtily —**con·de·scen·sion** \-'senchən\ n

con·di·ment \'kändəmənt\ n : pungent seasoning

con·di·tion \kən'dishən\ n 1 : necessary situation or stipulation 2 pl : state of affairs 3 : state of being ∼ vb 1 : limit by a condition 2 : put into proper condition —**con·di·tion·al** \kən'dish(ə)nəl\ adj —**con·di·tion·al·ly** \-ē\ adv

con·dole \kən'dōl\ vb **-doled; -dol·ing** : express sympathy —**con·do·lence** \kən'dōləns, 'kändə-\ n

con·do·min·i·um \‚kändə'minēəm\ n, pl **-ums** : individually owned apartment

con·done \kən'dōn\ vb **-doned; -doning** : overlook or forgive

con·dor \'kändər, -‚dȯr\ n : large western American vulture

con·du·cive \kən'd(y)üsiv\ adj : tending to help or promote

con·duct \'kän‚(‚)dəkt\ n 1 : management 2 : behavior ∼ \kən'dəkt\ vb 1 : guide 2 : manage or direct 3 : be a channel for 4 : behave —**con·duc·tion** \-'dəkshən\ n —**con·duc·tive** \-'dəktiv\ adj —**con·duc·tor** \-'dəktər\ n

con·duit \'kän‚d(y)üət, -d(w)ət\ n : channel (as for conveying fluid)

cone \'kōn\ n 1 : scaly fruit of pine and related trees 2 : solid figure having a circular base and tapering sides

Con·es·to·ga \‚känə'stōgə\ n : covered wagon

con·fec·tion \kən'fekshən\ n : sweet dish or candy —**con·fec·tion·er** \-sh(ə)nər\ n

con·fed·er·a·cy \kən'fed(ə)rəsē\ n 1 pl **-cies** : league 2 cap : 11 southern states that seceded from the U.S. in 1860 and 1861

con·fed·er·ate \-rət\ adj 1 : united in a league 2 cap : relating to the Confederacy ∼ n 1 : ally 2 cap : adherent of the Confederacy ∼ \-'fedə‚rāt\ vb **-at·ed; -at·ing** : unite —**con·fed·er·a·tion** \-‚fedə'rāshən\ n

con·fer \kən'fər\ vb **-rr-** 1 : give 2 : meet to exchange views —**con·fer·ee** \‚känfə'rē\ n —**con·fer·ence** \'känf(ə)rəns\ n

con·fess \kən'fes\ vb 1 : acknowledge or disclose one's misdeed, fault, or sin 2 : declare faith in —**con·fes·sion** \-'feshən\ n —**con·fes·sion·al** \-'fesh(ə)nəl\ n or adj

con·fes·sor \kən'fesər, 2 also 'kän‚fes-\ n 1 : one who confesses 2 : priest who hears confessions

con·fet·ti \kən'fetē\ n : bits of paper or ribbon thrown in celebration

con·fi·dant \'känfə‚dant, -‚dänt\ n : one to whom secrets are confided

con·fide \kən'fīd\ vb **-fid·ed; -fid·ing** 1 : share private thoughts 2 : reveal in confidence

con·fi·dence \'känfədəns\ n 1 : trust 2 : self-assurance 3 : something confided —**con·fi·dent** \-ᵊnt\ adj —**con·fi·den·tial** \‚känfə'denchəl\ adj

con·fig·u·ra·tion \kən‚figyə'rāshən\ n : arrangement

con·fine \-'fīn\ vb **-fined; -fin·ing** 1 : restrain or restrict to a limited area 2 : put in prison **confines** \'känfīnz\

pl : bounds —**con·fine·ment** *n* —**con·fin·er** *n*

con·firm \kən'fərm\ *vb* 1 : ratify 2 : verify 3 : admit as a full member of a church or synagogue —**con·fir·ma·tion** \ˌkänfər'māshən\ *n*

con·fis·cate \'känfəˌskāt\ *vb* -cat·ed; -cat·ing : take by authority —**con·fis·ca·tion** \ˌkänfə'skāshən\ *n*

con·fla·gra·tion \ˌkänflə'grāshən\ *n* : great fire

con·flict \'känˌflikt\ *n* 1 : war 2 : clash of ideas ~ \kən'flikt\ *vb* : clash

con·form \kən'fórm\ *vb* 1 : make or be like 2 : obey —**con·for·mi·ty** \kən'fórmətē\ *n*

con·found \kən'faúnd, kän-\ *vb* : confuse

con·front \kən'frənt\ *vb* : oppose or face —**con·fron·ta·tion** \ˌkänfrən'tāshən\ *n*

con·fuse \kən'fyüz\ *vb* -fused; -fus·ing 1 : make mentally uncertain 2 : jumble —**con·fu·sion** \-'fyüzhən\ *n*

con·fute \-'fyüt\ *vb* -fut·ed; -fut·ing : overwhelm by argument

con·geal \kən'jēl\ *vb* 1 : freeze 2 : become thick and solid

con·ge·nial \kən-\ *adj* : kindred or agreeable —**con·ge·ni·al·i·ty** *n*

con·gen·i·tal \kən-\ *adj* : existing from birth

con·gest \kən'jest\ *vb* : overcrowd or overfill —**con·ges·tion** \-'jeschən\ *n* —**con·ges·tive** \-'jestiv\ *adj*

con·glom·er·ate \kən'gläm(ə)rət\ *adj* : made up of diverse parts ~ \-əˌrāt\ *vb* -at·ed; -at·ing : form into a mass ~ \-(ə)rət\ *n* 1 : rock composed of fragments and a cementing material 2 : diversified corporation —**con·glom·er·a·tion** \-ˌglämə'rāshən\ *n*

con·grat·u·late \kən'grachəˌlāt\ *vb* -lat·ed; -lat·ing : express pleasure to for good fortune —**con·grat·u·la·tion** \-ˌgrachə'lāshən\ *n* —**con·grat·u·la·to·ry** \-'grachələˌtōrē\ *adj*

con·gre·gate \'käŋgriˌgāt\ *vb* -gat·ed; -gat·ing : assemble

con·gre·ga·tion \ˌkäŋgri'gāshən\ *n* 1 : assembly of people at worship 2 : religious group —**con·gre·ga·tion·al** \-sh(ə)nəl\ *adj*

con·gress \'käŋgrəs\ *n* : assembly of delegates or of senators and representatives —**con·gres·sio·nal** \kən'gresh(ə)nəl, kəŋ-\ *adj* —**con·gress·man** \'käŋgrəsmən\ *n* —**con·gress·wom·an** *n*

con·gru·ence \kən'grüəns, 'käŋgrəwəns\ *n* : likeness —**con·gru·ent** \-ənt\ *adj*

con·gru·ity \kən'grüətē, kän-\ *n* : correspondence between things —**con·gru·ous** \'käŋgrəwəs\ *adj*

con·ic \'känik\ *adj* : relating to or like a cone —**con·i·cal** \-ikəl\ *adj*

co·ni·fer \'känəfər, 'kōn-\ *n* : cone-bearing tree —**co·nif·er·ous** \kō'nif(ə)rəs\ *adj*

con·jec·ture \kən'jekchər\ *n* or *vb* : guess —**con·jec·tur·al** \-əl\ *adj*

con·join \kən-\ *vb* : join together

con·ju·gal \'känjigəl, kən'jü-\ *adj* : relating to marriage

con·ju·gate \'känjəˌgāt\ *vb* -gat·ed; -gat·ing : give the inflected forms of (a verb) —**con·ju·ga·tion** \ˌkänjə'gāshən\ *n*

con·junc·tion \kən'jəŋkshən\ *n* 1 : combination 2 : occurrence at the same time 3 : a word that joins other words together —**con·junc·tive** \-tiv\ *adj*

con·jure \'känjər, 'kən-\ *vb* -jured; -jur·ing 1 : summon by sorcery 2 : practice sleight of hand 3 : entreat —**con·jur·er, con·ju·ror** \'känjərər, 'kən-\ *n*

con·nect \kə'nekt\ *vb* : join or associate —**con·nec·tion** \-'nekshən\ *n* —**con·nec·tive** \-tiv\ *n or adj* —**con·nec·tor** *n*

con·nive \kə'nīv\ *vb* -nived; -niv·ing 1 : pretend ignorance of wrongdoing 2 : cooperate secretly —**con·niv·ance** *n*

con·nois·seur \ˌkänə'sər\ *n* : expert judge esp. of art

con·note \kə'nōt\ *vb* -not·ed; -not·ing : suggest additional meaning —**con·no·ta·tion** \ˌkänə'tāshən\ *n*

con·nu·bi·al \kə'n(y)übēəl\ *adj* : relating to marriage

con·quer \'käŋkər\ *vb* : defeat or overcome —**con·quer·or** \-kərər\ *n*

con·quest \'känˌkwest, 'käŋ-\ *n* 1 : act of conquering 2 : something conquered

con·science \'känchəns\ *n* : awareness of right and wrong

con·sci·en·tious \ˌkänchē'enchəs\ *adj* : honest and hard-working —**con·sci·en·tious·ly** *adv*

con·scious \'känchəs\ *adj* 1 : aware 2 : mentally awake or alert 3 : intentional —**con·scious·ly** *adv* —**con·scious·ness** *n*

con·script \kən'skript\ *vb* : draft for military service —**con·script** \'kän,skript\ *n* —**con·scrip·tion** \kən'skripshən\ *n*

con·se·crate \'känsəˌkrāt\ *vb* -crat·ed; -crat·ing 1 : declare sacred 2 : devote to a solemn purpose —**con·se·cra·tion** \ˌkänsə'krāshən\ *n*

con·sec·u·tive \kən'sek(y)ətiv\ *adj* : following in order —**con·sec·u·tive·ly** *adv*

con·sen·sus \-'sensəs\ *n* **1** : agreement in opinion **2** : collective opinion

con·sent \-'sent\ *vb* : give permission or approval —**consent** *n*

con·se·quence \'känsə,kwens\ *n* **1** : result or effect **2** : importance —**con·se·quent** \-kwənt, -,kwent\ *adj* —**con·se·quent·ly** *adv*

con·se·quen·tial \,känsə'kwenchəl\ *adj* : important

con·ser·va·tion \,känsər'vāshən\ *n* : planned management of natural resources —**con·ser·va·tion·ist** \-sh(ə)nəst\ *n*

con·ser·va·tive \kən'sərvətiv\ *adj* **1** : disposed to maintain the status quo **2** : cautious —**con·ser·va·tism** \-və,tizəm\ *n* —**conservative** *n*

con·ser·va·to·ry \kən'sərvə,tōrē\ *n, pl* **-ries** : school for art or music

con·serve \-'sərv\ *vb* **-served; -serv·ing** : keep from wasting ~ \'kän,sərv\ *n* : candied fruit or fruit preserves

con·sid·er \kən'sidər\ *vb* **1** : think about **2** : give thoughtful attention to **3** : think that —**con·sid·er·ate** \-'sid(ə)rət\ *adj* —**con·sid·er·ate·ly** *adv* —**con·sid·er·ate·ness** *n* —**con·sid·er·a·tion** \-,sidə'rāshən\ *n*

con·sid·er·able \-'sidər(ə)bəl, -'sidrəbəl\ *adj* **1** : significant **2** : noticeably large —**con·sid·er·ably** \-blē\ *adv*

con·sid·er·ing \-(ə)riŋ\ *prep* : taking notice of

con·sign \kən'sīn\ *vb* **1** : transfer **2** : send to an agent for sale —**con·sign·ee** \,känsə'nē, -,sī-; kən,sī-\ *n* —**con·sign·ment** \kən'sīnmənt\ *n* —**con·sign·or** \,känsə'nòr, -,sī-; kən,sī-\ *n*

con·sist \kən'sist\ *vb* **1** : be inherent —used with *in* **2** : be made up —used with *of*

con·sis·ten·cy \-'sistənsē\ *n, pl* **-cies** **1** : degree of thickness or firmness **2** : quality of being consistent

con·sis·tent \-tənt\ *adj* : being steady and regular —**con·sis·tent·ly** *adv*

¹con·sole \kən'sōl\ *vb* **-soled; -sol·ing** : soothe the grief of —**con·so·la·tion** \,känsə'lāshən\ *n*

²con·sole \'kän,sōl\ *n* : cabinet or part with controls

con·sol·i·date \kən'sälə,dāt\ *vb* **-dat·ed; -dat·ing** : unite or compact —**con·sol·i·da·tion** \-,sälə'dāshən\ *n*

con·som·mé \,känsə'mā\ *n* : clear soup

con·so·nance \'känsənəns\ *n* : agree-ment or harmony —**con·so·nant** \-s(ə)nənt\ *adj*

con·so·nant \-s(ə)nənt\ *n* **1** : speech sound marked by constriction or closure in the breath channel **2** : letter other than *a, e, i, o,* and *u* —**con·so·nan·tal** \,känsə'nant³l\ *adj*

con·sort \'kän,sòrt\ *n* : spouse ~ \kən'sòrt\ *vb* : keep company

con·spic·u·ous \kən'spikyəwəs\ *adj* : very noticeable —**con·spic·u·ous·ly** *adv*

con·spire \kən'spī(ə)r\ *vb* **-spired; -spir·ing** : secretly plan an unlawful act —**con·spir·a·cy** \-'spirəsē\ *n* —**con·spir·a·tor** \-'spirətər\ *n*

con·sta·ble \'känstəbəl, 'kän-\ *n* : police officer

con·stab·u·lary \kən'stabyə,lerē\ *n, pl* **-lar·ies** : police force

con·stant \'känstənt\ *adj* **1** : steadfast or faithful **2** : not varying **3** : continually recurring ~ *n* : something unchanging —**con·stan·cy** \-stənsē\ *n* —**con·stant·ly** *adv*

con·stel·la·tion \,känstə'lāshən\ *n* : group of stars

con·ster·na·tion \-stər'nāshən\ *n* : amazed dismay

con·sti·pa·tion \-stə'pāshən\ *n* : difficulty of defecation —**con·sti·pate** \'känstə,pāt\ *vb*

con·stit·u·ent \kən'stichəwənt\ *adj* **1** : component **2** : having power to elect ~ *n* **1** : component part **2** : one who may vote for a representative —**con·stit·u·en·cy** \-wənsē\ *n*

con·sti·tute \'känstə,t(y)üt\ *vb* **-tut·ed; -tut·ing 1** : establish **2** : be all or a basic part of

con·sti·tu·tion \,känstə't(y)üshən\ *n* **1** : physical composition or structure **2** : the basic law of an organized body or the document containing it —**con·sti·tu·tion·al** \-əl\ *adj* —**con·sti·tu·tion·al·i·ty** \-,t(y)üshə'nalətē\ *n*

con·strain \kən'strān\ *vb* **1** : compel **2** : confine **3** : restrain —**con·straint** \-'strānt\ *n*

con·strict \-'strikt\ *vb* : draw or squeeze together —**con·stric·tion** \-'strikshən\ *n* —**con·stric·tive** \-'striktiv\ *adj*

con·struct \kən'strəkt\ *vb* : build or make —**con·struc·tion** \-'strəkshən\ *n* —**con·struc·tive** \-tiv\ *adj*

con·strue \kən'strü\ *vb* **-strued; -stru·ing** : explain or interpret

con·sul \'känsəl\ *n* **1** : Roman magistrate **2** : government commercial official in a foreign country —**con·sul·ar** \-sələr\ *adj* —**con·sul·ate** \-lət\ *n* con·sult \kən'səlt\ vb 1 : ask advice or opinion of 2 : confer —con·sul·tant \-ənt\ n —con·sul·ta·tion \ˌkänsəl'tāshən\ n

con·sume \kən'süm\ vb -sumed; -sum·ing : eat or use up —con·sum·able adj —con·sum·er n

con·sum·mate \kən'səmət\ adj : complete or perfect ~ \'känsəˌmāt\ vb -mat·ed; -mat·ing : make complete —con·sum·ma·tion \ˌkänsə'māshən\ n

con·sump·tion \kən'səmpshən\ n 1 : act of consuming 2 : use of goods 3 : tuberculosis —con·sump·tive \-tiv\ adj or n

con·tact \'känˌtakt\ n 1 : a touching 2 : association or relationship 3 : connection or communication ~ vb 1 : come or bring into contact 2 : communicate with

con·ta·gion \kən'tājən\ n 1 : spread of disease by contact 2 : disease spread by contact —con·ta·gious \-jəs\ adj

con·tain \-'tān\ vb 1 : enclose or include 2 : have or hold within 3 : restrain —con·tain·er n —con·tain·ment n

con·tam·i·nate \kən'taməˌnāt\ vb -nat·ed; -nat·ing : soil or infect by contact or association —con·tam·i·na·tion \-ˌtamə'nāshən\ n

con·tem·plate \'käntəmˌplāt\ vb -plat·ed; -plat·ing : view or consider thoughtfully —con·tem·pla·tion \ˌkäntəm'plāshən\ n —con·tem·pla·tive \kən'templətiv; 'käntəmˌplāt-\ adj

con·tem·po·ra·ne·ous \kənˌtempə'rānēəs\ adj : contemporary

con·tem·po·rary \-'tempəˌrerē\ adj 1 : occurring or existing at the same time 2 : of the same age —contemporary n

con·tempt \kən'tempt\ n 1 : feeling of scorn 2 : state of being despised 3 : disobedience to a court or legislature —con·tempt·ible \-'temptəbəl\ adj

con·temp·tu·ous \-'tempchə(wə)s\ adj : feeling or expressing contempt —con·temp·tu·ous·ly adv

con·tend \-'tend\ vb 1 : strive against rivals or difficulties 2 : argue 3 : maintain or claim —con·tend·er n

¹con·tent \kən'tent\ adj : satisfied ~ vb : satisfy ~ n : ease of mind —con·tent·ed adj —con·tent·ed·ly adv —con·tent·ed·ness n —con·tent·ment \-mənt\ n

²con·tent \'känˌtent\ n 1 pl : something contained 2 pl : subject matter (as of a book) 3 : essential meaning 4 : proportion contained

con·ten·tion \kən'tenchən\ n : state of contending —con·ten·tious \-chəs\ adj

con·test \kən'test\ vb : dispute or challenge ~ \'känˌtest\ n 1 : struggle 2 : game —con·test·able \kən-'testəbəl\ adj —con·test·ably \-blē adv —con·tes·tant \-'testənt\ n

con·text \'känˌtekst\ n : words surrounding a word or phrase

con·tig·u·ous \kən'tigyəwəs\ adj : connected to or adjoining —con·ti·gu·i·ty \ˌkäntə'gyüətē\ n

con·ti·nence \'käntənəns\ n : self-restraint —con·ti·nent \-ənt\ adj

con·ti·nent \'käntənənt, 'käntnənt\ n : great division of land on the globe —con·ti·nen·tal \ˌkäntən'ent²l\ adj

con·tin·gen·cy \kən'tinjənsē\ n, pl -cies : possible event

con·tin·gent \-jənt\ adj : dependent on something else ~ n : a quota from an area or group

con·tin·u·al \kən'tinyəwəl\ adj 1 : continuous 2 : steadily recurring —con·tin·u·al·ly \-ē\ adv

con·tin·ue \kən'tinyü\ vb -tin·ued; -tin·u·ing 1 : remain in a place or condition 2 : endure 3 : resume after an intermission 4 : extend —con·tin·u·ance \-yəwəns\ n —con·tin·u·a·tion \-ˌtinyə'wāshən\ n

con·tin·u·ous \-'tinyəwəs\ adj : continuing without interruption —con·ti·nu·i·ty \ˌkäntə'n(y)üətē\ n —con·tin·u·ous·ly adv

con·tort \kən'tört\ vb : twist out of shape —con·tor·tion \-'törshən\ n

con·tour \'känˌtür\ n 1 : outline 2 pl : shape

con·tra·band \'käntrəˌband\ n : illegal goods

con·tra·cep·tion \ˌkäntrə'sepshən\ n : prevention of conception —con·tra·cep·tive \-'septiv\ adj or n

con·tract \'känˌtrakt\ n : binding agreement ~ \kən'trakt, 1 usu 'kän,trakt\ vb 1 : establish or undertake by contract 2 : become ill with 3 : drawn together so as to shorten 4 : shorten (a word) by omission —con·trac·tion \kən'trakshən\ n —con·trac·tor \'kän,traktər, kən'trak-\ n —con·trac·tu·al \kən'trakchə(wə)l\ adj

con·tra·dict \ˌkäntrə'dikt\ vb : state the contrary of —con·tra·dic·tion

\-'dikshən\ *n* —con·tra·dic·to·ry \-'dikt(ə)rē\ *adj*

con·tral·to \kən'traltō\ *n, pl* -tos : lowest female voice

con·trap·tion \kən'trapshən\ *n* : device or contrivance

con·trary \'kän,trerē; *4 often* kən'tre(ə)rē\ *adj* 1 : opposite in character, nature, or position 2 : mutually opposed 3 : unfavorable 4 : uncooperative or stubborn —con·trari·ly \-,trerəlē, -'trer-\ *adv* —con·trari·wise \-,wīz\ *adv* —contrary \'kän,trerē\ *n*

con·trast \'kän,trast\ *n* 1 : unlikeness shown by comparing 2 : unlike color or tone of adjacent parts ~ \kən'trast\ *vb* 1 : show differences 2 : compare so as to show differences

con·tra·vene \,käntrə'vēn\ *vb* -vened; -ven·ing : go or act contrary to

con·trib·ute \kən'tribyət\ *vb* -ut·ed; -ut·ing : give or help along with others —con·tri·bu·tion \,käntrə'byüshən\ *n* —con·trib·u·tor \kən'tribyətər\ *n* —con·trib·u·to·ry \-yə,tōrē\ *adj*

con·trite \'kän,trīt, kən'trīt\ *adj* : repentant —con·tri·tion \kən'trishən\ *n*

con·trive \kən'trīv\ *vb* -trived; -triv·ing 1 : devise or make with ingenuity 2 : bring about —con·triv·ance \-'trīvəns\ *n* —con·triv·er *n*

con·trol \kən'trōl\ *vb* -ll- 1 : exercise power over 2 : dominate or rule ~ *n* 1 : power to direct or regulate 2 : restraint 3 : regulating device —con·trol·la·ble *adj* —con·trol·ler \-'trōlər, 'kän,-\ *n*

con·tro·ver·sy \'käntrə,vərsē\ *n, pl* -sies : clash of opposing views —con·tro·ver·sial \,käntrə'vərshəl, -sēəl\ *adj*

con·tro·vert \'käntrə,vərt, ,käntrə'-\ *vb* : contradict —con·tro·vert·ible *adj*

con·tu·ma·cious \,känt(y)ə'māshəs\ *adj* : stubborn or insubordinate —con·tu·ma·cy \(,)kən't(y)üməsē, 'känt(y)ə-\ *n*

con·tu·me·ly \kən't(y)ümēlē, 'känt(y)ə,mēlē\ *n* : rudeness

con·tu·sion \kən't(y)üzhən\ *n* : bruise —con·tuse \-'t(y)üz\ *vb*

co·nun·drum \kə'nəndrəm\ *n* : riddle

con·va·lesce \,känvə'les\ *vb* -lesced; -lesc·ing : gradually recover health —con·va·les·cence \-³ns\ *n* —con·va·les·cent \-³nt\ *adj or n*

con·vec·tion \kən'vekshən\ *n* : circulation in fluids due to warmer portions rising and colder ones sinking —con-

vect \-'vekt\ *vb* —con·vec·tion·al \-'veksh(ə)nəl\ *adj* —con·vec·tive \-'vektiv\ *adj*

con·vene \kən'vēn\ *vb* -vened; -ven·ing : assemble or meet

con·ve·nience \-'vēnyəns\ *n* 1 : personal comfort or ease 2 : device that saves work

con·ve·nient \-nyənt\ *adj* 1 : suited to one's convenience 2 : near at hand —con·ve·nient·ly *adv*

con·vent \'känvənt, -,vent\ *n* : community of nuns

con·ven·tion \kən'venchən\ *n* 1 : agreement esp. between nations 2 : large meeting 3 : body of delegates 4 : accepted usage or way of behaving —con·ven·tion·al \-'vench(ə)nəl\ *adj* —con·ven·tion·al·ly *adv*

con·verge \kən'vərj\ *vb* -verged; -verg·ing : approach a single point —con·ver·gence \-'vərjəns\, con·ver·gen·cy \-jənsē\ *n* —con·ver·gent \-jənt\ *adj*

con·ver·sant \-'vərs³nt\ *adj* : having knowledge and experience

con·ver·sa·tion \,känvər'sāshən\ *n* : an informal talking together —con·ver·sa·tion·al \-sh(ə)nəl\ *adj*

¹con·verse \kən'vərs\ *vb* -versed; -vers·ing : engage in conversation —con·verse \'kän,vərs\ *n*

²con·verse \'kän,vərs, kän'vərs\ *adj* : opposite —con·verse \'kän,vərs\ *n* —con·verse·ly *adv*

con·ver·sion \kən'vərzhən\ *n* 1 : change 2 : adoption of religion

con·vert \kən'vərt\ *vb* 1 : turn from one belief or party to another 2 : change ~ \'kän,vərt\ *n* : one who has undergone religious conversion —con·vert·er, con·ver·tor \-ər\ *n* —con·vert·ible *adj*

con·vert·ible \kən'vərtəbəl\ *n* : automobile with a removable top

con·vex \kän'veks, 'kän,-, kən'-\ *adj* : curved or rounded like the outside of a sphere —con·vex·i·ty \kən'veksətē, kän'-\ *n*

con·vey \kən'vā\ *vb* -veyed; -vey·ing : transport or transmit —con·vey·ance \-'vāəns\ *n* —con·vey·er, con·vey·or \-ər\ *n*

con·vict \kən'vikt\ *vb* : find guilty ~ \'kän,vikt\ *n* : person in prison

con·vic·tion \kən'vikshən\ *n* 1 : act of convicting 2 : strong belief

con·vince \-'vins\ *vb* -vinced; -vinc·ing : cause to believe

con·viv·ial \-'vivyəl, -'vivēəl\ *adj* : cheerful or festive —con·viv·i·al·i·ty \-,vivē'alətē\ *n* con·voke \kən'vōk\ vb -voked; -vok·ing : call together to a meeting —con·vo·ca·tion \,känvə'kāshən\ n

con·vo·lut·ed \'känvə,lütəd\ adj 1 : intricately folded 2 : intricate

con·vo·lu·tion \,känvə'lüshən\ n 1 : a coiling together 2 : convoluted structure

con·voy \'kän,vȯi, kən'vȯi\ vb : accompany for protection ~ \'kän,vȯi\ n : group of vehicles moving together

con·vul·sion \kən'vəlshən\ n : violent involuntary muscle contraction —con·vulse \-'vəls\ vb —con·vul·sive \-'vəlsiv\ adj

coo \'kü\ n : sound of a pigeon —coo vb

cook \'kük\ n : one who prepares food ~ vb : prepare food —cook·book \-,buk\ n —cook·er n —cook·ery \-(ə)rē\ n —cook·ware n

cook·ie, cooky \'kükē\ n, pl -ies : small sweet flat cake

cool \'kül\ adj 1 : moderately cold 2 : not excited 3 : showing dislike ~ vb : make or become cool ~ n 1 : cool time or place 2 : composure —cool·ant \-ənt\ n —cool·er n —cool·ly \'kül(l)ē\ adv —cool·ness n

coo·lie \'külē\ n : unskilled Oriental laborer

coop \'küp, 'kup\ n : enclosure usu. for poultry ~ vb : confine in or as if in a coop

co-op \'kō,äp\ n : cooperative

coo·per \'küpər, 'kup-\ n : barrel maker —cooper vb

co·op·er·ate \kō'äpə,rāt\ vb : act jointly —co·op·er·a·tion \-,äpə'rāshən\ n

co·op·er·a·tive \kō'äp(ə)rətiv, -'äpə,rāt-\ adj : willing to work with others ~ n : enterprise owned and run by those using its services

co-opt \kō'äpt\ vb 1 : elect as a colleague 2 : take over

co·or·di·nate \-'ȯrd³nət, -'ȯrdnət\ adj : equal esp. in rank ~ n : any of a set of numbers used in specifying the location of a point on a surface or in space \-³n,āt\ vb -nat·ed; -nat·ing 1 : make or become coordinate 2 : work or act together harmoniously —co·or·di·na·tion \-,ȯrd³n'āshən\ n —co·or·di·na·tor n

coot \'küt\ n : dark-colored ducklike bird

cop \'käp\ n : police officer

¹cope \'kōp\ n : cloaklike ecclesiastical vestment

²cope vb coped; cop·ing : deal with difficulties

co·pi·lot \'kō-\ n : assistant airplane pilot

cop·ing \'kōpiŋ\ n : top layer of a wall

co·pi·ous \'kōpēəs\ adj : very abundant —co·pi·ous·ly adv —co·pi·ous·ness n

cop·per \'käpər\ n 1 : malleable reddish metallic chemical element 2 : penny —cop·pery adj

cop·per·head n : largely coppery brown venomous snake

co·pra \'kōprə\ n : dried coconut meat

copse \'käps\ n : thicket

cop·u·la \'käpyələ\ n : verb linking subject and predicate —cop·u·la·tive \-,lātiv\ adj

cop·u·late \'käpyə,lāt\ vb -lat·ed; -lat·ing : engage in sexual intercourse —cop·u·la·tion \,käpyə'lāshən\ n

copy \'käpē\ n, pl cop·ies 1 : imitation or reproduction of an original 2 : writing to be set for printing ~ vb cop·ied; copy·ing 1 : make a copy of 2 : imitate —copi·er \-ər\ n —copy·ist n

copy·right n : sole right to a literary or artistic work ~ vb : get a copyright on

co·quette \kō'ket\ n : flirt

cor·al \'kȯrəl\ n 1 : skeletal material of colonies of tiny sea polyps 2 : deep pink —coral adj

cord \'kȯrd\ n 1 : usu. heavy string 2 : long slender anatomical structure 3 : measure of firewood equal to 128 cu. ft. 4 : small electrical cable ~ vb 1 : tie or furnish with a cord 2 : pile in cords

cor·dial \'kȯrjəl\ adj : warmly welcoming ~ n : liqueur —cor·di·al·i·ty \-,kȯrjē'alətē, kȯrd'yal-\ n —cor·dial·ly \'kȯrjəlē\ adv

cor·don \'kȯrd³n\ n : encircling line of troops or police —cordon vb

cor·do·van \-əvən\ n : soft fine-grained leather

cor·du·roy \-ə,rȯi\ n 1 : heavy ribbed fabric 2 pl : trousers of corduroy

core \'kȯr\ n 1 : central part of some fruits 2 : inmost part ~ vb cored; cor·ing : take out the core of —cor·er n

cork \'kȯrk\ n 1 : tough elastic bark of a European oak (cork oak) 2 : stopper of cork ~ vb : stop up with a cork —corky adj

cork·screw n : device for drawing corks from bottles

cor·mo·rant \'kȯrm(ə)rənt, -ə,rant\ n : dark seabird

¹corn \'kȯrn\ *n* : cereal grass or its seeds ~ *vb* : cure or preserve in brine —**corn·meal** *n* —**corn·stalk** *n* —**corn·starch** *n*

²corn *n* : local hardening and thickening of skin

corn-cob *n* : axis on which the kernels of Indian corn are arranged

cor·nea \'kȯrnēə\ *n* : transparent part of the coat of the eyeball —**cor·ne·al** *adj*

cor·ner \'kȯrnər\ *n* **1** : point or angle formed by the meeting of lines or sides **2** : place where two streets meet **3** : inescapable position **4** : control of the supply of something ~ *vb* **1** : drive into a corner **2** : get a corner on **3** : turn a corner

cor·ner·stone *n* **1** : stone at a corner of a wall **2** : something basic

cor·net \kȯr'net\ *n* : trumpetlike instrument

cor·nice \'kȯrnəs\ *n* : horizontal wall projection

cor·nu·co·pia \ˌkȯrn(y)ə'kōpēə\ *n* : goat's horn filled with fruits and grain emblematic of abundance

co·rol·la \kə'rälə\ *n* : petals of a flower

cor·ol·lary \'kȯrəˌlerē\ *n, pl* **-lar·ies 1** : logical deduction **2** : consequence or result

co·ro·na \kə'rōnə\ *n* : shining ring around the sun seen during eclipses

cor·o·nary \'kȯrəˌnerē\ *adj* : relating to the heart or its blood vessels ~ *n* : thrombosis of an artery supplying the heart

cor·o·na·tion \ˌkȯrə'nāshən\ *n* : crowning of a monarch

cor·o·ner \'kȯrənər\ *n* : public official who investigates causes of suspicious deaths

¹cor·po·ral \'kȯrp(ə)rəl\ *adj* : bodily

²corporal *n* : noncommissioned officer ranking next below a sergeant

cor·po·ra·tion \ˌkȯrpə'rāshən\ *n* : legal creation with the rights and liabilities of a person —**cor·po·rate** \'kȯrp(ə)rət\ *adj*

cor·po·re·al \kȯr'pōrēəl\ *adj* : physical or material —**cor·po·re·al·ly** *adv*

corps \'kȯr\ *n, pl* **corps** \'kȯrz\ **1** : subdivision of a military force **2** : working group

corpse \'kȯrps\ *n* : dead body

cor·pu·lence \'kȯrpyələns\ *or* **cor·pu·len·cy** \-lənsē\ *n* : excessive fatness —**cor·pu·lent** \-lənt\ *adj*

cor·pus \'kȯrpəs\ *n, pl* **-po·ra** \-pərə\ **1** : corpse **2** : body of writings

cor·pus·cle \'kȯr(ˌ)pəsəl\ *n* : blood cell

cor·ral \kə'ral\ *n* : enclosure for animals —**corral** *vb*

cor·rect \-'rekt\ *vb* **1** : make right **2** : chastise ~ *adj* **1** : true or factual **2** : conforming to a standard —**cor·rec·tion** \-'rekshən\ *n* —**cor·rec·tive** \-'rektiv\ *adj* —**cor·rect·ly** \-'rek(t)lē\ *adv* —**cor·rect·ness** \-'rek(t)nəs\ *n*

cor·re·late \'kȯrəˌlāt\ *vb* **-lat·ed; -lat·ing** : show a connection between —**cor·re·late** \-lət, -ˌlāt\ *n* —**cor·re·la·tion** \ˌkȯrə'lāshən\ *n*

cor·rel·a·tive \kə'relətiv\ *adj* : regularly used together —**correlative** *n*

cor·re·spond \ˌkȯrə'spänd\ *vb* **1** : match **2** : communicate by letter —**cor·re·spon·dence** \-'spändəns\ *n*

cor·re·spon·dent \-'spändənt\ *n* **1** : person one writes to **2** : reporter

cor·ri·dor \'kȯrədər, -əˌdȯr\ *n* : passageway connecting rooms

cor·rob·o·rate \kə'räbəˌrāt\ *vb* **-rat·ed; -rat·ing** : support with evidence —**cor·rob·o·ra·tion** \-ˌräbə'rāshən\ *n*

cor·rode \kə'rōd\ *vb* **-rod·ed; -rod·ing** : wear away by chemical action —**cor·ro·sion** \-'rōzhən\ *n* —**cor·ro·sive** \-'rōsiv\ *adj or n*

cor·ru·gate \'kȯrəˌgāt\ *vb* **-gat·ed; -gat·ing** : form into ridges and grooves —**cor·ru·ga·tion** \ˌkȯrə'gāshən\ *n*

cor·rupt \kə'rəpt\ *vb* **1** : change from good to bad **2** : bribe ~ *adj* **1** : morally debased —**cor·rupt·ible** *adj* —**cor·rup·tion** \-'rəpshən\ *n*

cor·sage \kȯr'säzh, -'säj\ *n* : bouquet worn by a woman

cor·set \'kȯrsət\ *n* : woman's stiffened undergarment

cor·tege \kȯr'tezh, 'kȯrˌ-\ *n* : funeral procession

cor·tex \'kȯrˌteks\ *n, pl* **-ti·ces** \'kȯrtəˌsēz\ *or* **-tex·es** : outer or covering layer of an organism or part (as the brain) —**cor·ti·cal** \'kȯrtikəl\ *adj*

cor·ti·sone \'kȯrtəˌsōn, -zōn\ *n* : adrenal hormone

cos·met·ic \käz'metik\ *n* : beautifying preparation ~ *adj* : relating to beautifying

cos·mic \'käzmik\ *adj* **1** : relating to the cosmos **2** : vast or grand

cos·mo·naut \'käzməˌnȯt\ *n* : Soviet astronaut

cos·mo·pol·i·tan \ˌkäzmə'pälət³n\ *adj* : belonging to all the world —**cosmopolitan** *n*

cos·mos \'käzməs *also* -ˌmōs, -ˌmäs\ *n* : universe

cos·sack \\'käs,ak, -ək\\ *n* : Russian czarist cavalryman

cost \\'kȯst\\ *n* **1** : amount paid for something **2** : loss or penalty ~ *vb* **cost; cost·ing 1** : require so much in payment **2** : cause to pay, suffer, or lose —**cost·li·ness** \\-lēnəs\\ *n* —**cost·ly** \\-lē\\ *adj*

cos·tume \\'käs,t(y)üm\\ *n* : clothing

co·sy \\'kōzē\\ *var of* COZY

cot \\'kät\\ *n* : small bed

cote \\'kōt, 'kät\\ *n* : small shed or coop

co·te·rie \\'kōtə,rē, ,kōtə'-\\ *n* : exclusive group of persons

co·til·lion \\kō'tilyən\\ *n* : formal ball

cot·tage \\'kätij\\ *n* : small house

cot·ton \\'kätən\\ *n* : soft fibrous plant substance or thread or cloth made of it —**cot·ton·seed** *n* —**cot·tony** *adj*

cot·ton·mouth *n* : poisonous snake

couch \\'kauch\\ *vb* **1** : lie or place on a couch **2** : phrase ~ *n* : bed or sofa

cou·gar \\'kügər, -,gär\\ *n* : large tawny wild American cat

cough \\'kȯf\\ *vb* : force air from the lungs with short sharp noises —**cough** *n*

could \\kəd, (')kud\\ *past of* CAN

coun·cil \\'kaunsəl\\ *n* **1** : assembly or meeting **2** : body of lawmakers —**coun·cil·lor, coun·cil·or** \\-s(ə)lər\\ *n* —**coun·cil·man** \\-mən\\ *n* —**coun·cil·wom·an** *n*

coun·sel \\'kaunsəl\\ *n* **1** : advice **2** : deliberation together **3** *pl* **-sel** : lawyer ~ *vb* **-seled** *or* **-selled; -sel·ing** *or* **-sel·ling 1** : advise **2** : consult together —**coun·sel·or, coun·sel·lor** \\-s(ə)lər\\ *n*

¹count \\'kaunt\\ *vb* **1** : name or indicate one by one to find the total number **2** : recite numbers in order **3** : rely **4** : be of value or account ~ *n* **1** : act of counting or the total obtained by counting **2** : charge in an indictment —**count·able** *adj*

²count *n* : European nobleman

coun·te·nance \\'kaunt^ənəns, 'kauntnəns\\ *n* : face or facial expression ~ *vb* **-nanced; -nanc·ing** : allow or encourage

¹coun·ter \\'kauntər\\ *n* **1** : piece for reckoning or games **2** : surface over which business is transacted

²count·er *n* : one that counts

³coun·ter *vb* : oppose ~ *adv* : in an opposite direction ~ *n* : offsetting force or move ~ *adj* : contrary

coun·ter- *prefix* **1** : contrary or opposite **2** : opposing **3** : retaliatory

counteraccusa- tion	counteroffer
counteraggres- sion	counterpetition
	counterploy
counterargue	counterpower
counterassault	counterpressure
counterattack	counterpropa- ganda
counterbid	
counterblockade	counterproposal
counterblow	counterprotest
countercampaign	counterquestion
counterchallenge	counterraid
countercharge	counterrally
counterclaim	counterrebuttal
countercomplaint	counterreform
countercoup	counterresponse
countercriticism	counterretalia- tion
counterdemand	
counterdemonstra- tion	counterrevolu- tion
counterdemon- strator	counterstrategy
	counterstyle
countereffect	countersue
countereffort	countersugges- tion
counterembargo	
counterevidence	countersuit
counterguerrilla	countertendency
counterinflation- ary	counterterror
	counterterrorism
counterinfluence	counterterrorist
counterintrigue	counterthreat
countermeasure	counterthrust
countermove	countertrend
countermove- ment	

coun·ter·act *vb* : lessen the force of

coun·ter·bal·ance *n* : balancing influence or weight ~ *vb* : oppose or balance

coun·ter·clock·wise *adv* : opposite to the way a clock's hands move —**counterclockwise** *adj*

coun·ter·feit \\'kauntər,fit\\ *vb* **1** : copy in order to deceive **2** : pretend ~ *adj* : spurious ~ *n* : fraudulent copy —**coun·ter·feit·er** *n*

coun·ter·mand \\-,mand\\ *vb* : supersede with a contrary order

coun·ter·part *n* : one that is similar or corresponds

coun·ter·point *n* : music with interwoven melodies

coun·ter·sign *n* : secret signal ~ *vb* : add a confirming signature to

count·ess \\'kauntəs\\ *n* : wife or widow of a count or an earl or a woman holding that rank in her own right

count·less \\-ləs\\ *adj* : too many to be numbered

coun·try \\'kəntrē\\ *n, pl* **-tries 1** : nation

2 : rural area ~ *adj* : rural —**coun-try-man** \'\-mən\ *n*

coun-try-side *n* : rural area or its people

coun-ty \'kaúntē\ *n, pl* **-ties** : local government division esp. of a state

coup \'kü\ *n, pl* **coups** \'küz\ **1** : brilliant sudden action or plan **2** : sudden overthrow of a government

cou-pé, coupe \kü'pā, 'küp\ *n* : 2-door automobile with an enclosed body

cou-ple \'kəpəl\ *vb* **-pled; -pling** : link together ~ *n* **1** : pair **2** : two persons closely associated or married

cou-pling \'kəpliŋ\ *n* : connecting device

cou-pon \'k(y)ü,pän\ *n* : certificate redeemable for goods or a cash discount

cour-age \'kərij\ *n* : ability to conquer fear or despair —**cou-ra-geous** \kə'rājəs\ *adj*

cou-ri-er \'kúrēər, 'kərē-\ *n* : messenger

course \'kōrs\ *n* **1** : progress **2** : ground over which something moves **3** : part of a meal served at one time **4** : method of procedure **5** : subject taught in a series of classes ~ *vb* **coursed; cours-ing 1** : hunt with dogs **2** : run speedily —**of course 1** : as might be expected

court \'kōrt\ *n* **1** : residence of a sovereign **2** : sovereign and his officials and advisers **3** : area enclosed by a building **4** : space marked for playing a game **5** : place where justice is administered ~ *vb* : woo —**court-house** *n* —**court-room** *n* —**court-ship** \-,ship\ *n*

cour-te-ous \'kərtēəs\ *adj* : showing politeness and respect for others —**cour-te-ous-ly** *adv*

cour-te-san \'kōrtəzən, 'kərt-\ *n* : prostitute

cour-te-sy \'kərtəsē\ *n, pl* **-sies** : courteous behavior

court-ier \'kōrtēər, 'kōrtyər\ *n* : person in attendance at a royal court

court-ly \'kōrtlē\ *adj* **-li-er; -est** : polite or elegant —**court-li-ness** *n*

court-mar-tial *n, pl* **courts-martial** : military trial court —**court-martial** *vb*

court-yard *n* : enclosure open to the sky that is attached to a house

cous-in \'kəz°n\ *n* : child of one's uncle or aunt

cove \'kōv\ *n* : sheltered inlet or bay

cov-e-nant \'kəv(ə)nənt\ *n* : binding agreement —**cov-e-nant** \-kəv(ə)nənt, -,nənt\ *vb*

cov-er \'kəvər\ *vb* **1** : place something over or upon **2** : clothe **3** : protect or hide **4** : include or deal with ~ *n* : something that covers —**cov-er-age** \-(ə)rij\ *n*

cov-er-let \-lət\ *n* : bedspread

co-vert \'kō(,)vərt, 'kəvərt\ *adj* : secret ~ \'kəvərt, 'kō-\ *n* : thicket that shelters animals

cov-et \'kəvət\ *vb* : desire enviously —**cov-et-ous** *adj*

cov-ey \'kəvē\ *n, pl* **-eys 1** : bird with her young **2** : small flock (as of quail)

¹**cow** \'kaú\ *n* : adult female of a bovine animal —**cow-hide** *n*

²**cow** *vb* : intimidate

cow-ard \'kaú(ə)rd\ *n* : one who lacks courage —**cow-ard-ice** \-əs\ *n* —**cow-ard-ly** *adv or adj*

cow-boy *n* : a mounted ranch hand who tends cattle —**cow-girl** *n*

cow-er \'kaú(ə)r\ *vb* : shrink from fear or cold

cowl \'kaúl\ *n* : monk's hood

cow-lick \'kaú,lik\ *n* : turned-up tuft of hair that resists control

cow-slip \-,slip\ *n* : yellow flower

cox-swain \'käksən, -,swān\ *n* : person who steers a boat

coy \'kói\ *adj* : shy or pretending shyness

coy-ote \'kī,ōt, kī'ōt-ē\ *n, pl* **coy-otes** *or* **coyote** : small No. American wolf

coz-en \'kəz°n\ *vb* : cheat

co-zy \'kōzē\ *adj* **-zi-er; -est** : snug

crab \'krab\ *n* : short broad shellfish with pincers

crab-by \'krabē\ *adj* **-bi-er; -est** : cross

¹**crack** \'krak\ *vb* **1** : break with a sharp sound **2** : fail in tone **3** : break without completely separating ~ *n* **1** : sudden sharp noise **2** : witty remark **3** : narrow break **4** : sharp blow **5** : try

²**crack** *adj* : extremely proficient

crack-down *n* : disciplinary action —**crack down** *vb*

crack-er \-ər\ *n* : thin crisp bakery product

crack-le \'krakəl\ *vb* **-led; -ling 1** : make snapping noises **2** : develop fine cracks in a surface —**crackle** *n*

crack-pot \'krak,pät\ *n* : eccentric

crack-up *n* : crash

cra-dle \'krād°l\ *n* : baby's bed ~ *vb* **-dled; -dling 1** : place in a cradle **2** : hold securely

craft \'kraft\ *n* **1** : occupation requiring special skill **2** : craftiness **3** *pl usu* **craft** : structure designed to provide transportation **4** *pl usu* **craft** : small

boat —**crafts·man** \\'kraftsmən\ n
—**crafts·man·ship** \\-₁ship\ n

crafty \\'kraftē\ adj **craft·i·er; -est** : sly
—**craft·i·ness** n

crag \\'krag\ n : steep cliff —**crag·gy**
\\-ē\ adj

cram \\'kram\ vb **-mm-** 1 : eat greedily
2 : pack in tight 3 : study intensely
for a test

cramp \\'kramp\ n 1 : sudden painful
contraction of muscle 2 : sharp
abdominal pains ~ vb 1 : affect with
cramp 2 : restrain

cran·ber·ry \\'kran₁berē, -b(ə)rē\ n
: red acid berry of a trailing plant

crane \\'krān\ n 1 : tall wading bird 2
: machine for lifting heavy objects ~
vb **craned; cran·ing** : stretch one's
neck to see

cra·ni·um \\'krānēəm\ n, pl **-ni·ums** or
-nia \\-nēə\ : skull —**cra·ni·al** \\-əl\
adj

crank \\'krank\ n 1 : bent lever turned
to operate a machine 2 : eccentric ~
vb : start or operate by turning a
crank

cranky \\'krankē\ adj **crank·i·er; -est**
: irritable

cran·ny \\'kranē\ n, pl **-nies** : crevice

craps \\'kraps\ n : dice game

crash \\'krash\ vb 1 : break noisily 2
: fall and hit something with noise
and damage ~ n 1 : loud sound 2
: action of crashing 3 : failure

crass \\'kras\ adj : crude or unfeeling

crate \\'krāt\ n : wooden shipping container —**crate** vb

cra·ter \\'krātər\ n : volcanic depression

cra·vat \\krə'vat\ n : necktie

crave \\'krāv\ vb **craved; crav·ing** : long
for —**crav·ing** n

cra·ven \\'krāvən\ adj : cowardly —**cra·
ven** n

craw·fish \\'kró₁fish\ n : crayfish

crawl \\'król\ vb 1 : move slowly (as by
drawing the body along the ground)
2 : swarm with creeping things ~ n
: very slow pace

cray·fish \\'krā₁fish\ n : lobsterlike
freshwater crustacean

cray·on \\'krā₁än, -ən\ n : stick of chalk
or wax used for drawing or coloring
—**crayon** vb

craze \\'krāz\ vb **crazed; craz·ing** : make
or become insane ~ n : fad

cra·zy \\'krāzē\ adj **cra·zi·er; -est** 1
: mentally disordered 2 : wildly impractical —**cra·zi·ly** adv —**cra·zi·ness**
n

creak \\'krēk\ vb or n : squeak —**creaky**
adj

cream \\'krēm\ n 1 : yellowish fat-rich
part of milk 2 : thick smooth sauce,
confection, or cosmetic 3 : choicest
part ~ vb : beat into creamy consistency —**creamy** adj

cream·ery \\-(ə)rē\ n, pl **-er·ies** : place
where butter and cheese are made

crease \\'krēs\ n : line made by folding
—**crease** vb

cre·ate \\krē'āt\ vb **-at·ed; -at·ing**
: bring into being —**cre·ation**
\\krē'āshən\ n —**cre·ative** \\-iv\ adj
—**cre·ativ·i·ty** \\₁krē(₁)ā'tivətē,
₁krēə'-\ n —**cre·ator** \\krē'ātər\ n

crea·ture \\'krēchər\ n : lower animal
or human being

cre·dence \\'krēd⁰ns\ n : belief

cre·den·tials \\kri'denchəlz\ n : evidence of qualifications or authority

cred·i·ble \\'kredəbəl\ adj : believable
—**cred·i·bil·i·ty** \\₁kredə'bilətē\ n

cred·it \\'kredət\ n 1 : balance in a person's favor 2 : time given to pay for
goods 3 : belief 4 : esteem 5 : source
of honor ~ vb 1 : believe 2 : give
credit to

cred·it·able \\-əbəl\ adj : worthy of esteem or praise —**cred·it·ably** \\-blē\
adv

cred·i·tor \\-ər\ n : person to whom
money is owed

cred·u·lous \\'krejələs\ adj : easily convinced —**cre·du·li·ty** \\kri'd(y)ülətē\
n

creed \\'krēd\ n : statement of essential
beliefs

creek \\'krēk, 'krik\ n : small stream

creel \\'krēl\ n : basket for carrying fish

creep \\'krēp\ vb **crept** \\'krept\; **creep·
ing** 1 : crawl 2 : grow over a surface
like ivy —**creep** n —**creep·er** n

cre·mate \\'krē₁māt\ vb **-mat·ed; -mat·
ing** : burn up (a corpse) —**cre·ma·
tion** \\kri'māshən\ n —**cre·ma·to·ry**
\\'krēmə₁tōrē, 'krem-\ n

cre·o·sote \\'krēə₁sōt\ n : oily wood
preservative

crepe, crêpe \\'krāp\ n : light crinkled
fabric

cre·scen·do \\krə'shendō\ adv or adj
: growing louder —**crescendo** n

cres·cent \\'kres⁰nt\ n : shape of the
moon between new moon and first
quarter

crest \\'krest\ n 1 : tuft on a bird's head
2 : top of a hill or wave 3 : part of a
coat of arms ~ vb : rise to a crest

crest·fall·en adj : sad

cre·tin \\'krēt⁰n\ n : person with
marked mental deficiency —**cre·tin·
ism** \\-₁izəm\ n

cre·vasse \krĭ'vas\ n : deep fissure esp. in a glacier

crev·ice \'krevəs\ n : narrow fissure

crew \'krü\ n : body of workers (as on a ship) —**crew·man** \-mən\ n

crib \'krib\ n 1 : manger 2 : grain storage bin 3 : baby's bed ~ vb -**bb**- : put in a crib

crib·bage \-ij\ n : card game scored by moving pegs on a board (**cribbage board**)

crick \'krik\ n : muscle spasm

¹crick·et \'krikət\ n : insect noted for the chirping of the male

²cricket n : bat and ball game played on a field with wickets

cri·er \'krī(ə)r\ n : one who calls out announcements

crime \'krīm\ n : serious violation of law

crim·i·nal \'krimən²l\ adj : relating to or being a crime or its punishment ~ n : one who commits a crime

crimp \'krimp\ vb : cause to become crinkled, wavy, or bent —**crimp** n

crim·son \'krimzən\ n : deep red —**crimson** adj

cringe \'krinj\ vb **cringed**; **cring·ing** : shrink in fear

crin·kle \'kriŋkəl\ vb -**kled**; -**kling** : wrinkle —**crinkle** n —**crin·kly** \-k(ə)lē\ adj

crin·o·line \'krin³lən\ n 1 : stiff cloth 2 : full stiff skirt or petticoat

crip·ple \'kripəl\ n : disabled person ~ vb -**pled**; -**pling** : disable

cri·sis \'krīsəs\ n, pl **cri·ses** \-ˌsēz\ : decisive or critical moment

crisp \'krisp\ adj 1 : easily crumbled 2 : firm and fresh 3 : lively 4 : invigorating —**crisp** vb —**crisp·ly** adv —**crisp·ness** n —**crispy** adj

criss·cross \'kris,krós\ n : pattern of crossed lines ~ vb : mark with or follow a crisscross

cri·te·ri·on \krī'tirēən\ n, pl **-ria** \-ēə\ : standard

crit·ic \'kritik\ n : judge of literary or artistic works

crit·i·cal \-ikəl\ adj 1 : inclined to criticize 2 : being a crisis 3 : relating to criticism or critics —**crit·i·cal·ly** \-ik(ə)lē\ adv

crit·i·cize \-ə,sīz\ vb -**cized**; -**cizing** 1 : judge as a critic 2 : find fault —**crit·i·cism** \-ə,sizəm\ n

cri·tique \krə'tēk\ n : critical estimate

croak \'krōk\ n : hoarse harsh cry (as of a frog) —**croak** vb

cro·chet \krō'shā\ n : needlework done with a hooked needle —**crochet** vb

crock \'kräk\ n : thick earthenware pot or jar —**crock·ery** \-(ə)rē\ n

croc·o·dile \'kräkə,dīl\ n : reptile of tropical waters

cro·cus \'krōkəs\ n, pl **-cus·es** : herb with spring flowers

crone \'krōn\ n : ugly old woman

cro·ny \'krōnē\ n, pl **-nies** : chum

crook \'krúk\ n 1 : bent or curved tool or part 2 : thief ~ vb : curve sharply

crook·ed \'krúkəd\ adj 1 : bent 2 : dishonest —**crook·ed·ness** n

croon \'krün\ vb : sing softly —**croon·er** n

crop \'kräp\ n 1 : pouch in the throat of a bird or insect 2 : short riding whip 3 : something that can be harvested ~ vb -**pp**- 1 : trim 2 : appear unexpectedly —used with up

cro·quet \krō'kā\ n : lawn game of driving balls through wickets

cro·quette \-'ket\ n : mass of minced food deep fried

cro·sier \'krōzhər\ n : bishop's staff

cross \'krós\ n 1 : figure or structure consisting of an upright and a cross piece 2 : interbreeding of unlike strains ~ vb 1 : intersect 2 : cancel 3 : go or extend across 4 : interbreed ~ adj 1 : going across 2 : contrary 3 : marked by bad temper —**cross·ing** n —**cross·ly** adv

cross·bow \-ˌbō\ n : short bow mounted on a rifle stock

cross·breed \-'brēd; -'brēd-\ vb -**bred**; -**breed·ing** : hybridize

cross·ex·am·ine vb : question about earlier testimony —**cross·ex·am·i·na·tion** n

cross·eye n : abnormality in which the eye turns toward the nose —**cross·eyed** adj

cross·re·fer vb : refer to another place (as in a book) —**cross·ref·er·ence** n

cross·roads n : place where 2 roads cross

cross section n : representative portion

cross·walk n : path for pedestrians crossing a street

cross·ways adv : crosswise

cross·wise \-ˌwīz\ adv : so as to cross something —**crosswise** adj

crotch \'kräch\ n : angle formed by the parting of 2 legs or branches

crotch·et \'krächət\ n : odd notion —**crotch·ety** adj

crouch \'kraúch\ vb : stoop over —**crouch** n

croup \'krüp\ n : laryngitis of infants

crou·ton \'krü,tän\ n : bit of toast

¹crow \'krō\ n : large glossy black bird

²**crow** \\'krō\\ *vb* 1 : make the loud sound of the cock 2 : gloat ~ *n* : cry of the cock

crow·bar \\-ˌbär\\ *n* : metal bar used as a pry or lever

crowd \\'kraúd\\ *vb* : collect or cram together ~ *n* : large number of people

crown \\'kraún\\ *n* 1 : wreath of honor or victory 2 : royal headdress 3 : top or highest part ~ *vb* 1 : place a crown on 2 : honor —**crowned** \\'kraúnd\\ *adj*

cru·cial \\'krüshəl\\ *adj* : vitally important

cru·ci·ble \\'krüsəbəl\\ *n* : heat-resisting container

cru·ci·fix \\-ˌfiks\\ *n* : representation of Christ on the cross

cru·ci·fix·ion \\ˌkrüsə'fikshən\\ *n* : act of crucifying

cru·ci·fy \\-ˌfī\\ *vb* -**fied;** -**fy·ing** 1 : put to death on a cross 2 : persecute

crude \\'krüd\\ *adj* **crud·er;** -**est** 1 : not refined 2 : lacking grace or elegance ~ *n* : unrefined petroleum —**crude·ly** *adv* —**cru·di·ty** \\-ətē\\ *n*

cru·el \\'krüəl\\ *adj* -**el·er** *or* -**el·ler;** -**el·est** *or* -**el·lest** : causing suffering to others —**cru·el·ly** \\-ē\\ *adv* —**cru·el·ty** \\-tē\\ *n*

cru·et \\'krüət\\ *n* : bottle for salad dressings

cruise \\'krüz\\ *vb* **cruised; cruis·ing** 1 : sail to several ports 2 : travel at the most efficient speed —**cruise** *n*

cruis·er \\'krüzər\\ *n* 1 : warship 2 : police car

crumb \\'krəm\\ *n* : small fragment

crum·ble \\'krəmbəl\\ *vb* -**bled;** -**bling** : break into small pieces —**crum·bly** \\-b(ə)lē\\ *adj*

crum·ple \\-pəl\\ *vb* -**pled;** -**pling** 1 : crush together 2 : collapse

crunch \\'krənch\\ *vb* : chew or press with a crushing noise ~ *n* : crunching sound —**crunchy** *adj*

cru·sade \\krü'sād\\ *n* 1 *cap* : medieval Christian expedition to the Holy Land 2 : reform movement —**crusade** *vb* —**cru·sad·er** *n*

crush \\'krəsh\\ *vb* 1 : squeeze out of shape 2 : grind or pound to bits 3 : suppress ~ *n* 1 : severe crowding 2 : infatuation

crust \\'krəst\\ *n* 1 : hard outer part of bread or a pie 2 : hard surface layer —**crust·al** *adj* —**crusty** *adj*

crus·ta·cean \\ˌkrəs'tāshən\\ *n* : aquatic arthropod having a firm shell

crutch \\'krəch\\ *n* : support for use by the disabled in walking

crux \\'krəks, 'krüks\\ *n, pl* **crux·es** 1 : hard problem 2 : crucial point

cry \\'krī\\ *vb* **cried; cry·ing** 1 : call out 2 : weep ~ *n, pl* **cries** 1 : shout 2 : fit of weeping 3 : characteristic sound of an animal

crypt \\'kript\\ *n* : underground chamber

cryp·tic \\'kriptik\\ *adj* : enigmatic

cryp·tog·ra·phy \\krip'tägrəfē\\ *n* : coding and decoding of messages —**cryp·tog·ra·pher** \\-fər\\ *n*

crys·tal \\'krist°l\\ *n* 1 : transparent quartz 2 : something (as glass) like crystal 3 : body formed by solidification that has a regular repeating atomic arrangement —**crys·tal·line** \\-tələn\\ *adj*

crys·tal·lize \\-tə₁līz\\ *vb* -**lized;** -**liz·ing** : form crystals or a definite shape —**crys·tal·li·za·tion** \\ˌkristələ'zāshən\\ *n*

cub \\'kəb\\ *n* : young animal

cub·by·hole \\'kəbē₁hōl\\ *n* : small confined space

cube \\'kyüb\\ *n* 1 : solid having 6 equal square sides 2 : product obtained by taking a number 3 times as a factor ~ *vb* **cubed; cub·ing** 1 : raise to the 3d power 2 : form into a cube 3 : cut into cubes —**cu·bic** \\'kyübik\\ *adj*

cu·bi·cle \\-bikəl\\ *n* : small room

cu·bit \\-bət\\ *n* : unit of length equal to about 18 inches

cuck·old \\'kəkəld, 'kük-\\ *n* : man whose wife is unfaithful

cuck·oo \\'kükü, 'kúk-\\ *n, pl* -**oos** : brown European bird ~ *adj* : silly

cu·cum·ber \\'kyü(ˌ)kəmbər\\ *n* : fleshy fruit related to the gourds

cud \\'kəd\\ *n* : food chewed again by ruminating animals

cud·dle \\'kəd°l\\ *vb* -**dled;** -**dling** : lie close

cud·gel \\'kəjəl\\ *n* *or* *vb* : club

¹**cue** \\'kyü\\ *n* : signal —**cue** *vb*

²**cue** *n* : stick used in pool

¹**cuff** \\'kəf\\ *n* 1 : part of a sleeve encircling the wrist 2 : folded trouser hem

²**cuff** *vb* *or* *n* : slap

cui·sine \\kwi'zēn\\ *n* : manner of cooking

cu·li·nary \\'kələˌnerē, 'kyülə-\\ *adj* : of or relating to cookery

cull \\'kəl\\ *vb* : select

cul·mi·nate \\'kəlməˌnāt\\ *vb* -**nat·ed;** -**nat·ing** : rise to the highest point —**cul·mi·na·tion** \\ˌkəlmə'nāshən\\ *n*

cul·pa·ble \\'kəlpəbəl\\ *adj* : deserving blame

cul·prit \\'kəlprət\\ *n* : guilty person

cult \\'kəlt\\ *n* 1 : religious system 2 : faddish devotion —**cult·ist** *n*

cul·ti·vate \\'kəltəˌvāt\\ *vb* -**vat·ed;** -**vat-**

ing 1 : prepare for crops **2** : foster the growth of **3** : refine —**cul·ti·va·tion** \\,kəltə'vāshən\ n

cul·ture \'kəlchər\ n **1** : cultivation **2** : refinement of intellectual and artistic taste **3** : particular form or stage of civilization —**cul·tur·al** \'kəlch(ə)rəl\ adj —**cul·tured** \'kəlchərd\ adj

cul·vert \'kəlvərt\ n : drain crossing under a road or railroad

cum·ber \'kəmbər\ vb : burden —**cum·ber·some** adj —**cum·brous** \-brəs\ adj

cu·mu·la·tive \'kyümyələtiv, -,lāt-\ adj : increasing by additions

cu·mu·lus \-ləs\ n, pl **-li** \-,lī, -,lē\ : massive rounded cloud

cun·ning \'kəniŋ\ adj **1** : crafty **2** : clever **3** : appealing ~ n **1** : skill **2** : craftiness

cup \'kəp\ n **1** : small drinking vessel **2** : contents of a cup ~ vb **-pp-** : shape like a cup —**cup·ful** n

cup·board \'kəbərd\ n : small storage closet

cup·cake n : small cake

cu·pid·i·ty \kyu'pidətē\ n, pl **-ties** : excessive desire for money

cu·po·la \'kyüpələ, -,lō\ n : small rooftop structure

cur \'kər\ n : mongrel dog

cu·rate \'kyurət\ n : clergyman —**cu·ra·cy** \-əsē\ n

cu·ra·tor \kyu'rātər\ n : one in charge of a museum or zoo

curb \'kərb\ n **1** : restraint **2** : raised edging along a street ~ vb : hold back

curd \'kərd\ n : coagulated milk

cur·dle \'kərdᵊl\ vb **-dled; -dling 1** : form curds **2** : sour

cure \'kyur\ n **1** : recovery from disease **2** : remedy ~ vb **cured; cur·ing 1** : restore to health **2** : process for storage or use —**cur·able** adj

cur·few \'kər,fyü\ n **1** : requirement to be off the streets at a set hour

cu·rio \'kyurē,ō\ n, pl **-ri·os** : rare or unusual article

cu·ri·ous \'kyurēəs\ adj **1** : eager to learn **2** : strange —**cu·ri·os·i·ty** \,kyurē'äsətē\ n

curl \'kərl\ vb **1** : form into ringlets **2** : curve ~ n **1** : ringlet of hair **2** : something with a spiral form —**curl·er** n —**curly** adj

cur·lew \-(y)ü\ n, pl **-lews** or **-lew** : long-legged brownish bird

curli·cue \'kərli,kyü\ n : fanciful curve

cur·rant \'kərənt\ n **1** : small seedless raisin **2** : berry of a shrub

cur·ren·cy \'kərənsē\ n, pl **-cies 1** : general use or acceptance **2** : money

cur·rent \'kərənt\ adj : occurring in or belonging to the present ~ n **1** : swiftest part of a stream **2** : flow of electric charge

cur·ric·u·lum \kə'rikyələm\ n, pl **-la** \-lə\ : course of study

¹cur·ry \'kərē\ vb **-ried; -ry·ing** : brush (a horse) with a wire brush (**curry·comb**) —**curry favor** : seek favor by flattery

²curry n, pl **-ries** : blend of spices or a food seasoned with this

curse \'kərs\ n **1** : a calling down of evil or harm upon one **2** : afflicton ~ vb **cursed; curs·ing 1** : call down injury upon **2** : swear at **3** : afflict

cur·so·ry \'kərs(ə)rē\ adj : hastily done

curt \'kərt\ adj : rudely abrupt —**curt·ly** adv

cur·tail \(,)kər'tāl\ vb : shorten —**cur·tail·ment** n

cur·tain \'kərtᵊn\ n : hanging screen that can be drawn back or raised —**curtain** vb

curt·sy, curt·sey \'kərtsē\ n, pl **-sies** or **-seys** : courteous bow made by bending the knees —**curtsy** vb

cur·va·ture \'kərvə,chur\ n : amount or state of curving

curve \'kərv\ vb **curved; curv·ing** : bend from a straight line or course ~ n **1** : a bending without angles **2** : something curved

cush·ion \'kushən\ n **1** : soft pillow **2** : something that eases or protects ~ vb **1** : provide with a cushion **2** : soften the force of

cusp \'kəsp\ n : pointed end

cus·pid \'kəspəd\ n : a canine tooth

cus·pi·dor \'kəspə,dȯr\ n : spittoon

cus·tard \'kəstərd\ n : sweetened cooked mixture of milk and eggs

cus·to·dy \'kəstədē\ n, pl **-dies** : immediate care or charge —**cus·to·di·al** \,kəs'tōdēəl\ adj —**cus·to·di·an** \-ēən\ n

cus·tom \'kəstəm\ n **1** : habitual course of action **2** pl : import taxes ~ adj : made to personal order —**cus·tom·ar·i·ly** \,kəstə'merəlē\ adv —**cus·tom·ary** \'kəstə,merē\ adj —**cus·tom-built** \,kəstəm-\ cus·tom-made adj

cus·tom·er \'kəstəmər\ n : buyer

cut \'kət\ vb **cut; cut·ting 1** : penetrate or divide with a sharp edge **2** : experience the growth of (a tooth) through the gum **3** : shorten **4** : remove by severing **5** : intersect ~ n **1**

: something separated by cutting **2**
: reduction —**cut in** vb : thrust oneself between others

cu·ta·ne·ous \kyü'tānēəs\ adj : relating
to the skin

cute \'kyüt\ adj **cut·er**, **-est** : pretty

cu·ti·cle \'kyütikəl\ n : outer layer (as
of skin)

cut·lass \'kətləs\ n : short heavy
curved sword

cut·lery \-lərē\ n : cutting utensils

cut·let \-lət\ n : slice of meat

cut·ter \'kətər\ n **1** : tool or machine
for cutting **2** : small armed motor-
boat **3** : light sleigh

cut·throat n : murderer ~ adj : ruthless

-cy \sē\ n suffix **1** : action or practice **2**
: rank or office **3** : body **4** : state or
quality

cy·a·nide \'sīə,nīd, -nəd\ n : poisonous
chemical salt

cy·cle \'sīkəl, 4 also 'sikəl\ n **1** : period
of time for a series of repeated events
2 : recurring round of events **3** : long
period of time **4** : bicycle or motorcycle ~ vb **-cled**; **-cling** : ride a cycle

cy·clic \'sīklik, 'sik-\, **cy·cli·cal**
\-əl\ adj —**cy·clist** \'sīk(ə)ləst, 'sik-\
n

cy·clone \'sī,klōn\ n : tornado
—**cy·clon·ic** \sī'klänik\ adj

cy·clo·pe·dia, **cy·clo·pae·dia** \,sīklə-
'pēdēə\ n : encyclopedia

cyl·in·der \'siləndər\ n **1** : long round
body or figure **2** : rotating chamber
in a revolver **3** : piston chamber in an
engine —**cy·lin·dri·cal** \sə'lindrikəl\
adj

cym·bal \'simbəl\ n : one of a pair of
concave brass plates clashed together

cyn·ic \'sinik\ n : one who attributes
all actions to selfish motives —**cyn·i·**
cal \-ikəl\ adj —**cyn·i·cism**
\-ə,sizəm\ n

cy·no·sure \'sīnə,shür, 'sinə-\ n : center of attraction

cy·press \'sīprəs\ n : evergreen tree related to the pines

cyst \'sist\ n : abnormal bodily sac
—**cys·tic** \'sistik\ adj

czar \'zär\ n : ruler of Russia until
1917 —**czar·ist** n or adj

D

d \'dē\ n, pl **d's** or **ds** \'dēz\ : 4th letter
of the alphabet

¹dab \'dab\ n : gentle touch or stroke
~ vb **-bb-** : touch or apply lightly

²dab n : small amount

dab·ble \'dabəl\ vb **-bled**; **-bling 1**
: splash **2** : work without serious effort

dachs·hund \'däks,hunt\ : small dog
with a long body and short legs

dad \'dad\ n : father

dad·dy \'dadē\ n, pl **-dies** : father

daf·fo·dil \'dafə,dil\ n : narcissus with
trumpetlike flowers

daft \'daft\ adj : foolish —**daft·ness** n

dag·ger \'dagər\ n : knife for stabbing

dahl·ia \'dalyə, 'däl-\ n : tuberous herb
with showy flowers

dai·ly \'dālē\ adj **1** : occurring, done,
or used every day or every weekday
2 : computed in terms of one day ~
n, pl **-lies** : daily newspaper —**daily**
adv

dain·ty \'dāntē\ n, pl **-ties** : something
delicious ~ adj **-ti·er**; **-est** : deli-
cately pretty —**dain·ti·ly** adv —**dain·**
ti·ness n

dairy \'de(ə)rē\ n, pl **-ies** : farm that
produces or company that processes
milk —**dairy·ing** \'derēiŋ\ n —**dairy·**
maid n —**dairy·man** \-mən, -,man\ n

da·is \'dāəs, 'dī-\ n : raised platform
(as for a speaker)

dai·sy \'dāzē\ n, pl **-sies** : tall
leafy-stemmed plant bearing showy
flowers

dale \'dāl\ n : valley

dal·ly \'dalē\ vb **-lied**; **-ly·ing 1** : flirt **2**
: dawdle —**dal·li·ance** \-əns\ n

dal·ma·tian \dal'māshən\ n : large dog
having a spotted white coat

¹dam \'dam\ n : female parent of a
domestic animal

²dam n : barrier to hold back water
—**dam** vb

dam·age \-ij\ n **1** : loss or harm due to
injury **2** pl : compensation for loss or
injury ~ vb **-aged**; **-ag·ing** : do damage to

dam·ask \-əsk\ n : firm lustrous figured
fabric

dame \'dām\ n : woman of rank or
authority

damn \'dam\ vb **1** : condemn to hell **2**
: curse —**dam·na·ble** \-nəbəl\ adj
—**dam·na·tion** \dam'nāshən\ n
—**damned** adj

damp \'damp\ n : moisture ~ vb **1**
: reduce the draft in **2** : restrain **3**
: moisten ~ adj : moist —**damp·ness**
n

damp·en \'dampən\ vb **1** : diminish in

activity or vigor **2** : make or become damp

damp·er \'dampər\ *n* : movable plate to regulate a flue draft

dam·sel \'damzəl\ *n* : young woman

dance \'dans\ *vb* **danced; danc·ing** : move rhythmically to music ~ *n* : act of dancing or a gathering for dancing —**danc·er** *n*

dan·de·li·on \'dand³l̩ˌīən\ *n* : common yellow-flowered herb

dan·der \'dandər\ *n* : temper

dan·druff \'dandrəf\ *n* : whitish scurf on the scalp

dan·dy \'dandē\ *n, pl* **-dies 1** : man too concerned with clothes **2** : something excellent ~ *adj* **-di·er; -est** : very good

dan·ger \'dānjər\ *n* **1** : exposure to injury or evil **2** : something that may cause injury —**dan·ger·ous** \'dānj(ə)rəs\ *adj*

dan·gle \'dangəl\ *vb* **-gled; -gling 1** : hang and swing freely **2** : be left without support or connection **3** : allow or cause to hang

dank \'dank\ *adj* : unpleasantly damp

dap·per \'dapər\ *adj* : neat and stylishly dressed

dap·ple \-əl\ *vb* **-pled; -pling** : mark with colored spots

dare \'daər\ *vb* **dared; dar·ing 1** : have sufficient courage **2** : urge or provoke to contend —**dare** *n* —**dar·ing** \'da(ə)riŋ\ *n or adj*

dare·dev·il *n* : recklessly bold person

dark \'därk\ *adj* **1** : having little or no light **2** : not light in color **3** : gloomy ~ *n* : absence of light —**dark·en** \-ən\ *vb* —**dark·ly** *adv* —**dark·ness** *n*

dar·ling \'därliŋ\ *n* **1** : beloved **2** : favorite ~ *adj* **1** : dearly loved **2** : very pleasing

darn \'därn\ *vb* : mend with interlacing stitches —**darn·er** *n*

dart \'därt\ *n* **1** : small pointed missile **2** *pl* : game of throwing darts at a target **3** : tapering fold in a garment **4** : quick movement ~ *vb* : move suddenly or rapidly

dash \'dash\ *vb* **1** : knock or hurl violently or impetuously **2** : smash **3** : ruin **4** : perform or finish hastily **5** : move quickly ~ *n* **1** : sudden burst, splash, or stroke **2** : punctuation mark — **3** : tiny amount **4** : showiness or liveliness **5** : sudden rush **6** : short race

dash·board *n* : instrument panel

dash·ing \'dashiŋ\ *adj* : dapper and charming

das·tard \'dastərd\ *n* : one who sneakingly commits malicious acts

das·tard·ly \-lē\ *adj* : base or malicious

da·ta \'dātə, 'dat-, 'dät-\ *sing or pl* : factual information

¹date \'dāt\ *n* : edible fruit of a palm

²date *n* **1** : day, month, or year when something is done or made **2** : historical time period **3** : social engagement or the person one goes out with ~ *vb* **dat·ed; dat·ing 1** : determine or record the date of **2** : have a date with **3** : originate —**to date** : up to now

dat·ed \-əd\ *adj* : old-fashioned

da·tum \'dātəm, 'dat-, 'dät-\ *n, pl* **-ta** \-ə\ *or* **-tums** : piece of data

daub \'dob\ *vb* : smear ~ *n* : something daubed on —**daub·er** *n*

daugh·ter \'dotər\ *n* : human female offspring —**daugh·ter·ly** *adj*

daugh·ter-in-law *n, pl* **daugh·ters-in-law** : wife of one's son

daunt \'dont\ *vb* : lessen the courage of

daunt·less \-ləs\ *adj* : fearless

dav·en·port \'davənˌpōrt\ *n* : sofa

daw·dle \'dod³l\ *vb* **-dled; -dling 1** : waste time **2** : loiter

dawn \'don\ *vb* **1** : grow light as the sun rises **2** : begin to appear, develop, or be understood ~ *n* : first appearance (as of daylight)

day \'dā\ *n* **1** : period of light between one night and the next **2** : 24 hours **3** : specified date **4** : particular time or age **5** : period of work for a day —**day·light** *n* —**day·time** *n*

day·break *n* : dawn

day·dream *n* : fantasy of wish fulfillment —**daydream** *vb*

daylight saving time *n* : time one hour ahead of standard time

daze \'dāz\ *vb* **dazed; daz·ing 1** : stun by a blow **2** : dazzle —**daze** *n*

daz·zle \'dazəl\ *vb* **-zled; -zling 1** : overpower with light **2** : impress greatly —**dazzle** *n*

DDT \ˌdē(ˌ)dēˈtē\ *n* : long-lasting insecticide

dea·con \'dēkən\ *n* : subordinate church officer —**dea·con·ess** *n*

dead \'ded\ *adj* **1** : lifeless **2** : unresponsive or inactive **3** : exhausted **4** : obsolete **5** : precise ~ *n, pl* **dead 1** : one that is dead—usu. with *the* **2** : most lifeless time ~ *adv* **1** : completely **2** : directly —**dead·en** \'ded³n\ *vb*

dead·beat *n* : one who will not pay debts

dead end *n* : end of a street with no exit —**dead-end** *adj*

dead heat *n* : tie in a contest

dead·line *n* : time by which something must be finished

dead·lock *n* : struggle that neither side can win —**deadlock** *vb*

dead·ly \'dedlē\ *adj* **-li·er; -est** 1 : capable of causing death 2 : very accurate 3 : fatal to spiritual progress 4 : suggestive of death 5 : very great ~ *adv* : extremely —**dead·li·ness** *n*

dead·pan *adj* : expressionless —**deadpan** *vb*

dead·wood *n* : something useless

deaf \'def\ *adj* : unable or unwilling to hear —**deaf·en** \-ən\ *vb* —**deaf·ness** *n*

deaf-mute *n* : deaf person unable to speak

deal \'dēl\ *n* 1 : indefinite quantity 2 : distribution of playing cards 3 : negotiation or agreement 4 : treatment received 5 : bargain ~ *vb* **dealt** \'delt\; **deal·ing** \'dēliŋ\ 1 : distribute playing cards 2 : be concerned with 3 : take action 4 : sell —**deal·er** *n* —**deal·ing** *n*

dean \'dēn\ *n* 1 : head of a group of clergymen 2 : university or school administrator 3 : senior member

dear \'dir\ *adj* 1 : highly valued or loved 2 : expensive ~ *n* : loved one —**dear·ly** *adv* —**dear·ness** *n*

dearth \'dərth\ *n* : scarcity

death \'deth\ *n* 1 : end of life 2 : cause of loss of life 3 : state of being dead 4 : destruction or extinction —**deathless** *adj* —**death·ly** *adj or adv*

de·ba·cle \di'bäkəl, -'bakəl\ *n* : disaster or fiasco

de·bar \di'bär\ *vb* : bar from something

de·bark \-'bärk\ *vb* : disembark —**debar·ka·tion** \ˌdēˌbär'kāshən\ *n*

de·base \di'bās\ *vb* : disparage —**debase·ment** *n*

de·bate \-'bāt\ *vb* **-bat·ed; -bat·ing** : discuss a question by argument —**de·bat·able** *adj* —**debate** *n* —**debat·er** *n*

de·bauch \di'bȯch\ *vb* : seduce or corrupt —**de·bauch·ery** \-(ə)rē\ *n*

de·bil·i·tate \di'bilə,tāt\ *vb* **-tat·ed; -tating** : make ill or weak

de·bil·i·ty \-'bilətē\ *n, pl* **-ties** : physical weakness

deb·it \'debət\ *n* : account entry of a payment or debt ~ *vb* : record as a debit

deb·o·nair \ˌdebə'naər\ *adj* : gracefully charming

de·bris \də'brē, dā-; 'dāˌbrē\ *n, pl* **-bris** \-'brēz, -ˌbrēz\ : remains of something destroyed

debt \'det\ *n* 1 : sin 2 : something owed 3 : state of owing money —**debt·or** \-ər\ *n*

de·bunk \dē'bəŋk\ *vb* : expose as false

de·but \'dāˌbyü, dā'byü\ *n* 1 : first public appearance 2 : formal entrance into society —**debut** *vb* —**deb·u·tante** \'debyüˌtänt\ *n*

de·cade \'dekˌād, -əd; de'kād\ *n* : 10 years

dec·a·dence \'dekədəns; di'kād°ns\ *n* : deterioration —**dec·a·dent** \-ənt; -°nt\ *adj or n*

de·cal \'dēˌkal, di'kal, 'dekəl\ *n* : picture or design for transfer from prepared paper

de·camp \di'kamp\ *vb* : depart suddenly

de·cant \di'kant\ *vb* : pour gently

de·cant·er \-ər\ *n* : ornamental bottle for decanting and serving

de·cap·i·tate \di'kapə,tāt\ *vb* **-tat·ed; -tat·ing** : behead —**de·cap·i·ta·tion** \-ˌkapə'tāshən\ *n*

de·cay \di'kā\ *vb* 1 : decline in condition 2 : decompose —**decay** *n*

de·cease \-'sēs\ *n* : death —**decease** *vb*

de·ceit \-'sēt\ *n* 1 : deception 2 : dishonesty —**de·ceit·ful** \-fəl\ *adj* —**de·ceit·ful·ly** *adv* —**de·ceit·ful·ness** *n*

de·ceive \-'sēv\ *vb* **-ceived; -ceiv·ing** : trick or mislead —**de·ceiv·er** *n*

de·cel·er·ate \dē'selə,rāt\ *vb* **-at·ed; -at·ing** : slow down

De·cem·ber \di'sembər\ *n* : 12th month of the year having 31 days

de·cent \'dēs°nt\ *adj* 1 : good, right, or just 2 : clothed 3 : not obscene 4 : fairly good —**de·cen·cy** \-°nsē\ *n* —**de·cent·ly** *adv*

de·cep·tion \di'sepshən\ *n* 1 : act or fact of deceiving 2 : fraud —**de·cep·tive** \-'septiv\ *adj* —**de·cep·tive·ly** *adv*

de·cide \di'sīd\ *vb* **-cid·ed; -cid·ing** 1 : make a choice or judgment 2 : bring to a conclusion 3 : cause to decide

de·cid·ed *adj* 1 : unmistakable 2 : resolute —**de·cid·ed·ly** *adv*

de·cid·u·ous \di'sijwəs\ *adj* : having leaves that fall annually

dec·i·mal \'desəməl\ *n* : fraction in which the denominator is a power of 10 expressed by a point (**decimal point**) placed at the left of the numerator —**decimal** *adj* —**dec·i·mal·ly** \-ē\ *adv*

de·ci·pher \di'sīfər\ *vb* : make out the meaning of —**de·ci·pher·able** *adj*

de·ci·sion \-'sizhən\ *n* 1 : act or result of deciding 2 : determination

de·ci·sive \-'sīsiv\ *adj* 1 : having the power to decide 2 : conclusive 3 : showing determination —**de·ci·sive·ly** *adv* —**de·ci·sive·ness** *n*

deck \'dek\ *n* 1 : floor of a ship 2 : pack of playing cards ~ *vb* 1 : array or dress up 2 : knock down

de·claim \di'klām\ *vb* : speak loudly or impressively —**dec·la·ma·tion** \,deklə'māshən\ *n*

de·clare \di'klaər\ *vb* -clared; -clar·ing 1 : make known formally 2 : state emphatically —**dec·la·ra·tion** \,deklə'rāshən\ *n* —**de·clar·a·tive** \di'klarətiv\ *adj* —**de·clar·a·to·ry** \di'klarə,tōrē\ *adj* —**de·clar·er** *n*

de·clen·sion \di'klenchən\ *n* : inflectional forms esp. of a noun or pronoun

de·cline \di'klīn\ *vb* -clined; -clin·ing 1 : turn or slope downward 2 : wane 3 : refuse to accept 4 : inflect ~ *n* 1 : gradual wasting away 2 : change to a lower state or level 3 : a descending slope —**dec·li·na·tion** \,deklə'nāshən\ *n*

de·code \dē'kōd\ *vb* : decipher (a coded message)

de·com·pose \,dēkəm'pōz\ *vb* 1 : separate into parts 2 : decay —**de·com·po·si·tion** \,dē,kämpə'zishən\ *n*

de·con·ges·tant \,dēkən'jestənt\ *n* : agent that relieves congestion

de·cor, dé·cor \dā'kor, 'dā,kor\ *n* : room design or decoration

dec·o·rate \'dekə,rāt\ *vb* -rat·ed; -rat·ing 1 : add something attractive to 2 : honor with a medal —**dec·o·ra·tion** \,dekə'rāshən\ *n* —**dec·o·ra·tive** \'dek(ə)rətiv\ *adj* —**dec·o·ra·tor** \'dekə,rātər\ *n*

de·co·rum \di'kōrəm\ *n* : proper behavior —**dec·o·rous** \'dekərəs, di'kōrəs\ *adj* —**dec·o·rous·ly** *adv* —**dec·o·rous·ness** *n*

de·coy \'dē,koi, di'-\ *n* : something that tempts ~ *vb* : tempt

de·crease \di'krēs\ *vb* -creased; -creas·ing : grow or cause to grow less —**de·crease** \'dē,krēs\ *n*

de·cree \di'krē\ *n* : official order —**decree** *vb*

de·crep·it \di'krepət\ *adj* : impaired by age

de·cre·scen·do \,dākrə'shendō\ *adv or adj* : with a decrease in volume

de·cry \di'krī\ *vb* : criticize

ded·i·cate \'dedi,kāt\ *vb* -cat·ed; -cat·ing 1 : set apart for a purpose (as honor or worship) 2 : address to

someone as a compliment —**ded·i·ca·tion** \,dedi'kāshən\ *n* —**ded·i·ca·to·ry** \'dedikə,tōrē\ *adj*

de·duce \di'd(y)üs\ *vb* -duced; -duc·ing : derive by reasoning —**de·duc·ible** *adj*

de·duct \-'dəkt\ *vb* : subtract —**de·duct·ible** *adj*

de·duc·tion \-'dəkshən\ *n* 1 : subtraction 2 : reasoned conclusion —**de·duc·tive** \-'dəktiv\ *adj*

deed \'dēd\ *n* 1 : exploit 2 : document showing ownership ~ *vb* : convey by deed

deem \'dēm\ *vb* : think

deep \'dēp\ *adj* 1 : extending far or a specified distance down, back, within, or outward 2 : occupied 3 : dark and rich in color 4 : low in tone ~ *adv* 1 : deeply 2 : far along in time ~ *n* : deep place —**deep·en** \'dēpən\ *vb* —**deep·ly** *adv*

deep-seat·ed \-'sētəd\ *adj* : firmly established

deer \'diər\ *n, pl* **deer** : ruminant mammal with antlers in the male —**deer·skin** *n*

de·face \di'fās\ *vb* : mar the surface of —**de·face·ment** *n*

de·fame \di'fām\ *vb* -famed; -fam·ing : injure the reputation of —**def·a·ma·tion** \,defə'māshən\ *n* —**de·fam·a·to·ry** \di'famə,tōrē\ *adj*

de·fault \di'folt\ *n* : failure in a duty —**default** *vb* —**de·fault·er** *n*

de·feat \di'fēt\ *vb* 1 : frustrate 2 : win victory over ~ *n* 1 : loss of a battle or contest

def·e·cate \'defi,kāt\ *vb* -cat·ed; -cat·ing : discharge feces from the bowels —**def·e·ca·tion** \,defi'kāshən\ *n*

de·fect \'dē,fekt, di'fekt\ *n* : imperfection — \di'-\ *vb* : desert —**de·fec·tion** \-'fekshən\ *n* —**de·fec·tor** \-'fektər\ *n*

de·fec·tive \di'fektiv\ *adj* : faulty or deficient —**defective** *n*

de·fend \-'fend\ *vb* 1 : protect from danger or harm 2 : take the side of —**de·fend·er** *n*

de·fen·dant \-'fendənt\ *n* : person charged or sued in a court

de·fense, de·fence \di'fens\ *n* 1 : act of defending 2 : something that defends 3 : party, group, or team that opposes another —**de·fense·less** *adj* —**de·fen·si·ble** *adj* —**de·fen·sive** *adj*

¹de·fer \di'fər\ *vb* -rr- : postpone —**de·fer·ment** \di'fərmənt\ *n* —**de·fer·ra·ble** \-əbəl\ *adj*

²**de·fer** vb **-rr-** : yield to the opinion or wishes of another —**def·er·ence** \'def(ə)rəns\ n —**def·er·en·tial** \ˌdefə'renchəl\ adj

de·fi·ance \di'fīəns\ n : act or state of defying —**de·fi·ant** \-ənt\ adj

de·fi·cient \di'fishənt\ adj : lacking something necessary —**de·fi·cien·cy** \-'fishənsē\ n

def·i·cit \'defəsət\ n : shortage esp. in money

de·file \di'fīl\ vb **-filed; -fil·ing** 1 : make filthy or corrupt 2 : profane or dishonor —**de·file·ment** n

de·fine \di'fīn\ vb **-fined; -fin·ing** 1 : fix or mark the limits of 2 : clarify in outline 3 : set forth the meaning of —**de·fin·able** adj —**de·fin·ably** adv —**de·fin·er** n —**def·i·ni·tion** \ˌdefə'nishən\ n

def·i·nite \'defənət\ adj 1 : having distinct limits 2 : clear in meaning, intent, or identity 3 : typically designating an identified or immediately identifiable person or thing —**def·i·nite·ly** adv

de·fin·i·tive \di'finətiv\ adj 1 : conclusive 2 : authoritative

de·flate \di'flāt\ vb **-flat·ed; -flat·ing** 1 : release air or gas from 2 : reduce —**de·fla·tion** \-'flāshən\ n

de·flect \di'flekt\ vb : turn aside —**de·flec·tion** \-'flekshən\ n

de·fo·li·ate \dē'fōlē,āt\ vb **-at·ed; -at·ing** : deprive of leaves esp. prematurely —**de·fo·li·ant** \-lēənt\ n —**de·fo·li·a·tion** \-ˌfōlē'āshən\ n

de·form \di'fȯrm\ vb 1 : distort 2 : disfigure —**de·for·ma·tion** \ˌdēfȯr'māshən, ˌdefər-\ n —**de·for·mi·ty** \di'fȯrmətē\ n

de·fraud \di'frȯd\ vb : cheat

de·fray \-'frā\ vb : pay

de·frost \-'frȯst\ vb 1 : thaw out 2 : free from ice —**de·frost·er** n

deft \'deft\ adj : quick and skillful —**deft·ly** adv —**deft·ness** n

de·funct \di'fəŋkt\ adj : dead

de·fy \-'fī\ vb **-fied; -fy·ing** 1 : challenge 2 : boldly refuse to obey

de·gen·er·ate \di'jen(ə)rət\ adj : degraded or corrupt ~ n : degenerate person ~ \-ə,rāt\ vb : become degenerate —**de·gen·er·a·cy** \-(ə)rəsē\ n —**de·gen·er·a·tion** \-ˌjenə'rāshən\ n —**de·gen·er·a·tive** \-'jenə'rātiv\ adj

de·grade \di'grād\ vb 1 : reduce from a higher to a lower rank or degree 2 : debase —**de·grad·able** \-əbəl\ adj —**deg·ra·da·tion** \ˌdegrə'dāshən\ n

de·gree \di'grē\ n 1 : step in a series 2 : extent, intensity, or scope 3 : title given to a college graduate 4 : a 360th part of the circumference of a circle

de·hy·drate \dē'hī,drāt\ vb 1 : remove water from 2 : lose liquid —**de·hy·dra·tion** \ˌdēhī'drāshən\ n

de·i·fy \'dēə,fī\ vb **-fied; -fy·ing** : make a god of —**de·i·fi·ca·tion** \ˌdēəfə'kāshən\ n

deign \'dān\ vb : condescend

de·i·ty \'dēətē\ n, pl **-ties** 1 cap : God 2 : a god or goddess

de·ject·ed \di'jektəd\ adj : sad —**de·jec·tion** \-shən\ n

de·lay \di'lā\ n : a putting off of something ~ vb 1 : postpone 2 : stop or hinder for a time

de·lec·ta·ble \di'lektəbəl\ adj : delicious

del·e·gate \'deligət, -ˌgāt\ n : representative ~ \-ˌgāt\ vb **-gat·ed; -gat·ing** 1 : entrust to another 2 : appoint as one's delegate —**del·e·ga·tion** \ˌdeli'gāshən\ n

de·lete \di'lēt\ vb **-let·ed; -let·ing** : eliminate something written —**de·le·tion** \-'lēshən\ n

del·e·te·ri·ous \ˌdelə'tirēəs\ adj : harmful

de·lib·er·ate \di'lib(ə)rət\ adj 1 : determined after careful thought 2 : intentional 3 : not hurried ~ \-ə,rāt\ vb **-at·ed; -at·ing** 1 : consider carefully —**de·lib·er·ate·ly** adv —**de·lib·er·ate·ness** n —**de·lib·er·a·tion** \-ˌlibə'rāshən\ n —**de·lib·er·a·tive** \-'libə,rātiv, -'lib(ə)rət-\ adj

del·i·ca·cy \'delikəsē\ n, pl **-cies** 1 : something special and pleasing to eat 2 : fineness 3 : frailty

del·i·cate \'delikət\ adj 1 : subtly pleasing to the senses 2 : dainty and charming 3 : sensitive or fragile 4 : requiring fine skill or tact —**del·i·cate·ly** adv

del·i·ca·tes·sen \ˌdelikə'tesᵊn\ n : store that sells ready-to-eat food

de·li·cious \di'lishəs\ adj : very pleasing esp. in taste or aroma —**de·li·cious·ly** adv

de·light \di'līt\ n 1 : great pleasure 2 : source of great pleasure ~ vb 1 : take great pleasure 2 : satisfy greatly —**de·light·ful** \-fəl\ adj —**de·light·ful·ly** adv

de·lin·e·ate \di'linē,āt\ vb **-eat·ed; -eat·ing** : sketch or portray —**de·lin·ea·tion** \-ˌlinē'āshən\ n

de·lin·quent \-'liŋkwənt\ n : delinquent person ~ adj 1 : violating

duty or law **2** : overdue in payment —**de·lin·quen·cy** \-kwənsē\ n

de·lir·i·um \di'lirēəm\ n : mental disturbance —**de·lir·i·ous** \-ēəs\ adj

de·liv·er \di'livər\ vb **1** : set free **2** : hand over **3** : assist in birth **4** : say or speak **5** : send to an intended destination —**de·liv·er·ance** \-(ə)rəns\ n —**de·liv·er·er** n —**de·liv·ery** \-(ə)rē\ n

dell \'del\ n : small secluded valley

del·ta \'deltə\ n : triangle of land at the mouth of a river

de·lude \di'lüd\ vb **-lud·ed; -lud·ing** : mislead or deceive

del·uge \'delyüj\ n **1** : flood **2** : drenching rain ~ vb **-uged; -ug·ing 1** : flood **2** : overwhelm

de·lu·sion \di'lüzhən\ n : false belief

de·luxe \di'lùks, -'ləks, -'lüks\ adj : very luxurious or elegant

delve \'delv\ vb **delved; delv·ing 1** : dig **2** : seek information in records

dem·a·gogue, dem·a·gog \'demə,gäg\ n : politician who appeals to emotion and prejudice —**dem·a·gogu·ery** \-,gäg(ə)rē\ n —**dem·a·gogy** \-,gäge, -,gäjē\ n

de·mand \di'mand\ n **1** : act of asking esp. with authority **2** : something claimed as due **3** : ability and desire to buy **4** : urgent need ~ vb **1** : ask for with authority **2** : require

de·mar·cate \di'mär,kāt, 'dē,mär-\ vb **-cat·ed; -cat·ing** : mark the limits of —**de·mar·ca·tion** \,dē,mär'kāshən\ n

de·mean \di'mēn\ vb : degrade

de·mean·or \-'mēnər\ n : behavior

de·ment·ed \-'mentəd\ adj : crazy

de·mer·it \-'merət\ n : mark given an offender

demi·god \'demi,gäd\ n : mythological being less powerful than a god

de·mise \di'mīz\ n : death

demi·tasse \'demi,tas\ n : small cup of coffee

de·mo·bi·lize \di-, dē-\ vb : disband from military service —**de·mo·bi·li·za·tion** n

de·moc·ra·cy \di'mäkrəsē\ n, pl **-cies 1** : government in which the supreme power is held by the people **2** : political unit with democratic government

dem·o·crat \'demə,krat\ n : adherent of democracy

dem·o·crat·ic \,demə'kratik\ adj : relating to or favoring democracy —**dem·o·crat·ize** \di'mäkrə,tīz\ vb

de·mol·ish \di'mälish\ vb **1** : tear down or smash **2** : put an end to —**de·mo·li·tion** \,demə'lishən, ,dē-\ n

de·mon \'dēmən\ n : evil spirit —**de·mon·ic** \di'mänik\ adj

dem·on·strate \'demən,strāt\ vb **-strat·ed; -strat·ing 1** : show clearly or publicly **2** : prove **3** : explain —**de·mon·stra·ble** \di'mänstrəbəl\ adj —**dem·on·stra·tion** \,demən'strāshən\ n —**de·mon·stra·tive** \di'mänstrətiv\ adj or n —**dem·on·stra·tor** \'demən,strātər\ n

de·mor·al·ize \di'mòrə,līz\ vb : destroy the enthusiasm of

de·mote \-'mōt\ vb **-mot·ed; -mot·ing** : reduce to a lower rank

de·mur \-'mər\ vb **-rr-** : object —**de·mur** n

de·mure \-'myùr\ adj : modest —**de·mure·ly** adv

den \'den\ n **1** : animal's shelter **2** : hiding place **3** : cozy private little room

de·na·ture \dē'nāchər\ vb **-tured; -tur·ing** : make (alcohol) unfit for drinking

de·ni·al \di'nī(ə)l\ n : rejection of a request or of the validity of a statement

den·i·grate \'deni,grāt\ vb **-grat·ed; -grat·ing** : speak ill of

den·im \'denəm\ n **1** : durable twilled cotton fabric **2** pl : pants of denim

den·i·zen \-əzən\ n : inhabitant

de·nom·i·na·tion \di,nämə'nāshən\ n **1** : religious body **2** : value or size in a series —**de·nom·i·na·tion·al** \-sh(ə)nəl\ adj

de·nom·i·na·tor \-'nämə,nātər\ n : part of a fraction below the line

de·note \di'nōt\ vb **1** : mark out plainly **2** : mean —**de·no·ta·tion** \,dēnō'tāshən\ n —**de·no·ta·tive** \'dēnō,tātiv, di'nōtətiv\ adj

de·noue·ment \,dānü'mämⁿ\ n : final outcome (as of a drama)

de·nounce \di'nauns\ vb **-nounced; -nounc·ing 1** : criticize severely **2** : inform against

dense \'dens\ adj **dens·er; -est 1** : thick, compact, or crowded **2** : stupid —**dense·ly** adv —**dense·ness** n —**den·si·ty** \'densətē\ n

dent \'dent\ n : small depression —**dent** vb

den·tal \-ᵊl\ adj : relating to teeth or dentistry

den·ti·frice \'dentəfrəs\ n : preparation for cleaning teeth

den·tin \'dentᵊn\, **den·tine** \'den,tēn, ,den'-\ n : bonelike component of teeth

den·tist \'dentəst\ n : one who cares for and replaces teeth —**den·tist·ry** n

den·ture \'denchər\ *n* : artificial teeth

de·nude \di'n(y)üd\ *vb* **-nud·ed; -nud·ing** : strip of covering

de·nun·ci·a·tion \di,nənsē'āshən\ *n* : act of denouncing

de·ny \-'nī\ *vb* **-nied; -ny·ing 1** : declare untrue **2** : disavow **3** : refuse to grant

de·odor·ant \dē'ōdərənt\ *n* : preparation to prevent unpleasant odors —**de·odor·ize** \-,rīz\ *vb*

de·part \di'pärt\ *vb* **1** : go away or away from **2** : die —**de·par·ture** \-'pärchər\ *n*

de·part·ment \di'pärtmənt\ *n* **1** : area of responsibility or interest **2** : functional division —**de·part·men·tal** \di,pärt'ment²l, ,dē-\ *adj*

de·pend \di'pend\ *vb* **1** : rely for support **2** : be determined by or based on something else —**de·pend·abil·i·ty** \-,pendə'bilətē\ *n* —**de·pend·able** *adj* —**de·pen·dence** \di'pendəns\ *n* —**de·pen·den·cy** \-dənsē\ *n* —**de·pen·dent** \-ənt\ *adj or n*

de·pict \di'pikt\ *vb* : show by or as if by a picture —**de·pic·tion** \-'pikshən\ *n*

de·plete \di'plēt\ *vb* **-plet·ed; -plet·ing** : use up resources of —**de·ple·tion** \-'plēshən\ *n*

de·plore \-'plōr\ *vb* **-plored; -plor·ing** : regret strongly —**de·plor·able** \-əbəl\ *adj*

de·ploy \-'plòi\ *vb* : spread out for battle —**de·ploy·ment** \-mənt\ *n*

de·port \di'pōrt\ *vb* **1** : behave **2** : send out of the country —**de·por·ta·tion** \di,dē,pōr'tāshən\ *n* —**de·port·ment** \di'pōrtmənt\ *n*

de·pose \-'pōz\ *vb* **-posed; -pos·ing 1** : remove (a ruler) from office **2** : testify —**de·po·si·tion** \,depə'zishən, ,dē-\ *n*

de·pos·it \di'päzət\ *vb* **-it·ed; -it·ing 1** : put away for safekeeping : give as a pledge **3** : lay or put down — *n* **1** : state of being deposited **2** : something deposited **3** : act of depositing —**de·pos·i·tor** \-'päzətər\ *n*

de·pos·i·to·ry \di'päzə,tōrē\ *n, pl* **-ries** : place for deposit

de·pot **1** *usu* \'depō, 2 *usu* \'dēp-\ *n* **1** : place for storage **2** : bus or railroad station

de·prave \di'prāv\ *vb* **-praved; -prav·ing** : corrupt morally —**de·praved** *adj* —**de·prav·i·ty** \-'pravətē\ *n*

dep·re·cate \'depri,kāt\ *vb* **-cat·ed; -cat·ing 1** : express disapproval of **2** : belittle —**dep·re·ca·tion** \,depri'kāshən\ *n* —**dep·re·ca·to·ry** \'depri,kə,tōrē\ *adj*

de·pre·ci·ate \di'prēshē,āt\ *vb* **-at·ed; -at·ing 1** : lessen in value **2** : belittle —**de·pre·ci·a·tion** \-,prēshē'āshən\ *n*

dep·re·da·tion \,depra'dāshən\ *n* : a laying waste or plundering

de·press \di'pres\ *vb* **1** : press down **2** : lessen the activity or force of **3** : discourage **4** : decrease the market value of —**de·pres·sant** \-²nt\ *n or adj* —**de·pressed** *adj* —**de·pres·sive** \-iv\ *adj or n* —**de·pres·sor** \-ər\ *n*

de·pres·sion \di'preshən\ *n* **1** : act of depressing or state of being depressed **2** : period of low economic activity

de·prive \-'prīv\ *vb* **-prived; -priv·ing** : take or keep something away from —**de·pri·va·tion** \,depra'vāshən\ *n*

depth \'depth\ *n, pl* **depths** \'dep(th)s\ **1** : something that is deep **2** : distance down from a surface **3** : distance from front to back **4** : quality of being deep

dep·u·ta·tion \,depyə'tāshən\ *n* : delegation

dep·u·ty \'depyətē\ *n, pl* **-ties** : person appointed to act for another —**dep·u·tize** \- yə,tīz\ *vb*

de·rail \di'rāl\ *vb* : run off the rails —**de·rail·ment** *n*

de·range \-'rānj\ *vb* **-ranged; -rang·ing 1** : disarrange or upset **2** : make insane —**de·range·ment** *n*

der·by \'dərbē, *Brit* 'där-\ *n, pl* **-bies 1** : horse race **2** : stiff felt hat with dome-shaped crown

der·e·lict \'derə,likt\ *adj* **1** : abandoned **2** : negligent ~ *n* **1** : something abandoned **2** : bum —**der·e·lic·tion** \,derə'likshən\ *n*

de·ride \di'rīd\ *vb* **-rid·ed; -rid·ing** : make fun of —**de·ri·sion** \-'rizhən\ *n* —**de·ri·sive** \-'rīsiv\ *adj*

de·rive \di'rīv\ *vb* **-rived; -riv·ing 1** : obtain from a source or parent **2** : come from a certain source **3** : infer or deduce —**der·i·va·tion** \,derə'vāshən\ *n* —**de·riv·a·tive** \di'rivə,tiv\ *adj or n*

der·ma·tol·o·gy \,dərmə'täləjē\ *n* : study of the skin and its disorders —**der·ma·tol·o·gist** \-jəst\ *n*

de·rog·a·to·ry \di'rägə,tōrē\ *adj* : intended to lower the reputation

der·rick \'derik\ *n* **1** : hoisting apparatus **2** : framework over an oil well

de·scend \di'send\ *vb* **1** : move or climb down **2** : come down from a stock or source **3** : extend downward **4** : make a sudden attack —**de·scen·dant, de·scen·dent** \-ənt\ *adj or n* —**de·scent** \di'sent\ *n* de·scribe \-'skrīb\ vb -scribed; -scrib-ing : represent in words —de·scrib-able adj —de·scrib·ably adv —de·scrip·tion \-'skripshən\ n —de·scrip·tive \-'skriptiv\ adj

de·scry \di'skrī\ vb -scried; -scry-ing : catch sight of

des·e·crate \'desi,krāt\ vb -crat·ed; -crat·ing : treat (something sacred) with disrespect —des·e·cra·tion \,desi'krāshən\ n

de·seg·re·gate \dē-\ vb : eliminate esp. racial segregation in —de·seg·re·ga·tion n

¹des·ert \'dezərt\ n : dry barren region —desert adj

²de·sert \di'zərt\ n : what one deserves

³de·sert \di'zərt\ vb : abandon —de·sert·er n —de·ser·tion \-'zərshən\ n

de·serve \-'zərv\ vb -served; -serv·ing : be worthy of

des·ic·cate \'desi,kāt\ vb -cat·ed; -cat·ing : dehydrate —des·ic·ca·tion \,desi'kāshən\ n

de·sign \di'zīn\ vb 1 : create and work out the details of ~ n 1 : make a pattern or sketch of ~ n 1 : mental project or plan 2 : purpose 3 : preliminary sketch 4 : underlying arrangement of elements 5 : decorative pattern —de·sign·er n

des·ig·nate \'dezig,nāt\ vb -nat·ed; -nat·ing 1 : indicate, specify, or name 2 : appoint —des·ig·na·tion \,dezig'nāshən\ n

de·sire \di'zīr\ vb -sired; -sir·ing 1 : feel desire for 2 : request ~ n 1 : strong conscious impulse to have, be, or do something 2 : something desired —de·sir·abil·i·ty \-,zīrə'bilətē\ n —de·sir·able \-'zīrəbəl\ adj —de·sir·ous \-'zīrəs\ adj

de·sist \di'zist, -'sist\ vb : stop

desk \'desk\ n : table esp. for writing and reading

des·o·late \'desələt, 'dez-\ adj 1 : lifeless 2 : disconsolate ~ \-,lāt\ vb -lat·ed; -lat·ing : lay waste —des·o·la·tion \,desə'lāshən, ,dez-\ n

de·spair \di'spaar\ vb : lose all hope ~ n : loss of hope

des·per·a·do \,despə'rädō, -'räd-\ n, pl -does or -dos : desperate criminal

des·per·ate \'desp(ə)rət\ adj 1 : hopeless 2 : rash 3 : extremely intense —des·per·ate·ly adv —des·per·a·tion \,despə'rāshən\ n

de·spi·ca·ble \di'spikəbel, 'despik-\ adj : deserving scorn

de·spise \di'spīz\ vb -spised; -spis·ing : feel contempt for

de·spite \di'spīt\ prep : in spite of

de·spoil \-'spóil\ vb : strip of possessions or value

de·spon·den·cy \-'spändənsē\ n : dejection —de·spon·dent \-dənt\ adj

des·pot \'despət, -,pät\ n : tyrant —des·pot·ic \des'pätik\ adj —des·po·tism \'despa,tizəm\ n

des·sert \di'zərt\ n : sweet food, fruit, or cheese ending a meal

des·ti·na·tion \,destə'nāshən\ n : place where something or someone is going

des·tine \'destən\ vb -tined; -tin·ing 1 : designate, assign, or determine in advance 2 : direct

des·ti·ny \'destənē\ n, pl -nies : that which is to happen in the future

des·ti·tute \'destə,t(y)üt\ adj 1 : lacking something 2 : very poor —des·ti·tu·tion \,destə't(y)üshən\ n

de·stroy \di'strói\ vb : kill or put an end to

de·stroy·er \-'strói(ə)r\ n 1 : one that destroys 2 : small speedy warship

de·struc·tion \di-'strəkshən\ n 1 : action of destroying 2 : ruin —de·struc·ti·bil·i·ty \-,strəktə'bilətē\ n —de·struc·ti·ble \-'strəktəbəl\ adj —de·struc·tive \-'strəktiv\ adj

de·sul·to·ry \'desəl,tōrē\ adj : aimless

de·tach \di'tach\ vb : separate

de·tached \-'tacht\ adj 1 : separate 2 : aloof or impartial

de·tach·ment \-'tachmənt\ n 1 : separation 2 : troops or ships on special service 3 : aloofness 4 : impartiality

de·tail \di'tāl, 'dē,tāl\ n : small item or part ~ vb : give details of

de·tain \di'tān\ vb 1 : hold in custody 2 : delay

de·tect \di'tekt\ vb : discover —de·tect·able adj —de·tec·tion \-'tekshən\ n —de·tec·tor \-tər\ n

de·tec·tive \-'tektiv\ n : one who investigates crime

dé·tente \dātä°t\ n : relaxation of tensions between nations

de·ten·tion \di'tenchən\ n : confinement

de·ter \-'tər\ vb -rr- : discourage or prevent —de·ter·rence \-əns\ n —de·ter·rent \-ənt\ adj or n

de·ter·gent \di'tərjənt\ n : cleansing agent

de·te·ri·o·rate \di-'tirēə,rāt\ vb -rat·ed; -rat·ing : make or grow worse —de·te·ri·o·ra·tion \-,tirēə'rāshən\ n

de·ter·mi·na·tion \di,tərmə'nāshən\ n 1 : act of deciding or fixing 2 : firm purpose

de·ter·mine \di'tərmən\ vb -mined; -min·ing 1 : decide

on, establish, or settle **2** : find out **3** : be the cause of

de·test \'test\ *vb* : hate **—de·test·able** *adj* **—de·tes·ta·tion** \ˌdē.testˈtāshən\ *n*

det·o·nate \'detᵊnˌāt, 'detəˌnāt\ *vb* **-nat·ed; -nat·ing** : explode **—det·o·na·tion** \ˌdetᵊnˈāshən, ˌdetəˈnā-\ *n* **—det·o·na·tor** \-ᵊr\ *n*

de·tour \'dēˌtu̇r\ *n* : temporary indirect route **—detour** *vb*

de·tract \di'trakt\ *vb* : take away **—de·trac·tion** \-'trakshən\ *n* **—de·trac·tor** \-'traktər\ *n*

det·ri·ment \'detrəmənt\ *n* : damage **—det·ri·men·tal** \ˌdetrə'mentᵊl\ *adj* **—det·ri·men·tal·ly** *adv*

deuce \'d(y)üs\ *n* **1** : 2 in cards or dice **2** : tie in tennis **3** : devil—used as an oath

deut·sche mark \ˌdȯiché-\ *n* : monetary unit of West Germany

de·val·ue \dē-\ *vb* : reduce the value of **—de·val·u·a·tion** *n*

dev·as·tate \'devəˌstāt\ *vb* **-tat·ed; -tat·ing** : ruin **—dev·as·ta·tion** \ˌdevə'stāshən\ *n*

de·vel·op \di'veləp\ *vb* **1** : grow, increase, or evolve gradually **2** : cause to grow, increase, or reach full potential **—de·vel·op·er** *n* **—de·vel·op·ment** *n* **—de·vel·op·men·tal** \-ˌveləp'mentᵊl\ *adj*

de·vi·ate \'dēvēˌāt\ *vb* **-at·ed; -at·ing** : change esp. from a course or standard **—de·vi·ant** \-vēənt\ *adj or n* **—de·vi·ate** \-vēət, -vēˌāt\ *n* **—de·vi·a·tion** \ˌdēvē'āshən\ *n*

de·vice \di'vīs\ *n* **1** : specialized piece of equipment or tool **2** : design

dev·il \'devəl\ *n* **1** : personified supreme spirit of evil **2** : demon **3** : wicked person ~ *vb* **-iled** *or* **-illed; -il·ing** *or* **-il·ling** **1** : pester **2** : mash or chop (food) and season highly **—dev·il·ish** \'dev(ə)lish\ *adj* **—dev·il·ry** \'devalrē\, **dev·il·try** \-trē\ *n*

de·vi·ous \'dēvēəs\ *adj* : tricky

de·vise \di'vīz\ *vb* **-vised; -vis·ing 1** : invent **2** : plot **3** : give by will

de·void \di'vȯid\ *adj* : entirely lacking

de·vote \di'vōt\ *vb* **-vot·ed; -vot·ing** : set apart for a special purpose **—de·vot·ed** *adj* : ardent

de·vo·tee \ˌdevə'tē, -'tā\ *n* : zealous follower

de·vo·tion \di'vōshən\ *n* **1** : prayer —usu. pl. **2** : strong affection **—de·vo·tion·al** \-sh(ə)nəl\ *adj*

de·vour \di'vau̇(ə)r\ *vb* : consume ravenously **—de·vour·er** *n*

de·vout \-'vau̇t\ *adj* **1** : devoted to religion **2** : sincere **—de·vout·ly** *adv* **—de·vout·ness** *n*

dew \'d(y)ü\ *n* : moisture condensed at night **—dew·drop** *n* **—dewy** *adj*

dex·ter·ous, dex·trous \'dekst(ə)rəs\ *adj* : skillful with the hands **—dex·ter·i·ty** \dek'sterətē\ *n* **—dex·ter·ous·ly** *adv*

dex·trose \'dekˌstrōs\ *n* : plant or food sugar

di·a·be·tes \ˌdīə'bētēz, -'bētəs\ *n* : disorder in which the body has too little insulin and too much sugar **—di·a·bet·ic** \-'betik\ *adj or n*

di·a·bol·ic \-'bälik\, **di·a·bol·i·cal** \-ikəl\ *adj* : fiendish

di·a·crit·ic \-'kritik\ *n* : mark accompanying a letter and indicating a specific sound value **—di·a·crit·i·cal** \-'kritikəl\ *adj*

di·a·dem \'dīəˌdem\ *n* : crown

di·ag·no·sis \ˌdīig'nōsəs, -əg-\ *n, pl* **-no·ses** \-ˌsēz\ : identifying of a disease from its symptoms **—di·ag·nose** \'dīig,nōs, -əg-\ *vb* **—di·ag·nos·tic** \ˌdīig'nästik, -əg-\ *adj*

di·ag·o·nal \dī'ag(ə)nᵊl\ *adj* : extending from one corner to the opposite corner ~ *n* : diagonal line, direction, or arrangement **—di·ag·o·nal·ly** \-ē\ *adv*

di·a·gram \'dīəˌgram\ *n* : explanatory drawing or plan ~ *vb* **-gramed** *or* **-grammed; -gram·ing** *or* **-gram·ming** : represent by a diagram **—di·a·gram·mat·ic** \ˌdīəgrə'matik\ *adj*

di·al \'dī(ə)l\ *n* **1** : face of a clock, meter, or gauge **2** : control knob or wheel ~ *vb* **-aled** *or* **-alled; -al·ing** *or* **-al·ling** : turn a dial to call, operate, or select

di·a·lect \'dīəˌlekt\ *n* : variety of language confined to a region or group

di·a·logue, di·a·log \-ˌlȯg\ *n* : conversation

di·am·e·ter \dī'amətər\ *n* **1** : straight line through the center of a circle **2** : thickness

di·a·met·ric \ˌdīə'metrik\, **di·a·met·ri·cal** \-trikəl\ *adj* : completely opposite **—di·a·met·ri·cal·ly** \-(ə)lē\ *adv*

di·a·mond \'dī(ə)mənd\ *n* **1** : hard brilliant mineral that consists of crystalline carbon **2** : flat figure having 4 equal sides, 2 acute angles, and 2 obtuse angles **3** : playing card of a suit marked with a red diamond **4** : baseball field

di·a·per \'dī(ə)pər\ *n* : folded material drawn up between a baby's legs and fastened at the waist ~ *vb* : put a diaper on

di·a·phragm \'dīə,fram\ *n* **1** : muscular partition between the chest and abdominal cavity **2** : contraceptive device

di·ar·rhea, di·ar·rhoea \,dīə'rēə\ *n* : abnormal discharge of loose matter from the bowels

di·a·ry \'dīə,rē\ *n, pl* **-ries** : daily record of personal experiences —**di·a·rist** \'dīərəst\ *n*

di·a·tribe \'dīə,trīb\ *n* : denunciation

dice \'dīs\ *n, pl* **dice** : die or a game played with dice ~ *vb* **diced; dic·ing** : cut into small cubes

dick·er \'dikər\ *vb* : bargain

dic·tate \'dik,tāt\ *vb* **-tat·ed; -tat·ing** **1** : speak for a person or a machine to record **2** : command ~ *n* : order —**dic·ta·tion** \dik'tāshən\ *n*

dic·ta·tor \'dik,tātər\ *n* : person ruling absolutely and often brutally —**dic·ta·to·ri·al** \,diktətōrēəl\ *adj* —**dic·ta·tor·ship** \dik'tātər,ship, 'dik,-\ *n*

dic·tion \'dikshən\ *n* **1** : choice of the best word **2** : precise pronunciation

dic·tio·nary \-shə,nerē\ *n, pl* **-nar·ies** : reference book of words with information about their meaning

dic·tum \'diktəm\ *n, pl* **-ta** \-tə\ : authoritative or formal statement

did *past of* DO

di·dac·tic \dī'daktik\ *adj* : intended to teach a moral lesson

¹die \'dī\ *vb* **died; dy·ing** \'dīiŋ\ **1** : stop living **2** : pass out of existence **3** : stop or subside **4** : long

²die \'dī\ *n* **1** *pl* **dice** \'dīs\ : small marked cube used in gambling **2** *pl* **dies** \'dīz\ : form for stamping or cutting

die·sel \'dēzəl, -səl\ *n* : engine in which high compression causes ignition of the fuel

di·et \'dīət\ *n* : food and drink regularly consumed (as by a person) ~ *vb* : eat less or according to certain rules —**di·etary** \'dīə,terē\ *adj or n* —**di·et·er** *n*

di·etet·ics \,dīə'tetiks\ *n sing or pl* : science of nutrition —**di·etet·ic** *adj* —**di·eti·tian, di·eti·cian** \-'tishən\ *n*

dif·fer \'difər\ *vb* **1** : be unlike **2** : disagree —**dif·fer·ence** \'difərns, 'dif(ə)rəns\ *n*

dif·fer·ent \-rent, -(ə)rent\ *adj* : not the same —**dif·fer·ent·ly** *adv*

dif·fer·en·ti·ate \,difə'renchē,āt\ *vb* **-at·ed; -at·ing** **1** : make or become different **2** : distinguish —**dif·fer·en·ti·a·tion** \-,renchē'āshən\ *n*

dif·fi·cult \'difi(,)kəlt\ *adj* : hard to do, understand, or deal with

dif·fi·cul·ty \-(,)kəltē\ *n, pl* **-ties** **1** : difficult nature **2** : great effort **3** : something hard to do, understand, or deal with

dif·fi·dent \'difədənt\ *adj* : reserved —**dif·fi·dence** \-əns\ *n*

dif·fuse \dif'yüs\ *adj* **1** : wordy **2** : scattered ~ \-'yüz\ *vb* **-fused; -fus·ing** : pour out or spread widely —**dif·fu·sion** \-'yüzhən\ *n*

dig \'dig\ *vb* **dug** \'dəg\; **dig·ging** **1** : turn up soil **2** : hollow out or form by removing earth **3** : uncover by turning up earth **4** : discover **5** : poke ~ *n* **1** : thrust **2** : cutting remark

¹di·gest \'dī,jest\ *n* : body of information in shortened form

²di·gest \dī'jest, də-\ *vb* **1** : think over **2** : convert (food) into a form that can be absorbed **3** : summarize —**di·gest·ible** *adj* —**di·ges·tion** \-'jeschən\ *n* —**di·ges·tive** \-'jestiv\ *adj*

dig·it \'dijət\ *n* **1** : any of the figures 1 to 9 inclusive and usu. the symbol 0 **2** : finger or toe

dig·i·tal \-əl\ *adj* : providing information in numerical digits —**dig·i·tal·ly** *adv*

dig·ni·fy \'dignə,fī\ *vb* **-fied; -fy·ing** : give dignity to

dig·ni·tary \'dignə,terē\ *n, pl* **-taries** : person of high position

dig·ni·ty \'dignətē\ *n, pl* **-ties** **1** : quality or state of being worthy or honored **2** : formal reserve (as of manner)

di·gress \dī'gres, də-\ *vb* : wander from the main subject —**di·gres·sion** \-'greshən\ *n*

dike \'dīk\ *n* : earth bank or dam

di·lap·i·dat·ed \də'lapə,dātəd\ *adj* : fallen into partial ruin —**di·lap·i·da·tion** \-,lapə'dāshən\ *n*

di·late \dī'lāt, 'dī,lāt\ *vb* **-lat·ed; -lat·ing** : swell or expand —**dil·a·ta·tion** \,dilə'tāshən\ *n* —**di·la·tion** \dī-'lāshən\ *n*

dil·a·to·ry \'dilə,tōrē\ *adj* **1** : delaying **2** : not prompt

di·lem·ma \də'lemə\ *n* : choice between equally undesirable alternatives

dil·et·tante \'dilə,tänt, -,tant; ,dilə'tänt(ē), -'tant(ē)\ *n, pl* **-tantes** *or* **-tan·ti** \-'täntē, -'tantē\ : one who dabbles in a field of interest

dil·i·gent \'diləjənt\ *adj* : attentive and busy —**dil·i·gence** \-jəns\ *n* —**dil·i·gent·ly** *adv*

dill \'dil\ n : herb with aromatic leaves and seeds

dil·ly·dal·ly \'dilē,dalē\ vb : waste time by delay

di·lute \dī'lüt, də-\ vb -lut·ed; -lut·ing : lessen the consistency or strength of by mixing with something else ~ adj : weak —**di·lu·tion** \-'lüshən\ n

dim \'dim\ adj -mm- 1 : not bright or distinct 2 : having no luster 3 : not seeing or understanding clearly —**dim** vb —**dim·ly** adv —**dim·mer** n —**dim·ness** n

dime \'dīm\ n : U.S. coin worth 1/10 dollar

di·men·sion \də'menchən, dī-\ n 1 : measurement of extension (as in length, height, or breadth) 2 : extent —**di·men·sion·al** \-'mench(ə)nəl\ adj

di·min·ish \də'minish\ vb 1 : make less or cause to appear less 2 : dwindle

di·min·u·tive \də'minyətiv\ adj : extremely small

dim·ple \'dimpəl\ n : small depression esp. in the cheek or chin

din \'din\ n : loud noise

dine \'dīn\ vb **dined; din·ing** : eat dinner

din·er \'dīnər\ n 1 : person eating dinner 2 : railroad dining car or restaurant in the shape of one

din·ghy \'diŋ(k)ē, -gē\ n, pl **-ghies** : light rowboat

din·gy \'dinjē\ adj -gi·er; -est : not fresh, bright, or light —**din·gi·ness** n

din·ner \'dinər\ n : main daily meal

di·no·saur \'dīnə,sȯr\ n : extinct often huge reptile

dint \'dint\ n : force—in the phrase by dint of

di·o·cese \'dīəsəs, -,sēz, -,sēs\ n, pl **-ces·es** \-əz, 'dīə,sēz\ : territorial jurisdiction of a bishop —**di·oc·e·san** \dī'äsəsən, ,dīə'sēz°n\ adj or n

dip \'dip\ vb -pp- 1 : plunge into a liquid 2 : take out with a ladle 3 : lower and quickly raise again 4 : sink or slope downward suddenly ~ n 1 : plunge into water for sport 2 : sudden downward movement or incline —**dip·per** n

diph·the·ria \dif'thirēə, dip-\ n : acute contagious disease

diph·thong \'dif,thȯŋ, 'dip-\ n : two vowel sounds joined to form one speech sound (as ou in out)

di·plo·ma \də'plōmə\ n, pl **-mas** : record of graduation from a school

di·plo·ma·cy \-məsē\ n 1 : business of conducting negotiations between nations 2 : tact —**dip·lo·mat** \'dip-

lə,mat\ n —**dip·lo·mat·ic** \,diplə'matik\ adj

dire \'dī(ə)r\ adj **dir·er; -est** 1 : very horrible 2 : extreme

di·rect \də'rekt, dī-\ vb 1 : address 2 : cause to move or to follow a certain course 3 : show (someone) the way 4 : regulate the activities or course of 5 : request with authority ~ adj 1 : leading to or coming from a point without deviation or interruption 2 : frank —**direct** adv —**di·rect·ly** \-'rek(t)lē\ adv —**di·rect·ness** \-'rek(t)nəs\ n —**di·rec·tor** \-tər\ n

direct current n : electric current flowing in one direction only

di·rec·tion \də'rekshən, dī-\ n 1 : supervision 2 : order 3 : course along which something moves —**di·rec·tion·al** \-sh(ə)nəl\ adj

di·rec·tive \-tiv\ n : order

di·rec·to·ry \-t(ə)rē\ n, pl **-ries** : alphabetical list of names and addresses

dirge \'dərj\ n : funeral hymn

di·ri·gi·ble \'dirəjəbəl, də'rijə-\ n : airship

dirt \'dərt\ n 1 : mud, dust, or grime that makes something unclear 2 : soil

dirty \-ē\ adj **dirt·i·er; -est** 1 : not clear 2 : unfair 3 : indecent ~ vb **dirt·ied; dirty·ing** : make or become dirty —**dirt·i·ness** n

dis·able \dis'ābəl\ vb **-abled; -abling** : make unable to function —**dis·abil·i·ty** \,disə'bilətē\ n

dis·abuse \,disə'byüz\ vb : free from error

dis·ad·van·tage \,disəd'vantij\ n : something that hinders success —**dis·ad·van·ta·geous** adj

dis·af·fect \,dis-\ vb : cause discontent in —**dis·af·fec·tion** n

dis·agree \,dis-\ vb 1 : fail to agree 2 : differ in opinion —**dis·agree·ment** n

dis·agree·able \,dis-\ adj : unpleasant

dis·al·low \,dis-\ vb : refuse to admit or recognize

dis·ap·pear \,dis-\ vb 1 : pass out of sight 2 : cease to be —**dis·ap·pear·ance** n

dis·ap·point \,disə'pȯint\ vb : fail to fulfill the expectation or hope of —**dis·ap·point·ment** n

dis·ap·prove \,dis-\ vb 1 : condemn or reject 2 : feel or express dislike or rejection —**dis·ap·prov·al** n

dis·arm \dis'ärm\ vb 1 : take weapons from 2 : reduce armed forces 3 : make harmless or friendly —**dis·ar·ma·ment** \-'ärməmənt\ n

dis·ar·range \,dis-\ vb : throw into disorder —**dis·ar·range·ment** n

dis·ar·ray \ˌdis-\ *n* : disorder

di·sas·ter \diz'astər, dis-\ *n* : sudden great misfortune —**di·sas·trous** \-'astrəs\ *adj*

dis·avow \ˌdisə'vaů\ *vb* : deny responsibility for —**dis·avow·al** \-'vaů(ə)l\ *n*

dis·band \dis-\ *vb* : break up the organization of

dis·bar \dis-\ *vb* : expel from the legal profession —**dis·bar·ment** *n*

dis·be·lieve \ˌdis-\ *vb* : hold not to be true or real —**dis·be·lief** *n*

dis·burse \dis'bərs\ *vb* -**bursed; -bursing** : pay out —**dis·burse·ment** *n*

disc *var of* DISK

dis·card \dis'kärd, 'dis,kärd\ *vb* : get rid of as unwanted —**dis·card** \'dis,kärd\ *n*

dis·cern \dis'ərn, diz-\ *vb* : discover with the eyes or the mind —**dis·cern·ible** *adj* —**dis·cern·ment** *n*

dis·charge \dis'chärj, 'dis,chärj\ *vb* 1 : unload 2 : shoot 3 : set free 4 : dismiss from service 5 : let go or let off 6 : give forth fluid ~ \'dis,-, dis'-\ *n* 1 : act of discharging 2 : a flowing out (as of blood) 3 : dismissal

dis·ci·ple \dis'īpəl\ *n* : one who helps spread his master's teachings

dis·ci·pli·nar·i·an \ˌdisəplə'nerēən\ *n* : one who enforces order

dis·ci·pline \'disəplən\ *n* 1 : field of study 2 : training that corrects, molds, or perfects 3 : punishment 4 : control gained by obedience or training ~ *vb* -**plined; -plin·ing** 1 : punish 2 : train in self-control —**dis·ci·plin·ary** \'disəplə,nerē\ *adj*

dis·claim \dis'klām\ *vb* : disavow

dis·close \-'klōz\ *vb* : reveal —**dis·clo·sure** \-'klōzhər\ *n*

dis·col·or \dis'kələr\ *vb* 1 : change the color of 2 : stain —**dis·col·or·ation** \dis,kələ'rāshən\ *n*

dis·com·fit \dis'kəmfət\ *vb* : upset —**dis·com·fi·ture** \dis'kəmfə,chůr\ *n*

dis·com·fort \dis'kəmfərt\ *n* : lack of comfort

dis·con·cert \ˌdiskən'sərt\ *vb* : upset

dis·con·nect \ˌdiskə'nekt\ *vb* : undo the connection of

dis·con·so·late \dis'känsələt\ *adj* : hopelessly sad

dis·con·tent \ˌdiskən'tent\ *n* : uneasiness of mind —**dis·con·tent·ed** *adj*

dis·con·tin·ue \ˌdis-\ *vb* : end —**dis·con·tin·u·ance** *n*

dis·cord \'dis,kórd\ *n* : lack of harmony —**dis·cor·dant** \dis'kórd³nt\ *adj*

dis·count \'dis,kaůnt\ *n* : reduction from a regular price ~ \'dis,-, dis'-\ *vb* 1 : reduce the amount of 2 : disregard

dis·cour·age \dis'kərij\ *vb* -**aged; -aging** 1 : deprive of courage, confidence, or enthusiasm 2 : dissuade —**dis·cour·age·ment** *n*

dis·course \'dis,kórs, dis'-\ *n* 1 : conversation 2 : formal treatment of a subject ~ \dis'-\ *vb* -**coursed; -cours·ing** : talk at length

dis·cour·te·ous \dis-\ *adj* : lacking courtesy —**dis·cour·te·ous·ly** *adv* —**dis·cour·te·sy** *n*

dis·cov·er \dis'kəvər\ *vb* 1 : make known 2 : obtain the first sight or knowledge of —**dis·cov·er·er** *n* —**dis·cov·ery** \-(ə)rē\ *n*

dis·cred·it \dis'kredət\ *vb* 1 : disbelieve 2 : destroy confidence in ~ *n* 1 : loss of reputation 2 : disbelief —**dis·cred·it·able** *adj*

dis·creet \dis'krēt\ *adj* : capable of keeping a secret —**dis·creet·ly** *adv*

dis·crep·an·cy \dis'krepənsē\ *n, pl* -**cies** : difference or disagreement

dis·crete \dis'krēt, 'dis-\ *adj* : individually distinct

dis·cre·tion \dis'kreshən\ *n* 1 : discreet quality 2 : power of decision or choice —**dis·cre·tion·ary** *adj*

dis·crim·i·nate \dis'krimə,nāt\ *vb* -**nated; -nat·ing** 1 : distinguish 2 : show favor or disfavor unjustly —**dis·crim·i·na·tion** \-,krimə'nāshən\ *n* —**dis·crim·i·na·to·ry** \-'krimənə,tōrē\ *adj*

dis·cur·sive \dis'kərsiv\ *adj* : passing from one topic to another —**dis·cur·sive·ly** *adv* —**dis·cur·sive·ness** *n*

dis·cus \'diskəs\ *n, pl* -**cus·es** : disk hurled for distance in a contest

dis·cuss \dis'kəs\ *vb* : talk about or present —**dis·cus·sion** \-'kəshən\ *n*

dis·dain \dis'dān\ *n* : feeling of contempt ~ *vb* : look upon or reject with disdain —**dis·dain·ful** \-fəl\ *adj* —**dis·dain·ful·ly** *adv*

dis·ease \diz'ēz\ *n* : condition of a body that impairs its functioning —**dis·eased** \-'ēzd\ *adj*

dis·em·bark \ˌdisəm'bärk\ *vb* : get off a ship —**dis·em·bar·ka·tion** \dis,em-,bär'kāshən\ *n*

dis·em·bod·ied \ˌdisəm'bädēd\ *adj* : having no substance or reality

dis·en·chant \ˌdisⁿn'chant\ *vb* : to free from illusion —**dis·en·chant·ment** *n*

dis·en·gage \-ⁿn'gāj\ *vb* : release —**dis·en·gage·ment** *n*

dis·en·tan·gle \-ⁿn'taŋgəl\ *vb* : free from entanglement

dis·fa·vor \dis-\ *n* : disapproval

dis·fig·ure \dis-\ *vb* : spoil the appearance of —**dis·fig·ure·ment** *n*

dis·fran·chise \dis-\ *vb* : deprive of the right to vote —**dis·fran·chise·ment** *n*

dis·gorge \dis·'gòrj\ *vb* : spew forth

dis·grace \-'grās\ *vb* : bring disgrace to ~ *n* 1 : shame 2 : cause of shame —**dis·grace·ful** \-fəl\ *adj* —**dis·grace·ful·ly** *adv*

dis·grun·tle \dis-'grənt²l\ *vb* -**tled; -tling** : put in bad humor

dis·guise \-'gīz\ *vb* -**guised; -guis·ing** : hide the true identity or nature of ~ *n* : something that conceals

dis·gust \-'gəst\ *n* : strong aversion ~ *vb* : provoke disgust in —**dis·gust·ed·ly** *adv* —**dis·gust·ing·ly** *adv*

dish \'dish\ *n* 1 : vessel for serving food or the food it holds 2 : food prepared in a particular way ~ *vb* : put in a dish —**dish·cloth** *n* —**dish·rag** *n* —**dish·wash·er** *n* —**dish·wa·ter** *n*

dis·har·mo·ny \dis·'härmənē\ *n* : lack of harmony —**dis·har·mo·ni·ous** \ˌdis(ˌ)här'mōnēəs\ *adj*

dis·heart·en \dis·'härt²n\ *vb* : discourage

di·shev·el \dish·'evəl\ *vb* -**eled or -elled; -el·ing or -el·ling** : throw into disorder —**di·shev·eled, di·shev·elled** *adj*

dis·hon·est \dis-\ *adj* : not honest —**dis·hon·est·ly** *adv* —**dis·hon·es·ty** *n*

dis·hon·or \dis-\ *n or vb* : disgrace —**dis·hon·or·able** *adj* —**dis·hon·or·ably** *adj*

dis·il·lu·sion \ˌdisə'lüzhən\ *vb* : to free from illusion —**dis·il·lu·sion·ment** *n*

dis·in·cli·na·tion *n* : unwillingness —**dis·in·cline** \ˌdisʾn'klīn\ *vb*

dis·in·fect \ˌdisʾn'fekt\ *vb* : destroy disease germs in or on —**dis·in·fec·tant** \-'fektənt\ *adj or n* —**dis·in·fec·tion** \-'fekshən\ *n*

dis·in·her·it \ˌdisʾn'herət\ *vb* : prevent from inheriting property

dis·in·te·grate \dis·'intəˌgrāt\ *vb* : break into parts or small bits —**dis·in·te·gra·tion** \dis-ˌintə'grāshən\ *n*

dis·in·ter·est·ed \dis-\ *adj* 1 : not interested 2 : not prejudiced —**dis·in·ter·est·ed·ness** *n*

dis·joint·ed \dis·'jòintəd\ *adj* 1 : separated at the joint 2 : incoherent

disk \'disk\ *n* : something round and flat

dis·like \dis·'līk\ *vb* : regard with dislike ~ *n* : feeling that something is unpleasant and to be avoided

dis·lo·cate \'disloˌkāt, dis'-\ *vb* : move out of the usual or proper place —**dis·lo·ca·tion** \ˌdis(ˌ)lō'kāshən\ *n*

dis·lodge \dis-\ *vb* : force out of a place

dis·loy·al \dis-\ *adj* : not loyal —**dis·loy·al·ty** *n*

dis·mal \'dizməl\ *adj* : showing or causing gloom —**dis·mal·ly** *adv*

dis·man·tle \dis·'mant²l\ *vb* -**tled; -tling** : take apart

dis·may \dis·'mā\ *vb* -**mayed; -may·ing** : discourage —**dismay** *n*

dis·mem·ber \dis·'membər\ *vb* : cut into pieces —**dis·mem·ber·ment** *n*

dis·miss \dis·'mis\ *vb* 1 : send away 2 : remove from service 3 : put aside or out of mind —**dis·miss·al** *n*

dis·mount \dis-\ *vb* 1 : get down from something 2 : take apart

dis·obey \ˌdisə'bā\ *vb* : refuse to obey —**dis·obe·di·ence** \-'bēdēəns\ *n* —**dis·obe·di·ent** \-ənt\ *adj*

dis·or·der \dis·'òrdər\ *vb* : cause disorder of ~ *n* 1 : lack of order 2 : breach of public order 3 : abnormal state of body or mind —**dis·or·der·li·ness** *n* —**dis·or·der·ly** *adj*

dis·or·ga·nize \dis-\ *vb* : throw into disorder —**dis·or·ga·ni·za·tion** *n*

dis·own \dis·'ōn\ *vb* : repudiate

dis·par·age \-'parij\ *vb* -**aged; -ag·ing** : say bad things about —**dis·par·age·ment** *n*

dis·pa·rate \dis·'parət, 'disp(ə)rət\ *adj* : different in quality or character —**dis·par·i·ty** \dis'parətē\ *n*

dis·pas·sion·ate \dis·'pash(ə)nət\ *adj* : not influenced by strong feeling —**dis·pas·sion** \-ən\ *n*

dis·patch \dis·'pach\ *vb* 1 : send 2 : kill 3 : attend to rapidly ~ *n* 1 : message 2 : news item from a correspondent 3 : promptness and efficiency —**dis·patch·er** *n*

dis·pel \dis·'pel\ *vb* -**ll-** : clear away

dis·pen·sa·ry \-'pens(ə)rē\ *n, pl* -**ries** : place where medical or dental aid is provided

dis·pen·sa·tion \ˌdispən'sāshən\ *n* 1 : system of principles or rules 2 : exemption from a rule 3 : act of dispensing

dis·pense \dis·'pens\ *vb* -**pensed; -pens·ing** 1 : portion out 2 : make up and give out (remedies) —**dis·pens·able** *adj* —**dis·pens·er** *n* —**dispense with** : do without

dis·perse \dis·'pərs\ *vb* -**persed; -pers·ing** : scatter —**dis·per·sal** \-'ərsəl\ *n* —**dis·per·sion** \-'pərzhən\ *n*

dis·place \-'plās\ *vb* 1 : expel or force to flee from home or native land 2

: take the place of —**dis·place·ment** \-mənt\ n

dis·play \-'plā\ vb : present to view —**display** n

dis·please \-'plēz\ vb : arouse the dislike of —**dis·plea·sure** \-'plezhər\ n

dis·port \dis'pōrt\ vb 1 : amuse 2 : frolic

dis·pose \dis'pōz\ vb -posed; -pos·ing 1 : give a tendency to 2 : settle —**dis·pos·able** \-'pōzəbəl\ adj —**dis·pos·al** \-'pōzəl\ n —**dis·pos·er** n —**dispose of 1** : determine the fate, condition, or use of 2 : get rid of

dis·po·si·tion \,dispə'zishən\ n 1 : act or power of disposing of 2 : arrangement 3 : natural attitude

dis·pos·sess \,dispə'zes\ vb : deprive of possession or occupancy —**dis·pos·ses·sion** \-'zeshən\ n

dis·pro·por·tion \,dispro'pōrshən\ n : lack of proportion —**dis·pro·por·tion·ate** \-sh(ə)nət\ adj

dis·prove \dis-\ vb : prove false —**dis·proof** n

dis·pute \dis'pyüt\ vb -put·ed; -put·ing 1 : argue 2 : deny the truth or rightness of 3 : struggle against or over ~ n : debate or quarrel —**dis·put·able** \-əbəl, 'dispyət-\ adj —**dis·put·ably** \-blē\ adv —**dis·pu·ta·tion** \dispyə-'tāshən\ n

dis·qual·i·fy \dis-\ vb : make ineligible —**dis·qual·i·fi·ca·tion** n

dis·qui·et \dis-\ vb : make uneasy or restless ~ n : anxiety

dis·re·gard \,dis-\ vb : pay no attention to ~ n : neglect

dis·re·pair \,dis-\ n : need of repair

dis·rep·u·ta·ble \dis-\ adj : having a bad reputation

dis·re·pute \,dis-\ n : low regard

dis·re·spect \,dis-\ n : lack of respect —**dis·re·spect·ful** adj

dis·robe \dis-\ vb : undress

dis·rupt \dis'rəpt\ vb : throw into disorder —**dis·rup·tion** \-'rəpshən\ n —**dis·rup·tive** \-'rəptiv\ adj

dis·sat·is·fac·tion \dis,atəs'fakshən\ n : dissatisfied feeling

dis·sat·is·fy \dis'atəs,fī\ vb : fail to satisfy —**dis·sat·is·fied** adj

dis·sect \dis'ekt, dī'sekt\ vb : cut into parts esp. to examine —**dis·sec·tion** \-'ekshən, -'sek-\ n

dis·sem·ble \dis'embəl\ vb -bled; -bling : disguise feelings or intention —**dis·sem·bler** n

dis·sem·i·nate \dis'emə,nāt\ vb -nat·ed; -nat·ing : spread around —**dis·sem·i·na·tion** \-,em'ənāshən\ n

dis·sen·sion \dis'enchən\ n : discord

dis·sent \dis'ent\ vb : object or disagree ~ n : difference of opinion —**dis·sent·er** n —**dis·sen·tient** \-'enchənt\ adj or n

dis·ser·ta·tion \,disər'tāshən\ n : long written study of a subject

dis·ser·vice \dis'-\ n : injury

dis·si·dent \'disədənt\ n : one who differs openly —**dis·si·dence** \-əns\ n —**dissident** adj

dis·sim·i·lar \dis'imələr\ adj : different —**dis·sim·i·lar·i·ty** \dis,imə'larətē\ n

dis·si·pate \'disə,pāt\ vb -pat·ed; -pat·ing 1 : break up and drive off 2 : squander 3 : drink to excess —**dis·si·pa·tion** \disə'pāshən\ n

dis·so·ci·ate \dis'ōs(h)ē,āt\ vb -at·ed; -at·ing : separate from association —**dis·so·ci·a·tion** \dis,ōs(h)ē'āshən\ n

dis·so·lute \'disə,lüt\ adj : loose in morals or conduct

dis·so·lu·tion \,disə'lüshən\ n : act or process of dissolving

dis·solve \diz'älv\ vb 1 : break up or bring to an end 2 : pass or cause to pass into solution

dis·so·nance \'disənəns\ n : discord —**dis·so·nant** \-nənt\ adj

dis·suade \dis'wād\ vb -suad·ed; -suad·ing : persuade not to do something —**dis·sua·sion** \-'wāzhən\ n

dis·tance \'distəns\ n 1 : measure of separation in space or time 2 : reserve

dis·tant \-tənt\ adj 1 : separate in space 2 : remote in time, space, or relationship 3 : reserved

dis·taste \dis'tāst\ n : dislike —**dis·taste·ful** adj

dis·tem·per \dis'tempər\ n : virus disease of dogs

dis·tend \dis'tend\ vb : swell out —**dis·ten·sion, dis·ten·tion** \-'tenchən\ n

dis·till \dis'til\ vb : obtain by distillation —**dis·til·late** \'distə,lāt, -lət\ n —**dis·till·er** n —**dis·till·ery** \-'til(ə)rē\ n

dis·til·la·tion \,distə'lāshən\ n : the driving off of gas or vapor from liquids or solids by heating then condensing

dis·tinct \dis'tiŋkt\ adj 1 : distinguished from others 2 : clearly seen or heard —**dis·tinct·ly** adv —**dis·tinct·ness** n

dis·tinc·tion \-'tiŋkshən\ n 1 : act of distinguishing 2 : difference 3 : special recognition

dis·tinc·tive \-'tiŋktiv\ adj 1 : setting one apart 2 : characteristic —**dis·tinc·tive·ly** adv —**dis·tinc·tive·ness** n

dis·tin·guish \-'tiŋgwish\ vb 1 : perceive as different 2 : set apart 3 : discern 4 : make outstanding —**dis·tin·guish·able** adj —**dis·tin·guished** \-'gwisht\ adj

dis·tort \dis'tȯrt\ vb : twist out of shape, condition, or true meaning —**dis·tor·tion** \-'tȯrshən\ n

dis·tract \dis'trakt\ vb : divert the mind or attention of —**dis·trac·tion** \-'trakshən\ n

dis·traught \dis'trȯt\ adj : agitated with mental conflict

dis·tress \-'tres\ n 1 : suffering 2 : misfortune 3 : state of danger or great need ~ vb : subject to strain or distress —**dis·tress·ful** \-fəl\ adj

dis·trib·ute \-'tribyət\ vb -ut·ed; -ut·ing 1 : divide among many 2 : spread or hand out —**dis·tri·bu·tion** \,dis·trə'byüshən\ n —**dis·trib·u·tive** \dis'tribyətiv\ adj —**dis·trib·u·tor** \-ər\ n

dis·trict \'dis(,)trikt\ n : territorial division

dis·trust \'dis'trəst\ vb or n : mistrust —**dis·trust·ful** \-fəl\ adj

dis·turb \dis'tərb\ vb 1 : interfere with 2 : destroy the peace, composure, or order of —**dis·tur·bance** \-'tərbəns\ n —**dis·turb·er** n

dis·use \-'üs, -'yüs\ n : lack of use

ditch \'dich\ n : trench ~ vb 1 : dig a ditch in 2 : get rid of

dith·er \'dithər\ n : highly nervous or excited state

dit·to \'ditō\ n, pl -tos : more of the same

dit·ty \'ditē\ n, pl -ties : short simple song

di·uret·ic \,dī(y)ə'retik\ adj : tending to increase urine flow —**diuretic** n

di·ur·nal \dī'ərn²l\ adj 1 : daily 2 : of or occurring in the daytime

di·van \'dī,van, dī-'\ n : couch

dive \'dīv\ vb dived \'dīvd\ or dove \'dōv\; **dived; div·ing** 1 : plunge into water headfirst 2 : submerge 3 : descend quickly ~ n 1 : act of diving 2 : sharp decline —**div·er** n

di·verge \də'vərj, dī-\ vb -verged; -verg·ing 1 : move in different directions 2 : differ —**di·ver·gence** \-'vərjəns\ n —**di·ver·gent** \-jənt\ adj

di·vers \'dīvərz\ adj : various

di·verse \dī'vərs, də-, 'dī,vərs\ adj : involving different forms —**di·ver·si·fi·ca·tion** \də,vərsəfə'kāshən, dī-\ n —**di·ver·si·fy** \-'vərsə,fī\ vb —**di·ver·si·ty** \-sətē\ n

di·vert \də'vərt, dī-\ vb 1 : turn from a course or purpose 2 : distract 3 : amuse —**di·ver·sion** \-'vərzhən\ n

di·vest \dī'vest, də-\ vb : strip of clothing, possessions, or rights

di·vide \də'vīd\ vb -vid·ed; -vid·ing 1 : separate 2 : distribute 3 : share 4 : subject to mathematical division ~ n : watershed —**di·vid·er** n

div·i·dend \'divə,dend\ n 1 : individual share 2 : bonus 3 : number to be divided by another

div·i·na·tion \,divə'nāshən\ n : practice of trying to foretell future events

di·vine \də'vīn\ adj -vin·er; -est 1 : relating to or being God or a god 2 : supremely good ~ n : clergyman ~ vb -vined; -vin·ing 1 : infer 2 : prophesy —**di·vine·ly** adv —**di·vin·er** n —**di·vin·i·ty** \də'vinətē\ n

di·vis·i·ble \-'vizabəl\ adj : capable of being divided —**di·vis·i·bil·i·ty** \-,vizə'bilətē\ n

di·vi·sion \-'vizhən\ n 1 : distribution 2 : part of a whole 3 : disagreement 4 : process of finding out how many times one number is contained in another —**di·vi·sion·al** \-'vizh(ə)nəl\ adj

di·vi·sive \də'vīsiv, -'viziv\ adj : creating dissension

di·vi·sor \də'vīzər\ n : number by which a dividend is divided

di·vorce \də'vȯrs\ n : legal breaking up of a marriage —**divorce** vb

di·vor·cée \-'vȯr'sā, -'sē\ n : divorced woman

di·vulge \də'vəlj, dī-\ vb -vulged; -vulg·ing : reveal

diz·zy \'dizē\ adj -zi·er; -est : having a sensation of whirling 2 : causing or caused by giddiness —**diz·zi·ly** adv —**diz·zi·ness** n

do \(')dü\ vb did \(')did\; **done** \'dən\; **do·ing** \'düiŋ\; **does** \(')dəz\ vb 1 : work to accomplish (an action or task) 2 : behave 3 : prepare or fix up 4 : fare 5 : finish 6 : serve the needs or purpose of 7 —used as an auxiliary verb —**do away with** 1 : get rid of 2 : destroy —**do by** : act toward in a specified way —**do in** vb 1 : ruin 2 : kill

doc·ile \'däsəl\ adj : easily managed —**do·cil·i·ty** \dä'silətē\ n

¹dock \'däk\ vb 1 : shorten 2 : reduce

²dock n 1 : berth between 2 piers to receive ships 2 : loading wharf or platform ~ vb : bring or come into dock —**dock·hand** n —**dock·work·er** n

³dock n : place in a court for a prisoner

dock·et \'däkət\ *n* **1** : record of the proceedings in a legal action **2** : list of legal causes to be tried —**docket** *vb*

doc·tor \'däktər\ *n* **1** : person holding one of the highest academic degrees **2** : one (as a surgeon) skilled in healing arts ~ *vb* **1** : give medical treatment to **2** : repair or alter —**doc·tor·al** \-t(ə)rəl\ *adj*

doc·trine \'däktrən\ *n* : something taught —**doc·tri·nal** \-trən³l\ *adj*

doc·u·ment \'däkyəmənt\ *n* : paper that furnishes information or legal proof —**doc·u·ment** \-,ment\ *vb* —**doc·u·men·ta·tion** \,däkyəmən-'tāshən\ *n*

doc·u·men·ta·ry \,däkyə'ment(ə)rē\ *adj* **1** : of or relating to documents **2** : giving a factual presentation —**documentary** *n*

dod·der \'dädər\ *vb* : become feeble usu. from age

dodge \'däj\ *vb* **dodged; dodg·ing 1** : move quickly aside or out of the way of **2** : evade —**dodge** *n*

do·do \'dōdō\ *n, pl* **-does** *or* **-dos 1** : heavy flightless extinct bird **2** : stupid person

doe \'dō\ *n, pl* **does** *or* **doe** : adult female deer —**doe·skin** \-,skin\ *n*

do·er \'düər\ *n* : one that does

does *pres 3d sing of* DO

doff \'däf\ *vb* : remove

dog \'dóg\ *n* : flesh-eating domestic mammal ~ *vb* **1** : hunt down or track like a hound **2** : worry as if by dogs —**dog·catch·er** *n* —**dog·gy** \-ē\ *n or adj* —**dog·house** *n*

dog·ear \'dóg,iər\ *n* : turned-down corner of a page —**dog·eared** \-,iərd\ *adj*

dog·ged \'dógəd\ *adj* : stubbornly determined

dog·ma \'dógmə\ *n* : tenet or code of tenets

dog·ma·tism \-,tizəm\ *n* : unwarranted stubbornness of opinion —**dog·mat·ic** \dóg'matik\ *adj*

dog·wood *n* : flowering tree

doi·ly \'dóilē\ *n, pl* **-lies** : small decorative mat

do·ings \'düiŋz\ *n pl* : deeds

dol·drums \'dōldrəmz,'däl-\ *n pl* **1** : spell of listlessness or despondency **2** : windless ocean near the equator

dole \'dōl\ *n* : distribution esp. of money to the needy or unemployed ~ *vb* : give out in small portions

dole·ful \'dōlfəl\ *adj* : full of grief —**dole·ful·ly** *adv*

doll \'däll, 'dól\ *n* : small figure of a person used esp. as a child's toy

dol·lar \'dälər\ *n* : any of various basic monetary units (as in the U.S. and Canada)

dol·ly \'dälē\ *n, pl* **-lies** : wheeled frame for moving heavy objects

dol·phin \'dälfən\ *n* **1** : sea mammal related to the whales **2** : saltwater food fish

dolt \'dōlt\ *n* : stupid person —**dolt·ish** *adj*

-dom \dəm\ *n suffix* **1** : office or realm **2** : state or fact of being **3** : those belonging to a group

do·main \dō'mān, də-\ *n* **1** : territory over which someone reigns **2** : sphere of activity

dome \'dōm\ *n* : large hemispherical roof

do·mes·tic \də'mestik\ *adj* **1** : relating to the household or family **2** : relating and limited to one's own country **3** : tame ~ *n* : household servant —**do·mes·ti·cal·ly** \-tik(ə)lē\ *adv*

do·mes·ti·cate \-ti,kāt\ *vb* **-cat·ed; -cat·ing** : tame —**do·mes·ti·ca·tion** \-,mesti'kāshən\ *n*

do·mi·cile \'dämə,sīl, 'dō-; 'däməsəl\ *n* : home —**domicile** *vb*

dom·i·nance \'dämənəns\ *n* : control —**dom·i·nant** \-nənt\ *adj*

dom·i·nate \-,nāt\ *vb* **-nat·ed; -nat·ing 1** : have control over **2** : rise high above —**dom·i·na·tion** \,dämə'nā-shən\ *n*

dom·i·neer \,dämə'niər\ *vb* : exercise arbitrary control

do·min·ion \də'minyən\ *n* **1** : supreme authority **2** : governed territory

dom·i·no \'dämə,nō\ *n, pl* **-noes** *or* **-nos** : flat rectangular block used as a piece in a game (**dominoes**)

don \'dän\ *vb* **-nn-** : put on (clothes)

do·nate \'dō,nāt\ *vb* **-nat·ed; -nat·ing** : make a gift of —**do·na·tion** \dō'nāshən\ *n*

¹done \'dən\ *past part of* DO

²done *adj* **1** : finished or ended **2** : cooked sufficiently

don·key \'däŋkē, 'dəŋ-\ *n, pl* **-keys** : domestic ass

do·nor \'dōnər\ *n* : one that gives

doo·dle \'düd³l\ *vb* **-dled; -dling** : draw or scribble aimlessly —**doodle** *n*

doom \'düm\ *n* **1** : judgment **2** : fate **3** : ruin —**doom** *vb*

door \'dōr\ *n* : passage for entrance or a movable barrier that can open or close such a passage —**door·jamb** *n* —**door·knob** *n* —**door·mat** *n* —**door·step** *n* —**door·way** *n*

dope \'dōp\ *n* **1** : narcotic preparation **2** : stupid person **3** : information ~ *vb* **doped; dop·ing** : drug

dor·mant \'dormənt\ *adj* : not actively growing or functioning —**dor·man·cy** \-mənsē\ *n*

dor·mer \'dormər\ *n* : window built upright in a sloping roof

dor·mi·to·ry \'dormə,tōrē\ *n, pl* **-ries** : residence hall (as at a college)

dor·mouse \'dor,maús\ *n* : squirrellike rodent

dor·sal \'dorsəl\ *adj* : relating to or on the back —**dor·sal·ly** *adv*

do·ry \'dōrē\ *n, pl* **-ries** : flat-bottomed boat

dose \'dōs\ *n* : quantity (as of medicine) taken at one time ~ *vb* **dosed; dos·ing** : give medicine to —**dos·age** \'dōsij\ *n*

dot \'dät\ *n* **1** : small spot **2** : small round mark made with or as if with a pen ~ *vb* **-tt-** : mark with dots

dot·age \'dōtij\ *n* : senility

dote \'dōt\ *vb* **dot·ed; dot·ing 1** : act feebleminded **2** : be foolishly fond

dou·ble \'dabəl\ *adj* **1** : consisting of 2 members or parts **2** : being twice as great or as many **3** : folded in two ~ *n* **1** : something twice another **2** : one that resembles another ~ *adv* : doubly ~ *vb* **-bled; -bling 1** : make or become twice as great **2** : fold or bend **3** : clench

dou·blecross *vb* : deceive by trickery —**dou·ble-cross·er** *n*

dou·bly \'dablē\ *adv* : to twice the degree

doubt \'daút\ *vb* **1** : be uncertain about **2** : mistrust **3** : consider unlikely ~ *n* **1** : uncertainty **2** : mistrust **3** : inclination not to believe —**doubt·ful** \-fəl\ *adj* —**doubt·ful·ly** *adv* —**doubt·less** \-ləs\ *adv*

douche \'düsh\ *n* : jet of fluid for cleaning a body part

dough \'dō\ *n* : stiff mixture of flour and liquid —**doughy** \'dōē\ *adj*

dough·nut \-(,)nət\ *n* : small fried ring-shaped cake

dough·ty \'daútē\ *adj* **-ti·er; -est** : able, strong, or valiant

dour \'daú(ə)r, 'dúr\ *adj* **1** : severe **2** : gloomy or sullen

douse \'daús, 'daúz\ *vb* **doused; dous·ing 1** : plunge into or drench with water **2** : extinguish

¹dove \'dəv\ *n* : small wild pigeon

²dove \'dōv\ *past of* DIVE

dove·tail \'dəv,tāl\ *n* **1** : flaring tenon and its mortise ~ *vb* **1** : join by dovetails **2** : fit together neatly

dow·a·ger \'daúijər\ *n* : widow with wealth or a title **2** : dignified elderly woman

dowdy \'daúdē\ *adj* **dowd·i·er; -est** : lacking neatness and charm

dow·el \'daú(ə)l\ *n* : peg used for fastening two pieces

dow·er \'daú(ə)r\ *n* : property given a widow for life ~ *vb* : supply with a dower

¹down \'daún\ *adv* **1** : toward or in a lower position or state **2** : to a lying or sitting position **3** : as a cash deposit **4** : on paper ~ *adj* **1** : lying on the ground **2** : directed or going downward **3** : being at a low level ~ *prep* : toward the bottom of ~ *vb* **1** : cause to go down **2** : defeat

²down *n* : fluffy feathers

down·cast *adj* **1** : sad **2** : directed down

down·fall *n* : ruin or cause of ruin —**down·fall·en** \-,fólən\ *adj*

down·grade *n* : downward slope ~ *vb* : lower in grade or position

down·heart·ed *adj* : sad

down·pour *n* : heavy rain

down·right *adv* : thoroughly ~ *adj* : absolute or thorough

downs \'daúnz\ *n pl* : rolling treeless uplands

down·stairs *adv* : on or to a lower floor and esp. the main floor —**downstairs** *adj or n*

down-to-earth *adj* : practical

down·town *adv* : to, toward, or in the business center of a town —**downtown** *n or adj*

down·trod·den \-'träd³n\ *adj* : abused by superior power

down·ward \'daúnwərd\, **down·wards** \-wərdz\ *adv* : to a lower place or condition —**downward** *adj*

down·wind *adv or adj* : in the direction the wind is blowing

downy \'daúnē\ *adj* **-i·er; -est** : resembling or covered with down

dow·ry \'daú(ə)rē\ *n, pl* **-ries** : property a woman gives her husband in marriage

dox·ol·o·gy \däk'säləjē\ *n, pl* **-gies** : hymn of praise to God

doze \'dōz\ *vb* **dozed; doz·ing** : sleep lightly —**doze** *n*

doz·en \'dəz³n\ *n, pl* **-ens** or **-en** : group of 12 —**doz·enth** \-³nth\ *adj*

drab \'drab\ *adj* **-bb-** : dull —**drab·ness** *n*

draft \'draft, 'dráft\ *n* **1** : act of drawing or hauling **2** : act of drinking **3** : amount drunk at once **4** : preliminary outline or rough sketch **5** : selection from a pool or the selection process **6** : order for the payment of money **7** : air current ~ *vb* **1** : select usu. on a compulsory basis **2** : make a preliminary sketch, version, or plan of ~ *adj* : drawn from a container —**draft·ee** \draf'tē, dráf-\ *n* —**drafty** \'draftē\ *adj*

drafts·man \'draftsmən, 'dráft-\ *n* : one who draws plans

drag \'drag\ *n* **1** : something dragged over a surface or through water **2** : something that hinders progress or is boring **3** : act or an instance of dragging ~ *vb* -**gg**- **1** : haul **2** : move or work with difficulty **3** : pass slowly **4** : search or fish with a drag —**drag·ger** *n*

drag·net \-,net\ *n* **1** : trawl **2** : planned actions for finding a criminal

drag·on \'dragən\ *n* : fabled winged serpent

drag·on·fly *n* : large 4-winged insect

drain \'drān\ *vb* **1** : draw off or flow off gradually or completely **2** : exhaust ~ *n* : means or act of draining —**drain·age** \-ij\ *n* —**drain·er** *n* —**drain·pipe** *n*

drake \'drāk\ *n* : male duck

dra·ma \'drämə, 'dram-\ *n* **1** : composition for theatrical presentation esp. on a serious subject **2** : series of events involving conflicting forces —**dra·mat·ic** \drə'matik\ *adj* —**dra·mat·i·cal·ly** \-ik(ə)lē\ *adv* —**dram·a·tist** \'dramətəst, 'dräm-\ *n* —**dram·a·ti·za·tion** \,draməti'zāshən, ,dräm-\ *n* —**dra·ma·tize** \'dramə,tīz, 'dräm-\ *vb*

drank *past of* DRINK

drape \'drāp\ *vb* **draped; drap·ing** **1** : cover or adorn with folds of cloth **2** : cause to hang in flowing lines or folds ~ *n* : curtain

drap·ery \'drāp(ə)rē\ *n, pl* -**er·ies** : decorative fabric hung esp. as a heavy curtain

dras·tic \'drastik\ *adj* : extreme or harsh —**dras·ti·cal·ly** \-tik(ə)lē\ *adv*

draught \'dráft\ *chiefly Brit var of* DRAFT

draw \'drö\ *vb* **drew** \'drü\; **drawn** \'drön\; **draw·ing** **1** : move or cause to move (as by pulling) **2** : attract or provoke **3** : extract **4** : take or receive (as money) **5** : bend a bow in preparation for shooting **6** : leave a contest undecided **7** : sketch **8** : write out **9** : deduce ~ *n* **1** : act, process, or result of drawing **2** : tie —**draw out** *vb* **1** : cause to speak candidly —**draw up** *vb* **1** : write out **2** : pull oneself erect **3** : bring or come to a stop

draw·back *n* : disadvantage

draw·bridge *n* : bridge that can be raised

draw·er \'dró(ə)r\ *n* **1** : one that draws **2** : sliding boxlike compartment **3** *pl* : underpants

draw·ing \'dróin\ *n* **1** : occasion of choosing by lot **2** : act or art of making a figure, plan, or sketch with lines **3** : something drawn

drawl \'dröl\ *vb* : speak slowly —**drawl** *n*

dread \'dred\ *vb* : feel extreme fear or reluctance ~ *n* : great fear ~ *adj* : causing dread —**dread·ful** \-fəl\ *adj* —**dread·ful·ly** *adv*

dream \'drēm\ *n* **1** : series of thoughts or visions during sleep **2** : dreamlike vision **3** : something notable **4** : ideal ~ *vb* **1** : have a dream **2** : imagine —**dream·er** *n* —**dream·like** *adj* —**dreamy** *adj*

drea·ry \'drirē\ *adj* -**ri·er**, -**est** : dismal —**drea·ri·ly** \'drirəlē\ *adv*

¹dredge \'drej\ *n* : machine for removing earth esp. from under water ~ *vb* **dredged; dredg·ing** : dig up or search with a dredge —**dredg·er** *n*

²dredge *vb* **dredged; dredg·ing** : coat (food) with flour

dregs \'dregz\ *n* **1** : sediment **2** : most worthless part

drench \'drench\ *vb* : wet thoroughly

dress \'dres\ *vb* **1** : put clothes on **2** : decorate **3** : prepare (as a carcass) for use **4** : apply dressings, remedies, or fertilizer to ~ *n* **1** : apparel **2** : single garment of bodice and skirt ~ *adj* : suitable for a formal occasion —**dress·mak·er** *n* —**dress·mak·ing** *n*

dress·er \'dresər\ *n* : bureau with a mirror

dress·ing *n* **1** : act or process of dressing **2** : sauce or a seasoned mixture **3** : material to cover an injury

dressy \-ē\ *adj* **dress·i·er**, -**est** : showy in dress **2** : stylish

drew *past of* DRAW

drib·ble \'dribəl\ *vb* -**bled**; -**bling** **1** : fall or flow in drops **2** : drool —**dribble** *n*

drier *comparative of* DRY

driest *superlative of* DRY

drift \'drift\ *n* **1** : motion or course of something drifting **2** : mass blown up by wind **3** : general intention or meaning ~ *vb* **1** : float or be driven along (as by a current) **2** : wander without purpose **3** : pile up under force —**drift·er** *n* —**drift·wood** *n*

¹drill \'dril\ *vb* **1** : bore with a drill **2** : instruct by repetition **3** : boring tool **2** : strict training and instruction —**drill·er** n

²**drill** n : seed-planting implement

³**drill** n : twill-weave cotton fabric

drily var of DRYLY

drink \'driŋk\ vb **drank** \'draŋk\; **drunk** \'drəŋk\ or **drank**; **drink·ing** **1** : swallow liquid **2** : absorb **3** : drink alcoholic beverages esp. to excess ~ n **1** : beverage **2** : alcoholic liquor —**drink·able** adj —**drink·er** n

drip \'drip\ vb **-pp-** : fall or let fall in drops ~ n **1** : a dripping **2** : sound of falling drops

drive \'drīv\ vb **drove** \'drōv\; **driv·en** \'drivən\; **driv·ing 1** : urge or force onward **2** : direct the movement or course of **3** : compel **4** : cause to become **5** : propel forcefully ~ n **1** : trip in a vehicle **2** : driveway **3** : intensive campaign **4** : aggressive or dynamic quality **5** : basic need —**driv·er** n

drive-in adj : accommodating patrons in cars —**drive-in** n

driv·el \'drivəl\ vb **-eled** or **-elled**; **el·ing** or **el·ling 1** : drool **2** : talk stupidly ~ n : nonsense

drive·way n : private road from the street to a house

driz·zle \'drizəl\ n : fine misty rain —**drizzle** vb

droll \'drōl\ adj : humorous or whimsical —**droll·ery** \-ərē\ n —**drol·ly** \'drō(l)lē\ adv

drom·e·dary \'drämə,derē\ n, pl **-dar·ies** : speedy one-humped camel

drone \'drōn\ n **1** : male honeybee **2** : deep hum or buzz ~ vb **droned; dron·ing** : make a dull monotonous sound

drool \'drül\ vb : let liquid run from the mouth

droop \'drüp\ vb **1** : hang or incline downward **2** : lose strength or spirit —**droop** n

drop \'dräp\ n **1** : quantity of fluid in one spherical mass **2** pl : medicine used by drops **3** : decline or fall **4** : distance something drops ~ vb **-pp-** **1** : fall in drops **2** : let fall **3** : convey **4** : go lower or become less strong or less active —**drop·let** \-lət\ n —**drop back** vb : move toward the rear —**drop behind** vb : fail to keep up —**drop in** vb : pay an unexpected visit

drop·per n : device that dispenses liquid by drops

drop·sy \'dräpsē\ n : abnormal accumulation of serous fluid in the body

dross \'dräs\ n : waste matter

drought, drouth \'draut(h)\ n : long dry spell

¹**drove** \'drōv\ n : crowd of moving people or animals

²**drove** past of DRIVE

drown \'draun\ vb **1** : suffocate in water **2** : overpower or become overpowered

drowse \'drauz\ vb **drowsed; drows·ing** : doze —**drowse** n

drowsy \'drauzē\ adj **drows·i·er; -est** : sleepy —**drows·i·ly** adv —**drows·i·ness** n

drub \'drəb\ vb **-bb-** : beat severely

drudge \'drəj\ vb **drudged; drudg·ing** : do hard or boring work —**drudge** n —**drudg·ery** \-(ə)rē\ n

drug \'drəg\ n **1** : substance used as or in medicine **2** : narcotic ~ vb **-gg-** : affect with drugs —**drug·gist** \-əst\ n —**drug·store** n

dru·id \'drüəd\ n : ancient Celtic priest

drum \'drəm\ n **1** : musical instrument that is a skin-covered cylinder beaten with sticks **2** : drum-shaped object (as a container) ~ vb **-mm- 1** : beat a drum **2** : drive, force, or bring about by steady effort —**drum·beat** n —**drum·mer** n

drum·stick n **1** : stick for beating a drum **2** : lower segment of a fowl's leg

drunk \'drəŋk\ adj : having the faculties impaired by alcohol ~ n : one who is drunk —**drunk·ard** \'drəŋkərd\ n —**drunk·en** \-kən\ adj —**drunk·en·ly** adv —**drunk·en·ness** n

dry \'drī\ adj **dri·er** \'drī(ə)r\; **dri·est** \'drīəst\ **1** : lacking water or moisture **2** : thirsty **3** : marked by the absence of alcoholic beverages **4** : uninteresting **5** : not sweet ~ vb **dried; dry·ing** : make or become dry —**dry·ly** adv —**dry·ness** n

dry-clean vb : clean (fabrics) chiefly with solvents other than water —**dry cleaning** n

dry·er \'drī(ə)r\ n : device for drying

dry goods n pl : textiles, clothing, and notions

dry ice n : solidified carbon dioxide

du·al \'d(y)üəl\ adj : twofold —**du·al·ism** \-ə,lizəm\ n —**du·al·i·ty** \d(y)ü'alətē\ n

dub \'dəb\ vb **-bb-** : name

du·bi·ous \'d(y)übēəs\ adj **1** : uncertain **2** : questionable —**du·bi·ous·ly** adv —**du·bi·ous·ness** n

du·cal \'d(y)ükəl\ adj : relating to a duke or dukedom

duch·ess \'dəchəs\ n **1** : wife of a duke **2** : woman holding a ducal title

duchy \'-ē\ *n, pl* **-ies** : territory of a duke or duchess

¹duck \'dǝk\ *n, pl* : swimming bird related to the goose and swan ~ *vb* **1** : thrust or plunge under water **2** : lower the head or body suddenly **3** : evade —**duck·ling** \-liŋ\ *n*

²duck *n* : cotton fabric

duct \'dǝkt\ *n* : canal for conveying a fluid —**duct·less** \-lǝs\ *adj*

duc·tile \'dǝkt²l\ *adj* : able to be drawn out or shaped —**duc·til·i·ty** \,dǝk'tilǝtē\ *n*

dude \'d(y)üd\ *n* : dandy

dudgeon \'dǝjǝn\ *n* : ill humor

due \'d(y)ü\ *adj* **1** : owed **2** : appropriate **3** : attributable **4** : expected ~ *n* **1** : something due **2** *pl* : fee ~ *adv* **1** : directly

du·el \'d(y)üǝl\ *n* : combat between 2 persons —**duel** *vb* —**du·el·ist** *n*

du·et \d(y)ü'et\ *n* : musical composition for 2 performers

due to *prep* : because of

dug *past of* DIG

dug·out \'dǝg,aút\ *n* **1** : boat made by hollowing out a log **2** : shelter made by digging

duke \'d(y)ük\ *n* : nobleman of the highest rank —**duke·dom** *n*

dull \'dǝl\ *adj* **1** : mentally slow **2** : blunt **3** : not brilliant or interesting ~ *vb* : make or become dull —**dull·ard** \'dǝlǝrd\ *n* —**dull·ness, dul·ness** *n* —**dul·ly** \'dǝl(l)ē\ *adv*

du·ly \'d(y)ülē\ *adv* : in a due manner, time, or degree

dumb \'dǝm\ *adj* **1** : mute **2** : stupid —**dumb·ly** *adv*

dumb·bell \'dǝm,bel\ *n* **1** : short bar with weights on the ends **2** : stupid person

dumb·found, dum·found \,dǝm'faúnd\ *vb* : amaze

dum·my \'dǝmē\ *n, pl* **-mies** **1** : dumb person **2** : imitation of something (as a human figure)

dump \'dǝmp\ *vb* : unload or discard in a mass ~ *n* : place for dumping something (as refuse) —**in the dumps** : sad

dump·ling \'dǝmpliŋ\ *n* : small mass of boiled or steamed dough

dumpy \'dǝmpē\ *adj* **dump·i·er**; **-est** : short and thick in build

¹dun \'dǝn\ *adj* : brownish gray

²dun *vb* **-nn-** : hound for payment of a debt

dunce \'dǝns\ *n* : stupid person

dune \'d(y)ün\ *n* : hill of sand

dung \'dǝŋ\ *n* : manure

dun·ga·ree \,dǝŋgǝ'rē\ *n* **1** : blue denim **2** *pl* : work clothes made of dungaree

dun·geon \'dǝnjǝn\ *n* : underground prison

dunk \'dǝŋk\ *vb* : dip or submerge temporarily in liquid

duo \'d(y)ü(,)ō\ *n, pl* **du·os** : pair

du·o·de·num \,d(y)ü'dēnǝm, d(y)ü'ad³nǝm\ *n, pl* **-na** \-'dēnǝ, -³nǝ\ *or* **-nums** : part of the small intestine nearest the stomach —**du·o·de·nal** \-'dēn³l, -³nǝl\ *adj*

dupe \'d(y)üp\ *n* : one easily deceived or cheated —**dupe** *vb*

du·plex \'d(y)üpleks\ *adj* : double ~ *n* : 2-level apartment or 2-family house

du·pli·cate \'d(y)üplikǝt\ *adj* **1** : consisting of 2 identical items **2** : being just like another ~ *n* : exact copy ~ \-,kāt\ *vb* **-cat·ed**; **-cat·ing** **1** : make an exact copy of **2** : repeat or equal —**du·pli·ca·tion** \,d(y)üpli'kāshǝn\ *n* —**du·pli·ca·tor** \'d(y)üpli,kātǝr\ *n*

du·plic·i·ty \d(y)ü'plisǝtē\ *n, pl* **-ties** : deception

du·ra·ble \'d(y)ürǝbǝl\ *adj* : lasting a long time —**du·ra·bil·i·ty** \,d(y)ürǝ'bilǝtē\ *n*

du·ra·tion \d(y)ü'rāshǝn\ *n* : length of time something lasts

du·ress \'rés\ *n* : coercion

dur·ing \'d(y)üriŋ\ *prep* **1** : throughout **2** : at some point in

dusk \'dǝsk\ *n* : twilight —**dusky** *adj*

dust \'dǝst\ *n* : powdered matter ~ *vb* **1** : remove dust from **2** : sprinkle with fine particles —**dust·er** *n* —**dust·pan** *n* —**dusty** *adj*

du·ty \'d(y)ütē\ *n, pl* **-ties** **1** : action required by one's occupation or position **2** : moral or legal obligation **3** : tax —**du·te·ous** \-ǝs\ *adj* —**du·ti·able** \-ǝbǝl\ *adj* —**du·ti·ful** \'d(y)ütifǝl\ *adj*

dwarf \'dwórf\ *n, pl* **dwarfs** \'dwó(ǝ)rfs\ *or* **dwarves** \'dwórvz\ : one that is much below normal size ~ *vb* **1** : stunt **2** : cause to seem smaller —**dwarf·ish** *adj*

dwell \'dwel\ *vb* **dwelt** \'dwelt\ *or* **dwelled** \'dweld, 'dwelt\; **dwell·ing** **1** : reside **2** : keep the attention directed —**dwell·er** *n* —**dwell·ing** *n*

dwin·dle \'dwind³l\ *vb* **-dled**; **-dling** : become steadily less

dye \'dī\ *n* : coloring material ~ *vb* **dyed**; **dye·ing** : give a new color to

dying *pres part of* DIE

dyke *var of* DIKE

dy·nam·ic \dī'namik\ *adj* 1 : relating to physical force producing motion 2 : energetic or forceful

dy·na·mite \'dīnə₁mīt\ *n* : explosive made of nitroglycerin —**dynamite** *vb*

dy·na·mo \-₁mō\ *n, pl* -**mos** : electrical generator

dy·nas·ty \'dīnəstē, -₁nas-\ *n, pl* -**ties** : succession of rulers of the same family —**dy·nas·tic** \dī'nastik\ *adj*

dys·en·tery \'dis³n₁terē\ *n, pl* -**ter·ies** : disorder marked by diarrhea

dys·lex·ia \dis'leksēə\ *n* : disturbance of the ability to read —**dys·lex·ic** \-sik\ *adj*

dys·pep·sia \-'pepshə, -sēə\ *n* : indigestion —**dys·pep·tic** \-'peptik\ *adj or n*

dys·tro·phy \'distrəfē\ *n, pl* -**phies** : disorder involving nervous and muscular tissue

E

e \'ē\ *n, pl* **e's** *or* **es** \'ēz\ : 5th letter of the alphabet

each \'ēch\ *adj* : being one of the class named ~ *pron* : every individual one ~ *adv* : apiece

ea·ger \'ēgər\ *adj* : enthusiastic or anxious —**ea·ger·ly** *adv* —**ea·ger·ness** *n*

ea·gle \'ēgəl\ *n* : large bird of prey

-ean —see -AN

¹ear \'iər\ *n* : organ of hearing or the outer part of this —**ear·ache** *n* —**eared** *adj* —**ear·lobe** \-₁lōb\ *n*

²ear *n* : fruiting head of a cereal

ear·drum *n* : thin membrane that receives and transmits sound waves in the ear

earl \'ərl\ *n* : British nobleman —**earl·dom** \-dəm\ *n*

ear·ly \'ərlē\ *adj* -**li·er; -est** 1 : relating to or occurring near the beginning or before the usual time 2 : ancient —**early** *adv*

ear·mark *vb* : designate for a specific purpose

earn \'ərn\ *vb* 1 : receive as a return for service 2 : deserve

ear·nest \'ərnəst\ *n* : serious state of mind —**earnest** *adj* —**ear·nest·ly** *adv* —**ear·nest·ness** *n*

earn·ings \'ərniŋz\ *n pl* : something earned

ear·phone *n* : device that reproduces sound and is worn over or in the ear

ear·ring *n* : earlobe ornament

ear·shot *n* : range of hearing

earth \'ərth\ *n* 1 : soil or land 2 : planet inhabited by man —**earth·li·ness** *n* —**earth·ly** *adj* —**earth·ward** \-wərd\, **earth·wards** \-wərdz\ *adv*

earth·en \'ərthən\ *adj* : made of earth or baked clay —**earth·en·ware** \-₁waər\ *n*

earth·quake *n* : shaking or trembling of the earth

earth·worm *n* : long segmented worm

earthy \'ərthē\ *adj* **earth·i·er; -est** 1

: consisting of or resembling soil 2 : practical 3 : coarse —**earth·i·ness** *n*

ease \'ēz\ *n* 1 : comfort 2 : naturalness of manner 3 : freedom from difficulty ~ *vb* **eased; eas·ing** 1 : relieve from distress 2 : lessen the tension of 3 : make easier

ea·sel \'ēzəl\ *n* : frame to hold a painter's canvas upright

east \'ēst\ *adv* : to or toward the east ~ *adj* : situated toward or at or coming from the east ~ *n* 1 : direction of sunrise 2 *cap* : regions to the east —**east·er·ly** \'ēstərlē\ *adv or adj* —**east·ward** *adv or adj* —**east·wards** *adv*

Eas·ter \'ēstar\ *n* : church feast celebrating Christ's resurrection

east·ern \'ēstərn\ *adj* 1 *cap* : relating to a region designated East 2 : lying toward or coming from the east —**East·ern·er** *n*

easy \'ēzē\ *adj* **eas·i·er; -est** 1 : marked by ease 2 : lenient —**eas·i·ly** \'ēz(ə)lē\ *adv* —**eas·i·ness** \-zēnəs\ *n*

easy·go·ing *adj* : taking life easily

eat \'ēt\ *vb* **ate** \'āt\; **eat·en** \'ēt³n\; **eat·ing** 1 : take in as food 2 : use up or corrode —**eat·able** *adj or n* —**eat·er** *n*

eaves \'ēvz\ *n pl* : overhanging edge of a roof

eaves·drop *vb* : listen secretly —**eaves·drop·per** *n*

ebb \'eb\ *n* 1 : outward flow of the tide 2 : decline ~ *vb* 1 : recede from the flood state 2 : wane

eb·o·ny \'ebənē\ *n, pl* -**nies** : hard heavy wood of tropical trees ~ (**ebony trees**) ~ *adj* 1 : made of ebony 2 : black

ebul·lient \i'bulyənt, -'bəl-\ *adj* : exuberant —**ebul·lience** \-yəns\ *n*

ec·cen·tric \ik'sentrik\ *adj* 1 : odd in behavior 2 : being off center —**eccentric** *n* —**ec·cen·tri·cal·ly**

\-trik(ə)lē\ *adv* —**ec·cen·tric·i·ty** \ˌek₁senˈtrisətē\ *n*

ec·cle·si·as·tic \ik₁lēzēˈastik\ *n* : clergyman

ec·cle·si·as·ti·cal \-tikəl\ *adj* : relating to a church —**ecclesiastic** *adj*

ech·e·lon \ˈeshəˌlän\ *n* 1 : steplike arrangement 2 : level of authority

echo \ˈekō\ *n, pl* **ech·oes** : repetition of a sound caused by a reflection of the sound waves —**echo** *vb*

éclair \āˈklaar\ *n* : custard-filled pastry

eclec·tic \eˈklektik, i-\ *adj* : drawing or drawn from varied sources —**eclectic** *n*

eclipse \iˈklips\ *n* : total or partial obscuring of one celestial body by another —**eclipse** *vb*

ecol·o·gy \iˈkäləjē, e-\ *n, pl* **-gies** : science concerned with the interaction of organisms and their environment —**eco·log·i·cal** \ˌēkəˈläjikəl, ˌek-\ *adj* —**eco·log·i·cal·ly** *adv* —**ecol·o·gist** \iˈkäləjəst, e-\ *n*

eco·nom·ic \ˌekəˈnämik, ˌēkə-\ *adj* : relating to the satisfaction of man's material needs

eco·nom·ics \-ˈnämiks\ *n* : branch of knowledge dealing with goods and services —**econ·o·mist** \iˈkänəməst\ *n*

econ·o·mize \iˈkänəˌmīz\ *vb* **-mized; -miz·ing** : be thrifty

econ·o·my \-əmē\ *n, pl* **-mies** 1 : thrifty management of resources 2 : economic system —**eco·nom·i·cal** \ˌekəˈnämikəl, ˌēkə-\ *adj* —**eco·nom·i·cal·ly** *adv* —**economy** *adj*

ecru \ˈekrü, ˈākrü\ *n* : beige

ec·sta·sy \ˈekstəsē\ *n, pl* **-sies** : extreme emotional excitement —**ec·stat·ic** \ekˈstatik, ik-\ *adj* —**ec·stat·i·cal·ly** \-ik(ə)lē\ *adv*

ec·u·men·i·cal \ˌekyəˈmenikəl\ *adj* : promoting worldwide Christian unity

ec·ze·ma \igˈzēmə, ˈegzəmə, ˈeksə-\ *n* : itching skin inflammation

1-ed \d *after a vowel or* b, g, j, l, m, n, ŋ, r, th, v, z, zh; əd, id *after* d, t; t *after other sounds*\ *vb suffix or adj suffix* 1 —used to form the past participle of regular verbs 2 : having or having the characteristics of

2-ed *vb suffix* —used to form the past tense of regular verbs

ed·dy \ˈedē\ *n, pl* **-dies** : whirlpool —**eddy** *vb*

ede·ma \iˈdēmə\ *n* : dropsy —**edem·a·tous** \-ˈdemətəs\ *adj*

Eden \ˈēdᵊn\ *n* : paradise

edge \ˈej\ *n* 1 : cutting side of a blade 2 : line where something begins or ends ~ *vb* **edged; edg·ing** 1 : give or form an edge 2 : move gradually —**edg·er** *n*

edgy \ˈejē\ *adj* **edg·i·er; -est** : nervous —**edg·i·ness** *n*

ed·i·ble \ˈedəbəl\ *adj* : fit or safe to be eaten —**ed·i·bil·i·ty** \ˌedəˈbilətē\ *n* —**edible** *n*

edict \ˈēˌdikt\ *n* : decree

ed·i·fi·ca·tion \ˌedəfəˈkāshən\ *n* : instruction or information —**ed·i·fy** \ˈedəˌfī\ *vb*

ed·i·fice \ˈedəfəs\ *n* : large building

ed·it \ˈedət\ *vb* : revise and prepare for publication —**ed·i·tor** \-ər\ *n* —**ed·i·tor·ship** *n*

edi·tion \iˈdishən\ *n* 1 : form in which a text is published 2 : total number published at one time

ed·i·to·ri·al \ˌedəˈtōrēəl\ *adj* 1 : relating to an editor 2 : expressing opinion ~ *n* : article (as in a newspaper) expressing the views of an editor —**ed·i·to·ri·al·ize** \-ēəˌlīz\ *vb* —**ed·i·to·ri·al·ly** *adv*

ed·u·cate \ˈejəˌkāt\ *vb* **-cat·ed; -cat·ing** 1 : give instruction to 2 : develop mentally and morally —**ed·u·ca·ble** \ˈejəkəbəl\ *adj* —**ed·u·ca·tion** \ˌejəˈkāshən\ *n* —**ed·u·ca·tion·al** \-sh(ə)nəl\ *adj* —**ed·u·ca·tor** \-ər\ *n*

-ee *n suffix* 1 : recipient or beneficiary of 2 : person who performs

eel \ˈēl\ *n* : snakelike fish

-eer *n suffix* : one that is concerned with, conducts, or produces

ee·rie \ˈi(ə)rē\ *adj* **-ri·er; -est** : weird —**ee·ri·ly** \ˈi(ə)rəlē\ *adv*

ef·face \iˈfās, e-\ *vb* **-faced; -fac·ing** : obliterate by rubbing out —**ef·face·ment** *n*

ef·fect \iˈfekt\ *n* 1 : result 2 : meaning 3 : influence 4 *pl* : goods or possessions ~ *vb* : accomplish or produce —**in effect** : in substance

ef·fec·tive \iˈfektiv\ *adj* 1 : producing a strong or desired effect 2 : being in operation —**ef·fec·tive·ly** *adv* —**ef·fec·tive·ness** *n*

ef·fec·tu·al \iˈfekchə(wə)l\ *adj* : producing an intended effect —**ef·fec·tu·al·ly** *adv* —**ef·fec·tu·al·ness** *n*

ef·fem·i·nate \əˈfemənət\ *adj* : unsuitably womanish —**ef·fem·i·na·cy** \-nəsē\ *n*

ef·fer·vesce \ˌefərˈves\ *vb* **-vesced; -vesc·ing** 1 : bubble and hiss as gas escapes 2 : show exhilaration —**ef·fer·ves·cence** \-ˈvesᵊns\ *n* —**ef·fer-**

ves·cent \-ᵊnt\ adj — ef·fer·ves·cent·ly adv

ef·fete \e'fēt\ adj : decadent or worn out

ef·fi·ca·cious \₁efə'kāshəs\ adj : effective —ef·fi·ca·cy \'efikəsē\ n

ef·fi·cient \i'fishənt\ adj : working well with little waste —ef·fi·cien·cy \-ənsē\ n —ef·fi·cient·ly adv

ef·fi·gy \'efəjē\ n, pl -gies : image of a person

ef·fort \'efərt\ n 1 : a putting forth of strength 2 : use of resources toward a goal 3 : product of effort —ef·fort·less adj —ef·fort·less·ly adv

ef·fron·tery \i'frəntərē\ n, pl -ter·ies : insolence

ef·fu·sion \i'fyüzhən, e-\ n : a gushing forth —ef·fu·sive \-'fyüsiv\ adj —ef·fu·sive·ly adv

¹egg \'eg, 'āg\ vb : urge to action

²egg n 1 : rounded usu. hard-shelled reproductive body esp. of birds and reptiles from which the young hatches 2 : ovum —egg·shell n

egg·nog \-₁näg\ n : drink of eggs and cream

egg·plant n : edible purplish fruit of a plant related to the potato

ego \'ēgō\ n, pl egos : self-esteem

ego·cen·tric \₁ēgō'sentrik\ adj : self-centered

ego·tism \'ēgə₁tizəm\ n : exaggerated sense of self-importance —ego·tist \-təst\ n —ego·tis·tic \₁ēgə'tistik\, ego·tis·ti·cal \-tikəl\ adj —ego·tis·ti·cal·ly adv

egre·gious \i'grējəs\ adj : notably bad —egre·gious·ly adv

egress \'ē₁gres\ n : a way out

egret \'ēgrət, i'gret, 'ēgrət\ n : long-plumed heron

ei·der \'īdər\ n : northern sea duck that yields a soft down (eiderdown)

eight \'āt\ n 1 : one more than 7 2 : 8th in a set or series 3 : something having 8 units —eight adj or pron —eighth \'ātth\ adj or adv or n

eigh·teen \ā(t)'tēn\ n : one more than 17 —eigh·teen adj or pron —eigh·teenth \-'tēnth\ adj or n

eighty \'ātē\ n, pl eight·ies : 8 times 10 —eight·i·eth \'ātēəth\ adj or n —eighty adj or pron

ei·ther \'ēthər, 'ī-\ adj 1 : both 2 : being the one or the other of two ~ pron : one of two or more ~ conj : one or the other

ejac·u·late \i'jakyə₁lāt\ vb -lat·ed; -lat·ing 1 : say suddenly 2 : eject a fluid (as semen) —ejac·u·la·tion \-₁jakyə'lāshən\ n

eject \i'jekt\ vb : drive or throw out —ejec·tion \-'jekshən\ n

eke \'ēk\ vb eked; ek·ing : barely gain with effort —usu. with out

elab·o·rate \i'lab(ə)rət\ adj 1 : planned in detail 2 : complex and ornate ~ \-ə₁rāt\ vb -rat·ed; -rat·ing : work out in detail —elab·o·rate·ly adv —elab·o·rate·ness n —elab·o·ra·tion \-₁labə'rāshən\ n

elapse \i'laps\ vb elapsed; elaps·ing : slip by

elas·tic \i'lastik\ adj 1 : springy 2 : flexible ~ n 1 : elastic material 2 : rubber band —elas·tic·i·ty \-₁las'tisətē, ₁ē₁las-\ n

elate \i'lāt\ vb elat·ed; elat·ing : fill with joy —ela·tion \-'lāshən\ n

el·bow \'el₁bō\ n 1 : joint of the arm 2 : elbow-shaped bend or joint ~ vb : push aside with the elbow

el·der \'eldər\ adj : older ~ n 1 : one who is older 2 : church officer

el·der·ber·ry \'eldə(r)₁berē\ n : edible black or red fruit or a tree or shrub bearing these

el·der·ly \'eldərlē\ adj : past middle age

el·dest \'eldəst\ adj : oldest

elect \i'lekt\ adj : elected but not yet in office ~ n elect pl : exclusive group ~ vb : choose esp. by vote —elec·tion \i'lekshən\ n —elec·tive \i'lektiv\ n or adj —elec·tor \i'lektər\ n —elec·tor·al \-t(ə)rəl\ adj

elec·tor·ate \i'lekt(ə)rət\ n : body of persons entitled to vote

elec·tric \i'lektrik\ adj 1 : relating to or run by electricity 2 : thrilling —elec·tri·cal \-trikəl\ adj —elec·tri·cal·ly adv

elec·tri·cian \i₁lek'trishən\ n : one who installs or repairs electrical equipment

elec·tric·i·ty \i₁'tris(ə)tē\ n, pl -ties 1 : fundamental form of energy occurring naturally (as in lightning) or produced artificially 2 : electric current

elec·tri·fy \i'lektrə₁fī\ vb -fied; -fy·ing 1 : charge with electricity 2 : equip for use of electric power 3 : thrill —elec·tri·fi·ca·tion \-₁lektrəfə'kāshən\ n

elec·tro·car·dio·gram \i₁lektrō'kärdēə₁gram\ n : tracing made by an electrocardiograph

elec·tro·car·dio·graph \-₁graf\ n : instrument for recording the changes of electrical potential occurring during the heartbeat

elec·tro·cute \i'lektrə₁kyüt\ vb -cut·ed; -cut·ing : kill by an electric shock

—elec·tro·cu·tion \-ˌlektrəˈkyüshən\
n

elec·trode \iˈlekˌtrōd\ n : conductor at
a nonmetallic part of a circuit

elec·trol·y·sis \iˌlek'träləsəs\ n 1 : production of chemical changes by passage of an electric current through a
substance 2 : destruction of hair
roots with an electric current
—elec·tro·lyt·ic \-trə'litik\ adj

elec·tro·lyte \i'lektrəˌlīt\ n : nonmetallic electric conductor

elec·tro·mag·net \iˌlektrō'magnət\ n
: magnet created with electric current
—elec·tro·mag·net·ic \-ˌmag'netik\
adj   —elec·tro·mag·net·i·cal·ly
\-ik(ə)lē\ adv

elec·tron \i'lekˌträn\ n : negatively
charged particle within the atom

elec·tron·ic \iˌlek'tränik\ adj : relating
to electrons or electronics —elec·
tron·i·cal·ly \-ik(ə)lē\ adv

elec·tron·ics \-iks\ n : physics of electrons and their use

elec·tro·plate \i'lektrəˌplāt\ vb : coat
(as with metal) by electrolysis

el·e·gance \'eligəns\ n : refined grace-
fulness —el·e·gant \-gənt\ adj —el·
e·gant·ly adv

ele·gi·ac \ˌelə'jīak, -ˌak\ adj : expressing grief

el·e·gy \'eləjē\ n, pl -gies : poem expressing grief for one who is dead

el·e·ment \'eləmənt\ n 1 pl : weather
conditions 2 : natural environment 3
: constituent part 4 pl : simplest
principles 5 : substance not separable by ordinary chemical means —el·
e·men·tal \ˌelə'ment'l\ adj

el·e·men·ta·ry \ˌelə'ment(ə)rē\ adj 1
: simple 2 : relating to the basic subjects of education

el·e·phant \'eləfənt\ n : huge mammal
with a trunk and 2 ivory tusks

el·e·vate \'eləˌvāt\ vb -vat·ed; -vat·ing
1 : lift up 2 : exalt

el·e·va·tion \ˌelə'vāshən\ n : height or
a high place

el·e·va·tor \'eləˌvātər\ n 1 : cage or
platform for raising or lowering
something 2 : grain storehouse

elev·en \i'levən\ n 1 : one more than
10 2 : 11th in a set or series 3 : something having 11 units —eleven adj or
pron —elev·enth \-ənth\ adj or n

elf \'elf\ n, pl elves \'elvz\ : mischievous fairy —elf·in \'elfən\ adj —elf·
ish \'elfish\

elic·it \i'lisət\ vb : draw forth

el·i·gi·ble \'eləjəbəl\ adj : qualified to
participate or to be chosen —el·i·gi·
bil·i·ty \ˌeləjə'bilətē\ n —eligible n

elim·i·nate \i'limə,nāt\ vb -nat·ed;
-nat·ing : get rid of —elim·i·na·tion
\iˌlimə'nāshən\ n

elite \ā'lēt\ n : choice or select group

elix·ir \i'liksər\ n : medicinal solution

elk \'elk\ n : large deer

el·lipse \i'lips, e-\ n : oval —el·lip·tic
\-'liptik\, el·lip·ti·cal \-tikəl\ adj

el·lip·sis \-'lipsəs\ n, pl -lip·ses \-ˌsēz\
1 : omission of a word 2 : marks (as
. . .) to show omission —el·lip·ti·cal
\-tikəl\, el·lip·tic \-'liptik\ adj

elm \'elm\ n : tall shade tree

el·o·cu·tion \ˌelə'kyüshən\ n : art of
public speaking

elon·gate \i'lòn,gāt\ vb -gat·ed; -gat·
ing : make or grow longer —elon·ga·
tion \(ˌ)ē,lòn'gāshən\ n

elope \i'lōp\ vb eloped; elop·ing : run
away esp. to be married —elope·
ment \-mənt\ n

el·o·quent \'eləkwənt\ adj : forceful
and persuasive in speech —el·o·
quence \-kwəns\ n —el·o·quent·ly
adv

else \'els\ adv 1 : in a different way,
time, or place 2 : otherwise ~ adj 1
: other 2 : more

else·where adv : in or to another place

elu·ci·date \i'lüsə,dāt\ vb -dat·ed; -dat·
ing : explain —elu·ci·da·tion
\iˌlüsə'dāshən\ n

elude \ē'lüd\ vb elud·ed; elud·ing
: evade —elu·sive \-'lüsiv\ adj —elu·
sive·ly adv —elu·sive·ness n

elves pl of ELF

ema·ci·ate \i'māshē,āt\ vb -at·ed; -at·
ing : become or make very thin
—ema·ci·a·tion \iˌmāsh)ē'āshən\ n

em·a·nate \'emə,nāt\ vb -nat·ed; -nat·
ing : come forth —em·a·na·tion
\ˌemə'nāshən\ n

eman·ci·pate \i'mansə,pāt\ vb -pat·ed;
-pat·ing : set free —eman·ci·pa·tion
\iˌmansə'pāshən\ n —eman·ci·pa·
tor \i'mansə,pātər\ n

emas·cu·late \i'maskyə,lāt\ vb -lat·ed;
-lat·ing 1 : castrate 2 : weaken
—emas·cu·la·tion \iˌmaskyə'lāshən\ n

em·balm \im'bäm, -'bälm\ vb : preserve (a corpse) —em·balm·er n

em·bank·ment \im'baŋkmənt\ n : protective barrier of earth

em·bar·go \im'bärgō\ n, pl -goes : ban
on trade —embargo vb

em·bark \-'bärk\ vb 1 : go on board a
ship or airplane 2 : make a start
—em·bar·ka·tion \ˌem,bär'kāshən\
n

em·bar·rass \im'barəs\ vb : cause distress and self-consciousness —em·bar·rass·ment n

em·bas·sy \'embəsē\ n, pl -sies : residence and offices of an ambassador

em·bed \im'bed\ vb -dd- : fix firmly

em·bel·lish \-'belish\ vb : decorate —em·bel·lish·ment n

em·ber \'embər\ n : smoldering fragment from a fire

em·bez·zle \im'bezəl\ vb -zled; -zling : steal (money) by falsifying records —em·bez·zle·ment n —em·bez·zler \-(ə)lər\ n

em·bit·ter \im'bitər\ vb : make bitter

em·bla·zon \-'blāzⁿn\ vb : display conspicuously

em·blem \'embləm\ n : symbol —em·blem·at·ic \,emblə'matik\ adj

em·body \im'bädē\ vb -bod·ied; -body·ing : give definite form or expression to —em·bodi·ment \-'bädimənt\ n

em·boss \-'bäs, -'bòs\ vb : ornament with raised work

em·brace \-'brās\ vb -braced; -brac·ing 1 : clasp in the arms 2 : welcome 3 : include —embrace n

em·broi·der \-'bròidər\ vb : ornament with or do needlework —em·broi·dery \-(ə)rē\ n

em·broil \im'bròil\ vb : involve in conflict or difficulties

em·bryo \'embrē,ō\ n : living being in its earliest stages of development —em·bry·on·ic \,embrē'änik\ adj

emend \ē'mend\ vb : correct —emen·da·tion \,ē,men'dāshən\ n

em·er·ald \'em(ə)rəld\ n : green gem ~ adj : bright green

emerge \i'mərj\ vb emerged; emerg·ing : rise, come forth, or appear —emer·gence \-'mərjəns\ n —emer·gent \-jənt\ adj

emer·gen·cy \i'mərjənsē\ n, pl -cies : condition requiring prompt action

em·ery \'em(ə)rē\ n, pl -er·ies : dark granular mineral used for grinding

emet·ic \i'metik\ n : agent that induces vomiting —emetic adj

em·i·grate \'emə,grāt\ vb -grat·ed; -grat·ing : leave a country to settle elsewhere —em·i·grant \'igrənt\ n —em·i·gra·tion \,emə'grāshən\ n

em·i·nence \'emənəns\ n 1 : prominence or superiority 2 : person of high rank

em·i·nent \-nənt\ adj : prominent —em·i·nent·ly adv

em·is·sary \'emə,serē\ n, pl -sar·ies : agent

emit \ē'mit\ vb -tt- : give off or out —emis·sion \-'mishən\ n

emol·u·ment \i'mälyəmənt\ n : salary or fee

emote \i'mōt\ vb emot·ed; emot·ing : express emotion

emo·tion \i'mōshən\ n : intense feeling —emo·tion·al \-sh(ə)nəl\ adj —emo·tion·al·ly adv

em·per·or \'empərər\ n : ruler of an empire

em·pha·sis \'emfəsəs\ n, pl -pha·ses \-,sēz\ : stress

em·pha·size \-,sīz\ vb -sized; -siz·ing : stress

em·phat·ic \im'fatik, em-\ adj : uttered with emphasis —em·phat·i·cal·ly \-'fatik(ə)lē\ adv

em·pire \'em,pī(ə)r\ n : large state or a group of states

em·pir·i·cal \im'pirikəl\ adj : based on observation —em·pir·i·cal·ly \ik(ə)lē\ adv

em·ploy \im'plòi\ vb 1 : use 2 : occupy ~ n : paid occupation —em·ploy·ee, em·ploye \im,plò(i),ē, -'plò(i),ē\ n —em·ploy·er n —em·ploy·ment \-mənt\ n

em·pow·er \im'paů(ə)r\ vb : authorize

em·press \'emprəs\ n 1 : wife of an emperor 2 : woman holding an imperial title

emp·ty \'emptē\ adj 1 : containing nothing 2 : not occupied 3 : lacking value, sense, or purpose ~ vb -tied; -ty·ing : make or become empty —emp·ti·ness \-tēnəs\ n

emu \'ēmyü\ n : Australian bird related to the ostrich

em·u·late \'emyə,lāt\ vb -lat·ed; -lat·ing : try to equal or excel —em·u·la·tion \,emyə'lāshən\ n

emul·si·fy \i'məlsə,fī\ vb -fied; -fy·ing : convert into an emulsion —emul·si·fi·ca·tion \i,məlsəfə'kāshən\ n —emul·si·fi·er \-,fī(ə)r\ n

emul·sion \i'məlshən\ n : mixture of mutually insoluble liquids —emul·sive \-'məlsiv\ adj

-en \ən, ᵊn\ vb suffix 1 : become or cause to be 2 : cause or come to have

en·able \in'ābəl\ vb -abled; -abling : give power, capacity, or ability

en·act \in'akt\ vb 1 : make into law 2 : act out —en·act·ment n

enam·el \in'aməl\ n 1 : glasslike substance used for coating metal or pottery 2 : hard outer layer of a tooth 3 : glossy paint —enamel vb

en·am·or \in'amər\ vb : inflame with love

en·camp \in'kamp\ vb : make camp —en·camp·ment n

en·case \in'kās\ *vb* : enclose in or as if in a case

-ence \əns, °ns\ *n suffix* 1 : action or process 2 : quality or state

en·ceph·a·li·tis \in₁sefə'lītəs\ *n, pl* **-lit·i·des** \-'litə₁dēz\ : inflammation of the brain

en·chant \in'chant\ *vb* 1 : bewitch 2 : fascinate —**en·chant·er** *n* —**en·chant·ment** *n* —**en·chant·ress** \-'chantrəs\ *n*

en·cir·cle \in'sərkəl\ *vb* : surround

en·close \in'klōz\ *vb* 1 : shut up or surround 2 : include —**en·clo·sure** \in'klōzhər\ *n*

en·co·mi·um \en'kōmēəm\ *n, pl* **-mi·ums** *or* **-mia** \-mēə\ : high praise

en·com·pass \in'kəmpəs, -'käm-\ *vb* : surround or include

en·core \'än₁kōr\ *n* : further performance

en·coun·ter \in'kaüntər\ *vb* 1 : fight 2 : meet unexpectedly —**encounter** *n*

en·cour·age \in'kərij\ *vb* **-aged; -ag·ing** 1 : inspire with courage and hope 2 : foster —**en·cour·age·ment** *n*

en·croach \in'krōch\ *vb* : enter upon another's property or rights —**en·croach·ment** *n*

en·crust \in'krəst\ *vb* : form a crust on

en·cum·ber \in'kəmbər\ *vb* : burden —**en·cum·brance** \-brəns\ *n*

-en·cy \ənsē, °n-\ *n suffix* : -ence

en·cyc·li·cal \in'siklikəl, -'sī-\ *n* : papal letter to bishops

en·cy·clo·pe·dia \in₁sīklə'pēdēə\ *n* : reference work on many subjects —**en·cy·clo·pe·dic** \-'pēdik\ *adj*

end \'end\ *n* 1 : point at which something stops or no longer exists 2 : cessation 3 : purpose — *vb* 1 : stop or finish 2 : be at the end of —**end·ed** *adj* —**end·less** *adj* —**end·less·ly** *adv*

en·dan·ger \in'dānjər\ *vb* : bring into danger

en·dear \in'diər\ *vb* : make dear —**en·dear·ment** \-mənt\ *n*

en·deav·or \in'devər\ *vb or n* : attempt

end·ing \'endiŋ\ *n* : end

en·dive \'en₁dīv\ *n* : salad plant

en·do·crine \'endəkrən, -₁krīn, -₁krēn\ *adj* : producing secretions distributed by the bloodstream —**endocrine** *n*

en·dorse \in'dòrs\ *vb* **-dorsed; -dors·ing** 1 : sign one's name to 2 : approve —**en·dorse·ment** *n*

en·dow \in'daü\ *vb* 1 : furnish with funds 2 : furnish naturally —**en·dow·ment** *n*

en·dure \in'd(y)ùr\ *vb* **-dured; -dur·ing** 1 : last 2 : suffer patiently : tolerate —**en·dur·able** *adj* —**en·dur·ance** \-əns\ *n*

en·e·ma \'enəmə\ *n* : injection of liquid into the rectum

en·e·my \'enə₁mē\ *n, pl* **-mies** : one that attacks or tries to harm another

en·er·get·ic \₁enər'jetik\ *adj* : full of energy or activity —**en·er·get·i·cal·ly** \-ik(ə)lē\ *adv*

en·er·gize \'enər₁jīz\ *vb* **-gized; -giz·ing** : give energy to

en·er·gy \'enərjē\ *n, pl* **-gies** 1 : capacity for action 2 : vigorous action 3 : capacity for doing work

en·er·vate \'enər₁vāt\ *vb* **-vat·ed; -vat·ing** : make weak or listless —**en·er·va·tion** \₁enər'vāshən\ *n*

en·fold \in'fōld\ *vb* : surround or embrace

en·force \-'fōrs\ *vb* 1 : compel 2 : carry out —**en·force·able** \-əbəl\ *adj* —**en·force·ment** *n*

en·fran·chise \-'fran₁chīz\ *vb* **-chised; -chis·ing** : grant voting rights to —**en·fran·chise·ment** \-₁chīzmənt, -chəz-\ *n*

en·gage \in'gāj\ *vb* **-gaged; -gag·ing** 1 : participate or cause to participate 2 : bring or come into working contact 3 : bind by a pledge to marry 4 : hire 5 : bring or enter into conflict —**en·gage·ment** \-mənt\ *n*

en·gag·ing *adj* : attractive

en·gen·der \in'jendər\ *vb* **-dered; -der·ing** : create

en·gine \'enjən\ *n* 1 : machine that converts energy into mechanical motion 2 : locomotive

en·gi·neer \₁enjə'niər\ *n* 1 : one trained in engineering 2 : engine operator — *vb* : lay out or manage as an engineer

en·gi·neer·ing \-iŋ\ *n* : practical application of science and mathematics

en·grave \in'grāv\ *vb* **-graved; -grav·ing** : cut into a surface —**en·grav·er** *n* —**en·grav·ing** *n*

en·gross \-'grōs\ *vb* : occupy fully

en·gulf \-'gəlf\ *vb* : swallow up

en·hance \-'hans\ *vb* **-hanced; -hanc·ing** : improve in value —**en·hance·ment** *n*

enig·ma \i'nigmə\ *n* : puzzle or mystery —**enig·mat·ic** \₁enig'matik, ₁ē-\ *adj*

en·join \in'jòin\ *vb* 1 : command 2 : forbid

en·joy \-'jòi\ *vb* : take pleasure in —**en·joy·able** *adj* —**en·joy·ment** *n*

en·large \-'lärj\ *vb* **-larged; -larg·ing** : make or grow larger —**en·large·ment** *n* —**en·larg·er** *n* en·light·en \-'līt⁾n\ vb : give knowledge or spiritual insight to —en·light·en·ment n

en·list \-'list\ vb 1 : join the armed forces 2 : get the aid of —en·list·ee \-ˌlis'tē\ n —en·list·ment \-'lis(t)mənt\ n

en·liv·en \in-'līvən\ vb : give life or spirit to

en·mi·ty \'enmətē\ n, pl -ties : mutual hatred

en·no·ble \-'nōbəl\ vb -bled; -bling : make noble

en·nui \'än'wē\ n : boredom

enor·mi·ty \i'nórmətē\ n, pl -ties 1 : great wickedness 2 : huge size

enor·mous \i'nórməs\ adj : great in size, number, or degree —enor·mous·ly adv —enor·mous·ness n

enough \i'nəf, ⁹nəf\ adj : adequate ~ adv 1 : in an adequate manner 2 : in a tolerable degree ~ pron : adequate number, quantity, or amount

en·quire \in'kwī(ə)r\, en·qui·ry \'inˌkwī(ə)rē, in¹-; 'inkwərē, 'iŋ-\ var of inquire, inquiry

en·rage \in'rāj\ vb : fill with rage

en·rich \-'rich\ vb : make rich —en·rich·ment n

en·roll, en·rol \-'rōl\ vb -rolled; -rolling 1 : enter on a list 2 : become enrolled —en·roll·ment n

en route \än'rüt, en-, in-\ adv or adj : on or along the way

en·sconce \in'skäns\ vb -sconced; -sconc·ing : settle snugly

en·sem·ble \än'sämbəl\ n 1 : small group 2 : complete costume

en·shrine \in'shrīn\ vb 1 : put in a shrine 2 : cherish

en·sign \'ensən, 1 also 'enˌsīn\ n 1 : flag 2 : commissioned officer in the navy ranking next below a lieutenant junior grade

en·slave \in'slāv\ vb : make a slave of —en·slave·ment n

en·snare \-'snaər\ vb : snare

en·sue \-'sü\ vb -sued; -su·ing : follow as a consequence

en·sure \-'shúr\ vb -sured; -sur·ing : guarantee

en·tail \-'tāl\ vb : involve a necessary result

en·tan·gle \-'taŋgəl\ vb : tangle —en·tan·gle·ment n

en·ter \'entər\ vb 1 : go or come in or into 2 : start 3 : set down (as in a list)

en·ter·prise \'entərˌprīz\ n 1 : an undertaking 2 : business organization 3 : initiative

en·ter·pris·ing \-ˌprīziŋ\ adj : showing initiative

en·ter·tain \ˌentər'tān\ vb 1 : treat or receive as a guest 2 : hold in mind 3 : amuse —en·ter·tain·er n —en·ter·tain·ment n

en·thrall, en·thral \in'thról\ vb -thralled; -thrall·ing : hold spellbound

en·thu·si·asm \-'th(y)üzēˌazəm\ n : strong excitement of feeling or its cause —en·thu·si·ast \-ˌast, -əst, -əst\ n —en·thu·si·as·tic \-ˌth(y)üzē'astik\ adj —en·thu·si·as·ti·cal·ly \-tik(ə)lē\ adv

en·tice \-'tīs\ vb -ticed; -tic·ing : tempt —en·tice·ment n

en·tire \-'tī(ə)r\ adj : complete or whole —en·tire·ly adv —en·tire·ty \-'tīrətē, -'tī(ə)rtē\ n

en·ti·tle \-'tīt⁾l\ vb -tled; -tling 1 : name 2 : give a right to

en·ti·ty \'entətē\ n, pl -ties : something with separate existence

en·to·mol·o·gy \ˌentə'mäləjē\ n : study of insects —en·to·mo·log·i·cal \-mə'läjikəl\ adj —en·to·mol·o·gist \-'mäləjəst\ n

en·trails \'entrəlz, -ˌtrālz\ n pl : intestines

1en·trance \'entrəns\ n 1 : act of entering 2 : means or place of entering —en·trant \'entrənt\ n

2en·trance \in'trans\ vb -tranced; -tranc·ing : fascinate or delight

en·trap \in'trap\ vb : trap —en·trap·ment n

en·treat \-'trēt\ vb : ask earnestly —en·treaty \-'trētē\ n

en·trée, en·tree \'änˌtrā\ n : principal dish of the meal

en·trench \in'trench\ vb : establish in a strong position —en·trench·ment n

en·tre·pre·neur \ˌäntrəprə'nər\ n : organizer or promoter of an enterprise

en·trust \in'trəst\ vb : commit to another with confidence

en·try \'entrē\ n, pl -tries 1 : entrance 2 : an entering in a record or an item so entered

en·twine \in'twīn\ vb : twine together or around

enu·mer·ate \i'n(y)üməˌrāt\ vb -at·ed; -at·ing 1 : count 2 : list —enu·mer·a·tion \iˌn(y)ümə'rāshən\ n

enun·ci·ate \ē'nənsēˌāt\ vb -at·ed; -at·ing 1 : announce 2 : pronounce —enun·ci·a·tion \-ˌnənsē'āshən\ n

en·vel·op \in'veləp\ vb : surround —en·vel·op·ment n

en·ve·lope \'envəˌlōp, 'än-\ n : paper container for a letter

en·vi·ron·ment \in'vīrənmənt\ n : surroundings —en·vi·ron·men·tal \-,vīrən'mentᵊl\ adj

en·vi·ron·men·tal·ist \-ᵊləst\ n : one concerned about the human environment

en·vi·rons \in'vīrənz\ n pl : vicinity

en·vis·age \in'vizij\ vb -aged; -ag·ing : have a mental picture of

en·voy \'en,vȯi, 'än-\ n : diplomat

en·vy \'envē\ n 1 : resentful awareness of another's advantage 2 : object of envy ~ vb -vied; -vy·ing : feel envy toward or on account of —en·vi·able \-vēabəl\ adj —en·vi·ous \-vēəs\ adj

en·zyme \'en,zīm\ n : complex mostly protein product of living cells

eon \'ēən, ē,än\ var of AEON

ep·au·let \,epə'let\ n : shoulder ornament on a uniform

ephem·er·al \i'fem(ə)rəl\ adj : shortlived

ep·ic \'epik\ n : long poem about a hero —epic adj

ep·i·cure \'epi,kyu̇r\ n : person with fastidious taste esp. in food and wine —ep·i·cu·re·an \,epikyu̇'rēən, -'kyu̇rē-\ n or adj

ep·i·dem·ic \,epə'demik\ adj : affecting many persons at one time —epidemic n

epi·der·mis \,epə'dərməs\ n : outer layer of skin

ep·i·gram \'epə,gram\ n : short witty poem or saying —ep·i·gram·mat·ic \,epəgrə'matik\ adj

ep·i·lep·sy \'epə,lepsē\ n, pl -sies : nervous disorder marked by convulsive attacks —ep·i·lep·tic \,epə'leptik\ adj or n

epis·co·pal \i'piskəpəl\ adj : governed by bishops

ep·i·sode \'epə,sōd, -,zōd\ n : occurrence —ep·i·sod·ic \,epə'sädik, -'zäd-\ adj

epis·tle \i'pisəl\ n : letter

ep·i·taph \'epə,taf\ n : inscription in memory of a dead person

ep·i·thet \'epə,thet, -thət\ n : characterizing often abusive word or phrase

epit·o·me \i'pitəmē\ n 1 : summary 2 : ideal example —epit·o·mize \-,mīz\ vb

ep·och \'epək, 'ep,äk\ n : extended period —ep·och·al \'epəkəl, 'ep,äkəl\ adj

ep·oxy \'ep,äksē, ep'äksē\ n : synthetic resin used esp. in adhesives ~ vb -ox·ied or -oxyed; -oxy·ing : glue with epoxy

equa·ble \'ekwəbəl, 'ēkwə-\ adj : free from unpleasant extremes —equa-

bil·i·ty \,ekwə'bilətē, ,ē-\ n —equa·bly \-blē\ adv

equal \'ēkwəl\ adj : of the same quantity, value, quality, number, or status as another ~ n : one that is equal to ~ vb equaled or equalled; equal·ing or equal·ling : be or become equal to —equal·i·ty \i'kwälətē\ n —equal·ize \'ēkwə,līz\ vb —equal·ly \'ēkwəlē\ adv

equa·nim·i·ty \,ēkwə'nimətē, ek-\ n, pl -ties : calmness

equate \i'kwāt\ vb equat·ed; equat·ing : treat or regard as equal

equa·tion \i'kwāzhən, -shən\ n : mathematical statement that two things are equal.

equa·tor \i'kwātər\ n : imaginary circle that separates the northern and southern hemispheres —equa·to·ri·al \,ēkwə'tōrēəl, ,ek-\ adj

eques·tri·an \i'kwestrēən\ adj : relating to horses or horsemanship ~ n : horseback rider

equi·lat·er·al \,ēkwə'lat(ə)rəl\ adj : having equal sides

equi·lib·ri·um \,ēkwə'librēəm\ n, pl -ri·ums or -ria \-rēə\ : state of balance

equine \'ē,kwīn, 'ek,wīn\ adj : relating to the horse —equine n

equi·nox \'ēkwə,näks, 'ek-\ n : time when day and night are everywhere of equal length

equip \i'kwip\ vb -pp- : furnish with needed resources —equip·ment \-mənt\ n

equi·ta·ble \'ekwətəbəl\ adj : fair

eq·ui·ty \'ekwətē\ n, pl -ties 1 : justice 2 : value of a property less debt

equiv·a·lent \i'kwiv(ə)lənt\ adj : equal —equiv·a·lence \-ləns\ n —equivalent n

equiv·o·cal \i'kwivəkəl\ adj : ambiguous or uncertain

equiv·o·cate \i'kwivə,kāt\ vb -cat·ed; -cat·ing : use misleading language —equiv·o·ca·tion \-,kwivə'kāshən\ n

1-er \ər\ adj suffix or adv suffix —used to form the comparative degree of adjectives and adverbs esp. those of one or two syllables

2-er \ər\, -ier \ēər, yər\, -yer \yər\ n suffix 1 : one that is associated with 2 : one that performs or is the object of an action 3 : one that is

era \'irə, 'erə, 'ērə\ n : period of time associated with something

erad·i·cate \i'radə,kāt\ vb -cat·ed; -cating : do away with —erad·i·ca·ble \-əkəbəl\ adj

erase \i'rās\ *vb* **erased; eras·ing** : rub or scratch out **—eras·er** *n* **—era·sure** \i'rāshər\ *n*

ere \(ₗ)eər\ *prep or conj* : before

erect \i'rekt\ *adj* : not leaning or lying down **~** *vb* **1** : build **2** : bring to an upright position **—erec·tion** \i'rekshən\ *n*

er·mine \'ərmən\ *n* : weasel with white winter fur or its fur

erode \i'rōd\ *vb* **erod·ed; erod·ing** : wear away gradually

ero·sion \i'rōzhən\ *n* : process of eroding

erot·ic \i'rätik\ *adj* : sexually arousing **—erot·i·cal·ly** \-ik(ə)lē\ *adv*

err \'eər, 'ər\ *vb* : be or do wrong

er·rand \'erənd\ *n* : short trip taken to do something often for another

er·rant \-ənt\ *adj* **1** : traveling about **2** : going astray

er·rat·ic \ir'atik\ *adj* : irregular or eccentric **—er·rat·i·cal·ly** \-ik(ə)lē\ *adv*

er·ro·ne·ous \ir'ōnēəs, e'rō-\ *adj* : wrong **—er·ro·ne·ous·ly** *adv*

er·ror \'erər\ *n* **1** : something that is not accurate **2** : state of being wrong

er·satz \'er,zäts\ *adj* : synthetic or phony

erst·while \'ərst,hwīl\ *adv* : in the past **~** *adj* : former

er·u·di·tion \,er(y)ə'dishən\ *n* : great learning **—er·u·dite** \'er(y)ə,dīt\ *adj*

erupt \i'rəpt\ *vb* : burst forth esp. suddenly and violently **—erup·tion** \i'rəpshən\ *n* **—erup·tive** \-tiv\ *adj*

-ery \(ə)rē\ *n suffix* **1** : character or condition **2** : practice **3** : place of doing

¹-es \əz, iz *after* s, z, sh, ch; z *after* v *or a vowel*\ *n pl suffix* —used to form the plural of some nouns

²-es *vb suffix* —used to form the 3d person singular present of some verbs

es·ca·late \'eskə,lāt\ *vb* **-lat·ed; -lat·ing** : become quickly larger or greater **—es·ca·la·tion** \,eskə'lāshən\ *n*

es·ca·la·tor \'eskə,lātər\ *n* : moving stairs

es·ca·pade \'eskə,pād\ *n* : mischievous adventure

es·cape \is'kāp\ *vb* **-caped; -cap·ing** : get away or get away from **~** *n* **1** : flight from or avoidance of something unpleasant **2** : leakage **3** : means of escape **~** *adj* : providing means of escape **—es·cap·ee** \is,kā'pē, ,es(ₗ)kā-\ *n*

es·ca·role \'eskə,rōl\ *n* : salad green

es·carp·ment \is'kärpmənt\ *n* : cliff

es·chew \is'chü\ *vb* : shun

es·cort \'es,kȯrt\ *n* : one accompanying another **—es·cort** \is'kȯrt, es-\ *vb*

es·crow \'es,krō\ *n* : deposit to be delivered upon fulfillment of a condition

esoph·a·gus \i'säfəgəs\ *n, pl* **-gi** \-ₗgī, -ₗjī\ : muscular tube connecting the mouth and stomach

es·o·ter·ic \,esə'terik\ *adj* : mysterious or secret

es·pe·cial·ly \is'pesh(ə)lē\ *adv* : particularly or notably

es·pi·o·nage \'espēə,näzh, -nij\ *n* : practice of spying

es·pous·al \is'pauzəl\ *n* **1** : betrothal **2** : wedding **3** : a taking up as a supporter **—es·pouse** \-'pauz\ *vb*

espres·so \e'spresō\ *n, pl* **-sos** : strong steam-brewed coffee

es·py \is'pī\ *vb* **-pied; -py·ing** : catch sight of

es·quire \'es,kwī(ə)r\ *n* —used as a title of courtesy

-ess \əs, ,es\ *n suffix* : female

es·say \'es,ā\ *n* **1** : literary composition **~** *vb* \e'sā, 'es,ā\ : attempt **—es·say·ist** \'es,āəst\ *n*

es·sence \'es²ns\ *n* **1** : fundamental nature or quality **2** : extract **3** : perfume

es·sen·tial \i'senchəl\ *adj* : basic or necessary **—essential** *n* **—es·sen·tial·ly** *adv*

-est \əst, ist\ *adj or adv suffix* —used to form the superlative degree of adjectives and adverbs esp. those of 1 or 2 syllables

es·tab·lish \is'tablish\ *vb* **1** : bring into existence **2** : put on a firm basis **3** : cause to be recognized

es·tab·lish·ment \-mənt\ *n* **1** : business or a place of business **2** : an establishing or being established **3** : controlling group

es·tate \is'tāt\ *n* **1** : one's possessions **2** : large piece of land with a house

es·teem \is'tēm\ *n or vb* : regard

es·ter \'estər\ *n* : organic chemical compound

esthetic *var of* AESTHETIC

es·ti·ma·ble \'estəməbəl\ *adj* : worthy of esteem

es·ti·mate \'estə,māt\ *vb* **-mat·ed; -mat·ing** : judge the approximate value, size, or cost **~** \-mət\ *n* **1** : rough or approximate calculation **2** : statement of the cost of a job **—es·ti·ma·tion** \,estə'māshən\ *n* **—es·ti·ma·tor** \'estə,mātər\ *n*

es·trange \is'trānj\ *vb* **-tranged; -trang·ing** : make hostile **—es·trange·ment** *n*

es·tro·gen \'estrəjən\ *n* : hormone that produces female characteristics

es·tu·ary \'escha,werē\ *n, pl* **-ar·ies** : arm of the sea at a river's mouth

et cet·era \et'setərə, -'setrə\ *n* : and others esp. of the same kind

etch \'ech\ *vb* 1 : make lines on with acid 2 : produce by etching —**etch·er** *n* —**etch·ing** *n*

eter·nal \i'tərnᵊl\ *adj* : lasting forever —**eter·nal·ly** *adv*

eter·ni·ty \-nətē\ *n, pl* **-ties** : infinite duration

eth·ane \'eth,ān\ *n* : gaseous hydrocarbon

eth·a·nol \'etha,nȯl, -,nōl\ *n* : alcohol

ether \'ēthər\ *n* : light flammable liquid used as an anesthetic

ethe·re·al \i'thirēəl\ *adj* 1 : celestial 2 : exceptionally delicate

eth·i·cal \'ethikəl\ *adj* 1 : relating to ethics 2 : honorable —**eth·i·cal·ly** *adv*

eth·ics \-iks\ *n sing or pl* 1 : study of good and evil and moral duty 2 : moral principles or practice

eth·nic \'ethnik\ *adj* : relating to races or groups of people with common customs ~ *n* : member of a minority ethnic group

eth·nol·o·gy \eth'näləjē\ *n* : study of the races of mankind —**eth·no·log·ic** \,ethnə'läjik\, **eth·no·log·i·cal** \-ikəl\ *adj* —**eth·nol·o·gist** \eth'näləjəst\ *n*

eth·yl \'ethəl\ *n* : hydrocarbon radical

et·i·quette \'etikət, -,ket\ *n* : good manners

et·y·mol·o·gy \,etə'mäləjē\ *n, pl* **-gies** : history of a word 2 : study of etymologies —**et·y·mo·log·i·cal** \-mə'läjikəl\ *adj* —**et·y·mol·o·gist** \-'mäləjəst\ *n*

eu·ca·lyp·tus \,yükə'liptəs\ *n, pl* **-ti** \-,tī\ *or* **-tus·es** : Australian evergreen tree

Eu·cha·rist \'yükə)rəst\ *n* : Communion —**eu·cha·ris·tic** \,yükə'ristik\ *adj*

eu·lo·gy \'yüləjē\ *n, pl* **-gies** : speech in praise —**eu·lo·gis·tic** \,yülə'jistik\ *adj* —**eu·lo·gize** \'yülə,jīz\ *vb*

eu·nuch \'yünək\ *n* : castrated man

eu·phe·mism \'yüfə,mizəm\ *n* : substitution of a pleasant expression for an unpleasant or offensive one —**eu·phe·mis·tic** \,yüfə'mistik\ *adj*

eu·pho·ni·ous \yü'fōnēəs\ *adj* : pleasing to the ear —**eu·pho·ny** \'yüfənē\ *n*

eu·pho·ria \yü'fōrēə\ *n* : elation —**eu·phor·ic** \-'fȯrik\ *adj*

eu·tha·na·sia \,yütha'nāzh(ē)ə\ *n* : mercy killing

evac·u·ate \i'vakyə,wāt\ *vb* **-at·ed; -at·ing** 1 : discharge wastes from the body 2 : remove or withdraw from —**evac·u·a·tion** \i,vakyə'wāshən\ *n*

evade \i'vād\ *vb* **evad·ed; evad·ing** : manage to avoid

eval·u·ate \i'valyə,wāt\ *vb* **-at·ed; -at·ing** : appraise —**eval·u·a·tion** \i,valyə'wāshən\ *n*

evan·gel·i·cal \,ē,van'jelikəl, ,evən-\ *adj* : relating to the Christian gospel

evan·ge·lism \i'vanjə,lizəm\ *n* : the winning or revival of personal commitments to Christ —**evan·ge·list** \i'vanjələst\ *n* —**evan·ge·lis·tic** \i,vanjə'listik\ *adj*

evap·o·rate \i'vapə,rāt\ *vb* **-rat·ed; -rat·ing** 1 : pass off in or convert into vapor 2 : disappear quickly —**evap·o·ra·tion** \i,vapə'rāshən\ *n* —**evap·o·ra·tive** \i'vapə,rātiv\ *adj* —**evap·o·ra·tor** \-,rātər\ *n*

eva·sion \i'vāzhən\ *n* : act or instance of evading —**eva·sive** \i'vāsiv\ *adj* —**eva·sive·ness** *n*

eve \'ēv\ *n* : evening

even \'ēvən\ *adj* 1 : smooth 2 : equal or fair 3 : fully revenged 4 : divisible by 2 ~ *adv* 1 : already 2 —used for emphasis ~ *vb* : make or become even —**even·ly** *adv* —**even·ness** *n*

eve·ning \'ēvniŋ\ *n* : early part of the night

event \i'vent\ *n* 1 : occurrence 2 : noteworthy happening 3 : eventuality —**event·ful** *adj*

even·tu·al \i'vench(əw)əl\ *adj* : later —**even·tu·al·ly** *adv*

even·tu·al·i·ty \i,vencha'walətē\ *n, pl* **-ties** : possible occurrence or outcome

ev·er \'evər\ *adv* 1 : always 2 : at any time 3 : in any case

ev·er·green *adj* : having foliage that remains green —**evergreen** *n*

ev·er·last·ing \,evər'lastiŋ\ *adj* : lasting forever

ev·ery \'evrē\ *adj* 1 : being each one of a group 2 : all possible

ev·ery·body \'evri,bädē, -bəd-\ *pron* : every person

ev·ery·day *adj* : ordinary

ev·ery·one \-(,)wən\ *pron* : every person

ev·ery·thing *pron* : all that exists

ev·ery·where *adv* : in every place or part

evict \i'vikt\ *vb* : force (a person) to move from a property —**evic·tion** \i'vikshən\ *n* ev·i·dence \'evədəns\ n 1 : outward sign 2 : proof or testimony

ev·i·dent \-ənt\ adj : clear or obvious —ev·i·dent·ly \-ədəntlē, -ə,dent\ adv

evil \'ēvəl\ adj evil·er or evil·ler; evil·est or evil·lest : wicked ~ n 1 : sin 2 : source of sorrow or distress —evil·do·er \,ēvəl'düər\ n —evil·ly adv

evince \i'vins\ vb evinced; evinc·ing : show

evis·cer·ate \i'visə,rāt\ vb -at·ed; -at·ing : remove the viscera of —evis·cer·a·tion \i,visə'rāshən\ n

evoke \i'vōk\ vb evoked; evok·ing : call forth or up —evo·ca·tion \,ēvō'kāshən, ,evə-\ n —evoc·a·tive \i'väkətiv\ adj

evo·lu·tion \,evə'lüshən\ n : process of change by degrees —evo·lu·tion·ary \-shə,nerē\ adj

evolve \i'välv\ vb evolved; evolv·ing : develop or change by degrees

ewe \'yü\ n : female sheep

ew·er \'yüər\ n : vase-shaped jug

ex·act \ig'zakt\ vb : compel to furnish ~ adj : precisely correct —ex·act·ing adj —ex·ac·tion \-'zakshən\ n —ex·ac·ti·tude \-'zaktə,t(y)üd\ n —ex·act·ly adv —ex·act·ness n

ex·ag·ger·ate \ig'zajə,rāt\ vb -at·ed; -at·ing : say more than is true —ex·ag·ger·at·ed·ly adv —ex·ag·ger·a·tion \-,zajə'rāshən\ n —ex·ag·ger·a·tor \-'zajərātər\ n

ex·alt \ig'zölt\ vb : glorify —ex·al·ta·tion \,egzöl'tāshən, ,ek,söl-\ n

ex·am \ig'zam\ n : examination

ex·am·ine \-ən\ vb -ined; -in·ing 1 : inspect closely 2 : test by questioning —ex·am·i·na·tion \-,zamə'nāshən\ n

ex·am·ple \-'zampəl\ n 1 : representative sample 2 : model 3 : problem to be solved for teaching purposes

ex·as·per·ate \ig'zaspə,rāt\ vb -at·ed; -at·ing : thoroughly annoy —ex·as·per·a·tion \ig,zaspə'rāshən\ n

ex·ca·vate \'ekskə,vāt\ vb -vat·ed; -vat·ing : dig or hollow out —ex·ca·va·tion \ekskə'vāshən\ n —ex·ca·va·tor \'ekskə,vātər\ n

ex·ceed \ik'sēd\ vb 1 : go or be beyond the limit of 2 : do better than

ex·ceed·ing·ly, ex·ceed·ing adv : extremely

ex·cel \ik'sel\ vb -ll- : do extremely well or far better than

ex·cel·lence \'eksə)ləns\ n : quality of being excellent

ex·cel·len·cy \-ə)lənsē\ n, pl -cies —used as a title of honor

ex·cel·lent \'eks(ə)lənt\ adj : very good —ex·cel·lent·ly adv

ex·cept \ik'sept\ vb : omit ~ prep 1 : excluding 2 : but ~ conj : but —ex·cep·tion \-'sepshən\ n

ex·cep·tion·al \-'sepsh(ə)nəl\ adj : superior —ex·cep·tion·al·ly adv

ex·cerpt \'ek,sərpt, 'eg,zərpt\ n : brief passage ~ \ek'-, eg'-, 'ek,-, 'eg,-\ vb : select an excerpt

ex·cess \ik'ses, 'ek,ses\ n : amount left over —excess adj —ex·ces·sive \ik'sesiv\ adj —ex·ces·sive·ly adv

ex·change \iks'chānj, 'eks,chānj\ n 1 : the giving or taking of one thing in return for another 2 : marketplace esp. for securities ~ vb -changed; -chang·ing : transfer in return for some equivalent —ex·change·able \iks'chānjəbəl\ adj

¹ex·cise \'ek,sīz, -,sīs\ n : tax

²ex·cise \ik'sīz\ vb -cised; -cis·ing : cut out —ex·ci·sion \-'sizhən\ n

ex·cite \ik'sīt\ vb -cit·ed; cit·ing 1 : stir up 2 : kindle the emotions of —ex·cit·abil·i·ty \-,sītə'bilətē\ n —ex·cit·able \-'sītəbəl\ adj —ex·ci·ta·tion \,ek,sī'tāshən, -sə-\ n —ex·cit·ed·ly adv —ex·cite·ment \ik'sītmənt\ n

ex·claim \iks'klām\ vb : cry out esp. in delight —ex·cla·ma·tion \,eks·klə'māshən\ n —ex·clam·a·to·ry \iks'klamə,tōrē\ adj

exclamation point n : punctuation mark ! used esp. after an interjection or exclamation

ex·clude \iks'klüd\ vb -clud·ed; -clud·ing : leave out —ex·clu·sion \-'klüzhən\ n

ex·clu·sive \ik'klüsiv\ adj 1 : reserved for particular persons 2 : stylish 3 : sole —ex·clu·sive·ly adv —ex·clu·sive·ness n

ex·com·mu·ni·cate \,ekskə·'myünə,kāt\ vb : expel from a church —ex·com·mu·ni·ca·tion \-,myünə'kāshən\ n

ex·cre·ment \'ekskrəmənt\ n : bodily waste —ex·cre·men·tal \,eks·krə'mentəl\ adj

ex·crete \ik'skrēt\ vb -cret·ed; -cret·ing : eliminate wastes from the body —ex·cre·tion \-'skrēshən\ n —ex·cre·to·ry \'ekskrə,tōrē\ adj

ex·cru·ci·at·ing \ik'skrüshē,ātiŋ\ adj : intensely painful —ex·cru·ci·at·ing·ly adv

ex·cul·pate \'ek(,)skəl,pāt\ vb -pat·ed; -pat·ing : clear from alleged fault

ex·cur·sion \ik'skərzhən\ n : pleasure trip

ex·cuse \ik'skyüz\ *vb* **-cused; -cus·ing** 1 : pardon 2 : release from an obligation 3 : justify ~ \-'skyüs\ *n* 1 : justification 2 : apology

ex·e·cute \'eksi,kyüt\ *vb* **-cut·ed; -cut·ing** 1 : carry to completion 2 : enforce 3 : put to death —**ex·e·cu·tion** \,eksi'kyüshən\ *n* —**ex·e·cu·tion·er** \-sh(ə)nər\ *n*

ex·ec·u·tive \ig'zek(y)ətiv\ *adj* : relating to the carrying out of decisions, plans, or laws ~ *n* 1 : branch of government with executive duties 2 : administrator

ex·ec·u·tor \-(y)ətər\ *n* : one who settles an estate —**ex·ec·u·trix** \-(y)ə,triks\ *n*

ex·em·pla·ry \ig'zemplərē\ *adj* : so commendable as to serve as a model

ex·em·pli·fy \-plə,fī\ *vb* **-fied; -fy·ing** : serve as an example of —**ex·em·pli·fi·ca·tion** \-,zempləfə'kāshən\ *n*

ex·empt \ig'zempt\ *adj* : being free from some liability ~ *vb* : make exempt —**ex·emp·tion** \-'zempshən\ *n*

ex·er·cise \'eksər,sīz\ *n* 1 : a putting into action 2 : exertion to develop endurance or a skill 3 *pl* : public ceremony ~ *vb* **-cised; cis·ing** 1 : exert 2 : engage in exercise —**ex·er·cis·er** *n*

ex·ert \ig'zert\ *vb* : put into action —**ex·er·tion** \-'zərshən\ *n*

ex·hale \eks'hāl\ *vb* **-haled; -hal·ing** : breathe out —**ex·ha·la·tion** \,eks(h)ə'lāshən\ *n*

ex·haust \ig'zȯst\ *vb* 1 : draw out or develop completely 2 : use up 3 : tire or wear out ~ *n* : waste steam or gas from an engine or a system for withdrawing it —**ex·haus·tion** \-'zȯschən\ *n* —**ex·haus·tive** \-'zȯstiv\ *adj*

ex·hib·it \ig'zibət\ *vb* : display esp. publicly ~ *n* 1 : act of exhibiting 2 : something exhibited —**ex·hi·bi·tion** \,eksə'bishən\ *n* —**ex·hib·i·tor** \ig'zibətər\ *n*

ex·hil·a·rate \ig'zilə,rāt\ *vb* **-rat·ed; -rat·ing** : thrill —**ex·hil·a·ra·tion** \-,zilə'rāshən\ *n*

ex·hort \-'zȯrt\ *vb* : urge earnestly —**ex·hor·ta·tion** \,eks,ȯr'tāshən, ,egz-, -ər-\ *n*

ex·hume \igz'(y)üm, iks'(h)yüm\ *vb* **-humed; -hum·ing** : dig up (a buried corpse) —**ex·hu·ma·tion** \,eks(h)yü-māshən, ,egz(y)ü-\ *n*

ex·i·gen·cy \'eksjənsē, ig'zijən-\ *n, pl* **-cies** 1 : urgent need 2 *pl* : require-

ments of the situation —**ex·i·gent** \'eksjənt\ *adj*

ex·ile \'eg,zīl, 'ek,sīl\ *n* 1 : banishment 2 : person banished from his country —**exile** *vb*

ex·ist \ig'zist\ *vb* 1 : have real or actual being 2 : live —**ex·is·tence** \-əns\ *n* —**ex·is·tent** \-ənt\ *adj*

ex·it \'egzət, 'eksət\ *n* 1 : departure 2 : way out of an enclosed space —**exit** *vb*

ex·o·dus \'eksədəs\ *n* : mass departure

ex·on·er·ate \ig'zänə,rāt\ *vb* **-at·ed; -at·ing** : free from blame —**ex·on·er·a·tion** \-,zänə'rāshən\ *n*

ex·or·bi·tant \ig'zȯrbətənt\ *adj* : exceeding what is usual or proper

ex·or·cise \'ek,sȯr,sīz, -sər-\ *vb* **-cised; -cis·ing** : drive out (as an evil spirit) —**ex·or·cism** \-,sizəm\ *n* —**ex·or·cist** \-,sist\ *n*

ex·ot·ic \ig'zätik\ *adj* 1 : foreign 2 : strange and exciting —**exotic** *n* —**ex·ot·i·cal·ly** \-ə(ə)lē\ *adv* —**ex·ot·i·cism** \-'zätə,sizəm\ *n*

ex·pand \ik'spand\ *vb* : enlarge

ex·panse \-'spans\ *n* : very large area

ex·pan·sion \-'spanchən\ *n* 1 : act or process of expanding 2 : expanded part

ex·pan·sive \-'spansiv\ *adj* 1 : tending to expand 2 : warmly benevolent 3 : of large extent —**ex·pan·sive·ly** *adv* —**ex·pan·sive·ness** *n*

ex·pa·tri·ate \ek'spātrē,āt, -ət\ *n* : exile —**expatriate** \-,āt\ *vb*

ex·pect \ik'spekt\ *vb* 1 : look forward to 2 : consider probable or one's due —**ex·pec·tan·cy** \-ənsē\ *n* —**ex·pec·tant** \-ənt\ *adj* —**ex·pec·tant·ly** *adv* —**ex·pec·ta·tion** \,ek,spek'tāshən\ *n*

ex·pe·di·ent \ik'spēdēənt\ *adj* : convenient or advantageous rather than right or just ~ *n* : convenient often makeshift means to an end

ex·pe·dite \'ekspə,dīt\ *vb* **-dit·ed; -dit·ing** : carry out or handle promptly —**ex·pe·dit·er** *n*

ex·pe·di·tion \,ekspə'dishən\ *n* : long journey for work or research or the people making this

ex·pe·di·tious \-əs\ *adj* : prompt and efficient

ex·pel \ik'spel\ *vb* **-ll-** : force out

ex·pend \-'spend\ *vb* 1 : pay out 2 : use up —**ex·pend·able** *adj*

ex·pen·di·ture \-'spendichər, -də,chùr\ *n* : act of using or spending

ex·pense \ik'spens\ *n* : cost —**ex·pen·sive** \-'spensiv\ *adj* —**ex·pen·sive·ly** *adv*

ex·pe·ri·ence \ik'spirēəns\ n **1** : a participating in or living through an event **2** : an event that affects one **3** : knowledge from doing ∼ vb **-enced; -enc·ing** : undergo

ex·per·i·ment \ik'sperəmənt\ n : test to discover something ∼ vb : make experiments **—ex·per·i·men·tal** \-,sperə'mentᵊl\ adj **—ex·per·i·men·ta·tion** \-mən'tāshən\ n **—ex·per·i·ment·er** \-sperə,mentər\ n

ex·pert \'ek,spərt\ adj : thoroughly skilled ∼ n : person with special skill **—ex·pert·ly** adv **—ex·pert·ness** n

ex·per·tise \,ek(,)spər'tēz\ n : skill

ex·pi·ate \'ekspē,āt\ vb : make amends for **—ex·pi·a·tion** \,ekspē'āshən\ n

ex·pire \ik'spī(ə)r, ek-\ vb **-pired; -pir·ing 1** : breathe out **2** : die **3** : end **—ex·pi·ra·tion** \,ekspə'rāshən\ n

ex·plain \ik'splān\ vb **1** : make clear **2** : give the reason for **—ex·plain·able** \-əbəl\ adj **—ex·pla·na·tion** \,eksplə'nāshən\ n **—ex·plan·a·to·ry** \ik'splanə,tōrē\ adj

ex·ple·tive \'eksplətiv\ n : usu. profane exclamation

ex·pli·ca·ble \ek'splikəbəl, 'ek(,)splik-\ adj : capable of being explained **—ex·pli·ca·bly** \-blē\ adv

ex·plic·it \ik'splisət\ adj : absolutely clear or precise **—ex·plic·it·ly** adv **—ex·plic·it·ness** n

ex·plode \ik'splōd\ vb **-plod·ed; -plod·ing 1** : discredit **2** : burst or cause to burst violently

ex·ploit \'ek,sploit\ n : heroic act ∼ \ik'sploit\ vb **1** : utilize **2** : use unfairly **—ex·ploi·ta·tion** \,ek,sploi'tāshən\ n

ex·plore \ik'splōr\ vb **-plored; -plor·ing** : examine or range over thoroughly **—ex·plo·ra·tion** \,eksplə'rāshən\ n **—ex·plor·a·to·ry** \ik'splōrə,tōrē\ adj **—ex·plor·er** n

ex·plo·sion \ik'splōzhən\ n : process or instance of exploding

ex·plo·sive \-siv\ adj **1** : able to cause explosion **2** : likely to explode **—ex·plosive** n **—ex·plo·sive·ly** adv

ex·po·nent \ik'spōnənt, 'ek,spō-\ n **1** : mathematical symbol showing how many times a number is to be repeated as a factor **2** : advocate **—ex·po·nen·tial** \,ekspə'nenchəl\ adj **—ex·po·nen·tial·ly** adv

ex·port \ek'spōrt, 'ek,spōrt\ vb : send to foreign countries **—export** \'ek,spōrt\ n **—ex·por·ta·tion** \,ek,spōr'tāshən\ n **—ex·port·er** \ek'spōrtər, 'ek,spōrt-\ n

ex·pose \ik'spōz\ vb **-posed; -pos·ing 1** : deprive of shelter or protection **2** : subject (film) to light **3** : make known **—ex·po·sure** \-'spōzhər\ n

ex·po·sé, ex·pose \,ekspō'zā\ n : exposure of something discreditable

ex·po·si·tion \,ekspə'zishən\ n : public exhibition

ex·pound \ik'spaund\ vb : set forth or explain in detail

¹ex·press \-'spres\ adj **1** : clear **2** : specific **3** : traveling at high speed with few stops **—express** adv or n **—express·ly** adv

²express vb **1** : make known in words or appearance **2** : press out (as juice) **—ex·press·ible** \-əbəl\ adj **—express·ibly** \-əblē\ adv

ex·pres·sion \-'spreshən\ n **1** : utterance **2** : mathematical symbol **3** : significant word or phrase **4** : look on one's face **—ex·pres·sion·less** adj **—ex·pres·sive** \-'spresiv\ adj **—ex·pres·sive·ness** n

ex·press·way \ik'spres,wā\ n : high-speed divided highway

ex·pul·sion \-'spəlshən\ n : an expelling or being expelled

ex·pur·gate \'ekspər,gāt\ vb **-gat·ed; -gat·ing** : censor **—ex·pur·ga·tion** \,ekspər'gāshən\ n

ex·qui·site \ek'skwizət, 'ek(,)skwiz-\ adj **1** : flawlessly beautiful and delicate **2** : keenly discriminating

ex·tant \'ekstənt; ek'stant\ adj : existing

ex·tem·po·ra·ne·ous \ek,stempə-'rānēəs\ adj : impromptu **—ex·tem·po·ra·ne·ous·ly** adv

ex·tend \ik'stend\ vb **1** : stretch forth or out **2** : prolong **3** : enlarge **—ex·tend·able, ex·tend·ible** \-'stendəbəl\ adj

ex·ten·sion \-'stenchən\ n **1** : an extending or being extended **2** : additional part

ex·ten·sive \-'stensiv\ adj : of considerable extent **—ex·ten·sive·ly** adv

ex·tent \-'stent\ n : size, length, or degree of something

ex·ten·u·ate \ik'stenyə,wāt\ vb **-at·ed; -at·ing** : lessen the seriousness of **—ex·ten·u·a·tion** \-,stenyə'wāshən\ n

ex·te·ri·or \ek'stirēər\ adj : external ∼ n : external part or surface

ex·ter·mi·nate \ik'stərmə,nāt\ vb **-nat·ed; -nat·ing** : destroy utterly **—ex·ter·mi·na·tion** \-,stərmə'nāshən\ n **—ex·ter·mi·na·tor** \-'stərmə,nātər\ n

ex·ter·nal \ek'stərnᵊl\ adj : relating to or on the outside **—ex·ter·nal·ly** adv

ex·tinct \ik'stiŋkt\ *adj* : no longer existing —**ex·tinc·tion** \-'stiŋkshən\ *n*

ex·tin·guish \-'stiŋgwish\ *vb* : put out (as a fire) —**ex·tin·guish·able** *adj* —**ex·tin·guish·er** *n*

ex·tir·pate \'ekstər,pāt\ *vb* **-pat·ed; -pat·ing** : destroy

ex·tol \ik'stōl\ *vb* **-ll-** : praise highly

ex·tort \-'stȯrt\ *vb* : obtain by force or improper pressure —**ex·tor·tion** \-'stȯrshən\ *n* —**ex·tor·tion·er** *n* —**ex·tor·tion·ist** *n*

ex·tra \'ekstrə\ *adj* **1** : additional **2** : superior —**extra** *n or adv*

extra- *prefix* : outside or beyond

extra-atmo- spheric	extragalactic
extracampus	extragovern- mental
extraclassroom	extrahuman
extracommunity	extralegal
extraconstitu- tional	extramarital
extracontinental	extranational
extradepart- mental	extraplanetary
extradiocesan	extrascholastic
extrafamilial	extrasensory
	extraterrestrial
	extravehicular

ex·tract \ik'strakt\ *vb* **1** : pull out forcibly **2** : withdraw (as a juice) ~ \'ek,-\ *n* **1** : excerpt **2** : product (as a juice) obtained by extracting —**ex·tract·able** *adj* —**ex·trac·tion** \ik'strakshən\ *n* —**ex·trac·tor** \-tər\ *n*

ex·tra·cur·ric·u·lar \,ekstrəkə'rikyələr\ *adj* : lying outside the regular curriculum

ex·tra·dite \'ekstrə,dīt\ *vb* **-dit·ed; -dit·ing** : bring or deliver a suspect to a different jurisdiction for trial —**ex·tra·di·tion** \,ekstrə'dishən\ *n*

ex·tra·ne·ous \ek'strānēəs\ *adj* : not essential or relevant —**ex·tra·ne·ous·ly** *adv*

ex·traor·di·nary \ik'strȯrd⁵n,erē, ,ekstrə'ȯrd-\ *adj* : notably unusual or exceptional —**ex·traor·di·nari·ly** \ik,strȯrd⁵n'erəlē, ,ekstrə,ȯrd-\ *adv*

ex·trav·a·gant \ik'stravigənt\ *adj* : wildly excessive, lavish, or costly —**ex·trav·a·gance** \-gəns\ *n* —**ex·trav·a·gant·ly** *adv*

ex·trav·a·gan·za \-,stravə'ganzə\ *n* : spectacular event

ex·tra·vert, ex·tro·vert \'ekstrə,vərt\ *n* : person more interested in the world than in the inner self —**ex·tra·ver·sion** \,ekstrə'vərzhən\ *n* —**extravert** \'ekstrə,vərt\ *adj* —**ex·tra·vert·ed** \-əd\ *adj*

ex·treme \ik'strēm\ *adj* **1** : very great or intense **2** : very severe or drastic **3** : not moderate **4** : most remote ~ *n* **1** : extreme state **2** : something located at one end or the other of a range —**ex·treme·ly** *adv*

ex·trem·i·ty \-'stremətē\ *n, pl* **-ties 1** : most remote part **2** : human hand or foot **3** : extreme degree or state (as of need)

ex·tri·cate \'ekstrə,kāt\ *vb* **-cat·ed; -cat·ing** : set or get free from an entanglement or difficulty —**ex·tri·ca·ble** \ik'strikəbəl, ek-; 'ek(,)strik-\ *adj* **ex·tri·ca·tion** \,ekstrə'kāshən\ *n*

ex·u·ber·ant \ig'züb(ə)rənt\ *adj* : joyously unrestrained —**ex·u·ber·ance** \-b(ə)rəns\ *n* —**ex·u·ber·ant·ly** *adv*

ex·ude \ig'züd\ *vb* **-ud·ed; -ud·ing 1** : discharge slowly through pores **2** : give off —**ex·u·date** \'eks(y)ú,dāt\ *n* —**ex·u·da·tion** \,eks(y)ú'dāshən\ *n*

ex·ult \ig'zəlt\ *vb* : rejoice in triumph —**ex·ul·tant** \-'zəlt⁵nt\ *adj* —**ex·ul·tant·ly** *adv* —**ex·ul·ta·tion** \,ek(,)səl'tāshən, ,egz(,)zəl-\ *n*

-ey —see -Y

eye \'ī\ *n* **1** : organ of sight consisting of a globular structure (**eye·ball**) in a socket of the skull with thin movable covers (**eye·lids**) bordered with hairs (**eye·lash·es**) **2** : vision **3** : judgment **4** : something suggesting an eye ~ *vb* **eyed; eye·ing** or **ey·ing** : look at —**eye·brow** \-,braú\ *n* —**eyed** \'īd\ *adj* —**eye·strain** *n*

eye·drop·per *n* : dropper

eye·glass·es *n pl* : glasses

eye·let \'īlət\ *n* : small hole (as in cloth) for a lacing or rope

eye·open·er *n* : something startling —**eye·open·ing** *adj*

eye·piece *n* : lens at the eye end of an optical instrument

eye·sight *n* : sight

eye·sore *n* : unpleasant sight

eye·tooth *n* : upper canine tooth

eye·wit·ness *n* : person who actually sees something happen

ey·rie \'ī(ə)rē, or like AERIE\ *var of* AERIE

F

f \'ef\ *n, pl* **f's** *or* **fs** \'efs\ : 6th letter of the alphabet

fa·ble \'fābəl\ *n* 1 : legendary story 2 : story that teaches a lesson —**fa·bled** \-bəld\ *adj*

fab·ric \'fabrik\ *n* 1 : structure 2 : material made usu. by weaving or knitting fibers

fab·ri·cate \-ri͵kāt\ *vb* **-cat·ed; -cat·ing** 1 : construct 2 : invent —**fab·ri·ca·tion** \͵fabri'kāshən\ *n*

fab·u·lous \'fabyələs\ *adj* 1 : like, told in, or based on fable 2 : incredible or marvelous —**fab·u·lous·ly** *adv*

fa·cade \fə'säd\ *n* 1 : principal face of a building 2 : false or superficial appearance

face \'fās\ *n* 1 : front or principal surface (as of the head) 2 : presence 3 : facial expression 4 : grimace 5 : outward appearance ~ *vb* **fac·ing** 1 : challenge or resist firmly or brazenly 2 : cover with different material 3 : sit or stand with the face toward 4 : front on —**faced** \'fāst\ *adj* —**face·less** *adj* —**face·less·ness** *n* —**fa·cial** \'fāshəl\ *adj or n*

face·down *adv* : with the face downward

fac·et \'fasət\ *n* 1 : surface of a cut gem 2 : phase —**fac·et·ed** *adj*

fa·ce·tious \fə'sēshəs\ *adj* : jocular —**fa·ce·tious·ly** *adv* —**fa·ce·tious·ness** *n*

fac·ile \'fasəl\ *adj* 1 : easy 2 : fluent

fa·cil·i·tate \fə'silə͵tāt\ *vb* **-tat·ed; -tat·ing** : make easier

fa·cil·i·ty \fə'silətē\ *n, pl* **-ties** 1 : ease in doing or using 2 : something built or installed to serve a purpose or facilitate an activity

fac·ing \'fāsiŋ\ *n* : lining or covering or material for this

fac·sim·i·le \fak'siməlē\ *n* : exact copy

fact \'fakt\ *n* 1 : act or action 2 : something that exists or is real —**fac·tu·al** \'fakchə(wə)l\ *adj* —**fac·tu·al·ly** *adv*

fac·tion \'fakshən\ *n* : part of a larger group —**fac·tion·al** *adj* —**fac·tion·al·ism** \-sh(ə)nə͵lizəm\ *n*

fac·tious \'fakshəs\ *adj* : causing discord

fac·ti·tious \fak'tishəs\ *adj* : artificial

fac·tor \'faktər\ *n* 1 : something that has an effect 2 : gene 3 : number used in multiplying

fac·to·ry \'fakt(ə)rē\ *n, pl* **-ries** : place for manufacturing

fac·to·tum \fak'tōtəm\ *n* : employee with varied duties

fac·ul·ty \'fakəltē\ *n, pl* **-ties** 1 : ability to act 2 : power of the mind or body 3 : body of teachers or department of instruction

fad \'fad\ *n* : briefly popular practice or interest —**fad·dish** *adj* —**fad·dist** *n*

fade \'fād\ *vb* **fad·ed; fad·ing** 1 : wither 2 : lose or cause to lose freshness or brilliance 3 : grow dim 4 : vanish

fag \'fag\ *vb* **-gg-** 1 : drudge 2 : tire or exhaust

fag·ot, fag·got \'fagət\ *n* : bundle of twigs

Fahr·en·heit \'farən͵hīt\ *adj* : relating to a thermometer scale with the boiling point at 212 degrees and the freezing point at 32 degrees

fail \'fāl\ *vb* 1 : decline in health 2 : die away 3 : stop functioning 4 : be unsuccessful 5 : become bankrupt 6 : disappoint or abandon 7 : neglect ~ *n* : act of failing

fail·ing *n* : slight defect in character or conduct ~ *prep* : in the absence or lack of

faille \'fīl\ *n* : closely woven ribbed fabric

fail·ure \'fālyər\ *n* 1 : absence of expected action or performance 2 : bankruptcy 3 : deficiency 4 : one that has failed

faint \'fānt\ *adj* 1 : cowardly or spiritless 2 : weak and dizzy 3 : lacking vigor 4 : indistinct ~ *vb* : lose consciousness ~ *n* : act or condition of fainting —**faint·heart·ed** *adj* —**faint·ly** *adv* —**faint·ness** *n*

¹fair \'faər\ *adj* 1 : attractive in appearance 2 : not stormy or cloudy 3 : just or honest 4 : conforming with the rules 5 : open to legitimate pursuit or attack 6 : light in color 7 : adequate —**fair·ness** *n*

²fair *adv* : FAIRLY

³fair *n* : exhibition for judging or selling —**fair·ground** *n*

fair·ly \'fa(ə)rlē\ *adv* 1 : quite 2 : in a fair manner 3 : moderately

fairy \'fa(ə)rē\ *n, pl* **fairies** : imaginary being —**fairy tale** *n*

fairy·land \-͵land\ *n* 1 : land of fairies 2 : beautiful or charming place

faith \'fāth\ *n, pl* **faiths** \'fāths, 'fāthz\ 1 : allegiance 2 : belief and trust in God 3 : confidence 4 : system of religious beliefs —**faith·ful** \-fəl\ *adj* —**faith·ful·ly** *adv* —**faith·ful·ness** *n* —**faith·less** *adj* —**faith·less·ly** *adv* —**faith·less·ness** *n*

fake \'fāk\ *vb* **faked; fak·ing** 1 : falsify 2 : counterfeit 3 : pretend ~ *n* : copy, counterfeit, or trick ~ *adj* : not genuine —**fak·er** *n*

fa·kir \fə'kiər\ *n* : wandering beggar of India

fal·con \'falkən, 'fȯl(l)-\ *n* : long-winged hawk esp. used for hunting —**fal·con·ry** \-rē\ *n*

fall \'fȯl\ *vb* **fell** \'fel\; **fall·en** \fȯlən\; **fall·ing** 1 : go down by gravity 2 : hang freely 3 : go lower 4 : be defeated or ruined 5 : commit a sin 6 : happen at a certain time 7 : become gradually ~ *n* 1 : act of falling 2 : autumn 3 : downfall 4 *pl* : waterfall 5 : distance something falls

fal·la·cy \'faləsē\ *n, pl* **-cies** 1 : false idea 2 : false reasoning —**fal·la·cious** \fə'lāshəs\ *adj*

fal·li·ble \'faləbəl\ *adj* : capable of making a mistake

fall·out *n* : radioactive particles from a nuclear explosion

fal·low \'falō\ *n* : land plowed but not planted —**fallow** *vb or adj*

false \'fȯls\ *adj* **fals·er; fals·est** 1 : not genuine, true, faithful, or permanent 2 : misleading —**false·ly** *adv* —**false·ness** *n* —**fal·si·fi·ca·tion** \ˌfȯlsəfə'kāshən\ *n* —**fal·si·fy** \'fȯlsə̇ˌfī\ *vb* —**fal·si·ty** \'fȯlsətē\ *n*

false·hood \'fȯls, hu̇d\ *n* : lie

fal·set·to \fȯl'setō\ *n, pl* **-tos** : artificially high singing voice

fal·ter \'fȯltər\ *vb* **-tered; -ter·ing** 1 : move unsteadily 2 : hesitate —**fal·ter·ing·ly** *adv*

fame \'fām\ *n* : public reputation —**famed** \'fāmd\ *adj*

fa·mil·ial \fə'milyəl\ *adj* : relating to a family

¹**fa·mil·iar** \fə'milyər\ *n* 1 : companion 2 : guardian spirit

²**familiar** *adj* 1 : closely acquainted 2 : forward 3 : frequently seen or experienced —**fa·mil·iar·i·ty** \fəˌmilˈyaratē, -ˌmilē'(y)ar-\ *n* —**fa·mil·iar·ize** \fə'milyəˌrīz\ *vb* —**fa·mil·iar·ly** *adv*

fam·i·ly \'fam(ə)lē\ *n, pl* **-lies** 1 : persons of common ancestry 2 : group living together 3 : parents and children 4 : group of related individuals

fam·ine \'famən\ *n* : extreme scarcity of food

fam·ish \-ish\ *vb* : starve

fa·mous \'fāməs\ *adj* : widely known or celebrated

fa·mous·ly *adv* : very well

¹**fan** \'fan\ *n* : device for producing a current of air ~ *vb* **-nn-** 1 : move air with a fan 2 : direct a current of air upon 3 : stir to activity

²**fan** *n* : enthusiastic follower or admirer

fa·nat·ic \fə'natik\, **fa·nat·i·cal** \-ikəl\ *adj* : excessively enthusiastic or devoted —**fanatic** *n* —**fa·nat·i·cism** \-'natəˌsizəm\ *n*

fan·ci·er \'fansēər\ *n* : one devoted to raising a particular plant or animal

fan·cy \'fansē\ *n, pl* **-cies** 1 : liking 2 : whim 3 : imagination ~ *vb* **-cied; -cy·ing** 1 : like 2 : imagine ~ *adj* **-ci·er; -est** 1 : not plain 2 : of superior quality —**fan·ci·ful** \-sifəl\ *adj* —**fan·ci·ful·ly** \-f(ə)lē\ *adv* —**fan·ci·ly** *adv*

fan·dan·go \fan'daŋgō\ *n, pl* **-gos** : lively Spanish dance

fan·fare \'fan,faər\ *n* 1 : a sounding of trumpets 2 : showy display

fang \'faŋ\ *n* : long tooth of a venomous snake

fan·light *n* : semicircular window

fan·ta·sia \fan'tāzhə, -z(h)ēə, ˌfantə'zēə\ *n* : music written to fancy rather than to form

fan·tas·tic \fan'tastik\ *adj* 1 : imaginary or unrealistic 2 : exceedingly or unbelievably great —**fan·tas·ti·cal** \-tikəl\ *adj* —**fan·tas·ti·cal·ly** \-tik(ə)lē\ *adv*

fan·ta·sy \'fantəsē\ *n* 1 : imagination 2 : product (as a daydream) of the imagination 3 : fantasia —**fan·ta·size** \'fantəˌsīz\ *vb*

far \'fär\ *adv* **farther** \-thər\ *or* **further** \'fər-\; **farthest** *or* **furthest** \-thəst\ 1 : at or to a distance 2 : much 3 : to a degree 4 : to an advanced point or extent ~ *adv* **farther** *or* **further; farthest** *or* **furthest** 1 : more distant 2 : long 3 : being more distant

far·away *adj* : distant

farce \'färs\ *n* 1 : satirical comedy with an improbable plot 2 : ridiculous action —**far·ci·cal** \-sikəl\ *adj*

¹**fare** \'faər\ *vb* **fared; far·ing** : get along

²**fare** *n* 1 : price of transportation 2 : range of food

fare·well \faər'wel\ *n* 1 : wish of welfare at parting 2 : departure —**farewell** \ˌfaər,wəl\ *adj*

far·fetched *adj* : not probable or reasonable

fa·ri·na \fə'rēnə\ *n* : fine meal made from cereal grains

farm \'färm\ *n* : place where something is raised — *vb* 1 : use (land) as a farm 2 : raise something —**farm·er** *n* —**farm·hand** \-,hand\ *n* —**farm·house** *n* —**farm·ing** *n* —**farm·land** \-,land\ *n* —**farm·yard** *n*

farm·stead \'färm,sted\ *n* : buildings and service areas of a farm

far-off *adj* : remote in time or space

far·ri·er \'farēər\ *n* : blacksmith who shoes horses

far·row \'farō\ *vb* : give birth to a litter of pigs —**farrow** *n*

far·sight·ed *adj* 1 : better able to see distant things than near 2 : judicious or shrewd —**far·sight·ed·ness** *n*

far·ther \'färthər\ *adv* 1 : at or to a greater distance or more advanced point 2 : more completely ~ *adj* : more distant

far·ther·most *adj* : most distant

far·thest \'färthəst\ *adj* : most distant ~ *adv* 1 : to or at the greatest distance 2 : to the most advanced point 3 : by the greatest extent

fas·ci·cle \'fasikəl\ *n* 1 : small bundle 2 : division of a book published in parts —**fas·ci·cled** \-kəld\ *adj*

fas·ci·nate \'fas°n,āt\ *vb* -**nat·ed; -nat·ing** : transfix and hold spellbound —**fas·ci·na·tion** \,fas°n'āshən\ *n*

fas·cism \'fash,izəm\ *n* : dictatorship that exalts nation and race —**fas·cist** \-əst\ *n or adj* —**fas·cis·tic** \fa'shistik\ *adj*

fash·ion \'fashən\ *n* 1 : manner 2 : prevailing custom or style ~ *vb* : form or construct —**fash·ion·able** \-(ə)nəbəl\ *adj* —**fash·ion·ably** \-blē\ *adv*

¹**fast** \'fast\ *adj* 1 : firmly fixed, bound, or shut 2 : faithful 3 : moving or acting quickly 4 : indicating ahead of the correct time 5 : deep and undisturbed 6 : permanently dyed 7 : wild or promiscuous ~ *adv* 1 : so as to be secure or bound 2 : soundly or deeply 3 : swiftly

²**fast** *vb* : abstain from food or eat sparingly ~ *n* : act or time of fasting

fas·ten \'fas°n\ *vb* : attach esp. by pinning or tying —**fas·ten·er** *n* —**fas·ten·ing** *n*

fas·tid·i·ous \fas'tidēəs\ *adj* : hard to please —**fas·tid·i·ous·ly** *adv* —**fas·tid·i·ous·ness** *n*

fat \'fat\ *adj* -**tt**- 1 : having much fat 2 : thick ~ *n* : animal tissue rich in

greasy or oily matter —**fat·ness** *n* —**fat·ten** \'fat°n\ *vb* —**fat·ty** *adj or n*

fa·tal \'fāt°l\ *adj* : causing death or ruin —**fa·tal·i·ty** \fā'talətē, fə-\ *n* —**fa·tal·ly** *adv*

fa·tal·ism \'fāt°l,izəm\ *n* : belief that fate determines events —**fa·tal·ist** \-əst\ *n* —**fa·tal·is·tic** \,fāt°l'istik\ *adj*

fate \'fāt\ *n* 1 : cause beyond human control held to determine events 2 : end or outcome —**fat·ed** *adj* —**fate·ful** \-fəl\ *adj* —**fate·ful·ly** *adv*

fa·ther \'fäthər, 'fath-\ *n* 1 : male parent 2 *cap* : God 3 : originator —**father** *vb* —**fa·ther·hood** \-,hùd\ *n* —**fa·ther·land** \-,land\ *n* —**fa·ther·less** *adj* —**fa·ther·ly** *adj*

father-in-law *n, pl* **fathers-in-law** : father of one's spouse

fath·om \'fathəm\ *n* : nautical unit of length equal to 6 feet ~ *vb* 1 : measure by sounding 2 : understand —**fath·om·able** *adj* —**fath·om·less** *adj*

fa·tigue \fə'tēg\ *n* 1 : weariness from labor or use 2 : tendency to break under repeated stress ~ *vb* -**tigued; -tigu·ing** : tire out

fat·u·ous \'fach(ə)wəs\ *adj* : foolish or stupid —**fat·u·ous·ly** *adv* —**fat·u·ous·ness** *n*

fau·cet \'fòsət, 'fäs-\ *n* : fixture for drawing off a liquid

fault \'fòlt\ *n* 1 : weakness in character 2 : something wrong or imperfect 3 : responsibility for something wrong 4 : fracture in the earth's crust ~ *vb* : find fault in or with —**fault·find·er** *n* —**fault·find·ing** *n* —**fault·i·ly** \'fòltəlē\ *adv* —**fault·less** *adj* —**fault·less·ly** *adv* —**faulty** *adj*

fau·na \'fònə\ *n* : animals or animal life esp. of a region —**fau·nal** \-°l\ *adj*

faux pas \'fō'pä\ *n, pl* **faux pas** \-'pä(z)\ : social blunder

fa·vor \'fāvər\ *n* 1 : approval 2 : partiality 3 : act of kindness ~ *vb* : regard or treat with favor —**fa·vor·able** \'fāv(ə)rəbəl\ *adj* —**fa·vor·ably** \-blē\ *adv*

fa·vor·ite \'fāv(ə)rət\ *n* : one favored —**favorite** *adj* —**fa·vor·it·ism** \-,izəm\ *n*

¹**fawn** \'fòn\ *vb* : seek favor by groveling

²**fawn** *n* : young deer

faze \'fāz\ *vb* **fazed; faz·ing** : disturb the composure of

fear \'fiər\ *n* : unpleasant emotion caused by expectation or awareness of danger ~ *vb* : be afraid of —**fear-**

ful \fəl\ adj : **fear·ful·ly** adv —**fear·less** \-ləs\ adj —**fear·less·ly** adv —**fear·less·ness** n —**fear·some** \-səm\ adj

fea·si·ble \'fēzəbəl\ adj : capable of being done —**fea·si·bil·i·ty** \ˌfēzə'bilətē\ n —**fea·si·bly** \'fēzəblē\ adv

feast \'fēst\ n 1 : large or fancy meal 2 : religious festival ~ vb : eat plentifully

feat \'fēt\ n : notable deed

feath·er \'fethər\ n : one of the light horny outgrowths that form the external covering of a bird's body —**feather** vb —**feath·ered** \-ərd\ adj —**feath·er·less** adj —**feath·ery** adj

fea·ture \'fēchər\ n 1 : shape or appearance of the face 2 : part of the face 3 : prominent characteristic 4 : special attraction ~ vb : give prominence to —**fea·ture·less** adj

Feb·ru·ary \'feb(yə)ˌwerē, 'febrə-\ n : 2d month of the year having 28 and in leap days 29 days

fe·ces \'fēˌsēz\ n pl : intestinal body waste —**fe·cal** \-kəl\ adj

feck·less \'feklas\ adj : irresponsible

fe·cund \'fekənd, 'fē-\ adj : prolific —**fe·cun·di·ty** \fi'kəndətē, fe-\ n

fed·er·al \'fed(ə)rəl\ adj : of or constituting a government with power distributed between a central authority and constituent units —**fed·er·al·ism** \-rəˌlizəm\ n —**fed·er·al·ist** \-ləst\ n or adj —**fed·er·al·ly** adv

fed·er·ate \'fedəˌrāt\ vb -at·ed; -at·ing : join in a federation

fed·er·a·tion \ˌfedə'rāshən\ n : union of organizations

fe·do·ra \fi'dōrə\ n : soft felt hat

fed up adj : out of patience

fee \'fē\ n : fixed charge

fee·ble \'fēbəl\ adj -bler; -blest : weak or ineffective —**fee·ble·mind·ed** \ˌfēbəl'mīndəd\ adj —**fee·ble·mind·ed·ness** n —**fee·ble·ness** n —**fee·bly** \-blē\ adv

feed \'fēd\ vb **fed** \'fed\; **feed·ing** 1 : give food to 2 : eat 3 : furnish ~ n : food for livestock —**feed·er** n

feel \'fēl\ vb **felt** \'felt\; **feel·ing** 1 : perceive or examine through physical contact 2 : think or believe 3 : be conscious of 4 : seem esp. to the touch 5 : have sympathy ~ n 1 : sense of touch 2 : quality of a thing imparted through touch —**feel·er** n

feel·ing \'fēliŋ\ n 1 : sense of touch 2 : state of mind 3 pl : sensibilities 4 : opinion

feet pl of FOOT

feign \'fān\ : pretend

feint \'fānt\ n : mock attack intended to distract attention —**feint** vb

fe·lic·i·tate \fi'lisəˌtāt\ vb -tat·ed; -tat·ing : congratulate —**fe·lic·i·ta·tion** \-ˌlisə'tāshən\ n

fe·lic·i·tous \fi'lisətəs\ adj : aptly expressed —**fe·lic·i·tous·ly** adv

fe·lic·i·ty \-'lisətē\ n, pl -ties 1 : great happiness 2 : pleasing faculty esp. in art or language

fe·line \'fēˌlīn\ adj : relating to cats —**feline** n

¹**fell** \'fel\ vb : cut or knock down

²**fell** past of FALL

fel·low \'felō\ n 1 : companion or associate 2 : man or boy —**fel·low·ship** \-ˌship\ n

fel·low·man \ˌfelō'man\ n : kindred human being

fel·on \'felən\ n : one who has committed a felony

fel·o·ny \'felənē\ n, pl -nies : serious crime —**fe·lo·ni·ous** \fə'lōnēəs\ adj

¹**felt** \'felt\ n : cloth made of pressed wool and fur

²**felt** past of FEEL

fe·male \'fēˌmāl\ adj : relating to or being the sex that bears young —**female** n

fem·i·nine \'femənən\ adj : relating to the female sex —**fem·i·nin·i·ty** \ˌfemə'ninətē\ n

fem·i·nism \'feməˌnizəm\ n : organized activity on behalf of women's rights —**fem·i·nist** \-nəst\ n or adj

fe·mur \'fēmər\ n, pl **fe·murs** or **fem·o·ra** \'fem(ə)rə\ : long bone of the thigh —**fem·o·ral** \'fem(ə)rəl\ adj

fence \'fens\ n : enclosing barrier esp. of wood or wire ~ vb **fenced; fenc·ing** 1 : enclose with a fence 2 : practice fencing —**fenc·er** n

fenc·ing \'fensiŋ\ n 1 : combat with swords for sport 2 : material for building fences

fend \'fend\ vb : ward off

fend·er \'fendər\ n : guard over an automobile wheel

fen·nel \'fen³l\ n : herb related to the carrot

fer·ment \fər'ment\ vb : cause or undergo fermentation ~ \'fərˌment\ n : agitation

fer·men·ta·tion \ˌfərmən'tāshən, -ˌmen-\ n : chemical decomposition of an organic substance in the absence of oxygen

fern \'fərn\ n : flowerless seedless green plant

fe·ro·cious \fə'rōshəs\ adj : fierce or savage —**fe·ro·cious·ly** adv —**fe·ro·cious·ness** n —**fe·roc·i·ty** \-'räsətē\ n

fer·ret \'ferət\ *n* : white European polecat ~ *vb* : find out by searching

fer·ric \'ferik\ *adj* : relating to or containing iron

fer·rous \'ferəs\ *adj* : relating to or containing iron

fer·rule \'ferəl\ *n* : metal band or ring

fer·ry \'ferē\ *vb* -ried; -ry·ing : carry by boat over water ~ *n, pl* -ries : boat used in ferrying —**fer·ry·boat** *n*

fer·tile \'fərt°l\ *adj* 1 : producing plentifully 2 : capable of developing or reproducing —**fer·til·i·ty** \(,)fər'tilətē\ *n*

fer·til·ize \'fərt°l,īz\ *vb* -ized; -iz·ing : make fertile —**fer·til·iza·tion** \,fərt°lə'zāshən\ *n* —**fer·til·iz·er** *n*

fer·vid \'fərvəd\ *adj* : ardent or zealous —**fer·vid·ly** *adv*

fer·vor \'fərvər\ *n* : passion —**fer·ven·cy** \-vənsē\ *n* —**fer·vent** \-vənt\ *adj* —**fer·vent·ly** *adv*

fes·ter \'festər\ *n* : pus-filled sore ~ *vb* 1 : form pus 2 : become more bitter or malignant

fes·ti·val \'festəvəl\ *n* : time of celebration

fes·tive \-tiv\ *adj* : joyous or happy —**fes·tive·ly** *adv* —**fes·tiv·i·ty** \fes'tivətē\ *n*

fes·toon \fes'tün\ *n* : decorative chain or strip hanging in a curve —**festoon** *vb*

fe·tal \'fēt°l\ *adj* : of, relating to, or being a fetus

fetch \'fech\ *vb* 1 : go or come after and bring or take back 2 : sell for

fetch·ing \'fechiŋ\ *adj* : attractive —**fetch·ing·ly** *adv*

fête \'fāt, 'fet\ *n* : lavish party ~ *vb* **fêt·ed; fêt·ing** : honor or commemorate with a fête

fet·id \'fetəd\ *adj* : having an offensive smell

fe·tish \'fetish, 'fēt-\ *n* 1 : object believed to have magical powers 2 : object of unreasoning devotion or concern

fet·lock \'fet,läk\ *n* : projection on the back of a horse's leg above the hoof

fet·ter \'fetər\ *n* : chain or shackle for the feet —**fetter** *vb*

fet·tle \'fet°l\ *n* : state of fitness

fe·tus \'fētəs\ *n* : vertebrate not yet born or hatched

feud \'fyüd\ *n* : lasting conflict between families or clans —**feud** *vb*

feu·dal \'fyüd°l\ *adj* : of or relating to feudalism

feu·dal·ism \-,izəm\ *n* : medieval political order in which land is granted in return for service —**feu·dal·is·tic** \,fyüd°l'istik\ *adj*

fe·ver \'fēvər\ *n* 1 : abnormal rise in body temperature 2 : state of heightened emotion —**fe·ver·ish** *adj* —**fe·ver·ish·ly** *adv*

few \'fyü\ *pron* : not many ~ *adj* : some but not many —often with *a* ~ *n* : small number —often with *a*

few·er \-ər\ *pron* : smaller number of things

fez \'fez\ *n, pl* **fez·zes** : round flat-crowned hat

fi·an·cé \,fē,än'sā\ *n* : man one is engaged to

fi·an·cée \,fē,än'sā\ *n* : woman one is engaged to

fi·as·co \fē'askō\ *n, pl* -coes : ridiculous failure

fi·at \'fēət, -,at, -,ät; 'fīət, -,at\ *n* : decree

fib \'fib\ *n* : trivial lie —**fib** *vb* —**fib·ber** *n*

fi·ber, fi·bre \'fībər\ *n* 1 : threadlike substance or structure (as a muscle cell or fine root) 2 : element that gives texture or substance —**fi·brous** \-brəs\ *adj*

fi·ber·board *n* : construction material made of compressed fibers

fi·ber·glass *n* : glass in fibrous form in various products (as insulation)

fi·bril·la·tion \,fibrə'lāshən, ,fīb-\ *n* : rapid irregular contractions of muscle fibers (as of the heart) —**fib·ril·late** \'fibrə,lāt, 'fīb-\ *vb*

fib·u·la \'fibyələ\ *n, pl* -lae \-lē, -lī\ *or* -las : outer of the two leg bones below the knee —**fib·u·lar** \-lər\ *adj*

fick·le \'fikəl\ *adj* : unpredictably changeable —**fick·le·ness** *n*

fic·tion \'fikshən\ *n* : a made-up story or literature consisting of these —**fic·tion·al** \-sh(ə)nəl\ *adj*

fic·ti·tious \fik'tishəs\ *adj* : made up or pretended

fid·dle \'fid°l\ *n* : violin ~ *vb* -dled; -dling 1 : play on the fiddle 2 : move the hands restlessly —**fid·dler** \'fidlər, -°lər\ *n*

fid·dle·sticks *n* : nonsense —used as an interjection

fi·del·i·ty \fə'delətē, fī-\ *n, pl* -ties 1 : quality or state of being faithful 2 : quality of reproduction

fid·get \'fijət\ *n* 1 *pl* : restlessness 2 : one that fidgets ~ *vb* : move restlessly —**fid·gety** *adj*

fi·du·cia·ry \fə'd(y)üshē,erē, -shərē\ *adj* : held or holding in trust —**fiduciary** *n*

field \'fēld\ *n* **1** : open country **2** : cleared land **3** : land yielding some special product **4** : sphere of activity **5** : area for sports **6** : region or space in which a given effect (as magnetism) exists ~ *vb* : put into the field —**field** *adj* —**field·er** *n*

fiend \'fēnd\ *n* **1** : devil **2** : extremely wicked person —**fiend·ish** *adj* —**fiend·ish·ly** *adv*

fierce \'fiərs\ *adj* **fierc·er; -est 1** : violently hostile or aggressive **2** : intense **3** : menacing looking —**fierce·ly** *adv* —**fierce·ness** *n*

fi·ery \'fī(ə)rē\ *adj* **fi·er·i·er; -est 1** : burning **2** : hot or passionate —**fi·eri·ness** \'fī(ə)rēnəs\ *n*

fi·es·ta \fē'estə\ *n* : festival

fife \'fīf\ *n* : small flute

fif·teen \fif'tēn\ *n* : one more than 14 —**fifteen** *adj or pron* —**fif·teenth** \-'tēnth\ *adj or n*

fifth \'fifth\ *n* **1** : one that is number 5 in a countable series **2** : one of 5 equal parts of something —**fifth** *adj or adv*

fif·ty \'fiftē\ *n, pl* **-ties** : 5 times 10 —**fif·ti·eth** \-tēəth\ *adj or n* —**fifty** *adj or pron*

fif·ty-fif·ty *adv or adj* : shared equally

fig \'fig\ *n* : pear-shaped edible fruit

fight \'fīt\ *vb* **fought** \'fot\; **fight·ing 1** : contend against another in battle **2** : box **3** : struggle ~ *n* **1** : hostile encounter **2** : boxing match **3** : verbal disagreement —**fight·er** *n*

fig·ment \'figmənt\ *n* : something imagined or made up

fig·u·ra·tive \'fig(y)ərətiv\ *adj* : metaphorical —**fig·u·ra·tive·ly** *adv*

fig·ure \'figyər\ *n* **1** : symbol representing a number **2** *pl* : arithmetical calculations **3** : price **4** : shape or outline **5** : illustration **6** : pattern or design **7** : prominent person ~ *vb* **-ured; -ur·ing 1** : be important **2** : calculate —**fig·ured** *adj*

fig·u·rine \,fig(y)ə'rēn\ *n* : small statue

fil·a·ment \'filəmənt\ *n* : fine thread or threadlike part —**fil·a·men·tous** \,filə'mentəs\ *adj*

fil·bert \'filbərt\ *n* : edible nut of a European hazel

filch \'filch\ *vb* : steal furtively

¹file \'fīl\ *n* : tool for smoothing or sharpening ~ *vb* **filed; fil·ing** : rub or smooth with a file

²file *vb* **filed; fil·ing 1** : arrange in order **2** : enter or record officially ~ *n* : device for keeping papers in order

³file *n* : row of persons or things one behind the other ~ *vb* **filed; fil·ing** : march in file

fil·ial \'filēəl, 'filyəl\ *adj* : relating to a son or daughter

fil·i·bus·ter \'filə,bəstər\ *n* : long speeches to delay a legislative vote —**filibuster** *vb* —**fil·i·bus·ter·er** *n*

fil·i·gree \-,grē\ *n* : ornamental designs of fine wire —**fil·i·greed** \-,grēd\ *adj*

fill \'fil\ *vb* **1** : make or become full **2** : stop up **3** : feed **4** : satisfy **5** : occupy fully **6** : spread through ~ *n* **1** : full supply **2** : material for filling —**fill·er** *n* —**fill in** *vb* **1** : provide information to or for **2** : substitute

fil·let \'filət, fi'lā, 'fil(,)ā\ *n* : piece of boneless meat or fish ~ *vb* : cut into fillets

fill·ing *n* : material used to fill something

fil·ly \'filē\ *n, pl* **-lies** : young female horse

film \'film\ *n* **1** : thin skin or membrane **2** : thin coating or layer **3** : strip of material used in taking pictures **4** : movie ~ *vb* : make a movie of —**filmy** *adj*

film·strip : strip of film with photographs for still projection

fil·ter \'filtər\ *n* **1** : device for separating matter from a fluid **2** : device (as on a camera lens) that absorbs light ~ *vb* **1** : pass through a filter **2** : remove by means of a filter —**fil·ter·able** *adj* —**fil·tra·tion** \fil'trāshən\ *n*

filth \'filth\ *n* : repulsive dirt or refuse —**filth·i·ness** *n* —**filthy** \'filthē\ *adj*

fin \'fin\ *n* **1** : thin external process controlling movement in an aquatic animal **2** : fin-shaped part (as on an airplane) **3** : flipper —**finned** \'find\ *adj*

fi·na·gle \fə'nāgəl\ *vb* **-gled; -gling** : get by clever or tricky means —**fi·na·gler** *n*

fi·nal \'fīn³l\ *adj* **1** : not to be changed **2** : ultimate **3** : coming at the end —**final** *n* —**fi·nal·ist** \'fīn³ləst\ *n* —**fi·nal·i·ty** \fī'nalətē, fə-\ *n* —**fi·nal·ize** \-,īz\ *vb* —**fi·nal·ly** *adv*

fi·na·le \fə'nalē, fē'näl-\ *n* : last or climactic part

fi·nance \fə'nans, 'fī,nans\ *n* **1** *pl* : money resources **2** : management of money affairs ~ *vb* **-nanced; -nanc·ing 1** : raise funds for **2** : give necessary funds to **3** : sell on credit

fi·nan·cial \fə'nanchəl, fī-\ *adj* : relating to finance —**fi·nan·cial·ly** *adv*

fi·nan·cier \,finən'sir, ,fī,nan-\ *n* : person who invests large sums of money

finch \'finch\ n : songbird (as a sparrow or linnet)

find \'fīnd\ vb **found** \'faùnd\; **find·ing** 1 : discover or encounter 2 : obtain by effort 3 : experience or perceive 4 : gain or regain the use of 5 : decide on (a verdict) ~ n 1 : act or instance of finding 2 : something found —**find·er** n —**find·ing** n —**find out** vb : learn, discover, or verify something

fine \'fīn\ n : money paid as a penalty ~ vb **fined; fin·ing** : impose a fine on ~ adj **fin·er; -est** 1 : free from impurity 2 : small or thin 3 : not coarse 4 : superior in quality or appearance ~ adv : finely —**fine·ly** adv —**fine·ness** n

fin·ery \'fīn(ə)rē\ n, pl **-er·ies** : showy clothing and jewels

fi·nesse \fə'nes\ n 1 : delicate skill 2 : craftiness —**finesse** vb

fin·ger \'fiŋgər\ n 1 : one of the 5 divisions at the end of the hand and esp. one other than the thumb 2 : something like a finger 3 : part of a glove for a finger ~ vb 1 : touch with the fingers 2 : identify as if by pointing —**fin·gered** adj —**fin·ger·nail** n —**fin·ger·tip** n

fin·ger·ling \-gərliŋ\ n : small fish

fin·ger·print n : impression of the pattern of marks on the tip of a finger —**fingerprint** vb

fin·icky \'finikē\ adj : excessively particular in taste or standards

fin·ish \'finish\ vb 1 : come or bring to an end 2 : use or dispose of entirely 3 : put a final coat or surface on ~ n 1 : end 2 : final treatment given a surface —**fin·ish·er** n

fi·nite \'fī,nīt\ adj : having definite limits

fink \'fiŋk\ n : contemptible person

fiord var of FJORD

fir \'fər\ n : erect evergreen tree or its wood

fire \'fī(ə)r\ n 1 : light or heat and esp. the flame of something burning 2 : destructive burning of something (as a house) 3 : enthusiasm 4 : discharge of firearms ~ vb **fired; fir·ing** 1 : kindle 2 : stir up or enliven 3 : dismiss from employment 4 : shoot 5 : bake —**fire·bomb** n or vb —**fire·less** adj —**fire·proof** adj or vb —**fire·wood** n

fire·arm n : weapon (as a rifle) that works by an explosion of gunpowder

fire·ball n 1 : ball of fire 2 : brilliant meteor

fire·boat n : ship equipped for fighting fire

fire·box n 1 : chamber (as of a furnace) that contains a fire 2 : fire-alarm box

fire·break n : cleared land for checking a forest fire

fire·bug n : person who deliberately sets destructive fires

fire·crack·er n : small firework that makes noise

fire·fly n : night-flying beetle that produces a soft light

fire·man \-mən\ n 1 : member of a company organized to put out fires 2 : stoker

fire·place n : opening made in a chimney to hold an open fire

fire·plug n : hydrant

fire·side n 1 : place near the fire or hearth 2 : home ~ adj : having an informal quality

fire·trap n : place apt to catch on fire

fire·work n : device that explodes to produce noise or a display of light

¹**firm** \'fərm\ adj 1 : securely fixed in place 2 : strong or vigorous 3 : not subject to change 4 : resolute ~ vb : make or become firm —**firm·ly** adv —**firm·ness** n

²**firm** n : business enterprise

fir·ma·ment \'fərməmənt\ n : sky

first \'fərst\ adj 1 : being number one 2 : foremost ~ adv 1 : before any other 2 : for the first time ~ n 1 : number one 2 : one that is first —**first class** n —**first-class** adj or adv —**first·ly** adv —**first-rate** adj or adv

first aid n : emergency care

first lieutenant n : commissioned officer ranking next below a captain

first sergeant n : noncommissioned officer serving as the chief assistant to the commander of a military unit (as a company) 2 : rank in the army below a command sergeant major and in the marine corps below a sergeant major

firth \'fərth\ n : estuary

fis·cal \'fiskəl\ adj : relating to money

fish \'fish\ n, pl **fish** or **fish·es** : water animal with fin, gills, and usu. scales ~ vb 1 : try to catch fish 2 : grope —**fish·er** n —**fish·hook** n —**fish·ing** n

fish·er·man \-mən\ n : one who fishes

fish·ery \'fish(ə)rē\ n, pl **-er·ies** : fishing business or a place for this

fishy \'fishē\ adj **fish·i·er; -est** 1 : relating to or like fish 2 : questionable

fis·sion \'fishən, 'fizh-\ n : splitting of an atomic nucleus —**fis·sion·able** \-(ə)nəbəl\ adj —**fis·sion·al** \-ən³l\ adj

fis·sure \'fishər\ n : crack

fist \'fist\ *n* 1 : hand doubled up —**fist-ed** \'fistəd\ *adj* —**fist-ful** \-,fùl\ *n*

fist-i-cuffs \'fisti,kəfs\ *n pl* : fist fight

¹fit \'fit\ *n* : sudden attack of illness or emotion

²fit *adj* **-tt-** 1 : suitable 2 : qualified 3 : sound in body ~ *vb* **-tt-** 1 : be suitable to 2 : insert or adjust correctly 3 : make room for 4 : supply or equip 5 : belong ~ *n* 1 : state of fitting or being fitted —**fit·ly** *adv* —**fit·ness** *n* —**fit·ter** *n*

fit·ful \'fitfəl\ *adj* : restless —**fit·ful·ly** *adv*

fit·ting *adj* : suitable ~ *n* : a small part

five \'fiv\ *n* 1 : one more than 4 2 : 5th in a set or series 3 : something having 5 units —**five** *adj or pron*

fix \'fiks\ *vb* 1 : attach 2 : establish 3 : make right 4 : prepare 5 : improperly influence ~ *n* 1 : predicament 2 : determination of location —**fix·er** *n*

fix·a·tion \fik'sāshən\ *n* : obsessive attachment —**fix·ate** \'fik,sāt\ *vb*

fixed \'fikst\ *adj* 1 : stationary 2 : settled —**fixed·ly** \'fiksədlē\ *adv* —**fixed·ness** \-nəs\ *n*

fix·ture \'fikschər\ *n* : permanent part of something

fizz \'fiz\ *vb* : make a hissing sound ~ *n* : effervescence

fiz·zle \'fizəl\ *vb* **-zled; -zling** 1 : fizz 2 : fail ~ *n* : failure

fjord \fē'ȯrd\ *n* : inlet of the sea between cliffs

flab \'flab\ *n* : flabby flesh

flab·ber·gast \'flabər,gast\ *vb* : astound

flab·by \'flabē\ *adj* **-bi·er; -est** : not firm —**flab·bi·ness** *n*

flac·cid \'flaksəd, 'flasəd\ *adj* : not firm

¹flag \'flag\ *n* : flat stone

²flag *n* 1 : fabric that is a symbol (as of a country) 2 : something used to signal ~ *vb* **-gg-** : signal with a flag —**flag·pole** *n* —**flag·staff** *n*

³flag *vb* **-gg-** : lose strength or spirit

flag·el·late \'flajə,lāt\ *vb* **-lat·ed; -lat·ing** : whip —**flag·el·la·tion** \,flajə'lāshən\ *n*

flag·on \'flagən\ *n* : container for liquids

fla·grant \'flāgrənt\ *adj* : conspicuously bad —**fla·grant·ly** *adv*

flag·ship *n* : ship carrying a commander

flag·stone *n* : flag

flail \'flāl\ *n* : tool for threshing grain ~ *vb* : beat with or as if with a flail

flair \'flaər\ *n* : natural aptitude

flak \'flak\ *n, pl* **flak** : antiaircraft fire

flake \'flāk\ *n* : small flat piece ~ *vb*

flaked; flak·ing : separate or form into flakes

flam·boy·ant \flam'bȯiənt\ *adj* : showy —**flam·boy·ance** \-əns\ *n* —**flam·boy·ant·ly** *adv*

flame \'flām\ *n* 1 : glowing part of a fire 2 : state of combustion 3 : burning passion —**flame** *vb* —**flam·ing** *adj*

fla·min·go \flə'miŋgō\ *n, pl* **-gos** : long-legged long-necked tropical water bird

flam·ma·ble \'flaməbəl\ *adj* : easily ignited

flange \'flanj\ *n* : rim

flank \'flaŋk\ *n* 1 : side of something ~ *vb* 1 : attack or go around the side of 2 : be at the side of

flan·nel \'flanᵊl\ *n* : soft napped fabric

flap \'flap\ *n* 1 : slap 2 : something flat that hangs loose ~ *vb* **-pp-** 1 : move (wings) up and down 2 : swing back and forth noisily

flap·jack \-,jak\ *n* : pancake

flare \'flaər\ *vb* **flared; flar·ing** : become suddenly bright or excited ~ *n* : blaze of light

flash \'flash\ *vb* 1 : give off a sudden flame or burst of light 2 : appear or pass suddenly ~ *n* 1 : sudden burst of light or inspiration 2 : instant ~ *adj* : coming suddenly

flash·light *n* : small battery-operated light

flashy \'flashē\ *adj* **flash·i·er; -est** : showy —**flash·i·ly** *adv* —**flash·i·ness** *n*

flask \'flask\ *n* : flattened bottle

¹flat \'flat\ *adj* **-tt-** 1 : smooth 2 : broad and thin 3 : definite 4 : uninteresting 5 : deflated 6 : below the true pitch ~ *n* 1 : level surface of land 2 : flat note in music 3 : deflated tire ~ *adv* **-tt-** 1 : exactly 2 : below the true pitch ~ *vb* **-tt-** : make flat —**flat·ly** *adv* —**flat·ness** *n* —**flat·ten** \-ᵊn\ *vb*

²flat *n* 1 : story in a building 2 : apartment

flat·car *n* : railroad car without sides

flat·fish *n* : flattened fish with both eyes on the upper side

flat·foot *n, pl* **flat·feet** : foot condition in which the arch is flattened —**flat·foot·ed** *adj*

flat·ter \'flatər\ *vb* 1 : praise insincerely 2 : judge or represent too favorably —**flat·ter·er** *n* —**flat·tery** \'flatərē\ *n*

flat·u·lent \'flachələnt\ *adj* : full of gas —**flat·u·lence** \-ləns\ *n*

flat·ware *n* : eating utensils

flaunt \'flȯnt\ *vb* : display ostentatiously —**flaunt** *n*

fla·vor \'flāvər\ n **1** : quality that affects the sense of taste **2** : something that adds flavor ~ vb : give flavor to —**fla·vor·ful** adj —**fla·vor·ing** \'flāv(ə)riŋ\ n —**fla·vor·some** adj

flaw \'flȯ\ n : fault —**flaw·less** adj —**flaw·less·ly** adv

flax \'flaks\ n : plant from which linen is made

flax·en \'flaksən\ adj : made of or like flax

flay \'flā\ vb **1** : strip off the skin of **2** : criticize harshly

flea \'flē\ n : leaping bloodsucking insect

fleck \'flek\ vb or n : streak or spot

fledg·ling \'flejliŋ\ n : young bird

flee \'flē\ vb **fled** \'fled\; **flee·ing** : run away

fleece \'flēs\ n : sheep's wool ~ vb **fleeced; fleec·ing 1** : shear **2** : get money from dishonestly —**fleecy** adj

¹fleet \'flēt\ vb : pass rapidly ~ adj : swift —**fleet·ing** adj —**fleet·ness** n

²fleet n : group of ships

fleet admiral n : commissioned officer of the highest rank in the navy

flesh \'flesh\ n **1** : soft parts of an animal's body **2** : soft plant tissue (as fruit pulp) —**fleshed** \'flesht\ adj —**fleshy** adj

flesh·ly \'fleshlē\ adj : sensual

flew past of FLY

flex \'fleks\ vb : bend

flex·i·ble \'fleksəbəl\ adj **1** : capable of being flexed **2** : adaptable —**flex·i·bil·i·ty** \,fleksə'bilətē\ n —**flex·i·bly** \-əblē\ adv

flick \'flik\ n : light jerky stroke ~ vb **1** : strike lightly **2** : flutter

flick·er \'flikər\ vb **1** : waver **2** : burn unsteadily ~ n **1** : sudden movement **2** : wavering light

fli·er \'flī(ə)r\ n **1** : aviator **2** : advertising circular

¹flight \'flīt\ n **1** : act or instance of flying **2** : ability to fly **3** : a passing through air or space **4** : series of stairs —**flight·less** adj

²flight n : act or instance of running away

flighty \-ē\ adj **flight·i·er; -est 1** : capricious **2** : silly

flim-flam \'flim,flam\ n : trickery

flim·sy \'flim-zē\ adj **-si·er; -est 1** : not strong or well made **2** : not believable —**flim·si·ly** adv —**flim·si·ness** n

flinch \'flinch\ vb : shrink from pain

fling \'fliŋ\ vb **flung** \'fləŋ\; **fling·ing 1** : move brusquely **2** : throw ~ n **1** : act or instance of flinging **2** : attempt **3** : period of self-indulgence

flint \'flint\ n : hard quartz that gives off sparks when struck with steel —**flinty** adj

flip \'flip\ vb **-pp- 1** : cause to turn over quickly or many times **2** : move with a quick push ~ adj : insolent —**flip** n

flip·pant \'flipənt\ adj : not serious enough —**flip·pan·cy** \-ənsē\ n

flip·per \'flipər\ n : paddlelike limb (as of a seal) for swimming

flirt \'flərt\ vb **1** : be playfully romantic **2** : trifle ~ n : one who flirts —**flir·ta·tion** \,flər'tāshən\ n —**flir·ta·tious** \-shəs\ adj

flit \'flit\ vb **-tt-** : dart

float \'flōt\ n **1** : something that floats **2** : vehicle carrying an exhibit ~ vb **1** : rest on or in a fluid without sinking **2** : finance by issuing stock or bonds —**float·er** n

flock \'fläk\ n : group of animals (as birds) or people ~ vb : gather or move as a group

floe \'flō\ n : mass of floating ice

flog \'fläg\ vb **-gg-** : beat with a rod or whip —**flog·ger** n

flood \'fləd\ n **1** : great flow of water over the land **2** : overwhelming volume ~ vb : cover or fill esp. with water —**flood·wa·ter** n

floor \'flōr\ n **1** : bottom of a room on which one stands **2** : story of a building **3** : lower limit ~ vb **1** : furnish with a floor **2** : knock down or overwhelm —**floor·board** n —**floor·ing** \-iŋ\ n

floo·zy, floo·zie \'flüzē\ n, pl **-zies** : tawdry woman

flop \'fläp\ vb **-pp- 1** : flap **2** : slump heavily **3** : fail —**flop** n

flop·py \'fläpē\ adj **-pi·er; -est** : soft and flexible

flo·ra \'flōrə\ n : plants or plant life of a region

flo·ral \'flōrəl\ adj : relating to flowers

flor·id \'flȯrəd\ adj **1** : excessively flowery in style **2** : reddish

flo·rist \'flȯrəst\ n : flower dealer

flo·ta·tion \flō'tāshən\ n : process or instance of floating

flo·til·la \flō'tilə\ n : small fleet

flot·sam \'flätsəm\ n : floating wreckage

¹flounce \'flaůns\ vb **flounced; flounc·ing** : move with exaggerated jerky motions —**flounce** n

²flounce n : fabric border

¹floun·der \'flaůndər\ n, pl **flounder** or **flounders** : flatfish

²flounder vb **1** : struggle for footing **2** : proceed clumsily

flour \'flaü(ə)r\ *n* : finely ground meal ~ *vb* : coat with flour —**floury** *adj*

flour·ish \'flərish\ *vb* 1 : thrive 2 : wave threateningly ~ *n* 1 : embellishment 2 : ostentatious action

flout \'flaüt\ *vb* : scorn

flow \'flō\ *vb* 1 : move in a stream 2 : proceed smoothly and readily ~ *n* : uninterrupted stream

flow·er \'flaü(ə)r\ *n* 1 : showy plant shoot that bears seeds 2 : state of flourishing ~ *vb* 1 : produce flowers 2 : flourish —**flow·ered** *adj* —**flow·er·i·ness** *n* —**flow·er·less** *adj* —**flow·er·pot** *n* —**flow·ery** \-ē\ *adj*

flown *past part of* FLY

flu \'flü\ *n* 1 : influenza 2 : minor virus ailment

flub \'fləb\ *vb* **-bb-** : bungle —**flub** *n*

fluc·tu·ate \'flakchə₁wāt\ *vb* **-at·ed; -at·ing** : change rapidly esp. up and down —**fluc·tu·a·tion** \₁flakchə-'wāshən\ *n*

flue \'flü\ *n* : smoke duct

flu·ent \'flüənt\ *adj* : speaking with ease —**flu·en·cy** \-ənsē\ *n* —**flu·ent·ly** *adv*

fluff \'fləf\ *n* 1 : something soft and light 2 : blunder ~ *vb* 1 : make fluffy 2 : make a mistake —**fluffy** \-ē\ *adj*

flu·id \'flüəd\ *adj* : flowing ~ *n* : substance that can flow —**flu·id·i·ty** \flü'idətē\ *n*

fluid ounce *n* : unit of liquid measure equal to ¹/₁₆ pint

fluke \'flük\ *n* : stroke of luck

flume \'flüm\ *n* : channel for water

flung *past of* FLING

flunk \'fləŋk\ *vb* : fail in school work

flun·ky, flun·key \'fləŋkē\ *n, pl* **-kies** *or* **keys** : obsequious or insignificant person

flu·o·res·cence \₁flu̇(ə)r'esᵊns\ *n* : emission of light after initial absorption —**flu·o·resce** \-'es\ *vb* —**flu·o·res·cent** \-'esᵊnt\ *adj*

flu·o·ri·date \'flu̇rə₁dāt\ *vb* **-dat·ed; -dat·ing** : add a compound of fluorine to —**flu·o·ri·da·tion** \₁flu̇rə'dā-shən\ *n*

flu·o·ride \'flü(ə)r₁īd\ *n* : compound of fluorine

flu·o·rine \'flü(ə)r₁ēn, -ən\ *n* : toxic gaseous chemical element

flu·o·ro·car·bon \₁flu̇(ə)rō'kärbən\ *n* : compound containing fluorine and carbon

flu·o·ro·scope \'flu̇rə₁skōp\ *n* : instrument for internal examination —**flu·o·ro·scop·ic** \₁flu̇rə'skäpik\ *adj* —**flu·o·ros·co·pist** \'flü(ə)r-

'äskəpəst\ *n* —**flu·o·ros·co·py** \-pē\ *n*

flur·ry \'flərē\ *n, pl* **-ries** 1 : light snowfall 2 : bustle 3 : brief burst of activity

¹flush \'fləsh\ *vb* : cause (a bird) to fly from cover

²flush *n* 1 : sudden flow (as of water) 2 : surge of emotion 3 : blush ~ *vb* 1 : blush 2 : wash out with a rush of liquid ~ *adj* 1 : filled to overflowing 2 : of a reddish healthy color 3 : smooth or level 4 : abutting —**flush** *adv*

³flush *n* : cards of the same suit

flus·ter \'fləstər\ *vb* : upset —**fluster** *n*

flute \'flüt\ *n* 1 : pipelike musical instrument 2 : groove —**flut·ed** *adj* —**flut·ing** *n* —**flut·ist** \-əst\ *n*

flut·ter \'flətər\ *vb* 1 : flap the wings rapidly 2 : move with quick wavering or flapping motions 3 : behave in an agitated manner ~ *n* 1 : a fluttering 2 : state of confusion —**flut·tery** \-ərē\ *adj*

flux \'fləks\ *n* : state of continuous change

¹fly \'flī\ *vb* **flew** \'flü\; **flown** \'flōn\; **fly·ing** 1 : move through the air with wings 2 : float or soar 3 : flee 4 : move or pass swiftly 5 : operate an airplane

²fly *n, pl* **flies** : garment closure

³fly *n, pl* **flies** : winged insect

fly-by-night *adj* : transitory

fly·er *var of* FLIER

fly·pa·per *n* : sticky paper for catching flies

fly·speck *n* 1 : speck of fly dung 2 : something tiny

fly·wheel *n* : rotating wheel that regulates the speed of machinery

f-number *n* : number expressing the effectiveness of a camera lens

foal \'fōl\ *n* : young horse —**foal** *vb*

foam \'fōm\ *n* 1 : mass of bubbles on top of a liquid 2 : material of cellular form ~ *vb* : form foam —**foamy** *adj*

fob \'fäb\ *n* : short chain for a pocket watch

fo'c'sle *var of* FORECASTLE

fo·cus \'fōkəs\ *n, pl* **-cus·es** *or* **-ci** \-₁sī\ 1 : point at which reflected or refracted rays meet 2 : adjustment (as of eyeglasses) for clear vision 3 : central point ~ *vb* : bring to a focus —**fo·cal** \-kəl\ *adj* —**fo·cal·ly** *adv*

fod·der \'fädər\ *n* : food for livestock

foe \'fō\ *n* : enemy

fog \'fȯg, 'fäg\ *n* 1 : fine particles of water suspended in the lower atmosphere 2 : mental confusion ~ *vb*

-gg- : obscure or be obscured with fog —**fog·gy** *adj*

fog-horn *n* : warning horn sounded in a fog

fo·gy \'fōgē\ *n, pl* **-gies** : person with old-fashioned ideas

foi·ble \'foibəl\ *n* : minor character fault

¹**foil** \'foil\ *vb* : defeat ~ *n* : fencing sword

²**foil** *n* **1** : thin sheet of metal **2** : one that sets off another by contrast

foist \'foist\ *vb* : force another to accept

¹**fold** \'fōld\ *n* **1** : enclosure for sheep **2** : group with a common interest

²**fold** *vb* **1** : lay one part over another **2** : embrace ~ *n* : part folded

fold·er \'fōldər\ *n* **1** : one that folds **2** : circular **3** : folded cover or envelope for papers

fol·de·rol \'fäldə,räl\ *n* : nonsense

fo·li·age \'fōl(ē)ij\ *n* : plant leaves

fo·lio \'fōlē,ō\ *n, pl* **-li·os** : sheet of paper folded once

folk \'fōk\ *n, pl* **folk** *or* **folks 1** : people in general **2** *folks pl* : one's family — *adj* : relating to the common people

folk-lore *n* : customs and traditions of a people —**folk-lor-ist** *n*

folksy \'fōksē\ *adj* **folks·i·er; -est** : friendly and informal

fol·li·cle \'fälikəl\ *n* : small anatomical cavity or gland

fol·low \'fälō\ *vb* **1** : go or come after **2** : pursue **3** : obey **4** : proceed along **5** : keep one's attention fixed on **6** : result from —**fol·low·er** *n*

fol·low·ing \'fäləwiŋ\ *adj* : next ~ *n* : group of followers ~ *prep* : after

fol·ly \'fälē\ *n, pl* **-lies** : foolishness

fo·ment \fō'ment\ *vb* : incite —**fo·men·ta·tion** \,fōmən'tāshən, -,men-\ *n*

fond \'fänd\ *adj* **1** : strongly attracted **2** : affectionate **3** : dear —**fond·ly** \'fän(d)lē\ *adv* —**fond·ness** \-nəs\ *n*

fon·dle \'fänd²l\ *vb* **-dled; -dling** : touch lovingly

fon·due \fän'd(y)ü\ *n* : preparation of melted cheese

font \'fänt\ *n* **1** : baptismal basin **2** : fountain

food \'füd\ *n* : material eaten to sustain life

fool \'fül\ *n* **1** : stupid person **2** : jester ~ *vb* **1** : waste time **2** : meddle **3** : deceive —**fool·ery** \'fül(ə)rē\ *n* —**fool·ish** \'fülish\ *adj* —**fool·ish·ly** *adv* —**fool·ish·ness** *n* —**fool-proof** *adj*

fool·har·dy \'fül,härdē\ *adj* : rash —**fool·har·di·ness** *n*

foot \'fut\ *n, pl* **feet** \'fēt\ **1** : terminal part of a leg **2** : unit of length equal to ⅓ yard **3** : unit of verse meter **4** : bottom —**foot·age** \-ij\ *n* —**foot-path** *n* —**foot·print** *n* —**foot-race** *n* —**foot-rest** *n* —**foot-wear** *n*

foot·ball *n* : ball game played by 2 teams on a rectangular field

foot-bridge *n* : bridge for pedestrians

foot·ed \'futəd\ *adj* : having feet or such or so many feet

foot-hill *n* : hill at the foot of higher hills

foot-hold *n* : support for the feet

foot·ing *n* **1** : foothold **2** : basis

foot-lights *n pl* : stage lights along the floor

foot-lock·er *n* : small trunk

foot-loose *adj* : having no ties

foot·man \-mən\ *n* : male servant

foot·note *n* : note at the bottom of a page

foot·step *n* **1** : step **2** : distance covered by a step **3** : footprint

foot·stool *n* : stool to support the feet

foot·work *n* : skillful movement of the feet (as in boxing)

fop \'fäp\ *n* : dandy —**fop·pery** \-(ə)rē\ *n* —**fop·pish** *adj*

for \fər, (')for\ *prep* **1** : —used to show preparation or purpose **2** : because of **3** : —used to show a recipient **4** : in support of **5** : so as to support or help cure **6** : so as to be equal to **7** : concerning **8** : through the period of ~ *conj* : because

for·age \'forij\ *n* **1** : food for animals **2** : search for provisions ~ *vb* **-aged; -ag·ing 1** : hunt food **2** : make a search

for·ay \'for,ā\ *vb* : raid for plunder —**foray** *n*

¹**for·bear** \for'baər\ *vb* **-bore** \-'bōr\, **-borne** \-'bōrn\; **-bear·ing 1** : refrain from **2** : be patient —**for·bear·ance** \-'barəns\ *n*

²**forbear** *var of* **FOREBEAR**

for·bid \fər'bid\ *vb* **-bade** \-'bad, -'bād\ *or* **-bad** \-'bad\; **-bid·den** \-'bid²n\; **-bid·ding 1** : prohibit **2** : order not to do something

for·bid·ding *adj* : tending to discourage

force \'fors\ *n* **1** : exceptional strength or energy **2** : military strength **3** : body (as of persons) available for a purpose **4** : violence **5** : influence (as a push or pull) that causes motion ~ *vb* **forced; forc·ing 1** : compel **2** : gain against resistance **3** : break open —**force·ful** \-fəl\ *adj* —**force·ful·ly** *adv* —**in force 1** : in great numbers **2** : valid

for·ceps \\'fȯrsəps\ *n, pl* **forceps** : surgical instrument for grasping objects

forc·i·ble \\'fȯrsəbəl\ *adj* **1** : done by force **2** : showing force —**forc·i·bly** \-blē\ *adv*

ford \\'fȯrd\ *n* : place to wade across a stream ~ *vb* : wade across

fore \\'fȯr\ *adv* : in or toward the front ~ *adj* : being or coming before in time, place, or order ~ *n* : front

fore–and–aft *adj* : lengthwise

fore·arm \\'fȯr-\ *n* : part of the arm between the elbow and the wrist

fore·bear, for·bear \\'fȯr₁baǝr, 'fȯr-\ *n* : ancestor

fore·bode \fȯr'bōd, fȯr-\ *vb* : predict —**fore·bod·ing** *n*

fore·cast \\'fȯr₁kast\ *vb* **-cast** *or* **-cast·ed; -cast·ing** : predict —**forecast** *n* —**fore·cast·er** *n*

fore·cas·tle \\'fōksǝl\ *n* : forward part of a ship

fore·close \fȯr'klōz\ *vb* : take legal measures to terminate a mortgage —**fore·clo·sure** \-'klōzhǝr\ *n*

fa·fa·ther \\'fȯr-\ *n* : ancestor

fore·fin·ger \\'fȯr-\ *n* : finger next to the thumb

fore·foot \\'fȯr-\ *n* : front foot of a quadruped

fore·front \\'fȯr-\ *n* : foremost position or place

fore·gath·er *var of* FORGATHER

¹fore·go \fȯr'gō\ *vb* **-went; -gone; -go·ing** : precede

²forego *var of* FORGO

fore·go·ing *adj* : preceding

fore·gone *adj* : determined in advance

fore·ground \\'fȯr-\ *n* : part of a scene nearest the viewer

fore·hand \\'fȯr-\ *n* : a stroke with the palm of the hand turned in the direction of movement —**forehand** *adj*

fore·head \\'fȯrǝd, 'fȯr₁hed\ *n* : part of the face above the eyes

for·eign \\'fȯrǝn\ *adj* **1** : situated outside a place or country and esp. one's own country **2** : belonging to a different place or country **3** : not pertinent **4** : related to or dealing with other nations —**for·eign·er** \-ǝr\ *n*

fore·know \fȯr'nō\ *vb* **-knew; -known; -know·ing** : know beforehand —**fore·knowl·edge** *n*

fore·leg \\'fȯr-\ *n* : front leg

fore·lock \\'fȯr-\ *n* : front lock of hair

fore·man \\'fȯrmǝn\ *n* **1** : spokesman of a jury **2** : workman in charge

fore·most \\'fȯr-\ *adj* : first in time, place, or order —**foremost** *adv*

fore·noon \\'fȯr-\ *n* : morning

fo·ren·sic \fǝ'rensik\ *adj* : relating to courts or public speaking or debate

fo·ren·sics \-siks\ *n pl* : art or study of speaking or debating

fore·or·dain \₁fȯr-\ *vb* : decree beforehand

fore·quar·ter \\'fȯr-\ *n* : front half of one side of the body of a quadruped

fore·run·ner \\'fȯr-\ *n* : one that goes before

fore·see \fȯr'sē\ *vb* **-saw; -seen; -see·ing** : see or realize beforehand —**fore·see·able** *adj*

fore·shad·ow \\'fȯr-\ *vb* : hint or suggest beforehand

fore·sight \\'fȯr-\ *n* : care or provision for the future —**fore·sight·ed** *adj* —**fore·sight·ed·ness** *n*

for·est \\'fȯrǝst\ *n* : large thick growth of trees and underbrush —**for·est·ed** \\'fȯrǝstǝd\ *adj* —**for·est·er** \-ǝstǝr\ *n* —**for·est·land** \-₁land\ *n* —**for·est·ry** \-ǝstrē\ *n*

fore·stall \fȯr'stȯl, fȯr-\ *vb* : prevent by acting in advance

foreswear *var of* FORSWEAR

fore·taste \\'fȯr-\ *n* : advance indication or notion ~ *vb* : anticipate

fore·tell \fȯr'tel\ *vb* **-told; -tell·ing** : predict

fore·thought \\'fȯr-\ *n* : foresight

for·ev·er \fǝ'revǝr\ *adv* **1** : for a limitless time **2** : always

for·ev·er·more \-₁evǝr'mōr\ *adv* : forever

fore·warn \fȯr-\ *vb* : warn beforehand

fore·word \\'fȯr-\ *n* : preface

for·feit \\'fȯrfǝt\ *n* : something forfeited ~ *vb* : lose or lose the right to by an error or crime —**for·fei·ture** \-fǝ₁chúr\ *n*

for·gath·er, fore·gath·er \fȯr'gathǝr, fȯr-\ *vb* : assemble

¹forge \\'fȯrj\ *n* : smithy ~ *vb* **forged; forg·ing 1** : form (metal) by heating and hammering **2** : imitate falsely esp. to defraud —**forg·er** *n* —**forg·ery** \-(ǝ)rē\ *n*

²forge *vb* **forged; forg·ing** : move ahead steadily

for·get \fǝr'get\ *vb* **-got** \-'gät\; **-got·ten** \-'gätᵊn\ *or* **-got; -get·ting 1** : be unable to think of or recall **2** : fail to think of at the proper time —**for·get·ful** \-fǝl\ *adj* —**for·get·ful·ly** *adv*

for·get–me–not *n* : small herb with blue or white flowers

for·give \fǝr'giv\ *vb* **-gave** \-'gāv\; **-giv·en** \-'givǝn\; **-giv·ing** : pardon —**for·giv·able** *adj* —**for·give·ness** *n*

for·go, fore·go \fȯr'gō, fȯr-\ *vb* **-went; -gone; -go·ing** : give up

fork \'fȯrk\ *n* **1** : implement with prongs for lifting, holding, or digging **2** : forked part **3** : a dividing into branches or a place where something branches ~ *vb* **1** : divide into branches **2** : move with a fork —**forked** \'fȯrkt, 'fȯrkəd\ *adj*

fork-lift *n* : hoisting machine with a fork-shaped lever

for-lorn \fər'lȯrn\ *adj* **1** : deserted **2** : wretched —**for-lorn-ly** *adv*

form \'fȯrm\ *n* **1** : shape **2** : set way of doing or saying something **3** : document with blanks to be filled in **4** : behavior or performance with respect to what is expected **5** : mold **6** : variety **7** : one of the ways in which a word is changed to show difference in use ~ *vb* **1** : give form or shape to **2** : train **3** : develop **4** : constitute —**form-a-tive** \'fȯrmətiv\ *adj* —**form-less** \-ləs\ *adj*

for-mal \'fȯrməl\ *adj* : following established custom ~ *n* : formal social event —**for-mal-i-ty** \fȯr'malətē\ *n* —**for-mal-ize** \'fȯrmə,līz\ *vb* —**for-mal-ly** *adv*

form-al-de-hyde \fȯr'maldə,hīd\ *n* : colorless pungent gas used as a preservative and disinfectant

for-mat \'fȯr,mat\ *n* : general style or arrangement of something —**format** *vb*

for-ma-tion \fȯr'māshən\ *n* **1** : a giving form to something **2** : something formed **3** : arrangement

for-mer \'fȯrmər\ *adj* : coming before in time —**for-mer-ly** *adv*

for-mi-da-ble \'fȯrmədəbəl, fȯr'mid-\ *adj* **1** : causing fear or dread **2** : very difficult —**for-mi-da-bly** \-blē\ *adv*

for-mu-la \'fȯrmyələ\ *n, pl* **-las** *or* **-lae** \-,lē, -,lī\ **1** : set form of words for ceremonial use **2** : recipe **3** : milk mixture for a baby **4** : group of symbols or figures expressing a single rule or idea **5** : set form or method

for-mu-late \-,lāt\ *vb* **-lat-ed; -lat-ing** : state definitely and clearly —**for-mu-la-tion** \,fȯrmyə'lāshən\ *n*

for-ni-ca-tion \,fȯrnə'kāshən\ *n* : illicit sexual intercourse —**for-ni-cate** \'fȯrnə,kāt\ *vb* —**for-ni-ca-tor** \-,kātər\ *n*

for-sake \fər'sāk\ *vb* **-sook** \-'sük\; **-sak-en** \-'sākən\; **-sak-ing** : abandon

for-swear, fore-swear \fȯr'swaar, fȯr-, -'swear\ *vb* **-swore; -sworn; -swear-ing 1** : renounce under oath **2** : perjure

for-syth-ia \fər'sithēə\ *n* : shrub grown for its yellow flowers

fort \'fȯrt\ *n* **1** : fortified place **2** : permanent army post

forte \'fȯrt, 'fȯr,tā\ *n* : something in which a person excels

forth \'fȯrth\ *adv* : forward

forth-com-ing *adj* : coming or available soon

forth-right *adj* : direct —**forth-right-ly** *adv* —**forth-right-ness** *n*

forth-with *adv* : immediately

for-ti-fy \'fȯrtə,fī\ *vb* **-fied; -fy-ing** : make strong —**for-ti-fi-ca-tion** \,fȯrtəfə'kāshən\ *n*

for-ti-tude \'fȯrtə,t(y)üd\ *n* : ability to endure

fort-night \'fȯrt,nīt\ *n* : 2 weeks —**fort-night-ly** *adj or adv*

for-tress \'fȯrtrəs\ *n* : fort

for-tu-itous \fȯr't(y)üətəs\ *adj* : accidental

for-tu-nate \'fȯrch(ə)nət\ *adj* **1** : coming by good luck **2** : lucky —**for-tu-nate-ly** *adv*

for-tune \'fȯrchən\ *n* **1** : apparent cause of something that happens to one unexpectedly **2** : good or bad luck **3** : destiny **4** : wealth

for-tune-tel-ler \-,telər\ *n* : one who foretells a person's future —**for-tune-tell-ing** \-iŋ\ *n or adj*

for-ty \'fȯrtē\ *n, pl* **forties** **:** 4 time 10 —**for-ti-eth** \-ēəth\ *adj or n* —**forty** *adj or pron*

for-ty-nin-er \-'nīnər\ *n* : a person in the gold rush to California in 1849

fo-rum \'fȯrəm\ *n, pl* **-rums 1** : Roman marketplace **2** : medium for open discussion

for-ward \'fȯrwərd\ *adj* **1** : being near or at or belonging to the front **2** : brash ~ *adv* : toward what is in front ~ *n* : player near the front of his team ~ *vb* **1** : help onward **2** : send on —**for-ward-er** \-wərdər\ *n* —**for-ward-ness** *n*

for-wards \'fȯrwərdz\ *adv* : forward

fos-sil \'fäsəl\ *n* : preserved trace of an ancient plant or animal ~ *adj* : being or originating from a fossil —**fos-sil-ize** *vb*

fos-ter \'fȯstər\ *adj* : being, having, or relating to substitute parents ~ *vb* : help to grow or develop

fought *past of* FIGHT

foul \'faúl\ *adj* **1** : offensive **2** : clogged with dirt **3** : abusive **4** : wet and stormy **5** : unfair ~ *n* : a breaking of the rules in a game ~ *adv* : foully ~ *vb* **1** : make or become foul or filthy **2** : tangle —**foul-ly** *adv* —**foul-**

mouthed \\-'maüthd, -'maütht\ *adj*
—**foul-ness** *n*

fou-lard \fü'lärd\ *n* : lightweight silk

foul-up *n* : error or state of confusion
—**foul up** *vb* : bungle

1found \'faünd\ *past of* FIND

2found *vb* : establish —**found-er** *n*

3found *vb* : melt (metal) and pour into
a mold —**found-er** *n* —**found-ry**
\'faündrē\ *n*

foun-da-tion \faün'dāshən\ *n* 1 : act of
founding 2 : basis for something 3
: endowed institution 4 : supporting
structure —**foun-da-tion-al**
\-sh(ə)nəl\ *adj*

foun-der \'faündər\ *vb* : sink

found-ling \'faün(d)liŋ\ *n* : abandoned
infant that is found

fount \'faünt\ *n* : fountain

foun-tain \'faünt⁰n\ *n* 1 : spring of water 2 : source 3 : artificial jet of water

four \'fōr\ *n* 1 : one more than 3
2 : 4th in a set or series 3 : something
having 4 units —**four** *adj or pron*

four-fold *adj* : quadruple —**four-fold**
adv

four-score *adj* : 80

four-some \'fōrsəm\ *n* : group of 4

four-teen \fōr'tēn\ *n* : one more than
13 —**fourteen** *adj or pron* —**four-
teenth** \-'tēnth\ *adj or n*

fourth \'fōrth\ *n* 1 : one that is 4th 2
: one of 4 equal parts of something
—**fourth** *adj or adv*

fowl \'faül\ *n, pl* **fowl** *or* **fowls** 1 : bird 2
: chicken

fox \'fäks\ *n, pl* **fox-es** *or* **fox** 1 : small
mammal related to wolves 2 : clever
person ~ *vb* : trick —**foxy** \'fäksē\
adj

fox-glove *n* : flowering plant that provides digitalis

fox-hole \'fäks,hōl\ *n* : pit for protection against enemy fire

foy-er \'foiər, 'foi,(y)ā\ *n* : entrance
hallway

fra-cas \'frākəs, 'frak-\ *n, pl* **-cas-es**
\-əsəz\ : brawl

frac-tion \'frakshən\ *n* 1 : number indicating one or more equal parts of
a whole 2 : portion —**frac-tion-al**
\-sh(ə)nəl\ *adj* —**frac-tion-al-ly** *adv*

frac-tious \-shəs\ *adj* : hard to control

frac-ture \-chər\ *n* : a breaking of
something —**fracture** *vb*

frag-ile \'frajəl, -,il\ *adj* : easily broken
—**fra-gil-i-ty** \frə'jilətē\ *n*

frag-ment \'fragmənt\ *n* : part broken
off ~ *vb* \-,ment\ : break into parts
—**frag-men-tary** \'fragmən,terē\ *adj*
—**frag-men-ta-tion** \,fragmən'tāshən, -,men-\ *n*

fra-grant \'frāgrənt\ *adj* : sweet-smell-
ing —**fra-grance** \-grəns\ *n* —**fra-
grant-ly** *adv*

frail \'frāl\ *adj* : weak or delicate
—**frail-ty** \'frā(ə)ltē\ *n*

frame \'frām\ *vb* **framed; fram-ing** 1
: plan 2 : formulate 3 : construct or
arrange 4 : enclose in a frame 5
: make appear guilty ~ *n* 1 : makeup
of the body 2 : supporting or enclosing structure 3 : state or disposition
(as of mind) —**frame-work** *n*

franc \'fraŋk\ *n* : monetary unit (as of
France)

fran-chise \'fran,chīz\ *n* 1 : special
privilege 2 : the right to vote —**fran-
chi-see** \,franchī'zē, -chə-\ *n*

fran-gi-ble \'franjəbəl\ *adj* : breakable
—**fran-gi-bil-i-ty** \,franjə'bilətē\ *n*

1frank \'fraŋk\ *adj* : direct and sincere
—**frank-ly** *adv* —**frank-ness** *n*

2frank *vb* : mark (mail) with a sign
showing it can be mailed free ~ *n*
: sign on franked mail

frank-furt-er \'fraŋk(f)ərtər, -,fərt-\,
frank-furt-er
\'fraŋkfərt(r)ər, -,fərt-\, **frank-furt**,
frank-fort \-fərt\ *n* : cooked sausage

frank-in-cense \'fraŋkən,sens\ *n* : incense resin

fran-tic \'frantik\ *adj* : wildly excited
—**fran-ti-cal-ly** \-ik(ə)lē\ *adv* —**fran-
tic-ly** \-iklē\ *adv*

fra-ter-nal \frə'tərnəl\ *adj* : brotherly
2 : of a fraternity —**fra-ter-nal-ly** *adv*

fra-ter-ni-ty \frə'tərnətē\ *n, pl* **-ties**
: social club of males

frat-er-nize \'fratər,nīz\ *vb* **-nized; -niz-
ing** 1 : mingle as friends 2 : associate
with citizens or troops of a hostile
nation —**frat-er-ni-za-tion** \,fratər-
nə'zāshən\ *n*

frat-ri-cide \'fratrə,sīd\ *n* : killing of a
brother or sister —**frat-ri-cid-al**
\,fratrə'sīd⁰l\ *adj*

fraud \'frȯd\ *n* : trickery —**fraud-u-lent**
\'frȯjələnt\ *adj* —**fraud-u-lent-ly** *adv*

fraught \'frȯt\ *adj* : bearing promise or
menace

1fray \'frā\ *n* : fight

2fray *vb* 1 : wear by rubbing 2 : separate the threads of 3 : irritate

fraz-zle \'frazəl\ *vb* **-zled; -zling** : wear
out ~ *n* : exhaustion

freak \'frēk\ *n* 1 : something abnormal
or unusual 2 : enthusiast —**freak-ish**
adj —**freak out** *vb* : experience night-
marish hallucinations from drugs

freck-le \'frekəl\ *n* : brown spot on the
skin —**freckle** *vb*

free \'frē\ *adj* **fre-er; fre-est** 1 : having
liberty or independence 2 : not taxed
3 : given without charge 4 : volun-

tary **5** : not in use **6** : not fastened ∼ *adv* : without charge ∼ *vb* **freed**;

free·ing : set free —**free-born** *adj* —**free·dom** \'frēdəm\ *n* —**free·ly** *adv*

free-boo·ter \-,bütər\ *n* : pirate

free-for-all *n* : fight with no rules

free·load *vb* : live off another's generosity —**free·load·er** *n*

free·stand·ing *adj* : standing without support

free·way \'frē,wā\ *n* : limited-access expressway

free will *n* : independent power to choose —**free·will** *adj*

freeze \'frēz\ *vb* **froze** \'frōz\; **fro·zen** \'frōz°n\; **freez·ing 1** : harden into ice **2** : become chilled **3** : damage by frost **4** : stick fast **5** : become motionless **6** : fix at one stage or level ∼ *n* **1** : very cold weather **2** : state of being frozen —**freez·er** *n*

freeze-dry *vb* : preserve by freezing then drying —**freeze-dried** *adj*

freight \'frāt\ *n* **1** : carrying of goods or payment for this **2** : shipped goods ∼ *vb* : load or ship goods —**freight·er** *n*

french fry *vb* : fry in deep fat —**french fry** *n*

fre·net·ic \fri'netik\ *adj* : frenzied —**fre·net·i·cal·ly** \-ik(ə)lē\ *adv*

fren·zy \'frenzē\ *n, pl* -**zies** : violent agitation —**fren·zied** \-zēd\ *adj*

fre·quen·cy \'frēkwənsē\ *n, pl* -**cies 1** : frequent or regular occurrence **2** : number of cycles or sound waves per second

fre·quent \'frēkwənt\ *adj* : happening often ∼ \frē'kwent, 'frē-\ *vb* : go to habitually —**fre·quent·er** *n* —**fre·quent·ly** *adv*

fres·co \'freskō\ *n, pl* -**coes** or -**cos** : painting on fresh plaster

fresh \'fresh\ *adj* **1** : not salt **2** : invigorating **3** : not preserved **4** : not stale **5** : like new **6** : insolent —**fresh·en** \-ən\ *vb* —**fresh·ly** *adv* —**fresh·ness** *n*

fresh·et \-ət\ *n* : overflowing stream

fresh·man \-mən\ *n* : first-year student

fresh·wa·ter *adj* : of water that is not salt

fret \'fret\ *vb* **-tt- 1** : worry or become irritated **2** : fray **3** : agitate ∼ *n* **1** : worn spot **2** : irritation —**fret·ful** \'fretfəl\ *adj* —**fret·ful·ly** *adv* —**fret·ful·ness** *n*

fri·a·ble \'frīəbəl\ *adj* : easily pulverized

fri·ar \'frī(ə)r\ *n* : member of a religious order

fri·ary \-ē\ *n, pl* -**ar·ies** : monastery of friars

fric·as·see \'frikə,sē, ,frikə'-\ *n* : meat stewed in a gravy ∼ *vb* **-seed**; **-see·ing** : stew in gravy

fric·tion \'frikshən\ *n* **1** : a rubbing between 2 surfaces **2** : clash of opinions —**fric·tion·al** *adj*

Fri·day \'frīdē\ *n* : 6th day of the week

friend \'frend\ *n* : person one likes —**friend·less** \'fren(d)ləs\ *adj* —**friend·li·ness** \'fren(d)lēnəs\ *n* —**friend·ly** *adj* —**friend·ship** \'fren(d),ship\ *n*

frieze \'frēz\ *n* : ornamental band around a room

frig·ate \'frigət\ *n* : warship larger than a destroyer

fright \'frīt\ *n* : sudden fear —**fright·en** \-°n\ *vb* —**fright·ful** \-fəl\ *adj* —**fright·ful·ly** *adv* —**fright·ful·ness** *n*

frig·id \'frijəd\ *adj* : intensely cold —**fri·gid·i·ty** \fri'jidətē\ *n*

frill \'fril\ *n* **1** : ruffle **2** : pleasing but nonessential addition —**frilly** *adj*

fringe \'frinj\ *n* **1** : ornamental border of short hanging threads or strips **2** : border ∼ *vb* : furnish with or serve as a fringe

frisk \'frisk\ *vb* **1** : leap about **2** : search (a person) esp. for weapons

frisky \'friskē\ *adj* **frisk·i·er; -est** : frolicsome —**frisk·i·ly** *adv* —**frisk·i·ness** *n*

¹frit·ter \'fritər\ *n* : fried batter containing fruit or meat

²fritter *vb* : waste little by little

friv·o·lous \'friv(ə)ləs\ *adj* : not important or serious —**fri·vol·i·ty** \fri-v²alətē\ *n* —**friv·o·lous·ly** *adv*

frizz \'friz\ *vb* : curl tightly —**frizz** *n* —**frizzy** *adj*

fro \'frō\ *adv* : away

frock \'fräk\ *n* **1** : loose outer garment **2** : dress

frog \'frog, 'fräg\ *n* **1** : leaping amphibian **2** : hoarseness **3** : ornamental braid fastener **4** : small holder for flowers

frog·man \-,man, -mən\ *n* : underwater swimmer

frol·ic \'frälik\ *vb* **-icked**; **-ick·ing** : romp ∼ *n* : fun —**frol·ic·some** \-səm\ *adj*

from \(')frəm, 'främ\ *prep* —used to show a starting point

frond \'fränd\ *n* : fern leaf

front \'frənt\ *n* **1** : face **2** : behavior **3** : main side of a building **4** : forward part **5** : boundary between air masses ∼ *vb* **1** : face **2** : serve as a front —**fron·tal** \-°l\ *adj*

front·age \'frəntij\ *n* : length of boundary line on a street

fron·tier \₁frən'tiər\ *n* : outer edge of settled territory —**fron·tiers·man** \-'tiərzmən\ *n*

fron·tis·piece \'frəntə₁spēs\ *n* : illustration facing a title page

frost \'frȯst\ *n* 1 : freezing temperature 2 : ice crystals on a surface ~ *vb* 1 : cover with frost 2 : put icing on (a cake) —**frosty** *adj*

frost·bite \'frȯs(t)₁bīt\ *n* : partial freezing of part of the body —**frostbit·ten** \-₁bit³n\ *adj*

frost·ing *n* : icing

froth \'frȯth\ *n, pl* **froths** \'frȯths, 'frȯthz\ : bubbles on a liquid —**frothy** *adj*

fro·ward \'frō(w)ərd\ *adj* : willful

frown \'fraún\ *vb or n* : scowl

frow·sy \'fraúzē\ *adj* **-si·er; -est** : untidy

froze *past of* FREEZE

frozen *past part of* FREEZE

fru·gal \'frügəl\ *adj* : thrifty —**fru·gal·i·ty** \frü'galətē\ *n* —**fru·gal·ly** *adv*

fruit \'früt\ *n* 1 : usu. edible and sweet part of a seed plant 2 : result ~ *vb* : bear fruit —**fruit·cake** *n* —**fruit·ed** \-əd\ *adj* —**fruit·ful** *adj* —**fruit·ful·ness** *n* —**fruit·less** *adj* —**fruity** *adj*

fru·ition \frü'ishən\ *n* : completion

frumpy \'frəmpē\ *adj* **frump·i·er; -est** : dowdy

frus·trate \'frəs₁trāt\ *vb* **-trat·ed; -trat·ing** 1 : block 2 : cause to fail —**frus·trat·ing·ly** *adv* —**frus·tra·tion** \frəs'trāshən\ *n*

¹fry \'frī\ *vb* **fried; fry·ing** 1 : cook esp. with fat or oil 2 : be cooked by frying ~ *n, pl* **fries** 1 : something fried 2 : social gathering with fried food

²fry *n, pl* **fry** : recently hatched fish

fud·dle \'fəd³l\ *vb* **-dled; -dling** : muddle

fud·dy-dud·dy \'fədē₁dədē\ *n, pl* **-dies** : one who is old-fashioned or unimaginative

fudge \'fəj\ *vb* **fudged; fudg·ing** : cheat or exaggerate ~ *n* : creamy candy

fu·el \'fyüəl\ *n* : substance burned to produce heat or power ~ *vb* **-eled** *or* **-elled; -el·ing** *or* **-el·ling** : provide with or take in fuel

fu·gi·tive \'fyüjətiv\ *adj* 1 : running away or trying to escape 2 : not lasting —**fugitive** *n*

-ful \fəl\ *adj suffix* 1 : full of 2 : having the qualities of 3 : -able ~ *n suffix* : quantity that fills

ful·crum \'fúlkrəm, 'fəl-\ *n, pl* **-crums**

or **-cra** \-krə\ : support on which a lever turns

ful·fill, ful·fil \fúl'fil\ *vb* **-filled; -fill·ing** 1 : perform 2 : satisfy —**ful·fill·ment** *n*

¹full \'fúl\ *adj* 1 : filled 2 : complete 3 : rounded 4 : having an abundance of something ~ *adv* : entirely ~ *n* : utmost degree —**full·ness** \'fúlnəs\ *n* —**ful·ly** \-(l)ē\ *adv*

²full *vb* : shrink and thicken woolen cloth —**full·er** *n*

full-fledged \'fúl'flejd\ *adj* : fully developed

ful·some \'fúlsəm\ *adj* : offensive

fum·ble \'fəmbəl\ *vb* **-bled; -bling** : fail to hold something properly —**fumble** *n*

fume \'fyüm\ *n* : irritating gas ~ *vb* **fumed; fum·ing** 1 : give off fumes 2 : show annoyance

fu·mi·gate \'fyümə₁gāt\ *vb* **-gat·ed; -gat·ing** : treat with pest-killing fumes —**fu·mi·gant** \'fyümigant\ *n* —**fu·mi·ga·tion** \₁fyümə'gāshən\ *n*

fun \'fən\ *n* 1 : something providing amusement or enjoyment 2 : enjoyment

func·tion \'fəŋkshən\ *n* 1 : special purpose 2 : formal ceremony or social affair ~ *vb* 1 : serve 2 : operate —**func·tion·al** \-sh(ə)nəl\ *adj* —**func·tion·al·ly** *adv* —**func·tion·less** *adj*

func·tion·ary \-shə₁nerē\ *n, pl* **-ar·ies** : official

fund \'fənd\ *n* 1 : store 2 : sum of money intended for a special purpose 3 *pl* : available money ~ *vb* : provide funds for

fun·da·men·tal \₁fəndə'ment³l\ *adj* 1 : basic 2 : of central importance or necessity —**fundamental** *n* —**fun·da·men·tal·ly** *adv*

fu·ner·al \'fyün(ə)rəl\ *n* : ceremony for a dead person —**funeral** *adj* —**fu·ne·re·al** \fyü'nirēəl\ *adj*

fun·gi·cide \'fənjə₁sīd, 'fəŋgə-\ *n* : agent that kills fungi —**fun·gi·cid·al** \₁fənjə'sīd³l, ₁fəŋgə-\ *adj*

fun·gus \'fəŋgəs\ *n, pl* **fun·gi** \'fən₁jī, 'fən₁gī\ : lower plant that lacks chlorophyll —**fun·gal** \'fəŋgəl\ *adj* —**fun·gous** \-gəs\ *adj*

funk \'fəŋk\ *n* : state of paralyzed fear

funky \'fəŋkē\ *adj* **funk·i·er; -est** : unconventional and unsophisticated

fun·nel \'fən³l\ *n* 1 : cone-shaped utensil with a tube 2 : ship's smokestack ~ *vb* **-neled; -nel·ing** : move to a central point or into a central channel

fun·nies \ˈfənēz\ *n pl* : section of comic strips

fun·ny \ˈfanē\ *adj* **-ni·er; -est 1** : amusing **2** : strange

fur \ˈfər\ *n* **1** : hairy coat of a mammal **2** : article of clothing made with fur —**fur** *adj* —**furred** \ˈfərd\ *adj* —**fur·ry** \-ē\ *adj*

fur·bish \ˈfərbish\ *vb* : make lustrous or new looking

fu·ri·ous \ˈfyurēəs\ *adj* : fierce or angry —**fu·ri·ous·ly** *adv*

fur·long \ˈfər‚lȯŋ\ *n* : a unit of length equal to 220 yards

fur·lough \ˈfərlō\ *n* : authorized absence from duty —**furlough** *vb*

fur·nace \ˈfərnəs\ *n* : enclosed structure in which heat is produced

fur·nish \-nish\ *vb* **1** : provide with what is needed **2** : make available for use

fur·nish·ings \-iŋs\ *n pl* **1** : articles or accessories of dress **2** : furniture

fur·ni·ture \ˈfərnichər\ *n* : movable equipment necessary for a room

fu·ror \ˈfyùr‚ȯr\ *n* **1** : anger **2** : sensational craze

fur·ri·er \ˈfərēər\ *n* : dealer in furs —**fur·ri·ery** \-ē\ *n*

fur·row \ˈfərō\ *n* **1** : trench made by a plow **2** : wrinkle or groove —**furrow** *vb*

fur·ther \ˈfərthər\ *adv* **1** : at or to a more advanced point **2** : more ~ *adj* : additional ~ *vb* : promote —**fur·ther·ance** \-(ə)rəns\ *n*

fur·ther·more \ˈfərthə(r)‚mōr\ *adv* : in addition

fur·ther·most \-‚thər‚mōst\ *adj* : most distant

fur·thest \ˈfərthəst\ *adv or adj* : farthest

fur·tive \ˈfərtiv\ *adj* : slyly or secretly

done —**fur·tive·ly** *adv* —**fur·tive·ness** *n*

fu·ry \ˈfyùrē\ *n, pl* **-ries 1** : violent anger **2** : violence

¹fuse \ˈfyüz\ *n* **1** : tube lighted to transmit fire to an explosive **2** *usu* **fuze** : device for exploding a charge ~, **fuze** *vb* **fused** or **fuzed; fus·ing** or **fuz·ing** : equip with a fuse

²fuse *vb* **fused; fus·ing 1** : melt and run together **2** : unite ~ *n* : electrical safety device —**fus·ible** *adj*

fu·se·lage \ˈfyüsə‚läzh, -zə-\ *n* : main body of an airplane

fu·sil·lade \ˈfyüsə‚läd, -‚läd, ‚fyüsəˈ-, -zə-\ *n* : volley of fire

fu·sion \ˈfyüzhən\ *n* **1** : process of merging by melting **2** : union of atomic nuclei

fuss \ˈfəs\ *n* **1** : needless bustle or excitement **2** : unusual amount of attention or interest **3** : objection or protest ~ *vb* **1** : shower flattering attention **2** : pay undue attention to details

fuss·bud·get \-‚bəjət\ *n* : one who fusses about trifles

fussy \ˈfəsē\ *adj* **fuss·i·er; -est 1** : irritable **2** : fastidious —**fuss·i·ly** *adv* —**fuss·i·ness** *n*

fu·tile \ˈfyütᵊl, ˈfyü‚tīl\ *adj* : useless or vain —**fu·til·i·ty** \fyüˈtilətē\ *n*

fu·ture \ˈfyüchər\ *adj* : coming after the present ~ *n* **1** : time yet to come **2** : what will happen —**fu·tur·is·tic** \‚fyüchəˈristik\ *adj*

fuze *var of* FUSE

fuzz \ˈfəz\ *n* : fine particles or fluff

fuzzy \ˈfəzē\ *adj* **fuzz·i·er; -est 1** : covered with or like fuzz **2** : indistinct —**fuzz·i·ness** *n*

-fy \‚fī\ *vb suffix* : make —**fi·er** \‚fī(ə)r\ *n suffix*

G

g \ˈjē\ *n, pl* **g's** or **gs** \ˈjēz\ **1** : 7th letter of the alphabet **2** : unit of gravitational force

gab \ˈgab\ *vb* **-bb-** : chatter —**gab** *n* —**gab·by** \ˈgabē\ *adj*

gab·ar·dine \ˈgabər‚dēn\ *n* : durable twilled fabric

ga·ble \ˈgābəl\ *n* : triangular part of the end of a building —**ga·bled** \-bəld\ *adj*

gad \ˈgad\ *vb* **-dd-** : roam about —**gad·der** *n*

gad·fly *n* : persistently critical person

gad·get \ˈgajət\ *n* : device —**gad·get·ry** \ˈgajətrē\ *n*

gaff \ˈgaf\ *n* : metal hook for lifting fish —**gaff** *vb*

gaffe \ˈgaf\ *n* : social blunder

gag \ˈgag\ *vb* **-gg- 1** : prevent from speaking or crying out by stopping up the mouth **2** : retch or cause to retch ~ *n* **1** : something that stops up the mouth **2** : laugh-provoking remark or act

gage *var of* GAUGE

gag·gle \ˈgagəl\ *n* : flock of geese

gai·ety \\'gāətē\ *n, pl* **-eties** : gay spirits

gai·ly \\'gālē\ *adv* : in a gay manner

gain \\'gān\ *n* **1** : profit **2** : obtaining of profit or possessions **3** : increase ~ *vb* **1** : get possession of **2** : win **3** : arrive at **4** : increase or increase in **5** : profit —**gain·er** *n* —**gain·ful** *adj* —**gain·ful·ly** *adv*

gain·say \gān'sā\ *vb* **-said** \-'sād, -'sed\; **-say·ing; -says** \-'sāz, -'sez\ : deny or dispute —**gain·say·er** *n*

gait \\'gāt\ *n* : manner of walking or running —**gait·ed** *adj*

gal \\'gal\ *n* : girl

ga·la \\'gālə, 'galə, 'gälə\ *n* : festive celebration —**gala** *adj*

gal·axy \\'galəksē\ *n, pl* **-ax·ies** : any of the systems that include stars, nebulas, and dust and make up the universe —**ga·lac·tic** \gə'laktik\ *adj*

gale \\'gāl\ *n* **1** : strong wind **2** : outburst

¹gall \\'gȯl\ *n* **1** : bile **2** : insolence

²gall *n* **1** : sore on the skin caused by chafing **2** : swelling of plant tissue caused by parasites ~ *vb* **1** : chafe **2** : irritate or vex

gal·lant \gə'lant, -'länt; 'galənt\ *n* : man very attentive to women ~ \'galənt; gə'lant, -'länt\ *adj* **1** : splendid **2** : brave **3** : polite and attentive to women —**gal·lant·ly** *adv* —**gal·lant·ry** \'galəntrē\ *n*

gall·blad·der *n* : pouch attached to the liver in which bile is stored

gal·le·on \\'galēən\ *n* : former ship used for war and commerce esp. by the Spanish

gal·lery \\'gal(ə)rē\ *n, pl* **-ler·ies** **1** : outdoor balcony **2** : long narrow room or passage **3** : room or building for exhibiting art **4** : spectators —**gal·ler·ied** \-rēd\ *adj*

gal·ley \\'galē\ *n, pl* **-leys** **1** : old ship propelled by oars and sails **2** : kitchen of a ship or airplane

gal·li·um \\'galēəm\ *n* : bluish white metallic chemical element

gal·li·vant \\'galə₁vant\ *vb* **1** : be socially active esp. with members of the opposite sex **2** : travel about for pleasure

gal·lon \\'galən\ *n* : unit of liquid measure equal to 4 quarts

gal·lop \\'gaľəp\ *n* : fast 3-beat gait of a horse —**gallop** *vb* —**gal·lop·er** *n*

gal·lows \\'galōz\ *n, pl* **-lows** *or* **-lows·es** : upright frame for hanging criminals

gall·stone *n* : abnormal concretion in the gallbladder or bile passages

ga·lore \gə'lōr\ *adj* : in abundance

ga·losh \-'läsh\ *n* : overshoe —usu. pl.

gal·va·nize \\'galvə₁nīz\ *vb* **-nized; -niz·ing 1** : shock into action **2** : coat (iron or steel) with zinc —**gal·va·ni·za·tion** \₁galvənə'zāshən\ *n* —**gal·va·niz·er** *n*

gam·bit \\'gambət\ *n* **1** : opening tactic in chess **2** : risky stratagem

gam·ble \\'gambəl\ *vb* **-bled; -bling 1** : play a game for stakes **2** : bet **3** : take a chance ~ *n* : risky undertaking —**gam·bler** \-blər\ *n*

gam·bol \\'gambəl\ *vb* **-boled** *or* **-bolled; -bol·ing** *or* **-bol·ling** : skip about in play —**gambol** *n*

game \\'gām\ *n* **1** : playing activity **2** : competition according to rules **3** : animals hunted for sport or food ~ *vb* **gamed; gam·ing** : gamble ~ *adj* **1** : plucky **2** : lame —**game·ly** *adv* —**game·ness** *n*

game·cock *n* : male fighting cock

game·keep·er *n* : person in charge of game animals or birds

ga·mete \gə'mēt, 'gam₁ēt\ *n* : matured germ cell —**ga·met·ic** \gə'metik\ *adj*

ga·mine \gə'mēn\ *n* : charming tomboy

gam·ut \\'gamət\ *n* : entire range or series

gamy *or* **gam·ey** \\'gāmē\ *adj* **gam·i·er; -est** : having the flavor of game esp. when slightly tainted —**gam·i·ness** *n*

¹gan·der \\'gandər\ *n* : male goose

²gander *n* : glance

gang \\'gaŋ\ *n* **1** : group of persons working together **2** : group of criminals ~ *vb* : attack in a gang —with **up**

gan·gling \\'gaŋgliŋ\ *adj* : lanky

gan·gli·on \\'gaŋglēən\ *n, pl* **-glia** \-glēə\ : mass of nerve cells —**gan·gli·on·ic** \₁gaŋglē'änik\ *adj*

gang·plank *n* : platform used in boarding or leaving a ship

gan·grene \\'gaŋ₁grēn, gaŋ'-; 'gaŋ₁-, gaŋ'-\ *n* : local death of body tissue —**gangrene** *vb* —**gan·gre·nous** \'gaŋgrənəs\ *adj*

gang·ster \\'gaŋstər\ *n* : member of criminal gang

gang·way \-,wā\ *n* : passage in or out

gan·net \\'ganət\ *n* : large fish-eating marine bird

gan·try \\'gantrē\ *n, pl* **-tries** : frame structure supported over or around something

gap \\'gap\ *n* **1** : break in a barrier **2** : mountain pass **3** : empty space

gape \\'gāp, 'gap\ *vb* **gaped; gap·ing 1** : open widely **2** : stare with mouth open —**gape** *n*

ga·rage \gə'räzh, -'räj\ n : building for housing or repairing automobiles ~ vb -raged; -rag·ing : put or keep in a garage

garb \'gärb\ n : clothing ~ vb : dress

gar·bage \'gärbij\ n 1 : food waste 2 : trash

gar·ble \'gärbəl\ vb -bled; -bling : distort the meaning or sound of

gar·den \'gärd°n\ n 1 : plot for growing fruits, flowers, or vegetables 2 : public recreation area ~ vb : work in a garden —gar·den·er \'gärdnər, -°nər\ n

gar·de·nia \gär'dēnyə\ n : tree or shrub with fragrant white or yellow flowers or the flower

gar·gan·tuan \gär'ganch(ə)wən\ adj : having tremendous size or volume

gar·gle \'gärgəl\ vb -gled; -gling : rinse the throat with liquid —gargle n

gar·goyle \'gär,göil\ n : waterspout in the form of a grotesque human or animal

gar·ish \'ga(ə)rish\ adj : offensively bright or gaudy

gar·land \'gärlənd\ n : wreath of leaves or flowers ~ vb : form into or deck with a garland

gar·lic \'gärlik\ n : herb with pungent bulbs used in cooking —gar·licky \-likē\ adj

gar·ment \-mənt\ n : article of clothing

gar·ner \-nər\ vb : acquire by effort

gar·net \-nət\ n : deep red mineral

gar·nish \-nish\ vb : add decoration to (as food) —garnish n

gar·nish·ee \,gärnə'shē\ vb -eed; -ee·ing : take (as a debtor's wages) by legal authority

gar·nish·ment \'gärnishmənt\ n : attachment of property to satisfy a creditor

gar·ret \'garət\ n : attic

gar·ri·son \-əsən\ n : military post or the troops stationed there —garrison vb

gar·ru·lous \'garələs\ adj : talkative —gar·ru·li·ty \gə'rülətē\ n —gar·ru·lous·ly adv —gar·ru·lous·ness n

gar·ter \'gärtər\ n : band to hold up a stocking or sock

gas \'gas\ n, pl gas·es 1 : fluid (as hydrogen or air) that tends to expand indefinitely 2 : gasoline ~ vb gassed; gas·sing 1 : treat with gas 2 : fill with gasoline —gas·eous \-ēəs, 'gashəs\ adj

gash \'gash\ n : deep long cut —gash vb

gas·ket \'gaskət\ n : material to seal a joint against leakage

gas·light n : light of burning illuminating gas

gas·o·line \'gasə,lēn, ,gasə'-\ n : flammable liquid from petroleum

gasp \'gasp\ vb 1 : catch the breath with emotion 2 : breathe laboriously —gasp n

gas·tric \'gastrik\ adj : relating to or located near the stomach

gas·tron·o·my \gas'tränəmē\ n : art of good eating —gas·tro·nom·ic \,gas-trə'nämik\, gas·tro·nom·i·cal \-ikəl\ adj

gate \'gāt\ n : an opening for passage in a wall or fence —gate·post n —gate·way n

gate·way n : way in or out

gath·er \'gathər\ vb 1 : bring or come together 2 : harvest 3 : pick up little by little 4 : deduce —gath·er·er n —gath·er·ing n

gauche \'gōsh\ adj : crude or tactless

gaudy \'gödē\ adj gaud·i·er; -est : tastelessly showy —gaud·i·ly \'gödəlē\ adv —gaud·i·ness n

gauge \'gāj\ n : instrument for measuring ~ vb gauged; gaug·ing : measure

gaunt \'gönt\ adj : thin or emaciated —gaunt·ness n

¹gaunt·let \-lət\ n 1 : protective glove 2 : challenge to combat

²gauntlet n : ordeal

gauze \'göz\ n : thin often transparent fabric —gauzy adj

gave past of GIVE

gav·el \'gavəl\ n : mallet of a presiding officer or auctioneer

gawk \'gök\ vb : stare stupidly

gawky \-ē\ adj gawk·i·er; -est : clumsy

gay \'gā\ adj 1 : merry 2 : bright and lively 3 : homosexual —gay n

gaze \'gāz\ vb gazed; gaz·ing : fix the eyes in a steady intent look —gaze n —gaz·er n

ga·zelle \gə'zel\ n : small swift antelope

ga·zette \-'zet\ n : newspaper

gaz·et·teer \,gazə'tiər\ n : geographical dictionary

gear \'giər\ n 1 : clothing 2 : equipment 3 : toothed wheel that interlocks with another for transmitting motion ~ vb 1 : provide with gears 2 : make ready or adjust —gear·ing n

gear·shift n : mechanism by which automobile gears are shifted

geese pl of GOOSE

gei·sha \'gāshə, 'gē-\ n, pl -sha or -shas : Japanese girl trained to entertain men

gel·a·tin \'jelət°n\ n : sticky substance obtained from animal tissues by boiling —ge·lat·i·nous \jə'latnəs, -ᵊnəs\ adj

geld \'geld\ vb : castrate

geld·ing \-iŋ\ n : castrated horse

gem \'jem\ n : cut and polished valuable stone —gem·stone n

gen·der \'jendər\ n 1 : sex 2 : division of a class of words (as nouns) that determines agreement of other words

gene \'jēn\ n : complex chemical unit of a chromosome that carries heredity —gen·ic \'jēnik, 'jen-\ adj

ge·ne·al·o·gy \ˌjēnē'ăləjē, ˌjen-, -'al-\ n, pl -gies : study of family pedigrees —ge·ne·a·log·i·cal \-ēə'lăjikəl\ adj —ge·ne·a·log·i·cal·ly adv —ge·ne·al·o·gist \-ē'ăləjəst, -'al-\ n

genera pl of GENUS

gen·er·al \'jen(ə)rəl\ adj 1 : relating to the whole 2 : applicable to all of a group 3 : common or widespread ~ n 1 : something that involves or is applicable to the whole 2 : commissioned officer ranking next below a general of the army or a general of the air force 3 : commissioned officer of the highest rank in the marine corps —gen·er·al·ly adv —in general : for the most part

gen·er·al·i·ty \ˌjenə'ralətē\ n, pl -ties : general statement

gen·er·al·ize \'jen(ə)rəˌlīz\ vb -ized; -iz·ing : reach a general conclusion esp. on the basis of particular instances —gen·er·al·i·za·tion \-(ə)rələ'zāshən\ n

general of the air force : commissioned officer of the highest rank in the air force

general of the army : commissioned officer of the highest rank in the army

gen·er·ate \'jenəˌrāt\ vb -at·ed; -at·ing : create or produce

gen·er·a·tion \ˌjenə'rāshən\ n 1 : living beings constituting a single step in a line of descent 2 : production —gen·er·a·tive \'jenəˌrātiv, -(ə)rət-\ adj

gen·er·a·tor \'jenəˌrātər\ n 1 : one that generates 2 : machine that turns mechanical into electrical energy

ge·ner·ic \jə'nerik\ adj 1 : general 2 : not protected by a trademark 3 : relating to a genus —generic n

gen·er·ous \'jen(ə)rəs\ adj : freely giving or sharing —gen·er·os·i·ty \ˌjenə'răsətē\ n —gen·er·ous·ly adv —gen·er·ous·ness n

ge·net·ics \jə'netiks\ n : biology dealing with heredity and variation —ge·net·ic \-ik\ adj —ge·net·i·cal·ly adv —ge·net·i·cist \-'netəsəst\ n

ge·nial \'jēnyəl\ adj : cheerful —ge·nial·i·ty \ˌjēnē'alətē, jēn'yal-\ n —ge·nial·ly \'jēnyəlē\ adv

ge·nie \'jēnē\ n : supernatural spirit that often takes human form

gen·i·tal \'jenətᵊl\ adj : concerned with reproduction —gen·i·tal·ly \-təlē\ adv

gen·i·ta·lia \ˌjenə'tālyə\ n pl : external genital organs

gen·i·tals \'jenətᵊlz\ n pl : genitalia

ge·nius \'jēnyəs\ n 1 : single strongly marked capacity 2 : extraordinary intellectual power or a person having such power

geno·cide \'jenəˌsīd\ n : systematic destruction of a racial or cultural group

genre \'zhänrə, 'zhä°rə, 'zhä°(ə)r\ n : category esp. of literary composition

gen·teel \jen'tēl\ adj : polite or refined

gen·tile \'jenˌtīl\ n : person who is not Jewish —gentile adj

gen·til·i·ty \jen'tilətē\ n, pl -ties 1 : good birth and family 2 : good manners

gen·tle \'jentᵊl\ adj -tler, -tlest 1 : of a family of high social station 2 : not harsh, stern, or violent 3 : soft or delicate ~ vb -tled; -tling : make gentle —gen·tle·ness n —gent·ly adv

gen·tle·man \-mən\ n : man of good family or manners —gen·tle·man·ly adj

gen·tle·wom·an \-ˌwu̇mən\ n : woman of good family or breeding

gen·try \'jentrē\ n, pl -tries : people of good birth or breeding

gen·u·flect \'jenyəˌflekt\ vb : bend the knee in worship —gen·u·flec·tion \ˌjenyə'flekshən\ n

gen·u·ine \'jenyəwən\ adj : being the same in fact as in appearance —gen·u·ine·ly adv —gen·u·ine·ness n

ge·nus \'jēnəs\ n, pl gen·era \'jenərə\ : category of biological classification

ge·ode \'jēˌōd\ n : stone having a mineral-lined cavity

geo·de·sic \ˌjēə'desik, -'dēs-\ adj : made of a framework of light straight-sided polygons in tension

ge·og·ra·phy \jē'ägrəfē\ n : study of the earth and its climate, products, and inhabitants —ge·og·ra·pher \-fər\ n —geo·graph·ic \ˌjēə'grafik\, geo·graph·i·cal \-ikəl\ adj —geo·graph·i·cal·ly adv

ge·ol·o·gy \jē'äləjē\ n : study of the history of the earth and its life esp. as recorded in rocks —geo·log·ic \ˌjēə'läjik\, geo·log·i·cal \-ikəl\ adj —ge·ol·o·gist \jē'äləjəst\ n

ge·om·e·try \jē'ämətrē\ *n, pl* **-tries** : mathematics of the relations, properties, and measurements of solids, surfaces, lines, and angles —**ge·om·e·ter** \-ətər\ *n* —**ge·o·met·ric** \ˌjēə'metrik\, **ge·o·met·ri·cal** \-rikəl\ *adj*

geo·phys·ics \ˌjēə'fiziks\ *n* : physics of the earth —**geo·phys·i·cal** \-ikəl\ *adj* —**geo·phys·i·cist** \-'fizəsəst\ *n*

geo·ther·mal \ˌjēō'thərməl\, **geo·ther·mic** \-mik\ *adj* : of or relating to the heat of the earth's interior

ge·ra·ni·um \jə'rānēəm\ *n* : garden plant with clusters of white, pink, or scarlet flowers

ger·bil \'jərbəl\ *n* : burrowing desert rodent

ge·ri·at·ric \ˌjerē'atrik\ *adj* : relating to aging or the aged

ge·ri·at·rics \-triks\ *n* : medicine dealing with the aged and aging

germ \'jərm\ *n* **1** : microorganism **2** : source or rudiment

ger·mane \(ˌ)jər'mān\ *adj* : relevant

ger·ma·ni·um \-'mānēəm\ *n* : grayish white hard chemical element

ger·mi·cide \'jərmə₁sīd\ *n* : agent that destroys germs —**ger·mi·cid·al** \ˌjərmə'sīdᵊl\ *adj*

ger·mi·nate \'jərmə₁nāt\ *vb* **-nat·ed**; **-nat·ing** : begin to develop —**ger·mi·na·tion** \ˌjərmə'nāshən\ *n*

ger·ry·man·der \ˌjerē'mandər, 'jerē₁-, ₁gerē'-, 'gerē₁-\ *vb* : divide into election districts so as to give one political party an advantage —**gerrymander** *n*

ge·rund \'jerənd\ *n* : word having the characteristics of both verb and noun

ge·sta·po \gə'stäpō\ *n, pl* **-pos** : secret police

ges·ta·tion \je'stāshən\ *n* : pregnancy or incubation —**ges·tate** \'jes₁tāt\ *vb*

ges·ture \'jeschər\ *n* **1** : movement of the body or limbs that expresses something **2** : something said or done for its effect on the attitudes of others —**ges·tur·al** \-chərəl\ *adj* —**gesture** *vb*

ge·sund·heit \gə'zúnt₁hīt\ *interj* —used to wish good health to one who has just sneezed

get \'get\ *vb* **got** \'gät\; **got** *or* **got·ten** \'gätᵊn\; **getting** **1** : gain or be in possession of **2** : succeed in coming or going **3** : cause to come or go or to be in a certain condition or position **4** : become **5** : be subjected to **6** : understand **7** : be obliged —**get along** *vb* **1** : get by **2** : be on friendly terms —**get by** *vb* : meet one's needs

get·away \'getə₁wā\ *n* **1** : escape **2** : a starting or getting under way

gey·ser \'gīzər\ *n* : spring that intermittently shoots up hot water and steam

ghast·ly \'gastlē\ *adj* **-li·er**; **-est** : horrible or shocking

gher·kin \'gərkən\ *n* : small pickle

ghet·to \'getō\ *n, pl* **-tos** *or* **-toes** : part of a city in which members of a minority group live

ghost \'gōst\ *n* : disembodied soul —**ghost·ly** *adv*

ghost·write *vb* **-wrote**; **-writ·ten** : write for and in the name of another —**ghost·writ·er** *n*

ghoul \'gül\ *n* : legendary evil being that feeds on corpses —**ghoul·ish** *adj*

GI \(')jē'ī\ *n, pl* **GI's** *or* **GIs** : member of the U.S. armed forces

gi·ant \'jīənt\ *n* **1** : huge legendary being **2** : something very large or very powerful —**giant** *adj*

gib·ber \'jibər\ *vb* **-bered**; **-ber·ing** : speak rapidly and foolishly

gib·ber·ish \'jib(ə)rish\ *n* : unintelligible speech or language

gib·bon \'gibən\ *n* : manlike ape

gibe \'jīb\ *vb* **gibed**; **gib·ing** : jeer at —**gibe** *n*

gib·lets \'jibləts\ *n pl* : edible fowl viscera

gid·dy \'gidē\ *adj* **-di·er**; **-est** **1** : silly **2** : dizzy —**gid·di·ness** *n*

gift \'gift\ *n* **1** : something given **2** : talent —**gift·ed** *adj*

gi·gan·tic \jī'gantik\ *adj* : very big

gig·gle \'gigəl\ *vb* **-gled**; **-gling** : laugh in a silly manner —**giggle** *n* —**gig·gly** \-ə̇lē\ *adj*

gig·o·lo \'jigə₁lō\ *n, pl* **-los** : man living on the earnings of a woman

Gi·la monster \'hēlə-\ *n* : large venomous lizard

gild \'gild\ *vb* **gild·ed** \'gildəd\ *or* **gilt** \'gilt\; **gild·ing** : cover with or as if with gold —**gild·ing** *n*

gill \'gil\ *n* : organ of a fish for obtaining oxygen from water

gilt \'gilt\ *adj* : gold-colored ~ *n* : gold or goldlike substance on the surface of an object

gim·bal \'gimbəl, 'jim-\ *n* : device that allows something to incline freely

gim·let \'gimlət\ *n* : small boring tool

gim·mick \'gimik\ *n* : new and ingenious scheme, feature, or device —**gim·mick·ry** *n* —**gim·micky** \-ikē\ *adj*

gimpy \'gimpē\ *adj* : lame

¹**gin** \'jin\ *n* : machine to separate seeds from cotton —**gin** *vb*

²gin \'\ *n* : clear liquor flavored with juniper berries

gin·ger \'jinjər\ *n* : pungent aromatic spice from a tropical plant —**gin·ger·bread** *n*

gin·ger·ly *adj* : very cautious or careful —**gingerly** *adv*

ging·ham \'giŋəm\ *n* : cotton clothing fabric

gin·gi·vi·tis \,jinjə'vītəs\ *n* : inflammation of the gums

gink·go \'giŋ(,)kō\ *n, pl* **-goes** *or* **-gos** : tree of eastern China

gin·seng \'jin,saŋ, -,seŋ, -,(,)siŋ\ *n* : aromatic root of a Chinese herb

gi·raffe \jə'raf\ *n* : African mammal with a very long neck

gird \'gərd\ *vb* **gird·ed** \'gərdəd\ *or* **girt** \'gərt\; **gird·ing** 1 : encircle or fasten with or as if with a belt 2 : prepare

gird·er \'gərdər\ *n* : horizontal supporting beam

gir·dle \'-ᵊl\ *n* : woman's supporting undergarment —*vb* : surround

girl \'gərl\ *n* 1 : female child 2 : sweetheart —**girl·hood** \-,hủd\ *n* —**girl·ish** *adj*

girl·friend *n* : frequent or regular female companion of a boy or man

girth \'gərth\ *n* : measure around something

gist \'jist\ *n* : main point of a matter

give \'giv\ *vb* **gave** \'gāv\; **giv·en** \'givən\; **giv·ing** 1 : put into the possession or keeping of another 2 : pay 3 : perform 4 : contribute or donate 5 : produce 6 : utter 7 : yield to force, strain, or pressure ~ *n* : capacity or tendency to yield to force or strain —**give in** *vb* : surrender —**give out** *vb* : become used up or exhausted —**give up** *vb* 1 : let out of one's control 2 : cease from trying, doing, or hoping

give·away *n* 1 : unintentional betrayal 2 : something given free

giv·en \'givən\ *adj* 1 : prone or disposed 2 : having been specified

giz·zard \'gizərd\ *n* : muscular usu. horny-lined enlargement following the crop of a bird

gla·cial \'glāshəl\ *adj* : of or relating to glaciers —**gla·cial·ly** *adv*

gla·cier \'glāshər\ *n* : large body of ice moving slowly

glad \'glad\ *adj* **-dd-** 1 : experiencing or causing pleasure, joy, or delight 2 : very willing —**glad·den** \-ᵊn\ *vb* —**glad·ly** *adv* —**glad·ness** *n*

glade \'glād\ *n* : grassy open space in a forest

glad·i·a·tor \'gladē,ātər\ *n* : one who fought to the death for the entertainment of ancient Romans —**glad·i·a·to·ri·al** \,gladēə'tōrēəl\ *adj*

glad·i·o·lus \,gladē'ōləs\ *n, pl* **-li** \-(,)lē, -,lī\ : plant related to the irises

glance \'glans\ *vb* **glanced**; **glanc·ing** 1 : strike and fly off to one side 2 : give a quick look ~ *n* : quick look

gland \'gland\ *n* : group of cells that secretes a substance —**glan·du·lar** \'glanjələr\ *adj*

glans \'glanz\ *n, pl* **glan·des** \'glan,dēz\ : conical vascular body forming the extremity of the penis or clitoris

glare \'glaər\ *vb* **glared**; **glar·ing** 1 : shine with a harsh dazzling light 2 : gaze angrily ~ *n* 1 : harsh dazzling light 2 : angry stare —**glar·ing** \'gla(ə)riŋ\ *adj* —**glar·ing·ly** *adv*

glass \'glas\ *n* 1 : usu. transparent substance made by melting sand and other materials 2 : something made of glass 3 *pl* : lenses used to correct defects of vision —**glass** *adj* —**glass·ful** \-,fúl\ *n* —**glass·ware** \-,waər\ *n* —**glassy** *adj*

glass-blow·ing *n* : art of shaping a mass of molten glass by blowing air into it —**glass-blow·er** *n*

glau·co·ma \glaú'kōmə, glò-\ *n* : state of increased pressure within the eyeball

glaze \'glāz\ *vb* **glazed**; **glaz·ing** 1 : furnish with glass 2 : apply glaze to ~ *n* : glassy surface or coating

gla·zier \'glāzhər\ *n* : one who sets glass in window frames

gleam \'glēm\ *n* 1 : transient or partly obscured light 2 : faint trace ~ *vb* : send out gleams

glean \'glēn\ *vb* : collect little by little —**glean·able** *adj* —**glean·er** *n*

glee \'glē\ *n* : joy —**glee·ful** *adj*

glen \'glen\ *n* : valley

glib \'glib\ *adj* **-bb-** : speaking or spoken with ease —**glib·ly** *adv*

glide \'glīd\ *vb* **glid·ed**; **glid·ing** 1 : move or descend smoothly and effortlessly ~ *n* : smooth motion or descent

glid·er \'glīdər\ *n* : aircraft having no engine

glim·mer \'glimər\ *vb* : shine faintly or unsteadily ~ *n* 1 : faint light 2 : small amount

glimpse \\'glimps\\ *vb* **glimpsed; glimps-ing** : take a brief look at —**glimpse** *n*

glint \\'glint\\ *vb* : gleam or sparkle —**glint** *n*

glis-ten \\'glis^{ə}n\\ *vb* : shine or sparkle by reflection —**glisten** *n*

glit-ter \\'glitər\\ *vb* : shine with brilliant or metallic luster ~ *n* : small glittering ornaments —**glit-tery** *adj*

gloat \\'glōt\\ *vb* : think of something with pride or self-satisfaction

glob \\'gläb\\ *n* : large rounded lump

glob-al \\'glōbəl\\ *adj* : worldwide —**glob-al-ly** *adv*

globe \\'glōb\\ *n* **1** : sphere **2** : the earth or a model of it

glob-u-lar \\'gläbyələr\\ *adj* **1** : round **2** : made up of globules

glob-ule \\'gläbyül\\ *n* : tiny ball

glock-en-spiel \\'gläkən,s(h)pēl\\ *n* : portable musical instrument consisting of tuned metal bars

gloom \\'glüm\\ *n* **1** : darkness **2** : sadness —**gloom-i-ly** *adv* —**gloom-i-ness** *n* —**gloomy** *adj*

glop \\'gläp\\ *n* : messy mass or mixture

glo-ri-fy \\'glōra,fī\\ *vb* **-fied; -fy-ing 1** : make to seem glorious **2** : worship —**glo-ri-fi-ca-tion** \\,glōrəfə'kāshən\\ *n*

glo-ry \\'glōrē\\ *n, pl* **-ries 1** : praise or honor offered in worship **2** : cause for praise or renown **3** : magnificence **4** : heavenly bliss ~ *vb* **-ried; -ry-ing** : rejoice proudly —**glo-ri-ous** \\'glōrēəs\\ *adj* —**glo-ri-ous-ly** *adv*

¹gloss \\'gläs, 'glȯs\\ *n* : luster ~ *vb* : treat rapidly or superficially —**gloss-i-ly** \\-əlē\\ *adv* —**gloss-i-ness** \\-ēnəs\\ *n* —**glossy** \\-ē\\ *adj*

²gloss *n* : brief explanation or translation ~ *vb* : translate or explain

glos-sa-ry \\'gläsə(ə)rē, 'glȯs-\\ *n, pl* **-ries** : dictionary —**glos-sar-i-al** \\glä's-arēəl, glȯ-\\ *adj*

glove \\'gləv\\ *n* : hand covering with sections for each finger

glow \\'glō\\ *vb* **1** : shine with or as if with intense heat **2** : show exuberance ~ *n* : brightness or warmth of color or feeling

glow-er \\'glaù(ə)r\\ *vb* : stare angrily —**glower** *n*

glow-worm *n* : insect or insect larva that emits light

glu-cose \\'glü,kōs\\ *n* : sugar found esp. in blood, plant sap, and fruits

glue \\'glü\\ *n* : substance used for sticking things together —**glue** *vb* —**glu-ey** \\'glüē\\ *adj*

glum \\'gləm\\ *adj* **-mm- 1** : sullen **2** : dismal

glut \\'glət\\ *vb* **-tt-** : fill to excess —**glut** *n*

glu-ten \\'glüt^{ə}n\\ *n* : gluey protein substance in flour

glu-ti-nous \\'glüt^{ə}nəs\\ *adj* : sticky

glut-ton \\'glət^{ə}n\\ *n* : one who eats to excess —**glut-ton-ous** \\'glət^{ə}nəs\\ *adj* —**glut-tony** \\'glət^{ə}nē\\ *n*

glyc-er-in, glyc-er-ine \\'glis(ə)rən\\ *n* : syrupy liquid used as a solvent and moistener

gnarl \\'närl\\ *n* : hard knob on a tree ~ *vb* : twist or contort —**gnarled** \\'närld\\ *adj*

gnash \\'nash\\ *vb* : grind (as teeth) together

gnat \\'nat\\ *n* : small biting fly

gnaw \\'nȯ\\ *vb* : bite or chew on —**gnawer** \\'nȯ(ə)r\\ *n*

gnome \\'nōm\\ *n* : dwarf of folklore —**gnom-ish** *adj*

gnu \\'n(y)ü\\ *n, pl* **gnu** *or* **gnus** : large African antelope

go \\'gō\\ *vb* **went** \\'went\\; **gone** \\'gȯn, 'gän\\; **go-ing** \\'gȯin\\; **goes** \\'gōz\\ **1** : move, proceed, run, or pass **2** : leave **3** : extend or lead **4** : sell or amount —**with** *for* **5** : happen **6** —used in present participle to show intent or imminent action **7** : become **8** : fit or harmonize **9** : belong ~ *n, pl* **goes 1** : act or manner of going **2** : vigor **3** : attempt —**go back on** : betray —**go by the board** : be discarded —**go for** : favor —**go off** : explode —**go one better** : outdo —**go over 1** : examine **2** : study —**go to town** : be very successful —**on the go** : constantly active

goad \\'gōd\\ *n* : something that urges —**goad** *vb*

goal \\'gōl\\ *n* **1** : mark to reach in a race **2** : purpose **3** : object in a game through which a ball is propelled

goal-ie \\'gōlē\\ *n* : player who defends the goal

goal-keep-er *n* : goalie

goat \\'gōt\\ *n* : horned ruminant mammal related to the sheep —**goat-skin** *n*

goa-tee \\gō'tē\\ *n* : small pointed beard

gob \\'gäb\\ *n* : lump

¹gob-ble \\'gäbəl\\ *vb* **-bled; -bling** : eat greedily

²gobble *vb* **-bled; -bling** : make the noise of a turkey (**gobbler**)

gob-ble-dy-gook, gob-ble-de-gook \\,gäbəldē'gúk, -'gük\\ *n* : nonsense

gob-let \\'gäblət\\ *n* : large stemmed drinking glass

gob-lin \\-lən\\ *n* : ugly mischievous sprite

god \'gäd, 'gȯd\ *n* 1 *cap* : supreme being 2 : being with supernatural powers —**god-like** \-ə̇s\ *n* —**god-like** *adj* —**god-ly** *adj*

god-child *n* : person one sponsors at baptism —**god-daugh-ter** *n* —**god-son** *n*

god-less \-ləs\ *adj* : not believing in God —**god-less-ness** *n*

god-par-ent *n* : sponsor at baptism —**god-fa-ther** *n* —**god-moth-er** *n*

god-send \-,send\ *n* : something needed that comes unexpectedly

goes *pres 3d sing of* GO

go-get-ter \'gō,getər\ *n* : enterprising person —**go-get-ting** \-iŋ\ *adj or n*

gog-gle \'gägəl\ *vb* -gled; -gling : stare wide-eyed

gog-gles \-əlz\ *n pl* : protective glasses

go-ings-on \,gōiŋz'ȯn, -'än\ *n pl* : events

goi-ter \'gȯitər\ *n* : abnormally enlarged thyroid gland —**goi-trous** *adj*

gold \'gōld\ *n* : malleable yellow metallic chemical element —**gold-smith** \-,smith\ *n*

gold-brick \-,brik\ *n* : person who shirks duty —**goldbrick** *vb*

gold digger *n* : woman interested only in a man's money

gold-en \'gōldən\ *adj* 1 : made of, containing, or relating to gold 2 : having the color of gold 3 : precious or favorable

gold-en-rod \'gōldən,räd\ *n* : herb having tall stalks with tiny yellow flowers

gold-finch \'gōl(d),finch\ *n* : yellow American finch

gold-fish \-,fish\ *n* : small usu. orange or golden carp

golf \'gälf, 'gȯlf\ *n* : game played by hitting a small ball (**golf ball**) with clubs (**golf clubs**) into holes placed in a field (**golf course**) —**golf** *vb* —**golf-er** *n*

go-nad \'gō,nad\ *n* : sex gland

gon-do-la \'gändələ (*usual for* 1), gän'dō-\ *n* 1 : long narrow boat used on the canals of Venice 2 : car suspended from a cable

gon-do-lier \,gändə'liər\ *n* : gondola boatman

gone \'gȯn\ *adj* 1 : past 2 : involved

gon-er \'gȯnər\ *n* : hopeless case

gong \'gäŋ, 'gȯŋ\ *n* : metallic disk that sounds when struck

gon-or-rhea \,gänə'rēə\ *n* : bacterial inflammatory venereal disease of the genital tract —**gon-or-rhe-al** \-'rēəl\ *adj*

goo \'gü\ *n* : thick or sticky substance —**goo-ey** \-ē\ *adj*

good \'gùd\ *adj* **bet-ter** \'betər\; **best** \'best\ 1 : satisfactory 2 : salutary 3 : considerable 4 : desirable 5 : well-behaved, kind, or virtuous ~ *n* 1 : something good 2 : benefit 3 *pl* : personal property 4 *pl* : wares ~ *adv* : well —**good-heart-ed** \-'härtəd\ *adj* —**good-ish** *adj* —**good-look-ing** *adj* —**good-na-tured** *adj* —**good-ness** *n* —**good-tem-pered** \-'tempərd\ *adj* —**for good** : forever

good-bye, good-by \gùd'bī, gə(d)-\ *n* : parting remark

good-for-noth-ing *n* : idle worthless person

Good Friday *n* : Friday before Easter observed as the anniversary of the crucifixion of Christ

good-ly *adj* **-li-er; -est** : considerable

good-will *n* 1 : good intention 2 : kindly feeling

goody \-ē\ *n, pl* **good-ies** : something that is good esp. to eat

goody-goody *adj* : affectedly or annoyingly sweet or self-righteous —**goody-goody** *n*

goof \'güf\ *vb* 1 : blunder 2 : waste time—usu. with *off* or *around* —**goof** *n* —**goof-off** *n*

goofy \'güfē\ *adj* **goof-i-er; -est** : crazy —**goof-i-ness** *n*

goose \'güs\ *n, pl* **geese** \'gēs\ : large bird with webbed feet

goose-ber-ry \'güs,berē, 'güz-, -b(ə)rē\ *n* : berry of a shrub related to the currant

goose-flesh *n* : roughening of the skin caused usu. by cold or fear

goose pimples *n pl* : gooseflesh

go-pher \'gōfər\ *n* : burrowing rodent

¹**gore** \'gōr\ *n* : blood

²**gore** *vb* **gored; gor-ing** : pierce or wound with a horn or tusk

¹**gorge** \'gȯrj\ *n* : narrow ravine

²**gorge** *vb* **gorged; gorg-ing** : eat greedily

gor-geous \'gȯrjəs\ *adj* : supremely beautiful

go-ril-la \gə'rilə\ *n* : African manlike ape

gory \'gōrē\ *adj* **gor-i-er; -est** : bloody

gos-hawk \'gäs,hȯk\ *n* : long-tailed hawk with short rounded wings

gos-ling \'gäzliŋ, 'gȯz-\ *n* : young goose

gos-pel \'gäspəl\ *n* 1 : teachings of Christ and the apostles 2 : something accepted as infallible truth —**gospel** *adj*

gos·sa·mer \'gäsəmər, gäz(ə)mər\ *n* 1 : film of cobweb 2 : light filmy substance

gos·sip \'gäsəp\ *n* 1 : person who reveals personal information 2 : rumor or report of an intimate nature ~ *vb* : spread gossip —**gos·sipy** *adj*

got *past of* GET

Goth·ic \'gäthik\ *adj* : relating to a medieval style of architecture

gotten *past part of* GET

gouge \'gaúj\ *n* 1 : rounded chisel 2 : cavity or groove scooped out ~ *vb* **gouged; goug·ing** 1 : cut or scratch a groove in 2 : overcharge —**goug·er** *n*

gou·lash \'gü,läsh, -,lash\ *n* : beef stew with vegetables and paprika

gourd \'górd, 'gúrd\ *n* 1 : any of a group of vines including the cucumber, squash, and melon 2 : inedible hard-shelled fruit of a gourd

gour·mand \'gúr,mänd\ *n* : person who loves good food and drink

gour·met \'gúr,mā, gúr'mā\ *n* : connoisseur of food and drink

gout \'gaút\ *n* : disease marked by painful inflammation and swelling of the joints —**gouty** *adj*

gov·ern \'gəvərn\ *vb* 1 : control and direct policy in 2 : guide or influence strongly 3 : restrain —**gov·ern·ment** \-ər(n)mənt\ *n* —**gov·ern·men·tal** \,gəvər(n)'ment°l\ *adj*

gov·ern·ess \'gəvərnəs\ *n* : female teacher in a private home

gov·er·nor \'gəv(ə)nər, 'gəvərnər\ *n* 1 : head of a political unit 2 : automatic speed-control device —**gov·er·nor·ship** *n*

gown \'gaún\ *n* 1 : loose flowing outer garment 2 : woman's formal evening dress —**gown** *vb*

grab \'grab\ *vb* **-bb-** : take by sudden grasp —**grab** *n*

grace \'grās\ *n* 1 : unmerited divine assistance 2 : short prayer before or after a meal 3 : respite 4 : ease of movement or bearing ~ *vb* **graced; grac·ing** 1 : honor 2 : adorn —**grace·ful** \-fəl\ *adj* —**grace·ful·ly** *adv* —**grace·ful·ness** *n* —**grace·less** *adj*

gra·cious \'grāshəs\ *adj* : marked by kindness and courtesy or charm and taste —**gra·cious·ly** *adv* —**gra·cious·ness** *n*

grack·le \'grakəl\ *n* : American blackbird

gra·da·tion \grā'dāshən, grə-\ *n* : step, degree, or stage in a series

grade \'grād\ *n* 1 : stage in a series, order, or ranking 2 : division of school representing one year's work

3 : mark of accomplishment in school 4 : degree of slope ~ *vb* **grad·ed; grad·ing** 1 : arrange in grades 2 : make level or evenly sloping 3 : give a grade to —**grad·er** *n*

grade school *n* : school including the first 6 or 8 grades

gra·di·ent \'grādēənt\ *n* : slope

grad·u·al \'graj(əw)əl\ *adj* : going by steps or degrees —**grad·u·al·ly** *adv*

grad·u·ate \'graj(ə)wət, -,-jə,wāt\ *n* : holder of a diploma ~ *adj* : of or relating to studies beyond the bachelor's degree ~ \-ə,wāt\ *vb* **-at·ed; -at·ing** 1 : grant or receive a diploma 2 : mark with degrees of measurement —**grad·u·a·tion** \graj°'wā-shən\ *n*

graf·fi·to \gra'fētō, grə-\ *n, pl* **-ti** \-,(,)ē\ : inscription on a wall

graft \'graft\ *vb* : join one thing to another so that they grow together ~ *n* 1 : grafted plant 2 : the getting of money dishonestly or the money so gained —**graft·er** *n*

grain \'grān\ *n* 1 : seeds or fruits of cereal plants 2 : small hard particle 3 : arrangement of fibers in wood —**grained** \'grānd\ *adj* —**grain·field** *n* —**grainy** *adj*

gram, gramme \'gram\ *n* : metric unit of weight nearly equal to one cubic centimeter of water at its maximum density

gram·mar \'gramər\ *n* : study of words and their functions and relations in the sentence —**gram·mar·i·an** \grə'mereēən, -'mar-\ *n* —**gram·mat·i·cal** \-'matikəl\ *adj* —**gram·mat·i·cal·ly** *adv*

grammar school *n* : grade school

gra·na·ry \'grān(ə)rē, 'gran-\ *n, pl* **-ries** : storehouse for grain

grand \'grand\ *adj* 1 : large or striking in size or scope 2 : fine and imposing 3 : very good —**grand·ly** \'gran(d)lē\ *adv* —**grand·ness** \-nəs\ *n*

grand·child \'gran(d),chīld\ *n* : child of one's son or daughter —**grand·daugh·ter** *n* —**grand·son** *n*

gran·deur \'granjər\ *n* : quality or state of being grand

gran·dil·o·quence \gran'diləkwəns\ *n* : pompous speaking —**gran·dil·o·quent** \-kwənt\ *adj*

gran·di·ose \'grandē,ōs, ,grandē'-\ *adj* 1 : impressive 2 : affectedly splendid —**gran·di·ose·ly** *adv*

grand·par·ent \-,pareənt\ *n* : parent of one's father or mother —**grand·fa·ther** \-,fä*th*ər, -,fá*th*-\ *n* —**grand·mo·ther** \-,mə*th*ər\ *n*

grand·stand \-₁stand\ n : usu. roofed stand for spectators

grange \'grānj\ n : farmers association

gran·ite \'granət\ n : hard igneous rock —**gra·nit·ic** \grə'nitik\ adj

grant \'grant\ vb 1 : consent to 2 : give 3 : admit as true ~ n 1 : act of granting 2 : something granted —**grant·ee** \grant'ē\ n —**grant·er** \'grantər\ n —**grant·or** \-ər, -₁ȯrt\ n

gran·u·late \'granyə₁lāt\ vb -**lat·ed**; -**lat·ing** : form into grains or crystals —**gran·u·lat·ed** adj —**gran·u·la·tion** \₁granyə'lāshən\ n

gran·ule \'granyül\ n : small particle —**gran·u·lar** \-yələr\ adj —**gran·u·lar·i·ty** \₁granyə'larətē\ n

grape \'grāp\ n : smooth juicy edible berry of a woody vine (**grape·vine**)

grape·fruit n : large edible yellow-skinned citrus fruit

graph \'graf\ n : diagram that shows relationships between things —**graph** vb

graph·ic \'grafik\ adj 1 : vividly described 2 : relating to the arts (**graphic arts**) of representation and printing on flat surfaces —**graph·i·cal·ly** \-ik(ə)lē\ adv —**graph·ics** \-iks\ n

graph·ite \'graf₁īt\ n : soft carbon used for lead pencils and lubricants

grap·nel \'grapnəl\ n : small anchor with several claws

grap·ple \'grapəl\ vb -**pled**; -**pling** 1 : seize or hold with or as if with a hooked implement 2 : wrestle

grasp \'grasp\ vb 1 : take or seize firmly 2 : understand ~ n 1 : one's hold or control 2 : one's reach 3 : comprehension

grass \'gras\ n : plant with jointed stem and narrow leaves —**grassy** adj

grass·hop·per \-₁häpər\ n : leaping plant-eating insect

grass·land n : land covered with grasses

¹grate \'grāt\ n 1 : framework with bars across it 2 : frame of iron bars to hold burning fuel

²grate vb grat·ed; -ing 1 : pulverize by rubbing against something rough 2 : irritate —**grat·er** n —**grat·ing·ly** adv

grate·ful \'grātfəl\ adj : thankful or appreciative —**grate·ful·ly** adv —**grate·ful·ness** n

grat·i·fy \'gratə₁fī\ vb -**fied**; -**fy·ing** : give pleasure to —**grat·i·fi·ca·tion** \₁gratəfə'kāshən\ n

grat·ing \'grātiŋ\ n : grate

gra·tis \'gratəs, 'grāt-\ adv or adj : free

grat·i·tude \'gratə₁t(y)üd\ n : state of being grateful

gra·tu·itous \grə't(y)üətəs\ adj 1 : free 2 : uncalled-for

gra·tu·ity \-ətē\ n, pl -**ities** : tip

¹grave \'grāv\ n : place of burial —**grave·stone** n —**grave·yard** n

²grave adj grav·er; grav·est 1 : threatening great harm or danger 2 : solemn —**grave·ly** adv —**grave·ness** n

grav·el \'gravəl\ n : loose rounded fragments of rock —**grav·el·ly** adj

grav·i·tate \'gravə₁tāt\ vb -**tat·ed**; -**tat·ing** : move toward something

grav·i·ta·tion \₁gravə'tāshən\ n : natural force of attraction that tends to draw bodies together —**grav·i·ta·tion·al** \-sh(ə)nəl\ adj —**grav·i·ta·tion·al·ly** adv —**grav·i·ta·tive** \'gravə₁tātiv\ adj

grav·i·ty \'gravətē\ n, pl -**ties** 1 : serious importance 2 : attraction of bodies toward the center of the earth —**gravity** adj

gra·vy \'grāvē\ n, pl -**vies** : sauce made from thickened juices of cooked meat

gray \'grā\ adj 1 : of the color gray 2 : having gray hair ~ n : neutral color between black and white ~ vb : make or become gray —**gray·ish** adj —**gray·ness** n

¹graze \'grāz\ vb grazed; graz·ing : feed on herbage or pasture —**graz·er** n

²graze vb grazed; graz·ing : touch lightly in passing

grease \'grēs\ n : thick oily material or fat ~ \'grēs, 'grēz\ vb greased; greas·ing : smear or lubricate with grease —**greasy** \'grēsē, -zē\ adj

great \'grāt, South also 'gre(ə)t\ adj 1 : large in size or number 2 : larger than usual —**great·ly** adv —**great·ness** n

grebe \'grēb\ n : diving bird related to the loon

greed \'grēd\ n : selfish desire beyond reason —**greed·i·ly** \-ᵊlē\ adv —**greed·i·ness** \-ēnəs\ n —**greedy** \'grēdē\ adj

green \'grēn\ adj 1 : of the color green 2 : unripe 3 : inexperienced ~ vb : become green ~ n 1 : color between blue and yellow 2 pl : leafy parts of plants —**green·ish** adj —**green·ness** \'grēnnəs\ n

green·ery \'grēn(ə)rē\ n, pl -**er·ies** : green foliage or plants

green·horn n : inexperienced person

green·house n : glass structure for the growing of plants

greet \'grēt\ vb 1 : address with expressions of kind wishes 2 : react to —**greet·er** n

greet·ing \'grēt·iŋ\ n 1 : friendly address on meeting 2 pl : best wishes

gre·gar·i·ous \gri'garēəs, -'ger-\ adj : social or companionable —**gre·gar·i·ous·ly** adv —**gre·gar·i·ous·ness** n

grem·lin \'gremlən\ n : small mischievous demon

gre·nade \grə'nād\ n : small missile filled with explosive or chemicals

grew past of GROW

grey var of GRAY

grey·hound \'grā,haůnd\ n : tall slender dog noted for speed

grid \'grid\ n 1 : grate 2 : metal plate for conducting current in a storage battery

grid·dle \'gridᵊl\ n : flat metal surface for cooking

grid·iron \'grid,ī(ə)rn\ n 1 : grate for broiling 2 : football field

grief \'grēf\ n 1 : emotional suffering caused by or as if by bereavement 2 : disaster

griev·ance \'grēvəns\ n : complaint

grieve \'grēv\ vb **grieved**; **griev·ing** : feel or cause to feel grief or sorrow

griev·ous \'grēvəs\ adj 1 : oppressive 2 : causing grief or sorrow —**griev·ous·ly** adv

grill \'gril\ vb 1 : cook on a grill 2 : question intensely ~ n 1 : griddle 2 : informal restaurant

grille, grill \'gril\ n : grating forming a barrier or screen —**grill·work** n

grim \'grim\ adj -mm- 1 : harsh and forbidding in appearance 2 : relentless —**grim·ly** adv —**grim·ness** n

gri·mace \'griməs, grim'ās\ n : facial expression of disgust —**grimace** vb

grime \'grīm\ n : embedded or accumulated dirt —**grimy** adj

grin \'grin\ vb -nn- : smile so as to show the teeth —**grin** n

grind \'grīnd\ vb **ground** \'graůnd\; **grind·ing** 1 : reduce to powder 2 : wear down or sharpen by friction 3 : operate or produce by turning a crank ~ n : monotonous labor or routine —**grind·er** n —**grind·stone** \'grīn,stōn\ n

grip \'grip\ vb -pp- : seize or hold firmly ~ n 1 : grasp 2 : control 3 : device for holding

gripe \'grīp\ vb **griped**; **grip·ing** 1 : cause pains in the bowels 2 : complain —**gripe** n

grippe \'grip\ n : influenza

gris·ly \'grizlē\ adj -li·er; -est : horrible or grusome

grist \'grist\ n : grain to be ground or already ground —**grist·mill** n

gris·tle \'grisəl\ n : cartilage —**gris·tly** \-(s)lē\ adj

grit \'grit\ n 1 : hard sharp granule 2 : material composed of granules 3 : unyielding courage ~ vb -tt- : press with a grating noise —**grit·ty** adj

grits \'grits\ n pl : coarsely ground hulled grain

griz·zled \'grizəld\ adj : streaked with gray

groan \'grōn\ vb 1 : moan 2 : creak under a strain —**groan** n

gro·cer \'grōsər\ n : food dealer —**gro·cery** \'grōs(ə)rē\ n

grog \'gräg\ n : rum diluted with water

grog·gy \-ē\ adj -gi·er; -est : dazed and unsteady on the feet —**grog·gi·ly** adv —**grog·gi·ness** n

groin \'gròin\ n : juncture of abdomen and thigh

grom·met \'grämət, 'grəm-\ n : eyelet

groom \'grüm, 'gruʹm\ n 1 : one who cleans and brushes horses 2 : bridegroom ~ vb 1 : clean and care for (as a horse) 2 : make neat, attractive, or acceptable

groove \'grüv\ n 1 : long narrow channel 2 : fixed routine —**groove** vb

grope \'grōp\ vb **groped**; **grop·ing** : search for by feeling

gros·beak \'grōs,bēk\ n : finch with large conical bill

¹**gross** \'grōs\ adj 1 : glaringly noticeable 2 : bulky 3 : consisting of an overall total exclusive of deductions 4 : vulgar ~ n : the whole before any deductions ~ vb : earn as a total —**gross·ly** adv —**gross·ness** n

²**gross** n, pl **gross** : 12 dozen

gro·tesque \grō'tesk\ adj 1 : absurdly distorted or repulsive 2 : ridiculous —**gro·tesque·ly** adv

grot·to \'grätō\ n, pl -**toes** : cave

grouch \'graůch\ n : complaining person —**grouch** vb —**grouchy** adj

¹**ground** \'graůnd\ n 1 : bottom of a body of water 2 pl : sediment 3 : basis for something 4 : surface of the earth 5 : conductor that makes electrical connection with the earth or a framework ~ vb 1 : force or bring down to the ground 2 : instruct in fundamental principles 3 : connect with an electrical ground —**ground·less** adj

²**ground** past of GRIND

ground·hog n : woodchuck

ground·wa·ter n : underground water

ground·work n : foundation

group \'grüp\ n : number of associated

individuals ~ *vb* : gather or collect into groups

grou·per \'grüpər\ *n* : large fish of warm seas

grouse \'graus\ *n, pl* **grouse** : game bird

grout \'graut\ *n* : mortar for filling cracks —**grout** *vb*

grove \'grōv\ *n* : small group of trees

grov·el \'grävəl, 'grəv-\ *vb* **-eled** *or* **-elled; -el·ing** *or* **-el·ling** : abase oneself

grow \'grō\ *vb* **grew** \'grü\; **grown** \'grōn\; **grow·ing 1** : come into existence and develop to maturity **2** : be able to grow **3** : advance or increase **4** : become **5** : cultivate —**grow·er** \'grō(ə)r\ *n*

growl \'graul\ *vb* : utter a deep threatening sound —**growl** *n*

grown–up \'grōn,əp\ *n* : adult —**grown–up** *adj*

growth \'grōth\ *n* **1** : stage in growing **2** : process of growing **3** : result of something growing

grub \'grəb\ *vb* **-bb-** : root out by digging ~ *n* **1** : thick wormlike larva **2** : food

grub·by \'grəbē\ *adj* **-bi·er; -est** : dirty —**grub·bi·ness** *n*

grub·stake *n* : supplies for a prospector

grudge \'grəj\ *vb* **grudged; grudg·ing** : be reluctant to give ~ *n* : feeling of ill will

gru·el \'grüəl\ *n* : thin porridge

gru·el·ing, gru·el·ling \-əliŋ\ *adj* : requiring extreme effort

grue·some \'grüsəm\ *adj* : horribly repulsive

gruff \'grəf\ *adj* : rough in speech or manner —**gruff·ly** *adv*

grum·ble \'grəmbəl\ *vb* **-bled; -bling** : mutter in discontent —**grum·bler** \-b(ə)lər\ *n*

grumpy \-pē\ *adj* **grump·i·er; -est** : cross —**grump·i·ly** *adv* —**grump·i·ness** *n*

grun·ion \'grənyən\ *n* : fish of the California coast

grunt \'grənt\ *n* : deep guttural sound —**grunt** *vb*

gua·no \'gwänō\ *n* : excrement of seabirds used as fertilizer

guar·an·tee \,garən'tē\ *n* **1** : assurance of the fulfillment of a condition **2** : something given or held as a security **3** : promise to be responsible for **2** : state with certainty —**guar·an·tor** \,garən'tòr\ *n*

guar·an·ty \'garəntē\ *n, pl* **-ties 1** : promise to answer for another's failure to pay a debt **2** : guarantee **3** : pledge ~ *vb* **-tied; -ty·ing** : guarantee

guard \'gärd\ *n* **1** : defensive position **2** : act of protecting **3** : an individual or group that guards against danger **4** : protective or safety device ~ *vb* **1** : protect or watch over **2** : take precautions —**guard·house** *n* —**guard·room** *n*

guard·ian \'gärdēən\ *n* : one who has responsibility for the care of a person or property —**guard·ian·ship** *n*

gua·va \'gwävə\ *n* : shrubby tree or its mildly acid fruit

gu·ber·na·to·ri·al \,g(y)übə(r)nə'tōrēəl\ *adj* : relating to a governor

guer·ril·la, gue·ril·la \gə'rilə\ *n* : soldier engaged in small-scale harassing tactics

guess \'ges\ *vb* **1** : form an opinion from little evidence **2** : state correctly solely by chance **3** : think or believe —**guess** *n*

guest \'gest\ *n* **1** : person to whom hospitality (as of a house) is extended **2** : patron of a commercial establishment (as a hotel) **3** : person not a regular cast member who appears on a program

guf·faw \(,)gə'fò, 'gəf,ò\ *n* : loud burst of laughter —**guf·faw** \(,)gə'fò\ *vb*

guide \'gīd\ *n* **1** : one that leads or gives direction to another **2** : device on a machine to direct motion ~ *vb* : direct —**guid·able** *adj* —**guid·ance** \'gīd⁰ns\ *n* —**guide·book** *n*

guild \'gild\ *n* : association

guile \'gīl\ *n* : craftiness —**guile·ful** *adj* —**guile·less** *adj* —**guile·less·ness** *n*

guil·lo·tine \'gilə,tēn; ,gē(y)ə,'tēn, 'gē(y)ə,-\ *n* : machine for beheading persons —**guillotine** *vb*

guilt \'gilt\ *n* **1** : fact of having committed an offense **2** : feeling of responsibility for offenses —**guilt·i·ly** *adv* —**guilt·i·ness** *n* —**guilty** \'giltē\ *adj*

guin·ea \'ginē\ *n* **1** : old gold coin of United Kingdom **2** : 21 shillings

guinea pig *n* : small So. American rodent

guise \'gīz\ *n* : external appearance

gui·tar \gə'tär, gi-\ *n* : 6-stringed musical instrument played by plucking

gulch \'gəlch\ *n* : ravine

gulf \'gəlf\ *n* **1** : extension of an ocean or a sea into the land **2** : abyss

¹gull \'gəl\ n : seabird with webbed feet

²gull vb : make a dupe of ~ n : dupe —gull·ible adj

gul·let \'gələt\ n : throat

gul·ly \-ē\ n, pl -lies : trench worn by running water

gulp \'gəlp\ vb : swallow hurriedly or greedily —gulp n

¹gum \'gəm\ n : tissue along the jaw at the base of the teeth

²gum n 1 : sticky plant substance 2 : gum usu. of sweetened chicle prepared for chewing

gum·bo \'gəmbō\ n : thick soup

gum-drop n : gumlike candy

gump·tion \'gəmpshən\ n : initiative

gun \'gən\ n 1 : cannon 2 : portable firearm 3 : discharge of a gun 4 : something like a gun ~ vb -nn- : hunt with a gun —gun·fight n —gun·fight·er n —gun·fire n —gun·man \-mən\ n —gun·pow·der n —gun·shot n —gun·smith n

gun·boat n : small armed ship

gun·ner \'gənər\ n : person who uses a gun

gunnery sergeant n : noncommissioned officer in the marine corps ranking next below a first sergeant

gun·ny \'gənē\ n : coarse jute material for making sacks (gunnysacks)

gun·sling·er \-ˌsliŋər\ n : gunman in the old West

gun·wale, gun·nel \'gənᵊl\ n : upper edge of a boat's side

gup·py \'gəpē\ n, pl -pies : tiny tropical fish

gur·gle \'gərgəl\ vb -gled; -gling : make a sound like that of a flowing and gently splashing liquid —gurgle n

gu·ru \gə'rü, 'gü(ə)r(ˌ)ü\ n, pl -rus : personal religious teacher in Hinduism

gush \'gəsh\ vb : pour forth violently or enthusiastically —gush·er \'gəshər\ n

gushy \-ē\ adj gush·i·er; -est : effusively sentimental

gust \'gəst\ n 1 : sudden brief rush of wind 2 : sudden outburst —gust vb —gusty adj

gus·ta·to·ry \'gəstəˌtōrē\ adj : relating to the sense of taste

gus·to \'gəstō\ n : zest

gut \'gət\ n 1 pl : intestines 2 : digestive canal 3 pl : courage ~ vb -tt- : eviscerate

gut·ter \'gətər\ n : channel for carrying off rainwater

gut·tur·al \'gətərəl\ adj : sounded in the throat —guttural n

¹guy \'gī\ n : rope, chain, or rod attached to something to steady it —guy vb

²guy n : person

guz·zle \'gəzəl\ vb -zled; -zling : drink greedily

gym \'jim\ n : gymnasium

gym·na·si·um \jim'nāzēəm, -zhəm\ n, pl -si·ums or -sia \-zēə, -zhə\ : place for indoor sports

gym·nas·tics \jim'nastiks\ n : physical exercises performed in a gymnasium —gym·nast \'jim,nast\ n —gym·nas·tic adj

gy·ne·col·o·gy \ˌgīnəˈkäləjē, ˌjin-\ n : branch of medicine dealing with the diseases of women —gy·ne·co·log·ic \-ikə'läjik\, gy·ne·co·log·i·cal \-ikal\ adj —gy·ne·col·o·gist \-ə'käləjəst\ n

gyp \'jip\ n : cheat 2 : trickery —gyp vb

gyp·sum \'jipsəm\ n : calcium-containing mineral

gy·rate \'jī,rāt\ vb -rat·ed; -rat·ing : revolve around a center —gy·ra·tion \jī'rāshən\ n

gy·ro·com·pass \'jīrōˌkəmpəs, -ˌkäm-\ n : compass in which the axis of a spinning gyroscope points toward the north

gy·ro·scope \-ˌskōp\ n : wheel mounted to spin rapidly about an axis that is free to turn in various directions

H

h \'āch\ n, pl h's or hs \'āchəz\ : 8th letter of the alphabet

hab·er·dash·er \'habə(r)ˌdashər\ n : men's clothier —hab·er·dash·ery \-(ə)rē\ n

hab·it \'habət\ n 1 : monk's or nun's clothing 2 : usual behavior —hab·it·form·ing adj

hab·it·able \-əbəl\ adj : capable of being lived in

hab·i·tat \'habəˌtat\ n : place where a plant or animal naturally occurs

hab·i·ta·tion \ˌhabə'tāshən\ n 1 : occupancy 2 : dwelling place

ha·bit·u·al \həˈbich(əw)əl\ adj 1 : commonly practiced or observed 2

: doing, practicing, or acting by habit —**ha·bit·u·al·ly** *adv* —**ha·bit·u·al·ness** *n*

ha·bit·u·ate \ha'bicha,wāt\ *vb* **-at·ed; -at·ing** : accustom

ha·ci·en·da \,(h)äsē'endə\ *n* : ranch house

¹**hack** \'hak\ *vb* **1** : cut with repeated irregular blows **2** : cough in a short dry manner **3** : manage successfully —**hack** *n* —**hack·er** *n*

²**hack** *n* **1** : horse or vehicle for hire **2** : saddle horse **3** : writer for hire —**hack** *adj* —**hack·man** \-mən\ *n*

hack·le \'hakəl\ *n* **1** : long feather on the neck or lower back of a bird **2** *pl* : hairs that can be erected **3** *pl* : temper

hack·ney \-nē\ *n, pl* **-neys 1** : horse for riding or driving **2** : carriage for hire

hack·neyed \-nēd\ *adj* : trite

hack·saw *n* : saw for metal

had *past of* HAVE

had·dock \'hadək\ *n, pl* **haddock** : Atlantic food fish

Ha·des \'hād,(ḷ)ēz\ *n* **1** : mythological abode of the dead **2** *often not cap* : hell

haft \'haft\ *n* : handle of a weapon or tool

hag \'hag\ *n* **1** : witch **2** : ugly old woman

hag·gard \'hagərd\ *adj* : worn or emaciated —**hag·gard·ly** *adv*

hag·gle \'hagəl\ *vb* **-gled; -gling** : argue in bargaining —**hag·gler** *n*

¹**hail** \'hāl\ *n* **1** : precipitation in small lumps of ice **2** : something like a rain of hail ~ *vb* : rain hail —**hail·stone** *n* —**hail·storm** *n*

²**hail** *vb* : greet or salute ~ *n* : expression of greeting or praise —often used as an interjection

hair \'haər\ *n* : threadlike growth from the skin —**hair·brush** *n* —**hair·cut** *n* —**hair·dress·er** *n* —**haired** *adj* —**hair·i·ness** *n* —**hair·less** *adj* —**hair·pin** *n* —**hair·style** *n* —**hair·styl·ing** *n* —**hair·styl·ist** *n* —**hairy** *adj*

hair·breadth \-,bredth\, **hairs·breadth** \'haərz-\ *n* : tiny distance or margin

hair·do \-,dü\ *n, pl* **-dos** : style of wearing hair

hair·line *n* **1** : thin line **2** : outline of the hair on the head

hair·piece *n* : toupee

hair·rais·ing *adj* : causing terror or astonishment

hake \'hāk\ *n* : marine food fish

hal·cy·on \'halsēən\ *adj* : prosperous or most pleasant

¹**hale** \'hāl\ *adj* : healthy or robust

²**hale** *vb* **haled; hal·ing 1** : haul **2** : compel to go

half \'haf, 'häf\ *n, pl* **halves** \'havz, 'hävz\ : one of 2 equal parts ~ *adj* **1** : being a half or constituting a half **2** : partial —**half** *adv*

half-breed *n* : offspring of parents of different races —**half-breed** *adj*

half brother *n* : brother by one parent only

half·heart·ed \-'härtəd\ *adj* : without enthusiasm —**half·heart·ed·ly** *adv* —**half·heart·ed·ness** *n*

half-life *n* : time for half of something to undergo a process

half sister *n* : sister by one parent only

half·way *adj* : midway between 2 points —**half-way** *adv*

half-wit \-,wit\ *n* : foolish person —**half-wit·ted** \-'witəd\ *adj*

hal·i·but \'haləbət\ *n, pl* **halibut** : large edible marine flatfish

hal·i·to·sis \,halə'tōsəs\ *n* : bad breath

hall \'hól\ *n* **1** : large public or university building **2** : lobby **3** : auditorium

hal·le·lu·jah \,halə'lüyə\ *interj* —used to express praise, joy, or thanks

hall·mark \'hól,märk\ *n* : distinguishing characteristic

hal·low \'halō\ *vb* : consecrate —**hallowed** \-ōd, -əwəd\ *adj*

Hal·low·een \,halə'wēn, ,häl-\ *n* : evening of October 31 observed esp. by children in merrymaking and masquerading

hal·lu·ci·na·tion \hə,lüs'n'āshən\ *n* : perception of objects or events that are not real —**hal·lu·ci·nate** \hə-'lüs'n,āt\ *vb* —**hal·lu·ci·na·tive** \-'lüs'n,ātiv\ *adj* —**hal·lu·ci·na·to·ry** \-'nə,tōrē\ *adj*

hal·lu·ci·no·gen \hə'lüs'nəjən\ *n* : substance that induces hallucinations —**hal·lu·ci·no·gen·ic** \-,lüs'nə'jenik\ *adj*

hall·way *n* : entrance hall

ha·lo \'hālō\ *n, pl* **-los** *or* **-loes** : circle of light appearing to surround a shining body

¹**halt** \'hólt\ *adj* : lame

²**halt** *vb* : stop or cause to stop —**halt** *n*

hal·ter \'hóltər\ *n* **1** : rope or strap for leading or tying an animal **2** : brief blouse held up by straps ~ *n* : catch (an animal) with a halter

halt·ing \'hóltiŋ\ *adj* : uncertain —**halt·ing·ly** *adv*

halve \'hav, 'häv\ *vb* **halved; halv·ing 1** : divide into halves **2** : reduce to half

halves *pl of* HALF

ham \\ham\\ n 1 : thigh 2 : cut esp. of pork from the thigh 3 : showy actor 4 : amateur radio operator ~ vb -mm- : overplay a part —ham adj

ham·burg·er \\ham,bərgər\\, **ham·burg** \-,bərg\\ n : ground beef or a sandwich made with this

ham·let \\hamlət\\ n : small village

ham·mer \-ər\\ n 1 : hand tool for pounding 2 : gun part whose striking explodes the charge ~ vb 1 : beat, drive, or shape with a hammer 2 : produce by repeated blows

ham·mer·head n 1 : striking part of a hammer 2 : shark with a hammerlike head

ham·mock \\hamək\\ n : swinging bed hung by cords at each end

¹ham·per \-pər\\ vb : impede

²hamper n : large covered basket

ham·ster \-stər\\ n : stocky short-tailed rodent

ham·string \-,striŋ\\ vb -strung \-,strəŋ\\; -string·ing \-,striŋiŋ\\ 1 : cripple by cutting the leg tendons 2 : make ineffective or powerless

hand \\hand\\ n 1 : end of a front limb adapted for grasping 2 : side 3 : promise of marriage 4 : handwriting 5 : assistance or participation 6 : applause 7 : cards held by a player 8 : worker ~ vb : lead, assist, give, or pass with the hand —hand·clasp n —hand·craft vb —hand·ful n —hand·gun n —hand·less adj —hand·made adj —hand·rail n —hand·saw n —hand·wo·ven adj —hand·writ·ing n —hand·writ·ten adj

hand·bag n : woman's purse

hand·ball n : game played by striking a ball with the hand

hand·bill n : printed advertisement or notice distributed by hand

hand·book n : concise reference book

hand·cuffs n, pl : locking bracelets that bind the wrists together —handcuff vb

hand·i·cap \\handi,kap\\ n 1 : advantage given or disadvantage imposed to equalize a competition 2 : disadvantage —handicap vb —hand·i·cap·per n

hand·i·craft \\handi,kraft\\ n 1 : manual skill 2 : article made by hand —hand·i·craft n —hand·i·crafts·man \-,kraftsmən\\ n

hand·i·work \-,wərk\\ n : work done personally

hand·ker·chief \\haŋkərchəf, -,chēf\\ n, pl -chiefs \-chəfs, -,chēfs\\ : small piece of cloth carried for personal use

han·dle \\hand⁰l\\ n : part to be grasped ~ vb -dled; -dling 1 : touch, hold, or manage with the hands 2 : deal with 3 : deal or trade in —han·dle·bar n —han·dled \-d⁰ld\\ adj

hand-maid·en, hand-maid n : female attendant

hand·out n : something given out

hand·pick vb : select personally

hand·shake n : clasping of hands (as in greeting)

hand·some \\hansəm\\ adj 1 : sizable 2 : generous 3 : nice-looking —hand·some·ly adv —hand·some·ness n

hand·spring n : somersault on the hands

hand·stand n : a balancing stance upside down on the hands

handy \\handē\\ adj hand·i·er; -est 1 : conveniently near 2 : easily used 3 : dexterous —hand·i·ly adv —hand·i·ness n

handy·man \-,man\\ n : one who does odd jobs

hang \\haŋ\\ vb hung \\həŋ\\ or hanged \\haŋd\\; hang·ing 1 : fasten or remain fastened to an elevated point without support from below 2 : put or come to death by suspending with a rope around the neck ~ n 1 : way a thing hangs 2 : knack —hang·er n

han·gar \\haŋər\\ n : airplane shelter

hang·dog \\haŋ,dóg\\ adj : ashamed or guilty

hang·man \-mən\\ n : public executioner

hang·nail n : loose skin near a fingernail

hang·out n : place where one likes to spend time

hang·over n : sick feeling following heavy drinking

hank \\haŋk\\ n : coil or loop

han·ker \\haŋkər\\ vb : desire strongly —han·ker·ing n

han·ky-pan·ky \,haŋkē'paŋkē\\ n : underhand activity

han·som \\hansəm\\ n : 2-wheeled covered carriage

Ha·nuk·kah \\känəkə, 'hän-\\ n : 8-day Jewish holiday commemorating the rededication of the Temple of Jerusalem after its defilement by Antiochus of Syria

hap·haz·ard \hap'hazərd\\ adj : having no plan or order —hap·haz·ard·ly adv

hap·less \\hapləs\\ adj : unfortunate —hap·less·ly adv —hap·less·ness n

hap·pen \\hapən\\ vb 1 : take place 2 : be fortunate to encounter something unexpectedly —often used with infinitive

hap·pen·ing \-(ə)niŋ\ *n* : occurrence

hap·py \'hapē\ *adj* **-pi·er; -est** 1 : fortunate 2 : content, pleased, or joyous —**hap·pi·ly** \'ha‚pəlē\ *adv* —**hap·pi·ness** *n*

ha·rangue \hə'raŋ\ *n* : ranting or scolding speech —**harangue** *vb* —**ha·rangu·er** \-'raŋər\ *n*

ha·rass \hə'ras, 'harəs\ *vb* 1 : worry and impede (an enemy) by repeated raids 2 : annoy continually —**ha·rass·ment** *n*

har·bin·ger \'härbənjər\ *n* : one that announces or foreshadows what is coming

har·bor \-bər\ *n* : protected body of water suitable for anchorage ~ *vb* 1 : give refuge to 2 : hold as a thought or feeling

hard \'härd\ *adj* 1 : not easily penetrated 2 : firm or definite 3 : close or searching 4 : severe or unfeeling 5 : strenuous or difficult 6 : physically strong or intense —**hard** *adv* —**hard·ness** *n*

hard·en \'härdᵊn\ *vb* : make or become hard or harder —**hard·en·er** *n*

hard·head·ed \-'hedəd\ *adj* 1 : stubborn 2 : realistic —**hard·head·ed·ly** *adv* —**hard·head·ed·ness** *n*

hard·heart·ed \-'härtəd\ *adj* : lacking sympathy —**hard·heart·ed·ly** *adv* —**hard·heart·ed·ness** *n*

hard·ly \-lē\ *adv* 1 : only just 2 : certainly not

hard·ship \-,ship\ *n* : suffering or privation

hard·tack \-,tak\ *n* : hard biscuit

hard·ware \-,war\ *n* : cutlery or tools made of metal

hard·wood *n* : wood of a broad-leaved usu. deciduous tree —**hardwood** *adj*

har·dy \'härdē\ *adj* **-di·er; -est** : able to withstand adverse conditions —**har·di·ly** *adv* —**har·di·ness** *n*

hare \'har\ *n, pl* **hare** *or* **hares** : long-eared mammal related to the rabbit

hare·lip \-'lip\ *n* : deformity in which the upper lip is vertically split —**hare·lipped** \-'lipt\ *adj*

ha·rem \'harəm\ *n* : house or part of a house allotted to women in a Muslim household or the women and servants occupying it

hark \'härk\ *vb* : listen

har·le·quin \'härlik(w)ən\ *n* : clown

har·lot \'härlət\ *n* : prostitute

harm \'härm\ *n* 1 : physical or mental damage ~ *vb* : cause harm —**harm·ful** \-fəl\ *adj* —**harm·ful·ly** *adv* —**harm·ful·ness** *n* —**harm·less** *adj* —**harm·less·ly** *adv* —**harm·less·ness** *n*

har·mon·ic \här'mänik\ *adj* 1 : of or relating to musical harmony 2 : pleasing to hear —**har·mon·i·cal·ly** \-ik(ə)lē\ *adv*

har·mon·i·ca \här'mänikə\ *n* : small wind instrument with metallic reeds

har·mo·ny \'härmənē\ *n, pl* **-nies** 1 : musical combination of sounds 2 : pleasing arrangment of parts 3 : lack of conflict 4 : internal calm —**har·mo·ni·ous** \här'mōnēəs\ *adj* —**har·mo·ni·ous·ly** *adv* —**har·mo·ni·ous·ness** *n* —**har·mo·ni·za·tion** \‚härmənə'zāshən\ *n* —**har·mo·nize** \'härmə‚nīz\ *vb*

har·ness \'härnəs\ *n* : gear of a draft animal ~ *vb* 1 : put a harness on 2 : put to use

harp \'härp\ *n* : musical instrument with many strings plucked by the fingers ~ *vb* 1 : play on a harp 2 : dwell on a subject tiresomely —**harp·er** *n* —**harp·ist** *n*

har·poon \här'pün\ *n* : barbed spear used in hunting whales —**harpoon** *vb* —**har·poon·er** *n*

harp·si·chord \'härpsi‚kȯrd\ *n* : keyboard instrument with strings that are plucked

har·py \'härpē\ *n, pl* **-pies** : shrewish woman

har·row \'harō\ *n* : implement used to break up soil ~ *vb* 1 : cultivate with a harrow 2 : distress

har·ry \'harē\ *vb* **-ried; -ry·ing** : torment by or as if by constant attack

harsh \'härsh\ *adj* 1 : disagreeably rough 2 : severe —**harsh·ly** *adv* —**harsh·ness** *n*

hart \'härt\ *n* : stag

har·um-scar·um \‚harəm'skarəm\ *adv* : recklessly

har·vest \'härvəst\ *n* 1 : act or time of gathering in a crop 2 : mature crop —**harvest** *vb* —**har·vest·er** *n*

has *pres 3d sing of* HAVE

hash \'hash\ *vb* : chop into small pieces ~ *n* : chopped meat mixed with potatoes and browned

hash·ish \'hash‚ēsh, -(‚)ish\ *n* : unadulterated intoxicating resin from female hemp plants

hasp \'hasp\ *n* : hinged strap fastener esp. for a door

has·sle \'hasəl\ *n* 1 : quarrel 2 : struggle —**hassle** *vb*

has·sock \'hasək\ *n* : cushion used as a seat or leg rest

haste \'hāst\ *n* 1 : rapidity of motion 2 : rash action 3 : excessive eagerness

—hast·i·ly \'hāstəlē\ adv —hast·i·ness \-stēnəs\ n —hasty \-stē\ adj

has·ten \'hāsᵊn\ vb : hurry

hat \'hat\ n : covering for the head

¹hatch \'hach\ n : small door or opening —hatch·way n

²hatch vb : emerge from an egg —hatch·ery \-(ə)rē\ n

hatch·et \'hachət\ n : short-handled ax

hate \'hāt\ n : intense hostility and aversion ~ vb hat·ed; hat·ing 1 : express or feel hate 2 : dislike —hate·ful \-fəl\ adj —hate·ful·ly adv —hate·ful·ness n —hat·er n

ha·tred \'hātrəd\ n : hate

hat·ter \'hatər\ n : one that makes or sells hats

haugh·ty \'hótē\ adj -ti·er; -est : disdainfully proud —haugh·ti·ly adv —haugh·ti·ness n

haul \'hól\ vb 1 : draw or pull 2 : transport or carry ~ n 1 : amount collected 2 : load or the distance it is transported —haul·age \-ij\ n —haul·er n

haunch \'hónch\ n : hip or hindquarter —usu. pl.

haunt \'hónt\ vb 1 : visit often 2 : visit or inhabit as a ghost ~ n : place habitually frequented —haunt·er n —haunt·ing·ly adv

have \(')hav, (h)əv, v; in sense 2 before "to" usu 'haf\ vb had \(')had, (h)əd\; hav·ing \'havin\; has \(')haz, (h)əz, in sense 2 before "to" usu 'has\ 1 : hold in possession, service, or affection : be compelled or forced to 3 —used as an auxiliary with the past participle to form the present perfect, past perfect, or future perfect 4 : obtain or receive 5 : undergo 6 : cause to 7 : bear —have to do with : have in the way of connection or relation with or effect on

ha·ven \'hāvən\ n : place of safety

hav·oc \'havək\ n 1 : wide destruction 2 : great confusion

¹hawk \'hók\ n : small or medium-sized day-flying bird of prey —hawk·ish adj

²hawk vb : offer for sale by calling out in the street —hawk·er n

haw·ser \'hózər\ n : large rope

haw·thorn \'hó,thórn\ n : spiny shrub or tree with pink or white fragrant flowers

hay \'hā\ n : herbage mowed and cured for fodder —hay vb —hay·fork n —hay·loft n —hay·mow \-,maů\ n —hay·stack n

hay·cock \'hā,käk\ n : small pile of hay

hay·rick \-,rik\ n : large outdoor stack of hay

hay·seed \'hā,sēd\ n : bumpkin

hay·wire adj : being out of order

haz·ard \'hazərd\ n 1 : source of danger 2 : chance ~ vb : venture or risk —haz·ard·ous adj

¹haze \'hāz\ n : fine dust, smoke, or light vapor in the air that reduces visibility

²haze vb hazed; haz·ing : harass by abusive and humiliating tricks

ha·zel \'hāzəl\ n : shrub or small tree bearing edible nuts (hazel·nuts)

ha·zy \'hāzē\ adj haz·i·er; -est 1 : obscured by haze 2 : vague or indefinite —haz·i·ly adv —haz·i·ness n

he \(')hē, ē\ pron 1 : that male one 2 : a or the person

head \'hed\ n 1 : front or upper part of the body 2 : mind 3 : upper or higher end 4 : director or leader 5 : place of leadership or honor ~ adj : principal or chief ~ vb 1 : provide with or form a head 2 : put, stand, or be at the head 3 : point or proceed in a certain direction —head·ache n —head·band n —head·dress n —head·ed adj —head·first adv or adj —head·gear n —head·less adj —head·man \-'man, -,man\ n —head·rest n —head·ship n —head·wait·er n

head·ing \-in\ n 1 : direction in which a plane or ship heads 2 : something (as a title) standing at the top or beginning

head·land \'hedland, -,land\ n : promontory

head·light n : light on the front of an automobile

head·line n : introductory line of a newspaper story printed in large type

head·long \-'lón\ adv 1 : head foremost 2 : in a rash or reckless manner —head·long \-,lón\ adj

head·mas·ter n : male head of a private school

head·mis·tress n : female head of a private school

head·on adj : having the front facing in the direction of initial contact —head·on adv

head·phone n : an earphone held on by a band over the head

head·quar·ters n sing or pl : command or administrative center

head·stone n : stone at the head of a grave

head·strong adj : stubborn or willful

head·wa·ter n : source of a stream —usu. pl.

head·way *n* : forward motion

heady \'hedē\ *adj* **head·i·er; -est 1** : intoxicating **2** : shrewd

heal \'hēl\ *vb* : make or become sound or whole —**heal·er** *n*

health \'helth\ *n* : sound physical or mental condition

health·ful \-fəl\ *adj* : beneficial to health —**health·ful·ly** *adv* —**health·ful·ness** *n*

healthy \'helthē\ *adj* **health·i·er; -est** : enjoying or typical of good health —**health·i·ly** *adv* —**health·i·ness** *n*

heap \'hēp\ *n* : pile ~ *vb* : throw or lay in a heap

hear \'hiər\ *vb* **heard** \'hərd\; **hear·ing** \'hi(ə)riŋ\ **1** : perceive by the ear **2** : heed **3** : learn —**hear·er** \'hirər\ *n*

hear·ing *n* **1** : process or power of perceiving sound **2** : earshot **3** : session in which witnesses are heard

hear·ken \'härkən\ *vb* : give attention

hear·say *n* : rumor

hearse \'hərs\ *n* : vehicle for carrying the dead to the grave

heart \'härt\ *n* **1** : hollow muscular organ that keeps up the circulation of the blood **2** : playing card of a suit marked with a red heart **3** : whole personality or the emotional or moral part of it **4** : courage **5** : essential part —**heart·beat** *n* —**heart·ed** *adj*

heart·ache *n* : anguish of mind

heart·break *n* : crushing grief —**heart·break·ing** *adj* —**heart·bro·ken** *adj*

heart·burn *n* : burning distress behind the lower sternum

heart·en \'härt³n\ *vb* : encourage

hearth \'härth\ *n* **1** : area in front of a fireplace **2** : home —**hearth·stone** *n*

heart·less \-ləs\ *adj* : cruel

heart·rend·ing \-ˌrendiŋ\ *adj* : causing intense grief or anguish

heart·sick *adj* : very despondent —**heart·sick·ness** *n*

heart·strings *n pl* : deepest emotions

heart·throb *n* : sweetheart

heart·warm·ing *adj* : inspiring sympathetic feeling

heart·wood *n* : central portion of wood

hearty \'härtē\ *adj* **heart·i·er; -est 1** : vigorously healthy **2** : nourishing —**heart·i·ly** *adv* —**heart·i·ness** *n*

heat \'hēt\ *vb* : make or become warm or hot ~ *n* **1** : condition of being hot **2** : form of energy that causes a body to rise in temperature **3** : intensity of feeling —**heat·ed·ly** *adv* —**heat·er** *n* —**heat·less** *adj*

heath \'hēth\ *n* **1** : often evergreen shrubby plant of wet acid soils **2** : tract of wasteland —**heathy** *adj*

hea·then \'hēthən\ *n, pl* **-thens** *or* **-then** : uncivilized or godless person —**hea·then** *adj*

heath·er \'hethər\ *n* : evergreen heath with lavender flowers —**heath·ery** *adj*

heat·stroke *n* : disorder that follows prolonged exposure to excessive heat

heave \'hēv\ *vb* **heaved** *or* **hove** \'hōv\; **heav·ing 1** : rise or lift upward **2** : throw **3** : rise and fall ~ *n* **1** : an effort to lift or raise **2** : throw

heav·en \'hevən\ *n pl* : sky **2** : abode of the Deity and of the blessed dead **3** : place of supreme happiness —**heav·en·ly** *adj* —**heav·en·ward** *adv or adj*

heavy \'hevē\ *adj* **heav·i·er; -est 1** : having great weight **2** : hard to bear **3** : greater than the average —**heav·i·ly** *adv* —**heav·i·ness** *n* —**heavy·weight** *n*

heavy-du·ty *adj* : able to withstand unusual strain

heavy·set *adj* : stocky and compact in build

heck·le \'hekəl\ *vb* **-led; -ling** : harass with gibes —**heck·ler** \-(ə)lər\ *n*

hec·tic \'hektik\ *adj* : filled with excitement or confusion —**hec·ti·cal·ly** \-tik(ə)lē\ *adv*

hedge \'hej\ *n* **1** : fence or boundary of shrubs or small trees **2** : means of protection ~ *vb* **hedged; hedg·ing 1** : protect oneself against loss **2** : evade the risk of commitment —**hedg·er** *n*

hedge·hog *n* : spiny mammal (as a porcupine)

he·do·nism \'hēd³nˌizəm\ *n* : way of life devoted to pleasure —**he·do·nist** \-³nəst\ *n* —**he·do·nis·tic** \ˌhēd³n'istik\ *adj*

heed \'hēd\ *vb* : pay attention ~ *n* : attention —**heed·ful** \-fəl\ *adj* —**heed·ful·ly** *adv* —**heed·ful·ness** *n* —**heed·less** *adj* —**heed·less·ly** *adv* —**heed·less·ness** *n*

¹heel \'hēl\ *n* **1** : back of the foot **2** : crusty end of a loaf of bread **3** : solid piece forming the back of the sole of a shoe —**heel·less** \'hēlləs\ *adj*

²heel *vb* : tilt to one side

heft \'heft\ *n* : weight ~ *vb* : judge the weight of by lifting

hefty \'heftē\ *adj* **heft·i·er; -est** : big and bulky

he·ge·mo·ny \hi'jemənē\ *n* : preponderant influence esp. of one nation over others

heif·er \'hefər\ *n* : young cow

height \'hīt, 'hīth\ *n* **1** : highest part

or point **2** : distance from bottom to top **3** : altitude

height·en \'hīt°n\ *vb* : increase in amount or degree

hei·nous \'hānəs\ *adj* : shockingly evil —**hei·nous·ly** *adv* —**hei·nous·ness** *n*

heir \'aər\ *n* : one who inherits or is entitled to inherit property —**heir·ship** *n*

heir·ess \'arəs\ *n* : female heir esp. to great wealth

heir·loom \'aər‚lüm\ *n* : something handed on from one generation to another

held *past of* HOLD

he·li·cal \'helikəl, 'hē-\ *adj* : spiral

he·li·cop·ter \'helə‚käptər, 'hē-\ *n* : aircraft supported in the air by rotors

he·lio·trope \'hēlyə‚trōp\ *n* : garden herb with small fragrant white or purple flowers

he·li·um \'hēlēəm\ *n* : very light nonflammable gaseous chemical element

he·lix \'hēliks\ *n, pl* **-li·ces** \'helə‚sēz, 'hē-\ : something spiral

hell \'hel\ *n* **1** : nether world in which the dead continue to exist **2** : realm of the devil **3** : place or state of torment or destruction —**hell·ish** *adj*

hell·gram·mite \'helgrə‚mīt\ *n* : aquatic insect larva

hel·lion \'helyən\ *n* : troublesome person

hel·lo \hə'lō, he-\ *n, pl* **-los** : expression of greeting

helm \'helm\ *n* : lever or wheel for steering a ship —**helms·man** \'helmzmən\ *n*

hel·met \'helmət\ *n* : protective covering for the head

help \'help\ *vb* **1** : supply what is needed **2** : be of use **3** : refrain from or prevent ~ *n* **1** : something that helps or a source of help **2** : one who helps another —**help·er** *n* —**help·ful** \-fəl\ *adj* —**help·ful·ly** *adv* —**help·ful·ness** *n* —**help·less** *adj* —**help·less·ly** *adv* —**help·less·ness** *n*

help·ing \'helpiŋ\ *n* : portion of food

help·mate *n* **1** : helper **2** : wife

help·meet \-‚mēt\ *n* : helpmate

hel·ter-skel·ter \‚heltər'skeltər\ *adv* : in total disorder

hem \'hem\ *n* : border of an article of cloth doubled back and stitched down ~ *vb* **-mm- 1** : sew a hem **2** : surround restrictively —**hem·line** *n*

he·ma·tol·o·gy \‚hēmə'täləjē\ *n* : study of the blood and blood-forming organs —**hem·a·to·log·ic** \-mət°l'äjik\,

hem·a·to·log·i·cal \-ikəl\ *adj* —**he·ma·tol·o·gist** \-'täləjəst\ *n*

hemi·sphere \'hemə‚sfiər\ *n* : one of the halves of the earth divided by the equator into northern and southern parts (**northern hemisphere, southern hemisphere**) or by a meridian into eastern and western parts (**eastern hemisphere, western hemisphere**) —**hemi·spher·ic** \‚hemə'sfiərik, -'sfer-\, **hemi·spher·i·cal** \-'sfirikəl, -'sfer-\ *adj*

hem·lock \'hem‚läk\ *n* **1** : poisonous herb related to the carrot **2** : evergreen tree related to the pines

he·mo·glo·bin \'hēmə‚glōbən\ *n* : iron-containing compound found in red blood cells

he·mo·phil·ia \‚hēmə'filēə\ *n* : tendency to severe prolonged bleeding —**he·mo·phil·i·ac** \-ē‚ak\ *adj or n*

hem·or·rhage \'hem(ə)rij\ *n* : large discharge of blood —**hemorrhage** *vb* —**hem·or·rhag·ic** \‚hemə'rajik\ *adj*

hem·or·rhoids \'hem(ə)‚roidz\ *n pl* : swollen mass of dilated veins at or just within the anus

hemp \'hemp\ *n* : tall Asian herb grown for its tough fiber —**hemp·en** \'hempən\ *adj*

hen \'hen\ *n* : female domestic fowl

hence \'hens\ *adv* **1** : away **2** : therefore **3** : from this source or origin

hence·forth *adv* : from this point on

hence·for·ward *adv* : henceforth

hench·man \'henchmən\ *n* : trusted follower

hen·na \'henə\ *n* : reddish brown dye obtained from the leaves of a tropical shrub

hen·peck \'hen‚pek\ *vb* : subject (one's husband) to persistent nagging

he·pat·ic \hi'patik\ *adj* : relating to or resembling the liver

hep·a·ti·tis \‚hepə'tītəs\ *n, pl* **-ti·des** \-'titə‚dēz\ : inflammation of the liver or a disease of which this is a feature

her \(h)ər, ‚hər\ *adj* : of or relating to her or herself ~ \ər, (')hər\ *pron, objective case of* SHE

her·ald \'herəld\ *n* **1** : official crier or messenger **2** : harbinger ~ *vb* : give notice

her·ald·ry \'herəldrē\ *n, pl* **-ries** : practice of devising and granting arms —**he·ral·dic** \he'raldik, hə-\ *adj*

herb \'(h)ərb\ *n* **1** : seed plant that lacks woody tissue **2** : plant or plant part valued for medicinal or savory qualities —**her·ba·ceous** \‚(h)ər'bāshəs\ *adj* —**herb·age**

\'(h)ərbij\ n —**her·bal** \-bəl\ n or adj —**herb·al·ist** \-bələst\ n

her·bi·cide \'(h)ərbə,sīd\ n : agent that destroys plants —**her·bi·cid·al** \,(h)ərbə'sīd⁰l\ adj

her·biv·o·rous \,(h)ər'bivərəs\ adj : feeding on plants —**her·bi·vore** \'(h)ərbə,vōr\ n —**her·biv·o·rous·ly** adv

her·cu·le·an \,hərkyə'lēən, ,hər'kyü-lēən\ adj : of extraordinary power, size, or difficulty

herd \'hərd\ n : group of animals of one kind ~ vb : assemble or move in a herd —**herd·er** n —**herds·man** \'hərdzmən\ n

here \'hiər\ adv 1 : in or at this place 2 : now 3 : at or in this point or particular 4 : in the present life or state ~ n : this place —**here·abouts** \'hirə,baůts\, **here·about** \-,baůt\ adv

here·af·ter adv : in some future time or state ~ n : existence beyond earthly life

here·by adv : by means of this

he·red·i·tary \hə'redə,terē\ adj 1 : genetically passed or passable from parent to offspring 2 : passing by inheritance

he·red·i·ty \-ətē\ n : the passing of characteristics from parent to offspring

here·in adv : in this

here·of adv : of this

here·on adv : on this

her·e·sy \'herəsē\ n, pl -**sies** : opinion or doctrine contrary to church dogma —**her·e·tic** \-,tik\ n —**he·ret·i·cal** \hə'retikəl\ adj

here·to adv : to this document

here·to·fore \'hirtə,fōr\ adv : up to this time

here·un·der adv : under this

here·un·to adv : to this

here·upon adv : on this

here·with adv 1 : with this 2 : hereby

her·i·tage \'heratij\ n 1 : inheritance 2 : birthright

her·maph·ro·dite \(,)hər'mafrə,dīt\ n : animal or plant having both male and female reproductive organs —**hermaphrodite** n —**her·maph·ro·dit·ic** \-,mafrə'ditik\ adj

her·met·ic \hər'metik\ adj : sealed airtight —**her·met·i·cal·ly** \-ik(ə)lē\ adv

her·mit \'hərmət\ n : one who lives in solitude

her·nia \'hərnēə\ n, pl -**ni·as** or -**ni·ae** \-nē,ē, -nē,ī\ : a protruding of a bodily part through the weakened wall of its enclosure —**her·ni·al** adj

—**her·ni·ate** \-nē,āt\ vb —**her·ni·a·tion** \,hərnē'āshən\ n

he·ro \'hērō\ n, pl -**roes** : one that is much admired or shows great courage —**he·ro·ic** \hi'rōik\ adj —**he·ro·i·cal·ly** \-ik(ə)lē\ adv —**he·ro·ics** \-iks\ n pl —**he·ro·ism** \'herə,wizəm\ n

her·o·in \'herəwən\ n : strongly addictive narcotic

her·o·ine \'herəwən\ n : woman of heroic achievements or qualities

her·on \'herən\ n : long-legged long-billed wading bird

her·pes \'hərpēz\ n : virus disease characterized by the formation of blisters

her·pe·tol·o·gy \,hərpə'täləjē\ n : study of reptiles and amphibians —**her·pe·to·log·ic** \-pət⁰l'äjik\, **her·pe·to·log·i·cal** \-ikəl\ adj —**her·pe·tol·o·gist** \-pə'tälajəst\ n

her·ring \'heriŋ\ n, pl -**ring** or -**rings** : narrow-bodied Atlantic food fish

hers \'hərz\ pron : one or the ones belonging to her

her·self \(h)ər'self\ pron : she, her —used reflexively or for emphasis

hertz \'herts, 'härts\ n, pl **hertz** : unit of frequency equal to one cycle per second

hes·i·tant \'hezətənt\ adj : tending to hesitate —**hes·i·tan·cy** \-tənsē\ n —**hes·i·tant·ly** adv

hes·i·tate \'hezə,tāt\ vb -**tat·ed**; -**tat·ing** 1 : hold back esp. in doubt 2 : pause —**hes·i·ta·tion** \,hezə'tāshən\ n

het·er·o·ge·neous \,het(ə)rə'jēnēəs, -nyəs\ adj : consisting of dissimilar ingredients or constituents —**het·er·o·ge·neous·ly** adv —**het·er·o·ge·neous·ness** n

het·ero·sex·u·al \,hetərō'seksh(əw)əl\ adj : oriented toward the opposite sex —**heterosexual** n

hew \'hyü\ vb **hewed**; **hewed** or **hewn** \'hyün\; **hew·ing** 1 : cut or shape with or as if with an ax 2 : conform strictly —**hew·er** n

hex \'heks\ vb : put an evil spell on —**hex** n

hexa·gon \'heksə,gän\ n : 6-sided polygon —**hex·ag·o·nal** \hek'sagən⁰l\ adj

hey·day \'hā,dā\ n : time of flourishing

hi·a·tus \hī'ātəs\ n : lapse in continuity

hi·ba·chi \hi'bächē\ n : brazier

hi·ber·nate \'hībər,nāt\ vb -**nat·ed**; -**nat·ing** : pass the winter in a torpid or resting state —**hi·ber·na·tion** \'hībər'nāshən\ n —**hi·ber·na·tor** \'hībər,nātər\ n

hic·cup \'hik(,)əp\ *n* : spasmodic inhalation with sudden closing of the glottis accompanied by a peculiar sound —**hiccup** *vb*

hick \'hik\ *n* : awkward provincial person —**hick** *adj*

hick·o·ry \'hik(ə)rē\ *n, pl* -ries : No. American hardwood tree —**hickory** *adj*

¹hide \'hīd\ *vb* **hid** \'hid\; **hid·den** \'hid°n\ *or* **hid**; **hid·ing** : put to or remain out of sight

²hide *n* : animal skin

hid·e·ous \'hidēəs\ *adj* : very ugly —**hid·e·ous·ly** *adv* —**hid·e·ous·ness** *n*

hie \'hī\ *vb* **hied**; **hy·ing** *or* **hie·ing** : hurry

hi·er·ar·chy \'hī(ə),rärkē\ *n, pl* -chies : persons or things arranged in a graded series —**hi·er·ar·chi·cal** \,hīə'rärkikəl\ *adj*

hi·er·o·glyph·ic \,hī(ə)rə'glifik\ *n* : character in the picture writing of the ancient Egyptians

high \'hī\ *adj* **1** : having large extension upward **2** : elevated in pitch **3** : exalted in character **4** : of greater degree or amount than average **5** : expensive **6** : excited or stupefied by alcohol or a drug ~ *adv* : at or to a high place or degree ~ *n* **1** : elevated point or level **2** : automobile gear giving the highest speed

high·boy \-,bōi\ *n* : high chest of drawers on legs

high·brow \-,braú\ *n* : person of superior learning or culture —**high·brow** *adj*

high-flown *adj* : pretentious

high-hand·ed *adj* : willful and arrogant —**high-hand·ed·ly** *adv* —**high-hand·ed·ness** *n*

high·land \'hīlənd\ *n* : hilly country —**high·land·er** \-ləndər\ *n*

high·light *n* : event or detail of major importance ~ *vb* **1** : emphasize **2** : be a highlight of

high·ness \-nəs\ *n* **1** : quality or degree of being high **2** —used as a title (as for kings)

high-rise *adj* : having several stories

high school *n* : school usu. comprising the 9th to 12th or 10th to 12th grades

high-spir·it·ed *adj* : lively

high-strung \-'strəŋ\ *adj* : very nervous or sensitive

high·way *n* : public road

high·way·man \-mən\ *n* : one who robs travelers on a road

hi·jack, high·jack \'hī,jak\ *vb* : steal esp. by commandeering a vehicle —**hijack** *n* —**hi·jack·er** *n*

hike \'hīk\ *vb* **hiked; hik·ing 1** : raise quickly **2** : take a long walk ~ *n* **1** : long walk **2** : increase

hi·lar·i·ous \hil'areəs, hī'lar-\ *adj* : extremely funny —**hi·lar·i·ous·ly** *adv* —**hi·lar·i·ty** \-ətē\ *n*

hill \'hil\ *n* : place where the land rises —**hill·side** *n* —**hill·top** *n* —**hilly** *adj*

hill·bil·ly \'hil,bilē\ *n, pl* -lies : person from a backwoods area

hill·ock \'hilək\ *n* : small hill

hilt \'hilt\ *n* : handle of a sword

him \'im, 'him\ *pron, objective case of* HE

him·self \(h)im'self\ *pron* : he, him —used reflexively or for emphasis

¹hind \'hīnd\ *n* : female deer

²hind *adj* : back

hin·der \'hindər\ *vb* : obstruct or hold back

hind·most *adj* : farthest to the rear

hind·quar·ter *n* : back half of a complete side of a carcass

hin·drance \'hindrəns\ *n* : something that hinders

hind·sight *n* : understanding of an event after it has happened

Hin·du·ism \'hindü,izəm\ *n* : body of religious beliefs and practices native to India —**Hin·du** *n or adj*

hinge \'hinj\ *n* : jointed piece on which one piece (as a door) turns or swings ~ *vb* **hinged; hing·ing 1** : attach by or furnish with hinges **2** : depend

hint \'hint\ *n* **1** : indirect suggestion **2** : clue **3** : very small amount —**hint** *vb*

hin·ter·land \'hintər,land\ *n* : remote region

hip \'hip\ *n* : part of the body on either side just below the waist —**hip·bone** *n*

hip·pie, hip·py \'hipē\ *n, pl* -pies : usu. young person who rejects conventional society —**hip·pie·dom** *n* —**hip·pie·hood** *n*

hip·po·pot·a·mus \,hipə'pätəməs\ *n, pl* -mus·es *or* -mi \-,mī\ : large thick-skinned African river animal

hire \'hī(ə)r\ *n* **1** : payment for labor **2** : employment ~ *vb* **hired; hir·ing** : employ for pay

hire·ling \'hī(ə)rliŋ\ *n* : one who serves another only for gain

hir·sute \'hər,süt, 'hiər-\ *adj* : hairy

his \(h)iz, ,hiz\ *adj* : of or belonging to him ~ \'hiz\ *pron* : ones belonging to him

hiss \'his\ *vb* **1** : make a sharp sibilant sound **2** : show dislike by hissing —**hiss** *n*

his·to·ri·an \his'tōrēən\ *n* : writer of history

his·to·ry \'hist(ə)rē\ *n, pl* **-ries** 1 : chronological record of significant events 2 : study of past events —**his·tor·ic** \his'tòrik\, **his·tor·i·cal** \-ikəl\ *adj* —**his·tor·i·cal·ly** \-k(ə)lē\ *adv*

hit \'hit\ *vb* **hit; hit·ting** 1 : reach with a blow 2 : come or cause to come in contact 3 : affect detrimentally ~ *n* 1 : blow 2 : something very successful —**hit·ter** *n*

hitch \'hich\ *vb* 1 : move by jerks 2 : catch by a hook 3 : hitchhike ~ *n* 1 : jerk 2 : sudden halt

hitch·hike \'hich,hīk\ *vb* : travel by securing free rides from passing vehicles —**hitch·hik·er** *n*

hith·er \'hithər\ *adv* : to this place

hith·er·to \-,tü\ *adv* : up to this time

hive \'hīv\ *n* 1 : container housing honeybees 2 : colony of bees —**hive** *vb*

hives \'hīvz\ *n sing or pl* : allergic disorder

hoard \'hòrd\ *n* : hidden accumulation —**hoard** *vb* —**hoard·er** *n*

hoar·frost \'hòr,fròst\ *n* : frost

hoarse \'hòrs\ *adj* **hoars·er; -est** 1 : harsh in sound 2 : speaking in a harsh strained voice —**hoarse·ly** *adv* —**hoarse·ness** *n*

hoary \'hòrē\ *adj* **hoar·i·er; -est** : gray or white with age —**hoar·i·ness** *n*

hoax \'hōks\ *n* : act intended to trick or dupe —**hoax** *vb* —**hoax·er** *n*

hob·ble \'häbəl\ *vb* **-bled; -bling** : limp along ~ *n* : hobbling movement

hob·by \-ē\ *n, pl* **-bies** : interest engaged in for relaxation —**hob·by·ist** \-ēəst\ *n*

hob·gob·lin \-,gäblən\ *n* : mischievous goblin 2 : bogey

hob·nail \-,nāl\ *n* : short nail for studding shoe soles —**hob·nailed** \-,nāld\ *adj*

hob·nob \-,näb\ *vb* **-bb-** : associate socially

ho·bo \'hōbō\ *n, pl* **-boes** : tramp

¹**hock** \'häk\ *n* : joint or region in the hind limb of a quadruped corresponding to the human ankle

²**hock** *n or vb* : pawn

hock·ey \'häkē\ *n* : game played on ice or a field by 2 teams

hod \'häd\ *n* : carrier for bricks or mortar 2 : scuttle

hodge·podge \'häj,päj\ *n* : heterogeneous mixture

hoe \'hō\ *n* : long-handled tool for cultivating or weeding —**hoe** *vb*

hog \'hòg, 'häg\ *n* 1 : domestic adult swine 2 : glutton ~ *vb* : take selfishly —**hog·gish** *adj*

hogs·head \'hògz,hed, 'hägz-\ *n* : large cask or barrel

hog·wash *n* : nonsense

hoist \'hòist\ *vb* : lift ~ *n* 1 : lift 2 : apparatus for hoisting

¹**hold** \'hōld\ *vb* **held** \'held\; **hold·ing** 1 : possess 2 : restrain 3 : have a grasp on 4 : remain or keep in a particular situation or position 5 : contain 6 : regard 7 : cause to occur 8 : occupy esp. by appointment or election ~ *n* 1 : act or manner of holding 2 : restraining or controlling influence —**hold·er** *n* —**hold forth** : speak at length —**hold to** : adhere to —**hold with** : agree with

²**hold** *n* : cargo area of a ship

hold·ing \'hōldiŋ\ *n* : property owned —usu. *pl.*

hold·up *n* 1 : robbery at the point of a gun 2 : delay

hole \'hōl\ *n* 1 : opening into or through something 2 : hollow place (as a pit) 3 : den —**hole** *vb*

hol·i·day \'hälə,dā\ *n* 1 : day of freedom from work 2 : vacation —**holiday** *vb*

ho·li·ness \'hōlēnəs\ *n* : quality or state of being holy

hol·ler \'hälər\ *vb* : cry out —**holler** *n*

hol·low \-ō\ *adj* **-low·er** \-əwər\; **-est** 1 : sunken 2 : having a cavity within 3 : sounding like a noise made in an empty place 4 : empty of value or meaning ~ *vb* : make or become hollow ~ *n* 1 : surface depression 2 : cavity —**hol·low·ness** *n*

hol·ly \-ē\ *n, pl* **-lies** : evergreen tree or shrub

hol·ly·hock \-,häk, -,hòk\ *n* : tall perennial herb grown for its showy flowers

ho·lo·caust \'hälə,kòst, 'hō-, 'hò-\ *n* : thorough destruction esp. by fire

hol·stein \'hōl,stēn, -,stīn\ *n* : large black-and-white dairy cow

hol·ster \'hōlstər\ *n* : case for a pistol

ho·ly \'hōlē\ *adj* **-li·er; -est** 1 : sacred 2 : spiritually pure

hom·age \'(h)ämij\ *n* : reverent regard

home \'hōm\ *n* 1 : residence 2 : congenial environment 3 : place of origin or refuge ~ *vb* **homed; hom·ing** : go or return home —**home·bred** *adj* —**home·com·ing** *n* —**home·grown** *adj* —**home·land** \-,land\ *n* —**home·less** *adj* —**home·made** \-,(m)ād\ *adj*

home·ly \-lē\ *adj* **-li·er; -est** : plain or unattractive —**home·li·ness** *n*

home·mak·er *n* : one who manages a household —**home·mak·ing** *n*

home·sick *adj* : longing for home —**home·sick·ness** *n*

home·spun \-,spən\ *adj* : simple

home·stead \-,sted\ *n* : home and land (as a tract acquired from U.S. public lands) occupied and worked by a family —**home·stead·er** \-ər\ *n*

home·stretch *n* **1** : last part of a racetrack **2** : final stage

¹home·ward \-wərd\, **home·wards** \-wərdz\ *adv* : toward home

²homeward *adj* : in the direction of home

home·work *n* : school lessons to be done outside the classroom

hom·ey \'hōmē\ *adj* **hom·i·er; -est** : intimate in nature

ho·mi·cide \'hämə,sīd, 'hō-\ *n* : the killing of one human being by another —**hom·i·cid·al** \,hämə'sīd^əl\ *adj*

hom·i·ly \'häməlē\ *n, pl* **-lies** : sermon —**hom·i·let·ic** \,hämə'letik\ *adj*

hom·i·ny \'hämənē\ *n* : type of processed hulled corn

ho·mo·ge·neous \,hōmə'jēnēəs, -nyəs\ *adj* : of the same or a similar kind —**ho·mo·ge·ne·i·ty** \-jə'nēətē\ *n* —**ho·mo·ge·neous·ly** *adv* —**ho·mo·ge·neous·ness** *n*

ho·mog·e·nize \hō'mäjə,nīz, hə-\ *vb* **-nized; -niz·ing** : make the particles in (as milk or paint) of uniform size and even distribution —**ho·mog·e·niz·er** *n*

ho·mo·graph \'hämə,graf, 'hōmə-\ *n* : one of 2 or more words (as the noun *conduct* and the verb *conduct*) spelled alike but different in origin or meaning or pronunciation

hom·onym \'hämə,nim, 'hōmə-\ *n* **1** : homophone **2** : homograph **3** : one of 2 or more words (as *pool* of water and *pool* the game) spelled and pronounced alike but different in meaning

ho·mo·phone \'hämə,fōn, 'hōmə-\ *n* : one of 2 or more words (as *to, too,* and *two*) pronounced alike but different in origin or meaning or spelling

Ho·mo sa·pi·ens \,hōmō'sapēənz, -'sā-\ *n* : man or mankind

ho·mo·sex·u·al \,hōmə'seksh(əw)əl\ *adj* : oriented toward one's own sex —**homosexual** *n*

hone \'hōn\ *n* : sharpening stone —**hone** *vb* —**hon·er** *n*

hon·est \'änəst\ *adj* **1** : free from deception **2** : trustworthy **3** : frank —**hon·est·ly** *adv* —**hon·es·ty** \-əstē\ *n*

hon·ey \'hənē\ *n, pl* **-eys** : sweet sticky

substance made by bees (**hon·ey·bees**) from the nectar of flowers

hon·ey·comb *n* : mass of 6-sided wax cells built by honeybees or something like it ~ *vb* : make or become full of holes like a honeycomb

hon·ey·moon *n* : holiday taken by a newly married couple —**honeymoon** *vb*

hon·ey·suck·le \-,səkəl\ *n* : shrub or vine with flowers rich in nectar

honk \'häŋk, 'hȯŋk\ *n* : cry of a goose or a similar sound —**honk** *vb* —**honk·er** *n*

hon·or \'änər\ *n* **1** : good name **2** : outward respect or symbol of this **3** : privilege **4** : person of superior rank or position —used esp. as a title **5** : something or someone worthy of respect **6** : integrity ~ *vb* **1** : regard with honor **2** : confer honor on **3** : fulfill the terms of —**hon·or·able** \'än(ə)rəbəl\ *adj* —**hon·or·ably** \-blē\ *adv* —**hon·or·ari·ly** \,änə'rerəlē\ *adv* —**hon·or·ary** \'änə,rerē\ *adj*

hood \'hud\ *n* **1** : part of a garment that covers the head **2** : covering over an automobile engine compartment —**hood·ed** *adj*

-hood \,hud\ *n suffix* **1** : state, condition, or quality **2** : individuals sharing a state or character

hood·lum \'hudləm, 'hud-\ *n* : thug

hood·wink \'hud,wiŋk\ *vb* : deceive

hoof \'huf, 'huf\ *n, pl* **hooves** \'huvz, 'huvz\ or **hoofs** : horny covering of the toes of some mammals (as horses or cattle) —**hoofed** \'huft, 'huft\ *adj*

hook \'huk\ *n* : curved or bent device for catching, holding, or pulling ~ *vb* : seize or make fast with a hook —**hook·er** *n*

hoo·kah \'hukə, 'hu-\ *n* : pipe for smoking so arranged that the smoke passes through water

hook·worm *n* : parasitic intestinal worm

hoo·li·gan \'huligən\ *n* : thug

hoop \'hup, 'hup\ *n* : circular strip, figure, or object

hoot \'hut\ *vb* **1** : shout in contempt **2** : make the cry of an owl —**hoot** *n* —**hoot·er** *n*

¹hop \'häp\ *vb* **-pp-** : move by quick springy leaps —**hop** *n*

²hop *n* : vine whose dried flowers are used to flavor malt liquors

hope \'hōp\ *vb* **hoped; hop·ing** : desire with expectation of fulfillment ~ *n* **1** : act of hoping **2** : something hoped for —**hope·ful** \-fəl\ *adj* —**hope·ful-**

ly *adv* —**hope·ful·ness** *n* —**hope·less** *adj* —**hope·less·ly** *adv* —**hope·less·ness** *n*

hop·per \'häpər\ *n* : container that releases its contents through the bottom

horde \'hord\ *n* : throng or swarm

hore·hound \'hōr,haùnd\ *n* : aromatic bitter mint

ho·ri·zon \hə'rīz⁰n\ *n* : line marking the apparent junction of earth and sky

hor·i·zon·tal \,horə'zänt⁰l\ *adj* : parallel to the horizon —**hor·i·zon·tal·ly** *adv*

hor·mone \'hor,mōn\ *n* : cell product in body fluids that has a specific effect on other cells —**hor·mon·al** \hor'mōn²l\ *adj*

horn \'horn\ *n* 1 : one of the hard bony projections on the head of many hoofed animals 2 : brass wind instrument —**horned** *adj* —**horn·less** *adj* —**horny** *adj*

hor·net \'hornət\ *n* : large social wasp

ho·rol·o·gy \hə'räləjē\ *n* : science of measuring time or making clocks —**hor·o·log·i·cal** \,horə'läjikəl\ *adj* —**ho·rol·o·gist** \hə'räləjəst\ *n*

horo·scope \'horə,skōp\ *n* : astrological forecast

hor·ren·dous \ho'rendəs\ *adj* : horrible

hor·ri·ble \'horəbəl\ *adj* 1 : having or causing horror 2 : highly disagreeable —**hor·ri·ble·ness** *n* —**hor·ri·bly** \-blē\ *adv*

hor·rid \'horəd\ *adj* : horrible —**hor·rid·ly** *adv*

hor·ri·fy \-ə,fī\ *vb* **-fied; -fy·ing** : cause to feel horror

hor·ror \-ər\ *n* 1 : intense fear, dread, or dismay 2 : intense repugnance 3 : something horrible

hors d'oeuvre \òr'dərv\ *n*, *pl* **hors d'oeuvres** \-'dərv(z)\ : appetizer

horse \'hors\ *n* : large solid-hoofed domesticated mammal —**horse·back** *n or adv* —**horse·hair** *n* —**horse·hide** *n* —**horse·less** *adj* —**horse·man** \-mən\ *n* —**horse·man·ship** *n* —**horse·woman** *n* —**hors·ey, horsy** *adj*

horse·fly *n* : large fly with bloodsucking female

horse·play *n* : rough boisterous play

horse·pow·er *n* : unit of mechanical power

horse·rad·ish *n* : herb with a pungent root used as a condiment

horse·shoe \'hors(h),shü\ *n* : protective metal plate fitted to the rim of a horse's hoof

hor·ta·to·ry \'hortə,tōrē\ *adj* : giving exhortation

hor·ti·cul·ture \'hortə,kəlchər\ *n* : science of growing fruits, vegetables, and flowers —*vb* **hosed; hos·ing** —**hor·ti·cul·tur·al** \,hortə'kolch(ə)rəl\ *adj* —**hor·ti·cul·tur·ist** \-rəst\ *n*

ho·san·na \hō'zanə, -'zän-\ *interj* —used as a cry of acclamation and adoration

hose \'hōz\ *n* 1 *pl* **hose** : stocking or sock 2 *pl* **hos·es** : flexible tube for conveying fluids ~ *vb* **hosed; hos·ing** : spray, water, or wash with a hose

ho·siery \'hōzh(ə)rē, 'hōz(ə)-\ *n* : stockings or socks

hos·pice \'häspəs\ *n* : lodging (as for travelers) maintained by a religious order

hos·pi·ta·ble \hä'spitəbəl, 'häs(,)pit-\ *adj* : given to generous and cordial reception of guests —**hos·pi·ta·bly** \-blē\ *adv*

hos·pi·tal \'häs,pit⁰l\ *n* : institution where the sick or injured receive medical care —**hos·pi·tal·iza·tion** \,häs,pit⁰lə'zāshən\ *n* —**hos·pi·tal·ize** \'häs,pit⁰l,īz\ *vb*

hos·pi·tal·i·ty \,häspə'talətē\ *n*, *pl* **-ties** : hospitable treatment, reception, or disposition

¹**host** \'hōst\ *n* 1 : army 2 : multitude

²**host** *n* : one who receives or entertains guests —**host** *vb*

³**host** *n* : eucharistic bread

hos·tage \'hästij\ *n* : person held to guarantee that promises be kept or demands met

hos·tel \'häst⁰l\ *n* : lodging for youth —**hos·tel·er** *n*

hos·tel·ry \-rē\ *n*, *pl* **-ries** : hotel

host·ess \'hōstəs\ *n* : woman who is host

hos·tile \'häst²l, -,tīl\ *adj* : openly or actively unfriendly or opposed to someone or something —**hostile** *n* —**hos·tile·ly** *adv* —**hos·til·i·ty** \hä'stilətē\ *n*

hot \'hät\ *adj* **-tt-** 1 : having a high temperature 2 : giving a sensation of heat or burning 3 : ardent 4 : pungent —**hot** *adv* —**hot·ly** *adv* —**hot·ness** *n*

hot·bed *n* : environment that favors rapid growth

hot dog *n* : frankfurter

ho·tel \hō'tel\ *n* : building where lodging and personal services are provided

hot·head·ed *adj* : impetuous —**hot·head** *n* —**hot·head·ed·ly** *adv* —**hot·head·ness** *n*

hot·house \-ˌhau̇s\ *n* : glass-enclosed house for raising plants

hound \ˈhau̇nd\ *n* : long-eared hunting dog ~ *vb* : pursue relentlessly

hour \ˈau̇(ə)r\ *n* **1** : 24th part of a day **2** : time of day —**hour·ly** *adv or adj*

hour·glass *n* : glass vessel for measuring time

house \ˈhau̇s, *n, pl* **hous·es** \ˈhau̇zəz\ **1** : building to live in **2** : household **3** : legislative body **4** : business firm ~ \ˈhau̇z\ *vb* **housed; hous·ing** : provide with or take shelter —**house·boat** \ˈhau̇s-\ *n* —**house·clean** \ˈhau̇s-\ *vb* —**house·clean·ing** *n* —**house·ful** \-ˌfu̇l\ *n* —**house·keep·er** *n* —**house·keep·ing** *n* —**house·maid** *n* —**house·wares** *n pl* —**house·work** *n*

house·bro·ken *adj* : trained to excretory habits acceptable in indoor living

house·fly *n* : two-winged fly common about human habitations

house·hold \-ˌhōld\ *n* : those who dwell as a family under the same roof ~ *adj* **1** : domestic **2** : common or familiar —**house·hold·er** *n*

house·warm·ing *n* : party to celebrate moving into a house

house·wife \ˈhau̇s-ˌwīf\ *n* : married woman in charge of a household —**house·wife·li·ness** *n* —**house·wife·ly** *adj* —**house·wif·ery** \-ˌwif(ə)rē\ *n*

hous·ing \ˈhau̇ziŋ\ *n* **1** : dwellings for people **2** : protective covering

hove *past of* HEAVE

hov·el \ˈhəvəl, ˈhäv-\ *n* : small wretched house

hov·er \ˈhəvər, ˈhäv-\ *vb* **1** : remain suspended in the air **2** : move about in the vicinity

how \(ˈ)hau̇\ *adv* **1** : in what way or condition **2** : for what reason **3** : to what extent ~ *conj* : in what manner or condition

how·ev·er \hau̇ˈevər\ *conj* : in whatever manner ~ *adv* **1** : to whatever degree or in whatever manner **2** : in spite of that

how·it·zer \ˈhau̇ətsər\ *n* : short cannon

howl \ˈhau̇l\ *vb* : emit a loud long doleful sound like a dog —**howl** *n* —**howl·er** *n*

hoy·den \ˈhȯid³n\ *n* : girl or woman of saucy or carefree behavior

hub \ˈhəb\ *n* : central part (as of a wheel) —**hub·cap** *n*

hub·bub \ˈhəb‚əb\ *n* : uproar

hu·bris \ˈhyübrəs\ *n* : excessive pride

huck·le·ber·ry \ˈhəkəlˌberē\ *n* **1** : shrub related to the blueberry or its berry **2** : blueberry

huck·ster \ˈhəkstər\ *n* : peddler

hud·dle \ˈhəd³l\ *vb* **-dled; -dling** **1** : crowd together **2** : confer —**huddle** *n*

hue \ˈhyü\ *n* : attribute of colors that permits them to be classed as red, yellow, green, blue, or an intermediate color —**hued** \ˈhyüd\ *adj*

huff \ˈhəf\ *n* : fit of pique —**huffy** *adj*

hug \ˈhəg\ *vb* **-gg- 1** : press tightly in the arms **2** : stay close to —**hug** *n*

huge \ˈhyüj\ *adj* **hug·er; hug·est** : very large or extensive —**huge·ly** *adv* —**huge·ness** *n*

hu·la \ˈhülə\ *n* : Polynesian dance

hulk \ˈhəlk\ *n* **1** : bulky or unwieldy person or thing **2** : old ship unfit for service —**hulk·ing** *adj*

hull \ˈhəl\ *n* **1** : outer covering of a fruit or seed **2** : frame or body of a ship ~ *vb* : remove the hulls of —**hull·er** *n*

hul·la·ba·loo \ˈhələbəˌlü\ *n, pl* **-loos** : uproar

hum \ˈhəm\ *vb* **-mm-** : make a prolonged sound like that of the speech sound \m\ —**hum** *n* —**hum·mer** *n*

hu·man \ˈ(h)yümən\ *adj* **1** : of or relating to the species people belong to **2** : by, for, or like people —**human** *n* —**hu·man·kind** *n* —**hu·man·ly** *adv* —**hu·man·ness** *n*

hu·mane \(h)yüˈmān\ *adj* : showing compassion or consideration for others —**hu·mane·ly** *adv* —**hu·mane·ness** *n*

hu·man·ism \ˈ(h)yüməˌnizəm\ *n* : doctrine or way of life centered on human interests or values —**hu·man·ist** \-nəst\ *n or adj* —**hu·man·is·tic** \ˌ(h)yümə'nistik\ *adj*

hu·man·i·tar·i·an \(h)yüˌmanə'terēən\ *n* : person promoting human welfare —**humanitarian** *adj* —**hu·man·i·tar·i·an·ism** *n*

hu·man·i·ty \(h)yüˈmanətē\ *n, pl* **-ties** **1** : human or humane quality or state **2** : mankind

hu·man·ize \ˈ(h)yüməˌnīz\ *vb* **-ized; -iz·ing** : make human or humane —**hu·man·iza·tion** \ˌ(h)yümənə'zāshən\ *n*

hu·man·oid \ˈ(h)yüməˌnȯid\ *adj* : having human form —**humanoid** *n*

hum·ble \ˈ(h)əmbəl\ *adj* **-bler; -blest** **1** : not proud or haughty **2** : not pretentious ~ *vb* **-bled; -bling** : make humble —**hum·ble·ness** *n* —**hum·bler** *n* —**hum·bly** \-blē\ *adv*

hum·bug \ˈhəm‚bəg\ *n* : nonsense

hum·drum \-‚drəm\ *adj* : monotonous

hu·mid \ˈ(h)yüməd\ *adj* : containing or characterized by moisture —**hu·mid·**

i·fi·ca·tion \ˌhyüˌmidəfəˈkāshən\ n
—hu·mid·i·fi·er \-ˈmidəˌfī(ə)r\ n
—hu·mid·i·fy \-ˌfī\ vb —hu·mid·ly
adv

hu·mid·i·ty \(h)yüˈmidətē\ n, pl -ties
: humidified atmospheric moisture

hu·mi·dor \ˈ(h)yüməˌdòr\ n : humidified storage case

hu·mil·i·ate \(h)yüˈmilēˌāt\ vb -at·ed;
-at·ing : injure the self-respect of
—hu·mil·i·at·ing·ly adv —hu·mil·i·a·tion \-ˌmilēˈāshən\ n

hu·mil·i·ty \(h)yüˈmilətē\ n : humble
quality or state

hum·ming·bird \ˈhəmiŋˌbərd\ n : tiny
American bird

hum·mock \ˈhəmək\ n : mound or
knoll

hu·mor \ˈ(h)yümər\ n 1 : mood 2
: quality of being laughably ludicrous
or incongruous 3 : appreciation of
what is ludicrous or incongruous 4
: something intended to be funny ~
vb : comply with the wishes or mood
of —hu·mor·ist \-(ə)rəst\ n —hu·mor·less adj —hu·mor·less·ly adv
—hu·mor·less·ness n —hu·mor·ous
\ˈ(h)yüm(ə)rəs\ adj —hu·mor·ous·ly
adv —hu·mor·ous·ness n

hump \ˈhəmp\ n : rounded protuberance —humped adj

hump·back n : hunchback —hump·backed adj

hu·mus \ˈ(h)yüməs\ n : dark organic
part of soil

hunch \ˈhənch\ vb : assume or cause to
assume a bent or crooked posture ~
n : strong intuitive feeling

hunch·back n 1 : back with a hump 2
: person with a crooked back
—hunch·backed adj

hun·dred \ˈhəndrəd\ n, pl -dreds or
-dred : 10 times 10 —hundred adj
—hun·dredth \-drədth\ adj or n

hung past of HANG

hun·ger \ˈhəŋgər\ n 1 : craving or urgent need for food 2 : strong desire
—hunger vb —hun·gri·ly \-grəlē\ adv
—hun·gry adj

hunk \ˈhəŋk\ n : large piece

hun·ker \ˈhəŋkər\ vb : squat down

hunt \ˈhənt\ vb 1 : pursue for food or
sport 2 : try to find ~ n : act or
instance of hunting —hunt·er n

hur·dle \ˈhərdᵊl\ n 1 : barrier to leap
over 2 : obstacle —hurdle vb —hur·dler n

hurl \ˈhərl\ vb : throw with violence
—hurl n —hurl·er n

hur·rah \hu̇ˈrò, -ˈrä\ interj —used to
express joy or approval

hur·ri·cane \ˈhərəˌkān\ n : tropical
storm with winds of 74 miles per
hour or greater

hur·ry \ˈhərē\ vb -ried; -ry·ing : go or
cause to go with haste ~ n : extreme
haste —hur·ried·ly adv —hur·ried·ness n

hurt \ˈhərt\ vb hurt; hurt·ing 1 : feel or
cause pain 2 : do harm to ~ n 1
: bodily injury 2 : harm —hurt·ful
adj

hur·tle \ˈhərtᵊl\ vb -tled; -tling : move
with rapid force

hus·band \ˈhəzbənd\ n : married man
~ vb : manage prudently

hus·band·ry \-bəndrē\ n 1 : careful use
2 : agriculture

hush \ˈhəsh\ vb : make or become
quiet ~ n : silence

husk \ˈhəsk\ n : outer covering of a
seed or fruit ~ vb : strip the husk
from —husk·er n

¹hus·ky \ˈhəskē\ adj -ki·er; -est
: hoarse —hus·ki·ly adv —hus·ki·ness n

²husky adj -ki·er; -est : burly —husk·i·ness n

³husky n, pl -kies : working dog of the
arctic

hus·sy \ˈhəzē, ˈhəs-\ n, pl -sies 1 : brazen woman 2 : mischievous girl

hus·tle \ˈhəsəl\ vb -tled; -tling 1 : hurry
2 : work energetically —hustle n
—hus·tler \ˈhəslər\ n

hut \ˈhət\ n : small often temporary
dwelling

hutch \ˈhəch\ n 1 : cupboard with
open shelves 2 : pen for an animal

hy·a·cinth \ˈhī(ə)ˌsinth\ n : bulbous
herb grown for bell-shaped flowers

hy·brid \ˈhībrəd\ n : offspring of genetically differing parents —hybrid
adj —hy·brid·iza·tion \ˌhībrədəˈzāshən\ n —hy·brid·ize \ˈhībrədˌīz\ vb
—hy·brid·iz·er n

hy·drant \ˈhīdrənt\ n : pipe from
which water may be drawn to fight
fires

hy·drau·lic \hīˈdròlik\ adj : operated
by liquid forced through a small hole
—hy·drau·lics \-liks\ n

hy·dro·car·bon \ˌhīdrəˈkärbən\ n : organic compound of carbon and hydrogen

hy·dro·elec·tric \ˌhīdrōiˈlektrik\ adj
: producing electricity by waterpower
—hy·dro·elec·tri·cal·ly \-trik(ə)lē\
adv —hy·dro·elec·tric·i·ty
\-ˌlekˈtrisətē\ n

hy·dro·gen \ˈhīdrəjən\ n : gaseous colorless odorless flammable chemical element —hy·drog·e·nous \hī'dräjənəs\ adj

hydrogen bomb n : bomb with violent power from the energy released by the union of atomic nuclei

hy·dro·pho·bia \ˌhīdrə'fōbēə\ n : rabies

hy·dro·plane \'hīdrəˌplān\ n : speedboat whose hull rises out of the water

hy·drous \'hīdrəs\ adj : containing water

hy·e·na \hī'ēnə\ n : nocturnal carnivorous mammal of Asia and Africa

hy·giene \'hīˌjēn\ n : conditions or practices conducive to health —hy·gien·ic \ˌhījē'enik; hī'jen-, -ˌjēn-\ adj —hy·gien·i·cal·ly \-ik(ə)lē\ adv —hy·gien·ist \hī'jēnəst, -'jen-; 'hīˌjēn-\ n

hy·grom·e·ter \hī'grämətər\ n : instrument for measuring atmospheric humidity —hy·grom·e·try \-ətrē\ n

hying pres part of HIE

hymn \'him\ n : song of praise esp. to God —hymn vb —hym·nal \'himnəl\ n

hyper- prefix 1 : above or beyond 2 : excessively or excessive

hyperacid	hypermasculine
hyperacidity	hypermilitant
hyperactive	hypermoralistic
hyperacute	hypernationalistic
hyperaggressive	
hyperanxious	hyperreactive
hypercautious	hyperrealistic
hyperclean	hyperromantic
hyperconscientious	hypersensitive
	hypersensitiveness
hypercorrect	hypersensitivity
hypercritical	hypersexual
hyperemotional	hypersusceptible
hyperenergetic	hypersuspicious
hyperexcitable	hypertense
hyperfastidious	hypervigilant
hyperintense	

hy·per·bo·le \hī'pərbə(ˌ)lē\ n : extravagant exaggeration

hy·per·ten·sion \'hīpərˌtenchən\ n

: high blood pressure —hy·per·ten·sive \ˌhīpər'tensiv\ adj or n

hy·phen \'hīfən\ n : punctuation mark - used to divide or compound words —hyphen vb

hy·phen·ate \'hīfəˌnāt\ vb -at·ed; -at·ing : connect or divide with a hyphen —hy·phen·ation \ˌhīfə'nāshən\ n

hyp·no·sis \hip'nōsəs\ n, pl -no·ses \-ˌsēz\ : induced state like sleep in which the subject is responsive to suggestions of the inducer (**hyp·no·tist** \'hipnətəst\) —hyp·no·tism \'hipnəˌtizəm\ n —hyp·no·tiz·able \-ˌtīzəbəl\ adj —hyp·no·tize \-ˌtīz\ vb

hyp·not·ic \hip'nätik\ adj : relating to hypnosis —hypnotic n —hyp·not·i·cal·ly \-ik(ə)lē\ adv

hy·po·chon·dria \ˌhīpə'kändrēə\ n : morbid concern for one's health —hy·po·chon·dri·ac \-drē·ak\ adj or n

hy·poc·ri·sy \hip'äkrəsē\ n, pl -sies : a feigning to be what one is not —hyp·o·crite \'hipəˌkrit\ n —hyp·o·crit·i·cal \ˌhipə'kritikəl\ adj —hyp·o·crit·i·cal·ly adv

hy·po·der·mic \ˌhīpə'dərmik\ adj : used for or given by injection beneath the skin ~ n : hypodermic syringe

hy·pot·e·nuse \hī'pätən(y)üs, -ˌ(y)üz\ n : side of a right-angled triangle opposite the right angle

hy·poth·e·sis \hī'päthəsəs\ n, pl -e·ses \-ˌsēz\ : assumption made in order to test its consequences —hy·poth·e·size \-ˌsīz\ vb —hy·po·thet·i·cal \ˌhīpə'thetikəl\ adj —hy·po·thet·i·cal·ly adv

hys·ter·ec·to·my \ˌhistə'rektəmē\ n, pl -mies : surgical removal of the uterus —hys·ter·ec·to·mize \-ˌmīz\ vb

hys·te·ria \his'terēə, -tir-\ n : uncontrollable fear or emotion hys·ter·ic \-'terik\, hys·ter·i·cal \-ikəl\ adj —hys·ter·i·cal·ly adv

hys·ter·ics \-'teriks\ n pl : uncontrollable laughter or crying

I

i \'ī\ n, pl **i's** or **is** \'īz\ : 9th letter of the alphabet

I \(')ī\ pron : the speaker

-ia adj suffix : of, relating to, or characterized by

-ian —see -AN

ibis \'ībəs\ n, pl **ibis** or **ibis·es** : wading bird with a down-curved bill

-ible —see -ABLE

-ic \ik\ adj suffix 1 : of, relating to, or being 2 : containing 3 : characteristic of 4 : marked by 5 : caused by

-i·cal \ikəl\ *adj suffix* : -ic —**-i·cal·ly** \ik(ə)lē\ *adv suffix*

ice \ˈīs\ *n* **1** : frozen water **2** : frozen dessert ~ vb **iced; ic·ing 1** : freeze **2** : chill **3** : cover with icing

ice·berg \ˈīs̩bərg\ *n* : large floating mass of ice

ice·box *n* : refrigerator

ice·break·er *n* : ship equipped to cut through ice

ice cream *n* : sweet frozen food

ice-skate *vb* : skate on ice —**ice skater** *n*

ich·thy·ol·o·gy \ˌikthē'äləjē\ *n* : study of fishes —**ich·thy·ol·o·gist** \-jəst\ *n*

ici·cle \ˈī̩sikəl\ *n* : hanging mass of ice

ic·ing \ˈīsiŋ\ *n* : sweet usu. creamy coating for baked goods

icon \ˈī̩kän\ *n* : religious image

icon·o·clast \ī'känə̩klast\ *n* : attacker of cherished beliefs or institutions —**icon·o·clasm** \-̩klazəm\ *n*

icy \ˈīsē\ *adj* **ic·i·er; -est 1** : covered or consisting of ice **2** : very cold —**ic·i·ly** \-əlē\ *adv* —**ic·i·ness** *n*

id \ˈid\ *n* : unconscious part of the mind

idea \ī'dēə\ *n* **1** : something imagined in the mind **2** : purpose or plan

ide·al \ī'dē(ə)l\ *adj* **1** : imaginary **2** : perfect ~ *n* **1** : standard of excellence **2** : model **3** : aim —**ide·al·ly** *adv*

ide·al·ism \ī'dē(ə)̩lizəm\ *n* **1** : adherence to ideals **2** : tendency to see things as they should be —**ide·al·ist** \-ləst\ *n* —**ide·al·is·tic** \ī̩dē(ə)l'istik\ *adj*

ide·al·ize \ī'dē(ə)̩līz\ *vb* **-ized; -iz·ing** : think of or represent as ideal —**ide·al·iza·tion** \ī̩dē(ə)lə'zāshən\ *n*

iden·ti·cal \ī'dentikəl\ *adj* **1** : being the same **2** : exactly or essentially alike

iden·ti·fi·ca·tion \ī̩dentəfə'kāshən\ *n* **1** : act of identifying **2** : evidence of identity

iden·ti·fy \ī'dentə̩fī\ *vb* **-fied; -fy·ing 1** : associate **2** : establish the identity of

iden·ti·ty \ī'dentətē\ *n, pl* **-ties 1** : sameness of essential character **2** : individuality **3** : fact of being what is supposed

ide·ol·o·gy \ī̩dē'äləjē, ̩id-\ *n, pl* **-gies** : body of beliefs —**ide·o·log·i·cal** \ī̩dēə'läjikəl, ̩id-\ *adj*

id·i·om \ˈidēəm\ *n* **1** : language peculiar to a person or group **2** : expression with a special meaning —**id·i·om·at·ic** \ˌidēə'matik\ *adj* —**id·i·om·at·i·cal·ly** \-k(ə)lē\ *adv*

id·io·syn·cra·sy \ˌidēə'siŋkrəsē\ *n, pl* **-sies** : personal peculiarity —**id·io·syn·crat·ic** \-ōsin'kratik\ *adj*

id·i·ot \ˈidēət\ *n* : feebleminded or foolish person —**id·i·o·cy** \-əsē\ *n* —**id·i·ot·ic** \ˌidē'ätik\ *adj* —**id·i·ot·i·cal·ly** \-ik(ə)lē\ *adv*

idle \ˈī-d²l\ *adj* **idler; idlest 1** : worthless **2** : inactive **3** : lazy ~ *vb* **idled; idling** : spend time doing nothing —**idle·ness** *n* —**idler** *n* —**idly** \ˈīd(ə)lē\ *adv*

idol \ˈīd²l\ *n* **1** : image of a god **2** : object of devotion —**idol·ize** \-²līz\ *vb*

idol·a·ter \ī'dälətər\ *n* : worshiper of idols —**idol·a·trous** \-trəs\ *adj* —**idol·a·try** \-trē\ *n*

-ier —see -ER

if \(̩)if, əf\ *conj* **1** : in the event that **2** : whether **3** : even though

-i·fy \ə̩fī\ *vb suffix* : -fy

ig·loo \ˈiglü\ *n, pl* **-loos** : hut made of snow blocks

ig·nite \ig'nīt\ *vb* **-nit·ed; -nit·ing** : set afire or catch fire

ig·ni·tion \ig'nishən\ *n* **1** : a setting on fire **2** : process or means of igniting fuel

ig·no·ble \ig'nōbəl\ *adj* : not honorable —**ig·no·bly** \-blē\ *adv*

ig·no·min·i·ous \ˌignə'minēəs\ *adj* **1** : dishonorable **2** : humiliating —**ig·no·min·i·ous·ly** *adv* —**ig·no·mi·ny** \'ignə̩minē, ig'nämənē\ *n*

ig·no·ra·mus \ˌignə'rāməs\ *n* : ignorant person

ig·no·rant \ˈignərənt\ *adj* **1** : lacking knowledge **2** : stupid **3** : unaware —**ig·no·rance** \-rəns\ *n* —**ig·no·rant·ly** *adv*

ig·nore \ig'nōr\ *vb* **-nored; -nor·ing** : refuse to notice

igua·na \i'gwänə\ *n* : tropical American lizard

ilk \ˈilk\ *n* : kind

ill \ˈil\ *adj* **worse** \ˈwərs\; **worst** \ˈwərst\ **1** : sick **2** : bad **3** : inferior **4** : hostile ~ *adv* **worse; worst 1** : with displeasure **2** : harshly **3** : scarcely **4** : badly ~ *n* **1** : evil **2** : misfortune **3** : sickness

il·le·gal \il'(l)ēgəl\ *adj* : not lawful —**il·le·gal·i·ty** \ili'galətē\ *n* —**il·le·gal·ly** \il'(l)ēgəlē\ *adv*

il·leg·i·ble \il'(l)ejəbəl\ *adj* : not legible —**il·leg·i·bil·i·ty** \il̩(l)ejə'bilətē\ *n* —**il·leg·i·bly** \il'(l)ejəblē\ *adv*

il·le·git·i·mate \ˌili'jitəmət\ *adj* **1** : born of unmarried parents **2** : illegal —**il·le·git·i·ma·cy** \-əməsē\ *n* —**il·le·git·i·mate·ly** *adv*

il·lic·it \il'(l)isət\ *adj* : not lawful —**il-lic·it·ly** *adv*

il·lim·it·able \il'(l)imətəbəl\ *adj* : boundless —**il·lim-it·ably** \-blē\ *adv*

il·lit·er·ate \il'(l)it(ə)rət\ *adj* : unable to read or write —**il·lit·er·a·cy** \-(ə)rəsē\ *n* —**illiterate** *n*

ill-na·tured \-'nāchərd\ *adj* : cross —**ill-na·tured·ly** *adv*

ill·ness \'ilnəs\ *n* : sickness

il·log·i·cal \il'läjikəl\ *adj* : contrary to logic —**il·log·i·cal·ly** *adv*

ill-starred \il'stärd\ *adj* : unlucky

il·lu·mi·nate \il'ümə,nāt\ *vb* -**nat·ed; -nat·ing** **1** : light up **2** : make clear —**il·lu·mi·nat·ing·ly** \-,nātiŋlē\ *adv* —**il·lu·mi·na·tion** \-,ümə'nāshən\ *n*

ill-use \-'yüz\ *vb* : abuse —**ill-use** \-'yüs\ *n*

il·lu·sion \il'üzhən\ *n* **1** : mistaken idea **2** : misleading visual image

il·lu·sive \il'üsiv\ *adj* : illusory

il·lu·so·ry \il'üs(ə)rē, -'üz-\ *adj* : based on or producing illusion

il·lus·trate \'iləs,trāt\ *vb* -**trat·ed; -trat-ing** **1** : explain by example **2** : provide with pictures or figures —**il·lus-tra·tor** \-,trātər\ *n*

il·lus·tra·tion \,iləs'trāshən\ *n* **1** : example that explains **2** : pictorial explanation

il·lus·tra·tive \il'əstrətiv\ *adj* : designed to illustrate —**il·lus·tra·tive·ly** *adv*

il·lus·tri·ous \-'trēəs\ *adj* : notably or brilliantly outstanding —**il·lus·tri·ous·ness** *n*

ill will *n* : unfriendly feeling

im·age \'imij\ *n* **1** : likeness **2** : visual counterpart of an object formed by a lens or mirror **3** : mental picture —*vb* -**aged; -ag·ing** : create a representation of

im·ag·ery \'imij(ə)rē\ *n* **1** : images **2** : figurative language

imag·i·nary \im'aja,nerē\ *adj* : existing only in the imagination

imag·i·na·tion \im,aja'nāshən\ *n* **1** : act or power of forming a mental image **2** : creative ability —**imag-i-na·tive** \im'aj(ə)nativ, -a,nātiv\ *adj* —**imag·i·na·tive·ly** *adv*

imag·ine \im'ajən\ *vb* -**ined; -in·ing** : form a mental picture of something not present —**imag·in·able** \-'aj(ə)nəbəl\ *adj* —**imag·in·ably** \-blē\ *adv*

im·bal·ance \(')im'baləns\ *n* : lack of balance

im·be·cile \'imbəsəl, -,sil\ *n* : feeble-minded or foolish person —**imbecile**,

im·be·cil·ic \,imbə'silik\ *adj* —**im-be·cil·i·ty** \-'silətē\ *n*

im·bibe \im'bīb\ *vb* -**bibed; -bib·ing** : drink —**im·bib·er** *n*

im·bro·glio \im'brōlyō\ *n, pl* -**glios** : complicated situation

im·brue \im'brü\ *vb* -**brued; -bru·ing** : steep

im·bue \-'byü\ *vb* -**bued; -bu·ing** : fill (as with color or a feeling)

im·i·tate \'imə,tāt\ *vb* -**tat·ed; -tat·ing** **1** : follow as a model **2** : mimic —**im·i·ta·tive** \-,tātiv\ *adj* —**im·i·ta·tor** \-,ər\ *n*

im·i·ta·tion \,imə'tāshən\ *n* **1** : act of imitating **2** : copy —**imitation** *adj*

im·mac·u·late \im'akyələt\ *adj* : without stain or blemish —**im·mac·u·late·ly** *adv*

im·ma·te·ri·al \imə'tirēəl\ *adj* **1** : spiritual **2** : not relevant —**im·ma·te·ri·al·i·ty** \-,tirē'alətē\ *n*

im·ma·ture \imə't(y)ùr\ *adj* : not yet mature —**im·ma·tu·ri·ty** \-ətē\ *n*

im·mea·sur·able \(')im'ezh(ə)rəbəl\ *adj* : indefinitely extensive —**im·mea·sur·ably** \-blē\ *adv*

im·me·di·a·cy \im'ēdēəsē\ *n, pl* -**cies** : urgency

im·me·di·ate \-ēət\ *adj* **1** : direct **2** : being next in line **3** : made or done at once **4** : not distant —**im·me·di-ate·ly** *adv*

im·me·mo·ri·al \,imə'mōrēəl\ *adj* : old beyond memory

im·mense \im'ens\ *adj* : vast —**im·mense·ly** *adv* —**im·men·si·ty** \-'ensətē\ *n*

im·merse \im'ərs\ *vb* -**mersed; -mers-ing** **1** : plunge or dip esp. into liquid **2** : engross —**im·mer·sion** \-'ərzhən\ *n*

im·mi·grant \'imigrənt\ *n* : one that immigrates

im·mi·grate \'imə,grāt\ *vb* -**grat·ed; -grat·ing** : come into a place and take up residence —**im·mi·gra·tion** \,imə'grāshən\ *n*

im·mi·nent \'imənənt\ *adj* : ready to take place —**im·mi·nence** \-nəns\ *n* —**im·mi·nent·ly** *adv*

im·mo·bile \(')im'ōbəl\ *adj* : incapable of being moved —**im·mo·bil·i·ty** \,imō'bilətē\ *n* —**im·mo·bi·lize** \im'ōbəlīz\ *vb*

im·mod·er·ate \(')im'äd(ə)rət\ *adj* : not moderate —**im·mod·er·a·cy** \-(ə)rəsē\ *n* —**im·mod·er·ate·ly** *adv*

im·mod·est \(')im'ädəst\ *adj* : not modest —**im·mod·est·ly** *adv* —**im·mod·es·ty** \-əstē\ *n*

im·mo·late \\'imə,lāt\ *vb* **-lat·ed; lat·ing** : offer in sacrifice —**im·mo·la·tion** \,imə'lāshən\ *n*

im·mor·al \(')im'ôrəl\ *adj* : not moral —**im·mor·al·i·ty** \,imô'ralətē, ,imə-\ *n* —**im·mor·al·ly** *adv*

im·mor·tal \im'ôrt⁰l\ *adj* **1** : not mortal **2** : having lasting fame ~ *n* : one exempt from death or oblivion —**im·mor·tal·i·ty** \,imôr'talətē\ *n* —**im·mor·tal·ize** \im'ôrt⁰l,īz\ *vb*

im·mov·able \(')im'üvəbəl\ *adj* **1** : stationary **2** : unyielding —**im·mov·abil·i·ty** \(,)im,üvə'bilətē\ *n* —**im·mov·ably** *adv*

im·mune \im'yün\ *adj* : not liable esp. to disease —**im·mu·ni·ty** \im'yünətē\ *n* —**im·mu·ni·za·tion** \,imyənə'zāshən\ *n* —**im·mu·nize** \'imyə,nīz\ *vb*

im·mu·nol·o·gy \,imyə'näləjē\ *n* : science of immunity —**im·mu·no·log·ic** \-yən⁰l'äjik\, **im·mu·no·log·i·cal** \-ikəl\ *adj* —**im·mu·nol·o·gist** \,imyə'näləjəst\ *n*

im·mu·ta·ble \(')im'yütəbəl\ *adj* : unchangeable —**im·mu·ta·bil·i·ty** \(,)im,yütə'bilətē\ *n* —**im·mu·ta·bly** *adv*

imp \'imp\ *n* **1** : demon **2** : mischievous child

im·pact \im'pakt\ *vb* **1** : press close **2** : have an effect on ~ \'im,pakt\ *n* **1** : forceful contact **2** : influence

im·pact·ed \im'paktəd\ *adj* : wedged between the jawbone and another tooth

im·pair \im'paər\ *vb* : diminish in quantity or value —**im·pair·ment** *n*

im·pa·la \im'palə\ *n* : large antelope

im·pale \im'pāl\ *vb* **-paled; pal·ing** : pierce with something pointed —**im·pale·ment** *n*

im·pal·pa·ble \(')im'palpəbəl\ *adj* : incapable of being felt —**im·pal·pa·bly** *adv*

im·pan·el \im'pan⁰l\ *vb* : enter in or on a panel

im·part \im'pärt\ *vb* : give from or as if from a store

im·par·tial \(')im'pärshəl\ *adj* : not partial —**im·par·tial·i·ty** \(,)im,pärshē'alətē, -,pär'shal-\ *n* —**im·par·tial·ly** *adv*

im·pass·able \(')im'pasəbəl\ *adj* : not passable

im·passe \'im,pas\ *n* : inescapable predicament

im·pas·sioned \im'pashənd\ *adj* : filled with passion

im·pas·sive \(')im'pasiv\ *adj* : showing no feeling or interest —**im·pas·sive·ly** *adv* —**im·pas·siv·i·ty** \,im,pas'ivətē\ *n*

im·pa·tiens \im'pāshənz, -shəns\ *n* : annual herb with showy irregular flowers

im·pa·tient \(')im'pāshənt\ *adj* : not patient —**im·pa·tience** \-shəns\ *n* —**im·pa·tient·ly** *adv*

im·peach \im'pēch\ *vb* **1** : charge an official with misconduct **2** : cast doubt on —**im·peach·ment** *n*

im·pec·ca·ble \(')im'pekəbəl\ *adj* : faultless —**im·pec·ca·bly** *adv*

im·pe·cu·nious \,impi'kyünyəs, -nēəs\ *adj* : broke —**im·pe·cu·nious·ness** *n*

im·pede \im'pēd\ *vb* **-ped·ed; ped·ing** : interfere with

im·ped·i·ment \-'pedəmənt\ *n* **1** : hindrance **2** : speech defect

im·pel \-'pel\ *vb* **-pelled; -pel·ling** : urge forward

im·pend \-'pend\ *vb* : be about to occur

im·pen·e·tra·ble \(')im'penətrəbəl\ *adj* : incapable of being penetrated or understood —**im·pen·e·tra·bil·i·ty** \(,)im,penətrə'bilətē\ *n* —**im·pen·e·tra·bly** *adv*

im·pen·i·tent \(')im'penətənt\ *adj* : not penitent —**im·pen·i·tence** \-təns\ *n*

im·per·a·tive \im'perətiv\ *adj* **1** : expressing a command **2** : urgent ~ *n* **1** : imperative mood or verb form **2** : unavoidable fact, need, or obligation —**im·per·a·tive·ly** *adv*

im·per·cep·ti·ble \,impər'septəbəl\ *adj* : not perceptible —**im·per·cep·ti·bly** *adv*

im·per·fect \(')im'pərfikt\ *adj* : not perfect —**im·per·fec·tion** *n* —**im·per·fect·ly** *adv*

im·pe·ri·al \im'pirēəl\ *adj* **1** : relating to an empire or an emperor **2** : royal

im·pe·ri·al·ism \im'pirēə,lizəm\ *n* : policy of controlling other nations —**im·pe·ri·al·ist** \-ləst\ *n* or *adj* —**im·pe·ri·al·is·tic** \-,pirēə'listik\ *adj*

im·per·il \im'perəl\ *vb* **-iled** or **-illed; -il·ing** or **-il·ling** : endanger

im·pe·ri·ous \im'pirēəs\ *adj* : arrogant or domineering —**im·pe·ri·ous·ly** *adv*

im·per·ish·able \(')im'perishəbəl\ *adj* : not perishable

im·per·ma·nent \-'pərmənənt\ *adj* : not permanent —**im·per·ma·nent·ly** *adv*

im·per·me·able \-'pərmēəbəl\ *adj* : not permeable

im·per·mis·si·ble \,impər'misəbəl\ *adj* : not permissible

im·per·son·al \(')im'pərsnəl, -ᵊnəl\ adj : not involving human personality or emotion —**im·per·son·al·ly** \-ē\ adv

im·per·son·ate \im'pərsᵊn,āt\ vb -at·ed; -at·ing : assume the character of —**im·per·son·ation** \-,pərsᵊn'āshən\ n —**im·per·son·ator** \-'pərsᵊn,ātər\ n

im·per·ti·nent \(')im'pərtᵊnənt\ adj 1 : irrelevant 2 : insolent —**im·per·ti·nence** \-ᵊnəns\ n —**im·per·ti·nent·ly** adv

im·per·turb·able \,impər'tərbəbəl\ adj : calm and steady

im·per·vi·ous \(')im'pərvēəs\ adj : incapable of being penetrated or affected

im·pet·u·ous \im'pech(ə)wəs\ adj : impulsive —**im·pet·u·os·i·ty** \(,)im,pecha'wäsətē\ n —**im·pet·u·ous·ly** adv

im·pe·tus \'impətəs\ n : driving force

im·pi·ety \(')im'pīətē\ n : quality or state of being impious

im·pinge \im'pinj\ vb -pinged; -ping·ing : encroach —**im·pinge·ment** \-'pinjmənt\ n

im·pi·ous \im'pēəs, (')im'pī-\ adj : not pious

imp·ish \'impish\ adj : mischievous —**imp·ish·ly** adv —**imp·ish·ness** n

im·pla·ca·ble \(')im'plakəbəl, -'plā-\ adj : not capable of being appeased or changed —**im·pla·ca·bil·i·ty** \(,)im,plakə'bilətē, -,plā-\ n —**im·pla·ca·bly** \(')im'plakəblē\ adv

im·plant \im'plant\ vb 1 : set firmly or deeply 2 : fix in the mind or spirit

im·plau·si·ble \(')im'plòzəbəl\ adj : not plausible —**im·plau·si·bil·i·ty** \(,)im,plòzə'bilətē\ n

im·ple·ment \'impləmənt\ n : piece of equipment for performing a hand or mechanical operation ~ \-,ment\ vb : put into practice —**im·ple·men·ta·tion** \,impləmən'tāshən\ n

im·pli·cate \'implə,kāt\ vb -cat·ed; -cat·ing : involve

im·pli·ca·tion \,implə'kāshən\ n 1 : an implying 2 : something implied

im·plic·it \im'plisət\ adj 1 : understood though only implied 2 : complete and unquestioning —**im·plic·it·ly** adv

im·plode \im'plōd\ vb -plod·ed; -plod·ing : burst inward —**im·plo·sion** \-'plōzhən\ n —**im·plo·sive** \-'plōsiv\ adj

im·plore \im'plōr\ vb -plored; -plor·ing : entreat

im·ply \-'plī\ vb -plied; -ply·ing : express indirectly

im·po·lite \,impə'līt\ adj : not polite

im·pol·i·tic \(')im'pälə,tik\ adj : not politic

im·pon·der·a·ble \(')im'pänd(ə)rəbəl\ adj : incapable of being precisely evaluated —**imponderable** n

im·port \im'pōrt\ vb 1 : mean 2 : bring in from an external source ~ \'im-,pōrt\ n 1 : meaning 2 : importance 3 : something imported —**im·por·ta·tion** \,im,pōr'tāshən\ n —**im·port·er** n

im·por·tant \im'pōrtᵊnt\ adj : having great worth, significance, or influence —**im·por·tance** \-ᵊns\ n —**im·por·tant·ly** adv

im·por·tu·nate \im'pōrch(ə)nət\ adj : troublesomely persistent or urgent

im·por·tune \,impər't(y)ün, im'pōrchən\ vb -tuned; -tun·ing : urge or beg persistently —**im·por·tu·ni·ty** \,impər't(y)ünətē\ n

im·pose \im'pōz\ vb -posed; -pos·ing 1 : establish as compulsory 2 : take unwarranted advantage of —**im·po·si·tion** \,impə'zishən\ n

im·pos·ing \im'pōziŋ\ adj : impressive —**im·pos·ing·ly** adv

im·pos·si·ble \(')im'päsəbəl\ adj 1 : incapable of occurring 2 : hopeless —**im·pos·si·bil·i·ty** \(,)im,päsə'bilətē\ n —**im·pos·si·bly** \(')im'päsəblē\ adv

im·post \'im,pōst\ n : tax

im·pos·tor, im·pos·ter \im'pästər\ n : one who assumes an identity or title to deceive —**im·pos·ture** \-'päschər\ n

im·po·tent \'impətənt\ adj 1 : lacking power 2 : sterile —**im·po·tence** \-pətəns\ n —**im·po·ten·cy** \-ənsē\ n —**im·po·tent·ly** adv

im·pound \im'paůnd\ vb : seize and hold in legal custody —**im·pound·ment** n

im·pov·er·ish \im'päv(ə)rish\ vb : make poor —**im·pov·er·ish·ment** n

im·prac·ti·ca·ble \(')im'praktikəbl\ adj : not practicable

im·prac·ti·cal \-'praktikəl\ adj : not practical

im·pre·cise \,impri'sīs\ adj : not precise —**im·pre·cise·ly** adv —**im·pre·cise·ness** n —**im·pre·ci·sion** \-'sizhən\ n

im·preg·na·ble \im'pregnəbəl\ adj : able to resist attack —**im·preg·na·bil·i·ty** \(,)im,pregnə'bilətē\ n

im·preg·nate \im'preg,nāt\ vb -nat·ed; -nat·ing : make pregnant 2 : saturate with some other substance —**im·preg·na·tion** \,im,preg'nāshən\ n

im·pre·sa·rio \,impra'särē,ō\ n, pl -ri·os : one who sponsors an entertainment

¹**im·press** \im'pres\ vb 1 : apply with or produce by pressure 2 : press, stamp, or print in or upon 3 : produce a vivid impression of 4 : affect (as the mind) forcibly ~ \'im,-\ n 1 : product of pressure or influence 2 : impression or effect —**im·press·ible** adj

²**im·press** \im'pres\ vb : force into naval service —**im·press·ment** n

im·pres·sion \im'preshən\ n 1 : mark made by impressing 2 : marked influence or effect 3 : printed copy 4 : vague notion or recollection —**im·pres·sion·able** \-'presh(ə)nəbəl\ adj

im·pres·sive \im'presiv\ adj : making a marked impression —**im·pres·sive·ly** adv —**im·pres·sive·ness** n

im·pri·ma·tur \,impra'mä,tů(ə)r\ n : official approval (as of a publication by a censor)

im·print \im'print, 'im,-\ vb : stamp or mark by or as if by pressure ~ \'im,-\ n : something imprinted or printed

im·pris·on \im'priz²n\ vb : put in prison —**im·pris·on·ment** \im'priz-ənmənt\ n

im·prob·a·ble \(')im'präbəbəl\ adj : unlikely to be true or to occur —**im·prob·a·bil·i·ty** \(,)im,präbə'bilətē\ n —**im·prob·a·bly** adv

im·promp·tu \im'prämpt(y)ü\ adj : not planned beforehand —**impromptu** adv or n

im·prop·er \(')im'präpər\ adj : not proper —**im·prop·er·ly** adv

im·pro·pri·ety \,impra'prīətē\ n, pl -eties : state or instance of being improper

im·prove \im'prüv\ vb -proved; -prov·ing 1 : grow or make better 2 : make good use of —**im·prov·able** \-'prüvəbəl\ adj —**im·prove·ment** n

im·prov·i·dent \(')im'prävədənt\ adj : not providing for the future —**im·prov·i·dence** \-əns\ n

im·pro·vise \,impra'vīz, 'impra,vīz\ vb -vised; -vis·ing : make, invent, or arrange offhand —**im·pro·vi·sa·tion** \im,prävə'zāshən, ,imprəvə-\ n —**im·pro·vis·er, im·pro·vi·sor** \,impra'vīzər, 'impravī-\ n

im·pru·dent \(')im'prüd²nt\ adj : not prudent —**im·pru·dence** \-²ns\ n

im·pu·dent \'impyədənt\ adj : insolent —**im·pu·dence** \-²ns\ n —**im·pu·dent·ly** adv

im·pugn \im'pyün\ vb : attack as false

im·pulse \'im,pəls\ n 1 : moving force 2 : sudden inclination

im·pul·sion \im'pəlshən\ n : act of impelling

im·pul·sive \im'pəlsiv\ adj : acting on impulse —**im·pul·sive·ly** adv —**impul·sive·ness** n

im·pu·ni·ty \im'pyünətē\ n : exemption from punishment or harm

im·pure \(')im'pyūr\ adj : not pure —**im·pu·ri·ty** \-'pyūrətē\ n

im·pute \im'pyüt\ vb -put·ed; -put·ing : credit to or blame on a person or cause —**im·pu·ta·tion** \,impyə'tāshən\ n

in \('),in, ən, ³n\ prep 1 —used to indicate location, inclusion, situation, or manner 2 : into 3 : during ~ \'in\ adv : to or toward the inside ~ \'in\ adj : located inside

in- \('),in, ,in\ prefix 1 : not 2 : lack of

inability	incoherence
inaccessibility	incoherent
inaccessible	incoherently
inaccuracy	incohesive
inaccurate	incombustible
inaction	incommensurate
inactive	incommodious
inactivity	incommunicable
inadequacy	incompatibility
inadequate	incompatible
inadequately	incomplete
inadmissibility	incompletely
inadmissible	incompleteness
inadvisability	incomprehen-
inadvisable	sible
inapparent	inconceivable
inapplicable	inconceivably
inapposite	inconclusive
inappositely	incongruent
inappositeness	inconsecutive
inappreciative	inconsiderate
inapproachable	inconsiderately
inappropriate	inconsiderate-
inappropriately	ness
inappropriate-	inconsistency
ness	inconsistent
inapt	inconsistently
inarguable	inconspicuous
inartistic	inconspicuously
inartistically	inconstancy
inattentive	inconstant
inattentively	inconstantly
inattentiveness	inconsumable
inaudible	incontestable
inaudibly	incontestably
inauspicious	incorporeal
inauthentic	incorporeally
incapability	incorrect
incapable	incorrectly
incautious	incorrectness

incorruptible
inculpable
incurable
incurious
indecency
indecent
indecently
indecipherable
indecisive
indecisively
indecisiveness
indecorous
indecorously
indecorousness
indefensible
indefinable
indefinably
indescribable
indescribably
indestructibility
indestructible
indigestible
indiscernible
indiscreet
indiscretion
indisputable
indisputably
indistinct
indistinctly
indistinctness
indivisibility
indivisible
ineducable
ineffective
ineffectively
ineffectiveness
ineffectual
ineffectually
ineffectualness
inefficiency
inefficient
inefficiently
inelastic
inelasticity
inelegance
inelegant
ineligibility
ineligible
ineradicable
inessential
inexact
inexactly
inexpedient
inexpensive
inexperience
inexperienced
inexpert
inexpertly
inexpertness
inexplicable
inexplicably
inexplicit

inexpressible
inexpressibly
inextinguishable
inextricable
inextricably
infeasibility
infeasible
infelicitous
infelicity
infertile
infertility
inflexibility
inflexible
inflexibly
infrequent
infrequently
inglorious
ingloriously
ingratitude
inhumane
inhumanely
injudicious
injudiciously
injudiciousness
inoffensive
inoperable
inoperative
insalubrious
insensitive
insensitivity
inseparable
insignificant
insincere
insincerely
insincerity
insolubility
insoluble
instability
insubstantial
insufficiency
insufficient
insufficiently
insupportable
intangibility
intangible
intangibly
intolerable
intolerably
intolerance
intolerant
intractable
intransitive
invariable
invariably
inviable
invisibility
invisible
invisibly
involuntarily
involuntary
invulnerability
invulnerable
invulnerably

in·ad·ver·tent \ˌinad¹vertⁿnt\ *adj* : unintentional —**in·ad·ver·tence** \-ⁿs\ *n* —**in·ad·ver·ten·cy** \-ⁿsē\ *n* —**in·ad·ver·tent·ly** *adv*

in·alien·able \(¹)in¹ālyənəbəl, -¹ālēənə-\ *adj* : incapable of being transferred or given up —**in·alien·abil·i·ty** \(ˌ)in¹ālyənə¹bilətē, -¹ālēənə-\ *n* —**in·alien·ably** *adv*

inane \in¹ān\ *adj* **inan·er; -est** : silly or stupid —**inan·i·ty** \in¹anətē\ *n*

in·an·i·mate \(¹)in¹anəmət\ *adj* : not animate or animated —**in·an·i·mate·ly** *adv* —**in·an·i·mate·ness** *n*

in·a·ni·tion \ˌinə¹nishən\ *n* : weakness from lack of food and water

in·ap·pre·cia·ble \ˌinə¹prēshəbəl\ *adj* : too small to be perceived —**in·ap·pre·cia·bly** *adv*

in·ar·tic·u·late \ˌinär¹tikyələt\ *adj* : without the power of speech or effective expression —**in·ar·tic·u·late·ly** *adv*

in·as·much as \ˌinəzˌməchəz\ *conj* : because

in·at·ten·tion \ˌinə¹tenchən\ *n* : failure to pay attention

in·au·gu·ral \in¹ȯgyərəl, -g(ə)rəl\ *adj* : relating to an inauguration ~ *n* **1** : inaugural speech **2** : inauguration

in·au·gu·rate \in¹ȯg(y)əˌrāt\ *vb* **-rat·ed; -rat·ing 1** : install in office **2** : start —**in·au·gu·ra·tion** \-ˌȯg(y)ə¹rāshən\ *n*

in·board \¹inˌbȯrd\ *adv* : inside a boat or ship —**inboard** *adj*

in·born \¹in¹bȯrn\ *adj* : present from birth

in·bred \¹in¹bred\ *adj* : inborn

in·breed·ing \¹in¸brēdiŋ\ *n* : interbreeding of closely related individuals —**in·breed** \-¹brēd\ *vb*

in·cal·cu·la·ble \(¹)in¹kalkyələbəl\ *adj* : too large to be calculated —**in·cal·cu·la·bly** *adv*

in·can·des·cent \ˌinkən¹desⁿnt\ *adj* **1** : glowing with heat **2** : brilliant —**in·can·des·cence** \-ⁿs\ *n*

in·can·ta·tion \ˌinˌkan¹tāshən\ *n* : use of spoken or sung charms or spells as a magic ritual

in·ca·pac·i·tate \ˌinkə¹pasəˌtāt\ *vb* **-tat·ed; -tat·ing** : disable

in·ca·pac·i·ty \ˌinkə¹pasətē\ *n, pl* **-ties** : quality or state of being incapable

in·car·cer·ate \in¹kärsəˌrāt\ *vb* : imprison —**in·car·cer·a·tion** \(ˌ)inˌkärsə¹rāshən\ *n*

in·car·nate \in¹kärnət, -ˌnāt\ *adj* : having bodily form and substance —**incar·nate** \-ˌnāt\ *vb* —**in·car·na·tion** \-ˌkär¹nāshən\ *n*

in·cen·di·ary \in'sendē,erē\ *adj* **1** : pertaining to or used to ignite fire **2** : tending to excite —**incendiary** *n*

in·cense \'in,sens\ *n* : material burned to produce a fragrant odor or its smoke ∼ \in'sens\ *vb* -**censed;** -**cens·ing** : make very angry

in·cen·tive \in'sentiv\ *n* : inducement to do something

in·cep·tion \in'sepshən\ *n* : beginning

in·ces·sant \(')in'ses^{ə}nt\ *adj* : continuing without interruption —**in·ces·sant·ly** *adv*

in·cest \'in,sest\ *n* : sexual intercourse between close relatives —**in·ces·tu·ous** \in'seschəwəs\ *adj*

inch \'inch\ *n* : unit of length equal to 1/12 foot ∼ *vb* : move by small degrees

in·cho·ate \in'kōət, 'inkə,wāt\ *adj* : new and not fully formed or ordered

in·ci·dent \'insədənt\ *n* : occurrence —**in·ci·dence** \-əns\ *n* —**incident** *adj*

in·ci·den·tal \,insə'dent^{ə}l\ *adj* **1** : subordinate, nonessential, or attendant **2** : met by chance ∼ *n* **1** : something incidental **2** *pl* : minor expenses that are not itemized —**in·ci·den·tal·ly** *adv*

in·cin·er·ate \in'sinə,rāt\ *vb* -**at·ed;** -**at·ing** : burn to ashes —**in·cin·er·a·tor** \-,rāt·ər\ *n*

in·cip·i·ent \in'sipēənt\ *adj* : beginning to be or appear

in·cise \in'sīz\ *vb* -**cised;** -**cis·ing** : carve into

in·ci·sion \in'sizhən\ *n* : surgical wound

in·ci·sive \in'sīsiv\ *adj* : keen and discerning —**in·ci·sive·ly** *adv*

in·ci·sor \in'sīzər\ *n* : tooth for cutting

in·cite \in'sīt\ *vb* -**cit·ed;** -**cit·ing** : arouse to action —**in·cite·ment** *n*

in·ci·vil·i·ty \insə'vilətē\ *n* : rudeness

in·clem·ent \(')in'klemənt\ *adj* : stormy —**in·clem·en·cy** \-ənsē\ *n*

in·cline \in'klīn\ *vb* -**clined;** -**clin·ing 1** : bow **2** : tend toward an opinion **3** : slope ∼ *n* : slope —**in·cli·na·tion** \,inklə'nāshən\ *n*

in·close, inclosure *var of* ENCLOSE, ENCLOSURE

in·clude \in'klüd\ *vb* -**clud·ed;** -**clud·ing** : take in or comprise —**in·clu·sion** \in'klüzhən\ *n* —**in·clu·sive** \-'klü-siv\ *adj*

in·cog·ni·to \,in,käg'nētō, in'kägnə,tō\ *adv or adj* : with one's identity concealed

in·come \'in,kəm\ *n* : money gained (as from work or investment)

in·com·ing \'in,kəmiŋ\ *adj* : coming in

in·com·mu·ni·ca·do \,inkə,myünə-'kädō\ *adv or adj* : without means of communication

in·com·pa·ra·ble \(')in'kämp(ə)rəbəl\ *adj* : eminent beyond comparison

in·com·pe·tent \(')in'kämpətənt\ *adj* : lacking sufficient knowledge or skill —**in·com·pe·tence** \-pətəns\ *n* —**in·com·pe·ten·cy** \-ənsē\ *n* —**incompetent** *n*

in·con·gru·ous \(')in'käŋgrəwəs\ *adj* : inappropriate or out of place —**in·con·gru·i·ty** \,inkən'grüətē, -,kän-\ *n* —**in·con·gru·ous·ly** *adv*

in·con·se·quen·tial \,in,känsə-'kwenchəl\ *adj* : unimportant —**in·con·se·quence** \(')in'känsə,kwens\ *n* —**in·con·se·quen·tial·ly** *adv*

in·con·sid·er·able \,inkən'sidər(ə)bəl, -'sidrəbəl\ *adj* : trivial

in·con·sol·able \,inkən'sōləbəl\ *adj* : incapable of being consoled —**in·con·sol·ably** *adv*

in·con·ve·nience \,inkən'vēnyəns\ *n* **1** : discomfort **2** : something that causes trouble or annoyance ∼ *vb* : cause inconvenience to —**in·con·ve·nient** \,inkən'vēnyənt\ *adj* —**in·con·ve·nient·ly** *adv*

in·cor·po·rate \in'kórpə,rāt\ *vb* -**rat·ed;** -**rat·ing 1** : blend **2** : form into a legal body —**in·cor·po·rat·ed** *adj* —**in·cor·po·ra·tion** \-,kórpə'rāshən\ *n*

in·cor·ri·gi·ble \(')in'kórəjəbəl\ *adj* : incapable of being corrected or reformed —**in·cor·ri·gi·bil·i·ty** \(,)in,kórəjə'bilətē\ *n* —**in·cor·ri·gi·bly** \(')in'kórəjəblē\ *adv*

in·crease \in'krēs, 'in,krēs\ *vb* -**creased;** -**creas·ing** : make or become greater ∼ \'in,-, in'-\ *n* **1** : enlargement in size **2** : something added —**in·creas·ing·ly** \-'krēsiŋlē\ *adv*

in·cred·i·ble \(')in'kredəbəl\ *adj* : too extraordinary to be believed —**in·cred·i·bil·i·ty** \(,)in,kredə'bilətē\ *n* —**in·cred·i·bly** \(')in'kredəblē\ *adv*

in·cred·u·lous \in'krejələs\ *adj* : skeptical —**in·cre·du·li·ty** \,in-kri'd(y)ülətē\ *n* —**in·cred·u·lous·ly** *adv*

in·cre·ment \'iŋkrəmənt, 'in-\ *n* : increase or amount of increase —**in·cre·men·tal** \,iŋkrə'ment^{ə}l, ,in-\ *adj*

in·crim·i·nate \in'krimə,nāt\ *vb* -**nat·ed;** -**nat·ing** : show to be guilty of a crime —**in·crim·i·na·tion** \-,krimə'nāshən\ *n* —**in·crim·i·na·to·ry** \-'krim(ə)nə,tōrē\ *adj*

in·cu·bate \'iŋkyə,bāt, 'in-\ vb **-bat·ed; -bat·ing** : keep (as eggs) under conditions favorable for development —**in·cu·ba·tion** \,iŋkyə'bā-shən, ,in-\ n —**in·cu·ba·tor** \'iŋkyə,bātər, 'in-\ n

in·cul·cate \in'kəl,kāt, 'in,(')kəl-\ vb **-cat·ed; -cat·ing** : instill by repeated teaching —**in·cul·ca·tion** \,in,(')kəl'kāshən\ n

in·cum·bent \in'kəmbənt\ n : holder of an office ~ adj : obligatory —**in·cum·ben·cy** \-bənsē\ n

in·cur \in'kər\ vb **-rr-** : become liable or subject to

in·cur·sion \in'kərzhən\ n : invasion

in·debt·ed \in'detəd\ adj : owing something —**in·debt·ed·ness** n

in·de·ci·sion \,indi'sizhən\ n : inability to decide

in·deed \in'dēd\ adv : without question

in·de·fat·i·ga·ble \indi'fatigəbəl\ adj : not tiring —**in·de·fat·i·ga·bly** \-blē\ adv

in·def·i·nite \(')in'def(ə)nət\ adj 1 : not defining or identifying 2 : not precise 3 : having no fixed limit or amount —**in·def·i·nite·ly** adv

in·del·i·ble \in'delabəl\ adj : not capable of being removed or erased —**in·del·i·bly** adv

in·del·i·cate \(')in'delikət\ adj : improper —**in·del·i·ca·cy** \in'deləkəsē\ n

in·dem·ni·fy \in'demnə,fī\ vb **-fied; -fy·ing** : repay for a loss —**in·dem·ni·fi·ca·tion** \-,demnəfə'kāshən\ n

in·dem·ni·ty \in'demnətē\ n, pl **-ties** : security against loss or damage

¹in·dent \in'dent\ vb : leave a space at the beginning of a paragraph —**in·dent** n

²indent vb : force inward so as to form a depression or dent

in·den·ta·tion \,in,den'tashən\ n 1 : notch, recess, or dent 2 : action of indenting 3 : space at the beginning of a paragraph

in·den·ture \in'denchər\ n : contract binding one person to work for another for a given period —usu. in pl. ~ vb **-tured; -tur·ing** : bind by indentures

Independence Day n : July 4 observed as a legal holiday in commemoration of the adoption of the Declaration of Independence in 1776

in·de·pen·dent \,ində'pendənt\ adj 1 : not governed by another 2 : not requiring or relying on something or somebody else 3 : not easily influenced —**in·de·pen·dence** \-dəns\ n

—**independent** n —**in·de·pen·dent·ly** adv

n·de·ter·mi·nate \,indi'tərm(ə)nət\ adj : not definitely determined —**in·de·ter·mi·na·cy** \-(ə)nəsē\ n —**in·de·ter·mi·nate·ly** adv

in·dex \'in,deks\ n, pl **-dex·es** or **-di·ces** \-də,sēz\ 1 : alphabetical list of items (as topics in a book) 2 : a number that serves as a measure or indicator of something ~ vb 1 : provide with an index 2 : serve as an index of

index finger n : forefinger

in·di·cate \'ində,kāt\ vb **-cat·ed; -cat·ing** 1 : point out or to 2 : reveal or suggest 3 : state briefly —**in·di·ca·tion** \,ində'kāshən\ n —**in·di·ca·tor** \'ində,kātər\ n

in·dic·a·tive \in'dikətiv\ adj : serving to indicate

in·dict \in'dīt\ vb : charge with a crime —**in·dict·able** adj —**in·dict·ment** n

in·dif·fer·ent \in'difərnt, -'dif(ə)rənt\ adj 1 : having no preference 2 : showing neither interest nor dislike 3 : mediocre —**in·dif·fer·ence** \-'difərns, -'dif(ə)rəns\ n —**in·dif·fer·ent·ly** adv

in·dig·e·nous \in'dijənəs\ adj : native to a particular region

in·di·gent \'indijənt\ adj : needy —**in·di·gence** \-jəns\ n

in·di·ges·tion \,indi'jeschən, -də-\ n : discomfort from inability to digest food

in·dig·na·tion \,indig'nāshən\ n : anger aroused by something unjust or unworthy —**in·dig·nant** \in'dignənt\ adj —**in·dig·nant·ly** adv

in·dig·ni·ty \in'dignətē\ n, pl **-ties** 1 : offense against self-respect 2 : humiliating treatment

in·di·go \'indi,gō\ n, pl **-gos** or **-goes** 1 : blue dye 2 : dark blue or violet color

in·di·rect \,ində'rekt, -dī-\ adj : not straight or straightforward —**in·di·rec·tion** \-'rekshən\ n —**in·di·rect·ly** adv —**in·di·rect·ness** n

in·dis·crim·i·nate \,indis'krimənət\ adj 1 : not careful or discriminating 2 : haphazard —**in·dis·crim·i·nate·ly** adv

in·dis·pens·able \,indis'pensabəl\ adj : absolutely essential —**in·dis·pens·abil·i·ty** \-,pensə'bilətē\ n —**in·dis·pensable** n —**in·dis·pens·ably** \-'pensəblē\ adv

in·dis·posed \-'pōzd\ adj : slightly ill —**in·dis·po·si·tion** \(,)in,dispə-'zishən\ n

in·dis·sol·u·ble \ˌindis'älyəbəl\ *adj* : not capable of being dissolved or broken

in·di·vid·u·al \ˌində'vij(əw)əl\ *n* 1 : single member of a category 2 : person —**individual** *adj* —**in·di·vid·u·al·ly** *adv*

in·di·vid·u·al·i·ty \-ˌvijə'walətē\ *n* : special quality that distinguishes an individual

in·di·vid·u·al·ize \-'vijə(wə)ˌlīz\ *vb* -**ized; -iz·ing** 1 : make individual 2 : treat individually

in·doc·tri·nate \in'däktrəˌnāt\ *vb* -**nat·ed; -nat·ing** : instruct in fundamentals (as of a doctrine) —**in·doc·tri·na·tion** \ˌ)in,däktrə'nāshən\ *n*

in·do·lent \'indələnt\ *adj* : lazy —**in·do·lence** \-ləns\ *n*

in·dom·i·ta·ble \in'dämətəbəl\ *adj* : invincible —**in·dom·i·ta·bly** \-blē\ *adv*

in·door \ˌin,dȯr\ *adj* : relating to the interior of a building

in·doors \in'dȯrz\ *adv* : in or into a building

in·du·bi·ta·ble \(ˈ)in'd(y)übətəbəl\ *adj* : being beyond question —**in·du·bi·ta·bly** \-blē\ *adv*

in·duce \in'd(y)üs\ *vb* -**duced; -duc·ing** 1 : persuade 2 : bring about —**in·duce·ment** *n* —**in·duc·er** *n*

in·duct \in'dəkt\ *vb* 1 : put in office 2 : admit as a member 3 : enroll (as for military service) —**in·duct·ee** \ˌ)in,dək'tē\ *n*

in·duc·tion \in'dəkshən\ *n* 1 : act or instance of inducting 2 : reasoning from particular instances to a general conclusion

in·duc·tive \in'dəktiv\ *adj* : reasoning by induction

in·dulge \in'dəlj\ *vb* -**dulged; -dulg·ing** : yield to the desire of or for —**in·dul·gence** \-'dəljəns\ *n* —**in·dul·gent** \-jənt\ *adj* —**in·dul·gent·ly** *adv*

in·dus·tri·al \in'dəstrēəl\ *adj* : having to do with industry —**in·dus·tri·al·ist** \-əlast\ *n* —**in·dus·tri·al·iza·tion** \-ˌdəstrēələ'zāshən\ *n* —**in·dus·tri·al·ize** \-'dəstrēəˌlīz\ *vb* —**in·dus·tri·al·ly** \-ē\ *adv*

in·dus·tri·ous \in'dəstrēəs\ *adj* : diligent or busy —**in·dus·tri·ous·ly** *adv* —**in·dus·tri·ous·ness** *n*

in·dus·try \'in,(ˌ)dəstrē\ *n, pl* -**tries** 1 : diligence 2 : manufacturing enterprises or activity

ine·bri·ate \in'ēbrēˌāt\ *vb* -**at·ed; -at·ing** : make drunk ~ *n* : one who is drunk —**ine·bri·a·tion** \-ˌēbrē'ā-shən\ *n*

in·ef·fa·ble \(ˈ)in'efəbəl\ *adj* : incapable of being expressed in words —**in·ef·fa·bly** \-blē\ *adv*

in·ept \in'ept\ *adj* 1 : inappropriate or foolish 2 : generally incompetent —**in·ep·ti·tude** \in'eptəˌt(y)üd\ *n* —**in·ept·ly** *adv* —**in·ept·ness** *n*

in·equal·i·ty \ˌini'kwälətē\ *n* : quality of being unequal or uneven

in·ert \in'ərt\ *adj* 1 : powerless to move or act 2 : sluggish —**in·ert·ly** *adv* —**in·ert·ness** *n*

in·er·tia \in'ərsh(ē)ə\ *n* : tendency of matter to remain at rest or in motion —**in·er·tial** \-shəl\ *adj*

in·es·cap·a·ble \ˌinis'kāpəbəl\ *adj* : inevitable —**in·es·cap·a·bly** \-blē\ *adv*

in·es·ti·ma·ble \(ˈ)in'estəməbəl\ *adj* : incapable of being estimated —**in·es·ti·ma·bly** \-blē\ *adv*

in·ev·i·ta·ble \in'evətəbəl\ *adj* : incapable of being avoided or escaped —**in·ev·i·ta·bil·i·ty** \ˌ)in,evətə'bilətē\ *n* —**in·ev·i·ta·bly** \in'evətəblē\ *adv*

in·ex·cus·able \ˌinik'skyüzəbəl\ *adj* : being without excuse or justification —**in·ex·cus·ably** \-blē\ *adv*

in·ex·haust·ible \ˌinig'zȯstəbəl\ *adj* : incapable of being used up or tired out —**in·ex·haust·ibly** \-blē\ *adv*

in·ex·o·ra·ble \(ˈ)in'eks(ə)rəbəl\ *adj* : unyielding or relentless —**in·ex·o·ra·bly** *adv*

in·fal·li·ble \(ˈ)in'faləbəl\ *adj* : incapable of error —**in·fal·li·bil·i·ty** \ˌ)in,falə'bilətē\ *n* —**in·fal·li·bly** *adv*

in·fa·mous \'infəməs\ *adj* : having the worst kind of reputation —**in·fa·mous·ly** *adv*

in·fa·my \-mē\ *n, pl* -**mies** : evil reputation

in·fan·cy \'infənsē\ *n, pl* -**cies** 1 : early childhood 2 : early period of existence

in·fant \'infənt\ *n* : baby

in·fan·tile \'infənˌtīl, -ˌtəl, ...ˌtēl\ *adj* : relating to infants

in·fan·try \'infəntrē\ *n, pl* -**tries** : soldiers that fight on foot

in·fat·u·ate \in'fachəˌwāt\ *vb* -**at·ed; -at·ing** : inspire with foolish love or admiration —**in·fat·u·a·tion** \-ˌfachə'wāshən\ *n*

in·fect \in'fekt\ *vb* : contaminate with disease-producing matter —**in·fec·tion** \-'fekshən\ *n* —**in·fec·tious** \-shəs\ *adj* —**in·fec·tive** \-'fektiv\ *adj*

in·fer \in'fər\ *vb* -**rr-** : deduce —**in·fer·ence** \'inf(ə)rəns\ *n* —**in·fer·en·tial** \ˌinfə'renchəl\ *adj*

in·fe·ri·or \in'firēər\ adj : being lower in position, degree, rank, or merit —**inferior** n —**in·fe·ri·or·i·ty** \(,)in,firē'orətē\ n

in·fer·nal \in'fərn°l\ adj : of or like hell—often used as a general expression of disapproval —**in·fer·nal·ly** adv

in·fer·no \in'fərnō\ n, pl -nos : place or condition suggesting hell

in·fest \in'fest\ vb : swarm or grow in or over —**in·fes·ta·tion** \,in,fes'tā-shən\ n

in·fi·del \'infəd°l, -fə,del\ n : one who does not believe in a particular religion

in·fi·del·i·ty \,infə'delətē, -fī-\ n, pl -ties : lack of faithfulness

in·field \'in,fēld\ n : baseball field inside the base lines —**in·field·er** n

in·fil·trate \in'fil,trāt, 'in,(,)fil-\ vb -trat·ed; -trat·ing : enter or become established in without being noticed —**in·fil·tra·tion** \,in,(,)fil'trāshən\ n

in·fi·nite \'infənət\ adj 1 : having no limit or extending indefinitely 2 : vast —**infinite** n —**in·fi·nite·ly** adv —**in·fin·i·tude** \in'finə,t(y)üd\ n

in·fin·i·tes·i·mal \(,)infinə'tesəməl\ adj : very minute —**in·fin·i·tes·i·mal·ly** adv

in·fin·i·tive \in'finətiv\ n : verb form in English usu. used with to

in·fin·i·ty \in'finətē\ n, pl -ties 1 : quality or state of being infinite 2 : indefinitely great number or amount

in·firm \in'fərm\ adj : feeble from age —**in·fir·mi·ty** \-'fərmətē\ n

in·fir·ma·ry \in'fərm(ə)rē\ n, pl -ries : place for the care of the sick

in·flame \in'flām\ vb -flamed; -flam·ing 1 : excite to intense action or feeling 2 : affect or become affected with inflammation —**in·flam·ma·to·ry** \-'flamə,tōrē\ adj

in·flam·ma·ble \in'flaməbəl\ adj : flammable

in·flam·ma·tion \,inflə'māshən\ n : response to injury in which an affected area becomes red and painful and congested with blood

in·flate \in'flāt\ vb -flat·ed; -flat·ing 1 : swell or puff up (as with gas) 2 : expand or increase abnormally —**in·flat·able** adj

in·fla·tion \in'flāshən\ n 1 : act of inflating 2 : abnormal increase in the volume of money and credit with a continuing rise in prices —**in·fla·tion·ary** \-shə,nerē\ adj

in·flec·tion \in'flekshən\ n 1 : change in pitch or loudness of the voice 2 : change in form of a word —**in·flect** \-'flekt\ vb —**in·flec·tion·al** \-'flekshənəl\ adj

in·flict \in'flikt\ vb : give by or as if by hitting —**in·flic·tion** \-'flikshən\ n

in·flu·ence \'in,flüəns\ n 1 : power or capacity of causing an effect in indirect or intangible ways 2 : one that exerts influence ∼ vb -enced; -enc·ing : affect or alter by influence —**in·flu·en·tial** \,influ'enchəl\ adj

in·flu·en·za \,influ'enzə\ n : acute very contagious virus disease

in·flux \'in,fləks\ n : a flowing in

in·form \in'form\ vb : give information or knowledge to —**in·for·mant** \-'ant\ n —**in·form·er** n

in·for·mal \in'forməl\ adj 1 : without formality or ceremony 2 : for ordinary or familiar use —**in·for·mal·i·ty** \,infor'malətē, -fər-\ n —**in·for·mal·ly** adv

in·for·ma·tion \,infər'māshən\ n : knowledge obtained from investigation, study, or instruction —**in·for·ma·tion·al** \-sh(ə)nəl\ adj

in·for·ma·tive \in'formətiv\ adj : giving knowledge

in·frac·tion \in'frakshən\ n : violation

in·fra·red \,infrə'red\ adj : being, relating to, or using invisible heat rays having wavelengths longer than those of red light —**infrared** n

in·fringe \in'frinj\ vb -fringed; -fring·ing : violate another's right or privilege —**in·fringe·ment** n

in·fu·ri·ate \in'fyür,ēāt\ vb -at·ed; -at·ing : make furious —**in·fu·ri·at·ing·ly** \-,ātiŋlē\ adv

in·fuse \in'fyüz\ vb -fused; -fus·ing 1 : instill a principle or quality in 2 : steep in liquid without boiling —**in·fu·sion** \-'fyüzhən\ n

¹-ing \iŋ\ vb suffix or adj suffix —used to form the present participle and sometimes an adjective resembling a present participle

²-ing n suffix 1 : action or process 2 : something connected with or resulting from an action or process

in·ge·nious \in'jēnyəs\ adj : very clever —**in·ge·nious·ly** adv —**in·ge·nious·ness** n

in·ge·nue or **in·gé·nue** \'anjə,nü, 'än-; 'aⁿzhə-, 'äⁿ-\ n : naive young woman

in·ge·nu·i·ty \,injə'n(y)üətē\ n, pl -ities : skill or cleverness in planning or inventing

in·gen·u·ous \in'jenyəwəs\ adj : innocent and candid —**in·gen·u·ous·ly** adv —**in·gen·u·ous·ness** n

in·gest \in'jest\ vb : eat —**in·ges·tion** \-'jeschən\ n

in·gle·nook \'ingəl,nůk\ n : corner by the fireplace

in·got \'ingət\ n : block of metal

in·grained \in'grānd\ adj : deep-seated

in·grate \'in,grāt\ n : ungrateful person

in·gra·ti·ate \in'grāshē,āt\ vb -at·ed; -at·ing : gain favor for (oneself) —**in·gra·ti·at·ing** adj

in·gre·di·ent \in'grēdēənt\ n : one of the substances that make up a mixture

in·grown \'in,grōn\ adj : grown in and esp. into the flesh

in·hab·it \in'habət\ vb : live or dwell in —**in·hab·it·able** adj —**in·hab·it·ant** \-ətənt\ n

in·hale \in'hāl\ vb -haled; -hal·ing : breathe in —**in·hal·ant** \-ənt\ n —**in·ha·la·tion** \,in(h)ə'lāshən\ n —**in·hal·er** n

in·here \in'hiər\ vb -hered; -her·ing : be inherent

in·her·ent \in'hirənt, -'her-\ adj : being an essential part of something —**in·her·ent·ly** adv

in·her·it \in'herət\ vb : receive from one's ancestors —**in·her·i·tance** \-ətəns\ n —**in·her·i·tor** \-ətər\ n

in·hib·it \in'hibət\ vb : hold in check —**in·hi·bi·tion** \,in(h)ə'bishən\ n

in·hu·man \(')in'(hyü)mən\ adj : cruel or impersonal —**in·hu·man·i·ty** \-(h)yü'manətē\ n —**in·hu·man·ly** adv

in·im·i·cal \in'imikəl\ adj : hostile or harmful —**in·im·i·cal·ly** adv

in·im·i·ta·ble \(')in'imətəbəl\ adj : not capable of being imitated

in·iq·ui·ty \in'ikwətē\ n, pl -ties : wickedness —**in·iq·ui·tous** \-wətəs\ adj

ini·tial \in'ishəl\ adj 1 : of or relating to the beginning 2 : first ~ n : 1st letter of a word or name ~ vb -tialed or -tialled; -tial·ing or -tial·ling : put initials on —**ini·tial·ly** adv

ini·ti·ate \in'ishē,āt\ vb -at·ed; -at·ing 1 : start 2 : induct into membership —**initiate** \-ish(ē)ət\ n —**ini·ti·a·tion** \-,ishē'āshən\ n —**ini·tia·to·ry** \-'ishēə,tōrē\ adj

ini·tia·tive \in'ishətiv\ n 1 : first step 2 : readiness to undertake something on one's own

in·ject \in'jekt\ vb : force or introduce into something —**in·jec·tion** \-'jekshən\ n

in·junc·tion \in'jəŋkshən\ n : court

writ requiring one to do or to refrain from doing a specified act

in·jure \'injər\ vb -jured; -jur·ing : do damage, hurt, or a wrong to

in·ju·ry \'inj(ə)rē\ n, pl -ries 1 : act that injures 2 : hurt, damage, or loss sustained —**in·ju·ri·ous** \in'jůrēəs\ adj

in·jus·tice \(')in'jəstəs\ n : unjust act

ink \'iŋk\ n : usu. liquid and colored material for writing and printing ~ vb : put ink on —**ink·well** \-,wel\ n —**inky** adj

in·kling \'iŋkliŋ\ n : hint or idea

in·land \'in,land, -lənd\ n : interior of a country —**inland** adj

in·law \'in,lô\ n : relative by marriage

in·lay \(')in'lā, 'in,lā\ vb -laid \-'lād\; -lay·ing : set into a surface for decoration ~ \'in,lā\ n 1 : inlaid work 2 : shaped filling cemented into a tooth

in·let \'in,let, -lət\ n : bay or recess in a shore

in·mate \'in,māt\ n : person confined to an asylum or prison

in me·mo·ri·am \,inmə'mōrēəm\ prep : in memory of

in·most \'in,mōst\ adj : deepest within

inn \'in\ n : hotel

in·nards \'inərdz\ n pl : internal parts

in·nate \in'āt\ adj 1 : inborn 2 : inherent —**in·nate·ly** adv

in·ner \'inər\ adj : on the inside

in·ner·most \'inər,mōst\ adj : farthest inward

in·ner·sole \,inər'sōl\ n : insole

in·ning \'iniŋ\ n : baseball team's turn at bat

inn·keep·er \'in,kēpər\ n : owner of an inn

in·no·cent \'inəsənt\ adj 1 : free from guilt 2 : harmless 3 : not sophisticated —**in·no·cence** \-səns\ n —**innocent** n —**in·no·cent·ly** adv

in·noc·u·ous \in'äkyəwəs\ adj 1 : harmless 2 : inoffensive

in·no·va·tion \,inə'vāshən\ n : new idea or method —**in·no·va·tive** \'inə,vātiv\ adj —**in·no·va·tor** \-,vātər\ n

in·nu·en·do \,inyə'wendō\ n, pl -dos or -does : insinuation

in·nu·mer·a·ble \in'(y)üm(ə)rəbəl\ adj : countless

in·oc·u·late \in'äkyə,lāt\ vb -lat·ed; -lat·ing : treat with something esp. to establish immunity —**in·oc·u·la·tion** \-,äkyə'lāshən\ n

in·op·por·tune \(,)in,äpər't(y)ün\ adj : happening at the wrong time —**in·op·por·tune·ly** adv

in·or·di·nate \in'ȯrdnət, -ᵊnət\ adj : unusual or excessive —**in·or·di·nate·ly** adv

in·or·gan·ic \ˌin.ȯr'ganik\ adj : made of mineral matter

in·pa·tient \'in.ˌpāshənt\ n : patient who stays in a hospital

in·put \'in.ˌpu̇t\ n : something put in —**input** vb

in·quest \'in.ˌkwest\ n : inquiry esp. before a jury

in·quire \in'kwī(ə)r\ vb -**quired**; -**quir·ing** 1 : ask 2 : investigate —**in·quir·er** n —**in·quir·ing·ly** adv —**in·qui·ry** \'in.ˌkwī(ə)rē, in'kwī(ə)rē; 'inkwərē, 'iŋ-\ n

in·qui·si·tion \ˌinkwə'zishən, ˌiŋ-\ n 1 : official inquiry 2 : severe questioning —**in·quis·i·tor** \in'kwizətər\ n —**in·quis·i·to·ri·al** \-ˌkwizə'tōrēəl\ adj

in·quis·i·tive \in'kwizətiv\ adj : curious —**in·quis·i·tive·ly** adv —**in·quis·i·tive·ness** n

in·road \'in.ˌrōd\ n : encroachment

in·rush \'in.ˌrəsh\ n : influx

in·sane \(')in'sān\ adj 1 : not sane 2 : foolish —**in·sane·ly** adv —**in·san·i·ty** \in'sanətē\ n

in·sa·tia·ble \(')in'sāshəbəl\ adj : incapable of being satisfied

in·sa·ti·ate \(')in'sāsh(ē)ət\ adj : insatiable

in·scribe \in'skrīb\ vb 1 : write 2 : engrave 3 : dedicate (a book) to someone —**in·scrip·tion** \-'skripshən\ n

in·scru·ta·ble \in'skrütəbəl\ adj : mysterious —**in·scru·ta·bly** adv

in·seam \'in.ˌsēm\ n : inner seam (of a garment)

in·sect \'in.ˌsekt\ n : small usu. winged animal with 6 legs

in·sec·ti·cide \in'sektəˌsīd\ n : insect poison —**in·sec·ti·cid·al** \(ˌ)in.ˌsektə'sīdᵊl\ adj

in·se·cure \ˌinsi'kyu̇r\ adj 1 : uncertain 2 : unsafe 3 : fearful —**in·se·cure·ly** adv —**in·se·cu·ri·ty** \-'kyu̇rətē\ n

in·sem·i·nate \in'seməˌnāt\ vb -**nat·ed**; -**nat·ing** : introduce semen into —**in·sem·i·na·tion** \-ˌsemə'nāshən\ n

in·sen·si·ble \(')in'sensəbəl\ adj 1 : unconscious 2 : unable to feel 3 : unaware —**in·sen·si·bil·i·ty** \(ˌ)in.ˌsen·sə'bilətē\ n —**in·sen·si·bly** adv

in·sen·tient \(')in'sench(ē)ənt\ adj : lacking feeling —**in·sen·tience** \-ch(ē)əns\ n

in·sert \in'sərt\ vb : put in —**insert** \'in.ˌsərt\ n —**in·ser·tion** \in'sərshən\ n

in·set \'in.ˌset\ vb inset or in·set·ted; in·set·ting : set in —**inset** n

in·shore \'in'shȯr\ adj 1 : situated near shore 2 : moving toward shore —adv : toward shore

in·side \in'sīd, 'in.ˌsīd\ n 1 : inner side 2 pl : innards ~ prep 1 : in or into the inside of 2 : before the end of —adv 1 : on the inner side 2 : into the interior —**inside** adj —**in·sid·er** \in'sīdər\ n

inside of prep : inside

in·sid·i·ous \in'sidēəs\ adj : treacherous 2 : seductive —**in·sid·i·ous·ly** adv —**in·sid·i·ous·ness** n

in·sight \'in.ˌsīt\ n : understanding —**in·sight·ful** \'in.ˌsītfəl, in'sīt-\ adj

in·sig·nia \in'signēə\, **in·sig·ne** \-(ˌ)nē\ n, pl **-nia** or **-ni·as** : badge of authority or office

in·sin·u·ate \in'sinyəˌwāt\ vb -**at·ed**; -**at·ing** 1 : imply 2 : bring in artfully —**in·sin·u·a·tion** \(ˌ)in.ˌsinyə'wāshən\ n

in·sip·id \in'sipəd\ adj 1 : tasteless 2 : not stimulating —**in·si·pid·i·ty** \ˌinsə'pidətē\ n

in·sist \in'sist\ vb : be firmly demanding —**in·sis·tence** \in'sistəns\ n —**in·sis·tent** \-'tənt\ adj —**in·sis·tent·ly** adv

in·so·far as \ˌinsə'fär.əz\ conj : to the extent that

in·sole \'in.ˌsōl\ n : inside sole of a shoe

in·so·lent \'insələnt\ adj : contemptuously rude —**in·so·lence** \-ləns\ n

in·sol·vent \(')in'sälvənt\ adj : unable or insufficient to pay debts —**in·sol·ven·cy** \-vənsē\ n

in·som·nia \in'sämnēə\ n : inability to sleep

in·so·much \ˌinsə'məch\ adv : to such a degree

in·sou·ci·ance \in'süsēəns, aⁿsüsyäⁿs\ n : lighthearted indifference —**in·sou·ci·ant** \in'süsēənt, aⁿsüsyäⁿ\ adj

in·spect \in'spekt\ vb : view closely and critically —**in·spec·tion** \-'spekshən\ n —**in·spec·tor** \-tər\ n

in·spire \in'spī(ə)r\ vb -**spired**; -**spir·ing** 1 : inhale 2 : influence by example 3 : bring about 4 : stir to action —**in·spi·ra·tion** \ˌinspə'rāshən\ n —**in·spi·ra·tion·al** \-'rāsh(ə)nəl\ adj —**in·spir·er** n

in·stall, in·stal \in'stȯl\ vb -**stalled**; -**stall·ing** 1 : induct into office 2 : set up for use —**in·stal·la·tion** \ˌin.ˌstəˈlāshən\ n

in·stall·ment \in'stȯlmənt\ n : partial payment

in·stance \'instəns\ n 1 : request or instigation 2 : example

in·stant \'instənt\ n : moment ~ adj 1 : immediate 2 : ready to mix —**in·stan·ta·neous** \,instən'tānēəs\ adj —**in·stan·ta·neous·ly** adv —**in·stant·ly** adv

in·stead \in'sted\ adv : as a substitute or alternative

instead of \in,stedə(v), -,stid-\ prep : as a substitute for or alternative to

in·step \'in,step\ n : part of the foot in front of the ankle

in·sti·gate \'instə,gāt\ vb -gat·ed; -gat·ing : incite —**in·sti·ga·tion** \,instə'gāshən\ n —**in·sti·ga·tor** \'instə,gātər\ n

in·still \in'stil\ vb -stilled; -still·ing : impart gradually

in·stinct \'in,stiŋkt\ n 1 : natural talent 2 : natural inherited or subconsciously motivated behavior —**in·stinc·tive** \in'stiŋktiv\ adj —**in·stinc·tive·ly** adv

in·sti·tute \'instə,t(y)üt\ vb -tut·ed; -tut·ing 1 : establish 2 : start ~ n 1 : organization promoting a cause 2 : school

in·sti·tu·tion \,instə't(y)üshən\ n 1 : act of instituting 2 : custom 3 : corporation or society of a public character —**in·sti·tu·tion·al** \-'t(y)üsh(ə)nəl\ adj —**in·sti·tu·tion·al·ize** \-,īz\ vb —**in·sti·tu·tion·al·ly** \-ē\ adv

in·struct \in'strəkt\ vb : teach —**in·struc·tion** \in'strəkshən\ n —**in·struc·tion·al** \-sh(ə)nəl\ adj —**in·struc·tive** \in'strəktiv\ adj —**in·struc·tor** \in'strəktər\ n —**in·struc·tor·ship** n

in·stru·ment \'instrəmənt\ n 1 : means 2 : implement 3 : something that produces music 4 : legal document 5 : device for controlling or regulating something —**in·stru·men·tal** \,instrə'mentəl\ adj —**in·stru·men·tal·ist** \-əst\ n —**in·stru·men·tal·i·ty** \,instrəmən'talətē, -,men-\ n —**in·stru·men·ta·tion** \,instrəmən'tāshən, -,men-\ n

in·sub·or·di·nate \,insə'bordnət, -ən\ adj : not obeying —**in·sub·or·di·na·tion** \-,bórd'nā'āshən\ n

in·suf·fer·able \(')in'səf(ə)rəbəl\ adj : unbearable —**in·suf·fer·ably** \-blē\ adv

in·su·lar \'ins(y)ələr, 'inshələr\ adj 1 : relating to an island 2 : isolated 3 : narrow-minded —**in·su·lar·i·ty** \,ins(y)ə'larətē, ,inshə'lar-\ n

in·su·late \'insə,lāt\ vb -lat·ed; -lat·ing : protect from heat loss or electricity —**in·su·la·tion** \,insə'lāshən\ n —**in·su·la·tor** \'insə,lātər\ n

in·su·lin \'ins(ə)lən\ n : hormone used by diabetics

in·sult \in'səlt\ vb : treat with contempt ~ \'in,səlt\ n : insulting act or remark —**in·sult·ing·ly** \-iŋlē\ adv

in·su·per·able \in'süp(ə)rəbəl\ adj : too difficult —**in·su·per·ably** \-blē\ adv

in·sure \in'shùr\ vb 1 : guarantee against loss 2 : make certain —**in·sur·able** \-əbəl\ adj —**in·sur·ance** \-əns\ n —**in·sured** \in'shùrd\ n —**in·sur·er** n

in·sur·gent \in'sərjənt\ n : rebel —**in·sur·gence** \-jəns\ n —**in·sur·gen·cy** \-jənsē\ n —**in·sur·gent** adj

in·sur·mount·able \,insər'maúntəbəl\ adj : too great to be overcome —**in·sur·mount·ably** \-blē\ adv

in·sur·rec·tion \,insə'rekshən\ n : revolution —**in·sur·rec·tion·ist** n

in·tact \in'takt\ adj : undamaged

in·take \'in,tāk\ n 1 : opening through which something enters 2 : act of taking in 3 : amount taken in

in·te·ger \'intijər\ n : number that is not a fraction and does not include a fraction

in·te·gral \'intigrəl\ adj : essential

in·te·grate \'intə,grāt\ vb -grat·ed; -grat·ing 1 : unite 2 : end segregation of or at —**in·te·gra·tion** \,intə'grāshən\ n

in·teg·ri·ty \in'tegrətē\ n 1 : soundness 2 : adherence to a code of values 3 : completeness

in·tel·lect \'intəl,ekt\ n : power of knowing or thinking —**in·tel·lec·tu·al** \,intəl'ekch(əw)əl\ adj or n —**in·tel·lec·tu·al·ism** \-,cha(wə),lizəm\ n —**in·tel·lec·tu·al·ly** adv

in·tel·li·gence \in'teləjəns\ n 1 : ability to learn and understand 2 : information

in·tel·li·gent \in'teləjənt\ adj : having or showing intelligence —**in·tel·li·gent·ly** adv

in·tel·li·gi·ble \in'teləjəbəl\ adj : understandable —**in·tel·li·gi·bil·i·ty** \-,teləjə'bilətē\ n —**in·tel·li·gi·bly** adv

in·tem·per·ance \(')in'temp(ə)rəns\ n : lack of moderation —**in·tem·per·ate** \-p(ə)rət\ adj —**in·tem·per·ate·ness** n

in·tend \in'tend\ vb : have as a purpose

in·tend·ed \-'tendəd\ n : engaged person —**intended** adj in·tense \in'tens\ adj 1 : extreme 2 : deeply felt —in·tense·ly adv —in·ten·si·fi·ca·tion \-ˌtensəfə'kāshən\ n —in·ten·si·fy \-'tensəˌfī\ vb —in·ten·si·ty \in'tensətē\ n —in·ten·sive \in'tensiv\ adj —in·ten·sive·ly adv

¹in·tent \in'tent\ n : purpose —in·ten·tion \-'tenchən\ n —in·ten·tion·al \-'tench(ə)nəl\ adj —in·ten·tion·al·ly adv

²intent adj : concentrated —in·tent·ly adv —in·tent·ness n

in·ter \in'tər\ vb -rr- : bury

inter- prefix : between or among

interagency	interinstitutional
interatomic	interisland
interbank	interlibrary
interborough	intermolecular
interbusiness	intermountain
intercampus	interoceanic
interchurch	interoffice
intercity	interparticle
interclass	interparty
intercoastal	interpersonal
intercollegiate	interplanetary
intercolonial	interpopulation
intercommunal	interprovincial
intercommunity	interpupil
intercompany	interracial
intercontinental	interregional
intercounty	interreligious
intercultural	interscholastic
interdenomina-	intersectional
tional	interstate
interdepart-	interstellar
mental	intersystem
interdivisional	interterm
interelectronic	interterminal
interethnic	intertribal
interfaculty	intertroop
interfamily	intertropical
interfiber	interuniversity
interfraternity	interurban
intergalactic	intervalley
intergang	intervillage
intergovern-	interwar
mental	interzonal
intergroup	interzone
interhemispheric	
interindustry	

in·ter·ac·tion \ˌintər'akshən\ n : mutual influence —in·ter·act \-'act\ vb

in·ter·breed \ˌintər'brēd\ vb -bred \-'bred\; -breed·ing : breed together

in·ter·ca·late \in'tərkəˌlāt\ vb -lat·ed; -lat·ing : insert —in·ter·ca·la·tion \-ˌtərkə'lāshən\ n

in·ter·cede \ˌintər'sēd\ vb -ced·ed; -ced·ing : act to reconcile —in·ter·ces·sion \-'seshən\ n —in·ter·ces·sor

\-'sesər\ n —in·ter·ces·so·ry \-'ses(ə)rē\ adj

in·ter·cept \ˌintər'sept\ vb : interrupt the progress of —intercept \'intərˌsept\ n —in·ter·cep·tion \ˌintər'sepshən\ n —in·ter·cep·tor \-'septər\ n

in·ter·change \ˌintər'chānj\ vb 1 : exchange 2 : change places ~ \'intərˌchānj\ n 1 : exchange 2 : junction of highways —in·ter·change·able \ˌintər'chānjəbəl\ adj

in·ter·course \'intərˌkōrs\ n 1 : relations between persons or nations 2 : copulation

in·ter·de·pen·dent \ˌintərdi'pendənt\ adj : mutually dependent —in·ter·de·pen·dence \-dəns\ n

in·ter·dict \ˌintər'dikt\ vb : prohibit —in·ter·dic·tion \-'dikshən\ n

in·ter·est \'int(ə)rəst, -tə,rest\ n 1 : right 2 : benefit 3 : charge for borrowed money 4 pl : group financially involved in something 5 : readiness to pay special attention 6 : quality that causes interest ~ vb 1 : concern 2 : get the attention of —in·ter·est·ing adj —in·ter·est·ing·ly adv

in·ter·face \'intərˌfās\ n : common boundary —in·ter·fa·cial \ˌintər'fāshəl\ adj

in·ter·fere \ˌintə(r)'fiər\ vb -fered; -fer·ing 1 : collide or be in opposition 2 : try to run the affairs of others —in·ter·fer·ence \-'firəns\ n

in·ter·im \'intərəm\ n : time between —interim adj

in·te·ri·or \in'tirēər\ adj : being on the inside ~ n 1 : inside 2 : inland area

in·ter·ject \ˌintər'jekt\ vb : stick in between

in·ter·jec·tion \-'jekshən\ n : an exclamatory word —in·ter·jec·tion·al·ly \-sh(ə)nəlē\ adv

in·ter·lace \ˌintər'lās\ vb : cross or cause to cross one over another

in·ter·lard \ˌintər'lärd\ vb : intersperse

in·ter·lin·ear \ˌintər'linēər\ adj : between written or printed lines

in·ter·lock \ˌintər'läk\ vb 1 : interlace 2 : connect for mutual effect —in·ter·lock \'intərˌläk\ n

in·ter·lope \ˌintər'lōp\ vb -loped; -lop·ing 1 : encroach 2 : interfere —in·ter·lop·er n

in·ter·lude \'intərˌlüd\ n : intervening period

in·ter·mar·ry \ˌintər'marē\ vb 1 : marry each other 2 : marry within a group —in·ter·mar·riage \-'marij\ n

in·ter·me·di·ary \ˌintər'mēdēˌerē\ n, pl

-ar·ies : agent between individuals or groups —**intermediary** adj

in·ter·me·di·ate \ˌintər'mēdēət\ adj : between extremes —**intermediate** n

in·ter·ment \in'tərmənt\ n : burial

in·ter·mi·na·ble \(ˌ)in'tərmənəbəl\ adj : endless —**in·ter·mi·na·bly** adv

in·ter·min·gle \ˌintər'miŋgəl\ vb : mingle

in·ter·mis·sion \ˌintər'mishən\ n : break in a performance

in·ter·mit·tent \-'mit'nt\ adj : coming at intervals —**in·ter·mit·tent·ly** adv

in·ter·mix \ˌintər'miks\ vb : mix together —**in·ter·mix·ture** \-'mikschər\ n

¹**in·tern** \'in,tərn, in'tərn\ vb : confine —**in·tern·ee** \ˌin,tər'nē\ n —**in·tern·ment** n

²**in·tern, in·terne** \'in,tərn\ n : advanced student (as in medicine) gaining supervised experience ~ vb : act as an intern —**in·tern·ship** n

in·ter·nal \in'tərn°l\ adj 1 : inward 2 : inside of the body 3 : relating to or existing in the mind —**in·ter·nal·ly** adv

in·ter·na·tion·al \ˌintər'nash(ə)nəl\ adj : affecting 2 or more nations ~ n : something having international scope —**in·ter·na·tion·al·ism** \-,izəm\ n —**in·ter·na·tion·al·ize** \-,īz\ vb —**in·ter·na·tion·al·ly** adv

in·ter·nist \'in,tərnəst\ n : specialist in nonsurgical medicine

in·ter·play \'intər,plā\ n : interaction

in·ter·po·late \in'tərpə,lāt\ vb -lat·ed; -lat·ing : insert —**in·ter·po·la·tion** \-,tərpə'lāshən\ n

in·ter·pose \ˌintər'pōz\ vb -posed; -pos·ing 1 : place between 2 : intrude —**in·ter·po·si·tion** \-pə'zishən\ n

in·ter·pret \in'tərprət\ vb : explain the meaning of —**in·ter·pre·ta·tion** \in,tərprə'tāshən\ n —**in·ter·pre·ta·tive** \-'tərprə,tātiv\ adj —**in·ter·pret·er** n —**in·ter·pre·tive** \-'tərprətiv\ adj

in·ter·re·late \ˌintə(r)ri'lāt\ vb : have a mutual relationship —**in·ter·re·lat·ed·ness** \-'lātədnəs\ n —**in·ter·re·la·tion** \-'lāshən\ n —**in·ter·re·la·tion·ship** n

in·ter·ro·gate \in'terə,gāt\ vb -gat·ed; -gat·ing : question —**in·ter·ro·ga·tion** \-,terə'gāshən\ n —**in·ter·rog·a·tive** \ˌintə'rägətiv\ adj or n —**in·ter·ro·ga·tor** \-'terə,gātər\ n —**in·ter·rog·a·to·ry** \ˌintə'rägə,tōrē\ adj

in·ter·rupt \ˌintə'rəpt\ vb : intrude so as to hinder or end continuity —**in·ter·rupt·er** n —**in·ter·rup·tion**

\-'rəpshən\ n —**in·ter·rup·tive** \-'rəptiv\ adj

in·ter·sect \ˌintər'sekt\ vb 1 : cut across or divide 2 : cross —**in·ter·sec·tion** \-'sekshən\ n

in·ter·sperse \ˌintər'spərs\ vb -spersed; -spers·ing : insert at intervals —**in·ter·sper·sion** \-'spərzhən\ n

in·ter·stice \in'tərstəs\ n, pl -stic·es \-stə,sēz, -stəsəz\ : space between —**in·ter·sti·tial** \ˌintər'stishəl\ adj

in·ter·twine \ˌintər'twīn\ vb : twist together

in·ter·val \'intərvəl\ n 1 : time between 2 : space between

in·ter·vene \ˌintər'vēn\ vb -vened; -ven·ing 1 : happen between events 2 : intercede —**in·ter·ven·tion** \-'venchən\ n

in·ter·view \'intər,vyü\ n : a meeting to get information —**interview** vb —**in·ter·view·er** n

in·ter·weave \ˌintər'wēv\ vb -wove \-'wōv\, -wo·ven \-'wōvən\; -weav·ing : weave together —**in·ter·wo·ven** \-'wōvən\ adj

in·tes·tate \in'tes,tāt, -tət\ adj : not leaving a will

in·tes·tine \in'testən\ n : tubular part of the digestive system after the stomach including a long narrow upper part (**small intestine**) followed by a broader shorter lower part (**large intestine**) —**in·tes·ti·nal** \-'ton°l\ adj

in·ti·mate \'intə,māt\ vb -mat·ed; -mat·ing : hint ~ \'intəmət\ adj 1 : very friendly 2 : suggesting privacy 3 : very personal ~ n : close friend —**in·ti·ma·cy** \'intəməsē\ n —**in·ti·mate·ly** adv —**in·ti·ma·tion** \ˌintə'māshən\ n

in·tim·i·date \in'timə,dāt\ vb -dat·ed; -dat·ing : make fearful —**in·tim·i·da·tion** \-,timə'dāshən\ n

in·to \ˌintə, 'intü\ prep 1 : to the inside of 2 : to the condition of 3 : against

in·to·na·tion \ˌintə'nāshən\ n : way of singing or speaking

in·tone \in'tōn\ vb -toned; -ton·ing : chant

in·tox·i·cate \in'täksə,kāt\ vb -cat·ed; -cat·ing : make drunk —**in·tox·i·cant** \-sikənt\ n —**in·tox·i·ca·tion** \-,täksə'kāshən\ n

in·tra·mu·ral \ˌintrə'myürəl\ adj : within a school

in·tran·si·gent \in'transəjənt\ adj : uncompromising —**in·tran·si·gence** \-jəns\ n —**intransigent** n

in·tra·ve·nous \ˌintrə'vēnəs\ adj : by way of the veins —**in·tra·ve·nous·ly** adv

in·trep·id \in'trepəd\ adj : fearless —**in·tre·pid·i·ty** \,intrə'pidətē\ n

in·tri·cate \'intrikət\ adj : very complex and delicate —**in·tri·ca·cy** \-trikəsē\ n —**in·tri·cate·ly** adv

in·trigue \in'trēg\ vb -trigued; -trigu·ing 1 : scheme 2 : arouse curiosity of ~ n : secret scheme —**in·trigu·ing·ly** \-iŋlē\ adv

in·trin·sic \in'trinzik, -sik\ adj : essential 2 : actual —**in·trin·si·cal·ly** \-zik(ə)lē, -si-\ adv

in·tro·duce \,intrə'd(y)üs\ vb -duced; -duc·ing 1 : bring in esp. for the 1st time 2 : cause to be acquainted 3 : bring to notice 4 : put in —**in·tro·duc·tion** \-'dəkshən\ n —**in·tro·duc·to·ry** \-'dəkt(ə)rē\ adj

in·troit \'in,trōət, -,tróit\ n : part of the Mass or music for it

in·tro·spec·tion \,intrə'spekshən\ n : examination of one's own thoughts or feelings —**in·tro·spect** \-'spekt\ vb —**in·tro·spec·tive** \-'spektiv\ adj —**in·tro·spec·tive·ly** adv

in·tro·vert \'intrə,vərt\ n : shy or retiring person —**in·tro·ver·sion** \,intrə'vərzhən\ n —**introvert** —**in·tro·vert·ed** \'intrə,vərtəd\ adj

in·trude \in'trüd\ vb -trud·ed; -trud·ing 1 : thrust in 2 : encroach —**in·trud·er** n —**in·tru·sion** \-'trüzhən\ n —**in·tru·sive** \-'trüsiv\ adj —**in·tru·sive·ness** n

in·tu·ition \,int(y)ü'ishən\ n : quick and ready insight —**in·tu·it** \in't(y)üət\ vb —**in·tu·i·tive** \in't(y)üətiv\ adj —**in·tu·i·tive·ly** adv

in·un·date \'inən,dāt\ vb -dat·ed; -dat·ing : flood —**in·un·da·tion** \,inən'dāshən\ n

in·ure \in'(y)ür\ vb -ured; -ur·ing : accustom to accept something undesirable

in·vade \in'vād\ vb -vad·ed; -vad·ing : enter for conquest —**in·vad·er** n —**in·va·sion** \-'vāzhən\ n

¹in·val·id \in'valəd\ adj : not true or legal —**in·va·lid·i·ty** \,invə'lidətē\ n —**in·val·id·ly** adv

²in·va·lid \in'valəd\ adj : sickly ~ n : one chronically ill —**in·va·lid·ism** \-,izəm\ n

in·val·i·date \(')in'valə,dāt\ vb : make invalid

in·val·u·able \(')in'valyə(wə)bəl\ adj : extremely valuable

in·vec·tive \in'vektiv\ n : abusive language —**invective** adj

in·veigh \in'vā\ vb : protest or complain forcefully

in·vei·gle \in'vāgəl, -'vē-\ vb -gled; -gling : win over or get by flattery

in·vent \in'vent\ vb 1 : think up 2 : create for the 1st time —**in·ven·tion** \-'venchən\ n —**in·ven·tive** \-iv\ adj —**in·ven·tive·ness** n —**in·ven·tor** \-'ventər\ n

in·ven·to·ry \'invən,tōrē\ n, pl -ries 1 : list of goods 2 : stock —**inventory** vb

in·verse \(')in'vərs, 'in,vərs\ adj : opposite —**in·verse·ly** adv

in·vert \in'vərt\ vb 1 : turn upside down or inside out 2 : reverse —**in·ver·sion** \-'vərzhən\ n

in·ver·te·brate \(')in'vərtəbrət, -,brāt\ adj : lacking a backbone ~ n : invertebrate animal

in·vest \in'vest\ vb 1 : give power or authority to 2 : endow with a quality 3 : commit money to someone else's use in hope of profit —**in·vest·ment** \-'ves(t)mənt\ n —**in·ves·tor** \-'vestər\ n

in·ves·ti·gate \in'vestə,gāt\ vb -gat·ed; -gat·ing : study closely and systematically —**in·ves·ti·ga·tion** \-,vestə'gāshən\ n —**in·ves·ti·ga·tor** \-'vestə,gātər\ n

in·ves·ti·ture \in'vestə,chúr, -chər\ n : act of establishing in office

in·vet·er·ate \in'vet(ə)rət\ adj : acting out of habit —**in·vet·er·a·cy** \-(ə)rəsē\ n

in·vid·i·ous \in'vidēəs\ adj 1 : detestable 2 : injurious —**in·vid·i·ous·ly** adv

in·vig·o·rate \in'vigə,rāt\ vb -rat·ed; -rat·ing : give life and energy to —**in·vig·o·ra·tion** \-,vigə'rāshən\ n

in·vin·ci·ble \(')in'vinsəbəl\ adj : incapable of being conquered —**in·vin·ci·bil·i·ty** \,in,vinsə'bilətē\ n —**in·vin·ci·bly** \-'vinsəblē\ adv

in·vi·o·la·ble \(')in'vīələbəl\ adj : safe from violation or desecration —**in·vi·o·la·bil·i·ty** \(,)in,vīələ'bilətē\ n

in·vi·o·late \(')in'vīələt\ adj : not violated or profaned

in·vite \in'vīt\ vb -vit·ed; -vit·ing 1 : entice 2 : increase the likelihood of 3 : request the presence or participation of 4 : encourage —**in·vi·ta·tion** \,invə'tāshən\ n —**in·vit·ing** \in'vītiŋ\ adj

in·vo·ca·tion \,invə'kāshən\ n 1 : prayer 2 : incantation

in·voice \'in,vóis\ n : itemized bill for goods shipped ~ vb -voiced; -voic·ing : bill

in·voke \in'vōk\ vb -voked; -vok·ing 1

: call on for help **2** : cite as authority **3** : conjure **4** : carry out

in·volve \in'välv\ vb **-volved; -volv·ing 1** : draw in as a participant **2** : relate closely **3** : require as a necessary part **4** : occupy fully —**in·volve·ment** n

in·volved \-'välvd\ adj : intricate

¹in·ward \'inwərd\ adj : inside

²inward, in·wards \-wərdz\ adv : toward the inside, center, or inner being

in·ward·ly adv **1** : mentally or spiritually **2** : internally **3** : to oneself

io·dide \'īə‚dīd\ n : compound of iodine

io·dine \'īə‚dīn, -ədᵊn\ n : nonmetallic chemical element

io·dize \'īə‚dīz\ vb **-dized; -diz·ing** : treat with iodine or an iodide

ion \'īən, 'ī‚än\ n : electrically charged particle —**ion·ic** \ī'änik\ adj —**ion·iz·able** \'īə‚nīzəbəl\ adj —**ion·iza·tion** \‚īənə'zāshən\ n —**ion·ize** \'īə‚nīz\ vb —**ion·iz·er** \'īə‚nīzər\ n

-ion suffix **1** : act or process **2** : state or condition

ion·o·sphere \ī'änə‚sfiər\ n : layer of the atmosphere with charged particles —**ion·o·spher·ic** \ī‚änə'sfi(ə)rik, -'sfer-\ adj

io·ta \ī'ōtə\ n : small quantity

IOU \‚ī(‚)ō'yü\ n : acknowledgment of a debt

iras·ci·ble \ir'asəbəl, ī'ras-\ adj : marked by hot temper —**iras·ci·bil·i·ty** \-‚asə'bilətē, -‚ras-\ n

irate \ī'rāt\ adj : roused to intense anger —**irate·ly** adv

ire \'ī(ə)r\ n : anger

ir·i·des·cence \‚irə'desᵊns\ n : rainbowlike play of colors —**ir·i·des·cent** \-ᵊnt\ adj

iris \'īrəs\ n, pl **iris·es** or **iri·des** \'īrə‚dēz, 'ir-\ **1** : colored part around the pupil of the eye **2** : plant with long leaves and large showy flowers

irk \'ərk\ vb : make weary, irritated, or bored —**irk·some** \-səm\ adj —**irk·some·ly** adv

iron \'ī(ə)rn\ n **1** : metallic chemical element **2** : something made of metal **3** : heated device for pressing clothes ~ vb : press or smooth out with an iron —**iron·er** n —**iron·ware** n —**iron·work** n —**iron·work·er** n —**iron·works** n pl

iron-clad \-'klad\ adj **1** : sheathed in iron armor **2** : strict or exacting

iron·ing \'ī(ə)rniŋ\ n : clothes to be ironed

iron·wood \-‚wúd\ n : tree or shrub with very hard wood

iro·ny \'īrənē\ n, pl **-nies 1** : use of words to express the opposite of the literal meaning **2** : incongruity between the actual and expected result of events —**iron·ic** \ī'ränik\, **iron·i·cal** \-ikəl\ adj —**iron·i·cal·ly** \-ik(ə)lē\ adv

ir·ra·di·ate \ir'ādē‚āt\ vb **-at·ed; -at·ing** : treat with radiation —**ir·ra·di·a·tion** \-‚ādē'āshən\ n

ir·ra·tio·nal \(')ir'ash(ə)nəl\ adj : incapable of reasoning **2** : not based on reason —**ir·ra·tio·nal·i·ty** \(‚)ir‚ashə'nalətē\ n —**ir·ra·tio·nal·ly** adv

ir·rec·on·cil·able \(‚)ir‚ekən'sīləbəl\ adj : impossible to reconcile —**ir·rec·on·cil·abil·i·ty** \-‚sīlə'bilətē\ n

ir·re·cov·er·able \‚iri'kəv(ə)rəbəl\ adj : not capable of being recovered —**ir·re·cov·er·ably** \-blē\ adv

ir·re·deem·able \‚iri'dēməbəl\ adj : not redeemable

ir·re·duc·ible \‚iri'd(y)üsəbəl\ adj : not reducible —**ir·re·duc·ibly** \-blē\ adv

ir·re·fut·able \‚iri'fyütəbəl, (')ir'(r)e-fyət-\ adj : impossible to refute

ir·reg·u·lar \(')ir'egyələr\ adj : not regular or normal —**irregular** n —**ir·reg·u·lar·i·ty** \(‚)ir‚egyə'larətē\ n —**ir·reg·u·lar·ly** adv

ir·rel·e·vant \ir'eləvənt\ adj : not relevant —**ir·rel·e·vance** \-vəns\ n

ir·re·li·gious \‚iri'lijəs\ adj : not following religious practices

ir·rep·a·ra·ble \(')ir'ep(ə)rəbəl\ adj : impossible to make good, undo, or remedy

ir·re·place·able \‚iri'plāsəbəl\ adj : not replaceable

ir·re·press·ible \-'presəbəl\ adj : impossible to repress or control

ir·re·proach·able \-'prōchəbəl\ adj : blameless

ir·re·sist·ible \-'zistəbəl\ adj : impossible to successfully resist —**ir·re·sist·ibly** \-blē\ adv

ir·res·o·lute \(')ir'ezəlüt\ adj : uncertain —**ir·res·o·lute·ly** adv —**ir·res·o·lu·tion** \-‚ezə'lüshən\ n

ir·re·spec·tive of \‚iri'spektiv-\ prep : without regard to

ir·re·spon·si·ble \‚iri'spänsəbəl\ adj : not responsible —**ir·re·spon·si·bil·i·ty** \-‚spänsə'bilətē\ n —**ir·re·spon·si·bly** adv

ir·re·triev·able \‚iri'trēvəbəl\ adj : not retrievable

ir·rev·er·ence \(')ir'ev(ə)rəns\ n **1** : lack of reverence **2** : irreverent act or utterance —ir·rev·er·ent \-(ə)rənt\ adj

ir·re·vers·ible \,iri'vərsəbəl\ adj : incapable of being reversed

ir·rev·o·ca·ble \('ir'evəkəbəl\ adj : incapable of being revoked —ir·rev·o·ca·bly \-blē\ adv

ir·ri·gate \'irə,gāt\ vb -gat·ed; -gat·ing : supply with water by artificial means —ir·ri·ga·tion \,irə'gāshən\ n

ir·ri·tate \'irə,tāt\ vb -tat·ed; -tat·ing 1 : excite to anger 2 : make sore or inflamed —ir·ri·ta·bil·i·ty \,irə-tə'bilətē\ n —ir·ri·ta·ble \'irətəbəl\ adj —ir·ri·ta·bly \'irətəblē\ adv —ir·ri·tant \'irətənt\ adj or n —ir·ri·tat·ing·ly \,irə'tā-shən\ n

is pres 3d sing of BE

-ish \ish\ adj suffix 1 : characteristic of 2 : somewhat

isin·glass \'īz²n,glas, 'īzin-\ n : gelatin from the air bladders of fish 2 : mica

Is·lam \is'läm, iz-, -'lam\ n : religious faith of Muslims —Is·lam·ic \-ik\ adj

is·land \'īlənd\ n : body of land surrounded by water —is·land·er \'īləndər\ n

isle \'īl\ n : small island

is·let \'īlət\ n : small island

-ism \,izəm\ n suffix 1 : act or practice 2 : characteristic manner 3 : condition 4 : doctrine

iso·late \'īsə,lāt, 'isə-\ vb -lat·ed; -lat·ing : place or keep by itself —iso·la·tion \,īsə'lāshən, ,isə-\ n

iso·met·rics \,īsə'metriks\ n sing or pl : exercise against unmoving resistance —isometric adj

isos·ce·les \ī'säsə,lēz\ adj : having 2 equal sides

iso·tope \'īsə,tōp\ n : any of 2 or more species of atoms of the same chemical element —iso·to·pic \,īsə'täpik, -'tō-\ adj —iso·to·pi·cal·ly \-ik(ə)lē\ adv

is·sue \'ish(,)ü\ vb -sued; -su·ing 1 : go, come, or flow out 2 : descend from a specified ancestor 3 : emanate or result 4 : put forth or distribute officially ~ n 1 : action of issuing 2 : offspring 3 : result 4 : point of controversy 5 : act of giving out or printing 6 : quantity given out or printed —is·su·ance \'ishəwəns\ n —is·su·er n

-ist \əst\ n suffix 1 : one that does 2 : one that plays 3 : one that specializes in 4 : follower of a doctrine

isth·mus \'isməs\ n : narrow strip of land connecting 2 larger portions

it \'it, ət\ pron 1 : that one —used of a lifeless thing or an abstract entity 2 —used as an anticipatory subject or object ~ n : player who tries to catch others (as in a game of tag)

ital·ic \i'talik, i-, ī-\ n : style of type with slanting letters —italic adj —ital·i·ci·za·tion \i,talasə'zāshən, i-, ī-\ n —ital·i·cize \i'talə,sīz, i-, ī-\ vb

itch \'ich\ n 1 : uneasy irritating skin sensation 2 : skin disorder 3 : persistent desire —itch vb —itchy adj

item \'ītəm\ n 1 : particular in a list, account, or series 2 : piece of news —item·iza·tion \,ītəmə'zāshən\ n —item·ize \'ītə,mīz\ vb

itin·er·ant \ī'tinərənt, ə-\ adj : traveling from place to place

itin·er·ary \ī'tinə,rerē, ə-\ n, pl -ar·ies : route or outline of a journey

its \(,)its, əts\ adj : relating to it

it·self \it'self, ət-\ pron : it —used reflexively or for emphasis

-ity \ətē\ n suffix : quality, state, or degree

-ive \iv\ adj suffix : that performs or tends toward an action

ivo·ry \'īv(ə)rē\ n, pl -ries 1 : hard creamy-white material of elephants' tusks 2 : pale yellow color

ivy \'īvē\ n, pl ivies : trailing woody vine with evergreen leaves

-ize \,īz\ vb suffix 1 : cause to be, become, or resemble 2 : subject to an action 3 : treat or combine with 4 : engage in an activity

J

j \'jā\ n, pl j's or js \'jāz\ : 10th letter of the alphabet

jab \'jab\ vb -bb- : thrust quickly or abruptly ~ n : short straight punch

jab·ber \'jabər\ vb : talk rapidly or unintelligibly —jabber n

jack \'jak\ n 1 : mechanical device to raise a heavy body 2 : small flag 3 : small 6-pointed metal object used in a game (jacks) 4 : electrical socket ~ vb 1 : raise with a jack 2 : increase

jack·al \'jakəl, -,ȯl\ n : wild dog smaller than a wolf

jack·ass n : male ass

jack·et \'jakət\ *n* : garment for the upper body —**jack·et·ed** *adj*

jack·ham·mer \'jak,hamər\ *n* : pneumatic tool for drilling

jack·knife \'jak,nīf\ *n* : pocketknife

jack-o'-lan·tern \'jakə,lantərn\ *n* : lantern made of a carved pumpkin

jack·pot \'jak,pät\ *n* : sum of money won

jack·rab·bit \-,rabət\ *n* : large hare of western No. America

jade \'jād\ *n* : usu. green gemstone

jad·ed \'jādəd\ *adj* : dulled or bored by having too much

jag·ged \'jagəd\ *adj* : sharply notched

jag·uar \'jag(yə),wär\ *n* : black-spotted tropical American cat

jai alai \'hī,lī\ *n* : game with a ball propelled by a basket on the hand

jail \'jāl\ *n* : prison ~ *vb* : put in jail —**jail·break** *n* —**jail·er, jail·or** *n*

ja·lo·py \jə'läpē\ *n, pl* -**lopies** : dilapidated automobile

jal·ou·sie \'jaləsē\ *n* : door or window with louvers

jam \'jam\ *vb* -**mm-** 1 : press into a close or tight position 2 : cause to become wedged so as to be unworkable ~ *n* 1 : crowded mass that blocks or impedes 2 : difficult situation 3 : thick sweet food made of cooked fruit

jamb \'jam\ *n* : upright framing piece of a door

jam·bo·ree \,jambə'rē\ *n* : large festive gathering

jan·gle \'jaŋgəl\ *vb* -**gled; -gling** : make a harsh ringing sound —**jangle** *n*

jan·i·tor \'janətər\ *n* : person who has the care of a building —**jan·i·to·ri·al** \,janə'tōrēəl\ *adj*

Jan·u·ary \'janyə,werē\ *n* : 1st month of the year having 31 days

¹jar \'jär\ *vb* -**rr-** 1 : have a harsh or disagreeable effect 2 : vibrate or shake ~ *n* 1 : jolt 2 : painful effect

²jar *n* : broad-mouthed container

jar·gon \'järgən, -,gän\ *n* : special vocabulary of a group

jas·mine \'jazmən\ *n* : climbing shrub with fragrant flowers

jas·per \'jaspər\ *n* : red, yellow, or brown opaque quartz

jaun·dice \'jȯndəs\ *n* : yellowish discoloration of skin, tissues, and body fluids

jaun·diced \-dəst\ *adj* : exhibiting envy or hostility

jaunt \'jȯnt\ *n* : short pleasure trip

jaun·ty \'jȯntē\ *adj* -**ti·er; -est** : lively in manner or appearance —**jaun·ti·ly** \'jȯntᵊlē\ *adv* —**jaun·ti·ness** *n*

jav·e·lin \'jav(ə)lən\ *n* : light spear

jaw \'jȯ\ *n* 1 : either of the bony or cartilaginous structures that support the mouth 2 : one of 2 movable parts for holding or crushing ~ *vb* : talk indignantly or at length —**jaw·bone** \-,bōn, -,bōn\ *n* —**jawed** \'jȯd\ *adj*

jay \'jā\ *n* : noisy brightly colored bird

jay·bird *n* : jay

jay·walk *vb* : cross a street carelessly —**jay·walk·er** *n*

jazz \'jaz\ *vb* : enliven ~ *n* 1 : kind of American music involving improvisation 2 : empty talk —**jazzy** *adj*

jeal·ous \'jeləs\ *adj* : suspicious of a rival or of one believed to enjoy an advantage —**jeal·ous·ly** *adv* —**jeal·ou·sy** \-əsē\ *n*

jeans \'jēnz\ *n pl* : pants made of durable twilled cotton cloth

jeep \'jēp\ *n* : 4-wheel army vehicle

jeer \'jiər\ *vb* 1 : speak or cry out in derision 2 : ridicule ~ *n* : taunt

Je·ho·vah \ji'hōvə\ *n* : God

je·june \ji'jün\ *adj* : dull or childish

jell \'jel\ *vb* 1 : come to the consistency of jelly 2 : take shape

jel·ly \'jelē\ *n, pl* -**lies** : a substance (as food) with a soft somewhat elastic consistency —**jelly** *vb*

jel·ly·fish *n* : sea animal with a saucer-shaped jellylike body

jen·ny \'jenē\ *n, pl* -**nies** : female bird or donkey

jeop·ar·dy \'jepərdē\ *n* : exposure to death, loss, or injury —**jeop·ar·dize** \-ər,dīz\ *vb* —**jeop·ar·dous** \-ərdəs\ *adj*

jerk \'jərk\ *vb* 1 : give a sharp quick push, pull, or twist 2 : move with abrupt motions ~ *n* 1 : short quick pull or twist 2 : stupid or foolish person —**jerk·i·ly** *adv* —**jerky** *adj*

jer·kin \'jərkən\ *n* : close-fitting sleeveless jacket

jer·ry-built \'jerē,bilt\ *adj* : built cheaply and flimsily

jer·sey \'jərzē\ *n, pl* -**seys** 1 : plain knit fabric 2 : knitted shirt

jest \'jest\ *n* : witty remark —**jest** *vb*

jest·er \'jestər\ *n* : one employed to entertain a court

¹jet \'jet\ *n* : velvet-black coal used for jewelry

²jet *vb* -**tt-** 1 : spout or emit in a stream 2 : travel by jet ~ *n* 1 : forceful rush of fluid through a narrow opening 2 : jet-propelled airplane

jet-propelled *adj* : driven by an engine (**jet engine**) that produces propulsion (**jet propulsion**) by the rearward discharge of a jet of fluid

jet·sam \'jetsəm\ *n* : jettisoned goods

jet·ti·son \'jetəsən\ *vb* **1** : throw (goods) overboard for safety —**jettison** *n*

jet·ty \'jetē\ *n, pl* **-ties** : pier or wharf

Jew \'jü\ *n* : one whose religion is Judaism —**Jew·ish** *adj*

jew·el \'jüəl\ *n* **1** : ornament of precious metal **2** : gem ~ *vb* **-eled** *or* **-elled**; **-el·ing** *or* **-el·ling** : adorn with jewels —**jew·el·er** *or* **jew·el·ler** \-ər\ *n* —**jew·el·ry** \-rē\ *n*

jib \'jib\ *n* : triangular sail

jibe \'jīb\ *vb* **jibed; jib·ing** : be in agreement

jif·fy \'jifē\ *n, pl* **-fies** : short time

jig \'jig\ *n* : lively dance ~ *vb* **-gg-** : dance a jig

jig·ger \'jigər\ *n* : measure used in mixing drinks

jig·gle \'jigəl\ *vb* **-gled; -gling** : move with quick little jerks —**jiggle** *n*

jig·saw \'jig,so\ *n* : machine saw with a narrow blade that moves up and down

jilt \'jilt\ *vb* : woman who jilts a man ~ *vb* : drop (one's lover) unfeelingly

jim·my \'jimē\ *n, pl* **-mies** : small crowbar ~ *vb* **-mied; -my·ing** : pry open

jim·son·weed \'jimsən,wēd\ *n* : coarse poisonous weed

jin·gle \'jiŋgəl\ *vb* **-gled; -gling** : make a light tinkling sound ~ *n* **1** : light tinkling sound **2** : short verse or song

jin·go·ism \'jiŋgō,izəm\ *n* : extreme chauvinism or nationalism —**jin·go·ist** \-əst\ *n* —**jin·go·is·tic** \,jiŋgō'istik\ *adj*

jinx \'jiŋks\ *n* : one that brings bad luck —**jinx** *vb*

jit·ney \'jitnē\ *n, pl* **-neys** : small bus

jit·ters \'jitərz\ *n pl* : extreme nervousness —**jit·tery** \-ərē\ *adj*

job \'jäb\ *n* **1** : something that has to be done **2** : regular employment —**job·hold·er** *n* —**job·less** *adj*

job·ber \'jäbər\ *n* : middleman

jock·ey \'jäkē\ *n, pl* **-eys** : one who rides a horse in a race ~ *vb* **-eyed; -ey·ing** : manipulate or maneuver adroitly

jo·cose \jō'kōs\ *adj* : jocular

joc·u·lar \'jäkyələr\ *adj* : marked by jesting —**joc·u·lar·i·ty** \,jäkyə'larətē\ *n*

jo·cund \'jäkənd\ *adj* : full of mirth or gaiety

jodh·purs \'jädpərz\ *n pl* : riding breeches

¹jog \'jäg\ *vb* **-gg-** **1** : give a slight shake or push to **2** : run or ride at a slow pace ~ *n* **1** : slight shake **2** : slow pace —**jog·ger** *n*

²jog *n* : brief abrupt change in direction or line

join \'join\ *vb* **1** : come or bring together **2** : become a member of —**join·er** *n*

joint \'joint\ *n* **1** : point of contact between bones **2** : place where 2 parts connect **3** : often disreputable place ~ *adj* : common to 2 or more —**joint·ed** *adj* —**joint·ly** *adv*

joist \'joist\ *n* : beam supporting a floor or ceiling

joke \'jōk\ *n* : something said or done to provoke laughter ~ *vb* **joked, joking** : make jokes —**jok·er** *n* —**jok·ing·ly** \'jōkiŋlē\ *adv*

jol·li·ty \'jälətē\ *n, pl* **-ties** : gaiety or merriment

jol·ly \'jälē\ *adj* **-li·er, -est** : full of high spirits

jolt \'jōlt\ *vb* **1** : move with a sudden jerky motion **2** : give a jolt to ~ *n* **1** : abrupt jerky blow or movement **2** : sudden shock —**jolt·er** *n*

jon·quil \'jänkwəl\ *n* : narcissus with white or yellow flowers

josh \'jäsh\ *vb* : tease or joke

jos·tle \'jäsəl\ *vb* **-tled; -tling** : push or shove

jot \'jät\ *n* : least bit ~ *vb* **-tt-** : write briefly and hurriedly

jounce \'jauns\ *vb* **jounced; jounc·ing** : jolt —**jounce** *n*

jour·nal \'jərn⁰l\ *n* **1** : brief account of daily events **2** : periodical (as a newspaper)

jour·nal·ism \'jərn⁰l,izəm\ *n* : business of reporting or printing news —**jour·nal·ist** \-əst\ *n* —**jour·nal·is·tic** \,jərn⁰l'istik\ *adj*

jour·ney \'jərnē\ *n, pl* **-neys** : a going from one place to another ~ *vb* **-neyed; -ney·ing** : make a journey

jour·ney·man \-mən\ *n* : worker who has learned a trade and works for another person

joust \'jaust\ *n* : combat on horseback between 2 knights with lances —**joust** *vb*

jo·vial \'jōvēəl\ *adj* : marked by good humor —**jo·vi·al·i·ty** \,jōvē'alətē\ *n* —**jo·vi·al·ly** \'jōvēəlē\ *adv*

¹jowl \'jaul\ *n* **1** : lower jaw **2** : cheek

²jowl *n* : loose flesh about the lower jaw or throat

joy \'joi\ *n* **1** : feeling of happiness **2** : source of happiness —**joy** *vb* —**joy·ful** *adj* —**joy·ful·ly** *adv* —**joy·less** *adj*

—**joy·ous** \'jóiəs\ *adj* —**joy·ous·ly** *adv* —**joy·ous·ness** *n*

joy·ride *n* : reckless ride for pleasure —**joy·rid·er** *n* —**joy·rid·ing** *n*

ju·bi·lant \'jübələnt\ *adj* : expressing great joy —**ju·bi·lant·ly** *adv* —**ju·bi·la·tion** \,jübə'lāshən\ *n*

ju·bi·lee \'jübə,lē\ *n* 1 : 50th anniversary 2 : season or occasion of celebration

Ju·da·ism \'jüdə,izəm\ *n* : religion developed among the ancient Hebrews —**Ju·da·ic** \ju'dāik\ *adj*

judge \'jəj\ *vb* **judged; judg·ing** 1 : form an opinion 2 : decide as a judge ~ *n* 1 : public official authorized to decide questions brought before a court 2 : one who gives an authoritative opinion —**judge·ship** *n*

judg·ment, judge·ment \'jəjmənt\ *n* 1 : decision or opinion after judging 2 : capacity for judging

ju·di·ca·ture \'jüdikə,chúr\ *n* : administration of justice

ju·di·cial \ju'dishəl\ *adj* : relating to judicature or the judiciary —**ju·di·cial·ly** *adv*

ju·di·cia·ry \ju'dishē,erē, -'dishərē\ *n* : system of courts of law or the judges of them —**judiciary** *adj*

ju·di·cious \ju'dishəs\ *adj* : having or characterized by sound judgment —**ju·di·cious·ly** *adv* —**ju·di·cious·ness** *n*

ju·do \'jüdō\ *n* : form of wrestling —**judo·ist** *n*

jug \'jəg\ *n* : large deep container with a narrow mouth and a handle

jug·ger·naut \'jəgər,nót\ *n* : massive inexorable force or object

jug·gle \'jəgəl\ *vb* **-gled; -gling** \-(ə)liŋ\ 1 : keep several objects in motion in the air at the same time 2 : manipulate for an often tricky purpose —**jug·gler** \'jəglər\ *n*

jug·u·lar \'jəgyələr\ *adj* : in or on the throat or neck

juice \'jüs\ *n* 1 : extractable fluid contents of cells or tissues 2 : electricity —**juic·er** *n* —**juic·i·ly** \'jüsəlē\ *adv* —**juic·i·ness** \-sēnəs\ *n* —**juicy** \'jüsē\ *adj*

ju·jube \'jü,jüb, 'jüjú,bē\ *n* : gummy candy

juke·box \'jük,bäks\ *n* : coin-operated record player

ju·lep \'jüləp\ *n* : mint-flavored bourbon drink

Ju·ly \ju'lī\ *n* : 7th month of the year having 31 days

jum·ble \'jəmbəl\ *vb* **-bled; -bling** : mix in a disorderly mass —**jumble** *n*

jum·bo \'jəmbō\ *n, pl* **-bos** : very large version —**jumbo** *adj*

jump \'jəmp\ *vb* 1 : rise into or through the air esp. by muscular effort 2 : pass over 3 : give a start 4 : rise or increase sharply ~ *n* 1 : a jumping 2 : sharp sudden increase 3 : initial advantage

¹jump·er \'jəmpər\ *n* : one that jumps

²jumper *n* : sleeveless one-piece dress

jumpy \'jəmpē\ *adj* **jump·i·er; -est** : nervous or jittery

junc·tion \'jəŋkshən\ *n* 1 : a joining 2 : place or point of meeting

junc·ture \'jəŋkchər\ *n* 1 : joint or connection 2 : critical time or state of affairs

June \'jün\ *n* : 6th month of the year having 30 days

jun·gle \'jəŋgəl\ *n* : thick tangled mass of tropical vegetation

ju·nior \'jünyər\ *n* : person who is younger or of lower rank than another 2 : student in the next-to-last year ~ *adj* : younger or lower in rank

ju·ni·per \'jünəpər\ *n* : evergreen shrub or tree

¹junk \'jəŋk\ *n* 1 : discarded articles 2 : shoddy product ~ *vb* : discard or scrap —**junky** *adj*

²junk *n* : flat-bottomed ship of Chinese waters

jun·ket \'jəŋkət\ *n* : trip made by an official at public expense

jun·ta \'hún·tə, 'jən·tə, 'hən·tə\ *n* : group of persons controlling a government

ju·ris·dic·tion \,júrəs'dikshən\ *n* 1 : right or authority to interpret and apply the law 2 : limits within which authority may be exercised —**ju·ris·dic·tion·al** \-sh(ə)nəl\ *adj*

ju·ris·pru·dence \-'prüd°ns\ *n* 1 : system of laws 2 : science or philosophy of law

ju·rist \'júrəst\ *n* : lawyer or judge

ju·ror \'júrər\ *n* : member of a jury

ju·ry \'júrē\ *n, pl* **-ries** : body of persons sworn to give a verdict on a matter

just \'jəst\ *adj* 1 : reasonable 2 : correct or proper 3 : morally or legally right 4 : deserved ~ \(,)jəst, (,)jist\ *adv* 1 : exactly 2 : very recently 3 : barely 4 : only —**just·ly** *adv* —**just·ness** *n*

jus·tice \'jəstəs\ *n* 1 : administration of what is just 2 : judge 3 : administration of law 4 : fairness

jus·ti·fy \'jəstə,fī\ *vb* **-fied; -fy·ing**

: prove to be just, right, or reasonable —**jus·ti·fi·able** \-fī-ə-bəl\ *adj* —**jus·ti·fi·ca·tion** \ˌjəstəfə'kāshən\ *n*

jut \'jət\ *vb* -**tt**- : stick out

jute \'jüt\ *n* : strong glossy fiber from a tropical herb

ju·ve·nile \'jüvə,nīl, -vənᵊl\ *adj* : relating to children or young people —*n* : young person

jux·ta·pose \'jəkstə,pōz\ *vb* -**posed**; -**pos·ing** : place side by side —**jux·ta·po·si·tion** \ˌjəkstəpə'zishən\ *n*

K

k \'kā\ *n, pl* **k's** *or* **ks** \'kāz\ : 11th letter of the alphabet

kai·ser \'kīzər\ *n* : German ruler

kale \'kāl\ *n* : curly cabbage

ka·lei·do·scope \kə'līdə,skōp\ *n* : device containing loose bits of colored glass reflecting in many patterns —**ka·lei·do·scop·ic** \-,līdə'skäpik\, **ka·lei·do·scop·i·cal** \-ikal\ *adj* —**ka·lei·do·scop·i·cal·ly** *adv*

kan·ga·roo \,kaŋgə'rü\ *n, pl* -**roos** : large leaping Australian mammal

ka·o·lin \'kāələn\ *n* : fine white clay

kar·at \'karət\ *n* : unit of gold content

ka·ra·te \kə'rätē\ *n* : art of self-defense by crippling kicks and punches

ka·ty·did \'kātē,did\ *n* : large American grasshopper

kay·ak \'kī,ak\ *n* : Eskimo canoe

ka·zoo \kə'zü\ *n, pl* -**zoos** : toy musical instrument

keel \'kēl\ *n* : central lengthwise strip on the bottom of a ship —**keeled** \'kēld\ *adj*

keen \'kēn\ *adj* 1 : sharp 2 : severe 3 : enthusiastic 4 : mentally alert —**keen·ly** *adv* —**keen·ness** \'kēnnəs\ *n*

keep \'kēp\ *vb* **kept** \'kept\; **keep·ing** 1 : perform 2 : guard 3 : maintain 4 : retain in one's possession 5 : detain 6 : continue in good condition 7 : refrain ~ *n* 1 : fortress 2 : means by which one is kept —**keep·er** *n*

keep·ing \'kēpiŋ\ *n* : conformity

keep·sake \'kēp,sāk\ *n* : souvenir

keg \'keg\ *n* : small cask or barrel

kelp \'kelp\ *n* : coarse brown seaweed

ken \'ken\ *n* : range of sight or understanding

ken·nel \'kenᵊl\ *n* : dog shelter —**kennel** *vb*

ker·chief \'kərchəf, -,chēf\ *n* : square of cloth worn as a head covering

ker·nel \'kərnᵊl\ *n* 1 : inner softer part of a seed or nut 2 : whole seed of a cereal 3 : central part

ker·o·sene, ker·o·sine \'kerə,sēn, ,kerə'-, 'kar-, ,kar-\ *n* : thin petroleum oil

ketch·up *var of* CATSUP

ket·tle \'ketᵊl\ *n* : vessel for boiling liquids

ket·tle·drum \-,drum\ *n* : brass or copper drum with a top of animal skin

¹**key** \'kē\ *n* 1 : metal piece to open a lock 2 : explanation 3 : lever pressed by a finger in playing an instrument or operating a machine 4 : leading individual or principle 5 : system of musical tones or pitch ~ *vb* 1 : attune 2 : make nervous ~ *adj* : basic —**key·hole** *n*

²**key** *n* : low island or reef

key·board *n* : arrangement of keys

key·note \-,nōt\ *n* 1 : 1st note of a scale 2 : central fact, idea, or mood ~ *vb* 1 : set the keynote of 2 : deliver the major speech

key·punch *n* : keyboard machine to punch cards —**key·punch** *vb* —**key·punch·er** *n*

key·stone *n* : wedge-shaped piece at the crown of an arch

kha·ki \'kakē, 'käk-\ *n* : light yellowish brown

khan \'kän, 'kan\ *n* : Mongol leader

kib·butz \kib'ùts, -'üts\ *n, pl* -**but·zim** \-,üt'sēm, -,üt-\ : Israeli collective farm or settlement

ki·bitz·er \'kibətsər, kə'bit-\ *n* : one who offers unwanted advice —**kib·itz** \'kibəts\ *vb*

kick \'kik\ *vb* 1 : strike out or hit with the foot 2 : object strongly 3 : recoil ~ *n* 1 : thrust with the foot 2 : recoil of a gun 3 : stimulating effect —**kick·er** *n*

kid \'kid\ *n* 1 : young goat 2 : child ~ *vb* -**dd**- 1 : deceive as a joke 2 : tease —**kid·der** *n* —**kid·ding·ly** *adv* —**kid·dish** \'kidish\ *adj*

kid·nap \'kid,nap\ *vb* -**napped** *or* -**naped** \-,napt\; -**nap·ping** *or* -**nap·ing** : carry a person away by illegal force —**kid·nap·per, kid·nap·er** *n*

kid·ney \'kidnē\ *n, pl* -**neys** : either of a pair of organs that excrete urine

kill \'kil\ *vb* 1 : deprive of life 2 : finish 3 : use up (time) ~ *n* : act of killing —**kill·er** *n*

kiln \'kil(n)\ n : heated enclosure for burning, firing, or drying —**kiln** vb

ki·lo \'kēlō\ n, pl **-los** 1 : kilogram 2 : kilometer

kilo·cy·cle \'kilə,sīkəl\ n : kilohertz

ki·lo·gram \'kēlə,gram, 'kilə-\ n : 1000 grams

ki·lo·hertz \'kilə,hərts, 'kēlə-, -,herts\ n : 1000 hertz

ki·lo·me·ter \kil'ämətər, 'kilə,mēt-\ n : 1000 meters

ki·lo·volt \'kilə,vōlt\ n : 1000 volts

kilo·watt \'kilə,wät\ n : 1000 watts

kilt \'kilt\ n : knee-length pleated skirt

kil·ter \'kiltər\ n : proper condition

ki·mo·no \kə'mōnə\ n, pl **-nos** : loose robe

kin \'kin\ n 1 : one's relatives 2 : kinsman

kind \'kīnd\ n 1 : essential quality 2 : group with common traits 3 : variety ~ adj 1 : of a sympathetic nature 2 : arising from sympathy —**kind-heart·ed** adj —**kind·ness** n

kin·der·gar·ten \'kindər,gärt⁰n\ n : class for young children —**kin·der·gart·ner** \-,gärtnər\ n

kin·dle \'kind⁰l\ vb **-dled; -dling** 1 : set on fire or start burning 2 : stir up

kin·dling \'kind(ə)liŋ, 'kinlən\ n : material for starting a fire

kind·ly \'kīndlē\ adj **-li·er; -est** : of a sympathetic nature ~ adv 1 : sympathetically 2 : courteously —**kind·li·ness** n

kin·dred \'kindrəd\ n 1 : related individuals 2 : kin ~ adj : of a like nature

kin·folk \'kin,fōk, **kinfolks** n pl : kin

king \'kiŋ\ n : male sovereign —**king·dom** \-dəm\ n —**king·less** adj —**king·ly** adj —**king·ship** n

king·fish·er \-,fishər\ n : bright-colored crested bird

kink \'kiŋk\ n 1 : short tight twist or curl 2 : cramp —**kinky** adj

kin·ship n : relationship

kins·man \'kinzmən\ n : male relative

kins·wom·an \-,wùmən\ n : female relative

kip·per \'kipər\ n : dried or smoked fish —**kipper** vb

kiss \'kis\ vb : touch with the lips as a mark of affection —**kiss** n

kit \'kit\ n : set of articles (as tools or parts)

kitch·en \'kichən\ n : room with cooking facilities

kite \'kīt\ n 1 : small hawk 2 : covered framework flown at the end of a string

kith \'kith\ n : familiar friends

kit·ten \'kit⁰n\ n : young cat —**kit·ten·ish** adj

¹**kit·ty** \'kitē\ n, pl **-ties** : kitten

²**kitty**, pl **-ties** : fund or pool (as in a card game)

kit·ty-cor·ner, kit·ty-cor·nered var of CATERCORNER

ki·wi \'kē(,)wē\ n : flightless New Zealand bird

klep·to·ma·nia \,kleptə'mānēə\ n : neurotic impulse to steal —**klep·to·ma·ni·ac** \-nē,ak\ n

knack \'nak\ n 1 : clever way of doing something 2 : natural aptitude

knap·sack \'nap,sak\ n : case for carrying supplies

knave \'nāv\ n : rogue —**knav·ery** \-'nāv(ə)rē\ n —**knav·ish** \'nāvish\ adj

knead \'nēd\ vb 1 : work and press with the hands 2 : massage —**knead·er** n

knee \'nē\ n : joint in the middle part of the leg —**kneed** \'nēd\ adj

knee·cap \'nē,kap\ n : bone forming the front of the knee

kneel \'nēl\ vb **knelt** \'nelt\ or **kneeled; kneel·ing** : fall or rest on the knees

knell \'nel\ n : stroke of a bell

knew past of KNOW

knick·ers \'nikərz\ n pl : pants gathered at the knee

knick-knack \'nik,nak\ n : small decorative object

knife \'nīf\ n, pl **knives** \'nīvz\ : sharp blade with a handle ~ vb **knifed; knif·ing** : stab or cut with a knife

knight \'nīt\ n 1 : mounted warrior of feudal times 2 : man honored by a sovereign ~ vb : make a knight of —**knight·hood** n —**knight·ly** adv

knit \'nit\ vb **knit** or **knit·ted; knit·ting** 1 : link firmly or closely 2 : form a fabric by interlacing yarn or thread ~ n : knitted garment —**knit·ter** n

knob \'näb\ n : rounded protuberance or handle —**knobbed** \'näbd\ adj —**knob·by** \'näbē\ adj

knock \'näk\ vb 1 : strike with a sharp blow 2 : collide 3 : find fault with ~ n : sharp blow —**knock out** vb : make unconscious

knock·er n : device hinged to a door to knock with

knoll \'nōl\ n : small round hill

knot \'nät\ n 1 : interlacing (as of string) that forms a lump 2 : base of a woody branch in the stem 3 : group 4 : one nautical mile per hour ~ vb

-tt- : tie in or with a knot —**knot·ty** adj

know \'nō\ vb **knew** \'n(y)ü\; **known** \'nōn\; **know·ing** 1 : perceive directly or understand 2 : be familiar with —**know·able** adj —**know·er** n

know·ing \'nōiŋ\ adj : shrewdly and keenly alert —**know·ing·ly** adv

knowl·edge \'nälij\ n 1 : understanding gained by experience 2 : range of information —**knowl·edge·able** adj

knuck·le \'nəkəl\ n : rounded knob at a finger joint —**knuck·le·bone** n

ko·ala \kōälə, kə'wäl-\ n : furry Australian animal

kohl·ra·bi \kōl'räbē, -'räb-\ n, pl -bies : cabbage that forms no head

Ko·ran \kə'ran, -'rän\ n : book of writings accepted by Muslims as revelations made to Muhammad by Allah

ko·sher \'kōshər\ adj : ritually fit for use according to Jewish law

kow·tow \kaü'taü, 'kaü,taü\ vb : show excessive deference

kryp·ton \'krip,tän\ n : gaseous chemical element

ku·dos \'k(y)ü,däs, -,dōz\ n : fame and renown

kum·quat \'kəm,kwät\ n : small citrus fruit

L

l \'el\ n, pl **l's** or **ls** \'elz\ : 12th letter of the alphabet

lab \'lab\ n : laboratory

la·bel \'lābəl\ n 1 : identification slip 2 : identifying word or phrase ~ vb -**beled** or -**belled**; -**bel·ing** or -**bel·ling** : put a label on

la·bi·al \'lābēəl\ adj : of or relating to the lips

la·bor \'lābər\ n 1 : physical or mental effort 2 : physical activities of childbirth 3 : task 4 : people who work for wages ~ vb : work esp. with great effort —**la·bor·er** n

lab·o·ra·to·ry \'lab(ə)rə,tōrē\ n, pl -ries : place for experimental testing and analysis

Labor Day n : 1st Monday in September observed as a legal holiday in recognition of the workingman

la·bo·ri·ous \lə'bōrēəs\ adj : requiring great effort —**la·bo·ri·ous·ly** adv

lab·y·rinth \'labə,rinth\ n : maze —**lab·y·rin·thine** \,labə'rinthən\ adj

lace \'lās\ n 1 : cord or string for tying 2 : fine net usu. figured fabric ~ vb **laced**; **lac·ing** 1 : tie 2 : adorn with lace —**lacy** \'lāsē\ adj

lac·er·ate \'lasə,rāt\ vb -**at·ed**; -**at·ing** : tear roughly —**lac·er·a·tion** \,lasə'rāshən\ n

lach·ry·mose \'lakrə,mōs\ adj : tearful

lack \'lak\ vb : be missing or deficient in ~ n : deficiency

lack·a·dai·si·cal \,lakə'dāzikəl\ adj : lacking spirit —**lack·a·dai·si·cal·ly** \-k(ə)lē\ adv

lack·ey \'lakē\ n, pl -**eys** 1 : liveried retainer 2 : toady

lack·lus·ter \'lak,ləstər\ adj : dull

la·con·ic \lə'känik\ adj : sparing of words —**la·con·i·cal·ly** \-ik(ə)lē\ adv

lac·quer \'lakər\ n : glossy surface coating —**lacquer** vb

la·crosse \lə'krós\ n : ball game played with long-handled rackets

lac·tate \'lak,tāt\ vb -**tat·ed**; -**tat·ing** : secrete milk —**lac·ta·tion** \lak'tā-shən\ n

lac·tic \'laktik\ adj : relating to milk

la·cu·na \lə'k(y)ünə\ n, pl -**nae** \-(,)nē\ or -**nas** : blank space or missing part

lad \'lad\ n : boy

lad·der \'ladər\ n : device with steps or rungs for climbing

lad·en \'lād⁰n\ adj : loaded

la·dle \'lād⁰l\ n : spoon with a deep bowl —**ladle** vb

la·dy \'lādē\ n, pl -**dies** 1 : woman of rank or authority 2 : woman

la·dy·bird \'lādē,bərd\ n : ladybug

la·dy·bug \-,bəg\ n : brightly colored beetle

lag \'lag\ vb -**gg-** : fail to keep up ~ n 1 : a falling behind 2 : interval

la·ger \'lägər\ n : beer

lag·gard \'lagərd\ adj : slow ~ n : one that lags —**lag·gard·ly** adv or adj —**lag·gard·ness** n

la·gniappe \'lan,yap\ n : bonus

la·goon \lə'gün\ n : shallow sound, channel, or pond near or connecting with a larger body of water

laid past of LAY

lain past part of LIE

lair \'laər\ n : den

lais·sez-faire \,les,ā'faər\ n : doctrine opposing government interference in business

la·ity \'lāətē\ n : people who are not clergy

lake \'lāk\ n : inland body of water

la·ma \'lämə\ n : Buddhist monk

lamb \'lam\ *n* : young sheep or its flesh used as food

lam·baste, lam·bast \lam'bāst, -'bast\ *vb* 1 : beat 2 : censure

lam·bent \'lambənt\ *adj* : light or bright —**lam·ben·cy** \-bənsē\ *n* —**lam·bent·ly** *adv*

lame \'lām\ *adj* **lam·er; lam·est** 1 : having a limb disabled 2 : weak ~ *vb* **lamed; lam·ing** : make lame —**lame·ly** *adv* —**lame·ness** *n*

la·mé \lä'mā, la-\ *n* : cloth with tinsel threads

lame-brain \'lām,brān\ *n* : fool

la·ment \lə'ment\ *vb* 1 : mourn 2 : express sorrow for ~ *n* : mourning —**lam·en·ta·ble** \'laməntəbəl, lə'mentə-\ *adj* —**lam·en·ta·bly** \-blē\ *adv* —**lam·en·ta·tion** \,lamən'tā-shən\ *n*

lamp \'lamp\ *n* : device for producing light or heat

lam·poon \lam'pün\ *n* : satire —**lampoon** *vb*

lam·prey \'lamprē\ *n, pl* **-preys** : suckling eellike water animal

lance \'lans\ *n* : spear ~ *vb* **lanced; lanc·ing** : pierce or open with a lancet

lance corporal *n* : enlisted man in the marine corps ranking above a private first class and below a corporal

lan·cet \'lansət\ *n* : pointed surgical instrument

land \'land\ *n* 1 : solid part of the surface of the earth 2 : country ~ *vb* 1 : go ashore 2 : catch or gain 3 : touch the ground or a surface —**land·less** *adj*

land·fill *n* : dump

land·hold·er \-,hōldər\ *n* : owner of land —**land·hold·ing** *adj or n*

land·ing \'landiŋ\ *n* 1 : action of one that lands 2 : place for loading passengers and cargo 3 : level part of a staircase

land·locked *adj* : enclosed by land

land·lord *n* : owner of property —**land·la·dy** *n*

land·lub·ber \-,ləbər\ *n* : one with little sea experience

land·mark \'lan(d),märk\ *n* 1 : object that marks a boundary or serves as a guide 2 : event that marks a turning point

: beautify a piece of land (as by decorative planting)

land·slide *n* 1 : slipping down of a mass of earth 2 : overwhelming victory

land·ward \'landwərd\ *adj* : toward the land —**landward** *adv*

lane \'lān\ *n* : narrow way

lan·guage \'laŋgwij\ *n* : words and the methods of combining them for communication

lan·guid \'laŋgwəd\ *adj* 1 : weak 2 : sluggish —**lan·guid·ly** *adv* —**lan·guid·ness** *n*

lan·guish \'laŋgwish\ *vb* : become languid or discouraged

lan·guor \'laŋ(g)ər\ *n* : listless indolence —**lan·guor·ous** *adj* —**lan·guor·ous·ly** *adv*

lank \'laŋk\ *adj* 1 : thin 2 : limp

lanky \'laŋkē\ *adj* **lank·i·er; -est** : tall and thin

lan·o·lin \'lan?lən\ *n* : fatty wax used in ointments

lan·tern \'lantərn\ *n* : enclosed portable light

¹**lap** \'lap\ *n* 1 : front part of the lower trunk and thighs of a seated person 2 : overlapping part 3 : one complete circuit ~ *vb* **-pp-** : fold over or around

²**lap** *vb* **-pp-** 1 : scoop up with the tongue 2 : splash gently

lap·dog *n* : small dog

la·pel \lə'pel\ *n* : fold of the front of a coat

lap·i·dary \'lapə,derē\ *n* : one who cuts and polishes gems ~ *adj* : relating to gems

lapse \'laps\ *n* 1 : slight error 2 : termination of a right or privilege 3 : interval ~ *vb* **lapsed; laps·ing** 1 : slip 2 : subside 3 : cease

lar·board \'lärbərd\ *n* : port side

lar·ce·ny \'lärsnē, -?nē\ *n, pl* **-nies** : theft —**lar·ce·nous** \'lärsnəs, -?nəs\ *adj*

larch \'lärch\ *n* : conical evergreen

lard \'lärd\ *n* : pork fat

lar·der \'lärdər\ *n* : pantry

large \'lärj\ *adj* **larg·er; larg·est** : greater than average —**large·ly** *adv* —**large·ness** *n*

lar·gess, lar·gesse \lär'zhes, -'jes; 'lär,jes\ *n* : liberal giving

lar·i·at \'lareət\ *n* : lasso

¹**lark** \'lärk\ *n* : small songbird

²**lark** *vb or n* : romp

lar·va \'lärvə\ *n, pl* **-vae** \-(,)vē\ : wormlike form of an insect —**lar·val** \-vəl\ *adj*

lar·yn·gi·tis \,larən'jītəs\ *n* : inflammation of the larynx

lar·ynx \'lariŋks\ *n, pl* **-ryn·ges** \lə'rin͟jēz\ *or* **-ynx·es** : upper part of the trachea —**la·ryn·ge·al** \ˌlarən'jēal, lə'rinjēal\ *adj*

las·civ·i·ous \lə'sivēəs\ *adj* : lewd —**las·civ·i·ous·ness** *n*

la·ser \'lāzər\ *n* : device that produces an intense light beam

¹lash \'lash\ *vb* : whip ~ *n* **1** : stroke esp. of a whip **2** : eyelash

²lash *vb* : bind with a rope or cord

lass \'las\ *n* : girl

lass·ie \'lasē\ *n* : girl

las·si·tude \'lasəˌt(y)üd\ *n* **1** : fatigue **2** : listlessness

las·so \'lasō, la'sü\ *n, pl* **-sos** *or* **-soes** : rope with a noose for catching livestock —**lasso** *vb*

¹last \'last\ *vb* : continue in existence or operation

²last *adj* **1** : following all the rest **2** : previous ~ *adv* **1** : at the end **2** : most recently **3** : in conclusion ~ *n* : something that is last —**at last** : finally —**last·ly** *adv*

³last *n* : form on which a shoe is shaped

latch \'lach\ *vb* : catch or get hold ~ *n* : catch that holds a door closed

late \'lāt\ *adj* **lat·er; lat·est 1** : coming or staying after the proper time **2** : advanced toward the end **3** : recently deceased **4** : recent —**late** *adv* —**late·com·er** \-ˌkəmər\ *n* —**late·ly** *adv* —**late·ness** *n*

la·tent \'lāt³nt\ *adj* : potential —**la·ten·cy** \-³nsē\ *n*

lat·er·al \'lat(ə)rəl\ *adj* : on or toward the side —**lat·er·al·ly** *adv*

la·tex \'lāˌteks\ *n, pl* **-ti·ces** \'lātəˌsēz, 'lat-\ *or* **-tex·es** : emulsion of synthetic rubber or plastic

lath \'lath, 'lath\ *n, pl* **laths** *or* **lath** : building material (as a thin strip of wood) used as a base for plaster —**lath·ing** \-iŋ\ *n*

lathe \'lāth\ *n* : machine that rotates material for shaping

lath·er \'lathər\ *n* : foam ~ *vb* : form or spread lather

lat·i·tude \'latəˌt(y)üd\ *n* **1** : distance north or south from the earth's equator **2** : freedom of action

la·trine \lə'trēn\ *n* : toilet

lat·ter \'latər\ *adj* **1** : more recent **2** : being the second of 2 —**lat·ter·ly** *adv*

lat·tice \'latəs\ *n* : framework of crossed strips

laud *vb or n* : praise —**laud·able** *adj* —**laud·ably** *adv*

laugh \'laf, 'läf\ *vb* : show mirth, joy, or scorn with a smile and explosive sound —**laugh** *n* —**laugh·able** *adj* —**laugh·ing·ly** \-iŋlē\ *adv*

laugh·ing·stock \'lafiŋˌstäk, 'läf-\ *n* : object of ridicule

laugh·ter \'laftər, 'läf-\ *n* : action or sound of laughing

¹launch \'lönch\ *vb* **1** : hurl or send off **2** : set afloat **3** : start —**launch** *n* —**launch·er** *n*

²launch *n* : small open boat

laun·der \'löndər\ *vb* : wash or iron fabrics —**laun·der·er** *n* —**laun·dress** \-drəs\ *n* —**laun·dry** \-drē\ *n*

lau·re·ate \'lörēət\ *n* : recipient of honors —**lau·re·ate·ship** *n*

lau·rel \'lörəl\ *n* **1** : small evergreen tree **2** : honor

la·va \'lävə, 'lav-\ *n* : volcanic molten rock

lav·a·to·ry \'lavəˌtōrē\ *n, pl* **-ries** : bathroom

lav·en·der \'lavəndər\ *n* **1** : aromatic plant used for perfume **2** : pale purple

lav·ish \'lavish\ *adj* : expending or expending profusely ~ *vb* : expend or give freely —**lav·ish·ly** *adv*

law \'lö\ *n* **1** : established rule of conduct **2** : body of such rules **3** : principle of construction or procedure **4** : rule stating uniform behavior under uniform conditions **5** : lawyer's profession —**law·break·er** *n* —**law·giv·er** *n* —**law·less** *adj* —**law·less·ly** *adv* —**law·mak·er** *n* —**law·man** \-mən\ *n* —**law·suit** *n*

law·ful \'löfəl\ *adj* : permitted by law —**law·ful·ly** *adv*

lawn \'lön\ *n* : grass-covered yard

law·yer \'löyər\ *n* : legal practitioner

lax \'laks\ *adj* : not strict or tense —**lax·i·ty** \'laksətē\ *n* —**lax·ly** *adv*

lax·a·tive \'laksətiv\ *n* : drug relieving constipation

¹lay \'lā\ *vb* **laid** \'lād\; **lay·ing 1** : put on a surface **2** : produce eggs **3** : bet **4** : impose as a duty or burden **5** : place (as stress) on something **6** : put forward ~ *n* : way something lies or is laid

²lay *past of* LIE

³lay *n* : song

⁴lay *adj* : of the laity —**lay·man** \-mən\ *n* —**lay·wom·an** \-ˌwùmən\ *n*

lay·er \'lāər\ *n* **1** : one that lays **2** : one thickness over or under another

lay·off \'lāˌöf\ *n* : temporary dismissal of a worker

lay·out \'lāˌaut\ *n* **1** : arrangement **2** : outfit

la·zy \'lāzē\ *adj* **-zi·er; -est** : disliking

activity or exertion —**la·zi·ly** \'lāzəlē\ adv —**la·zi·ness** n

lea \'lē, 'lā\ n : meadow

leach \'lēch\ vb : remove (a soluble part) with a solvent

¹lead \'lēd\ vb **led** \'led\; **lead·ing** 1 : direct or run on a course 2 : direct the activity of 3 : go at the head of 4 : bring or tend to a definite result ~ n : position in front —**lead·er** n —**lead·er·less** adj —**lead·er·ship** n

²lead \'led\ n 1 : heavy bluish white chemical element 2 : marking substance in a pencil —**lead·en** \'led²n\ adj

leaf \'lēf\ n, pl **leaves** \'lēvz\ 1 : green outgrowth of a plant stem 2 : leaflike thing ~ vb 1 : produce leaves 2 : turn book pages —**leaf·age** \'lēfij\ n —**leafed** \'lēft\ adj —**leaf·less** adj —**leafy** adj —**leaved** \'lēfd\ adj

leaf·let \'lēflət\ n : pamphlet

¹league \'lēg\ n : unit of distance equal to about 3 miles

²league n : association for a common purpose —**league** vb —**leagu·er** n

leak \'lēk\ vb 1 : enter or escape through a leak 2 : become or make known ~ n : opening that accidentally admits or lets out a substance —**leak·age** \'lēkij\ n —**leaky** adj

¹lean \'lēn\ vb 1 : bend from a vertical position 2 : rely on for support 3 : incline in opinion —**lean** n

²lean adj : lacking in flesh 2 : lacking richness —**lean·ness** \'lēnnəs\ n

leap \'lēp\ vb **leaped** or **leapt** \'lēpt, 'lept\; **leap·ing** : jump —**leap** n

leap year n : 366-day year

learn \'lərn\ vb 1 : gain understanding or skill by study or experience 2 : memorize 3 : find out —**learn·er** n

learn·ed \-əd\ adj : having great learning

learn·ing \-iŋ\ n : knowledge gained by study

lease \'lēs\ n : contract transferring real estate for a term and usu. for rent ~ vb **leased; leas·ing** : grant by or hold under a lease

leash \'lēsh\ n : line to hold an animal —**leash** vb

least \'lēst\ adj 1 : lowest in importance or position 2 : smallest 3 : scantiest ~ n : one that is least ~ adv : in the smallest or lowest degree

leath·er \'lethər\ n : dressed animal skin —**leather** adj —**leath·ern** \-ərn\ adj —**leath·ery** adj

¹leave \'lēv\ vb **left** \'left\; **leav·ing** 1 : bequeath 2 : allow or cause to remain 3 : have as a remainder 4 : go

away ~ n 1 : permission 2 : authorized absence 3 : departure

²leave vb **leaved; leav·ing** : leaf

leav·en \'levən\ n : substance for producing fermentation ~ vb : raise dough with a leaven

leaves pl of LEAF

lech·ery \'lechərē\ n : inordinate indulgence in sex —**lech·er** \'lechər\ n —**lech·er·ous** adj —**lech·er·ous·ness** n

lec·ture \'lekchər\ n : instructive talk —**lec·ture** vb —**lec·tur·er** n —**lec·ture·ship** n

led past of LEAD

ledge \'lej\ n : shelflike projection

led·ger \'lejər\ n : account book

lee \'lē\ n : side sheltered from the wind —**lee** adj

leech \'lēch\ n : segmented freshwater worm

leek \'lēk\ n : onionlike herb

leer \'liər\ n : suggestive look —**leer** vb

leery \'li(ə)rē\ adj : suspicious or wary

lees \'lēz\ n pl : dregs

lee·ward \'lēwərd, 'lüərd\ adj : situated away from the wind ~ n : the lee side —**leeward** adv

lee·way \'lē,wā\ n : allowable margin

¹left \'left\ adj : on the same side of the body as the heart ~ n : left hand —**left** adv

²left past of LEAVE

leg \'leg\ n 1 : limb of an animal that supports the body or something like it 2 : clothing to cover the leg ~ vb -**gg**- : walk or run —**legged** \'legəd\ adj —**leg·less** adj

leg·a·cy \'legəsē\ n, pl -**cies** : inheritance

le·gal \'lēgəl\ adj 1 : relating to law or lawyers 2 : lawful —**le·gal·is·tic** \,lēgə'listik\ adj —**le·gal·i·ty** \li'galətē\ n —**le·gal·ize** \'lēgə,līz\ vb —**le·gal·ly** \-gəlē\ adv

le·gate \'legət\ n : official representative

le·ga·tion \li'gāshən\ n 1 : diplomatic mission 2 : official residence and office of a diplomat

leg·end \'lejənd\ n : story handed down from the past 2 : inscription —**leg·end·ary** \-ən,derē\ adj

leg·er·de·main \,lejərdə'mān\ n : sleight of hand

leg·gings, leg·gins \'legənz, -inz\ n pl : leg coverings

leg·i·ble \'lejəbəl\ adj : capable of being read —**leg·i·bil·i·ty** \,lejə'bilətē\ n —**leg·i·bly** \'lejəblē\ adv le·gion \'lējən\ n 1 : large military force 2 : multitude 3 : association of former servicemen —le·gion·ary \-ẏerē\ n —le·gion·naire \ˌlējən'aər\ n

leg·is·late \'lejəˌslāt\ vb -lat·ed; -lat·ing : enact or bring about with laws —leg·is·la·tion \ˌlejə'slāshən\ n —leg·is·la·tive \'lejəˌslātiv\ adj —leg·is·la·tor \-ər\ n

leg·is·la·ture \'lejəˌslāchər\ n : organization with authority to make laws

le·git·i·mate \li'jitəmət\ adj 1 : lawfully begotten 2 : genuine 3 : conforming with law or accepted standards —le·git·i·ma·cy \-məsē\ n —le·git·i·mate·ly adv

le·gume \'legˌyüm, li'gyüm\ n : plant bearing pods —le·gu·mi·nous \li'gyümənəs\ adj

lei \'lā(ˌē)\ n : necklace of flowers

lei·sure \'lēzhər, 'lezh-, 'lāzh-\ n 1 : free time 2 : comfort 3 : convenience —lei·sure·ly adj

lem·ming \'lemiŋ\ n : short-tailed rodent

lem·on \'lemən\ n : yellow citrus fruit —lem·ony adj

lem·on·ade \ˌlemə'nād\ n : sweetened lemon beverage

lend \'lend\ vb lent \'lent\; lend·ing 1 : give for temporary use 2 : furnish —lend·er n

length \'leŋth\ n 1 : longest dimension 2 : duration in time 3 : piece to be joined to others —length·en \'leŋthən\ vb —length·wise adv or adj —lengthy adj

le·nient \'lēnēənt, -nyənt\ adj : mild and tolerant disposition or effect —le·ni·en·cy \-nēənsē, -nyənsē,\ n —le·ni·ent·ly adv

len·i·ty \'lenətē\ n : leniency

lens \'lenz\ n 1 : curved piece for forming an image in an optical instrument 2 : transparent body in the eye that focuses light rays

Lent \'lent\ n : 40-day period of penitence and fasting from Ash Wednesday to Easter —Lent·en \-ən\ adj

len·til \'lent-ᵊl\ n : Old World legume

le·o·nine \'lēəˌnīn\ adj : like a lion

leop·ard \'lepərd\ n : large tawny black-spotted cat

le·o·tard \'lēəˌtärd\ n : close-fitting garment

lep·er \'lepər\ n : person with leprosy

lep·re·chaun \'leprəˌkän\ n : mischievous Irish elf

lep·ro·sy \'leprəsē\ n : chronic bacterial disease —lep·rous \-rəs\ adj

les·bi·an \'lezbēən\ n : female homosexual —lesbian adj —les·bi·an·ism \-ˌizəm\ n

le·sion \'lēzhən\ n : abnormal area in the body due to injury or disease

less \'les\ adj 1 : fewer 2 : of lower rank, degree, or importance 3 : smaller ~ adv : to a lesser degree ~ n, pl less : smaller portion ~ prep : minus —less·en \-ᵊn\ vb

-less \ləs\ adj suffix 1 : not having 2 : unable to act or be acted on

les·see \le'sē\ n : tenant under a lease

less·er \'lesər\ adj 1 : smaller 2 : inferior

les·son \'lesᵊn\ n 1 : reading or exercise to be studied by a pupil 2 : something learned

les·sor \'lesˌór, le'sòr\ n : one who transfers property by a lease

lest \'lest\ conj : for fear that

¹let \'let\ n : hindrance or obstacle

²let vb let; let·ting 1 : cause to 2 : rent 3 : permit

-let \lət\ n suffix : small one

le·thal \'lēthəl\ adj : deadly —le·thal·ly adv

leth·ar·gy \'lethərjē\ n : state of being lazy or indifferent —le·thar·gic \li'thärjik\ adj

let·ter \'letər\ n 1 : unit of an alphabet 2 : written or printed communication 3 pl : literature or learning 4 : literal meaning ~ vb : mark with letters —let·ter·er n

let·tuce \'letəs\ n : garden plant with crisp leaves

leu·ke·mia \lü'kēmēə\ n : cancerous blood disease —leu·ke·mic \-mik\ adj or n

lev·ee \'levē\ n : embankment to prevent flooding

lev·el \'levəl\ n 1 : device for establishing a flat surface 2 : horizontal surface 3 : position in a scale ~ vb -eled or -elled; -el·ing or -el·ling 1 : make flat or level 2 : aim 3 : raze ~ adj 1 : having a smooth surface 2 : of the same height or rank —lev·el·er n —lev·el·ly adv —lev·el·ness n

le·ver \'levər, 'lē-\ n : bar for prying or dislodging something —le·ver·age \'lev(ə)rij, 'lēv-\ n

le·vi·a·than \li'vīəthən\ n 1 : large sea animal 2 : enormous thing

lev·i·ty \'levətē\ n : unseemly frivolity

levy \'levē\ n, pl lev·ies : imposition or collection of a tax ~ vb lev·ied; levy·ing 1 : impose or collect legally 2 : enlist for military service 3 : wage

lewd \'lüd\ adj 1 : sexually unchaste 2

: salacious —**lewd·ly** *adv* —**lewd·ness**
n

lex·i·cog·ra·phy \ˌleksəˈkägrəfē\ *n*
: dictionary making —**lex·i·cog·ra·pher** \-fər\ *n* —**lex·i·co·graph·i·cal** \-kōˈgrafikəl\ *or* **lex·i·co·graph·ic** \-ik\ *adj*

lex·i·con \ˈleksəˌkän\ *n*, *pl* **-i·ca** \-sikə\ *or* **-icons** : dictionary

li·a·ble \ˈlīəbəl\ *adj* 1 : legally obligated 2 : probable 3 : susceptible —**li·a·bil·i·ty** \ˌlīəˈbilətē\ *n*

li·ai·son \ˈlēəˌzän, lēˈā-\ *n* 1 : close bond 2 : communication between groups

li·ar \ˈlīər\ *n* : one who lies

li·bel \ˈlībəl\ *n* : action, crime, or an instance of injuring a person's reputation esp. by something written ~ *vb* **-beled** *or* **-belled**; **-bel·ing** *or* **-bel·ling** : make or publish a libel —**li·bel·er** *n* —**li·bel·ist** *n* —**li·bel·ous, li·bel·lous** \-bələs\ *adj*

lib·er·al \ˈlib(ə)rəl\ *adj* : not stingy, narrow, or conservative —**liberal** *n* —**lib·er·al·ism** \-ˌizəm\ *n* —**lib·er·al·i·ty** \ˌlibəˈralətē\ *n* —**lib·er·al·ize** \ˈlib(ə)rəˌlīz\ *vb* —**lib·er·al·ly** \-rəlē\ *adv*

lib·er·ate \ˈlibəˌrāt\ *vb* **-at·ed**; **-at·ing** : set free —**lib·er·a·tion** \ˌlibəˈrāshən\ *n* —**lib·er·a·tor** \ˈlibəˌrātər\ *n*

lib·er·tine \ˈlibərˌtēn\ *n* : one who leads a dissolute life

lib·er·ty \ˈlibərtē\ *n*, *pl* **-ties** 1 : quality or state of being free 2 : action going beyond normal limits

li·bi·do \ləˈbēdō, -ˈbid\ *n*, *pl* **-dos** : sexual drive —**li·bid·i·nal** \ləˈbidʰnəl\ *adj* —**li·bid·i·nous** \-əs\ *adj*

li·brary \ˈlīˌbrerē\ *n*, *pl* **-brar·ies** 1 : place where books are kept for use 2 : collection of books —**li·brar·i·an** \līˈbrerēən\ *n*

li·bret·to \ləˈbretō\ *n*, *pl* **-tos** *or* **-ti** \-ē\ : text of an opera —**li·bret·tist** \-əst\ *n*

lice *pl of* LOUSE

li·cense, li·cence \ˈlīs³ns\ *n* 1 : legal permission to engage in some activity 2 : document or tag evidencing a license granted 3 : irresponsible use of freedom —**license** *vb* —**li·cens·ee** \ˌlīs³nˈsē\ *n*

li·cen·tious \līˈsenchəs\ *adj* : disregarding sexual restraints —**li·cen·tious·ly** *adv* —**li·cen·tious·ness** *n*

li·chen \ˈlīkən\ *n* : complex lower plant made up of an alga and a fungus —**li·chen·ous** *adj*

lic·it \ˈlisət\ *adj* : lawful

lick \ˈlik\ *vb* 1 : draw the tongue over 2 : beat ~ *n* 1 : stroke of the tongue 2 : small amount

lic·o·rice \ˈlik(ə)rish, -rəs\ *n* : dried root of a European leguminous plant or candy flavored with an extract from it

lid \ˈlid\ *n* 1 : movable cover 2 : eyelid

¹lie \ˈlī\ *vb* **lay** \ˈlā\; **lain** \ˈlān\; **ly·ing** \ˈlīiŋ\ 1 : be in, rest in, or assume a horizontal position 2 : occupy a certain relative position ~ *n* : position in which something lies

²lie *vb* **lied; ly·ing** \ˈlīiŋ\ : tell a lie ~ *n* : untrue statement

liege \ˈlēj\ *n* : feudal superior or vassal

lien \ˈlēn, ˈlēən\ *n* : legal claim on the property of another

lieu·ten·ant \lüˈtenənt\ *n* 1 : representative 2 : first lieutenant or second lieutenant 3 : commissioned officer in the navy ranking next below a lieutenant commander —**lieu·ten·an·cy** \-ənsē\ *n*

lieutenant colonel *n* : commissioned officer (as in the army) ranking next below a colonel

lieutenant commander *n* : commissioned officer in the navy ranking next below a commander

lieutenant general *n* : commissioned officer (as in the army) ranking next below a general

lieutenant junior grade *n*, *pl* **lieutenants junior grade** : commissioned officer in the navy ranking next below a lieutenant

life \ˈlīf\ *n*, *pl* **lives** \ˈlīvz\ 1 : quality that distinguishes a vital and functional being from a dead body or inanimate matter 2 : physical and mental experiences of an individual 3 : biography 4 : period of existence 5 : way of living 6 : liveliness —**life·less** *adj* —**life·like** *adj*

life·blood *n* : basic source of strength and vitality

life·boat *n* : boat for use in saving lives at sea

life·guard *n* : one employed to safeguard bathers

life·long *adj* : continuing through life

life·sav·ing *n* : art or practice of saving lives —**life·sav·er** \-ˌsāvər\ *n*

life·time *n* : duration of an individual's existence

lift \ˈlift\ *vb* 1 : move upward or cause to move upward 2 : put an end to —**lift** *n*

lift-off \ˈlifˌtȯf\ *n* : vertical takeoff by a rocket

lig·a·ment \\'ligəmənt\ *n* : band of tough tissue that holds bones together

lig·a·ture \\'ligə,chùr, -chər\ *n* : something that binds or ties

¹light \\'līt\ *n* **1** : radiation that makes vision possible **2** : daylight **3** : source of light **4** : public knowledge **5** : aspect **6** : celebrity **7** : flame for lighting ~ *vb* **light·ed** *or* **lit; light·ing** **1** : make or become light **2** : cause to burn —**light·er** *n* —**light·ness** *n* —**light·proof** *adj*

²light *adj* : not heavy, serious, or abundant —**light** *adv* —**light·ly** *adv* —**light·ness** *n*

³light *vb* **light·ed** *or* **lit** \\'lit\; **light·ing** : settle or dismount

light·en \\'lītᵊn\ *vb* **1** : make light or bright **2** : give out flashes of lightning

²lighten *vb* **1** : relieve of a burden **2** : become lighter

light·heart·ed \-'härtəd\ *adj* : GAY —**light·heart·ed·ly** *adv* —**light·heart·ed·ness** *n*

light·house *n* : structure with a powerful light for guiding sailors

light·ning \\'lītniŋ\ *n* : flashing discharge of atmospheric electricity

light-year \\'līt,yiər\ *n* : distance traveled by light in one year equal to about 5.878 trillion miles

lig·nite \\'lig,nīt\ *n* : brownish black soft coal

¹like \\'līk\ *vb* **liked; lik·ing** **1** : enjoy **2** : desire ~ *n* : preference —**lik·able, like·able** \\'līkəbəl\ *adj*

²like *adj* : similar ~ *prep* **1** : similar or similarly to **2** : typical of **3** : such as ~ *n* : counterpart ~ *conj* : as or as if —**like·ness** *n* —**like·wise** *adv*

-like \,līk\ *adj comb form* : resembling, suggesting, or characteristic of

like·li·hood \\'līklē,hùd\ *n* : probability

like·ly \\'līklē\ *adj* **-li·er; -est** **1** : probable **2** : believable ~ *adv* : in all probability

lik·en \\'līkən\ *vb* : compare

lik·ing \\'līkiŋ\ *n* : favorable regard

li·lac \\'līlək, -,lak, -,läk\ *n* : shrub with clusters of fragrant pink, purple, or white flowers

lilt \\'lilt\ *n* : rhythmical swing or flow

lily \\'lilē\ *n, pl* **lil·ies** : tall bulbous herb with funnel-shaped flowers

lima bean \\'līmə-\ *n* : bushy or tall bean grown for its flat edible seed or the seed

limb \\'lim\ *n* **1** : projecting appendage used in moving or grasping **2** : tree branch —**limb·less** *adj*

lim·ber \\'limbər\ *adj* : supple or agile ~ *vb* : make or become limber

lim·bo \\'limbō\ *n, pl* **-bos** : place or state of confinement or oblivion

¹lime \\'līm\ *n* : caustic white oxide of calcium

²lime *n* : small green lemonlike citrus fruit —**lime·ade** \-,ād\ *n*

lime·light *n* : center of public attention

lim·er·ick \\'lim(ə)rik\ *n* : light poem of 5 lines

lime·stone *n* : rock that yields lime when burned

lim·it \\'limət\ *n* **1** : boundary **2** : something that restrains or confines ~ *vb* **1** : set limits on —**lim·i·ta·tion** \,limə'tāshən\ *n* —**lim·it·less** *adj*

lim·ou·sine \\'limə,zēn, ,limə'-\ *n* : large luxurious sedan

limp \\'limp\ *vb* : walk lamely ~ *n* : limping movement or gait ~ *adj* : lacking firmness and body —**limp·ly** *adv* —**limp·ness** *n*

lim·pid \\'limpəd\ *adj* : clear or transparent

lin·den \\'lindən\ *n* : tree with large heart-shaped leaves

¹line \\'līn\ *vb* **lined; lin·ing** : cover the inner surface of —**lin·ing** *n*

²line *n* **1** : cord, rope, or wire **2** : row of something like a row **3** : note **4** : course of action or thought **5** : state of agreement **6** : occupation **7** : limit **8** : transportation system **9** : long narrow mark ~ *vb* **lined; lin·ing** **1** : mark with a line **2** : place in a line **3** : form a line

lin·eage \\'linēij\ *n* : descent from a common ancestor

lin·eal \\'linēəl\ *adj* **1** : linear **2** : in a direct line of ancestry

lin·ea·ments \\'linēəmənts\ *n pl* : features or contours esp. of a face

lin·ear \\'linēər\ *adj* **1** : straight **2** : long and narrow

lin·en \\'linən\ *n* **1** : cloth or thread made of flax **2** : household articles made of cloth

lin·er \\'līnər\ *n* **1** : one that lines **2** : ship or airplane belonging to a line

line·up \\'līn,əp\ *n* **1** : line of persons for inspection or identification **2** : list of players in a game

-ling \liŋ\ *n suffix* **1** : one connected with or having the quality of **2** : young, small, or inferior one

lin·ger \\'liŋgər\ *vb* : be slow to leave or act

lin·ge·rie \,länjə'rā, ,läⁿzhə-, -'rē\ *n* : women's underwear

lin·go \\'liŋgō\ *n, pl* **-goes** : usu. strange language

lin·guist \'liŋgwəst\ *n* **1** : person skilled in speech or languages **2** : student of language —**lin·guis·tic** \liŋ'gwistik\ *adj* —**lin·guis·tics** *n pl*

lin·i·ment \'linəmənt\ *n* : liquid medication rubbed on the skin

link \'liŋk\ *n* **1** : connecting structure (as a ring of a chain) **2** : bond —**link** *vb* —**link·age** \-ij\ *n* —**link·er** *n*

li·no·leum \lə'nōlēəm\ *n* : floor covering with hard surface

lin·seed \'lin,sēd\ *n* : seeds of flax yielding an oil (**linseed oil**)

lint \'lint\ *n* : fine fluff or loose short fibers from fabric

lin·tel \'lint⁹l\ *n* : horizontal piece over a door or window

li·on \'līən\ *n* : large cat of Africa and Asia —**li·on·ess** \-nəs\ *n*

li·on·ize \'līə,nīz\ *vb* **-ized; -iz·ing** : treat as very important —**li·on·iza·tion** \,līənə'zāshən\ *n*

lip \'lip\ *n* **1** : either of the 2 fleshy folds surrounding the mouth **2** : edge of something hollow —**lipped** \'lipt\ *adj* —**lip·read·ing** *n*

lip·stick \'lip,stik\ *n* : stick of cosmetic to color lips

liq·ue·fy \'likwə,fī\ *vb* **-fied; -fy·ing** : reduce to liquid —**liq·ue·fac·tion** \,likwə'fakshən\ *n* —**liq·ue·fi·able** \-'fīəbəl\ *adj* —**liq·ue·fi·er** \-'likwə,fīər\ *n*

li·queur \li'kər\ *n* : sweet or aromatic alcoholic liquor

liq·uid \'likwəd\ *adj* **1** : flowing freely like water **2** : neither solid nor gaseous **3** : of or convertible to cash —**liquid** *n* —**li·quid·i·ty** \lik'widətē\ *n*

liq·ui·date \'likwə,dāt\ *vb* **-dat·ed; -dat·ing** : pay off **2** : dispose of —**liq·ui·da·tion** \,likwə'dāshən\ *n*

li·quor \'likər\ *n* : liquid substance and esp. a distilled alcoholic beverage

lisp \'lisp\ *vb* : pronounce *s* and *z* imperfectly —**lisp** *n*

lis·some \'lisəm\ *adj* : supple or agile

¹list \'list\ *n* : series of names or items —*vb* **1** : make a list of **2** : put on a list

²list *vb* : tilt or lean over —*n* : slant

lis·ten \'lis⁹n\ *vb* **1** : pay attention in order to hear **2** : heed —**lis·ten·er** \'lisnər, -⁹nər\ *n*

list·less \'listləs\ *adj* : having no desire to act —**list·less·ly** *adv* —**list·less·ness** *n*

lit \'lit\ *past of* LIGHT

lit·a·ny \'lit⁹nē\ *n, pl* **-nies** : prayer said as a series of responses to a leader

li·ter \'lētər\ *n* : unit of liquid measure equal to about 1.06 quarts

lit·er·al \'lit(ə)rəl\ *adj* : being exactly as stated —**lit·er·al·ly** *adv*

lit·er·ary \'litə,rerē\ *adj* : relating to literature

lit·er·ate \'lit(ə)rət\ *adj* : able to read and write —**lit·er·a·cy** \'lit(ə)rəsē\ *n*

lit·er·a·ture \'lit(ə)rə,chúr, -chər\ *n* : writings of enduring interest

lithe \'līth, 'lith\ *adj* **1** : supple **2** : graceful —**lithe·some** \-səm\ *adj*

lith·o·graph \'lithə,graf\ *n* : print from drawing on stone —**li·thog·ra·pher** \lith'ägrəfər, 'lithə,grafər\ *n* —**lith·o·graph·ic** \,lithə'grafik\ *adj* —**li·thog·ra·phy** \lith'ägrəfē\ *n*

lit·i·gate \'litə,gāt\ *vb* **-gat·ed; -gat·ing** : carry on a lawsuit —**lit·i·gant** \'litigənt\ *n* —**lit·i·ga·tion** \,litə'gāshən\ *n* —**li·ti·gious** \lə'tijəs, li-\ *adj* —**li·ti·gious·ness** *n*

lit·mus \'litməs\ *n* : coloring matter that turns red in acid solutions and blue in alkaline

lit·ter \'litər\ *n* **1** : animal offspring of one birth **2** : stretcher **3** : rubbish ~ *vb* **1** : give birth to young **2** : strew with litter

lit·tle \'lit⁹l\ *adj* **lit·tler** \'litlər, -⁹lər\ *or* **less** \'les\ *or* **less·er** \'lesər\; **lit·tlest** \'litləst, -⁹ləst\ *or* **least** \'lēst\ **1** : not big **2** : not much **3** : not important ~ *adv* **less** \'les\; **least** \'lēst\ **1** : slightly **2** : not often ~ *n* : small amount —**lit·tle·ness** *n*

lit·ur·gy \'litərjē\ *n, pl* **-gies** : rite of worship —**li·tur·gi·cal** \lə'tərjikəl\ *adj* —**li·tur·gi·cal·ly** \-k(ə)lē\ *adv* —**lit·ur·gist** \'litərjəst\ *n*

liv·able \'livəbəl\ *adj* : suitable for living in or with —**liv·a·bil·i·ty** \,livə'bilətē\ *n*

¹live \'liv\ *vb* **lived; liv·ing 1** : be alive **2** : conduct one's life **3** : subsist **4** : reside

²live \'līv\ *adj* **1** : having life **2** : burning **3** : connected to electric power **4** : not exploded **5** : of continuing interest **6** : involving the actual presence of real people

live·li·hood \'līvlē,húd\ *n* : means of subsistence

live·long \'liv,lóŋ\ *adj* : whole

live·ly \'līvlē\ *adj* **-li·er; -est** : full of life and vigor —**live·li·ness** *n*

liv·en \'līvən\ *vb* : enliven

liv·er \'livər\ *n* : organ that secretes bile —**liv·ered** \'livərd\ *adj*

liv·ery \'liv(ə)rē\ *n, pl* **-er·ies 1** : uniform for household servants **2** : care of horses for pay —**liv·er·ied** \-rēd\ *adj* —**liv·ery·man** \-mən\ *n*

lives *pl of* LIFE

live·stock \'līv‚stäk\ *n* : farm animals

liv·id \'livəd\ *adj* **1** : discolored by bruising **2** : pale **3** : enraged

liv·ing \'livin\ *adj* : having life ~ *n* : livelihood

liz·ard \'lizərd\ *n* : scaly reptile

lla·ma \'lämə\ *n* : So. American mammal related to the camel

lo \'lō\ *interj* —used to call attention

load \'lōd\ *n* **1** : cargo **2** : supported weight **3** : burden ~ *vb* **1** : put a load on **2** : burden **3** : put ammunition in

¹loaf \'lōf\ *n, pl* **loaves** \'lōvz\ : mass of bread

²loaf *vb* : waste time —**loaf·er** *n*

loam \'lōm, 'lüm\ *n* : soil —**loamy** *adj*

loan \'lōn\ *n* **1** : money borrowed at interest **2** : something lent temporarily **3** : permission to use ~ *vb* : lend

loath \'lōth, 'lōth\ *adj* : very reluctant

loathe \'lōth\ *vb* **loathed; loath·ing** : hate

loath·ing \'lōthiŋ\ *n* : extreme disgust

loath·some \'lōthsəm, 'lōth-\ *adj* : repulsive

lob \'läb\ *vb* **-bb-** : throw or hit in a high arc —**lob** *n*

lob·by \'läbē\ *n, pl* **-bies** **1** : public waiting room at the entrance of a building **2** : persons lobbying ~ *vb* **-bied; -by·ing** : try to influence legislators —**lob·by·ist** *n*

lobe \'lōb\ *n* : rounded part —**lo·bar** \'lōbər\ *adj* —**lobed** \'lōbd\ *adj*

lo·bot·o·my \lō'bätəmē\ *n, pl* **-mies** : severance of nerve fibers in the brain

lob·ster \'läbstər\ *n* : marine crustacean with 2 large pincerlike claws

lo·cal \'lōkəl\ *adj* : confined to or serving a limited area —**local** *n* —**lo·cal·ly** *adv*

lo·cale \lō'kal\ *n* : setting for an event

lo·cal·i·ty \lō'kalətē\ *n, pl* **-ties** : particular place

lo·cal·ize \'lōkə‚līz\ *vb* **-ized; -iz·ing** : confine to a definite place —**lo·cal·i·za·tion** \‚lōkələ'zāshən\ *n*

lo·cate \'lō‚kāt, lō'kāt\ *vb* **-cat·ed; -cat·ing** **1** : settle **2** : find a site for **3** : discover the place of —**lo·ca·tion** \lō'kāshən\ *n*

¹lock \'läk\ *n* : tuft or strand of hair

²lock *n* **1** : fastener using a bolt **2** : enclosure in a canal to raise or lower boats ~ *vb* **1** : make fast with a lock **2** : confine **3** : interlock

lock·er \'läkər\ *n* : storage compartment

lock·et \'läkət\ *n* : small case worn on a necklace

lock·jaw *n* : tetanus

lock·out *n* : closing of a plant by an employer during a labor dispute

lock·smith \-‚smith\ *n* : one who makes or repairs locks

lo·co·mo·tion \‚lōkə'mōshən\ *n* : power of moving —**lo·co·mo·tive** \-'mōtiv\ *adj*

lo·co·mo·tive \-'mōtiv\ *n* : vehicle that moves railroad cars

lo·co·weed \'lōkō‚wēd\ *n* : western plant poisonous to livestock

lo·cust \'lōkəst\ *n* **1** : migratory grasshopper **2** : cicada **3** : tree with hard wood

lo·cu·tion \lō'kyüshən\ *n* : way of saying something

lode \'lōd\ *n* : ore deposit

lode·stone *n* : magnetic rock

lodge \'läj\ *vb* **lodged; lodg·ing** **1** : provide quarters for **2** : come to rest **3** : file ~ *n* : special house (as for hunters) **2** : animal's den **3** : branch of a fraternal organization —**lodg·er** \'läjər\ *n* —**lodg·ing** *n* —**lodg·ment, lodge·ment** \-mənt\ *n*

loft \'loft\ *n* **1** : attic **2** : upper floor (as of a warehouse)

lofty \'loftē\ *adj* **loft·i·er; -est** : tall or high —**loft·i·ly** *adv* —**loft·i·ness** *n*

¹log \'lȯg, 'läg\ *n* **1** : unshaped timber **2** : daily record of a ship's or plane's progress ~ *vb* **-gg-** **1** : cut trees for lumber **2** : enter in a log

²log *n* : logarithm

log·a·rithm \'lȯgə‚rithəm, 'läg-\ *n* : exponent to which a base number is raised to produce a given number —**log·a·rith·mic** \‚lȯgə'rithmik, ‚läg-\ *adj*

loge \'lōzh\ *n* : box in a theater

log·ger \-ər\ *n* : one engaged in logging

log·ger·head \'lȯgər‚hed, 'läg-\ *n* : large Atlantic sea turtle —**at loggerheads** : in disagreement

log·ic \'läjik\ *n* **1** : science of reasoning **2** : sound reasoning —**log·i·cal** \-ikəl\ *adj* —**log·i·cal·ly** *adv* —**lo·gi·cian** \lō'jishən\ *n*

lo·gis·tics \lō'jistiks\ *n sing or pl* : procurement and movement of people and supplies —**lo·gis·tic** *adj*

logo \'lōgō, 'lȯg-, 'läg-\ *n, pl* **log·os** \-ōz\ : advertising symbol

loin \'lȯin\ *n* **1** : part of the body on each side of the spine between the hip and lower ribs **2** *pl* : abdominal regions

loi·ter \'lȯitər\ *vb* : remain around a place idly —**loi·ter·er** *n*

loll \\'läl\\ *vb* : lounge

lol·li·pop, lol·ly·pop \\'läli,päp\\ *n* : hard candy on a stick

lone \\'lōn\\ *adj* **1** : alone or isolated **2** : only —**lone·li·ness** *n* —**lone·ly** —**lon·er** \\'lōnər\\ *n*

lone·some \\-səm\\ *adj* : sad from lack of company —**lone·some·ly** *adv* —**lone·some·ness** *n*

long \\'lòng\\ *adj* **lon·ger** \\'lòngər\\; **lon·gest** \\'lòngəst\\ **1** : extending far or for a considerable time **2** : having a specified length **3** : tedious **4** : well supplied—used with *on* ~ *adv* : for a long time ~ *n* : long period ~ *vb* : feel a strong desire —**long·ing** \\lòniŋ\\ *n* —**long·ing·ly** *adv*

lon·gev·i·ty \\län'jevətē\\ *n* : long life

long·hand *n* : handwriting

long·horn *n* : cattle with long horns

lon·gi·tude \\'länjə,t(y)üd\\ *n* : angular distance east or west from a meridian

lon·gi·tu·di·nal \\,länjə't(y)üdnəl, -ǝnəl\\ *adj* : lengthwise —**lon·gi·tu·di·nal·ly** *adv*

long·shore·man \\'lòng'shòrmən\\ *n* : one who loads and unloads ships

look \\'lük\\ *vb* **1** : see **2** : seem **3** : direct one's attention **4** : face ~ *n* **1** : movement of the eyes to see something **2** : appearance of the face **3** : aspect —**look after** : take care of —**look for 1** : expect **2** : search for

look·out *n* **1** : one who watches **2** : careful watch

¹loom \\'lüm\\ *n* : frame or machine for weaving

²loom *vb* : appear large and indistinct or impressive

loon \\'lün\\ *n* : black-and-white diving bird

loo·ny, loo·ney \\'lünē\\ *adj* **-ni·er; -est** : crazy

loop \\'lüp\\ *n* **1** : doubling of a line that leaves an opening **2** : something like a loop —**loop** *vb*

loop·hole \\'lüp,hōl\\ *n* : means of evading

loose \\'lüs\\ *adj* **loos·er; -est 1** : not fixed tight **2** : not restrained **3** : not dense **4** : slack **5** : not exact ~ *adv* **loosed; loos·ing 1** : release **2** : untie or relax —**loose** *adv* —**loose·ly** *adv* —**loos·en** \\'lüs³n\\ *vb* —**loose·ness** *n*

loot \\'lüt\\ *n or vb* : plunder —**loot·er** *n*

lop \\'läp\\ *vb* **-pp-** : cut off

lope \\'lōp\\ *n* : bounding gait —**lope** *vb*

lop·sid·ed \\'läp'sīdəd\\ *adj* **1** : leaning to one side **2** : not symmetrical —**lop·sid·ed·ly** *adv* —**lop·sid·ed·ness** *n*

lo·qua·cious \\lō'kwāshəs\\ *adj* : very talkative —**lo·quac·i·ty** \\-'kwasətē\\ *n*

lord \\'lòrd\\ *n* **1** : one with authority over others **2** : British nobleman

lord·ly \\-lē\\ *adj* **-li·er; -est** : haughty

lord·ship \\-,ship\\ *n* : rank of a lord

Lord's Supper *n* : Communion

lore \\'lōr\\ *n* : traditional knowledge

lose \\'lüz\\ *vb* **lost** \\'lòst\\; **los·ing** \\'lüziŋ\\ **1** : have pass from one's possession **2** : be deprived of **3** : waste **4** : be defeated in **5** : fail to keep to or hold —**los·er** *n*

loss \\'lòs\\ *n* **1** : something lost **2** *pl* : killed, wounded, or captured soldiers **3** : failure to win

lost \\'lòst\\ *adj* **1** : not used, won, or claimed **2** : unable to find the way

lot \\'lät\\ *n* **1** : object used in deciding something by chance **2** : share **3** : fate **4** : plot of land **5** : much

loth \\'lōth, 'lōth\\ *var of* LOATH

lo·tion \\'lōshən\\ *n* : liquid to rub on the skin

lot·tery \\'lätərē\\ *n, pl* **-ter·ies** : drawing of lots with prizes going to winners

lo·tus \\'lōtəs\\ *n* **1** : legendary fruit that causes forgetfulness **2** : water lily

loud \\'laüd\\ *adj* **1** : high in volume of sound **2** : noisy **3** : obtrusive in color or pattern —**loud** *adv* —**loud·ly** *adv* —**loud·ness** *n*

loud·speak·er *n* : device that amplifies sound

lounge \\'laünj\\ *vb* **lounged; loung·ing** : act or move lazily ~ *n* : room with comfortable furniture

lour \\'laü(ə)r\\ *var of* LOWER

louse \\'laüs\\ *n, pl* **lice** \\'līs\\ : parasitic insect

lousy \\'laüzē\\ *adj* **lous·i·er; -est 1** : infested with lice **2** : not good —**lous·i·ly** *adv* —**lous·i·ness** *n*

lout \\'laüt\\ *n* : stupid awkward person —**lout·ish** *adj* —**lout·ish·ly** *adv*

lou·ver, lou·vre \\'lüvər\\ *n* : opening having parallel slanted slats for ventilation or such a slat

love \\'ləv\\ *n* **1** : strong affection **2** : warm attachment **3** : beloved person ~ *vb* **loved; lov·ing 1** : feel affection for **2** : enjoy greatly —**lov·able** \\-əbəl\\ *adj* —**love·less** *adj* —**lov·er** *n* —**lov·ing·ly** *adv*

love·lorn \\-,lòrn\\ *adj* : deprived of love or of a lover

love·ly \\'ləvlē\\ *adj* **-li·er; -est** : beautiful —**love·li·ness** *n*

¹low \\'lō\\ *vb or n* : moo

²low *adj* **low·er; low·est 1** : not high or tall **2** : below the normal level **3** : not loud **4** : humble **5** : sad **6** : less usual **7** : falling short of a standard **8** : unfavorable ~ *n* **1** : something low **2** : automobile gear giving the slowest speed —**low** *adv* —**low-ness** *n*

low-brow \'lō,braù\ *n* : person without intellectual interests or culture

¹**low-er** \'laù(ə)r\ *vb* **1** : scowl **2** : become dark and threatening

²**low-er** \'lō(ə)r\ *adj* : relatively low (as in rank)

³**low-er** \'lō(ə)r\ *vb* **1** : drop **2** : let descend **3** : reduce in value

low-land \'lōlənd, -,land\ *n* : low flat country

low-ly \'lōlē\ *adj* **-li-er; -est** : humble —**low-li-ness** *n*

loy-al \'lȯi(ə)l\ *adj* : faithful to a country, cause, or friend —**loy-al-ist** *n* —**loy-al-ly** *adv* —**loy-al-ty** \'lȯi(ə)ltē\ *n*

loz-enge \'läz²nj\ *n* : small medicated candy

LSD \,el,es'dē\ *n* : hallucinogenic drug

lu-bri-cant \'lübrikənt\ *n* : material to reduce friction

lu-bri-cate \-,kāt\ *vb* **-cat-ed; -cat-ing** : apply a lubricant to —**lu-bri-ca-tion** \,lübrə'kāshən\ *n* —**lu-bri-ca-tor** \'lübrə,kātər\ *n*

lu-cid \'lüsəd\ *adj* **1** : clear-minded **2** : easily understood —**lu-cid-i-ty** \lü'sidətē\ *n* —**lu-cid-ly** *adv* —**lu-cid-ness** *n*

luck \'lək\ *n* **1** : chance **2** : good fortune —**luck-i-ly** *adv* —**luck-i-ness** *n* —**luck-less** *adj* —**lucky** *adj*

lu-cra-tive \'lükrətiv\ *adj* : profitable —**lu-cra-tive-ly** *adv* —**lu-cra-tive-ness** *n*

lu-di-crous \'lüdəkrəs\ *adj* : comically ridiculous —**lu-di-crous-ly** *adv* —**lu-di-crous-ness** *n*

lug \'ləg\ *vb* **-gg-** : drag or carry laboriously

lug-gage \'ləgij\ *n* : baggage

lu-gu-bri-ous \lü'gübrēəs\ *adj* : mournful —**lu-gu-bri-ous-ly** *adv* —**lu-gu-bri-ous-ness** *n*

luke-warm \'lük'wȯrm\ *adj* **1** : moderately warm **2** : not enthusiastic

lull \'ləl\ *vb* : make or become quiet or relaxed ~ *n* : temporary calm

lul-la-by \'lələ,bī\ *n, pl* **-bies** : song to lull children to sleep

lum-ba-go \,ləm'bāgō\ *n* : rheumatic back pain

lum-ber \'ləmbər\ *n* : timber dressed for use ~ *vb* : cut logs —**lum-ber-man** *n* —**lum-ber-yard** *n*

lum-ber-jack \-,jak\ *n* : logger

lu-mi-nary \'lümə,nerē\ *n, pl* **-nar-ies** : very famous person

lu-mi-nes-cence \,lümə'nes²ns\ *n* : low-temperature emission of light —**lu-mi-nes-cent** \-²nt\ *adj*

lu-mi-nous \'lümənəs\ *adj* : emitting light —**lu-mi-nance** \-nəns\ *n* —**lu-mi-nos-i-ty** \,lümə'näsətē\ *n* —**lu-mi-nous-ly** *adv*

lump \'ləmp\ *n* **1** : mass of irregular shape **2** : abnormal swelling ~ *vb* : heap together —**lump-ish** *adj* —**lumpy** *adj*

lu-na-cy \'lünəsē\ *n, pl* **-cies** : insanity

lu-nar \'lünər\ *adj* : of the moon

lu-na-tic \'lünə,tik\ *adj* : insane —**lunatic** *n*

lunch \'lənch\ *n* : noon meal ~ *vb* : eat lunch

lun-cheon \'lənchən\ *n* : usu. formal lunch

lung \'ləŋ\ *n* : breathing organ in the chest —**lunged** \'ləŋd\ *adj*

lunge \'lənj\ *n* **1** : sudden thrust **2** : sudden move forward —**lunge** *vb*

lurch \'lərch\ *n* : sudden swaying —**lurch** *vb*

lure \'lùr\ *n* **1** : something that attracts **2** : artificial fish bait ~ *vb* **lured; luring** : attract

lu-rid \'lùrəd\ *adj* **1** : gruesome **2** : sensational —**lu-rid-ly** *adv*

lurk \'lərk\ *vb* : lie in wait

lus-cious \'ləshəs\ *adj* **1** : pleasingly sweet in taste or smell **2** : sensually appealing —**lus-cious-ly** *adv* —**lus-cious-ness** *n*

lush \'ləsh\ *adj* : covered with abundant growth

lust \'ləst\ *n* **1** : intense sexual desire **2** : intense longing —**lust** *vb* —**lust-ful** *adj*

luster, lustre \'ləstər\ *n* **1** : brightness from reflected light **2** : magnificence —**lus-ter-less** *adj* —**lus-trous** \-trəs\ *adj*

lusty \'ləstē\ *adj* **lust-i-er; -est** : full of vitality —**lust-i-ly** *adv* —**lust-i-ness** *n*

lute \'lüt\ *n* : pear-shaped stringed instrument —**lute-nist, lu-ta-nist** \'lüt²nəst\ *n*

lux-u-ri-ant \,ləg'zhùrēənt, ,lək'shùr-\ *adj* **1** : growing plentifully **2** : rich and varied —**lux-u-ri-ance** \-ēəns\ *n* —**lux-u-ri-ant-ly** *adv*

lux-u-ri-ate \-ē,āt\ *vb* **-at-ed; -at-ing** : revel

lux-u-ry \'ləksh(ə)rē, 'ləgzh-\ *n, pl* **-ries** **1** : great comfort **2** : something desirable but costly **3** : something adding to pleasure or comfort —**lux-u-ri-ous**

\,lȯg'zhu̇rēəs, \,lək'shu̇r-\ *adj* —**lux-u-ri-ous-ly** *adv*

-ly \lē\ *adj suffix, after 1 usu* ē; *(corresponding adjectives may end in* əl, *as* "double"); *-ically is* ik(ə)lē\ *adv suffix* **1** : in a specified way **2** : from a specified point of view

ly-ce-um \lī'sēəm, 'līsē-\ *n* : hall for public lectures

lye \'lī\ *n* : corrosive alkaline substance

lying *pres part of* LIE

lymph \'limf\ *n* : bodily liquid consist-ing chiefly of blood plasma and white blood cells —**lym-phat-ic** \lim'fatik\ *adj*

lynch \'linch\ *vb* : put to death by mob action —**lynch-er** *n*

lynx \'liŋks\ *n, pl* **lynx** *or* **lynx-es** : wildcat

lyre \'lī(ə)r\ *n* : ancient Greek stringed instrument

lyr-ic \'lirik\ *adj* **1** : suitable for singing **2** : expressing direct personal emotion ~ *n* **1** : lyric poem **2** *pl* : words of a song —**lyr-i-cal** \-ikəl\ *adj*

M

m \'em\ *n, pl* **m's** *or* **ms** \'emz\ : 13th letter of the alphabet

ma'am \'mam, *after* "yes" *often* əm\ *n* : madam

ma-ca-bre \mə'käb(rə), -'käbər, -'käbrə\ *adj* : gruesome

mac-ad-am \mə'kadəm\ *n* : pavement of cemented broken stone —**mac-ad-am-ize** \-,īz\ *vb*

mac-a-ro-ni \,makə'rōnē\ *n* : tubes of dried wheat paste used as food

mac-a-roon \,makə'rün\ *n* : cookie of ground almonds or coconut

ma-caw \mə'kȯ\ *n* : large long-tailed parrot

¹**mace** \'mās\ *n* **1** : heavy spiked club **2** : ornamental staff as a symbol of authority

²**mace** *n* : spice from the fibrous coating of the nutmeg

ma-chete \mə'shetē\ *n* : large heavy knife

mach-i-na-tion \,makə'nāshən, ,mashə-\ *n* : plot or scheme —**mach-i-nate** \'makə,nāt, 'mash-\ *vb*

ma-chine \mə'shēn\ *n* : combination of mechanical or electrical parts ~ *vb* -**chined; -chin-ing** : modify by machine-operated tools —**ma-chin-able** *adj* —**ma-chin-ery** \-(ə)rē\ *n* —**ma-chin-ist** *n*

mack-er-el \'mak(ə)rəl\ *n, pl* **-el** *or* **-els** : No. Atlantic food fish

mack-i-naw \'makə,nȯ\ *n* : short heavy plaid coat

mac-ra-me \,makrə'mā\ *n* : coarse lace or fringe made by knotting

mac-ro \'mak(,)rō\ *adj* : very large

mac-ro-cosm \'makrə,käzəm\ *n* : universe

mad \'mad\ *adj* -**dd**- **1** : insane or rabid **2** : rash and foolish **3** : angry **4** : carried away by enthusiasm —**mad-den** \'mad⁰n\ *vb* —**mad-den-ing-ly** \'madniŋlē, -⁰niŋ-\ *adv* —**mad-ly** *adv* —**mad-ness** *n*

mad-am \'madəm\ *n, pl* **mes-dames** \mā'däm\ —used in polite address to a woman

ma-dame \mə'dam, *before a surname also* ,madəm\ *n, pl* **mes-dames** \mā'däm\ —used as a title for a woman not of English-speaking nationality

mad-cap \'mad,kap\ *adj* : wild or zany —**madcap** *n*

made *past of* MAKE

Ma-dei-ra \mə'dirə\ *n* : amber-colored dessert wine

ma-de-moi-selle \,mad(ə)m(w)ə'zel, mam'zel\ *n, pl* **ma-de-moi-selles** \-'zelz\ *or* **mes-de-moi-selles** \,mād(ə)m(w)ə'zel\ : an unmarried girl or woman —used as a title for a woman esp. of French nationality

mad-house *n* **1** : insane asylum **2** : place of great uproar or confusion

mad-man \-,man, -mən\ *n* : lunatic —**mad-wom-an** *n*

mad-ri-gal \'madrigəl\ *n* : elaborate song for several voice parts

mael-strom \'mālstrəm\ *n* : whirlpool

mae-stro \'mīstrō\ *n, pl* **-stros** *or* **-stri** \-,strē\ : eminent composer or conductor

Ma-fia \'mäfēə\ *n* : secret criminal organization

ma-fi-o-so \,mäfē'ō(,)sō\ *n, pl* **-si** \-(,)sē\ : member of the Mafia

mag-a-zine \'magə,zēn\ *n* **1** : storehouse **2** : publication issued at regular intervals **3** : cartridge container in a gun

ma-gen-ta \mə'jentə\ *n* : deep purplish red

mag-got \'magət\ *n* : wormlike fly larva —**mag-goty** *adj*

mag·ic \\'majik\\ *n* **1** : art of using supernatural powers **2** : extraordinary power or influence **3** : sleight of hand —**magic**, **mag·i·cal** \\-ikəl\\ —**mag·i·cal·ly** \\-ik(ə)lē\\ *adv* —**ma·gi·cian** \\mə'jishən\\ *n*

mag·is·te·ri·al \\majə'stirēəl\\ *adj* : authoritative or relating to a magistrate

mag·is·trate \\'majə,strāt\\ *n* : judge —**mag·is·tra·cy** \\-strəsē\\ *n*

mag·ma \\'magmə\\ *n* : molten rock —**mag·mat·ic** \\mag'matik\\ *adj*

mag·nan·i·mous \\mag'nanəməs\\ *adj* : noble or generous —**mag·na·nim·i·ty** \\,magnə'nimətē\\ *n* —**mag·nan·i·mous·ly** *adv* —**mag·nan·i·mous·ness** *n*

mag·ne·sia \\mag'nēshə, -zhə\\ *n* : oxide of magnesium used as a laxative

mag·ne·sium \\mag'nēzēəm, -zhəm\\ *n* : silver-white metallic chemical element

mag·net \\'magnət\\ *n* **1** : body that attracts iron **2** : something that attracts —**mag·net·ic** \\mag'netik\\ *adj* —**mag·net·i·cal·ly** \\-ik(ə)lē\\ *adv* —**mag·ne·tism** \\'magnə,tizəm\\ *n*

mag·ne·tite \\'magnə,tīt\\ *n* : black iron ore

mag·ne·tize \\'magnə,tīz\\ *vb* -**tized**; -**tiz·ing** **1** : attract like a magnet **2** : give magnetic properties to —**mag·ne·tiz·able** *adj* —**mag·ne·ti·za·tion** \\,magnətə'zāshən\\ *n* —**mag·ne·tiz·er** *n*

mag·nif·i·cent \\mag'nifəsənt\\ *adj* : splendid —**mag·nif·i·cence** \\-səns\\ *n* —**mag·nif·i·cent·ly** *adv*

mag·ni·fy \\'magnə,fī\\ *vb* -**fied**; -**fy·ing** **1** : intensify **2** : enlarge —**mag·ni·fi·ca·tion** \\,magnəfə'kāshən\\ *n* —**mag·ni·fi·er** \\'magnə,fī(ə)r\\ *n*

mag·ni·tude \\'magnə,t(y)üd\\ *n* **1** : greatness of size or extent **2** : quantity

mag·no·lia \\mag'nōlyə\\ *n* : shrub with large fragrant flowers

mag·pie \\'mag,pī\\ *n* : long-tailed black-and-white bird

ma·hog·a·ny \\mə'hägənē\\ *n, pl* -**nies** : tropical evergreen tree or its reddish brown wood

maid \\'mād\\ *n* **1** : unmarried young woman **2** : female servant

maid·en \\'mādən\\ *n* : unmarried young woman ~ *adj* **1** : unmarried **2** : first —**maid·en·hood** \\-,hůd\\ *n* —**maid·en·ly** *adj*

maid·en·hair \\-,haər\\ *n* : fern with delicate feathery fronds

¹mail \\'māl\\ *n* **1** : something sent or carried in the postal system **2** : postal system ~ *vb* : send by mail —**mail·box** *n* —**mail·man** \\-,man, -mən\\ *n*

²mail *n* : armor of metal links or plates

maim \\'mām\\ *vb* : seriously wound or disfigure

main \\'mān\\ *n* **1** : force **2** : ocean **3** : principal pipe, duct, or circuit of a utility system ~ *adj* : chief —**main·ly** *adv*

main·land \\'mān,land, -lənd\\ *n* : part of a country on a continent

main·stay *n* : chief support

main·stream *n* : prevailing current or direction of activity or influence —**mainstream** *adj*

main·tain \\mān'tān\\ *vb* **1** : keep in an existing state (as of repair) **2** : sustain **3** : declare —**main·tain·abil·i·ty** \\-,tānə'bilətē\\ *n* —**main·tain·able** \\-'tānəbəl\\ *adj* —**main·te·nance** \\'māntənəns, -ənens\\ *n*

mai·tre d'hô·tel \\,mātrədō'tel, ,me-\\ *n* : head of a dining room staff

maize \\'māz\\ *n* : corn

maj·es·ty \\'majəstē\\ *n, pl* -**ties** **1** : sovereign power or dignity —used as a title **2** : grandeur or splendor —**ma·jes·tic** \\mə'jestik\\, **ma·jes·ti·cal** \\-tikəl\\ *adj* —**ma·jes·ti·cal·ly** \\-tik(ə)lē\\ *adv*

ma·jor \\'mājər\\ *adj* **1** : larger or greater **2** : noteworthy or conspicuous ~ *n* **1** : commissioned officer (as in the army) ranking next below a lieutenant colonel **2** : main field of study ~ *vb* -**jored**; -**jor·ing** : pursue an academic major

ma·jor·do·mo \\,mājər'dōmō\\ *n, pl* -**mos** : head steward

major general *n* : commissioned officer (as in the army) ranking next below a lieutenant general

ma·jor·i·ty \\mə'jorətē\\ *n, pl* -**ties** **1** : age of full civil rights **2** : quantity more than half

make \\'māk\\ *vb* **made** \\'mād\\; **mak·ing 1** : cause to exist, occur, or appear **2** : fashion or manufacture **3** : formulate in the mind **4** : constitute **5** : prepare **6** : cause to be or become **7** : carry out or perform **8** : compel **9** : gain **10** : have an effect —used with *for* ~ *n* : brand —**mak·er** *n* —**make do** *vb* : get along with what is available —**make good** *vb* **1** : repay **2** : succeed —**make out** *vb* **1** : draw up or write **2** : discern or understand **3** : fare —**make up** *vb* **1** : invent **2** : become reconciled **3** : compensate for

make–be·lieve \n : a pretending to believe ~ *adj* : imagined or pretended

make·shift \n : temporary substitute —**makeshift** *adj*

make·up \-,əp\ n 1 : way in which something is constituted 2 : cosmetics

mal·ad·just·ed \,malə'jəstəd\ adj : poorly adjusted (as to one's environment) —**mal·ad·just·ment** \-'jəs(t)mənt\ n

mal·adroit \,malə'dròit\ adj : clumsy or inept

mal·a·dy \'maladē\ n, pl **-dies** : disease or disorder

mal·aise \mə-'lāz, ma-\ n : sense of being unwell

mal·a·mute \'malə,myüt\ n : powerful heavy-coated dog

mal·a·prop·ism \'malə,präp,izəm\ n : humorous misuse of a word

ma·lar·ia \mə'lerēə\ n : disease transmitted by a mosquito —**ma·lar·i·al** \-əl\ adj

ma·lar·key \mə'lärkē\ n : foolishness

mal·con·tent \,malkən'tent\ adj : dissatisfied with the state of affairs —**malcontent** n

male \'māl\ adj 1 : relating to the sex that performs a fertilizing function 2 : masculine ~ n : male individual —**male·ness** n

male·dic·tion \,malə'dikshən\ n : curse

male·fac·tor \'malə,faktər\ n : one who commits an offense esp. against the law

ma·lef·i·cent \mə'lefəsənt\ adj : harmful —**ma·lef·i·cence** \-səns\ n

ma·lev·o·lent \mə'levələnt\ adj : malicious or spiteful —**ma·lev·o·lence** \-ləns\ n

mal·fea·sance \mal'fēz³ns\ n : misconduct by a public official

mal·for·ma·tion \,malfòr'māshən\ n : distortion or faulty formation —**mal·formed** \-'fòrmd\ adj

mal·func·tion \mal'fəŋkshən\ vb : fail to operate properly —**malfunction** n

mal·ice \'maləs\ n : ill will —**ma·li·cious** \mə'lishəs\ adj —**ma·li·cious·ly** adv

ma·lign \mə'līn\ adj 1 : wicked 2 : malignant ~ vb : speak evil of

ma·lig·nant \mə'lignənt\ adj 1 : harmful 2 : likely to cause death —**ma·lig·nan·cy** \-nənsē\ n —**ma·lig·nant·ly** adv —**ma·lig·ni·ty** \-nətē\ n

mall \'mòl\ n 1 : shaded promenade 2 : concourse providing access to rows of shops

mal·lard \'malərd\ n, pl **-lard** or **-lards** : common wild duck

mal·lea·ble \'malēəbəl\ adj : easily shaped —**mal·lea·bil·i·ty** \,malēə'bilətē\ n

mal·let \'malət\ n : hammerlike tool

mal·nour·ished \mal'nərisht\ adj : poorly nourished

mal·nu·tri·tion \,maln(y)ü'trishən\ n : inadequate nutrition

mal·odor·ous \mal'ōdərəs\ adj : foulsmelling —**mal·odor·ous·ly** adv —**mal·odor·ous·ness** n

mal·prac·tice \-'praktəs\ n : failure of professional duty

malt \'mòlt\ n : sprouted grain used in brewing

mal·treat \mal'trēt\ vb : treat badly —**mal·treat·ment** n

ma·ma, mam·ma \'mämə\ n : mother

mam·mal \'maməl\ n : vertebrate animal that nourishes its young with milk —**mam·ma·li·an** \mə'mālēən, ma-\ adj or n

mam·ma·ry \'mamərē\ adj : relating to the milk-secreting glands

mam·moth \'maməth\ n : large hairy extinct elephant ~ adj : enormous

man \'man\ n, pl **men** \'men\ 1 : human being 2 : adult male 3 : mankind — vb **-nn-** 1 : station people to work on or at 2 : physically operate —**man·hood** n —**man·hunt** n —**man·like** adj —**man·li·ness** n —**man·ly** adj or adv —**man·made** adj —**man·nish** adj —**man·nish·ly** adv —**man·nish·ness** n —**man·size, man·sized** adj

man·a·cle \'manikəl\ n : shackle for the hands —**manacle** vb

man·age \'manij\ vb **-aged; -ag·ing** 1 : control 2 : direct or carry on business or affairs 3 : cope —**man·age·abil·i·ty** \,manijə'bilətē\ n —**man·age·able** \'manijəbəl\ adj —**man·age·able·ness** n —**man·age·ably** \-blē\ adv —**man·age·ment** \'manijmənt\ n —**man·age·men·tal** \,manij'ment³l\ adj —**man·ag·er** \'manijər\ n —**man·a·ge·ri·al** \,manə'jirēəl\ adj

man·da·rin \'mandərən\ n : Chinese imperial official

man·date \'man,dāt\ n : authoritative command

man·da·to·ry \'mandə,tōrē\ adj : obligatory

man·di·ble \'mandəbəl\ n : lower jaw —**man·dib·u·lar** \man'dibyələr\ adj

man·do·lin \,mandə'lin, 'mand³lən\ n : stringed musical instrument

man·drake \'man,drāk\ n : herb with a large forked root

mane \\'mān\\ *n* : animal's neck hair —**maned** \\'mānd\\ *adj*

ma·neu·ver \\mə'n(y)üvər\\ *n* **1** : planned movement of troops or ships **2** : military training exercise **3** : procedure involving expert physical movement **4** : skillful often evasive action or management —**maneuver** *vb* —**ma·neu·ver·abil·i·ty** \\-ˌn(y)üvərə'bilətē\\ *n*

man·ful \\'manfəl\\ *adj* : courageous —**man·ful·ly** *adv*

man·ga·nese \\'maŋgəˌnēz, -ˌnēs\\ *n* : gray metallic chemical element —**man·ga·ne·sian** \\ˌmaŋgə'nēzhən, -shən\\ *adj*

mange \\'mānj\\ *n* : skin disease of domestic animals —**mangy** \\'mānjē\\ *adj*

man·ger \\'mānjər\\ *n* : feeding trough for livestock

man·gle \\'maŋgəl\\ *vb* **-gled; -gling 1** : mutilate **2** : bungle —**man·gler** \\-g(ə)lər\\ *n*

man·go \\'maŋgō\\ *n, pl* **-goes** *or* **-gos** : yellowish red tropical fruit

man·grove \\'man,grōv, 'maŋ-\\ *n* : tropical tree growing in salt marsh

man·han·dle *vb* : handle roughly

man·hole *n* : entry to a sewer

ma·nia \\'mānēə, -nyə\\ *n* **1** : insanity **2** : excessive enthusiasm —**ma·ni·ac** \\-nē,ak\\ *n* —**ma·ni·a·cal** \\mə'nīəkəl\\ *adj* —**man·ic** \\'manik\\ *adj or n*

man·i·cure \\'manəˌkyu̇r\\ *n* : treatment for the fingernails ~ *vb* **-cured; -cur·ing 1** : do manicure work on **2** : trim precisely —**man·i·cur·ist** \\-ˌkyu̇rəst\\ *n*

¹man·i·fest \\'manəˌfest\\ *adj* : clear to the senses or to the mind ~ *vb* : make evident —**man·i·fes·ta·tion** \\ˌmanəfə'stāshən\\ *n* —**man·i·fest·ly** *adv*

²manifest *n* : invoice of cargo or list of passengers

man·i·fes·to \\ˌmanə'festō\\ *n, pl* **-tos** *or* **-toes** : public declaration of policy or views

man·i·fold \\'manəˌfōld\\ *adj* : marked by diversity or variety ~ *n* : pipe fitting with several outlets for connections

manila paper \\mə'nilə-\\ *n* : durable brownish paper

ma·nip·u·late \\mə'nipyəˌlāt\\ *vb* **-lat·ed; -lat·ing 1** : treat or operate manually or mechanically **2** : influence esp. by cunning —**ma·nip·u·la·tion** \\mə,nipyə'lāshən\\ *n* —**ma·nip·u·la·tive**

\\-'nipyəˌlātiv\\ *adj* —**ma·nip·u·la·tor** \\-ˌlātər\\ *n*

man·kind \\'man'kīnd\\ *n* : human race

man·na \\'manə\\ *n* : something valuable that comes unexpectedly

manned \\'mand\\ *adj* : carrying or performed by a man

man·ne·quin \\'manikən\\ *n* : dummy used to display clothes

man·ner \\'manər\\ *n* **1** : kind **2** : usual way of acting **3** : artistic method **4** *pl* : social conduct

man·nered \\-ərd\\ *adj* **1** : having manners of a specified kind **2** : artificial

man·ner·ism \\'manə,rizəm\\ *n* : individual peculiarity of action

man·ner·ly \\-lē\\ *adj* : polite —**man·ner·li·ness** *n*

man-of-war \\ˌmanə(v)'wȯr\\ *n, pl* **men-of-war** \\ˌmen-\\ : warship

man·or \\'manər\\ *n* : country estate —**ma·no·ri·al** \\mə'nōrēəl\\ *adj* —**ma·no·ri·al·ism** \\-ə,lizəm\\ *n*

man·pow·er *n* : supply of people available for service

man·sard \\'man,särd\\ *n* : roof with two slopes on all sides and the lower slope the steeper

manse \\'mans\\ *n* : parsonage

man·ser·vant *n, pl* **men·ser·vants** : a male servant

man·sion \\'manchən\\ *n* : very big house

man·slaugh·ter *n* : unintentional killing of a person

man·tel \\'mantᵊl\\ *n* : shelf above a fireplace

man·tis \\'mantəs\\ *n, pl* **-tis·es** *or* **-tes** \\'man,tēz\\ : large insect with stout forelegs

man·tle \\'mantᵊl\\ *n* **1** : sleeveless cloak **2** : something that covers, enfolds, or envelopes ~ *vb* **-tled; -tling** : cover

man·tra \\'mantrə\\ *n* : mystical chant

man·u·al \\'manyə(wə)l\\ *adj* : involving the hands or physical force ~ *n* : handbook —**man·u·al·ly** *adv*

man·u·fac·ture \\ˌman(y)ə'fakchər\\ *n* : process of making wares by hand or by machinery ~ *vb* **-tured; -tur·ing** : make from raw materials —**man·u·fac·tur·er** *n*

ma·nure \\mə'n(y)u̇r\\ *n* : animal excrement used as fertilizer —**ma·nu·ri·al** \\-ēəl\\ *adj*

man·u·script \\'manyə,skript\\ *n* : something written or typed

many \\'menē\\ *adj* **more** \\'mȯr\\; **most** \\'mōst\\ : consisting of a large number —**many** *n or pron*

map \\'map\\ *n* : representation of a geographical area ~ *vb* **-pp- 1** : make a map of **2** : plan in detail —**map·pa·ble** \-əbəl\ *adj* —**map·per** *n*

ma·ple \'māpəl\ *n* : tree with hard light-colored wood

mar \'mär\ *vb* -**rr**- : damage

mar·a·schi·no \₁marə'skēnō, -'shē-\ *n*, *pl* -**nos** : preserved cherry

mar·a·thon \'marə₁thän\ *n* **1** : long-distance race **2** : test of endurance

ma·raud \mə'rȯd\ *vb* : plunder —**ma·raud·er** *n*

mar·ble \'märbəl\ *n* **1** : crystallized limestone **2** : small glass ball used in a children's game (**marbles**)

mar·bling \-b(ə)liŋ\ *n* : intermixture of fat and lean in meat

march \'märch\ *vb* : move with regular steps or in a purposeful manner ~ *n* **1** : distance covered in a march **2** : measured stride **3** : forward movement **4** : music for marching —**march·er** *n*

March *n* : 3d month of the year having 31 days

mar·chio·ness \'märshənəs\ *n* **1** : wife or widow of a marquess **2** : woman holding the rank of a marquess

Mar·di Gras \'märdē₁grä\ *n* : Tuesday before the beginning of Lent often observed with parades and merrymaking

mare \'maər\ *n* : female horse

mar·ga·rine \'märj(ə)rən, -ə₁rēn\ *n* : butter substitute made usu. from vegetable oils

mar·gin \'märjən\ *n* **1** : edge **2** : spare amount, measure, or degree —**mar·gin·al** \-ᵊl\ *adj* —**mar·gin·al·ly** *adv*

mari·gold \'marə₁gōld, 'mer-\ *n* : garden plant with showy flower heads

mar·i·jua·na, **mar·i·hua·na** \₁marə'(h)wänə\ *n* : intoxicating drug obtained from the hemp plant

ma·ri·na \mə'rēnə\ *n* : place for mooring boats

mar·i·nate \'marə₁nāt\ *vb* -**nat·ed; -nat·ing** : soak in a savory sauce

ma·rine \mə'rēn\ *adj* **1** : relating to the sea **2** : relating to marines ~ *n* : infantry soldier associated with a navy

mar·i·ner \'marənər\ *n* : sailor

mar·i·o·nette \₁marēə'net, ₁mer-\ *n* : puppet

mar·i·tal \'marətᵊl\ *adj* : relating to marriage

mar·i·time \'marə₁tīm\ *adj* : relating to the sea or commerce on the sea

mar·jo·ram \'märj(ə)rəm\ *n* : aromatic mint used as a seasoning

¹mark \'märk\ *n* **1** : something aimed at **2** : something (as a line) designed

to record position **3** : visible sign **4** : written symbol **5** : grade **6** : lasting impression **7** : blemish ~ *vb* **1** : designate or set apart by a mark or make a mark on **2** : characterize **3** : remark —**mark·er** *n*

²mark *n* : monetary unit of East Germany

marked \'märkt\ *adj* : noticeable —**mark·ed·ly** \'märkədlē\ *adv*

mar·ket \'märkət\ *n* **1** : buying and selling of goods or the place this happens **2** : demand for commodities : store ~ *vb* : sell —**mar·ket·able** *adj*

mar·ket·place *n* **1** : market **2** : world of trade or economic activity

marks·man \'märksmən\ *n* : good shooter —**marks·man·ship** *n*

mar·lin \'märlən\ *n* : large oceanic fish

mar·ma·lade \'märmə₁lād\ *n* : jam with pieces of fruit and rind

mar·mo·set \'märmə₁set\ *n* : small bushy-tailed monkey

mar·mot \'märmət\ *n* : burrowing rodent

¹ma·roon \mə'rün\ *vb* : isolate without hope of escape

²maroon *n* : dark red

mar·quee \mär'kē\ *n* : canopy over an entrance

mar·quess \'märkwəs\ *n* : British noble ranking next below a duke

mar·quis \'märkwəs, mär'kē\ *n* : marquess

mar·quise \mär'kēz\ *n*, *pl* **mar·quises** \-'kēz(əz)\ : marchioness

mar·riage \'marij\ *n* **1** : state of being married **2** : wedding ceremony —**mar·riage·able** *adj*

mar·row \'marō\ *n* : soft tissue in the cavity of bone

mar·ry \'marē\ *vb* -**ried; -ry·ing 1** : join as husband and wife **2** : take or give in marriage —**mar·ried** *adj* or *n*

marsh \'märsh\ *n* : soft wet land —**marshy** *adj*

mar·shal \'märshəl\ *n* **1** : leader of ceremony **2** : usu. high military or administrative officer ~ *vb* -**shaled** *or* -**shalled; -shal·ing** *or* -**shal·ling 1** : arrange in order, rank, or positon **2** : lead with ceremony

marsh·mal·low \'märsh₁melō, -₁mal\ *n* : spongy candy

mar·su·pi·al \mär'süpēəl\ *n* : Australian mammal that nourishes young in an abdominal pouch —**marsupial** *adj*

mart \'märt\ *n* : market

mar·ten \'märtᵊn\ *n*, *pl* -**ten** *or* -**tens** : weasellike mammal

mar·tial \'märshəl\ *adj* : relating to war or an army **2** : warlike

mar·tin \'märt°n\ *n* : small swallow

mar·ti·net \,märt°n'et\ *n* : strict disciplinarian

mar·tyr \'märtər\ *n* : one who dies or makes a great sacrifice for a cause ~ *vb* : make a martyr of —**mar·tyr·dom** \-dəm\ *n*

mar·vel \'märvəl\ *vb* **-veled** *or* **-velled**; **-vel·ing** *or* **-vel·ling** : feel surprise or wonder ~ *n* : something amazing —**mar·vel·ous**, **mar·vel·lous** \'märv(ə)ləs\ *adj* —**mar·vel·ous·ly** *adv* —**mar·vel·ous·ness** *n*

Marx·ism \'märk,sizəm\ *n* : political and social principles of Karl Marx —**Marx·ist** \-səst\ *n or adj*

mas·cara \mas'karə\ *n* : eye cosmetic

mas·cot \'mas,kät, -kət\ *n* : one believed to bring good luck

mas·cu·line \'maskyələn\ *adj* : relating to the male sex —**mas·cu·lin·i·ty** \,maskyə'linətē\ *n*

mash \'mash\ *n* 1 : crushed steeped grain for fermenting 2 : soft pulpy mass ~ *vb* 1 : reduce to a pulpy mass 2 : smash —**mash·er** *n*

mask \'mask\ *n* : disguise for the face ~ *vb* 1 : disguise 2 : cover to protect —**mask·er** *n*

mas·och·ism \'masə,kizəm, 'maz-\ *n* : pleasure in being abused —**mas·och·ist** \-kəst\ *n* —**mas·och·is·tic** \,masə'kistik, ,maz-\ *adj*

ma·son \'mās°n\ *n* : workman who builds with stone or brick —**ma·son·ry** \-rē\ *n*

mas·quer·ade \,maskə'rād\ *n* 1 : costume party 2 : disguise ~ *vb* **-ad·ed**; **-ad·ing** 1 : disguise oneself 2 : take part in a costume party —**mas·quer·ad·er** *n*

mass \'mas\ *n* 1 : large amount of matter or number of things 2 : expanse or magnitude 3 : great body of people —usu. pl. ~ *vb* : form into a mass —**mass·less** \-ləs\ *adj* —**mass·less·ness** *n* —**massy** *adj*

Mass *n* : worship service of the Roman Catholic Church

mas·sa·cre \'masikər\ *n* : wholesale slaughter —**massacre** *vb*

mas·sage \mə'säzh, -'säj\ *n* : a rubbing of the body —**massage** *vb*

mas·seur \ma'sər\ *n* : man who massages

mas·seuse \-'sə(r)z, -'süz\ *n* : woman who massages

mas·sive \'masiv\ *adj* 1 : being a large mass 2 : large in scope —**mas·sive·ly** *adv* —**mas·sive·ness** *n*

mast \'mast\ *n* : tall pole supporting sails —**mast·ed** *adj*

mas·ter \'mastər\ *n* 1 : male teacher 2 : holder of an academic degree between a bachelor's and a doctor's 3 : one highly skilled 4 : one in authority ~ *vb* 1 : subdue 2 : become proficient in —**mas·ter·ful** \-fəl\ *adj* —**mas·ter·ful·ly** *adv* —**mas·ter·ly** *adj* —**mas·ter·ship** \-,ship\ *n* —**mas·tery** \'mast(ə)rē\ *n*

master chief petty officer *n* : petty officer of the highest rank in the navy

master gunnery sergeant *n* : noncommissioned officer in the marine corps ranking above a master sergeant

mas·ter·piece \'mastər,pēs\ *n* : great piece of work

master sergeant *n* 1 : noncommissioned officer in the army ranking next below a sergeant major 2 : noncommissioned officer in the air force ranking next below a senior master sergeant 3 : noncommissioned officer in the marine corps ranking next below a master gunnery sergeant

mas·ter·work *n* : masterpiece

mas·tic \'mastik\ *n* : pasty glue

mas·ti·cate \'mastə,kāt\ *vb* **-cat·ed**; **-cat·ing** : chew —**mas·ti·ca·tion** \,mastə'kāshən\ *n*

mas·tiff \'mastəf\ *n* : large dog

mast·odon \'mastə,dän\ *n* : extinct elephantlike animal

mas·toid \'mas,tȯid\ *n* : bone behind the ear —**mastoid** *adj*

mas·tur·ba·tion \,mastər'bāshən\ *n* : stimulation of sex organs by hand —**mas·tur·bate** \'mastər,bāt\ *vb*

¹mat \'mat\ *n* 1 : coarse woven or plaited fabric 2 : mass of tangled strands 3 : thick pad ~ *vb* **-tt-** : form into a mat

²mat, matt, matte \'mat\ *adj* : not shiny ~ *n* 1 : border around a picture 2 : dull finish

mat·a·dor \'matə,dȯr\ *n* : bullfighter

¹match \'mach\ *n* 1 : one equal to another 2 : 2 things that go well together 3 : game 4 : marriage ~ *vb* 1 : set in competition 2 : marry 3 : be or provide the equal of 4 : fit or go together —**match·less** *adj* —**match·er** *n*

²match *n* : piece of wood or paper material with a combustible tip

mate \'māt\ *n* 1 : companion 2 : subordinate officer on a ship 3 : one of a pair ~ *vb* **mat·ed**; **mat·ing** 1 : fit together 2 : come together as a pair

ma·te·ri·al \mə'tirēəl\ *adj* 1 : natural 2 : relating to matter 3 : important 4 : of a physical or worldly nature ~ *n*

: stuff something is made of —**ma·te·ri·al·ly** adv

ma·te·ri·al·ism \mə'tirēə,lizəm\ n 1 : theory that matter is the only reality 2 : preoccupation with material and not spiritual things —**ma·te·ri·al·ist** \-last\ n or adj —**ma·te·ri·al·is·tic** \-,tirēə'listik\ adj

ma·te·ri·al·ize \mə'tirēə,līz\ vb **-ized; -iz·ing** : take or cause to take bodily form —**ma·te·ri·al·i·za·tion** \mə-,tirēələ'zāshən\ n

ma·té·ri·el \mə,tirē'el\ n : military supplies

ma·ter·nal \mə'tərnəl\ adj : motherly —**ma·ter·nal·ly** adv

ma·ter·ni·ty \mə'tərnətē\ n, pl **-ties** 1 : state of being a mother 2 : hospital's childbirth facility —**maternity** adj

math \'math\ n : mathematics

math·e·mat·ics \,mathə'matiks\ n pl : science of numbers and of space configurations —**math·e·mat·i·cal** \-ikəl\ adj —**math·e·mat·i·cal·ly** adv —**math·e·ma·ti·cian** \,mathə-mə'tishən\ n

mat·i·née \,mat²n'ā\ n : afternoon performance

mat·ins \'mat²nz\ n : morning prayers

ma·tri·arch \'mātrē,ärk\ n : woman who rules a family —**ma·tri·ar·chal** \,mātrē'ärkəl\ adj —**ma·tri·ar·chy** \'mātrē,ärkē\ n

ma·tri·cide \'matrə,sīd, 'mā-\ n : murder of one's mother —**ma·tri·cid·al** \,matrə'sīd²l, ,mā-\ adj

ma·tric·u·late \mə'trikyə,lāt\ vb **-lat·ed; -lat·ing** : enroll in school —**ma·tric·u·la·tion** \-,trikyə'lāshən\ n

mat·ri·mo·ny \'matrə,mōnē\ n : marriage —**mat·ri·mo·ni·al** \,matrə'mō-nēəl\ adj —**mat·ri·mo·ni·al·ly** adv

ma·trix \'mātriks\ n, pl **-tri·ces** \'mā-trə,sēz, 'ma-\ or **-trix·es** \'mā-triksəz\ 1 : something within which something else originates or develops 2 : mold

ma·tron \'mātrən\ n 1 : dignified matron woman 2 : woman supervisor —**ma·tron·ly** adj

matt, matte var of MAT

mat·ter \'matər\ n 1 : subject of interest 2 pl : circumstances 3 : trouble 4 : physical substance ~ vb : be important

mat·tock \'matək\ n : a digging tool

mat·tress \'matrəs\ n : pad to sleep on

ma·ture \mə'túr\ adj **-tur·er; -est** 1 : carefully considered 2 : fully grown or developed 3 : due for payment ~ vb **-tured; -tur·ing** : become mature —**mat·u·ra·tion** \,machə'rāshən\ n —**mat·u·ra·tion·al** \-sh(ə)nəl\ adj —**ma·tur·a·tive** \'mə'ch(y)ùrətiv\ adj —**ma·tu·ri·ty** \-ətē\ n

maud·lin \'mȯdlən\ adj : stupidly sentimental

maul \'mȯl\ n : heavy wooden hammer ~ vb 1 : beat 2 : handle roughly

mau·so·le·um \,mȯsə'lēəm, ,mȯzə-\ n, pl **-leums** or **-lea** \-'lēə\ : large above-ground tomb

mauve \'mōv, 'mȯv\ n : lilac color

ma·ven, ma·vin \'māvən, 'māvin\ n : expert

mav·er·ick \'mav(ə)rik\ n 1 : unbranded range animal 2 : nonconformist

maw \'mȯ\ n 1 : stomach 2 : throat, esophagus, or jaws

mawk·ish \'mȯkish\ adj : sickly sentimental —**mawk·ish·ly** adv —**mawk·ish·ness** n

max·im \'maksəm\ n : proverb

max·i·mum \'maks(ə)məm\ n, pl **-ma** \-səmə\ or **-mums** \-s(ə)məmz\ 1 : greatest quantity 2 : upper limit 3 : largest number —**maximum** adj —**max·i·mize** \-sə,mīz\ vb

may \('mā\ verbal auxiliary, past **might** \('mīt\; pres sing & pl **may** 1 : have permission 2 : be likely to 3 —used to express desire, purpose, or contingency

May \'mā\ n : 5th month of the year having 31 days

may·ap·ple n : woodland herb having edible fruit

may·be \'mābē, 'mebē\ adv : perhaps

may·flow·er n : spring-blooming herb

may·fly n : fly with an aquatic larva

may·hem \'mā,hem, 'māəm\ n : crippling or mutilation of a person

may·on·naise \'māə,nāz\ n : thick salad dressing

may·or \'māər\ n : chief city official —**may·or·al** \-əl\ adj —**may·or·al·ty** \-əltē\ n —**may·or·ess** \'māərəs\ n

maze \'māz\ n : confusing network of passages —**mazy** adj

ma·zur·ka \mə'zərkə\ n : Polish dance

me \(')mē\ pron, objective case of **I**

mead \'mēd\ n : alcoholic beverage brewed from honey

mead·ow \'medō\ n : low-lying usu. level grassland —**mead·ow·land** \-,land\ n —**mead·owy** \'medəwē\ adj

mead·ow·lark n : songbird with a yellow breast

mea·ger, mea·gre \'mēgər\ adj 1 : thin 2 : scanty —**mea·ger·ly** adv —**mea·ger·ness** n

¹meal \'mēl\ *n* **1** : food to be eaten at one time **2** : act of eating —**meal-time** *n*

²meal *n* : ground grain —**mealy** *adj*

¹mean \'mēn\ *adj* **1** : humble **2** : worthy of or showing little regard **3** : stingy **4** : malicious —**mean·ly** *adv* —**mean·ness** *n*

²mean \'mēn\ *vb* **meant** \'ment\; **mean·ing** \'mēniŋ\ **1** : intend **2** : serve to convey, show, or indicate **3** : be important

³mean *n* **1** : middle point **2** *pl* : something that helps gain an end **3** *pl* : material resources **4** : sum of several quantities divided by the number of quantities ~ *adj* : being a mean

me·an·der \mē'andər\ *vb* -**dered**; -**der·ing** \-d(ə)riŋ\ **1** : follow a winding course **2** : wander aimlessly —**meander** *n*

mean·ing \'mēniŋ\ *n* : idea conveyed or intended to be conveyed —**mean·ing·ful** \-fəl\ *adj* —**mean·ing·ful·ly** *adv* —**mean·ing·less** *adj*

mean·time \'mēn,tīm\ *n* : intervening time —**meantime** *adv*

mean·while \-,hwīl\ *n* : meantime —**meanwhile** *adv*

mea·sles \'mēzəlz\ *n pl* : disease that is marked by red spots on the skin

mea·sly \'mēz(ə)lē\ *adj* -**sli·er**; -**est** : contemptibly small in amount

mea·sure \'mezhər, 'māzh-\ *n* **1** : moderate amount **2** : dimensions or amount **3** : something to show amount **4** : unit or system of measurement **5** : act of measuring **6** : means to an end ~ *vb* -**sured**; -**sur·ing 1** : regulate by a standard **2** : find out or mark off size or amount of **3** : have a specified measurement —**mea·sur·able** \'mezh(ə)rəbəl, 'māzh-\ *adj* —**mea·sur·ably** \-blē\ *adv* —**mea·sure·less** *adj* —**mea·sure·ment** *n* —**mea·sur·er** *n*

meat \'mēt\ *n* **1** : food **2** : animal flesh used as food —**meat·ball** *n* —**meaty** *adj*

me·chan·ic \mi'kanik\ *adj* **1** : manual **2** : like a machine ~ *n* : worker who repairs machines

me·chan·i·cal \mi'kanikəl\ *adj* **1** : relating to machines or mechanics **2** : involuntary —**me·chan·i·cal·ly** *adv*

me·chan·ics \-iks\ *n sing or pl* **1** : branch of physics dealing with energy and forces in relation to bodies **2** : mechanical details

mech·a·nism \'mekə,nizəm\ *n* **1** : piece of machinery **2** : technique for gaining a result **3** : basic processes producing a phenomenon —**mech·a·nis·tic** \,mekə'nistik\ *adj* —**mech·a·nis·ti·cal·ly** \-tik(ə)lē\ *adv* —**mech·a·ni·za·tion** \,mekənə'zāshən\ *n* —**mech·a·nize** \'mekə,nīz\ *vb* —**mech·a·niz·er** *n*

med·al \'medʔl\ *n* **1** : religious pin or pendant **2** : coinlike commemorative metal piece

me·dal·lion \mə'dalyən\ *n* : large medal

med·dle \'medʔl\ *vb* -**dled**; -**dling** : interfere —**med·dler** \'medlər, -ʔlər\ *n* —**med·dle·some** \'medʔlsəm\ *adj*

me·dia \'mēdēə\ *n pl* : communications organizations

me·di·an \'mēdēən\ *n* : middle value in a range —**median** *adj*

me·di·ate \'mēdē,āt\ *vb* -**at·ed**; -**at·ing** : help settle a dispute —**me·di·a·tion** \,mēdē'āshən\ *n* —**me·di·a·tor** \'mēdē,ātər\ *n*

med·ic \'medik\ *n* : medical worker esp. in the military

med·i·ca·ble \'medikəbəl\ *adj* : curable —**med·i·ca·bly** \-blē\ *adv*

med·ic·aid \'medi,kād\ *n* : government program of medical aid for the poor

med·i·cal \'medikəl\ *adj* : relating to medicine —**med·i·cal·ly** \-k(ə)lē\ *adv*

med·i·care \'medi,kear\ *n* : government program of medical care for the aged

med·i·cate \'medə,kāt\ *vb* -**cat·ed**; -**cat·ing** : treat with medicine —**med·i·ca·tion** \,medə'kāshən\ *n*

med·i·cine \'medəsən\ *n* **1** : preparation used to treat disease **2** : science dealing with the cure of disease —**me·dic·i·nal** \mə'disnəl, -ʔnəl\ *adj* —**me·dic·i·nal·ly** *adv*

me·di·eval, me·di·ae·val \,mēdē'ēvəl, ,med-, ,mid-\ *adj* : of or relating to the Middle Ages —**me·di·e·val·ism** \-,izəm\ *n* —**me·di·e·val·ist** \-əst\ *n*

me·di·o·cre \,mēdē'ōkər\ *adj* : not very good —**me·di·oc·ri·ty** \-'äkrətē\ *n*

med·i·tate \'medə,tāt\ *vb* -**tat·ed**; -**tat·ing** : contemplate —**med·i·ta·tion** \,medə'tāshən\ *n* —**med·i·ta·tive** \'medə,tātiv\ *adj* —**med·i·ta·tive·ly** *adv*

me·di·um \'mēdēəm\ *n, pl* -**diums** or -**dia** \-ēə\ **1** : middle position or degree **2** : means of effecting or conveying something **3** : surrounding substance **4** : means of communication **5** : mode of artistic expression —**medium** *adj*

med·ley \'medlē\ *n, pl* -**leys** : series of songs performed as one

meek \'mēk\ adj 1 : mild-mannered 2 : weak —**meek·ly** adv —**meek·ness** n

meer·schaum \'miərshəm, -ˌshóm\ n : claylike tobacco pipe

¹meet \'mēt\ vb met \'met\; meet·ing 1 : run into 2 : join 3 : oppose 4 : assemble 5 : satisfy 6 : be introduced to ~ n : sports team competition

²meet adj : proper

meet·ing \'mētiŋ\ n : a getting together —**meet·ing-house** n

mega·cy·cle \'megəˌsīkəl\ n : megahertz

mega-hertz \-ˌhorts, -ˌhearts\ n : one million hertz

mega·phone \'megəˌfōn\ n : coneshaped device to intensify or direct the voice

mel·an·choly \'melənˌkälē\ n : depression —**mel·an·chol·ic** \ˌmelən'kälik\ adj —**melancholy** adj

mel·a·no·ma \ˌmelə'nōmə\ n, pl -mas also -ma·ta \-mətə\ : usu. malignant tumor

me·lee \'māˌlā, mā'lā\ n : brawl

me·lio·rate \'mēlyəˌrāt, 'mēlēə-\ vb -rat·ed; -rat·ing : improve —**me·lio·ra·tion** \ˌmēlyə'rāshən, ˌmēlēə-\ n —**me·lio·ra·tive** \'mēlyəˌrātiv, 'mēlēə-\ adj

mel·lif·lu·ous \me'liflǝwǝs, mǝ-\ adj : sweetly flowing —**mel·lif·lu·ous·ly** adv —**mel·lif·lu·ous·ness** n

mel·low \'melō\ adj 1 : grown gentle or mild 2 : rich and full —**mellow** vb —**mel·low·ness** n

melo·dra·ma \'melǝˌdrämǝ, -ˌdram-\ n : overly theatrical play —**melo·dra·mat·ic** \ˌmelǝdrǝ'matik\ adj —**melo·dra·ma·tist** \ˌmelǝ'dramǝtǝst, -'dräm-\ n

mel·o·dy \'melǝdē\ n, pl -dies 1 : agreeable sound 2 : succession of musical notes —**me·lod·ic** \mǝ'lädik\ adj —**me·lod·i·cal·ly** \-ik(ǝ)lē\ adv —**me·lo·di·ous** \mǝ'lōdēǝs\ adj —**me·lo·di·ous·ly** adv —**me·lo·di·ous·ness** n

mel·on \'melǝn\ n : gourdlike fruit

melt \'melt\ vb 1 : change from solid to liquid usu. by heat 2 : dissolve or disappear gradually 3 : move or be moved emotionally

mem·ber \'membǝr\ n 1 : part of a person, animal, or plant 2 : one of a group 3 : part of a whole —**mem·ber·ship** \-ˌship\ n

mem·brane \'memˌbrān\ n : thin layer esp. of animal or plant tissue —**mem·bra·nous** \-brǝnǝs\ adj

me·men·to \mi'mentō\ n, pl -tos or -toes : souvenir

memo \'memō\ n, pl mem·os : memorandum

mem·oirs \'memˌwärz\ n pl : autobiography

mem·o·ra·bil·ia \ˌmemǝrǝ'bilēǝ, -'bilyǝ\ n pl 1 : memorable things 2 : mementos

mem·o·ra·ble \'mem(ǝ)rǝbǝl\ adj : worth remembering —**mem·o·ra·bil·i·ty** \ˌmemǝrǝ'bilǝtē\ n —**mem·o·ra·ble·ness** \'mem(ǝ)rǝbǝlnǝs\ n —**mem·o·ra·bly** \-blē\ adv

mem·o·ran·dum \ˌmemǝ'randǝm\ n, pl -dums or -da \-dǝ\ : informal note

me·mo·ri·al \mǝ'mōrēǝl\ n : something (as a monument) meant to keep remembrance alive —**memorial** adj —**me·mo·ri·al·ize** vb

Memorial Day n : last Monday in May or formerly May 30 observed as a legal holiday in commemoration of dead servicemen

mem·o·ry \'mem(ǝ)rē\ n, pl -ries 1 : power of remembering 2 : something remembered 3 : commemoration 4 : time within which past events are remembered —**mem·o·ri·za·tion** \ˌmem(ǝ)rǝ'zāshǝn\ n —**mem·o·rize** \'memǝˌrīz\ vb —**mem·o·riz·er** n

men pl of MAN

men·ace \'menǝs\ n : threat of danger ~ vb -aced; -ac·ing 1 : threaten 2 : endanger —**men·ac·ing·ly** adv

me·nag·er·ie \mǝ'naj(ǝ)rē\ n : collection of wild animals

mend \'mend\ vb 1 : improve 2 : repair 3 : heal —**mend** n —**mend·er** n

men·da·cious \men'dāshǝs\ adj : dishonest —**men·da·cious·ly** adv —**men·dac·i·ty** \-'dasǝtē\ n

men·di·cant \'mendikǝnt\ n : beggar —**men·di·can·cy** \-kǝnsē\ n —**mendicant** adj

men·ha·den \men'hādᵊn, mǝn-\ n, pl -den : fish related to the herring

me·nial \'mēnēǝl, -nyǝl\ adj 1 : relating to servants 2 : humble ~ n : domestic servant —**me·ni·al·ly** adv

men·in·gi·tis \ˌmenǝn'jītǝs\ n, pl -git·i·des \-'jitǝˌdēz\ : disease of the brain and spinal cord

meno·pause \'menǝˌpòz\ n : time when menstruation ends —**meno·paus·al** \ˌmenǝ'pòzǝl\ adj

men·stru·a·tion \ˌmenstrǝ'wāshǝn, menˌstrā-\ n : monthly discharge of blood from the uterus —**men·stru·al** \'menstrǝ(wǝ)l\ adj —**men·stru·ate** \'menstrǝˌwāt, -ˌstrāt\ vb

-ment \mənt\ *n suffix* **1** : result or means of an action **2** : action or process **3** : place of an action **4** : state or condition

men·tal \'ment⁰l\ *adj* : relating to the mind or its disorders —**men·tal·i·ty** \men'taləte\ *n* —**men·tal·ly** *adv*

men·thol \'men,thōl, -,thól\ *n* : soothing substance from oil of peppermint —**men·tho·lat·ed** \-thə,lātəd\ *adj*

men·tion \'menchən\ *vb* : refer to —**mention** *n*

men·tor \'men,tòr, 'mentər\ *n* : instructor

menu \'menyü, 'mān-\ *n* : restaurant's list of food

me·ow \mē'aù\ *n* : characteristic cry of a cat —**meow** *vb*

mer·can·tile \'mərkən,tēl, -,tīl\ *adj* : relating to merchants or trade

mer·ce·nary \'mərs⁰n,erē\ *n, pl* -**nar·ies** : hired soldier ∼ *adj* : serving only for money —**mer·ce·nar·i·ly** \,mərs⁰n'erəlē\ *adv* —**mer·ce·nari·ness** \'mərs⁰nerēnəs\ *n*

mer·cer \'mərsər\ *n* : textile dealer

mer·chan·dise \'mərchən,dīz, -,dīs\ *n* : goods bought and sold ∼ *vb* -**dised**; -**dis·ing** : buy and sell —**mer·chan·dis·er** *n*

mer·chant \'mərchənt\ *n* : one who buys and sells

merchant marine *n* : commercial ships

mer·cu·ri·al \,mər'kyúrēəl\ *adj* : unpredictable —**mer·cu·ri·al·ly** *adv* —**mer·cu·ri·al·ness** *n*

mer·cu·ry \'mərkyərē\ *n* : liquid metallic chemical element —**mer·cu·ric** \,mər'kyúrik\ *adj* —**mer·cu·rous** \,mər'kyúrəs, 'mərkyərəs\ *adj*

mer·cy \'mərsē\ *n, pl* -**cies** **1** : show of pity or leniency **2** : divine blessing —**mer·ci·ful** \-sifəl\ *adj* —**mer·ci·ful·ly** *adv* —**mer·ci·less** \-siləs\ *adj* —**mer·ci·less·ly** *adv* —**mercy** *adj*

mere \'miər\ *adj* **mer·est** : simple —**mere·ly** *adv*

merge \'mərj\ *vb* **merged**; **merg·ing** **1** : unite **2** : blend —**merg·er** \'mərjər\ *n*

me·rid·i·an \mə'ridēən\ *n* : imaginary circle on the earth's surface passing through the poles —**meridian** *adj*

me·ringue \mə'raŋ\ *n* : dessert topping of baked beaten egg whites

me·ri·no \mə'rēnō\ *n, pl* -**nos** **1** : kind of sheep **2** : fine soft woolen yarn

mer·it \'merət\ *n* **1** : praiseworthy quality **2** *pl* : rights and wrongs of a legal case ∼ *vb* : deserve —**mer·i·to·ri·ous** \,merə'tōrēəs\ *adj* —**mer·i·to·ri·ous·ly** *adv* —**mer·i·to·ri·ous·ness** *n*

mer·maid \'mər,mād\ *n* : legendary female sea creature

mer·ry \'merē\ *adj* -**ri·er**; -**est** : full of high spirits —**mer·ri·ly** *adv* —**mer·ri·ment** \'merimənt\ *n* —**mer·ry·mak·er** \'merē,mākər\ *n* —**mer·ry·mak·ing** \'merē,mākiŋ\ *n*

merry-go-round *n* : revolving amusement ride

me·sa \'māsə\ *n* : steep flat-topped hill

mesdames *pl of* MADAM *or* MADAME *or of* MRS.

mesdemoiselles *pl of* MADEMOISELLE

mesh \'mesh\ *n* **1** : one of the openings in a net **2** : net fabric **3** : working contact ∼ *vb* : fit together properly —**meshed** \'mesht\ *adj*

mes·mer·ize \'mezmə,rīz\ *vb* -**ized**; -**iz·ing** : hypnotize —**mes·mer·ic** \mez'merik\ *adj* —**mes·mer·ism** \'mezmə,rizəm\ *n*

mess \'mes\ *n* **1** : meal eaten by a group **2** : confused, dirty, or offensive state **3** : state of disorder or distress ∼ *vb* **1** : make dirty or untidy **2** : putter **3** : interfere

mes·sage \'mesij\ *n* : news, information, or a command sent by one person to another

mes·sen·ger \'mes⁰njər\ *n* : one who carries a message or does an errand

Mes·si·ah \mə'sīə\ *n* **1** : expected deliverer of the Jews **2** : Jesus Christ **3** *not cap* : great leader

messieurs *pl of* MONSIEUR

Messrs. *pl of* MR.

mes·ti·zo \me'stēzō\ *n, pl* -**zos** : person of mixed blood

met *past of* MEET

me·tab·o·lism \mə'tabə,lizəm\ *n* : sum of the processes of life support and esp. the processes by which a substance is assimilated or eliminated by the body —**met·a·bol·ic** \,metə'bälik\ *adj* —**me·tab·o·lize** \mə'tabə,līz\ *vb*

met·al \'met⁰l\ *n* : lustrous, fusible, ductile substance —**me·tal·lic** \mə'talik\ *adj* —**met·al·ware** *n* —**met·al·work** *n* —**met·al·work·er** *n* —**met·al·work·ing** *n*

met·al·lur·gy \'met⁰l,ərjē\ *n* : science of metals —**met·al·lur·gi·cal** \,met⁰l'ərjikəl\ *adj* —**met·al·lur·gi·cal·ly** *adv* —**met·al·lur·gist** \'met⁰l,ərjəst\ *n*

meta·mor·pho·sis \,metə'mòrfəsəs\ *n, pl* -**pho·ses** \-,sēz\ : sudden and drastic change (as of form) —**met·a·mor·phose** \-,fōz, -,fōs\ *vb*

met·a·phor \'metə,fòr, -fər\ *n* : use of a word denoting one kind of object or idea in place of another to suggest a likeness between them —**met·a·phor·i·cal** \,meta'fôrikəl\ adj

meta·phys·ics \,metə'fiziks\ n : study of the causes and nature of things —**meta·phys·i·cal** \-'fizakəl\ adj —**meta·phy·si·cian** \-fə'zishən\ n

mete \'mēt\ vb met·ed; met·ing : allot

me·te·or \'mētēər, -ē,ȯr\ n : small piece of matter in the solar system

me·te·or·ic \,mētē'ȯrik\ adj 1 : relating to a meteor 2 : sudden and brilliant —**me·te·or·i·cal·ly** \-i'kle\ adv

me·te·or·ite \'mētēə,rīt\ n : meteor that reaches the earth —**me·te·or·it·ic** \,mētēə'ritik\ adj

me·te·o·rol·o·gy \,mētēə'rälajē\ n : science of weather —**me·te·o·ro·log·i·cal** \-ē,ȯrə'läjikəl\ adj —**me·te·o·rol·o·gist** \-ēə'räljist\ n

¹me·ter \'mētər\ n : rhythm in verse or music

²met·er \'mētər\ n : unit of length equal to 39.37 inches

³me·ter \'mētər\ n : measuring instrument

meth·a·done \'methə,dōn\, **meth·a·don** \-,dän\ n : synthetic addictive narcotic

meth·ane \'meth,ān\ n : colorless odorless flammable gas

meth·a·nol \'methə,nȯl, -,nōl\ n : volatile flammable poisonous liquid

meth·od \'methəd\ n 1 : procedure for achieving an end 2 : orderly arrangement or plan —**me·thod·i·cal** \mə'thädikəl\ adj —**me·thod·i·cal·ly** \-k(ə)lē\ adv —**me·thod·i·cal·ness** n

me·tic·u·lous \mə'tikyələs\ adj : extremely careful in attending to details —**me·tic·u·lous·ly** adv —**me·tic·u·lous·ness** n

met·ric \'metrik\, **met·ri·cal** \-trikəl\ adj : relating to meter or the metric system —**met·ri·cal·ly** adv

met·ri·ca·tion \,metri'kāshən\ n : conversion into or expression in the metric system

metric system n : system of weights and measures using the meter and kilogram

met·ro·nome \'metrə,nōm\ n : instrument that produces regular repeated ticks

me·trop·o·lis \mə'träp(ə)ləs\ n : major city —**met·ro·pol·i·tan** \,metrə'päpət'n\ adj

met·tle \'met'l\ n : spirit or courage —**met·tle·some** \-səm\ adj

mez·za·nine \'mez'n,ēn, ,mez'n'ēn\ n 1 : shopping level between 2 main floors 2 : lowest balcony

mez·zo·so·pra·no \,metsōsə'pranō, ,me(d)z-\ n : voice between soprano and contralto

mi·as·ma \mī'azmə\ n : noxious vapor —**mi·as·mic** \-mik\ adj

mi·ca \'mīkə\ n : mineral separable into thin transparent sheets

mice pl of MOUSE

mi·cro \'mīkrō\ adj : very small

mi·crobe \'mī,krōb\ n : disease-causing microorganism —**mi·cro·bi·al** \mī'krōbēəl\ adj

mi·cro·bi·ol·o·gy \,mīkrōbī'äləjē\ n : biology dealing with microscopic life —**mi·cro·bi·o·log·i·cal** \-'mī,krō,bīə'läjikəl\ adj —**mi·cro·bi·ol·o·gist** \-'mīkrōbī'äləjist\ n

mi·cro·cosm \'mīkrə,käzəm\ n 1 : miniature universe 2 : human nature as an epitome of the world

mi·cro·film \'mīkrə,film\ n : small film recording printed matter —**microfilm** vb

mi·crom·e·ter \mī'krämətər\ n : instrument for measuring minute distances

mi·cro·min·ia·ture \,mīkrō'minēə,chùr, -'mini,chùr, -,chər\ adj : suitable for use with parts reduced to a very small size —**mi·cro·min·ia·tur·iza·tion** \-,minēə,chùrə'zāshən, -,mini,chùr-, -,chər-\ n —**mi·cro·min·ia·tur·ized** \-'minēəchə,rīzd, -'minichə-\ adj

mi·cron \'mī,krän\ n : 1/1000 millimeter

mi·cro·or·gan·ism \,mīkrō'ȯrgə,nizəm\ n : tiny being

mi·cro·phone \'mīkrə,fōn\ n : instrument for transmitting or recording sound by changing sound waves into variations of an electric current

mi·cro·scope \-,skōp\ n : optical device for magnifying tiny objects —**mi·cro·scop·ic** \,mīkrə'skäpik\, **mi·cro·scop·i·cal** \-ikəl\ adj —**mi·cro·scop·i·cal·ly** adv —**mi·cros·co·py** \mī'kräs-kəpē\ n

mi·cro·wave \'mīkrə,wāv\ n : short radio wave

mid \'mid\ adj : middle —**mid·point** n —**mid·stream** n —**mid·sum·mer** n —**mid·town** n or adj —**mid·week** n —**mid·win·ter** n —**mid·year** n

mid·air n : a point well above the ground

mid·day n : noon

mid·dle \'mid'l\ adj 1 : equally distant from the extremes 2 : being at neither extreme ~ n : middle part or point

Middle Ages n pl : period from about A.D. 500 to about 1500

mid·dle·man \-ˌman\ *n* : dealer or agent between the producer and consumer

mid·dling \'midliŋ, -lən\ *adj* 1 : of middle or medium size, degree, or quality 2 : mediocre

midge \'mij\ *n* : very tiny fly

midg·et \'mijət\ *n* : very small person or thing

mid·land \'midlənd, -ˌland\ *n* : interior of a country

mid·most *adj* : being nearest the middle —**midmost** *adv*

mid·night *n* : 12 o'clock at night

mid·riff \'mid,rif\ *n* : mid-region of the torso

mid·ship·man \'mid,shipmən, (ˌ)mid'ship-\ *n* : student naval officer

midst \'midst\ *n* : position close to or surrounded by others —**midst** *prep*

mid·way \'mid,wā\ *n* : concessions and amusements at a carnival ∼ *adv* : in the middle

mid·wife \'mid,wīf\ *n* : woman who aids at childbirth —**mid·wife·ry** \-ˌwīf(ə)rē\ *n*

mien \'mēn\ *n* : appearance

miff \'mif\ *vb* : upset or peeve

¹might \(ˈ)mīt\ *past of* MAY —used to express permission or possibility or as a polite alternative to *may*

²might \'mīt\ *n* : power or resources

mighty \'mītē\ *adj* **might·i·er; -est** 1 : very strong 2 : great —**might·i·ly** *adv* —**might·i·ness** *n* —**mighty** *adv*

mi·graine \'mī,grān\ *n* : severe headache and often nausea

mi·grant \'mīgrənt\ *n* : one who moves frequently to find work

mi·grate \'mī,grāt\ *vb* **-grat·ed; -grat·ing** 1 : move from one place to another 2 : pass periodically from one region or climate to another —**mi·gra·tion** \mī'grāshən\ *n* —**mi·gra·tion·al** \-sh(ə)nəl\ *adj* —**mi·gra·to·ry** \'mīgrəˌtōrē\ *adj*

mild \'mīld\ *adj* 1 : gentle in nature or behavior 2 : moderate in action or effect —**mild·ly** *adv* —**mild·ness** *n*

mil·dew \'mil,d(y)ü\ *n* : whitish fungal growth —**mildew** *vb*

mile \'mīl\ *n* : unit of length equal to 5280 feet

mile·age \'mīlij\ *n* 1 : allowance per mile for traveling expenses 2 : amount or rate of use expressed in miles

mile·stone *n* : significant point in development

mi·lieu \mēl'yə(r), -'yü\ *n, pl* **-lieus** *or*

-lieux \-'yə(r)(z), -'yüz\ : surroundings or setting

mil·i·tant \'milətənt\ *adj* : aggressively active or hostile —**mil·i·tan·cy** \-tənsē\ *n* —**militant** *n* —**mil·i·tant·ly** *adv*

mil·i·ta·rism \'milətə,rizəm\ *n* : dominance of military ideals or of a policy of aggressive readiness for war —**mil·i·tar·ist** \-ˌrəst\ *n* —**mil·i·ta·ris·tic** \,milətə'ristik\ *adj*

mil·i·tary \'milə,terē\ *adj* 1 : relating to soldiers, arms, or war 2 : relating to or performed by armed forces ∼ *n* : armed forces or the people in them —**mil·i·tar·i·ly** \,milə'terəlē\ *adv*

mil·i·tate \'milə,tāt\ *vb* **-tat·ed; -tat·ing** : have an effect

mi·li·tia \mə'lishə\ *n* : civilian soldiers —**mi·li·tia·man** \-mən\ *n*

milk \'milk\ *n* : nutritive fluid secreted by female mammals for feeding their young ∼ *vb* : draw off the milk of —**milk·er** *n* —**milk·i·ness** \-ēnəs\ *n* —**milky** *adj*

milk·man \-ˌman, -mən\ *n* : man who sells or delivers milk

milk·weed \-ˌwēd\ *n* : herb with milky juice

¹mill \'mil\ *n* 1 : building in which grain is ground into flour 2 : manufacturing plant 3 : machine used esp. for forming or processing ∼ *vb* 1 : subject to a process in a mill 2 : move in a circle —**mill·er** *n*

²mill *n* : 1/10 cent

mil·len·ni·um \mə'lenēəm\ *n, pl* **-nia** \-ēə\ *or* **-niums** : a period of 1000 years

mil·let \'milət\ *n* : cereal and forage grass with small seeds

mil·li·gram \'milə,gram\ *n* : 1/1000 gram

mil·li·li·ter \-ˌlētər\ *n* : 1/1000 liter

mil·li·me·ter \-ˌmētər\ *n* : 1/1000 meter

mil·li·ner \'milənər\ *n* : person who makes or sells women's hats —**mil·li·nery** \'milə,nerē\ *n*

mil·lion \'milyən\ *n, pl* **millions** *or* **million** : 1000 thousands —**million** *adj* —**mil·lionth** \-yənth\ *adj or n*

mil·lion·aire \,milyə'naər, 'milyə,naər\ *n* : person worth a million or more (as of dollars)

mil·li·pede \'milə,pēd\ *n* : long-bodied arthropod with 2 pairs of legs on most segments

mill·stone *n* : either of 2 round flat stones used for grinding grain

mime \'mīm, 'mēm\ *n* 1 : mimic 2 : art of telling a story by body movements —**mime** *vb*

mim·eo·graph \\'mimēə₁graf\\ *n* : machine for making many stencil copies —**mimeograph** *vb*

mim·ic \\'mimik\\ *n* : one that mimics ~ *vb* **-icked; -ick·ing 1** : imitate closely **2** : ridicule by imitation —**mim·ic·ry** \\'mimikrē\\ *n*

min·a·ret \\₁minə'ret\\ *n* : tower attached to a mosque

mince \\'mins\\ *vb* **minced; minc·ing 1** : cut into small pieces **2** : choose (one's words) carefully **3** : walk in a prim affected manner —**minc·ing** *adj*

mind \\'mīnd\\ *n* **1** : memory **2** : the part of an individual that feels, perceives, and esp. reasons **3** : intention **4** : normal mental condition **5** : opinion **6** : intellectual ability ~ *vb* **1** : attend to **2** : obey **3** : be concerned about **4** : be careful —**mind·ed** *adj* —**mind·less** \\'mīndləs\\ *adj* —**mind·less·ly** *adv* —**mind·less·ness** *n*

mind·ful \\-fəl\\ *adj* : aware or attentive —**mind·ful·ly** *adv* —**mind·ful·ness** *n*

¹mine \\'mīn\\ *pron* : one or the ones belonging to me

²mine \\'mīn\\ *n* **1** : excavation from which mineral substances are taken **2** : encased explosive for destroying enemy vehicles or vessels ~ *vb* **mined; min·ing 1** : get ore from **2** : place military mines in —**min·er** *n*

min·er·al \\'min(ə)rəl\\ *n* **1** : crystalline substance not of animal or vegetable origin **2** : useful natural substance (as coal) obtained from the ground —**mineral** *adj* —**min·er·al·ize** \\-₁līz\\ *vb*

min·er·al·o·gy \\₁minə'räləjē, -'ral-\\ *n* : science dealing with minerals —**min·er·al·og·i·cal** \\₁min(ə)rə'läjikəl\\ *adj* —**min·er·al·o·gist** \\₁minə'räləjəst, -'ral-\\ *n*

min·gle \\'miŋgəl\\ *vb* **-gled; -gling** : bring together or mix

mini- *comb form* : miniature or of small dimensions

minibook	minicourse
miniboom	minicrisis
minibrain	minidrama
minibudget	minidress
minibus	minifair
minicab	minifarm
minicalculator	minifestival
minicamera	minifeud
minicar	miniflaw
miniclock	minigarden
minicoat	minigrant
minicomponent	minigroup
minicomputer	miniguide
miniconvention	minihospital

minileague	minischool
minilecture	minisearch
minimarket	minisedan
minimiracle	miniseries
minimuseum	miniski
minination	miniskirt
mininetwork	minislump
mininovel	minisociety
mini-opera	ministate
minipanic	ministrike
minipark	minisub
miniplan	minisubmarine
minipool	minisurvey
miniprice	minisystem
miniproblem	miniterritory
minipump	minitheater
minirebellion	minitrain
minirecession	minivacation
miniriot	minivan
minirobot	miniversion
minirose	miniwar
miniscandal	minizoo

min·ia·ture \\'minēə₁chùr, 'mini₁chùr, -chər\\ *n* : tiny copy or very small version —**miniature** *adj* —**min·ia·tur·ist** \\-₁chùrəst, -chər-\\ *n* —**min·ia·tur·ize** \\-₁chə(r)₁rīz, -ichə-\\ *vb*

min·i·mal \\'minəməl\\ *adj* : relating to or being a minimum —**min·i·mal·ly** *adv*

min·i·mize \\'minə₁mīz\\ *vb* **-mized; -miz·ing 1** : reduce to a minimum **2** : estimate at a minimum

min·i·mum \\'minəməm\\ *n, pl* **-ma** \\-mə\\ *or* **-mums** : lowest quantity or amount —**minimum** *adj*

min·ion \\'minyən\\ *n* **1** : servile dependent **2** : subordinate official

min·is·ter \\'minəstər\\ *n* **1** : Protestant clergyman **2** : high officer of state **3** : diplomatic representative ~ *vb* : give aid or service —**min·is·te·ri·al** \\₁minə'stirēəl\\ *adj* —**min·is·tra·tion** *n*

min·is·try \\'minəstrē\\ *n, pl* **-tries 1** : office or duties of a minister **2** : body of ministers **3** : government department headed by a minister

mink \\'miŋk\\ *n, pl* **mink** *or* **minks** : weasellike mammal or its soft brown fur

min·now \\'minō\\ *n, pl* **-nows** : small freshwater fish

mi·nor \\'mīnər\\ *adj* : less in size, importance, or value ~ *n* **1** : person not yet of legal age **2** : secondary field of academic specialization

mi·nor·i·ty \\mə'nòrətē, mī-\\ *n, pl* **-ties 1** : time or state of being a minor **2** : smaller number (as of votes) **3**

: part of a population differing from others (as in race or religion)

min·strel \\'minstrəl\\ n 1 : medieval singer of verses 2 : performer in a program usu. of Negro songs and jokes —**min·strel·sy** \\-sē\\ n

¹mint \\'mint\\ n 1 : place where coins are made 2 : vast sum —**mint** vb —**mint·age** \\-ij\\ n —**mint·er** n

²mint n : herb with fragrant foliage —**minty** adj

min·u·et \\,minyə'wet\\ n : slow graceful dance

mi·nus \\'mīnəs\\ prep 1 : diminished by 2 : lacking ~ n : negative quantity or quality

mi·nus·cule \\'minəs,kyül, min'əs-\\ or **min·is·cule** \\'minəs-\\ adj : very small

¹min·ute \\'minət\\ n 1 : 60th part of an hour or of a degree 2 : short time 3 pl : official record of a meeting

²mi·nute \\mī'n(y)üt, mə-\\ adj **-nut·er; -est** 1 : very small 2 : marked by close attention to details —**mi·nute·ly** adv —**mi·nute·ness** n

mir·a·cle \\'mirikəl\\ n 1 : event that cannot be explained by known laws of nature 2 : marvel —**mi·rac·u·lous** \\mə'rakyələs\\ adj —**mi·rac·u·lous·ly** adv

mi·rage \\mə'räzh\\ n : reflection visible at sea or in deserts of some distant object

mire \\'mī(ə)r\\ n : heavy deep mud ~ vb **mired; mir·ing** : stick or sink in mire —**miry** adj

mir·ror \\'mirər\\ n : smooth substance (as of glass) that reflects images ~ vb : reflect in or as if in a mirror

mirth \\'mərth\\ n : gladness and laughter —**mirth·ful** \\-fəl\\ adj —**mirth·ful·ly** adv —**mirth·ful·ness** n —**mirth·less** adj

mis·an·thrope \\'misⁿn,thrōp\\ n : one who hates mankind —**mis·an·throp·ic** \\,misⁿn'thräpik\\ adj —**mis·an·thro·py** \\mis'anthrəpē\\ n

mis·ap·pre·hend \\,mis-\\ vb : misunderstand —**mis·ap·pre·hen·sion** n

mis·ap·pro·pri·ate \\,mis-\\ vb : take dishonestly for one's own use —**mis·ap·pro·pri·a·tion** n

mis·be·have \\,mis-\\ vb : behave improperly —**mis·be·hav·er** n —**mis·be·hav·ior** n

mis·cal·cu·late \\,mis-\\ vb : calculate wrongly —**mis·cal·cu·la·tion** \\,mis-\\ n

mis·car·ry \\,mis-\\ vb : give birth prematurely before the fetus can survive

2 : go wrong or be unsuccessful —**mis·car·riage** n

mis·ce·ge·na·tion \\,misə,jə'nāshən, ,misijə'nā-\\ n : marriage between members of different races

mis·cel·la·neous \\,misə'lānēəs\\ adj 1 : consisting of many things of different kinds —**mis·cel·la·neous·ly** adv —**mis·cel·la·neous·ness** n

mis·cel·la·ny \\'misə,lānē\\ n, pl **-nies** : collection of various things

mis·chance \\mis-\\ n : bad luck

mis·chief \\'mischəf\\ n : conduct esp. of a child that annoys or causes minor damage

mis·chie·vous \\'mischəvəs\\ adj 1 : causing annoyance or minor injury 2 : irresponsibly playful —**mis·chie·vous·ly** adv —**mis·chie·vous·ness** n

mis·con·ceive \\,mis-\\ vb : interpret incorrectly —**mis·con·cep·tion** n

mis·con·duct \\,mis-\\ n 1 : mismanagement 2 : bad behavior

mis·con·strue \\,mis-\\ vb : misinterpret —**mis·con·struc·tion** n

mis·cre·ant \\'miskrēənt\\ n : one who behaves criminally or viciously —**miscreant** adj

mis·deed \\mis-\\ n : wrong deed

mis·de·mean·or \\,misdi'mēnər\\ n : crime less serious than a felony

mi·ser \\'mīzər\\ n : person who hoards money —**mi·ser·li·ness** \\-lēnəs\\ n —**mi·ser·ly** adj

mis·er·a·ble \\'mizərbəl, 'miz(ə)rəbəl\\ adj 1 : wretchedly deficient 2 : causing extreme discomfort —**mis·er·a·ble·ness** n —**mis·er·a·bly** \\-blē\\ adv

mis·ery \\'miz(ə)rē\\ n, pl **-er·ies** : suffering and want caused by distress or poverty

mis·fire \\mis-\\ n 1 : fail to fire 2 : miss an intended effect —**misfire** n

mis·fit \\'mis,fit, mis'fit\\ n : person poorly adjusted to his environment

mis·for·tune \\mis-\\ n 1 : bad luck 2 : unfortunate condition or event

mis·giv·ing \\mis-\\ n : doubt or concern

mis·guid·ed \\mis-\\ adj : mistaken, uninformed, or deceived

mis·hap \\'mis,hap\\ n : accident

mis·in·form \\,misⁿn'fôrm\\ vb : give false information to —**mis·in·for·ma·tion** \\,mis-\\ n

mis·in·ter·pret \\,misⁿn'tərprət\\ vb : understand or explain wrongly —**mis·in·ter·pre·ta·tion** \\-,tərprə'tāshən\\ n

mis·judge \\mis-\\ vb : judge incorrectly or unjustly —**mis·judg·ment** n

mis·lay \\mis-\\ vb **-laid; -lay·ing** : misplace

mis·lead \mis-\ *vb* **-led; -lead·ing** : lead in a wrong direction or into error —**mis·lead·ing·ly** *adv*

mis·man·age \mis-\ *vb* : manage badly —**mis·man·age·ment** *n*

mis·no·mer \mis'nōmər\ *n* : wrong name

mi·sog·y·nist \mə'säjənəst\ *n* : one who hates or distrusts women —**mi·sog·y·ny** \-nē\ *n*

mis·place \mis-\ *vb* : put in an unremembered place or in the wrong place

mis·print \'mis,print, mis'-\ *n* : error in something printed

mis·pro·nounce \mis-\ *vb* : pronounce incorrectly —**mis·pro·nun·ci·a·tion** *n*

mis·quote \mis-\ *vb* : quote incorrectly —**mis·quo·ta·tion** \mis-\ *n*

mis·read \mis-\ *vb* **-read; -read·ing** : read or interpret incorrectly

mis·rep·re·sent \mis-\ *vb* : represent falsely or unfairly —**mis·rep·re·sen·ta·tion** *n*

mis·rule \mis-\ *vb* : govern badly ~ *n* **1** : bad or corrupt government **2** : disorder

¹**miss** \'mis\ *vb* **1** : fail to hit, reach, or contact **2** : notice the absence of **3** : fail to obtain **4** : avoid **5** : omit —**miss** *n*

²**miss** *n* : young unmarried woman or girl —often used as a title

mis·sal \'misəl\ *n* : book containing what is said at mass during the year

mis·shap·en \mis(h)'shāpən\ *adj* : distorted

mis·sile \'misəl\ *n* : object (as a stone or weapon) propelled **2** : self-propelled rocket weapon

miss·ing \'misiŋ\ *adj* : absent or lost

mis·sion \'mishən\ *n* **1** : ministry sent by a church to spread its teaching **2** : group of diplomats sent to another country **3** : task

mis·sion·ary \'mishə,nerē\ *adj* : relating to religious missions ~ *n, pl* **-ar·ies** : person sent to spread religious faith

mis·sive \'misiv\ *n* : letter

mis·spell \mis-\ *vb* : spell incorrectly —**mis·spell·ing** *n*

mis·state \mis-\ *vb* : state incorrectly —**mis·state·ment** *n*

mis·step \mis-\ *n* **1** : wrong step **2** : mistake

mist \'mist\ *n* : particles of water falling as fine rain

mis·take \mə'stāk\ *n* **1** : misunderstanding or wrong belief **2** : wrong action or statement —**mistake** *vb*

mis·tak·en \-'stākən\ *adj* : having a wrong opinion or incorrect information —**mis·tak·en·ly** *adv*

mis·ter \'mistər\ *n* : sir —used without a name in addressing a man

mis·tle·toe \'misəl,tō\ *n* : parasitic green plant

mis·treat \mis'trēt\ *vb* : treat badly —**mis·treat·ment** *n*

mis·tress \'mistrəs\ *n* **1** : woman in control **2** : woman with whom a man lives unmarried

mis·tri·al \mis'trī(ə)l\ *n* : trial that has no legal effect

mis·trust \-'trəst\ *n* : lack of confidence ~ *vb* : have no confidence in —**mis·trust·ful** \-fəl\ *adj* —**mis·trust·ful·ly** *adv* —**mis·trust·ful·ness** *n*

misty \'mistē\ *adj* **mist·i·er, -est** : obscured by mist —**mist·i·ly** *adv* —**mist·i·ness** *n*

mis·un·der·stand \mis,əndər'stand\ *vb* **1** : fail to understand **2** : interpret incorrectly

mis·un·der·stand·ing \-'standiŋ\ *n* **1** : wrong interpretation **2** : disagreement

mis·use \mis'ūz, mis(h)'yūz\ *vb* **1** : use incorrectly **2** : mistreat —**mis·use** \-'ūz, -'yūs\ *n*

mite \'mīt\ *n* **1** : tiny spiderlike animal **2** : small amount

mi·ter, mi·tre \'mītər\ *n* **1** : bishop's headdress **2** : angular joint in wood ~ *vb* **-tered** *or* **-tred; -ter·ing** *or* **-tring** \'mītəriŋ\ : bevel the ends of for a miter joint

mit·i·gate \'mitə,gāt\ *vb* **-gat·ed; -gat·ing** : make less severe —**mit·i·ga·tion** \,mitə'gāshən\ *n* —**mit·i·ga·tive** \'mitə,gātiv\ *adj* —**mit·i·ga·tor** \-,gātər\ *n* —**mit·i·ga·to·ry** \-gə,tōrē\ *adj*

mi·to·sis \mī'tōsəs\ *n, pl* **-to·ses** \-,sēz\ : process of forming 2 cell nuclei from one —**mi·tot·ic** \-'tätik\ *adj*

mitt \'mit\ *n* : mittenlike baseball glove

mit·ten \'mitᵊn\ *n* : hand covering without finger sections

mix \'miks\ *vb* : combine or join into one mass or group ~ *n* : commercially prepared food mixture —**mix·able** *adj* —**mix·er** *n* —**mix up** *vb* : confuse

mix·ture \'miks·chər\ *n* : act or product of mixing

mix-up *n* : instance of confusion

mne·mon·ic \ni'mänik\ *adj* : assisting memory

moan \'mōn\ *n* : low prolonged sound of pain or grief —**moan** *vb*

moat \'mōt\ *n* : deep wide trench around a castle

mob \'mäb\ *n* 1 : large disorderly crowd 2 : criminal gang ~ *vb* -**bb**- : crowd around and attack or annoy

mo·bile \'mōbəl, -,bēl, -,bīl\ *adj* : capable of moving or being moved ~ \'mō,bēl\ *n* : suspended art construction with freely moving parts —**mo·bil·i·ty** \mō'bilətē\ *n*

mo·bi·lize \'mōbə,līz\ *vb* -**lized; -liz·ing** : assemble and make ready for war duty —**mo·bi·li·za·tion** \,mōbə-lə'zāshən\ *n* —**mo·bi·liz·er** \'mō-bə,līzər\ *n*

moc·ca·sin \'mäkəsən\ *n* 1 : heelless shoe 2 : venomous U.S. snake

mock \'mäk, 'mȯk\ *vb* 1 : ridicule 2 : mimic in derision ~ *adj* 1 : simulated 2 : phony —**mock·er** *n* —**mock·ery** \-(ə)rē\ *n* —**mock·ing·ly** *adv*

mock·ing·bird \'mäkiŋ,bərd, 'mȯk-\ *n* : songbird that mimics other birds

mode \'mōd\ *n* 1 : particular form or variety 2 : style —**mod·al** \-ᵊl\ *adj* —**mod·ish** \'mōdish\ *adj*

mod·el \'mädᵊl\ *n* 1 : structural design 2 : miniature representation 3 : something worthy of copying 4 : one who poses for an artist or displays clothes 5 : type or design ~ *vb* -**eled** *or* -**elled; -el·ing** *or* -**el·ling** 1 : shape 2 : work as a model ~ *adj* 1 : serving as a pattern 2 : being a miniature representation of

mod·er·ate \'mädə)rət\ *adj* : avoiding extremes ~ \'mädə,rāt\ *vb* -**at·ed; -at·ing** 1 : lessen the intensity of 2 : act as a moderator —**moderate** *n* —**mod·er·ate·ly** *adv* —**mod·er·ate·ness** *n* —**mod·er·a·tion** \,mädə'rā-shən\ *n*

mod·er·a·tor \'mädə,rātər\ *n* : one who presides

mod·ern \'mädərn\ *adj* : relating to or characteristic of the present —**modern** *n* —**mo·der·ni·ty** \mə'dərnətē\ *n* —**mod·ern·iza·tion** \,mädərnə'zā-shən\ *n* —**mod·ern·ize** \'mädər,nīz\ *vb* —**mod·ern·iz·er** \'mädər,nīzər\ *n* —**mod·ern·ly** *adv* —**mod·ern·ness** *n*

mod·est \'mädəst\ *adj* 1 : having a moderate estimate of oneself 2 : reserved or decent in thoughts or actions 3 : limited in size, amount, or aim —**mod·est·ly** *adv* —**mod·es·ty** \-əstē\ *n*

mod·i·cum \'mädikəm\ *n* : small amount

mod·i·fy \'mädə,fī\ *vb* -**fied; -fy·ing** 1 : limit the meaning of 2 : change —**mod·i·fi·ca·tion** \,mädəfə'kāshən\ *n* —**mod·i·fi·er** \'mädə,fī(ə)r\ *n*

mod·u·lar \'mäjələr\ *adj* : built with standardized units —**mod·u·lar·ized** \-lə,rīzd\ *adj*

mod·u·late \'mäjə,lāt\ *vb* -**lat·ed; -lat·ing** 1 : keep in proper measure or proportion 2 : vary a radio wave —**mod·u·la·tion** \,mäjə'lāshən\ *n* —**mod·u·la·tor** \'mäjə,lātər\ *n* —**mod·u·la·to·ry** \-lə,tōrē\ *adj*

mod·ule \'mäjül\ *n* : standardized unit —**molar** *adj*

mo·gul \'mōgəl, mō'gəl\ *n* : important person

mo·hair \'mō,haər\ *n* : fabric made from the hair of the Angora goat

moist \'moist\ *adj* : slightly or moderately wet —**moist·en** \'moisᵊn\ *vb* —**moist·en·er** \'moisnər, -ᵊnər\ *n* —**moist·ly** *adv* —**moist·ness** *n*

mois·ture \'moischər\ *n* : small amount of liquid that causes dampness

mo·lar \'mōlər\ *n* : grinding tooth —**molar** *adj*

mo·las·ses \mə'lasəz\ *n* : thick brown syrup from raw sugar

¹**mold** \'mōld\ *n* : crumbly organic soil

²**mold** *n* : frame or cavity for forming ~ *vb* : shape in or as if in a mold —**mold·er** *n*

³**mold** *n* : surface growth of fungus ~ *vb* : become moldy —**mold·i·ness** \'mōldēnəs\ *n* —**moldy** *adj*

mol·der \'mōldər\ *vb* : crumble

mold·ing \'mōldiŋ\ *n* : decorative surface, plane, or strip

¹**mole** \'mōl\ *n* : spot on the skin

²**mole** *n* : small burrowing mammal —**mole·hill** *n*

mol·e·cule \'mäli,kyül\ *n* : small particle of matter —**mo·lec·u·lar** \mə'lek-yələr\ *adj*

mole·skin \-,skin\ *n* : heavy cotton fabric

mo·lest \mə'lest\ *vb* : annoy esp. by improper or rough handling —**mo·les·ta·tion** \,mōl,es'tāshən\ *n* —**mo·lest·er** *n*

mol·li·fy \'mälə,fī\ *vb* -**fied; -fy·ing** : soothe in temper —**mol·li·fi·ca·tion** \,mäləfə'kāshən\ *n*

mol·lusk, mol·lusc \'mäləsk\ *n* : shelled aquatic invertebrate —**mol·lus·can** \mə'ləskən\ *adj*

mol·ly·cod·dle \'mälē,kädᵊl\ *vb* -**dled; -dling** : pamper

molt \'mōlt\ *vb* : shed hair, feathers, outer skin, or horns periodically —**molt** *n* —**molt·er** *n*

mol·ten \'mōlt⁹n\ *adj* : fused or lique-fied by heat

mom \'mäm, 'məm\ *n* : mother

mo·ment \'mōmənt\ *n* **1** : tiny portion of time **2** : time of excellence **3** : importance

mo·men·tari·ly \'mōmən'terəlē\ *adv* **1** : for a moment **2** : at any moment

mo·men·tary \'mōmən,terē\ *adj* : continuing only a moment —**mo·men·tar·i·ness** *n*

mo·men·tous \mō'mentəs\ *adj* : very important —**mo·men·tous·ly** *adv* —**mo·men·tous·ness** *n*

mo·men·tum \-əm\ *n, pl* **-ta** \-ə\ *or* **-tums** : force of a moving body

mon·arch \'mänərk, -,ärk\ *n* **1** : ruler **2** : large orange and black migratory butterfly —**mo·nar·chi·cal** \mə'närkikəl\, **mo·nar·chic** \-'närkik\ *adj*

mon·ar·chy \'mänərkē\ *n, pl* **-chies** : realm of a monarch

mon·as·tery \'mänə,sterē\ *n, pl* **-ter·ies** : house for monks —**mon·as·te·ri·al** \,mänə'stirēəl\ *adj*

mo·nas·tic \mə'nastik\ *adj* : relating to monasteries, monks, or nuns —**monastic** *n* —**mo·nas·ti·cal·ly** \-tik(ə)lē\ *adv* —**mo·nas·ti·cism** \-tə,sizəm\ *n*

Mon·day \'məndē\ *n* : 2d day of the week

mon·e·tary \'mänə,terē, 'mən-\ *adj* : relating to money

mon·ey \'mänē\ *n, pl* **-eys** *or* **-ies** \'mänēz\ **1** : something (as coins or paper currency) used in buying **2** : wealth —**mon·eyed** \-ēd\ *adj* —**mon·ey·lend·er** *n*

mon·ger \'məngər, 'mäŋ-\ *n* : dealer

mon·gol·ism \'mäŋgə,lizəm\ *n* : congenital idiocy —**Mon·gol·oid** \-gə,lȯid\ *adj or n*

mon·goose \'män,güs, 'mäŋ-\ *n, pl* **-goos·es** : small agile mammal of India

mon·grel \'məŋgrəl, 'mäŋ-\ *n* : off-spring of mixed breed

mon·i·tor \'mänətər\ *n* **1** : student assistant **2** : television screen ~ *vb* : watch or observe esp. for quality

monk \'məŋk\ *n* : member of a religious order living in a monastery —**monk·ish** *adj* —**monk·ish·ly** *adv* —**monk·ish·ness** *n*

mon·key \'məŋkē\ *n, pl* **-keys** : small long-tailed arboreal primate ~ *vb* **1** : fool **2** : tamper

mon·key·shines \-,shīnz\ *n pl* : pranks

monks·hood \'məŋks,hůd\ *n* : poisonous herb with showy flowers

mon·o·cle \'mänikəl\ *n* : eyeglass for one eye

mo·nog·a·my \mə'näɡəmē\ *n* : marriage with one person at a time —**mo·nog·am·ic** \,mänə'ɡamik\ *adj* —**mo·nog·a·mist** \mə'näɡəməst\ *n* —**mo·nog·a·mous** \-məs\ *adj*

mono·gram \'mänə,ɡram\ *n* : sign of identity made of initials —**monogram** *vb*

mono·graph \-,ɡraf\ *n* : learned treatise

mono·lin·gual \,mänə'liŋɡwəl\ *adj* : using only one language

mono·lith \'män⁹l,ith\ *n* **1** : single great stone **2** : single uniform massive whole —**mono·lith·ic** \,män⁹l'ithik\ *adj*

mono·logue \'män⁹l,ȯɡ\ *n* : long speech —**mono·logu·ist** \-,ȯɡəst\, **mo·nol·o·gist** \mə'näləjəst, 'män⁹l,ȯɡəst\ *n*

mono·nu·cle·o·sis \,mänō,n(y)ü-klē'ōsəs\ *n* : acute infectious disease

mo·nop·o·ly \mə'näp(ə)lē\ *n, pl* **-lies 1** : exclusive ownership or control of a commodity **2** : one controlling a monopoly —**mo·nop·o·list** \-list\ *n* —**mo·nop·o·lis·tic** \mə,näpə'listik\ *adj* —**mo·nop·o·li·za·tion** \-lə'zāshən\ *n* —**mo·nop·o·lize** \mə'näpə,līz\ *vb*

mono·rail \'mänə,rāl\ *n* : single rail for a wheeled vehicle or a vehicle or system using it

mono·syl·la·ble \-,siləbəl\ *n* : word of one syllable —**mono·syl·lab·ic** \-sə'labik\ *adj*

mono·the·ism \'mänə(,)thē,izəm\ *n* : doctrine or belief that there is only one deity —**mono·the·ist** \-,thēəst\ *n*

mono·tone \'mänə,tōn\ *n* : succession of words in one unvarying tone

mo·not·o·nous \mə'nät⁹nəs\ *adj* **1** : sounded in one unvarying tone **2** : tediously uniform —**mo·not·o·nous·ly** *adv* —**mo·not·o·nous·ness** *n* —**mo·not·o·ny** \-⁹nē\ *n*

mon·ox·ide \mə'näk,sīd\ *n* : oxide containing one atom of oxygen in the molecule

mon·sieur \məs(h)(')yə(r), mə'si(ə)r\ *n, pl* **mes·sieurs** \məs(h)(')yə(r)(z), más-; mə'si(ə)r(z)\ : man of high rank or station —used as a title for a man esp. of French nationality

mon·si·gnor \män'sēnyər\ *n, pl* **monsignors** *or* **mon·si·gno·ri** \,män-,sēn'yȯrē\ : Roman Catholic prelate —used as a title

mon·soon \män'sün\ *n* : periodic rainy season —**mon·soon·al** \-⁹l\ *adj*

mon·ster \'mänstər\ *n* **1** : abnormal or terrifying animal **2** : ugly, wicked, or cruel person —**mon·stros·i·ty**

\mān'strāsətē\ *n* —**mon·strous**
\'mänstrəs\ *adj* —**mon·strous·ly** *adv*

mon·tage \män'täzh\ *n* : composite photo

month \'mənth\ *n* : 12th part of a year —**month·ly** *adv or adj or n*

mon·u·ment \'mänyəmənt\ *n* : structure erected in remembrance —**mon·u·men·tal** \,mänyə'ment³l\ *adj* —**mon·u·men·tal·ly** *adv*

moo \'mü\ *vb* : make the noise of a cow —**moo** *n*

mood \'müd\ *n* : state of mind or emotion

moody \'müdē\ *adj* **mood·i·er; -est** 1 : sad 2 : subject to changing moods and esp. to bad moods —**mood·i·ly** \'müd³lē\ *adv* —**mood·i·ness** \-ēnəs\ *n*

moon \'mün\ *n* : earth's satellite —**moon·beam** *n* —**moon·light** *n* —**moon·lit** *adj*

moon·light \-,līt\ *vb* **-ed; -ing** : hold a 2d job —**moon·light·er** *n*

moon·shine *n* 1 : moonlight 2 : illegally distilled liquor

¹**moor** \'mür\ *n* : open usu. swampy wasteland —**moor·land** \-lənd, -,land\ *n*

²**moor** *vb* : fasten with line or anchor

moor·ing \-iŋ\ *n* : place where boat can be moored

moose \'müs\ *n, pl* **moose** : large heavy-antlered deer

moot \'müt\ *adj* : open to question

mop \'mäp\ *n* : floor-cleaning implement ~ *vb* **-pp-** : use a mop on

mope \'mōp\ *vb* **moped; mop·ing** : be sad or listless

mo·ped \'mō,ped\ *n* : low-powered motorbike

mo·raine \mə'rān\ *n* : glacial deposit of earth and stones

mor·al \'mòrəl\ *adj* 1 : relating to principles of right and wrong 2 : conforming to a standard of right behavior 3 : relating to or acting on the mind, character, or will ~ *n* 1 : point of a story 2 *pl* : moral practices or teachings —**mor·al·ist** \'mòrələst\ *n* —**mor·al·is·tic** \,mòrə'listik\ *adj* —**mor·al·i·ty** \mə'ralətē\ *n* —**mor·al·ize** \'mòrə,līz\ *vb* —**mor·al·ly** *adv*

mo·rale \mə'ral\ *n* : emotional attitude

mo·rass \mə'ras\ *n* : swamp

mor·a·to·ri·um \,mòrə'tōrēəm\ *n, pl* **-ri·ums** *or* **-ria** \-ēə\ : suspension of activity

mo·ray \mə'rā, 'mòr,ā\ *n* : savage eel

mor·bid \'mòrbəd\ *adj* 1 : relating to disease 2 : gruesome —**mor·bid·i·ty**

\mòr'bidətē\ *n* —**mor·bid·ly** *adv* —**mor·bid·ness** *n*

mor·dant \'mòrd³nt\ *adj* : incisive —**mor·dant·ly** *adv*

more \'mōr\ *adj* 1 : greater 2 : additional ~ *adv* 1 : in addition 2 : to a greater degree ~ *n* 1 : greater quantity 2 : additional amount ~ *pron* : additional ones

more·over \mōr'ōvər\ *adv* : in addition

mo·res \'mòr,āz, -(,)ēz\ *n, pl* : customs

morgue \'mòrg\ *n* : mortuary for persons found dead

mor·i·bund \'mòrə(,)bənd\ *adj* : dying —**mor·i·bun·di·ty** \,mòrə'bəndətē\ *n*

morn \'mòrn\ *n* : morning

morn·ing \-niŋ\ *n* : time from sunrise to noon

mo·ron \'mōr,än\ *n* : mentally deficient person —**mo·ron·ic** \mə'ränik\ *adj* —**mo·ron·i·cal·ly** \-ik(ə)lē\ *adv*

mo·rose \mə'rōs\ *adj* : sullen —**mo·rose·ly** *adv* —**mo·rose·ness** *n*

mor·phine \'mòr,fēn\ *n* : addictive painkilling drug

mor·row \'märō\ *n* : next day

Morse code \'mòrs-\ *n* : code of dots and dashes or long and short sounds used for transmitting messages

mor·sel \'mòrsəl\ *n* : small piece or quantity

mor·tal \'mòrt³l\ *adj* 1 : causing or subject to death 2 : extreme —**mortal** *n* —**mor·tal·i·ty** \mòr'talətē\ *n* —**mor·tal·ly** \'mòrt³lē\ *adv*

mor·tar \'mòr,tar\ *n* 1 : strong bowl 2 : short-barreled cannon 3 : masonry material that hardens —**mortar** *vb*

mort·gage \'mòrgij\ *n* : transfer of property rights as security for a loan —**mortgage** *vb* —**mort·gag·ee** \,mòrgi'jē\ *n* —**mort·gag·or** \,mòrgi'jòr\ *n*

mor·ti·fy \'mòrta,fī\ *vb* **-fied; -fy·ing** 1 : subdue by abstinence or self-inflicted pain 2 : humiliate —**mor·ti·fi·ca·tion** \,mòrtəfə'kāshən\ *n*

mor·tu·ary \'mòrchə,werē\ *n, pl* **-ar·ies** : place in which dead bodies are kept until burial

mo·sa·ic \mō'zāik\ *n* : inlaid stone decoration

Mos·lem \'mäzləm\ *var of* MUSLIM

mosque \'mäsk\ *n* : building where Muslims worship

mos·qui·to \mə'skētō\ *n, pl* **-toes** : biting insect

moss \'mòs\ *n* : green seedless plant —**mossy** *adj*

most \'mōst\ *adj* : majority of 2 : greatest ~ *adv* : to the greatest or a very great degree ~ n : greatest amount ~ pron : greatest number or part

-most \ˌmōst\ adj suffix : most : most toward

most·ly \ˈmōstlē\ adv : mainly

mote \ˈmōt\ n : small particle

mo·tel \mōˈtel\ n : hotel with outdoor parking area

moth \ˈmȯth\ n : small pale insect related to the butterflies

moth·er \ˈməthər\ n 1 : female parent 2 : source ~ vb 1 : give birth to 2 : cherish or protect —mother·hood \-ˌhůd\ n —mother·land \-ˌland\ n —mother·less adj —moth·er·ly adj

moth·er-in-law \ˈməth(ə)rənˌlȯ, ˈməthərnˌlȯ\ n, pl mothers-in-law : spouse's mother

mo·tif \mōˈtēf\ n : dominant theme

mo·tion \ˈmōshən\ n 1 : proposal for action 2 : act or instance of moving ~ vb : direct by a motion —motion·less adj —mo·tion·less·ly adv —mo·tion·less·ness n

motion picture n : movie

mo·ti·vate \ˈmōtəˌvāt\ vb -vat·ed; -vat·ing : provide with a motive —mo·ti·va·tion \ˌmōtəˈvāshən\ n

mo·tive \ˈmōtiv\ n : cause of a person's action ~ adj 1 : moving to action 2 : relating to motion —mo·tive·less adj

mot·ley \ˈmätlē\ adj : of diverse colors or elements

mo·tor \ˈmōtər\ n : unit that supplies power or motion ~ vb : travel by automobile —mo·tor·ist \-əst\ n —mo·tor·ize \ˈmōtəˌrīz\ vb

mo·tor·bike n : lightweight motorcycle

mo·tor·boat n : engine-driven boat

mo·tor·car n : automobile

mo·tor·cy·cle \-ˌsīkəl\ n : 2-wheeled automotive vehicle —mo·tor·cy·clist n

mo·tor·truck n : automotive truck

mot·tle \ˈmätᵊl\ vb -tled; -tling : mark with spots of different color

mot·to \ˈmätō\ n, pl -toes : brief guiding rule

mould \ˈmōld\ var of MOLD

mound \ˈmaůnd\ n : pile (as of earth)

¹mount \ˈmaůnt\ n : mountain

²mount \ˈmaůnt\ vb 1 : increase in amount 2 : get up on 3 : put in position ~ n 1 : frame or support 2 : horse to ride —mount·able adj —mount·er n

moun·tain \ˈmaůntᵊn\ n : elevated land higher than a hill —moun·tain·ous \ˈmaůntnəs, -ᵊnəs\ adj —moun·tain·top n

moun·tain·eer \ˌmaůntᵊnˈiər\ n

: mountain resident or climber —mountaineer vb

mourn \ˈmōrn\ vb : feel or express grief —mourn·er n —mourn·ful \-fəl\ adj —mourn·ful·ly adv —mourn·ful·ness n —mourn·ing n

mouse \ˈmaůs\ n, pl mice \ˈmīs\ : small rodent —mouse·trap n or vb

mous·tache \ˈməsˌtash, (ˌ)məsˈtash\ var of MUSTACHE

mouth \ˈmaůth\ n : opening through which an animal takes in food ~ \ˈmaůth\ vb : speak —mouthed \ˈmaůthd, ˈmaůtht\ adj —mouth·ful \-ˌfůl\ n

mouth·piece n 1 : part (as of a musical instrument) held in or to the mouth 2 : spokesman

mou·ton \ˈmüˌtän\ n : processed sheepskin

move \ˈmüv\ vb moved; mov·ing 1 : go or cause to go to another point 2 : change residence 3 : change or cause to change position 4 : take or cause to take action 5 : make a formal request 6 : stir the emotions ~ n : act or instance of moving —mov·able, move·able \-əbəl\ adj —move·ment n —mov·er n

mov·ie \ˈmüvē\ n : projected picture in which persons and objects seem to move

¹mow \ˈmaů\ n : part of a barn where hay or straw is stored

²mow \ˈmō\ vb mowed; mowed or mown \ˈmōn\; mow·ing : cut with a machine —mow·er n

Mr. \ˌmistər\ n, pl Messrs. \ˌmesərz\ —conventional title for a man

Mrs. \ˌmisəz, -əs, esp South \ˌmizəz, -əs, or (ˌ)miz, or before first names (ˌ)mis\ n, pl Mes·dames \mā'däm, -'dam\ —conventional title for a married woman

Ms. \(ˈ)miz\ n —conventional title for a woman

much \ˈməch\ adj more \ˈmōr\; most \ˈmōst\ : great in quantity, extent, or degree ~ adv more; most : to a great degree or extent ~ n : great quantity, extent, or degree

mu·ci·lage \ˈmyüs(ə)lij\ n : weak glue —mu·ci·lag·i·nous \ˌmyüsəˈlajənəs\ adj

muck \ˈmək\ n : manure, dirt, or mud —mucky adj

mu·cus \ˈmyükəs\ n : slippery protective secretion of membranes (mucous membranes) lining body cavities —mu·cous \-kəs\ adj

mud \\'məd\\ *n* : soft wet earth —**mud-di-ly** \\'məd?lē\\ *adv* —**mud-di-ness** \\-ēnəs\\ *n* —**mud-dy** *adj or vb*

mud-dle \\'məd?l\\ *vb* -**dled**; -**dling** 1 : make, be, or act confused 2 : make a mess of —**muddle** *n* —**mud-dle-head-ed** \\,məd?l'hedəd\\ *adj*

mu-ez-zin \\m(y)ü'ez?n\\ *n* : Muslim who calls the hour of daily prayer

¹muff \\'məf\\ *n* : tubular hand covering

²muff *vb* : bungle —**muff** *n*

muf-fin \\'məfən\\ *n* : soft biscuit baked in a cup-shaped container

muf-fle \\'məfəl\\ *vb* -**fled**; -**fling** 1 : wrap up 2 : dull the sound of —**muf-fler** \\'məflər\\ *n*

muf-ti \\'məftē\\ *n* : civilian clothes

¹mug \\'məg\\ *n* : drinking cup ~ *vb* -**gg**- : make faces

²mug *vb* -**gg**- : assault with intent to rob —**mug-ger** *n*

mug-gy \\'məgē\\ *adj* -**gi-er**; -**est** : hot and humid —**mug-gi-ness** *n*

Mu-ham-mad-an \\mō'haməd?n, -'häm-; mü-\\ *n* : Muslim —**Mu-ham-mad-an-ism** \\-,izəm\\ *n*

mu-lat-to \\m(y)ü'latō, -lät-\\ *n, pl* -**toes** *or* -**tos** : 1st-generation offspring of a Negro and a white

mul-ber-ry \\'məl,berē\\ *n* : tree with small edible fruit

mulch \\'məlch\\ *n* : protective ground covering —**mulch** *vb*

mulct \\'məlkt\\ *n or vb* : fine

¹mule \\'myül\\ *n* 1 : offspring of a male ass and a female horse 2 : stubborn person —**mul-ish** \\'myülish\\ *adj* —**mul-ish-ly** *adv* —**mul-ish-ness** *n*

²mule *n* : backless shoe

mull \\'məl\\ *vb* : ponder

mul-let \\'mələt\\ *n, pl* -**let** *or* -**lets** : marine food fish

multi- *comb form* 1 : many or multiple 2 : many times over

multiarmed	multidivisional
multibarreled	multidwelling
multibillion	multifaceted
multibranched	multifamily
multibuilding	multifilament
multicenter	multifunction
multichambered	multifunctional
multichannel	multigrade
multicolored	multiheaded
multidenomina-	multihospital
tional	multihued
multidimensional	multilane
multidirectional	multilevel
multidisciplinary	multimillion
multidiscipline	multimillionaire

multipart	multispeed
multiparty	multistage
multiplant	multistep
multipolar	multistory
multiproblem	multisyllabic
multiproduct	multitalented
multipurpose	multitrack
multiracial	multiunion
multiroomed	multiunit
multisense	multiuse
multiservice	multiwarhead
multisided	multiyear

mul-ti-far-i-ous \\,məltə'farēəs\\ *adj* : diverse —**mul-ti-far-i-ous-ly** *adv*

mul-ti-lat-er-al \\,məltəˈlatərəl, -,tī-, -'latrəl\\ *adj* : having many sides or participants

mul-ti-lin-gual \\-'lingwəl\\ *adj* : involving several languages —**mul-ti-lin-gual-ism** \\-,gwə,lizəm\\ *n*

mul-ti-ple \\'məltəpəl\\ *adj* : several or many 2 : complex ~ *n* : product of one number by another

multiple sclerosis *n* : brain or spinal disease affecting muscle control

mul-ti-pli-ca-tion \\,məltəplə'kāshən\\ *n* 1 : increase 2 : short method of repeated addition

mul-ti-plic-i-ty \\,məltə'plisətē\\ *n, pl* -**ties** : great number or variety

mul-ti-ply \\'məltə,plī\\ *vb* -**plied**; -**ply-ing** 1 : increase in number 2 : perform multiplication —**mul-ti-pli-er** \\-,plī(ə)r\\ *n*

mul-ti-tude \\'məltə,t(y)üd\\ *n* : great number —**mul-ti-tu-di-nous** \\,məltə't(y)üdnəs, -°nəs\\ *adj*

¹mum \\'məm\\ *adj* : silent

²mum *n* : chrysanthemum

mum-ble \\'məmbəl\\ *vb* -**bled**; -**bling** : speak indistinctly —**mumble** *n* —**mum-bler** *n*

mum-mer \\'məmər\\ *n* 1 : actor esp. in a pantomime 2 : disguised merry-maker —**mum-mery** *n*

mum-my \\'məmē\\ *n, pl* -**mies** : embalmed body —**mum-mi-fi-ca-tion** \\,məmifə'kāshən\\ *n* —**mum-mi-fy** \\'məmi,fī\\ *vb*

mumps \\'məmps\\ *n sing or pl* : virus disease with swelling esp. of the salivary glands

munch \\'mənch\\ *vb* : chew

mun-dane \\,mən'dān, 'mən,-\\ *adj* 1 : relating to the world 2 : lacking concern for the ideal or spiritual —**mun-dane-ly** *adv*

mu-nic-i-pal \\myu̇'nisəpəl\\ *adj* : of or relating to a town or city —**mu-nic-i-**

pal·i·ty \myü,nisə'palətē\ n —mu·nic·i·pal·ly adv

mu·nif·i·cent \myü'nifəsənt\ adj : generous —mu·nif·i·cence \-səns\ n

mu·ni·tions \myü'nishənz\ n pl : armaments

mu·ral \'myürəl\ adj : relating to a wall ~ n : wall painting —mu·ra·list n

mur·der \'mərdər\ n : unlawful killing of a person ~ vb : commit a murder —mur·der·er n —mur·der·ess \-əs\ n —mur·der·ous \-əs\ adj —mur·der·ous·ly adv

murk \'mərk\ n : darkness —murk·i·ly \'mərkəlē\ adv —murk·i·ness \-kēnəs\ n —murky adj

mur·mur \'mərmər\ n 1 : muttered complaint 2 : low indistinct sound —murmur vb —mur·mur·er n —murmur·ous adj

mus·ca·tel \,məskə'tel\ n : sweet wine

mus·cle \'məsəl\ n 1 : body tissue capable of contracting 2 : strength ~ vb -cled; -cling : force one's way —mus·cled adj —mus·cu·lar \'məskyələr\ adj —mus·cu·lar·i·ty \,məskyə'larətē\ n

muscular dystrophy n : disease marked by progressive wasting of muscles

mus·cu·la·ture \'məskyələ,chür\ n : bodily muscles

¹**muse** \'myüz\ vb mused; mus·ing : ponder —mus·ing·ly adv

²**muse** n : source of inspiration

mu·se·um \myü'zēəm\ n : institution displaying objects of interest

mush \'məsh\ n 1 : corn meal boiled in water or something of similar consistency 2 : sentimental nonsense —mushy adj

mush·room \'məsh,rüm, -,rům\ n : caplike organ of a fungus ~ vb : grow rapidly

mu·sic \'myüzik\ n : vocal or instrumental sounds —mu·si·cal \-zikəl\ adj or n —mu·si·cal·ly adv

mu·si·cian \myü'zishən\ n : composer or performer of music —mu·si·cian·ly adj —mu·si·cian·ship n

musk \'məsk\ n : strong-smelling substance from an Asiatic deer used in perfume —musk·i·ness \'məskēnəs\ n —musky adj

mus·kel·lunge \'məskə,lənj\ n, pl -lunge : large No. American pike

mus·ket \'məskət\ n : shoulder firearm —mus·ke·teer \,məskə'tiər\ n

musk·mel·on \'məsk,melən\ n : small edible melon

musk-ox \'məsk,äks\ n : shaggy-coated wild ox of the arctic

musk·rat \'məs,krat\ n, pl -rat or -rats : No. American water rodent

Mus·lim \'məzləm\ n : adherent of the religion founded by Muhammad

mus·lin \'məzlən\ n : cotton fabric

muss \'məs\ n : untidy state ~ vb : disarrange —muss·i·ly \'məsəlē\ adv —muss·i·ness \-ēnəs\ n —mussy adj

mus·sel \'məsəl\ n : edible mollusk

must \'məst\ vb —used as an auxiliary esp. to express a command, obligation, or necessity ~ \'məst\ n : something necessary

mus·tache \'məs,tash, (,)məs'-\ n : hair of the human upper lip

mus·tang \'məs,taŋ\ n : wild horse of Western America

mus·tard \'məstərd\ n : pungent yellow seasoning

mus·ter \'məstər\ vb 1 : assemble 2 : rouse ~ n : assembled group

musty \'məstē\ adj mus·ti·er; -est : stale —must·i·ly adv —must·i·ness n

mu·ta·ble \'myütəbəl\ adj : changeable —mu·ta·bil·i·ty \,myütə'bilətē\ n

mu·tant \'myüt³nt\ adj : relating to or produced by mutation —mutant n

mu·tate \'myü,tāt\ vb -tat·ed; -tat·ing : undergo mutation —mu·ta·tive \'myü,tātiv, myütət-\ adj

mu·ta·tion \myü'tāshən\ n : change in a hereditary character —mu·ta·tion·al adj

mute \'myüt\ adj mut·er; -est 1 : unable to speak 2 : silent ~ n 1 : one who is speechless 2 : muffling device ~ vb muted; mut·ing : muffle —mute·ly adv —mute·ness n

mu·ti·late \'myüt³l,āt\ vb -lat·ed; -lat·ing : damage seriously (as by cutting off or altering an essential part) —mu·ti·la·tion \,myüt³l'āshən\ n —mu·ti·la·tor \'myüt³l,ātər\ n

mu·ti·ny \'myüt(ə)nē\ n, pl -nies : rebellion —mu·ti·neer \,myüt³n'iər\ n —mu·ti·nous \'myüt³nəs\ adj —mu·ti·nous·ly adv

mutt \'mət\ n : mongrel

mut·ter \'mətər\ vb 1 : speak indistinctly or softly 2 : grumble —mutter n

mut·ton \'mət³n\ n : flesh of a mature sheep —mut·tony adj

mu·tu·al \'myüchə(wə)l\ adj : given or felt by one another in equal amount 2 : common —mu·tu·al·ly adv

muz·zle \'məzəl\ n 1 : nose and jaws of

an animal 2 : muzzle covering to immobilize an animal's jaws 3 : discharge end of a gun ~ vb -zled; -zling : restrain with or as if with a muzzle

my \\('\\)mī\\ adj 1 : relating to me or myself 2 —used interjectionally esp. to express surprise

my·na, my·nah \\'mīnə\\ n : Asian starling

my·o·pia \\mī'ōpēə\\ n : nearsightedness —**my·o·pic** \\-'ōpik, -'äpik\\ adj —**my·o·pi·cal·ly** \\-(ə)lē\\ adv

myr·i·ad \\'mirēəd\\ n : indefinitely large number —**myriad** adj

myrrh \\'mər\\ n : aromatic plant gum

myr·tle \\'mərt²l\\ n : shiny evergreen

my·self \\mī'self, mə-\\ pron : I, me —used reflexively or for emphasis

mys·tery \\'mist(ə)rē\\ n, pl -ter·ies 1 : religious truth 2 : something not understood 3 : puzzling or secret quality or state —**mys·te·ri·ous**

\\mis'tirēəs\\ adj —**mys·te·ri·ous·ly** adv —**mys·te·ri·ous·ness** n

mys·tic \\'mistik\\ adj : mystical or mysterious ~ n : one who has mystical experiences —**mys·ti·cism** \\-tə,sizəm\\ n

mys·ti·cal \\'mistikəl\\ adj 1 : spiritual 2 : relating to direct communion with God

mys·ti·fy \\'mistə,fī\\ vb -fied; -fy·ing : perplex —**mys·ti·fi·ca·tion** \\,mistəfə'kāshən\\ n

mys·tique \\mis'tēk\\ n : beliefs and attitudes associated with something

myth \\'mith\\ n 1 : legendary narrative explaining a belief or phenomenon 2 : imaginary person or thing —**myth·i·cal** \\-ikəl\\ adj

my·thol·o·gy \\mith'äləjē\\ n, pl -gies : body of myths —**myth·o·log·i·cal** \\,mithə'läjikəl\\ adj —**my·thol·o·gist** \\mith'äləjəst\\ n

N

n \\'en\\ n, pl **n's** or **ns** \\'enz\\ : 14th letter of the alphabet

nab \\'nab\\ vb -bb- : seize or arrest

na·dir \\'nā,dior, 'nādər\\ n : lowest point

¹**nag** \\'nag\\ n : old or decrepit horse

²**nag** vb -gg- 1 : scold or urge continually 2 : be persistently annoying ~ n : one who nags habitually

na·iad \\'nāəd, 'nī-, -,ad\\ n, pl -iads or -ia·des \\-ə,dēz\\ : mythological water nymph

nail \\'nāl\\ n 1 : horny sheath at the end of each finger and toe 2 : pointed metal fastener ~ vb : fasten with a nail —**nail·er** n

na·ive, na·ive \\nä'ēv\\ adj -iv·er; -est 1 : innocent and unsophisticated 2 : easily deceived —**na·ive·ly** adv —**na·ive·ness** n

na·ive·té, na·ive·te \\,nä,ēv(ə)'tā, nä'ēvə,-\\ n : quality or state of being naive

na·ked \\'nākəd, 'nekəd\\ adj 1 : having no clothes on 2 : uncovered 3 : plain or obvious 4 : unaided —**na·ked·ly** adv —**na·ked·ness** n

nam·by-pam·by \\,nambē'pambē\\ adj : weak or indecisive

name \\'nām\\ n 1 : word by which a person or thing is known 2 : disparaging word for someone 3 : distinguished reputation ~ vb named; **nam·ing** 1 : give a name to 2 : mention or identify by name 3 : nominate or appoint ~ adj 1 : relating to a name 2 : prominent —**name·able** adj —**name·less** adj —**name·less·ly** adv

name·ly \\'nāmlē\\ adv : that is to say

name·sake \\-,sāk\\ n : one named after another

¹**nap** \\'nap\\ vb -pp- 1 : sleep briefly 2 : be off guard ~ n : short sleep

²**nap** n : soft downy surface —**nap·less** adj —**napped** \\'napt\\ adj

na·palm \\'nā,pä(l)m\\ n : gasoline in the form of a jelly

nape \\'nāp, 'nap\\ n : back of the neck

naph·tha \\'naftha, 'nap-\\ n : flammable solvent

nap·kin \\'napkən\\ n : small cloth for use at the table

nar·cis·sism \\'närsə,sizəm\\ n : self-love —**nar·cis·sist** \\-səst\\ n or adj

nar·cis·sus \\när'sisəs\\ n, pl -cis·sus or -cis·sus·es or -cis·si \\-'sis,ī, -,ē\\ : plant with flowers usu. borne separately

nar·cot·ic \\när'kätik\\ n : painkilling addictive drug —**narcotic** adj

nar·rate \\'nar,āt\\ vb nar·rat·ed; nar·rat·ing : tell (a story) —**nar·ra·tion** \\na'rāshən\\ n —**nar·ra·tive** \\'närətiv\\ n or adj —**nar·ra·tor** \\'nar,ātər\\ n

nar·row \\'narō\\ adj 1 : of less than standard width 2 : limited 3 : not liberal 4 : barely successful ~ vb

: make narrow —**nar·row·ly** adv
—**nar·row·ness** n

nar·row-mind·ed \\,narō'mīndəd\ adj
: shallow, provincial, or bigoted

nar·rows \\'narōz\ n pl : narrow passages

nar·whal \\'när,hwäl, 'närwəl\ n : sea mammal with a tusk

nasal \\'nāzəl\ adj : relating to or uttered through the nose —**na·sal·ly** adv

nas·tur·tium \\nə'stərshəm, na-\ n : herb with showy flowers

nas·ty \\'nastē\ adj **nas·ti·er; -est** 1 : filthy 2 : indecent 3 : malicious or spiteful —**nas·ti·ly** \\'nastəlē\ adv —**nas·ti·ness** \\-ēnəs\ n

na·tal \\'nāt³l\ adj : relating to birth

na·tion \\'nāshən\ n 1 : people of similar characteristics 2 : community with its own territory and government —**na·tion·al** \\'nash(ə)nəl\ adj or n —**na·tion·al·ly** adv —**na·tion·hood** n

na·tion·al·ism \\'nash(ə)nəl,izəm\ n : devotion to national interests, unity, and independence —**na·tion·al·ist** \\-əst\ n or adj —**na·tion·al·is·tic** \\,nash(ə)nəl'istik\ adj

na·tion·al·i·ty \\,nash(ə)nalətē\ n, pl **-ties** 1 : national character 2 : membership in a nation 3 : political independence 4 : ethnic group

na·tion·al·ize \\'nash(ə)nəl,īz\ vb **-ized; -iz·ing** 1 : make national 2 : place under government control —**na·tion·al·iza·tion** \\,nash(ə)nələ'zāshən\ n

na·tive \\'nātiv\ adj 1 : belonging to a person at or by way of birth 2 : born or produced in a particular place ~ n : one who belongs to a country by birth

Na·tiv·i·ty \\nə'tivətē, nā-\ n, pl **-ties** 1 : birth of Christ 2 : Christmas 3 not cap : birth

nat·ty \\'natē\ adj **-ti·er; -est** : smartly dressed —**nat·ti·ly** \\'nat³lē\ adv —**nat·ti·ness** \\-ēnəs\ n

nat·u·ral \\'nach(ə)rəl\ adj 1 : relating to or determined by nature 2 : not artificial 3 : simple and sincere 4 : lifelike —**nat·u·ral·ness** n

nat·u·ral·ism \\'nach(ə)rə,lizəm\ n : realism in art and literature —**nat·u·ral·is·tic** \\,nach(ə)rə'listik\ adj

nat·u·ral·ist \\-ləst\ n 1 : one who practices naturalism 2 : student of animals or plants

nat·u·ral·ize \\-,līz\ vb **-ized; -iz·ing** 1 : become or cause to become established 2 : confer citizenship on

—**nat·u·ral·iza·tion** \\,nach(ə)-rələ'zāshən\ n

nat·u·ral·ly \\'nach(ə)rəlē, 'nachərlē\ adv 1 : in a natural way 2 : as might be expected

na·ture \\'nāchər\ n 1 : basic quality of something 2 : kind 3 : disposition 4 : physical universe 5 : natural environment —**natured** adj

naught \\'nȯt, 'nät\ n 1 : nothing 2 : zero

naugh·ty \\'nȯtē, 'nät-\ adj **-ti·er; -est** 1 : disobedient or misbehaving 2 : improper —**naught·i·ly** \\'nȯt³lē, 'nät-\ adv —**naught·i·ness** \\-ēnəs\ n

nau·sea \\'nȯzēə, -shə\ n 1 : sickness of the stomach with a desire to vomit 2 : extreme disgust —**nau·seous** \\-shəs, -zēəs\ adj

nau·se·ate \\'nȯz(h)ē,āt, -s(h)ē-\ vb **-at·ed; -at·ing** : affect or become affected with nausea —**nau·se·at·ing·ly** \\-,ātiŋlē\ adv

nau·ti·cal \\'nȯtikəl\ adj : relating to ships and sailing —**nau·ti·cal·ly** \\-k(ə)lē\ adv

nau·ti·lus \\'nȯt³ləs\ n, pl **-lus·es** or **-li** \\-³l,ī, -,ē\ : sea mollusk

na·val \\'nāvəl\ adj : relating to a navy

nave \\'nāv\ n : central part of a church

na·vel \\'nāvəl\ n : depression in the abdomen

nav·i·ga·ble \\'navigəbəl\ adj : capable of being navigated —**nav·i·ga·bil·i·ty** \\,navigə'bilətē\ n —**nav·i·ga·bly** \\'navigəblē\ adv

nav·i·gate \\'navə,gāt\ vb **-gat·ed; -gat·ing** 1 : sail on or through 2 : direct the course of —**nav·i·ga·tion** \\,navə'gāshən\ n —**nav·i·ga·tor** \\'navəgātər\ n

na·vy \\'nāvē\ n, pl **-vies** 1 : fleet 2 : nation's organization for sea warfare

nay \\'nā\ adv : no—used in oral voting ~ n : negative vote

Na·zi \\'nätsē, 'nat-\ n : member of a German fascist party from 1933 to 1945 —**Nazi** adj —**Na·zism** \\'nät,sizəm, 'nat-\, **Na·zi·ism** \\-sē,izəm\ n

near \\'nir\ adv : at or close to ~ prep : close to ~ adj 1 : not far away 2 : very much alike ~ vb : approach —**near·ly** adv —**near·ness** n

near·by \\nir'bī, -,bī\ adv or adj : near

near·sight·ed \\'nir'sītəd\ adj : seeing well at short distances only —**near·sight·ed·ly** adv —**near·sight·ed·ness** n

neat \\'nēt\ adj 1 : not diluted 2 : tastefully simple 3 : orderly and clean —**neat** adv —**neat·ly** adv —**neat·ness** n

neb·u·la \'nebyələ\ n, pl **-las** or **-lae** \-lē, -lī\ : vast mass of interstellar gas —**neb·u·lar** \-lər\ adj

neb·u·lous \-ləs\ adj : indistinct

nec·es·sary \'nesə,serē\ n, pl **-saries** : indispensable item —adj **1** : inevitable **2** : compulsory **3** : positively needed —**nec·es·sar·i·ly** \,nesə'serəlē\ adv

ne·ces·si·tate \ni'sesə,tāt\ vb **-tat·ed; -tat·ing** : make necessary

ne·ces·si·ty \ni'sesətē\ n, pl **-ties 1** : very great need **2** : something that is necessary **3** : poverty **4** : circumstances that force a course of action or that cannot be changed

neck \'nek\ n **1** : body part connecting the head and trunk **2** : part of a garment at the neck **3** : narrow part ~ vb : kiss and caress —**necked** \'nekt\ adj

neck·er·chief \'nekərchəf, -,chēf\ n, pl **-chiefs** \-chəfs, -,chēfs\ : cloth worn tied about the neck

neck·lace \'nekləs\ n : ornamental chain for the neck

neck·tie n : ornamental cloth tied under a collar

ne·crol·o·gy \nə'kräləjē\ n, pl **-gies** : obituary list

nec·ro·man·cy \'nekrə,mansē\ n : art of conjuring —**nec·ro·man·cer** \-sər\ n

ne·cro·sis \nə'krōsəs, ne-\ n, pl **-cro·ses** \-,sēz\ : death of body tissue —**ne·crot·ic** \-'krätik\ adj

nec·tar \'nektər\ n : sweet plant secretion

nec·tar·ine \,nektə'rēn\ n : smooth-skinned peach

née, nee \'nā\ adj—used to identify a married woman by maiden name

need \'nēd\ n **1** : obligation **2** : lack of something or what is lacking **3** : poverty ~ vb **1** : be in want **2** : have cause for **3** : be under obligation —**need·ful** \-fəl\ adj —**need·less** adj —**need·less·ly** adv —**needy** adj

nee·dle \'nēd[ə]l\ n **1** : pointed sewing implement or something like it **2** : movable bar in a compass **3** : hollow instrument for injecting or withdrawing material ~ vb **-dled; -dling** : incite to action by repeated gibes —**nee·dle·work** \-,wərk\ n

nee·dle·point \'nēd[ə]l,pȯint\ n **1** : lace work **2** : embroidery on canvas —**needlepoint** adj

ne·far·i·ous \ni'farēəs\ adj : very wicked —**ne·far·i·ous·ly** adv

ne·gate \ni'gāt\ vb **-gat·ed; -gat·ing 1**

: deny **2** : nullify —**ne·ga·tion** \-'gāshən\ n

neg·a·tive \'negətiv\ adj **1** : marked by denial or refusal **2** : showing a lack of something suspected or desirable **3** : less than zero **4** : having more electrons than protons **5** : having light and shadow images reversed ~ n **1** : negative word or vote **2** : negative photographic image —**neg·a·tive·ly** adv

ne·glect \ni'glekt\ vb **1** : disregard **2** : leave unattended to ~ n **1** : act of neglecting **2** : condition of being neglected —**ne·glect·ful** adj

neg·li·gee \,neglə'zhā\ n : woman's loose robe

neg·li·gent \'neglijənt\ adj : marked by neglect —**neg·li·gence** \-jəns\ n —**neg·li·gent·ly** adv

neg·li·gi·ble \'neglijəbəl\ adj : insignificant

ne·go·ti·ate \ni'gōshē,āt\ vb **-at·ed; -at·ing 1** : confer with another to settle a matter **2** : obtain cash for **3** : get through successfully —**ne·go·tia·ble** \-sh(ē)əbəl\ adj —**ne·go·ti·a·tion** \-,gōsh(ē)ē'āshən\ n —**ne·go·ti·a·tor** \-'gōshē,ātər\ n

Ne·gro \'nēgrō\ n, pl **-groes** : member of the black race —**Negro** adj —**Negroid** \'nē,grȯid\ n or adj, often not cap

neigh \'nā\ n : cry of a horse —**neigh** vb

neigh·bor \'nābər\ n **1** : one living nearby **2** : fellowman ~ vb : be near or next to —**neigh·bor·hood** \-,húd\ n —**neigh·bor·li·ness** n —**neigh·bor·ly** adv

nei·ther \'nēthər, 'nī-\ pron or adj : not the one or the other ~ conj **1** : not either **2** : nor

nem·e·sis \'neməsəs\ n, pl **-e·ses** \-ə,sēz\ **1** : old and usu. frustrating rival **2** : retaliation

ne·ol·o·gism \nē'älə,jizəm\ n : new word

ne·on \'nē,än\ n : gaseous colorless chemical element —**neon** adj

neo·phyte \'nēə,fīt\ n : beginner

neph·ew \'nefyü, chiefly Brit 'nev-\ n : a son of one's brother, sister, brother-in-law, or sister-in-law

nep·o·tism \'nepə,tizəm\ n : favoritism shown in hiring a relative

nerve \'nərv\ n **1** : strand of body tissue that connects the brain with other parts of the body **2** : self-control **3** : daring **4** pl : nervousness —**nerved** \'nərvd\ adj —**nerve·less** adj

ner·vous \'nərvəs\ *adj* 1 : relating to or made up of nerves 2 : easily excited 3 : fearful —**ner·vous·ly** *adv* —**ner·vous·ness** *n*

nervy \'nərvē\ *adj* **nerv·i·er, -est** : insolent or presumptuous

-ness \nəs\ *n suffix* : condition or quality

nest \'nest\ *n* 1 : shelter prepared by a bird for its eggs 2 : place where eggs (as of insects or fish) are laid and hatched 3 : snug retreat 4 : set of objects fitting one inside or under another ~ *vb* : build or occupy a nest

nes·tle \'nesəl\ *vb* **-tled; -tling** : settle snugly (as in a nest)

¹net \'net\ *n* : fabric with spaces between strands or something made of this ~ *vb* **-tt-** : cover with or catch in a net

²net *adj* : remaining after deductions ~ *vb* **-tt-** : have as profit

neth·er \'nethər\ *adj* : situated below

net·tle \'net²l\ *n* : coarse herb with stinging hairs ~ *vb* **-tled; -tling** : provoke or vex —**net·tle·some** *adj*

net·work *n* : system of crossing or connected elements

neu·ral \'n(y)ùrəl\ *adj* : relating to a nerve

neu·ral·gia \n(y)ù'raljə\ *n* : pain along a nerve —**neu·ral·gic** \-jik\ *adj*

neu·ri·tis \n(y)ù'rītəs\ *n, pl* **-rit·i·des** \-'ritə,dēz\ *or* **-ri·tis·es** : inflammation of a nerve —**neu·rit·ic** \-'ritik\ *adj or n*

neu·rol·o·gy \n(y)ù'räləjē\ *n* : study of the nervous system —**neu·ro·log·i·cal** \,n(y)ùrə'läjikəl\, **neu·ro·log·ic** \-ik\ *adj* —**neu·ro·log·i·cal·ly** *adv* —**neu·rol·o·gist** \n(y)ù'räləjəst\ *n*

neu·ro·sis \n(y)ù'rōsəs\ *n, pl* **-ro·ses** \-,sēz\ : nervous disorder

neu·rot·ic \n(y)ù'rätik\ *adj* : relating to neurosis ~ *n* : unstable person —**neu·rot·i·cal·ly** \-ik(ə)lē\ *adv*

neu·ter \'n(y)ütər\ *adj* : neither masculine nor feminine

neu·tral \'n(y)ütrəl\ *adj* 1 : not favoring either side 2 : being neither one thing nor the other 3 : not decided in color 4 : not electrically charged ~ *n* 1 : one that is neutral 2 : position of gears that are not engaged —**neu·tral·iza·tion** \,n(y)ütrələ'zāshən\ *n* —**neu·tral·ize** \'n(y)ütrə,līz\ *vb*

neu·tral·i·ty \n(y)ü'tralətē\ *n* : state of being neutral

neu·tron \'n(y)ü,trän\ *n* : uncharged atomic particle

nev·er \'nevər\ *adv* 1 : not ever 2 : not in any degree, way, or condition

nev·er·more *adv* : never again

nev·er·the·less *adv* : in spite of that

new \'n(y)ü\ *adj* 1 : not old or familiar 2 : different from the former 3 : recently discovered or learned 4 : not accustomed 5 : refreshed or regenerated 6 : being such for the first time ~ *adv* : newly —**new·ish** *adj* —**new·ness** *n*

new·born *adj* 1 : recently born 2 : born anew ~ *n, pl* **-born** *or* **-borns** : newborn individual

new·ly \'n(y)ülē\ *adv* : recently

news \'n(y)üz\ *n* : report of recent events —**news·let·ter** *n* —**news·maga·zine** *n* —**news·man** \-mən, -,man\ *n* —**news·pa·per** *n* —**news·pa·per·man** \-,man\ *n* —**news·stand** *n* —**news·wor·thy** *adj*

news·cast \-,kast\ *n* : broadcast of news —**news·cast·er** \-,kastər\ *n*

news·print *n* : cheap paper made from wood pulp

newsy \'n(y)üzē\ *adj* **news·i·er; -est** : filled with news

newt \'n(y)üt\ *n* : small salamander

New Year *n* : New Year's Day

New Year's Day *n* : January 1 observed as a legal holiday

next \'nekst\ *adj* : immediately preceding or following ~ *adv* 1 : in the time or place nearest 2 : at the first time yet to come ~ *prep* : nearest to

nex·us \'neksəs\ *n, pl* **-us·es** \-səsəz\ *or* **-us** \-səs, -,süs\ : connection or bond

nib \'nib\ *n* : pen point

nib·ble \'nibəl\ *vb* **-bled; -bling** : bite gently or bit by bit ~ *n* : small bite

nice \'nīs\ *adj* **nic·er; nic·est** 1 : fastidious 2 : very precise or delicate 3 : pleasing 4 : respectable —**nice·ly** *adv* —**nice·ness** *n*

nice·ty \'nīsətē\ *n, pl* **-ties** 1 : dainty or elegant thing 2 : fine detail 3 : exactness

niche \'nich\ *n* 1 : recess in a wall 2 : fitting place, work, or use

nick \'nik\ *n* 1 : small broken area or chip 2 : critical moment ~ *vb* : make a nick in

nick·el \'nikəl\ *n* 1 : hard silver-white metallic chemical element used in alloys 2 : U.S. 5-cent piece ~ *vb* **-eled** *or* **-elled; -el·ing** *or* **-el·ling** : plate with nickel

nick·name \'nik,nām\ *n* : informal substitute name —**nickname** *vb*

nic·o·tine \'nikə,tēn\ *n* : poisonous substance in tobacco

niece \'nēs\ *n* : a daughter of one's brother, sister, brother-in-law, or sister-in-law

nig·gard·ly \\'nigərdlē\\ *adj* : stingy —**nig·gard** *n* —**nig·gard·li·ness** *n*

nig·gling \\'nig(ə)liŋ\\ *adj* : petty and annoying

nigh \\'nī\\ *adv or adj or prep* : near

night \\'nīt\\ *n* **1** : period between dusk and dawn **2** : the coming of night —**night** *adj* —**night·ly** *adj or adv* —**night·time** *n*

night·clothes *n pl* : garments worn in bed

night·club \\-,kləb\\ *n* : place for drinking and entertainment open at night

night crawler *n* : earthworm

night·fall *n* : the coming of night

night·gown *n* : gown worn for sleeping

night·in·gale \\'nītⁿ,gāl, -iŋ-\\ *n* : Old World thrush that sings at night

night·mare \\'nīt,mar\\ *n* **1** : frightening dream —**nightmare** *adj* —**night·mar·ish** \\-,marish\\ *adj*

night·shade \\'nīt,shād\\ *n* : group of plants with berries of which some forms are used as food while others are poisonous

nil \\'nil\\ *n* : nothing

nim·ble \\'nimbəl\\ *adj* **-bler; -blest 1** : agile **2** : clever —**nim·ble·ness** *n* —**nim·bly** \\-blē\\ *adv*

nine \\'nīn\\ *n* **1** : one more than 8 **2** : 9th in a set or series —**nine** *adj or pron* —**ninth** \\'nīnth\\ *adj or n*

nine·pins *n* : bowling game using 9 pins

nine·teen \\'nīn'tēn\\ *n* : one more than 18 —**nineteen** *adj or pron* —**nine·teenth** \\-'tēnth\\ *adj or n*

nine·ty \\'nīntē\\ *n, pl* **-ties** : 9 times 10 —**nine·ti·eth** \\-ēəth\\ *adj or n* —**ninety** *adj or pron*

nin·ny \\'ninē\\ *n, pl* **ninnies** : fool

¹nip \\'nip\\ *vb* **-pp- 1** : catch hold of and squeeze tightly **2** : pinch or bite off **3** : destroy the growth or fulfillment of ~ *n* **1** : biting cold **2** : tang **3** : pinch or bite

²nip *n* : small quantity of liquor ~ *vb* **-pp-** : take liquor in nips

nip·per \\'nipər\\ *n* **1** : one that nips **2** *pl* : pincers **3** : large claw of a crustacean **4** : small boy

nip·ple \\'nipəl\\ *n* : tip of the breast or something resembling it

nip·py \\'nipē\\ *adj* **-pi·er; -est 1** : pungent **2** : chilly

nir·va·na \\nir'vänə\\ *n* : state of blissful oblivion

nit \\'nit\\ *n* : parasitic insect egg

ni·ter \\'nītər\\ *n* : nitrate of potassium or sodium used in gunpowder or fertilizer or in curing meat

ni·trate \\'nī,trāt, -trət\\ *n* : chemical salt used esp. in curing meat

ni·tric \\'nītrik\\ *adj* : relating to nitrogen

ni·trite \\-,trīt\\ *n* : chemical salt used in curing meat

ni·tro \\-trō\\ *n, pl* **-tros** : nitroglycerin

ni·tro·gen \\'nītrəjən\\ *n* : tasteless odorless gaseous chemical element —**ni·trog·e·nous** \\nī'träjənəs\\ *adj* —**ni·trous** \\'nītrəs\\ *adj*

ni·tro·glyc·er·in, ni·tro·glyc·er·ine \\,nītrō'glis(ə)rən\\ *n* : heavy oily explosive liquid

nit-wit \\'nit,wit\\ *n* : stupid person

no \\(')nō\\ *adv* **1** —used to express the negative **2** : in no respect or degree **3** : not so **4** —used as an interjection of surprise or doubt ~ *adj* **1** : not any **2** : not a ~ *n, pl* **noes** *or* **nos** \\'nōz\\ **1** : refusal **2** : negative vote

no·bil·i·ty \\nō'bilətē\\ *n* **1** : quality or state of being noble **2** : noble rank **3** : class of people of noble rank

no·ble \\'nōbəl\\ *adj* **-bler; -blest 1** : illustrious **2** : aristocratic **3** : stately **4** : of outstanding character ~ *n* : nobleman —**no·ble·ness** *n* —**no·bly** *adv*

no·ble·man \\-mən\\ *n* : member of the nobility

no·body \\'nō,bädē, -bədē\\ *pron* : no person ~ *n, pl* **-bod·ies** : person of no influence or social standing

noc·tur·nal \\näk'tərnⁿl\\ *adj* : relating to, occurring at, or active at night

noc·turne \\'näk,tərn\\ *n* : dreamy pensive instrumental composition

nod \\'näd\\ *vb* **-dd- 1** : bend the head downward or forward (as in bowing or going to sleep or as a sign of assent) **2** : move up and down **3** : show by a nod of the head —**nod** *n*

node \\'nōd\\ *n* : stem part from which a leaf arises —**nod·al** \\-²l\\ *adj*

nod·ule \\'näjül\\ *n* : small lump or swelling —**nod·u·lar** \\'näjələr\\ *adj*

no·el \\nō'el\\ *n* **1** : Christmas carol **2** *cap* : Christmas season

noes *pl of* NO

nog·gin \\'nägən\\ *n* **1** : small mug **2** : person's head

no·how \\'nō,haú\\ *adv* : in no manner

noise \\'nóiz\\ *n* **1** : loud or unpleasant sound ~ *vb* **noised; nois·ing** : spread by rumor —**noise·mak·er** *n* —**nois·i·ly** \\'nóizəlē\\ *adv* —**nois·i·ness** \\-zēnəs\\ *n* —**noisy** \\'nóizē\\ *adj*

noi·some \\'nóisəm\\ *adj* : harmful or offensive

no·mad \\'nō,mad\\ *n* : one who has no permanent home —**nomad** *adj* —**no·mad·ic** \\nō'madik\\ *adj*

no·men·cla·ture \\'nōmən,klāchər\\ *n* : system of names

nom·i·nal \\'nämən\əl\ *adj* **1** : being something in name only **2** : very small or negligible —**nom·i·nal·ly** *adv*

nom·i·nate \\'nämə,nāt\ *vb* **-nat·ed; -nat·ing** : propose or choose as a candidate —**nom·i·na·tion** \\,nämə'nā-shən\ *n*

nom·i·na·tive \\'näm(ə)nətiv\ *adj* : relating to or being a grammatical case marking typically the subject of a verb —**nominative** *n*

nom·i·nee \\,nämə'nē\ *n* : person nominated

non- \\('\)nän,'nän\ *prefix* : not, reverse of, or absence of

nonabrasive
nonabsorbent
nonacademic
nonaccredited
nonacid
nonaddictive
nonadherence
nonadhesive
nonadjacent
nonadjustable
nonaffiliated
nonaggression
nonalcoholic
nonaligned
nonappearance
nonautomatic
nonbeliever
nonbinding
nonbreakable
noncancerous
noncandidate
noncarbonated
non-Catholic
nonchargeable
non-Christian
nonchurchgoer
noncitizen
nonclassical
nonclassified
noncombat
noncombatant
noncombustible
noncommercial
noncommuni-
cable
non-Communist
noncompliance
nonconclusive
nonconflicting
nonconforming
nonconsecutive
nonconstructive
nonconsumable
noncontagious
noncontributing
noncontrollable

noncontroversial
noncorrosive
noncriminal
noncritical
noncumulative
noncurrent
nondeductible
nondefense
nondeferrable
nondegradable
nondelivery
nondemocratic
nondenomina-
tional
nondestructive
nondiscrimi-
nation
nondiscrimi-
natory
noneducational
nonelastic
nonelected
nonelective
nonelectric
nonelectronic
nonemotional
nonenforceable
nonenforcement
nonessential
nonexchangeable
nonexistence
nonexistent
nonexplosive
nonfat
nonfatal
nonfattening
nonfictional
nonflammable
nonflowering
nonfunctional
nongovernmental
nongraded
nonhazardous
nonhereditary
nonindustrial
nonindustrialized

noninfectious
noninflationary
nonintegrated
nonintellectual
noninterference
nonintoxicating
noninvolvement
non-Jewish
nonlegal
nonlethal
nonliterary
nonliving
nonmagnetic
nonmalignant
nonmedical
nonmember
nonmetal
nonmetallic
nonmilitary
nonmusical
nonnarcotic
nonnative
nonnegotiable
nonobjective
nonobservance
nonorthodox
nonparallel
nonparticipant
nonparticipating
nonpaying
nonpayment
nonperformance
nonperishable
nonpermanent
nonphysical
nonpoisonous
nonpolitical
nonpolluting
nonporous
nonpregnant
nonproductive
nonprofessional
nonprofit
nonracial
nonradioactive
nonrated
nonrealistic
nonrecoverable
nonrecurring
nonrefillable

nonrefundable
nonregistered
nonreligious
nonrenewable
nonrepresent-
ative
nonresident
nonresponsive
nonrestricted
nonreusable
nonreversible
nonscientific
nonscientist
nonsegregated
non-self-gov-
erning
nonsexist
nonsexual
nonsignificant
nonskier
nonsmoker
nonsmoking
nonspeaking
nonspecialist
nonspecific
nonstaining
nonstandard
nonstrategic
nonstriker
nonstriking
nonstudent
nonsubscriber
nonsugar
nonsurgical
nonswimmer
nontaxable
nonteaching
nontechnical
nontoxic
nontraditional
nontransferable
nontropical
nontypical
nonunion
nonuser
nonvenomous
nonverbal
nonvoter
nonwhite
nonworker

non·age \\'nänij, 'nōnij\ *n* : period of youth and esp. legal minority

nonce \\'näns\ *n* : present occasion ~ *adj* : occurring, used, or made only once

non·cha·lant \\,nänshə'länt\ *adj* : showing indifference —**non·cha·lance** \\-'läns\ *n* —**non·cha·lant·ly** *adv*

non·com·mis·sioned officer \\,nän-kə,mishənd-\ *n* : subordinate officer in the armed forces appointed from enlisted personnel

non·com·mit·tal \ˌnänkə¹mitᵊl\ *adj* : indicating neither consent or dissent

non·con·duc·tor \ˌnän-\ *n* : substance that is a very poor conductor

non·con·form·ist \ˌnän-\ *n* : one who does not conform to an established belief or mode of behavior —**non·con·for·mi·ty** *n*

non·de·script \ˌnändi¹skript\ *adj* : not easily described

none \¹nən\ *pron* : not any ~ *adv* : not at all

non·en·ti·ty \nä¹nentətē\ *n* : one of no consequence

none·the·less \ˌnənthə¹les\ *adv* : nevertheless

non·pa·reil \ˌnänpə¹rel\ *adj* : having no equal ~ *n* 1 : one who has no equal 2 : chocolate candy disk

non·par·ti·san \ˌnän-\ *adj* : not influenced by political party bias

non·per·son \ˌnän-\ *n* : person without ordinary rights or respect

non·plus \ˌnän¹pləs\ *vb* **-ss-** : perplex

non·pro·lif·er·a·tion \ˌnän-\ *n* : aimed at ending increased use of nuclear arms

non·sched·uled \ˌnän-\ *adj* : licensed to carry by air without a regular schedule

non·sense \¹nänˌsens, -sⁿns\ *n* : foolish or meaningless words or actions —**non·sen·si·cal** \nän¹sensikəl\ *adj* —**non·sen·si·cal·ly** \-k(ə)lē\ *adv*

non·sup·port \ˌnän-\ *n* : failure in a legal obligation to provide for someone's needs

non·vi·o·lence \ˌnän-\ *n* : avoidance of violence esp. in political demonstrations —**non·vi·o·lent** *adj*

noo·dle \¹nüdᵊl\ *n* : ribbon-shaped dried food paste

nook \¹nük\ *n* 1 : inside corner 2 : private place

noon \¹nün\ *n* : middle of the day —**noon** *adj*

noon·day \-ˌdā\ *n* : noon

no one *pron* : no person

noon·time *n* : noon

noose \¹nüs\ *n* : rope loop that slips down tight

nor \nər, (¹)nór\ *conj* —used esp. after *neither* to introduce and negate the 2d member of a series

norm \¹nórm\ *n* : standard usu. derived from an average

nor·mal \¹nórməl\ *adj* : average, regular, or standard —**nor·mal·cy** \-sē\ *n* —**nor·mal·i·ty** \nór¹malətē\ *n*

mal·iza·tion \ˌnórmələ¹zāshən\ *n* —**nor·mal·ize** \¹nórməˌlīz\ *vb* —**nor·mal·ly** *adv*

north \¹nórth\ *adv* : to or toward the north ~ *adj* : situated toward, at, or coming from the north ~ *n* 1 : direction to the left of one facing east 2 *cap* : regions to the north —**north·er·ly** \¹nórthərlē\ *adv or adj* —**north·ern** \-ərn\ *adj* —**North·ern·er** *n* —**north·ern·most** \-ˌmóst\ *adj* —**north·ward** \-wərd\ *adv or adj* —**north·wards** \-wərdz\ *adv*

north·east \nórth¹ēst\ *n* 1 : direction between north and east 2 *cap* : regions to the northeast —**northeast** *adj or adv* —**north·east·er·ly** \-ərlē\ *adv or adj* —**north·east·ern** \-ərn\ *adj*

northern lights *n pl* : aurora borealis

north pole *n* : northernmost point of the earth

north·west \-¹west\ *n* 1 : direction between north and west 2 *cap* : regions to the northwest —**northwest** *adj or adv* —**north·west·er·ly** \-ərlē\ *adv or adj* —**north·west·ern** \-ərn\ *adj*

nose \¹nōz\ *n* 1 : part of the face containing the nostrils 2 : sense of smell 3 : front part ~ *vb* **nosed; nos·ing** 1 : detect by smell 2 : push aside with the nose 3 : defeat narrowly 4 : pry 5 : inch ahead —**nose·bleed** *n* —**nosed** \¹nōzd\ *adj*

nose·gay \-ˌgā\ *n* : small bunch of flowers

nosh \¹näsh\ *vb* : eat a snack —**nosh** *n*

nos·tal·gia \nä¹staljə, nə-\ *n* : wistful yearning for something past —**nos·tal·gic** \-jik\ *adj*

nos·tril \¹nästrəl\ *n* : opening of the nose

nos·trum \-trəm\ *n* : questionable medicine

nosy, nos·ey \¹nōzē\ *adj* **nos·i·er; -est** : tending to pry

not \(¹)nät\ *adv* —used to make a statement negative

no·ta·ble \¹nōtəbəl\ *adj* 1 : noteworthy 2 : distinguished ~ *n* : notable person —**no·ta·bil·i·ty** *n* —**no·ta·bly** \-blē\ *adv*

no·ta·rize \¹nōtəˌrīz\ *vb* **-rized; -riz·ing** : attest as a notary public

no·ta·ry public \¹nōtərē-\ *n, pl* **-aries public** *or* **-ry publics** : public official who attests writings to make them legally authentic

no·ta·tion \nō¹tāshən\ *n* 1 : note 2 : act, process, or method of marking things down

notch \¹näch\ *n* : V-shaped hollow —**notch** *vb*

note \\'nōt\\ vb **not·ed; not·ing 1** : notice **2** : write down ~ n **1** : musical tone **2** : written comment or record : notice or heed —**note-book** n

not·ed \\'nōtəd\\ adj : famous

note-wor·thy \\-₁wərthē\\ adj : worthy of special mention

noth·ing \\'nəthiŋ\\ pron **1** : no thing **2** : no part **3** : one of no value or importance ~ adv : not at all ~ n **1** : something that does not exist **2** : zero **3** : one of little or no importance —**noth-ing-ness** n

no·tice \\'nōtəs\\ n **1** : warning or announcement **2** : attention ~ vb **-ticed; -tic·ing** : take notice of —**no-tice·able** adj —**no-tice·ably** adv

no·ti·fy \\'nōtə₁fī\\ vb **-fied; -fy·ing** : give notice of or to —**no·ti·fi·ca·tion** \\₁nōtəfə'kāshən\\ n

no·tion \\'nōshən\\ n **1** : idea or opinion **2** : whim **3** pl : small sewing or personal articles

no·to·ri·ous \\nō'tōrēəs\\ adj : widely and unfavorably known —**no·to·ri·ety** \\₁nōtə'rīətē\\ n —**no·to·ri·ous·ly** adv

not·with·stand·ing \\₁nätwith'standiŋ, -with-\\ prep : in spite of ~ adv : nevertheless ~ conj : although

nou·gat \\'nügət\\ n : nuts or fruit pieces in a sugar paste

nought \\'nót, 'nät\\ var of NAUGHT

noun \\'naún\\ n : word that is the name of a person, place, or thing

nour·ish \\'nərish\\ vb : promote the growth of —**nour-ish-ing** adj —**nour·ish·ment** n

no·va \\'nōvə\\ n, pl **-vas** or **-vae** \\-₁vē, -₁vī\\ : star that suddenly brightens and then fades

nov·el \\'nävəl\\ adj : new or strange ~ n : long invented prose story —**nov·el·ist** \\-(ə)ləst\\ n

nov·el·ty \\'nävəltē\\ n, pl **-ties 1** : something new or unusual **2** : newness **3** : small manufactured article—usu. pl.

No·vem·ber \\nō'vembər\\ n : 11th month of the year having 30 days

nov·ice \\'nävəs\\ n **1** : one preparing to take vows in a religious order **2** : one who is inexperienced or untrained

no·vi·tiate \\nō'vishət, nə-\\ n : period or state of being a novice

now \\(')naú\\ adv **1** : at the present time or moment **2** : forthwith **3** : under these circumstances ~ conj : in view of the fact ~ n **1** : the present time

now·a·days \\'naú(ə)₁dāz\\ adv : now

no·where \\-₁hwear\\ adv : not anywhere —**nowhere** n

nox·ious \\'näkshəs\\ adj : harmful

noz·zle \\'näzəl\\ n : device to direct or control flow of fluid

nu·ance \\n(y)ü₁äns, n(y)ü'äns\\ n : subtle distinction or variation

nub \\'nəb\\ n **1** : knob or lump **2** : gist —**nub·by** adj

nu·bile \\'n(y)übəl, -₁bīl\\ adj : of marriageable condition or age

nu·cle·ar \\'n(y)üklēər\\ adj : relating to the atomic nucleus or atomic energy

nu·cle·us \\'n(y)ükleəs\\ n, pl **-clei** \\-klē₁ī\\ : central mass or part (as of a cell or an atom)

nude \\'n(y)üd\\ adj **nud·er; nud·est** : naked ~ n : nude human figure —**nu·di·ty** \\'n(y)üdətē\\ n

nudge \\'nəj\\ vb **nudged; nudg·ing** : touch or push gently —**nudge** n

nud·ism \\'n(y)üd₁izəm\\ n : practice of going nude —**nud·ist** \\'n(y)üdəst\\ n

nug·get \\'nəgət\\ n : lump of gold

nui·sance \\'n(y)üs²ns\\ n : something annoying

null \\'nəl\\ adj : having no legal or binding force —**nul·li·ty** \\'nələtē\\ n

nul·li·fy \\'nələ₁fī\\ vb **-fied; -fy·ing** : make null or valueless —**nul·li·fi·ca·tion** \\₁nələfə'kāshən\\ n

numb \\'nəm\\ adj : lacking feeling —**numb** vb —**numb·ly** adv —**numb·ness** n

num·ber \\'nəmbər\\ n **1** : total of individuals taken together **2** : group not specif. enumerated **3** : unit of a mathematical system **4** : numeral **5** : one in a sequence ~ vb **1** : count **2** : assign a number to **3** : comprise in number —**num·ber·less** adj

nu·mer·al \\'n(y)üm(ə)rəl\\ n : word or symbol representing a number

nu·mer·a·tor \\'n(y)ümə₁rātər\\ n : part of a fraction above the line

nu·mer·ic \\n(y)ü'merik\\ adj : numerical

nu·mer·i·cal \\n(y)ü'merikəl\\ adj **1** : of or relating to numbers **2** : denoting a number or expressed in numbers —**nu·mer·i·cal·ly** \\-k(ə)lē\\ adv

nu·mer·ol·o·gy \\₁n(y)ümə'räləjē\\ n : occult study of numbers —**nu·mer·ol·o·gist** \\-jəst\\ n

nu·mer·ous \\'n(y)üm(ə)rəs\\ adj : consisting of a great number

nu·mis·mat·ics \\₁n(y)üməz'matiks\\ n : study or collection of monetary objects —**nu·mis·mat·ic** \\-ik\\ adj —**nu·mis·ma·tist** \\n(y)ü'mizmətəst\\ n

num·skull \\'nəm₁skəl\\ n : stupid person

nun \\'nən\\ n : woman belonging to a religious order —**nun·nery** \\-(ə)rē\\ n

nup·tial \'nəpshəl\ *adj* : relating to marriage or a wedding ~ *n* : marriage or wedding—usu. pl.

nurse \'nərs\ *n* 1 : one hired to care for children 2 : person trained to care for sick people ~ *vb* **nursed; nurs·ing** 1 : suckle 2 : care for

nurs·ery \'nərs(ə)rē\ *n, pl* **-er·ies** 1 : place where children are cared for 2 : place where young plants are grown

nursing home *n* : private establishment where care is provided for persons who are unable to care for themselves

nur·ture \'nərchər\ *n* 1 : training or upbringing 2 : food or nourishment ~ *vb* **-tured; -tur·ing** 1 : care for or feed 2 : educate

nut \'nət\ *n* 1 : dry hard-shelled fruit or seed with a firm inner kernel 2 : metal block with a screw hole through it 3 : foolish, eccentric, or crazy person 4 : enthusiast —**nut·crack·er** *n* —**nut·shell** *n* —**nut·ty** *adj*

nut·hatch \'nət₁hach\ *n* : small bird

nut·meg \'nət₁meg, -₁māg\ *n* : nutlike aromatic seed of a tropical tree

nu·tri·ent \'n(y)ütrēənt\ *n* : something giving nourishment —**nutrient** *adj*

nu·tri·ment \-trəmənt\ *n* : nutrient

nu·tri·tion \n(y)ü'trishən\ *n* : act or process of nourishing esp. with food —**nu·tri·tion·al** \-'trish(ə)nəl\ *adj* —**nu·tri·tious** \-'trishəs\ *adj* —**nu·tri·tive** \'n(y)ütrətiv\ *adj*

nuts \'nəts\ *adj* 1 : enthusiastic 2 : crazy

nuz·zle \'nəzəl\ *vb* **-zled; -zling** 1 : touch with or as if with the nose 2 : snuggle

ny·lon \'nī₁län\ *n* 1 : tough synthetic material used esp. in textiles 2 *pl* : stockings made of nylon

nymph \'nimf\ *n* 1 : lesser goddess in ancient mythology 2 : immature insect

nym·pho·ma·nia \₁nimfə'mānēə, -nyə\ *n* : excessive sexual desire by a female —**nym·pho·ma·ni·ac** \-nē₁ak\ *n or adj*

O

o \'ō\ *n, pl* **o's** *or* **os** \'ōz\ : 15th letter of the alphabet

O *var of* OH

oaf \'ōf\ *n* : stupid or awkward person —**oaf·ish** \'ōfish\ *adj*

oak \'ōk\ *n, pl* **oaks** *or* **oak** : tree bearing a thin-shelled nut or its wood —**oak·en** \'ōkən\ *adj*

oa·kum \'ōkəm\ *n* : loosely twisted tarred hemp or jute fiber for caulking ships

oar \'ōr\ *n* : implement used to propel a boat

oar·lock \-₁läk\ *n* : device for holding an oar

oa·sis \ō'āsəs\ *n, pl* **oa·ses** \-₁sēz\ : fertile area in a desert

oat \'ōt\ *n* : cereal grass or its edible seed —**oat·cake** *n* —**oat·en** \-ᵊn\ *adj* —**oat·meal** *n*

oath \'ōth\ *n, pl* **oaths** \'ōthz, 'ōths\ 1 : solemn appeal to God as a pledge of sincerity 2 : profane utterance

ob·du·rate \'äbd(y)ərət\ *adj* : stubbornly resistant —**ob·du·ra·cy** \-rəsē\ *n*

obe·di·ent \ō'bēdēənt\ *adj* : willing to obey —**obe·di·ence** \-əns\ *n* —**obe·di·ent·ly** *adv*

obei·sance \ō'bāsəns, -'bēs-\ *n* : bow of respect or submission

obe·lisk \'äbə₁lisk\ *n* : 4-sided tapering pillar

obese \ō'bēs\ *adj* : extremely fat —**obe·si·ty** \-'bēsətē\ *n*

obey \ō'bā\ *vb* **obeyed; obey·ing** 1 : follow the commands or guidance of 2 : behave in accordance with

ob·fus·cate \'äbfə₁skāt\ *vb* **-cat·ed; -cat·ing** : confuse —**ob·fus·ca·tion** \₁äbfəs'kāshən\ *n*

obit·u·ary \ə'bichə₁werē\ *n, pl* **-ar·ies** : death notice

¹ob·ject \'äbjikt\ *n* 1 : something that may be seen or felt 2 : purpose 3 : noun or equivalent toward which the action of a verb is directed or which follows a preposition

²ob·ject \əb'jekt\ *vb* : offer opposition or disapproval —**ob·jec·tion** \-'jekshən\ *n* —**ob·jec·tion·able** \-sh(ə)nəbəl\ *adj* —**ob·jec·tor** \-'jektər\ *n*

ob·jec·tive \əb'jektiv\ *adj* 1 : relating to an object or end 2 : existing outside an individual's thoughts or feelings 3 : treating facts without distortion 4 : relating to or being a grammatical case marking objects ~ *n* : aim or end of action —**ob·jec·tive·ly** *adv* —**ob·jec·tive·ness** *n* —**ob·jec·tiv·i·ty** \₁äb₁jek'tivətē\ *n*

ob·li·gate \ˈäblə₁gāt\ *vb* -**gat·ed;** -**gat·ing** : bind legally or morally —**obli·ga·tion** \₁äblə¹gāshən\ *n* —**oblig·a·to·ry** \ə¹bligə₁tōrē, ¹äbligə-\ *adj*

oblige \ə¹blīj\ *vb* **obliged; oblig·ing** 1 : compel 2 : do a favor for —**oblig·ing** *adj* —**oblig·ing·ly** *adv*

oblique \ō¹blēk, -¹blīk\ *adj* 1 : lying at a slanting angle 2 : indirect —**oblique·ly** *adv* —**oblique·ness** *n* —**obliq·ui·ty** \-¹blikwətē\ *n*

oblit·er·ate \ə¹blitə₁rāt\ *vb* -**at·ed;** -**at·ing** : completely remove or destroy —**oblit·er·a·tion** \-₁blitə¹rāshən\ *n*

obliv·i·on \ə¹blivēən\ *n* 1 : state of having lost conscious awareness 2 : state of being unknown or forgotten

obliv·i·ous \-ēəs\ *adj* : not aware or mindful—with *to* or *of* —**obliv·i·ous·ly** *adv* —**obliv·i·ous·ness** *n*

oblong \¹äb₁lȯŋ\ *adj* : longer in one direction than in the other with opposite sides parallel —**oblong** *n*

ob·lo·quy \¹äbləkwē\ *n, pl* -**quies** 1 : strongly condemning utterance 2 : bad repute

ob·nox·ious \äb¹näkshəs, əb-\ *adj* : repugnant —**ob·nox·ious·ly** *adv* —**ob·nox·ious·ness** *n*

oboe \¹ōbō\ *n* : slender woodwind instrument with a reed mouthpiece —**obo·ist** \¹ō₁bōəst\ *n*

ob·scene \äb¹sēn, əb-\ *adj* : repugnantly indecent —**ob·scene·ly** *adv* —**ob·scen·i·ty** \-¹senətē\ *n*

ob·scure \äb¹skyur, əb-\ *adj* 1 : dim or hazy 2 : not well known 3 : vague ~ *vb* : make indistinct or unclear —**ob·scure·ly** *adv* —**ob·scu·ri·ty** \-¹skyurətē\ *n*

ob·se·quies \¹äbsəkwēz\ *n pl* : funeral or burial rite

ob·se·qui·ous \əb¹sēkwēəs\ *adj* : excessively attentive or flattering —**ob·se·qui·ous·ly** *adv* —**ob·se·qui·ous·ness** *n*

ob·ser·va·to·ry \əb¹zərvə₁tōrē\ *n, pl* -**ries** : place for observing astronomical phenomena

ob·serve \əb¹zərv\ *vb* -**served;** -**serv·ing** 1 : conform to 2 : celebrate 3 : see, watch, or notice 4 : remark —**ob·serv·able** *adj* —**ob·ser·vance** \-¹zərvəns\ *n* —**ob·ser·vant** \-vənt\ *adj* —**ob·ser·va·tion** \₁äbsər¹vāshən, -zər-\ *n*

ob·sess \əb¹ses\ *vb* : preoccupy intensely or abnormally —**ob·ses·sion** \äb¹seshən, əb-\ *n* —**ob·ses·sive** \-¹sesiv\ *adj and n*

ob·so·les·cent \₁äbsə¹les²nt\ *adj* : going out of use —**ob·so·les·cence** \-²ns\ *n*

ob·so·lete \₁äbsə¹lēt, ¹äbsə₁-\ *adj* : no longer in use

ob·sta·cle \¹äbstikəl\ *n* : something that stands in the way or opposes

ob·stet·rics \əb¹stetriks\ *n sing or pl* : branch of medicine that deals with childbirth —**ob·stet·ri·cal** \-rikəl\ *adj* —**ob·ste·tri·cian** \₁äbstə¹trishən\ *n*

ob·sti·nate \¹äbstənət\ *adj* : stubborn —**ob·sti·na·cy** \-nəsē\ *n* —**ob·sti·nate·ly** *adv*

ob·strep·er·ous \äb¹strep(ə)rəs\ *adj* : uncontrollably noisy or defiant —**ob·strep·er·ous·ness** *n*

ob·struct \əb¹strəkt\ *vb* : block or impede —**ob·struc·tion** \-¹strəkshən\ *n* —**ob·struc·tive** \-¹strəktiv\ *adj* —**ob·struc·tor** \-tər\ *n*

ob·tain \əb¹tān\ *vb* 1 : gain by effort 2 : be generally recognized —**ob·tain·able** *adj*

ob·trude \äb¹trüd\ *vb* -**trud·ed;** -**trud·ing** 1 : thrust out 2 : intrude —**ob·tru·sion** \-¹trüzhən\ *n* —**ob·tru·sive** \-¹trüsiv\ *adj* —**ob·tru·sive·ly** *adv* —**ob·tru·sive·ness** *n*

ob·tuse \äb¹t(y)üs, əb-\ *adj* 1 : slow-witted 2 : exceeding 90 but less than 180 degrees —**ob·tuse·ly** *adv* —**ob·tuse·ness** *n*

ob·verse \¹äb₁vərs, äb¹-\ *n* : principal side (as of a coin)

ob·vi·ate \¹äbvē₁āt\ *vb* -**at·ed;** -**at·ing** : make unnecessary —**ob·vi·a·tion** \₁äbvē¹āshən\ *n*

ob·vi·ous \¹äbvēəs\ *adj* : plain or unmistakable —**ob·vi·ous·ly** *adv* —**ob·vi·ous·ness** *n*

oc·ca·sion \ə¹kāzhən\ *n* 1 : favorable opportunity 2 : cause 3 : time of an event 4 : special event ~ *vb* : cause —**oc·ca·sion·al** \-¹kāzh(ə)nəl\ *adj* —**oc·ca·sion·al·ly** *adv*

oc·ci·den·tal \₁äksə¹dent²l\ *adj* : western —**Occidental** *n*

oc·cult \ə¹kəlt, ¹äk₁əlt\ *adj* : secret or mysterious

oc·cu·pan·cy \¹äkyəpənsē\ *n, pl* -**cies** : an occupying

oc·cu·pant \-pənt\ *n* : one who occupies

oc·cu·pa·tion \₁äkyə¹pāshən\ *n* 1 : vocation 2 : action or state of occupying —**oc·cu·pa·tion·al** \-sh(ə)nəl\ *adj* —**oc·cu·pa·tion·al·ly** *adv*

oc·cu·py \¹äkyə₁pī\ *vb* -**pied;** -**py·ing** 1 : engage the attention of 2 : fill up 3 : sit or lie in 4 : reside in —**oc·cu·pi·er** \-₁pī(ə)r\ *n*

oc·cur \ə¹kər\ *vb* -**rr-** 1 : be found or

met with 2 : take place 3 : come to mind

oc·cur·rence \ə'kərəns\ n : something that takes place

ocean \'ōshən\ n 1 : whole body of salt water 2 : large body of water —**ocean·front** n —**ocean·go·ing** adj —**oce·an·ic** \ˌōshē'anik\ adj

ocean·og·ra·phy \ˌōshə'nägrəfē\ n : science dealing with the ocean —**ocean·og·ra·pher** \-fər\ n —**ocean·o·graph·ic** \-nə'grafik\ adj

oce·lot \'äsəˌlät, 'ōsə-\ n : medium-sized American wildcat

ocher, ochre \'ōkər\ n : red or yellow pigment

o'clock \ə'kläk\ adv : according to the clock

oc·ta·gon \'äktəˌgän\ n : 8-sided polygon —**oc·tag·o·nal** \äk'tagənᵊl\ adj

oc·tave \'äktiv\ n : musical interval of 8 steps or the notes within this interval

Oc·to·ber \äk'tōbər\ n : 10th month of the year having 31 days

oc·to·pus \'äktəpəs\ n, pl **-pus·es** or **-pi** \-ˌpī\ : sea mollusk with 8 arms

oc·u·lar \'äkyələr\ adj : relating to the eye

oc·u·list \'äkyələst\ n 1 : ophthalmologist 2 : optometrist

odd \'äd\ adj 1 : being only one of a pair or set 2 : not divisible by two without a remainder 3 : additional to what is usual or to the number mentioned 4 : queer —**odd·ly** adv —**odd·ness** n

odd·i·ty \'ädətē\ n, pl **-ties** : something odd

odds \'ädz\ n pl 1 : difference by which one thing is favored 2 : equalizing allowance 3 : disagreement

ode \'ōd\ n : solemn lyric poem

odi·ous \'ōdēəs\ adj : hated —**odi·ous·ly** adv —**odi·ous·ness** n

odi·um \'ōdēəm\ n 1 : merited loathing 2 : disgrace

odor \'ōdər\ n : quality that affects the sense of smell —**odor·less** adj —**odor·ous** adj

od·ys·sey \'ädəsē\ n, pl **-seys** : long wandering

o'er \'ō(ə)r\ adv or prep : OVER

of \(')əv, 'äv\ prep 1 : from 2 : distinguished by 3 : because of 4 : made or written by 5 : made with, being, or containing 6 : belonging to or connected with 7 : about 8 : that is 9 : concerning 10 : before

off \'óf\ adv 1 : from a place 2 : unattached or removed 3 : to a state of being no longer in use 4 : away from

work 5 : at a distance in time or space ~ \(')óf\ prep 1 : away from esp. the surface or top of 2 : at the expense of 3 : not engaged in or abstaining from 4 : below the usual level of ~ \(')óf\ adj 1 : not operating, up to standard, or correct 2 : remote 3 : provided for

of·fal \'ófəl\ n 1 : waste 2 : viscera and trimmings of a butchered animal

of·fend \ə'fend\ vb 1 : sin or act in violation 2 : hurt, annoy, or insult —**of·fend·er** n

of·fense, of·fence \ə'fens, 'äf,ens\ n : attack, misdeed, or insult

of·fen·sive \ə'fensiv, 'äf,en-\ adj : causing offense ~ n : attack —**of·fen·sive·ly** adv —**of·fen·sive·ness** n

of·fer \'ófər\ vb 1 : present for acceptance 2 : propose 3 : put up (an effort) ~ n 1 : proposal 2 : bid —**of·fer·ing** n

of·fer·to·ry \'ófə(r)ˌtōrē\ n, pl **-ries** : presentation of offerings or its musical accompaniment

off·hand adv or adj : without previous thought or preparation

of·fice \'ófəs\ n 1 : position of authority (as in government) 2 : rite 3 : place where a business is transacted —**of·fice·hold·er** n

of·fi·cer \'ófəsər\ n 1 : one charged with law enforcement 2 : one who holds an office of trust or authority 3 : one who holds a commission in the armed forces

of·fi·cial \ə'fishəl\ n : one in office ~ adj : authorized or authoritative —**of·fi·cial·dom** \-dəm\ n —**of·fi·cial·ly** adv

of·fi·ci·ate \ə'fishēˌāt\ vb **-at·ed; -at·ing** : perform a ceremony or function

of·fi·cious \ə'fishəs\ adj : volunteering one's services unnecessarily —**of·fi·cious·ly** adv —**of·fi·cious·ness** n

off·ing \'ófin\ n : future

off·set \'óf,set\ vb **-set; -set·ting** : provide an opposite or equaling effect to

off·shoot \'óf,shüt\ n : outgrowth

off·shore adv : at a distance from the shore ~ adj : moving away from or situated off the shore

off·spring \'óf,sprin\ n, pl **offspring** : one coming into being through animal or plant reproduction

of·ten \'óf(t)ən\ adv : many times —**of·ten·times** adv

ogle \'ōgəl\ vb **ogled; ogling** : stare at lustily —**ogle** n —**ogler** \-(ə)lər\ n

ogre \'ōgər\ n 1 : monster 2 : dreaded person —**ogress** \'ōg(ə)rəs\ n

oh \('\)ō\ *interj* **1**—used to express an emotion **2**—used in direct address

ohm \'ōm\ *n* : unit of electrical resistance —**ohm·ic** \'ō-mik\ *adj* —**ohm·me·ter** \'ō(m),mētər\ *n*

oil \'oil\ *n* **1** : greasy liquid substance **2** : petroleum ~ *vb* : treat, furnish, or lubricate with oil —**oil·er** *n* —**oil·i·ness** \'oilēnəs\ *n* —**oily** \'oilē\ *adj*

oil-cloth *n* : cloth treated with oil or paint and used for coverings

oil-skin *n* : oiled waterproof cloth

oink \'oiŋk\ *n* : natural noise of a hog —**oink** *vb*

oint·ment \'ointmənt\ *n* : oily medicinal preparation

OK *or* **okay** \ō'kā\ *adv or adj* : all right ~ *vb* **OK'd** *or* **okayed**; **OK'·ing** *or* **okay·ing** : approve ~ *n* : approval

okra \'ōkrə, *South also* -krē\ *n* : leafy vegetable with edible green pods

old \'ōld\ *adj* **1** : of long standing **2** : of a specified age **3** : relating to a past era **4** : having existed a long time —**old·ish** \'ōldish\ *adj*

old·en \'ōldən\ *adj* : of or relating to a bygone era

old-fash·ioned \'ōld(d)'fashənd\ *adj* **1** : out-of-date **2** : conservative

old maid *n* : spinster

old-tim·er \'ōld(d)'tīmər\ *n* **1** : veteran **2** : one who is old

ole·an·der \'ōlē,andər\ *n* : poisonous evergreen shrub

oleo·mar·ga·rine \,ōlēō'märj(ə)rən, -'märjə,rēn\ *n* : margarine

ol·fac·to·ry \äl'fakt(ə)rē, ōl-\ *adj* : relating to the sense of smell

oli·gar·chy \'älə,gärkē, 'ōlə-\ *n, pl* **-chies 1** : government by a few people **2** : those holding power in an oligarchy —**oli·garch** \'älə,gärk\ *n* —**oli·gar·chic** \,älə'gärkik, ,ōlə-\, **oli·gar·chi·cal** \-kikəl\ *adj*

ol·ive \'äliv, -əv\ *n* **1** : evergreen tree bearing small edible fruit or the fruit **2** : dull yellow to yellowish green color

om·buds·man \'äm,budzmən, äm'budz-\ *n, pl* **-men** \-mən\ : complaint investigator

om·elet, om·elette \'äm(ə)lət\ *n* : beaten eggs lightly fried and folded

omen \'ōmən\ *n* : sign or warning for the future

om·i·nous \'ämənəs\ *adj* : threatening —**om·i·nous·ly** *adv* —**om·i·nous·ness** *n*

omit \ō'mit\ *vb* **-tt-** **1** : leave out **2** : fail to perform —**omis·sion** \'mishən\ *n*

om·nip·o·tent \äm'nipətənt\ *adj* : almighty —**om·nip·o·tence** \-əns\ *n*

om·ni·pres·ent \,ämni'prez²nt\ *adj* : ever-present —**om·ni·pres·ence** \-²ns\ *n*

om·ni·scient \äm'nishənt\ *adj* : all-knowing —**om·ni·science** \-əns\ *n* —**om·ni·scient·ly** *adv*

om·niv·o·rous \äm'niv(ə)rəs\ *adj* **1** : eating both meat and vegetables **2** : avid —**om·niv·o·rous·ly** *adv* —**om·niv·o·rous·ness** *n*

on \('\)òn, (')än\ *prep* **1** : in or to a position over and in contact with **2** : at or to **3** : about **4** : from **5** : with regard to **6** : in a state or process **7** : during the time of ~ \'òn, 'än\ *adv* **1** : in or into contact with **2** : forward **3** : into operation

once \'wəns\ *adv* **1** : one time only **2** : at any one time **3** : formerly ~ *n* : one time ~ *conj* : as soon as —**at once 1** : simultaneously **2** : immediately **3** : both

once-over *n* : swift examination

on·com·ing \'òn,\ *adj* : approaching

one \'wən\ *adj* **1** : being a single thing **2** : being one in particular **3** : united ~ *pron* **1** : a single member **2** : a person in general ~ *n* **1** : 1st in a series **2** : single person or thing —**one·ness** *n*

oner·ous \'änərəs, 'ōnə-\ *adj* : oppressive

one·self \(,)wən'self\ *pron* : one's own self—usu. used reflexively or for emphasis

one-sid·ed \-'sīdəd\ *adj* **1** : unequal **2** : partial

one·time *adj* : former

one-way *adj* : made for or used in only one direction

on·go·ing *adj* : continuing

on·ion \'ənyən\ *n* : plant grown for its pungent edible bulb

on·ly \'ōnlē\ *adj* : alone in its class ~ *adv* **1** : nothing more than **2** : without respect to anyone or anything else ~ *conj* : but

on·set *n* : start

on·shore \'än,\ *adj* **1** : moving toward shore **2** : lying on or near the shore —**on·shore** *adv*

on·slaught \'än,slòt, 'òn-\ *n* : attack

on·to \'òntə, ,än-; 'òntü, 'än-\ *prep* : to a position or point on

onus \'ōnəs\ *n* : burden (as of obligation or blame)

on·ward \'ònwərd, 'än-\ *adv or adj* : forward

on·yx \'äniks\ *n* : quartz used as a gem

1ooze \'üz\ *n* : soft mud —**oozy** \'üzē\ *adj*

2ooze *vb* **oozed; ooz·ing** : flow or leak out slowly

opac·i·ty \ō'pasətē\ *n* : quality or state of being opaque or an opaque spot

opal \'ōpəl\ *n* : gem with delicate colors

opaque \ō'pāk\ *adj* **1** : impervious to light **2** : not easily understood **3** : dull-witted —**opaque·ly** *adv* —**opaque·ness** *n*

open \'ōpən\ *adj* **1** : not shut or shut up **2** : not secret or hidden **3** : frank or generous **4** : extended **5** : free from controls **6** : not decided —*vb* **1** : make or become open **2** : make or become functional **3** : start —*n* : outdoors —**open·er** \'ōp(ə)nər\ *n* —**open·ly** *adv* —**open·ness** *n*

open-hand·ed \-'handəd\ *adj* : generous

open·ing \'ōp(ə)niŋ\ *n* **1** : act or instance of causing to be open **2** : something that is open **3** : opportunity

op·era \'äp(ə)rə\ *n* : drama set to music —**op·er·at·ic** \'äpə'ratik\ *adj*

op·er·a·ble \'äp(ə)rəbəl\ *adj* : usable or in working condition **2** : suitable for surgical treatment

op·er·ate \'äpə,rāt\ *vb* **-at·ed; -at·ing 1** : perform work **2** : perform an operation **3** : manage —**op·er·a·tor** \-,rātər\ *n*

op·er·a·tion \,äpə'rāshən\ *n* **1** : act or process of operating **2** : surgical work on a living body **3** : military action or mission —**op·er·a·tion·al** \-sh(ə)nəl\ *adj*

op·er·a·tive \'äp(ə)rətiv, 'äpə,rāt-\ *adj* : working or having an effect

op·er·et·ta \,äpə'retə\ *n* : light opera

oph·thal·mol·o·gy \,äf,thal'mäləjē, ,äp-\ *n* : branch of medicine dealing with the eye —**oph·thal·mol·o·gist** \-jəst\ *n*

opi·ate \'ōpēət, -pē,āt\ *n* : preparation or derivative of opium

opin·ion \ə'pinyən\ *n* **1** : belief **2** : judgment **3** : formal statement by an expert

opin·ion·at·ed \-yə,nātəd\ *adj* : stubborn in one's opinions

opi·um \'ōpēəm\ *n* : addictive narcotic drug that is the dried juice of a poppy

opos·sum \ə'päsəm\ *n* : common tree-dwelling mammal

op·po·nent \ə'pōnənt\ *n* : one that opposes

op·por·tune \,äpər't(y)ün\ *adj* **1** : suitable **2** : occurring at a suitable time —**op·por·tune·ly** *adv*

op·por·tun·ism \-'t(y)ü,nizəm\ *n* : a taking advantage of opportunities —**op·por·tun·ist** \-nəst\ *n* —**op·por·tu·nis·tic** \-t(y)ü'nistik\ *adj*

op·por·tu·ni·ty \-'t(y)ünətē\ *n, pl* **-ties** : favorable time

op·pose \ə'pōz\ *vb* **-posed; -pos·ing 1** : place opposite or against something **2** : resist —**op·po·si·tion** \,äpə'zishən\ *n*

op·po·site \'äpəzət\ *n* : one that is opposed —*adj* **1** : set facing opposite something that is at the other side or end **2** : opposed or contrary —*adv* : on opposite sides —*prep* : across from —**op·po·site·ly** *adv* —**op·po·site·ness** *n*

op·press \ə'pres\ *vb* **1** : persecute **2** : weigh down —**op·pres·sion** \ə'preshən\ *n* —**op·pres·sive** \-siv\ *adj* —**op·pres·sive·ly** *adv* —**op·pres·sor** \-'presər\ *n*

op·pro·bri·ous \ə'prōbrēəs\ *adj* : expressing or deserving opprobrium —**op·pro·bri·ous·ly** *adv*

op·pro·bri·um \-brēəm\ *n* **1** : something that brings disgrace **2** : infamy

opt \'äpt\ *vb* : choose

op·tic \'äptik\ *adj* : relating to vision or the eye

op·ti·cal \'äptikəl\ *adj* : relating to optics, vision, or the eye

op·ti·cian \äp'tishən\ *n* : maker of or dealer in eyeglasses

op·tics \'äptiks\ *n pl* : science of light and vision

op·ti·mal \'äptəməl\ *adj* : most favorable —**op·ti·mal·ly** *adv*

op·ti·mism \'äptə,mizəm\ *n* : tendency to hope for the best —**op·ti·mist** \-məst\ *n* —**op·ti·mis·tic** \,äptə'mistik-\ *adj* —**op·ti·mis·ti·cal·ly** \-tik(ə)lē\ *adv*

op·ti·mum \'äptəməm\ *n, pl* **-ma** \-mə\ : amount or degree of something most favorable to an end

op·tion \'äpshən\ *n* **1** : ability to choose **2** : right to buy or sell a stock **3** : alternative —**op·tion·al** \-sh(ə)nəl\ *adj*

op·tom·e·try \äp'tämətrē\ *n* : profession of examining the eyes —**op·tom·e·trist** \-trəst\ *n*

op·u·lent \'äpyələnt\ *adj* : lavish —**op·u·lence** \-ləns\ *n*

opus \'ōpəs\ *n, pl* **opera** \'ōpərə, 'äpə-\ : work esp. of music

or \ər,(,)ór\ *conj*—used to indicate an alternative

-or \ər\ *n suffix* : one that performs an action

or·a·cle \'orəkəl\ *n* 1 : one held to give divinely inspired answers or revelations 2 : wise person or an utterance of such a person —**orac·u·lar** \o'rak-yələr\ *adj*

oral \'orəl, 'or-\ *adj* 1 : spoken 2 : relating to the mouth —**oral·ly** *adv*

or·ange \'orinj\ *n* 1 : reddish yellow citrus fruit 2 : color between red and yellow —**or·ange·ade** \,orinj'ād\ *n*

orang·utan, orang·ou·tan \ə'raŋə,taŋ, -,tan\ *n* : reddish brown ape

ora·tion \ə'rāshən\ *n* : elaborate formal speech

or·a·tor \'orətər\ *n* : one who delivers an oration

or·a·to·rio \,orə'tōrē,ō\ *n, pl* **-ri·os** : major choral work

or·a·to·ry \'orə,tōrē\ *n* : art of public speaking —**or·a·tor·i·cal** \,orə'tòr-ikəl\ *adj*

orb \'orb\ *n* 1 : sphere 2 : celestial body —**or·bic·u·lar** \or'bikyələr\ *adj*

or·bit \'orbət\ *n* : path made by one body revolving around another ~ *vb* : revolve around —**or·bit·al** \-ʔl\ *adj* —**or·bit·er** *n*

or·chard \'orchərd\ *n* : place where fruit or nut trees are grown —**or·chard·ist** \-əst\ *n*

or·ches·tra \'orkəstrə\ *n* 1 : group of musicians 2 : front seats of a theater's main floor —**or·ches·tral** \or'kestrəl\ *adj*

or·ches·trate \'orkə,strāt\ *vb* **-trat·ed; -trat·ing** : compose or arrange for an orchestra —**or·ches·tra·tion** \,orkə'strāshən\ *n*

or·chid \'orkəd\ *n* : plant with showy 3-petal flowers or its flower

or·dain \or'dān\ *vb* 1 : admit to the clergy 2 : decree

or·deal \or'dē(ə)l, 'or,dē(ə)l\ *n* : severely trying experience

or·der \'ordər\ *n* 1 : rank, class, or special group 2 : arrangement 3 : rule of law 4 : authoritative regulation or instruction 5 : working condition 6 : special request for a purchase or what is purchased ~ *vb* 1 : arrange 2 : give an order to 3 : place an order for

or·der·ly \-lē\ *adj* 1 : being in order or tidy 2 : well behaved ~ *n, pl* **-lies** 1 : officer's attendant 2 : hospital attendant —**or·der·li·ness** *n*

or·di·nal \'ordnəl, -ʔn·əl\ *n* : number indicating order in a series

or·di·nance \-nəns, -ʔnəns\ *n* : municipal law

or·di·nary \'ordʔn,erē\ *adj* : of common occurrence, quality, or ability —**or·di·nar·i·ly** \,ordʔn'erəlē\ *adv*

or·di·na·tion \,ordʔn'āshən\ *n* : act of ordaining

ord·nance \'ordnəns\ *n* : military supplies

ore \'or\ *n* : mineral containing a valuable constituent

or·gan \'orgən\ *n* 1 : air-powered or electronic keyboard instrument 2 : animal or plant structure with special function 3 : periodical

or·gan·ic \or'ganik\ *adj* 1 : relating to a bodily organ 2 : relating to living things 3 : relating to or containing carbon or its compounds —**or·gan·i·cal·ly** \-ik(ə)lē\ *adv*

or·gan·ism \'orgə,nizəm\ *n* : living person, animal, or plant

or·gan·ist \'orgənəst\ *n* : organ player

or·ga·nize \'orgə,nīz\ *vb* **-nized; -niz·ing** : form parts into a functioning whole —**or·ga·ni·za·tion** \,org(ə)-nə'zāshən\ *n* —**or·ga·niz·er** *n*

or·gasm \'or,gazəm\ *n* : climax of sexual excitement

or·gy \'orjē\ *n, pl* **-gies** : unrestrained indulgence

ori·ent \'orē,ent\ *vb* 1 : set in a definite position 2 : acquaint with a situation —**ori·en·ta·tion** \,orēən'tāshən\ *n*

ori·en·tal \,orē'entʔl\ *adj* : Eastern —**Oriental** *n*

or·i·fice \'orəfəs\ *n* : opening

or·i·gin \'orəjən\ *n* 1 : ancestry 2 : rise, beginning, or derivation from a source —**orig·i·nate** \ə'rijə,nāt\ *vb* —**orig·i·na·tor** \-ər\ *n*

orig·i·nal \ə'rij(ə)nəl\ *n* : something from which a copy is made ~ *adj* 1 : first 2 : not copied from something else 3 : inventive —**orig·i·nal·i·ty** \ə,rijə'nalətē\ *n* —**orig·i·nal·ly** *adv*

ori·ole \'orē,ōl\ *n* : American songbird

or·na·ment \'ornəmənt\ *n* : something that adorns ~ *vb* : provide with ornament —**or·na·men·tal** \,orn-nə'mentʔl\ *adj* —**or·na·men·ta·tion** \-mən'tāshən\ *n*

or·nate \or'nāt\ *adj* : elaborately decorated —**or·nate·ly** *adv* —**or·nate·ness** *n*

or·nery \'orn(ə)rē, 'än-\ *adj* : irritable

or·ni·thol·o·gy \,ornə'thäləjē\ *n, pl* **-gies** : study of birds —**or·ni·tho·log·i·cal** \-thə'läjikəl\ *adj* —**or·ni·thol·o·gist** \-'thäləst\ *n*

or·phan \'orfən\ *n* : child whose parents are dead —**orphan** *vb* —**or·phan·age** \-(ə)nij\ *n*

or·tho·don·tics \ˌȯrtha'däntiks\ *n* : dentistry dealing with straightening teeth —**or·tho·don·tist** \-'däntəst\ *n*

or·tho·dox \'ȯrtha,däks\ *adj* 1 : conforming to established doctrine 2 *cap* : of or relating to a Christian church originating in the Eastern Roman Empire —**or·tho·doxy** \-,däksē\ *n*

or·thog·ra·phy \ȯr'thägrəfē\ *n* : spelling —**or·tho·graph·ic** \ˌȯrtha'grafik\ *adj*

or·tho·pe·dics \ˌȯrtha'pēdiks\ *n sing or pl* : correction or prevention of skeletal deformities —**or·tho·pe·dic** \-ik\ *adj* —**or·tho·pe·dist** \-'pēdəst\ *n*

-o·ry \ˌȯrē, ȯrē, (ə)rē\ *adj suffix* 1 : of, relating to, or characterized by 2 : serving for, producing, or maintaining

os·cil·late \'äsə,lāt\ *vb* **-lat·ed; -lat·ing** : swing back and forth —**os·cil·la·tion** \ˌäsə'lāshən\ *n*

os·mo·sis \äz'mōsəs, äs-\ *n* : diffusion esp. of water through a membrane —**os·mot·ic** \-'mätik\ *adj*

os·prey \'äsprē, -ˌprā\ *n, pl* **-preys** : large hawk

os·ten·si·ble \ä'stensəbəl\ *adj* : seeming —**os·ten·si·bly** \-blē\ *adv*

os·ten·ta·tion \ˌästən'tāshən\ *n* : pretentious display —**os·ten·ta·tious** \-shəs\ *adj* —**os·ten·ta·tious·ly** *adv*

os·te·op·a·thy \ˌästē'äpəthē\ *n* : system of healing that emphasizes manipulation (as of joints) —**os·te·o·path** \'ästēə,path\ *n* —**os·te·o·path·ic** \ˌästēə'pathik\ *adj*

os·tra·cize \'ästrə,sīz\ *vb* **-cize; -ciz·ing** : exclude by common consent —**os·tra·cism** \-,sizəm\ *n*

os·trich \'ästrich, 'ȯs-\ *n* : very large flightless bird

oth·er \'əthər\ *adj* 1 : being the one left 2 : alternate 3 : additional ~ *pron* 1 : remaining one 2 : different one

oth·er·wise *adv* 1 : in a different way 2 : in different circumstances 3 : in other respects —**otherwise** *adj*

ot·ter \'ätər\ *n* : mammal with webbed feet

ot·to·man \'ätəmən\ *n* : upholstered footstool

ought \'ȯt\ *verbal auxiliary*—used to express obligation, advisability, or expectation

ounce \'aúns\ *n* 1 : unit of weight equal to about 28.3 grams 2 : unit of capacity equal to about 29.6 milliliters

our \är, (')aú(ə)r\ *adj* : of or relating to us

ours \('))aú(ə)rz, ärz\ *pron* : one belonging to us

our·selves \är'selvz, aú(ə)r-\ *pron* : we, us—used reflexively or for emphasis

-ous \əs\ *adj suffix* : having or having the qualities of

oust \'aúst\ *vb* : expel or eject

oust·er \'aústər\ *n* : expulsion

out \'aút\ *adv* 1 : away from the inside or center 2 : beyond control 3 : to extinction, exhaustion, or completion 4 : in or into the open ~ *vb* : become known — *adj* 1 : situated outside 2 : absent — *prep* 1 : out through 2 : outward on or along —**out·bound** *adj* —**out·build·ing** *n*

out·board \'aút,bȯrd\ *adv* : outside a boat or ship —**outboard** *adj*

out·break \'aút,brāk\ *n* : sudden occurrence

out·burst \-,bərst\ *n* : violent expression of feeling

out·cast \-,kast\ *n* : person cast out by society

out·come \-,kəm\ *n* : result

out·crop \'aút,kräp\ *n* : part of a rock stratum that appears above the ground —**outcrop** *vb*

out·cry \-,krī\ *n* : loud cry

out·dat·ed \aút'dātəd\ *adj* : out-of-date

out·dis·tance *vb* : go far ahead of

out·do \aút'dü\ *vb* **-did** \-'did\; **-done** \-'dən\; **-do·ing** \-'düiŋ\; **-does** \-'dəz\ : do better than

out·doors \aút'dōrz\ *adv* : in or into the open air ~ *n* : open air —**out·door** *adj*

out·er \aútər\ *adj* 1 : external 2 : farther out —**out·er·most** *adj*

out·field \'aút,fēld\ *n* : baseball field beyond the infield —**out·field·er** \-,fēldər\ *n*

out·fit \'aút,fit\ *n* 1 : equipment for a special purpose 2 : group ~ *vb* **-tt-** : equip —**out·fit·ter** *n*

out·go \'aút,gō\ *n, pl* **outgoes** : expenditure

out·go·ing \'aút,gōiŋ\ *adj* 1 : retiring from a position 2 : friendly

out·grow \aút'grō\ *vb* **-grew** \-'grü\; **-grown** \-'grōn\; **-grow·ing** 1 : grow faster than 2 : grow too large for

out·growth \'aút,grōth\ *n* 1 : product of growing out 2 : consequence

out·ing \'aútiŋ\ *n* : excursion

out·land·ish \aút'landish\ *adj* : very strange —**out·land·ish·ly** *adv*

out·last *vb* : last longer than

out·law \'aút,lȯ\ *n* : lawless person ~ *vb* : make illegal —**out·law·ry** \-,lȯ(ə)rē\ *n*

out·lay \\'autˌlā\ *n* : expenditure

out·let \\'autˌlet, -lət\ *n* **1** : exit **2** : means of release **3** : market for goods **4** : electrical device that gives access to wiring

out·line \\'autˌlīn\ *n* **1** : line marking the outer limits **2** : summary ~ *vb* **1** : draw the outline of **2** : indicate the chief parts of

out·live \auṫ'liv\ *vb* : live longer than

out·look \\'auṫˌlu̇k\ *n* **1** : viewpoint **2** : prospect for the future

out·ly·ing \\'auṫˌlīiŋ\ *adj* : far from a central point

out·mod·ed \auṫ'mōdəd\ *adj* : out-of-date

out·num·ber \-'nəmbər\ *vb* : exceed in number

out of *prep* **1** : out from within **2** : beyond the limits of **3** : among —used to indicate absence or loss **5** : because of **6** : from or with

out-of-date *adj* : no longer in fashion or in use

out·pa·tient *n* : person treated at a hospital who does not stay

out·post *n* : remote military post

out·put *n* : amount produced ~ *vb* **-put·ted** *or* **-put; -put·ting** : produce

out·rage \\'auṫˌrāj\ *n* **1** : violent or shameful act **2** : injury or insult ~ *vb* **-raged; -rag·ing 1** : subject to violent injury **2** : make very angry —**out·ra·geous** \auṫ'rājəs\ *adj* —**out·ra·geous·ly** *adv*

out·right *adv* **1** : completely **2** : instantly ~ *adj* **1** : complete **2** : given without reservation

out·set *n* : beginning

out·side \auṫ'sīd, 'auṫ-\ *n* **1** : place beyond a boundary **2** : exterior **3** : utmost limit ~ *adj* **1** : outer **2** : coming from without **3** : remote ~ *adv* : on or to the outside ~ *prep* **1** : on or to the outside of **2** : beyond the limits of

outside of *prep* **1** : outside **2** : besides

out·sid·er \-'sīdər\ *n* : one who does not belong to a group

out·skirts *n pl* : outlying parts (as of a city)

out·smart \auṫ-\ *vb* : outwit

out·spo·ken *adj* : direct and open in speech —**out·spo·ken·ness** *n*

out·stand·ing *adj* **1** : unpaid **2** : very good —**out·stand·ing·ly** *adv*

out·strip \auṫ'strip\ *vb* **1** : go faster than **2** : surpass

¹out·ward \'auṫwərd\ *adj* **1** : being toward the outside **2** : showing outwardly

²outward, out·wards \-wərdz\ *adv* : toward the outside —**out·ward·ly** *adv*

out·wit \auṫ'wit\ *vb* : get the better of by superior cleverness

ova *pl of* OVUM

oval \'ōvəl\ *adj* : egg-shaped —**oval** *n*

ova·ry \'ōv(ə)rē\ *n, pl* **-ries 1** : egg-producing organ **2** : seed-producing part of a flower —**ovar·i·an** \ō'varēən, -'ver-\ *adj*

ova·tion \ō'vāshən\ *n* : enthusiastic applause

ov·en \'əvən\ *n* : chamber (as in a stove) for baking

over \'ōvər\ *adv* **1** : across **2** : upside down **3** : in excess or addition **4** : above **5** : at an end **6** : again ~ *prep* **1** : above in position or authority **2** : more than **3** : along, through, or across **4** : because of ~ *adj* **1** : upper **2** : remaining **3** : ended

over- *prefix* **1** : so as to exceed or surpass **2** : excessive or excessively

overabundance	overconfidence
overabundant	overconfident
overacceptance	overconscien-
overachiever	tious
overactive	overconsume
overaggressive	overconsumption
overambitious	overcontrol
overamplify	overcook
overanalyze	overcorrect
overanxiety	overcritical
overanxious	overcrowd
overapologetic	overdecorate
overarousal	overdepend
overarouse	overdependent
overassertive	overdevelop
overbake	overdose
overbid	overdramatic
overbill	overdramatize
overbold	overdress
overborrow	overdrink
overbright	overdue
overbroad	overeager
overbuild	overeat
overburden	overeducate
overbusy	overelaborate
overbuy	overemotional
overcapacity	overemphasis
overcapitalize	overemphasize
overcareful	overenergetic
overcautious	overenthusiastic
overcharge	overestimate
overcivilized	overexaggerate
overclean	overexaggeration
overcommit	overexcite
overcompensate	overexcitement
overcomplicate	overexercise
overconcern	overexert

overexertion
overexhaust
overexpand
overexpansion
overexplain
overexploit
overexpose
overextend
overextension
overexuberant
overfamiliar
overfatigue
overfeed
overfertilize
overfill
overfond
overgenerous
overglamorize
overgraze
overharvest
overhasty
overheat
overidealize
overimaginative
overimbibe
overimpressed
overindebted
overindulge
overindulgence
overindulgent
overinflate
overinfluence
overinsistent
overintense
overintensity
overinvest
overinvolve
overladen
overlarge
overlend
overliberal
overload
overlong
overloud
overmedicate
overmodest
overmuch
overobvious
overoptimistic
overorganize
overpack
overparticular
overpatriotic
overpay
overpayment
overpermissive
overplay

overpopulated
overpossessive
overpraise
overprescribe
overpressure
overprice
overprivileged
overproduce
overproduction
overpromise
overprotect
overprotective
overpublicize
overqualified
overrate
overreact
overreaction
overrefine
overregulate
overregulation
overreliance
overrepresent
overrespond
overripe
oversaturate
oversell
oversensitive
overserious
oversexed
oversimple
oversimplify
oversolicitous
overspecialize
overspend
overstaff
overstimulate
overstock
overstrain
overstress
overstretch
overstrict
oversubtle
oversupply
oversuspicious
oversweeten
overtax
overtighten
overtip
overtired
overtrain
overtreat
overuse
overutilize
overvalue
overweight
overwork
overzealous

over-all \ˌōvərˈȯl\ adj : including everything

over-alls \ˈōvərˌȯlz\ n pl : work garment

over-awe vb : restrain by awe

over-bear-ing \-ˈba(ə)riŋ\ adj : arrogant

over-blown \-ˈblōn\ adj : pretentious

over-board adv : over the side into the water

over-cast adj : clouded over ~ n : cloud covering

over-coat n : outer coat

over-come vb -came \-ˈkäm\; -come; -com-ing 1 : defeat 2 : make helpless or exhausted

over-do vb -did; -done; -do-ing; -does : do too much

over-draft n : overdrawn sum

over-draw vb -drew; -drawn; -draw-ing : write checks for more than one's bank balance

over-flow \ˌōvərˈflō\ vb 1 : flood 2 : flow over —**over-flow** \ˈōvərˌflō\ n

over-grow vb -grew; -grown; -grow-ing : grow over

over-hand adj : made with the hand brought down from above —**over-hand** adv

over-hang vb -hung; -hang-ing : jut out over ~ n : something that overhangs

over-haul vb 1 : repair 2 : overtake

over-head \ˌōvərˈhed\ adv : aloft ~ \ˈōvərˌ-\ adj : situated above ~ \ˈōvərˌ-\ n : general business expenses

over-hear vb -heard; -hear-ing : hear without the speaker's knowledge

over-joy vb : fill with joy

over-land \-ˌland, -lənd\ adv or adj : by, on, or across land

over-lap vb : lap over

over-lay \ˌōvərˈlā\ vb -laid; -lay-ing : lay over or across —**over-lay** \ˈōvərˌlā\ n

over-look \ˌōvərˈlu̇k\ vb 1 : look down on 2 : fail to see 3 : ignore 4 : pardon 5 : supervise ~ \ˈōvərˌ-\ n : observation point

over-ly \ˈōvərlē\ adv : excessively

over-night adv : through the night —**overnight** adj

over-pass n : bridge over a road

over-pow-er vb 1 : conquer 2 : overwhelm

over-reach \ˌōvə(r)ˈrēch\ vb : try or seek too much

over-ride vb -rode; -rid-den; -rid-ing : neutralize action of

over-rule vb : rule against or set aside

over-run vb -ran; -run-ning 1 : swarm or

¹**over-age** \ˌōvərˈāj\ adj : too old
²**over-age** \ˈōv(ə)rij\ n : surplus

flow over **2** : go beyond ~ *n* : an exceeding of estimated costs

over·seas *adv or adj* : beyond or across the sea

over·see \ˌōvərˈsē\ *vb* -saw; -seen; -see·ing : supervise —**over·seer** \ˈōvərˌsiər\ *n*

over·shad·ow *vb* : exceed in importance

over·shoe *n* : protective outer shoe

over·shoot *vb* -shot; -shoot·ing : shoot or pass beyond

over·sight *n* : inadvertent omission or error

over·sleep *vb* -slept; -sleep·ing : sleep longer than intended

over·spread *vb* -spread; -spread·ing : spread over or above

over·state *vb* : exaggerate —**over·state·ment** *n*

over·stay *vb* : stay too long

over·step *vb* : exceed

overt \ōˈvərt, ˈōˌvərt\ *adj* : not secret

over·take *vb* -took; -tak·en; -tak·ing : catch up with

over·throw \ˌōvərˈthrō\ *vb* -threw; -thrown; -throw·ing **1** : upset **2** : bring to defeat —**over·throw** \ˈōvərˌ-\ *n*

over·time *n* : extra working time —**overtime** *adv*

over·tone *n* **1** : higher tone in a complex musical tone **2** : suggestion

over·ture \ˈōvərˌchu̇r, -chər\ *n* **1** : opening offer **2** : musical introduction

over·turn *vb* **1** : turn over **2** : overthrow

over·view *n* : brief survey

over·ween·ing \ˌōvərˈwēniŋ\ *adj* **1** : arrogant **2** : excessive

over·whelm \ˌōvərˈhwelm\ *vb* : overcome completely —**over·whelm·ing·ly** \-ˈhwelmiŋlē\ *adv*

over·wrought \ˌōvə(r)ˈrȯt\ *adj* : extremely excited

ovoid \ˈōˌvȯid\, **ovoi·dal** \ōˈvȯidᵊl\ *adj* : egg-shaped

ovu·late \ˈävyəˌlāt, ˈōv-\ *vb* -lat·ed; -lat·ing : produce eggs —**ovu·la·tion** \ˌävyəˈlāshən, ˌōv-\ *n*

ovum \ˈōvəm\ *n, pl* **ova** \-və\ : female germ cell

owe \ˈō\ *vb* **owed; ow·ing 1** : have an obligation to pay **2** : be indebted to or for

owing to *prep* : because of

owl \ˈau̇l\ *n* : nocturnal bird of prey —**owl·ish** *adj* —**owl·ish·ly** *adv*

own \ˈōn\ *adj* : belonging to oneself ~ *vb* **1** : have as property **2** : acknowledge ~ *pron* : one or ones belonging to oneself —**own·er** *n* —**own·er·ship** *n*

ox \ˈäks\ *n, pl* **ox·en** \ˈäksən\ : bovine mammal and esp. a castrated bull

ox·ide \ˈäkˌsīd\ *n* : compound of oxygen

ox·i·dize \ˈäksəˌdīz\ *vb* -dized; -diz·ing : combine with oxygen —**ox·i·da·tion** \ˌäksəˈdāshən\ *n* —**ox·i·diz·able** \ˌäksəˈdīzəbəl\ *adj* —**ox·i·diz·er** *n*

ox·y·gen \ˈäksijən\ *n* : gaseous chemical element —**ox·y·gen·ic** \ˌäksiˈjenik\ *adj*

oys·ter \ˈȯistər\ *n* : bivalve mollusk —**oys·ter·ing** \ˈȯist(ə)riŋ\ *n* —**oys·ter·man** \-mən\ *n*

ozone \ˈōˌzōn\ *n* : faintly blue form of oxygen

P

p \ˈpē\ *n, pl* **p's** *or* **ps** \ˈpēz\ : 16th letter of the alphabet

pace \ˈpās\ *n* **1** : walking step **2** : rate of progress ~ *vb* **paced; pac·ing 1** : go at a pace **2** : cover with slow steps **3** : set the pace of

pace·mak·er *n* : electrical device to regulate heartbeat

pachy·derm \ˈpakiˌdərm\ *n* : elephant

pa·cif·ic \pəˈsifik\ *adj* : calm or peaceful

pac·i·fism \ˈpasəˌfizəm\ *n* : opposition to war or violence —**pac·i·fist** \-fəst\ *n or adj* —**pac·i·fis·tic** \ˌpasəˈfistik\ *adj*

pac·i·fy \ˈpasəˌfī\ *vb* -fied; -fy·ing : make calm —**pac·i·fi·ca·tion** \ˌpasəfəˈkāshən\ *n* —**pac·i·fi·er** \ˈpasəˌfī(ə)r\ *n*

pack \ˈpak\ *n* **1** : compact bundle **2** : group of animals ~ *vb* **1** : put into a container **2** : fill tightly or completely **3** : send without ceremony —**pack·er** *n*

pack·age \ˈpakij\ *n* : items bundled together ~ *vb* -aged; -ag·ing : enclose in a package

pack·et \ˈpakət\ *n* : small package

pact \ˈpakt\ *n* : agreement

pad \ˈpad\ *n* **1** : cushioning part or thing **2** : floating leaf of a water plant **3** : tablet of paper ~ *vb* -dd- **1** : furnish with a pad **2** : expand with needless matter —**pad·ding** *n*

pad·dle \'pad³l\ *n* : implement with a flat blade ~ *vb* -**dled**; -**dling** : move, beat, or stir with a paddle

pad·dock \'padək\ *n* : enclosed area for racehorses

pad·dy \'padē\ *n, pl* -**dies** : wet land where rice is grown

pad·lock *n* : lock with a U-shaped catch —**padlock** *vb*

pa·dre \'pädrā\ *n* : priest

pae·an \'pēən\ *n* : song of praise

pa·gan \'pāgən\ *n or adj* : heathen —**pa·gan·ism** \-,izəm\ *n*

¹page \'pāj\ *n* : messenger ~ *vb* **paged**; **pag·ing** : summon by repeated calls

²page *n* : single leaf (as of a book) or one side of the leaf

pag·eant \'pajənt\ *n* : elaborate spectacle or procession —**pag·eant·ry** \-əntrē\ *n*

pa·go·da \pə'gōdə\ *n* : tower with roofs curving upward

paid *past of* PAY

pail \'pāl\ *n* : cylindrical container with a handle —**pail·ful** \-,ful\ *n*

pain \'pān\ *n* 1 : punishment or penalty 2 : suffering of body or mind 3 *pl* : great care ~ *vb* : cause or experience pain —**pain·ful** \-fəl\ *adj* —**pain·ful·ly** *adv* —**pain·kill·er** *n* —**pain·kill·ing** *adj* —**pain·less** *adj* —**pain·less·ly** *adv*

pains·tak·ing \'pān,stākiŋ\ *adj* : taking pains —**painstaking** *n* —**pains·tak·ing·ly** *adv*

paint \'pānt\ *vb* 1 : apply color or paint to 2 : portray esp. in color ~ *n* : mixture of pigment and liquid —**paint·brush** *n* —**paint·er** *n* —**paint·ing** *n*

pair \'paər\ *n* : a set of two ~ *vb* : put or go together as a pair

pa·ja·mas \pə'jäməz, -'jam-\ *n pl* : loose suit for sleeping

pal \'pal\ *n* : close friend

pal·ace \'paləs\ *n* 1 : residence of a sovereign 2 : mansion —**pa·la·tial** \pə'lāshəl\ *adj*

pal·a·din \'palədən\ *n* : knight

pal·at·able \'palətəbəl\ *adj* : agreeable to the taste

pal·ate \'palət\ *n* 1 : roof of the mouth 2 : taste —**pal·a·tal** \-ət³l\ *adj*

pa·la·ver \pə'lavər, -'läv-\ *n* : talk —**palaver** *vb*

¹pale \'pāl\ *adj* **pal·er; pal·est** 1 : lacking in color or brightness 2 : light in color or shade ~ *vb* **paled; pal·ing** : make or become pale —**pale·ness** *n*

²pale *n* 1 : fence stake 2 : enclosed place

pal·ette \'palət\ *n* : board on which paints are laid and mixed

pal·frey \'pólfrē\ *n, pl* -**freys** : saddle horse

pal·i·sade \,palə'sād\ *n* 1 : high fence 2 : line of cliffs

¹pall \'pól\ *n* : cloth draped over a coffin

²pall *vb* : lose in interest or attraction

pall·bear·er *n* : one who attends the coffin at a funeral

pal·let \'palət\ *n* : makeshift bed

²pallet *n* : portable storage platform

pal·li·ate \'palē,āt\ *vb* -**at·ed; -at·ing** 1 : ease without curing 2 : cover or conceal by excusing —**pal·li·a·tion** \,palē'āshən\ *n* —**pal·li·a·tive** \'palē,ātiv\ *adj or n*

pal·lid \'paləd\ *adj* : pale

pal·lor \'palər\ *n* : paleness

¹palm \'päm, 'pälm\ *n* 1 : tall tropical tree crowned with large leaves 2 : symbol of victory

²palm *n* : underside of the hand ~ *vb* 1 : conceal in the hand 2 : impose by fraud

palm·ist·ry \'päməstrē, 'pälmə-\ *n* : reading a person's character or future in his palms —**palm·ist** \'päməst, 'pälməst\ *n*

palmy \'pämē, 'pälmē\ *adj* **palm·i·er; -est** : flourishing

pal·o·mi·no \,palə'mēnō\ *n, pl* -**nos** : light-colored horse

pal·pa·ble \'palpəbəl\ *adj* 1 : capable of being touched 2 : obvious —**pal·pa·bly** \-blē\ *adv*

pal·pi·tate \'palpə,tāt\ *vb* -**tat·ed; -tat·ing** : pulsate —**pal·pi·ta·tion** \,palpə'tāshən\ *n*

pal·sy \'pólzē\ *n, pl* -**sies** 1 : paralysis 2 : condition marked by tremor —**pal·sied** \-zēd\ *adj*

pal·try \'póltrē\ *adj* -**tri·er; -est** : trivial

pam·pa \'pampə\ *n, pl* **-pas** \-pəz, -pəs\ : grassy So. American plain

pam·per \'pampər\ *vb* : spoil or indulge

pam·phlet \'pamflət\ *n* : unbound publication —**pam·phle·teer** \,pamflə'tiər\ *n*

pan \'pan\ *n* 1 : broad, shallow, and open container ~ *vb* 1 : wash gravel in a pan to search for gold 2 : criticize severely

pan·a·cea \,panə'sēə\ *n* : universal remedy

pan·cake *n* : fried flat cake

pan·cre·as \'paŋkrēəs, 'pan-\ *n* : gland that produces insulin —**pan·cre·at·ic** \,paŋkrē'atik, ,pan-\

pan·da \'pandə\ *n* : black-and-white bearlike animal

pan·de·mo·ni·um \ˌpandə'mōnēəm\ *n* : wild uproar

pan·der \'pandər\ *n* **1** : pimp **2** : one who caters to others' desires or weaknesses ~ *vb* : act as a pander

pane \'pān\ *n* : sheet of glass

pan·e·gyr·ic \ˌpanə'jirik\ *n* : eulogistic oration —**pan·e·gyr·ist** \-'jirəst\ *n*

pan·el \'pan°l\ *n* **1** : list of persons (as jurors) **2** : discussion group **3** : flat piece of construction material **4** : board with instruments or controls ~ *vb* -**eled** *or* -**elled**; -**el·ing** *or* -**el·ling** : decorate with panels —**pan·el·ing** *n* —**pan·el·ist** \-əst\ *n*

pang \'paŋ\ *n* : sudden sharp pain

pan·han·dle \'pan,hand°l\ *vb* -**dled**; -**dling** : ask for money on the street —**pan·han·dler** \-dlər, -°l-dlər\ *n*

pan·ic \'panik\ *n* : sudden overpowering fright ~ *vb* -**icked**; -**ick·ing** : affect or be affected with panic —**pan·icky** \-ikē\ *adj*

pan·o·ply \'panəplē\ *n, pl* -**plies 1** : full suit of armor **2** : impressive array

pan·ora·ma \ˌpanə'ramə, -'räm-\ *n* : view in every direction —**pan·oram·ic** \-'ramik\ *adj*

pan·sy \'panzē\ *n, pl* -**sies** : low-growing garden herb with showy flowers

pant \'pant\ *vb* **1** : breathe with great effort **2** : yearn ~ *n* : panting sound

pan·ta·loons \ˌpant°l'ünz\ *n pl* : pants

pan·ther \'panthər\ *n* : large wild cat

pant·ies \'pantēz\ *n pl* : undergarment with closed crotch and short legs

pan·to·mime \'pantə,mīm\ *n* **1** : play without words **2** : expression by bodily or facial movements ~ *vb* : represent by pantomime

pan·try \'pantrē\ *n, pl* -**tries** : storage room for food and dishes

pants \'pants\ *n pl* **1** : 2-legged outer garment **2** : panties

pap \'pap\ *n* : soft food

pa·pa·cy \'pāpəsē\ *n, pl* -**cies** : office of pope

pa·pal \'pāpəl\ *adj* : relating to the pope

pa·pa·ya \pə'pīə\ *n* : tropical tree with large edible fruit

pa·per \'pāpər\ *n* **1** : pliable substance used to write or print on, to wrap things in, or to cover walls **2** : printed or written document **3** : newspaper —**paper** *adj or vb* —**pa·per·hang·er** *n* —**pa·per·hang·ing** *n* —**pa·per·weight** *n* —**pa·pery** \'pāp(ə)rē\ *adj*

pa·per·board *n* : cardboard

pa·pier-mâ·ché \ˌpāpərmā'shā, ˌpap,yāmə-, -mä-\ *n* : molding material of waste paper

pa·poose \pa'püs, pə-\ *n* : young child of American Indian parents

pa·pri·ka \pə'prēkə, pa-\ *n* : mild red spice

pa·py·rus \pə'pīrəs\ *n, pl* -**rus·es** *or* -**ri** \-(,)rē, -,rī\ **1** : tall grasslike plant **2** : paper from papyrus

par \'pär\ *n* **1** : stated value **2** : common level **3** : accepted standard or normal condition —**par** *adj*

par·a·ble \'parəbəl\ *n* : simple story illustrating a moral truth

para·chute \'parə,shüt\ *n* : large umbrella-shaped device for making a descent from an airplane —**para·chute** *vb* —**para·chut·ist** \-,shütəst\ *n*

pa·rade \pə'rād\ *n* **1** : pompous display **2** : ceremonial formation and march ~ *vb* -**rad·ed**; -**rad·ing 1** : march in a parade **2** : show off

par·a·digm \'parə,dīm, -,dim\ *n* : model

par·a·dise \'parə,dīs, -,dīz\ *n* : place of bliss

par·a·dox \'parə,däks\ *n* : statement that seems contrary to common sense yet is perhaps true —**par·a·dox·i·cal** \ˌparə'däksikəl\ *adj* —**par·a·dox·i·cal·ly** *adv*

par·af·fin \'parəfən\ *n* : white waxy substance used esp. for making candles and sealing foods —**paraffin** *vb* —**par·af·fin·ic** \ˌparə'finik\ *adj*

par·a·gon \'parə,gän, -gən\ *n* : model of perfection

para·graph \'parə,graf\ *n* : unified division of a piece of writing ~ *vb* : divide into paragraphs

par·a·keet \'parə,kēt\ *n* : small slender parrot

par·al·lel \'parə,lel\ *adj* **1** : lying or moving in the same direction but always the same distance apart **2** : similar ~ *n* **1** : parallel line, curve, or surface **2** : line of latitude **3** : similarity ~ *vb* **1** : compare **2** : correspond to —**par·al·lel·ism** \-,izəm\ *n*

par·al·lel·o·gram \ˌparə'lelə,gram\ *n* : 4-sided polygon with opposite sides equal and parallel

pa·ral·y·sis \pə'raləsəs\ *n, pl* -**y·ses** \-,sēz\ : loss of function and esp. of voluntary motion —**par·a·lyt·ic** \ˌparə'litik\ *adj or n*

par·a·lyze \'parə,līz\ *vb* -**lyzed**; -**lyz·ing** : affect with paralysis —**par·a·lyz·ing·ly** *adv*

pa·ram·e·ter \pə'ramətər\ *n* : characteristic element —**para·met·ric** \ˌparə'metrik\ *adj*

par·a·mount \'parəˌmaunt\ *adj* : superior to all others

par·amour \'parəˌmur\ *n* : illicit lover

para·noia \ˌparə'nóiə\ *n* : mental disorder marked by irrational suspicion —**para·noid** \ˌparəˌnóid\ *adj or n*

par·a·pet \'parəpət, -ˌpet\ *n* : protecting rampart in a fort

par·a·pher·na·lia \ˌparəfə(r)'nālyə\ *n sing or pl* : equipment

para·phrase \'parəˌfrāz\ *n* : restatement of a text giving the meaning in different words —**paraphrase** *vb*

para·ple·gia \ˌparə'plēj(ē)ə\ *n* : paralysis of the lower trunk and legs —**para·ple·gic** \-jik\ *adj or n*

par·a·site \'parəˌsīt\ *n* : organism living on another —**par·a·sit·ic** \ˌparə'sitik\ *adj* —**par·a·sit·ism** \'parəsəˌtizəm, -ˌsīˌtiz-\ *n*

para·sol \'parəˌsól\ *n* : umbrella used to keep off the sun

para·troops \-ˌtrüps\ *n pl* : troops trained to parachute from an airplane —**para·troop·er** \-ˌtrüpər\ *n*

par·boil \'pärˌbóil\ *vb* : boil briefly

par·cel \'pärsəl\ *n* 1 : lot 2 : package ~ *vb* **-celed** *or* **-celled; -cel·ing** *or* **-cel·ling** : divide into portions

parch \'pärch\ *vb* : toast or shrivel with dry heat

parch·ment \'pärchmənt\ *n* : animal skin prepared to write on

par·don \'pärdᵊn\ *n* : excuse of an offense ~ *vb* : free from penalty —**par·don·able** \'pärdnəbəl, -ᵊnəbəl\ *adj* —**par·don·er** \-nər, -ᵊnər\ *n*

pare \'paər\ *vb* **pared; par·ing** 1 : trim off an outside part 2 : reduce as if by paring —**par·er** *n*

par·e·gor·ic \ˌparə'górik\ *n* : tincture of opium and camphor

par·ent \'parənt\ *n* : one that begets offspring —**par·ent·age** \-ij\ *n* —**pa·ren·tal** \pə'rentᵊl\ *adj* —**par·ent·hood** *n*

pa·ren·the·sis \pə'renthəsəs\ *n, pl* **-the·ses** \-ˌsēz\ 1 : word or phrase inserted in a passage 2 : one of a pair of punctuation marks ( ) —**par·en·thet·ic** \ˌparən'thetik\, **par·en·thet·i·cal** \-ikəl\ *adj* —**par·en·thet·i·cal·ly** \-k(ə)lē\ *adv*

par·fait \pär'fā\ *n* : layered cold dessert

pa·ri·ah \pə'rīə\ *n* : outcast

par·ish \'parish\ *n* : local church community

pa·rish·io·ner \pə'rish(ə)nər\ *n* : member of a parish

par·i·ty \'parətē\ *n, pl* **-ties** : equality

park \'pärk\ *n* : land reserved for recreation or beauty ~ *vb* : leave a vehicle standing

par·ka \'pärkə\ *n* : usu. hooded heavy jacket

park·way \'pärkˌwā\ *n* : broad thoroughfare

par·lance \'pärləns\ *n* : manner of speaking

par·lay \'pärˌlā\ *n* : the risking of a stake plus its winnings —**parlay** *vb*

par·ley \'pärlē\ *n, pl* **-leys** : conference about a dispute —**parley** *vb*

par·lia·ment \'pärləmənt\ *n* : legislative assembly —**par·lia·men·tar·i·an** *n* —**par·lia·men·ta·ry** \ˌpärlə·ˈment(ə)rē\ *adj*

par·lor \'pärlər\ *n* 1 : reception room 2 : place of business

pa·ro·chi·al \pə'rōkēəl\ *adj* 1 : relating to a church parish 2 : provincial —**pa·ro·chi·al·ism** \-əˌlizəm\ *n*

par·o·dy \'parədē\ *n, pl* **-dies** : humorous or satirical imitation —**parody** *vb*

pa·role \pə'rōl\ *n* : conditional release of a prisoner —**parole** *vb* —**pa·rol·ee** \-ˌrō'lē, -'rōˌlē\ *n*

par·ox·ysm \'parəkˌsizəm, pə'räk-\ *n* : spasm —**par·ox·ys·mal** \ˌparək·ˈsizməl, pəˌräk-\ *adj*

par·que·try \'pärkətrē\ *n, pl* **-tries** : inlaid woodwork

par·ra·keet *var of* PARAKEET

par·rot \'parət\ *n* : bright-colored tropical bird

par·ry \'parē\ *vb* **-ried; -ry·ing** 1 : ward off a blow 2 : evade adroitly —**parry** *n*

parse \'pärs, 'pärz\ *vb* **parsed; pars·ing** : analyze grammatically

par·si·mo·ny \'pärsəˌmōnē\ *n* : extreme frugality —**par·si·mo·ni·ous** \ˌpärsə'mōnēəs\ *adj* —**par·si·mo·ni·ous·ly** *adv*

pars·ley \'pärslē\ *n* : garden plant used as a seasoning

pars·nip \'pärsnəp\ *n* : carrotlike vegetable

par·son \'pärsᵊn\ *n* : minister

par·son·age \'pärsnij, -ᵊnij\ *n* : parson's house

part \'pärt\ *n* 1 : one of the units into which a larger whole is divided 2 : function or role ~ *vb* 1 : take leave 2 : separate 3 : go away 4 : give up

par·take \pär'tāk, pər-\ *vb* **-took; -tak·en; -tak·ing** : have or take a share —**par·tak·er** *n*

par·tial \'pärshəl\ *adj* 1 : favoring one over another 2 : affecting a part only —**par·tial·i·ty** \ˌpärsh(ē)'alətē\ *n* —**par·tial·ly** \'pärsh(ə)lē\ *adv*

par·tic·i·pate \pər'tisə,pāt, pär-\ *vb* -**pat·ed; -pat·ing** : take part in something —**par·tic·i·pant** \-pənt\ *adj* or *n* —**par·tic·i·pa·tion** \-ˌtisə'pāshən\ *n* —**par·tic·i·pa·to·ry** \-'tisəpə,tōrē\ *adj*

par·ti·ci·ple \'pärtə,sipəl\ *n* : verb form with functions of both verb and adjective —**par·ti·cip·i·al** \ˌpärtə'sipēəl\ *adj*

par·ti·cle \'pärtikəl\ *n* : small bit

par·tic·u·lar \pə(r)'tikyələr\ *adj* 1 : relating to a specific person or thing 2 : individual 3 : hard to please ~ *n* : detail —**par·tic·u·lar·ly** *adv*

par·ti·san, par·ti·zan \'pärtəzən, -sən\ *n* 1 : adherent 2 : guerrilla —**partisan** *adj* —**par·ti·san·ship** *n*

par·tite \'pär,tīt\ *adj* : divided into parts

par·ti·tion \pər'tishən, pär-\ *n* 1 : distribution 2 : something that divides —**partition** *vb*

part·ly \'pärtlē\ *adv* : in some degree

part·ner \'pärtnər\ *n* 1 : associate 2 : companion 3 : business associate —**part·ner·ship** *n*

part of speech : class of words distinguished esp. according to function

par·tridge \'pärtrij\ *n*, *pl* **-tridge** or **-tridg·es** : stout-bodied game bird

par·tu·ri·tion \ˌpärtə'rishən, ˌpärchə-, ˌpärtyū-\ *n* : childbirth

par·ty \'pärtē\ *n*, *pl* **-ties** 1 : political organization 2 : participant 3 : company of persons esp. with a purpose 4 : social gathering

par·ve·nu \'pärvə,n(y)ü\ *n* : social upstart

pass \'pas\ *vb* 1 : move past, over, or through 2 : go away or die 3 : allow to elapse 4 : go unchallenged 5 : transfer or undergo transfer 6 : render a judgment 7 : occur 8 : enact 9 : undergo testing successfully 10 : be regarded 11 : decline ~ *n* 1 : low place in a mountain range 2 : act of passing 3 : accomplishment 4 : permission to leave, enter, or move about —**pass·able** *adj* —**pass·er** *n* —**pass·er·by** *n*

pas·sage \'pasij\ *n* 1 : process of passing 2 : means of passing 3 : voyage 4 : right to pass 5 : literary selection —**pas·sage·way** *n*

pass·book *n* : bankbook

pas·sé \pa'sā\ *adj* : out-of-date

pas·sen·ger \'pasᵊnjər\ *n* : traveler in a conveyance

pass·ing \'pasiŋ\ *n* : death

pas·sion \'pashən\ *n* 1 : strong feeling esp. of anger, love, or desire 2 : object of affection or enthusiasm —**pas·sion·ate** \'pash(ə)nət\ *adj* —**pas·sion·ate·ly** *adv* —**pas·sion·less** *adj*

Pass·over \'pas,ōvər\ *n* : Jewish holiday celebrated in March or April in commemoration of the Hebrews' liberation from slavery in Egypt

pass·port \'pas,pōrt\ *n* : government document needed for travel abroad

pass·word *n* : word or phrase spoken to pass a guard

past \'past\ *adj* 1 : ago 2 : just gone by 3 : having existed before the present 4 : expressing past time ~ *prep* or *adv* : beyond ~ *n* : time gone by 2 : verb tense expressing time gone by 3 : past life

pas·ta \'pästə\ *n* : fresh or dried shaped dough

paste \'pāst\ *n* 1 : smooth ground food 2 : moist adhesive ~ *vb* **pasted; past·ing** : attach with paste —**pasty** *adj*

paste·board *n* : cardboard

pas·tel \pas'tel\ *n* : light color —**pastel** *adj*

pas·teur·ize \'pascha,rīz, 'pästə-\ *vb* -**ized; -iz·ing** : heat (as milk) so as to kill germs —**pas·teur·i·za·tion** \ˌpaschərə'zāshən, ˌpästə-\ *n* —**pas·teur·iz·er** *n*

pas·time \'pas,tīm\ *n* : amusement

pas·tor \'pastər\ *n* : clergyman serving a church or parish —**pas·tor·ate** \-t(ə)rət\ *n*

pas·to·ral \'pastə(ə)rəl\ *adj* 1 : relating to rural life 2 : of or relating to spiritual guidance or a pastor ~ *n* : literary work dealing with rural life

pas·try \'pāstrē\ *n*, *pl* **-tries** : sweet baked goods

pas·ture \'paschər\ *n* : land used for grazing ~ *vb* **-tured; -tur·ing** : graze

pat \'pat\ *n* 1 : light tap 2 : small mass ~ *vb* **-tt-** : tap gently ~ *adj* or *adv* 1 : apt or glib 2 : unyielding

patch \'pach\ *n* 1 : piece used for mending 2 : small area distinct from surrounding area ~ *vb* 1 : mend with a patch 2 : make of fragments 3 : repair hastily

patch·work *n* : something made of pieces of different materials, shapes, or colors

pate \'pāt\ *n* : crown of the head

pa·tel·la \pə'telə\ *n, pl* **-lae** \-'tel(ˌ)ē, -ˌī\ *or* **-las** : kneecap

¹pat·ent *adj* **1** \'pat²nt, 'pāt-\ : obvious **2** \'pat-\ : protected by a patent

²pat·ent \'pat-\ *n* : document conferring or securing a right — *vb* : secure by patent — **pat·en·tee** \ˌpat²n't'tē\

pa·ter·nal \pə'tərn³l\ *adj* **1** : fatherly **2** : related through or inherited from a father — **pa·ter·nal·ly** *adv*

pa·ter·ni·ty \pə'tərnətē\ *n* : fatherhood

path \'path, 'páth\ *n* **1** : trodden way **2** : route or course — **path·find·er** *n* — **path·way** *n* — **path·less** *adj*

pa·thet·ic \pə'thetik\ *adj* : pitiful — **pa·thet·i·cal·ly** \-ik(ə)lē\ *adv*

pa·thol·o·gy \pə'thäləjē\ *n, pl* **-gies 1** : study of disease **2** : abnormality — **path·o·log·i·cal** \ˌpathə'läjikəl\ *adj* — **pa·thol·o·gist** \pə'thäləjəst\ *n*

pa·thos \'pāˌthäs\ *n* : element evoking pity

pa·tience \'pāshəns\ *n* : habit or fact of being patient

pa·tient \'pāshənt\ *adj* : bearing pain or trials without complaint — *n* : person under medical care — **pa·tient·ly** *adv*

pa·ti·na \'patənə, pə'tēnə\ *n, pl* **-nas** \-nəz\ *or* **-nae** \-ˌnē, -ˌnī\ : green film formed on copper and bronze

pa·tio \'patēˌō, 'pät-\ *n, pl* **-ti·os 1** : courtyard **2** : paved recreation area near a house

pa·tri·arch \'pātrēˌärk\ *n* **1** : man revered as father or founder **2** : venerable old man — **pa·tri·ar·chal** \ˌpātrē'ärkəl\ *adj* — **pa·tri·ar·chy** \-ˌärkē\ *n*

pa·tri·cian \pə'trishən\ *n* : person of high birth — **patrician** *adj*

pat·ri·cide \'patrəˌsīd\ *n* : murder of one's father

pat·ri·mo·ny \'patrəˌmōnē\ *n* : something inherited — **pat·ri·mo·ni·al** \ˌpatrə'mōnēəl\ *adj*

pa·tri·ot \'pātrēət, -ˌät\ *n* : one who loves his country — **pa·tri·ot·ic** \ˌpātrē'ätik\ *adj* — **pa·tri·ot·i·cal·ly** \-ik(ə)lē\ *adv* — **pa·tri·o·tism** \'pātrēəˌtizəm\ *n*

pa·trol \pə'trōl\ *n* : a going around for observation or security **2** : group on patrol — *vb* **-ll-** : carry out a patrol

pa·trol·man \-mən\ *n* : police officer

pa·tron \'pātrən\ *n* **1** : special protector **2** : wealthy supporter **3** : customer

pa·tron·age \'patrənij, 'pā-\ *n* **1** : support or influence of a patron **2** : trade of customers **3** : control of government appointments

pa·tron·ize \'pātrəˌnīz, 'pa-\ *vb* **-ized; -iz·ing 1** : be a customer of **2** : treat with condescension

¹pat·ter \'patər\ *vb* : talk glibly or mechanically — *n* : rapid talk

²patter *vb* : pat or tap rapidly — *n* : quick succession of pats or taps

pat·tern \'patərn\ *n* **1** : model for imitation or for making things **2** : artistic design **3** : noticeable formation or set of characteristics — *vb* : form according to a pattern

pat·ty \'patē\ *n, pl* **-ties** : small flat cake

pau·ci·ty \'pósətē\ *n* : shortage

paunch \'pónch\ *n* : large belly — **paunchy** *adj*

pau·per \'pópər\ *n* : person without means of support — **pau·per·ism** \-pəˌrizəm\ *n* — **pau·per·ize** \-pəˌrīz\ *vb*

pause \'póz\ *n* : temporary stop — *vb* **paused; paus·ing** : stop briefly

pave \'pāv\ *vb* **paved; pav·ing** : cover to smooth or firm the surface — **pave·ment** \-mənt\ *n* — **pav·ing** *n*

pa·vil·ion \pə'vilyən\ *n* **1** : large tent **2** : light structure used for entertainment

paw \'pó\ *n* : foot of a 4-legged clawed animal — *vb* **1** : handle clumsily or rudely **2** : touch or strike with a paw, hoof, or foot

pawn \'pón\ *n* **1** : goods deposited as security for a loan **2** : state of being pledged — *vb* **3** : deposit as a pledge — **pawn·bro·ker** *n* — **pawn·shop** *n*

pay \'pā\ *vb* **paid** \'pād\; **pay·ing 1** : make due return for goods or services **2** : discharge indebtedness for **3** : require **4** : give or make freely or as fitting **5** : be profitable — *n* **1** : status of being paid **2** : something paid — **pay·able** *adj* — **pay·check** *n* — **pay·ee** \pā'ē\ *n* — **pay·er** *n* — **pay·ment** *n*

pea \'pē\ *n* : round edible seed of a leguminous vine

peace \'pēs\ *n* **1** : state of calm and quiet **2** : absence of war or strife — **peace·able** \-əbəl\ *adj* — **peace·ably** \-blē\ *adv* — **peace·ful** \-fəl\ *adj* — **peace·ful·ly** *adv* — **peace·keep·er** *n* — **peace·keep·ing** *n* — **peace·mak·er** *n* — **peace·time** *n*

peach \'pēch\ *n* : sweet juicy fruit of a flowering tree

pea·cock \'pēˌkäk\ *n* : brilliantly colored male pheasant

peak \'pēk\ *n* **1** : pointed or projecting part **2** : top of a hill **3** : highest level ~ *vb* : reach a maximum —**peak** *adj*

peak·ed \'pēkəd\ *adj* : sickly

peal \'pēl\ *n* : loud sound (as of ringing bells) ~ *vb* : give out peals

pea·nut \'pē(,)nət\ *n* : annual herb that bears underground pods or the pod or the edible seed inside

pear \'paər\ *n* : fleshy fruit of a tree related to the apple

pearl \'pərl\ *n* : gem formed within an oyster —**pearly** \'pərlē\ *adj*

peas·ant \'pez²nt\ *n* : tiller of the land —**peas·ant·ry** \-²ntrē\ *n*

peat \'pēt\ *n* : decayed organic deposit often dried for fuel —**peaty** *adj*

peb·ble \'pebəl\ *n* : small stone —**pebbly** *adj*

pe·can \pi'kän, -'kan\ *n* : hickory tree bearing a smooth-shelled nut or the nut

pec·ca·dil·lo \,pekə'dilō\ *n, pl* **-loes** *or* **-los** : slight offense

¹peck \'pek\ *n* : unit of dry measure equal to 8 quarts

²peck *vb* : strike or pick up with the bill ~ *n* : quick sharp stroke

pec·tin \'pektən\ *n* : water-soluble plant substance that causes fruit jellies to set —**pec·tic** \-tik\ *adj*

pec·to·ral \'pekt(ə)rəl\ *adj* : relating to the breast or chest

pec·u·late \'pekyə,lāt\ *vb* **-lat·ed; -lat·ing** : embezzle —**pec·u·la·tion** \,pekyə'lāshən\ *n*

pe·cu·liar \pi'kyülyər\ *adj* **1** : characteristic of only one **2** : strange —**pe·cu·liar·i·ty** \-,kyül'yarət̄ē, -ē'ar-\ *n* —**pe·cu·liar·ly** *adv*

pe·cu·ni·ary \pi'kyünē,erē\ *adj* : relating to money

ped·a·go·gy \'pedə,gōjē, -,gäj-\ *n* : art or profession of teaching —**ped·a·gog·ic** \,pedə'gäjik, -'gōj-\, **ped·a·gog·i·cal** \-ikəl\ *adj* —**ped·a·gogue** \'pedə,gäg\ *n*

¹ped·al \'ped²l\ *n* : lever worked by the foot ~ *adj* : relating to the foot ~ *vb* : use a pedal

ped·ant \'ped²nt\ *n* : learned bore —**pe·dan·tic** \pi'dantik\ *adj* —**ped·ant·ry** \'ped²ntrē\ *n*

ped·dle \'ped²l\ *vb* **-dled; -dling** : offer for sale —**ped·dler, ped·lar** \'pedlər\ *n*

ped·es·tal \'pedəst²l\ *n* : support or foot of something standing upright

pe·des·tri·an \pə'destrēən\ *adj* **1** : ordinary **2** : walking ~ *n* : person who walks

pe·di·at·rics \,pēdē'atriks\ *n* : branch of medicine dealing with children —**pe·di·at·ric** \-trik\ *adj* —**pe·di·a·tri·cian** \,pēdēə'trishən\ *n*

ped·i·gree \'pedə,grē\ *n* : line of ancestors or a record of it

ped·i·ment \'pedəmənt\ *n* : triangular gablelike decoration on a building

peek \'pēk\ *vb* **1** : look furtively **2** : glance —**peek** *n*

peel \'pēl\ *vb* **1** : strip the skin or rind from **2** : lose the outer layer ~ *n* : skin or rind —**peel·ing** *n*

¹peep \'pēp\ *vb or n* : cheep

²peep *vb* **1** : look slyly **2** : begin to emerge ~ *n* : brief look —**peep·er** *n* —**peep·hole** *n*

¹peer \'piər\ *n* **1** : one's equal **2** : nobleman —**peer·age** \-ij\ *n*

²peer *vb* : look intently or curiously

peer·less \-ləs\ *adj* : having no equal

peeve \'pēv\ *vb* **peeved; peev·ing** : make resentful ~ *n* : complaint —**peev·ish** \-ish\ *adj* —**peev·ish·ly** *adv* —**peev·ish·ness** *n*

peg \'peg\ *n* : small pinlike piece ~ *vb* **-gg-** **1** : put a peg into **2** : fix or mark with or as if with pegs

pei·gnoir \pān'wär, pen-\ *n* : negligee

pelf \'pelf\ *n* : money

pel·i·can \'pelikən\ *n* : large-billed seabird

pel·la·gra \pə'lagrə, -'läg-\ *n* : protein-deficiency disease

pel·let \'pelət\ *n* : little ball —**pel·let·al** \-²l\ *adj* —**pel·let·ize** \-,īz\ *vb*

pell-mell \'pel'mel\ *adv* : in confusion or haste

pel·lu·cid \pə'lüsəd\ *adj* : very clear

pelt \'pelt\ *n* : skin of a fur-bearing animal

²pelt *vb* : strike with blows or missiles

pel·vis \'pelvəs\ *n, pl* **-vis·es** \-vəsəz\ *or* **-ves** \-,vēz\ : cavity formed by the hip bones —**pel·vic** \-vik\ *adj*

pem·mi·can \'pemikən\ *n* : dried meat

¹pen \'pen\ *n* : enclosure for animals ~ *vb* **-nn-** : shut in a pen

²pen *n* : tool for writing with ink ~ *vb* **-nn-** : write

pe·nal \'pēn²l\ *adj* : relating to punishment

pe·nal·ize \'pēn²l,īz, 'pen-\ *vb* **-ized; -iz·ing** : put a penalty on

pen·al·ty \'pen²ltē\ *n, pl* **-ties** **1** : punishment for crime **2** : disadvantage, loss, or hardship due to an action

pen·ance \'penəns\ *n* : act performed to show repentance

pence \'pens\ *pl of* PENNY

pen·chant \'penchənt\ *n* : strong inclination

pen·cil \'pensəl\ *n* : writing or drawing tool with a solid marking substance as its core ~ *vb* **-ciled** *or* **-cilled; -ciling** *or* **-cil·ling** : draw or write with a pencil

pen·dant \'pendənt\ *n* : hanging ornament

pen·dent, pen·dant \'pendənt\ *adj* : hanging

pend·ing \'pendiŋ\ *prep* : while awaiting ~ *adj* : not yet decided

pen·du·lous \'penjələs, -də-\ *adj* : hanging loosely

pen·du·lum \-ləm\ *n* : weight that swings from a fixed point

pen·e·trate \'penə,trāt\ *vb* **-trat·ed; -trat·ing** 1 : enter into 2 : permeate 3 : see into —**pen·e·tra·ble** \-trəbəl\ *adj* —**pen·e·tra·tion** \,penə'trāshən\ *n* —**pen·e·tra·tive** \'penə,trātiv\ *adj*

pen·guin \'peŋgwən, 'pen-\ *n* : short-legged flightless seabird

pen·i·cil·lin \,penə'silən\ *n* : anitbiotic produced by a mold

pen·in·su·la \pə'ninsələ, -'ninchə-\ *n* : land extending out into the water —**pen·in·su·lar** \-lər\ *adj*

pe·nis \'pēnəs\ *n, pl* **-nes** \-,nēz\ *or* **-nis·es** : male organ of copulation

pen·i·tent \'penətənt\ *adj* : feeling sorrow for sins or offenses ~ *n* : penitent person —**pen·i·tence** \-təns\ *n* —**pen·i·ten·tial** \,penə'tenchəl\ *adj*

pen·i·ten·tia·ry \,penə'tench(ə)rē\ *n, pl* **-ries** : state or federal prison

pen·man·ship \'penmən,ship\ *n* : art or practice of writing

pen·nant \'penənt\ *n* : nautical or championship flag

pen·ny \'penē\ *n, pl* **-nies** \-ēz\ *or* **pence** \'pens\ 1 : monetary unit equal to 1/100 pound 2 *pl* **-nies** : cent —**pen·ni·less** \'peniləs\ *adj*

pen·sion \'penchən\ *n* : retirement income ~ *vb* : pay a pension to —**pen·sion·er** *n*

pen·sive \'pensiv\ *adj* : thoughtful —**pen·sive·ly** *adv*

pent \'pent\ *adj* : confined

pent·a·gon \'pentə,gän\ *n* : 5-sided polygon —**pen·tag·o·nal** \pen'tagənᵊl\ *adj*

pen·tam·e·ter \pen'tamətər\ *n* : line of 5 metrical feet

pent·house \'pent,hau̇s\ *n* : rooftop apartment

pe·nu·ri·ous \pə'n(y)u̇rēəs\ *adj* 1 : marked by penury 2 : stingy

pen·u·ry \'penyərē\ *n* : poverty

pe·on \'pē,än, -ən\ *n, pl* **-ons** *or* **-ones** \pā'ōnēz\ : landless laborer in Spanish America —**pe·on·age** \-ənij\ *n*

pe·o·ny \'pēənē\ *n, pl* **-nies** : garden plant having large flowers

peo·ple \'pēpəl\ *n, pl* **people** 1 *pl* : human beings in general 2 *pl* : human beings in a certain group (as a family) or community 3 *pl* **peoples** : tribe, nation, or race ~ *vb* **-pled; -pling** : constitute the population of

pep \'pep\ *n* : brisk energy ~ *vb* **pepped; pep·ping** : put pep into —**pep·py** *adj*

pep·per \'pepər\ *n* 1 : pungent seasoning from the berry (**peppercorn**) of a shrub 2 : vegetable grown for its hot or sweet fruit ~ *vb* : season with pepper —**pep·pery** \-(ə)rē\ *adj*

pep·per·mint \-,mint, -mənt\ *n* : pungent aromatic mint

pep·tic \'peptik\ *adj* : relating to digestion or the effect of digestive juices

per \'pər\ *prep* 1 : by means of 2 : for each 3 : according to

per·am·bu·late \pə'rambyə,lāt\ *vb* **-lat·ed; -lat·ing** : travel over esp. on foot —**per·am·bu·la·tion** \-,rambyə'lāshən\ *n*

per·cale \(,)pər'kāl, 'pər-; (,)pər'kal\ *n* : fine woven cotton cloth

per·ceive \pər'sēv\ *vb* **-ceived; -ceiv·ing** 1 : realize 2 : become aware of through the senses —**per·ceiv·able** *adj*

per·cent \pər'sent\ *adj* : in each hundred ~ *n, pl* **-cent** *or* **-cents** 1 : one part in a hundred 2 : percentage

per·cent·age \pər'sentij\ *n* : part of a whole expressed in hundredths

per·cep·ti·ble \pər'septəbəl\ *adj* : capable of being perceived —**per·cep·ti·bly** \-blē\ *adv*

per·cep·tion \pər'sepshən\ *n* 1 : act or result of perceiving 2 : ability to perceive

per·cep·tive \pər'septiv\ *adj* : showing perception —**per·cep·tive·ly** *adv*

¹**perch** \'pərch\ *n* : roost for birds ~ *vb* : roost

²**perch** *n, pl* **perch** *or* **perch·es** : freshwater spiny-finned food fish

per·co·late \'pərkə,lāt\ *vb* **-lat·ed; -lat·ing** : trickle or cause to trickle down through a substance —**per·co·la·tor** \-,lātər\ *n*

per·cus·sion \pər'kəshən\ *n* 1 : sharp blow 2 : musical instrument sounded by striking

pe·remp·to·ry \pə'rempt(ə)rē\ *adj* 1 : imperative 2 : domineering —**pe·remp·to·ri·ly** \-t(ə)rəlē\ *adv*

pe·ren·ni·al \pə'renēəl\ *adj* 1 : present at all seasons of the year 2 : continuing to live from year to year 3 : recurring regularly ~ *n* : plant that lives for a number of years —**pe·ren·ni·al·ly** *adv*

per·fect \'pərfikt\ *adj* 1 : being without fault or defect 2 : exact 3 : complete ~ *vb* : make perfect —**per·fect·ibil·i·ty** \,pər,fektə'bilətē, ,pərfik-\ *n* —**per·fect·ible** \pər'fektəbəl, 'pərfik\ *adj* —**per·fect·ly** *adv* —**per·fect·ness** *n*

per·fec·tion \pər'fekshən\ *n* 1 : quality or state of being perfect 2 : highest degree of excellence —**per·fec·tion·ist** \-sh(ə)nəst\ *n*

per·fi·dy \'pərfədē\ *n* : treachery —**per·fid·i·ous** \pər'fidēəs\ *adj* —**per·fid·i·ous·ly** *adv*

per·fo·rate \'pərfə,rāt\ *vb* -rat·ed; -rat·ing : make a hole in —**per·fo·ra·tion** \,pərfə'rāshən\ *n*

per·force \pə(r)'fōrs\ *adv* : of necessity

per·form \pə(r)'fōrm\ *vb* 1 : adhere to the terms of 2 : carry out 3 : give a performance —**per·form·er** *n*

per·for·mance \pər'fōr,məns\ *n* 1 : act or process of performing 2 : public presentation

per·fume \'pər,fyüm, pər'-\ *n* 1 : pleasant odor 2 : preparation used for scenting ~ \pər'-, 'pər,-\ *vb* -fumed; -fum·ing : add a pleasing smell to

per·func·to·ry \pər'fəŋkt(ə)rē\ *adj* : done merely as a duty —**per·func·to·ri·ly** \-t(ə)rəlē\ *adv*

per·haps \pər'(h)aps, 'praps\ *adv* : possibly but not certainly

per·il \'perəl\ *n* : danger —**per·il·ous** *adj* —**per·il·ous·ly** *adv*

pe·rim·e·ter \pə'rimətər\ *n* : outer boundary of a body or figure

pe·ri·od \'pirēəd\ *n* 1 : punctuation mark . used esp. to mark the end of a declarative sentence or an abbreviation 2 : division of time 3 : stage or division in a process or development

pe·ri·od·ic \,pirē'ädik\ *adj* : occurring at regular intervals —**pe·ri·od·i·cal·ly** \-ik(ə)lē\ *adv*

pe·ri·od·i·cal \,pirē'ädikəl\ *n* : newspaper or magazine

pe·riph·ery \pə'rif(ə)rē\ *n, pl* -er·ies : outer boundary —**pe·riph·er·al** \-(ə)rəl\ *adj*

peri·scope \'perə,skōp\ *n* : optical instrument for viewing from a submarine

per·ish \'perish\ *vb* : die or spoil —**per·ish·able** \-əbəl\ *adj or n*

per·ju·ry \'pərj(ə)rē\ *n* : voluntary violation of an oath to tell the truth —**per·jure** \'pərjər\ *vb* —**per·jur·er** *n*

¹**perk** \'pərk\ *vb* 1 : thrust (as the head) up jauntily 2 : make trim or brisk 3 : gain vigor or spirit —**perky** *adj*

²**perk** *vb* : percolate

¹**per·ma·nent** \'pərmənənt\ *adj* : lasting —**per·ma·nence** \-nəns\ *n* —**per·ma·nen·cy** \-nənsē\ *n* —**per·ma·nent·ly** *adv*

²**permanent** *n* : long-lasting hair wave or straightening

per·me·able \'pərmēəbəl\ *adj* : permitting liquids or gases to seep through —**per·me·a·bil·i·ty** \,pərmēə'bilətē\ *n*

per·me·ate \'pərmē,āt\ *vb* -at·ed; -at·ing 1 : seep through 2 : pervade —**per·me·ation** \,pərmē'āshən\ *n*

per·mis·si·ble \pər'misəbəl\ *adj* : that may be permitted

per·mis·sion \pər'mishən\ *n* : formal consent

per·mis·sive \pər'misiv\ *adj* : granting freedom esp. to excess —**per·mis·sive·ness** *n*

per·mit \pər'mit\ *vb* -mit·ted; -mit·ting 1 : give approval for 2 : make possible ~ \'pər,-, pər'-\ *n* : license

per·ni·cious \pər'nishəs\ *adj* : harmful —**per·ni·cious·ly** *adv*

per·ox·ide \pə'räk,sīd\ *n* : compound (as hydrogen peroxide) in which oxygen is joined to oxygen

per·pen·dic·u·lar \,pərpən'dikyələr\ *adj* 1 : vertical 2 : meeting another line at a right angle —**perpendicular** *n* —**per·pen·dic·u·lar·i·ty** \-,dikyə'larətē\ *n* —**per·pen·dic·u·lar·ly** *adv*

per·pe·trate \'pərpə,trāt\ *vb* -trat·ed; -trat·ing : be guilty of doing —**per·pe·tra·tion** \,pərpə'trāshən\ *n* —**per·pe·tra·tor** \'pərpə,trātər\ *n*

per·pet·u·al \pər'pech(əw)əl\ *adj* 1 : continuing forever 2 : occurring continually —**per·pet·u·al·ly** *adv*

per·pe·tu·i·ty \,pərpə't(y)üətē\ *n*

per·pet·u·ate \pər'pechə,wāt\ *vb* -at·ed; -at·ing : make perpetual —**per·pet·u·a·tion** \-,pechə'wāshən\ *n*

per·plex \pər'pleks\ *vb* : confuse —**per·plex·i·ty** \-ətē\ *n*

per·qui·site \'pərkwəzət\ *n* : privilege or profit beyond regular pay

per·se·cute \'pərsi,kyüt\ *vb* -cut·ed; -cut·ing : harass in such a way as to injure or afflict —**per·se·cu·tion** \,pərsi'kyüshən\ *n* —**per·se·cu·tor** \'pərsi,kyütər\ *n*

per·se·vere \,pərsə'viər\ *vb* -vered; -ver·ing : persist —**per·se·ver·ance** \-'virəns\ *n*

per·sist \pər'sist, -'zist\ *vb* 1 : go on resolutely in spite of difficulties 2 : continue to exist —**per·sis·tence** \-'sistəns, -'zis-\ *n* —**per·sis·ten·cy** \-tənsē\ *n* —**per·sis·tent** \-tənt\ *adj* —**per·sis·tent·ly** *adv*

per·son \'pərs³n\ *n* 1 : human being 2 : human being's body or individuality 3 : reference to the speaker, one spoken to, or one spoken of

per·son·able \'pərsnəbəl, -³nəbəl\ *adj* : having a pleasing personality

per·son·age \'pərsnij, -³nij\ *n* : person of rank or distinction

per·son·al \'pərsnəl, -³nəl\ *adj* 1 : relating to or affecting a particular person 2 : done in person 3 : affecting an individual's body 4 : indicating grammatical person —**per·son·al·ly** *adv*

per·son·al·i·ty \pərs³n'alətē\ *n, pl* -ties 1 : offensive personal remark 2 : manner and disposition of an individual 3 : distinctive person

per·son·al·ize \'pərsnə‚līz, -³nə‚līz\ *vb* -ized; -iz·ing : mark as belonging to a particular person

per·son·i·fy \pər'sänə‚fī\ *vb* -fied; -fy·ing 1 : represent as a human being 2 : be the embodiment of —**per·son·i·fi·ca·tion** \-‚sänəfə'kāshən\ *n*

per·son·nel \‚pərs³n'el\ *n* : body of persons employed in an organization

per·spec·tive \pər'spektiv\ *n* 1 : apparent depth and distance in painting 2 : view of things in their true relationship or importance

per·spi·cac·i·ty \‚pərspə'kasətē\ *n* : acuteness of understanding or judgment —**per·spi·ca·cious** \-'kāshəs\ *adj*

per·spire \pər'spīr\ *vb* -spired; -spir·ing : sweat —**per·spi·ra·tion** \‚pərspə-'rāshən\ *n*

per·suade \pər'swād\ *vb* -suad·ed; -suad·ing : cause to do or believe by argument or entreaty —**per·sua·sive** \-'swāsiv, -ziv\ *adj* —**per·sua·sive·ly** *adv* —**per·sua·sive·ness** *n*

per·sua·sion \pər'swāzhən\ *n* : act or process of persuading

pert \'pərt\ *adj* : flippant or irreverent

per·tain \pər'tān\ *vb* 1 : belong 2 : relate

per·ti·na·cious \‚pərt³n'āshəs\ *adj* : obstinately persistent —**per·ti·nac·i·ty** \-'asətē\ *n*

per·ti·nent \'pərt³nənt\ *adj* : relevant —**per·ti·nence** \-əns\ *n*

per·turb \pər'tərb\ *vb* : make uneasy —**per·tur·ba·tion** \‚pərtər'bāshən\ *n*

pe·ruse \pə'rüz\ *vb* -rused; -rus·ing : read attentively —**pe·rus·al** \-'rüzəl\ *n*

per·vade \pər'vād\ *vb* -vad·ed; -vad·ing : spread through every part of —**per·va·sive** \-'vāsiv, -ziv\ *adj*

per·verse \pər'vərs\ *adj* 1 : corrupt 2 : unreasonably contrary —**per·verse·ly** *adv* —**per·verse·ness** *n* —**per·ver·sion** \pər'vərzhən\ *n* —**per·ver·si·ty** \pər'vərsətē\ *n*

per·vert \pər'vərt\ *vb* : corrupt or distort ~ \'pər‚-\ *n* : one that is perverted

pe·so \'pāsō\ *n, pl* -sos : monetary unit (as of Mexico)

pes·si·mism \'pesə‚mizəm\ *n* : inclination to expect the worst —**pes·si·mist** \-məst\ *n* —**pes·si·mis·tic** \‚pesə-'mistik\ *adj*

pest \'pest\ *n* 1 : nuisance 2 : plant or animal detrimental to man —**pes·ti·cide** \'pestə‚sīd\ *n*

pes·ter \'pestər\ *vb* -tered; -ter·ing : harass persistently with petty matters

pes·ti·lence \'pestələns\ *n* : plague —**pes·ti·lent** \-lənt\ *adj*

pes·tle \'pesəl, 'pest³l\ *n* : implement for grinding substances in a mortar

pet \'pet\ *n* 1 : domesticated animal kept for pleasure rather than utility 2 : favorite ~ *vb* : stroke gently or lovingly

pet·al \'pet³l\ *n* : modified leaf of a flower head

pe·tite \pə'tēt\ *adj* : having a small trim figure

pe·ti·tion \pə'tishən\ *n* : formal written request ~ *vb* : make a petition —**pe·ti·tion·er** *n*

pe·trel \'petrəl\ *n* : small seabird

pet·ri·fy \'petrə‚fī\ *vb* -fied; -fy·ing 1 : change into stony material 2 : make rigid or inactive (as from fear) —**pet·ri·fac·tion** \‚petrə'fakshən\ *n*

pe·tro·leum \pə'trōlēəm\ *n* : raw oil obtained from the ground

pet·ti·coat \'petē‚kōt\ *n* : skirt worn under a dress

pet·ty \'petē\ *adj* -ti·er; -est 1 : being small or minor and of no importance 2 : narrow-minded or unsympathetic —**pet·ti·ly** \'petəlē\ *adv* —**pet·ti·ness** *n*

petty officer *n* : subordinate officer in the navy or coast guard appointed from among the enlisted men

petty officer first class *n* : petty officer ranking below a chief petty officer

petty officer second class *n* : petty officer ranking below a petty officer first class

pet·ty officer third class n : petty officer ranking below a petty officer second class

pet·u·lant \'pechələnt\ adj : irritable —**pet·u·lance** \-ləns\ n —**pet·u·lant·ly** adv

pe·tu·nia \pi't(y)ünyə\ n : garden plant with bright flowers

pew \'pyü\ n : bench with a back used in a church

pew·ter \'pyütər\ n : alloy of tin used for kitchen or table utensils

pH \(')pē'āch\ n : number expressing relative acidity and alkalinity

pha·lanx \'fā,laŋks\ n, pl **-lanx·es** or **-lan·ges** \'fā'lan,jēz\ 1 : body (as of troops) in compact formation 2 pl phalanges : digital bone of the hand or foot

phal·lus \'faləs\ n, pl **-li** \'fal,ī\ or **-lus·es** : penis —**phal·lic** adj

phantasy var of FANTASY

phan·tom \'fantəm\ n : something that only appears to be real —**phantom** adj

pha·raoh \'fe(ə)rō, 'fārō\ n : ruler of ancient Egypt

phar·i·see \'farə,sē\ n : a self-righteous or hypocritical person —**phar·i·sa·ic** \,farə'sāik\ adj

phar·ma·ceu·ti·cal \,färmə'sütikəl\ adj 1 : relating to pharmacy or pharmacists 2 : medicinal —**pharmaceutical** n

phar·ma·col·o·gy \,färmə'käləjē\ n : science of drugs esp. as related to medicinal uses —**phar·ma·co·log·ic** \-kə'läjik\, **phar·ma·co·log·i·cal** \-ikəl\ adj —**phar·ma·col·o·gist** \-'käləjəst\ n

phar·ma·cy \'färməsē\ n, pl **-cies** 1 : art or practice of preparing and dispensing drugs 2 : drugstore —**phar·ma·cist** \-səst\ n

phar·ynx \'fariŋks\ n, pl **pha·ryn·ges** \fə'rin,jēz\ : space behind the mouth into which the nostrils, esophagus, and windpipe open —**pha·ryn·ge·al** \fə'rinj(ē)əl, ,farən'jēəl\ adj

phase \'fāz\ n 1 : particular appearance or stage in a recurring series of changes 2 : stage in a process

pheas·ant \'fez³nt\ n, pl **-ant** or **-ants** : long-tailed brilliantly colored game bird

phe·nom·e·non \fi'nämə,nän, -nən\ n, pl **-na** \-nə\ or **-nons** 1 : observable fact or event 2 pl **-nons** : prodigy —**phe·nom·e·nal** \-'nämən³l\ adj

phi·lan·der \fə'landər\ vb : make love without serious intent —**phi·lan·der·er** n

phi·lan·thro·py \fə'lanthrəpē\ n, pl **-pies** : charitable act or gift or an organization that distributes such gifts —**phil·an·throp·ic** \,filən'thräpik\ adj —**phi·lan·thro·pist** \-'lanthrəpəst\ n

phi·lat·e·ly \fə'lat³lē\ n : collection and study of postage stamps —**phi·lat·e·list** \-³ləst\ n

phil·har·mon·ic \,filär'mänik, ,filh(ä)r-\ adj : relating to a symphony orchestra

phi·lis·tine \'filə,stēn; fə'listən\ n : one who is smugly indifferent to ideas or art —**philistine** adj

philo·den·dron \,filə'dendrən\ n, pl **-drons** or **-dra** \-drə\ : plant grown for its showy leaves

phi·los·o·pher \fə'läsəfər\ n 1 : reflective thinker 2 : student of or specialist in philosophy

phi·los·o·phy \fə'läsəfē\ n, pl **-phies** 1 : critical study of fundamental beliefs 2 : sciences and liberal arts exclusive of medicine, law, and theology 3 : system of ideas 4 : sum of personal convictions 5 : calmness —**philo·soph·ic** \,filə'säfik\, **phil·o·soph·i·cal** \-ikəl\ adj —**phil·o·soph·i·cal·ly** \-k(ə)lē\ adv —**phi·los·o·phize** \fə'läsə,fīz\ vb

phle·bi·tis \fli'bītəs\ n : inflammation of a vein

phlegm \'flem\ n : thick mucus in the nose and throat

phleg·mat·ic \fleg'matik\ adj : slow and stolid

phlox \'fläks\ n, pl **phlox** or **phlox·es** : herb grown for its flower clusters

pho·bia \'fōbēə\ n : irrational persistent fear

phoe·nix \'fēniks\ n : legendary bird held to burn itself to death and rise fresh and young from its ashes

phone \'fōn\ n : telephone ∼ vb **phoned**; **phon·ing** : call on a telephone

pho·neme \'fō,nēm\ n : smallest distinguishable unit of speech —**pho·ne·mic** \fō'nēmik\ adj

pho·net·ics \fə'netiks\ n : study of speech sounds —**pho·net·ic** \-ik\ adj —**pho·ne·ti·cian** \fōnə'tishən\ n

pho·no·graph \'fōnə,graf\ n : instrument that reproduces sounds from a grooved disc —**pho·no·graph·ic** \,fōnə'grafik\ adj —**pho·no·graph·i·cal·ly** \-ik(ə)lē\ adv

pho·ny, pho·ney \'fōnē\ adj **-ni·er; -est** : not sincere or genuine —**phony** n

phos·phate \'fäs,fāt\ n : chemical salt used in fertilizers —**phos·phat·ic** \fäs'fatik\ adj

phos·phor \'fäsfər\ n : phosphorescent substance

phos·pho·res·cence \,fäsfə'res°ns\ n : luminescence without heat —**phos·pho·res·cent** \-°nt\ adj —**phos·pho·res·cent·ly** adv

phos·pho·rus \'fäsf(ə)rəs\ n : poisonous waxy chemical element —**phos·phor·ic** \fäs'fōrik, -'fär-\ adj —**phos·pho·rous** \'fäsf(ə)rəs; fäs'fōrəs, -'fōr-\ adj

pho·to \'fōtō\ n, pl **-tos** : photograph —**photo** vb or adj

pho·to·elec·tric \,fōtōi'lektrik\ adj : relating to an electrical effect due to the interaction of light with matter —**pho·to·elec·tri·cal·ly** \-trik(ə)lē\ adv

pho·to·gen·ic \,fōtə'jenik\ adj : suitable for being photographed

pho·to·graph \'fōtə,graf\ n : picture taken by photography —**photograph** vb —**pho·tog·ra·pher** \fə'tägrəfər\ n

pho·tog·ra·phy \fə'tägrəfē\ n : process of using light to produce images on a sensitized surface —**pho·to·graph·ic** \,fōtə'grafik\ adj —**pho·to·graph·i·cal·ly** \-ik(ə)lē\ adv

pho·to·syn·the·sis \,fōtō'sinthəsəs\ n : formation of carbohydrates by chlorophyll-containing plants exposed to sunlight —**pho·to·syn·the·size** \-,sīz\ vb —**pho·to·syn·thet·ic** \-sin'thetik\ adj

phrase \'frāz\ n 1 : brief expression 2 : group of related words that express a thought ~ vb **phrased; phras·ing** : express in a particular manner

phrase·ol·o·gy \,frāzē'äləjē\ n, pl **-gies** : manner of phrasing

phy·lum \'fīləm\ n, pl **-la** \-lə\ : major division of the plant or animal kingdom

phys·ic \'fizik\ n : medicine that purges

phys·i·cal \'fizikəl\ adj 1 : relating to nature 2 : material as opposed to mental or spiritual 3 : relating to the body —**phys·i·cal·ly** \-k(ə)lē\ adv

phy·si·cian \fə'zishən\ n : doctor of medicine

phys·i·cist \'fizəsəst\ n : specialist in physics

phys·ics \'fiziks\ n : science that deals with matter and motion

phys·i·og·no·my \,fizē'ä(g)nəmē\ n, pl **-mies** : facial appearance esp. as a reflection of inner character

phys·i·ol·o·gy \,fizē'äləjē\ n 1 : science dealing with the functioning of living matter and beings 2 : functional processes in an organism —**phys·i·o·log·i·cal** \-ēə'läjikəl\, **phys·i·o·log·ic** \-ik\ adj —**phys·i·ol·o·gist** \-ē'äləjəst\ n

phy·sique \fə'zēk\ n : build of a person's body

pi \'pī\ n, pl **pis** \'pīz\ : symbol π denoting the ratio of the circumference of a circle to its diameter or the ratio itself

pi·a·nist \pē'anəst, 'pēənəst\ n : one who plays the piano

pi·ano \pē'anō\ n, pl **-anos** : musical instrument with strings sounded by hammers arranged from a keyboard

pi·az·za \pē'azə, -'atsə\ n, pl **-zas** or **-ze** \-'ät(,)sä, -'ät-\ : open square in a town

pi·ca·yune \,pikē'(y)ün\ adj : trivial or petty

pic·co·lo \'pikə,lō\ n, pl **-los** : small shrill flute

¹**pick** \'pik\ vb 1 : break up with a pointed instrument 2 : remove bit by bit 3 : gather by plucking 4 : select 5 : rob 6 : provoke 7 : unlock with a wire 8 : eat sparingly ~ n 1 : act of choosing 2 : choicest one —**pick·er** n —**pick up** vb 1 : improve 2 : put in order

²**pick** n : pointed digging tool

pick·ax n : pick

pick·er·el \'pik(ə)rəl\ n, pl **-el** or **-els** : small pike

pick·et \'pikət\ n 1 : pointed stake (as for a fence) 2 : worker demonstrating on strike ~ vb : demonstrate as a picket

pick·le \'pikəl\ n : brine or vinegar solution for preserving foods or a food preserved in a pickle —**pickle** vb

pick·pock·et n : one who steals from pockets

pick-up \'pik,əp\ n 1 : revival or acceleration 2 : light truck with an open body

pic·nic \'pik,nik\ n : outing with food usu. eaten in the open ~ vb **-nicked; -nick·ing** : go on a picnic

pic·to·ri·al \pik'tōrēəl\ adj : relating to pictures

pic·ture \'pikchər\ n 1 : representation by painting, drawing, or photography 2 : vivid description 3 : image or copy 4 : movie ~ vb **-tured; -tur·ing** : form a mental image of

pic·tur·esque \ˌpikchə'resk\ *adj* : attractive or charming enough to be suitable for a picture —**pic·tur·esque·ness** *n*

pie \'pī\ *n* : pastry crust and a filling

pie·bald \'pī,bȯld\ *adj* : blotched with white and black

piece \'pēs\ *n* **1** : part of a whole **2** : one of a group or set ~ *vb* **pieced**; **piec·ing** : join into a whole

piece·meal \'pēs,mēl\ *adv or adj* : gradually

pied \'pīd\ *adj* : colored in blotches

pier \'piər\ *n* **1** : support for a bridge span **2** : deck or wharf built out over water **3** : pillar

pierce \'piərs\ *vb* **pierced**; **pierc·ing** : enter or thrust into or through **2** : penetrate **3** : see through

pi·ety \'pīətē\ *n, pl* **-eties** : devotion to religion

pig \'pig\ *n* **1** : young swine **2** : dirty or greedy individual **3** : a casting (as of iron) run directly from a furnace into a mold —**pig·let** \-lət\ *n* —**pig·pen** *n* —**pig·sty** *n*

pi·geon \'pijən\ *n* : stout-bodied short-legged bird

pi·geon·hole *n* : small open compartment for letters or documents ~ *vb* **1** : place in a pigeonhole **2** : classify

pig·gish \'pigish\ *adj* : greedy

pig·gy·back \'pigē,bak\ *adv or adj* : up on the back and shoulders

pig·head·ed \-'hedəd\ *adj* : stubborn

pig·ment \'pigmənt\ *n* : coloring matter —**pig·men·ta·tion** *n*

pigmy *var of* PYGMY

pig·tail *n* : tight braid of hair

¹pike \'pīk\ *n, pl* **pike** *or* **pikes** : large freshwater fish

²pike : former weapon consisting of a long wooden staff with a steel point —**pike·staff** *n*

³pike *n* : turnpike

pi·las·ter \'pī,lastər, pə'las-\ *n* : slightly projecting upright column

¹pile \'pīl\ *n* **1** : supporting pillar driven into the ground

²pile *n* : quantity of things thrown on one another ~ *vb* **piled**; **pil·ing** : heap up or accumulate

³pile *n* : surface of fine hairs or threads —**piled** *adj*

piles \'pīls\ *n pl* : hemorrhoids

pil·fer \'pilfər\ *vb* : steal in small quantities at a time

pil·grim \'pilgrəm\ *n* **1** : one who travels to a shrine or holy place in devotion **2** *cap* : one of the founding settlers in America in 1620

pil·grim·age \-grəmij\ *n* : pilgrim's journey

pill \'pil\ *n* : small rounded mass of medicine —**pill·box** *n*

pil·lage \'pilij\ *vb* **-laged**; **-lag·ing** : take booty —**pillage** *n*

pil·lar \'pilər\ *n* : upright usu. supporting column or shaft —**pil·lared** *adj*

pil·lo·ry \'pil(ə)rē\ *n, pl* **-ries** : wooden frame for public punishment with holes for the head and hands ~ *vb* **-ried**; **-ry·ing 1** : set in a pillory **2** : expose to public scorn

pil·low \'pilō\ *n* : soft cushion for the head —**pil·low·case** *n*

pi·lot \'pīlət\ *n* **1** : helmsman **2** : person licensed to take ships into and out of a port **3** : guide **4** : one that flies an aircraft or spacecraft ~ *vb* : act as pilot of —**pi·lot·age** \-ij\ *n* —**pi·lot·less** *adj*

pi·men·to \pə'mentō\ *n, pl* **-tos** *or* **-to 1** : pimiento **2** : allspice

pi·mien·to \pə'm(y)entō\ *n, pl* **-tos** : mild red sweet pepper fruit

pimp \'pimp\ *n* : man who solicits clients for a prostitute —**pimp** *vb*

pim·ple \'pimpəl\ *n* : small inflamed swelling on the skin —**pim·ply** \-p(ə)lē\ *adj*

pin \'pin\ *n* **1** : fastener made of a small pointed piece of wire **2** : ornament or emblem fastened to clothing with a pin **3** : wooden object used as a target in bowling ~ *vb* **-nn- 1** : fasten with a pin **2** : hold fast or immobile —**pin·hole** *n*

pin·afore \'pinə,fōr\ *n* : sleeveless dress or apron fastened at the back

pin·cer \'pinsər\ *n, pl* **1** : gripping tool with 2 jaws **2** : pincerlike claw

pinch \'pinch\ *vb* **1** : squeeze between the finger and thumb or between the jaws of a tool **2** : compress painfully ~ *n* **1** : critical point **2** : painful effect **3** : act of pinching **4** : very small quantity

pin·cush·ion *n* : cushion for storing pins

¹pine \'pīn\ *vb* **pined**; **pin·ing 1** : lose health through distress **2** : yearn for intensely

²pine *n* : evergreen cone-bearing tree or its wood

pine·ap·ple *n* : tropical plant bearing an edible juicy fruit

pin·feath·er *n* : new feather just coming through the skin

¹pin·ion \'pinyən\ *vb* : restrain by binding the arms

²pinion *n* : small gear

pink \'piŋk\ *n* **1** : plant with narrow leaves and showy flowers **2** : light red

3 : highest degree —**pink** *adj* —**pink-ish** *adj*

pink·eye \'piŋk,ī\ *n* : contagious eye inflammation

pin·na·cle \'pinikəl\ *n* : highest point

pi·noch·le \'pē,nəkəl\ *n* : card game played with a 48-card deck

pin·point *vb* : locate, hit, or aim with great precision

pint \'pīnt\ *n* : 1/2 quart

pin·to \'pin,tō\ *n, pl* **pintos** : spotted horse

pin·worm *n* : small parasitic intestinal worm

pi·o·neer \,pīə'niər\ *n* **1** : one that originates or helps open up a new line of thought or activity **2** : early settler ~ *vb* : act as a pioneer

pi·ous \'pīəs\ *adj* **1** : conscientious in religious practices **2** : affectedly religious —**pi·ous·ly** *adv*

pipe \'pīp\ *n* **1** : tube that produces music when air is forced through **2** : bagpipe **3** : long tube for conducting a fluid **4** : smoking tool ~ *vb* **piped; pip·ing 1** : play on a pipe **2** : speak in a high voice **3** : convey by pipes —**pip·er** *n*

pipe·line *n* **1** : line of pipe **2** : channel for information

pip·ing \'pīpiŋ\ *n* **1** : music of pipes **2** : narrow fold of material used to decorate edges or seams

pi·quant \'pēkənt\ *adj* **1** : tangy **2** : provocative or charming —**pi·quan·cy** \-kənsē\ *n*

pique \'pēk\ *n* : resentment ~ *vb* **piqued; piqu·ing 1** : offend **2** : arouse

pi·qué, pi·que \pi'kā\ *n* : durable ribbed clothing fabric

pi·ra·cy \'pīrəsē\ *n, pl* **-cies 1** : robbery on the seas **2** : unauthorized use of another's production or invention

pi·ra·nha \pə'ranyə, -'rän(y)ə\ *n* : small voracious So. American fish

pi·rate \'pīrət\ *n* : one who commits piracy —**pirate** *vb* —**pi·rat·i·cal** \pə'ratikəl, pī-\ *adj*

pir·ou·ette \,pirə'wet\ *n* : full turn on the toe or ball of one foot in ballet —**pirouette** *vb*

pis *pl of* **PI**

pis·ta·chio \pə'stash(ē,)ō, -'stäsh-\, *n, pl* **-chios** : small tree bearing a greenish edible seed or its seed

pis·til \'pist²l\ *n* : female reproductive organ in a flower —**pis·til·late** \'pistə,lāt\ *adj*

pis·tol \'pist²l\ *n* : firearm held with one hand

pis·ton \'pistən\ *n* : sliding piece that

receives and transmits motion usu. inside a cylinder

¹pit \'pit\ *n* **1** : hole or shaft in the ground **2** : sunken or enclosed place for a special purpose **3** : hell **4** : hollow or indentation ~ *vb* **-tt- 1** : form pits in **2** : become marred with pits

²pit *n* : stony seed of some fruits ~ *vb* **-tt-** : remove the pit from

¹pitch \'pich\ *n* : resin from conifers —**pitchy** *adj*

²pitch *vb* **1** : erect and fix firmly in place **2** : throw **3** : set at a particular level **4** : fall headlong ~ *n* **1** : action or manner of pitching **2** : degree of slope **3** : relative highness of a tone —**pitched** *adj*

pitch·blende \'pich,blend\ *n* : mineral source of uranium

¹pitch·er \'pichər\ *n* : container for liquids

²pitcher *n* : one that pitches

pitch·fork *n* : long-handled fork for pitching hay

pit·e·ous \'pitēəs\ *adj* : arousing pity —**pit·e·ous·ly** *adv*

pit·fall \'pit,fol\ *n* : hidden danger

pith \'pith\ *n* **1** : spongy plant tissue **2** : essential or meaningful part —**pithy** *adj*

piti·able \'pitēəbəl\ *adj* : pitiful

piti·ful \'pitifəl\ *adj* **1** : arousing or deserving pity **2** : contemptible —**piti·ful·ly** \-f(ə)lē\ *adv*

pit·tance \'pit²ns\ *n* : small portion or amount

pi·tu·itary \pə't(y)üə,terē\ *adj* : relating to or being a small gland attached to the brain

pity \'pitē\ *n, pl* **pit·ies 1** : sympathetic sorrow **2** : something to be regretted ~ *vb* **pit·ied; pity·ing** : feel pity for —**piti·less** *adj* —**piti·less·ly** *adv*

piv·ot \'pivət\ *n* : fixed pin on which something turns ~ *vb* : turn on or as if on a pivot —**pivot** *adj* —**piv·ot·al** *adj*

pix·ie, pixy \'piksē\ *n, pl* **pix·ies** : mischievous sprite

piz·za \'pētsə\ *n* : thin pie of bread dough spread with a spiced mixture (as of tomatoes, cheese, and meat)

piz·ze·ria \,pētsə'rēə\ *n* : pizza restaurant

plac·ard \'plakərd, -,ärd\ *n* : poster ~ *vb* : display placards in or on

pla·cate \'plā,kāt, 'plak,āt\ *vb* **-cat·ed; -cat·ing** : appease —**plac·a·ble** \'plakəbəl, 'plākə-\ *adj*

place \'plās\ *n* **1** : space or room **2** : indefinite area **3** : a particular building, locality, area, or part **4**

: relative position in a scale or sequence **5** : seat **6** : job ~ *vb* **placed**; **plac·ing 1** : put in a place **2** : identify —**place·ment** *n*

pla·cen·ta \plə'sentə\ *n, pl* **-tas** *or* **-tae** \-(,)ē\ : structure by which a mammal is nourished before birth —**pla·cen·tal** \-'sent^əl\ *adj*

plac·id \'plasəd\ *adj* : undisturbed or peaceful —**pla·cid·i·ty** \plə'sidətē\ *n* —**plac·id·ly** *adv*

pla·gia·rize \'plājə,rīz\ *vb* **-rized**; **-riz·ing** : use (words or ideas) of another as if your own —**pla·gia·rism** \-,rizəm\ *n* —**pla·gia·rist** \-rəst\ *n*

plague \'plāg\ *n* **1** : disastrous evil **2** : destructive contagious bacterial disease ~ *vb* **plagued**; **plagu·ing 1** : afflict with disease or disaster **2** : harass

plaid \'plad\ *n* : woolen fabric with a pattern of crossing stripes or the pattern itself —**plaid** *adj*

¹plain \'plān\ *n* : expanse of relatively level treeless country

²plain *adj* **1** : lacking ornament **2** : not concealed or disguised **3** : easily understood **4** : frank **5** : not fancy or pretty —**plain·ly** *adv* —**plain·ness** \'plānnəs\ *n*

plaint \'plānt\ *n* : complaint

plain·tiff \'plāntəf\ *n* : complaining party in a lawsuit

plain·tive \'plāntiv\ *adj* : expressive of suffering or woe —**plain·tive·ly** *adv*

plait \'plāt, 'plat\ *n* **1** : pleat **2** : braid of hair or straw —**plait** *vb*

plan \'plan\ *n* **1** : drawing or diagram **2** : method for accomplishing something ~ *vb* **-nn- 1** : form a plan of **2** : intend —**plan·less** *adj* —**plan·ner** *n*

¹plane \'plān\ *vb* **planed**; **plan·ing** : smooth or level off with a plane ~ *n* : smoothing or shaping tool —**plan·er** *n*

²plane *n* **1** : level surface **2** : level of existence, consciousness, or development **3** : airplane ~ *adj* **1** : flat **2** : dealing with flat surfaces or figures

plan·et \'planət\ *n* : celestial body that revolves around the sun —**plan·e·tary** \-ə,terē\ *adj*

plan·e·tar·i·um \,planə'terēəm\ *n, pl* **-iums** *or* **-ia** \-ēə\ : building or room housing a device to project images of celestial bodies

plank \'plaŋk\ *n* **1** : heavy thick board **2** : article in the platform of a political party —**plank·ing** *n*

plank·ton \'plaŋktən\ *n* : tiny aquatic animal and plant life —**plank·ton·ic** \plaŋk'tänik\ *adj*

plant \'plant\ *vb* **1** : set in the ground to grow **2** : place firmly or forcibly ~ *n* **1** : living thing without sense organs that cannot move about **2** : land, buildings, and machinery used esp. in manufacture

¹plan·tain \'plant^ən\ *n* : short-stemmed herb with tiny greenish flowers

²plantain *n* : banana plant with starchy greenish fruit

plan·ta·tion \plan'tāshən\ *n* : agricultural estate worked by resident laborers

plant·er \'plantər\ *n* **1** : plantation owner **2** : plant container

plaque \'plak\ *n* : commemorative tablet

plas·ma \'plazmə\ *n* : watery part of blood —**plas·mat·ic** \plaz'matik\ *adj*

plas·ter \'plastər\ *n* **1** : medicated dressing **2** : hardening paste for coating walls and ceilings ~ *vb* : cover with plaster —**plas·ter·er** *n* —**plas·tery** *adj*

plas·tic \'plastik\ *adj* : capable of being molded ~ *n* : material that can be formed into rigid objects, films, or filaments —**plas·tic·i·ty** \plas'tisətē\ *n*

plate \'plāt\ *n* **1** : flat thin piece of plated metalware **2** : shallow usu. circular dish **3** : denture or the part of it that fits to the mouth **4** : something printed from an engraving ~ *vb* **plat·ed**; **plat·ing** : overlay with metal —**plat·ing** *n*

pla·teau \pla'tō\ *n, pl* **-teaus** *or* **-teaux** \-'tōz\ : large level area raised above adjacent land

plat·form \'plat,fȯrm\ *n* **1** : raised flooring or stage **2** : declaration of principles for a political party

plat·i·num \'platnəm, -^ənəm\ *n* : heavy silver-white metallic chemical element

plat·i·tude \'platə,t(y)üd\ *n* : trite remark —**plat·i·tu·di·nous** \,platə't(y)üdnəs, -^ənəs\ *adj*

pla·toon \plə'tün\ *n* : small military unit

platoon sergeant *n* : noncommissioned officer in the army ranking below a first sergeant

plat·ter \'platər\ *n* : large serving plate

platy·pus \'platipəs\ *n* : small aquatic egg-laying mammal

plau·dit \'plȯdət\ *n* : act of applause

plau·si·ble \'plȯzəbəl\ *adj* : reasonable or believable —**plau·si·bil·i·ty** \,plȯzə'bilətē\ *n* —**plau·si·bly** \-blē\ *adv*

play \'plā\ *n* **1** : action in a game **2** : recreational activity **3** : stage representation of a drama **4** : light or fitful movement **5** : free movement ~ *vb* **1** : engage in recreation **2** : move or toy with aimlessly **3** : perform music **4** : act in a drama —**play·act·ing** *n* —**play·er** *n* —**play·ful** \-fəl\ *adj* —**play·ful·ly** *adv* —**play·ful·ness** *n* —**play·go·er** *n* —**play·let** \-lət\ *n* —**play·pen** *n* —**play·suit** *n*

play·ground *n* : place for children to play

play·house *n* **1** : theater **2** : small house for children to play in

playing card *n* : one of a set of 24 to 78 cards marked to show its rank and suit and used to play a game of cards

play·mate *n* : companion in play

play·off *n* : contest or series of contests to determine a champion

play·thing *n* : toy

play·wright \-₁rīt\ *n* : writer of plays

pla·za \'plazə, 'pläz-\ *n* : public square

plea \'plē\ *n* **1** : defendant's answer to charges **2** : urgent request

plead \'plēd\ *vb* **plead·ed** *or* **pled** \'pled\; **plead·ing 1** : argue for or against in court **2** : answer to a charge or indictment **3** : appeal earnestly —**plead·er** *n*

pleas·ant \'plez²nt\ *adj* **1** : giving pleasure **2** : marked by pleasing behavior or appearance —**pleas·ant·ly** *adv* —**pleas·ant·ness** *n*

pleas·ant·ries \-³ntrēz\ *n pl* : pleasant and casual conversation

please \'plēz\ *vb* **pleased; pleas·ing 1** : give pleasure or satisfaction to **2** : desire or intend **3** : be willing to

pleas·ing \'plēziŋ\ *adj* : giving pleasure —**pleas·ing·ly** *adv*

plea·sur·able \'plezh(ə)rəbəl\ *adj* : pleasant —**plea·sur·ably** \-blē\ *adv*

plea·sure \'plezhər\ *n* **1** : desire or inclination **2** : enjoyment **3** : source of delight

pleat \'plēt\ *vb* : arrange in pleats ~ *n* : fold in cloth

ple·be·ian \pli'bēən\ *n* : one of the common people ~ *adj* : ordinary

pleb·i·scite \'plebə₁sīt, -sət\ *n* : vote of the people (as of a country) on a proposal submitted to them

pledge \'plej\ *n* **1** : something given as security **2** : promise or vow ~ *vb* **pledged; pledg·ing 1** : offer as or bind by a pledge **2** : promise

ple·na·ry \'plēnərē, 'plen-\ *adj* : full

pleni·po·ten·tia·ry \₁plenəpə-'tench(ə)rē, -'tenchē₁erē\ *n* : diplo-

matic agent having full authority —**plenipotentiary** *adj*

plen·i·tude \'plenə₁t(y)üd\ *n* **1** : completeness **2** : abundance

plen·te·ous \'plentēəs\ *adj* : existing in plenty

plen·ti·ful \'plentifəl\ *adj* : abundant —**plen·ti·ful·ly** *adv*

plen·ty \'plentē\ *n* : more than adequate number or amount

pleth·o·ra \'plethərə\ *n* : excess

pleu·ri·sy \'plurəsē\ *n* : inflammation of the chest membrane

pli·able \'plīəbəl\ *adj* : flexible

pli·ant \'plīənt\ *adj* : flexible —**pli·an·cy** \-ənsē\ *n*

pli·ers \'plī(ə)rz\ *n pl* : pinching or gripping tool

¹plight \'plīt\ *vb* : pledge

²plight *n* : bad state

plod \'pläd\ *vb* **-dd- 1** : walk heavily or slowly **2** : work laboriously and monotonously —**plod·der** *n* —**plod·ding·ly** \-iŋlē\ *adv*

plot \'plät\ *n* **1** : small area of ground **2** : ground plan **3** : main story development (as of a book or movie) **4** : secret plan for doing something ~ *vb* **-tt- 1** : make a plot or plan of **2** : plan or contrive —**plot·ter** *n*

plo·ver \'pləvər, 'plōvər\ *n, pl* **-ver** *or* **-vers** : shorebird related to the sandpiper

plow, plough \'plau\ *n* **1** : tool used to turn soil **2** : plowlike device ~ *vb* **1** : break up with a plow **2** : cleave or move through like a plow —**plow·able** *adj* —**plow·er** *n* —**plow·man** \-mən, -₁man\ *n*

plow·share \-₁she(ə)r\ *n* : plow part that cuts the earth

ploy \'ploi\ *n* : clever plan or maneuver

pluck \'plək\ *vb* **1** : pull off or out **2** : tug or twitch ~ *n* **1** : act or instance of plucking **2** : spirit or courage

plucky \'pləkē\ *adj* **pluck·i·er; -est** : courageous or spirited

plug \'pləg\ *n* **1** : something for sealing an opening **2** : electrical connector at the end of a cord **3** : piece of favorable publicity ~ *vb* **-gg- 1** : stop or make tight or secure by inserting a plug **2** : publicize

plum \'pləm\ *n* **1** : smooth-skinned juicy fruit **2** : fine reward

plum·age \'plümij\ *n* : feathers of a bird

plumb \'pləm\ *n* : weight on the end of a line to show vertical direction ~ *adv* **1** : vertically **2** : completely ~ *vb*

: sound or test with a plumb ~ *adj* : vertical

plumb·er \'pləmər\ *n* : one who repairs usu. water pipes and fixtures

plumb·ing \'pləmiŋ\ *n* : system of water pipes in a building

plume \'plüm\ *n* : large, conspicuous, or showy feather ~ *vb* **plumed; plum·ing 1** : provide or deck with feathers **2** : indulge in pride —**plumed** \'plümd\ *adj* —**plumy** \'plümē\ *adj*

plum·met \'pləmət\ *vb* : drop straight down

¹plump \'pləmp\ *vb* : drop suddenly or heavily ~ *adv* **1** : suddenly and heavily **2** : directly

²plump *adj* : having a full rounded form —**plump·ness** *n*

plun·der \'pləndər\ *vb* : rob or take goods by force (as in war) ~ *n* : something taken in plundering —**plun·der·er** *n*

plunge \'plənj\ *vb* **plunged; plung·ing 1** : thrust or dive into something **2** : begin an action suddenly **3** : dive or throw oneself forward or down ~ *n* : act or instance of plunging —**plung·er** *n*

plu·ral \'plùrəl\ *adj* : relating to a word form denoting more than one —**plural** *n*

plu·ral·i·ty \plù'ralətē\ *n, pl* **-ties** : greatest number of votes cast when not a majority

plu·ral·ize \'plùrə₁līz\ *vb* **-ized; -iz·ing** : make plural —**plu·ral·iza·tion** \₁plùrələ'zāshən\ *n*

plus \'pləs\ *prep* : with the addition of ~ *n* **1** : sign + (**plus sign**) in mathematics to require addition **2** : added or positive quantity **3** : advantage ~ *adj* : being more or in addition

plush \'pləsh\ *n* : fabric with a long pile ~ *adj* : luxurious —**plush·ly** *adv* —**plushy** *adj*

plu·toc·ra·cy \plü'täkrəsē\ *n, pl* **-cies 1** : government by the wealthy **2** : a controlling class of rich men —**plu·to·crat** \'plütə₁krat\ *n* —**plu·to·crat·ic** \₁plütə'kratik\ *adj*

plu·to·ni·um \plü'tōnēəm\ *n* : radioactive chemical element

¹ply \'plī\ *n, pl* **plies** : fold, thickness, or strand of which something is made

²ply *vb* **plied; ply·ing 1** : use or work at **2** : keep supplying something to **3** : travel over regularly

ply·wood *n* : sheets of wood glued and pressed together

pneu·mat·ic \n(y)ù'matik\ *adj* **1** : moved by air pressure **2** : filled with compressed air —**pneu·mat·i·cal·ly** \-ik(ə)lē\ *adv*

pneu·mo·nia \n(y)ù'mōnyə\ *n* : inflammatory lung disease

¹poach \'pōch\ *vb* : cook in simmering liquid

²poach *vb* : hunt or fish illegally —**poach·er** *n*

pock \'päk\ *n* : small swelling on the skin or its scar —**pock·mark** *n* —**pock-marked** *adj*

pock·et \'päkət\ *n* **1** : small open bag sewn into a garment **2** : container or receptacle **3** : isolated area or group ~ *vb* : put in a pocket —**pock·et·ful** \-₁fùl\ *n*

pock·et·book *n* **1** : purse **2** : financial resources

pock·et·knife *n* : knife with a folding blade for the pocket

pod \'päd\ *n* **1** : dry fruit that splits open when ripe **2** : detachable spacecraft compartment

po·di·a·try \pə'dīətrē, pō-\ *n* : branch of medicine dealing with the foot —**po·di·a·trist** \pə'dīətrəst, pō-\ *n*

po·di·um \'pōdēəm\ *n, pl* **-di·ums** or **-dia** \-ēə\ : dais

po·em \'pōəm\ *n* : composition in verse

po·et \'pōət\ *n* : writer of poetry

po·et·ry \'pōətrē\ *n* **1** : metrical writing **2** : poems —**po·et·ic** \pō'etik\, **po·et·i·cal** \-ikəl\ *adj*

po·grom \pə'gräm, 'pōgrəm, 'pägrəm\ *n* : organized massacre

poi·gnant \'pòinyənt\ *adj* **1** : emotionally painful **2** : deeply moving —**poi·gnan·cy** \-nyənsē\ *n*

poin·set·tia \pòin'setēə, -'setə\ *n* : showy tropical American plant

point \'pòint\ *n* **1** : individual often essential detail **2** : purpose **3** : particular place, time, or stage **4** : sharp end **5** : projecting piece of land **6** : dot or period **7** : division of the compass **8** : unit of counting ~ *vb* **1** : sharpen **2** : indicate direction by extending a finger **3** : direct attention to **4** : aim —**point·less** *adj*

point-blank *adj* **1** : so close to a target that a missile fired goes straight to it **2** : direct —**point-blank** *adv*

point·er \'pòintər\ *n* **1** : one that points out **2** : large short-haired hunting dog **3** : hint or tip

poise \'pòiz\ *vb* **poised; pois·ing** : balance ~ *n* : self-possessed calmness

poi·son \'pòiz²n\ *n* : chemical that can injure or kill ~ *vb* **1** : injure or kill with poison **2** : apply poison to **3** : affect destructively —**poi·son·er**

\\-nər, -ᵊnər\\ n —**poi·son·ous**
\\'pȯiznəs, -ᵊnəs\\ adj

poke \\'pōk\\ vb **poked; pok·ing 1** : prod
2 : dawdle ~ n : quick thrust
¹pok·er \\'pōkər\\ n : rod for stirring a
fire

²po·ker n : card game

po·lar \\'pōlər\\ adj : relating to a geographical or magnetic pole

po·lar·ize \\'pōlə,rīz\\ vb **-ized; -iz·ing
1** : cause to have magnetic poles —**po-
lar·iza·tion** \\,pōlərə'zāshən\\ n

¹pole \\'pōl\\ n : long slender piece of
wood or metal

²pole n **1** : either end of the earth's axis
2 : battery terminal **3** : either end of a
magnet

pole·cat \\'pōl,kat\\ n, pl **polecats** or
polecat 1 : European carnivorous
mammal **2** : skunk

po·lem·ics \\pə'lemiks\\ n sing or pl
: practice of disputation —**polemic,
po·lem·i·cal** \\-ikəl\\ adj —**po·lem·i-
cist** \\-səst\\ n

police \\pə'lēs\\ n, pl **-lice 1** : department of government that keeps pub-
lic order and enforces the laws **2**
: members of the police ~ vb **-liced;
-lic·ing** : regulate and keep in order
—**po·lice·man** \\-mən\\ n —**po·lice-
wom·an** n

¹pol·i·cy \\'päləsē\\ n, pl **-cies** : course
of action selected to guide decisions

²policy n, pl **-cies** : insurance contract
—**pol·i·cy·hold·er** n

po·lio \\'pōlē,ō\\ n : poliomyelitis —**po-
lio** adj

po·lio·my·e·li·tis \\-,mīə'lītəs\\ n : acute
virus disease marked by fever, paralysis, and atrophy of skeletal muscles

pol·ish \\'pälish\\ vb **1** : make smooth
and glossy **2** : develop or refine ~ n
1 : shiny surface **2** : refinement

po·lite \\pə'līt\\ adj **-lit·er; -est** : marked
by correct social conduct —**po·lite·ly**
adv —**po·lite·ness** n

pol·i·tic \\'pälə,tik\\ adj : shrewdly tact-
ful

pol·i·tics \\'pälə,tiks\\ n sing or pl
: practice of government and managing of public affairs —**po·lit·i·cal**
\\pə'litikəl\\ adj —**pol·i·ti·cian**
\\,pälə'tishən\\ n

pol·ka \\'pōlkə\\ n : lively couple dance
—**polka** vb

poll \\'pōl\\ n **1** : head **2** : place where
votes are cast —usu. pl. **3** : a sam-
pling of opinion ~ vb **1** : cut off **2**
: receive or record votes **3** : question
in a poll —**poll·ster** \\-stər\\ n

pol·len \\'pälən\\ n : spores of a seed
plant

pol·li·na·tion \\,pälə'nāshən\\ n : the
carrying of pollen to fertilize the seed
—**pol·li·nate** \\'pälə,nāt\\ vb —**pol·li-
na·tor** \\-ər\\ n

pol·li·wog, pol·ly·wog \\'pälē,wäg\\ n
: tadpole

pol·lute \\pə'lüt\\ vb **-lut·ed; -lut·ing**
: make impure esp. by contaminating
with man-made waste —**pol·lut·ant**
\\-'lütᵊnt\\ n —**pol·lut·er** n —**pol·lu-
tion** \\-'lüshən\\ n

po·lo \\'pōlō\\ n : game played by 2
teams on horseback using long-handled mallets to drive a wooden ball

pol·troon \\päl'trün\\ n : coward

poly·es·ter \\'pälē,estər\\ n : synthetic
fiber

po·lyg·a·my \\pə'ligəmē\\ n : marriage
to several spouses at the same time
—**po·lyg·a·mist** \\-məst\\ n —**po·lyg-
a·mous** \\-məs\\ adj

poly·gon \\'päli,gän\\ n : closed plane
figure with straight sides —**po·lyg·o-
nal** \\pə'ligənᵊl\\ adj

poly·syl·la·ble \\'päli,siləbəl\\ n : a word
of more than 3 syllables —**poly·syl-
lab·ic** \\,pälisə'labik\\ adj

poly·tech·nic \\,päli'teknik\\ adj : relating to many arts or sciences

poly·the·ism \\'pälithē,izəm\\ n : worship of many gods —**poly·the·ist**
\\-,thēəst\\ adj or n

po·made \\pō'mäd, -'mād\\ n : perfumed hair ointment

pome·gran·ate \\'päm(ə),granət\\ n
: tropical reddish fruit with many
seeds

pom·mel \\'pəməl, 'päm-\\ n **1** : knob
on the hilt of a sword **2** : knob at the
front of a saddle ~ \\'pəməl\\ vb
-meled or **-melled; -mel·ing** or **-mel-
ling** : pummel

pomp \\'pämp\\ n **1** : brilliant display **2**
: ostentation

pomp·ous \\'pämpəs\\ adj : pretentiously dignified —**pom·pos·i·ty**
\\päm'päsətē\\ n —**pomp·ous·ly** adv

pon·cho \\'pänchō\\ n, pl **-chos** : blan-
ketlike cloak

pond \\'pänd\\ n : small body of water

pon·der \\'pändər\\ vb : weigh in the
mind

pon·der·ous \\'pänd(ə)rəs\\ adj **1** : very
heavy **2** : clumsy **3** : oppressively
dull

pon·tiff \\'päntəf\\ n : bishop **2** : pope
—**pon·tif·i·cal** \\pän'tifikəl\\ adj

pon·tif·i·cate \\pän'tifə,kät\\ vb **-cat·ed;
-cat·ing** : talk pompously

pon·toon \pän'tün\ n : flat-bottomed boat or float

po·ny \'pōnē\ n, pl **-nies** : small horse

poo·dle \'püdᵊl\ n : dog with a curly coat

¹pool \'pül\ n 1 : small body of water 2 : puddle

²pool n 1 : game of pocket billiards 2 : amount contributed by participants in a joint venture ~ vb : contribute to a common fund

poop \'püp\ n : enclosed super-structure at the stern of a ship

poor \'pur\ adj 1 : lacking material possessions 2 : less than adequate **—poor·ly** adv

pop \'päp\ vb **-pp-** 1 : move suddenly 2 : burst with or make a sharp sound 3 : protrude ~ n 1 : sharp explosive sound 2 : flavored soft drink

pop·corn \'päp,korn\ n : corn whose kernels burst open into a white mass when heated

pope \'pōp\ n, often cap : head of the Roman Catholic Church

pop·lar \'päplər\ n : slender quick-growing tree

pop·lin \'päplən\ n : strong plain-woven fabric with crosswise ribs

pop·over \'päp,ōvər\ n : egg-rich bis-cuit that expands into a hollow shell as it bakes

pop·py \'päpē\ n, pl **-pies** : herb with showy flowers

pop·u·lace \'päpyələs\ n 1 : common people 2 : population

pop·u·lar \'päpyələr\ adj 1 : relating to the general public 2 : widely accepted 3 : commonly liked **—pop·u·lar·i·ty** \,päpyə'larətē\ n **—pop·u·lar·ize** \'päpyələ,rīz\ vb **—pop·u·lar·ly** \-lərlē\ adv

pop·u·late \'päpyə,lāt\ vb **-lat·ed; -lat·ing** : inhabit or occupy

pop·u·la·tion \,päpyə'lāshən\ n : people or number of people in a country or area

pop·u·list \'päpyələst\ n : advocate of the rights of the common people **—pop·u·lism** \-,lizəm\ n

pop·u·lous \'päpyələs\ adj : densely populated **—pop·u·lous·ness** n

por·ce·lain \'pōrs(ə)lən\ n : fine-grained ceramic ware

porch \'porch\ n : covered entrance

por·cine \'por,sīn\ adj : relating to or suggesting swine

por·cu·pine \'porkyə,pīn\ n : mammal with sharp quills

¹pore \'pōr\ vb **pored; por·ing** : read attentively

²pore n : tiny hole **—pored** adj

pork \'pork\ n : pig meat

por·nog·ra·phy \por'nägrəfē\ n : depic-tion of erotic behavior meant chiefly to cause sexual excitement **—por·no·graph·ic** \,pornə'grafik\ adj

po·rous \'pōrəs\ adj : permeable to fluids **—po·ros·i·ty** \pə'räsətē\ n

por·poise \'porpəs\ n 1 : small whale with a blunt snout 2 : dolphin

por·ridge \'porij\ n : soft boiled cereal

por·rin·ger \'poranjər\ n : low one-handled metal bowl or cup for chil-dren

¹port \'port\ n 1 : harbor 2 : city with a harbor

²port n 1 : inlet or outlet (as in an engine) for a fluid 2 : porthole

³port n : left side of a ship or airplane looking forward **—port** adj

⁴port n : sweet wine

por·ta·ble \'portəbəl\ adj : capable of being carried **—portable** n

por·tage \'portij, por'täzh\ n : carrying of boats overland between navigable bodies of water or the route where this is done **—portage** vb

por·tal \'portᵊl\ n : entrance

por·tend \por'tend\ vb : give a warning of beforehand

por·tent \'por,tent\ n : something that foreshadows a coming event **—por·ten·tous** \por'tentəs\ adj

por·ter \'portər\ n : baggage carrier

por·ter·house \-,haus\ n : choice cut of steak

port·fo·lio \port'folē,ō\ n, pl **-lios** 1 : portable case for papers 2 : inves-tor's securities

port·hole \'port,hōl\ n : opening in the side of a ship or aircraft

por·ti·co \'porti,kō\ n, pl **-coes** or **-cos** : colonnade forming a porch

por·tion \'pōrshən\ n : part or share of a whole ~ vb : divide into or allot portions

port·ly \'portlē\ adj **-li·er; -est** : some-what stout

por·trait \'portrət, -,trāt\ n : picture of a person **—por·trait·ist** \-əst\ n **—por·trai·ture** \'portrə,chur\ n

por·tray \por'trā\ vb 1 : make a picture of 2 : describe in words 3 : play the role of **—por·tray·al** n

pose \'pōz\ vb **posed; pos·ing** 1 : as-sume a posture or attitude 2 : pro-pose 3 : pretend to be what one is not ~ n 1 : sustained posture 2 : pre-tense **—pos·er** n

posh \'päsh\ adj : elegant

po·si·tion \pə'zishən\ n 1 : stand taken on a question 2 : place or location 3 : status 4 : job **—position** vb

pos·i·tive \'päzətiv\ adj 1 : definite 2 : confident 3 : relating to or being an adjective or adverb form that denotes no increase 4 : greater than zero 5 : having a deficiency of electrons 6 : affirmative —**pos·i·tive·ly** adv —**pos·i·tive·ness** n

pos·se \'päse\ n : emergency assistants of a sheriff

pos·sess \pə'zes\ vb 1 : have as property or as a quality 2 : control —**pos·ses·sion** \-'zeshən\ n —**pos·ses·sor** \-'zesər\ n

pos·ses·sive \pə'zesiv\ adj 1 : relating to a grammatical case denoting ownership 2 : jealous —**possessive** n —**pos·ses·sive·ness** n

pos·si·ble \'päsəbəl\ adj 1 : that can be done 2 : potential —**pos·si·bil·i·ty** \,päsə'bilətē\ n —**pos·si·bly** adv

pos·sum \'päsəm\ n : opossum

¹post \'pōst\ n : upright stake serving to support or mark ~ vb : put up or announce by a notice

²post vb 1 : mail 2 : inform

³post n 1 : sentry's station 2 : assigned task 3 : army camp ~ vb : station

post- prefix : after or subsequent to

postadolescence	postinoculation
postadolescent	postmarital
postattack	postmenopausal
postbaccalaureate	postnatal
	postnuptial
postbiblical	postproduction
postcollege	postpubertal
postcolonial	postpuberty
postelection	postradiation
postexercise	postrecession
postfertilization	postretirement
postflight	postrevolutionary
postgame	postseason
postgraduate	postsecondary
postgraduation	postsurgical
postharvest	posttreatment
posthospital	posttrial
postimperial	postvaccination
postinaugural	postwar
postindustrial	

post·age \'pōstij\ n : fee for mail

post·al \'pōst²l\ adj : relating to the mail

post·card n : card for mailing a message

post·er \'pōstər\ n : large usu. printed notice

pos·te·ri·or \pō'stirēər, pä-\ adj 1 : later 2 : situated behind ~ n : buttocks

pos·ter·i·ty \pä'sterətē\ n : succeeding generations

post·haste \'pōst'hāst\ adv : speedily

post·hu·mous \'päschəməs\ adj : occurring after one's death

post·man \'pōs(t)mən, -,man\ n : mailman

post·mark n : official mark on mail —**postmark** vb

post·mas·ter n : chief of a post office

post me·ri·di·em \'pōs(t)mə'ridēəm, -ē,em\ adj : being after noon

post·mor·tem \(')pōs(t)'mortəm\ adj : occurring or done after death ~ n : medical examination of a corpse

post office n : agency or building for mail service

post·op·er·a·tive \(')pōst'äp(ə)rətiv, -'äpə,rāt-\ adj : following surgery

post·paid adv : with postage paid by the sender

post·par·tum \(')pōst'pärtəm\ adj : following childbirth —**postpartum** adv

post·pone \-'pōn\ vb -poned; -pon·ing : hold back to a later time —**postpone·ment** n

post·script \'pō(s),skript\ n : added note

pos·tu·lant \'päschələnt\ n : candidate for a religious order

pos·tu·late \'päschə,lāt\ vb -lat·ed; -lat·ing : assume as true ~ n : assumption

pos·ture \'päschər\ n : bearing of the body ~ vb -tured; -tur·ing : strike a pose

po·sy \'pōzē\ n, pl -sies : flower or bunch of flowers

pot \'pät\ n 1 : rounded container 2 : marijuana ~ vb -tt- : place in a pot —**pot·ful** n

po·ta·ble \'pōtəbəl\ adj : drinkable

pot·ash \'pät,ash\ n : white chemical salt

po·tas·si·um \pə'tasēəm\ n : silvery white metallic chemical element

po·ta·to \pə'tātō\ n, pl -toes : edible plant tuber

pot·bel·ly n : paunch —**pot·bel·lied** adj

po·tent \'pōt²nt\ adj : powerful or effective —**po·ten·cy** \-²nsē\ n

po·ten·tate \'pōt²n,tāt\ n : powerful ruler

po·ten·tial \pə'tenchəl\ adj : capable of becoming actual ~ n 1 : something that can become actual 2 : degree of electrification with reference to a standard —**po·ten·ti·al·i·ty** \pə,tenchē'alətē\ n —**po·ten·tial·ly** adv

poth·er \'päthər\ n : fuss

po·tion \'pōshən\ n : liquid medicine or poison

pot·luck n : whatever food is available

pot·pour·ri \ˌpōpu̇ˈrē\ *n* : miscellaneous collection

pot-shot *n* **1** : casual or easy shot **2** : random critical remark

pot·ter \ˈpätər\ *n* : pottery maker

pot·tery \ˈpätərē\ *n, pl* **-ter·ies** : objects (as dishes) made from clay

pouch \ˈpau̇ch\ *n* **1** : small bag **2** : bodily sac

poul·tice \ˈpōltəs\ *n* : warm medicated dressing —**poultice** *vb*

poul·try \ˈpōltrē\ *n* : domesticated fowl

pounce \ˈpau̇ns\ *vb* **pounced; pounc·ing** : spring or swoop upon and seize

¹pound \ˈpau̇nd\ *n* **1** : unit of weight equal to 16 ounces **2** : monetary unit (as of the United Kingdom) —**pound·age** \-ij\ *n*

²pound *vb* **1** : crush by beating **2** : strike heavily **3** : throb

³pound *n* : shelter for stray animals

pour \ˈpōr\ *vb* **1** : flow or supply copiously **2** : rain hard

pout \ˈpau̇t\ *vb* : look sullen —**pout** *n*

pov·er·ty \ˈpävərtē\ *n* **1** : lack of money or possessions **2** : poor quality

pow·der \ˈpau̇dər\ *n* : dry material of fine particles ~ *vb* **1** : sprinkle or cover with powder **2** : reduce to powder —**pow·dery** *adj*

pow·er \ˈpau̇(ə)r\ *n* **1** : position of authority **2** : ability to act **3** : one that has power **4** : physical might **5** : force or energy used to do work ~ *vb* : supply with power —**pow·er·ful** \-fəl\ *adj* —**pow·er·ful·ly** *adv* —**pow·er·less** *adj*

pow-wow \ˈpau̇ˌwau̇\ *n* : conference

pox \ˈpäks\ *n, pl* **pox** *or* **pox·es** : disease marked by skin rash

prac·ti·ca·ble \ˈpraktikəbəl\ *adj* : feasible —**prac·ti·ca·bil·i·ty** \ˌpraktikəˈbilətē\ *n*

prac·ti·cal \ˈpraktikəl\ *adj* **1** : relating to practice **2** : virtual **3** : capable of being put to use **4** : inclined to action as opposed to speculation —**prac·ti·cal·i·ty** \ˌpraktiˈkalətē\ *n* —**prac·ti·cal·ly** \ˈpraktik(ə)lē\ *adv*

prac·tice, prac·tise \ˈpraktəs\ *vb* **-ticed** *or* **-tised; -tic·ing** *or* **-tis·ing** **1** : perform repeatedly to become proficient **2** : do or perform customarily **3** : be professionally engaged in ~ *n* **1** : actual performance **2** : habit **3** : exercise for proficiency **4** : exercise of a profession

prac·ti·tio·ner \prakˈtish(ə)nər\ *n* : one who practices a profession

prag·ma·tism \ˈpragməˌtizəm\ *n*

: practical approach to problems —**prag·mat·ic** \pragˈmatik\ *adj*

prai·rie \ˈpre(ə)rē\ *n* : broad grassy rolling tract of land

praise \ˈprāz\ *vb* **praised; prais·ing** **1** : express approval of **2** : glorify —**praise** *n* —**praise·wor·thy** *adj*

prance \ˈprans\ *vb* **pranced; pranc·ing** **1** : spring from the hind legs **2** : swagger —**prance** *n* —**pranc·er** *n*

prank \ˈprank\ *n* : playful or mischievous act —**prank·ster** \-stər\ *n*

prate \ˈprāt\ *vb* **prat·ed; prat·ing** : talk long and foolishly

prat·fall \ˈprat,-\ *n* : fall on the buttocks

prat·tle \ˈprat³l\ *vb* **-tled; -tling** : babble —**prattle** *n*

prawn \ˈprȯn\ *n* : shrimplike crustacean

pray \ˈprā\ *vb* **1** : entreat **2** : ask earnestly for something **3** : address a divinity

prayer \ˈpraər\ *n* **1** : earnest request **2** : an addressing of a divinity **3** : words used in praying

praying mantis *n* : mantis

pre- *prefix* : before, prior to, or in advance

preadapt	precolonial
preaddress	precombustion
preadmission	precompute
preadolescence	preconceive
preadolescent	preconception
preadult	preconcerted
prealert	precondition
prealign	preconference
preallocate	preconstruct
preanesthetic	preconvention
prearraignment	precook
prearrange	precool
prearrangement	precut
preassemble	predawn
preassign	predefine
preaudit	predelinquent
preauthorize	predeparture*
prebattle	predesignate
prebiblical	predesignation
prebirth	predetermine
prebreakfast	predischarge
prebuilt	predrill
precalculate	predug
precalculus	preedit
precampaign	preelection
precancel	preelectric
precancellation	preelectronic
precivilization	preemployment
preclean	preestablish
preclear	preexist
preclearance	preexistence
precollege	preexistent

prefight
prefilter
preform
pregame
preheat
preimmunization
preimmunize
preinaugural
preindustrial
preinoculate
preinoculation
preinterview
prejudge
prekindergarten
prelaunch
preload
premarital
premenopausal
premenstrual
premix
premodern
premodify
premoisten
premold
prenatal
prenotification
prenotify
prenuptial
preopening
preoperational
preordain
prepack
prepackage
prepay
preplan
preprocess
preproduction

preprofessional
preprogram
prepubertal
prepublication
prepunch
prepurchase
prerecord
preregister
preregistration
prerehearsal
prerelease
pre-Renaissance
preretirement
prerevolutionary
prerinse
preseason
preselect
preset
preshrink
presoak
presort
prestamp
presterilize
prestrike
presurgical
presweeten
pretape
preteen
pretelevision
pretournament
pretreat
pretreatment
pretrial
pretrip
prewar
prewash
prewrap

preach \'prēch\ *vb* 1 : deliver a sermon 2 : advocate earnestly —**preach·er** *n* —**preach·ment** *n*

pre·am·ble \'prē,ambəl\ *n* : introduction

pre·car·i·ous \pri'karēəs\ *adj* : dangerously insecure —**pre·car·i·ous·ly** *adv* —**pre·car·i·ous·ness** *n*

pre·cau·tion \pri'kȯshən\ *n* : care taken beforehand —**pre·cau·tion·ary** \-shə,nerē\ *adj*

pre·cede \pri'sēd\ *vb* -ced·ed; -ced·ing : be, go, or come ahead of —**prec·e·dence** \'presədəns, pri'sēd°ns\ *n*

prec·e·dent \'presədənt\ *n* : something said or done earlier that serves as an example

pre·ced·ing \pri'sēdiŋ\ *adj* : that precedes

pre·cept \'prē,sept\ *n* : rule of action or conduct

pre·cep·tor \pri'septər, 'prē,sep-\ *n* : tutor

pre·cinct \'prē,siŋkt\ *n* 1 : district of a city 2 *pl* : vicinity

pre·cious \'preshəs\ *adj* 1 : of great value 2 : greatly cherished 3 : affected

prec·i·pice \'presəpəs\ *n* : steep cliff

pre·cip·i·tate \pri'sipə,tāt\ *vb* -tat·ed; -tat·ing 1 : cause to happen quickly or abruptly 2 : cause to separate out of a liquid ~ *n* : solid matter precipitated from a liquid ~ \-'sipətət, -ə,tāt\ *adj* : unduly hasty —**pre·cip·i·tate·ly** *adv* —**pre·cip·i·tate·ness** *n* —**pre·cip·i·tous** \pri'sipətəs\ *adj* —**pre·cip·i·tous·ly** *adv*

pre·cip·i·ta·tion \pri,sipə'tāshən\ *n* 1 : rash haste 2 : rain, snow, or hail

pré·cis \prā'sē\ *n, pl* **pré·cis** \-'sēz\ : concise summary of essential points

pre·cise \pri'sīs\ *adj* 1 : definite 2 : highly accurate —**pre·cise·ly** *adv* —**pre·cise·ness** *n*

pre·ci·sion \pri'sizhən\ *n* : quality or state of being precise

pre·clude \pri'klüd\ *vb* -clud·ed; -clud·ing : make impossible

pre·co·cious \pri'kōshəs\ *adj* : exceptionally advanced —**pre·co·cious·ly** *adv* —**pre·coc·i·ty** \pri'käsətē\ *n*

pre·cur·sor \pri'kərsər\ *n* : harbinger

pred·a·to·ry \'predə,tōrē\ *adj* : preying upon others —**pred·a·tor** \'predətər\ *n*

pre·de·ces·sor \'predə,sesər, 'prēd-\ *n* : one who has previously held a position

pre·des·tine \prē'destən\ *vb* : settle beforehand

pre·dic·a·ment \pri'dikəmənt\ *n* : difficult situation

pred·i·cate \'predikət\ *n* : part of a sentence that states something about the subject ~ \'predə,kāt\ *vb* -cat·ed; -cat·ing 1 : affirm 2 : establish —**pred·i·ca·tion** \,predə'kāshən\ *n*

pre·dict \pri'dikt\ *vb* : declare in advance —**pre·dict·able** \-'diktəbəl\ *adj* —**pre·dict·ably** \-blē\ *adv* —**pre·dic·tion** \-'dikshən\ *n*

pre·di·lec·tion \,predəl'ekshən, ,prēd-\ *n* : favorable inclination

pre·dis·pose \,prēdis'pōz\ *vb* : cause to be favorable to something beforehand —**pre·dis·po·si·tion** \,prē,dispə'zishən\ *n*

pre·dom·i·nate \pri'dämə,nāt\ *vb* : be superior —**pre·dom·i·nance** \-nəns\ *n* —**pre·dom·i·nant** \-nənt\ *adj* —**pre·dom·i·nant·ly** *adv*

pre·em·i·nent \prē'emənənt\ *adj* : having highest rank —**pre·em·i·nence** \-nəns\ *n* —**pre·em·i·nent·ly** *adv*

pre·empt \prē'empt\ vb 1 : seize for oneself 2 : take the place of —**pre·emp·tion** \-'empshən\ n

preen \'prēn\ vb : dress or smooth up (as feathers)

pre·fab·ri·cat·ed \'prē'fabrə,kātəd\ adj : manufactured for rapid assembly elsewhere —**pre·fab·ri·ca·tion** \,prē,fabri'kāshən\ n

pref·ace \'prefəs\ n : introductory comments ~ vb -aced; -ac·ing : introduce with a preface —**pref·a·to·ry** \'prefə,tōrē\ adj

pre·fect \'prē,fekt\ n : chief officer or judge —**pre·fec·ture** \-,fekchər\ n

pre·fer \pri'fər\ vb -rr- 1 : like better 2 : bring (as a charge) against a person —**pref·er·a·ble** \'pref(ə)rəbəl\ adj —**pref·er·a·bly** adv —**pref·er·ence** \-(ə)rəns\ n —**pref·er·en·tial** \,prefə'renchəl\ adj

pre·fer·ment \pri'fərmənt\ n : promotion

pre·fig·ure \prē'figyər\ vb : foreshadow

¹pre·fix \'prē,fiks, prē'fiks\ vb : place before

²pre·fix \'prē,fiks\ n : affix at the beginning of a word

preg·nant \'pregnənt\ adj 1 : containing unborn young 2 : meaningful —**preg·nan·cy** \-nənsē\ n

pre·hen·sile \prē'hensəl, -,sīl\ adj : adapted for grasping

pre·his·tor·ic \prē(h)is'tôrik\, **pre·his·tor·i·cal** \-ikəl\ adj : relating to the period before written history

prej·u·dice \'prejədəs\ n 1 : damage esp. to one's rights 2 : unreasonable attitude for or against something ~ vb -diced; -dic·ing 1 : damage 2 : cause to have prejudice —**prej·u·di·cial** \,prejə'dishəl\ adj

prel·ate \'prelət\ n : clergyman of high rank —**prel·a·cy** \-əsē\ n

pre·lim·i·nary \pri'limə,nerē\ n, adj : something that precedes or introduces —**preliminary** adj

pre·lude \'prel,(y)üd, 'prā,lüd\ n : introductory performance, event, or musical piece

pre·ma·ture \,prēmə't(y)u̇ər, -'chu̇(ə)r\ adj : coming before the usual or proper time —**pre·ma·ture·ly** adv

pre·med·i·tate \pri'medə,tāt\ vb : plan beforehand —**pre·med·i·ta·tion** \-,medə'tāshən\ n

pre·mier \pri'm(y)i̇ər, 'prēmēər\ adj : first in rank or importance ~ n : prime minister —**pre·mier·ship** n

pre·miere \pri'myeər, -'miər\ n : 1st performance ~ vb -miered; -mier·ing : give a 1st performance of

prem·ise \'preməs\ n 1 : statement made or implied as a basis of argument 2 pl : piece of land with the structures on it

pre·mi·um \'prēmēəm\ n 1 : bonus 2 : sum over the stated value 3 : sum paid for insurance 4 : high value

pre·mo·ni·tion \,prēmə'nishən, ,premə-\ n : feeling that something is about to happen —**pre·mon·i·to·ry** \pri'mänə,tōrē\ adj

pre·oc·cu·pied \prē'äkyə,pīd\ adj : lost in thought

pre·oc·cu·py \-,pī\ vb : occupy the attention of —**pre·oc·cu·pa·tion** \prē,äkyə'pāshən\ n

pre·pare \pri'paər\ vb -pared; -par·ing 1 : make or get ready 2 : put together or compound —**prep·a·ra·tion** \,prepə'rāshən\ n —**pre·par·a·to·ry** \pri'parə,tōrē\ adj —**pre·pared·ness** \-'paərədnəs\ n

pre·pon·der·ate \pri'pändə,rāt\ vb -at·ed; -at·ing : exceed in weight, power, importance, or numbers —**pre·pon·der·ance** \-(ə)rəns\ n —**pre·pon·der·ant** \-(ə)rənt\ adj —**pre·pon·der·ant·ly** adv

prep·o·si·tion \,prepə'zishən\ n : word that combines with a noun or pronoun to form a phrase —**prep·o·si·tion·al** \-'zish(ə)nəl\ adj

pre·pos·sess·ing \,prēpə'zesiŋ\ adj : tending to create a favorable impression

pre·pos·ter·ous \pri'päst(ə)rəs\ adj : absurd

pre·req·ui·site \prē'rekwəzət\ n : something required beforehand —**prerequisite** adj

pre·rog·a·tive \pri'rägətiv\ n : special right or power

pre·sage \'presij, pri'sāj\ vb -saged; -sag·ing 1 : give a warning of 2 : predict —**presage** \'presij\ n

pres·by·ter \'prezbətər\ n : priest or minister

pre·science \'prēsh(ē)əns, 'presh-\ n : foreknowledge of events —**pre·scient** \-(ē)ənt\ adj

pre·scribe \pri'skrīb\ vb -scribed; -scrib·ing 1 : lay down as a guide 2 : direct the use of as a remedy

pre·scrip·tion \pri'skripshən\ n : written direction for the preparation and use of a medicine or the medicine prescribed

pres·ence \'prez²ns\ n 1 : fact or condition of being present 2 : appearance or bearing

¹pres·ent \'prez²nt\ n : something

given or received without compensation

²pre·sent \pri'zent\ vb 1 : introduce 2 : bring before the public 3 : make a gift to or of 4 : bring before a court for inquiry —pre·sent·able adj —pre·sen·ta·tion \,prē,zen'tāshən, ,prez°n-\ n —pre·sent·ment \pri'zentmənt\ n

³pres·ent \'prez°nt\ adj : now existing, in progress, or attending ~ n : present time

pre·sen·ti·ment \pri'zentəmənt\ n : premonition

pres·ent·ly \'prez°ntlē\ adv 1 : soon 2 : now

present participle n : participle that typically expresses present action

pre·serve \pri'zərv\ vb -served; -serv·ing 1 : keep safe from danger or spoilage 2 : maintain ~ n 1 : preserved fruit —often in pl. 2 : area for protection of natural resources —pres·er·va·tion \,prezər'vāshən\ n —pre·ser·va·tive \pri'zərvətiv\ adj or n —pre·server·er \-'zərvər\ n

pre·side \pri'zīd\ vb -sid·ed; -sid·ing 1 : act as chairman 2 : exercise control

pres·i·dent \'prezədənt\ n : one chosen to preside 2 : chief official (as of a company or nation) —pres·i·den·cy \-ənsē\ n —pres·i·den·tial \,prezə'denchəl\ adj

press \'pres\ n 1 : crowded condition 2 : machine or device for exerting pressure and esp. for printing 3 : pressure 4 : printing or publishing establishment 5 : news media and esp. newspapers ~ vb 1 : lie against and exert pressure on 2 : smooth with an iron or squeeze with something heavy 3 : urge 4 : crowd 5 : force one's way —press·er n

press·ing adj : urgent

pres·sure \'preshər\ n 1 : burden of distress or urgent business 2 : direct application of force —pressure vb —pres·sur·iza·tion \,presh(ə)rə'zāshən\ n —pres·sur·ize \-īz\ vb

pres·ti·dig·i·ta·tion \,prestə,dijə'tāshən\ n : sleight of hand

pres·tige \pres'tēzh, -'tēj\ n : estimation in the eyes of people —pres·ti·gious \-'tijəs\ adj

pres·to \'prestō\ adv or adj : quickly

pre·sume \pri'züm\ vb -sumed; -sum·ing 1 : assume authority without right to do so 2 : take for granted —pre·sum·able \-'züməbəl\ adj —pre·sum·ably \-blē\ adv

pre·sump·tion \pri'zəmpshən\ n 1 : presumptuous attitude or conduct 2 : belief supported by probability —pre·sump·tive \-'tiv\ adj

pre·sump·tu·ous \pri'zəmpchə(wə)s\ adj : too bold or forward

pre·sup·pose \,prēsə'pōz\ vb : take for granted —pre·sup·po·si·tion \(,)prē,səpə'zishən\ n

pre·tend \pri'tend\ vb 1 : act as if something is real or true when it is not 2 : act in a way that is false 3 : lay claim —pre·tend·er n

pre·tense, pre·tence \'prē,tens, pri'tens\ n 1 : insincere effort 2 : deception —pre·ten·sion \pri'tenchən\ n

pre·ten·tious \pri'tenchəs\ adj : overly showy or self-important —pre·ten·tious·ly adv —pre·ten·tious·ness n

pre·ter·nat·u·ral \,prētər'nach(ə)rəl\ adj 1 : exceeding what is natural 2 : inexplicable by ordinary means —pre·ter·nat·u·ral·ly adv

pre·text \'prē,tekst\ n : falsely stated purpose

pret·ty \'pritē, 'pùrt-\ adj -ti·er; -est : pleasing by delicacy or attractiveness ~ \'pùrtē, part-, prit-\ adv : in some degree ~ \'pritē, 'pùrtē\ vb -tied; -ty·ing : make pretty —pret·ti·ly \'prit?lē\ adv —pret·ti·ness n

pret·zel \'pretsəl\ n : twisted cracker that is glazed and salted

pre·vail \pri'vāl\ vb 1 : triumph 2 : urge successfully 3 : be frequent —pre·vail·ing·ly \-inlē\ adv

prev·a·lent \'prevələnt\ adj : widespread —prev·a·lence \-ləns\ n

pre·var·i·cate \pri'varə,kāt\ vb -cat·ed; -cat·ing : deviate from the truth —pre·var·i·ca·tion \-,varə'kāshən\ n —pre·var·i·ca·tor \-'varə,kātər\ n

pre·vent \pri'vent\ vb : keep from happening or acting —pre·vent·able adj —pre·ven·tion \-'venchən\ n —pre·ven·tive \-'ventiv\, pre·ven·ta·tive \-'ventətiv\ adj or n

pre·view \'prē,vyü\ vb : view or show beforehand —preview n

pre·vi·ous \'prēvēəs\ adj : having gone, happened, or existed before —pre·vi·ous·ly adv

prey \'prā\ n, pl preys 1 : animal taken for food by another 2 : victim ~ vb 1 : seize and devour animals as prey 2 : have a harmful effect on

price \'prīs\ n : cost ~ vb priced; pric·ing : set a price on

price·less \-ləs\ adj : too precious to have a price

prick \'prik\ n 1 : tear or small wound

made by a point **2** : something sharp or pointed ~ *vb* : pierce slightly with a sharp point —**prick·er** *n*

prick·le \'prikəl\ *n* **1** : small sharp spine or thorn **2** : slight stinging pain ~ *vb* **-led; -ling** : tingle —**prick·ly** \'priklē\ *adj*

pride \'prīd\ *n* : quality or state of being proud ~ *vb* **prid·ed; prid·ing** : indulge in pride —**pride·ful** *adj*

priest \'prēst\ *n* : person having authority to perform the sacred rites of a religion —**priest·ess** \-əs\ *n* —**priest·hood** *n* —**priest·li·ness** \-lēnəs\ *n* —**priest·ly** *adj*

prig \'prig\ *n* : one who irritates by rigid or pointed observance of proprieties —**prig·gish** \-ish\ *adj* —**prig·gish·ly** *adv*

prim \'prim\ *adj* **-mm-** : stiffly formal and proper —**prim·ly** *adv* —**prim·ness** *n*

pri·mal \'prīməl\ *adj* : original or primitive

pri·ma·ry \'prī,merē, 'prīm(ə)rē\ *adj* : first in order of time, rank, or importance ~ *n, pl* **-ries** : preliminary election —**pri·mar·i·ly** \prī'merəlē\ *adv*

primary school *n* : elementary school

pri·mate *n* **1** \'prī,māt, -mət\ : highest-ranking bishop **2** \-,māt\ : mammal of the group that includes man and monkeys

prime \'prīm\ *n* : earliest or best part or period ~ *adj* : standing first (as in significance or quality) ~ *vb* **primed; prim·ing 1** : fill or load **2** : lay a preparatory coating on

prime minister *n* : chief executive of a parliamentary government

¹**prim·er** \'primər\ *n* : small introductory book

²**prim·er** \'prīmər\ *n* **1** : device for igniting an explosive **2** : material for priming a surface

pri·me·val \prī'mēvəl\ *adj* : relating to the earliest ages

prim·i·tive \'primətiv\ *adj* : relating to or characteristic of an early stage of development ~ *n* : one that is primitive —**prim·i·tive·ly** *adv* —**prim·i·tive·ness** *n* —**prim·i·tiv·i·ty** \,primə'tivətē\ *n*

pri·mor·di·al \prī'mòrdēəl\ *adj* : primeval

primp \'primp\ *vb* : dress or groom in a finicky manner

prim·rose \'prim,rōz\ *n* : low herb with clusters of showy flowers

prince \'prins\ *n* **1** : ruler **2** : son of a king or queen —**prince·ly** *adj*

prin·cess \'prinsəs, -,ses\ *n* **1** : daughter of a king or queen **2** : wife of a prince

prin·ci·pal \'prinsəpəl\ *adj* : most important ~ *n* **1** : leading person **2** : head of a school **3** : sum lent at interest —**prin·ci·pal·ly** *adv*

prin·ci·pal·i·ty \,prinsə'palətē\ *n, pl* **-ties** : territory of a prince

prin·ci·ple \'prinsəpəl\ *n* **1** : general or fundamental law **2** : rule or code of conduct or devotion to such a code

print \'print\ *n* **1** : mark made by pressure **2** : printed state or form **3** : printed matter **4** : copy made by printing **5** : cloth with a figure stamped on it ~ *vb* **1** : produce impressions of (as from type) **2** : write in letters like those of printer's type —**print·able** *adj* —**print·er** *n*

print·ing \'printiŋ\ *n* : art or business of printing

print·out \'print,aut\ *n* : printed record produced by a computer —**print out** \(')print'aut\ *vb*

¹**pri·or** \'prī(ə)r\ *n* : head of a religious house —**pri·or·ess** \'prīərəs\ *n* —**pri·o·ry** \'prī(ə)rē\ *n*

²**pri·or** *adj* : coming before in time, order, or importance —**pri·or·i·ty** \prī'òrətē\ *n*

prism \'prizəm\ *n* : transparent 3-sided object that separates light into colors —**pris·mat·ic** \priz'matik\ *adj*

pris·on \'prizʰn\ *n* : place where criminals are confined

pris·on·er \'priznər, -ʰnər\ *n* : person on trial or in prison

pris·sy \'prisē\ *adj* **-si·er; -est** : prim —**pris·si·ness** *n*

pris·tine \'pris,tēn\ *adj* : pure

pri·va·cy \'prīvəsē\ *n, pl* **-cies** : quality or state of being apart from others

pri·vate \'prīvət\ *adj* **1** : belonging to a particular individual or group **2** : carried on independently **3** : withdrawn from company or observation ~ *n* : enlisted man of the lowest rank in the marine corps or one of the two lowest ranks in the army —**pri·vate·ly** *adv*

pri·va·teer \,prīvə'tiər\ *n* : private ship armed to attack enemy ships and commerce

private first class *n* : enlisted man ranking next below a corporal in the army and next below a lance corporal in the marine corps

pri·va·tion \prī'vāshən\ *n* : lack of what is needed for existence

priv·i·lege \'priv(ə)lij\ *n* : right granted

as an advantage or favor —**priv·i·leged** adj

privy \'privē\ adj : private or secret — n : outdoor toilet —**priv·i·ly** \'privəlē\ adv

¹prize \'prīz\ n 1 : something offered or striven for in competition or in contests of chance 2 : something very desirable —**prize** adj —**prize·win·ner** n

²prize vb **prized; priz·ing** : value highly

³prize \'prīz\ vb **prized; priz·ing** : pry

prize·fight n : professional boxing match —**prize·fight·er** n —**prize·fight·ing** n

¹pro \'prō\ n : favorable argument or person — adv : in favor

²pro n or adj : professional

prob·a·ble \'präbəbəl\ adj : seeming true or real or to have a good chance of happening —**prob·a·bil·i·ty** \,präbə'bilətē\ n —**prob·a·bly** \'präbəblē, 'präblē\ adv

pro·bate \'prō,bāt\ n : judicial determination of the validity of a will — vb **-bat·ed; -bat·ing** : establish by probate

pro·ba·tion \prō'bāshən\ n 1 : period of testing and trial 2 : freedom of a convict during good behavior under supervision —**pro·ba·tion·ary** \-shə,nerē\ adj —**pro·ba·tion·er** n

probe \'prōb\ n 1 : slender instrument for examining a cavity 2 : investigation ~ vb **probed; prob·ing** 1 : examine with a probe 2 : investigate

pro·bi·ty \'prōbətē\ n : honest behavior

prob·lem \'präbləm\ n 1 : question to be solved 2 : source of perplexity or vexation —**problem** adj —**prob·lem·at·ic** \,präblə'matik\ adj —**prob·lem·at·i·cal** \-ikəl\ adj

pro·bos·cis \prə'bäsəs\ n, pl **-cis·es** also **-ci·des** \-ə,dēz\ : long flexible snout

pro·ce·dure \prə'sējər\ n 1 : way of doing something 2 : series of steps in regular order —**pro·ce·dur·al** \-'sēj(ə)rəl\ adj

pro·ceed \prō'sēd\ vb 1 : come forth 2 : go on in an orderly way 3 : begin and carry on an action 4 : advance

pro·ceed·ing n 1 : procedure 2 pl : something said or done or its official record

pro·ceeds \'prō,sēdz\ n pl : total money taken in

pro·cess \'präs,es, 'prōs-\ n, pl **-cess·es** \-,esəz, -əsəz, -ə,sēz\ 1 : natural phenomenon marked by gradual changes 2 : series of actions or operations directed toward a result 3 : summons 4 : projecting part ~ vb : subject to a process —**pro·ces·sor** \-ər\ n

pro·ces·sion \prə'seshən\ n : group moving along in an orderly way

pro·ces·sion·al \-'sesh(ə)nəl\ n : music for a procession

pro·claim \prō'klām\ vb : announce publicly or with conviction —**proc·la·ma·tion** \,präklə'māshən\ n

pro·cliv·i·ty \prō'klivətē\ n, pl **-ties** : inclination

pro·cras·ti·nate \prə'krastə,nāt\ vb **-nat·ed; -nat·ing** : put something off until later —**pro·cras·ti·na·tion** \-,krastə'nāshən\ n —**pro·cras·ti·na·tor** \-'krastə,nātər\ n

pro·cre·ate \'prōkrē,āt\ vb **-at·ed; -at·ing** : produce offspring —**pro·cre·ation** \,prōkrē'āshən\ n —**pro·cre·ative** \'prōkrē,ātiv\ adj —**pro·cre·ator** \-,ātər\ n

proc·tor \'präktər\ n : supervisor of students (as at an examination) —**proctor** vb —**proc·to·ri·al** \präk'tōrēəl\ adj

pro·cure \prə'kyūr\ vb **-cured; -cur·ing** : get possession of —**pro·cur·able** \-'kyūrəbəl\ adj —**pro·cure·ment** n —**pro·cur·er** n

prod \'präd\ vb **-dd-** : push with or as if with a pointed instrument —**prod** n

prod·i·gal \'prädigəl\ adj : recklessly extravagant or wasteful —**prodigal** n —**prod·i·gal·i·ty** \,prädə'galətē\ n

pro·di·gious \prə'dijəs\ adj : extraordinary in size or degree —**pro·di·gious·ly** adv

prod·i·gy \'prädəjē\ n, pl **-gies** : extraordinary person or thing

pro·duce \prə'd(y)üs\ vb **-duced; -duc·ing** 1 : present to view 2 : give birth to 3 : bring into existence ~ \'präd,(y)üs, 'prōd- also -(y)üs\ n 1 : product 2 : agricultural products for sale —**pro·duc·er** \prə'd(y)üsər\ n

prod·uct \'präd,(,)əkt\ n 1 : number resulting from multiplication 2 : something produced

pro·duc·tion \prə'dəkshən\ n : act, process, or result of producing —**pro·duc·tive** \-'dəktiv\ adj —**pro·duc·tive·ness** n —**pro·duc·tiv·i·ty** \(,)prō,dək'tivətē, ,präd,(,)ək-\ n

pro·fane \prō'fān\ vb **-faned; -fan·ing** : treat with irreverence ~ adj 1 : not concerned with religion 2 : serving to debase what is holy —**pro·fane·ly** adv —**pro·fane·ness** \-'fānnəs\ n —**pro·fan·i·ty** \prō'fanətē\ n pro·fess \prə'fes\ vb 1 : declare openly 2 : confess one's faith in —pro·fessed·ly \-'adlē\ adv

pro·fes·sion \prə'feshən\ n 1 : open declaration of belief 2 : occupation requiring specialized knowledge and academic training

pro·fes·sion·al \prə'fesh(ə)nəl\ adj 1 : of, relating to, or engaged in a profession 2 : playing sport for pay —professional n —pro·fes·so·ri·al·ism n —pro·fes·sion·al·ize vb —pro·fes·sion·al·ly adv

pro·fes·sor \prə'fesər\ n : university or college teacher —pro·fes·so·ri·al \,prōfə'sōrēəl, ,prăfə-\ adj —pro·fes·sor·ship n

prof·fer \'präfər\ vb -fered; -fer·ing : offer —proffer n

pro·fi·cient \prə'fishənt\ adj : very good at something —pro·fi·cien·cy \-ənsē\ n —proficient n —pro·fi·cient·ly adv

pro·file \'prō,fīl\ n : picture in outline —profile vb

prof·it \'präfət\ n 1 : valuable return 2 : excess of the selling price of goods over cost ~ vb : gain a profit —prof·it·able \'präfətəbəl, 'präftəbəl\ adj —prof·it·ably adv —prof·it·less adj

prof·i·teer \,präfə'tiər\ n : one who makes an unreasonable profit —profiteer vb

prof·li·gate \'präfligət, -lə,gāt\ adj 1 : shamelessly immoral 2 : wildly extravagant —prof·li·ga·cy \-gəsē\ n —profligate n —prof·li·gate·ly adv

pro·found \prə'faůnd\ adj 1 : marked by intellectual depth or insight 2 : deeply felt —pro·found·ly adv —pro·fun·di·ty \-'fəndətē\ n

pro·fuse \prə'fyůs\ adj : pouring forth liberally —pro·fuse·ly adv —pro·fu·sion \-'fyůzhən\ n

pro·gen·i·tor \prō'jenətər\ n : direct ancestor

prog·e·ny \'präjənē\ n, pl -nies : offspring

prog·no·sis \präg'nōsəs\ n, pl -no·ses \-,sēz\ : forecast esp. of the course of a disease

prog·nos·ti·cate \präg'nästə,kāt\ vb -cat·ed; -cat·ing : predict from signs or symptoms —prog·nos·ti·ca·tion \-,nästə'kāshən\ n —prog·nos·ti·ca·tor \-'nästə,kātər\ n

pro·gram, pro·gramme \'prō,gram, -grəm\ n 1 : outline of the order to be pursued or the subjects included (as in a performance) 2 : plan of procedure 3 : coded instructions for a computer ~ vb -grammed or

-gramed; -gram·ming or -gram·ing 1 : enter in a program 2 : provide a computer with a program —pro·gram·ma·bil·i·ty \(,)prō,gramə'bilətē\ n —pro·gram·ma·ble \'prō,graməbəl\ adj —pro·gram·mer \'prō,gramər, -grəmər\ n

prog·ress \'prägrəs, -,res\ n : movement forward or to a better condition ~ \prə'gres\ vb 1 : move forward 2 : improve —pro·gres·sive \-'gresiv\ adj —pro·gres·sive·ly adv

pro·gres·sion \prə'greshən\ n 1 : act of progressing 2 : continuous connected series

pro·hib·it \prō'hibət\ vb : prevent by authority

pro·hi·bi·tion \,prōə'bishən\ n 1 : act of prohibiting 2 : legal restriction on sale or manufacture of alcoholic beverages —pro·hi·bi·tion·ist \-'bish(ə)nəst\ n —pro·hib·i·tive \prō'hibətiv\ adj —pro·hib·i·tive·ly adv —pro·hib·i·to·ry \-'hibə,tōrē\ adj

proj·ect \'präj,ekt, -ikt\ n : planned undertaking ~ \prə'jekt\ vb 1 : design or plan 2 : protrude 3 : throw forward —pro·jec·tion \-'jekshən\ n

pro·jec·tile \prə'jekt³l\ n : missile hurled by external force

pro·jec·tor \-'jektər\ n : device for projecting pictures on a screen

pro·le·tar·i·an \,prōlə'terēən\ n : member of the proletariat —proletarian adj

pro·le·tar·i·at \-ēət\ n : laboring class

pro·lif·er·ate \prə'lifə,rāt\ vb -at·ed; -at·ing : grow or increase in number rapidly —pro·lif·er·a·tion \-,lifə'rāshən\ n

pro·lif·ic \prə'lifik\ adj : producing abundantly —pro·lif·i·cal·ly \-ik(ə)lē\ adv

pro·logue \'prō,lòg, -,läg\ n : preface

pro·long \prə'lòn\ vb : lengthen in time or extent —pro·lon·ga·tion \,prō,lòn'gāshən\ n

prom \'präm\ n : formal school dance

prom·e·nade \,prämə'nād, -'näd\ n 1 : leisurely walk 2 : place for strolling —promenade vb

prom·i·nence \'präm(ə)nəns\ n 1 : quality, state, or fact of being readily noticeable or distinguished 2 : something that stands out —prom·i·nent \-nənt\ adj —prom·i·nent·ly adv

pro·mis·cu·ous \prə'miskyəwəs\ adj : not restricted to one sexual partner —prom·is·cu·i·ty \,prämis'kyůətē, ₚprō̇·mis-\ n —**pro·mis·cu·ous·ly** adv —**pro·mis·cu·ous·ness** n

prom·ise \'präməs\ n 1 : statement that one will do or not do something 2 : basis for expectation —**promise** vb —**prom·is·so·ry** \-ə,sōrē\ adj

prom·is·ing \'präməsiŋ\ adj : likely to succeed —**prom·is·ing·ly** adv

prom·on·to·ry \'prämən,tōrē\ n, pl -ries : point of land jutting into the sea

pro·mote \prə'mōt\ vb -mot·ed; -mot·ing 1 : advance in rank 2 : contribute to the growth, development, or prosperity of —**pro·mot·er** n —**pro·mo·tion** \-'mōshən\ n —**pro·mo·tion·al** \-'mōsh(ə)nəl\ adj

¹**prompt** \'prämpt\ vb 1 : incite 2 : give a cue to (an actor or singer) —**prompt·er** n

²**prompt** adj : ready and quick —**prompt·ly** adv —**prompt·ness** n

prone \'prōn\ adj 1 : having a tendency 2 : lying face downward —**prone·ness** \'prōnnəs\ n

prong \'prȯŋ\ n : sharp point of a fork —**pronged** \'prȯŋd\ adj

pro·noun \'prō,naȯn\ n : word used as a substitute for a noun

pro·nounce \prə'naȯns\ vb -nounced; -nounc·ing 1 : utter officially or as an opinion 2 : say or speak esp. correctly —**pro·nounce·able** adj —**pro·nounce·ment** n —**pro·nun·ci·a·tion** \-,nənsē'āshən\ n

pro·nounced \-'naȯnst\ adj : strongly marked

¹**proof** \'prüf\ n 1 : evidence of a truth or fact 2 : trial impression or print

²**proof** adj : designed for or successful in resisting or repelling

proof·read vb : read and mark corrections in (printer's proof) —**proof·read·er** n

prop \'präp\ vb -pp- 1 : support 2 : sustain —**prop** n

pro·pa·gan·da \,präpə'gandə, ,prōpə-\ n : the spreading of ideas or information to further or damage a cause —**prop·a·gan·dist** \-dəst\ n —**pro·pa·gan·dize** \-,dīz\ vb

prop·a·gate \'präpə,gāt\ vb -gat·ed; -gat·ing 1 : reproduce biologically 2 : cause to spread —**prop·a·ga·tion** \,präpə'gāshən\ n

pro·pane \'prō,pān\ n : heavy flammable gaseous fuel

pro·pel \prə'pel\ vb -ll- : drive forward —**pro·pel·lant, pro·pel·lent** n or adj

pro·pel·ler \prə'pelər\ n : hub with revolving blades that drives a craft

pro·pen·si·ty \prə'pensətē\ n, pl -ties : particular interest or inclination

prop·er \'präpər\ adj 1 : suitable or right 2 : limited to a specified thing 3 : correct 4 : strictly adhering to standards of good manners, dignity, or good taste —**prop·er·ly** adv

prop·er·ty \'präpərtē\ n, pl -ties 1 : quality peculiar to an individual 2 : something owned 3 : piece of real estate 4 : ownership

proph·e·cy \'präfəsē\ n, pl -cies : prediction

proph·e·sy \-,sī\ vb -sied; -sy·ing : predict —**proph·e·si·er** \-,sī(ə)r\ n

proph·et \'präfət\ n : one who utters revelations or predicts events —**proph·et·ess** \-əs\ n —**pro·phet·ic** \prə'fetik\, **pro·phet·i·cal** \-ikəl\ adj —**pro·phet·i·cal·ly** \-ik(ə)lē\ adv

pro·pin·qui·ty \prə'piŋkwətē\ n : nearness

pro·pi·ti·ate \prō'pishē,āt\ vb -at·ed; -at·ing : gain or regain the favor of —**pro·pi·ti·a·tion** \-,pish(ē)ā'shən\ n —**pro·pi·tia·to·ry** \-'pish(ē)ə,tōrē\ adj

pro·pi·tious \prə'pishəs\ adj : favorable

pro·po·nent \prə'pōnənt\ n : one who argues in favor of something

pro·por·tion \prə'pōrshən\ n 1 : relation of one part to another or to the whole with respect to magnitude, quantity, or degree 2 : symmetry 3 : share ~ vb : adjust in size in relation to others —**pro·por·tion·al** \-sh(ə)nəl\ adj —**pro·por·tion·al·ly** adv —**pro·por·tion·ate** \-sh(ə)nət\ adj —**pro·por·tion·ate·ly** adv

pro·pose \prə'pōz\ vb -posed; -pos·ing 1 : plan or intend 2 : make an offer of marriage 3 : present for consideration —**pro·pos·al** \-'pōzəl\ n —**pro·pos·er** n

prop·o·si·tion \,präpə'zishən\ n : something proposed ~ vb : suggest sexual intercourse to one

pro·pound \prə'paȯnd\ vb : set forth for consideration

pro·pri·etor \prə'prīətər\ n : owner —**pro·pri·etary** \prə'prīə,terē\ adj —**pro·pri·etor·ship** n —**pro·pri·etress** \-'prīətrəs\ n

pro·pri·ety \prə'prīətē\ n, pl -eties : standard of acceptability in social conduct

pro·pul·sion \prə'pəlshən\ n 1 : action of propelling 2 : driving power —**pro·pul·sive** \-siv\ adj

pro·sa·ic \prō'zāik\ adj : dull

pro·scribe \prō'skrīb\ vb -scribed; -scrib·ing : prohibit —pro·scrip·tion \-'skripshən\ n

prose \'prōz\ n : ordinary language

pros·e·cute \'präsi,kyüt\ vb -cut·ed; -cut·ing 1 : follow to the end 2 : seek legal punishment of —pros·e·cu·tion \,präsi'kyüshən\ n —pros·e·cu·tor \'präsi,kyütər\ n

pros·e·lyte \'präsə,līt\ n : new convert —pros·e·ly·tize \-'präsələ,tīz\ vb

pros·pect \'präs,pekt\ n 1 : extensive view 2 : something awaited 3 : potential buyer ~ vb : look for mineral deposits —pro·spec·tive \prə'spektiv, 'präs,pek-\ adj —pro·spec·tive·ly adv —pros·pec·tor \-,pektər, -'pek-\ n

pro·spec·tus \prə'spektəs\ n : introductory description of an enterprise

pros·per \'präspər\ vb : thrive or succeed —pros·per·ous \-p(ə)rəs\ adj

pros·per·i·ty \präs'perətē\ n : economic well-being

pros·tate \'präs,tāt\ n : glandular body about the base of the male urethra —prostate adj

pros·the·sis \präs'thēsəs, 'prästhə-\ n, pl -the·ses \-,sēz\ : artificial replacement for a body part —pros·thet·ic \präs'thetik\ adj

pros·ti·tute \'prästə,t(y)üt\ vb -tut·ed; -tut·ing : put to corrupt or unworthy purposes ~ n : one who engages in sexual intercourse for pay —pros·ti·tu·tion \,prästə't(y)üshən\ n

pros·trate \'präs,trāt\ adj : stretched out with face on the ground ~ vb -trat·ed; -trat·ing 1 : fall or throw (oneself) into a prostrate position 2 : reduce to helplessness —pros·tra·tion \präs'trāshən\ n

pro·tect \prə'tekt\ vb : shield from injury —pro·tec·tor \-tər\ n

pro·tec·tion \prə'tekshən\ n 1 : act of protecting 2 : one that protects —pro·tec·tive \-'tektiv\ adj

pro·tec·tor·ate \-(t)ə)rət\ n : state dependent upon the authority of another state

pro·té·gé \'prōtə,zhā\ n : one under the care and protection of an influential person —pro·té·gée \-,zhā\ n

pro·tein \'prō,tēn, 'prōtēən\ n : complex combination of amino acids present in living matter

pro·test \'prō,test\ n 1 : organized public demonstration of disapproval 2 : strong objection ~ \prə'test\ vb 1 : assert positively 2 : object strongly —prot·es·ta·tion \,prätəs'tāshən\ n —pro·test·er, pro·tes·tor \-ər\ n

Prot·es·tant \'prätəstənt\ n : Christian not of a Catholic or Orthodox church —Prot·es·tant·ism \'prätəstənt,izəm\ n

pro·to·col \'prōtə,kòl\ n : diplomatic etiquette

pro·ton \'prō,tän\ n : positively charged particle

pro·to·plasm \'prōtə,plazəm\ n : complex colloidal living substance of plant and animal cells —pro·to·plas·mic \,prōtə'plazmik\ adj

pro·to·type \'prōtə,tīp\ n : original model

pro·to·zo·an \,prōtə'zōən\ n : single-celled lower invertebrate animal

pro·tract \prō'trakt\ vb : prolong

pro·trac·tor \-'traktər\ n : instrument for constructing and measuring angles

pro·trude \prō'trüd\ vb -trud·ed; -trud·ing : stick out or cause to stick out —pro·tru·sion \-'trüzhən\ n —pro·tru·sive \-'trüsiv\ adj

pro·tu·ber·ance \prō't(y)üb(ə)rəns\ n : something that protrudes —pro·tu·ber·ant adj

proud \'praud\ adj 1 : having or showing excessive self-esteem 2 : highly pleased 3 : having proper self-respect 4 : glorious —proud·ly adv

prove \'prüv\ vb proved; proved or prov·en \'prüvən\; prov·ing 1 : test by experiment or by a standard 2 : establish the truth of by argument or evidence 3 : turn out esp. after trial or test —prov·able \'prüvəbəl\ adj

prov·en·der \'prävəndər\ n : dry food for domestic animals

prov·erb \'präv,ərb\ n : short meaningful popular saying —pro·ver·bi·al \prə'vərbēəl\ adj

pro·vide \prə'vīd\ vb -vid·ed; -vid·ing 1 : take measures beforehand 2 : make a stipulation 3 : supply what is needed —pro·vid·er n

pro·vid·ed conj : if

prov·i·dence \'prävədəns\ n 1 often cap : divine guidance 2 cap : God 3 : quality of being provident

prov·i·dent \-ədənt\ adj : making provision for the future 2 : thrifty —prov·i·dent·ly adv

prov·i·den·tial \,prävə'denchəl\ adj 1 : relating to Providence 2 : opportune

prov·ince \'prävəns\ n 1 : administrative district 2 pl : all of a country outside the metropolis 3 : sphere

pro·vin·cial \prə'vinchəl\ *adj* 1 : relating to a province 2 : not cosmopolitan —**pro·vin·cial·ism** \-,izəm\ *n*

pro·vi·sion \prə'vizhən\ *n* 1 : act of providing 2 : stock of food —usu. in pl. 3 : stipulation ~ *vb* : supply with provisions

pro·vi·sion·al \-'vizh(ə)nəl\ *adj* : provided for a temporary need

pro·vi·so \prə'vīzō\ *n, pl* -sos *or* -soes : article or clause that introduces a condition

pro·voke \prə'vōk\ *vb* -voked; -vok·ing 1 : incite to anger 2 : stir up on purpose —**prov·o·ca·tion** \,prävə'kāshən\ *n* —**pro·voc·a·tive** \prə'väkətiv\ *adj*

prow \'prau̇\ *n* : bow of a ship

prow·ess \'prau̇əs\ *n* 1 : valor 2 : extraordinary ability

prowl \'prau̇l\ *vb* : roam about stealthily —**prowl** *n* —**prowl·er** *n*

prox·i·mate \'präksəmət\ *adj* : very near

prox·im·i·ty \präk'simətē\ *n* : nearness

proxy \'präksē\ *n, pl* **prox·ies** : authority to act for another —**proxy** *adj*

prude \'prüd\ *n* : one who shows extreme modesty —**prud·ery** \'prüdərē\ *n* —**prud·ish** \'prüdish\ *adj*

pru·dent \'prüd°nt\ *adj* 1 : shrewd 2 : cautious 3 : thrifty —**pru·dence** \-°ns\ *n* —**pru·den·tial** \prü'denchəl\ *adj* —**pru·dent·ly** *adv*

¹prune \'prün\ *n* : dried plum

²prune *vb* **pruned; prun·ing** : cut off unwanted parts

pru·ri·ent \'prürēənt\ *adj* : lewd —**pru·ri·ence** \-ēəns\ *n*

¹pry \'prī\ *vb* **pried; pry·ing** : look closely or inquisitively

²pry *vb* **pried; pry·ing** : raise, move, or pull apart with a lever

psalm \'säm, 'sälm\ *n* : sacred song or poem —**psalm·ist** *n*

pseud·onym \'süd°n,im\ *n* : fictitious name —**pseud·on·y·mous** \sü'dänəməs\ *adj*

pso·ri·a·sis \sə'rīəsəs\ *n* : chronic skin disease

psy·che \'sīkē\ *n* : soul or mind

psy·chi·a·try \sə'kīətrē, sī-\ *n* : branch of medicine dealing with mental disorders —**psy·chi·at·ric** \,sīkē'atrik\ *adj* —**psy·chi·a·trist** \sə'kīətrəst, sī-\ *n*

psy·chic \'sīkik\ *adj* 1 : relating to the psyche 2 : sensitive to supernatural forces ~ *n* : person sensitive to supernatural forces —**psy·chi·cal·ly** \-k(ə)lē\ *adv*

psy·cho·anal·y·sis \,sīkōə'naləsəs\ *n* : study of the normally hidden content of the mind esp. to resolve conflicts —**psy·cho·an·a·lyst** \-'an°ləst\ *n* —**psy·cho·an·a·lyt·ic** \-,an°l'itik\ *adj* —**psy·cho·an·a·lyze** \-'an°l,īz\ *vb*

psy·chol·o·gy \sī'käləjē\ *n, pl* -gies 1 : science of mind and behavior 2 : mental and behavioral aspect (as of an individual) —**psy·cho·log·i·cal** \,sīkə'läjikəl\ *adj* —**psy·cho·log·i·cal·ly** \-ik(ə)lē\ *adv* —**psy·chol·o·gist** \sī'käləjəst\ *n*

psy·cho·path \'sīkə,path\ *n* : mentally ill or unstable person —**psy·cho·path·ic** \,sīkə'pathik\ *adj*

psy·cho·sis \sī'kōsəs\ *n, pl* -cho·ses \-,sēz\ : mental derangement (as paranoia) —**psy·chot·ic** \-'kätik\ *adj or n*

psy·cho·so·mat·ic \,sīkōsə'matik\ *adj* : caused by the interaction of mind and body

psy·cho·ther·a·py \,sīkō'therəpē\ *n* : treatment of mental disorder by psychological means —**psy·cho·ther·a·pist** \-,pəst\ *n*

pto·maine \'tō,mān\ *n* : bacterial decay product

pu·ber·ty \'pyübərtē\ *n* : time of sexual maturity —**pu·ber·tal** \-bərt°l\ *adj*

pu·bic \'pyübik\ *adj* : relating to the lower abdominal region

pub·lic \'pəblik\ *adj* 1 : relating to the people as a whole 2 : civic 3 : not private 4 : open to all 5 : well-known ~ *n* : people as a whole —**pub·lic·ly** *adv*

pub·li·ca·tion \,pəblə'kāshən\ *n* 1 : process of publishing 2 : published work

pub·lic·i·ty \(,)pə'blisətē\ *n* 1 : news information given out to gain public attention 2 : public attention

pub·li·cize \'pəblə,sīz\ *vb* -cized; -ciz·ing : give publicity to —**pub·li·cist** \-səst\ *n*

pub·lish \'pəblish\ *vb* 1 : announce publicly 2 : reproduce for sale esp. by printing —**pub·lish·er** *n*

puck·er \'pəkər\ *vb* : pull together into folds or wrinkles —**pucker** *n* : wrinkle

pud·ding \'pu̇diŋ\ *n* : creamy dessert

pud·dle \'pəd°l\ *n* : very small pool of water

pudgy \'pəjē\ *adj* **pudg·i·er, -est** : short and plump

pu·er·ile \'pyu̇ərəl\ *adj* : childish —**pu·er·il·i·ty** \,pyu̇ə'rilətē\ *n*

puff \'pəf\ *vb* 1 : blow in short gusts 2 : pant 3 : enlarge ~ *n* 1 : short discharge (as of air) **2** : slight swelling **3** : something light and fluffy —**puffy** *adj*

pug \'pəg\ *n* : small stocky dog

pu·gi·lism \'pyüjə,lizəm\ *n* : boxing —**pu·gi·list** \-ləst\ *n* —**pu·gi·lis·tic** \,pyüjə'listik\ *adj*

pug·na·cious \,pəg'nāshəs\ *adj* : prone to fighting —**pug·nac·i·ty** \-'nasətē\ *n*

puke \'pyük\ *vb* **puked; puk·ing** : vomit —**puke** *n*

pul·chri·tude \'pəlkrə,t(y)üd\ *n* : beauty —**pul·chri·tu·di·nous** \,pəlkrə't(y)üdnəs, -³nəs\ *adj*

pull \'pul\ *vb* **1** : exert force so as to draw (something) toward or out **2** : move **3** : stretch or tear ~ *n* **1** : act of pulling **2** : influence **3** : device for pulling something —**pull·er** *n*

pul·let \'pulət\ *n* : young hen

pul·ley \'pulē\ *n, pl* **-leys** : wheel with a grooved rim

Pull·man \'pulmən\ *n* : railroad car with berths

pull·over \,pul,ōvər\ *adj* : put on by being pulled over the head —**pull·over** \'pul,ōvər\ *n*

pul·mo·nary \'pulmə,nerē, 'pəl-\ *adj* : relating to the lungs

pulp \'pəlp\ *n* **1** : soft part of a fruit or vegetable **2** : soft moist mass (as of mashed wood) —**pulpy** *adj*

pul·pit \'pul,pit\ *n* : raised desk used in preaching

pul·sate \'pəl,sāt\ *vb* **-sat·ed; -sat·ing** : expand and contract rhythmically —**pul·sa·tion** \,pəl'sāshən\ *n*

pulse \'pəls\ *n* : arterial throbbing caused by heart contractions —**pulse** *vb*

pul·ver·ize \'pəlvə,rīz\ *vb* **-ized; -iz·ing** : beat or grind into a powder

pu·ma \'p(y)ümə\ *n* : cougar

pum·ice \'pəməs\ *n* : light porous volcanic glass used in polishing

pum·mel \'pəməl\ *vb* **-meled** *or* **-melled; -mel·ing** *or* **-mel·ling** \-(ə)liŋ\ : beat

¹pump \'pəmp\ *n* : device for moving or compressing fluids ~ *vb* **1** : raise (as water) with a pump **2** : fill by means of a pump —with *up* **3** : move like a pump —**pump·er** *n*

²pump *n* : woman's low shoe

pum·per·nick·el \'pəmpər,nikəl\ *n* : dark rye bread

pump·kin \'pəŋkən, 'pəm(p)kən\ *n* : large yellow fruit of a vine related to the gourd

pun \'pən\ *n* : humorous use of a word in a way that suggests two interpretations —**pun** *vb*

¹punch \'pənch\ *vb* **1** : strike with the fist **2** : perforate with a punch ~ *n* : quick blow with the fist —**punch·er** *n*

²punch *n* : tool for piercing or stamping

³punch *n* : mixed beverage often including fruit juice

punc·til·i·ous \(,)pəŋk'tilēəs\ *adj* : marked by precise accordance with conventions

punc·tu·al \'pəŋkchə(wə)l\ *adj* : prompt —**punc·tu·al·i·ty** \,pəŋkchə'walətē\ *n* —**punc·tu·al·ly** *adv*

punc·tu·ate \'pəŋkchə,wāt\ *vb* **-at·ed; -at·ing** : mark with punctuation

punc·tu·a·tion \,pəŋkchə'wāshən\ *n* : standardized marks inserted in written matter to clarify the meaning or their use

punc·ture \'pəŋkchər\ *n* : act or result of puncturing ~ *vb* **-tured; -tur·ing** : make a hole in

pun·dit \'pəndət\ *n* **1** : learned man **2** : expert

pun·gent \'pənjənt\ *adj* : having a sharp or stinging odor or taste —**pun·gen·cy** \-jənsē\ *n* —**pun·gent·ly** *adv*

pun·ish \'pənish\ *vb* : impose a penalty on or for —**pun·ish·able** *adj* —**pun·ish·ment** *n*

pu·ni·tive \'pyünətiv\ *adj* : inflicting punishment

pun·kin *var of* PUMPKIN

¹punt \'pənt\ *n* : long narrow flat-bottomed boat ~ *vb* : propel (a boat) by pushing with a pole

²punt *vb* : kick a ball dropped from the hands ~ *n* : act of punting a ball

pu·ny \'pyünē\ *adj* **-ni·er; -est** : slight in power or size

pup \'pəp\ *n* : young dog

pu·pa \'pyüpə\ *n, pl* **-pae** \-(,)pē, -,pī\ *or* **-pas** : insect (as a moth) when it is in a case or cocoon —**pu·pal** \'pəl\ *adj*

¹pu·pil \'pyüpəl\ *n* : young person in school

²pupil *n* : dark central opening of the iris of the eye

pup·pet \'pəpət\ *n* : small doll moved by hand or by strings —**pup·pe·teer** \,pəpə'tiər\ *n*

pup·py \'pəpē\ *n, pl* **-pies** : young dog

pur·chase \'pərchəs\ *vb* **-chased; -chas·ing** : obtain in exchange for money ~ *n* **1** : act of purchasing **2** : something purchased **3** : secure grasp —**pur·chas·er** *n*

pure \'pyür\ *adj* **pur·er; pur·est** : free

of foreign matter, contamination, or corruption

pu·ree \pyü'rā, -'rē\ *n* : thick liquid mass of food

pur·ga·to·ry \'pərgə,tōrē\ *n, pl* **-ries** : intermediate state after death for purification by expiating sins —**pur·ga·tor·i·al** \,pərgə'tōrēəl\ *adj*

purge \'pərj\ *vb* **purged; purg·ing** 1 : purify esp. from sin 2 : have or cause free evacuation from the bowels 3 : rid (as a political party) by a purge ~ *n* 1 : act or result of purging 2 : something that purges —**pur·ga·tive** \'pərgətiv\ *adj or n*

pu·ri·fy \'pyürə,fī\ *vb* **-fied; -fy·ing** : make or become pure —**pu·ri·fi·ca·tion** \,pyürəfə'kāshən\ *n* —**pu·ri·fi·er** \-,fī(ə)r\ *n*

Pu·rim \'pür,(,)im\ *n* : a Jewish holiday celebrated in February or March in commemoration of the deliverance of the Jews from the massacre plotted by Haman

pu·ri·tan \'pyürət³n\ *n* : one who practices or preaches a very strict moral code —**pu·ri·tan·i·cal** \,pyürə'tanikəl\ *adj*

pu·ri·ty \'pyürətē\ *n* : quality or state of being pure

purl \'pərl\ *n* : stitch in knitting ~ *vb* : knit in purl stitch

pur·loin \(,)pər'lóin, 'pər,lóin\ *vb* : steal

pur·ple \'pərpəl\ *n* : bluish red color —**pur·plish** \'pərp(ə)lish\ *adj*

pur·port \(,)pər'pōrt\ *vb* : convey outwardly as the meaning ~ \'pər,pōrt\ *n* : meaning —**pur·port·ed·ly** \-ədlē\ *adv*

pur·pose \'pərpəs\ *n* 1 : something (as a result) aimed at 2 : resolution ~ *vb* **-posed; -pos·ing** : intend —**pur·pose·ful** \-fəl\ *adj* —**pur·pose·ful·ly** *adv* —**pur·pose·less** *adj* —**pur·pose·ly** *adv*

purr \'pər\ *n* : low murmur typical of a contented cat —**purr** *vb*

¹purse \'pərs\ *n* 1 : bag or pouch for money and small objects 2 : financial resource 3 : prize money

²purse *vb* **pursed; purs·ing** : pucker

pur·su·ance \pər'süəns\ *n* : act of carrying into effect

pursuant to \-'süənt-\ *prep* : according to

pur·sue \pər'sü\ *vb* **-sued; -su·ing** 1 : follow in order to overtake 2 : seek to accomplish 3 : engage in —**pur·su·er** *n*

pur·suit \pər'süt\ *n* 1 : act of pursuing 2 : occupation

pur·vey \(,)pər'vā\ *vb* **-veyed; -vey·ing** : supply (as provisions) usu. as a business —**pur·vey·ance** \-əns\ *n* —**pur·vey·or** \-ər\ *n*

pus \'pəs\ *n* : thick yellowish fluid (as in a boil)

push \'push\ *vb* 1 : press against to move forward 2 : urge on or provoke ~ *n* 1 : vigorous effort 2 : act of pushing —**push·cart** *n*

pushy \'pushē\ *adj* **push·i·er; -est** : objectionably aggressive

pu·sil·lan·i·mous \,pyüsə'lanəməs\ *adj* : cowardly

pussy \'püsē\ *n, pl* **puss·ies** : cat

pus·tule \'pəschül\ *n* : pus-filled pimple

put \'put\ *vb* **put; put·ting** 1 : bring to a specified position or condition 2 : subject to pain, suffering, or death 3 : impose or cause to exist 4 : express 5 : cause to be used or employed —**put out** *vb* : bother or inconvenience —**put up with** : endure

pu·tre·fy \'pyütrə,fī\ *vb* **-fied; -fy·ing** : make or become putrid —**pu·tre·fac·tion** \,pyütrə'fakshən\ *n* —**pu·tre·fac·tive** \-tiv\ *adj*

pu·trid \'pyütrəd\ *adj* : rotten —**pu·trid·i·ty** \pyü'tridətē\ *n*

put·ter \'pətər\ *vb* : occupy oneself with casual or unimportant work

put·ty \'pətē\ *n, pl* **-ties** : doughlike cement —**putty** *vb*

puz·zle \'pəzəl\ *vb* **-zled; -zling** 1 : confuse 2 : attempt to solve —with *out* or *over* ~ *n* : something that confuses or tests ingenuity —**puz·zle·ment** *n* —**puz·zler** \-(ə)lər\ *n*

pyg·my \'pigmē\ *n, pl* **-mies** : dwarf —**pygmy** *adj*

py·lon \'pī,län, -lən\ *n* : tower or tall post

pyr·a·mid \'pirə,mid\ *n* : structure with a square base and 4 triangular sides meeting at a point —**py·ra·mi·dal** \pə'ramədəl, ,pirə'mid-\ *adj*

pyre \'pī(ə)r\ *n* : material heaped for a funeral fire

py·ro·ma·nia \,pīrō'mānēə\ *n* : irresistible impulse to start fires —**py·ro·ma·ni·ac** \-ē,ak\ *n*

py·ro·tech·nics \,pīrə'tekniks\ *n pl* : spectacular display (as of fireworks) —**py·ro·tech·nic** \-nik\ *adj*

py·thon \'pī,thän, -thən\ *n* : very large constricting snake

Q

q \'kyü\ *n, pl* **q's** *or* **qs** \'kyüz\ : 17th letter of the alphabet

¹quack \'kwak\ *vb* : make a cry like that of a duck —**quack** *n*

²quack *n* : one who pretends to have medical or healing skill —**quack** *adj* —**quack·ery** \-ərē\ *n* —**quack·ish** *adj*

quad·ran·gle \'kwäd,raŋgəl\ *n* : flat geometrical figure having 4 angles and 4 sides —**quad·ran·gu·lar** \kwä'draŋgyələr\ *adj*

quad·rant \'kwädrənt\ *n* : 1/4 of a circle

quad·ri·lat·er·al \,kwädrə'lat(ə)rəl\ *adj* : having 4 sides ~ *n* : 4-sided polygon

qua·drille \kwä'dril, k(w)ə-\ *n* : square dance of 5 or 6 figures in various rhythms

quad·ru·ped \'kwädrə,ped\ *n* : animal having 4 feet —**qua·dru·pe·dal** \kwä'drüpəd²l, ,kwädrə'ped-\ *adj*

qua·dru·ple \kwä'drüpəl, -'drəp-; 'kwädrəp-\ *vb* **-pled; -pling** \-(ə)liŋ\ : multiply by 4 ~ *adj* : being 4 times as great or as many

qua·dru·plet \kwä'drəplət, -'drüp-; 'kwädrəp-\ *n* : one of 4 offspring born at one birth

quaff \'kwäf, 'kwaf\ *vb* : drink deeply or repeatedly —**quaff** *n*

quag·mire \'kwag,mī(ə)r, 'kwag-\ *n* : soft land or bog

qua·hog \'kō,hóg, 'kwó-, 'kwō-, -,häg\ *n* : thick-shelled clam

¹quail \'kwāl\ *n, pl* **quail** *or* **quails** : short-winged stout-bodied game bird

²quail *vb* : lose courage or cower in fear

quaint \'kwānt\ *adj* : pleasingly old-fashioned or odd —**quaint·ly** *adv* —**quaint·ness** *n*

quake \'kwāk\ *vb* **quaked; quak·ing** : shake or tremble ~ *n* : earthquake

qual·i·fi·ca·tion \,kwäləfə'kāshən\ *n* 1 : limitation or stipulation 2 : special skill or experience for a job

qual·i·fy \'kwälə,fī\ *vb* **-fied; -fy·ing** 1 : modify or limit 2 : fit by skill or training for some purpose 3 : become eligible —**qual·i·fied** *adj* —**qual·i·fi·er** \-,fī(ə)r\ *n*

qual·i·ty \'kwälətē\ *n, pl* **-ties** 1 : peculiar and essential character, nature, or feature 2 : excellence or distinction

qualm \'kwäm, 'kwälm, 'kwóm\ *n* : scruple

quan·da·ry \'kwänd(ə)rē\ *n, pl* **-ries** : state of perplexity or doubt

quan·ti·ty \'kwäntətē\ *n, pl* **-ties** 1 : something that can be measured or numbered 2 : considerable amount

quar·an·tine \'kwórən,tēn\ *n* 1 : restraint on the movements of persons or goods to prevent the spread of pests or disease 2 : place or period of quarantine —**quarantine** *vb*

quar·rel \'kwór(ə)l\ *n* : basis of conflict —**quarrel** *vb* —**quar·rel·some** \-səm\ *adj*

¹quar·ry \'kwórē\ *n, pl* **quarries** : prey

²quarry *n, pl* **-ries** : excavation for obtaining stone —**quarry** *vb*

quart \'kwórt\ *n* : unit of liquid measure equal to .95 liter or of dry measure equal to 1.10 liters

quar·ter \'kwórtər\ *n* 1 : 1/4 part 2 : 1/4 of a dollar 3 : city district 4 *pl* : place to live esp. for a time 5 : mercy ~ *vb* : divide into 4 equal parts

quar·ter·ly \'kwórtərlē\ *adv or adj* : at 3-month intervals ~ *n, pl* **-lies** : periodical published 4 times a year

quar·ter·mas·ter *n* 1 : ship's helmsman 2 : army supply officer

quar·tet \kwór'tet\ *n* 1 : music for 4 performers 2 : group of 4

quar·to \'kwórtō\ *n, pl* **-tos** : book printed on pages cut 4 from a sheet

quartz \'kwórts\ *n* : transparent crystalline mineral

quash \'kwäsh, 'kwósh\ *vb* 1 : set aside by judicial action 2 : suppress summarily and completely

qua·si \'kwä,zī, -sī; 'kwāzē, 'kwäs-; 'kwäzē\ *adj* : similar or nearly identical

qua·train \'kwä,trān\ *n* : unit of 4 lines of verse

qua·ver \'kwāvər\ *vb* : tremble or trill —**quaver** *n*

quay \'kē, 'k(w)ā\ *n* : wharf

quea·sy \'kwēzē\ *adj* **-si·er; -est** : nauseated —**quea·si·ly** \-zəlē\ *adv* —**quea·si·ness** \-zēnəs\ *n*

queen \'kwēn\ *n* 1 : wife or widow of a king 2 : female monarch 3 : woman of rank, power, or attractiveness 4 : fertile female of a social insect —**queen·ly** *adj*

queer \'kwiər\ *adj* : differing from the

usual or normal —queer·ly adv
—queer·ness n

quell \'kwel\ vb : put down

quench \'kwench\ vb 1 : put out 2
: satisfy (a thirst) —quench·able adj
—quench·less adj

quer·u·lous \'kwer(y)ələs\ adj : fretful
or whining —quer·u·lous·ly adv
—quer·u·lous·ness n

que·ry \'kwi(ə)rē, 'kwe(ə)r-\ n, pl -ries
: question —query vb

quest \'kwest\ n or vb : search

ques·tion \'kweschən\ n 1 : something
asked 2 : subject for discussion 3
: dispute ~ vb 1 : ask questions 2
: doubt or dispute 3 : subject to
analysis —ques·tion·er n

ques·tion·able \'kweschənabəl\ adj 1
: not certain 2 : of doubtful truth or
morality

question mark n : a punctuation mark ?
used esp. at the end of a sentence to
indicate a direct question

ques·tion·naire \,kweschə'na(ə)r\ n
: set of questions

queue \'kyü\ n 1 : braid of hair 2 : line
of persons or vehicles ~ vb queued;
queu·ing or queue·ing : line up

quib·ble \'kwibəl\ n : minor objection
—quibble vb

quick \'kwik\ adj 1 : rapid 2 : alert or
perceptive ~ n : sensitive area (as
under a fingernail) —quick adv
—quick·ly adv —quick·ness n

quick·en \'kwikən\ vb 1 : come to life
2 : hurry

quick·sand n : deep mass of sand and
water

quick·sil·ver n : mercury

qui·es·cent \kwī'es²nt\ adj : being at
rest —qui·es·cence \-əns\ n

qui·et \'kwīət\ adj 1 : marked by little
motion or activity 2 : gentle 3 : free
from noise 4 : not showy 5 : secluded
~ vb : pacify —quiet adv or n —qui·
et·ly adv —qui·et·ness n

qui·etude \'kwīə,t(y)üd\ n : quietness
or repose

quill \'kwil\ n 1 : a large stiff feather 2
: porcupine's spine

quilt \'kwilt\ n : padded bedspread ~
vb : stitch or sew in layers with padding in between

quince \'kwins\ n : hard yellow apple-
like fruit

qui·nine \'kwī,nīn\ n : bitter drug used
against malaria

quin·tes·sence \kwin'tes²ns\ n 1 : pur-
est essence of something 2 : most
typical example —quin·tes·sen·tial
\,kwintə'senchal\ adj

quin·tet \kwin'tet\ n 1 : music for 5
performers 2 : group of 5

quin·tu·ple \kwin't(y)üpəl, -'təp-;
'kwintəp-\ adj 1 : having 5 units or
members 2 : being 5 times as great or
as many —quintuple n or vb

quin·tu·plet \kwin'təplət, -'t(y)üp-;
'kwintəp-\ n : one of 5 offspring at
one birth

quip \'kwip\ vb -pp- : make a clever
remark —quip n

quire \'kwī(ə)r\ n : 24 or 25 sheets of
paper of the same size and quality

quirk \'kwərk\ n : peculiarity of action
or behavior —quirky adj

quit \'kwit\ vb quit; quit·ting 1 : stop 2
: leave —quit·ter n

quite \'kwīt\ adv 1 : completely 2 : to a
considerable extent

quits \'kwits\ adj : even or equal with
another (as by repaying a debt)

¹quiv·er \'kwivər\ n : case for arrows

²quiver vb : shake or tremble —quiver n

quix·ot·ic \kwik'sätik\ adj : idealistic
to an impractical degree

quiz \'kwiz\ n, pl quiz·zes : short test
~ vb -zz- : question closely

quiz·zi·cal \'kwizikəl\ adj 1 : teasing 2
: curious

quoit \'k(w)ȯit, 'kwȯit\ n : ring thrown
at a peg in a game (quoits)

quon·dam \'kwändəm, -,dam\ adj
: former

quo·rum \'kwȯrəm\ n : required number of members present

quo·ta \'kwȯtə\ n : proportional part
or share

quotation mark n : one of a pair of
punctuation marks " " or ' ' used esp.
to indicate the beginning and the end
of a quotation

quote \'kwōt\ vb quot·ed; quot·ing 1
: speak or write another's words 2
: state (a price) —quot·able adj
—quo·ta·tion \kwō'tāshən\ n
—quote n

quo·tient \'kwōshənt\ n : number resulting from division

R

r \\'är\\ *n, pl* **r's** *or* **rs** \\'ärz\\ : 18th letter of the alphabet

rab·bet \\'rabət\\ *n* : groove in a board

rab·bi \\'rab,ī\\ *n* : Jewish religious leader —**rab·bin·ic** \\rə'binik\\, **rab·bin·i·cal** \\-ikəl\\ *adj*

rab·bin·ate \\'rabənət, -,nāt\\ *n* : office of a rabbi

rab·bit \\'rabət\\ *n, pl* **-bit** *or* **-bits** : long-eared burrowing mammal

rab·ble \\'rabəl\\ *n* : mob

rab·id \\'rabəd\\ *adj* 1 : violent 2 : fanatical 3 : affected with rabies —**rab·id·ly** *adv*

ra·bies \\'rābēz\\ *n, pl* **rabies** : acute deadly virus disease

rac·coon \\ra'kün\\ *n, pl* **-coon** *or* **-coons** : tree-dwelling mammal with a bushy ringed tail

¹race \\'rās\\ *n* 1 : strong current of water 2 : contest of speed 3 : election campaign ~ *vb* **raced; rac·ing** 1 : run in a race 2 : rush —**race·course** *n* —**rac·er** *n* —**race·track** *n*

²race *n* 1 : family, tribe, people, or nation of the same stock 2 : division of mankind based on hereditary traits —**ra·cial** \\'rāshəl\\ *adj* —**ra·cial·ly** *adv*

race·horse *n* : horse used for racing

rac·ism \\'rās,izəm\\ *n* : discrimination based on the belief that some races are by nature superior —**rac·ist** \\-əst\\ *n*

rack \\'rak\\ *n* 1 : framework for display or storage 2 : instrument that stretches the body for torture ~ *vb* : torture with or as if with a rack

¹rack·et \\'rakət\\ *n* : bat with a tight netting across one frame

²racket *n* 1 : confused noise 2 : fraudulent scheme —**rack·e·teer** \\,rakə'tiər\\ *n* —**rack·e·teer·ing** *n*

ra·con·teur \\,rak,än'tər\\ *n* : storyteller

racy \\'rāsē\\ *adj* **rac·i·er; -est** : risqué —**rac·i·ly** *adv* —**rac·i·ness** *n*

ra·dar \\'rā,där\\ *n* : radio device for determining distance, shape, or position of distant objects

ra·di·al \\'rādēəl\\ *adj* : having parts arranged like rays coming from a common center —**ra·di·al·ly** *adv*

ra·di·ant \\'rādēənt\\ *adj* 1 : glowing 2 : beaming with happiness 3 : transmitted by radiation —**ra·di·ance** \\-əns\\ *n* —**ra·di·an·cy** \\-ənsē\\ *n* —**ra·di·ant·ly** *adv*

ra·di·ate \\'rādē,āt\\ *vb* **-at·ed; -at·ing** 1 : issue rays or in rays 2 : spread from a center —**ra·di·a·tion** \\,rādē'āshən\\ *n*

ra·di·a·tor \\'rādē,ātər\\ *n* : cooling or heating device

rad·i·cal \\'radikəl\\ *adj* 1 : fundamental 2 : extreme ~ *n* 1 : person favoring extreme changes 2 : group of atoms replaceable by one atom —**rad·i·cal·ism** \\-,izəm\\ *n* —**rad·i·cal·ly** *adv*

radii *pl of* **RADIUS**

ra·dio \\'rādē,ō\\ *n, pl* **-di·os** 1 : transmission or reception of sound by means of electromagnetic waves 2 : radio receiving set ~ *vb* : send a message to by radio —**radio** *adj*

ra·dio·ac·tiv·i·ty \\,rādēō,ak'tivətē\\ *n* : property of an element that emits energy through nuclear disintegration —**ra·dio·ac·tive** \\-'aktiv\\ *adj*

ra·di·ol·o·gy \\,rādē'äləjē\\ *n* : medical use of radiation —**ra·di·ol·o·gist** \\-jəst\\ *n*

rad·ish \\'radish\\ *n* : pungent fleshy root usu. eaten raw

ra·di·um \\'rādēəm\\ *n* : metallic radioactive chemical element

ra·di·us \\'rādēəs\\ *n, pl* **-dii** \\-ē,ī\\ 1 : line from the center of a circle or sphere to the circumference or surface 2 : area defined by a radius

raff·ish \\'rafish\\ *adj* : flashily vulgar —**raff·ish·ly** *adv* —**raff·ish·ness** *n*

raf·fle \\'rafəl\\ *n* : lottery among people who have bought tickets ~ *vb* **-fled; -fling** : offer in a raffle

¹raft \\'raft\\ *n* : flat floating platform ~ *vb* : travel or transport by raft

²raft *n* : large amount or number

raf·ter \\'raftər\\ *n* : usu. sloping timber of a roof

¹rag \\'rag\\ *n* : waste piece of cloth

²rag *n* : composition in ragtime

rag·a·muf·fin \\'ragə,məfən\\ *n* : ragged dirty person

rage \\'rāj\\ *n* 1 : violent anger 2 : vogue ~ *vb* **raged; rag·ing** 1 : be extremely angry or violent 2 : be out of control

rag·ged \\'ragəd\\ *adj* 1 : torn —**rag·ged·ly** *adv* —**rag·ged·ness** *n*

ra·gout \\ra'gü\\ *n* : meat stew

rag·time *n* : syncopated rhythm

rag·weed \'rag-ˌwēd\ n : coarse weedy herb with allergenic pollen

raid \'rād\ n : sudden usu. surprise attack —**raid** vb —**raid·er** n

¹rail \'rāl\ n 1 : bar serving as a guard or barrier 2 : bar forming a track for wheeled vehicles 3 : railroad

²rail vb : scold someone vehemently —**rail·er** n

rail·ing \'rāliŋ\ n : rail or a barrier of rails

rail·lery \'rālərē\ n, pl **-ler·ies** : good-natured ridicule

rail·road \'rāl,rōd\ n : road for a train laid with iron rails and wooden ties ~ vb : force something hastily —**rail·road·er** n —**rail·road·ing** n

rail·way \-ˌwā\ n : railroad

rai·ment \'rāmənt\ n : clothing

rain \'rān\ n 1 : water falling in drops from the clouds 2 : shower of objects ~ vb : fall as or like rain —**rain·coat** n —**rain·drop** n —**rain·fall** n —**rain·mak·er** n —**rain·mak·ing** n —**rain·storm** n —**rain·water** n —**rainy** adj

rain·bow \-ˌbō\ n : arc of colors formed by the sun shining through moisture

raise \'rāz\ vb **raised; rais·ing** 1 : lift 2 : arouse 3 : erect 4 : collect 5 : breed, grow, or bring up 6 : increase 7 : make light ~ n : increase esp. in pay —**rais·er** n

rai·sin \'rāz²n\ n : dried grape

ra·ja, ra·jah \'räjə\ n : Indian prince

¹rake \'rāk\ n : tool for smoothing or sweeping ~ vb **raked; rak·ing** 1 : gather, loosen, or smooth with or as if with a rake 2 : sweep with gunfire

²rake n : dissolute man —**rak·ish** \'rākish\ adj

rakish \'rākish\ adj : smart or jaunty —**rak·ish·ly** adv —**rak·ish·ness** n

ral·ly \'ralē\ vb **-lied; -ly·ing** 1 : bring or come together 2 : revive or recover ~ n, pl **-lies** 1 : act of rallying 2 : mass meeting

ram \'ram\ n 1 : male sheep 2 : beam used in battering down walls or doors ~ vb **-mm-** 1 : force or drive in or through 2 : strike against violently

ram·ble \'rambəl\ vb **-bled; -bling** : wander —**ramble** n —**ram·bler** \-blər\ n

ram·bunc·tious \ram'bəŋkshəs\ adj : unruly

ram·i·fi·ca·tion \ˌraməfə'kāshən\ n : consequence

ram·i·fy \'ramə,fī\ vb **-fied; -fy·ing** : branch out

ramp \'ramp\ n : sloping passage or connecting roadway

ram·page \'ram,pāj, (ˈ)ram'pāj\ vb **-paged; -pag·ing** : rush about wildly ~ \'ram,-\ n : violent or riotous action or behavior

ram·pant \'rampənt\ adj : widespread —**ram·pant·ly** adv

ram·part \'ram,pärt\ n : embankment of a fortification

ram·rod n : rod used to load or clean a gun

ram·shack·le \'ram,shakəl\ adj : shaky

ran past of RUN

ranch \'ranch\ n 1 : establishment for the raising of cattle, sheep, or horses 2 : specialized farm ~ vb : operate a ranch —**ranch·er** n —**ranch·land** \-ˌland\ n

ran·cid \'ransəd\ adj : smelling or tasting as if spoiled —**ran·cid·i·ty** \ran'sidətē\ n —**ran·cid·ness** n

ran·cor \'raŋkər\ n : deep hatred —**ran·cor·ous** adj

ran·dom \'randəm\ adj : occurring by chance —**ran·dom·ly** adv —**ran·dom·ness** n —**at random** : without definite aim or method

ran·dom·ize \'randə,mīz\ vb **-ized; -iz·ing** : distribute or treat in a random way —**ran·dom·iza·tion** \ˌrandəmə'zāshən\ n

rang past of RING

range \'rānj\ n 1 : series of things in a row 2 : open land for grazing 3 : cooking stove 4 : variation within limits 5 : place for target practice 6 : extent ~ vb **ranged; rang·ing** 1 : set in a row or in order 2 : roam at large, freely, or over 3 : vary within limits —**range·land** \-ˌland\ n

rang·er \'rānjər\ n : lawman or soldier who patrols a large area

rangy \'rānjē\ adj **rang·i·er; -est** : being slender with long limbs —**rang·i·ness** n

¹rank \'raŋk\ adj 1 : vigorous in growth 2 : unpleasantly strong-smelling —**rank·ly** adv —**rank·ness** n

²rank n 1 : line of soldiers 2 : orderly arrangement 3 : grade of official standing 4 : position within a group ~ vb 1 : arrange in formation or according to class 2 : take or give a relative position

rank and file n : general membership

ran·kle \'raŋkəl\ vb **-kled; -kling** 1 : become inflamed 2 : cause anger, irritation, or bitterness

ran·sack \'ran,sak\ vb : search through and rob

ran·som \'ransəm\ n : something demanded for the freedom of a captive

~ *vb* : gain the freedom of by paying a price —**ran·som·er** *n*

rant \'rant\ *vb* : talk or scold violently —**rant·er** *n* —**rant·ing·ly** *adv*

¹**rap** \'rap\ *n* : sharp blow or rebuke ~ *vb* -**pp-** : strike or criticize sharply

²**rap** *vb* -**pp-** : talk freely

ra·pa·cious \rə'pāshəs\ *adj* 1 : excessively greedy 2 : ravenous —**ra·pa·cious·ly** *adv* —**ra·pa·cious·ness** *n* —**ra·pac·i·ty** \-'pasətē\ *n*

¹**rape** \'rāp\ *n* : herb grown as a forage crop and for its seeds (**rape·seed**)

²**rape** *vb* **raped; rap·ing** : force to have sexual intercourse —**rape** *n* —**rap·er** *n* —**rap·ist** \'rāpəst\ *n*

rap·id \'rapəd\ *adj* : very fast —**ra·pid·i·ty** \rə'pidətē\ *n* —**rap·id·ly** *adv*

rap·ids \-ədz\ *n pl* : place in a stream where the current is swift

ra·pi·er \'rāpēər\ *n* : narrow 2-edged sword

rap·ine \'rapən, -,īn\ *n* : plunder

rap·port \ra'pōr\ *n* : harmonious relationship

rapt \'rapt\ *adj* : engrossed —**rapt·ly** *adv* —**rapt·ness** *n*

rap·ture \'rapchər\ *n* : spiritual or emotional ecstasy —**rap·tur·ous** \-chərəs\ *adj*

¹**rare** \'rar\ *adj* **rar·er; rar·est** : having a portion relatively uncooked

²**rare** *adj* **rar·er; rar·est** 1 : not dense 2 : unusually fine 3 : seldom met with —**rare·ly** *adv* —**rare·ness** *n* —**rar·i·ty** \'rarətē\ *n*

rar·efy \'rarə,fī\ *vb* -**fied; -fy·ing** : make or become rare, thin, or less dense —**rar·efac·tion** \,rarə'fakshən\ *n*

rar·ing \'ra(ə)rən, -iŋ\ *adj* : full of enthusiasm

ras·cal \'raskəl\ *n* : mean, dishonest, or mischievous person —**ras·cal·i·ty** \ras-'kal-ət-ē\ *n* —**ras·cal·ly** \'raskəlē\ *adj*

¹**rash** \'rash\ *adj* : too hasty in decision or action —**rash·ly** *adv* —**rash·ness** *n*

²**rash** *n* : a breaking out of the skin with red spots

rasp \'rasp\ *vb* 1 : rub with or as if with a rough file 2 : speak in a grating tone ~ *n* : coarse file

rasp·ber·ry \'raz,berē, -b(ə)rē\ *n* : edible red or black berry

rat \'rat\ *n* : destructive rodent larger than the mouse

ratch·et \'rachət\ *n* : notched device for allowing motion in one direction

rate \'rāt\ *n* 1 : quantity, amount, or degree measured in relation to some other quantity 2 : rank ~ *vb* **rat·ed;**

rat·ing 1 : estimate or determine the rank or quality of 2 : deserve —**rat·er** *n*

rath·er \'rathər, 'rath-, 'rāth-\ *adv* 1 : preferably 2 : on the other hand 3 : more properly 4 : somewhat

rat·i·fy \'ratə,fī\ *vb* -**fied; -fy·ing** : approve and accept formally —**rat·i·fi·ca·tion** \,ratəfə'kāshən\ *n*

rat·ing \'rātiŋ\ *n* : classification according to grade

ra·tio \'rāsh(ē)ō\ *n, pl* -**tios** : relation in number, quantity, or degree between things

ra·tion \'rashən, 'rāshən\ *n* : share or allotment (as of food) ~ *vb* : use or allot sparingly

ra·tio·nal \'rash(ə)nəl\ *adj* 1 : having reason or sanity 2 : relating to reason —**ra·tio·nal·ly** *adv*

ra·tio·nale \,rashə'nal\ *n* 1 : explanation of principles of belief or practice 2 : underlying reason

ra·tio·nal·ize \-,īz\ *vb* -**ized; -iz·ing** : justify (as one's behavior or weaknesses) esp. to oneself —**ra·tio·nal·iza·tion** \,rash(ə)nələ'zāshən\ *n*

rat·tan \ra'tan, rə-\ *n* : palm with long stems used esp. for canes and wickerwork

rat·tle \'ratᵊl\ *vb* -**tled; -tling** 1 : make a series of clattering sounds 2 : say briskly 3 : confuse or upset ~ *n* 1 : series of clattering sounds 2 : toy that rattles

rat·tler \'ratlər\ *n* : rattlesnake

rat·tle·snake *n* : American venomous snake with a rattle at the end of the tail

rau·cous \'rōkəs\ *adj* : harsh or boisterous —**rau·cous·ly** *adv* —**rau·cous·ness** *n*

rav·age \'ravij\ *n* : destructive effect ~ *vb* -**aged; -ag·ing** : lay waste —**rav·ag·er** *n*

rave \'rāv\ *vb* **raved; rav·ing** 1 : talk wildly in or as if in delirium 2 : talk with extreme enthusiasm ~ *n* 1 : act of raving 2 : enthusiastic praise

rav·el \'ravəl\ *vb* -**eled** *or* -**elled; -el·ing** *or* -**el·ling** 1 : unravel 2 : tangle ~ *n* 1 : something tangled 2 : loose thread

ra·ven \'rāvən\ *n* : large black bird ~ *adj* : black and shiny

rav·en·ous \'rav(ə)nəs\ *adj* : very hungry —**rav·en·ous·ly** *adv* —**rav·en·ous·ness** *n*

ra·vine \rə'vēn\ *n* : narrow steep-sided valley

rav·ish \'ravish\ *vb* 1 : seize and take away by violence 2 : overcome with

264

joy or delight 3 : rape —**rav·ish·er** *n*
—**rav·ish·ment** *n*
raw \'rȯ\ *adj* **raw·er** \'rȯ(ə)r\; **raw·est**
\'rȯəst\ 1 : not cooked 2 : not pro-
cessed 3 : not trained 4 : having the
skin rubbed off 5 : cold and damp 6
: vulgar —**raw·ness** *n*
raw·hide \'rȯ,hīd\ *n* : untanned skin of
cattle
ray \'rā\ *n* 1 : thin beam of radiant
energy (as light) 2 : tiny bit
ray·on \'rā,än\ *n* : fabric made from
cellulose fiber
raze \'rāz\ *vb* **razed; raz·ing** : destroy
or tear down
ra·zor \'rāzər\ *n* : sharp cutting instrument used to shave off hair
re- \rē, ˌrē, 'rē\ *prefix* 1 : again or
anew 2 : back or backward

reaccelerate	reassociate
reaccept	reattach
reacclimatize	reattain
reaccredit	reawaken
reaccumulate	rebalance
reachieve	rebaptize
reacquaint	rebid
reacquire	rebind
reactivate	reborn
reactivation	rebroadcast
readapt	rebuild
readdict	rebury
readdress	recalculate
readjust	recapture
readjustable	recast
readjustment	recertification
readmit	recertify
readopt	rechannel
reaffirm	recharge
realign	recheck
realignment	rechristen
reallocate	recirculate
reanalysis	recirculation
reanalyze	reclassification
reanesthetize	reclassify
reappear	recolonize
reappearance	recombine
reapply	recompute
reappoint	reconceive
reapportion	reconnect
reappraisal	reconquer
reappraise	reconquest
reapprove	reconsider
reargue	reconsideration
rearrange	reconsolidate
rearrest	reconstruct
reassemble	recontaminate
reassert	reconvene
reassess	reconvict
reassessment	recopy
reassign	recross
reassignment	redeal

redecorate	reinstall
rededicate	reinstitute
rededication	reintegrate
redefine	reintegration
redeposit	reinter
redesign	reintroduce
redesignate	reinvent
redevelop	reinvestigate
rediscover	reinvestigation
rediscovery	reinvigorate
redissolve	rejudge
redistribute	rekindle
redraft	reknit
redraw	relabel
reemerge	relandscape
reemergence	relaunch
reemphasize	relearn
reenergize	relight
reengage	reline
reenlist	reload
reenlistment	remarriage
reenroll	remarry
reenter	remelt
reequip	remobilize
reestablish	remoisten
reestablishment	remold
reestimate	remotivate
reevaluate	rename
reevaluation	renegotiate
reexamination	reoccupy
reexamine	reoccur
refilm	reoccurrence
refinance	reoperate
refire	reorchestrate
refloat	reorganization
reflood	reorganize
refocus	reorient
refold	repack
reformulate	repaint
refreeze	repave
regrow	rephotograph
regrowth	replan
rehear	replaster
reheat	replay
rehire	replot
rehospitalization	repolish
rehospitalize	repopulate
reidentify	repressurize
reignite	reprice
reimplant	reprint
reimpose	reprocess
reincorporate	reprogram
reincarnate	repropose
reindict	reread
reinfection	rerecord
reinfest	reregister
reinflate	reroof
reinject	reroute
reinjection	resalable
reinoculate	resale
reinsert	reschedule
reinsertion	reseal
reinspect	

resegregate
resell
resentence
reset
resettle
resew
reshoot
reshow
resod
resolder
resolidify
restage
restart
restate
restatement
restimulate
restock
restructure
restudy
restyle
resubmit
resupply
resurface
resurvey
resuspend
resynthesis
resynthesize

retarget
reteach
retell
retest
rethink
retighten
retitle
retrain
retranslate
retransmit
retransplant
retrap
retry
retune
retype
reupholster
reutilize
revaccinate
revaccination
revisit
rewash
rewax
reweave
rewind
rewire
rewrap

reach \'rēch\ *vb* **1** : stretch out **2** : touch or try to touch or grasp **3** : extend to or arrive at **4** : communicate with — *n* **1** : act of reaching **2** : distance or extent of reaching —**reach·able** *adj* —**reach·er** *n*

re·act \rē'akt\ *vb* **1** : act in response to some influence or stimulus **2** : undergo chemical reaction —**re·active** \-'aktiv\ *adj*

re·ac·tion \rē'akshən\ *n* **1** : action or emotion caused by and directly related or counter to another action **2** : chemical change

re·ac·tion·ary \-shə₁nerē\ *adj* : relating to or favoring return to an earlier political order or policy — *n, pl* **-aries** : reactionary person

re·ac·tor \rē'aktər\ *n* **1** : one that reacts **2** : apparatus for the controlled release of atomic energy

read \'rēd\ *vb* **read** \'red\; **read·ing** \'rēdiŋ\ **1** : understand written language **2** : utter aloud printed words **3** : interpret **4** : study **5** : indicate — *adj* \'red\ : informed by reading —**read·a·bil·i·ty** \₁rēdə'bilətē\ *n* —**read·able** *adj* —**read·ably** *adv* —**read·er** *n* —**read·er·ship** *n*

read·ing \'rēdiŋ\ *n* **1** : something read or for reading **2** : particular version, interpretation, or performance **3** : indication of data made by an instrument

ready \'redē\ *adj* **readi·er; -est 1** : prepared or available for use or action **2** : willing to do something — *vb* **read·ied; ready·ing** : make ready — *n* : state of being ready —**read·i·ly** *adv* —**read·i·ness** *n*

re·al \'rē(ə)l\ *adj* **1** : actually existing **2** : genuine — *adv* : very —**re·al·ness** *n* —**for real 1** : in earnest **2** : genuine

real estate *n* : property in houses and land

re·al·ism \'rēə₁lizəm\ *n* **1** : disposition to deal with facts practically **2** : faithful portrayal of reality —**re·al·ist** \-ləst\ *adj or n* —**re·al·is·tic** \₁rēə'listik\ *adj* —**re·al·is·ti·cally** \-tik(ə)lē\ *adv*

re·al·i·ty \rē'alətē\ *n, pl* **-ties 1** : quality or state of being real **2** : something real

re·al·ize \'rēə₁līz\ *vb* **-ized; -iz·ing 1** : make actual **2** : obtain **3** : be aware of —**re·al·iz·able** *adj* —**re·al·i·za·tion** \₁rēələ'zāshən\ *n*

re·al·ly \'rē(ə)lē\ *adv* : in truth

realm \'relm\ *n* **1** : kingdom **2** : sphere

¹**ream** \'rēm\ *n* : quantity of paper that is 480, 500, or 516 sheets

²**ream** *vb* : enlarge or clean (a hole) with a specially shaped tool (**reamer**)

reap \'rēp\ *vb* : cut or clear (as a crop) with a scythe or machine —**reap·er** *n*

¹**rear** \'riər\ *vb* **1** : raise upright **2** : breed or bring up **3** : rise on the hind legs

²**rear** *n* **1** : back **2** : position at the back of something — *adj* : being at the back —**rear·ward** \-wərd\ *adj or adv*

rear admiral *n* : commissioned officer in the navy or coast guard ranking next below a vice admiral

rea·son \'rēz²n\ *n* **1** : explanation or justification **2** : motive for action or belief **3** : power or process of thinking — *vb* **1** : use the faculty of reason **2** : try to persuade another —**rea·son·er** *n* —**rea·son·ing** \'rēz-niŋ, -²niŋ\ *n*

rea·son·able \'rēznəbəl, -²nəbəl\ *adj* **1** : being within the bounds of reason **2** : inexpensive —**rea·son·able·ness** *n* —**rea·son·ably** \-blē\ *adv*

re·as·sure \₁rēə'shùr\ *vb* : restore one's confidence —**re·as·sur·ance** \-'shùrəns\ *n* —**re·as·sur·ing·ly** *adv*

re·bate \'rē₁bāt\ *n* : return of part of a payment —**rebate** *vb*

reb·el \'rebəl\ *n* : one that resists authority — *vb* \ri'bel\ **-belled; -bel·ling 1** : resist authority **2** : feel or exhibit anger —**rebel** \'rebəl\

re·bel·lion \ri'belyən\ *n* : resistance to authority and esp. to one's government

re·bel·lious \-yas\ *adj* 1 : engaged in rebellion 2 : inclined to resist authority —**re·bel·lious·ly** *adv* —**re·bel·lious·ness** *n*

re·birth \'rē'bərth\ *n* 1 : new or second birth 2 : revival

re·bound \'rē'baund, ri-\ *vb* 1 : spring back on striking something 2 : recover from a reverse ~ \'rē,-\ *n* 1 : action of rebounding 2 : immediate reaction to a reverse

re·buff \ri'bəf\ *vb* : refuse or repulse rudely —**rebuff** *n*

re·buke \-'byük\ *vb* -**buked; -buk·ing** : reprimand sharply —**rebuke** *n*

re·bus \'rēbəs\ *n* : riddle representing syllables or words with pictures

re·but \ri'bət\ *vb* -**but·ted; -but·ting** : refute —**re·but·ter** *n*

re·but·tal \-'əl\ *n* : opposing argument

re·cal·ci·trant \ri'kalsətrənt\ *adj* 1 : stubbornly resisting authority 2 : resistant to handling or treatment —**re·cal·ci·trance** \-trəns\ *n*

re·call \ri'kól\ *vb* 1 : call back 2 : remember 3 : revoke ~ \ri'-, 'rē,-\ *n* 1 : a summons to return 2 : remembrance 3 : act of revoking

re·cant \ri'kant\ *vb* : take back (something said) publicly

re·ca·pit·u·late \,rēkə'pichə,lāt\ *vb* -**lat·ed; -lat·ing** : summarize —**re·ca·pit·u·la·tion** \-,pichə'lāshən\ *n*

re·cede \ri'sēd\ *vb* -**ced·ed; -ced·ing** 1 : move back or away 2 : slant backward

re·ceipt \-'sēt\ *n* 1 : act of receiving 2 : something (as payment) received —usu. in pl. 3 : writing acknowledging something received

re·ceive \ri'sēv\ *vb* -**ceived; -ceiv·ing** 1 : take in or accept 2 : greet or entertain (visitors) 3 : pick up radio waves and convert into sounds or pictures —**re·ceiv·able** *adj*

re·ceiv·er \ri'sēvər\ *n* 1 : one that receives 2 : one having charge of property or money involved in a lawsuit 3 : apparatus for receiving radio waves —**re·ceiv·er·ship** *n*

re·cent \'rēs°nt\ *adj* 1 : lately made or used 2 : of the present time or time just past —**re·cent·ly** *adv* —**re·cent·ness** *n*

re·cep·ta·cle \ri'septikəl\ *n* : container

re·cep·tion \ri'sepshən\ *n* 1 : act of receiving 2 : social gathering at which guests are formally welcomed

re·cep·tion·ist \-sh(ə)nəst\ *n* : one who greets callers

re·cep·tive \ri'septiv\ *adj* : open and responsive to ideas, impressions, or suggestions —**re·cep·tive·ly** *adv* —**re·cep·tive·ness** *n* —**re·cep·tiv·i·ty** \,rē,sep'tivətē\ *n*

re·cess \'rē,ses, ri'ses\ *n* 1 : indentation in a line or surface 2 : suspension of a session for rest ~ *vb* 1 : make a recess in or put into a recess 2 : interrupt a session for a recess

re·ces·sion \ri'seshən\ *n* 1 : departing procession 2 : period of reduced economic activity

rec·i·pe \'resə(,)pē\ *n* : instructions for making something

re·cip·i·ent \ri'sipēənt\ *n* : one that receives

re·cip·ro·cal \ri'siprəkəl\ *adj* 1 : affecting each in the same way 2 : so related that one is equivalent to the other —**re·cip·ro·cal·ly** \-k(ə)lē\ *adv* —**re·ci·proc·i·ty** \,resə'präsətē\ *n*

re·cip·ro·cate \-,kāt\ *vb* -**cat·ed; -cat·ing** : make a return for something done or given —**re·cip·ro·ca·tion** \-,siprə'kāshən\ *n*

re·cit·al \ri'sīt°l\ *n* 1 : public reading or recitation 2 : music or dance concert or exhibition by pupils —**re·cit·al·ist** \-°ləst\ *n*

rec·i·ta·tion \,resə'tāshən\ *n* : a reciting or recital

re·cite \ri'sīt\ *vb* -**cit·ed; -cit·ing** 1 : repeat verbatim 2 : recount —**re·cit·er** *n*

reck·less \'rekləs\ *adj* : lacking caution —**reck·less·ly** *adv* —**reck·less·ness** *n*

reck·on \'rekən\ *vb* 1 : count or calculate 2 : consider —**reck·on·er** *n*

reck·on·ing *n* 1 : act or instance of reckoning 2 : calculation of a ship's position 3 : settling of accounts

re·claim \ri'klām\ *vb* : obtain from a waste product or by-product —**re·claim·able** *adj* —**rec·la·ma·tion** \,reklə'māshən\ *n*

re·cline \ri'klīn\ *vb* -**clined; -clin·ing** : lean backward or lie down

re·cluse \'rek,lüs, ri'klüs\ *n* : one who lives in seclusion

rec·og·ni·tion \,rekig'nishən, -əg-\ *n* : act of recognizing or state of being recognized

re·cog·ni·zance \ri'kä(g)nəzəns\ *n* : promise recorded before a court

rec·og·nize \'rekig,nīz, -əg-\ *vb* -**nized; -niz·ing** 1 : identify as previously known 2 : take notice of 3 : acknowledge esp. with appreciation —**rec·og-**

niz·able \'rekəg,nīzəbəl, -ig-\ *adj*
—**rec·og·niz·ably** \-blē\ *adv*

re·coil \ri'kȯil\ *vb* : draw or spring back ~ \'rē,-, ri'-\ *n* : action of recoiling

rec·ol·lect \,rekə'lekt\ *vb* : remember

rec·ol·lec·tion \,rekə'lekshən\ *n* 1 : act or power of recollecting 2 : something recollected

rec·om·mend \,rekə'mend\ *vb* 1 : present as deserving of acceptance or trial 2 : advise —**rec·om·mend·able** \-'mendəbəl\ *adj* **rec·om·men·da·to·ry** \-də,tōrē, -,tȯr-\ *adj* —**rec·om·mend·er** *n*

rec·om·men·da·tion \,rekəmən'dāshən\ *n* 1 : act of recommending 2 : statement or letter recommending someone

rec·om·pense \'rekəm,pens\ *vb* **-pensed; -pens·ing** : give compensation to ~ *n* : compensation

rec·on·cile \'rekən,sīl\ *vb* **-ciled; -cil·ing** 1 : cause to be friendly again 2 : adjust or settle 3 : bring to acceptance —**rec·on·cil·able** *adj* —**rec·on·cile·ment** *n* —**rec·on·cil·i·a·tion** \,rekən,silē'āshən\ *n*

re·con·nais·sance \ri'känəzəns, -səns\ *n* : exploratory survey of enemy territory

re·con·noi·ter \,rēkə'nȯitər, ,rekə-\ *vb* : make a reconnaissance of

re·con·dite \'rekən,dīt\ *adj* 1 : hard to understand 2 : little known

re·cord \ri'kȯrd\ *vb* 1 : set down in writing 2 : register permanently 3 : indicate 4 : preserve (as sound or images) for later reproduction ~ \'rekərd\ *n* 1 : something recorded 2 : best performance

re·cord·er \ri'kȯrdər\ *n* 1 : one who records transactions officially 2 : wind instrument with finger holes 3 : recording device

¹**re·count** \ri'kȧunt\ *vb* : relate in detail

²**re·count** \'rē'-\ *vb* : count again —**count** \'rē,-, -'rē'-\ *n*

re·coup \ri'küp\ *vb* : make up for (an expense or loss)

re·course \'rē,kȯrs, ri'-\ *n* : source of aid or a turning to such a source

re·cov·er \ri'kəvər\ *vb* 1 : regain position, poise, or health 2 : recoup —**cov·er·able** *adj* —**re·cov·ery** \-'kəv(ə)rē\ *n*

rec·re·ation \,rekrē'āshən\ *n* : a refreshing of strength or spirits as a change from work or study —**rec·re·ation·al** \-sh(ə)nəl\ *adj* —**rec·re·ative** \'rekrē,ātiv\ *adj*

re·crim·i·na·tion \ri,krimə'nāshən\ *n* : accusation —**re·crim·i·nate** *vb* —**re·crim·i·na·to·ry** \-'krimə(ə)nə,tōrē\ *adj*

re·cruit \ri'krüt\ *n* : newly enlisted member ~ *vb* : enlist the membership or services of —**re·cruit·er** *n* —**re·cruit·ment** *n*

rect·an·gle \'rek,tangəl\ *n* : 4-sided figure with 4 right angles —**rect·an·gu·lar** \rek'tangyələr\ *adj*

rec·ti·fy \'rektə,fī\ *vb* **-fied; -fy·ing** : make or set right —**rec·ti·fi·ca·tion** \,rektəfə'kāshən\ *n* —**rec·ti·fi·er** \'rektə,fī(ə)r\ *n*

rec·ti·tude \'rektə,t(y)üd\ *n* : moral integrity

rec·tor \'rektər\ *n* : clergyman in charge of a parish —**rec·tor·ate** \-t(ə)rət\ *n* —**rec·to·ri·al** \rek'tōrēəl\ *adj*

rec·to·ry \'rekt(ə)rē\ *n, pl* **-ries** : rector's residence

rec·tum \'rektəm\ *n, pl* **-tums** *or* **-ta** \-tə\ : last part of the intestine joining colon and anus —**rec·tal** \-təl\ *adj*

re·cum·bent \ri'kəmbənt\ *adj* : lying down

re·cu·per·ate \ri'k(y)üpə,rāt\ *vb* **-at·ed; -at·ing** : recover (as from illness) —**re·cu·per·a·tion** \-,k(y)üpə'rāshən\ *n* —**re·cu·per·a·tive** \-'k(y)üpərātiv\ *adj*

re·cur \ri'kər\ *vb* **-rr-** 1 : return in thought or talk 2 : happen or occur again —**re·cur·rence** \-'kərəns\ *n* —**re·cur·rent** \-ənt\ *adj*

red \'red\ *n* 1 : color of blood or of the ruby 2 *cap* : communist —**red** *adj* —**red·dish** *adj* —**red·ness** *n*

red·den \'redᵊn\ *vb* : make or become red or reddish

re·deem \ri'dēm\ *vb* 1 : regain, free, or rescue by paying a price 2 : atone for 3 : free from sin 4 : convert into something of value —**re·deem·able** *adj* —**re·deem·er** *n*

re·demp·tion \-'dempshən\ *n* : act of redeeming —**re·demp·tive** \-tiv\ *adj* —**re·demp·to·ry** \-t(ə)rē\ *adj*

red·head \-,hed\ *n* : one having red hair —**red·head·ed** \-'hedəd\ *adj*

red·o·lent \'redᵊlənt\ *adj* 1 : having a fragrance 2 : suggestive —**red·o·lence** \-əns\ *n* —**red·o·lent·ly** *adv*

re·doubt \ri'daȯt\ *n* : small fortification

re·doubt·able \-əbəl\ *adj* : arousing dread

re·dound \ri'daȯnd\ *vb* : have an effect

re·dress \ri'dres\ *vb* : set right ~ *n* 1 : relief or remedy 2 : compensation

red tape *n* : complex obstructive official routine

re·duce \ri'd(y)üs\ *vb* **-duced; -duc·ing** 1 : lessen 2 : put in a lower rank 3 : lose weight —**re·duc·er** *n* —**re·duc·ible** \-'d(y)üsəbəl\ *adj*

re·duc·tion \ri'dəkshən\ *n* 1 : act of reducing 2 : amount lost in reducing 3 : something made by reducing

re·dun·dant \ri'dəndənt\ *adj* : using more words than necessary —**re·dun·dan·cy** \-dənsē\ *n* —**re·dun·dant·ly** *adv*

red·wood *n* : tall coniferous timber tree

reed \'rēd\ *n* 1 : tall slender grass of wet areas 2 : elastic strip that vibrates to produce tones in certain wind instruments —**reedy** *adj*

reef \'rēf\ *n* : ridge of rocks or sand at or near the surface of the water —**reefy** *adj*

reek \'rēk\ *n* : strong or disagreeable fume or odor ~ *vb* : give off a reek —**reeky** *adj*

¹**reel** \'rēl\ *n* : revolvable device on which something flexible may be wound or quantity of something wound on it ~ *vb* 1 : wind on a reel 2 : pull in by reeling. —**reel·able** *adj* —**reel·er** *n*

²**reel** *vb* 1 : whirl or waver as from a blow 2 : walk or move unsteadily ~ *n* : reeling motion

³**reel** *n* : lively dance

re·fer \ri'fər\ *vb* **-rr-** 1 : direct or send to some person or place 2 : submit for consideration or action 3 : have connection 4 : mention or allude to something —**re·fer·able** \'ref(ə)rəbəl, ri'fərə-\ *adj* —**re·fer·ral** \ri'fərəl\ *n*

ref·er·ee \,refə'rē\ *n* 1 : one to whom an issue is referred for settlement 2 : sports official ~ *vb* **-eed; -ee·ing** : act as referee

ref·er·ence \'refərns, 'ref(ə)rəns\ *n* 1 : act of referring 2 : a bearing on a matter 3 : consultation for information 4 : person who can speak for one's character or ability or a recommendation given by such a person

ref·er·en·dum \,refə'rendəm\ *n, pl* **-da** \-də\ *or* **-dums** : a seeking of voters' approval for a legislative proposal

re·fill \'rē'fil\ *vb* : fill again —**re·fill** \'rē-, -fil\ *n* —**re·fill·able** *adj*

re·fine \ri'fīn\ *vb* **-fined; -fin·ing** 1 : free from impurities or waste matter 2 : improve or perfect 3 : free or become free of what is coarse or un-

couth —**re·fine·ment** \-mənt\ *n* —**re·fin·er** *n*

re·fin·ery \ri'fīn(ə)rē\ *n, pl* **-er·ies** : place for refining (as of sugar)

re·flect \ri'flekt\ *vb* 1 : bend or cast back (as light or heat) 2 : bring as a result 3 : cast reproach or blame 4 : ponder —**re·flec·tion** \-'flekshən\ *n* —**re·flec·tive** \-tiv\ *adj* —**re·flec·tor** \-tər\ *n*

re·flex \'rē,fleks\ *n* : automatic response to a stimulus ~ *adj* 1 : bent back 2 : relating to a reflex —**re·flex·ly** *adv*

re·flex·ive \ri'fleksiv\ *adj* : of or relating to an action directed back upon the doer or the grammatical subject —**reflexive** *n* —**re·flex·ive·ly** *adv* —**re·flex·ive·ness** *n*

re·form \ri'fôrm\ *vb* : make or become better esp. by correcting bad habits —**reform** *n* —**re·form·able** *adj* —**re·for·ma·tive** \-'fôrmətiv\ *adj* —**re·form·er** *n*

re·for·ma·to·ry \ri'fôrmə,tōrē\ *n, pl* **-ries** : penal institution for reforming young offenders

re·fract \ri'frakt\ *vb* : subject to refraction

re·frac·tion \-'frakshən\ *n* : the bending of a ray (as of light) when it passes from one medium into another —**re·frac·tive** \-tiv\ *adj*

re·frac·to·ry \ri'frakt(ə)rē\ *adj* : obstinate or unmanageable

re·frain \ri'frān\ *vb* : hold oneself back ~ *n* : verse recurring regularly in a song —**re·frain·ment** *n*

re·fresh \ri'fresh\ *vb* 1 : make or become fresh or fresher 2 : supply or take refreshment —**re·fresh·er** *n* —**re·fresh·ing·ly** *adv*

re·fresh·ment \-mənt\ *n* 1 : act of refreshing 2 *pl* : light meal

re·frig·er·ate \ri'frijə,rāt\ *vb* **-at·ed; -at·ing** : chill or freeze (food) for preservation —**re·frig·er·ant** \-(ə)rənt\ *adj or n* —**re·frig·er·a·tion** \-,frijə'rāshən\ *n* —**re·frig·er·a·tor** \-'frijə,rātər\ *n*

ref·uge \'ref,yüj\ *n* 1 : protection from danger 2 : place that provides protection

ref·u·gee \,refyü'jē\ *n* : one who flees for safety

re·fund \ri'fənd, 'rē,fənd\ *vb* : give or put back (money) —**re·fund** \'rē-\ *n* 1 : act of refunding 2 : sum refunded —**re·fund·able** *adj*

re·fur·bish \ri'fərbish\ *vb* : renovate

¹**re·fuse** \ri'fyüz\ *vb* **-fused; -fus·ing**

: decline to accept, do, or give —re-fus-al \-'fyüzəl\ n

²ref-use \'ref₁yüs, -₁yüz\ n : worthless matter

re-fute \ri'fyüt\ vb -fut-ed; -fut-ing : prove to be false —ref-u-ta-tion \₁refyü'tāshən\ n —re-fut-er \ri'fyütər\ n

re-gain \ri'gān\ vb : get again

re-gal \'rēgəl\ adj 1 : befitting a king 2 : stately —re-gal-ly adv

re-gale \ri'gāl\ vb -galed; -gal-ing 1 : entertain richly or agreeably 2 : delight —re-gale-ment n

re-ga-lia \ri'gālyə\ n pl 1 : symbols of royalty 2 : insignia of an office or order 3 : finery

re-gard \ri'gärd\ n 1 : consideration 2 : feeling of approval and liking 3 : friendly greetings 4 : relation ~ vb 1 : pay attention to 2 : show respect for 3 : have an opinion of 4 : look at 5 : relate to —re-gard-ful adj —re-gard-less adj

re-gard-ing prep : concerning

re-gard-less of \ri'gärdləs-\ prep : in spite of

re-gen-er-ate \ri'jen(ə)rət\ adj 1 : formed or created again 2 : spiritually reborn ~ vb 1 : reform completely 2 : get new life —re-gen-er-a-tion \-₁jenə'rāshən\ n —re-gen-er-a-tive \-'jenə₁rātiv\ adj —re-gen-er-a-tor \-₁rātər\ n

re-gent \'rējənt\ n 1 : person who rules during the childhood, absence, or incapacity of the sovereign 2 : member of a governing board —re-gen-cy \-jənsē\ n

re-gime \rā'zhēm, ri-\ n : government in power

reg-i-men \'rejəmən\ n : systematic course of treatment

reg-i-ment \'rejəmənt\ n : military unit ~ \-₁ment\ vb : organize rigidly for control —reg-i-men-tal \₁rejə'ment³l\ adj —reg-i-men-ta-tion \-mən'tāshən\ n

re-gion \'rējən\ n : indefinitely defined area —re-gion-al \'rēj(ə)nəl\ adj —re-gion-al-ly adv

reg-is-ter \'rejəstər\ n 1 : record of items or details or a book for keeping such a record 2 : device to regulate ventilation 3 : counting or recording device 4 : range of a voice or instrument ~ vb 1 : enter in a register 2 : record automatically 3 : get special care for mail by paying more postage

reg-is-trar \'rejə₁strär\ n : official keeper of records

reg-is-tra-tion \₁rejə'strāshən\ n 1 : act of registering 2 : entry in a register

re-gress \ri'gres\ vb : go or cause to go back or to a lower level —re-gres-sion \-'greshən\ n —re-gres-sive adj —re-gres-sor \-'gresər\ n

re-gret \ri'gret\ vb -tt- 1 : mourn the loss or death of 2 : be keenly sorry for ~ n 1 : sorrow or the expression of sorrow 2 pl : message declining an invitation —re-gret-ful \-fəl\ adj —re-gret-ful-ly adv —re-gret-ta-ble \-əbəl\ adj —re-gret-ta-bly \-blē\ adv —re-gret-ter n

reg-u-lar \'regyələr\ adj 1 : conforming to what is usual, normal, or average 2 : steady, uniform, or unvarying —regular n —reg-u-lar-i-ty \₁regyə'larətē\ n —reg-u-lar-ize \'regyələ₁rīz\ vb —reg-u-lar-ly adv

reg-u-late \'regyə₁lāt\ vb -lat-ed; -lat-ing 1 : govern according to rule 2 : adjust to a standard —reg-u-la-tive \-₁lātiv\ adj —reg-u-la-tor \-₁lātər\ n —reg-u-la-to-ry \-lə₁tōrē\ adj

reg-u-la-tion \₁regyə'lāshən\ n 1 : act of regulating 2 : rule dealing with details of procedure

re-gur-gi-tate \rē'gərjə₁tāt\ vb -tat-ed; -tat-ing : vomit —re-gur-gi-ta-tion \-₁gərjə'tāshən\ n

re-ha-bil-i-tate \₁rē(h)ə'bilə₁tāt\ vb -tat-ed; -tat-ing 1 : reinstate 2 : make good or usable again —re-ha-bil-i-ta-tion \-₁bilə'tāshən\ n —re-ha-bil-i-ta-tive \-₁tātiv\ adj

re-hears-al \ri'hərsəl\ n : practice session or performance

re-hearse \-'hərs\ vb -hearsed; -hears-ing 1 : repeat or recount 2 : engage in a rehearsal of —re-hears-er n

reign \'rān\ n 1 : sovereign's authority or rule ~ vb : rule as a sovereign

re-im-burse \₁rēəm'bərs\ vb -bursed; -burs-ing : repay —re-im-burs-able adj —re-im-burse-ment n

rein \'rān\ n 1 : line of a bridle to control an animal 2 : restraining influence ~ vb : direct by reins

re-in-car-na-tion \₁rē₁in₁kär'nāshən\ n : rebirth of the soul —re-in-car-nate \₁rēin'kär₁nāt\ vb

rein-deer \'rān₁diər\ n : large deer of northern regions

re-in-force \₁rēən'fōrs\ vb : strengthen or support —re-in-force-ment n —re-in-forc-er n

re-in-state \₁rēən'stāt\ vb : restore to a former position —re-in-state-ment n

re-it-er-ate \rē'itə₁rāt\ vb : say again —re-it-er-a-tion \-₁itə'rāshən\ n

re·ject \ri'jekt\ vb 1 : refuse to acknowledge or grant 2 : refuse to accept or keep ~ \'re-\ n : rejected person or thing —**re·jec·tion** \-'jekshən\ n

re·joice \ri'jȯis\ vb -joiced; -joic·ing : feel joy —**re·joic·er** n —**re·joic·ing** n

re·join vb 1 \'re¹jȯin\ : join again 2 \ri¹-\ : say in answer

re·join·der \ri'jȯindər\ n : answer

re·ju·ve·nate \ri'jüvə₁nāt\ vb -nat·ed; -nat·ing : make young again —**re·ju·ve·na·tion** \-₁jüvə'nāshən\ n

re·lapse \ri'laps, 're₁laps\ n : recurrence of illness after a period of improvement ~ \ri¹-\ vb : suffer a relapse

re·late \ri'lāt\ vb -lat·ed; -lat·ing 1 : give a report of 2 : show a connection between 3 : have a relationship —**re·lat·able** adj —**re·lat·er** n

re·la·tion \-'lāshən\ n 1 : account 2 : connection : relationship 4 : reference 5 pl : dealings

re·la·tion·ship \-₁ship\ n : the state of being related or interrelated

rel·a·tive \'relətiv\ n : person connected with another by blood or marriage ~ adj : considered in comparison with something else —**rel·a·tive·ly** adv —**rel·a·tive·ness** n

re·lax \ri'laks\ vb 1 : make or become less tense or rigid 2 : make less severe 3 : seek rest or recreation —**re·lax·er** n

re·lax·ation \₁rē₁lak'sāshən\ n 1 : lessening of tension 2 : recreation

re·lay \'rē₁lā\ n : fresh supply (as of horses or people) arranged to relieve others ~ \'rē₁-, ri¹-\ vb -layed; -lay·ing : pass along in stages

re·lease \ri'lēs\ vb -leased; -leas·ing 1 : free from confinement or oppression 2 : relinquish 3 : permit publication or performance ~ n 1 : relief from trouble 2 : discharge from an obligation 3 : act of releasing or what is released

rel·e·gate \'relə₁gāt\ vb -gat·ed; -gat·ing 1 : remove to some less prominent position 2 : assign to a particular class or sphere —**rel·e·ga·tion** \₁relə'gāshən\ n

re·lent \ri'lent\ vb : become less severe

re·lent·less \-ləs\ adj : mercilessly severe or persistent —**re·lent·less·ly** adv —**re·lent·less·ness** n

rel·e·vance \'reləvəns\ n : relation to the matter at hand —**rel·e·vant** \-vənt\ adj —**rel·e·vant·ly** adv

re·li·able \ri'līəbəl\ adj : fit to be trusted —**re·li·a·bil·i·ty** \-₁līə'bilətē\ n —**re·li·able·ness** n —**re·li·ably** \-'līəblē\ adv

re·li·ance \ri'līəns\ n : act or result of relying —**re·li·ant** \-ənt\ adj

rel·ic \'relik\ n 1 : object venerated because of its association with a saint or martyr 2 : remaining trace

re·lief \ri'lēf\ n 1 : lightening of something oppressive 2 : aid in the form of money or necessities (as for the elderly)

re·lieve \ri'lēv\ vb -lieved; -liev·ing 1 : free from a burden or distress 2 : release from a post or duty 3 : break the monotony of —**re·liev·er** n

re·li·gion \ri'lijən\ n 1 : service and worship of God 2 : organized system of faith and worship —**re·li·gion·ist** n

re·li·gious \-'lijəs\ adj 1 : relating or devoted to the divine 2 : relating to religious beliefs or observances —**re·li·gious·ly** adv

re·lin·quish \-'liŋkwish, -'lin-\ vb 1 : renounce 2 : let go of —**re·lin·quish·ment** n

rel·ish \'relish\ n 1 : keen enjoyment 2 : highly seasoned sauce (as of pickles) ~ vb : enjoy —**rel·ish·able** adj

re·live \(')rē'liv\ vb : live over again (as in the imagination)

re·lo·cate \(')rē'lō₁kāt, ₁rēlō'kāt\ vb : move to a new location —**re·lo·ca·tion** \₁rēlō'kāshən\ n

re·luc·tance \ri'ləktəns\ n : state of being reluctant

re·luc·tant \-tənt\ adj : holding back (as from acting) —**re·luc·tant·ly** adv

re·ly \ri'lī\ vb -lied; -ly·ing : place faith or confidence—often with on

re·main \ri'mān\ vb 1 : be left after others have been removed 2 : be something yet to be done 3 : stay behind 4 : continue unchanged

re·main·der \-'māndər\ n : that which is left over

re·mains \-'mānz\ n pl 1 : remaining part or trace 2 : dead body

re·mark \ri'märk\ vb : express as an observation ~ n : passing comment

re·mark·able \-'märkəbəl\ adj : extraordinary —**re·mark·able·ness** n —**re·mark·ably** \-blē\ adv

re·me·di·al \ri'mēdēəl\ adj : intended to remedy or improve —**re·me·di·al·ly** adv

rem·e·dy \'remədē\ n, pl -dies 1 : medicine that cures 2 : something that corrects an evil or compensates for a loss ∼ *vb* -**died;** -**dy·ing** : provide or serve as a remedy for

re·mem·ber \ri'membər\ *vb* **1** : recall to mind **2** : keep from forgetting **3** : convey greetings from

re·mem·brance \-brəns\ *n* **1** : act of remembering **2** : something that serves to bring to mind

re·mind \ri'mīnd\ *vb* : cause to remember —**re·mind·er** *n*

rem·i·nisce \,remə'nis\ *vb* -**nisced;** -**nisc·ing** : indulge in reminiscence

rem·i·nis·cence \-'nisⁿns\ *n* **1** : recalling of a past experience **2** : account of a memorable experience

rem·i·nis·cent \-ⁿnt\ *adj* **1** : relating to reminiscence **2** : serving to remind —**rem·i·nis·cent·ly** *adv*

re·miss \ri'mis\ *adj* : negligent or careless in performance of duty —**re·miss·ly** *adv* —**re·miss·ness** *n*

re·mis·sion \ri'mishən\ *n* **1** : act of forgiving **2** : a period of relief from or easing of symptoms of a disease

re·mit \ri'mit\ *vb* -**tt-** **1** : pardon **2** : send money in payment

re·mit·tance \ri'mitⁿns\ *n* : sum of money remitted

rem·nant \'remnənt\ *n* : small part or trace remaining

re·mod·el \'re'mädⁿl\ *vb* : alter the structure of

re·mon·strance \ri'mänstrəns\ *n* : act or instance of remonstrating

re·mon·strate \ri'män,strāt\ *vb* -**strated;** -**strat·ing** : speak in protest, reproof, or opposition —**re·mon·stra·tion** \ri,män'strāshən, remən-\ *n* —**re·mon·stra·tor** \ri'män,strātər\ *n*

re·morse \ri'mȯrs\ *n* : distress arising from a sense of guilt —**re·morse·ful** *adj* —**re·morse·less** *adj*

re·mote \ri'mōt\ *adj* -**mot·er;** -**est 1** : far off in place or time **2** : hard to reach or find **3** : slight **4** : distant in manner —**re·mote·ly** *adv* —**re·mote·ness** *n*

re·move \ri'müv\ *vb* -**moved;** -**mov·ing 1** : move by lifting or taking off or away **2** : get rid of —**re·mov·able** *adj* —**re·mov·al** \-vəl\ *n* —**re·mov·er** *n*

re·mu·ner·ate \ri'myünə,rāt\ *vb* -**at·ed;** -**at·ing** : pay —**re·mu·ner·a·tion** —**re·mu·ner·a·tor** \-,rātər\ *n* —**re·mu·ner·a·to·ry** \-rə,tȯrē\ *adj*

re·mu·ner·a·tive \ri'myünərətiv, -,rāt-\ *adj* : gainful —**re·mu·ner·a·tive·ly** *adv* —**re·mu·ner·a·tive·ness** *n*

re·nais·sance \,renə'säns, -'zäns\ *n* : rebirth or revival

re·nal \'rēnⁿl\ *adj* : relating to the kidneys

rend \'rend\ *vb* **rent** \'rent\; **rend·ing** : tear apart forcibly

ren·der \'rendər\ *vb* **1** : extract by heating **2** : hand over or give up **3** : do (a service) for another **4** : cause to be or become

ren·dez·vous \'rändi,vü, -dā-\ *n*, *pl* **ren·dez·vous** \-,vüz\ **1** : place appointed for a meeting **2** : meeting at an appointed place ∼ *vb* -**voused;** -**vous·ing** : meet at a rendezvous

ren·di·tion \ren'dishən\ *n* : version

ren·e·gade \'reni,gād\ *n* : one who deserts one faith or cause for another

re·nege \ri'neg, -'neg, -'nēg, -'näg\ *vb* -**neged;** -**neg·ing** : go back on a promise —**re·neg·er** *n*

re·new \ri'n(y)ü\ *vb* **1** : make or become new, fresh, or strong again **2** : begin again **3** : grant or obtain an extension of —**re·new·able** *adj* —**re·new·al** *n* —**re·new·er** *n*

re·nounce \ri'naúns\ *vb* -**nounced;** -**nounc·ing** : give up, refuse, or resign —**re·nounce·ment** *n*

ren·o·vate \'renə,vāt\ *vb* -**vat·ed;** -**vat·ing** : make like new again —**ren·o·va·tion** \,renə'vāshən\ *n* —**ren·o·va·tor** \'renə,vātər\ *n*

re·nown \ri'naún\ *n* : state of being widely known and honored —**re·nowned** \-'naúnd\ *adj*

¹**rent** \'rent\ *n* : money paid or due for the use of another's property ∼ *vb* : hold or give possession and use of for rent —**rent·al** *n* or *adj* —**rent·er** *n*

²**rent** : a tear in cloth

re·nun·ci·a·tion \ri,nənsē'āshən\ *n* : act of renouncing

¹**re·pair** \ri'paər\ *vb* : go

²**re·pair** : restore to good condition ∼ *n* **1** : act or instance of repairing **2** : condition —**re·pair·er** *n* —**re·pair·man** \-,man\ *n*

rep·a·ra·tion \,repə'rāshən\ *n* : money paid for redress—usu. pl.

rep·ar·tee \,repər'tē\ *n* : clever replies

re·past \ri'past, 're',past\ *n* : meal

re·pa·tri·ate \re'pātrē,āt\ *vb* -**at·ed;** -**at·ing** : send back to one's own country —**re·pa·tri·ate** \-trēət, -trē,āt\ *n* —**re·pa·tri·a·tion** \-,pātrē'āshən\ *n*

re·pay \ri'pā\ *vb* -**paid;** -**pay·ing** : pay back —**re·pay·able** *adj* —**re·pay·ment** *n*

re·peal \ri'pēl\ *vb* : annul by legislative action —**repeal** *n* —**re·peal·er** *n*

re·peat \ri'pēt\ *vb* : say or do again ∼ *n* **1** : act of repeating **2** : something repeated —**re·peat·able** *adj* —**re·peat·ed·ly** *adv* —**re·peat·er** *n*

re·pel \ri'pel\ vb **-pelled; -pel·ling** 1 : drive away 2 : disgust —**re·pel·lent** \-'pelənt\ adj or n

re·pent \ri'pent\ vb 1 : turn from sin 2 : regret —**re·pen·tance** \ri'pentⁿns\ n —**re·pen·tant** \-ⁿnt\ adj

re·per·cus·sion \,rēpər'kəshən, ,repər-\ n : effect of something done or said

rep·er·toire \'repə(r),twär\ n : pieces or parts a company or performer can present

rep·er·to·ry \'repə(r),tōrē\ n, pl **-ries** 1 : repertoire 2 : theater with a resident company doing several plays

rep·e·ti·tion \,repə'tishən\ n : act or instance of repeating

rep·e·ti·tious \-'tishəs\ adj : tediously repeating —**rep·e·ti·tious·ly** adv —**rep·e·ti·tious·ness** n

re·pet·i·tive \ri'petətiv\ adj : repetitious —**re·pet·i·tive·ly** adv —**re·pet·i·tive·ness** n

re·pine \ri'pīn\ vb **re·pined; re·pin·ing** : feel or express discontent

re·place \ri'plās\ vb 1 : restore to a former position 2 : take the place of 3 : put something new in the place of —**re·place·able** adj —**re·place·ment** n —**re·plac·er** n

re·plen·ish \ri'plenish\ vb : stock or supply anew —**re·plen·ish·ment** n

re·plete \ri'plēt\ adj : full —**re·plete·ness** n —**re·ple·tion** \-'plēshən\ n

rep·li·ca \'replikə\ n : copy

rep·li·cate \'replə,kāt\ vb **-cat·ed; -cat·ing** : duplicate or repeat —**rep·li·cate** \-likət\ n

re·ply \ri'plī\ vb **-plied; -ply·ing** : say or do in answer ~ n, pl **-plies** : answer

re·port \ri'pōrt\ n 1 : rumor 2 : statement of information (as events or causes) 3 : explosive noise ~ vb 1 : give an account of 2 : present an account of (an event) as news 3 : present oneself 4 : make known to authorities —**re·port·age** \ri'pōrtij, ,repər'täzh, ,rep,ȯr'-\ n —**re·port·ed·ly** adv —**re·port·er** n —**re·por·to·ri·al** \,repə(r)'tōrēəl\ adj

re·pose \ri'pōz\ vb **-posed; -pos·ing** : lay or lie at rest ~ n 1 : state of resting 2 : calm or peace —**re·pose·ful** adj

re·pos·i·to·ry \ri'päzə,tōrē\ n, pl **-ries** : place where something is stored

re·pos·sess \,rēpə'zes\ vb : regain possession and legal ownership of —**re·pos·ses·sion** \-'zeshən\ n

rep·re·hend \,repri'hend\ vb : express disapproval of —**rep·re·hen·si·ble**

\-'hensəbəl\ adj —**rep·re·hen·si·bly** adv —**rep·re·hen·sion** \-'henchən\ n

rep·re·sent \,repri'zent\ vb 1 : serve as a sign or symbol of 2 : act or speak for 3 : describe as having a specified quality or character —**rep·re·sen·ta·tion** \,repri,zen'tāshən\ n

rep·re·sen·ta·tive \,repri'zentativ\ adj 1 : standing or acting for another 2 : carried on by elected representatives ~ n 1 : typical example 2 : one that represents another 3 : member of usu. the lower house of a legislature —**rep·re·sen·ta·tive·ly** adv —**rep·re·sen·ta·tive·ness** n

re·press \ri'pres\ vb : restrain or suppress —**re·pres·sion** \-'preshən\ n —**re·pres·sive** \-'presiv\ adj

re·prieve \ri'prēv\ vb **-prieved; -priev·ing** : delay the punishment or execution of —**reprieve** n

rep·ri·mand \'reprə,mand\ n : formal reproof —**reprimand** vb

re·pri·sal \ri'prīzəl\ n : act in retaliation

re·prise \ri'prēz\ n : musical repetition

re·proach \ri'prōch\ n 1 : disgrace 2 : rebuke ~ vb : express disapproval to —**re·proach·ful** adj —**re·proach·ful·ly** adv —**re·proach·ful·ness** n

rep·ro·bate \'reprə,bāt\ n : scoundrel —**reprobate** adj

rep·ro·ba·tion \,reprə'bāshən\ n : strong disapproval

re·pro·duce \,rēprə'd(y)üs\ vb 1 : produce again or anew 2 : bear offspring —**re·pro·duc·ible** \-'d(y)üsəbəl\ adj —**re·pro·duc·tion** \-'dəkshən\ n —**re·pro·duc·tive** \-'dəktiv\ adj

re·proof \ri'prüf\ n : blame or censure for a fault

re·prove \ri'prüv\ vb **-proved; -prov·ing** : express disapproval to or of —**re·prov·er** n

rep·tile \'reptⁿl, -,tīl\ n : air-breathing scaly vertebrate —**rep·til·i·an** \rep'tilēən\ adj or n

re·pub·lic \ri'pəblik\ n : country with representative government

re·pub·li·can \-likən\ adj 1 : relating to or resembling a republic 2 : supporting a republic —**republican** n —**re·pub·li·can·ism** n

re·pu·di·ate \ri'pyüdē,āt\ vb **-at·ed; -at·ing** : refuse to have anything to do with —**re·pu·di·a·tion** \-,pyüdē'āshən\ n —**re·pu·di·a·tor** \-'pyüdē,ātər\ n

re·pug·nant \ri'pəgnənt\ adj : contrary to one's tastes or principles —**re·pug·nance** \-nəns\ n —**re·pug·nant·ly** adv

re·pulse \ri'pəls\ vb -pulsed; -puls·ing 1 : drive or beat back 2 : rebuff 3 : be repugnant to —repulse n —re·pul·sion \-'pəlshən\ n

re·pul·sive \-siv\ adj : arousing aversion or disgust —re·pul·sive·ly adv —re·pul·sive·ness n

rep·u·ta·ble \'repyətəbəl\ adj : having a good reputation —rep·u·ta·bly \-blē\ adv

rep·u·ta·tion \,repyə'tāshən\ n : one's character or public esteem

re·pute \ri'pyüt\ vb -put·ed; -put·ing : think of as being ~ n : reputation —re·put·ed adj —re·put·ed·ly adv

re·quest \ri'kwest\ n : act or instance of asking for something or a thing asked for ~ vb 1 : make a request of 2 : ask for —re·quest·er n

re·qui·em \'rekwēəm, 'rāk-\ n : Mass for a dead person or a musical setting for this

re·quire \ri'kwī(ə)r\ vb -quired; -quir·ing 1 : insist on 2 : call for as essential —re·quire·ment n

req·ui·site \'rekwəzət\ adj : necessary —requisite n

req·ui·si·tion \,rekwə'zishən\ n : formal application or demand —requisition vb

re·quite \ri'kwīt\ vb -quit·ed; -quit·ing : make return for or to —re·quit·al \-'kwīt²l\ n

re·scind \ri'sind\ vb : repeal or cancel —re·scind·er n —re·scis·sion \-'sizhən\ n

res·cue \'reskyü\ vb -cued; -cu·ing : set free from danger or confinement —rescue n —res·cu·er n

re·search \ri'sərch, 'rē,sərch\ n : careful or diligent search esp. for new knowledge —research vb —re·search·er n

re·sem·ble \ri'zembəl\ vb -sem·bled; -sem·bling : be like or similar to —re·sem·blance \-'zemblans\ n

re·sent \ri'zent\ vb : feel or show annoyance at —re·sent·ful adj —re·sent·ful·ly adv —re·sent·ment n

res·er·va·tion \,rezər'vāshən\ n 1 : act of reserving or something reserved 2 : limiting condition

re·serve \ri'zərv\ vb -served; -serv·ing 1 : store for future use 2 : set aside for special use ~ n 1 : something reserved 2 : restraint in words or bearing 3 : military forces withheld from action or not part of the regular services —re·served adj

res·er·voir \'rezə(r)v,wär, -ə(r)v₁(w)ȯr, -ər,vȯil\ n : place where something (as water) is kept in store

re·side \ri'zīd\ vb -sid·ed; -sid·ing 1 : make one's home 2 : be present

res·i·dence \'rezədəns\ n 1 : act or fact of residing in a place 2 : place where one lives —res·i·dent \-ənt\ adj or n —res·i·den·tial \,rezə'denchəl\ adj

res·i·due \'rezə,d(y)ü\ n : part remaining —re·sid·u·al \ri'zij(ə)wəl\ adj

re·sign \ri'zīn\ vb 1 : give up deliberately 2 : give (oneself) over without resistance —res·ig·na·tion \,rezig'nāshən\ n

re·signed \ri'zīnd\ adj : submissive —re·sign·ed·ly \-'zīnədlē\ adv

re·sil·ience \ri'zilyəns\ n : ability to recover or adjust easily

re·sil·ien·cy \-yənsē\ n : resilience

re·sil·ient \-yənt\ adj : elastic

res·in \'rez²n\ n : substance from the gum or sap of trees —res·in·ous adj

re·sist \ri'zist\ vb 1 : withstand the force or effect of 2 : fight against —re·sist·ible, re·sist·able \-'zistəbəl\ adj —re·sist·less adj

re·sis·tance \ri'zistəns\ n 1 : act of resisting 2 : opposition to electric current

re·sis·tant \-tənt\ adj : giving resistance

res·o·lute \'rezə,lüt\ adj : having a fixed purpose —res·o·lute·ly adv —res·o·lute·ness n

res·o·lu·tion \,rezə'lüshən\ n 1 : process of resolving 2 : firmness of purpose 3 : statement of the opinion, will, or intent of a body

re·solve \ri'zälv\ vb -solved; -solv·ing 1 : find an answer to 2 : make a formal resolution ~ n 1 : something resolved 2 : steadfast purpose —re·solv·able adj

res·o·nant \'rez²nənt\ adj 1 : continuing to sound 2 : relating to intensification or prolongation of sound (as by a vibrating body) —res·o·nance \-ons\ n —res·o·nant·ly adv

re·sort \ri'zȯrt\ n 1 : source of help 2 : place to go for vacation ~ vb 1 : go often or habitually 2 : have recourse

re·sound \ri'zaūnd\ vb : become filled with sound

re·sound·ing \-iŋ\ adj : impressive —re·sound·ing·ly adv

re·source \'rē,sȯrs, ri'sȯrs\ n 1 : new or reserve source 2 pl : available funds 3 : ability to handle situations —re·source·ful adj —re·source·ful·ness n

re·spect \ri'spekt\ n 1 : relation to something 2 : high or special regard 3 : detail ~ vb : consider deserving of high regard —re·spect·er n —re·

spect·ful \-fəl\ adj —re·spect·ful·ly adv —re·spect·ful·ness n

re·spect·able \ri'spektəbəl\ adj 1 : worthy of respect 2 : fair in size, quantity, or quality —re·spect·abil·i·ty \-,spektə'bilətē\ n —re·spect·ably \-'spektəblē\ adv

re·spec·tive \-tiv\ adj : individual and specific

re·spec·tive·ly \-lē\ adv 1 : as relating to each 2 : each in the order given

res·pi·ra·tion \,respə'rāshən\ n 1 : act or process of breathing 2 : energy-yielding oxidation in living matter —re·spi·ra·to·ry \'resp(ə)rə,tōrē, ri'spīrə-\ adj —re·spire \ri'spī(ə)r\ vb

res·pi·ra·tor \'respə,rātər\ n : device for artificial respiration

re·spite \'respət\ n : temporary delay or rest

re·splen·dent \ri'splendənt\ adj : shining brilliantly —re·splen·dence \-dəns\ n —re·splen·dent·ly adv

re·spond \ri'spänd\ vb 1 : answer 2 : react —re·spon·dent \-'spändənt\ n or adj —re·spond·er n

re·sponse \ri'späns\ n 1 : act of responding 2 : answer

re·spon·si·ble \ri'spänsəbəl\ adj 1 : answerable for acts or decisions 2 : able to fulfill obligations 3 : having important duties —re·spon·si·bil·i·ty \ri,spänsə'bilətē\ n —re·spon·si·ble·ness n —re·spon·si·bly \-blē\ adv

re·spon·sive \-siv\ adj : quick to respond —re·spon·sive·ly adv —re·spon·sive·ness n

¹rest \'rest\ n 1 : sleep 2 : freedom from work or activity 3 : state of inactivity 4 : something used as a support ~ vb 1 : get rest 2 : cease action or motion 3 : give rest to 4 : sit or lie fixed or supported 5 : depend —rest·ful adj —rest·ful·ly adv

²rest n : remainder

res·tau·rant \'rest(ə)rənt, -tə,ränt\ n : public eating place

res·ti·tu·tion \,restə't(y)üshən\ n : act or fact of restoring something or repaying someone

res·tive \'restiv\ adj : uneasy or fidgety —res·tive·ly adv —res·tive·ness n

rest·less \'restləs\ adj 1 : lacking or giving no rest 2 : never resting or ceasing 3 : lacking in repose —rest·less·ly adv —rest·less·ness n

re·store \ri'stōr\ vb -stored; -stor·ing 1 : give back 2 : put back into use or into a former state —re·stor·able adj —res·to·ra·tion \,restə'rāshən\ n

—re·stor·a·tive \ri'stōrətiv\ n or adj —re·stor·er n

re·strain \ri'strān\ vb : limit or keep under control —re·strain·able adj —re·strained \-'strānd\ adj —re·strain·ed·ly \-'strānədlē\ adv —re·strain·er n

re·straint \-'strānt\ n 1 : act of restraining 2 : restraining force 3 : control over feelings

re·strict \ri'strikt\ vb 1 : confine within bounds 2 : limit use of —re·stric·tion \-'strikshən\ n —re·stric·tive \-'striktiv\ adj —re·stric·tive·ly adv

re·sult \ri'zəlt\ vb 1 : come about because of something else 2 : end ~ n 1 : thing that results 2 : something obtained by calculation or investigation —re·sul·tant \-'zəlt⁹nt\ adj or n

re·sume \ri'züm\ vb -sumed; -sum·ing : return to or take up again after interruption —re·sump·tion \-'zəmpshən\ n

ré·su·mé \'rezə,mā, ,rezə'-\ n : summary of one's career and qualifications

re·sur·gence \ri'sərjəns\ n : a rising again —re·sur·gent \-jənt\ adj

res·ur·rect \,rezə'rekt\ vb 1 : raise from the dead 2 : bring to attention or use again —res·ur·rec·tion \-'rekshən\ n

re·sus·ci·tate \ri'səsə,tāt\ vb -tat·ed; -tat·ing : revive from a deathlike condition —re·sus·ci·ta·tion \ri,səsə'tāshən, ,rē-\ n —re·sus·ci·ta·tor \-,tātər\ n

re·tail \'rē,tāl\ vb : sell in small quantities directly to the consumer ~ n : business of selling to consumers —retail adj or adv —re·tail·er n

re·tain \ri'tān\ vb 1 : keep or hold onto 2 : engage the services of

re·tain·er n 1 : household servant 2 : retaining fee

re·tal·i·ate \ri'talē,āt\ vb -at·ed; -at·ing : get revenge —re·tal·i·a·tion \-,talē'āshən\ n —re·tal·i·a·to·ry \-'talyə,tōrē\ adj

re·tard \ri'tärd\ vb : hold back —re·tar·da·tion \,rē,tär'dāshən, ri-\ n —re·tard·er n

re·tard·ed \ri'tärdəd\ adj : slow or limited in intellectual development

retch \'rech, 'rēch\ vb : try to vomit

re·ten·tion \ri'tenchən\ n 1 : state of being retained 2 : ability to retain —re·ten·tive \-'tentiv\ adj

ret·i·cent \'retəsənt\ adj : inclined to be silent or secretive —ret·i·cence \-səns\ n —ret·i·cent·ly adv

ret·i·na \'ret⁰n⁰\ *n, pl* **-nas** *or* **-nae** \-⁰n₁ē\ : sensory membrane lining the eye —**ret·i·nal** \'ret⁰nəl\ *adj*

ret·i·nue \'ret⁰n₁(y)ü\ *n* : attendants or followers of a distinguished person

re·tire \ri'tī(ə)r\ *vb* **-tired; -tir·ing** 1 : withdraw for privacy 2 : end a career 3 : go to bed —**re·tir·ee** \ri₁tī'rē\ *n* —**re·tire·ment** *n*

re·tir·ing \ri'tī(ə)riŋ\ *adj* : shy or reserved

¹re·tort \ri'tȯrt\ *vb* : say in reply — *n* 1 : quick, witty, or cutting answer

²re·tort \ri'tȯrt, 'rē₁tȯrt\ *n* : vessel in which substances are distilled or broken up by heat

re·trace \(')rē'trās\ *vb* 1 : trace again 2 : go over again in reverse

re·tract \ri'trakt\ *vb* 1 : to draw back or in 2 : withdraw a charge or promise —**re·tract·able** *adj* —**re·trac·tion** \-'trakshən\ *n*

re·treat \ri'trēt\ *n* 1 : act of withdrawing 2 : place of privacy or safety or meditation and study ~ *vb* : make a retreat

re·trench \ri'trench\ *vb* : cut down (as expenses) —**re·trench·ment** *n*

ret·ri·bu·tion \₁retrə'byüshən\ *n* : retaliation —**re·trib·u·tive** \ri'tribyətiv\ *adj* —**re·trib·u·to·ry** \-yə₁tōrē\ *adj*

re·trieve \ri'trēv\ *vb* **-trieved; -triev·ing** 1 : search for and bring in game 2 : recover —**re·triev·able** *adj* —**re·triev·al** \-'trēvəl\ *n*

re·triev·er \-'trēvər\ *n* : dog for retrieving game

ret·ro·ac·tive \₁retrō'aktiv\ *adj* : made effective as of a prior date —**ret·ro·ac·tive·ly** *adv*

ret·ro·grade \'retrə₁grād\ *adj* 1 : moving backward 2 : becoming worse

ret·ro·gress \₁retrə'gres\ *vb* : move backward —**ret·ro·gres·sion** \-'greshən\ *n*

ret·ro·spect \'retrə₁spekt\ *n* : review of past events —**ret·ro·spec·tion** \₁retrə'spekshən\ *n* —**ret·ro·spec·tive** \-'spektiv\ *adj* —**ret·ro·spec·tive·ly** *adv*

re·turn \ri'tərn\ *vb* 1 : go or come back 2 : pass, give, or send back to an earlier possessor 3 : answer 4 : bring in as a profit 5 : give or do in return ~ *n* 1 : act of returning or something returned 2 *pl* : report of balloting results 3 : statement of taxable income 4 : profit —**return** *adj* —**re·turn·able** *adj* —**re·turn·er** *n*

re·union \rē'yünyən\ *n* 1 : act of re-

uniting 2 : meeting of persons who have been separated

re·vamp \(')rē'vamp\ *vb* : give a new form to old materials

re·veal \ri'vēl\ *vb* 1 : make known 2 : show plainly

re·veil·le \'revəlē\ *n* : military signal sounded about sunrise

rev·el \'revəl\ *vb* **-eled** *or* **-elled; -el·ing** *or* **-el·ling** 1 : take part in a revel 2 : take great delight ~ *n* : wild party or celebration —**rev·el·er, rev·el·ler** \-ər\ *n* —**rev·el·ry** \-rē\ *n*

rev·e·la·tion \₁revə'lāshən\ *n* 1 : act of revealing 2 : something enlightening or astonishing

re·venge \ri'venj\ *vb* **-venged; -veng·ing** : inflict harm or injury in return for a wrong ~ *n* 1 : act of revenging 2 : desire to return evil —**re·venge·ful** *adj* —**re·veng·er** *n*

rev·e·nue \'revə₁n(y)ü\ *n* : money collected by a government

re·ver·ber·ate \ri'vərbə₁rāt\ *vb* **-at·ed; -at·ing** : resound in a series of echoes —**re·ver·ber·a·tion** \-₁vərbə'rāshən\ *n*

re·vere \ri'viər\ *vb* **-vered; -ver·ing** : show honor and devotion to —**rev·er·ence** \'rev(ə)rəns\ *n* —**rev·er·ent** \-rənt\ *adj* —**rev·er·ent·ly** *adv*

rev·er·end \'rev(ə)rənd\ *adj* : worthy of reverence ~ *n* : clergyman

rev·er·ie, rev·ery \'rev(ə)rē\ *n, pl* **-er·ies** : daydream

re·verse \ri'vərs\ *adj* 1 : opposite to a previous or normal condition 2 : acting in an opposite way ~ *vb* **-versed; -vers·ing** 1 : turn upside down or completely around 2 : change to the contrary or in the opposite direction ~ *n* 1 : something contrary 2 : change for the worse 3 : back of something —**re·ver·sal** \-səl\ *n* —**re·verse·ly** *adv* —**re·vers·ible** \-'vərsəbəl\ *adj*

re·vert \ri'vərt\ *vb* : return to an original type or condition —**re·ver·sion** \-'vərzhən\ *n*

re·view \ri'vyü\ *n* 1 : formal inspection 2 : general survey 3 : critical evaluation 4 : second or repeated study or examination ~ *vb* 1 : examine or study again 2 : reexamine judicially 3 : view in retrospect 4 : write a critical examination of 5 : inspect —**re·view·er** *n*

re·vile \ri'vīl\ *vb* **-viled; -vil·ing** : abuse verbally —**re·vile·ment** *n* —**re·vil·er** *n*

re·vise \ri'vīz\ *vb* **-vised; -vis·ing** 1 : look over something written to correct or improve **2** : make a new version of —**re·vis·able** *adj* —**revise** *n* —**re·vis·er, re·vi·sor** \-'vīzər\ *n* —**re·vi·sion** \-'vizhən\ *n*

re·viv·al \-'vīvəl\ *n* **1** : act of reviving or state of being revived **2** : evangelistic meeting

re·vive \-'vīv\ *vb* **-vived; -viv·ing 1** : return to consciousness or life **2** : bring back into use —**re·viv·er** *n*

re·vo·ca·tion \,revə'kāshən\ *n* : act or instance of revoking

re·voke \ri'vōk\ *vb* **-voked; -vok·ing** : annul by recalling —**re·vok·er** *n*

re·volt \-'vōlt\ *vb* **1** : throw off allegiance **2** : cause or experience disgust or shock — *n* : rebellion or revolution —**re·volt·er** *n*

rev·o·lu·tion \,revə'lüshən\ *n* **1** : rotation **2** : progress in an orbit **3** : cycle **4** : overthrow of a ruler or government —**rev·o·lu·tion·ary** \-shə,narē\ *adj or n*

rev·o·lu·tion·ize \-shə,nīz\ *vb* **-ized; -iz·ing** : change radically —**rev·o·lu·tion·iz·er** *n*

re·volve \ri'välv\ *vb* **-volved; -volv·ing 1** : ponder **2** : move in an orbit **3** : rotate —**re·volv·able** *adj*

re·volv·er \ri'välvər\ *n* : pistol with a revolving cylinder

re·vue \ri'vyü\ *n* : theatrical production of brief numbers

re·vul·sion \ri'vəlshən\ *n* : complete dislike or repugnance

re·ward \ri'wórd\ *vb* : give a reward to or for — *n* : something offered for service or achievement

rhap·so·dy \'rapsədē\ *n, pl* **-dies 1** : extravagantly rapturous discourse **2** : flowing free-form musical composition —**rhap·sod·ic** \rap'sädik\ *adj* —**rhap·sod·i·cal·ly** \-ik(ə)lē\ *adv* —**rhap·so·dize** \'rapsə,dīz\ *vb*

rhet·o·ric \'retərik\ *n* : art of speaking or writing effectively —**rhe·tor·i·cal** \ri'tórikəl\ *adj* —**rhet·o·ri·cian** \,retə'rishən\ *n*

rheu·ma·tism \'rümə,tizəm, 'rüm-\ *n* : disorder marked by inflammation or pain in muscles or joints —**rheu·mat·ic** \rü'matik\ *adj*

rhine·stone \'rīn,stōn\ *n* : a colorless imitation gem

rhi·no \'rīnō\ *n, pl* **-no** *or* **-nos** : rhinoceros

rhi·noc·er·os \rī'näs(ə)rəs\ *n, pl* **-noc·er·os·es** *or* **-noc·er·os** *or* **-noc·eri** \-'näsə,rī\ : large thick-skinned mammal with 1 or 2 horns on the snout

rho·do·den·dron \,rōdə'dendrən\ *n* : flowering evergreen shrub

rhom·bus \'rämbəs\ *n, pl* **-bus·es** *or* **-bi** \-,bī\ : parallelogram with equal sides and usu. oblique angles

rhu·barb \'rü,bärb\ *n* : garden plant with edible stalks

rhyme \'rīm\ *n* **1** : correspondence in terminal sounds **2** : verse that rhymes — *vb* **rhymed; rhym·ing** : make or have rhymes

rhythm \'riṯhəm\ *n* : regular succession of sounds or motions —**rhyth·mic** \'riṯhmik\, **rhyth·mi·cal** \-mikəl\ —**rhyth·mi·cal·ly** *adv*

rhythm and blues *n* : popular music based on blues and black folk music

rib \'rib\ *n* **1** : curved bone joined to the spine **2** : riblike thing — *vb* **-bb- 1** : furnish or mark with ribs **2** : tease —**rib·ber** *n*

rib·ald \'ribəld\ *adj* : coarse or vulgar —**rib·ald·ry** \-əldrē\ *n*

rib·bon \'ribən\ *n* **1** : narrow strip of fabric used esp. for decoration **2** : strip of inked cloth (as in a typewriter)

ri·bo·fla·vin \,rībō'flāvən, 'rībə,-\ *n* : growth-promoting vitamin

rice \'rīs\ *n, pl* **rice** : edible seeds of an annual cereal grass

rich \'rich\ *adj* **1** : having a lot of money or possessions **2** : valuable **3** : containing much sugar, fat, or seasoning **4** : abundant **5** : deep and pleasing in color or tone **6** : fertile —**rich·ly** *adv* —**rich·ness** *n*

rich·es \'richəz\ *n pl* : wealth

rick·ets \'rikəts\ *n* : childhood bone disease

rick·ety \'rikətē\ *adj* : shaky

rick·sha, rick·shaw \'rik,shav\ *n* : small covered 2-wheeled vehicle pulled by one man

ric·o·chet \'rikə,shā, *Brit also* -,shet\ *vb* **-cheted** \-,shād\ *or* **-chet·ted** \-,shet·əd\; **-chet·ing** \-,shāiŋ\ *or* **-chet·ting** \-,shetiŋ\ : skip with or as if with glancing rebounds —**ricochet** *n*

rid \'rid\ *vb* **rid; rid·ding** : make free of something unwanted —**rid·dance** \'rid²ns\ *n*

rid·den \'rid²l\ *adj* : overburdened with

¹rid·dle \'rid²l\ *n* : puzzling question — *vb* **-dled; -dling** : speak in riddles

²riddle *vb* **-dled; -dling** : fill full of holes

ride \'rīd\ *vb* **rode** \'rōd\; **rid·den** \'rid²n\; **rid·ing** \'rīdiŋ\ **1** : be carried along by an animal or vehicle **2** : sit on and cause to move **3** : travel over a surface 4 : tease or nag ~ n 1 : trip on an animal or in a vehicle 2 : mechanical device ridden for amusement

rid·er \'rīd-ər\ n 1 : one that rides 2 : attached clause or document —**rid·er·less** adj

ridge \'rij\ n 1 : range of hills 2 : raised line or strip 3 : point of intersection of 2 sloping surfaces —**ridgy** adj

rid·i·cule \'rid-ə,kyül\ vb -culed; -cul·ing : laugh at or make fun of —**ridi·cule** n

ri·dic·u·lous \rə'dikyələs\ adj : arousing ridicule —**ri·dic·u·lous·ly** adv —**ri·dic·u·lous·ness** n

rife \'rīf\ adj : abounding —**rife** adv —**rife·ness** n

riff·raff \'rif,raf\ n : mob

¹ri·fle \'rīfəl\ vb -fled; -fling : ransack esp. in order to steal —**ri·fler** \-f(ə)lər\ n

²rifle n : long shoulder weapon with spiral grooves in the bore —**ri·fle·man** \-mən\ n —**ri·fling** n

rift \'rift\ n : separation —**rift** vb

¹rig \'rig\ vb -gg- 1 : fit out with rigging 2 : set up esp. as a makeshift ~ n 1 : distinctive shape, number, and arrangement of sails and masts of a ship 2 : equipment 3 : carriage with its horses

²rig vb -gg- : manipulate esp. by deceptive or dishonest means

rig·ging \'rigiŋ, -ən\ n : lines that hold and move masts, sails, and spars of a ship

right \'rīt\ adj 1 : meeting a standard of conduct 2 : correct 3 : genuine 4 : normal 5 : opposite of left ~ n 1 : something that is correct, just, proper, or honorable 2 : something to which one has a just claim 3 : something that is on the right side ~ adv 1 : according to what is right 2 : immediately 3 : completely 4 : on or to the right ~ vb 1 : restore to a proper state 2 : bring or become upright again —**right·er** n —**right·ness** n —**right·ward** \-wərd\ adj

right angle n : angle bounded by 2 lines perpendicular to each other —**right·an·gled** \'rīt'aŋgəld\ adj

righ·teous \'rīchəs\ adj : acting or being in accordance with what is just or moral —**right·eous·ly** adv —**right·eous·ness** n

right·ful \'rītfəl\ adj : lawful —**right·ful·ly** \-ē\ adv —**right·ful·ness** n

right·ly \'rītlē\ adv 1 : justly 2 : properly 3 : correctly

rig·id \'rijəd\ adj : lacking flexibility —**ri·gid·i·ty** \rə'jidətē\ n —**rig·id·ly** adv

rig·ma·role \'rig(ə)mə,rōl\ n : meaningless talk or procedure

rig·or \'rigər\ n : severity —**rig·or·ous** adj —**rig·or·ous·ly** adv

rig·or mor·tis \,rigər'mórtəs\ n : temporary stiffness of muscles occurring after death

rile \'rīl\ vb riled; ril·ing : anger

rill \'ril\ n : small brook

rim \'rim\ n : edge esp. of something curved ~ vb -mm- 1 : furnish with a rim 2 : run around the rim of

¹rime \'rīm\ n : frostlike ice formed on exposed objects —**rimy** \'rīmē\ adj

²rime var of RHYME

rind \'rīnd\ n : usu. hard or tough outer layer

¹ring \'riŋ\ n 1 : circular band used as an ornament or for holding or fastening 2 : something circular 3 : place for contest or display 4 : group with a selfish or dishonest aim ~ vb : surround —**ringed** adj —**ring-like** adj

²ring vb rang \'raŋ\; rung \'rəŋ\; ring·ing 1 : sound resonantly when struck 2 : cause to make a metallic sound by striking ~ n 1 : resonant sound or tone 2 : act or instance of ringing

ring·er \'riŋər\ n 1 : one that sounds by ringing 2 : illegal substitute

ring·lead·er \'riŋ,lēdər\ n : leader esp. of troublemakers

ring·let n : long curl

ring·worm n : a contagious fungous skin disease

rink \'riŋk\ n : enclosed place for skating

rinse \'rins\ vb rinsed; rins·ing 1 : cleanse usu. with water only 2 : treat (hair) with a rinse ~ n : liquid used for rinsing —**rins·er** n

ri·ot \'rīət\ n 1 : violent public disorder 2 : random or disorderly profusion —**riot** vb —**ri·ot·er** n —**ri·ot·ous** adj

rip \'rip\ vb -pp- : cut or tear open ~ n : rent made by ripping —**rip·per** n

ripe \'rīp\ adj rip·er; rip·est : fully grown, developed, or prepared —**ripe·ly** adv —**rip·en** \'rīpən\ vb —**ripe·ness** n

rip-off n : theft —**rip off** vb

rip·ple \'ripəl\ vb -pled; -pling 1 : become lightly ruffled on the surface 2 : sound like rippling water —**ripple** n

rise \'rīz\ vb rose \'rōz\; ris·en \'riz²n\; ris·ing \'rīziŋ\ 1 : get up from sitting, kneeling, or lying 2 : rebel 3 : appear above the horizon 4 : ascend 5 : gain a higher position or rank **6** : increase ~ *n* **1** : act of rising **2** : origin **3** : elevation **4** : increase **5** : upward slope **6** : area of high ground —**ris·er** \\'rīzər\\ *n*

ris·i·ble \\'rizabəl\\ *adj* **1** : able or inclined to laugh **2** : arousing laughter —**ris·i·bil·i·ty** \\,rizə'bilətē\\ *n*

risk \\'risk\\ *n* : exposure to loss or injury —**risk** *vb* —**risk·i·ness** *n* —**risky** *adj*

ris·qué \\ris'kā\\ *adj* : nearly indecent

rite \\'rīt\\ *n* **1** : set form of conducting a ceremony **2** : liturgy of a church **3** : ceremonial action

rit·u·al \\'richəwəl\\ *n* : rite —**ritual** *adj* —**rit·u·al·ism** \\-,izəm\\ *n* —**rit·u·al·is·tic** \\,richəwəl'istik\\ *adj* —**rit·u·al·is·ti·cal·ly** \\-tik(ə)lē\\ *adv* —**rit·u·al·ly** \\'richəwəlē\\ *adv*

ri·val \\'rīvəl\\ *n* **1** : competitor **2** : peer ~ *vb* -**valed** *or* -**valled**; -**val·ing** *or* -**val·ling 1** : be in competition with **2** : equal —**rival** *adj* —**ri·val·ry** \\-rē\\ *n*

riv·er \\'rivər\\ *n* : natural stream larger than a brook —**riv·er·bank** *n* —**riv·er·bed** *n* —**riv·er·boat** *n* —**riv·er·side** *n*

riv·et \\'rivət\\ *n* : headed metal bolt ~ *vb* : fasten with a rivet —**riv·et·er** *n*

riv·u·let \\'riv(y)ələt\\ *n* : small stream

roach \\'rōch\\ *n* : cockroach

road \\'rōd\\ *n* : open way for vehicles, persons, and animals —**road·bed** *n* —**road·way** *n*

road·block *n* : obstruction on a road

road·run·ner *n* : large fast-running bird

road·side *n* : strip of land along a road —**roadside** *adj*

roam \\'rōm\\ *vb* : wander

roan \\'rōn\\ *adj* : having a dark coat with white hairs interspersed ~ *n* : animal with a roan coat or its color

roar \\'rōr\\ *vb* : utter a full loud prolonged sound —**roar** *n* —**roar·er** *n*

roast \\'rōst\\ *vb* **1** : cook by dry heat **2** : criticize severely ~ *n* : piece of meat suitable for roasting —**roast** *adj* —**roast·er** *n*

rob \\'räb\\ *vb* -**bb- 1** : steal from **2** : commit robbery —**rob·ber** *n*

rob·bery \\'räb(ə)rē\\ *n, pl* -**ber·ies** : theft of something from a person by use of violence or threat

robe \\'rōb\\ *n* **1** : long flowing outer garment **2** : covering for the lower body ~ *vb* **robed; rob·ing** : clothe with or as if with a robe

rob·in \\'räbən\\ *n* : No. American thrush with a reddish breast

ro·bot \\'rō,bät, -bət\\ *n* **1** : machine that looks and acts like a human

being **2** : efficient but insensitive person

ro·bust \\rō'bəst, 'rō(,)bəst\\ *adj* : strong and vigorously healthy —**ro·bust·ly** *adv* —**ro·bust·ness** *n*

¹rock \\'räk\\ *vb* : sway or cause to sway back and forth ~ *n* **1** : rocking movement **2** : popular music marked by repetition and a strong beat

²rock *n* : mass of hard mineral material —**rock** *adj* —**rocky** *adj*

rock·er *n* : curved piece on which a chair or cradle rocks

rock·et \\'räkət\\ *n* **1** : self-propelled firework or missile **2** : jet engine ~ *vb* : rise abruptly and rapidly —**rock·et·ry** \\-ətrē\\ *n*

rod \\'räd\\ *n* **1** : straight slender stick **2** : unit of length equal to 5½ yards

rode *past of* RIDE

ro·dent \\'rōd³nt\\ *n* : small gnawing mammal

ro·deo \\'rōdē,ō, rə'dāō\\ *n, pl* -**de·os** : contest of cowboy skills

roe \\'rō\\ *n* : fish eggs

rogue \\'rōg\\ *n* : dishonest or mischievous person —**ro·guery** \\'rōgərē\\ *n* —**ro·guish** \\'rōgish\\ *adj* —**ro·guish·ly** *adv* —**ro·guish·ness** *n*

roil \\'rôil, *for 2 also* 'rīl\\ *vb* **1** : make cloudy or muddy by stirring up **2** : make angry

role \\'rōl\\ *n* **1** : part to play **2** : function

roll \\'rōl\\ *n* **1** : official record or list of names **2** : something rolled up or rounded **3** : bread baked in a small rounded mass **4** : sound of rapid drum strokes **5** : heavy reverberating sound **6** : rolling movement ~ *vb* **1** : move by turning over and over **2** : move on wheels **3** : flow in a continuous stream **4** : swing from side to side **5** : shape or become shaped in rounded form **6** : press with a roller

roll·er *n* **1** : revolving cylinder **2** : rod on which something is rolled up

roller skate *n* : a skate with wheels instead of a runner —**roller-skate** *vb* —**roller skater** *n*

rol·lick·ing \\'rälikiŋ\\ *adj* : gay or boisterous

Ro·man Catholic \\,rōmən-\\ *n* : member of a Christian church led by a pope —**Roman Catholic** *adj* —**Roman Catholicism** *n*

ro·mance \\rō'mans, 'rō,mans\\ *n* **1** : medieval tale of knightly adventure **2** : love story **3** : love affair ~ *vb* -**manced; -manc·ing 1** : have romantic fancies **2** : have a love affair with —**ro·manc·er** *n*

ro·man·tic \rō'mantik\ *adj* 1 : visionary or imaginative 2 : appealing to one's emotions —**ro·man·ti·cal·ly** \-ik(ə)lē\ *adv*

romp \'rämp\ *vb* : play actively and noisily —**romp** *n*

roof \'rüf, 'rúf\ *n, pl* **roofs** \'rüfs, 'rúfs; 'rüvz, 'rúvz\ : upper covering part of a building ~ *vb* : cover with a roof —**roofed** \'rüft, 'rúft\ *adj* —**roof·ing** *n* —**roof·less** *adj* —**roof·top** *n*

¹**rook** \'rúk\ *n* : crowlike bird

²**rook** *vb* : cheat

rook·ie \'rúkē\ *n* : novice

room \'rüm, 'rúm\ *n* 1 : sufficient space 2 : partitioned part of a building ~ *vb* : occupy lodgings —**room·er** *n* —**room·ful** *n* —**roomy** *adj*

room·mate *n* : one sharing the same lodgings

roost \'rüst\ *n* : support on which birds perch ~ *vb* : settle on a roost

roost·er \'rüstər, 'rús-\ *n* : adult male domestic fowl

¹**root** \'rüt, 'rút\ *n* 1 : leafless underground part of a seed plant 2 : rootlike thing or part 3 : source 4 : essential core ~ *vb* : form, fix, or become fixed by roots —**root·less** *adj* —**root·let** \-lət\ *n* —**root·like** *adj*

²**root** *vb* : turn up with the snout

³**root** \'rüt, 'rút\ *vb* : applaud or encourage noisily —**root·er** *n*

rope \'rōp\ *n* : large strong cord of strands of fiber ~ *vb* **roped; rop·ing** 1 : tie with a rope 2 : lasso

ro·sa·ry \'rōzərē\ *n, pl* **-ries** 1 : string of beads used in praying 2 : Roman Catholic devotion

¹**rose** *past of* RISE

²**rose** \'rōz\ *n* 1 : prickly shrub with bright flowers 2 : purplish red —**rose** *adj* —**rose·bud** *n* —**rose·bush** *n*

rose·mary \'rōz₁merē\ *n, pl* **-mar·ies** : fragrant shrubby mint

ro·sette \rō'zet\ *n* : rose-shaped ornament

Rosh Ha·sha·nah \₁rōsh(h)ə'shōnə\ *n* : Jewish New Year observed as a religious holiday in September or October

ros·in \'räz°n\ *n* : brittle resin

ros·ter \'rästər\ *n* : list of names

ros·trum \'rästrəm\ *n, pl* **-trums** *or* **-tra** \-trə\ : speaker's platform

rosy \'rōzē\ *adj* **ros·i·er; -est** 1 : of the color rose 2 : hopeful —**ros·i·ly** *adv* —**ros·i·ness** *n*

rot \'rät\ *vb* **-tt-** : undergo decomposition ~ *n* 1 : decay 2 : disease in which tissue breaks down

ro·ta·ry \'rōtərē\ *adj* 1 : turning on an axis 2 : having a rotating part

ro·tate \'rō₁tāt\ *vb* **-tat·ed; -tat·ing** 1 : turn about an axis or a center 2 : alternate in a series —**ro·ta·tion** \rō'tāshən\ *n* —**ro·ta·tor** \'rō₁tātər\ *n*

rote \'rōt\ *n* : repetition from memory

ro·tor \'rōtər\ *n* 1 : part that rotates 2 : system of rotating horizontal blades for supporting a helicopter

rot·ten \'rät°n\ *adj* 1 : having rotted 2 : corrupt 3 : extremely unpleasant or inferior —**rot·ten·ness** \-°n(n)əs\ *n*

ro·tund \rō'tənd\ *adj* : rounded —**ro·tun·di·ty** \-'təndətē\ *n*

ro·tun·da \rō'təndə\ *n* : building or room with a dome

roué \rú'ā\ *n* : man given to debauched living

rouge \'rüzh, 'rüj\ *n* : cosmetic for the cheeks —**rouge** *vb*

rough \'rəf\ *adj* 1 : not smooth 2 : not calm 3 : harsh, violent, or rugged 4 : crudely or hastily done ~ *n* : rough state or something in that state ~ *vb* 1 : roughen 2 : manhandle 3 : make roughly —**rough·ly** *adv* —**rough·ness** *n*

rough·age \'rəfij\ *n* : coarse bulky food

rough·en \'rəfən\ *vb* : make or become rough

rough·neck \'rəf₁nek\ *n* : rowdy

rou·lette \rú'let\ *n* : gambling game using a whirling numbered wheel

¹**round** \'raúnd\ *adj* 1 : having every part the same distance from the center 2 : cylindrical 3 : complete 4 : approximate 5 : blunt 6 : moving in or forming a circle ~ *n* 1 : round thing 2 : curved part 3 : series of recurring actions or events 4 : period of time or a unit of action 5 : fired shot 6 : cut of beef ~ *vb* 1 : make or become round 2 : go around 3 : finish 4 : express as an approximation —**round·ish** *adj* —**round·ly** *adv* —**round·ness** *n*

²**round** *prep or adv* : around

round·about *adj* : indirect

round·up \'raúnd₁əp\ *n* 1 : gathering together of range cattle 2 : summary —**round up** *vb*

rouse \'raúz\ *vb* **roused; rous·ing** 1 : wake from sleep 2 : excite to activity

rout \'raút\ *n* 1 : state of wild confusion 2 : disastrous defeat ~ *vb* : defeat decisively

route \'rüt, 'raút\ *n* : line of travel ~ *vb* **rout·ed; rout·ing** : send by a selected route

rou·tine \rü´tēn\ n : procedure or course of action regularly followed —**routine** adj —**rou·tine·ly** adv

rove \´rōv\ vb **roved; rov·ing** : wander without definite direction —**rov·er** n

¹row \´rō\ vb **1** : propel a boat with oars **2** : travel or convey in a rowboat ~ n : act of rowing —**row·boat** n —**row·er** \´rō(ə)r\ n

²row n : number of objects in a line

³row \´rau̇\ n : noisy quarrel —**row** vb

row·dy \´rau̇dē\ adj **-di·er; -est** : coarse or boisterous in behavior —**row·di·ness** n —**rowdy** n —**row·dy·ism** n

roy·al \´rȯiəl\ adj : relating to or befitting a king —**roy·al·ly** adv

roy·al·ty \´rȯialtē\ n, pl **-ties 1** : state of being royal **2** : royal person **3** : payment for use of property

rub \´rəb\ vb **-bb- 1** : use pressure and friction on a body **2** : scour, polish, erase, or smear by pressure and friction **3** : chafe with friction ~ n **1** : act of rubbing **2** : difficulty

rub·ber \´rəbər\ n **1** : one that rubs **2** : waterproof elastic substance or something made of it —**rubber** adj —**rub·ber·ize** \-ˌīz\ vb —**rub·bery** adj

rub·bish \´rəbish\ n : waste or trash

rub·ble \´rəbəl\ n : broken stones or bricks

ru·ble \´rübəl\ n : monetary unit of the U.S.S.R.

ru·by \´rübē\ n, pl **-bies** : precious red stone

rud·der \´rədər\ n : steering device at the rear of a boat or aircraft

rud·dy \´rədē\ adj **-di·er; -est** : reddish —**rud·di·ness** n

rude \´rüd\ adj **rud·er; rud·est 1** : roughly made **2** : impolite —**rude·ly** adv —**rude·ness** n

ru·di·ment \´rüdəmənt\ n **1** : something not fully developed **2** : elementary principle —**ru·di·men·ta·ry** \ˌrüdə´ment(ə)rē\ adj

rue \´rü\ vb **rued; ru·ing** : feel regret for ~ n : regret —**rue·ful** \-fəl\ adj —**rue·ful·ly** adv —**rue·ful·ness** n

ruf·fi·an \´rəfēən\ n : brutal person

ruf·fle \´rəfəl\ vb **-fled; -fling 1** : draw into or provide with pleats **2** : roughen the surface of **3** : irritate ~ n : strip of fabric pleated on one edge

rug \´rəg\ n : piece of heavy fabric used as a floor covering

rug·ged \´rəgəd\ adj **1** : having a rough uneven surface **2** : severe **3** : strong —**rug·ged·ly** adv —**rug·ged·ness** n

ru·in \´rüən\ n **1** : complete collapse or destruction **2** : remains of something

destroyed—usu. in pl. **3** : cause of destruction ~ vb **1** : destroy **2** : damage beyond repair **3** : bankrupt

ru·in·ous \´rüənəs\ adj : causing ruin —**ru·in·ous·ly** adv

rule \´rül\ n **1** : guide or principle for governing action **2** : usual way of doing something **3** : government **4** : straight strip (as of wood or metal) marked off in units for measuring ~ vb **ruled; rul·ing 1** : govern **2** : give as a decision —**rul·er** n

rum \´rəm\ n : liquor distilled from a fermented sugarcane product

rum·ble \´rəmbəl\ vb **-bled; -bling** : make a low heavy rolling sound —**rum·ble** n

ru·mi·nant \´rümənənt\ n : hoofed mammal (as a cow or deer) that chews the cud —**ruminant** adj

rum·mage \´rəmij\ vb **-maged; -mag·ing** : poke around looking for something —**rum·mag·er** n

rum·my \´rəmē\ n : card game

ru·mor \´rümər\ n **1** : common talk **2** : widespread statement not authenticated —**rumor** vb

rump \´rəmp\ n : rear part of an animal

rum·ple \´rəmpəl\ vb **-pled; -pling** : tousle or wrinkle —**rumple** n

rum·pus \´rəmpəs\ n : disturbance

run \´rən\ vb **ran** \´ran\; **run; run·ning 1** : go rapidly or hurriedly **2** : enter a race or election **3** : operate **4** : continue in force **5** : flow rapidly **6** : take a certain direction **7** : manage **8** : incur ~ n **1** : act of running **2** : brook **3** : continuous series **4** : usual kind **5** : freedom of movement **6** : lengthwise ravel

run-around n : evasive or delaying action

run·away \´rənəˌwā\ n : fugitive ~ adj **1** : fugitive **2** : out of control

run-down adj : being in poor condition

¹rung past part of RING

²rung \´rəŋ\ n : a round of a chair or ladder

run·ner \´rənər\ n **1** : one that runs **2** : lengthwise supporting part of a sled, skate, or drawer

run·ner-up n, pl **run·ners-up** : competitor who finishes next to the winner

run·ning \´rəniŋ\ adj **1** : flowing **2** : continuous

runt \´rənt\ n : small person or animal —**runty** adj

run·way \´rənˌwā\ n : strip on which aircraft land and take off

ru·pee \rü´pē, ´rü-\ n : monetary unit (as of India)

rup·ture \'rəpchər\ n 1 : breaking or tearing apart 2 : hernia ~ vb -tured; -tur·ing : cause or undergo rupture

ru·ral \'rürəl\ adj : relating to the country or agriculture

ruse \'rüs, 'rüz\ n : trick

¹rush \'rəsh\ n : grasslike marsh plant

²rush vb 1 : move forward or act with too great haste 2 : perform in a short time ~ n : violent forward motion ~ adj : requiring speed —**rush·er** n

rus·set \'rəsət\ n 1 : reddish brown color 2 : winter apple —russet adj

rust \'rəst\ n 1 : reddish coating on exposed metal (as iron) 2 : reddish orange color —rust vb —rusty adj

rus·tic \'rəstik\ adj 1 : rural 2 : boorish 3 : simple ~ n : rustic person —**rus·ti·cal·ly** \-k(ə)lē\ adv —**rus·tic·i·ty** \₁rəs'tisətē\ n

rus·tle \'rəsəl\ vb -tled; -tling 1 : make or cause a rustle 2 : forage food 3 : steal cattle from the range ~ n : succession of small sounds —**rus·tler** \-(ə)lər\ n

rut \'rət\ n 1 : track worn by wheels or feet 2 : set routine —**rut·ted** adj

ruth·less \'rüthləs\ adj : having no pity —**ruth·less·ly** adv —**ruth·less·ness** n

-ry \rē\ n suffix : -ery

rye \'rī\ n : cereal grass grown for grain

S

s \'es\ n, pl **s's** or **ss** \'esəz\ : 19th letter of the alphabet

¹-s \s after sounds f, k, k̲, p, t, th; əz after sounds ch, j, s, sh, z, zh; z after other sounds\ —used to form the plural of most nouns

²-s vb suffix —used to form the 3d person singular present of most verbs

Sab·bath \'sabəth\ n 1 : Saturday observed as a day of worship by Jews and some Christians 2 : Sunday observed as a day of worship by Christians

sa·ber, sa·bre \'sābər\ n : cavalry sword

sa·ble \'sābəl\ n 1 : black 2 : dark brown mammal or its fur

sab·o·tage \'sabə₁täzh\ n : deliberate destruction or hampering ~ vb -taged; -tag·ing : wreck through sabotage

sab·o·teur \₁sabə'tər\ n : person who commits sabotage

sac \'sak\ n : baglike part

sac·cha·rin \'sak(ə)rən\ n : very sweet white substance

sac·cha·rine \-(ə)rən\ adj : nauseatingly sweet

sa·chet \sa'shā\ n : small bag with perfumed powder (**sachet powder**)

¹sack \'sak\ n : bag

²sack vb : plunder a captured place

sack·cloth n : rough garment worn as a sign of penitence

sac·ra·ment \'sakrəmənt\ n : formal religious act or rite —**sac·ra·men·tal** \₁sakrə'mentᵊl\ adj

sa·cred \'sākrəd\ adj 1 : set apart for or worthy of worship 2 : worthy of

reverence 3 : relating to religion —**sa·cred·ly** adv —**sa·cred·ness** n

sac·ri·fice \'sakrə₁fīs\ n 1 : the offering of something precious to a deity or the thing offered 2 : loss or deprivation ~ vb -ficed; -fic·ing : offer or give up as a sacrifice —**sac·ri·fi·cial** \₁sakrə'fishəl\ adj —**sac·ri·fi·cial·ly** adv

sac·ri·lege \'sakrəlij\ n : violation of something sacred —**sac·ri·le·gious** \₁sakrə'lijəs, -'lējəs\ adj —**sac·ri·le·gious·ly** adv

sac·ro·sanct \'sakrō₁sankt\ adj : sacred

sad \'sad\ adj -dd- 1 : affected with grief or sorrow 2 : causing sorrow —**sad·den** \'sadᵊn\ vb —**sad·ly** adv —**sad·ness** n

sad·dle \'sadᵊl\ n : seat for riding on horseback ~ vb -dled; -dling : put a saddle on

sa·dism \'sā₁dizəm, 'sad₁iz-\ n : delight in cruelty —**sa·dist** \'sādəst, 'sad-\ n —**sa·dis·tic** \sə'distik\ adj —**sa·dis·ti·cal·ly** \-tik(ə)lē\ adv

sa·fa·ri \sə'färē, -'far-\ n : hunting expedition in Africa

safe \'sāf\ adj safe·er; saf·est 1 : freed or secure from danger 2 : providing safety ~ n : container to keep valuables safe —**safe·keep·ing** n —**safe·ly** adv

safe·guard n : measure or device for preventing accidents —**safeguard** vb

safe·ty \'sāftē\ n, pl -ties 1 : freedom from danger 2 : protective device

saf·flow·er \'saf₁laü(ə)r\ n : herb with seeds rich in edible oil

saf·fron \'safrən\ n : orange powder from a crocus flower used in cooking

sag \'sag\ vb -gg- : droop, sink, or settle —**sag** n

sa·ga \'sägə\ n : story of heroic deeds

sa·ga·cious \sə'gāshəs\ adj : shrewd —**sa·gac·i·ty** \-'gasətē\ n

¹sage \'sāj\ adj : wise or prudent ~ n : wise man —**sage·ly** adv

²sage n : shrublike mint

sage·brush n : low shrub of the western U.S.

said past of SAY

sail \'sāl\ n 1 : a fabric used to catch the wind and push a ship 2 : trip on a sailboat ~ vb 1 : travel on a ship 2 : glide through the air —**sail·boat** n —**sail·or** \'sālər\ n

sail·fish n : large fish with a very large dorsal fin

saint \'sānt, before a name (¸)sānt or sənt\ n : holy or godly person —**saint·ed** \-əd\ adj —**saint·hood** \-¸hud\ n —**saint·li·ness** n —**saint·ly** adj

¹sake \'sāk\ n 1 : purpose or reason 2 : one's good or benefit

²sa·ke, sa·ki \'säkē\ n : Japanese rice wine

sa·la·cious \sə'lāshəs\ adj : sexually suggestive

sal·ad \'saləd\ n : dish usu. of raw lettuce, vegetables, or fruit

sal·a·man·der \'salə¸mandər\ n : lizardlike amphibian

sa·la·mi \sə'lämē\ n : highly seasoned dried sausage

sal·a·ry \'sal(ə)rē\ n, pl -ries : regular payment for services

sale \'sāl\ n 1 : transfer of ownership of property for money 2 : selling at bargain prices —**sal·able, sale·able** \'sāləbəl\ adj —**sales·man** \-mən\ n —**sales·woman** n

sa·lient \'sālyənt\ adj : standing out conspicuously

sa·line \'sā¸lēn, -¸līn\ adj : containing salt —**sa·lin·i·ty** \sā'linətē, sə-\ n

sa·li·va \sə'līvə\ n : liquid secreted into the mouth —**sal·i·vary** \'salə¸verē\ adj —**sal·i·vate** \-¸vāt\ vb —**sal·i·va·tion** \¸salə'vāshən\ n

sal·low \'salō\ adj : of a yellowish sickly color

sal·ly \'salē\ n, pl -lies 1 : rushing attack against troops 2 : witty remark —**sally** vb

salm·on \'samən\ n, pl **salmon** : soft-finned food fish

sa·lon \sə'län, 'sal¸än, sa'lōⁿ\ n : elegant room or shop

sa·loon \sə'lün\ n 1 : large room or ballroom on a passenger ship 2 : barroom

salt \'sȯlt\ n 1 : white crystalline substance that consists of sodium and chlorine 2 : compound formed usu. from acid and metal —**salt** vb or adj —**salt·i·ness** n —**salty** adj

salt·wa·ter adj : relating to or living in salt water

sa·lu·bri·ous \sə'lübrēəs\ adj : good for health

sal·u·tary \'salyə¸terē\ adj : health-giving or beneficial

sal·u·ta·tion \¸salyə'tāshən\ n : greeting

sa·lute \sə'lüt\ vb -lut·ed; -lut·ing : honor by ceremony or formal movement —**salute** n

sal·vage \'salvij\ n : something saved from destruction ~ vb -vaged; -vag·ing : rescue or save

sal·va·tion \sal'vāshən\ n : saving of a person from sin or danger

salve \'sav, 'sȧv\ n : medicinal ointment ~ vb salved; salv·ing : soothe

sal·ver \'salvər\ n : small tray

sal·vo \'salvō\ n, pl -vos or -voes : simultaneous discharge of guns

same \'sām\ adj : being the one referred to ~ pron : the same one or ones ~ adv : in the same manner —**same·ness** n

sam·ple \'sampəl\ n : piece or item that shows the quality of the whole ~ vb -pled; -pling : judge by a sample

sam·pler \'samplər\ n : piece of needlework testing skill in embroidery

san·a·to·ri·um \¸sanə'tōrēəm\ n, pl -riums or -ria \-ēə\ : hospital for the chronically ill

sanc·ti·fy \'saŋktə¸fī\ vb -fied; -fy·ing : make holy —**sanc·ti·fi·ca·tion** \¸saŋktəfə'kāshən\ n

sanc·ti·mo·nious \¸saŋktə'mōnēəs\ adj : hypocritically pious

sanc·tion \'saŋkshən\ n 1 : authoritative approval 2 : coercive measure —usu. pl ~ vb : approve

sanc·ti·ty \'saŋktətē\ n, pl -ties : quality or state of being holy or sacred

sanc·tu·ary \'saŋkchə¸werē\ n, pl -ar·ies 1 : consecrated place 2 : place of refuge

sand \'sand\ n : loose granular particles of rock ~ vb : smooth with an abrasive —**sand·bank** n —**sand·storm** n —**sandy** adj

san·dal \'sand³l\ n : shoe consisting of a sole strapped to the foot

sand·pa·per n : abrasive paper —**sand·paper** vb

sand·pip·er \-¸pīpər\ n : long-billed shorebird

sand·stone \ n : rock made of naturally cemented sand

sand·wich \'san(ˌ)wich\ n : 2 or more slices of bread with a filling between them ~ vb : squeeze or crowd in

sane \'sān\ adj **san·er; san·est 1** : mentally healthy **2** : sensible —**sane·ly** adv

sang past of SING

san·gui·nary \'saŋgwə,nerē\ adj : bloody

san·guine \'saŋgwən\ adj **1** : reddish **2** : cheerful

san·i·tar·i·um \ˌsanə'terēəm\ n, pl **-iums** or **-ia** \-ēə\ : sanatorium

san·i·tary \'sanəterē\ adj **1** : relating to health **2** : free from filth or infective matter

san·i·ta·tion \ˌsanə'tāshən\ n : protection of health by maintenance of sanitary conditions

san·i·ty \'sanətē\ n : soundness of mind

sank past of SINK

¹sap \'sap\ n **1** : vital fluid **2** : watery fluid that circulates through a vascular plant —**sap·less** adj —**sap·py** adj

²sap vb **-pp- 1** : undermine **2** : weaken or exhaust gradually

sa·pi·ent \'sāpēənt, 'sap-\ adj : wise —**sa·pi·ence** \-əns\ n

sap·ling \'sapliŋ\ n : young tree

sap·phire \'saf,ī(ə)r\ n : hard transparent blue precious stone

sap·suck·er \'sap,səkər\ n : small American woodpecker

sar·casm \'sär,kazəm\ n **1** : cutting remark **2** : ironical criticism or reproach —**sar·cas·tic** \sär'kastik\ adj —**sar·cas·ti·cal·ly** \-tik(ə)lē\ adv

sar·coph·a·gus \sär'käfəgəs\ n, pl **-gi** \-ˌgī, -ˌjī\ : large stone coffin

sar·dine \sär'dēn\ n : small fish preserved esp. in oil for use as food

sar·don·ic \sär'dänik\ adj : bitterly disdainful —**sar·don·i·cal·ly** \-ik(ə)lē\ adv

sa·rong \sə'ròŋ, -'räŋ\ n : loose skirt worn esp. by people of the Pacific islands

sar·sa·pa·ril·la \ˌsas(ə)pə'rilə, ˌsärs-\ n : root of a tropical American plant used esp. for flavoring

sar·to·ri·al \sär'tōrēəl\ adj : relating to a tailor or men's clothes

¹sash \'sash\ n **1** : broad band worn around the waist or over the shoulder

²sash n, pl **sash 1** : frame for a pane of glass in a door or window **2** : movable part of a window

sas·sa·fras \'sasəˌfras\ n : No. Ameri-

can tree or its dried bark used in medicine and as flavoring

sassy \'sasē\ adj **sass·i·er; -est** : saucy

sat past of SIT

Sa·tan \'sātᵊn\ n : devil

satch·el \'sachəl\ n : small bag

sate \'sāt\ vb **sat·ed; sat·ing** : satisfy to the full

sat·el·lite \'satᵊl,īt\ n **1** : one that is dependent **2** : body that revolves around a larger celestial body

sa·ti·ate \'sāshē,āt\ vb **-at·ed; -at·ing 1** : satisfy fully **2** : surfeit —**sa·ti·ety** \sə'tīətē\ n

sat·in \'satᵊn\ n : glossy fabric

sat·ire \'sa,tī(ə)r\ n **1** : literary ridicule done with humor —**sa·tir·ic** \sə'tirik\, **sa·tir·i·cal** \-ikəl\ adj —**sa·tir·i·cal·ly** adv —**sat·i·rist** \'satərəst\ n —**sat·i·rize** \-ə,rīz\ vb

sat·is·fac·tion \ˌsatəs'fakshən\ n : state of being satisfied —**sat·is·fac·to·ri·ly** \-'fakt(ə)rəlē\ adv —**sat·is·fac·to·ry** \-'fakt(ə)rē\ adj

sat·is·fy \'satəs,fī\ vb **-fied; -fy·ing 1** : make happy **2** : pay what is due to or on —**sat·is·fy·ing·ly** adv

sat·u·rate \'sachə,rāt\ vb **-rat·ed; -rat·ing** : soak or charge thoroughly —**sat·u·ra·tion** \ˌsachə'rāshən\ n

Sat·ur·day \'satərdē\ n : 7th day of the week

sat·ur·nine \'satər,nīn\ adj : sardonic or sullen

sa·tyr \'sātər, 'sat-\ n : partly horselike or goatlike deity of Greek mythology

sauce \'sòs\ n : dressing for salads or meats —**sauce·pan** n

sau·cer \'sòsər\ n : small shallow dish under a cup

saucy \'sasē, 'sòsē\ adj **sauc·i·er; -est** : insolent —**sauc·i·ly** adv —**sauc·i·ness** n

sau·er·kraut \'sau(ə)r,kraut\ n : finely cut and fermented cabbage

sau·na \'saúnə\ n : steam or dry heat bath or a room or cabinet used for such a bath

saun·ter \'sòntər, 'sänt-\ vb : stroll

sau·sage \'sòsij\ n : minced and highly seasoned meat

sau·té \sò'tā, sō-\ vb **-téed** or **-téd; -té·ing** : fry in a little fat —**sauté** n

sav·age \'savij\ adj **1** : wild **2** : cruel ~ n : person belonging to a primitive society —**sav·age·ly** adv —**sav·age·ness** n —**sav·age·ry** n

¹save \'sāv\ vb **saved; sav·ing 1** : rescue from danger **2** : guard from destruction **3** : redeem from sin **4** : put aside as a reserve —**sav·er** n

²save \(ˌ)sāv\ prep : except

sav·ior, sav·iour \'sāvyər\ *n* 1 : one who saves 2 *cap* : Jesus Christ

sa·vor \'sāvər\ *n* : special flavor ∼ *vb* : taste with pleasure —**sa·vory** *adj*

¹**saw** *past of* SEE

²**saw** \'sò\ *n* : cutting tool with teeth ∼ *vb* **sawed; sawed** *or* **sawn; saw·ing** : cut with a saw —**saw·dust** \-ı(ı)dəst\ *n* —**saw·mill** *n* —**saw·yer** \-yər\ *n*

saw-horse *n* : support for wood being sawed

sax·o·phone \'saksə₁fōn\ *n* : wind instrument with a reed mouthpiece and usu. a bent metal body

say \'sā\ *vb* **said** \'sed\; **say·ing** \'sāiŋ\; **says** \'sez\ 1 : express in words 2 : state positively ∼ *n, pl* **says** 1 : expression of opinion 2 : power of decision

say·ing \'sāiŋ\ *n* : commonly repeated statement

scab \'skab\ *n* 1 : protective crust over a sore or wound 2 : worker taking a striker's job ∼ *vb* **-bb-** 1 : become covered with a scab 2 : work as a scab —**scab·by** *adj*

scab·bard \'skabərd\ *n* : sheath for the blade of a weapon

scaf·fold \'skafəld, -ıold\ *n* 1 : raised platform for workmen 2 : platform on which a criminal is executed

scald \'skòld\ *vb* 1 : burn with hot liquid or steam 2 : heat to the boiling point

¹**scale** \'skāl\ *n* : weighing device ∼ *vb* **scaled; scal·ing** : weigh

²**scale** *n* 1 : thin plate esp. on the body of a fish or reptile 2 : thin coating or layer ∼ *vb* **scaled; scal·ing** : strip of scales —**scaled** \'skāld\ *adj* —**scale·less** *adj* —**scaly** *adj*

³**scale** *n* 1 : graduated series 2 : size of a sample (as a model) in proportion to the size of the actual thing 3 : standard of estimation or judgment 4 : series of musical tones ∼ *vb* **scaled; scal·ing** 1 : go up by a ladder 2 : arrange in a graded series

scal·lion \'skalyən\ *n* : bulbless onion

scal·lop \'skäləp, 'skal-\ *n* 1 : marine mollusk 2 : rounded projection on a border

scalp \'skalp\ *n* : skin and flesh of the head ∼ *vb* 1 : tear the scalp from 2 : sell again at a greatly increased price —**scalp·er** *n*

scal·pel \'skalpəl\ *n* : surgical knife

scamp \'skamp\ *n* : rascal

scam·per \'skampər\ *vb* : run nimbly —**scamper** *n*

scan \'skan\ *vb* **-nn-** 1 : read (verses) so

as to show meter 2 : examine closely or hastily —**scan** *n* —**scan·ner** *n*

scan·dal \'skandᵊl\ *n* 1 : disgraceful situation 2 : malicious gossip —**scan·dal·ize** *vb* —**scan·dal·ous** *adj*

scant \'skant\ *adj* : barely sufficient ∼ *vb* : stint —**scant·i·ly** *adv* —**scanty** *adj*

scape·goat \'skāp₁gōt\ *n* : one that bears the blame for others

scap·u·la \'skapyələ\ *n, pl* **-lae** \-ılē\ *or* **-las** : shoulder blade

scar \'skär\ *n* : mark where a wound has healed —**scar** *vb*

scar·ab \'skarəb\ *n* : large dark beetle or an ornament representing one

scarce \'skears\ *adj* **scarc·er; scarc·est** 1 : not plentiful 2 : rare —**scar·ci·ty** \'skersətē\ *n*

scarce·ly \'skearslē\ *adv* 1 : barely 2 : almost not

scare \'skear\ *vb* **scared; scar·ing** : frighten ∼ *n* : fright —**scary** *adj*

scare·crow \'skear₁krō\ *n* : figure for scaring birds from crops

scarf \'skärf\ *n, pl* **scarves** \'skärvz\ *or* **scarfs** : cloth worn about the shoulders or the neck

scar·let \'skärlət\ *n* : bright red —**scarlet** *adj*

scarlet fever *n* : acute contagious disease marked by fever, sore throat, and red rash

scath·ing \'skāthiŋ\ *adj* : bitterly severe

scat·ter \'skatər\ *vb* 1 : spread about irregularly 2 : disperse

scav·en·ger \'skavənjər\ *n* 1 : person that collects refuse or waste 2 : animal that feeds on decayed matter —**scav·enge** \'skavənj\ *vb*

sce·nar·io \sə'narē₁ō\ *n, pl* **-i·os** : plot of a movie

scene \'sēn\ *n* 1 : single situation in a play or movie 2 : stage setting 3 : view 4 : display of emotion —**scenic** \'sēnik\ *adj*

scen·ery \'sēn(ə)rē\ *n, pl* **-er·ies** 1 : painted setting for a stage 2 : picturesque view

scent \'sent\ *vb* 1 : smell 2 : fill with odor ∼ *n* 1 : odor 2 : sense of smell 3 : perfume

scep·ter \'septər\ *n* : staff signifying authority

scep·tic \'skeptik\ *var of* SKEPTIC

sched·ule \'skejül, *esp Brit* 'shedyül\ *n* : list showing sequence of events ∼ *vb* **-uled; -ul·ing** : make a schedule of

scheme \'skēm\ *n* 1 : crafty plot 2 : systematic design ∼ *vb* **schemed;**

schem·ing : form a plot —**sche·mat·ic** \ski'matik\ *adj* —**schem·er** *n*

schism \'sizəm, 'skiz-\ *n* : split —**schis·mat·ic** \siz'matik, skiz-\ *n or adj*

schizo·phre·nia \,skitsə'frēnēə\ *n* : severe mental disorder —**schiz·oid** \'skit,sȯid\ *adj or n* —**schizo·phren·ic** \,skitsə'frenik\ *adj or n*

schol·ar \'skälər\ *n* : student or learned person —**schol·ar·ly** *adj*

schol·ar·ship \-,ship\ *n* 1 : qualities or learning of a scholar 2 : money given to a student to pay for education

scho·las·tic \skə'lastik\ *adj* : relating to schools, scholars, or scholarship

1school \'skül\ *n* 1 : institution for learning 2 : pupils in a school 3 : group with shared beliefs ~ *vb* : teach —**school·boy** *n* —**school·girl** *n* —**school·house** *n* —**school·mate** *n* —**school·room** *n* —**school·teacher** *n*

2school *n* : large number of fish swimming together

schoo·ner \'skünər\ *n* : sailing ship

sci·ence \'sīəns\ *n* : branch of systematic study esp. of the physical world —**sci·en·tif·ic** \,sīən'tifik\ *adj* —**sci·en·tif·i·cal·ly** \-ik)lē\ *adv* —**sci·en·tist** \'sīəntəst\ *n*

scin·til·late \'sint³l,āt\ *vb* -**lat·ed**; -**lat·ing** : flash —**scin·til·la·tion** \,sint³l'āshən\ *n*

sci·on \'sīən\ *n* 1 : shoot of a plant 2 : descendant

scis·sors \'sizərz\ *n pl* : small shears

scle·ro·sis \sklə'rōsəs\ *n* : hardening of an artery —**scle·rot·ic** \-'rätik\ *adj*

scoff \'skäf\ *vb* : mock —**scoff·er** *n*

scold \'skōld\ *n* : person who scolds ~ *vb* : criticize severely

scoop \'süp\ *n* : shovellike utensil ~ *vb* 1 : take out with a scoop 2 : dig out

scoot \'süt\ *vb* : go suddenly and swiftly

scoot·er \'skütər\ *n* : child's foot-propelled vehicle

1scope \'skōp\ *n* 1 : extent 2 : room for development

2scope *n* : viewing device (as a microscope)

scorch \'skȯrch\ *vb* : burn the surface of

score \'skōr\ *n, pl* **scores** 1 *or pl* **score** : twenty 2 : cut 3 : record of points made (as in a game) 4 : debt 5 : music of a composition ~ *vb* **scored**; **scor·ing** 1 : record 2 : mark with lines 3 : gain in a game 4 : assign a grade to 5 : compose a score for —**score·less** *adj* —**scor·er** *n*

scorn \'skȯrn\ *n* : emotion involving both anger and disgust ~ *vb* : hold in contempt —**scorn·er** *n* —**scorn·ful** \-fəl\ *adj* —**scorn·ful·ly** *adv*

scor·pi·on \'skȯrpēən\ *n* : poisonous spider-like animal

scoun·drel \'skaündrəl\ *n* : mean worthless person

1scour \'skaü(ə)r\ *vb* : examine thoroughly

2scour *vb* : rub (as with a gritty substance) in order to clean

scourge \'skərj\ *n* 1 : whip 2 : punishment ~ *vb* **scourged**; **scourg·ing** 1 : lash 2 : punish severely

scout \'skaüt\ *vb* : inspect or observe to get information ~ *n* : person sent out to get information

scow \'skaü\ *n* : large flat-bottomed boat with square ends

scowl \'skaül\ *vb* : make a face in expression of displeasure —**scowl** *n*

scrag·gly \'skraglē\ *adj* : irregular or unkempt

scram \'skram\ *vb* -**mm-** : go away at once

scram·ble \'skrambəl\ *vb* -**bled**; -**bling** 1 : clamber clumsily around 2 : struggle for possession of something 3 : mix together 4 : stir during frying —**scramble** *n*

1scrap \'skrap\ *n* 1 : fragment 2 : discarded material ~ *vb* -**pp-** : get rid of as useless

2scrap *vb* -**pp-** : fight —**scrap** *n* —**scrap·per** *n*

scrap·book *n* : blank book in which mementos are kept

scrape \'skrāp\ *vb* **scraped**; **scrap·ing** 1 : remove by drawing a knife over 2 : clean or smooth by rubbing 3 : get (money) together 4 : get along with difficulty ~ *n* 1 : act of scraping 2 : predicament —**scrap·er** *n*

scratch \'skrach\ *vb* 1 : scrape or dig with or as if with claws or nails 2 : cause to move gratingly ~ *n* : mark or sound made in scratching —**scratchy** *adj*

scrawl \'skrȯl\ *vb* : write hastily and carelessly —**scrawl** *n*

scraw·ny \'skrȯnē\ *adj* -**ni·er**; -**est** : very thin

scream \'skrēm\ *vb* : cry out loudly and shrilly ~ *n* : loud shrill cry

screech \'skrēch\ *vb or n* : shriek

screen \'skrēn\ *n* 1 : device or partition used to protect or decorate 2 : surface on which pictures appear (as in movies) ~ *vb* 1 : shield with a screen 2 : separate with or as if with a screen

screw \'skrü\ *n* 1 : grooved fastening

device **2** : propeller ~ *vb* **1** : fasten by means of a screw **2** : move spirally

screw·driv·er \\'skrü,drīvər\ *n* : tool for turning screws

scrib·ble \\'skribəl\ *vb* **-bled; -bling** : write hastily or carelessly —**scribble** *n* —**scrib·bler** \-(ə)lər\ *n*

scribe \\'skrīb\ *n* : one who writes or copies writing

scrimp \\'skrimp\ *vb* : economize greatly

scrip \\'skrip\ *n* **1** : paper money for less than a dollar **2** : certificate entitling one to something (as stock)

script \\'skript\ *n* : text (as of a play)

scrip·ture \\'skripchər\ *n* : sacred writings of a religion —**scrip·tur·al** \\'skripchərəl\ *adj*

scroll \\'skrōl\ *n* **1** : roll of paper for writing a document **2** : spiral or coiled design

scro·tum \\'skrōtəm\ *n, pl* **-ta** \-ə\ *or* **-tums** : pouch containing the testes

scrounge \\'skraunj\ *vb* **scrounged; scroung·ing** : collect by or as if by foraging

¹scrub \\'skrəb\ *n* : stunted tree or shrub or a growth of these —**scrub** *adj* —**scrub·by** *adj*

²scrub *vb* **-bb-** **1** : rub in washing **2** : wash by rubbing —**scrub** *n*

scruff \\'skrəf\ *n* : loose skin of the back of the neck

scru·ple \\'skrüpəl\ *n* : reluctance due to ethical considerations —**scruple** *vb* —**scru·pu·lous** \-pyələs\ *adj* —**scru·pu·lous·ly** *adv*

scru·ti·ny \\'skrüt³nē\ *n, pl* **-nies** : careful inspection —**scru·ti·nize** \-³n,īz\ *vb*

scud \\'skəd\ *vb* **-dd-** : move speedily

scuff \\'skəf\ *vb* : scratch, scrape, or wear away —**scuff** *n*

scuf·fle \\'skəfəl\ *vb* **-fled; -fling 1** : struggle at close quarters **2** : shuffle one's feet —**scuffle** *n*

scull \\'skəl\ *n* **1** : oar for sculling **2** : racing shell propelled with sculls ~ *vb* : propel a boat by an oar over the stern

scul·lery \\'skəl(ə)rē\ *n, pl* **-ler·ies** : small room near the kitchen for cleaning

sculp·ture \\'skəlpchər\ *n* : work of art carved or molded ~ *vb* **-tured; -tur·ing** : form as sculpture —**sculp·tor** \-tər\ *n* —**sculp·tur·al** \-chərəl\ *adj*

scum \\'skəm\ *n* : filthy film on a liquid

scurf \\'skərf\ *n* : thin dry scales of skin

scur·ri·lous \\'skərələs\ *adj* : coarsely jesting

scur·ry \\'skərē\ *vb* **-ried; -ry·ing** : scamper

scur·vy \\'skərvē\ *n* : vitamin-deficiency disease

¹scut·tle \\'skət³l\ *n* : pail for coal

²scuttle *vb* **-tled; -tling** : cut a hole in a ship to sink it

³scuttle *vb* **-tled; -tling** : scamper

scythe \\'sīth\ *n* : mowing tool —**scythe** *vb*

sea \\'sē\ *n* **1** : large body of salt water **2** : ocean **3** : rough water —**sea** *adj* —**sea-coast** *n* —**sea-food** *n* —**sea lev-el** *n* —**sea·port** *n* —**sea·shore** *n* —**sea·water** *n*

sea·bird *n* : bird frequenting the open ocean

sea·board *n* : country's seacoast

sea·far·er \-,farər\ *n* : seaman —**sea·far·ing** \-,farin\ *adj or n*

sea horse *n* : small fish with a horselike head

¹seal \\'sēl\ *n* : large sea mammal of cold regions —**seal·skin** *n*

²seal *n* **1** : device for stamping a design **2** : something that closes ~ *vb* **1** : affix a seal to **2** : close up securely **3** : determine finally —**seal·ant** \-ənt\ *n* —**seal·er** *n*

sea lion *n* : large Pacific seal with external ears

seam \\'sēm\ *n* **1** : line of junction of 2 edges **2** : layer of a mineral ~ *vb* : join by sewing —**seam·less** *adj*

sea·man \\'sēmən\ *n* **1** : one who helps to handle a ship **2** : enlisted man in the navy ranking next below a petty officer 3d class —**sea·man·ship** *n*

seaman apprentice *n* : enlisted man in the navy ranking next below a seaman

seaman recruit *n* : enlisted man of the lowest rank in the navy

seam·stress \\'sēmstrəs\ *n* : woman who sews

seamy \\'sēmē\ *adj* **seam·i·er; -est** : unpleasant or sordid

sé·ance \\'sā,äns\ *n* : meeting for communicating with spirits

sea·plane *n* : airplane that can take off from and land on the water

sear \\'siər\ *vb* : scorch

search \\'sərch\ *vb* **1** : look through **2** : seek —**search** *n* —**search·er** *n* —**search·light** *n*

sea·sick *adj* : nauseated by the motion of a ship —**sea·sick·ness** *n*

¹sea·son \\'sēz³n\ *n* **1** : division of the year **2** : customary time for something —**sea·son·al** \\'sēznəl, -ən³l\ *adj* —**sea·son·al·ly** *adv*

²season *vb* **1** : add spice to (food) **2**

: make strong or fit for use —**sea·son·ing** \\-niŋ, ³niŋ\ n

sea·son·able \'sēznəbəl\ adj : occurring at a suitable time —**sea·son·ably** \-blē\ adv

seat \'sēt\ n 1 : place to sit 2 : chair, bench, or stool for sitting on 3 : place that serves as a capital or center ~ n 1 : place in or on a seat 2 : provide seats for

sea·weed n : marine alga

sea·wor·thy adj : strong enough to hold up to a sea voyage

se·cede \si'sēd\ vb **-ced·ed; -ced·ing** : withdraw from a body (as a nation)

se·clude \si'klüd\ vb **-clud·ed; -clud·ing** : shut off alone —**se·clu·sion** \si'klüzhən\ n

¹sec·ond \'sekənd\ adj : next after the 1st ~ n 1 : one that is second 2 : one who assists (as in a duel) —**second, sec·ond·ly** adv

²second n 1 : 60th part of a minute of time or of a degree 2 : moment

sec·ond·ary \'sekən,derē\ adj 1 : second in rank or importance 2 : coming after the primary or elementary

sec·ond-hand adj 1 : not original 2 : used before

second lieutenant n : commissioned officer ranking next below a first lieutenant

se·cret \'sēkrət\ adj 1 : hidden 2 : kept from general knowledge —**se·cre·cy** \-krəsē\ n —**secret** n —**se·cre·tive** \'sēkrətiv, si'krēt-\ adj —**se·cret·ly** adv

sec·re·tar·i·at \,sekrə'terēət\ n 1 : body of secretaries in an office 2 : administrative department

sec·re·tary \'sekrə,terē\ n, pl **-tar·ies** 1 : one hired to handle correspondence and other tasks for a superior 2 : official in charge of correspondence or records 3 : head of a government department —**sec·re·tar·i·al** \,sekrə'terēəl\ adj

¹se·crete \si'krēt\ vb **-cret·ed; -cret·ing** : produce as a secretion

²se·crete \si'krēt, 'sēkrət\ vb **-cret·ed; -cret·ing** : hide

se·cre·tion \si'krēshən\ n 1 : act or process of secreting 2 : product of glandular activity

sect \'sekt\ n : religious group

sec·tar·i·an \sek'terēən\ adj 1 : relating to a sect 2 : limited in character or scope ~ n : member of a sect

sec·tion \'sekshən\ n : distinct part —**sec·tion·al** \-sh(ə)nəl\ adj

sec·tor \'sektər\ n 1 : part of a circle between 2 radii 2 : distinctive part

sec·u·lar \'sekyələr\ adj 1 : not sacred 2 : not monastic

se·cure \si'kyůr\ adj **-cur·er, -est** : free from danger or loss ~ vb 1 : fasten safely 2 : get —**se·cure·ly** adv

se·cu·ri·ty \si'kyůrətē\ n, pl **-ties** 1 : safety 2 : something given to guarantee payment 3 pl : bond or stock certificates

se·dan \si'dan\ n 1 : chair carried by 2 men 2 : enclosed automobile

se·date \si'dāt\ adj : quiet and dignified —**se·date·ly** adv

sed·a·tive \'sedətiv\ adj : serving to relieve tension ~ n : sedative drug —**se·da·tion** \si'dāshən\ n

sed·en·tary \'sedən,terē\ adj : characterized by much sitting

sedge \'sej\ n : grasslike marsh plant

sed·i·ment \'sedəmənt\ n : material that settles to the bottom of a liquid or is deposited by water or a glacier —**sed·i·men·ta·ry** \,sedə'ment(ə)rē\ adj —**sed·i·men·ta·tion** \-,mən-'tāshən, -,men-\ n

se·di·tion \si'dishən\ n : revolution against a government —**se·di·tious** \-əs\ adj

se·duce \si'd(y)üs\ vb **-duced; -duc·ing** 1 : lead astray 2 : entice to unlawful sexual intercourse —**se·duc·er** n —**se·duc·tion** \-'dəkshən\ n —**se·duc·tive** \-tiv\ adj

sed·u·lous \'sejələs\ adj : diligent

¹see \'sē\ vb saw \'sô\, seen \'sēn\; **see·ing** 1 : perceive by the eye 2 : notice or heed 3 : understand 4 : make sure 5 : meet with or escort

²see n : jurisdiction of a bishop

seed \'sēd\ n, pl seed or seeds 1 : part by which a plant is propagated 2 : source ~ vb 1 : sow 2 : remove seeds from —**seed·less** adj

seed·ling \-liŋ\ n : plant grown from seed

seedy \-ē\ adj **seed·i·er, -est** 1 : full of seeds 2 : inferior

seek \'sēk\ vb sought \'sôt\; **seek·ing** 1 : search for 2 : try to reach or obtain —**seek·er** n

seem \'sēm\ vb : give the impression of being —**seem·ing·ly** adv

seem·ly \-lē\ adj **seem·li·er, -est** : proper

seep \'sēp\ vb : leak through fine pores or cracks —**seep·age** \'sēpij\ n

seer \'sir\ n : one who foresees or predicts events

seer·suck·er \'sir,səkər\ n : light puckered fabric

see·saw \'sē,sô\ n : board balanced in the middle —**seesaw** vb

seethe \'sēth\ vb **seethed; seeth·ing** : become violently agitated

seg·ment \'segmənt\ n : division of a thing —**seg·ment·ed** \-,mentəd\ adj

seg·re·gate \'segri,gāt\ vb -**gat·ed; -gat·ing** : cut off from others —**seg·re·ga·tion** \,segri'gāshən\ n

seine \'sān\ n : large weighted fishing net ~ vb : fish with a seine

seis·mic \'sīzmik, 'sīs-\ adj : relating to an earthquake

seis·mo·graph \'-mə,graf\ n : apparatus for detecting earthquakes

seize \'sēz\ vb **seized; seiz·ing** : take by force —**sei·zure** \'sēzhər\ n

sel·dom \'seldəm\ adv : not often

se·lect \sə'lekt\ adj 1 : favored 2 : discriminating ~ vb : take by preference —**se·lec·tive** \-'lektiv\ adj

se·lec·tion \sə'lekshən\ n : act of selecting or thing selected

se·lect·man \si'lek(t),man, -mən\ n : New England town official

self \'self\ n, pl **selves** \'selvz\ : essential person distinct from others

self- comb form 1 : oneself or itself 2 : of oneself or itself 3 : by oneself or automatic 4 : to, for, or toward oneself

self-addressed	self-determina-
self-adminis-	tion
tered	self-determined
self-analysis	self-discipline
self-appointed	self-doubt
self-assertive	self-educated
self-assurance	self-employed
self-assured	self-employment
self-awareness	self-esteem
self-cleaning	self-evident
self-closing	self-explanatory
self-complacent	self-expression
self-conceit	self-fulfilling
self-confessed	self-fulfillment
self-confidence	self-governing
self-confident	self-government
self-contained	self-help
self-contempt	self-image
self-contradic-	self-importance
tion	self-important
self-contradic-	self-imposed
tory	self-improve-
self-control	ment
self-created	self-indulgence
self-criticism	self-indulgent
self-defeating	self-inflicted
self-defense	self-interest
self-denial	self-love
self-denying	self-operating
self-destruction	self-pity
self-destructive	self-portrait

self-possessed	self-sacrifice
self-possession	self-satisfaction
self-preservation	self-satisfied
self-proclaimed	self-service
self-propelled	self-serving
self-propelling	self-starting
self-protection	self-styled
self-reliance	self-sufficiency
self-reliant	self-sufficient
self-respect	self-supporting
self-respecting	self-winding
self-restraint	

self-cen·tered adj : concerned only with one's own self

self-con·scious adj : ill at ease —**self-con·scious·ly** adv —**self-con·scious·ness** n

self·ish \'selfish\ adj : taking care of oneself without regard for others —**self·ish·ly** adv —**self·ish·ness** n

self·less \'selfləs\ adj : having no concern for self —**self·less·ness** n

self-made adj : rising by one's own efforts

self-righ·teous adj : strongly convinced of one's own righteousness

self·same \'self,sām\ adj : precisely the same

sell \'sel\ vb **sold** \'sōld\; **sell·ing** 1 : transfer (property) esp. for money 2 : deal in as a business 3 : be sold —**sell·er** n

selves pl of SELF

se·man·tic \si'mantik\ adj : relating to meaning —**se·man·tics** \-iks\ n sing or pl

sema·phore \'semə,fōr\ n 1 : visual signaling apparatus 2 : signaling by flags

sem·blance \'sembləns\ n : appearance

se·men \'sēmən\ n : male reproductive fluid

se·mes·ter \sə'mestər\ n : half a school year

semi- \,semi, sem-, -,ī\ prefix 1 : half 2 : partial

semi·co·lon \'semi,kōlən\ n : punctuation mark ;

semi·con·duc·tor \,semi-, -,ī-\ n : electronic device used to regulate flow of electricity —**semi·con·duct·ing** adj

semi·fi·nal \,semi-\ adj : being next to the final —**semifinal** \'semi-\ n

semi·for·mal \,semi-\ adj : being or suitable for an occasion of moderate formality

sem·i·nal \'semən^əl\ adj 1 : relating to seed or semen 2 : causing or influencing later development

sem·i·nar \'semə,när\ n : conference or conferencelike study

sem·i·nary \'semə,nerē\ n, pl -**nar·ies**

: school and esp. a theological school —**sem·i·nar·i·an** \,semə'nerēən\ *n*

sen·ate \'senət\ *n* : upper branch of a legislature —**sen·a·tor** \-ət\ *n* —**sen·a·to·ri·al** \,senə'tōrēəl\ *adj*

send \'send\ *vb* **sent** \'sent\; **send·ing** **1** : cause to go 2 : propel —**send·er** *n*

se·nile \'sēn,īl, 'sen-\ *adj* : mentally deficient through old age —**se·nil·i·ty** \si'nilətē\ *n*

se·nior \'sēnyər\ *adj* : older or higher ranking —**senior** *n* —**se·nior·i·ty** \,sēn'yōrətē\ *n*

senior chief petty officer *n* : petty officer in the navy ranking next below a master chief petty officer

senior master sergeant *n* : noncommissioned officer in the air force ranking next below a chief master sergeant

sen·sa·tion \sen'sāshən\ *n* **1** : bodily feeling 2 : condition of excitement or the cause of it —**sen·sa·tion·al** \-sh(ə)nəl\ *adj*

sense \'sens\ *n* **1** : meaning 2 : faculty of perceiving something physical 3 : sound mental capacity ~ *vb* **sensed**; **sens·ing** : perceive by the senses —**sense·less** *adj* —**sense·less·ly** *adv*

sen·si·bil·i·ty \,sensə'bilətē\ *n, pl* **-ties** : delicacy of feeling

sen·si·ble \'sensəbəl\ *adj* **1** : capable of sensing or being sensed 2 : aware or conscious 3 : intelligent —**sen·si·bly** \-blē\ *adv*

sen·si·tive \'sensətiv\ *adj* **1** : subject to excitation by or responsive to stimuli 2 : having power of feeling 3 : easily affected —**sen·si·tive·ness** *n* —**sen·si·tiv·i·ty** \,sensə'tivətē\ *n*

sen·si·tize \'sensə,tīz\ *vb* **-tized; -tiz·ing** : make or become sensitive

sen·so·ry \'sens(ə)rē\ *adj* : relating to sensation or the senses

sen·su·al \'sench(ə)wəl, 'senshəl\ *adj* **1** : pleasing the senses 2 : devoted to the pleasures of the senses —**sen·su·al·ist** *n* —**sen·su·al·i·ty** \,sench(ə)'walətē\ *n* —**sen·su·al·ly** *adv*

sen·su·ous \'sench(ə)wəs\ *adj* : having strong appeal to the senses —**sen·su·ous·ly** *adv* —**sen·su·ous·ness** *n*

sent *past of* SEND

sen·tence \'sent⁰ns, -⁰nz\ *n* **1** : judgment of a court 2 : grammatically self-contained speech unit ~ *vb* **-tenced; -tenc·ing** : impose a sentence on

sen·ten·tious \sen'tenchəs\ *adj* : using pompous language

sen·tient \'sench(ē)ənt\ *adj* : capable of feeling

sen·ti·ment \'sentəmənt\ *n* **1** : belief 2 : feeling

sen·ti·men·tal \,sentə'ment⁰l\ *adj* : influenced by tender feelings —**sen·ti·men·tal·ism** *n* —**sen·ti·men·tal·ist** *n* —**sen·ti·men·tal·i·ty** \-,men'talətē, -mən-\ *n* —**sen·ti·men·tal·ize** \-'ment⁰l,īz\ *vb* —**sen·ti·men·tal·ly** *adv*

sen·ti·nel \'sentnəl, -⁰nəl\ *n* : sentry

sen·try \'sentrē\ *n, pl* **-tries** : one who stands guard

se·pal \'sēpəl, 'sep-\ *n* : one of the modified leaves comprising a flower calyx

sep·a·rate \'sepə,rāt\ *vb* **-rat·ed; -rat·ing 1** : set or keep apart 2 : become divided or detached ~ \'sep(ə)rət\ *adj* **1** : not connected or shared 2 : distinct from each other —**sep·a·ra·ble** \'sep(ə)rəbəl\ *adj* —**sep·a·rate·ly** *adv* —**sep·a·ra·tion** \,sepə'rāshən\ *n* —**sep·a·ra·tor** \'sepə,rātər\ *n*

se·pia \'sēpēə\ *n* : brownish gray

Sep·tem·ber \sep'tembər\ *n* : 9th month of the year having 30 days

sep·tic \'septik\ *adj* : relating to or using the action of bacteria

sep·ul·cher, sep·ul·chre \'sepəlkər\ *n* : burial vault —**se·pul·chral** \sə'pəlkrəl\ *adj*

se·quel \'sēkwəl\ *n* **1** : consequence or result 2 : continuation of a story

se·quence \'sēkwəns\ *n* : continuous or connected series —**se·quen·tial** \si'kwenchəl\ *adj*

se·ques·ter \si'kwestər\ *vb* : segregate

se·quin \'sēkwən\ *n* : spangle

se·quoia \si'kwòiə\ *n* : huge California coniferous tree

sera *pl of* SERUM

ser·aph \'serəf\ *n, pl* **-a·phim** \-ə,fim\ *or* **-aphs** : angel —**se·raph·ic** \sə'rafik\ *adj*

sere \'siər\ *adj* : dried up or withered

ser·e·nade \,serə'nād\ *n* : music sung esp. to a lady —**serenade** *vb*

ser·en·dip·i·ty \,seren'dipətē\ *n* : good luck in finding things not sought for —**ser·en·dip·i·tous** \-əs\ *adj*

se·rene \sə'rēn\ *adj* : tranquil —**se·rene·ly** *adv* —**se·ren·i·ty** \sə'renətē\ *n*

serf \'sərf\ *n* : peasant obligated to work the land —**serf·dom** \-dəm\ *n*

serge \'sərj\ *n* : twilled woolen cloth

ser·geant \'särjənt\ *n* : noncommissioned officer (as in the army) ranking next below a staff sergeant

sergeant first class *n* : noncommissioned officer in the army ranking next below a master sergeant

ser·geant major *n, pl* **sergeants major** *or* **sergeant majors 1** : noncommissioned officer serving as chief administrative assistant in a headquarters **2** : noncommissioned officer in the marine corps ranking above a first sergeant

se·ri·al \'sirēəl\ *n* : story told a little bit at a time —**serial** *adj* —**se·ri·al·ly** *adv*

se·ries \'si(ə)rēz\ *n, pl* **series** : number of things in order

se·ri·ous \'sirēəs\ *adj* **1** : subdued in appearance or manner **2** : sincere **3** : of great importance —**se·ri·ous·ly** *adv* —**se·ri·ous·ness** *n*

ser·mon \'sərmən\ *n* : lecture on religion or behavior

ser·pent \'sərpənt\ *n* : snake —**ser·pen·tine** \-pən₁tēn, -₁tīn\ *adj*

ser·rated \'ser₁ātəd\ *adj* : saw-toothed

se·rum \'sirəm\ *n, pl* **-rums** *or* **-ra** \-ə\ : watery part of blood —**se·rous** \-əs\ *adj*

ser·vant \'sərvənt\ *n* : person employed for domestic work

serve \'sərv\ *vb* **served; serv·ing 1** : work through or perform a term of service **2** : be of use **3** : prove adequate **4** : hand out (food or drink) **5** : be of service to —**serv·er** *n*

ser·vice \'sərvəs\ *n* **1** : act or means of serving **2** : required duty **3** : meeting for worship **4** : branch of public employment or the persons in it **5** : set of dishes or silverware **6** : benefit ~ *vb* **-viced; -vic·ing** : do repair work on —**serv·ice·able** *adj* —**serv·ice·man** \-₁man, -mən\ *n*

ser·vile \'sərvəl, -₁vīl\ *adj* : behaving like a slave —**ser·vil·i·ty** \₁sər'vilətē\ *n*

ser·vi·tude \'sərvə₁t(y)üd\ *n* : slavery

ses·a·me \'sesəmē\ *n* : East Indian annual herb or its seeds

ses·sion \'seshən\ *n* : meeting

set \'set\ *vb* **set; set·ting 1** : cause to sit **2** : place **3** : settle, arrange, or adjust **4** : cause to be or do **5** : become fixed or solid **6** : sit on eggs to hatch them **7** : sink below the horizon ~ *adj* : settled — *n* **1** : group classed together **2** : setting for the scene of a play or film **3** : electronic apparatus **4** : collection of mathematical elements —**set forth** : begin a trip —**set off** : begin a trip —**set out** : begin a trip or undertaking —**set up** *vb* **1** : assemble or erect **2** : cause

set·back *n* : reverse

set·tee \se'tē\ *n* : bench or sofa

set·ter \'setər\ *n* : large long-coated hunting dog

set·ting \'setiŋ\ *n* : background or surroundings

set·tle \'setᵊl\ *vb* **-tled; -tling 1** : come to rest **2** : sink gradually **3** : become established in a place or a home **4** : adjust or arrange **5** : calm **6** : dispose of (as by paying) **7** : decide or agree on —**set·tle·ment** \-mənt\ *n* —**set·tler** \'setlər, -ᵊlər\ *n*

sev·en \'sevən\ *n* : one more than 6 —**seven** *adj or pron* —**sev·enth** \-ənth\ *adj or adv or n*

sev·en·teen \₁sevən'tēn\ *n* : one more than 16 —**seventeen** *adj or pron* —**sev·en·teenth** \-'tēnth\ *adj or n*

sev·en·ty \'sevəntē\ *n, pl* **-ties** : 7 times 10 —**sev·en·ti·eth** \-tēəth\ *adj or n* —**seventy** *adj or pron*

sev·er \'sevər\ *vb* **-ered; -er·ing** : cut off or apart —**sev·er·ance** \-(ə)rəns\ *n*

sev·er·al \'sev(ə)rəl\ *adj* **1** : distinct **2** : consisting of an indefinite but not large number —**sev·er·al·ly** \-ē\ *adv*

se·vere \sə'vi(ə)r\ *adj* **-ver·er; -est 1** : allowing no evasion or compromise **2** : restrained or unadorned **3** : painful or distressing **4** : hard to endure —**se·vere·ly** *adv* —**se·ver·i·ty** \-'verətē\ *n*

sew \'sō\ *vb* **sewed; sewn** \'sōn\ *or* **sewed; sew·ing** : fasten by stitches made with thread and needle —**sew·ing** *n*

sew·age \'süij\ *n* : liquid household waste

¹sew·er \'sō(ə)r\ *n* : one that sews

²sew·er \'süər\ *n* : pipe or channel to carry off waste matter

sex \'seks\ *n* **1** : either of 2 divisions of organisms distinguished respectively as male and female or the qualities which differentiate them **2** : copulation —**sexed** \'sekst\ *adj* —**sex·less** *adj* —**sex·u·al** \'seksh(əw)əl\ *adj* —**sex·u·al·i·ty** \₁sekshə'walətē\ *n* —**sex·u·al·ly** *adv* —**sexy** *adj*

sex·ism \'sek₁sizəm\ *n* : discrimination based on sex and esp. against women —**sex·ist** \'seksəst\ *adj or n*

sex·tant \'sekstənt\ *n* : instrument for navigation

sex·tet \sek'stet\ *n* **1** : music for 6 performers **2** : group of 6

sex·ton \'sekstən\ *n* : church caretaker

shab·by \'shabē\ *adj* **-bi·er; -est 1** : worn and faded **2** : dressed in worn clothes **3** : not generous or fair —**shab·bi·ly** *adv* —**shab·bi·ness** *n*

shack \'shak\ *n* : hut

shack·le \'shakəl\ *n* : metal device to bind legs or arms ~ *vb* **-led; -ling** : fasten with shackles

shad \'shad\ *n* : Atlantic food fish

shade \'shād\ *n* **1** : space sheltered from the light esp. of the sun **2** : gradation of color **3** : small difference **4** : something that shades ~ *vb* **shad·ed; shad·ing** : shelter from light and heat —**shady** *adj*

shad·ow \'shadō\ *n* **1** : shade cast upon a surface by something blocking light **2** : trace **3** : gloomy influence ~ *vb* **1** : cast a shadow **2** : follow closely —**shad·owy** *adj*

shaft \'shaft\ *n* **1** : long slender cylindrical part **2** : deep vertical opening (as of a mine)

shag \'shag\ *n* : shaggy tangled mat

shag·gy \'shagē\ *adj* **-gi·er; -est 1** : covered with long hair or wool **2** : not neat and combed

shah \'shä, 'shȯ\ *n* : monarch in Iran

shake \'shāk\ *vb* **shook** \'shůk\; **shak·en** \'shākən\; **shak·ing 1** : move or cause to move quickly back and forth **2** : distress **3** : clasp (hands) as friendly gesture —**shake** *n* —**shak·er** \-ər\ *n*

shake-up *n* : reorganization

shaky \'shākē\ *adj* **shak·i·er; -est** : not sound, stable, or reliable —**shak·i·ly** *adv* —**shak·i·ness** *n*

shale \'shāl\ *n* : stratified rock

shall \shəl, (')shal\ *vb, past* **should** \shəd, (')shúd\; *pres sing & pl* **shall** —used as an auxiliary to express a command, futurity, or determination

shal·low \'shalō\ *adj* **1** : not deep **2** : not intellectually profound

shal·lows \-ōz\ *n pl* : area of shallow water

sham \'sham\ *adj or n or vb* : fake

sham·ble \'shambal\ *vb* **-bled; -bling** : shuffle along —**sham·ble** *n*

sham·bles \'shambəlz\ *n* : state of disorder

shame \'shām\ *n* **1** : distress over guilt or disgrace **2** : cause of shame or regret ~ *vb* **shamed; sham·ing 1** : make ashamed **2** : disgrace —**shame·ful** \-fəl\ *adj* —**shame·ful·ly** \-ē\ *adv* —**shame·less** *adj* —**shame·less·ly** *adv*

shame·faced \'shām'fāst\ *adj* : ashamed

sham·poo \sham'pü\ *vb* : wash one's hair ~ *n, pl* **-poos** : act of or preparation used in shampooing

sham·rock \'sham,räk\ *n* : plant with 3-lobed leaves

shank \'shank\ *n* : part of the leg between the knee and ankle

shan·ty \'shantē\ *n, pl* **-ties** : hut

shape \'shāp\ *vb* **shaped; shap·ing** : form esp. in a particular structure or appearance ~ *n* **1** : distinctive appearance or arrangement of parts **2** : condition —**shape·less** \-ləs\ *adj*

shard \'shärd\ *n* : broken piece

share \'sheər\ *n* **1** : portion belonging to one **2** : interest in a company's stock ~ *vb* **shared; shar·ing 1** : divide or use with others —**share·hol·der** *n* —**shar·er** *n*

share·crop·per \-ˌkräpər\ *n* : farmer who works another's land in return for a share of the crop —**share·crop** *vb*

shark \'shärk\ *n* : voracious sea fish

sharp \'shärp\ *adj* **1** : having a good point or cutting edge **2** : alert, clever, or sarcastic **3** : vigorous or fierce **4** : having prominent angles or a sudden change in direction **5** : distinct **6** : higher than the true pitch ~ *adv* : exactly ~ *n* : sharp note —**sharp·ly** *adv* —**sharp·ness** *n*

sharp·en \'shärpən\ *vb* : make sharp —**sharp·en·er** \'shärp(ə)nər\ *n*

sharp·shoot·er *n* : expert marksman —**sharp·shoot·ing** *n*

shat·ter \'shatər\ *vb* : smash or burst into fragments

shave \'shāv\ *vb* **shaved; shaved** *or* **shav·en** \'shāvən\; **shav·ing 1** : cut off with a razor **2** : make bare by cutting the hair from **3** : slice very thin ~ *n* : act of instance of shaving —**shav·er** *n*

shawl \'shȯl\ *n* : loose covering for the head or shoulders

she \(')shē\ *pron* : that female one

sheaf \'shēf\ *n, pl* **sheaves** \'shēvz\ : bundle esp. of grain stalks

shear \'shiər\ *vb* **sheared; sheared** *or* **shorn** \'shȯrn\; **shear·ing 1** : trim wool from **2** : cut off with scissorlike action

shears \'shiərz\ *n pl* : cutting tool with 2 blades fastened so that the edges slide by each other

sheath \'shēth\ *n, pl* **sheaths** \'shēthz, 'shēths\ : covering (as for a blade)

sheathe \'shēth\ *vb* **sheathed; sheath·ing** : put into a sheath

shed \'shed\ *vb* **shed; shed·ding 1** : give off (as tears or hair) **2** : cause to flow or diffuse ~ *n* : small storage building

sheen \'shēn\ *n* : subdued luster

sheep \'shēp\ *n, pl* **sheep** : domesti-

cated mammal covered with wool
—**sheep-skin** *n*

sheep-ish \'shēpish\ *adj* : embarrassed
by awareness of a fault

sheer \'shiər\ *adj* **1** : pure **2** : very
steep **3** : very thin or transparent
—**sheer** *adv*

sheet \'shēt\ *n* : broad flat piece (as of
cloth or paper)

sheikh, sheik \'shēk, 'shāk\ *n* : Arab
chief —**sheikh-dom, sheik-dom**
\-dəm\ *n*

shelf \'shelf\ *n, pl* **shelves** \'shelvz\ **1**
: flat narrow structure used for stor-
age or display **2** : sandbank or rock
ledge

shell \'shel\ *n* **1** : hard or tough outer
covering **2** : case holding explosive
powder and projectile for a weapon
3 : light racing boat with oars ~ *vb* **1**
: remove the shell of **2** : bombard
—**shelled** \'sheld\ *adj* —**shell-er** *n*

shel-lac \shə'lak\ *n* : varnish ~ *vb* **-lacked; -lack-ing 1** : coat with shel-
lac **2** : defeat —**shel-lack-ing** *n*

shell-fish *n* : water animal with a shell

shel-ter \'sheltər\ *n* : something that
gives protection ~ *vb* : give refuge to

shelve \'shelv\ *vb* **shelved; shelv-ing 1**
: place or store on shelves **2** : dismiss
or put aside

she-nan-i-gans \shə'naniganz\ *n pl*
: mischievous or deceitful conduct

shep-herd \'shepərd\ *n* : one that tends
sheep ~ *vb* : act as a shepherd or
guardian —**shep-herd-ess** \-əs\ *n*

sher-bet \'shərbət\, **sher-bert** \-bərt\ *n*
: fruit-flavored frozen dessert

sher-iff \'sherəf\ *n* : county law officer

sher-ry \'sherē\ *n, pl* **-ries** : type of
wine

shield \'shēld\ *n* **1** : broad piece of
armor carried on the arm **2** : something that protects —**shield** *vb*

shier *comparative of* SHY

shiest *superlative of* SHY

shift \'shift\ *vb* **1** : change place, position, or direction **2** : get by ~ *n* **1**
: transfer **2** : scheduled work period
3 : loose-fitting dress

shift-less \'shif(t)ləs\ *adj* : lazy —**shift-
less-ness** *n*

shifty \'shiftē\ *adj* **shift-i-er; -est**
: tricky or untrustworthy

shil-le-lagh \shə'lālē\ *n* : club or stick

shil-ling \'shilin\ *n* : former British
coin

shil-ly–shal-ly \'shilē,shalē\ *vb* **-shall-
ied; -shally-ing 1** : hesitate **2** : dawdle

shim-mer \'shimər\ *vb or n* : glimmer

shin \'shin\ *n* : front part of the leg

below the knee ~ *vb* **-nn-** : climb by
sliding the body close along

shine \'shīn\ *vb* **shone** \-shōn\ *or*
shined; *shin-ing* **1** : give off or cause
to give off light **2** : be outstanding **3**
: polish ~ *n* : brilliance

shin-gle \'shingəl\ *n* **1** : small thin
piece used in covering roofs or exterior walls ~ *vb* **-gled; -gling** : cover
with shingles

shin-gles \'shingəlz\ *n pl* : acute inflammation of spinal nerves

shin-ny \'shinē\ *vb* **-nied; -ny-ing** : shin

shiny \'shīnē\ *adj* **shin-i-er; -est**
: bright or polished

ship \'ship\ *n* **1** : large craft for navigation **2** : aircraft or spacecraft ~ *vb*
-pp- 1 : put on a ship **2** : transport by
carrier —**ship-board** *n* —**ship-build-er**
n —**ship-per** *n* —**ship-yard** *n*

-ship \,ship\ *n suffix* **1** : state, condition, or quality **2** : rank or profession
3 : skill **4** : something showing a
state or quality

ship-ment \-mənt\ *n* : goods shipped

ship-ping \'shipin\ *n* **1** : ships **2** : transportation of goods

ship-shape *adj* : tidy

ship-wreck *n* : destruction or loss of a
ship —**shipwreck** *vb*

shire \'shī(ə)r, in place-name compounds \shiər, shər\ *n* : British
county

shirk \'shərk\ *vb* : evade —**shirk-er** *n*

shirr \'shər\ *vb* **1** : gather (cloth) by
drawing up parallel lines of stitches
2 : bake (eggs) in a dish

shirt \'shərt\ *n* : garment for covering
the torso —**shirt-less** *adj*

shiv-er \'shivər\ *vb* : tremble —**shiver** *n*

shoal \'shōl\ *n* : shallow place (as in a
river)

¹shock \'shäk\ *n* : pile of sheaves set
up in the field

²shock *n* **1** : forceful impact **2** : violent
mental or emotional disturbance **3**
: effect of a charge of electricity **4**
: depression of the vital bodily processes ~ *vb* **1** : strike with surprise,
horror, or disgust **2** : subject to an
electrical shock —**shock-proof** *adj*

³shock *n* : bushy mass (as of hair)

shod-dy \'shädē\ *adj* **-di-er; -est**
: cheaply or poorly made or done
—**shod-di-ly** \'shäd²lē\ *adv* —**shod-
di-ness** *n*

shoe \'shü\ *n* **1** : covering for the human foot **2** : horseshoe ~ *vb* **shod**
\'shäd\; **shoe-ing** : put horseshoes
on —**shoe-lace** *n* —**shoe-mak-er** *n*

shone *past of* SHINE

shook *past of* SHAKE

shoot \'shüt\ vb **shot** \'shät\; **shoot·ing** 1 : propel (as an arrow or bullet) 2 : wound or kill with a missile 3 : discharge (a weapon) 4 : drive (as a ball) at a goal 5 : photograph ~ n : new plant growth —**shoot·er** n

shop \'shäp\ n : place where things are made or sold ~ vb -**pp**- : visit stores —**shop·keep·er** n —**shop·per** n

shop·lift vb : steal goods from a store —**shop·lift·er** \-,liftər\ n

¹shore \'shōr\ n : land along the edge of water —**shore·less** adj

²shore vb **shored**; **shor·ing** : prop up ~ n : something that props

shore·bird n : bird of the seashore

shorn past part of SHEAR

short \'shȯrt\ adj 1 : not long or tall or extending far 2 : brief in time 3 : curt 4 : not having or being enough ~ adv : curtly ~ n 1 pl : short drawers or trousers 2 : short circuit —**short·en** \-ᵊn\ vb —**short·ly** adv —**short·ness** n

short·age \'shȯrtij\ n : deficiency

short·cake n : dessert of biscuit with sweetened fruit

short·change vb : cheat esp. by giving too little change

short circuit n : abnormal electric connection —**short-circuit** vb

short·com·ing n : failing

short·cut \-,kət\ n 1 : more direct route than that usu. taken 2 : quicker way of doing something

short·hand n : method of speed writing

short-lived \'shȯrt'līvd, -,livd\ adj : of short life or duration

short·sight·ed adj : lacking foresight

shot \'shät\ n 1 : act of shooting 2 : attempt (as at making a goal) 3 : small pellets forming a charge 4 : range or reach 5 : photograph 6 : injection of medicine 7 : portion (as of liquor) taken at one time —**shot·gun** n

should \shəd, (')shu̇d\ past of SHALL —used as an auxiliary to express condition, obligation, or probability

shoul·der \'shōldər\ n 1 : part of the body where the arm joins the trunk 2 : part that projects or lies to the side ~ vb : push with or take upon the shoulder

shoulder blade n : the flat triangular bone at the back of the shoulder

shout \'shau̇t\ vb : give voice loudly —**shout** n

shove \'shəv\ vb **shoved**; **shov·ing** : push along, aside, or away —**shove** n

shov·el \'shəvəl\ n : broad tool for digging or lifting ~ vb -**eled** or -**elled**; -**el·ing** or -**el·ling** : take up or dig with a shovel

show \'shō\ vb **showed** \'shōd\; **shown** \'shōn\ or **showed**; **show·ing** 1 : present to view 2 : reveal or demonstrate 3 : indicate 4 : conduct or escort 5 : act in (a specified manner) 6 : appear or be noticeable ~ n 1 : demonstrative display 2 : spectacle 3 : theatrical, radio, or television program —**show·case** n —**show off** vb 1 : display proudly 2 : act so as to attract attention —**show up** vb : arrive

show·down n : final settlement of a contested issue

show·er \'shau̇(ə)r\ n 1 : brief fall of rain 2 : bath in which water sprinkles down on the person 3 : party at which someone gets gifts ~ vb 1 : fall in a shower 2 : bathe in a shower —**show·ery** adj

showy \'shōē\ adj **show·i·er**; -**est** : very noticeable or overly elaborate —**show·i·ly** adv —**show·i·ness** n

shrap·nel \'shrapnᵊl\ n, pl **shrapnel** : metal fragments of a bomb

shred \'shred\ n : narrow strip cut or torn off ~ vb -**dd**- : cut or tear into shreds

shrew \'shrü\ n 1 : scolding woman 2 : mouselike mammal —**shrew·ish** \-ish\ adj

shrewd \'shrüd\ adj : showing cleverness or good judgment —**shrewd·ly** adv —**shrewd·ness** n

shriek \'shrēk\ n 1 : shrill cry —**shriek** vb

shrill \'shril\ adj : piercing and high-pitched —**shril·ly** adv

shrimp \'shrimp\ n : small sea crustacean

shrine \'shrīn\ n 1 : tomb of a saint 2 : hallowed place

shrink \'shriŋk\ vb **shrank** \'shraŋk\; **shrunk** or **shrunk·en** \'shrəŋkən\ 1 : draw back or away 2 : become smaller —**shrink·able** adj

shrink·age \'shriŋkij\ n : amount something shrinks

shriv·el \'shrivəl\ vb -**eled** or -**elled**; -**el·ing** or -**el·ling** : shrink or wither into wrinkles

shroud \'shrau̇d\ n 1 : cloth put over a corpse 2 : cover or screen ~ vb : veil or screen from view

shrub \'shrəb\ n : low woody plant —**shrub·by** adj

shrub·bery \'shrəb(ə)rē\ n, pl -**ber·ies** : growth of shrubs

shrug \'shrəg\ vb -**gg**- : hunch the shoulders up in doubt, indifference, or dislike —**shrug** n

shuck \\'shək\\ vb : strip of a shell or husk —**shuck** n

shud·der \\'shədər\\ vb : tremble —**shudder** n

shuf·fle \\'shəfəl\\ vb -fled; -fling 1 : mix together 2 : walk with a sliding movement —**shuffle** n

shuf·fle·board \\'shəfəl,börd\\ n : game of sliding disks into a scoring area

shun \\'shən\\ vb -nn- : keep away from

shunt \\'shənt\\ vb : turn off to one side

shut \\'shət\\ vb shut; shut·ting 1 : bar passage into or through (as by moving a lid or door) 2 : suspend activity —**shut out** : exclude —**shut up** : stop or cause to stop talking

shut-in n : invalid

shut·ter \\'shətər\\ n 1 : movable cover for a window 2 : camera part that exposes film

shut·tle \\'shətᵊl\\ n 1 : part of a weaving machine that carries thread back and forth 2 : vehicle traveling back and forth over a short route ~ vb -tled; -tling : move back and forth frequently

shut·tle·cock \\'shətᵊl,käk\\ n : feathered object in badminton

shy \\'shī\\ adj shi·er or shy·er \\'shī(ə)r\\; shi·est or shy·est \\'shīəst\\ 1 : sensitive and hesitant in dealing with others 2 : wary 3 : lacking ~ vb shied; shy·ing : move back from fright —**shy·ly** adv —**shy·ness** n

sib·i·lant \\'sibələnt\\ adj : having the sound of the s or the sh in sash —**sibilant** n

sib·ling \\'sibliŋ\\ n : brother or sister

sick \\'sik\\ adj 1 : not in good health 2 : nauseated 3 : relating to or meant for the sick —**sick·bed** n —**sick·en** \\-ən\\ vb —**sick·ly** adj —**sick·ness** n

sick·le \\'sikəl\\ n : curved short-handled blade

side \\'sīd\\ n 1 : part to left or right of an object or the torso 2 : edge or surface away from the center or at an angle to top and bottom or ends 3 : contrasting or opposing position or group —**sid·ed** adj

side·board n : piece of dining-room furniture for table service

side·burns \\-,bərnz\\ n pl : whiskers in front of the ears

side·long \\,sīd'löŋ\\ adv or adj : to or along the side

si·de·re·al \\sī'dirēəl, sə-\\ adj : measured by the apparent motion of fixed stars

side·show n : minor show at a circus

side·step vb 1 : step aside 2 : avoid

side·swipe \\-,swīp\\ vb : strike with a glancing blow —**sideswipe** n

side-track vb : lead aside or astray

side·walk n : paved walk at the side of a road

side·ways \\-,wāz\\ adv or adj 1 : to or from the side 2 : with one side to the front

sid·ing \\'sīdiŋ\\ n 1 : short railroad track 2 : material for covering the outside of a building

si·dle \\'sīdᵊl\\ vb -dled; -dling : move sideways or unobtrusively

siege \\'sēj\\ n : persistent attack (as on a fortified place)

si·es·ta \\sē'estə\\ n : midday nap

sieve \\'siv\\ n : utensil with holes to separate particles

sift \\'sift\\ vb 1 : pass through a sieve 2 : examine carefully —**sift·er** n

sigh \\'sī\\ n : audible release of the breath (as to express weariness) —**sigh** vb

sight \\'sīt\\ n 1 : something seen or worth seeing 2 : process, power, or range of seeing 3 : device used in aiming 4 : view or glimpse ~ vb : get sight of —**sight·ed** adj —**sight·less** adj —**sight·see·ing** adj —**sight·seer** n

sign \\'sīn\\ n 1 : symbol 2 : gesture expressing a command or thought 3 : public notice to advertise or warn 4 : trace ~ vb 1 : mark with or make a sign 2 : write one's name on —**sign·er** n

sig·nal \\'signᵊl\\ n 1 : sign of command or warning 2 : electronic transmission ~ vb -naled or -nalled; -nal·ing or -nal·ling : communicate or notify by signals

sig·na·to·ry \\'signə,tōrē\\ n, pl -ries : person or government that signs jointly with others

sig·na·ture \\'signə,chùr\\ n : one's name written by oneself

sig·net \\'signət\\ n : small seal

sig·nif·i·cance \\sig'nifikəns\\ n 1 : meaning 2 : importance —**sig·nif·i·cant** \\-kənt\\ adj —**sig·nif·i·cant·ly** adv

sig·ni·fy \\'signə,fī\\ vb -fied; -fy·ing 1 : show by a sign 2 : mean —**sig·ni·fi·ca·tion** \\,signəfə'kāshən\\ n

si·lence \\'sīləns\\ n : state of being without sound ~ vb -lenced; -lenc·ing : keep from making noise or sound —**si·lenc·er** n

si·lent \\'sīlənt\\ adj : having or producing no sound —**si·lent·ly** adv

sil·hou·ette \\,silə'wet\\ n : outline filled

in usu. with black ~ -ett·ed; -ett·ing : represent by a silhouette

sil·i·ca \'silikə\ n : mineral found as quartz and opal

sil·i·con \'silikən, 'silə,kän\ n : nonmetallic chemical element

silk \'silk\ n **1** : fine strong lustrous protein fiber from moth larvae (**silk·worms** \-,wərmz\) **2** : thread or cloth made from silk —**silk·en** \'silkən\ adj —**silky** adj

sill \'sil\ n : bottom part of a window frame or a doorway

sil·ly \'silē\ adj **sil·li·er; -est** : foolish or stupid —**sil·li·ness** n

si·lo \'sīlō\ n, pl **-los** : building for storing animal feed

silt \'silt\ n : fine earth carried by rivers ~ vb : obstruct or cover with silt

sil·ver \'silvər\ n **1** : white ductile metallic chemical element **2** : silverware ~ adj : having the color of silver —**sil·very** adj

sil·ver·ware \-,waər\ n : utensils of silver, silver-plated metal, or stainless steel

sim·i·lar \'simələr\ adj : resembling each other in some ways —**sim·i·lar·i·ty** \,simə'larətē\ n —**sim·i·lar·ly** \'simələrlē\ adv

sim·i·le \'simə(,)lē\ n : comparison of unlike things using like or as

si·mil·i·tude \sə'milə,t(y)üd\ n : likeness

sim·mer \'simər\ vb : stew gently

sim·per \'simpər\ vb : give a silly smile —**simper** n

sim·ple \'simpəl\ adj **-pler; -plest** **1** : not combined **2** : not other than **3** : not complex or fancy **4** : naive —**sim·ple·ness** n —**sim·ply** \-plē\ adv

sim·ple·ton \'simpəltən\ n : fool

sim·plic·i·ty \sim'plisətē\ n : state or fact of being simple

sim·pli·fy \'simplə,fī\ vb **-fied; -fy·ing** : make easier —**sim·pli·fi·ca·tion** \,simpləfə'kāshən\ n

sim·u·late \'simyə,lāt\ vb **-lat·ed; -lat·ing** : create the effect or appearance of —**sim·u·la·tion** \,simyə'lāshən\ n

si·mul·ta·ne·ous \,sīməl'tānēəs, ,siməl-\ adj : occurring or operating at the same time —**si·mul·ta·ne·ous·ly** adv —**si·mul·ta·ne·ous·ness** n

sin \'sin\ n : offense against God ~ vb **-nn-** : commit a sin —**sin·ful** \-fəl\ adj —**sin·less** adj —**sin·ner** n

since \'(')sins\ adv **1** : from a past time until now **2** : backward in time ~ prep **1** : in the period after **2** : continuously from ~ conj **1** : from the time when **2** : because

sin·cere \sin'siər\ adj : genuine or honest —**sin·cere·ly** adv —**sin·cer·i·ty** \-'serətē\ n

si·ne·cure \'sīni,kyúər, 'sini-\ n : well-paid job that requires little work

sin·ew \'sinyü\ n **1** : tendon **2** : physical strength —**sin·ewy** adj

sing \'siŋ\ vb **sang** \'saŋ\ or **sung** \'səŋ\; **sung; sing·ing** : produce musical tones with the voice —**sing·er** n

singe \'sinj\ vb **singed; singe·ing** : scorch lightly

sin·gle \'siŋgəl\ adj **1** : one only **2** : unmarried ~ n : separate one —**sin·gle·ness** n —**sin·gly** \-glē\ adv —**single out** vb : select or set aside

sin·gu·lar \'siŋgyələr\ adj **1** : relating to a word form denoting one **2** : outstanding or superior **3** : queer —**singular** n —**sin·gu·lar·i·ty** \,siŋgyə'larətē\ n —**sin·gu·lar·ly** \'siŋgyələrlē\ adv

sin·is·ter \'sinəstər\ adj : threatening evil

sink \'siŋk\ vb **sank** \'saŋk\ or **sunk** \'səŋk\; **sunk; sink·ing** **1** : submerge or descend **2** : grow worse **3** : make by digging or boring **4** : invest ~ n : basin with a drain

sink·er \'siŋkər\ n : weight to sink a fishing line

sin·u·ous \'sinyəwəs\ adj : winding in and out —**sin·u·os·i·ty** \,sinyə'wäsətē\ n —**sin·u·ous·ly** adv

si·nus \'sīnəs\ n : skull cavity connecting with the nostrils

sip \'sip\ vb **-pp-** : drink in small quantities —**sip** n

si·phon \'sīfən\ n : bent tube through which a liquid is drawn by suction —**siphon** vb

sir \'(,)sər\ n **1** —used before the first name of a knight or baronet **2** —used in addressing a man without using his name

sire \'sī(ə)r\ n : father ~ vb **sired; sir·ing** : beget

si·ren \'sīrən\ n **1** : seductive woman **2** : wailing warning whistle —**siren** adj

sir·loin \'sər,lóin\ n : cut of beef

sirup var of **SYRUP**

si·sal \'sīsəl, -zəl\ n : strong rope fiber

sis·sy \'sisē\ n, pl **-sies** : timid or effeminate boy

sis·ter \'sistər\ n : female sharing one or both parents with another person —**sis·ter·hood** \-,húd\ n —**sis·ter·ly** adj

sis·ter-in-law \'sistə(r)ən,lò\ n, pl **sis·ters-in-law** \-tərzən-\ : sister of one's husband or wife or wife of one's brother

sit \\'sit\\ *vb* **sat** \\'sat\\; **sit·ting 1** : rest on the buttocks or haunches **2** : roost **3** : hold a session **4** : pose for a portrait **5** : have a location **6** : rest or fix in place — **sit·ter** *n*

site \\'sīt\\ *n* : place

sit·u·at·ed \\'sichə,wātəd\\ *adj* : located

sit·u·a·tion \\,sichə'wāshən\\ *n* **1** : location **2** : condition **3** : job

six \\'siks\\ *n* : one more than 5 — **six** *adj or pron* — **sixth** \\'siksth\\ *adj or adv or n*

six·teen \\siks'tēn\\ *n* : one more than 15 — **sixteen** *adj or pron* — **six·teenth** \\-'tēnth\\ *adj or n*

six·ty \\'sikstē\\ *n, pl* **sixties** : 6 times 10 — **six·ti·eth** \\- əth\\ *adj or n* — **sixty** *adj or pron*

siz·able, size·able \\'sīzəbəl\\ *adj* : quite large — **siz·ably** \\-blē\\ *adv*

size \\'sīz\\ *n* : measurement of the amount of space something takes up ~ *vb* : grade according to size

siz·zle \\'sizəl\\ *vb* **-zled; -zling** : fry with a hissing sound — **sizzle** *n*

skate \\'skāt\\ *n* **1** : metal runner on a shoe for gliding over ice **2** : roller skate — **skate** *vb* — **skat·er** *n*

skein \\'skān\\ *n* : loosely twisted quantity (as of yarn)

skel·e·ton \\'skelət^ən\\ *n* : bony framework — **skel·e·tal** \\-ət^əl\\ *adj*

skep·tic \\'skeptik\\ *n* : one who is critical or doubting — **skep·ti·cal** \\-tikəl\\ *adj* — **skep·ti·cism** \\-tə,sizəm\\ *n*

sketch \\'skech\\ *n* **1** : rough drawing **2** : small story or essay — **sketch** *vb* — **sketchy** *adj*

skew·er \\'skyüər\\ *n* : pin for holding roasting meat — **skewer** *vb*

ski \\'skē\\ *n, pl* **skis** : long strip bound to the shoe for gliding over snow or water — **ski** *vb* — **ski·er** *n*

skid \\'skid\\ *n* **1** : plank for supporting something or on which it slides **2** : act of skidding ~ *vb* **-dd-** : slide sideways

skiff \\'skif\\ *n* : small open boat

skill \\'skil\\ *n* : developed or learned ability — **skilled** \\'skild\\ *adj* — **skill·ful** \\-fəl\\ *adj* — **skill·ful·ly** *adv* — **skill·ful·ness** *n*

skil·let \\'skilət\\ *n* : pan for frying

skim \\'skim\\ *vb* **-mm- 1** : take off from the top of a liquid **2** : read or move over swiftly ~ *adj* : having the cream removed — **skim·mer** *n*

skimp \\'skimp\\ *vb* : give too little of something — **skimpy** *adj*

skin \\'skin\\ *n* **1** : outer layer of an animal body **2** : rind ~ *vb* **-nn-** : take the skin from — **skin·less** *adj* — **skinned** *adj* — **skin·tight** *adj*

skin·flint \\'skin,flint\\ *n* : stingy person

skin·ny \\'skinē\\ *adj* **-ni·er; -est** : very thin

skip \\'skip\\ *vb* **-pp- 1** : move with leaps **2** : read past or ignore — **skip** *n*

skip·per \\'skipər\\ *n* : ship's master — **skipper** *vb*

skir·mish \\'skərmish\\ *n* : minor combat — **skirmish** *vb*

skirt \\'skərt\\ *n* : garment or part of a garment that hangs below the waist ~ *vb* : pass around the edge of

skit \\'skit\\ *n* : brief usu. humorous play

skit·tish \\'skitish\\ *adj* : easily frightened

skulk \\'skəlk\\ *vb* : move furtively

skull \\'skəl\\ *n* : bony case that protects the brain

skunk \\'skəŋk\\ *n* : mammal that can forcibly eject an ill-smelling fluid

sky \\'skī\\ *n, pl* **skies** **1** : upper air **2** : heaven — **sky·ey** \\'skīē\\ *adj* — **sky·line** \\-,līn\\ *n* — **sky·ward** \\-wərd\\ *adv or adj*

sky·lark \\-,lärk\\ *n* : European lark noted for its song

sky·light *n* : window in a roof or ceiling

sky·rock·et *n* : shooting firework ~ *vb* : rise suddenly

sky·scrap·er \\-,skrāpər\\ *n* : very tall building

slab \\'slab\\ *n* : thick slice

slack \\'slak\\ *adj* **1** : careless **2** : not taut **3** : not busy ~ *n* **1** : part hanging loose **2** *pl* : casual trousers — **slack·ly** *adv* — **slack·ness** *n*

slag \\'slag\\ *n* : waste from melting of ores

slain *past part of* SLAY

slake \\'slāk\\ *vb* **slaked; slak·ing** : quench

slam \\'slam\\ *n* : heavy jarring impact ~ *vb* **-mm-** : shut, strike, or throw violently and loudly

slan·der \\'slandər\\ *n* : malicious gossip ~ *vb* : hurt (someone) with slander — **slan·der·er** *n* — **slan·der·ous** *adj*

slang \\'slaŋ\\ *n* : informal nonstandard vocabulary — **slangy** *adj*

slant \\'slant\\ *vb* **1** : slope **2** : present with a special viewpoint ~ *n* : sloping direction, line, or plane

slap \\'slap\\ *vb* **-pp-** : strike sharply with the open hand — **slap** *n*

slash \\'slash\\ *vb* **1** : cut with sweeping strokes **2** : reduce sharply ~ *n* : gash

slat \\'slat\\ *n* : thin narrow flat strip

slate \\'slāt\\ *n* **1** : dense fine-grained

layered rock **2** : roofing tile or writing tablet of slate **3** : list of candidates ~ vb **slat·ed; slat·ing** : designate

slat·tern \'slatərn\ n : untidy woman —**slat·tern·ly** adv or adj

slaugh·ter \'slótər\ n **1** : butchering of livestock for market **2** : great and cruel destruction of lives ~ vb : commit slaughter upon —**slaugh·ter·house** n

slave \'slāv\ n : one owned and forced into service by another ~ vb **slaved; slav·ing** : work as or like a slave —**slave** adj —**slav·ery** \'slāv(ə)rē\ n

sla·ver \'slavər, 'slāv-\ vb or n : slobber

slav·ish \'slāvish\ adj : of or like a slave —**slav·ish·ly** adv

slay \'slā\ vb **slew** \'slü\; **slain** \'slān\; **slay·ing** : kill —**slay·er** n

slea·zy \'slēzē, 'slā-\ adj **-zi·er; -est** : shabby or shoddy

sled \'sled\ n : vehicle on runners —**sled** vb

¹sledge \'slej\ n : sledgehammer

²sledge n : heavy sled

sledge·ham·mer n : heavy long-handled hammer —**sledgehammer** adj or vb

sleek \'slēk\ adj : smooth or glossy —**sleek** vb

sleep \'slēp\ n : natural suspension of consciousness ~ vb **slept** \'slept\; **sleep·ing** : rest in a state of sleep —**sleep·er** n —**sleep·less** adj

sleep·walk·er n : one who walks during sleep

sleepy \'slēpē\ adj **sleep·i·er; -est** **1** : ready for sleep **2** : quietly inactive —**sleep·i·ly** \'slēpəlē\ adv —**sleep·i·ness** \-pēnəs\ n

sleet \'slēt\ n : partly frozen rain —**sleet** vb —**sleety** adj

sleeve \'slēv\ n : part of a garment for the arm —**sleeve·less** adj

sleigh \'slā\ n : horse-drawn sled with seats ~ vb : drive or ride in a sleigh

sleight of hand \'slīt-\ : skillful manual manipulation or a trick requiring it

slen·der \'slendər\ adj **1** : thin esp. in physique **2** : scanty

sleuth \'slüth\ n : detective

slew \'slü\ past of SLAY

slice \'slīs\ n : thin flat piece ~ vb **sliced; slic·ing** : cut a slice from

slick \'slik\ adj **1** : very smooth **2** : clever —**slick** vb

slick·er \'slikər\ n : waterproof raincoat

slide \'slīd\ vb **slid** \'slid\; **slid·ing** \'slīdiŋ\ : move smoothly along or down a surface ~ n **1** : act of sliding

2 : surface on which something slides **3** : transparent picture for projection

slier comparative of SLY

sliest superlative of SLY

slight \'slīt\ adj **1** : slender **2** : frail **3** : small in degree ~ vb **1** : ignore or treat as unimportant —**slight** n —**slight·ly** adv

slim \'slim\ adj **-mm- 1** : slender **2** : scanty ~ vb **-mm-** : make or become slender

slime \'slīm\ n : dirty slippery film (as on water) —**slimy** adj

sling \'sliŋ\ vb **slung** \'sləŋ\; **sling·ing** : hurl with or as if with a sling ~ n **1** : strap for swinging and hurling stones **2** : looped strap or bandage to lift or support

sling·shot n : forked stick with elastic bands for shooting small stones or shot

slink \'sliŋk\ vb **slunk** \'sləŋk\; **slink·ing** : move stealthily or sinuously —**slinky** adj

¹slip \'slip\ vb **-pp- 1** : escape quietly or secretly **2** : slide along smoothly **3** : make a mistake **4** : to pass without being noticed or done **5** : fall off from a standard ~ n **1** : ship's berth **2** : sudden mishap **3** : mistake **4** : woman's undergarment

²slip n **1** : plant shoot **2** : small strip (as of paper)

slip·per \'slipər\ n : shoe that slips on easily

slip·pery \'slip(ə)rē\ adj **-peri·er; -est** **1** : slick enough to slide on **2** : tricky —**slip·peri·ness** n

slip·shod \'slip'shäd\ adj : careless

slit \'slit\ vb **slit; slit·ting** : make a slit in ~ n : long narrow cut

slith·er \'slithər\ vb : glide along like a snake —**slith·ery** adj

sliv·er \'slivər\ n : splinter

slob \'släb\ n : untidy person

slob·ber \'släbər\ vb : dribble saliva —**slobber** n

slo·gan \'slōgən\ n : word or phrase expressing the aim of a cause

sloop \'slüp\ n : sailing boat with one mast

slop \'släp\ n : food waste for animal feed ~ vb **-pp-** : spill

slope \'slōp\ vb **sloped; slop·ing** : deviate from the vertical or horizontal ~ n : upward or downward slant

slop·py \'släpē\ adj **-pi·er; -est 1** : muddy **2** : untidy

slot \'slät\ n : narrow opening

sloth \'slóth, 'slōth\ n, pl **sloths** \with ths or thz\ **1** : laziness **2** : slow-moving mammal —**sloth·ful** adj

slouch \'slaůch\ n 1 : drooping posture 2 : lazy or incompetent person ~ vb : walk or stand with a slouch

¹slough \'slü\ n : swamp or muddy place

²slough \'sləf\, **sluff** vb : cast off (a skin)

slov·en·ly \'sləvənlē\ adj : untidy

slow \slō\ adj 1 : sluggish or stupid 2 : moving, working, or happening at less than the usual speed ~ vb 1 : make slow 2 : go slower —**slow** adv —**slow·ly** adv —**slow·ness** n

sludge \'sləj\ n : slushy mass (as of treated sewage)

slug \'sləg\ n 1 : mollusk related to the snails 2 : bullet 3 : metal disk ~ vb -gg- : strike forcibly —**slug·ger** n

slug·gish \'sləgish\ adj : slow in movement or flow —**slug·gish·ly** adv —**slug·gish·ness** n

sluice \'slüs\ n : channel for water ~ vb sluiced; sluic·ing : wash in running water

slum \'sləm\ n 1 : thickly populated area marked by poverty

slum·ber \'sləmbər\ vb or n : sleep

slump \'sləmp\ vb 1 : sink suddenly 2 : slouch —**slump** n

slung past of SLING

slunk past of SLINK

¹slur \'slər\ vb -rr- : run (words or notes) together —**slur** n

²slur n : malicious or insulting remark —**slur** vb

slurp \'slərp\ vb : eat or drink noisily —**slurp** n

slush \'sləsh\ n : partly melted snow —**slushy** adj

slut \'slət\ n 1 : untidy woman 2 : prostitute —**slut·tish** \'slətish\ adj

sly \'slī\ adj sli·er \'slī(ə)r\; sli·est \'slīəst\ : given to or showing secrecy and deception —**sly·ly** adv —**sly·ness** n

¹smack \'smak\ n : characteristic flavor ~ vb : have a taste or hint

²smack vb 1 : move (the lips) so as to make a sharp noise 2 : kiss or slap with a loud noise ~ n 1 : sharp noise made by the lips 2 : noisy slap

³smack adv : squarely and sharply

⁴smack n : fishing ship

small \'smȯl\ adj 1 : little in size or amount 2 : few in number 3 : trivial —**small·ish** adj —**small·ness** n

small·pox \'smȯl̩päks\ n : contagious virus disease marked by fever and eruption

smart \'smärt\ vb 1 : cause or feel stinging pain 2 : endure distress ~ adj 1 : intelligent or resourceful 2

: stylish —**smart** n —**smart·ly** adv —**smart·ness** n

smash \'smash\ vb : break or be broken into pieces ~ n 1 : smashing blow 2 : act or sound of smashing

smat·ter·ing \'smatəriŋ\ n 1 : superficial knowledge 2 : small scattered number or amount

smear \'smiər\ n : greasy stain ~ vb 1 : spread (something sticky) 2 : smudge 3 : slander

smell \'smel\ vb smelled \'smeld\ or smelt \'smelt\; smell·ing 1 : perceive the odor of 2 : have or give off an odor ~ n 1 : special sense by which one perceives odor 2 : odor —**smelly** adj

¹smelt \'smelt\ n, pl smelts or smelt : small food fish

²smelt vb : melt or fuse (ore) in order to separate the metal —**smelt·er** n

smile \'smīl\ n : facial expression with the mouth turned up usu. to show pleasure —**smile** vb

smirk \'smərk\ vb : wear a conceited smile —**smirk** n

smite \'smīt\ vb smote \'smōt\; smit·ten \'smitᵊn\ or smote; smit·ing \'smītiŋ\ 1 : strike heavily or kill 2 : affect strongly

smith \'smith\ n : worker in metals and esp. a blacksmith

smithy \'smithē\ n, pl smith·ies : a smith's workshop

smock \'smäk\ n : loose dress or protective coat

smog \'smäg, 'smȯg\ n : fog and smoke —**smog·gy** adj

smoke \'smōk\ n : sooty gas from burning ~ vb smoked; smok·ing 1 : give off smoke 2 : inhale and exhale the fumes of burning tobacco 3 : cure (as meat) with smoke —**smoke·less** adj —**smok·er** n —**smoky** adj

smoke·stack n : chimney through which smoke is discharged

smol·der, smoul·der \'smōldər\ vb 1 : burn and smoke without flame 2 : be suppressed but active —**smolder** n

smooth \'smüth\ adj 1 : having a surface without bends, curves, or irregularities 2 : not jarring or jolting ~ vb : make smooth —**smooth·ly** adv —**smooth·ness** n

smor·gas·bord \'smȯrgəs̩bȯrd\ n : buffet consisting of many foods

smoth·er \'smᵊthər\ vb 1 : kill by depriving of air 2 : cover thickly

smudge \'sməj\ vb smudged; smudg·ing : soil or blur by rubbing ~ n 1 : thick smoke 2 : dirty spot

smug \'sməg\ *adj* **-gg-** : content in one's own virtue or accomplishment —**smug·ly** *adv* —**smug·ness** *n*

smug·gle \'sməgəl\ *vb* **-gled; -gling** : import or export secretly or illegally —**smug·gler** \-glər\ *n*

smut \'smət\ *n* **1** : something that smudges **2** : indecent language or matter **3** : fungous disease of plants —**smut·ty** *adj*

snack \'snak\ *n* : light meal

snag \'snag\ *n* : unexpected difficulty ~ *vb* **-gg-** : become caught on something that sticks out

snail \'snāl\ *n* : small mollusk with a spiral shell

snake \'snāk\ *n* : long-bodied limbless crawling reptile —**snake·bite** *n*

snap \'snap\ *vb* **-pp-** **1** : bite at something **2** : utter angry words **3** : break suddenly with a sharp sound ~ *n* **1** : act or sound of snapping **2** : fastening that closes with a click **3** : something easy to do —**snap·per** *n* —**snap·pish** *adj* —**snap·py** *adj*

snap·drag·on *n* : garden plant with spikes of showy flowers

snap·shot \'snap̩shät\ *n* : casual photograph

snare \'snar\ *n* : trap for catching game ~ *vb* : capture or hold with or as if with a snare

¹snarl \'snärl\ *n* : tangle ~ *vb* : cause to become knotted

²snarl *vb or n* : growl

snatch \'snach\ *vb* **1** : try to grab something suddenly **2** : seize or take away suddenly ~ *n* **1** : act of snatching **2** : something brief or fragmentary

sneak \'snēk\ *vb* : move or take in a furtive manner ~ *n* : one who acts in a furtive manner —**sneak·ing·ly** *adv* —**sneaky** *adj*

sneak·er \'snēkər\ *n* : sports shoe

sneer \'snir\ *vb* : smile scornfully —**sneer** *n*

sneeze \'snēz\ *vb* **sneezed; sneez·ing** : force the breath out with sudden and involuntary violence —**sneeze** *n*

snick·er \'snikər\ *n* : partly suppressed laugh —**snicker** *vb*

snide \'snīd\ *adj* : subtly ridiculing

sniff \'snif\ *vb* **1** : draw air audibly up the nose **2** : detect by smelling —**sniff** *n*

snip \'snip\ *n* : fragment snipped off ~ *vb* **-pp-** : cut off by bits

¹snipe \'snīp\ *n, pl* **snipes** *or* **snipe** : bird of marshy areas

²snipe *vb* **sniped; snip·ing** : shoot at an enemy from a concealed position —**snip·er** *n*

snips \'snips\ *n pl* : scissorslike tool

sniv·el \'snivəl\ *vb* **-eled** *or* **-elled; -eling** *or* **-el·ling** **1** : have a running nose **2** : whine —**snivel** *n*

snob \'snäb\ *n* : one who acts superior to others —**snob·bery** \-(ə)rē\ *n* —**snob·bish** *adj* —**snob·bish·ly** *adv* —**snob·bish·ness** *n*

snoop \'snüp\ *vb* : pry in a furtive way ~ *n* : prying person

snooze \'snüz\ *vb* **snoozed; snooz·ing** : take a nap —**snooze** *n*

snore \'snōr\ *vb* **snored; snor·ing** : breathe with a hoarse noise while sleeping —**snore** *n*

snort \'snort\ *vb* : force air noisily through the nose —**snort** *n*

snout \'snaut\ *n* : long projecting muzzle (as of a swine)

snow \'snō\ *n* : crystals formed from water vapor ~ *vb* : fall as snow —**snow·ball** *n* —**snow·bank** *n* —**snow·drift** *n* —**snow·fall** *n* —**snow·plow** *n* —**snow·storm** *n* —**snowy** *adj*

snow·shoe *n* : frame of wood strung with thongs used for walking on snow

snub \'snəb\ *vb* **-bb-** : ignore or avoid through disdain —**snub** *n*

¹snuff \'snəf\ *vb* : put out (a candle) —**snuff·er** *n*

²snuff *vb* : draw forcibly into the nose ~ *n* : pulverized tobacco

snug \'snəg\ *adj* **-gg-** **1** : warm, secure, and comfortable **2** : fitting closely —**snug·ly** *adv* —**snug·ness** *n*

snug·gle \'snəgəl\ *vb* **-gled; -gling** : curl up comfortably

so \(')sō\ *adv* **1** : in the manner or to the extent indicated **2** : in the same way **3** : therefore **4** : finally **5** : thus ~ *conj* : for that reason

soak \'sōk\ *vb* **1** : lie in a liquid **2** : absorb ~ *n* : act of soaking

soap \'sōp\ *n* : cleaning substance —**soap** *vb* —**soapy** *adj*

soar \'sōr\ *vb* : fly upward on or as if on wings

sob \'säb\ *vb* **-bb-** : weep with convulsive heavings of the chest —**sob** *n*

so·ber \'sōbər\ *adj* **1** : not drunk **2** : serious or solemn —**so·ber·ly** *adv*

so·bri·ety \sə'brīətē, sō-\ *n* : quality or state of being sober

soc·cer \'säkər\ *n* : game played by kicking a ball

so·cia·ble \'sōshəbəl\ *adj* : friendly —**so·cia·bil·i·ty** \ˌsōshə'bilətē\ *n* —**so·cia·bly** \'sōshəblē\ *adv*

so·cial \'sōshəl\ *adj* **1** : relating to pleasant companionship **2** : naturally living or growing in groups **3** : relating to human society ~ n : social gathering —**so·cial·ly** adv

so·cial·ism \'sōshə‚lizəm\ n : social organization based on government control of the production and distribution of goods —**so·cial·ist** \'sōsh(ə)ləst\ n or adj —**so·cial·is·tic** \‚sōshə'listik\ adj

so·cial·ize \'sōshə‚līz\ vb -**ized**; -**iz·ing** 1 : regulate by socialism 2 : adapt to social needs 3 : participate in a social gathering —**so·cial·iza·tion** \‚sōsh(ə)lə'zāshən\ n

social work n : services concerned with aiding the poor and socially maladjusted —**social worker** n

so·ci·ety \sə'sīətē\ n, pl -**et·ies** 1 : companionship 2 : community life 3 : rich or fashionable class 4 : voluntary group

so·ci·ol·o·gy \‚sōs(h)ē'äləjē\ n : study of social relationships —**so·ci·o·log·i·cal** \-ē-ə'läjikəl\ adj —**so·ci·ol·o·gist** \-'äləjəst\ n

¹**sock** \'säk\ n, pl **socks** or **sox** : short stocking

²**sock** vb or n : punch

sock·et \'säkət\ n : hollow part that holds something

sod \'säd\ n : turf ~ vb -**dd**- : cover with sod

so·da \'sōdə\ n 1 : carbonated water or a soft drink 2 : ice cream drink made with soda

sod·den \'sädᵊn\ adj 1 : lacking spirit 2 : soaked or soggy

so·di·um \'sōdēəm\ n : soft waxy silver white metallic chemical element

so·fa \'sōfə\ n : wide padded chair

soft \'sȯft\ adj 1 : not hard, rough, or harsh 2 : nonalcoholic —**soft·ly** adv —**soft·ness** n

soft·ball : game like baseball

soft·en \'sȯfən\ vb : make or become soft —**soft·en·er** \-(ə)nər\ n

sog·gy \'sägē\ adj -**gier**; -**est** : heavy with moisture —**sog·gi·ness** \-ēnəs\ n

¹**soil** \'sȯil\ vb : make or become dirty ~ n : embedded dirt

²**soil** n : loose surface material of the earth

so·journ \'sō‚jərn, sō'jərn\ vb : reside temporarily —**so·journ** n

so·lace \'säləs\ n or vb : comfort

so·lar \'sōlər\ adj : relating to the sun or the energy in sunlight

sold past of SELL

sol·der \'sädər, 'sȯd-\ n : metallic alloy melted to join metallic surfaces ~ vb : cement with solder

sol·dier \'sōljər\ n : person in military service ~ vb : serve as a soldier —**sol·dier·ly** adj or adv

¹**sole** \'sōl\ n : bottom of the foot or a shoe —**soled** adj

²**sole** n : flatfish caught for food

³**sole** adj : single or only —**sole·ly** \'sōl(l)lē\ adv

sol·emn \'säləm\ adj 1 : dignified and ceremonial 2 : highly serious 3 : of great importance or responsibility —**so·lem·ni·ty** \sə'lemnətē\ n —**sol·emn·ly** adv —**sol·emn·ness** n

so·lic·it \sə'lisət\ vb : ask for —**so·lic·i·ta·tion** \-‚lisə'tāshən\ n

so·lic·i·tor \sə'lisətər\ n 1 : one that solicits 2 : lawyer

so·lic·i·tous \sə'lisətəs\ adj : showing or expressing concern —**so·lic·i·tous·ly** adv —**so·lic·i·tude** \-'lisə‚t(y)üd\ n

sol·id \'säləd\ adj 1 : not hollow 2 : having 3 dimensions 3 : hard 4 : of good quality 5 : of one character ~ n 1 : 3-dimensional figure 2 : substance in solid form —**solid** adv —**so·lid·i·ty** \sə'lidətē\ n —**sol·id·ly** adv —**sol·id·ness** n

sol·i·dar·i·ty \‚sälə'darətē\ n : unity of purpose

so·lid·i·fy \sə'lidə‚fī\ vb -**fied**; -**fy·ing** : make or become solid —**so·lid·i·fi·ca·tion** \-‚lidəfə'kāshən\ n

so·lil·o·quy \sə'liləkwē\ n, pl -**quies** : dramatic monologue —**so·lil·o·quize** \-‚kwīz\ vb

sol·i·taire \'sälə‚taər\ n 1 : solitary gem 2 : card game for one person

sol·i·tary \-‚terē\ adj 1 : alone 2 : secluded 3 : single

sol·i·tude \-‚t(y)üd\ n : state of being alone

so·lo \'sōlō\ n, pl -**los** : performance by only one person ~ adv : alone —**solo** adj or vb —**so·lo·ist** n

sol·stice \'sälstəs\ n : time of the year when the sun is farthest north or south of the equator

sol·u·ble \'sälyəbəl\ adj 1 : capable of being dissolved 2 : capable of being solved —**sol·u·bil·i·ty** \‚sälyə'bilətē\ n

so·lu·tion \sə'lüshən\ n 1 : answer to a problem 2 : homogeneous liquid mixture

solve \'sälv\ vb **solved**; **solv·ing** : find a solution for —**solv·able** adj

sol·vent \'sälvənt\ adj 1 : able to pay all debts 2 : dissolving or able to dissolve ~ n : substance that dissolves or disperses another substance —**sol·ven·cy** \-vənsē\ n

som·ber, som·bre \\'sämbər\ *adj* 1 : dark 2 : grave —**som·ber·ly** *adv*

som·bre·ro \säm'bre(ə)rō\ *n, pl* -ros : broad-brimmed hat

some \(')səm\ *adj* 1 : one unspecified 2 : unspecified or indefinite number of 3 : at least a few or a little ~ \'səm\ *pron* : a certain number or amount

-some \səm\ *adj suffix* : characterized by a thing, quality, state, or action

some·body \'səm,bädē, -bəd-\ *pron* : some person

some·day \'səm,dā\ *adv* : at some future time

some·how \-,haů\ *adv* : by some means

some·one \-(,)wən\ *pron* : some person

som·er·sault \'səmər,sölt\ *n* : body flip —**somersault** *vb*

some·thing \'səmthiŋ\ *pron* : some undetermined or unspecified thing

some·time \'səm,tīm\ *adv* : at a future, unknown, or unnamed time

some·times \-,tīmz\ *adv* : occasionally

some·what \-,hwät, -,hwət\ *adv* : in some degree

some·where \-,hwear\ *adv* : in, at, or to an unknown or unnamed place

som·no·lent \'sämnələnt\ *adj* : sleepy —**som·no·lence** \-ləns\ *n*

son \'sən\ *n* : male offspring

so·nar \'sō,när\ *n* : apparatus that locates underwater objects by reflected vibrations

so·na·ta \sə'nätə\ *n* : instrumental composition

song \'söŋ\ *n* : music and words to be sung

song·bird \'söŋ-\ *n* : bird with musical tones

son·ic \'sänik\ *adj* : relating to sound waves or the speed of sound

son–in–law \'sən-\ *n, pl* **sons–in–law** : husband of one's daughter

son·net \'sänət\ *n* : poem of 14 lines

so·no·rous \sə'nōrəs, 'sänərəs\ *adj* 1 : loud, deep, or rich in sound 2 : impressive —**so·nor·i·ty** \sə'nörətē\ *n*

soon \'sün\ *adv* 1 : before long 2 : promptly 3 : early

soot \'sůt, 'sət, 'süt\ *n* : fine black substance formed by combustion —**sooty** *adj*

soothe \'süth\ *vb* **soothed; sooth·ing** : calm or comfort —**sooth·er** *n*

sooth·say·er \'süth,sāər\ *n* : prophet —**sooth·say·ing** \-iŋ\ *n*

sop \'säp\ *n* : conciliatory bribe, gift, or concession ~ *vb* -**pp-** 1 : dip in a liquid 2 : soak 3 : mop up

so·phis·ti·cat·ed \sə'fistə,kātəd, sə-\ *adj* 1 : complex 2 : wise, cultured, or shrewd in human affairs —**so·phis·ti·ca·tion** \-,fistə'kāshən\ *n*

soph·ist·ry \'säfəstrē\ *n* : subtly fallacious reasoning or argument —**soph·ist** \'säfəst\ *n* —**so·phis·tic** \sə'fistik, sə-\, **so·phis·ti·cal** \-tikəl\ *adj*

soph·o·more \'säfəm,ōr, 'säf,mōr\ *n* : 2-year student

so·po·rif·ic \,säpə'rifik, ,sōp-\ *adj* : causing sleep or drowsiness

so·pra·no \sə'pranō\ *n, pl* -**nos** : highest singing voice

sor·cery \'sörs(ə)rē\ *n* : witchcraft —**sor·cer·er** \-rər\ *n* —**sor·cer·ess** \-rəs\ *n*

sor·did \'sördəd\ *adj* : vulgar, degrading, or corrupt —**sor·did·ly** *adv* —**sor·did·ness** *n*

sore \'sōr\ *adj* **sor·er; sor·est** 1 : causing pain or distress 2 : severe or intense 3 : angry ~ *n* : sore usu. infected spot on the body —**sore·ly** *adv* —**sore·ness** *n*

sor·ghum \'sörgəm\ *n* : forage grass

so·ror·i·ty \sə'rörətē\ *n, pl* -**ties** : club usu. for college women

sor·rel \'sörəl\ *n* : herb with sour juice

sor·row \'särō\ *n* : deep distress and regret or a cause of this —**sor·row·ful** \-fəl\ *adj* —**sor·row·ful·ly** \-f(ə)lē\ *adv*

sor·ry \'särē\ *adj* -**ri·er, -est** 1 : feeling sorrow, regret, or penitence 2 : dismal

sort \'sört\ *n* 1 : kind 2 : nature ~ *vb* : classify —**out of sorts** : grouchy

sor·tie \'sörtē, sör'tē\ *n* : military attack esp. against besiegers

SOS \,es(,)ō'es\ *n* : call for help

so-so \'sō'sō\ *adj or adv* : barely acceptable

sot \'sät\ *n* : drunkard —**sot·tish** *adj*

souf·flé \sü'flā\ *n* : baked dish made light with beaten egg whites

sought *past of* SEEK

soul \'sōl\ *n* 1 : immaterial essence of an individual life 2 : essential nature 3 : person —**soul·less** \-ləs\ *adj*

soul·ful \'sōlfəl\ *adj* : full of or expressing deep feeling —**soul·ful·ly** *adv*

¹sound \'saůnd\ *adj* 1 : free from fault, error, or illness 2 : firm or hard 3 : showing good judgment —**sound·ly** *adv* —**sound·ness** *n*

²sound *n* 1 : sensation experienced by hearing 2 : noise ~ *vb* 1 : make or cause to make a noise 2 : seem —**sound·proof** *adj or vb*

³sound *n* : wide strait ~ *vb* 1 : measure the depth of (water) 2 : investigate

soup \'süp\ *n* : broth usu. containing pieces of solid food —**soupy** *adj*

sour \'saů(ə)r\ *adj* 1 : having an acid or tart taste 2 : disagreeable ~ *vb*

: become or make sour —**sour·ish** adj
—**sour·ly** adv —**sour·ness** n

source \'sōrs\ n 1 : point of origin 2
: one that provides something needed

souse \'saủs\ vb **soused; sous·ing** 1
: pickle 2 : plunge into a liquid 3
: intoxicate ~ n 1 : something pickled 2 : drunkard

south \'saủth\ adv : to or toward the
south ~ adj 1 : situated toward, at, or
coming from the south ~ n 1 : direction to the right of sunrise 2 cap : regions to the south —**south·er·ly**
\'sə<u>th</u>ərlē\ adv or adj —**south·ern**
\'sə<u>th</u>ərn\ adj —**South·ern·er** n
—**South·ern·most** \-ˌmōst\ adj
—**south·ward** \'saủthwərd\ adv or
adj —**south·wards** \-wərdz\ adv

south·east \saủth'ēst, naut saủ'ēst\ n 1
: direction between south and east 2
cap : regions to the southeast —**south-
east** adj or adv —**south·east·er·ly** adv or adj —**south·east·ern**
\-ərn\ adj

south pole n : the southernmost point
of the earth

south·west \saủth'west, naut saủ'west\
n 1 : direction between south and
west 2 cap : regions to the southwest
—**southwest** adj or adv —**south·west·er·ly** adv or adj —**south·west·ern**
\-ərn\ adj

sou·ve·nir \ˌsüvəˌniər\ n : something
that is a reminder of a place or event

sov·er·eign \'sävɡərən\ n 1 : supreme
ruler 2 : gold coin of the United
Kingdom ~ adj 1 : supreme 2 : independent —**sov·er·eign·ty** \-tē\ n

¹**sow** \'saủ\ n : female swine

²**sow** \'sō\ vb **sowed; sown** \'sōn\ or
sowed, sow·ing 1 : plant or strew
with seed 2 : scatter abroad —**sow·er**
\'sō(ə)r\ n

sox pl of SOCK

soy·bean \'sói'bēn, -ˌbēn\ n : legume
with edible seeds

spa \'spä\ n : resort at a mineral spring

space \'spās\ n 1 : period of time 2
: area in, around, or between 3 : region beyond earth's atmosphere 4
: accommodations ~ vb **spaced; spac·ing** : separate —**space·craft** n
—**space·flight** n —**space·ship** n

spa·cious \'spāshəs\ adj : large or
roomy —**spa·cious·ly** adv —**spa·cious·ness** n

¹**spade** \'spād\ n : shovel with a flat
blade ~ vb **spad·ed; spad·ing** : dig
with a spade —**spade·ful** n

²**spade** n : playing card of a suit
marked with a black figure like an
inverted heart

spa·ghet·ti \spə'getē\ n : pasta strings

span \'span\ n 1 : amount of time 2
: distance between supports ~ vb
-nn- : extend across

span·gle \'spangəl\ n : small disk of
shining metal —**spangle** vb

span·iel \'spanyəl\ n : small dog with
drooping ears

spank \'spank\ vb : strike the buttocks
of with the open hand

¹**spar** \'spär\ n : pole or boom

²**spar** vb **-rr-** : practice boxing

spare \'spaər\ adj 1 : held in reserve 2
: thin or scanty ~ vb **spared; spar·ing**
1 : reserve or avoid using 2 : avoid
punishing or killing —**spare** n

spar·ing \'spa(ə)riŋ\ adj : thrifty
—**spar·ing·ly** adv

spark \'spärk\ n 1 : tiny hot and glowing particle 2 : smallest beginning or
germ 3 : visible electrical discharge
~ vb 1 : emit or produce sparks 2
: stir to activity

spar·kle \'spärkəl\ vb **-kled; -kling** 1
: flash 2 : effervesce ~ n : gleam
—**spark·ler** \-k(ə)lər\ n

spar·row \'sparō\ n : small singing bird

sparse \'spärs\ adj **spars·er; spars·est**
: thinly scattered —**sparse·ly** adv

spasm \'spazəm\ n 1 : involuntary
muscular contraction 2 : sudden, violent, and temporary effort or feeling
—**spas·mod·ic** \spaz'mädik\ adj

spas·tic \'spastik\ adj : relating to or
marked by muscular spasm —**spastic**
n

¹**spat** \'spat\ past of SPIT

²**spat** n : petty dispute

spa·tial \'späshəl\ adj : relating to
space —**spa·tial·ly** \-ē\ adv

spat·ter \'spatər\ vb : splash with
drops of liquid —**spatter** n

spat·u·la \'spachələ\ n : flexible knife-
like utensil

spawn \'spón\ vb 1 : produce eggs or
offspring 2 : bring forth ~ n : egg
cluster

spay \'spā\ vb : remove the ovaries
from (an animal)

speak \'spēk\ vb **spoke** \'spōk\; **spo·ken** \'spōkən\; **speak·ing** 1 : utter
words 2 : express orally 3 : address
an audience 4 : use (a language) in
speaking —**speak·er** n

spear \'spiər\ n : long pointed weapon
~ vb : strike or pierce with a spear
—**spear·head** n : leading force, element,
or influence —**spearhead** vb

spear·mint \'spiər-\ n : aromatic garden mint

spe·cial \'speshəl\ adj 1 : unusual or
unique 2 : particularly favored 3 : set

aside for a particular use —**special** *n*
—**spe·cial·ly** *adv*

spe·cial·ist \'spesh(ə)ləst\ *n* **1** : one devoted to a branch of learning or activity **2** : any of four enlisted ranks in the army corresponding to the grades of corporal through sergeant first class

spe·cial·ize \'speshə‚līz\ *vb* **-ized; -iz·ing** : concentrate one's efforts —**spe·cial·iza·tion** \‚speshələ'zāshən\ *n*

spe·cial·ty \'speshəltē\ *n, pl* **-ties** : area or field in which one specializes

spe·cie \'spēshē, -sē\ *n* : money in coin

spe·cies \'spēshēz, -sēz\ *n, pl* **spe·cies** : biological grouping of closely related organisms

spe·cif·ic \spi'sifik\ *adj* : definite or exact —**spe·cif·i·cal·ly** \-(ə)lē\ *adv*

spec·i·fi·ca·tion \‚spesəfə'kāshən\ *n* **1** : item specified **2** : detailed description of work to be done —usu. pl.

spec·i·fy \'spesə‚fī\ *vb* **-fied; -fy·ing** : mention precisely or by name

spec·i·men \-əmən\ *n* : typical example

spe·cious \'spēshəs\ *adj* : apparently but really not genuine or correct

speck \'spek\ *n* : tiny particle or blemish —**speck** *vb*

speck·led \'spekəld\ *adj* : marked with spots

spec·ta·cle \'spektikəl\ *n* **1** : impressive public display **2** *pl* : eyeglasses

spec·tac·u·lar \spek'takyələr\ *adj* : sensational or showy

spec·ta·tor \'spek‚tātər\ *n* : one who looks on

spec·ter, spec·tre \'spektər\ *n* **1** : ghost **2** : haunting vision

spec·tral \'spektrəl\ *adj* : relating to or resembling a specter or spectrum

spec·trum \'spektrəm\ *n, pl* **-tra** \-trə\ *or* **-trums** : series of colors formed when white light is dispersed into its components

spec·u·late \'spekyə‚lāt\ *vb* **-lat·ed; -lat·ing** **1** : think about things yet unknown **2** : risk money in a business deal in hope of high profit —**spec·u·la·tion** \‚spekyə'lāshən\ *n* —**spec·u·la·tive** \'spekyə‚lātiv\ *adj* —**spec·u·la·tor** \-‚lātər\ *n*

speech \'spēch\ *n* **1** : power, act, or manner of speaking **2** : talk given to an audience —**speech·less** *adj*

speed \'spēd\ *n* **1** : quality of being fast **2** : rate of motion or performance ~ *vb* **sped** \'sped\ *or* **speed·ed; speed·ing** : go at or travel at excessive rate of speed —**speed·boat** *n* —**speed·er** *n* —**speed·i·ly** \'spēd^ə lē\ *adv* —**speed·up** \-‚əp\ *n* —**speedy** *adj*

speed·om·e·ter \spi'dämətər\ *n* : instrument for indicating speed

¹spell \'spel\ *n* : influence of or like magic

²spell *vb* **1** : name, write, or print the letters of (a word) **2** : mean —**spell·er** *n*

³spell *vb* : substitute for or relieve (someone) ~ *n* **1** : turn at work **2** : period of time

spell·bound *adj* : held by a spell

spend \'spend\ *vb* **spent** \'spent\; **spend·ing** **1** : pay out **2** : occupy oneself during (a period of time) —**spend·er** *n*

spend·thrift \'spen(d)‚thrift\ *n* : wasteful person

sperm \'spərm\ *n, pl* **sperm** *or* **sperms** : semen or a germ cell in it

spew \'spyü\ *vb* : gush out in a stream

sphere \'sfir\ *n* **1** : figure with every point on its surface at an equal distance from the center **2** : round body **3** : range of action or influence —**spher·i·cal** \'sfirikəl, 'sfer-\ *adj*

spher·oid \'sfi(ə)r‚ȯid, 'sfe(ə)r-\ *n* : spherelike figure

spice \'spīs\ *n* **1** : aromatic plant product for seasoning food **2** : interesting quality —**spice** *vb* —**spicy** *adj*

spi·der \'spīdər\ *n* : small insectlike animal with 8 legs —**spi·dery** *adj*

spig·ot \'spigət, 'spikət\ *n* : faucet

spike \'spīk\ *n* : very large nail ~ *vb* **spiked; spik·ing** : fasten or pierce with a spike —**spiked** \'spīkt\ *adj*

spill \'spil\ *vb* : cause or allow unintentionally to fall, flow, or run out ~ *n* **1** : act of spilling **2** : something spilled —**spill·able** *adj*

spill·way *n* : passage for surplus water

spin \'spin\ *vb* **spun** \'spən\; **spin·ning** **1** : draw out fiber and twist into thread **2** : form thread from a sticky body fluid **3** : revolve or cause to revolve extremely fast ~ *n* : rapid rotating motion —**spin·ner** *n*

spin·ach \'spinich\ *n* : garden herb with edible leaves

spi·nal \'spīn³l\ *adj* : relating to the backbone —**spi·nal·ly** *adv*

spinal cord *n* : thick strand of nervous tissue that extends from the brain along the back within the backbone

spin·dle \'spind³l\ *n* **1** : stick used for spinning thread **2** : shaft around which something turns

spin·dly \'spin(d)lē\ *adj* : tall and slender

spine \'spīn\ *n* **1** : backbone **2** : stiff sharp projection on a plant or animal —**spine·less** *adj* —**spiny** *adj*

spin·et \\'spinət\\ *n* : small piano

spin·ster \\'spinstər\\ *n* : woman who never married

spi·ral \\'spīrəl\\ *adj* : circling or winding around a single point or line —**spiral** *n or vb* —**spi·ral·ly** *adv*

spire \\'spī(ə)r\\ *n* : steeple —**spiry** *adj*

spir·it \\'spirət\\ *n* **1** : life-giving force **2** *cap* : presence of God **3** : ghost **4** : mood **5** : vivacity or enthusiasm **6** *pl* : alcoholic liquor ~ *vb* : carry off secretly —**spir·it·ed** *adj* —**spir·it·less** *adj*

spir·i·tu·al \\'spirich(əw)əl\\ *adj* **1** : relating to the spirit or sacred matters **2** : deeply religious ~ *n* : religious folk song —**spir·i·tu·al·i·ty** \\₁spiricha°wal̇ətē\\ *n* —**spir·i·tu·al·ly** *adv*

spir·i·tu·al·ism \\'spirich(əw)ə₁lizəm\\ *n* : belief that spirits communicate with the living —**spir·i·tu·al·ist** \\-ləst\\ *n* —**spir·i·tu·al·is·tic** \\₁spirich(əw)ə-'listik\\ *adj*

¹spit \\'spit\\ *n* **1** : rod for holding and turning meat over a fire **2** : point of land that runs into the water

²spit *vb* **spit** *or* **spat** \\'spat\\; **spit·ting 1** : eject saliva from the mouth ~ *n* **1** : saliva **2** : perfect likeness

spite \\'spīt\\ *n* : grudge with a wish to injure ~ *vb* **spit·ed;** **spit·ing** : treat insultingly —**spite·ful** \\-fəl\\ *adj* —**spite·ful·ly** *adv* —**in spite of** : in defiance or contempt of

spit·tle \\'spit°l\\ *n* : saliva

spit·toon \\spi'tün\\ *n* : receptacle for spit

splash \\'splash\\ *vb* : scatter a liquid on —**splash** *n*

splat·ter \\'splatər\\ *vb* : spatter —**splat·ter** *n*

splay \\'splā\\ *vb* **1** : spread out **2** : slope or slant outward —**splay** *n or adj*

spleen \\'splēn\\ *n* **1** : organ for maintenance of the blood **2** : spite or anger

splen·did \\'splendəd\\ *adj* **1** : impressive in beauty or brilliance **2** : outstanding —**splen·did·ly** *adv*

splen·dor \\'splendər\\ *n* **1** : brilliance **2** : magnificence

splice \\'splīs\\ *vb* **spliced;** **splic·ing** : join (2 things) end to end —**splice** *n*

splint \\'splint\\ *n* **1** : thin strip of wood **2** : something that keeps an injured body part in place

splin·ter \\'splintər\\ *n* : thin needlelike piece ~ *vb* : break into splinters

split \\'split\\ *vb* **split, split·ting** : divide lengthwise or along a grain —**split** *n*

splotch \\'spläch\\ *n* : blotch

splurge \\'splərj\\ *vb* **splurged; splurg·ing** : indulge oneself —**splurge** *n*

splut·ter \\'splətər\\ *n* : sputter —**splut·ter** *vb*

spoil \\'spȯil\\ *n* : plunder ~ *vb* **spoiled** \\'spȯild, 'spȯilt\\ *or* **spoilt** \\'spȯilt\\; **spoil·ing 1** : pillage **2** : ruin **3** : rot —**spoil·age** \\'spȯilij\\ *n* —**spoil·er** *n*

¹spoke \\'spōk\\ *past of* SPEAK

²spoke *n* : rod from the hub to the rim of a wheel

spo·ken *past part of* SPEAK

spokes·man \\'spōksmən\\ *n* : one who speaks for others —**spokes·wom·an** \\-₁wûmən\\ *n*

sponge \\'spənj\\ *n* **1** : porous mass that forms the skeleton of some marine animals **2** : spongelike material used for wiping ~ *vb* **sponged; spong·ing 1** : wipe with a sponge **2** : live at another's expense —**spongy** \\'spənjē\\ *adj*

spon·sor \\'spänsər\\ *n* : one who assumes responsibility for another or who provides financial support —**sponsor** *vb* —**spon·sor·ship** *n*

spon·ta·ne·ous \\spän'tānēəs\\ *adj* : done, produced, or occurring naturally or without planning —**spon·ta·ne·i·ty** \\₁späntən'ēatē\\ *n* —**spon·ta·ne·ous·ly** \\spän'tānēəslē\\ *adv*

spoof \\'spüf\\ *vb* : make good-natured fun of —**spoof** *n*

spook \\'spük\\ *n* : ghost ~ *vb* : frighten —**spooky** *adj*

spool \\'spül\\ *n* : cylinder on which something is wound

spoon \\'spün\\ *n* : utensil consisting of a shallow bowl with a handle —**spoon** *vb* —**spoon·ful** \\-₁fûl\\ *n*

spoor \\'spu̇r, 'spȯr\\ *n* : track or trail esp. of a wild animal

spo·rad·ic \\spə'radik\\ *adj* : occasional —**spo·rad·i·cal·ly** \\-i(k)əlē\\ *adv*

spore \\'spȯr\\ *n* : primitive usu. one-celled reproductive body

sport \\'spȯrt\\ *vb* **1** : frolic **2** : wear or display ostentatiously ~ *n* **1** : physical activity engaged in for pleasure **2** : jest **3** : likable person **4** : one showing mutation —**sport·ive** \\-iv\\ *adj* —**sporty** *adj*

sports·cast \\'spȯrts₁kast\\ *n* : broadcast of a sports event —**sports·cast·er** \\-₁kastər\\ *n*

sports·man \\-mən\\ *n* : one who enjoys hunting and fishing

sports·man·ship \\-mən₁ship\\ *n* : ability to be gracious in winning or losing

spot \\'spät\\ *n* **1** : blemish **2** : distinctive small part **3** : location ~ *vb* **-tt- 1** : mark with spots **2** : see or recognize ~ *adj* : made at random or in limited numbers —**spot·less** *adj* —**spot·less·ly** *adv*

spot·light *n* **1** : intense beam of light **2** : center of public interest —**spotlight** *vb*

spot·ty \'spätē\ *adj* **-ti·er; -est** : uneven in quality

spouse \'spaůs\ *n* : one's husband or wife

spout \'spaůt\ *vb* **1** : shoot forth in a stream **2** : say pompously ~ *n* **1** : opening through which liquid spouts **2** : jet of liquid

sprain \'sprān\ *n* : twisting injury to a joint ~ *vb* : injure with a sprain

sprat \'sprat\ *n* : small or young herring

sprawl \'sprȯl\ *vb* : lie or sit with limbs spread out —**sprawl** *n*

¹spray \'sprā\ *n* : branch or arrangement of flowers

²spray *n* **1** : mist **2** : device that discharges liquid as a mist —**spray** *vb* —**spray·er** *n*

spread \'spred\ *vb* **spread; spread·ing 1** : open up or unfold **2** : scatter or smear over a surface **3** : cause to be known or to exist over a wide area ~ *n* **1** : extent to which something is spread **2** : cloth cover **3** : something intended to be spread —**spread·er** *n*

spree \'sprē\ *n* : burst of indulging in something

sprig \'sprig\ *n* : small shoot or twig

spright·ly \'sprītlē\ *adj* **-li·er; -est** : lively —**spright·li·ness** *n*

spring \'spriŋ\ *vb* **sprang** \'spraŋ\ *or* **sprung** \'spraŋ\, **sprung, spring·ing 1** : move or shoot up quickly or by elastic force **2** : make known suddenly ~ *n* **1** : source **2** : flow of water from underground **3** : season between winter and summer **4** : elastic body or device (as a coil of wire) **5** : leap **6** : elastic power —**springy** *adj*

sprin·kle \'spriŋkəl\ *vb* **-kled; -kling** : scatter in small drops or particles ~ *n* : light rainfall —**sprin·kler** \-k(ə)lər\ *n*

sprint \'sprint\ *n* : short run at top speed —**sprint** *vb* —**sprint·er** *n*

sprite \'sprīt\ *n* : elf or elfish being

sprock·et \'spräkət\ *n* : tooth on a wheel (**sprocket wheel**) shaped so as to interlock with a chain

sprout \'spraůt\ *vb* : send out new growth ~ *n* : plant shoot

¹spruce \'sprüs\ *n* : conical evergreen tree

²spruce *adj* **spruc·er; spruc·est** : neat

and stylish in appearance ~ *vb* **spruced; spruc·ing** : make or become neat

spry \'sprī\ *adj* **spri·er** *or* **spry·er** \'sprī(ə)r\; **spri·est** *or* **spry·est** \'sprīəst\ : agile and active

spume \'spyüm\ *n* : froth

spun *past of* SPIN

spunk \'spəŋk\ *n* : courage —**spunky** *adj*

spur \'spər\ *n* **1** : pointed device used to urge on a horse **2** : something that urges to action **3** : projecting part ~ *vb* **-rr-** : urge on —**spurred** *adj*

spu·ri·ous \'spyůrēəs\ *adj* : not genuine

spurn \'spərn\ *vb* : reject

¹spurt \'spərt\ *n* : burst of effort, speed, or activity ~ *vb* : make a spurt

²spurt *vb* : gush out ~ *n* : sudden gush

sput·ter \'spətər\ *vb* **1** : talk hastily and indistinctly in excitement **2** : make popping sounds —**sputter** *n*

spu·tum \'spyütəm\ *n, pl* **-ta** \-ə\ : expectorated saliva and mucus

spy \'spī\ *vb* **spied; spy·ing** : watch or try to gather information about someone secretly —**spy** *n*

squab \'skwäb\ *n, pl* **squabs** *or* **squab** : young pigeon

squab·ble \'skwäbəl\ *n or vb* : dispute

squad \'skwäd\ *n* : small group

squad·ron \'skwädrən\ *n* : small military unit

squal·id \'skwäləd\ *adj* : filthy or wretched

squall \'skwȯl\ *n* : sudden violent brief storm —**squally** *adj*

squa·lor \'skwälər\ *n* : quality or state of being squalid

squan·der \'skwändər\ *vb* : waste

square \'skwaər\ *n* **1** : instrument for measuring right angles **2** : flat figure that has 4 equal sides and 4 right angles **3** : open area in a city **4** : product of number multiplied by itself ~ *adj* **squar·er; squar·est 1** : being a square in form **2** : having sides meet at right angles **3** : multiplied by itself **4** : being a square unit of area **5** : honest **6** : even or tied ~ *vb* **squared; squar·ing 1** : form into a square **2** : multiply a number by itself **3** : conform **4** : settle —**square·ly** *adv*

¹squash \'skwäsh, 'skwȯsh\ *vb* **1** : press flat **2** : suppress

²squash *n, pl* **squash·es** *or* **squash** : garden vegetable

squat \'skwät\ *vb* **-tt- 1** : stoop or sit on one's heels **2** : settle on land one does not own ~ *n* : act or posture of squatting ~ *adj* **squat·ter, squat·test** : short and thick in stature —**squat·ter** *n*

squaw \'skwo\ *n* : Indian woman

squawk \'skwok\ *n* : harsh loud cry —**squawk** *vb*

squeak \'skwēk\ *vb* : make a thin high-pitched sound —**squeak** *n* —**squeaky** *adj*

squeal \'skwēl\ *vb* 1 : make a shrill sound or cry 2 : protest —**squeal** *n*

squea·mish \'skwēmish\ *adj* : easily nauseated or disgusted

squeeze \'skwēz\ *vb* **squeezed; squeez·ing** 1 : apply pressure to 2 : extract by pressure —**squeeze** *n* —**squeez·er** *n*

squelch \'skwelch\ *vb* : suppress (as with a retort) —**squelch** *n*

squid \'skwid\ *n, pl* **squid** *or* **squids** : 10-armed long-bodied sea mollusk

squint \'skwint\ *vb* : look with the eyes partly closed —**squint** *n or adj*

squire \'skwī(ə)r\ *n* 1 : knight's aide 2 : country landholder 3 : lady's devoted escort ~ *vb* **squired; squir·ing** : escort

squirm \'skwərm\ *vb* : wriggle

squir·rel \'skwər(ə)l\ *n* : rodent with a long bushy tail

squirt \'skwərt\ *vb* : eject liquid in a spurt —**squirt** *n*

stab \'stab\ *n* 1 : wound given by a pointed weapon 2 : quick thrust 3 : attempt ~ *vb* **-bb-** : pierce or wound with or as if with a pointed weapon

¹**sta·ble** \'stābəl\ *n* : building for livestock ~ *vb* **-bled; -bling** : keep in a stable

²**stable** *adj* **sta·bler; sta·blest** 1 : firmly established 2 : mentally well-balanced 3 : steady —**sta·bil·i·ty** \stə'bilətē\ *n* —**sta·bi·li·za·tion** \ˌstābələ'zāshən\ *n* —**sta·bi·lize** \'stābə‚līz\ *vb* —**sta·bi·liz·er** *n*

stac·ca·to \stə'kätō\ *adj* : disconnected

stack \'stak\ *n* : large pile ~ *vb* : pile up

sta·di·um \'stādēəm\ *n* : outdoor sports arena

staff \'staf\ *n, pl* **staffs** \'stafs, stavz\ *or* **staves** \'stavz, 'stāvz\ 1 : rod or supporting cane 2 : people assisting a leader 3 : 5 horizontal lines on which music is written ~ *vb* : supply with workers —**staff·er** *n*

staff sergeant *n* : noncommissioned officer ranking in the army next below a sergeant first class, in the air force next below a technical sergeant, and

in the marine corps next below a gunnery sergeant

stag \'stag\ *n, pl* **stags** *or* **stag** : male deer ~ *adj* : only for men ~ *adv* : without a date

stage \'stāj\ *n* 1 : raised platform for a speaker or performers 2 : theater 3 : step in a process ~ *vb* **staged; stag·ing** : produce (a play) —**stagy** \'stājē\ *adj*

stage-coach *n* : passenger coach

stag·ger \'stagər\ *vb* 1 : reel or cause to reel from side to side 2 : overlap or alternate —**stagger** *n* —**stag·ger·ing·ly** *adv*

stag·nant \'stagnənt\ *adj* : not moving or active —**stag·nate** \-‚nāt\ *vb* —**stag·na·tion** \stag'nāshən\ *n*

¹**staid** \'stād\ *adj* : sedate

²**staid** *past of* STAY

stain \'stān\ *vb* 1 : discolor 2 : dye (as wood) 3 : disgrace ~ *n* 1 : discolored area 2 : dishonor 3 : coloring preparation —**stain·less** *adj*

stair \'staər\ *n* 1 : step in a series for going from one level to another 2 *pl* : flight of steps —**stair·way** *n*

stair·case *n* : series of steps with their framework

stake \'stāk\ *n* 1 : small post driven into the ground 2 : bet 3 : prize in a contest ~ *vb* **staked; stak·ing** 1 : mark or secure with a stake 2 : place as a bet

sta·lac·tite \stə'lak‚tīt\ *n* : icicle-shaped deposit hanging in a cavern

sta·lag·mite \stə'lag‚mīt\ *n* : icicle-shaped deposit on the floor of a cavern

stale \'stāl\ *adj* **stal·er; stal·est** : not fresh —**stale** *vb*

stale·mate \'stāl‚māt\ *n* : deadlock —**stalemate** *vb*

¹**stalk** \'stok\ *vb* 1 : walk stiffly or haughtily 2 : to approach (game) stealthily

²**stalk** *n* : plant stem —**stalked** \'stokt\ *adj*

¹**stall** \'stol\ *n* 1 : compartment in a stable 2 : booth where articles are sold

²**stall** *vb* : bring or come to a stand-still unintentionally

³**stall** *vb* : delay, evade, or keep a situation going to gain advantage or time

stal·lion \'stalyən\ *n* : male horse

stal·wart \'stolwərt\ *n* : strong or brave

sta·men \'stāmən\ *n* : flower organ that produces pollen

stam·i·na \'stamənə\ *n* : endurance

stam·mer \'stamər\ *vb* : hesitate in speaking —**stammer** *n*

stamp \'stamp *also* 'stämp *or* 'stömp\ *vb* **1** : pound with the sole of the foot or a heavy implement **2** : impress with a mark **3** : cut out with a die **4** : attach a postage stamp to ~ *n* **1** : device for stamping **2** : act of stamping **3** : government seal showing a tax or fee has been paid

stam·pede \stam'pēd\ *n* : headlong rush of frightened animals ~ *vb* **-ped·ed; -ped·ing** : flee in panic

stance \'stans\ *n* : way of standing

¹stanch \'stönch, 'stänch\ *vb* : stop the flow of (as blood)

²stanch *var of* STAUNCH

stan·chion \'stanchən\ *n* : upright support

stand \'stand\ *vb* **stood** \'stùd\; **stand·ing 1** : be at rest in or assume an upright position **2** : remain unchanged **3** : be steadfast **4** : maintain a relative position or rank **5** : set upright **6** : undergo or endure ~ *n* **1** : act or place of standing, staying, or resisting **2** : sales booth **3** : structure for holding something upright **4** : group of plants growing together **5** *pl* : tiered seats **6** : opinion or viewpoint

stan·dard \'standərd\ *n* **1** : symbolic figure or flag **2** : model, rule, or guide **3** : upright support —**standard** *adj* —**stan·dard·iza·tion** \,standərdə-'zāshən\ *n* —**stan·dard·ize** \'standərd,īz\ *vb*

standard time *n* : time established over a region or country

stand·ing \'standiŋ\ *n* **1** : relative position or rank **2** : duration

stand·still *n* : state of rest

stank *past of* STINK

stan·za \'stanzə\ *n* : division of a poem

¹sta·ple \'stāpəl\ *n* : U-shaped wire fastener —**staple** *vb* —**sta·pler** \-p(ə)lər\ *n*

²staple *n* : chief commodity or item —**staple** *adj*

star \'stär\ *n* **1** : celestial body visible as a point of light **2** : 5- or 6-pointed figure representing a star **3** : leading performer ~ *vb* **-rr- 1** : mark with a star **2** : play the leading role —**star·dom** \'stärdəm\ *n* —**star·less** *adj* —**star·light** *n* —**star·ry** *adj*

star·board \'stärbərd\ *n* : right side of a ship or airplane looking forward —**starboard** *adj*

starch \'stärch\ *n* : nourishing carbohydrate from plants also used in adhesives and laundering ~ *vb* : stiffen with starch —**starchy** *adj*

stare \'staər\ *vb* **stared; star·ing** : look intently with wide-open eyes —**stare** *n* —**star·er** *n*

stark \'stärk\ *adj* **1** : absolute **2** : severe or bleak —**stark** *adv* —**stark·ly** *adv*

star·ling \'stärliŋ\ *n* : bird related to the crows

start \'stärt\ *vb* **1** : twitch or jerk (as from surprise) **2** : perform or show performance of the first part of an action or process ~ *n* **1** : sudden involuntary motion **2** : beginning —**start·er** *n*

star·tle \'stärt°l\ *vb* **-tled; -tling** : frighten or surprise suddenly

starve \'stärv\ *vb* **starved; starv·ing 1** : suffer or die from hunger **2** : kill with hunger —**star·va·tion** \stär'vāshən\ *n*

state \'stāt\ *n* **1** : condition of being **2** : condition of mind **3** : nation or a political unit within it ~ *vb* **stat·ed; stat·ing 1** : express in words **2** : establish —**state·hood** \-,hùd\ *n*

state·ly \'stātlē\ *adj* **-li·er; -est** : having impressive dignity —**state·li·ness** *n*

state·ment \'stātmənt\ *n* **1** : something stated **2** : financial summary

state·room *n* : private room on a ship

states·man \'stātsmən\ *n* : one skilled in government or diplomacy —**states·man·like** *adj* —**states·man·ship** *n*

stat·ic \'statik\ *adj* **1** : relating to bodies or forces at rest **2** : not moving **3** : relating to stationary charges of electricity ~ *n* : noise on radio or television from electrical disturbances

sta·tion \'stāshən\ *n* **1** : place of duty **2** : regular stopping place on a transportation route **3** : social standing **4** : place where radio or television programs originate ~ *vb* : assign to a station

sta·tion·ary \'stāshə,nerē\ *adj* **1** : not moving or not movable **2** : not changing

sta·tio·nery \'stāshə,nerē\ *n* : letter paper and envelopes

sta·tis·tic \stə'tistik\ *n* : single item of statistics

sta·tis·tics \-tiks\ *n pl* : numerical facts collected for study —**sta·tis·ti·cal** \-tikəl\ *adj* —**sta·tis·ti·cal·ly** *adv* —**stat·is·ti·cian** \,statə'stishən\ *n*

stat·u·ary \'stachə,werē\ *n, pl* **-ar·ies** : collection of statues

stat·ue \'stachü\ *n* : sculptured likeness of a being —**stat·u·et·te** \,stachə'wet\ n

stat·u·esque \,stachə'wesk\ adj : well-proportioned or of dignified bearing

stat·ure \'stachər\ n 1 : height 2 : status gained by achievement

sta·tus \'stātəs, 'stat-\ n : relative situation or condition

status quo \-'kwō\ n : existing state of affairs

stat·ute \'stachüt\ n : law —**stat·u·to·ry** \'stachə,tōrē\ adj

staunch \'stonch\ adj : steadfast —**staunch·ly** adv

stave \'stāv\ n : narrow strip of wood ~ vb **staved** or **stove** \'stōv\; **stav·ing** 1 : break a hole in 2 : drive away

staves pl of STAFF

stay \'stā\ n : support ~ vb **stayed**; **stay·ing** 1 : prop up 2 : satisfy for a time

²**stay** vb **stayed** \'stād\ or **staid** \'stād\; **stay·ing** 1 : pause 2 : lodge 3 : remain 4 : stop or postpone ~ n : a staying

stead \'sted\ n : one's place, job, or function —**in good stead** : to advantage

stead·fast \-,fast\ adj : faithful or determined —**stead·fast·ly** adv —**stead·fast·ness** n

steady \'stedē\ adj **steadi·er; -est** 1 : firm in position or sure in movement 2 : calm or reliable 3 : constant 4 : regular ~ vb **stead·ied; steady·ing** : make or become steady —**steadi·ly** \'sted³lē\ adv —**steadi·ness** n —**steady** adv

steak \'stāk\ n : thick slice of meat

steal \'stēl\ vb **stole** \'stōl\; **sto·len** \'stōlən\; **steal·ing** 1 : take and carry away wrongfully and with intent to keep 2 : move secretly or slowly

stealth \'stelth\ n : secret or underhand procedure —**stealth·i·ly** adv —**stealthy** adj

steam \'stēm\ n : vapor of boiling water ~ vb : give off steam —**steam·boat** n —**steam·ship** n —**steamy** adj

steed \'stēd\ n : horse

steel \'stēl\ n : tough carbon-containing iron ~ vb : make able to resist —**steel** adj —**steely** adj

¹**steep** \'stēp\ adj : having a very sharp slope or great elevation —**steep·ly** adv —**steep·ness** n

²**steep** vb : soak in a liquid

stee·ple \'stēpəl\ n : usu. tapering church tower

stee·ple·chase n : race over hurdles

¹**steer** \'stir\ n : castrated ox

²**steer** vb 1 : direct the course of (as a ship or car) 2 : guide

steer·age \'sti(ə)rij\ n : section in a ship for passengers paying the lowest fares

stein \'stīn\ n : mug

stel·lar \'stelər\ adj : relating to stars or resembling a star

¹**stem** \'stem\ n : main upright part of a plant ~ vb -**mm-** 1 : derive 2 : make progress against —**stem·less** adj —**stemmed** adj

²**stem** vb -**mm-** : stop the flow of

stench \'stench\ n : stink

sten·cil \'stensəl\ n : printing sheet cut with letters to let ink pass through —**stencil** vb

ste·nog·ra·phy \stə'nägrəfē\ n : art or process of writing in shorthand —**ste·nog·ra·pher** \-fər\ n —**steno·graph·ic** \,stenə'grafik\ adj

sten·to·ri·an \sten'tōrēən\ adj : extremely loud

step \'step\ n 1 : single action of a leg in walking or running 2 : rest for the foot in going up or down 3 : degree, rank, or stage 4 : way of walking ~ vb -**pp-** 1 : move by steps 2 : press with the foot

step- \'step-\ comb form : related by a remarriage (as of a parent) and not by blood

step·lad·der n : light portable set of steps in a hinged frame

steppe \'step\ n : dry grassy land esp. of Asia

-ster \stər\ n suffix 1 : one that does, makes, or uses 2 : one that is associated with or takes part in 3 : one that is

ste·reo \'sterēō, 'stir-\ n, pl -**reos** : stereophonic sound system —**stereo** adj

ste·reo·phon·ic \,sterēə'fänik, ,stir-\ adj : relating to a 3-dimensional effect of reproduced sound

ste·reo·typed \'sterēə,tīp, 'stir-\ adj : represented as lacking originality or individuality

ster·ile \'sterəl\ adj 1 : unable to bear fruit, crops, or offspring 2 : free from disease germs —**ste·ril·i·ty** \stə'rilətē\ n —**ster·il·iza·tion** \,sterələ'zāshən\ n —**ster·il·ize** \-ə,līz\ vb —**ster·il·iz·er** n

ster·ling \'stərliŋ\ adj 1 : having a fixed standard of purity represented by an alloy of 925 parts of silver with 75 parts of copper 2 : made of sterling silver 3 : excellent

¹**stern** \'stərn\ adj : severe —**stern·ly** adv —**stern·ness** n

²**stern** n : back end of a boat

ster·num \'stərnəm\ *n, pl* **-nums** *or* **-na** \-nə\ : long flat chest bone joining the 2 sets of ribs

stetho·scope \'stethə,skōp\ *n* : instrument used for listening to sounds in the chest

ste·ve·dore \'stēvə,dōr\ *n* : worker who loads and unloads ships

stew \'st(y)ü\ *n* : dish of boiled meat and vegetables —**stew** *vb*

stew·ard \'st(y)üərd\ *n* **1** : manager of an estate or an organization **2** : person on a ship or airliner who looks after passenger comfort —**stew·ard·ess** \-əs\ *n* —**stew·ard·ship** *n*

¹stick \'stik\ *n* **1** : cut or broken branch **2** : long thin piece of wood or something resembling it

²stick *vb* **stuck** \'stək\; **stick·ing 1** : stab **2** : thrust or project **3** : hold fast to something **4** : attach **5** : become jammed or fixed

stick·er \'stikər\ *n* : gummed label

stick·ler \'stik(ə)lər\ *n* : one who insists on exactness or completeness

sticky \'stikē\ *adj* **stick·i·er; -est 1** : adhesive **2** : gluey

stiff \'stif\ *adj* **1** : not bending easily **2** : tense **3** : formal **4** : strong **5** : severe —**stiff·ly** *adv* —**stiff·ness** *n*

stiff·en \'stifən\ *vb* : make or become stiff —**stiff·en·er** \-(ə)nər\ *n*

sti·fle \'stīfəl\ *vb* **-fled; -fling 1** : smother or suffocate **2** : suppress

stig·ma \'stigmə\ *n, pl* **-ma·ta** \stig'mätə, 'stigmətə\ *or* **-mas** : mark of disgrace —**stig·ma·tize** \'stigmə,tīz\ *vb*

stile \'stīl\ *n* : steps for crossing a fence

sti·let·to \stə'letō\ *n, pl* **-tos** *or* **-toes** : slender dagger

¹still \'stil\ *adj* **1** : motionless **2** : silent ~ *vb* : make or become still ~ *adv* **1** : without motion **2** : up to and during this time **3** : in spite of that ~ *n* : silence —**still·ness** *n*

²still *n* : apparatus used in distillation

still·born \'stil'bȯrn\ *adj* : born dead —**still·birth** *n*

stilt \'stilt\ *n* : one of a pair of poles for walking

stilt·ed \'stiltəd\ *adj* : pompous

stim·u·lant \'stimyələnt\ *n* : substance that temporarily increases the activity of an organism —**stimulant** *adj*

stim·u·late \-,lāt\ *vb* **-lat·ed; -lat·ing** : make active —**stim·u·la·tion** \,stimyə'lāshən\ *n*

stim·u·lus \'stimyələs\ *n, pl* **-li** \-,lī\ : something that stimulates

sting \'stiŋ\ *vb* **stung** \'stəŋ\; **sting·ing 1** : prick painfully **2** : hurt with an

intense burning pain ~ *n* : act of stinging —**sting·er** *n*

stin·gy \'stinjē\ *adj* **stin·gi·er; -est** : not generous —**stin·gi·ness** *n*

stink \'stiŋk\ *vb* **stank** \'staŋk\ *or* **stunk** \'stəŋk\; **stunk; stink·ing** : have a strong offensive odor —**stink** *n* —**stink·er** *n*

stint \'stint\ *vb* : be sparing or stingy ~ *n* **1** : restraint **2** : quantity or period of work

sti·pend \'stī,pend, -pənd\ *n* : money paid periodically

stip·ple \'stipəl\ *vb* **-pled; -pling** : engrave, paint, or draw with dots instead of lines —**stipple** *n*

stip·u·late \'stipyə,lāt\ *vb* **-lat·ed; -lat·ing** : demand as a condition —**stip·u·la·tion** \,stipyə'lāshən\ *n*

stir \'stər\ *vb* **-rr- 1** : move slightly **2** : prod or push into activity **3** : mix by continued circular movement ~ *n* : act or result of stirring

stir·rup \'stərəp\ *n* : saddle loop for the foot

stitch \'stich\ *n* **1** : loop formed by a needle in sewing **2** : sudden sharp pain ~ *vb* **1** : fasten or decorate with stitches **2** : sew

stock \'stäk\ *n* **1** : block or part of wood **2** : original from which others derive **3** : farm animals **4** : supply of goods kept by a merchant **5** : money invested in a large business **6** *pl* : instrument of punishment like a pillory but having holes for the feet or feet and hands ~ *vb* : provide with stock

stock·ade \stä'kād\ *n* : defensive or confining enclosure

stock·ing \'stäkiŋ\ *n* : close-fitting covering for the foot and leg

stock·pile *n* : reserve supply —**stockpile** *vb*

stock·yard \'stäk,yärd\ *n* : yard for livestock to be slaughtered or shipped

stocky \'stäkē\ *adj* **stock·i·er; -est** : short and relatively thick

stodgy \'stäjē\ *adj* **stodg·i·er; -est** : dull

sto·ic \'stōik\, **sto·i·cal** \-ikəl\ *adj* : showing indifference to pain —**stoic** *n* —**sto·i·cal·ly** \-ik(ə)lē\ *adv* —**sto·icism** \'stōə,sizəm\ *n*

stoke \'stōk\ *vb* **stoked; stok·ing** : stir up a fire or supply fuel to a furnace —**stok·er** *n*

¹stole \'stōl\ *past of* STEAL

²stole *n* : long wide scarf

stolen *past part of* STEAL

stol·id \'stäləd\ *adj* : having or showing little or no emotion —**sto·lid·i·ty** \stä'lidətē\ *n* —**stol·id·ly** \'stälədlē\ *adv*

stom·ach \'stəmək, -ik\ *n* 1 : saclike digestive organ 2 : abdomen 3 : appetite or desire —**stom·ach·ache** *n*

stomp \'stämp, 'stómp\ *vb* : stamp

stone \'stōn\ *n* 1 : hardened earth or mineral matter 2 : small piece of rock 3 : seed that is hard or has a hard covering ~ *vb* **stoned**; **ston·ing** : pelt or kill with stones —**stony** *adj*

stood *past of* STAND

stool \'stül\ *n* 1 : seat usu. without back or arms 2 : footstool 3 : discharge of feces

¹stoop \'stüp\ *vb* 1 : bend over 2 : lower oneself ~ *n* 1 : act of bending over 2 : bent position of shoulders

²stoop *n* : small porch at a house door

stop \'stäp\ *vb* -**pp**- 1 : block a hole or opening 2 : end or cause to end 3 : pause for rest or a visit in a journey ~ *n* 1 : plug 2 : act or place of stopping 3 : delay in a journey —**stop·light** *n* —**stop·page** \-ij\ *n* —**stop·per** *n*

stop·gap *n* : temporary measure or thing

stor·age \'stōrij\ *n* : safekeeping of goods (as in a warehouse)

store \'stōr\ *vb* **stored**; **stor·ing** : put aside for future use ~ *n* 1 : something stored 2 : retail business establishment —**store·house** *n* —**store·keep·er** *n* —**store·room** *n*

stork \'stórk\ *n* : large wading bird

storm \'stórm\ *n* 1 : heavy fall of rain or snow 2 : violent outbreak ~ *vb* 1 : rain or snow heavily 2 : rage 3 : make an attack against —**stormy** *adj*

¹sto·ry \'stōrē\ *n, pl* -**ries** 1 : narrative 2 : report —**sto·ry·tell·er** *n* —**sto·ry·tell·ing** *adj* or *n*

²story *n, pl* -**ries** : floor of a building

stout \'staüt\ *adj* 1 : firm or strong 2 : thick or bulky —**stout·ly** *adv* —**stout·ness** *n*

¹stove \'stōv\ *n* : apparatus for providing heat (as for cooking or heating)

²stove *past of* STAVE

stow \'stō\ *vb* 1 : pack in a compact mass 2 : put or hide away

strad·dle \'strad³l\ *vb* -**dled**; -**dling** : stand over or sit on with legs on opposite sides —**straddle** *n*

strafe \'sträf\ *vb* **strafed**; **straf·ing** : fire upon with machine guns from a low-flying airplane

strag·gle \'stragəl\ *vb* -**gled**; -**gling** : wander or become separated from others —**strag·gler** \-(ə)lər\ *n*

straight \'strāt\ *adj* 1 : having no bends, turns, or twists 2 : just,

proper, or honest 3 : neat and orderly ~ *adv* : in a straight manner

straight·en \'strāt³n\ *vb* : make or become straight

straight·for·ward \strāt'fórwərd\ *adj* : frank or honest

straight·way *adv* : immediately

¹strain \'strān\ *n* 1 : lineage 2 : trace

²strain *vb* 1 : exert to the utmost 2 : filter or remove by filtering 3 : injure by improper use ~ *n* 1 : excessive tension or exertion 2 : bodily injury from excessive effort —**strain·er** *n*

strait \'strāt\ *n* 1 : narrow channel connecting 2 bodies of water 2 *pl* : distress

strait·en \'strāt³n\ *vb* 1 : hem in 2 : make distressing or difficult

¹strand \'strand\ *vb* 1 : drive or cast upon the shore 2 : leave helpless

²strand *n* 1 : twisted fiber of a rope 2 : length of something ropelike

strange \'strānj\ *adj* **strang·er**; **strang·est** 1 : unusual or queer 2 : new —**strange·ly** *adv* —**strange·ness** *n*

strang·er \'strānjər\ *n* : person with whom one is not acquainted

stran·gle \'strangəl\ *vb* -**gled**; -**gling** : choke to death —**stran·gler** \-g(ə)lər\ *n*

stran·gu·la·tion \,strangyə'lāshən\ *n* : act or process of strangling

strap \'strap\ *n* : narrow strip of flexible material used esp. for fastening ~ *vb* 1 : secure with a strap 2 : beat with a strap —**strap·less** *adj*

strap·ping \'strapin\ *adj* : robust

strat·a·gem \'stratəjəm, -jem\ *n* : deceptive scheme or maneuver

strat·e·gy \'stratəjē\ *n, pl* -**gies** : carefully worked out plan of action —**stra·te·gic** \strə'tējik\ *adj* —**strat·e·gist** \'stratəjəst\ *n*

strat·i·fy \'stratə,fī\ *vb* -**fied**; -**fy·ing** : form or arrange in layers —**strat·i·fi·ca·tion** \,stratəfə'kāshən\ *n*

strato·sphere \'stratə,sfiər\ *n* : earth's atmosphere from about 7 to 37 miles above the earth's surface —**strato·spher·ic** \,stratə'sfi(ə)rik, -'sfer-\ *adj*

stra·tum \'strātəm, 'strat-\ *n, pl* -**ta** \'strātə, 'strat-\ : layer

straw \'stró\ *n* 1 : grass stems after grain is removed 2 : tube for drinking ~ *adj* : made of straw

straw·ber·ry \'stró,berē, berə\ *n* : red pulpy fruit

stray \'strā\ *vb* : wander from a course or herd ~ *n* : person or animal that strays ~ *adj* : separated from or not related to anything close by

streak \'strēk\ n 1 : mark of a different color 2 : narrow band of light 3 : trace 4 : run (as of luck) or series ~ vb 1 : form streaks in or on 2 : move fast

stream \'strēm\ n 1 : flow of water on land 2 : steady flow (as of water or air) ~ vb 1 : flow in a stream 2 : pour out streams

stream·er \'strēmər\ n : long ribbon or ribbonlike flag

stream·lined \-,līnd, -'līnd\ adj 1 : made with contours to reduce air or water resistance 2 : simplified 3 : modernized —**streamline** vb

street \'strēt\ n : thoroughfare esp. in a city or town

street·car n : passenger vehicle running on rails in the streets

strength \'streŋth\ n 1 : quality of being strong 2 : toughness 3 : intensity

strength·en \'streŋthən\ vb : make, grow, or become stronger —**strength·en·er** \'streŋth(ə)nər\ n

stren·u·ous \'strenyəwəs\ adj : requiring or showing energetic effort —**stren·u·ous·ly** adv

stress \'stres\ n 1 : pressure or strain that tends to distort a body 2 : relative prominence or importance given to one thing among others 3 : state of physical or mental tension or something inducing it ~ vb : put stress on

stretch \'strech\ vb 1 : spread or reach out 2 : draw out in length or breadth 3 : make taut 4 : exaggerate 5 : become extended without breaking ~ n : act of extending beyond normal limits

stretch·er \'strechər\ n : cot with handles for carrying a disabled person

strew \'strü\ vb strewed; strewed or strewn \'strün\; strew·ing 1 : scatter 2 : cover by scattering something over

strick·en \'strikən\ adj : afflicted with disease

strict \'strikt\ adj 1 : severe and unyielding 2 : precise —**strict·ly** adv —**strict·ness** n

stric·ture \'strikchər\ n : hostile criticism

stride \'strīd\ vb strode \'strōd\; strid·den \'strid³n\; strid·ing \'strīdiŋ\ : walk or run with long steps ~ n : long step 2 : manner of striding

stri·dent \'strīd³nt\ adj : loud and harsh

strife \'strīf\ n : conflict

strike \'strīk\ vb struck \'strək\; struck; strik·ing \'strīkiŋ\ 1 : hit sharply 2 : delete 3 : produce by impressing 4 : cause to sound 5 : afflict 6 : occur to or impress 7 : cause (a match) to ignite by rubbing 8 : refrain from working 9 : find 10 : take on (as a pose) ~ n 1 : act or instance of striking 2 : work stoppage 3 : military attack —**strik·er** n —**strike out** vb : start out vigorously —**strike up** vb : start

strik·ing \'strīkiŋ\ adj : very noticeable —**strik·ing·ly** adv

string \'striŋ\ n 1 : line usu. of twisted threads 2 : series 3 pl : stringed instruments ~ vb strung \'strəŋ\; string·ing 1 : thread on or with a string 2 : hang or fasten by a string

stringed \'striŋd\ adj : having strings

strin·gent \'strinjənt\ adj : severe

stringy \'striŋē\ adj string·i·er; -est : tough or fibrous

¹strip \'strip\ vb -pp- 1 : take the covering or clothing from 2 : undress —**strip·per** n

²strip n : long narrow flat piece

stripe \'strīp\ n 1 : distinctive line or long narrow section ~ vb striped \'strīpt\; strip·ing : make stripes on

striped \'strīpt, 'strīpəd\ adj : having stripes or streaks

strive \'strīv\ vb strove \'strōv\; striv·en \'strivən\ or strived; striv·ing \'strīviŋ\ 1 : struggle 2 : try hard

strode past of STRIDE

stroke \'strōk\ vb stroked; strok·ing : rub gently ~ n 1 : act of swinging or striking 2 : sudden action

stroll \'strōl\ vb : walk leisurely —**stroll** n —**stroll·er** n

strong \'stroŋ\ adj 1 : capable of exerting great force or of withstanding stress or violence 2 : healthy 3 : zealous —**strong·ly** adv

strong·hold n : fortified place

stron·tium \'stränch(ē)əm, 'stränteəm\ n : soft malleable metallic chemical element

struck past of STRIKE

struc·ture \'strəkchər\ n 1 : building 2 : arrangement of elements ~ vb -tured; -tur·ing : make into a structure —**struc·tur·al** \-chərəl, -shrəl\ adj

strug·gle \'strəgəl\ vb -gled; -gling 1 : make strenuous efforts to overcome an adversary 2 : proceed with great effort ~ n 1 : strenuous effort 2 : intense competition for superiority

strum \'strəm\ vb -mm- : play (a musical instrument) by brushing the strings with the fingers

strum·pet \'strəmpət\ n : prostitute

strung past of STRING

strut \'strət\ vb -tt- : walk in a proud or showy manner ~ n 1 : proud walk 2 : supporting bar or rod

strych·nine \'strik,nīn, -nən, -,nēn\ n : bitter poisonous substance

stub \'stəb\ n : short end or section ~ vb -bb- : strike against something

stub·ble \'stəbəl\ n : short growth left after cutting —**stub·bly** adj

stub·born \'stəbərn\ adj 1 : unreasonably determined not to yield 2 : hard to control —**stub·born·ly** adv —**stub·born·ness** n

stub·by \'stəbē\ adj : short, blunt, and thick

stuc·co \'stəkō\ n, pl -cos or -coes : plaster for coating outside walls ~ vb : coat with stucco

stuck past of STICK

stuck-up \'stək'əp\ adj : conceited

¹**stud** \'stəd\ n : male horse kept for breeding

²**stud** n 1 : upright wall support 2 : projecting nail, pin, or rod ~ vb -dd- : supply or dot with studs

stu·dent \'st(y)üdᵊnt\ n : one who studies

stud·ied \'stədēd\ adj : premeditated

stu·dio \'st(y)üdē,ō\ n, pl -dios 1 : artist's workroom 2 : place where movies are made or television or radio shows are broadcast

stu·di·ous \'st(y)üdēəs\ adj : devoted to study —**stu·di·ous·ly** adv

study \'stədē\ n, pl stud·ies 1 : act or process of learning about something 2 : branch of learning 3 : careful examination 4 : room for reading or studying ~ vb stud·ied; study·ing : apply the attention and mind to a subject

stuff \'stəf\ n 1 : personal property 2 : raw or fundamental material 3 : unspecified often worthless material or things ~ vb : fill esp. by packing tightly —**stuff·ing** n

stuffy \'stəfē\ adj stuff·i·er; -est 1 : lacking fresh air 2 : unimaginative or pompous

stul·ti·fy \'stəltə,fī\ vb -fied; -fy·ing : cause to appear foolish —**stul·ti·fi·ca·tion** \,stəltəfə'kāshən\ n

stum·ble \'stəmbəl\ vb -bled; -bling 1 : lose one's balance or fall in walking or running 2 : speak or act clumsily 3 : come by chance —**stumble** n

stump \'stəmp\ n : part left when something is cut off ~ vb : confuse —**stumpy** adj

stun \'stən\ vb -nn- 1 : make senseless

or dizzy by or as if by a blow 2 : bewilder

stung past of STING

stunk past of STINK

stun·ning \'stəniŋ\ adj : strikingly beautiful —**stun·ning·ly** adv

¹**stunt** \'stənt\ vb : hinder the normal growth of

²**stunt** n : spectacular feat

stu·pe·fy \'st(y)üpə,fī\ vb -fied; -fy·ing 1 : make insensible by or as if by drugs 2 : amaze —**stu·pe·fac·tion** \,st(y)üpə'fakshən\ n

stu·pen·dous \st(y)ü'pendəs\ adj : very big or impressive —**stu·pen·dous·ly** adv

stu·pid \'st(y)üpəd\ adj : not sensible or intelligent —**stu·pid·i·ty** \st(y)ü'pidətē\ n —**stu·pid·ly** adv

stu·por \'st(y)üpər\ n : state of being conscious but not aware or sensible —**stu·por·ous** adj

stur·dy \'stərdē\ adj -di·er; -est : strong —**stur·di·ly** \'stərd°lē\ adv —**stur·di·ness** n

stur·geon \'stərjən\ n : fish whose roe is caviar

stut·ter \'stətər\ vb or n : stammer

¹**sty** \'stī\ n, pl sties : pig pen

²**sty, stye** \'stī\ n, pl sties or styes : inflamed swelling on the edge of an eyelid

style \'stīl\ n 1 : distinctive way of speaking, writing, or acting 2 : elegant or fashionable way of living ~ vb styled; styl·ing 1 : name 2 : give a particular design or style to —**styl·ish** \'stīlish\ adj —**styl·ish·ly** adv —**styl·ish·ness** n —**styl·ist** \-əst\ n —**styl·ize** \'stī(ə),līz\ vb

sty·lus \'stīləs\ n, pl -li \'stī(ə)ī,lī\ 1 : pointed writing tool 2 : phonograph needle

sty·mie \'stīmē\ -mied; -mie·ing : block or frustrate

suave \'swäv\ adj : well-mannered and gracious —**suave·ly** adv

¹**sub** \'səb\ n or vb : substitute

²**sub** n : submarine

sub- \,səb, 'səb, 'səb\ prefix 1 : under or beneath 2 : subordinate or secondary 3 : subordinate portion of 4 : with repetition of a process so as to form, stress, or deal with subordinate parts or relations 5 : somewhat 6 : nearly

subacute	subaverage
subagency	subbase
subagent	subbasement
subarctic	subbranch
subarea	subcabinet
subatmospheric	subcategory

subclass
subclassification
subclassify
subcommission
subcommunity
subcomponent
subconcept
subcontract
subcontractor
subculture
subdean
subdepartment
subdistrict
subentry
subequatorial
subfamily
subfreezing
subgroup
subhead
subheading
subhuman
subindex
subindustry
sublease
sublethal
sublevel
subliterate
subnetwork

suboceanic
suborder
subpar
subpart
subplot
subpolar
subprincipal
subprocess
subprogram
subproject
subregion
subsea
subsection
subsense
subspecialty
subspecies
substage
subsurface
subsystem
subteen
subtemperate
subtheme
subtopic
subtotal
subtreasury
subtype
subunit

possibility or contingency —**subjunc·tive** *n*

sub·let \\ˈsəbˈlet\\ *vb* **-let; -let·ting** : rent (a property) from a lessee

sub·lime \\səˈblīm\\ *adj* : splendid —**sub·lim·i·ty** \\-ˈblimətē\\ *n*

sub·ma·rine \\ˈsəbməˌrēn, ˌsəbməˈ-\\ *adj* : existing, acting, or growing under the sea ~ *n* : underwater boat

sub·merge \\səbˈmərj\\ *vb* **-merged; -merg·ing** : put or plunge under the surface of water —**sub·mer·gence** \\-ˈmərjəns\\ *n* —**sub·mers·ible** \\səbˈmərsəbəl\\ *adj* —**sub·mer·sion** \\-ˈmərzhən\\ *n*

sub·mit \\səbˈmit\\ *vb* **-tt-** 1 : yield 2 : give or offer —**sub·mis·sion** \\-ˈmishən\\ *n* —**sub·mis·sive** \\-ˈmisiv\\ *adj*

sub·nor·mal \\səbˈnorməl\\ *adj* : falling below what is normal

sub·or·di·nate \\səˈbordnət, -ᵊnət\\ *adj* : lower in rank ~ *n* : one that is subordinate ~ \\səˈbordᵊnˌāt\\ *vb* **-nat·ed; -nat·ing** : place in a lower rank or class —**sub·or·di·na·tion** \\-ˌbordᵊnˈāshən\\ *n*

sub·poe·na \\səˈpēnə\\ *n* : summons to appear in court ~ *vb* **-naed; -na·ing** : summon with a subpoena

sub·scribe \\səbˈskrīb\\ *vb* **-scribed; -scrib·ing** 1 : give consent or approval 2 : agree to support or to receive and pay for —**sub·scrib·er** *n*

sub·scrip·tion \\səbˈskripshən\\ *n* : order for regular receipt of a publication

sub·se·quent \\ˈsəbsikwənt, -saˌkwent\\ *adj* : following after —**sub·se·quent·ly** \\-ˌkwentlē, -kwənt-\\ *adv*

sub·ser·vi·ence \\səbˈsərvēəns\\ *n* : obsequious submission —**sub·ser·vi·en·cy** \\-ənsē\\ *n* —**sub·ser·vi·ent** \\-ənt\\ *adj*

sub·side \\səbˈsīd\\ *vb* **-sid·ed; -sid·ing** : die down in intensity

sub·sid·iary \\səbˈsidēˌerē\\ *adj* 1 : furnishing support 2 : controlled by a main company —**subsidiary** *n*

sub·si·dize \\ˈsəbsəˌdīz\\ *vb* **-dized; -diz·ing** : aid with a subsidy

sub·si·dy \\ˈsəbsədē\\ *n, pl* **-dies** : gift of supporting funds

sub·sist \\səbˈsist\\ *vb* : acquire the necessities of life —**sub·sis·tence** \\-ˈsistəns\\ *n*

sub·stance \\ˈsəbstəns\\ *n* 1 : essence or essential part 2 : physical material 3 : wealth

sub·stan·dard \\ˌsəbˈstandərd, ˈsəb-\\ *adj* : falling short of a standard or norm

sub·con·scious \\ˌsəbˈkänchəs, ˈsəb-\\ *adj* : existing without conscious awareness ~ *n* : part of the mind concerned with subconscious activities —**sub·con·scious·ly** *adv* —**sub·con·scious·ness** *n*

sub·di·vide \\ˌsəbdəˈvīd, ˈsəbdəˌvīd\\ *vb* 1 : divide into several parts 2 : divide (a tract of land) into building lots —**sub·di·vi·sion** \\-ˈvizhən, -ˌvizh-\\ *n*

sub·due \\səbˈd(y)ü\\ *vb* **-dued; -du·ing** 1 : bring under control 2 : reduce the intensity

sub·ject \\ˈsəbjikt\\ *n* 1 : person under the authority of another 2 : something being discussed or studied 3 : word or word group about which something is said in a sentence ~ *adj* 1 : being under one's authority 2 : prone 3 : dependent on some condition or act ~ \\səbˈjekt\\ *vb* 1 : bring under control 2 : cause to undergo —**sub·jec·tion** \\-ˈjekshən\\ *n*

sub·jec·tive \\(ˌ)səbˈjektiv\\ *adj* : deriving from an individual viewpoint or bias —**sub·jec·tive·ly** *adv* —**sub·jec·tiv·i·ty** \\-jekˈtivətē\\ *n*

sub·ju·gate \\ˈsəbjiˌgāt\\ *vb* **-gat·ed; -gat·ing** : bring under one's control —**sub·ju·ga·tion** \\ˌsəbjiˈgāshən\\ *n*

sub·junc·tive \\səbˈjəŋktiv\\ *adj* : relating to a verb form which expresses

sub·stan·tial \səb'stanchəl\ adj 1 : plentiful 2 : considerable —**sub·stan·tial·ly** adv

sub·stan·ti·ate \səb'stanchē,āt\ vb -at·ed; -at·ing 1 : verify —**sub·stan·ti·a·tion** \-,stanchē'āshən\ n

sub·sti·tute \'səbstə,t(y)üt\ n : replacement ~ vb -tut·ed; -tut·ing : put or serve in place of another —**substitute** adj —**sub·sti·tu·tion** \,səbstə't(y)üshən\ n

sub·ter·fuge \'səbtər,fyüj\ n : deceptive trick

sub·ter·ra·nean \,səbtə'rānēən, subter·ra·neous \-nēəs\ adj : lying or being underground

sub·ti·tle \'səb,tīt⁰l\ n : movie caption

sub·tle \'sət⁰l\ adj -tler \'sətlər, -⁰lər\; -tlest \-ləst, -⁰ləst\ 1 : hardly noticeable 2 : clever —**sub·tle·ty** \-tē\ n —**sub·tly** \-tlē, -⁰lē\ adv

sub·tract \səb'trakt\ vb : take away (as one number from another) —**sub·trac·tion** \-'trakshən\ n

sub·urb \'səb,ərb\ n : residential area adjacent to a city —**sub·ur·ban** \sə'bərbən\ adj or n —**sub·ur·ban·ite** \- bə,nīt\ n

sub·vert \səb'vərt\ vb : overthrow or ruin —**sub·ver·sion** \-'vərzhən\ n —**sub·ver·sive** \-'vərsiv\ adj

sub·way \'səb,wā\ n : underground electric railway

suc·ceed \sək'sēd\ vb 1 : follow (someone) in a job, role, or title 2 : attain a desired object or end

suc·cess \-'ses\ n 1 : satisfactory completion of something 2 : gaining of wealth and fame 3 : one that succeeds —**suc·cess·ful** \-fəl\ adj —**suc·cess·ful·ly** adv

suc·ces·sion \sək'seshən\ n 1 : order, act, or right of succeeding 2 : series

suc·ces·sive \-'sesiv\ adj : following in order —**suc·ces·sive·ly** adv

suc·ces·sor \-'sesər\ n : one that succeeds another

suc·cinct \(,)sək'siŋkt, sə'siŋkt\ adj : brief —**suc·cinct·ly** adv —**suc·cinct·ness** n

suc·cor \'səkər\ n or vb : help

suc·co·tash \'səkə,tash\ n : beans and corn cooked together

suc·cu·lent \'səkyələnt\ adj : juicy —**suc·cu·lence** \-ləns\ n —**succulent** n

suc·cumb \sə'kəm\ vb 1 : give up 2 : die

such \(,)səch, (,)sich\ adj 1 : of this or that kind 2 : having a specified quality —**such** pron or adv

suck \'sək\ vb 1 : draw in liquid with the mouth 2 : draw liquid from by or as if by mouth —**suck** n

suck·er \'səkər\ n 1 : one that sucks or clings 2 : shoot from the roots or lower part of a plant 3 : easily deceived person

suck·le \'səkəl\ vb -led; -ling : give or draw milk from the breast or udder

suck·ling \'səkliŋ\ n : young unweaned mammal

su·crose \'sü,krōs, -,krōz\ n : cane or beet sugar

suc·tion \'səkshən\ n 1 : act of sucking 2 : act or process of drawing in by partially exhausting the air

sud·den \'səd⁰n\ adj 1 : happening quickly or unexpectedly 2 : steep 3 : hasty —**sud·den·ly** adv —**sud·den·ness** n

suds \'sədz\ n pl : soapy water esp. when frothy —**sudsy** \'sədzē\ adj

sue \'sü\ vb sued; su·ing 1 : petition 2 : bring legal action against

suede, suède \'swād\ n : leather with a napped surface

su·et \'süət\ n : hard beef fat

suf·fer \'səfər\ vb 1 : experience pain, loss, or hardship 2 : permit —**suf·fer·er** n

suf·fer·ing \-(ə)riŋ\ n : pain or hardship

suf·fice \sə'fīs\ vb -ficed; -fic·ing 1 : be sufficient

suf·fi·cient \sə'fishənt\ adj : adequate —**suf·fi·cien·cy** \-ənsē\ n —**suf·fi·cient·ly** adv

suf·fix \'səf,iks\ n : letters added at the end of a word —**suffix** \'səfiks, (,)sə'fiks\ vb —**suf·fix·a·tion** \,səf,ik'sāshən\ n

suf·fo·cate \'səfə,kāt\ vb -cat·ed; -cat·ing : suffer or die or cause to die from lack of air —**suf·fo·cat·ing·ly** adv —**suf·fo·ca·tion** \,səfə'kāshən\ n

suf·frage \'səfrij\ n : right to vote

suf·fuse \sə'fyüz\ vb -fused; -fus·ing : spread over or through

sug·ar \'shúgər\ n : sweet substance ~ vb : mix, cover, or sprinkle with sugar —**sug·ar·cane** n —**sug·ary** adj

sug·gest \sə(g)'jest\ vb 1 : put into someone's mind 2 : remind one by association of ideas —**sug·gest·ible** \-'jestəbəl\ adj —**sug·ges·tion** \-'jeschən\ n

sug·ges·tive \-'jestiv\ adj : suggesting something improper —**sug·ges·tive·ly** adv —**sug·ges·tive·ness** n

sui·cide \'süə,sīd\ n 1 : act of killing oneself purposely 2 : one who commits suicide —**su·i·cid·al** \,süə'sīd⁰l\ adj

suit \'süt\ *n* **1** : action in court to recover a right or claim **2** : number of things used or worn together **3** : one of the 4 sets of playing cards ~ *vb* **1** : be appropriate or becoming to **2** : meet the needs of —suit·abil·i·ty \,süta'bilatē\ *n* —suit·able \'sütabəl\ *adj* —suit·ably *adv*

suit·case *n* : flat rectangular traveling bag

suite \'swēt, *for 2 also* 'süt\ *n* **1** : group of rooms **2** : set of matched furniture

suit·or \'sütər\ *n* : one who seeks to marry a woman

sul·fur, sul·phur \'səlfər\ *n* : nonmetallic yellow chemical element —sul·fu·re·ous \,səl'fyürēəs\ *adj* —sul·fu·ric \-'fyürik\ *adj* —sul·fu·rous \-'fyürəs, 'səlf(y)ərəs\ *adj*

sulk \'səlk\ *vb* : be moodily silent —sulk *n*

sulky \'səlkē\ *adj* : inclined to sulk ~ *n* : light 2-wheeled cart —sulk·i·ly \'səlkəlē\ *adv* —sulk·i·ness \-kēnəs\ *n*

sul·len \'sələn\ *adj* **1** : gloomily silent **2** : dismal —sul·len·ly *adv* —sul·len·ness *n*

sul·ly \'səlē\ *vb* -lied; -ly·ing : cast doubt or disgrace on

sul·tan \'səltən\ *n* : sovereign of a Muslim state —sul·tan·ate \-,āt\ *n*

sul·try \'səltrē\ *adj* -tri·er; -est : very hot and moist

sum \'səm\ *n* **1** : amount **2** : gist **3** : result of addition ~ *vb* -mm- : find the sum of

su·mac, su·mach \'s(h)ü,mak\ *n* : shrub with spikes of berries

sum·ma·ry \'səmərē\ *adj* **1** : concise **2** : done without delay or formality ~ *n, pl* -ries : concise statement —sum·mar·i·ly \(,)sə'merəlē, 'səmərəlē\ *adv* —sum·ma·rize \'səmə,rīz\ *vb*

sum·ma·tion \(,)sə'māshən\ *n* : a summing up esp. in court

sum·mer \'səmər\ *n* : season in which the sun shines most directly —sum·mery *adj*

sum·mit \'səmət\ *n* : highest point

sum·mon \'səmən\ *vb* **1** : send for or call together **2** : order to appear in court —sum·mon·er *n*

sum·mons \'səmənz\ *n, pl* sum·mons·es : an order to answer charges in court

sump·tu·ous \'səmpchə(wə)s\ *adj* : lavish

sun \'sən\ *n* **1** : shining celestial body around which the planets revolve **2** : light of the sun ~ *vb* -nn- : expose to the sun —sun·beam *n* —sun·burn *n* —sun·glass·es *n pl* —sun·light *n*

—sun·ny *adj* —sun·rise *n* —sun·set *n* —sun·shine *n* —sun·tan *n*

sun·dae \'səndē\ *n* : ice cream with topping

Sun·day \'səndē\ *n* : 1st day of the week

sun·di·al \-,dī(ə)l\ *n* : device for showing time by the sun's shadow

sun·dries \'səndrēz\ *n, pl* : various small articles

sun·dry \-drē\ *adj* : several

sun·fish *n* : perchlike freshwater fish

sun·flow·er *n* : tall plant grown for its oil-rich seeds

sung *past of* SING

sunk *past of* SINK

sunk·en \'səŋkən\ *adj* **1** : submerged **2** : fallen in

sun·spot *n* : dark spot on the sun

sun·stroke *n* : heatstroke from the sun

sup \'səp\ *vb* -pp- : eat the evening meal

super \'süpər\ *adj* : very fine

super- \'süpər, ,sü-\ *prefix* **1** : higher in quantity, quality, or degree than **2** : in addition **3** : exceeding a norm **4** : in excessive degree or intensity **5** : surpassing others of its kind **6** : situated above, on, or at the top of **7** : more inclusive than **8** : superior in status or position

superabundance	supermodern
superabundant	superpatriot
superambitious	superpatriotic
superathlete	superpatriotism
superbomb	superplane
superclean	superpolite
supercold	superport
supercolossal	superpowerful
superconvenient	superrefined
supercop	superrich
superdense	supersalesman
supereffective	superscout
superefficiency	supersecrecy
superefficient	supersecret
superenthusiasm	supersensitive
superenthusiastic	supership
	supersize
superfast	supersized
supergood	superslick
supergovernment	supersmooth
	supersoft
supergroup	superspecial
superhard	superspecialist
superhero	superspy
superheroine	superstate
superhuman	superstrength
superintellectual	superstrong
superintelligence	supersuccessful
superintelligent	supersystem
superman	

supertanker   supertough
superthick   superweak
superthin   superweapon
supertight   superwoman

su·perb \su̇'pərb\ *adj* : outstanding —su·perb·ly *adv*

su·per·cil·i·ous \,su̇pər'silēəs\ *adj* : haughtily contemptuous

su·per·fi·cial \,su̇pər'fishəl\ *adj* : relating to what is only apparent —su·per·fi·ci·al·i·ty \-,fishē'alətē\ *n* —su·per·fi·cial·ly *adv*

su·per·flu·ous \su̇'pərfləwəs\ *adj* : more than necessary —su·per·flu·i·ty \,su̇pər'flüətē\ *n*

su·per·im·pose \,su̇pərim'pōz\ *vb* : lay over and above something

su·per·in·tend \,su̇p(ə)rin'tend\ *vb* : have charge and oversight of —su·per·in·ten·dence \-'tendəns\ *n* —su·per·in·ten·den·cy \-'dənsē\ *n* —su·per·in·ten·dent \-dənt\ *n*

su·pe·ri·or \su̇'pirēər\ *adj* 1 : higher, better, or more important 2 : haughty —superior *n* —su·pe·ri·or·i·ty \-,pirē'ȯrətē\ *n*

su·per·la·tive \su̇'pərlətiv\ *adj* 1 : relating to or being an adjective or adverb form that denotes an extreme level 2 : surpassing others —superlative *n* —su·per·la·tive·ly *adv*

su·per·mar·ket \'su̇pər,märkət\ *n* : self-service grocery store

su·per·nat·u·ral \,su̇pər'nach(ə)rəl\ *adj* : beyond the observable physical world —su·per·nat·u·ral·ly *adv*

su·per·sede \,su̇pər'sēd\ *vb* -sed·ed; -sed·ing : take the place of

su·per·son·ic \,su̇pər'sänik\ *adj* : relating to speeds 1 to 5 times the speed of sound

su·per·sti·tion \,su̇pər'stishən\ *n* : beliefs based on ignorance, fear of the unknown, or trust in magic —su·per·sti·tious \-əs\ *adj*

su·per·struc·ture \'su̇pər,strəkchər\ *n* : something built on a base or as a vertical extension

su·per·vene \,su̇pər'vēn\ *vb* -vened; -ven·ing : occur unexpectedly —su·per·ve·nient \-'vēnyənt\ *adj*

su·per·vise \'su̇pər,vīz\ *vb* -vised; -vis·ing : have charge of —su·per·vi·sion \,su̇pər'vizhən\ *n* —su·per·vi·sor \'su̇pər,vīzər\ *n* —su·per·vi·so·ry \,su̇pər'vīz(ə)rē\ *adj*

su·pine \su̇'pīn\ *adj* 1 : lying on the back 2 : indifferent or abject

sup·per \'səpər\ *n* : evening meal

sup·plant \sə'plant\ *vb* : take the place of

sup·ple \'səpəl\ *adj* -pler; -plest : able to bend easily

sup·ple·ment \'səpləmənt\ *n* : something that adds to or makes up for a lack —supplement *vb* —sup·ple·men·tal \,səplə'ment°l\ *adj* —sup·ple·men·ta·ry \-'ment(ə)rē\ *adj*

sup·pli·ant \'səplēənt\ *n* : one who supplicates

sup·pli·cate \'səplə,kāt\ *vb* -cat·ed; -cat·ing 1 : pray to God 2 : ask earnestly and humbly —sup·pli·cant \-likənt\ *n* —sup·pli·ca·tion \,səplə'kāshən\ *n*

sup·ply \sə'plī\ *vb* -plied; -ply·ing : furnish ~ *n*, *pl* -plies 1 : amount needed or available 2 *pl* : provisions —sup·pli·er \-'plī(ə)r\ *n*

sup·port \sə'pōrt\ *vb* 1 : take sides with 2 : provide with food, clothing, and shelter 3 : hold up or serve as a foundation for —support *n* —sup·port·able *adj* —sup·port·er *n*

sup·pose \sə'pōz\ *vb* -posed; -pos·ing 1 : assume to be true 2 : expect 3 : think probable —sup·po·si·tion \,səpə'zishən\ *n*

sup·pos·i·to·ry \sə'päzə,tōrē\ *n*, *pl* -ries : medicated material for insertion (as into the rectum)

sup·press \sə'pres\ *vb* 1 : put an end to by authority 2 : keep from being known —sup·pres·sion \-'preshən\ *n*

sup·pu·rate \'səpyə,rāt\ *vb* -rat·ed; -rat·ing : form or give off pus —sup·pu·ra·tion \,səpyə'rāshən\ *n*

su·prem·a·cy \su̇'preməsē\ *n*, *pl* -cies : supreme power or authority

su·preme \su̇'prēm\ *adj* 1 : highest in rank or authority 2 : greatest possible —su·preme·ly *adv*

Supreme Being *n* : God

sur·charge \'sər,chärj\ *n* 1 : excessive load or burden 2 : extra fee or cost

sure \'shu̇r\ *adj* sur·er; sur·est 1 : confident 2 : reliable 3 : not to be disputed 4 : bound to happen ~ *adv* : surely —sure·ly *adv* —sure·ness *n*

sure·ty \'shu̇rətē\ *n*, *pl* -ties 1 : guarantee 2 : one who gives a guarantee for another person

surf \'sərf\ *n* : waves that break on the shore ~ *vb* : ride the surf —surf·board *n* —surf·er *n* —surf·ing *n*

sur·face \'sərfəs\ *n* 1 : the outside of an object or body 2 : outward aspect ~ *vb* -faced; -fac·ing : rise to the surface

sur·feit \'sərfət\ *n* 1 : excess 2 : excessive indulgence (as in food or drink) 3 : disgust caused by excess ~ *vb*

: feed, supply, or indulge to the point of surfeit

surge \'sərj\ *vb* **surged; surg·ing** : rise and fall in or as if in waves ~ *n* : sudden increase

sur·geon \'sərjən\ *n* : physician who specializes in surgery

sur·gery \'sərj(ə)rē\ *n, pl* **-ger·ies** : medical treatment involving cutting open the body

sur·gi·cal \-jikəl\ *adj* : relating to surgeons or surgery —**sur·gi·cal·ly** *adv*

sur·ly \'sərlē\ *adj* **-li·er; -est** : cross —**sur·li·ness** *n*

sur·mise \sər'mīz\ *vb* **-mised; -mis·ing** : guess —**surmise** *n*

sur·mount \-'maùnt\ *vb* **1** : defeat **2** : get to or be the top of

sur·name \'sər,nām\ *n* : family name

sur·pass \sər'pas\ *vb* : go beyond or exceed —**sur·pass·ing·ly** *adv*

sur·plice \'sərpləs\ *n* : loose white outer ecclesiastical vestment

sur·plus \'sər,pləs\ *n* : quantity left over

sur·prise \sə(r)'prīz\ *vb* **-prised; -pris·ing 1** : come upon or affect unexpectedly **2** : amaze —**surprise** *n* —**sur·pris·ing** *adj* —**sur·pris·ing·ly** *adv*

sur·ren·der \sə'rendər\ *vb* : give up oneself or a possession to another ~ *n* : act of surrendering

sur·rep·ti·tious \,sərəp'tishəs\ *adj* : done, made, or acquired by stealth —**sur·rep·ti·tious·ly** *adv*

sur·rey \'sərē\ *n, pl* **-reys** : horse-drawn carriage

sur·round \sə'raùnd\ *vb* : enclose on all sides

sur·round·ings \sə'raùndiŋz\ *n pl* : objects, conditions, or area around something

sur·veil·lance \sər'vāləns, -'vālyəns, -'vāəns\ *n* : careful watch

sur·vey \sər'vā\ *vb* **-veyed; -vey·ing 1** : look over and examine closely **2** : make a survey of (as a tract of land) ~ \'sər,-\ *n, pl* **-veys** : inspection **2** : process of measuring (as land) —**sur·vey·or** \-ər\ *n*

sur·vive \sər'vīv\ *vb* **-vived; -viv·ing 1** : remain alive or in existence **2** : outlive or outlast —**sur·viv·al** *n* —**sur·vi·vor** \-'vīvər\ *n*

sus·cep·ti·ble \sə'septəbəl\ *adj* : likely to allow or be affected by something —**sus·cep·ti·bil·i·ty** \-,septə'bilətē\ *n*

sus·pect \'səs,pekt, sə'spekt, *adj* : regarded with suspicion ~ \'səs,pekt\ *n* : one who is suspected (as of a crime) ~ \sə'spekt\ *vb* **1** : have

doubts of **2** : believe guilty without proof **3** : guess

sus·pend \sə'spend\ *vb* **1** : temporarily stop or keep from a function or job **2** : withhold (judgment) temporarily **3** : hang

sus·pend·er \sə'spendər\ *n* : one of 2 supporting straps for trousers which pass over the shoulders

sus·pense \sə'spens\ *n* : excitement and uncertainty as to outcome —**suspense·ful** *adj*

sus·pen·sion \sə'spenchən\ *n* : act of suspending or the state or period of being suspended

sus·pi·cion \sə'spishən\ *n* : act of suspecting something **2** : trace

sus·pi·cious \-əs\ *adj* **1** : arousing suspicion **2** : inclined to suspect —**sus·pi·cious·ly** *adv*

sus·tain \sə'stān\ *vb* **1** : provide with nourishment **2** : keep going **3** : hold up **4** : suffer **5** : support or prove

sus·te·nance \'səstənəns\ *n* **1** : nourishment **2** : something that sustains or supports

swab \'swäb\ *n* **1** : mop **2** : wad of absorbent material for applying medicine ~ *vb* **-bb-** : use a swab on

swad·dle \'swäd²l\ *vb* **-dled; -dling** \'swädliŋ, ²liŋ\ : bind (an infant) in bands of cloth

swag·ger \'swagər\ *vb* **-gered; -ger·ing 1** : walk with a conceited swing **2** : boast —**swagger** *n*

1swal·low \'swälō\ *n* : small migratory bird

2swallow *vb* **1** : take into the stomach through the throat **2** : envelop or take in **3** : accept too easily **4** : endure **5** : retract or repress —**swallow** *n*

swam *past of* SWIM

swamp \'swämp\ *n* : wet spongy land ~ *vb* : deluge (as with water) —**swampy** *adj*

swan \'swän\ *n* : white long-necked swimming bird

swap \'swäp\ *vb* **-pp-** : trade —**swap** *n*

swarm \'swórm\ *n* **1** : mass of honeybees leaving a hive to start a new colony **2** : large crowd moving together ~ *vb* : gather in a swarm

swar·thy \'swórthē, -thē\ *adj* **-thi·er; -est** : dark in complexion

swash·buck·ler \'swäsh,bəklər\ *n* : boasting blustering soldier or daredevil —**swash·buck·ling** \-,bək(ə)liŋ\ *adj*

swat \'swät\ *vb* **-tt-** : hit sharply —**swat** *n* —**swat·ter** *n*

swatch \'swäch\ *n* : sample piece (as of fabric)

swath \'swäth, 'swȯth\, **swathe** \'swäth, 'swȯth, 'swāth\, \'swäth, 'swȯth, 'swāth\ *n* : row or path cut (as through grass)

swathe \'swäth, 'swȯth, 'swāth\ *vb* **swathed; swath·ing** : wrap with or as if with a bandage

sway \'swā\ *vb* 1 : swing gently from side to side 2 : influence ~ *n* 1 : gentle swinging from side to side 2 : controlling power or influence

swear \'swaȯr\ *vb* **swore** \'swōr\; **sworn** \'swȯrn\; **swear·ing** 1 : make or cause to make a solemn statement or promise under oath 2 : use profane language —**swear·er** *n* —**swear·ing** *n*

sweat \'swet\ *vb* **sweat** or **sweat·ed; sweat·ing** 1 : excrete salty moisture from glands of the skin 2 : form drops of moisture on the surface 3 : work or cause to work hard ~ *n* 1 : liquid exuded through pores from glands (**sweat glands**) of the skin 2 : moisture gathering on a surface in drops —**sweaty** *adj*

sweat·er \'swetɚr\ *n* : knitted jacket or pullover

sweep \'swēp\ *vb* **swept** \'swept\; **sweep·ing** 1 : remove or clean by a brush or a single forceful wipe (as of the hand) 2 : move over with speed and force (as of the hand) 3 : move or extend in a wide curve ~ *n* 1 : a clearing off or away 2 : single forceful wipe or swinging movement 3 : scope —**sweep·er** *n* —**sweep·ing** *adj*

sweep·stakes \'swēp,stāks\ *n, pl* **sweepstakes** : contest in which the entire prize may go to the winner

sweet \'swēt\ *adj* 1 : being or causing the pleasing taste typical of sugar 2 : not stale or spoiled 3 : not salted 4 : pleasant 5 : regarded with love or fondness ~ *n* : something sweet —**sweet·ly** *adv* —**sweet·ness** *n*

sweet·en \'swēt³n\ *vb* : make sweet —**sweet·en·er** \'swētnɚr, -³nɚr\ *n*

sweet·heart *n* : person one loves

sweet potato *n* : sweet yellow edible root of a tropical vine

swell \'swel\ *vb* **swelled; swelled** or **swol·len** \'swōlən\; **swell·ing** 1 : enlarge 2 : bulge 3 : fill or be filled with emotion ~ *n* 1 : increase 2 : long crestless wave —**swell·ing** *n*

swel·ter \'sweltɚr\ *vb* : be uncomfortable from excessive heat

swept *past of* SWEEP

swerve \'swɚrv\ *vb* **swerved; swerv·ing** :

: move abruptly aside from a course —**swerve** *n*

¹swift \'swift\ *adj* 1 : moving with great speed 2 : occurring suddenly —**swift·ly** *adv* —**swift·ness** *n*

²swift *n* : small insect-eating bird

swig \'swig\ *vb* -**gg**- : drink in gulps —**swig** *n*

swill \'swil\ *vb* : swallow greedily ~ *n* 1 : animal food of refuse and liquid 2 : garbage

swim \'swim\ *vb* **swam** \'swam\; **swum** \'swəm\; **swim·ming** 1 : propel oneself in water 2 : float in or be surrounded with a liquid 3 : have a sensation of dizziness ~ *n* : act or period of swimming —**swim·mer** *n*

swin·dle \'swind³l\ *vb* -**dled; -dling** \-d³lū, -d³lin\ : cheat (someone) of money or property —**swindle** *n* —**swin·dler** \-(d)lɚr, -d³lɚr\ *n*

swine \'swīn\ *n, pl* **swine** : short-legged hoofed mammal with a snout —**swin·ish** \'swīnish\ *adj*

swing \'swiŋ\ *vb* **swung** \'swəŋ\; **swing·ing** 1 : move rapidly in an arc 2 : sway or cause to sway back and forth 3 : hang so as to sway or sag 4 : turn on a hinge or pivot 5 : accomplish through effort or influence ~ *n* 1 : act or instance of swinging 2 : swinging movement (as in trying to hit something) 3 : suspended seat for swinging —**swing** *adj* —**swing·er** *n*

swipe \'swīp\ *n* : strong sweeping blow ~ *vb* **swiped; swip·ing** 1 : strike or wipe with a sweeping motion 2 : steal esp. with a quick movement

swirl \'swɚrl\ *vb* : eddy —**swirl** *n*

swish \'swish\ *n* : hissing, sweeping, or brushing sound —**swish** *vb*

switch \'swich\ *n* 1 : slender flexible whip or twig 2 : blow with a switch 3 : shift, change, or reversal 4 : device that opens or closes an electrical circuit ~ *vb* 1 : punish or urge on with a switch 2 : change or reverse roles, positions, or subjects 3 : operate a switch of

switch·board *n* : panel of switches to control electrical circuits

swiv·el \'swivəl\ *vb* -**eled** or -**elled; -eling** or -**el·ing** : swing or turn on a pivot —**swivel** *n*

swollen *past part of* SWELL

swoon \'swün\ *n* : faint —**swoon** *vb*

swoop \'swüp\ *vb* : make a swift diving attack —**swoop** *n*

sword \'sȯrd\ *n* : sharp cutting weapon with a long blade

sword·fish *n* : large ocean fish with a long swordlike projection

swore *past of* SWEAR

sworn *past part of* SWEAR

swum *past part of* SWIM

swung *past of* SWING

syc·a·more \'sikə,mōr\ *n* : shade tree

sy·co·phant \'sikəfənt\ *n* : servile flatterer —**syc·o·phan·tic** \,sikə'fantik\ *adj*

syl·la·ble \'siləbəl\ *n* : unit of a spoken word —**syl·lab·ic** \sə'labik\ *adj*

syl·la·bus \'siləbəs\ *n, pl* **-bi** \-,bī\ *or* **-bus·es** : summary of main topics (as of a course of study)

syl·van \'silvən\ *adj* **1** : living or located in a wooded area **2** : abounding in woods

sym·bol \'simbəl\ *n* : something that represents or suggests another thing —**sym·bol·ic** \sim'bälik\, **sym·bol·i·cal** \-ikəl\ *adj* —**sym·bol·i·cal·ly** *adv*

sym·bol·ism \'simbə,lizəm\ *n* : representation of meanings with symbols

sym·bol·ize \'simbə,līz\ *vb* **-ized; -iz·ing** : serve as a symbol of —**sym·bol·iza·tion** \,simbələ'zāshən\ *n*

sym·me·try \'simətrē\ *n, pl* **-tries** : regularity and balance in the arrangement of parts —**sym·met·ri·cal** \sə'metrikəl\ *adj* —**sym·met·ri·cal·ly** \-k(ə)lē\ *adv*

sym·pa·thize \'simpə,thīz\ *vb* **-thized; -thiz·ing** : feel or show sympathy —**sym·pa·thiz·er** *n*

sym·pa·thy \'simpəthē\ *n, pl* **-thies 1** : ability to understand or share the feelings or interests of another **2** : expression of sorrow for another's misfortune —**sym·pa·thet·ic** \,simpə'thetik\ *adj* —**sym·pa·thet·i·cal·ly** \-ik(ə)lē\ *adv*

sym·pho·ny \'simfənē\ *n, pl* **-nies** : composition for an orchestra or the orchestra itself —**sym·phon·ic** \sim'fänik\ *adj*

sym·po·sium \sim'pōzēəm\ *n, pl* **-sia** \-zēə\ *or* **-siums** : conference at which a topic is discussed

symp·tom \'simptəm\ *n* : unusual feeling or reaction that is a sign of disease —**symp·tom·at·ic** \,simptə'matik\ *adj*

syn·a·gogue \'sinə,gäg\ *n* : Jewish house of worship

syn·chro·nize \'siŋkrə,nīz, 'sin-\ *vb* **-nized; -niz·ing 1** : occur or cause to occur at the same instant **2** : cause to agree in time —**syn·chro·ni·za·tion** \,siŋkrənə'zāshən, ,sin-\ *n*

syn·co·pa·tion \,siŋkə'pāshən, ,sin-\ *n* : shifting of the regular musical accent to the weak beat —**syn·co·pate** \'siŋkə,pāt, 'sin-\ *vb*

syn·di·cate \'sindikət\ *n* : business association —\-də,kāt\ *vb* **-cat·ed; -cat·ing 1** : form a syndicate **2** : publish through a syndicate

syn·drome \'sin,drōm\ *n* : particular group of symptoms

syn·onym \'sinə,nim\ *n* : word with the same meaning as another —**syn·on·y·mous** \sə'nänəməs\ *adj* —**syn·on·y·my** \-mē\ *n*

syn·op·sis \sə'näpsəs\ *n, pl* **-op·ses** \-,sēz\ : condensed statement or outline

syn·tax \'sin,taks\ *n* : way in which words are put together —**syn·tac·tic** \sin'taktik\ *adj* —**syn·tac·ti·cal** \-tikəl\ *adj*

syn·the·sis \'sinthəsəs\ *n, pl* **-the·ses** \-,sēz\ : combination of parts or elements into a whole —**syn·the·size** \-,sīz\ *vb*

syn·thet·ic \sin'thetik\ *adj* : artificially made —**synthetic** *n* —**syn·thet·i·cal·ly** \-ik(ə)lē\ *adv*

syph·i·lis \'sif(ə)ləs\ *n* : venereal disease —**syph·i·lit·ic** \,sifə'litik\ *adj or n*

sy·ringe \sə'rinj, 'sirinj\ *n* : plunger device for injecting or withdrawing liquids

syr·up \'sərəp, 'sirəp\ *n* : thick sticky sweet liquid —**syr·upy** *adj*

sys·tem \'sistəm\ *n* **1** : arrangement of units that function together **2** : regular order —**sys·tem·at·ic** \,sistə'matik\, **sys·tem·at·i·cal** \-ikəl\ *adj* —**sys·tem·at·i·cal·ly** *adv* —**sys·tem·atize** \'sistəmə,tīz\ *vb*

sys·tem·ic \sis'temik\ *adj* : relating to the whole body

T

t \'tē\ *n, pl* **t's, ts** \'tēz\ : 20th letter of the alphabet

tab \'tab\ *n* **1** : short projecting flap **2** *pl* : careful watch

tab·by \'tabē\ *n, pl* **-bies** : domestic cat

tab·er·na·cle \'tabər₁nakəl\ *n* : house of worship

ta·ble \'tābəl\ *n* **1** : piece of furniture having a smooth slab fixed on legs **2** : supply of food **3** : condensed list —**ta·ble·cloth** *n* —**ta·ble·top** *n* —**ta·ble·ware** *n* —**tab·u·lar** \'tabyələr\ *adj*

tab·leau \'tab₁lō\ *n, pl* **-leaux** \-₁lōz\ *also* **-leaus 1** : graphic description **2** : depiction of a scene by people in costume

ta·ble·spoon *n* **1** : large serving spoon **2** : measuring spoon holding ½ fluidounce —**ta·ble·spoon·ful** \-₁fùl\ *n*

tab·let \'tablət\ *n* **1** : flat slab suited for an inscription **2** : collection of sheets of paper glued together at one edge **3** : disk-shaped pill

tab·loid \'tab₁lòid\ *n* : newspaper of small page size

ta·boo \tə'bü, ta-\ *adj* : banned esp. as immoral or dangerous —**taboo** *n or vb*

tab·u·late \'tabyə₁lāt\ *vb* **-lat·ed; -lat·ing** : put in the form of a table —**tab·u·la·tion** \₁tabyə'lāshən\ *n* —**tab·u·la·tor** \'tabyə₁lātər\ *n*

tac·it \'tasət\ *adj* : implied but not expressed —**tac·it·ly** *adv* —**tac·it·ness** *n*

tac·i·turn \'tasə₁tərn\ *adj* : not inclined to talk —**tac·i·tur·ni·ty** \₁tasə'tərnatē\ *n*

tack \'tak\ *n* **1** : small sharp nail **2** : course of action ~ *vb* **1** : fasten with tacks **2** : add on

tack·le \'takəl, *naut often* 'tāk-\ *n* **1** : equipment **2** : arrangement of ropes and pulleys **3** : act of tackling ~ *vb* **-led; -ling 1** : seize or throw down **2** : start dealing with

¹tacky \'takē\ *adj* **tack·i·er; -est** : sticky to the touch

²tacky *adj* **tack·i·er; -est** : cheap or gaudy

tact \'takt\ *n* : sense of the proper thing to say or do —**tact·ful** \-fəl\ *adj* —**tact·ful·ly** *adv* —**tact·less** *adj* —**tact·less·ly** *adv*

tac·tic \'taktik\ *n* : action as part of a plan

tac·tics \'taktiks\ *n sing or pl* **1** : science of maneuvering forces in com-

bat **2** : skill of using available means to reach an end —**tac·ti·cal** \-tikəl\ *adj* —**tac·ti·cian** \tak'tishən\ *n*

tac·tile \'takt²l, -₁tīl\ *adj* : relating to or perceptible through the sense of touch

tad·pole \'tad₁pōl\ *n* : larval frog or toad with tail and gills

taf·fe·ta \'tafətə\ *n* : crisp lustrous fabric (as of silk)

taf·fy \'tafē\ *n, pl* **-fies** : candy stretched until pliable

¹tag \'tag\ *n* : piece of hanging or attached material ~ *vb* **-gg- 1** : provide or mark with a tag **2** : follow closely

²tag *n* : children's game of trying to catch one another ~ *vb* : touch a person in tag

tail \'tāl\ *n* **1** : rear end or a growth extending from the rear end of an animal **2** : back or last part **3** : the reverse of a coin ~ *vb* : follow —**tailed** \'tāld\ *adj* —**tail·less** *adj*

tail·light *n* : red warning light at the back of a vehicle

tai·lor \'tālər\ *n* : one who makes or alters garments ~ *vb* **1** : fashion or alter (clothes) **2** : make or adapt for a special purpose

tail·spin *n* : spiral dive by an airplane

taint \'tānt\ *vb* : affect or become affected with something bad and esp. decay ~ *n* : trace of decay or corruption

take \'tāk\ *vb* **took** \'tùk\; **tak·en** \'tākən\; **tak·ing 1** : get into one's possession **2** : become affected by **3** : receive into one's body (as by eating) **4** : pick out or remove **5** : use for transportation **6** : need or make use of **7** : lead, carry, or cause to go to another place **8** : undertake and do, make, or perform ~ *n* : amount taken —**tak·er** *n* —**take advantage of** : profit by —**take exception** : object —**take off** *vb* **1** : remove **2** : go away **3** : mimic **4** : begin flight —**take over** *vb* : assume control or possession of or responsibility for —**take·over** *n*

take·off *n* : act or instance of taking off

talc \'talk\ *n* : soft mineral used in making toilet powder (**tal·cum pow·der** \'talkəm-\)

tale \'tāl\ *n* **1** : story or anecdote **2** : falsehood

tal·ent \'talənt\ *n* : natural mental, creative, or artistic ability —**tal·ent·ed** adj

tal·is·man \'taləsmən, -əz-\ n, pl **-mans** : object thought to act as a charm

talk \'tȯk\ vb 1 : express one's thoughts in speech 2 : discuss 3 : influence to a position or course of action by talking ~ n 1 : act of talking 2 : formal discussion 3 : rumor 4 : informal lecture —**talk·ative** \-ətiv\ adj —**talk·er** n

tall \'tȯl\ adj : extending to a great or specified height —**tall·ness** n

tal·low \'talō\ n : hard white animal fat used esp. in soap and lubricants

tal·ly \'talē\ n, pl **-lies** : recorded amount ~ vb **-lied; -ly·ing** 1 : add or count up 2 : match

tal·on \'talən\ n : bird's claw

tam \'tam\ n : tam-o'-shanter

tam·bou·rine \,tambə'rēn\ n : small drum with loose disks at the sides

tame \'tām\ adj **tam·er; tam·est** 1 : changed from being wild to being controllable by man 2 : docile 3 : dull ~ vb **tamed; tam·ing** : make or become tame —**tam·able, tame·able** adj —**tame·ly** adv —**tame·ness** n —**tam·er** n

tam-o'-shan·ter \'tamə,shantər\ n : Scottish woolen cap with a wide flat circular crown

tamp \'tamp\ vb : drive down or in by a series of light blows

tam·per \'tampər\ vb : interfere so as to change for the worse

tan \'tan\ vb **-nn-** 1 : change (hide) into leather esp. by soaking in a liquid containing tannin 2 : make or become brown (as by exposure to the sun) ~ n 1 : brown skin color induced by the sun 2 : light yellowish brown —**tan·ner** n —**tan·nery** \'tan(ə)rē\ n

tan·dem \'tandəm\ adv : one behind another

tang \'taŋ\ n : sharp distinctive flavor —**tangy** adj

tan·gent \'tanjənt\ adj : touching a curve or surface ~ n 1 : tangent line, curve, or surface 2 : abrupt change of course —**tan·gen·tial** \tan'jenchəl\ adj

tan·ger·ine \'tanjə,rēn, ,tanjə'-\ n : deep orange citrus fruit

tan·gi·ble \'tanjəbəl\ adj 1 : able to be touched 2 : substantially real —**tan·gi·bil·i·ty** \,tanjə'bilətē\ n —**tan·gi·bly** adv

tan·gle \'taŋgəl\ vb **-gled; -gling** : unite in intricate confusion ~ n : tangled twisted mass

tan·go \'taŋgō\ n, pl **-gos** : dance of Spanish-American origin —**tango** vb

tank \'taŋk\ n 1 : large artificial receptacle for liquids 2 : armored military vehicle —**tank·ful** n

tan·kard \'taŋkərd\ n : tall one-handled drinking vessel

tank·er \'taŋkər\ n : vehicle or vessel with tanks for transporting a liquid

tan·nin \'tanən\ n : substance of plant origin used in tanning and dyeing

tan·ta·lize \'tant²l,īz\ vb **-lized; -liz·ing** : tease or torment by keeping something desirable just out of reach —**tan·ta·liz·er** n —**tan·ta·liz·ing·ly** adv

tan·ta·mount \'tantə,maunt\ adj : equivalent in value or meaning

tan·trum \'tantrəm\ n : fit of bad temper

¹tap \'tap\ n 1 : faucet 2 : act of tapping ~ vb **-pp-** 1 : pierce so as to draw off fluid 2 : connect into —**tap·per** n

²tap vb **-pp-** 1 : rap lightly 2 : make (as a hole) by repeated light blows ~ n : light stroke or its sound

tape \'tāp\ n 1 : narrow flexible strip (as of cloth, plastic, or metal) 2 : tape measure ~ vb **taped; tap·ing** 1 : fasten with tape 2 : record on tape

tape measure n : strip of tape marked in units for use in measuring

ta·per \'tāpər\ n 1 : slender wax candle 2 : gradual lessening of width in a long object ~ vb 1 : make or become smaller toward one end 2 : diminish gradually

tap·es·try \'tapəstrē\ n, pl **-tries** : heavy handwoven ruglike wall hanging

tape·worm n : long flat intestinal worm

tap·i·o·ca \,tapē'ōkə\ n : a granular starch used esp. in puddings

tar \'tär\ n 1 : thick dark sticky liquid distilled (as from coal) ~ vb **-rr-** : treat or smear with tar

ta·ran·tu·la \tə'ranch(ə)lə, -'rant²lə\ n : large hairy usu. harmless spider

tar·dy \'tärdē\ adj **-di·er; -est** : late —**tar·di·ly** \'tärd²lē\ adv —**tar·di·ness** n

tar·get \'tärgət\ n 1 : mark to shoot at 2 : goal to be achieved ~ vb 1 : make a target of 2 : establish as a goal

tar·iff \'tarəf\ n 1 : duty or rate of duty imposed on imported goods 2 : schedule of tariffs, rates, or charges

tar·nish \'tärnish\ vb : make or become dull or discolored —**tarnish** n

tar·pau·lin \tär'pólən, 'tärpə-\ *n* : waterproof protective covering

tar·ry \'tarē\ *vb* **-ried; -ry·ing** : be slow in leaving

¹tart \'tärt\ *adj* **1** : pleasantly sharp to the taste **2** : caustic —**tart·ly** *adv* —**tart·ness** *n*

²tart *n* : small pie

tar·tan \'tärtᵊn\ *n* : woolen fabric with a plaid design

tar·tar \'tärtər\ *n* : hard crust on the teeth —**tar·tar·ic** \tär'tarik\ *adj*

task \'task\ *n* : assigned work

task·mas·ter *n* : one that burdens another with labor

tas·sel \'tasəl, 'täs-\ *n* : hanging ornament made of a bunch of cords fastened at one end

taste \'tāst\ *vb* **tast·ed; tast·ing 1** : test or determine the flavor of **2** : eat or drink in small quantities **3** : have a specific flavor ~ *n* **1** : small amount tasted **2** : bit **3** : special sense that identifies sweet, sour, bitter, or salty qualities **4** : individual preference **5** : critical appreciation of quality —**taste·ful** \-fəl\ *adj* —**taste·ful·ly** *adv* —**taste·less** *adj* —**taste·less·ly** *adv* —**tast·er** *n* —**tasty** *adj*

tat·ter \'tatər\ *n* **1** : part torn and left hanging **2** *pl* : tattered clothing ~ *vb* : make or become ragged

tat·tle \'tatᵊl\ *vb* **-tled; -tling** : inform on someone —**tat·tler** \'tatlər, -ᵊlər\ *n*

tat·tle·tale *n* : one that tattles

tat·too \ta'tü\ *vb* : mark the skin with indelible designs or figures —**tattoo** *n*

taught *past of* TEACH

taunt \'tónt\ *n* : sarcastic challenge or insult —**taunt** *vb* —**taunt·er** *n*

taut \'tót\ *adj* : tightly drawn —**taut·ly** *adv* —**taut·ness** *n*

tav·ern \'tavərn\ *n* : establishment where liquors are sold to be drunk on the premises

taw·dry \'tódrē\ *adj* **-dri·er; -est** : cheap and gaudy

taw·ny \'tónē\ *adj* **-ni·er; -est** : brownish orange

tax \'taks\ *vb* **1** : impose a tax on **2** : charge **3** : put under stress ~ *n* **1** : charge by authority for public purposes **2** : strain —**tax·able** *adj* —**tax·a·tion** \tak'sāshən\ *n* —**tax·pay·er** *n* —**tax·pay·ing** *adj*

taxi \'taksē\ *n, pl* **tax·is** \-sēz\ : automobile transporting passengers for a fare ~ *vb* **tax·ied; taxi·ing** *or* **taxy·ing; tax·is** *or* **tax·ies 1** : transport or go by taxi **2** : move along the ground before takeoff or after landing

taxi·cab \'taksē,kab\ *n* : taxi

taxi·der·my \'taksə,dərmē\ *n* : art of stuffing and mounting animal skins —**taxi·der·mist** \-məst\ *n*

tea \'tē\ *n* : cured leaves of an oriental shrub or a drink made from these —**tea·cup** *n* —**tea·pot** *n*

teach \'tēch\ *vb* **taught** \'tót\; **teach·ing 1** : tell or show the fundamentals or skills of something **2** : cause to know the consequences **3** : impart knowledge of —**teach·able** *adj* —**teach·er** *n* —**teach·ing** *n*

teak \'tēk\ *n* : East Indian timber tree or its wood

tea·ket·tle \'tē,ketᵊl, -,kit-\ *n* : covered kettle with a handle and spout for boiling water

teal \'tēl\ *n, pl* **teal** *or* **teals** : small short-necked wild duck

team \'tēm\ *n* **1** : draft animals harnessed together **2** : number of people organized for a game or work ~ *vb* : form or work together as a team —**team** *adj* —**team·mate** *n* —**team·work** *n*

team·ster \'tēmstər\ *n* : one that drives a team or truck

¹tear \'tiər\ *n* : drop of salty liquid that moistens the eye —**tear·ful** \-fəl\ *adj* —**tear·ful·ly** *adv*

²tear \'taər\ *vb* **tore** \'tōr\; **torn** \'tōrn\; **tear·ing 1** : separate or pull apart by force **2** : move or act with violence or haste ~ *n* : act or result of tearing

tease \'tēz\ *vb* **teased; teas·ing** : annoy by goading, coaxing, or tantalizing ~ *n* **1** : act of teasing or state of being teased **2** : one that teases

tea·spoon \'tē,spün\ *n* **1** : small spoon for stirring or sipping **2** : measuring spoon holding ⅙ fluidounce —**tea·spoon·ful** \-,fül\ *n*

teat \'tit, 'tēt\ *n* : protuberance through which milk is drawn from an udder or breast

tech·ni·cal \'teknikəl\ *adj* **1** : having or relating to special mechanical or scientific knowledge **2** : by strict interpretation of rules —**tech·ni·cal·ly** \-k(ə)lē\ *adv*

tech·ni·cal·i·ty \,teknə'kalətē\ *n, pl* **-ties** : detail meaningful only to a specialist

technical sergeant : noncommissioned officer in the air force ranking next below a master sergeant

tech·ni·cian \tek'nishən\ *n* : person with the technique of a specialized skill

tech·nique \tek'nēk\ n : manner of accomplishing something

tech·nol·o·gy \tek'näləjē\ n, pl -gies : applied science —**tech·no·log·i·cal** \,teknə'läjikəl\ adj

te·dious \'tēdēəs, 'tējəs\ adj : wearisome from length or dullness —**te·dious·ly** adv —**te·dious·ness** n

te·di·um \'tēdēəm\ n : tedious state or quality

tee \'tē\ n : mound or peg on which a golf ball is placed before beginning play —**tee** vb

teem \'tēm\ vb : become filled to overflowing

teen·age \'tēn,āj\, **teen·aged** \-,ājd\ adj : relating to people in their teens —**teen·ag·er** \-,ājər\ n

teens \'tēnz\ n pl : years 13 to 19 in a person's life

tee·pee var of TEPEE

tee·ter \'tētər\ vb 1 : move unsteadily 2 : seesaw —**teeter** n

teeth pl of TOOTH

teethe \'tēth\ vb teethed; teeth·ing : grow teeth

tele·cast \'teli,kast\ vb -cast; -cast·ing : broadcast by television —**telecast** n —**tele·cast·er** n

tele·gram \'telə,gram\ n : message sent by telegraph

tele·graph \-,graf\ n : system for communication by electrical transmission of coded signals ~ vb : send by telegraph —**te·leg·ra·pher** \tə'legrəfər\ n —**te·leg·ra·phist** \-fast\ n

te·lep·a·thy \tə'lepəthē\ n : apparent communication without known sensory means —**tele·path·ic** \,telə'pathik\ adj —**tele·path·i·cal·ly** \-ik(ə)lē\ adv

tele·phone \'telə,fōn\ n : instrument or system for electrical transmission of spoken words ~ vb -phoned; -phon·ing : communicate with by telephone —**tele·phon·er** n

tele·scope \-,skōp\ n : tube-shaped optical instrument for viewing distant objects ~ vb -scoped; -scop·ing : slide or cause to slide inside another similar section —**tele·scop·ic** \,telə'skäpik\ adj

tele·vise \'telə,vīz\ vb -vised; -vis·ing : broadcast by television

tele·vi·sion \-,vizhən\ n : transmission and reproduction of images by radio waves

tell \'tel\ vb told \'tōld\; tell·ing 1 : count 2 : relate in detail 3 : reveal 4 : give information or an order to 5 : determine

tell·er \'telər\ n 1 : one that relates or counts 2 : bank employee handling money

te·mer·i·ty \tə'merətē\ n, pl -ties : boldness

tem·per \'tempər\ vb 1 : dilute or soften 2 : toughen ~ n 1 : characteristic attitude or feeling 2 : toughness 3 : disposition or control over one's emotions

tem·per·a·ment \'temp(ə)rəmənt\ n : characteristic frame of mind —**tem·per·a·men·tal** \,temp(ə)rə'ment[ə]l\ adj

tem·per·ance \'temp(ə)rəns\ n : moderation in or abstinence from indulgence and esp. the use of intoxicating drink

tem·per·ate \'temp(ə)rət\ adj : moderate

tem·per·a·ture \'tempər,chür, -p(ə)rə,chür, -chər\ n 1 : degree of hotness or coldness 2 : fever

tem·pest \'tempəst\ n : violent storm —**tem·pes·tu·ous** \tem'peschəwəs\ adj

¹**tem·ple** \'tempəl\ n : place of worship

²**temple** n : flattened space on each side of the forehead

tem·po \'tempō\ n, pl -pi \-(,)pē\ or -pos : rate of speed

tem·po·ral \'temp(ə)rəl\ adj : relating to time or to secular concerns

tem·po·rary \'tempə,rerē\ adj : lasting for a short time only —**tem·po·rar·i·ly** \,tempə'rerəlē\ adv

tempt \'tempt\ vb 1 : coax or persuade to do wrong 2 : attract or provoke —**tempt·er** n —**tempt·ing·ly** adv —**tempt·ress** \'temptrəs\ n

temp·ta·tion \temp'tāshən\ n 1 : act of tempting 2 : something that tempts

ten \'ten\ n 1 : one more than 9 2 : 10th in a set or series 3 : thing having 10 units —**ten** adj or pron —**tenth** \'tenth\ adj or adv or n

ten·a·ble \'tenəbəl\ adj : capable of being held or defended —**ten·a·bil·i·ty** \,tenə'bilətē\ n

te·na·cious \tə'nāshəs\ adj 1 : holding fast 2 : retentive —**te·na·cious·ly** adv —**te·nac·i·ty** \tə'nasətē\ n

ten·ant \'tenənt\ n : one who occupies a rented dwelling —**ten·an·cy** \-ənsē\ n

¹**tend** \'tend\ vb : take care of or supervise something

²**tend** vb 1 : move in a particular direction 2 : show a tendency

ten·den·cy \'tendənsē\ n, pl -cies : likelihood to move, think, or act in a particular way

¹ten·der \\'tendər\ *adj* **1** : soft or delicate **2** : expressing or responsive to love or sympathy **3** : sensitive (as to touch) **—ten·der·ly** *adv* **—ten·der·ness** *n*

²tend·er \\'tendər\ *n* **1** : one that tends **2** : vehicle attached to a locomotive **3** : transport to a larger ship

³ten·der \\'tendər\ *n* **1** : offer of a bid for a contract **2** : something that may be offered in payment **—tender** *vb*

ten·der·ize \\'tendə,rīz\ *vb* **-ized; -iz·ing** : make (meat) tender **—ten·der·iz·er** \\'tendə,rīzər\ *n*

ten·der·loin \\'tendər,lóin\ *n* : tender beef or pork strip from near the backbone

ten·don \\'tendən\ *n* : cord of tissue attaching muscle to bone **—ten·di·nous** \-dənəs\ *adj*

ten·dril \\'tendrəl\ *n* : slender coiling growth of some climbing plants

ten·e·ment \\'tenəmənt\ *n* **1** : house divided into apartments **2** : shabby dwelling

te·net \\'tenət\ *n* : principle of belief

ten·nis \\'tenəs\ *n* : racket-and-ball game played across a net

ten·or \\'tenər\ *n* **1** : general drift or meaning **2** : highest natural adult male voice

ten·pin \\'ten,pin\ *n* : bottle-shaped pin bowled at in a game **(tenpins)**

¹tense \\'tens\ *n* : distinct verb form that indicates time

²tense *adj* **tens·er; tens·est 1** : stretched tight **2** : marked by nervous tension **—tense** *vb* **—tense·ly** *adv* **—tense·ness** *n* **—ten·si·ty** \\'tensətē\ *n*

ten·sile \\'tensəl, -,sīl\ *adj* : relating to tension

ten·sion \\'tenchən\ *n* **1** : tense condition **2** : state of mental unrest or of potential hostility or opposition

tent \\'tent\ *n* : collapsible shelter

ten·ta·cle \\'tentikəl\ *n* : long flexible projection of an insect or mollusk **—ten·ta·cled** \-kəld\ *adj* **—ten·tac·u·lar** \ten'takyələr\ *adj*

ten·ta·tive \\'tentətiv\ *adj* : subject to change or discussion **—ten·ta·tive·ly** *adv*

ten·u·ous \\'tenyəwəs\ *adj* **1** : not dense or thick **2** : flimsy or weak **—te·nu·i·ty** \te'nüyüətē, tə-\ *n* **—ten·u·ous·ly** *adv* **—ten·u·ous·ness** *n*

ten·ure \\'tenyər\ *n* : act, right, manner, or period of holding something **—ten·ured** \-yərd\ *adj*

te·pee \\'tē,pē\ *n* : conical tent

tep·id \\'tepəd\ *adj* : moderately warm

term \\'tərm\ *n* **1** : period of time **2** : mathematical expression **3** : special word or phrase **4** *pl* : conditions **5** *pl* : relations ~ *vb* : name

ter·mi·nal \\'tərmən⁰l\ *n* **1** : end **2** : device for making an electrical connection **3** : station at end of a transportation line **—terminal** *adj*

ter·mi·nate \\'tərmə,nāt\ *vb* **-nat·ed; -nat·ing** : bring or come to an end **—ter·mi·na·ble** \-nəbəl\ *adj* **—ter·mi·na·tion** \,tərmə'nāshən\ *n*

ter·mi·nol·o·gy \,tərmə'näləjē\ *n* : terms used in a particular subject

ter·mi·nus \\'tərmənəs\ *n, pl* **-ni** \-,nī\ *or* **-nus·es 1** : end **2** : end of a transportation line

ter·mite \\'tər,mīt\ *n* : wood-eating insect

tern \\'tərn\ *n* : small sea gull

ter·race \\'terəs\ *n* **1** : balcony or patio **2** : bank with a flat top ~ *vb* **-raced; -rac·ing** : landscape in a series of banks

ter·ra-cot·ta \,terə'kätə\ *n* : reddish brown earthenware

ter·rain \tə'rān\ *n* : features of the land

ter·ra·pin \\'terəpən\ *n* : No. American turtle

ter·rar·i·um \tə'rareəm\ *n, pl* **-ia** \-ēə\ *or* **-i·ums** : container for keeping plants or animals

ter·res·tri·al \tə'rest(r)ēəl\ *adj* **1** : relating to the earth or its inhabitants **2** : living or growing on land

ter·ri·ble \\'terəbəl\ *adj* **1** : exciting terror **2** : distressing **3** : intense **4** : of very poor quality **—ter·ri·bly** \-blē\ *adv*

ter·ri·er \\'terēər\ *n* : small dog

ter·rif·ic \tə'rifik\ *adj* **1** : exciting terror **2** : extraordinary

ter·ri·fy \\'terə,fī\ *vb* **-fied; -fy·ing** : fill with terror **—ter·ri·fy·ing·ly** *adv*

ter·ri·to·ry \\'terə,tōrē\ *n, pl* **-ries** : particular geographical region **—ter·ri·to·ri·al** \,terə'tōrēəl\ *adj*

ter·ror \\'terər\ *n* : intense fear and panic or a cause of it

ter·ror·ism \-,izəm\ *n* : systematic covert warfare to produce terror for political coercion **—ter·ror·ist** \-əst\ *adj or n*

ter·ror·ize \-,īz\ *vb* **-ized; -iz·ing 1** : fill with terror **2** : coerce by threat or violence

ter·ry \\'terē\ *n, pl* **-ries** : absorbent fabric with a loose pile of uncut loops

terse \\'tərs\ *adj* **ters·er; ters·est** : concise **—terse·ly** *adv* **—terse·ness** *n*

ter·tia·ry \\'tərshē,erē\ *adj* : of 3d rank, importance, or value

test \'test\ n : examination or evaluation ~ vb : examine by a test —**test·er** n

tes·ta·ment \'testəmənt\ n 1 cap : division of the Bible 2 : will —**tes·ta·men·ta·ry** \ˌtestə'ment(ə)rē\ adj

tes·ti·cle \'testikəl\ n : testis

tes·ti·fy \'testəˌfī\ vb -**fied**; -**fy·ing** 1 : give testimony 2 : serve as evidence

tes·ti·mo·ni·al \ˌtestə'mōnēəl\ n 1 : favorable recommendation 2 : tribute —**testimonial** adj

tes·ti·mo·ny \'testəˌmōnē\ n, pl -**nies** : statement given as evidence in court

tes·tis \'testəs\ n, pl -**tes** \-ˌtēz\ : male reproductive gland

tes·ty \'testē\ adj -**ti·er**; -**est** : easily annoyed

tet·a·nus \'tet°nəs\ n : bacterial disease producing violent muscular spasm —**tet·a·nal** \-°nal\ adj

tête-à-tête \ˌtātə'tāt\ adv : privately ~ n : private conversation ~ adj : private

teth·er \'tethər\ n : leash ~ vb : restrain with a leash

text \'tekst\ n 1 : author's words 2 : main body of printed or written matter on a page 3 : textbook 4 : scriptural passage used as the theme of a sermon 5 : topic —**tex·tu·al** \'tekschə(wə)l\ adj

text·book \'teks(t)ˌbuk\ n : book on a school subject

tex·tile \'tekˌstīl, 'tekst°l\ n : fabric

tex·ture \'tekschər\ n 1 : feel and appearance of something 2 : structure

than \thən, (ˌ)than\ conj or prep —used in comparisons

thank \'thaŋk\ vb : express gratitude to

thank·ful \-fəl\ adj : giving thanks —**thank·ful·ly** adv —**thank·ful·ness** n

thank·less adj : not appreciated

thanks \'thaŋks\ n pl : expression of gratitude

Thanks·giv·ing \thaŋks'giviŋ\ n : 4th Thursday in November observed as a legal holiday for giving thanks for divine goodness

that \(ˌ)that\ pron, pl **those** \'thōz\ 1 : something indicated or understood 2 : the one farther away ~ adj, pl **those** : being the one mentioned or understood or farther away ~ \thət, (ˌ)that\ conj or pron —used to introduce a clause ~ \'that\ adv : to such an extent

thatch \'thach\ vb : cover with thatch ~ n : covering of matted straw

thaw \'thȯ\ vb : melt or cause to melt —**thaw** n

the \thə, before vowel sounds usu thē\ definite article : that particular one ~ adv —used before a comparative

the·ater, the·atre \'thēətər\ n 1 : building or room for viewing a play or movie 2 : dramatic arts

the·at·ri·cal \thē'atrikəl\ adj 1 : relating to the theater 2 : involving exaggerated emotion

thee \(ˌ)thē\ pron, obejctive case of THOU

theft \'theft\ n : act of stealing

their \thər, (ˌ)ther\ adj : relating to them

theirs \'therz\ pron : their one or ones

the·ism \'thēˌizəm\ n : belief in the existence of a god or gods —**the·ist** \-əst\ n or adj —**the·is·tic** \thē'istik\ adj

them \thəm, (ˌ)them\ pron, objective case of THEY

theme \'thēm\ n 1 : subject matter 2 : essay 3 : melody developed in a piece of music —**the·mat·ic** \thi'matik\ adj

them·selves \thəm'selvz, them-\ pron pl : they, them —used reflexively or for emphasis

then \(ˌ)then\ adv 1 : at that time 2 : soon after that 3 : in addition 4 : in that case 5 : consequently ~ \'than\ n : that time ~ adj : existing at that time

thence \'thens, 'thens\ adv : from that place or fact

the·oc·ra·cy \thē'äkrəsē\ n, pl -**cies** : government by officials regarded as divinely inspired —**the·o·crat·ic** \ˌthēə'kratik\ adj

the·ol·o·gy \thē'äləjē\ n, pl -**gies** : study of religion —**the·o·lo·gian** \ˌthēə'lōjən\ n —**the·o·log·i·cal** \-'läjikəl\ adj

the·o·rem \'thēərəm, 'thirəm\ n : provable statement of truth

the·o·ret·i·cal \ˌthēə'retikəl\ adj : relating to or being theory —**the·o·ret·i·cal·ly** adv

the·o·rize \'thēəˌrīz\ vb -**rized**; -**riz·ing** : put forth theories —**the·o·rist** n

the·o·ry \'thēərē, 'thirē\ n, pl -**ries** 1 : general principles of a subject 2 : plausible or scientifically acceptable explanation 3 : judgment, guess, or opinion

ther·a·peu·tic \ˌthera'pyütik\ adj : offering or relating to remedy —**ther·a·peu·ti·cal·ly** \-i(k(ə)lē\ adv

ther·a·py \'therəpē\ n, pl -**pies** : treatment for mental or physical disorder —**ther·a·pist** \-pəst\ n

there \'thaər, 'theər\ adv 1 : in, at, or to that place 2 : in that respect ~ \(ₗ)tha(ə)r, (ₗ)the(ə)r, thər\ pron —used to introduce a sentence or clause ~ \'thaər, 'theər\ n : that place or point

there·abouts, **there·about** \ₗtharə'baut(s), 'tharə,-, ₗtherə,-, 'therə,-\ adv : near that place, time, number, or quantity

there·af·ter \thar'aftər, ther-\ adv : after that

there·by \tha(ə)r'bī, the(ə)r-, 'tha(ə)r,bī, 'the(ə)r,bī\ adv 1 : by that 2 : connected with or with reference to that

there·fore \'tha(ə)r,fōr, 'the(ə)r-\ adv : for that reason

there·in \thar'in, ther-\ adv 1 : in or into that place, time, or thing 2 : in that respect

there·of \-'əv, -'av\ adv 1 : of that or it 2 : from that

there·upon \'tharə,pón, 'ther-, -,pän; ,tharə'pón, ,ther-\ adv 1 : on that matter 2 : therefore 3 : immediately after that

there·with \tha(ə)r'with, the(ə)r-, -'with\ adv : with that

ther·mal \'thərməl\ adj : relating to, caused by, or conserving heat —**ther·mal·ly** adv

ther·mo·dy·nam·ics \ₗthərmə-dī'namiks\ n : physics of heat

ther·mom·e·ter \thə(r)'mämətər\ n : instrument for measuring temperature —**ther·mo·met·ric** \ₗthərmə'metrik\ adj —**ther·mo·met·ri·cal·ly** \-rik(ə)lē\ adv

ther·mos \'thərməs\ n : double-walled bottle used to keep liquids hot or cold

ther·mo·stat \'thərmə,stat\ n : automatic temperature control —**ther·mo·stat·ic** \ₗthərmə'statik\ adj —**ther·mo·stat·i·cal·ly** \-ik(ə)lē\ adv

the·sau·rus \thi'sórəs\ n, pl **-sau·ri** \-'sòr,ī\ or **-sau·rus·es** \-'sòrəsəz\ : book of words and esp. synonyms

these pl of THIS

the·sis \'thēsəs\ n, pl **the·ses** \'thē,sēz\ 1 : proposition to be argued for 2 : essay embodying results of original research

thes·pi·an \'thespēən\ adj : dramatic ~ n : actor

they \'thā\ pron 1 : those ones 2 : people in general

thi·a·mine \'thīəmən, -,mēn\ also **thi·a·min** \-mən\ n : essential vitamin

thick \'thik\ adj 1 : having relatively great mass from front to back or top

to bottom 2 : viscous ~ n : most crowded or thickest part —**thick·ly** adv —**thick·ness** n

thick·en \'thikən\ vb : make or become thick —**thick·en·er** \-(ə)nər\ n

thick·et \'thikət\ n : dense growth of bushes or small trees

thick-skinned \-'skind\ adj : insensitive to criticism

thief \'thēf\ n, pl **thieves** \'thēvz\ : one that steals

thieve \'thēv\ vb **thieved**; **thiev·ing** : steal —**thiev·ery** n

thigh \'thī\ n : upper part of the leg

thigh·bone \'thī'bōn, -,bōn\ n : femur

thim·ble \'thimbəl\ n : protective cap for the finger in sewing —**thim·ble·ful** n

thin \'thin\ adj **-nn-** 1 : having relatively little mass from front to back or top to bottom 2 : not closely set or placed 3 : relatively free flowing 4 : lacking substance, fullness, or strength ~ vb **-nn-** : make or become thin —**thin·ly** adv —**thin·ness** n

thing \'thing\ n 1 : matter of concern 2 : event or act 3 : object 4 pl : possessions

think \'think\ vb **thought** \'thòt\; **think·ing** 1 : form or have in the mind 2 : have as an opinion 3 : ponder 4 : devise by thinking 5 : imagine —**think·er** n

thin-skinned adj : extremely sensitive to criticism

third \'thərd\ adj : being number 3 in a countable series ~ n 1 : one that is third 2 : one of 3 equal parts —**third**, **third·ly** adv

third dimension n : thickness or depth —**third-dimensional** adj

thirst \'thərst\ n 1 : dryness in mouth and throat 2 : intense desire ~ vb : feel thirst —**thirsty** adj

thir·teen \ₗthər'tēn, 'thər-\ n : one more than 12 —**thirteen** adj or pron —**thir·teenth** \-'tēnth\ adj or n

thir·ty \'thərtē\ n, pl **thirties** : 3 times 10 —**thir·ti·eth** \-ēəth\ adj or n —**thirty** adj or pron

this \(')this\ pron, pl **these** \'thēz\ : something close or under immediate discussion ~ adj, pl **these** : being the one near, present, just mentioned, or more immediately under observation ~ \'this\ adv : to such an extent or degree

this·tle \'thisəl\ n : tall prickly herb

thith·er \'thithər\ adv : to that place

thong \'thòn\ n : strip of leather or hide

tho·rax \'thōr,aks\ *n, pl* **-rax·es** *or* **-ra·ces** \'thōrə,sēz\ **1** : part of the body between neck and abdomen **2** : middle of 3 divisions of an insect body —**tho·rac·ic** \thə'rasik\ *adj*

thorn \'thòrn\ *n* : sharp spike on a plant or a plant bearing these —**thorny** *adj*

thor·ough \'thərō\ *adj* : omitting or overlooking nothing —**thor·ough·ly** *adv* —**thor·ough·ness** *n*

thor·ough·bred \'thərə,bred\ *n* **1** *cap* : light speedy racing horse **2** : one of excellent quality —**thoroughbred** *adj*

thor·ough·fare \'thərə,faər\ *n* : public road

those *pl of* THAT

thou \(')thaù\ *pron, archaic* : you

though \'thō\ *adv* : however ~ \(,)thō\ *conj* **1** : despite the fact that **2** : granting that

thought \'thòt\ *past of* THINK ~ *n* **1** : process of thinking **2** : serious consideration **3** : idea

thought·ful \-fəl\ *adj* **1** : absorbed in or showing thought **2** : considerate of others —**thought·ful·ly** *adv* —**thought·ful·ness** *n*

thought·less \-ləs\ *adj* **1** : careless or reckless **2** : lacking concern for others —**thought·less·ly** *adv* —**thought·less·ness** *n*

thou·sand \'thaùz²nd\ *n, pl* **-sands** *or* **-sand** : 10 times 100 —**thousand** *adj* —**thou·sandth** \-³nth\ *adj or n*

thrash \'thrash\ *vb* **1** : thresh **2** : beat **3** : move about violently —**thrash·er** *n*

thread \'thred\ *n* **1** : fine line of fibers **2** : train of thought **3** : ridge around a screw ~ *vb* **1** : pass thread through **2** : put together on a thread **3** : make one's way through or between

thread·bare *adj* **1** : worn so that the thread shows **2** : trite

threat \'thret\ *n* **1** : expression of intention to harm **2** : thing that threatens

threat·en \'thret²n\ *vb* **1** : utter threats **2** : show signs of being near or impending —**threat·en·ing·ly** *adv*

three \'thrē\ *n* **1** : one more than 2 **2** : 3d in a set or series —**three** *adj or pron*

three·fold \'thrē,fōld, -'fōld\ *adj* : triple —**three·fold** \-'fōld\ *adv*

three·score *adj* : being 3 times 20

thresh \'thresh, 'thrash\ *vb* : beat to separate grain —**thresh·er** *n*

thresh·old \'thresh,ōld\ *n* **1** : sill of a door **2** : beginning stage

threw *past of* THROW

thrice \'thrīs\ *adv* : 3 times

thrift \'thrift\ *n* : careful management or saving of money —**thrift·i·ly** \'thriftəlē\ *adv* —**thrift·less** *adj* —**thrifty** *adj*

thrill \'thril\ *vb* **1** : have or cause to have a sudden sharp feeling of excitement **2** : tremble —**thrill** *n* —**thrill·er** *n* —**thrill·ing·ly** *adv*

thrive \'thrīv\ *vb* **throve** \'thrōv\ *or* **thrived**; **thriv·en** \'thrivən\ **1** : grow vigorously **2** : prosper

throat \'thrōt\ *n* **1** : front part of the neck **2** : passage to the stomach —**throat·ed** *adj* —**throaty** *adj*

throb \'thräb\ *vb* **-bb-** : pulsate —**throb** *n*

throe \'thrō\ *n* **1** : pang or spasm **2** *pl* : hard or painful struggle

throne \'thrōn\ *n* : chair representing power or sovereignty

throng \'thròŋ\ *n or vb* : crowd

throt·tle \'thrät²l\ *vb* **-tled**; **-tling** : choke ~ *n* : valve regulating volume of fuel and air delivered to engine cylinders

through \(')thrü\ *prep* **1** : into or out at the other side of **2** : by way of **3** : among, between, or all around **4** : because of **5** : throughout the time of ~ \'thrü\ *adv* **1** : from one end or side to the other **2** : from beginning to end **3** : to the core **4** : into the open ~ \'thrü\ *adj* **1** : going directly from origin to destination **2** : finished

through·out \thrü'aùt\ *adv* **1** : everywhere **2** : from beginning to end ~ *prep* **1** : in or to every part of **2** : during the whole of

throve *past of* THRIVE

throw \'thrō\ *vb* **threw** \'thrü\; **thrown** \'thrōn\, **throw·ing** **1** : propel through the air **2** : cause to fall or fall off **3** : put suddenly in a certain position or condition **4** : move quickly as if throwing **5** : put on or off hastily —**throw** *n* —**throw·er** \'thrō(ə)r\ *n* —**throw up** *vb* : vomit

thrush \'thrəsh\ *n* : songbird

thrust \'thrəst\ *vb* **thrust**; **thrust·ing** **1** : shove forward **2** : stab or pierce —**thrust** *n*

thud \'thəd\ *n* : dull sound of something falling —**thud** *vb*

thug \'thəg\ *n* : ruffian or gangster

thumb \'thəm\ *n* **1** : short thick division of the hand opposing the fingers **2** : glove part for the thumb ~ *vb* : leaf through with the thumb —**thumb·nail** *n*

thump \'thəmp\ *vb* : strike with something thick or heavy causing a dull heavy sound —**thump** n

thun·der \'thəndər\ n : sound following lightning —**thunder** vb —**thun·der·clap** n —**thun·der·ous** \'thənd(ə)rəs\ adj —**thun·der·ous·ly** adv

thun·der·bolt \-,bōlt\ n : discharge of lightning with thunder

thun·der·show·er \'thəndər,shau̇(ə)r\ n : shower with thunder and lightning

thun·der·storm n : storm with thunder and lightning

Thurs·day \'thərzdē\ n : 5th day of the week

thus \'thəs\ adv 1 : in this or that way 2 : to this degree or extent 3 : because of this or that

thwart \'thwȯrt\ vb : block or defeat

thy \(,)thī\ adj, archaic : your

thyme \'tīm, 'thīm\ n : cooking herb

thy·roid \'thī,rȯid\, **thy·roi·dal** \'thī'rȯid^əl\ adj : relating to a large endocrine gland (**thyroid gland**)

thy·self \thī'self\ pron, archaic : yourself

ti·ara \tē'arə, -'er-, -'är-\ n : decorative formal headband

tib·ia \'tibēə\ n, pl -i·ae \-,ē,ē\ : bone between the knee and ankle

¹tic \'tik\ n : twitching of facial muscles

¹tick \'tik\ n : small 8-legged blood-sucking animal

²tick n 1 : light rhythmic tap or beat 2 : check mark ~ vb 1 : make ticks 2 : mark with a tick 3 : operate

tick·er \'tikər\ n 1 : something (as a watch) that ticks 2 : telegraph instrument that prints on paper tape

tick·et \'tikət\ n 1 : tag showing price, payment of a fee or fare, or a traffic offense 2 : list of candidates ~ vb : put a ticket on

tick·ing \'tikiŋ\ n : fabric covering of a mattress

tick·le \'tikəl\ vb -led; -ling 1 : please or amuse 2 : touch lightly causing uneasiness, laughter, or spasmodic movements —**tickle** n

tick·lish \'tik(ə)lish\ adj 1 : sensitive to tickling 2 : requiring delicate handling —**tick·lish·ly** adv —**tick·lish·ness** n

tid·al wave \,tīd^əl-\ n : high sea wave following an earthquake

tid·bit \'tid,bit\ n : choice morsel

tide \'tīd\ n : alternate rising and falling of the sea ~ vb tid·ed; tid·ing : be enough to allow (one) to get by for a time —**tid·al** \'tīd^əl\ adj —**tide·wa·ter** n

tid·ings \'tīdiŋz\ n pl : news or message

ti·dy \'tīdē\ adj -di·er; -est 1 : well ordered and cared for 2 : large or substantial —**ti·di·ness** n —**tidy** vb

tie \'tī\ n 1 : line or ribbon for fastening, uniting, or closing 2 : cross support to which railroad rails are fastened 3 : uniting force 4 : equality in score or tally of a deadlocked contest 5 : necktie ~ vb tied; ty·ing or tie·ing 1 : fasten or close by wrapping and knotting a tie 2 : form a knot in 3 : gain the same score or tally as an opponent

tier \'tiər\ n : one of a steplike series of rows

tiff \'tif\ n : petty quarrel —**tiff** vb

ti·ger \'tīgər\ n : large black-striped flesh-eating mammal —**ti·ger·ish** \-g(ə)rish\ adj —**ti·gress** \-grəs\ n

tight \'tīt\ adj 1 : fitting close together esp. so as not to allow air or water to enter 2 : held very firmly 3 : taut 4 : fitting too snugly 5 : difficult 6 : stingy 7 : evenly contested 8 : low in supply —**tight** adv —**tight·en** \-^ən\ vb —**tight·ly** adv —**tight·ness** n

tights \'tīts\ n pl : skintight garments

tight·wad \'tīt,wäd\ n : stingy person

tile \'tīl\ n : thin piece of stone or fired clay used on roofs, floors, or walls ~ vb : cover with tiles —**til·ing** \-iŋ\ n

¹till \(,)til\ prep or conj : until

²till \'til\ vb : cultivate (soil) —**till·able** adj

³till \'til\ n : money drawer

til·ler \'tilər\ n : lever for turning a boat's rudder

tilt \'tilt\ vb : cause to incline ~ n : slant

tim·ber \'timbər\ n 1 : cut wood for building 2 : large squared piece of wood 3 : wooded land or trees for timber ~ vb : cover, frame, or support with timbers —**tim·bered** adj —**tim·ber·land** \-,land\ n

tim·bre \'tambər, 'tim-\ n : sound quality

time \'tīm\ n 1 : period during which something exists or continues or can be accomplished 2 : point at which something happens 3 : customary hour 4 : age 5 : tempo 6 : moment, hour, day, or year as indicated by a clock or calendar 7 : one's experience during a particular period ~ vb timed; tim·ing 1 : arrange or set the time of 2 : determine or record the time, duration, or rate of —**time·keep·er** n —**time·less** adj —**time·less·ness** n —**time·li·ness** n —**time·ly** adv —**tim·er** n

time·piece n : device to show time

times \ˌtīmz\ prep : multiplied by

time-ta-ble \ˈtīmˌtābəl\ n : table of departure and arrival times

tim-id \ˈtiməd\ adj : lacking in courage or self-confidence —**ti-mid-i-ty** \təˈmidətē\ n

tim-o-rous \ˈtim(ə)rəs\ adj : fearful —**tim-o-rous-ly** adv —**tim-o-rous-ness** n

tim-pa-ni \ˈtimpənē\ n pl : set of kettledrums —**tim-pa-nist** \-nəst\ n

tin \ˈtin\ n 1 : soft white metallic chemical element 2 : metal food can

tinc-ture \ˈtiŋkchər\ n : alcoholic solution of a medicine

tin-der \ˈtindər\ n : substance used to kindle a fire

tine \ˈtīn\ n : one of the points of a fork

tin-foil \ˈtinˌfȯil\ n : thin metal sheeting

tinge \ˈtinj\ vb **tinged; tinge-ing** or **ting-ing** \ˈtinjiŋ\ 1 : color slightly 2 : affect with a slight odor ~ n 1 : slight coloring or flavor

tin-gle \ˈtingəl\ vb **-gled; -gling** : feel a ringing, stinging, or thrilling sensation —**tingle** n

tin-ker \ˈtiŋkər\ vb : experiment in repairing something —**tin-ker-er** n

tin-kle \ˈtiŋkəl\ vb **-kled; -kling** : make or cause to make a high ringing sound —**tinkle** n

tin-sel \ˈtinsəl\ n : decorative thread or strip of glittering metal or paper

tint \ˈtint\ n 1 : slight or pale coloration 2 : color shade ~ vb : give a tint to

ti-ny \ˈtīnē\ adj **-ni-er; -est** : very small

¹**tip** \ˈtip\ n : pointed end of something ~ vb **-pp-** 1 : furnish with a tip 2 : cover the tip of

²**tip** vb **-pp-** 1 : overturn 2 : lean ~ n : act or state of tipping

³**tip** n : small sum given for a service performed ~ vb : give a tip to

⁴**tip** n : piece of confidential information ~ vb **-pp-** : give confidential information to

tip-off \ˈtipˌȯf\ n : indication

tip-ple \ˈtipəl\ vb **-pled; -pling** : drink intoxicating liquor esp. habitually or excessively —**tip-pler** n

tip-sy \ˈtipsē\ adj **-si-er; -est** : unsteady or foolish from alcohol

tip-toe \ˈtipˌtō\ n : the toes of the feet ~ adv or adj : supported on tiptoe ~ vb **-toed; -toe-ing** : walk quietly or on tiptoe

tip-top n : highest point ~ adj : excellent

ti-rade \ˈtīˌrād, ˈtī-\ n : prolonged speech of abuse

¹**tire** \ˈtī(ə)r\ vb **tired; tir-ing** 1 : make or become weary 2 : wear out the patience of —**tire-less** adj —**tire-less-ly** adv —**tire-less-ness** n —**tire-some** \-səm\ adj —**tire-some-ly** adv —**tire-some-ness** n

²**tire** n : rubber cushion encircling a car wheel

tired \ˈtī(ə)rd\ adj : weary

tis-sue \ˈtishü\ n 1 : soft absorbent paper 2 : layer of cells forming a basic structural element of an animal or plant body

ti-tan-ic \tīˈtanik, tə-\ adj : gigantic

ti-ta-ni-um \tīˈtānēəm, tə-\ n : gray light strong metallic chemical element

tithe \ˈtīth\ n : tenth part paid or given esp. for the support of a church —**tithe** vb —**tith-er** n

tit-il-late \ˈtitᵊlˌāt\ vb **-lat-ed; -lat-ing** : excite pleasurably —**tit-il-la-tion** \ˌtitᵊlˈāshən\ n

ti-tle \ˈtītᵊl\ n 1 : legal ownership 2 : distinguishing name 3 : designation of honor, rank, or office 4 : championship —**ti-tled** adj

tit-ter \ˈtitər\ n : nervous or affected laugh —**titter** n

tit-u-lar \ˈtich(ə)lər\ adj 1 : existing in title only 2 : relating to or bearing a title

TNT \ˌtēˌenˈtē\ n : high explosive

to \tə, (ˈ)tü\ prep 1 : in the direction of 2 : at, on, or near 3 : resulting in 4 : before or until 5 —used to show a relationship or object of a verb 6 —used with an infinitive ~ \ˈtü\ adv 1 : forward 2 : to a state of consciousness

toad \ˈtōd\ n : tailless leaping amphibian

toad-stool \-ˌstül\ n : mushroom esp. when inedible or poisonous

toady \ˈtōdē\ n, pl **toad-ies** : one who flatters to gain favors —**toady** vb

toast \ˈtōst\ vb 1 : make (as a slice of bread) crisp and brown 2 : drink in honor of someone or something 3 : warm ~ n 1 : toasted sliced bread 2 : act of drinking in honor of someone —**toast-er** n

to-bac-co \təˈbakō\ n, pl **-cos** : broadleaved herb or its leaves prepared for smoking or chewing

to-bog-gan \təˈbägən\ n : long flat-bottomed light sled ~ vb : coast on a toboggan

to-day \təˈdā\ adv 1 : on or for this day

2 : at the present time ~ *n* : present day or time

tod·dle \'täd³l\ *vb* -dled; -dling : walk with tottering steps like a young child —**toddle** *n* —**tod·dler** \'tädlər, -³lər\ *n*

to-do \tə-'dü\ *n, pl* **to-dos** \-'düz\ : disturbance or fuss

toe \'tō\ *n* : one of the 5 end divisions of the foot —**toe·nail** *n*

to·ga \'tōgə\ *n* : loose outer garment of ancient Rome

to·geth·er \tə-'geₜ͟hər\ *adv* **1** : in or into one place or group **2** : in or into contact or association **3** : at one time **4** : as a group —**to·geth·er·ness** *n*

toil \'tȯil\ *vb* : work hard and long —**toil** *n* —**toil·er** *n* —**toil·some** *adj*

toi·let \'tȯilət\ *n* **1** : dressing and grooming oneself **2** : bathroom **3** : water basin to urinate and defecate in

toils \'tȯilz\ *n pl* : net or trap

to·ken \'tōkən\ *n* **1** : outward sign or expression of something **2** : small part representing the whole **3** : piece resembling a coin

told *past of* TELL

tol·er·a·ble \'tälⱶ(ə)rəbəl\ *adj* **1** : capable of being endured **2** : moderately good —**tol·er·a·bly** \-blē\ *adv*

tol·er·ance \'täl(ə)rəns\ *n* **1** : lack of opposition for beliefs or practices differing from one's own **2** : capacity for enduring **3** : allowable deviation —**tol·er·ant** *adj* —**tol·er·ant·ly** *adv*

tol·er·ate \'tälⱶ,rāt\ *vb* -at·ed; -at·ing **1** : allow to be or to be done without opposition **2** : endure or resist the action of —**tol·er·a·tion** \,tälə'rāshən\ *n*

¹toll \'tōl\ *n* **1** : fee paid for a privilege or service **2** : cost of achievement in loss or suffering —**toll·booth** *n* —**toll·gate** *n*

²toll *vb* **1** : cause the sounding of (a bell) **2** : sound with slow measured strokes ~ *n* : sound of a tolling bell

tom·a·hawk \'tämi,hȯk\ *n* : light ax used as a weapon by Indians

to·ma·to \tə'mātō, -'mät-\ *n, pl* -toes : tropical American herb or its fruit

tomb \'tüm\ *n* : house, vault, or grave for burial

tom·boy \'täm,bȯi\ *n* : girl with boyish behavior

tomb·stone *n* : stone marking a grave

tom·cat \'täm,kat\ *n* : male cat

tome \'tōm\ *n* : large or weighty book

to·mor·row \tə'märō\ *adv* : on or for the day after today —**tomorrow** *n*

tom-tom \'täm,täm\ *n* : small-headed drum beaten with the hands

ton \'tən\ *n* : unit of weight equal to 2000 pounds

tone \'tōn\ *n* **1** : vocal or musical sound **2** : sound of definite pitch **3** : manner of speaking that expresses an emotion or attitude **4** : color quality **5** : healthy condition **6** : general character or quality —**tone down** *vb* : soften or muffle —**ton·al** \-³l\ *adj* —**to·nal·i·ty** \tō'nalətē\ *n*

tongs \'täŋz, 'tȯŋz\ *n pl* : grasping device of 2 joined or hinged pieces

tongue \'təŋ\ *n* **1** : fleshy movable organ of the mouth **2** : language **3** : something long and flat and fastened at one end —**tongued** \'təŋd\ *adj* —**tongue·less** *adj*

ton·ic \'tänik\ *n* : something (as a drug) that invigorates or restores health —**tonic** *adj*

to·night \tə'nīt\ *adv* : on this night ~ *n* : present or coming night

ton·sil \'tänsəl\ *n* : either of a pair of oval masses in the throat —**ton·sil·lec·to·my** \,tänsə'lektəmē\ *n* —**ton·sil·li·tis** \-'lītəs\ *n*

too \(')tü\ *adv* **1** : in addition **2** : excessively

took *past of* TAKE

tool \'tül\ *n* **1** : hand implement used when working with the hands ~ *vb* : shape or finish with a tool

toot \'tüt\ *vb* : sound or cause to sound esp. in short blasts —**toot** *n*

tooth \'tüth\ *n, pl* **teeth** \'tēth\ **1** : one of the hard structures in the jaws for chewing **2** : one of the projections on the edge of a gear wheel —**tooth·ache** *n* —**tooth·brush** *n* —**toothed** \'tütht\ *adj* —**tooth·less** *adj* —**tooth·paste** *n* —**tooth·pick** *n*

tooth·some \'tüthsəm\ *adj* **1** : delicious **2** : attractive

¹top \'täp\ *n* **1** : highest part or level of something **2** : lid or covering ~ *vb* -pp- **1** : cover with a top **2** : surpass **3** : go over the top of ~ *adj* : being at the top —**topped** *adj*

²top *n* : spinning toy

to·paz \'tō,paz\ *n* : hard gem

top·coat *n* : lightweight overcoat

top·ic \'täpik\ *n* : subject for discussion or study

top·i·cal \-ikəl\ *adj* **1** : relating to or arranged by topics **2** : relating to current or local events —**top·i·cal·ly** \-k(ə)lē\ *adv*

top·most \'täp,mōst\ *adj* : highest of all

top-notch \-'näch\ *adj* : of the highest quality

to·pog·ra·phy \tə'pägrəfē\ *n* **1** : art of mapping the physical features of a place **2** : outline of the form of a place —**to·pog·ra·pher** \-fər\ *n* —**top·o·graph·ic** \ˌtäpə'grafik, ˌtōp-\ **top·o·graph·i·cal** \-ikəl\ *adj*

top·ple \'täpəl\ *vb* **-pled; -pling** : fall or cause to fall

top·sy-tur·vy \ˌtäpsē'tərvē\ *adv or adj* **1** : upside down **2** : in utter confusion

torch \'tórch\ *n* : flaming light —**torch·bear·er** *n* —**torch·light** *n*

tore *past of* TEAR

tor·ment \'tór,ment\ *n* : extreme pain or anguish or a source of this ~ *vb* **1** : cause severe anguish to **2** : harass —**tor·men·tor** \-ər\ *n*

torn *past part of* TEAR

tor·na·do \tór'nādō\ *n, pl* **-does** *or* **-dos** : violent destructive whirling wind

tor·pe·do \tór'pēdō\ *n, pl* **-does** : self-propelling explosive submarine missile ~ *vb* : hit with a torpedo

tor·pid \'tórpəd\ *adj* **1** : having lost motion or the power of exertion **2** : lacking vigor —**tor·pid·i·ty** \tór'pidətē\ *n*

tor·por \'tórpər\ *n* : extreme sluggishness or lethargy

torque \'tórk\ *n* : turning force

tor·rent \'tórənt\ *n* **1** : rushing stream **2** : tumultuous outburst

tor·ren·tial \tó'renchəl, tə-\ *adj* : relating to or like a torrent

tor·rid \'tórəd\ *adj* **1** : parched with heat **2** : impassioned

tor·sion \'tórshən\ *n* : a twisting or being twisted —**tor·sion·al** \'tórsh(ə)nəl\ *adj* —**tor·sion·al·ly** *adv*

tor·so \'tórsō\ *n, pl* **-sos** *or* **-si** \-ˌsē\ : trunk of the human body

tor·til·la \tór'tē(y)ə\ *n* : round flat cornmeal bread

tor·toise \'tórtəs\ *n* : sea turtle

tor·tu·ous \'tórch(ə)wəs\ *adj* **1** : winding **2** : tricky

tor·ture \'tórchər\ *n* **1** : use of pain to punish or force **2** : agony ~ *vb* **-tured; -tur·ing** : inflict torture on —**tor·tur·er** *n*

toss \'tós, 'täs\ *vb* **1** : move to and fro or up and down violently **2** : throw with a quick light motion **3** : move restlessly —**toss** *n*

toss–up *n* **1** : a deciding by flipping a coin **2** : even chance

tot \'tät\ *n* : small child

to·tal \'tōt^əl\ *n* : entire amount ~ *vb* **-taled** *or* **-talled; -tal·ing** *or* **-tal·ling** **1**

: add up **2** : amount to —**total** *adj* —**to·tal·ly** *adv*

to·tal·i·tar·i·an \tō,talə'terēən\ *adj* : relating to a political regime based on subordination of the individual to the state and strict control of all aspects of life —**totalitarian** *n* —**to·tal·i·tar·i·an·ism** \-əˌnizəm\ *n*

to·tal·i·ty \tō'talətē\ *n, pl* **-ties** : whole amount or entirety

tote \'tōt\ *vb* **toted; tot·ing** : carry

to·tem \'tōtəm\ *n* : often carved figure used as a family or tribe emblem

tot·ter \'tätər\ *vb* **1** : sway as if about to fall **2** : stagger

touch \'təch\ *vb* **1** : make contact with so as to feel **2** : be or cause to be in contact **3** : take into the hands or mouth **4** : treat or mention a subject **5** : relate or concern **6** : move to sympathetic feeling ~ *n* **1** : light stroke **2** : act or fact of touching or being touched **3** : sense of feeling **4** : trace **5** : state of being in contact

touch·down \'təch,daún\ *n* : scoring of 6 points in football

touch·stone *n* : test or criterion of genuineness or quality

touchy \'təchē\ *adj* **touch·i·er; -est 1** : easily offended **2** : requiring tact

tough \'təf\ *adj* **1** : strong but elastic **2** : not easily chewed **3** : severe or disciplined **4** : difficult to influence or overcome ~ *n* : rowdy or belligerent person —**tough·ly** *adv* —**tough·ness** *n*

tough·en \'təfən\ *vb* : make or become tough

tou·pee \tü'pā\ *n* : small wig for a bald spot

tour \'túr, 1 *is also* 'taú(ə)r\ *n* **1** : period of time spent at work or on an assignment **2** : journey with a return to the starting point ~ *vb* : travel over to see the sights —**tour·ist** \'túrəst\ *n*

tour·na·ment \'túrnəmənt, 'tər-\ *n* **1** : medieval jousting competition **2** : championship series of games

tour·ney \-nē\ *n, pl* **-neys** : tournament

tour·ni·quet \'túrnikət, -ˌkā\ *n* : twisted bandage for stopping blood flow

tou·sle \'taúzəl\ *vb* **-sled; -sling** : dishevel (as someone's hair)

tout \'taút, 'tüt\ *vb* : praise or publicize loudly

tow \'tō\ *vb* : pull along behind —**tow** *n*

to·ward, to·wards \(')tō(ə)rd(z), tə'wòrd(z)\ *prep* **1** : in the direction of **2** : with respect to **3** : in part payment on tow·el \'tau̇(ə)l\ n : absorbent cloth or paper for wiping or drying

tow·er \'tau̇(ə)r\ n : tall structure ~ vb : rise to a great height —tow·ered \'tau̇(ə)rd\ adj —tow·er·ing adj

tow·head \'tō,hed\ n : person having white or light blond hair —tow·head·ed \-,hedəd\ adj

town \'tau̇n\ n 1 : small residential area 2 : city —towns·peo·ple \'tau̇nz,pēpəl\ n pl

town·ship \'tau̇n,ship\ n 1 : unit of local government 2 : 36 square miles of U.S. public land

tox·ic \'täksik\ adj : poisonous —tox·ic·i·ty \täk'sisətē\ n

tox·in \'täksən\ n : poison produced by an organism

toy \'tȯi\ n : something for a child to play with ~ vb : amuse oneself or play with something ~ adj 1 : designed as a toy 2 : very small

¹trace \'trās\ vb traced; trac·ing 1 : mark over the lines of (a drawing) 2 : follow the trail or the development of ~ n 1 : track 2 : tiny amount or residue —trace·able adj —trac·er n

²trace n : line of a harness

tra·chea \'trākēə\ n, pl -che·ae \-kē,ē\ : windpipe —tra·che·al \-kēəl\ adj

track \'trak\ n 1 : trail left by wheels or footprints 2 : racing course 3 : train rails 4 : awareness of a progression 5 : looped belts propelling a vehicle ~ vb 1 : follow the tracks of 2 : make tracks on —track·er n

track-and-field adj : relating to athletic contests of running, jumping, and throwing events

¹tract \'trakt\ n : pamphlet of propaganda

²tract n 1 : stretch of land 2 : system of body organs

trac·ta·ble \'traktəbəl\ adj : easily controlled

trac·tion \'trakshən\ n : gripping power to permit movement —trac·tion·al \-sh(ə)nəl\ adj —trac·tive \'traktiv\ adj

trac·tor \'traktər\ n 1 : farm vehicle used esp. for pulling 2 : truck for hauling a trailer

trade \'trād\ n 1 : one's regular business 2 : occupation requiring skill 3 : the buying and selling of goods 4 : act of trading ~ vb trad·ed; trad·ing 1 : give in exchange for something 2 : buy and sell goods 3 : be a regular customer —trades·peo·ple \'trādz,pēpəl\ n pl

trade·mark \'trād,märk\ n : word or mark identifying a manufacturer —trademark

trades·man \'trādzmən\ n : shopkeeper

tra·di·tion \trə'dishən\ n : belief or custom passed from generation to generation —tra·di·tion·al \-'dish(ə)nəl\ adj —tra·di·tion·al·ly adv

tra·duce \trə'd(y)üs\ vb -duced; -duc·ing : lower the reputation of —tra·duc·er n

traf·fic \'trafik\ n 1 : business dealings 2 : movement along a route ~ vb : do business —traf·fick·er n —traffic light n

trag·e·dy \'trajədē\ n, pl -dies 1 : serious drama describing a conflict and having a sad end 2 : disastrous event

trag·ic \'trajik\ adj : being a tragedy —trag·i·cal·ly \-ik(ə)lē\ adv

trail \'trāl\ vb 1 : hang down and drag along the ground 2 : draw along behind 3 : follow the track of 4 : dwindle ~ n 1 : something that trails 2 : path or evidence left by something

trail·er \'trālər\ n : vehicle intended to be hauled

train \'trān\ n 1 : trailing part of a gown 2 : retinue or procession 3 : connected series 4 : group of railroad cars moving together ~ vb 1 : cause to grow as desired 2 : make or become prepared or skilled 3 : point —train·ee n —train·er n —train·load n —train·man \-mən\ n

trait \'trāt\ n : distinguishing quality

trai·tor \'trātər\ n : one who betrays a trust or commits treason —trai·tor·ous adj —trai·tress \'trātrəs\ n

tra·jec·to·ry \trə'jekt(ə)rē\ n, pl -ries : curving path of something moving through air or space

tram·mel \'traməl\ vb -meled or -melled; -mel·ing or -mel·ling \-(ə)liŋ\ : impede —trammel n

tramp \'tramp, 2 is also \'trämp, 'trȯmp\ vb 1 : walk or hike 2 : tread on ~ n : beggar or vagrant

tram·ple \'trampəl\ vb -pled; -pling : walk or step on so as to bruise or crush —trample n —tram·pler n

tram·po·line \,trampə'lēn, 'trampə,-\ n : resilient canvas-and-springs surface used for bouncing —tram·po·lin·er n —tram·po·lin·ist \-əst\ n

trance \'trans\ n 1 : sleeplike condition 2 : state of mystical absorption

tran·quil \'traŋkwəl, 'tran-\ adj : quiet and undisturbed —tran·quil·ize, tran·quil·lize \-kwə,līz\ vb —tran·quil·iz·er n —tran·quil·li·ty,

quil·i·ty \tran'kwilətē, traŋ-\ n —**tran·quil·ly** adv

trans·act \trans'akt, tranz-\ vb : conduct (business)

trans·action \-'akshən\ n 1 : business deal 2 pl : records of proceedings

tran·scend \trans'end\ vb : rise above or surpass —**tran·scen·dent** \-'endənt\ adj —**tran·scen·den·tal** \ˌtransˌen'dentᵊl, -ən-\ adj

tran·scribe \trans'krīb\ vb -scribed; -scrib·ing : make a copy, arrangement, or recording of —**tran·scrip·tion** \trans'kripshən\ n

tran·script \'trans,kript\ n : official copy

tran·sept \'trans,ept\ n : part of a church that crosses the nave at right angles

trans·fer \trans'fər, 'trans,fər\ vb -rr- 1 : move from one person, place, or situation to another 2 : convey ownership of 3 : print or copy by contact 4 : change to another vehicle or transportation line ~ \'trans,fər\ n 1 : act or process of transferring 2 : one that transfers or is transferred 3 : ticket permitting one to transfer —**trans·fer·able** \trans'fərəbəl\ adj —**trans·fer·al** \-əl\ n —**trans·fer·ence** \-əns\ n

trans·fig·ure \trans'figyər\ vb -ured; -ur·ing 1 : change the form or appearance of 2 : glorify —**trans·fig·u·ra·tion** \ˌtransˌfig(y)ə'rāshən\ n

trans·fix \trans'fiks\ vb 1 : pierce through 2 : hold motionless

trans·form \-'förm\ vb 1 : to change in structure, appearance, or character 2 : change (an electric current) in potential or type —**trans·for·ma·tion** \ˌtransfər'māshən\ n —**trans·form·er** \trans'förmər\ n

trans·fuse \trans'fyüz\ vb -fused; -fus·ing 1 : diffuse into or through 2 : transfer (as blood) into a vein —**trans·fu·sion** \-'fyüzhən\ n

trans·gress \trans'gres, tranz-\ vb : sin —**trans·gres·sion** \-'greshən\ n —**trans·gres·sor** \-'gresər\ n

tran·sient \'tranchənt\ adj : not lasting or staying long —**transient** n —**tran·sient·ly** adv

tran·sis·tor \tranz'istər, trans-\ n : small semiconductor —**tran·sis·tor·ize** \-tə,rīz\ vb

tran·sit \'transət, 'tranz-\ n 1 : movement over, across, or through 2 : local and esp. public transportation 3 : surveyor's instrument

tran·si·tion \trans'ishən, tranz-\ n : passage from one state, stage, or

subject to another —**tran·si·tion·al** \-'ish(ə)nəl\ adj

tran·si·to·ry \'transə,tōrē, 'tranz-\ adj : of brief duration

trans·late \trans'lāt, tranz-\ vb -lat·ed; -lat·ing : change into another language —**trans·lat·able** adj —**trans·la·tion** \-'lāshən\ n —**trans·la·tor** \-'lātər\ n

trans·lu·cent \trans'lüsᵊnt, tranz-\ adj : diffusing light so that objects beyond cannot be distinguished —**trans·lu·cence** \-ᵊns\ n —**trans·lu·cen·cy** \-ᵊnsē\ n —**trans·lu·cent·ly** adv

trans·mis·sion \-'mishən\ n 1 : act or process of transmitting 2 : system of gears between a car engine and drive wheels

trans·mit \-'mit\ vb -tt- 1 : transfer from one person or place to another 2 : pass on by inheritance 3 : broadcast —**trans·mis·si·ble** \-'misəbəl\ adj —**trans·mit·ta·ble** \-'mitəbəl\ adj —**trans·mit·tal** \-'mitᵊl\ n —**trans·mit·ter** n

tran·som \'transəm\ n : window above a door

trans·par·ent \trans'parənt\ adj 1 : clear enough to see through 2 : obvious —**trans·par·en·cy** \-ᵊnsē\ n —**trans·par·ent·ly** adv

tran·spire \trans'pī(ə)r\ vb -spired; -spir·ing : take place —**tran·spi·ra·tion** \ˌtranspə'rāshən\ n

trans·plant \trans'plant\ vb 1 : dig up and move to another place 2 : transfer from one body part or person to another —**transplant** \'trans,-\ n —**trans·plan·ta·tion** \ˌtrans,plan-'tāshən\ n

trans·port \trans'pōrt\ vb 1 : carry or deliver to another place 2 : carry away by emotion ~ \'trans,-\ n 1 : act of transporting 2 : rapture 3 : ship or plane for carrying troops or supplies —**trans·por·ta·tion** \ˌtranspor'tāshən\ n —**trans·port·er** n

trans·pose \trans'pōz\ vb -posed; -pos·ing : change the position, sequence, or key —**trans·po·si·tion** \ˌtranspə'zishən\ n

trans·ship \tran(ch)'ship, trans-\ vb : transfer from one mode of transportation to another —**trans·ship·ment** n

trans·verse \trans'vərs, tranz-\ adj : lying across —**trans·verse** \'trans,vərs, 'tranz-\ n —**trans·verse·ly** adv

trap \'trap\ n 1 : device for catching animals 2 : something by which one is caught unawares **3** : device to allow one thing to pass through while keeping other things out ~ *vb* **-pp-** : catch in a trap —**trap·per** *n*

trap·door *n* : door in a floor or roof

tra·peze \tra'pēz\ *n* : suspended bar used by acrobats

trap·e·zoid \'trapə,zȯid\ *n* : plane 4-sided figure with 2 parallel sides —**trap·e·zoi·dal** \,trapə'zȯid°l\ *adj*

trap·pings \'trapiŋz\ *n pl* **1** : ornamental covering **2** : outward decoration or dress

trash \'trash\ *n* : something that is no good —**trashy** *adj*

trau·ma \'trȯma, 'trò-\ *n, pl* **-ma·ta** \-məta\ *or* **-mas** : bodily or mental injury —**trau·mat·ic** \trə'matik, trò-, traù-\ *adj*

tra·vail \trə'vāl, 'trav,āl\ *n* : painful work or exertion ~ *vb* : labor hard

trav·el \'travəl\ *vb* **-eled** *or* **-elled; -el·ing** *or* **-el·ling 1** : take a trip or tour **2** : move or be carried from point to point ~ *n* : journey —often pl. —**trav·el·er, trav·el·ler** *n*

tra·verse \'travərs, trə'vərs, travərs\ *vb* **-versed; -vers·ing** : go or extend across or over —**tra·verse** \'travərs\ *n*

trav·es·ty \'travəstē\ *n, pl* **-ties** : terrible distortion or imitation of something —**travesty** *vb*

trawl \'trȯl\ *vb* : fish or catch with a trawl ~ *n* : large cone-shaped net —**trawl·er** *n*

tray \'trā\ *n* : shallow flat-bottomed receptacle for holding or carrying something

treach·er·ous \'trech(ə)rəs\ *adj* : disloyal or dangerous —**treach·er·ous·ly** *adv*

treach·ery \'trech(ə)rē\ *n, pl* **-er·ies** : betrayal of a trust

tread \'tred\ *vb* **trod** \'träd\; **trod·den** \'träd°n\ *or* **trod; tread·ing 1** : step on or over **2** : walk **3** : press or crush with the feet ~ *n* **1** : way of walking **2** : sound made in walking **3** : part on which a thing runs

trea·dle \'tred°l\ *n* : foot pedal operating a machine

tread·mill *n* **1** : mill worked by walking persons or animals **2** : wearisome routine

trea·son \'trēz°n\ *n* : attempt to overthrow the government —**trea·son·able** \'trēznəbəl, -°nəbəl\ *adj* —**trea·son·ous** \-nəs, -°nəs\ *adj*

trea·sure \'trezhər, 'trāzh-\ *n* **1** : wealth stored up **2** : something of

great value ~ *vb* **-sured; -sur·ing** : keep as precious

trea·sur·er \'trezhrər, trezhərər, 'trāzh-\ *n* : officer who handles funds

trea·sury \'trezh(ə)rē, 'trāzh-\ *n, pl* **-sur·ies** : place or office for keeping and distributing funds

treat \'trēt\ *vb* **1** : have as a topic **2** : pay for the food or entertainment of **3** : act toward or regard in a certain way **4** : give medical care for —*n* **1** : food or entertainment paid for by another **2** : something special and enjoyable —**treat·ment** \-mənt\ *n*

trea·tise \'trētəs\ *n* : systematic written exposition or argument

trea·ty \'trētē\ *n, pl* **-ties** : agreement between governments

tre·ble \'trebəl\ *n* **1** : highest part in music **2** : upper half of the musical range ~ *adj* : triple in number or amount ~ *vb* **-bled; -bling** : make triple —**tre·bly** *adv*

tree \'trē\ *n* : tall woody plant ~ *vb* **treed; tree·ing** : force up a tree —**tree·less** *adj*

trek \'trek\ *n* : difficult trip ~ *vb* **-kk-** : make a trek

trel·lis \'treləs\ *n* : structure of crossed strips

trem·ble \'trembəl\ *vb* **-bled; -bling 1** : shake from fear or cold **2** : move or sound as if shaken

tre·men·dous \tri'mendəs\ *adj* : amazingly large, powerful, or excellent —**tre·men·dous·ly** *adv*

trem·or \'tremər\ *n* : a trembling

trem·u·lous \'tremyələs\ *adj* : trembling or quaking —**trem·u·lous·ly** *adv*

trench \'trench\ *n* : long narrow cut in land

tren·chant \'trenchənt\ *adj* : sharply perceptive

trend \'trend\ *n* : prevailing tendency, direction, or style

trep·i·da·tion \,trepə'dāshən\ *n* : nervous apprehension

tres·pass \'trespəs, -,pas\ *n* **1** : sin **2** : unauthorized entry onto someone's property ~ *vb* **1** : sin **2** : enter illegally —**tres·pass·er** *n*

tress \'tres\ *n* : long lock of hair

tres·tle \'tresəl\ *n* **1** : support with a horizontal piece and spreading legs **2** : framework bridge

tri·ad \'trī,ad, -əd\ *n* : union of 3

tri·al \'trī(ə)l\ *n* **1** : hearing and judgment of a matter in court **2** : source of great annoyance **3** : test use or experimental effort —**trial** *adj*

tri·an·gle \'trī,aŋgəl\ *n* : plane figure with 3 sides and 3 angles —**tri·an·gu-**

lar \trī'aŋgyələr\ *adj* —**tri·an·gu·lar·ly** *adv*

tribe \'trīb\ *n* : social group of numerous families —**trib·al** \'trībəl\ *adj* —**tribes·man** \'trībzmən\ *n*

trib·u·la·tion \ˌtribyə'lāshən\ *n* : suffering from oppression

tri·bu·nal \trī'byün²l, trib'yün-\ *n* 1 : court 2 : something that decides

trib·u·tary \'tribyə‚terē\ *n, pl* **-tar·ies** : stream that flows into a river or lake —**tributary** *adj*

trib·ute \'trib(‚)yüt, -yət\ *n* 1 : payment to acknowledge submission 2 : tax 3 : gift or act showing respect

trick \'trik\ *n* 1 : scheme to deceive 2 : prank 3 : deceptive or ingenious feat 4 : mannerism 5 : knack 6 : turn of duty ~ *vb* : deceive by cunning —**trick·ery** \-(ə)rē\ *n* —**trick·ster** \-stər\ *n*

trick·le \'trikəl\ *vb* **-led; -ling** : run in drops or a thin stream —**trickle** *n*

tricky \'trikē\ *adj* **trick·i·er; -est** 1 : inclined to trickery 2 : requiring skill or caution

tri·cy·cle \'trī‚sikəl\ *n* : 3-wheeled bicycle

tri·dent \'trīd²nt\ *n* : 3-pronged spear

tri·en·ni·al \trī'enēəl\ *adj* : lasting, occurring, or done every 3 years —**triennial** *n*

tri·fle \'trīfəl\ *n* : something of little value or importance ~ *vb* **-fled; -fling** 1 : speak or act in a playful or flirting way 2 : toy —**tri·fler** *n*

tri·fling \'trīfliŋ\ *adj* : trivial

trig·ger \'trigər\ *n* : finger-piece of a firearm lock that releases the hammer ~ *vb* : set into motion —**trigger** *adj* —**trig·gered** \-ərd\ *adj*

trig·o·nom·e·try \ˌtrigə'nämətrē\ *n* : mathematics dealing with triangular measurement —**trig·o·no·met·ric** \-nə'metrik\, **trig·o·no·met·ri·cal** \-rikəl\ *adj*

trill \'tril\ *n* 1 : rapid alternation between 2 adjacent tones 2 : rapid vibration in speaking ~ *vb* : utter in or with a trill

tril·lion \'trilyən\ *n* : 1000 billions —**trillion** *adj* —**tril·lionth** \-yənth\ *adj or n*

tril·o·gy \'triləjē\ *n, pl* **-gies** : 3-part literary or musical composition

trim \'trim\ *vb* **-mm-** 1 : decorate 2 : make neat or reduce by cutting ~ *adj* **-mm-** : neat and compact ~ *n* 1 : state or condition 2 : ornaments —**trim·ly** *adv* —**trim·mer** *n* —**trim·ness** *n*

trim·ming \'trimiŋ\ *n* 1 : something

that ornaments or completes 2 *pl* : scraps left after cutting

Trin·i·ty \'trinətē\ *n* : divine unity of Father, Son, and Holy Spirit

trin·ket \'triŋkət\ *n* : small ornament

trio \'trēō\ *n, pl* **tri·os** 1 : music for 3 performers 2 : group of 3

trip \'trip\ *vb* **-pp-** 1 : step lightly 2 : stumble or cause to stumble 3 : make or cause to make a mistake 4 : release (as a spring or switch) ~ *n* 1 : journey 2 : stumble 3 : drug-induced experience

tri·par·tite \trī'pär‚tīt\ *adj* : having 3 parts or parties

tripe \'trīp\ *n* 1 : animal's stomach used as food 2 : trash

tri·ple \'tripəl\ *vb* **-pled; -pling** : make 3 times as great ~ *n* : group of 3 ~ *adj* 1 : having 3 units 2 : being 3 times as great or as many

trip·let \'triplət\ *n* 1 : group of 3 2 : one of 3 offspring born together

trip·li·cate \'triplikət\ *adj* : made in 3 identical copies ~ *n* : one of 3 copies

tri·pod \'trī‚päd\ *n* : a stand with 3 legs —**tripod**, **tri·po·dal** \'tripəd²l, 'trī‚päd-\ *adj*

tri·sect \'trī‚sekt, trī'-\ *vb* : divide into 3 usu. equal parts —**tri·sec·tion** \'trī‚sekshən\ *n*

trite \'trīt\ *adj* **trit·er; trit·est** : too much used

tri·umph \'trīəmf\ *n, pl* **-umphs** \-əmfs, -əm(p)s\ : victory or great success ~ *vb* : obtain or celebrate victory —**tri·um·phal** \trī'əmfəl\ *adj* —**tri·um·phant** \-fənt\ *adj* —**tri·um·phant·ly** *adv*

tri·um·vi·rate \trī'əmvərət\ *n* : ruling body of 3 persons

triv·et \'trivət\ *n* 1 : 3-legged stand 2 : stand to hold a hot dish

triv·ia \'trivēə\ *n sing or pl* : unimportant details

triv·i·al \'trivēəl\ *adj* : of little importance —**triv·i·al·i·ty** \ˌtrivē'alətē\ *n*

trod *past of* TREAD

trod·den *past part of* TREAD

troll \'trōl\ *n* : dwarf or giant of folklore inhabiting caves or hills

trol·ley, trol·ly \'trälē\ *n, pl* **-leys or -lies** : streetcar run by overhead electric wires

trol·lop \'träləp\ *n* : untidy or immoral woman

trom·bone \träm'bōn, 'träm‚-\ *n* : musical instrument with a long sliding tube —**trom·bon·ist** \-'bōnəst, -‚bō-\ *n*

troop \'trüp\ *n* 1 : cavalry unit 2 *pl* : soldiers 3 : collection of people or things ~ *vb* : move or gather in crowds

troop·er \'trüpər\ *n* **1** : cavalry soldier **2** : policeman on horseback or state policeman

tro·phy \'trōfē\ *n, pl* **-phies** : prize gained by a victory

trop·ic \'träpik\ *n* **1** : either of the 2 parallels of latitude one 23½ degrees north of the equator (**tropic of Can·cer** \-'kansər\) and one 23½ degrees south of the equator (**tropic of Cap·ri·corn** \-'kaprə,kȯrn\) **2** *pl* : region lying between the tropics —**tropic, trop·i·cal** \-ikəl\ *adj*

trot \'trät\ *n* : moderately fast gait esp. of a horse with diagonally paired legs moving together ~ *vb* **-tt-** : go at a trot —**trot·ter** *n*

troth \'träth, 'trȯth, 'trōth\ *n* **1** : pledged faithfulness **2** : betrothal

trou·ba·dour \'trübə,dȯr\ *n* : medieval lyric poet

trou·ble \'trəbəl\ *vb* **-bled; -bling 1** : disturb **2** : afflict **3** : make an effort ~ *n* **1** : cause of mental or physical distress **2** : effort —**trou·ble·mak·er** *n* —**trou·ble·some** *adj* —**trou·ble·some·ly** *adv*

trough \'trȯf, 'trȯth, *by bakers often* 'trō\ *n, pl* **troughs** \'trȯfs, 'trȯvz; 'trȯths, 'trȯ(th)z; 'trȯz\ **1** : narrow container for animal feed or water **2** : long channel or depression (as between waves)

trounce \'traúns\ *vb* **trounced; trounc·ing** : thrash, punish, or defeat severely

troupe \'trüp\ *n* : group of stage performers —**troup·er** *n*

trou·sers \'traúzərz\ *n pl* : long pants for men or boys —**trouser** *adj*

trous·seau \'trüsō, trü'sō\ *n, pl* **-seaux** \-sōz, -'sōz\ *or* **-seaus** : bride's special collection of clothing and personal items

trout \'traút\ *n, pl* **trout** : freshwater food and game fish

trow·el \'traú(ə)l\ *n* **1** : tool for spreading or smoothing **2** : garden scoop —**trowel** *vb*

troy \'trȯi\ *n* : system of weights based on a pound of 12 ounces

tru·ant \'trüənt\ *n* **1** : one who shirks duty **2** : one absent from school without permission —**tru·an·cy** \-ənsē\ *n* —**truant** *adj*

truce \'trüs\ *n* : agreement to halt fighting

truck \'trək\ *n* **1** : wheeled frame for moving heavy objects **2** : automotive vehicle for transporting heavy loads ~ *vb* : transport on a truck —**truck·er** *n* —**truck·load** *n*

truck·le \'trəkəl\ *vb* **-led; -ling** : yield slavishly to another

tru·cu·lent \'trəkyələnt\ *adj* : aggressively self-assertive —**truc·u·lence** \-ləns\, —**truc·u·len·cy** \-lənsē\ *n* —**tru·cu·lent·ly** *adv*

trudge \'trəj\ *vb* **trudged; trudg·ing** : walk or march steadily and with difficulty

true \'trü\ *adj* **tru·er; tru·est 1** : loyal **2** : in agreement with fact or reality **3** : genuine ~ *adv* **1** : truthfully **2** : accurately —**tru·ly** *adv*

true-blue *adj* : loyal

truf·fle \'trəfəl, 'trüf-\ *n* : edible fruit of an underground fungus

tru·ism \'trü,izəm\ *n* : obvious truth

trump \'trəmp\ *n* : card of a designated suit any of whose cards will win over other cards ~ *vb* : take with a trump

trumped-up \'trəm(p)t'əp\ *adj* : made-up

trum·pet \'trəmpət\ *n* : tubular brass wind instrument with a flaring end ~ *vb* **1** : blow a trumpet **2** : proclaim loudly —**trum·pet·er** *n*

trun·cate \'trəŋ,kāt, 'trən-\ *vb* **-cat·ed; -cat·ing** : cut short —**trun·ca·tion** \,trəŋ'kāshən\ *n*

trun·dle \'trəndᵊl\ *vb* **-dled; -dling** : roll along

trunk \'trəŋk\ *n* **1** : main part (as of a body or tree) **2** : long muscular nose of an elephant **3** : storage chest **4** : storage space in a car **5** *pl* : shorts

truss \'trəs\ *vb* : bind tightly ~ *n* **1** : set of structural parts forming a framework **2** : appliance worn to hold a hernia in place

trust \'trəst\ *n* **1** : reliance on another **2** : assured hope **3** : credit **4** : property held or managed in behalf of another **5** : combination of firms that reduces competition **6** : something entrusted to another's care **7** : custody ~ *vb* **1** : depend **2** : hope **3** : entrust **4** : have faith in —**trust·ful** \-fəl\ *adj* —**trust·ful·ly** *adv* —**trust·ful·ness** *n* —**trust·wor·thi·ness** *n* —**trust·wor·thy** *adj*

trust·ee \,trəs'tē\ *n* : person holding property in trust —**trust·ee·ship** *n*

trusty \'trəstē\ *adj* **trust·i·er; -est** : dependable

truth \'trüth\ *n, pl* **truths** \'trüthz, 'trüths\ **1** : real state of things **2** : true or accepted statement **3** : agreement with fact or reality —**truth·ful** \-fəl\ *adj* —**truth·ful·ly** *adv* —**truth·ful·ness** *n*

try \'trī\ *vb* **tried; try·ing 1** : conduct the trial of **2** : put to a test **3** : strain **4** : make an effort at ~ *n, pl* **tries** : act of trying

try·out *n* : competitive test of performance esp. for athletes or actors —**try out** *vb*

tryst \'trist, 'trīst\ *n* : secret rendezvous of lovers

tsar \'zär, 'tsär\ *var of* CZAR

T-shirt \'tē₁shərt\ *n* : collarless pullover shirt with short sleeves

tub \'təb\ *n* **1** : wide bucketlike vessel **2** : bathtub

tu·ba \'t(y)übə\ *n* : large low-pitched brass wind instrument

tube \'t(y)üb\ *n* **1** : hollow cylinder **2** : round container from which a substance can be squeezed **3** : airtight circular tube of rubber inside a tire **4** : device with a space through which electricity is conducted used esp. in radio —**tubed** \'t(y)übd\ *adj* —**tube·less** *adj*

tu·ber \'t(y)übər\ *n* : fleshy underground growth (as of a potato) —**tu·ber·ous** \-rəs\ *adj*

tu·ber·cu·lo·sis \t(y)ü₁bərkyə'lōsəs\ *n, pl* **-lo·ses** \-₁sēz\ : bacterial disease esp. of the lungs —**tu·ber·cu·lar** \-'bərkyələr\ *adj* —**tu·ber·cu·lous** \-ləs\ *adj*

tub·ing \'t(y)übiŋ\ *n* : series or arrangement of tubes

tu·bu·lar \'t(y)übyələr\ *adj* : of or like a tube

tuck \'tək\ *vb* **1** : pull up into a fold **2** : put into a snug often concealing place **3** : make snug in bed —**with** *in* ~ **1** : fold in a cloth

tuck·er \'təkər\ *vb* : fatigue

Tues·day \'t(y)üzdē\ *n* : 3d day of the week

tuft \'təft\ *n* : clump (as of hair or feathers) —**tuft·ed** \'təftəd\ *adj*

tug \'təg\ *vb* **-gg- 1** : pull hard **2** : move by pulling ~ *n* **1** : act of tugging **2** : tugboat

tug·boat *n* : boat for towing or pushing ships through a harbor

tug-of-war \₁təgə(v)'wȯr\ *n, pl* **tugs-of-war** : pulling contest between 2 teams

tu·ition \t(y)ü'ishən\ *n* : cost of instruction

tu·lip \'t(y)üləp\ *n* : herb with cup-shaped flowers

tum·ble \'təmbəl\ *vb* **-bled; -bling 1** : perform gymnastic feats of rolling and turning **2** : fall or cause to fall suddenly **3** : toss ~ *n* : act of tumbling

tum·bler \'təmblər\ *n* **1** : acrobat **2** : drinking glass **3** : obstruction in a lock that can be moved (as by a key)

tu·mid \'t(y)üməd\ *adj* : turgid —**tu·mid·i·ty** \t(y)ü'midətē\ *n*

tum·my \'təmē\ *n, pl* **-mies** : belly

tu·mor \'t(y)ümər\ *n* : abnormal and useless growth of tissue —**tu·mor·ous** *adj*

tu·mult \'t(y)ü₁məlt\ *n* **1** : confusion of loud sounds and movement **2** : violent agitation of mind or feelings —**tu·mul·tu·ous** \t(y)ü'məlch(ə)wəs, -'məlchəs\ *adj*

tun \'tən\ *n* : large cask

tu·na \'t(y)ünə\ *n, pl* **-na, -nas** : large sea food fish

tun·dra \'təndrə\ *n* : treeless arctic plain

tune \'t(y)ün\ *n* **1** : melody **2** : correct musical pitch **3** : harmonious relationship ~ *vb* **tuned; tun·ing 1** : bring or come into harmony **2** : adjust in musical pitch **3** : adjust a receiver so as to receive a broadcast **4** : put in first-class working order —**tune·ful** \-fəl\ *adj* —**tun·er** *n*

tung·sten \'təŋstən\ *n* : metallic element used for electrical purposes and in hardening alloys (as steel)

tu·nic \'t(y)ünik\ *n* **1** : ancient knee-length garment **2** : hip-length blouse or jacket

tun·nel \'tən³l\ *n* : underground passageway ~ *vb* **-neled** *or* **-nelled; -nel·ing** *or* **-nel·ling** : make a tunnel through or under something

tur·ban \'tərbən\ *n* : wound headdress worn esp. by Muslims

tur·bid \'tərbəd\ *adj* **1** : dark with stirred-up sediment **2** : confused —**tur·bid·i·ty** \₁tər'bidətē\ *n* —**tur·bid·ly** \'tərbədlē\ *adv* —**tur·bid·ness** *n*

tur·bine \'tərbən, -₁bīn\ *n* : engine turned by the force of gas or water on fan blades

tur·bo·jet \'tərbō₁jet\ *n* : airplane powered by a jet engine having a turbine-driven air compressor

tur·bo·prop \'tərbō₁präp\ *n* : airplane powered by a propeller turned by a jet engine–driven turbine

tur·bu·lent \'tərbyələnt\ *adj* : causing violence or disturbance **2** : marked by agitation or tumult —**tur·bu·lence** \-ləns\ *n* —**tur·bu·lent·ly** *adv*

tu·reen \tə'rēn, tyu̇-\ *n* : deep bowl for serving soup

turf \'tərf\ *n, pl* **turfs** \'tərfs\ *or* **turves** \'tərvz\ : upper layer of soil bound by grass and roots

tur·gid \'tərjəd\ *adj* **1** : swollen **2** : too highly embellished in style —**tur·gid·i·ty** \,tər'jidətē\ *n*

tur·key \'tərkē\ *n, pl* **-keys** : large American bird raised for food

tur·moil \'tər,mȯil\ *n* : extremely agitated condition

turn \'tərn\ *vb* **1** : move or cause to move around an axis **2** : twist (a mechanical part) to operate **3** : wrench **4** : cause to face or move in a different direction **5** : reverse the sides or surfaces of **6** : upset **7** : go around **8** : become or cause to become **9** : seek aid from a source ~ *n* **1** : act or instance of turning **2** : change **3** : place at which something turns **4** : place, time, or opportunity to do something in order —**turn down** : decline to accept —**turn in 1** : deliver or report to authorities **2** : go to bed —**turn off** : stop the functioning of —**turn out 1** : expel **2** : produce **3** : come together **4** : prove to be in the end —**turn up 1** : discover or appear **2** : happen unexpectedly

turn·coat *n* : traitor

tur·nip \'tərnəp\ *n* : edible root of an herb

turn·out \'tərn,aůt\ *n* **1** : gathering of people for a special purpose **2** : size of a gathering

turn·over *n* **1** : upset or reversal **2** : filled pastry **3** : volume of business **4** : movement (as of goods or people) into, through, and out of a place

turn·pike \'tərn,pīk\ *n* : expressway on which tolls are charged

turn·stile \-,stīl\ *n* : post with arms pivoted on the top that allows people to pass one by one

turn·ta·ble *n* : platform that turns a phonograph record

tur·pen·tine \'tərpən,tīn\ *n* : oil used as a solvent and in paint that is distilled from pine trees

tur·pi·tude \'tərpə,t(y)üd\ *n* : inherent baseness

tur·quoise \'tər,k(w)ȯiz\ *n* : blue or greenish gray gemstone

tur·ret \'tərət\ *n* **1** : little tower on a building **2** : revolving tool holder or gun housing

tur·tle \'tərt³l\ *n* : reptile with the trunk enclosed in a bony shell

tur·tle·dove *n* : wild pigeon

tur·tle·neck *n* : high close-fitting collar that can be turned over or a sweater with this collar

turves *pl of* TURF

tusk \'təsk\ *n* : long protruding tooth (as of an elephant) —**tusked** \'təskt\ *adj*

tus·sle \'təsəl\ *n or vb* : struggle

tu·te·lage \'t(y)üt³lij\ *n* **1** : act of protecting **2** : instruction esp. of an individual

tu·tor \'t(y)ütər\ *n* : private teacher ~ *vb* : teach usu. individually

tux·e·do \,tək'sēdō\ *n, pl* **-dos** *or* **-does** : semiformal evening clothes for a man

TV \'tē'vē\ *n* : television

twain \'twān\ *n* : two

twang \'twaŋ\ *n* **1** : harsh sound like that of a plucked bowstring **2** : nasal speech or resonance ~ *vb* : sound or speak with a twang

tweak \'twēk\ *vb* : pinch and pull playfully —**tweak** *n*

tweed \'twēd\ *n* **1** : rough woolen fabric **2** *pl* : tweed clothing

tweet \'twēt\ *n* : chirping note —**tweet** *vb*

twee·zers \'twēzərz\ *n pl* : small pincerlike tool

twelve \'twelv\ *n* **1** : one more than 11 **2** : 12th in a set or series **3** : something having 12 units —**twelfth** \'twelfth\ *adj or n* —**twelve** *adj or pron*

twen·ty \'twentē\ *n, pl* **-ties** : 2 times 10 —**twen·ti·eth** \-ēəth\ *adj or n* —**twenty** *adj or pron*

twice \'twīs\ *adv* **1** : on 2 occasions **2** : 2 times

twig \'twig\ *n* : small branch —**twig·gy** *adj*

twi·light \'twī,līt\ *n* : light from the sky at dusk or dawn —**twilight** *adj*

twill \'twil\ *n* : fabric with a weave that gives an appearance of diagonal lines in the fabric

twilled \'twild\ *adj* : made with a twill weave

twin \'twin\ *adj* **1** : born with one another or as a pair at one birth **2** : made up of 2 similar parts ~ *n* : either of 2 offspring born together

twine \'twīn\ *n* : strong twisted thread ~ *vb* **twined; twin·ing 1** : twist together **2** : coil about a support —**twin·er** *n* —**twiny** *adj*

twinge \'twinj\ *vb* **twinged; twing·ing** *or* **twinge·ing** : affect with or feel a sudden sharp pain ~ *n* : sudden sharp stab (as of pain)

twin·kle \'twiŋkəl\ *vb* **-kled; -kling** : shine with a flickering light ~ *n* **1** : wink **2** : intermittent shining —**twin·kler** \-k(ə)lər\ *n*

twirl \'twərl\ *vb* : whirl round ~ *n* **1** : act of twirling **2** : coil —**twirl·er** *n*

twist \'twist\ *vb* **1** : unite by winding (threads) together **2** : wrench **3** : move in or have a spiral shape **4** : follow a winding course ~ *n* **1** : act or result of twisting **2** : unexpected development

twist·er \'twistər\ *n* : tornado

twit \'twit\ *vb* -tt- : taunt

twitch \'twich\ *vb* : move or pull with a sudden motion ~ *n* : act of twitching

twit·ter \'twitər\ *vb* : make chirping noises ~ *n* : small intermittent noise

two \'tü\ *n, pl* **twos** **1** : one more than one **2** : the 2d in a set or series **3** : something having 2 units —**two** *adj or pron*

two·fold \'tü-₁fōld, -'fōld\ *adj* : double —**two·fold** \-'fōld\ *adv*

two·some \'tüsəm\ *n* : couple

-ty *n suffix* : quality, condition, or degree

ty·coon \tī'kün\ *n* : powerful and successful businessman

tying *pres part of* TIE

tyke \'tīk\ *n* : small child

tym·pa·num \'timpənəm\ *n, pl* **-na** \-nə\ : eardrum or the cavity which it closes externally —**tym·pan·ic** \tim'panik\ *adj*

type \'tīp\ *n* **1** : class, kind, or group set apart by common characteristics **2** : special design of printed letters ~ *vb* **typed; typ·ing** **1** : produce on a typewriter **2** : identify or classify as a particular type

type·writ·er *n* : keyboard machine that produces printed material by striking with raised letters through an inked ribbon —**type·write** *vb*

ty·phoid \'tī₁fȯid, tī'-\ *adj* : relating to or being a communicable bacterial disease (**typhoid fever**)

ty·phoon \tī'fün\ *n* : hurricane of the western Pacific ocean

ty·phus \'tīfəs\ *n* : severe disease with fever, delirium, and rash

typ·i·cal \'tipikəl\ *adj* : having the essential characteristics of a group —**typ·i·cal·ly** *adv* —**typ·i·cal·ness** *n*

typ·i·fy \'tipə₁fī\ *vb* -**fied; -fy·ing** : be typical of

typ·ist \'tīpəst\ *n* : one who operates a typewriter

ty·pog·ra·phy \tī'pägrəfē\ *n* **1** : art of printing with type **2** : style, arrangement, or appearance of matter printed from type —**ty·po·graph·ic** \₁tīpə'grafik\, **ty·po·graph·i·cal** \-ikəl\ *adj* —**ty·po·graph·i·cal·ly** *adv*

ty·ran·ni·cal \tə'ranikəl, tī-\ *adj* : relating to a tyrant —**ty·ran·ni·cal·ly** *adv*

tyr·an·nize \'tirə₁nīz\ *vb* -**nized; -niz·ing** : rule or deal with in the manner of a tyrant —**tyr·an·niz·er** *n*

tyr·an·ny \'tirənē\ *n, pl* **-nies** : unjust use of absolute governmental power

ty·rant \'tīrənt\ *n* : harsh ruler having absolute power

ty·ro \'tīrō\ *n, pl* **-ros** : beginner

tzar \'zär, '(t)sär\ *var of* CZAR

U

u \'yü\ *n, pl* **u's** *or* **us** \'yüz\ : 21st letter of the alphabet

ubiq·ui·tous \yü'bikwətəs\ *adj* : everpresent —**ubiq·ui·tous·ly** *adv* —**ubiq·ui·ty** \-wətē\ *n*

ud·der \'ədər\ *n* : animal sac containing milk glands and nipples

ug·ly \'əglē\ *adj* **ug·li·er, -est** **1** : offensive to look at **2** : mean or quarrelsome —**ug·li·ness** *n*

uku·le·le \₁yükə'lālē\ *n* : small 4-string guitar

ul·cer \'əlsər\ *n* : eroded sore —**ul·cer·ous** *adj*

ul·cer·ate \'əlsə₁rāt\ *vb* -**at·ed; -at·ing** : cause or become affected with an ulcer —**ul·cer·a·tion** \₁əlsə'rāshən\ *n* —**ul·cer·a·tive** \'əlsə₁rātiv\ *adj*

ul·na \'əlnə\ *n* : inner bone of the forearm

ul·te·ri·or \₁əl'tirēər\ *adj* : not revealed

ul·ti·mate \'əltəmət\ *adj* : final, maximum, or extreme —**ultimate** *n* —**ul·ti·mate·ly** *adv*

ul·ti·ma·tum \₁əltə'mātəm, -'mät-\ *n, pl* **-tums** *or* **-ta** \-ə\ : final proposition or demand carrying or implying a threat

ul·tra·vi·o·let \₁əltrə'vīələt\ *adj* : having a wavelength shorter than visible light

um·bil·i·cus \₁əmbə'līkəs, ₁əm'bili-\ *n, pl* **-li·ci** \-bə'lī₁kī, -₁sī; -'bilə₁kī, -₁kē\ *or* **-li·cus·es** : small depression on the abdominal wall marking the site of the cord (**umbilical cord**) that joins the unborn fetus to its mother —**um·bil·i·cal** \₁əm'bilikəl\ *adj*

um·brage \'əmbrij\ *n* : resentment

um·brel·la \₁əm'brelə\ *n* : collapsible fabric device to protect from sun or rain um·pire \'əm,pī(ə)r\ n 1 : arbitrator 2 : sport official —umpire vb

ump·teen \'əmp'tēn\ adj : very numerous —umpteenth \-'tēnth\ adj

un- \,ən, 'ən\ prefix 1 : not 2 : opposite of

unable	uncontrolled
unabridged	unconventional
unacceptable	unconventionally
unaccompanied	unconverted
unaccounted	uncooked
unacquainted	uncooperative
unaddressed	uncoordinated
unadorned	uncovered
unadulterated	uncultivated
unafraid	undamaged
unaided	undated
unalike	undeclared
unambiguous	undefeated
unambitious	undemocratic
unannounced	undependable
unanswered	undeserving
unanticipated	undesirable
unappetizing	undetected
unappreciated	undetermined
unapproved	undeveloped
unassisted	undeviating
unattended	undignified
unattractive	undisturbed
unauthorized	undivided
unavailable	undomesticated
unavoidable	undrinkable
unbearable	unearned
unbelievable	uneducated
unbelievably	unemotional
unbiased	unending
unbranded	unendurable
unbreakable	unenforceable
uncensored	unenlightened
unchallenged	unethical
unchangeable	unexcitable
unchanged	unexciting
unchanging	unexpected
uncharacteristic	unexpectedly
uncharged	unexplainable
unchaste	unexplored
uncivilized	unfair
unclaimed	unfairly
unclear	unfairness
uncleared	unfavorable
unclothed	unfavorably
uncluttered	unfeigned
uncombed	unfilled
uncomfortable	unfinished
uncomfortably	unflattering
uncomplimentary	unforeseeable
unconfirmed	unforeseen
uncontested	unforgivable

unforgiving	unneighborly
unfulfilled	unnoticeable
unfurnished	unnoticed
ungenerous	unobjectionable
ungentlemanly	unobservable
ungraceful	unobservant
ungrammatical	unobtainable
unharmed	unobtrusive
unhealthful	unobtrusively
unhurt	unofficial
unidentified	unopened
unimaginable	unopposed
unimaginative	unorganized
unimportant	unoriginal
unimpressed	unorthodox
uninformed	unpaid
uninhabited	unpardonable
uninjured	unpatriotic
uninsured	unpaved
unintelligent	unpleasant
unintelligible	unpleasantly
unintelligibly	unpleasantness
unintended	unpopular
unintentional	unpopularity
unintentionally	unposed
uninterested	unpredictable
uninteresting	unpredictably
uninterrupted	unprejudiced
uninvited	unprepared
unjust	unpretentious
unjustifiable	unproductive
unjustified	unprofitable
unjustly	unprotected
unknowing	unproved
unknowingly	unproven
unknown	unprovoked
unleavened	unpunished
unlicensed	unqualified
unlikable	unquenchable
unlike	unquestioning
unlikelihood	unreachable
unlikely	unreadable
unlikeness	unready
unlimited	unrealistic
unlovable	unreasonable
unmanageable	unreasonably
unmarked	unrefined
unmarried	unrelated
unmerciful	unreliable
unmercifully	unremembered
unmerited	unrepentant
unmolested	unrequited
unmotivated	unresolved
unmoving	unresponsive
unnamed	unrestrained
unnavigable	unrestricted
unnecessarily	unrewarding
unnecessary	unripe
unneeded	unsafe

unsalted	unsure
unsanitary	unsuspecting
unsatisfactory	unsweetened
unsatisfied	unsympathetic
unsatisfying	untamed
unscented	untanned
unscheduled	unthankful
unseasoned	untidy
unseen	untouched
unselfish	untrained
unselfishly	untreated
unselfishness	untrue
unshaped	untrustworthy
unshaved	untruthful
unshaven	unusable
unskillful	unusual
unskillfully	unvarying
unsolicited	unverified
unsolved	unwanted
unsophisticated	unwarranted
unsound	unwary
unsoundly	unwavering
unsoundness	unweaned
unspecified	unwed
unspoiled	unwelcome
unsteadily	unwholesome
unsteadiness	unwilling
unsteady	unwillingly
unstructured	unwillingness
unsubstantiated	unwise
unsuccessful	unwisely
unsuitable	unworkable
unsuitably	unworthily
unsuited	unworthiness
unsupervised	unworthy
unsupported	unyielding

un·ac·cus·tomed \ˌ‚ən-\ *adj* **1** : not customary **2** : not accustomed

un·af·fect·ed \ˌ‚ən-\ *adj* **1** : not influenced or changed by something **2** : natural and sincere —**un·af·fect·ed·ly** *adv*

unan·i·mous \yu̇ˈnanəməs\ *adj* **1** : showing no disagreement **2** : formed with the agreement of all —**una·nim·i·ty** \ˌyünəˈnimətē\ *n* —**unan·i·mous·ly** *adv*

un·armed \ˌ‚ən-\ *adj* : not armed or armored

un·as·sum·ing \ˌ‚ən-\ *adj* : not bold or arrogant

un·at·tached \ˌ‚ən-\ *adj* **1** : not attached **2** : not married or engaged

un·awares \ˌ‚ənəˈwaərz\ *adv* **1** : without warning **2** : unintentionally

un·bal·anced \ˌ‚ən-\ *adj* **1** : not balanced **2** : mentally unstable

un·beat·en \ˌ‚ən-\ *adj* : not beaten

un·be·com·ing \ˌ‚ən-\ *adj* : not proper or suitable —**un·be·com·ing·ly** *adv*

un·bend \ˌ‚ən-\ *vb* **-bent; -bend·ing** : make or become more relaxed and friendly

un·bend·ing \ˌ‚ən-\ *adj* : formal and inflexible

un·bind \ˌ‚ən-, ˈ‚ən-\ *vb* **-bound; -bind·ing 1** : remove bindings from **2** : release

un·bolt \ˌ‚ən-, ˈ‚ən-\ *vb* : open or unfasten by withdrawing a bolt

un·born \ˌ‚ən-, ˈ‚ən-\ *adj* : not yet born

un·bo·som \ˌ‚ən-, ˈ‚ən-\ *vb* : disclose thoughts or feelings

un·bowed \ˌ‚ənˈbau̇d, ˈ‚ən-\ *adj* : not defeated or subdued

un·bri·dled \ˌ‚ənˈbrīd³ld, ˈ‚ən-\ *adj* : unrestrained

un·bro·ken \ˌ‚ən-, ˈ‚ən-\ *adj* **1** : not damaged **2** : not interrupted

un·buck·le \ˌ‚ən-, ˈ‚ən-\ *vb* : unfasten the buckle of

un·bur·den \ˌ‚ən-, ˈ‚ən-\ *vb* : relieve (oneself) of anxieties

un·but·ton \ˌ‚ən-, ˈ‚ən-\ *vb* : unfasten the buttons of

un·called-for \ˌ‚ən-\ *adj* : too harsh or rude for the occasion

un·can·ny \ˌ‚ənˈkanē\ *adj* **1** : weird **2** : suggesting superhuman powers —**un·can·ni·ly** \-ˈkanᵊlē\ *adv*

un·ceas·ing \ˌ‚ən-\ *adj* : never ceasing —**un·ceas·ing·ly** *adv*

un·cere·mo·ni·ous \ˌ‚ən-\ *adj* : acting without ordinary courtesy —**un·cere·mo·ni·ous·ly** *adv*

un·cer·tain \ˌ‚ən-\ *adj* **1** : not determined, sure, or definitely known **2** : subject to chance or change —**un·cer·tain·ly** *adv* —**un·cer·tain·ty** *n*

un·chris·tian \ˌ‚ən-, ˈ‚ən-\ *adj* : not consistent with Christian teachings

un·cle \ˈ‚əŋkəl\ *n* **1** : brother of one's father or mother **2** : husband of one's aunt

un·clean \ˌ‚ən-, ˈ‚ən-\ *adj* : not clean or pure —**un·clean·ness** *n*

un·clog \ˌ‚ən-, ˈ‚ən-\ *vb* : remove an obstruction from

un·coil \ˌ‚ən-, ˈ‚ən-\ *vb* : release or become released from a coiled state

un·com·mit·ted \ˌ‚ən-\ *adj* : not pledged to a particular allegiance or course of action

un·com·mon \ˌ‚ən-, ˈ‚ən-\ *adj* **1** : rare **2** : superior —**un·com·mon·ly** *adv*

un·com·pro·mis·ing \ˌ‚ən-, ˈ‚ən-\ *adj* : not making or accepting a compromise

un·con·cerned \ˌən-\ *adj* **1** : disinterested **2** : not anxious —**un·con·cern·ed·ly** *adv*

un·con·di·tion·al \ˌən-\ *adj* : not limited in any way —**un·con·di·tion·al·ly** *adv*

un·con·scio·na·ble \ˌən-, ˈən-\ *adj* : shockingly unjust or unscrupulous —**un·con·scio·na·bly** *adv*

un·con·scious \ˌən-, ˈən-\ *adj* **1** : not awake or aware of one's surroundings **2** : not consciously done ~ *n* : part of one's mental life that one is not aware of —**un·con·scious·ly** *adv* —**un·con·scious·ness** *n*

un·con·sti·tu·tion·al \ˌən-\ *adj* : not according to or consistent with a constitution

un·con·trol·la·ble \ˌən-\ *adj* : incapable of being controlled —**un·con·trol·la·bly** *adv*

un·count·ed \ˌən-\ *adj* : countless

un·couth \ˌən-ˈküth, ˈən-\ *adj* : rude and vulgar

un·cov·er \ˌən-, ˈən-\ *vb* **1** : reveal **2** : expose by removing a covering

unc·tion \ˈəŋkshən\ *n* **1** : rite of anointing **2** : exaggerated or insincere earnestness

unc·tu·ous \ˈəŋkchə(wə)s\ *adj* **1** : oily **2** : excessively or insincerely ingratiating —**unc·tu·ous·ly** *adv*

un·cut \ˌən-, ˈən-\ *adj* **1** : not cut down, into, off, or apart **2** : not shaped by cutting **3** : not abridged

un·daunt·ed \ˌən-, ˈən-\ *adj* : not discouraged —**un·daunt·ed·ly** *adv*

un·de·cid·ed \ˌən-\ *adj* **1** : not settled **2** : not having made up one's mind

un·de·ni·able \ˌən-\ *adj* : plainly true —**un·de·ni·ably** *adv*

un·der \ˈəndər\ *adv* : below or beneath something ~ \ˌəndər, ˈəndər\ *prep* **1** : lower than and sheltered by **2** : below the surface of **3** : covered or concealed by **4** : subject to the authority of **5** : less than ~ \ˈəndər\ *adj* **1** : lying below or beneath **2** : subordinate **3** : less than usual, proper, or desired

un·der·brush \ˈəndər,brəsh\ *n* : shrubs and small trees growing beneath large trees

un·der·clothes \ˈəndər,klō(th)z\ *n pl* : underwear

un·der·cloth·ing \-ˌklōthiŋ\ *n* : underwear

un·der·cov·er \ˌəndər-\ *adj* : employed or engaged in secret investigation

un·der·cur·rent \ˈəndər-\ *n* : hidden tendency or opinion

un·der·cut \ˌəndər-\ *vb* **-cut; -cut·ting** : offer to sell or to work at a lower rate than

un·der·de·vel·oped \ˌəndər-\ *adj* : not normally or adequately developed esp. economically

un·der·dog \ˈəndər-\ *n* : contestant given least chance of winning

un·der·done \ˌəndər-\ *adj* : not thoroughly done or cooked

un·der·es·ti·mate \ˌəndər-\ *vb* : estimate too low

un·der·ex·pose \ˌəndər-\ *vb* : give less than normal exposure to —**un·der·ex·po·sure** *n*

un·der·feed \ˌəndər-\ *vb* **-fed; -feed·ing** : feed inadequately

un·der·foot \ˌəndər-\ *adv* **1** : under the feet **2** : in the way of another

un·der·gar·ment \ˈəndər-\ *n* : garment to be worn under another

un·der·go \ˌəndər-\ *vb* **-went** \-ˈwent\; **-gone; -go·ing 1** : endure **2** : pass through (as an experience)

un·der·grad·u·ate \ˌəndər-\ *n* : university or college student

un·der·ground \ˌəndər-\ *adv* **1** : beneath the surface of the earth **2** : in secret ~ \ˈəndər-\ *adj* **1** : being or growing under the surface of the ground **2** : secret ~ \ˈəndər-\ *n* : secret political movement or group

un·der·growth \ˈəndər-\ *n* : low growth on the floor of a forest

un·der·hand \ˈəndər-\ *adv or adj* **1** : with secrecy and deception **2** : with the hand kept below the waist

un·der·hand·ed \ˌəndər-\ *adj or adv* : underhand —**un·der·hand·ed·ly** *adv* —**un·der·hand·ed·ness** *n*

un·der·line \ˈəndər-\ *vb* **1** : draw a line under **2** : stress —**underline** *n*

un·der·ling \ˈəndərliŋ\ *n* : inferior

un·der·ly·ing \ˌəndər-ˈlīiŋ\ *adj* : basic

un·der·mine \ˌəndər-\ *vb* **1** : excavate beneath **2** : weaken or wear away secretly or gradually

un·der·neath \ˌəndərˈnēth\ *prep* : directly under ~ *adv* **1** : below a surface or object **2** : on the lower side

un·der·nour·ished \ˌəndər-\ *adj* : insufficiently nourished —**un·der·nour·ish·ment** *n*

un·der·pants \ˈəndər,pants\ *n pl* : pants worn as underwear

un·der·pass \-ˌpas\ *n* : passage underneath

un·der·pin·ning \ˈəndər,piniŋ\ *n* : support

un·der·priv·i·leged \ˌəndər-\ *adj* : poor

un·der·rate \ˌəndə(r)ˈrāt\ *vb* : rate or value too low

un·der·score \'əndər-\ vb or n : underline

un·der·sea \ˌəndər'sē\ adj : being, carried on, or used beneath the surface of the sea ~ \ˌəndər'sē\, **un·der·seas** \-'sēz\ adv : beneath the surface of the sea

un·der·sec·re·tary \ˌəndər-\ n : deputy secretary

un·der·sell \ˌəndər-\ vb -**sold**; -**sell·ing** : sell articles cheaper than

un·der·shirt \'əndər,shərt\ n : shirt worn as underwear

un·der·shorts \'əndər,shorts\ n pl : short underpants

un·der·side \'əndər,sīd, ˌəndər'sīd\ n : side or surface lying underneath

un·der·sized \ˌəndər'sīzd\ adj : unusually small

un·der·stand \ˌəndər'stand\ vb -**stood** \-'stůd\; -**stand·ing 1** : be aware of the meaning of **2** : deduce **3** : have a sympathetic attitude —**un·der·stand·able** \-'standəbəl\ adj —**un·der·stand·ably** \-blē\ adv

un·der·stand·ing \ˌəndər'standiŋ\ n **1** : intelligence **2** : ability to comprehend and judge **3** : mutual agreement ~ adj : sympathetic

un·der·state \ˌəndər-\ vb **1** : represent as less than is the case **2** : state with restraint —**un·der·state·ment** n

un·der·stood \ˌəndər'stůd\ adj **1** : agreed upon **2** : implicit

un·der·study \'əndər-, ˌəndər-\ vb : study another actor's part in order to substitute —**understudy** \'əndər-\ n

un·der·take \ˌəndər-\ vb -**took**, -**tak·en**; -**tak·ing 1** : attempt (a task) or assume (a responsibility) **2** : guarantee

un·der·tak·er \'əndər,tākər\ n : one in the funeral business

un·der·tak·ing \'əndər-, ˌəndər-\ n **1** : something (as work) that is undertaken **2** : promise

under-the-counter adj : illicit

un·der·tone \'əndər-\ n : low or subdued tone or utterance

un·der·tow \-,tō\ n : current beneath the waves that flows seaward

un·der·val·ue \ˌəndər-\ vb : value too low

un·der·wa·ter \ˌəndər-\ adj : being or used below the surface of the water —**underwater** adv

under way adv : in motion or in progress

un·der·wear \'əndər-\ n : clothing worn next to the skin and under ordinary clothes

un·der·world \'əndər-\ n **1** : place of departed souls **2** : world of organized crime

un·der·write \'əndə(r)-, ˌəndə(r)-\ vb -**wrote**; -**writ·ten**; -**writ·ing** \-, rītiŋ, -'rīt-\ **1** : provide insurance for **2** : guarantee financial support of —**un·der·writ·er** n

un·dies \'əndēz\ n pl : underwear

un·do \ˌən-, 'ən-\ vb -**did**; -**done**; -**do·ing 1** : unfasten **2** : reverse **3** : ruin —**un·do·ing** n

un·doubt·ed \ˌən-, 'ən-\ adj : certain —**un·doubt·ed·ly** adv

un·dress \ˌən-, 'ən-\ vb : remove one's clothes

un·due \ˌən-, 'ən-\ adj : excessive —**un·du·ly** adv

un·du·late \'ənjə,lāt\ vb -**lat·ed**; -**lat·ing** : rise and fall regularly

un·dy·ing \ˌən-, 'ən-\ adj : immortal or perpetual

un·earth \ˌən-, 'ən-\ vb : dig up or discover

un·earth·ly \ˌən-, 'ən-\ adj : supernatural

un·easy \ˌən-, 'ən-\ adj **1** : awkward or embarrassing **2** : disturbed or worried —**un·eas·i·ly** adv —**un·eas·i·ness** n

un·em·ployed \ˌən-, 'ən-\ adj : not having a job —**un·em·ploy·ment** n

un·equal \ˌən-, 'ən-\ adj : not equal or uniform —**un·equal·ly** adv

un·equaled \ˌən-, 'ən-\ adj : having no equal

un·equiv·o·cal \ˌən-\ adj : leaving no doubt —**un·equiv·o·cal·ly** adv

un·err·ing \ˌən-, 'ən-\ adj : infallible —**un·err·ing·ly** adv

un·even \ˌən-, 'ən-\ adj **1** : not smooth **2** : not regular or consistent —**un·even·ly** adv —**un·even·ness** n

un·event·ful \ˌən-, 'ən-\ adj : lacking interesting or noteworthy incidents

un·fail·ing \ˌən-, 'ən-\ adj : steadfast —**un·fail·ing·ly** adv

un·faith·ful \ˌən-, 'ən-\ adj : not loyal —**un·faith·ful·ly** adv —**un·faith·ful·ness** n

un·fa·mil·iar \ˌən-\ adj **1** : not well known **2** : not acquainted —**un·fa·mil·iar·i·ty** n

un·fas·ten \ˌən-, 'ən-\ vb : release a catch or lock

un·feel·ing \ˌən-, 'ən-\ adj : lacking feeling or compassion —**un·feel·ing·ly** adv

un·fit \ˌən-, 'ən-\ adj : not suitable —**un·fit·ness** n

un·flap·pa·ble \ˌən'flapəbəl, 'ən-\ adj : not easily upset or panicked

un·fold \ˌ-ən-, -'ən-\ *vb* **1** : open the folds of **2** : reveal **3** : develop

un·for·get·ta·ble \ˌ-ən-, -'ən-\ *adj* : memorable —**un·for·get·ta·bly** *adv*

un·for·tu·nate \ˌ-ən-, -'ən-\ *adj* **1** : not lucky or successful **2** : deplorable —**unfortunate** *n* —**un·for·tu·nate·ly** *adv*

un·found·ed \ˌ-ən-, -'ən-\ *adj* : lacking a sound basis

un·freeze \ˌ-ən-, -'ən-\ *vb* -**froze; -frozen; -freez·ing** : thaw

un·friend·ly \ˌ-ən-, -'ən-\ *adj* : not friendly or kind —**un·friend·li·ness** *n*

un·furl \ˌ-ən-, -'ən-\ *vb* : unfold or unroll

un·gain·ly \ˌ-ən-, -'ən-\ *adj* : clumsy —**un·gain·li·ness** *n*

un·god·ly \ˌ-ən-ˈgädlē, -ˈgód-, -'ən-\ *adj* : wicked —**un·god·li·ness** *n*

un·grate·ful \ˌ-ən-, -'ən-\ *adj* : not thankful for favors —**un·grate·ful·ly** \-ē\ *adv* —**un·grate·ful·ness** *n*

un·guent \ˈəngwənt, -'ən-\ *n* : ointment

un·hand \ˌ-ən-, -'ən-\ *vb* : let go

un·hap·py \ˌ-ən-, -'ən-\ *adj* **1** : unfortunate **2** : sad —**un·hap·pi·ly** *adv* —**un·hap·pi·ness** *n*

un·healthy \ˌ-ən-, -'ən-\ *adj* **1** : not wholesome **2** : not well

un·heard-of \ˌ-ən-ˈhərdəv, -ən-, -ˌäv\ *adj* : unprecedented

un·hinge \ˌ-ən-, -'ən-\ *vb* **1** : take from the hinges **2** : make unstable (as one's mind)

un·hitch \ˌ-ən-, -'ən-\ *vb* : unfasten (something hitched)

un·ho·ly \ˌ-ən-, -'ən-\ *adj* : sinister or shocking —**un·ho·li·ness** *n*

un·hook \ˌ-ən-, -'ən-\ *vb* : release from a hook

uni·cel·lu·lar \ˌyüni-ˈselyələr\ *adj* : of or having a single cell

uni·corn \ˈyüniˌkórn\ *n* : legendary animal with one horn in the middle of the forehead

uni·cy·cle \ˈyüniˌsīkəl\ *n* : pedal-powered vehicle with only a single wheel

uni·di·rec·tion·al \ˌyünidə'reksh(ə)nəl, -dī-\ *adj* : working in only a single direction

uni·form \ˈyünəˌfòrm\ *adj* : not changing or showing any variation ~ *n* : distinctive dress worn by members of a particular group —**uni·for·mi·ty** \ˌyünəˈfòrmətē\ *n* —**uni·form·ly** *adv*

uni·fy \ˈyünəˌfī\ *vb* -**fied; -fy·ing** : make into a coherent whole —**uni·fi·ca·tion** \ˌyünəfə'kāshən\ *n*

uni·lat·er·al \ˌyüni'lat(ə)rəl\ *adj* : having, affecting, or done by one side only —**uni·lat·er·al·ly** *adv*

un·im·peach·able \ˌ-ən-, -'ən-\ *adj* : blameless **2** : not to be doubted

un·in·hib·it·ed \ˌ-ən-, -'ən-\ *adj* : free of restraint —**un·in·hib·it·ed·ly** *adv*

union \ˈyünyən\ *n* **1** : act or instance of joining 2 or more things into one or the state of being so joined **2** : confederation of nations or states **3** : organization of workers (**labor union, trade union**)

union·ize \ˈyünyəˌnīz\ *vb* -**ized; -iz·ing** : form into a labor union —**union·iza·tion** \ˌyünyənə'zāshən\ *n*

unique \yü'nēk\ *adj* **1** : being the only one of its kind **2** : very unusual —**unique·ly** *adv* —**unique·ness** *n*

uni·son \ˈyünəsən, -nəzən\ *n* **1** : sameness in pitch **2** : exact agreement

unit \ˈyünət\ *n* **1** : smallest whole number **2** : definite amount or quantity used as a standard of measurement **3** : single part of a whole —**unit** *adj*

unite \yü'nīt\ *vb* -**ed; -ing** : put or join together

uni·ty \ˈyünətē\ *n, pl* -**ties 1** : quality or state of being united or a unit **2** : harmony

uni·ver·sal \ˌyünə'vərsəl\ *adj* : relating to or affecting everyone or everything **2** : present or occurring everywhere —**uni·ver·sal·ly** *adv*

uni·verse \ˈyünəˌvərs\ *n* : the complete system of all things that exist

uni·ver·si·ty \ˌyünə'vərs(ə)tē\ *n, pl* -**ties** : institution of higher learning

un·kempt \ˌ-ən-, -'ən-\ *adj* : not neat or combed

un·kind \ˌ-ən-, -'ən-\ *adj* : mean or severe —**un·kind·ly** *adv* —**un·kind·ness** *n*

un·law·ful \ˌ-ən-, -'ən-\ *adj* : illegal —**un·law·ful·ly** *adv*

un·leash \ˌ-ən-, -'ən-\ *vb* : free from control or restraint

un·less \ən̩ˌles, -ən-\ *conj* : except on condition that

un·load \ˌ-ən-, -'ən-\ *vb* **1** : take (cargo) from a vehicle, vessel, or plane **2** : take a load from **3** : discard

un·lock \ˌ-ən-, -'ən-\ *vb* **1** : unfasten through release of a lock **2** : release or reveal

un·lucky \ˌ-ən-, -'ən-\ *adj* **1** : experiencing bad luck **2** : likely to bring misfortune —**un·luck·i·ly** *adv*

un·mis·tak·able \ˌ-ən-, -'ən-\ *adj* : not capable of being mistaken or misunderstood —**un·mis·tak·ably** *adv*

un·moved \ˌ-ən-, -'ən-\ *adj* : not emotionally affected **2** : remaining in the same place or position

un·nat·u·ral \ˌən-, ˈən-\ *adj* **1** : not natural or spontaneous **2** : abnormal —**un·nat·u·ral·ly** *adv* —**un·nat·u·ral·ness** *n*

un·nerve \ˌən-, ˈən-\ *vb* : deprive of courage

un·oc·cu·pied \ˌən-, ˈən-\ *adj* **1** : not busy **2** : not occupied

un·pack \ˌən-, ˈən-\ *vb* **1** : remove (things packed) from a container **2** : remove the contents of (a package)

un·par·al·leled \ˌən-, ˈən-\ *adj* : having no equal

un·plug \ˌən-, ˈən-\ *vb* **1** : unclog **2** : disconnect from an electric circuit by removing a plug

un·prec·e·dent·ed \ˌən-, ˈən-\ *adj* : unlike or superior to anything known before

un·prin·ci·pled \ˌən-, ˈən-\ *adj* : unscrupulous

un·ques·tion·able \ˌən-, ˈən-\ *adj* : acknowledged as beyond doubt —**un·ques·tion·ably** *adv*

un·rav·el \ˌən-, ˈən-\ *vb* **1** : separate the threads of **2** : solve

un·re·al \ˌən-, ˈən-\ *adj* : not real or genuine —**un·re·al·i·ty** \ˌən-\ *n*

un·rea·son·ing \ˌən-, ˈən-\ *adj* : not using or being guided by reason

un·re·lent·ing \ˌən-, ˈən-\ *adj* : not yielding or easing —**un·re·lent·ing·ly** *adv*

un·rest \ˌən-, ˈən-\ *n* : turmoil

un·ri·valed, un·ri·valled \ˌən-, ˈən-\ *adj* : having no rival

un·roll \ˌən-, ˈən-\ *vb* **1** : unwind a roll of **2** : become unrolled

un·ruf·fled \ˌən-, ˈən-\ *adj* : not agitated or upset

un·ru·ly \ˌənˈrülē, ˈən-\ *adj* : not easily controlled or disciplined —**un·rul·i·ness** *n*

un·scathed \ˌənˈskāthd, ˈən-\ *adj* : unharmed

un·sci·en·tif·ic \ˌən-, ˈən-\ *adj* : not in accord with the principles and methods of science

un·screw \ˌən-, ˈən-\ *vb* : loosen or remove by withdrawing screws or by turning

un·scru·pu·lous \ˌən-, ˈən-\ *adj* : being or acting in total disregard of conscience, ethical principles, or rights of others —**un·scru·pu·lous·ly** *adv* —**un·scru·pu·lous·ness** *n*

un·seal \ˌən-, ˈən-\ *vb* : break or remove the seal of

un·sea·son·able \ˌən-, ˈən-\ *adj* : not appropriate or usual for the season —**un·sea·son·ably** *adv*

un·seem·ly \ˌən-, ˈən-\ *adj* : not polite or in good taste

un·set·tle \ˌən-, ˈən-\ *vb* : disturb —**un·set·tled** *adj*

un·skilled \ˌən-, ˈən-\ *adj* : not having or requiring a particular skill

un·snap \ˌən-, ˈən-\ *vb* : loosen by undoing a snap

un·speak·able \ˌənˈspēkəbəl, ˈən-\ *adj* : extremely bad —**un·speak·ably** \-blē\ *adv*

un·sta·ble \ˌən-, ˈən-\ *adj* **1** : not mentally or physically balanced **2** : tending to change

un·stop \ˌən-, ˈən-\ *vb* **1** : unclog **2** : remove a stopper from

un·strung \ˌənˈstrəŋ, ˈən-\ *adj* : nervously tired or anxious

un·sung \ˌənˈsəŋ, ˈən-\ *adj* : not celebrated in song or verse

un·tan·gle \ˌən-, ˈən-\ *vb* **1** : free from a state of being tangled **2** : find a solution to

un·think·able \ˌənˈthiŋkəbəl, ˈən-\ *adj* : not to be thought of or considered possible

un·think·ing \ˌən-, ˈən-\ *adj* : careless —**un·think·ing·ly** *adv*

un·tie \ˌən-, ˈən-\ *vb* -**tied**; -**ty·ing** *or* -**tie·ing** : open by releasing ties

un·til \(ˌ)ən,til\ *prep* : up to the time of ~ *conj* : to the time that

un·time·ly \ˌən-, ˈən-\ *adj* **1** : premature **2** : coming at an unfortunate time

un·to \ˈəntə, ˈən(ˌ)tü\ *prep* : to

un·told \ˌən-, ˈən-\ *adj* **1** : not told **2** : too numerous to count

un·to·ward \ˌənˈtō(ə)rd, ˈən-\ *adj* **1** : difficult to manage **2** : inconvenient

un·truth \ˌən-, ˈən-\ *n* **1** : lack of truthfulness **2** : lie

un·used *adj* **1** \ˌənˈyüst, ˈən-, -ˈyüzd\ : not accustomed **2** \-ˈyüzd\ : not used

un·well \ˌən-, ˈən-\ *adj* : sick

un·wieldy \ˌənˈwēldē, ˈən-\ *adj* : too big or awkward to manage easily

un·wind \ˌən-, ˈən-\ *vb* -**wound**; -**wind·ing** **1** : undo something that is wound **2** : become unwound **3** : relax

un·wit·ting \ˌən-, ˈən-\ *adj* **1** : not intended **2** : not knowing —**un·wit·ting·ly** *adv*

un·wont·ed \ˌən-, ˈən-\ *adj* **1** : unusual **2** : not accustomed by experience

un·wrap \ˌən-, ˈən-\ *vb* : remove the wrappings from

un·writ·ten \ˌən-, ˈən-\ *adj* : made or passed on only in speech or through tradition

un·zip \ˌən-, ˈən-\ *vb* : zip open

up \ˈəp\ adv **1** : in or to a higher position or level **2** : from beneath a surface or behind **3** : in or into an upright position **4** : out of bed **5** : to or with greater intensity **6** : into existence, evidence, or knowledge **7** : away **8** —used to indicate a degree of success, completion, or finality **9** : in or into parts ~ adj **1** : in the state of having risen **2** : raised to or at a higher level **3** : moving, inclining, or directed upward **4** : in a state of greater intensity **5** : at an end ~ vb **upped** or in 1 **up; upped; up·ping; ups** or in 1 **up 1** : act abruptly **2** : move or cause to move upward ~ prep **1** : to, toward, or at a higher point of **2** : along or toward the beginning of

up·braid \ˌəpˈbrād\ vb : criticize or scold

up·bring·ing \ˈəpˌbriŋ-\ n : process of bringing up and training

up·com·ing \ˌəpˈkəmiŋ\ adj : approaching

up·date \ˌəpˈdāt\ vb : bring up to date —**update** \ˈəpˌdāt\ n

up·end \ˌəp-\ vb : stand or rise on end

up·grade \ˈəpˌgrād\ n **1** : upward slope **2** : increase \ˈəpˌ-, ˌəpˈ-\ ~ vb : raise to a higher position

up·heav·al \ˌəpˈhēvəl\ n **1** : a heaving up (as of part of the earth's crust) **2** : violent change

up·hill \ˈəpˈhil\ adv : upward on a hill or incline ~ \ˈəpˌ-\ adj **1** : going up **2** : difficult

up·hold \ˌəp-\ vb **-held; -hold·ing** : support or defend —**up·hold·er** n

up·hol·ster \ˌəpˈhōlstər\ n **1** : cover (furniture) with padding and fabric (**up·hol·stery** \-st(ə)rē\) —**up·hol·ster·er** n

up·keep \ˈəpˌkēp\ n : act or cost of keeping up or maintaining

up·land \ˈəpland, -ˌland\ n : high land —**upland** adj

up·lift \ˌəpˈlift\ vb **1** : lift up **2** : improve the condition or spirits of —**up·lift** \ˈəpˌ-\ n

up·on \ˈpȯn, -ˈpȧn\ prep : on

up·per \ˈəpər\ adj : higher in position, rank, or order ~ n : top part of a shoe

up·per·most \ˈəpərˌmōst\ adv : in or into the highest or most prominent position —**uppermost** adj

up·right \ˈəpˌrīt\ adj **1** : vertical **2** : erect in posture **3** : morally correct ~ n : something in an upright position —**upright** adv —**up·right·ly** adv —**up·right·ness** n

up·ris·ing \ˈəpˌrīziŋ\ n : revolt

up·roar \ˈəpˌrȯr\ n : state of commotion or violent disturbance

up·roar·i·ous \ˌəpˈrȯrēəs\ adj **1** : marked by uproar **2** : extremely funny —**up·roar·i·ous·ly** adv

up·root \ˌəp-\ vb : remove by or as if by pulling up by the roots

up·set \ˌəpˈset\ vb **-set; -set·ting 1** : force or be forced out of the usual position **2** : disturb emotionally or physically ~ \ˈ-ˌ\ n **1** : act of throwing into disorder **2** : minor physical disorder

up·shot \ˈəpˌshät\ n : final result

up·side down \ˌəpˌsīdˈdau̇n\ adv **1** : turned so that the upper and lower parts are reversed **2** : in or into confusion or disorder —**upside-down** adj

up·stairs \ˈəpˈ-\ adv : up the stairs or to the next floor ~ adj : situated on the floor above ~ n sing or pl : part of a building above the ground floor

up·stand·ing \ˌəpˈstandiŋ, ˈəpˌ-\ adj : honest

up·start \ˈəpˌstärt\ n : one who claims more personal importance than is warranted —**up·start** \ˌəp-\ adj

up·swing \ˈəpˌswiŋ\ n : marked increase (as in activity)

up·tight \ˈəpˈtīt\ adj **1** : tense **2** : angry **3** : rigidly conventional

up-to-date adj : current —**up-to-date·ness** n

up·town \ˈəpˈ-\ adv : toward, to, or in the upper part of town —**up·town** adj

up·ward \ˈəpwərd\, **up·wards** \-wərdz\ adv **1** : in a direction from lower to higher **2** : toward a higher or greater state or number ~ adj : directed toward or situated in a higher place

up·wind \ˈəpˈwind\ adv or adj : in the direction from which the wind is blowing

ura·ni·um \yu̇ˈrānēəm\ n : metallic radioactive chemical element

ur·ban \ˈərbən\ adj : characteristic of a city

ur·bane \ˌərˈbān\ adj : polished in manner —**ur·ban·i·ty** \ˌərˈbanətē\ n

ur·chin \ˈərchən\ n : mischievous youngster

-ure n suffix : act or process

ure·thra \yu̇ˈrēthrə\ n, pl **-thras** or **-thrae** \-(ˌ)thrē\ : canal that carries off urine from the bladder —**ure·thral** \-thrəl\ adj

urge \ˈərj\ vb **urged; urging 1** : earnestly plead for or insist on (an action) **2** : try to persuade **3** : impel to a course of activity ~ *n* : force or impulse that moves one to action

ur·gent \'ərjənt\ *adj* 1 : calling for immediate attention 2 : urging insistently —**ur·gen·cy** \-jənsē\ *n* —**urgent·ly** *adv*

uri·nal \'yurən³l\ *n* : receptacle to urinate in

uri·nate \'yurə,nāt\ *vb* -nat·ed; -nat·ing : discharge urine —**uri·na·tion** \,yurə'nāshən\ *n*

urine \'yurən\ *n* : liquid waste material from the kidneys —**uri·nary** \-ə,nerē\ *adj*

urn \'ərn\ *n* 1 : vaselike or cuplike vessel on a pedestal 2 : large coffee pot

us \(')əs\ *pron, objective case of* WE

us·able \'yüzəbəl\ *adj* : suitable or fit for use —**us·abil·i·ty** \,yüzə'bilətē\ *n*

us·age \'yüsij, -zij\ *n* 1 : customary practice 2 : way of doing or of using something

use \'yüs\ *n* 1 : act or practice of putting something into action 2 : state of being used 3 : way of using 4 : privilege, ability, or power to use something 5 : utility or function 6 : occasion or need to use ~ \'yüz\ *vb* **used** \'yüzd; "used to" usu 'yüstə\; **us·ing** \'yüziŋ\ 1 : accustom 2 : put into action or service 3 : consume 4 : behave toward 5 —used in the past tense with *to* to indicate a former practice —**use·ful** \'yüsfəl\ *adj* —**use·ful·ly** *adv* —**use·ful·ness** *n* —**use·less** \'yüsləs\ *adj* —**use·less·ly** *adv* —**use·less·ness** *n* —**us·er** *n*

used \'yüzd\ *adj* : not new

ush·er \'əshər\ *n* : one who escorts people to their seats ~ *vb* : conduct

to a place —**ush·er·ette** \,əshə'ret\ *n*

usu·al \'yüzhə(wə)l\ *adj* : being what is expected according to custom or habit —**usu·al·ly** \'yüzh(ə)wəlē, 'yüzh(ə)lē\ *adv*

usurp \yü'sərp, -'zərp\ *vb* : seize and hold by force or without right —**usur·pa·tion** \,yüsər'pāshən, -zər-\ *n* —**usurp·er** *n*

usu·ry \'yüzh(ə)rē\ *n, pl* -ries 1 : lending of money at excessive interest or the rate or amount of such interest —**usu·rer** \-zhərər\ *n* —**usu·ri·ous** \yü'zhürēəs\ *adj*

uten·sil \yü'tensəl\ *n* 1 : eating or cooking tool 2 : useful article

uter·us \'yütərəs\ *n, pl* **uteri** \-,rī\ : organ for containing and nourishing an unborn offspring —**uter·ine** \-,rīn, -rən\ *adj*

util·i·tar·i·an \yü,tilə'terēən\ *adj* : being of meant to be useful rather than beautiful

util·i·ty \yü'tilətē\ *n, pl* -ties 1 : usefulness 2 : regulated business providing a public service (as electricity)

uti·lize \'yüt³l,īz\ *vb* -lized; -liz·ing : make use of —**uti·li·za·tion** \,yüt³lə'zāshən\ *n*

ut·most \'ət,mōst\ *adj* 1 : most distant 2 : of the greatest or highest degree or amount —**utmost** *n*

uto·pia \yü'tōpēə\ *n* : place of ideal perfection —**uto·pi·an** \-pēən\ *adj or n*

ut·ter \'ətər\ *adj* : absolute ~ *vb* : express with the voice —**ut·ter·ly** *adv*

ut·ter·ance \'ətərəns, 'ətrəns\ *n* : what one says

V

v \'vē\ *n, pl* **v's** *or* **vs** \'vēz\ : 22d letter of the alphabet

va·can·cy \'vākənsē\ *n, pl* -cies 1 : state of being vacant 2 : unused or unoccupied place or office

va·cant \-kənt\ *adj* 1 : not occupied, filled, or in use 2 : foolish or without expression —**va·cant·ly** *adv*

va·cate \-,kāt\ *vb* -cat·ed; -cat·ing 1 : annul 2 : leave unfilled or unoccupied

va·ca·tion \vā'kāshən, və-\ *n* : extended period of rest from routine —**vacation** *vb* —**va·ca·tion·er** *n*

vac·ci·nate \'vaksə,nāt\ *vb* -nat·ed; -nat·ing : inoculate

vac·ci·na·tion \,vaksə'nāshən\ *n* : act of or the scarl left by vaccinating

vac·cine \vak'sēn, 'vak,-\ *n* : substance to induce immunity to a disease —**vaccine** *adj*

vac·il·late \'vasə,lāt\ *vb* -lat·ed; -lat·ing : waver between courses or opinions —**vac·il·la·tion** \,vasə'lāshən\ *n*

vac·u·ous \'vakyəwəs\ *adj* 1 : empty 2 : dull or inane —**va·cu·ity** \va'kyüətē, və-\ *n* —**vac·u·ous·ly** *adv* —**vac·u·ous·ness** *n*

vac·u·um \'vakyüəm, -(,)yüm, -yəm\ *n, pl* **vac·u·ums** *or* **vac·ua** \-yəwə\ : empty space with no air ~ *vb* : clean with a vacuum cleaner

vacuum cleaner n : appliance that cleans by suction

vag·a·bond \'vagə,bänd\ n : wanderer with no home —**vagabond** adj

va·ga·ry \'vāgərē, və'ge(ə)rē\ n, pl -ries : whim

va·gi·na \və'jīnə\ n, pl -nae \-(,)nē\ or -nas : canal that leads out from the uterus —**vag·i·nal** \'vajən²l\ adj

va·grant \'vāgrənt\ n : person with no home and no job —**va·gran·cy** \-grənsē\ n —**vagrant** adj

vague \'vāg\ adj **vagu·er; vagu·est** : not clear, definite, or distinct —**vague·ly** adv —**vague·ness** n

vain \'vān\ adj **1** : of no value **2** : unsuccessful **3** : conceited —**vain·ly** adv —**in vain** : without result or success

va·lance \'valəns, 'val-\ n : border drapery

vale \'vāl\ n : valley

vale·dic·to·ri·an \,valə,dik'tōrēən\ n : student giving the farewell address at commencement

vale·dic·to·ry \-'dikt(ə)rē\ adj : bidding farewell —**valedictory** n

va·lence \'vāləns\ n : degree of combining power of a chemical element

val·en·tine \'valən,tīn\ n : sweetheart or a card sent to a sweetheart or friend on St. Valentine's Day

va·let \'valət, 'valā, va'lā\ n : male personal servant

val·iant \'valyənt\ adj : brave or heroic —**val·iant·ly** adv

val·id \'valəd\ adj **1** : proper and legally binding **2** : founded on truth or fact —**va·lid·i·ty** \və'lidətē, va-\ n —**val·id·ly** adv —**val·id·ness** n

val·i·date \'valə,dāt\ vb **-dat·ed; -dat·ing** : establish as valid —**val·i·da·tion** \,valə'dāshən\ n

va·lise \və'lēs\ n : bag for a traveler's clothing and personal articles

val·ley \'valē\ n, pl -leys : long depression between ranges of hills

val·or \'valər\ n : bravery or heroism —**val·or·ous** \,valərəs\ adj

valu·able \'valyə(wə)bəl\ adj **1** : worth a lot of money **2** : being of great importance or use —**valuable** n

val·u·a·tion \,valyə'wāshən\ n **1** : act or process of valuing **2** : market value of a thing

val·ue \'valyü\ n **1** : fair return or equivalent for something exchanged **2** : how much something is worth **3** : distinctive quality (as of a color or sound) **4** : guiding principle or ideal—usu. pl. ~ vb **val·ued; valu·ing 1** : estimate the worth of **2** : appreci-

ate the importance of —**valued** adj —**val·ue·less** adj —**val·u·er** n

valve \'valv\ n : structure or device to control flow of a liquid or gas —**valved** \'valvd\ adj —**valve·less** adj

vam·pire \'vam,pī(ə)r\ n **1** : legendary night-wandering dead body that sucks human blood **2** : bat that feeds on the blood of animals

¹van \'van\ n : vanguard

²van n : enclosed truck

va·na·di·um \və'nādēəm\ n : soft ductile metallic chemical element

van·dal \'vand²l\ n : one who willfully defaces or destroys property —**van·dal·ism** \-,izəm\ n —**van·dal·ize** \-,īz\ vb

vane \'vān\ n : bladelike device designed to be moved by force of the air or water

van·guard \'van,gärd\ n **1** : troops moving at the front of an army **2** : forefront of an action or movement

va·nil·la \və'nilə\ n : tropical orchid with pods yielding a flavoring substance

van·ish \'vanish\ vb : disappear suddenly

van·i·ty \'vanətē\ n, pl -ties **1** : futility or something that is futile **2** : undue pride in oneself **3** : makeup table

van·quish \'vaŋkwish, 'van-\ vb **1** : overcome in battle or in a contest **2** : gain mastery over

van·tage \'vantij\ n : position of advantage or prospective

va·pid \'vapəd, 'vāpəd\ adj : lacking spirit, liveliness, or zest —**va·pid·i·ty** \va'pidətē\ n —**vap·id·ly** \'vapədlē\ adv —**vap·id·ness** n

va·por \'vāpər\ n **1** : fine separated particles floating in and clouding the air **2** : gaseous form of an ordinarily liquid substance ~ vb : give off vapor —**va·por·ish** \-(ə)rish\ adj —**va·por·ous** \-(ə)rəs\ adj

va·por·ize \'vāpə,rīz\ vb **-ized; -iz·ing** : convert into vapor —**va·por·iza·tion** \,vāpərə'zāshən\ n —**va·por·iz·er** n

vari·able \'verēəbəl\ adj : apt to vary —**vari·abil·i·ty** \,verēə'bilətē\ n —**variable** n —**vari·able·ness** n —**vari·ably** adv

vari·ance \'verēəns\ n **1** : instance or degree of variation **2** : legal permission to build contrary to a zoning law

vari·ant \-ənt\ n : something that differs from others of its kind —**variant** adj

vari·a·tion \,verē'āshən\ n : instance or extent of varying

var·i·cose \'var·ə₁kōs\ *adj* : abnormally swollen

var·ied \'verēd\ *adj* : showing variety —**var·ied·ly** *adv*

var·ie·gate \'verē·ə₁gāt, 'veri₁gāt\ *vb* -gat·ed; -gat·ing : diversify in appearance esp. with different colors —**var·ie·gat·ed** *adj* —**var·ie·ga·tion** \₁verēə'gāshən, ₁veri'gā-\ *n*

va·ri·ety \və'rīətē\ *n, pl* -et·ies : 1 state of being different 2 : collection of different things 3 : something that differs from others of its kind

var·i·ous \'verēəs\ *adj* : being many and unlike —**var·i·ous·ly** *adv*

var·nish \'värnish\ *n* : liquid that dries to a hard glossy protective coating ~ *vb* : cover with varnish

var·si·ty \'värsətē, -stē\ *n, pl* -ties : principal team representing a school

vary \'verē\ *vb* **var·ied; vary·ing** 1 : alter 2 : make or be of different kinds

vas·cu·lar \'vaskyələr\ *adj* : relating to a channel for the conveyance of a body fluid (as blood or sap)

vase \'vās, 'vāz\ *n* : tall usu. ornamental container to hold flowers and water

vas·sal \'vasəl\ *n* 1 : one acknowledging another as feudal lord 2 : one in a dependent position —**vas·sal·age** \-əlij\ *n*

vast \'vast\ *adj* : very great in size, extent, or amount —**vast·ly** *adv* —**vast·ness** *n*

vat \'vat\ *n* : large tub- or barrel-shaped container

vaude·ville \'vòd(ə)vəl, 'väd-, 'vòd-, -(ə)₁vil\ *n* : stage entertainment of unrelated acts

¹vault \'vòlt\ *n* 1 : masonry arch 2 : usu. underground storage or burial room ~ *vb* : form or cover with a vault —**vault·ed** *adj* —**vaulty** *adj*

²vault *vb* : spring over esp. with the help of the hands or a pole ~ *n* : act of vaulting —**vault·er** *n* —**vault·ing** *adj*

vaunt \'vònt\ *vb* : boast ~**vaunt** *n*

veal \'vēl\ *n* : flesh of a young calf

veer \'viər\ *vb* : change course esp. gradually —**veer** *n*

veg·e·ta·ble \'vej(ə)təbəl\ *adj* 1 : relating to or obtained from plants 2 : like that of a plant ~ *n* 1 : plant 2 : plant grown for food

veg·e·tar·i·an \₁vejə'terēən\ *n* : person who eats no meat —**vegetarian** *adj* —**veg·e·tar·i·an·ism** \-ēə₁nizəm\ *n*

veg·e·tate \'vejə₁tāt\ *vb* -tat·ed; -tat·ing : lead a dull inert life

veg·e·ta·tion \₁vejə'tāshən\ *n* : plant life —**veg·e·ta·tion·al** \-sh(ə)nəl\ *adj*

ve·he·ment \'vēəmənt\ *adj* : showing strong esp. violent feeling —**ve·he·mence** \-məns\ *n* —**ve·he·ment·ly** *adv*

ve·hi·cle \'vē₁(h)ikəl, 'vēəkəl\ *n* 1 : medium through which something is expressed, applied, or administered 2 : structure for transporting something esp. on wheels —**ve·hic·u·lar** \vē'hikyələr\ *adj*

veil \'vāl\ *n* 1 : sheer material to hide something or to cover the face and head 2 : something that hides ~ *vb* : cover with a veil

vein \'vān\ *n* 1 : rock fissure filled with deposited mineral matter 2 : vessel that carries blood toward the heart 3 : sap-carrying tube in a leaf 4 : distinctive nature or mode of expression —**veined** \'vānd\ *adj*

ve·loc·i·ty \və'läs(ə)tē\ *n, pl* -ties : speed

ve·lour, ve·lours \və'lùr\ *n, pl* **velours** \-'lùrz\ : fabric with a velvetlike pile

vel·vet \'velvət\ *n* : fabric with a short soft pile —**velvet** *adj* —**velvety** *adj*

ve·nal \'vēn³l\ *adj* : capable of being corrupted esp. by money —**ve·nal·i·ty** \vi'nalətē\ *n* —**ve·nal·ly** *adv*

vend \'vend\ *vb* : sell —**vend·ible** *adj* —**ven·dor** \'vendər\ *n*

ven·det·ta \ven'detə\ *n* : feud between clans

ve·neer \və'niər\ *n* 1 : thin layer of fine wood glued over a cheaper wood 2 : superficial display ~ *vb* : overlay with a veneer

ven·er·a·ble \'venər(ə)bəl, 'venrəbəl\ *adj* : deserving of respect

ven·er·ate \'venə₁rāt\ *vb* -at·ed; -at·ing : respect esp. with reverence —**ven·er·a·tion** \₁venə'rāshən\ *n*

venereal disease \və₁nirēəl-\ *n* : contagious disease spread through copulation

ven·geance \'venjəns\ *n* : punishment in retaliation for an injury or offense

venge·ful \'venjfəl\ *adj* : filled with a desire for revenge —**venge·ful·ly** *adv*

ve·ni·al \'vēnēəl, -nyəl\ *adj* : capable of being forgiven

ven·i·son \'venəsən, -əzən\ *n* : deer meat

ven·om \'venəm\ *n* 1 : poison secreted by certain animals 2 : ill will —**ven·om·ous** \-əməs\ *adj*

vent \'vent\ *vb* 1 : provide with or let out at a vent 2 : give expression to ~ *n* : opening for passage or for relieving pressure

ven·ti·late \'vent⁰l,āt\ *vb* -lat·ed; -lat·ing : allow fresh air to circulate through —**ven·ti·la·tion** \,vent⁰l'āshən\ *n* —**ven·ti·la·tor** \'vent⁰l,ātər\ *n*

ven·tri·cle \'ventrikəl\ *n* : heart chamber that pumps blood into the arteries of the brain

ven·tril·o·quist \ven'trilə,kwəst\ *n* : one who can make the voice appear to come from another source —**ven·tril·o·quism** \-,kwizəm\ *n* —**ven·tril·o·quy** \-kwē\ *n*

ven·ture \'venchər\ *vb* -tured; -tur·ing 1 : risk or take a chance on 2 : put forward (an opinion) ~ *n* : speculative business enterprise

ven·ture·some \-səm\ *adj* : brave or daring —**ven·ture·some·ly** *adv* —**ven·ture·some·ness** *n*

ven·ue \'venyü\ *n* : scene of an action or event

ve·rac·i·ty \və'rasətē\ *n, pl* -ties : truthfulness or accuracy —**ve·ra·cious** \və'rāshəs\ *adj*

ve·ran·da, ve·ran·dah \və'randə\ *n* : large open porch

verb \'vərb\ *n* : word that expresses action or existence

ver·bal \'vərbəl\ *adj* 1 : having to do with or expressed in words 2 : oral 3 : relating to or formed from a verb —**ver·bal·iza·tion** \,vərbələ'zāshən\ *n* —**ver·bal·ize** \'vərbə,līz\ *vb* —**ver·bal·ly** \-ē\ *adv*

verbal auxiliary *n* : auxiliary verb

ver·ba·tim \(,)vər'bātəm\ *adv or adj* : using the same words

ver·biage \'vərbēij\ *n* : excess of words

ver·bose \(,)vər'bōs\ *adj* : using more words than are needed —**ver·bos·i·ty** \-'bäsətē\ *n*

ver·dant \'vərd⁰nt\ *adj* : green with growing plants —**ver·dant·ly** *adv*

ver·dict \'vər,(,)dikt\ *n* : decision of a jury

ver·dure \'vərjər\ *n* : green growing vegetation or its color

verge \'vərj\ *vb* **verged; verg·ing** 1 : be almost on the point of happening or doing something ~ *n* 1 : edge 2 : threshold

ver·i·fy \'verə,fī\ *vb* -fied; -fy·ing : establish the truth, accuracy, or reality of —**ver·i·fi·able** *adj* —**ver·i·fi·ca·tion** \,verəfə'kāshən\ *n*

ver·i·ly \'verəlē\ *adv* : truly or confidently

ver·i·ta·ble \'verətəbəl\ *adj* : actual —often used to suggest the aptness of a metaphor —**ver·i·ta·bly** *adv*

ver·i·ty \'verətē\ *n, pl* -ties : truth

ver·mi·cel·li \,vərmə'chelē, -'sel-\ *n* : thin spaghetti

ver·min \'vərmən\ *n, pl* **vermin** : small animal pest

ver·nac·u·lar \və(r)'nakyələr\ *adj* : relating to a native language or dialect and esp. its normal spoken form ~ *n* : vernacular language

ver·nal \'vərn⁰l\ *adj* : relating to spring

ver·sa·tile \'vərsət⁰l\ *adj* : having many abilities or uses —**ver·sa·til·i·ty** \,vərsə'tilətē\ *n*

verse \'vərs\ *n* 1 : line or stanza of poetry 2 : poetry 3 : short division of a chapter in the Bible

versed \'vərst\ *adj* : familiar from experience, study, or practice

ver·sion \'vərzhən\ *n* 1 : translation of the Bible 2 : account or description from a particular point of view

ver·sus \'vərsəs\ *prep* : opposed to or against

ver·te·bra \'vərtəbrə\ *n, pl* -**brae** \-,brā, -(,)brē\ *or* -**bras** : segment of the backbone —**ver·te·bral** \(,)vər'tēbrəl, 'vərtə-\ *adj*

ver·te·brate \'vərtəbrət, -,brāt\ *n* : animal with a backbone —**vertebrate** *adj*

ver·tex \'vər,teks\ *n, pl* **ver·tex·es** *or* **ver·ti·ces** \'vərtə,sēz\ *n* 1 : point of intersection of lines or surfaces 2 : highest point

ver·ti·cal \'vərtikəl\ *adj* : rising straight up from a level surface —**vertical** *n* —**ver·ti·cal·ly** *adv* —**ver·ti·cal·ness** *n*

ver·ti·go \'vərti,gō\ *n, pl* -**goes** *or* -**gos** : dizziness

verve \'vərv\ *n* : liveliness or vividness

very \'verē\ *adj* **veri·er; -est** 1 : exact 2 : exactly suitable 3 : precisely the same ~ *adv* 1 : to a high degree

ves·i·cle \'vesikəl\ *n* : membranous cavity —**ve·sic·u·lar** \və'sikyələr\ *adj*

ves·pers \'vespərz\ *n pl* : late afternoon or evening worship service

ves·sel \'vesəl\ *n* 1 : a container (as a barrel, bottle, pan, or cup) for a liquid 2 : craft for navigation esp. on water 3 : tube in which a body fluid is circulated

¹**vest** \'vest\ *vb* 1 : give a particular authority, right, or property to 2 : clothe with or as if with a garment

²**vest** *n* : sleeveless garment worn under a suit coat

ves·ti·bule \'vestə,byül\ *n* : enclosed entrance —**ves·tib·u·lar** \ve'stibyələr\ *adj*

ves·tige \'vestij\ n : visible trace or remains —**ves·ti·gial** \ve'stijēəl\ adj —**ves·ti·gial·ly** adv

vest·ment \'ves(t)mənt\ n : clergyman's garment

ves·try \'vestrē\ n, pl **-tries** : church storage room for garments and articles

vet·er·an \'vet(ə)rən\ n 1 : former member of the armed forces 2 : person with long experience —**veteran** adj

Veterans Day n : 4th Monday in October or formerly November 11 observed as a legal holiday in commemoration of the end of war in 1918 and 1945

vet·er·i·nar·i·an \₁vet(ə)rən'erēən, ₁vetᵊn-\ n : doctor of animals —**vet·er·i·nary** \'vet(ə)rən₁erē, 'vetᵊn-\ adj

ve·to \'vētō\ n, pl **-toes** 1 : power to forbid and esp. the power of a chief executive to prevent a bill from becoming law 2 : exercise of the veto ~ vb 1 : forbid 2 : reject a legislative bill

vex \'veks\ vb **vexed**; **vex·ing** : trouble, distress, or annoy —**vex·a·tion** \vek'sāshən\ n —**vex·a·tious** \-shəs\ adj

via \₁vīə, ₁vēə\ prep : by way of

vi·a·ble \'vīəbəl\ adj 1 : capable of surviving or growing 2 : practical or workable —**vi·a·bil·i·ty** \₁vīə'bilətē\ n —**vi·a·bly** \'vīəblē\ adv

vi·a·duct \'vīə₁dəkt\ n : high road or railway bridge

vi·al \'vī(ə)l\ n : small bottle

vi·brant \'vībrənt\ adj 1 : vibrating 2 : pulsing with vigor or activity 3 : sounding from vibration —**vi·bran·cy** \-brənsē\ n

vi·brate \'vī₁brāt\ vb **-brat·ed**; **-brat·ing** 1 : move or cause to move quickly back and forth or side to side 2 : respond sympathetically —**vi·bra·tion** \vī'brāshən\ n —**vi·bra·tor** \'vī₁brātər\ n —**vi·bra·tory** \'vībrə₁tōrē\ adj

vic·ar \'vikər\ n : parish clergyman —**vi·car·i·al** \vī'karēəl\ adj —**vic·ar·i·ate** \-ēət\ n

vi·car·i·ous \vī'kerēəs, -'kar-\ adj : experienced imaginatively or sympathetically —**vi·car·i·ous·ly** adv —**vi·car·i·ous·ness** n

vice \'vīs\ n 1 : immoral habit 2 : depravity

vice- \(')vīs, vīs\ prefix : one that takes the place of

vice-chairman
vice-chairmanship
vice-chancellor
vice-chancellorship
vice-consul
vice-mayor
vice-premier
vice-presidency
vice-president
vice-presidential
vice-principal
vice-regent

vice admiral n : commissioned officer in the navy or coast guard ranking above a rear admiral

vice·roy \'vīs₁roi\ n : provincial governor who represents the sovereign

vice ver·sa \₁vīsi'vərsə, (')vīs'vər-\ adv : with the order reversed

vi·cin·i·ty \və'sinətē\ n, pl **-ties** : surrounding area

vi·cious \'vishəs\ adj 1 : wicked 2 : savage 3 : malicious —**vi·cious·ly** adv —**vi·cious·ness** n

vi·cis·si·tude \və'sisə₁t(y)üd, vī-\ n : irregular, unexpected, or surprising change —usu. used in pl.

vic·tim \'viktəm\ n : person killed, hurt, or abused

vic·tim·ize \'viktə₁mīz\ vb **-ized**; **-iz·ing** : make a victim of —**vic·tim·i·za·tion** \₁viktəmə'zāshən\ n —**vic·tim·iz·er** \'viktə₁mīzər\ n

vic·tor \'viktər\ n : winner

Vic·to·ri·an \vik'tōrēən\ adj : relating to the reign of Queen Victoria of England or the art, taste, or standards of her time ~ n : one of the Victorian period

vic·to·ri·ous \vik'tōrēəs\ adj : having won a victory —**vic·to·ri·ous·ly** adv

vic·to·ry \'vikt(ə)rē\ n, pl **-ries** : success in defeating an enemy or opponent or in overcoming difficulties

vict·uals \'vit²lz\ n pl : food

vid·eo \'vidē₁ō\ adj : relating to the television image

vid·eo·tape \'vidēō₁tāp\ vb : make a recording of (a television production) on special tape —**video-tape** n

vie \'vī\ vb **vied**; **vy·ing** : contend —**vi·er** \'vī(ə)r\ n

view \'vyü\ n 1 : process of seeing or examining 2 : opinion 3 : area of landscape that can be seen 4 : range of vision 5 : purpose or object ~ vb 1 : look at 2 : think about or consider

view·point n : position from which something is considered

vig·il \'vijəl\ n 1 : day of devotion before a religious feast 2 : act or time of keeping awake 3 : long period of keeping watch (as over a sick or dying person)

vig·i·lant \'vijələnt\ adj : alert esp. to

avoid danger —**vig·i·lance** \-ləns\ n —**vig·i·lant·ly** adv

vig·i·lan·te \₁vijə'lantē\ n : one of a group independent of the law working to suppress crime

vi·gnette \vin'yet\ n : short descriptive literary piece

vig·or \'vigər\ n 1 : energy or strength 2 : intensity or force —**vig·or·ous** \'vig(ə)rəs\ adj —**vig·or·ous·ly** adv —**vig·or·ous·ness** n

vile \'vīl\ adj **vil·er; vil·est** : thoroughly bad or contemptible —**vile·ly** adv —**vile·ness** n

vil·i·fy \'vilə₁fī\ vb **-fied; -fy·ing** : speak evil of —**vil·i·fi·ca·tion** \₁viləfə'kāshən\ n —**vil·i·fi·er** \'vilə₁fī(ə)r\ n

vil·la \'vilə\ n : country estate

vil·lage \'vilij\ n : small country town —**vil·lag·er** n

vil·lain \'vilən\ n : bad person —**vil·lain·ess** \-ənəs\ n —**vil·lainy** n

vil·lain·ous \-ənəs\ adj : evil or corrupt —**vil·lain·ous·ly** adv —**vil·lain·ous·ness** n

vim \'vim\ n : energy

vin·di·cate \'vində₁kāt\ vb **-cat·ed; -cat·ing** 1 : avenge 2 : exonerate 3 : justify —**vin·di·ca·tion** \₁vində'kāshən\ n —**vin·di·ca·tor** \'vində₁kātər\ n

vin·dic·tive \vin'diktiv\ adj : seeking or meant for revenge —**vin·dic·tive·ly** adv —**vin·dic·tive·ness** n

vine \'vīn\ n : climbing or trailing plant

vin·e·gar \'vinigər\ n : acidic liquid obtained by fermentation —**vin·e·gary** \-g(ə)rē\ adj

vine·yard \'vinyərd\ n : plantation of grapevines

vin·tage \'vintij\ n 1 : season's yield of grapes or wine 2 : period of origin ~ adj : of enduring interest

vi·nyl \'vīn²l\ n : strong plastic

vi·o·la \vē'ōlə\ n : instrument of the violin family tuned lower than the violin —**vi·o·list** \-ləst\ n

vi·o·late \'vīə₁lāt\ vb **-lat·ed; -lat·ing** 1 : act with disrespect or disregard of 2 : rape 3 : desecrate —**vi·o·la·tor** \'vīə'lāshən\ n —**vi·o·la·tor** \'vīə₁lātər\ n

vi·o·lence \'vīələns\ n : intense physical force that causes or is intended to cause injury or destruction —**vi·o·lent** \-lənt\ adj —**vi·o·lent·ly** adv

vi·o·let \'vīələt\ n 1 : small flowering plant 2 : reddish blue —**violet** n

vi·o·lin \₁vīə'lin\ n : bowed stringed instrument —**vi·o·lin·ist** \-əst\ n

VIP \₁vē₁ī'pē\ n, pl **VIPs** \-'pēz\ : very important person

vi·per \'vīpər\ n 1 : venomous snake 2 : treacherous or malignant person

vi·ra·go \və'rägō, -'rā-; 'virə₁gō\ n, pl **-goes** or **-gos** : shrew

vi·ral \'vīrəl\ adj : relating to or caused by a virus

vir·gin \'vərjən\ n : unmarried or chaste woman ~ adj 1 : chaste 2 : natural and unspoiled —**vir·gin·al** \-əl\ adj —**vir·gin·al·ly** adv —**vir·gin·i·ty** \vər'jinətē\ n

vir·gule \'vərgyül\ n : mark / used esp. to denote "or" or "per"

vir·ile \'virəl\ adj : masculine —**vi·ril·i·ty** \və'rilətē\ n

vir·tu·al \'vərchə(wə)l\ adj : being almost the same —**vir·tu·al·ly** adv

vir·tue \'vərchü\ n 1 : moral excellence 2 : effective or commendable quality 3 : chastity

vir·tu·os·i·ty \₁vərchə'wäsətē\ n, pl **-ties** : great skill (as in music)

vir·tu·o·so \₁vərchə'wōsō, -zō\ n, pl **-sos** or **-si** \-sē, -zē\ : highly skilled performer esp. of music —**virtuoso** adj

vir·tu·ous \'vərch(ə)wəs\ adj 1 : morally good 2 : chaste —**vir·tu·ous·ly** adv

vir·u·lent \'vir(y)ələnt\ adj 1 : bitterly hostile 2 : extremely severe or infectious —**vir·u·lence** \-ləns\ n —**vir·u·len·cy** \-lənsē\ n —**vir·u·lent·ly** adv

vi·rus \'vīrəs\ n : tiny disease-causing agent

vi·sa \'vēzə, -sə\ n : authorization to enter a foreign country

vis·age \'vizij\ n : face

vis·cera \'visərə\ n pl : internal bodily organs esp. of the trunk

vis·cer·al \'visərəl\ adj 1 : bodily 2 : instinctive 3 : deeply or crudely emotional —**vis·cer·al·ly** adv

vis·cid \'visəd\ adj : viscous —**vis·cid·i·ty** \vis'idətē\ n —**vis·cid·ly** adv

vis·cos·i·ty \vis'käsətē\ n, pl **-ties** : quality of being viscous

vis·count \'vī₁kaúnt\ n : British nobleman ranking below an earl and above a baron —**vis·count·ess** \-əs\ n

vis·cous \viskəs\ adj : having a thick or sticky consistency

vise \'vīs\ n : device for clamping something being worked on

vis·i·bil·i·ty \₁vizə'bilətē\ n, pl **-ties** : degree or range to which something can be seen

vis·i·ble \'vizəbəl\ adj 1 : capable of

being seen **2** : manifest —**vis·i·bly** *adv*

vi·sion \'vizhən\ *n* **1** : vivid picture seen in a dream or trance or in the imagination **2** : foresight **3** : power of seeing ~ *vb* : imagine

vi·sion·ary \'vizhə,nerē\ *adj* **1** : given to dreaming or imagining **2** : illusory **3** : not practical ~ *n* : one with great dreams or projects

vis·it \'vizət\ *vb* **1** : go or come to see **2** : stay with for a time as a guest **3** : cause or be a reward, affliction, or punishment ~ *n* : short stay as a guest —**vis·it·able** *adj* —**vis·i·tor** \-ər\ *n*

vis·i·ta·tion \,vizə'tāshən\ *n* **1** : official visit **2** : divine punishment or favor **3** : severe trial

vi·sor \'vīzər\ *n* **1** : front piece of a helmet **2** : part (as on a cap or car windshield) that shades the eyes

vis·ta \'vistə\ *n* : distant view

vi·su·al \'vizh(əw)əl\ *adj* : relating to sight **2** : visible —**vi·su·al·ly** *adv*

vi·su·al·ize \'vizh(ə)wə,līz\ *vb* **-ized; -iz·ing** : form a mental image of —**vi·su·al·iza·tion** \,vizhə(wə)lə'zāshən\ *n* —**vi·su·al·iz·er** \'vizh(ə)wə,līzər\ *n*

vi·tal \'vīt²l\ *adj* **1** : relating to or characteristic of life **2** : full of life and vigor **3** : basic **4** : very important —**vi·tal·ly** *adv*

vi·tal·i·ty \vī'talətē\ *n, pl* **-ties 1** : life force **2** : energy

vi·ta·min \'vītəmən\ *n* : natural organic substance essential to health

vi·ti·ate \'vishē,āt\ *vb* **-at·ed; -at·ing 1** : spoil or impair **2** : invalidate —**vi·ti·a·tion** \,vishē'āshən\ *n* —**vi·ti·a·tor** \'vishē,ātər\ *n*

vit·re·ous \'vitrēəs\ *adj* : relating to or resembling glass

vit·ri·fy \'vitrə,fī\ *vb* **-fied; -fy·ing** : change into a glassy substance by heat and fusion —**vit·ri·fi·ca·tion** \,vitrəfə'kāshən\ *n*

vit·ri·ol \'vitrēəl\ *n* : something caustic, corrosive, or biting —**vit·ri·ol·ic** \,vitrē'älik\ *adj*

vi·tu·per·ate \vī't(y)üpə,rāt, və-\ *vb* **-at·ed; -at·ing** : abuse in words —**vi·tu·per·a·tion** \-,t(y)üpə'rāshən\ *n* —**vi·tu·per·a·tive** \-'t(y)üp(ə)rətiv, -pə,rāt-\ *adj* —**vi·tu·per·a·tive·ly** *adv*

vi·va·cious \və'vāshəs, vī-\ *adj* : lively —**vi·va·cious·ly** *adv* —**vi·va·cious·ness** *n* —**vi·vac·i·ty** \-'vasətē\ *n*

viv·id \'vivəd\ *adj* **1** : lively **2** : brilliant **3** : intense or sharp —**viv·id·ly** *adv* —**viv·id·ness** *n*

viv·i·fy \'vivə,fī\ *vb* **-fied; -fy·ing** : give life or vividness to

vivi·sec·tion \,vivə'sekshən, 'vivə,-\ *n* : experimental operation on a living animal

vix·en \'viksən\ *n* **1** : female fox **2** : scolding woman

vo·cab·u·lary \vō'kabyə,lerē\ *n, pl* **-lar·ies 1** : list or collection of words **2** : terminology of a person or subject

vo·cal \'vōkəl\ *adj* **1** : relating to or produced by or for the voice **2** : speaking out freely and usu. emphatically

vocal cords *n pl* : membranous folds in the larynx that are important in making vocal sounds

vo·cal·ist \'vōkələst\ *n* : singer

vo·cal·ize \-,līz\ *vb* **-ized; -iz·ing** : give vocal expression to

vo·ca·tion \vō'kāshən\ *n* : regular employment —**vo·ca·tion·al** \-sh(ə)nəl\ *adj*

vo·cif·er·ous \vō'sif(ə)rəs\ *adj* : noisy and insistent —**vo·cif·er·ous·ly** *adv*

vod·ka \'vädkə\ *n* : colorless distilled grain liquor

vogue \'vōg\ *n* : brief but intense popularity

voice \'vois\ *n* **1** : sound produced through the mouth by humans and many animals **2** : power of speaking **3** : right of choice or opinion ~ *vb* **voiced; voic·ing** : express in words —**voiced** \'voist\ *adj*

void \'void\ *adj* **1** : containing nothing **2** : lacking —*with of* **3** : not legally binding ~ *n* **1** : empty space **2** : feeling of hollowness ~ *vb* **1** : discharge (as body waste) **2** : make (as a contract) void —**void·able** *adj* —**void·er** *n*

vol·a·tile \'välət²l\ *adj* **1** : readily vaporizing at a relatively low temperature **2** : explosive or easily stirred to violence **3** : changeable —**vol·a·til·i·ty** \,välə'tilətē\ *n* —**vol·a·til·ize** \'välət²l,īz\ *vb*

vol·ca·no \väl'kānō\ *n, pl* **-noes** *or* **-nos** : opening in the earth's crust from which molten rock and steam come out —**vol·ca·nic** \-'kanik\ *adj*

vo·li·tion \vō'lishən\ *n* : free will —**vo·li·tion·al** \-'lish(ə)nəl\ *adj*

vol·ley \'välē\ *n, pl* **-leys 1** : flight of missiles (as arrows or bullets) **2** : simultaneous shooting of many weapons

vol·ley·ball *n* : game of batting a large ball over a net

vol·plane \'väl,plān\ *vb* **-planed; -plan·ing** : glide in an airplane

volt \ˈvōlt\ *n* : unit for measuring the force that moves an electric current

volt·age \ˈvōltij\ *n* : measure of volts

vol·u·ble \ˈvälyəbəl\ *adj* : fluent and smooth in speech —**vol·u·bil·i·ty** \ˌvälyəˈbilətē\ *n* —**vol·u·bly** \ˈvälyəblē\ *adv*

vol·ume \ˈvälyəm\ *n* 1 : book 2 : space occupied as measured by cubic units 3 : amount 4 : intensity of a sound

vo·lu·mi·nous \vəˈlümənəs\ *adj* : large or bulky

vol·un·tary \ˈvälənˌterē\ *adj* 1 : done, made, or given freely and without expecting compensation 2 : relating to or controlled by the will —**vol·un·tari·ly** *adv*

vol·un·teer \ˌvälənˈtiər\ *n* : person who offers to help or work without expecting payment or reward ~ *vb* 1 : offer or give voluntarily 2 : offer oneself as a volunteer

vo·lup·tuous \vəˈləpchə(wə)s\ *adj* 1 : luxurious 2 : having a full and sexually attractive figure —**vo·lup·tuous·ly** *adv* —**vo·lup·tuous·ness** *n*

vom·it \ˈvämət\ *vb* : throw up the contents of the stomach —**vomit** *n*

voo·doo \ˈvüdü\ *n, pl* **voodoos** 1 : religion derived from African ancestor worship and involving sorcery 2 : one who practices voodoo 3 : charm or fetish used in voodoo —**voodoo** *adj* —**voo·doo·ism** \ˌizəm\ *n*

vo·ra·cious \vȯˈrāshəs, və-\ *adj* : greedy or exceedingly hungry —**vo·ra·cious·ly** *adv* —**vo·ra·cious·ness** *n* —**vo·rac·i·ty** \ˈrasətē\ *n*

vor·tex \ˈvȯrˌteks\ *n, pl* **vor·ti·ces** \ˈvȯrtəˌsēz\ : whirling liquid

vo·ta·ry \ˈvōtərē\ *n, pl* -**ries** 1 : devoted participant, adherent, admirer, or worshiper

vote \ˈvōt\ *n* 1 : individual expression of preference in choosing or reaching a decision 2 : right to indicate one's preference or the preference expressed ~ *vb* **vot·ed; vot·ing** 1 : cast a vote 2 : choose or defeat by vote —**vote·less** *adj* —**vot·er** *n*

vo·tive \ˈvōtiv\ *adj* : offered or performed in fulfillment of a vow or in petition, gratitude, or devotion

vouch \ˈvauch\ *vb* : give a guarantee or personal assurance

vouch·er \ˈvauchər\ *n* : written record or receipt that serves as proof of a transaction

vouch·safe \ˈvauchˈsāf\ *vb* -**safed; -saf·ing** : grant

vow \ˈvau\ *n* : solemn promise to do something or to live or act a certain way —**vow** *vb*

vow·el \ˈvau(ə)l\ *n* 1 : speech sound produced without obstruction or friction in the mouth 2 : letter representing such a sound

voy·age \ˈvȯiij\ *n* : long journey esp. by water or through space ~ *vb* -**aged; -ag·ing** : make a voyage —**voy·ag·er** *n*

vul·ca·nize \ˈvəlkəˌnīz\ *vb* -**nized; -niz·ing** : treat (as rubber) to make more elastic or stronger —**vul·ca·ni·za·tion** \ˌvəlkənəˈzāshən\ *n*

vul·gar \ˈvəlgər\ *adj* 1 : relating to the common people 2 : lacking refinement 3 : offensive in manner or language —**vul·gar·ism** \-ˌrizəm\ *n* —**vul·gar·ize** \-ˌrīz\ *vb* —**vul·gar·ly** *adv*

vul·gar·i·ty \ˌvəlˈgaratē\ *n, pl* -**ties** 1 : state of being vulgar 2 : vulgar language or act

vul·ner·a·ble \ˈvəln(ə)rəbəl\ *adj* : susceptible to attack or damage —**vul·ner·a·bil·i·ty** \ˌvəln(ə)rəˈbilətē\ *n* —**vul·ner·a·bly** *adv*

vul·ture \ˈvəlchər\ *n* : large flesh-eating bird

vul·va \ˈvəlvə\ *n, pl* -**vae** \-ˌvē, -ˌvī\ : external genital parts of the female

vy·ing *pres part of* VIE

W

w \ˈdəbəl(ˌ)yü\ *n* : 23d letter of the alphabet

wab·ble \ˈwäbəl\ *var of* WOBBLE

wad \ˈwäd\ *n* 1 : little mass 2 : soft mass of fibrous material 3 : pliable plug to retain a powder charge ~ *vb* 1 : form into a wad 2 : stuff with a wad

wad·dle \ˈwädᵊl\ *vb* -**dled; -dling** : walk with short steps swaying from side to side —**waddle** *n*

wade \ˈwād\ *vb* **wad·ed; wad·ing** 1 : step in or through (as water) 2 : move with difficulty —**wade** *n* —**wad·er** *n*

wa·fer \ˈwāfər\ *n* 1 : thin crisp cake or cracker 2 : waferlike thing

waf·fle \ˈwäfəl\ *n* : crisped cake of batter cooked in a hinged utensil (**waffle iron**)

waft \\'wäft, 'waft\\ *vb* : cause to move lightly by wind or waves —**waft** *n*

wag \\'wag\\ *vb* -**gg**- : sway or swing from side to side or to and fro ~ *n* 1 : wit 2 : act of wagging —**wag·gish** *adj*

wage \\'wāj\\ *vb* **waged; wag·ing** : engage in ~ *n* 1 : payment for labor or services 2 : compensation

wa·ger \\'wājər\\ *n or vb* : bet

wag·gle \\'wagəl\\ *vb* -**gled; -gling** : wag —**waggle** *n*

wag·on \\'wagən\\ *n* 1 : 4-wheeled vehicle drawn by animals 2 : child's 4-wheeled cart

waif \\'wāf\\ *n* : homeless child

wail \\'wāl\\ *vb* 1 : mourn 2 : make a sound like a mournful cry —**wail** *n*

wain·scot \\'wānskət, -,skōt, -,skät\\ *n* : usu. paneled wooden lining of an interior wall —**wainscot** *vb*

waist \\'wāst\\ *n* 1 : narrowed part of the body between chest and hips 2 : waistline part —**waist·line** *n*

wait \\'wāt\\ *vb* 1 : remain in readiness or expectation 2 : delay 3 : attend as a waiter ~ *n* 1 : concealment 2 : act or period of waiting

wait·er \\'wātər\\ *n* : man who waits on tables

wait·ress \\'wātrəs\\ *n* : woman who waits on tables

waive \\'wāv\\ *vb* **waived; waiv·ing** : give up claim to

waiv·er \\'wāvər\\ *n* : act of waiving right, claim, or privilege

¹wake \\'wāk\\ *vb* **waked** \\'wākt\\ *or* **woke** \\'wōk\\; **waked** *or* **wo·ken** \\'wōkən\\ *or* **woke; wak·ing** : keep watch 2 : bring or come back to consciousness after sleep ~ 1 : state of being awake 2 : watch held over a dead body

²wake *n* : track left by a ship

wake·ful \\'wākfəl\\ *adj* : not sleeping or able to sleep —**wake·ful·ness** *n*

wak·en \\'wākən\\ *vb* : wake

wale \\'wāl\\ *n* : streak or ridge made on the skin 2 : ridge on cloth

walk \\'wȯk\\ *vb* 1 : move or cause to move on foot 2 : pass over, through, or along by walking ~ *n* 1 : a going on foot 2 : place or path for walking 3 : distance to be walked 4 : way of living 5 : way of walking 6 : slow 4-beat gait of a horse —**walk·er** *n*

wall \\'wȯl\\ *n* 1 : structure for defense or for enclosing something 2 : upright enclosing part of a building or room 3 : something like a wall ~ *vb*

: provide, separate, surround, or close with a wall —**walled** \\'wȯld\\ *adj*

wal·la·by \\'wäləbē\\ *n, pl* -**bies** : small or medium-sized kangaroo

wal·let \\'wälət\\ *n* : pocketbook with compartments

wall·flow·er *n* 1 : mustardlike plant with showy fragrant flowers 2 : one who remains on the sidelines of social activity

wal·lop \\'wäləp\\ *n* 1 : powerful blow 2 : ability to hit hard ~ *vb* 1 : defeat soundly 2 : hit hard

wal·low \\'wälō\\ *vb* 1 : roll about in deep mud 2 : live with excessive pleasure ~ *n* : place for wallowing

wall·pa·per *n* : decorative paper for walls —**wallpaper** *vb*

wal·nut \\'wȯl,(,)nət\\ *n* 1 : edible nut with a furrowed shell and adherent husk 2 : tree on which this nut grows or its brown wood 3 : hickory nut or tree

wal·rus \\'wȯlrəs, 'wäl-\\ *n, pl* -**rus** *or* -**rus·es** : large seallike mammal of northern seas

waltz \\'wȯlts\\ *n* : gliding dance to music having 3 beats to the measure of the music —**waltz** *vb*

wam·pum \\'wämpəm\\ *n* : strung shell beads used by No. American Indians as money

wan \\'wän\\ *adj* -**nn**- : sickly or pale —**wan·ly** *adv* —**wan·ness** *n*

wand \\'wänd\\ *n* : slender staff

wan·der \\'wändər\\ *vb* 1 : move about aimlessly 2 : stray 3 : become delirious —**wan·der·er** *n*

wan·der·lust \\'wändər,ləst\\ *n* : strong urge to wander

wane \\'wān\\ *vb* **waned; wan·ing** 1 : grow smaller or less 2 : lose power, prosperity, or influence —**wane** *n*

wan·gle \\'wangəl\\ *vb* -**gled; -gling** : obtain by sly or indirect means

want \\'wȯnt\\ *vb* 1 : lack 2 : need 3 : desire earnestly ~ *n* 1 : deficiency 2 : dire need 3 : something wanted

want·ing \\-iŋ\\ *adj* 1 : not present or in evidence 2 : falling below standards 3 : lacking in ability ~ *prep* 1 : lacking 2 : diminished by

wan·ton \\'wȯntⁿn\\ *adj* 1 : excessively merry 2 : lewd 3 : having no regard for justice or for others' feelings, rights, or safety ~ *n* : lewd or immoral person ~ *vb* : be wanton —**wan·ton·ly** *adv* —**wan·ton·ness** *n*

wa·pi·ti \\'wäpətē\\ *n, pl* -**ti** *or* -**tis** : elk

war \\'wȯr\\ *n* 1 : armed fighting between nations 2 : state of hostility or conflict **3** : struggle between opposing forces or for a particular end ~ *vb* **-rr-** : engage in warfare —**war·less** \-ləs\ *adj* —**war·time** *n*

war·ble \'wȯrbəl\ *n* **1** : melodious succession of low pleasing sounds **2** : musical trill ~ *vb* **-bled; -bling** : sing or utter in a trilling way

war·bler \'wȯrblər\ *n* **1** : small thrush-like singing bird **2** : small bright-colored insect-eating bird

ward \'wȯrd\ *n* **1** : a guarding or being under guard or guardianship **2** : division of a prison or hospital **3** : electoral or administrative division of a city **4** : person under protection of a guardian or a law court ~ *vb* : turn aside —**ward·ship** *n*

1-ward \wərd\ *adj suffix* **1** : that moves, tends, faces, or is directed toward **2** : that occurs or is situated in the direction of

2-ward, -wards \wərdz\ *adv suffix* **1** : in a (specified) direction **2** : toward a (specified) point, position, or area

war·den \'wȯrdᵊn\ *n* **1** : guardian **2** : official charged with supervisory duties or enforcement of laws **3** : official in charge of a prison

ward·er \'wȯrdər\ *n* : watchman or warden

ward·robe \'wȯrd,rōb\ *n* **1** : clothes closet **2** : collection of wearing apparel

ware \waər\ *n* **1** : articles for sale —often *pl.* **2** : items of fired clay

ware·house \-,haús\ *n* : place for storage of merchandise —**warehouse** *vb* —**ware·house·man** \-mən\ *n* —**ware·hous·er** \-haúzər, -sər\ *n*

war·fare \'wȯr,faər\ *n* **1** : military operations between enemies **2** : struggle

war·head \-,hed\ *n* : part of a missile (as a bomb) holding the charge

war·like *adj* : fond of or threatening war

warm \'wȯrm\ *adj* **1** : having or giving out moderate or adequate heat **2** : serving to retain heat **3** : showing strong feeling **4** : giving a pleasant impression of warmth, cheerfulness, or friendliness ~ *vb* **1** : make or become warm **2** : give warmth or energy to **3** : become increasingly ardent, interested, or competent —**warm·er** *n* —**warm·ly** *adv*

war·mon·ger \'wȯr,məŋgər, -,mäŋ-\ *n* : one who attempts to stir up war

warmth \'wȯrmth\ *n* **1** : quality or state of being warm **2** : enthusiasm

warn \'wȯrn\ *vb* **1** : put on guard **2**

: notify in advance —**warn·ing** \-iŋ\ *n or adj*

warp \'wȯrp\ *n* **1** : lengthwise threads in a woven fabric **2** : twist ~ *vb* **1** : twist out of shape **2** : lead astray **3** : distort

war·rant \'wȯrənt, 'wär-\ *n* **1** : authorization **2** : legal writ authorizing action ~ *vb* **1** : declare or maintain positively **2** : guarantee **3** : approve **4** : justify

warrant officer *n* **1** : officer in the armed forces ranking next below a commissioned officer **2** : commissioned officer in the navy or coast guard ranking below an ensign

war·ran·ty \'wȯrəntē, 'wär-\ *n, pl* **-ties** : guarantee of the integrity of a product

war·ren \'wȯrən, 'wär-\ *n* : area for the keeping of small game as rabbits

war·rior \'wȯryər, 'wȯrēər; 'wärē-, 'wäryər\ *n* : man engaged or experienced in warfare

war·ship \'wȯr,ship\ *n* : armed military ship

wart \'wȯrt\ *n* **1** : small projection on the skin caused by a virus **2** : wart-like protuberance

wary \'wa(ə)rē\ *adj* **wari·er; -est** : careful in guarding against danger or deception

was *past 1st & 3d sing of* BE

wash \'wȯsh, 'wäsh\ *vb* **1** : cleanse with or as if with a liquid (as water) **2** : wet thoroughly with liquid **3** : flow along the border of **4** : flow in a stream **5** : move or remove by or as if by the action of water **6** : cover or daub lightly with a liquid **7** : undergo laundering ~ *n* **1** : act of washing or being washed **2** : articles to be washed **3** : surging action of water or disturbed air

wash·able \-əbəl\ *adj* : capable of being washed without damage

wash·board *n* : grooved board to scrub clothes on

wash·bowl *n* : large bowl for water for washing hands and face

wash·cloth *n* : cloth used for washing one's face and body

wash·er \'wȯshər, 'wäsh-\ *n* **1** : machine for washing **2** : ring used around a bolt or screw to ensure tightness or relieve friction

wash·ing \'wȯshiŋ, 'wäsh-\ *n* : articles to be washed

Washington's Birthday *n* : the 3d Monday in February or formerly February 22 observed as a legal holiday

wash·out *n* **1** : washing out or away of

earth **2** : place where earth is washed away **3** : failure

wash-room *n* : room with washing and toilet facilities

wasp \'wäsp, 'wȯsp\ *n* : slender-bodied winged insect related to the bees and having a formidable sting

wasp-ish \'wäspish, 'wȯs-\ *adj* : irritable

was-sail \'wäsəl, wä'sāl\ *n* **1** : toast to someone's health **2** : liquor drunk on festive occasions **3** : riotous drinking —**wassail** *vb*

waste \'wāst\ *n* **1** : sparsely settled or barren region **2** : act or an instance of wasting **3** : refuse (as garbage or rubbish) **4** : material (as feces) produced but not used by a living body ~ *vb* **wast-ed; wast-ing 1** : ruin **2** : spend or use carelessly **3** : lose substance or energy ~ *adj* **1** : wild and uninhabited **2** : being of no further use —**wast-er** *n* —**waste-ful \-fəl** *adj* —**waste-ful-ly** *adv* —**waste-ful-ness** *n*

waste-bas-ket \'wās(t)ₒbaskət\ *n* : receptacle for refuse

waste-land \'wāstₒland, -lənd\ *n* : barren uncultivated land

wast-rel \'wāstrəl, 'wästrəl\ *n* : one who wastes

watch \'wäch, 'wȯch\ *vb* **1** : be or stay awake intentionally **2** : be on the lookout for danger **3** : observe **4** : keep oneself informed about ~ *n* **1** : act of keeping awake to guard **2** : close observation **3** : one that watches **4** : period of duty on a ship or those on duty during this period **5** : timepiece carried on the person —**watch-er** *n*

watch-dog *n* **1** : dog kept to guard property **2** : one that protects

watch-ful \-fəl** *adj* : steadily attentive —watch-ful-ly** *adv* —**watch-ful-ness** *n*

watch-man \-mən\ *n* : person assigned to watch

watch-word *n* **1** : secret word used as a signal **2** : slogan

wa-ter \'wȯtər, 'wät-\ *n* **1** : liquid that descends as rain and forms rivers, lakes, and seas **2** : liquid containing or resembling water ~ *vb* **1** : supply with or get water **2** : dilute with or as if with water **3** : form or secrete watery matter

water buffalo *n* : common oxlike often domesticated Asian buffalo

wa-ter-col-or *n* **1** : paint whose liquid part is water **2** : picture made with watercolors

wa-ter-course *n* : stream of water

wa-ter-cress \-ₒkres\ *n* : perennial salad plant found chiefly in clear running water

wa-ter-fall *n* : steep descent of the water of a stream

wa-ter-fowl *n* **1** : bird that frequents the water **2** *pl* : swimming game birds

wa-ter-front *n* : land fronting a body of water

water lily *n* : aquatic plant with floating leaves and showy flowers

wa-ter-logged \-ₒlȯgd, -ₒlägd\ *adj* : filled or soaked with water

wa-ter-mark *n* **1** : mark showing how high water has risen **2** : a marking in paper visible under light ~ *vb* : mark (paper) with a watermark

wa-ter-mel-on *n* : large fruit with sweet juicy usu. red pulp

water moccasin *n* : venomous snake of the southern U.S.

wa-ter-pow-er *n* : power of moving water used to run machinery

wa-ter-proof *adj* : not letting water through ~ *vb* : make waterproof —**wa-ter-proof-ing** *n*

wa-ter-shed \-ₒshed\ *n* : dividing ridge between two drainage areas or one of these areas

water ski *n* : ski used on water when the wearer is towed —**wa-ter-ski** *vb* —**wa-ter-ski-er** *n*

wa-ter-spout *n* **1** : pipe from which water is spouted **2** : tornado over a body of water

wa-ter-tight *adj* **1** : so tight as not to let water in **2** : so worded that its meaning cannot be misunderstood or its purpose defeated

wa-ter-way *n* : navigable body of water

wa-ter-works *n pl* : system by which water is supplied (as to a city)

wa-tery \'wȯtərē, 'wät-\ *adj* **1** : relating to water **2** : containing, full of, or giving out water **3** : being like water **4** : soft and soggy

watt \'wät\ *n* : unit of electric power —**watt-age** \'wätij\ *n*

wat-tle \'wät⁰l\ *n* **1** : framework of flexible branches used for fencing **2** : fleshy process hanging usu. about the head or neck (as of a bird) —**wat-tled** \-⁰ld\ *adj*

wave \'wāv\ *vb* **waved; wav-ing 1** : flutter **2** : signal with the hands **3** : wave to and fro with the hand **4** : curve up and down like a wave ~ *n* **1** : moving swell on the surface of water **2** : wavelike shape **3** : waving motion **4** : surge **5** : disturbance that transfers energy from point to point —**wave-let \-lət** *n* —**wave-like** *adj* —**wavy** *adj*

wave·length \'wāv,leŋth\ n : distance from crest to crest in the line of advance of a wave

wa·ver \'wāvər\ vb 1 : fluctuate in opinion, allegiance, or direction 2 : flicker 3 : falter —**waver** n —**wa·ver·er** n —**wa·ver·ing·ly** adv

¹wax \'waks\ n 1 : yellowish plastic substance secreted by bees 2 : substance resembling beeswax ~ vb : treat or rub with wax esp. for polishing

²wax vb 1 : grow larger 2 : become

wax·en \'waksən\ adj : made of or resembling wax

waxy \'waksē\ adj **wax·i·er; -est** : made of, full of, or resembling wax

way \'wā\ n 1 : thoroughfare for travel or passage 2 : route 3 : course of action 4 : method 5 : detail 6 : usual or characteristic state of affairs 7 : condition 8 : distance 9 : progress along a course —**by way of** 1 : for the purpose of 2 : by the route through —**out of the way** : remote —**under way** : in motion or progress

way·bill n : paper that accompanies a shipment and gives details of goods, route, and charges

way·far·er \'wā,farər\ n : traveler esp. on foot —**way·far·ing** \-,fariŋ\ adj

way·lay \'wā,lā\ vb **-laid** \-,lād\; **-lay·ing** 1 : lie in wait for 2 : stop (someone) to converse

way·side n : side of a road

way·ward \'wāwərd\ adj 1 : disobedient 2 : unpredictable 3 : opposite to what is desired

we \(')wē\ pron —used of a group that includes the speaker or writer

weak \'wēk\ adj 1 : lacking strength or vigor 2 : deficient in vigor of mind or character 3 : deficient in the usual ingredients 4 : not having or exerting authority —**weak·en** \'wēkən\ vb —**weak·ly** adv

weak·ling \-liŋ\ n : person who is physically, mentally, or morally weak

weak·ly \'wēklē\ adj : feeble

weak·ness \-nəs\ n 1 : quality or state of being weak 2 : fault 3 : object of special liking

wealth \'welth\ n 1 : abundant possessions or resources 2 : profusion

wealthy \'welthē\ adj **wealth·i·er; -est** : having wealth

wean \'wēn\ vb 1 : accustom (a young mammal) to take food otherwise than by nursing 2 : free from dependence

weap·on \'wepən\ n 1 : something (as a gun) that may be used to fight with 2

: means by which one contends against another

wear \'waər\ vb **wore** \'wōr\; **worn** \'wōrn\; **wear·ing** 1 : use as an article of clothing or adornment 2 : carry on the person 3 : show an appearance of 4 : decay by use or by scraping 5 : lessen the strength of 6 : endure use ~ n 1 : act of wearing 2 : clothing 3 : lasting quality 4 : result of use —**wear·able** \'warəbəl\ adj —**wear·er** n —**wear out** ~ vb 1 : make or become useless by wear 2 : tire

wea·ri·some \'wirēsəm\ adj : causing weariness

wea·ry \'wi(ə)rē\ adj **-ri·er; -est** 1 : worn out in strength, freshness, or patience 2 : expressing or characteristic of weariness ~ vb **-ried; -ry·ing** : make or become weary —**wea·ri·ly** adv —**wea·ri·ness** n

wea·sel \'wēzəl\ n : small slender flesh-eating mammals

weath·er \'wethər\ n : condition of the atmosphere ~ vb 1 : expose to or endure the action of weather 2 : endure

weath·er-beat·en adj : altered by exposure to the weather

weath·er·man \-,man\ n : one who forecasts and reports the weather

weath·er·proof adj : able to withstand exposure to weather —**weather-proof** vb

weather vane n : movable device that shows the way the wind blows

weave \'wēv\ vb **wove** \'wōv\ or **weaved; wo·ven** \'wōvən\ or **weaved; weav·ing** 1 : form by interlacing strands of material 2 : contrive 3 : make a coherent whole 4 : follow a winding course ~ n : pattern or method of weaving —**weav·er** n

web \'web\ n 1 : cobweb 2 : animal or plant membrane 3 : network ~ vb **-bb-** : cover or provide with a web

webbed \'webd\ adj : having or being toes or fingers united by a web

web·bing \'webiŋ\ n : strong closely woven tape

wed \'wed\ vb **-dd-** 1 : marry 2 : unite

wed·ding \'wediŋ\ n : marriage ceremony and celebration

wedge \'wej\ n : V-shaped object used for splitting, raising, forcing open, or tightening ~ vb **wedged; wedg·ing** 1 : tighten or split with a wedge 2 : force into a narrow space

wed·lock \'wed,läk\ n : marriage

Wednes·day \'wenzdē\ n : 4th day of the week

wee \'wē\ *adj* : very small

weed \'wēd\ *n* : unwanted plant ~ *vb* : remove weeds or other unwanted items —**weed·er** *n* —**weedy** *adj*

weeds *n pl* : mourning clothes

week \'wēk\ *n* 1 : 7 successive days 2 : calendar period of 7 days beginning with Sunday and ending with Saturday 3 : the working or school days of the calendar week

week·day \'wēk,dā\ *n* : any day except Sunday and often Saturday

week·end \-,end\ *n* : Saturday and Sunday ~ *vb* : spend the weekend

week·ly \'wēklē\ *adj* : occurring, done, produced, or issued every week ~ *adv* : once a week ~ *n, pl* **-lies** : weekly publication —**weekly** *adv*

weep \'wēp\ *vb* **wept** \'wept\; **weep·ing** : shed tears —**weep·er** *n* —**weepy** *adj*

wee·vil \'wēvəl\ *n* : small injurious beetle with a long head usu. curved into a snout —**wee·vily, wee·vil·ly** \'wēv(ə)lē\ *adj*

weft \'weft\ *n* : woof

weigh \'wā\ *vb* 1 : determine the heaviness of 2 : have a specified weight 3 : consider carefully 4 : heave up (an anchor) 5 : press down or burden

weight \'wāt\ *n* 1 : amount that something weighs 2 : relative heaviness 3 : heavy object 4 : burden or pressure 5 : importance ~ *vb* 1 : load with a weight 2 : oppress —**weight·less** \-ləs\ *adj* —**weight·less·ness** *n* —**weighty** \'wātē\ *adj*

weird \'wiərd\ *adj* 1 : unearthly or mysterious 2 : strange —**weird·ly** *adv* —**weird·ness** *n*

wel·come \'welkəm\ *vb* **-comed; -com·ing** : accept or greet cordially ~ *adj* : received or permitted gladly ~ *n* : cordial greeting or reception

weld \'weld\ *vb* : unite by heating, hammering, or pressing ~ *n* : union by welding —**weld·er** *n*

wel·fare \'wel,faər\ *n* 1 : prosperity 2 : relief

¹well \'wel\ *n* 1 : spring 2 : hole sunk in the earth to obtain a natural deposit (as of oil) 3 : source of supply 4 : open space containing water vertically through floors ~ *vb* : flow forth

²well *adv* **bet·ter** \'betər\; **best** \'best\ 1 : in a good or proper manner 2 : satisfactorily 3 : fully 4 : considerably ~ *adj* 1 : satisfactory 2 : prosperous 3 : desirable 4 : healthy

well-ad·vised \,weləd'vīzd\ *adj* : prudent

well-bred \-'bred\ *adj* : having good manners

well-done *adj* 1 : properly performed 2 : cooked thoroughly

well-heeled \-'hēld\ *adj* : financially well-off

well-mean·ing *adj* : having good intentions

well-nigh *adv* : nearly

well-off *adj* : being in good condition esp. financially

well-read \-'red\ *adj* : well informed through reading

well-round·ed \-'raûndəd\ *adj* : broadly developed

well·spring *n* : source

well-to-do \,weltə'dü\ *adj* : prosperous

well-worn \-'wōrn\ *adj* 1 : worn by much use 2 : trite

welsh \'welsh, 'welch\ *vb* : default dishonorably

Welsh rabbit *n* : melted often seasoned cheese poured over toast or crackers

Welsh rare·bit \-'raərbət\ *n* : Welsh rabbit

welt \'welt\ *n* 1 : narrow strip of leather between a shoe upper and sole 2 : ridge raised on the skin usu. by a blow ~ *vb* : hit hard

wel·ter \'weltər\ *vb* 1 : toss about 2 : wallow ~ *n* : confused jumble

wen \'wen\ *n* : cyst formed by blockage of a skin gland

wench \'wench\ *n* : young woman

wend \'wend\ *vb* : direct one's course

went *past of* GO

wept *past of* WEEP

were 2d sing, past pl, or past subjunctive of BE

were·wolf \'wiər,wûlf, 'wər-, 'wear-\ *n, pl* **-wolves** \-,wûlvz\ : person held to be able to change into a wolf

west \'west\ *adv* : to or toward the west ~ *adj* : situated toward or at or coming from the west ~ *n* 1 : direction of sunset 2 *cap* : regions to the west —**west·er·ly** \'westərlē\ *adv or adj* —**west·ward** \-wərd\ *adv or adj* —**west·wards** \-wərdz\ *adv*

west·ern \'westərn\ *adj* 1 *cap* : of a region designated West 2 : lying toward or coming from the west —**West·ern·er** *n*

wet \'wet\ *adj* **-tt-** 1 : consisting of or covered or soaked with liquid 2 : not dry ~ *n* : moisture ~ *vb* **-tt-** : make or become moist —**wet·ly** *adv* —**wet·ness** *n*

whack \'hwak\ *vb* : strike sharply ~ *n* 1 : sharp blow 2 : proper working order 3 : chance 4 : try

¹whale \'hwāl\ *n, pl* **whales** *or* **whale** : large marine mammal ~ *vb* **whaled**; **whal·ing** : hunt for whales —**whale·boat** *n* —**whal·er** *n*

²whale *vb* **whaled**; **whal·ing** : strike or hit vigorously

whale·bone *n* : horny substance attached to the upper jaw of some whales (**whalebone whales**)

wharf \'hwȯrf\ *n, pl* **wharves** \'hwȯrvz\ : structure alongside which boats lie to load or unload

what \'(')hwät\ *pron* **1** —used to inquire the identity or nature of something **2** : that which **3** : whatever ~ *adv* : to what degree or in what respect ~ *adj* **1** —used to inquire about the identity or nature of something **2** : how remarkable or surprising **3** : whatever

what·ev·er \hwät'evər\ *pron* **1** : anything or everything that **2** : no matter what ~ *adj* : of any kind at all

what·so·ev·er \ˌhwätsə'wevər\ *pron or adj* : whatever

wheal \'hwēl\ *n* : a wale or welt on the skin

wheat \'hwēt\ *n* : cereal grain that yields flour —**wheat·en** *adj*

whee·dle \'hwēd⁰l\ *vb* -**dled**; -**dling** : coax or tempt by flattery

wheel \'hwēl\ *n* **1** : disk or circular frame capable of turning on a central axis **2** : device of which the main part is a wheel ~ *vb* **1** : convey or move on wheels or a wheeled vehicle **2** : rotate **3** : turn so as to change direction —**wheeled** *adj* —**wheel·er** *n* —**wheel·less** *adj*

wheel·bar·row \-ˌbarō\ *n* : one-wheeled vehicle for carrying small loads

wheel·base *n* : distance in inches between the front and rear axles of an automotive vehicle

wheel·chair *n* : chair mounted on wheels esp. for the use of invalids

wheeze \'hwēz\ *vb* **wheezed**; **wheez·ing** : breathe with difficulty and with a whistling sound —**wheeze** *n* —**wheezy** *adj*

whelk \'hwelk\ *n* : large sea snail

whelp \'hwelp\ *n* : one of the young of various carnivorous mammals (as a dog) ~ *vb* : bring forth whelps

when \'(')hwen, hwən\ *adv* —used to inquire about or designate a particular time ~ *conj* **1** : at or during the time that **2** : every time that **3** : if **4** : although ~ \ˌhwen\ *pron* : what time

whence \'(')hwens\ *adv* **1** : from what

place, source, or cause **2** : from or out of which

when·ev·er \hwen'evər, hwən-\ *conj or adv* : at whatever time

where \'(')hwear\ *adv* **1** : at, in, or to what place **2** : at, in, or to what situation, position, direction, circumstances, or respect ~ *conj* **1** : at, in, or to what place, position, or circumstance **2** : at, in, or to which place ~ \'hwear\ *n* **1** : place **2** : what place

where·abouts \-ˌbaüts\ *adv* : about where ~ *n sing or pl* : place where a person or thing is

where·as \hwer'az\ *conj* **1** : because **2** : while on the contrary

where·by *conj* : by, through, or in accordance with which

where·fore \'hwear₁fȯr\ *adv* **1** : why **2** : therefore ~ *n* : cause

where·in \hwer'in\ *adv* : in what respect

where·of \-'əv, -'äv\ *conj* : of what, which, or whom

where·up·on \'hwera₁pȯn, -₁pän\ *conj* —used to introduce a result or consequence

wher·ev·er \hwer'evər\ *adv* : where ~ *conj* : at, in, or to whatever place or circumstance

where·with·al \'hwerwith₁ȯl, -with-\ *n* : resources and esp. money

whet \'hwet\ *vb* -**tt**- **1** : sharpen by rubbing (as with a stone) **2** : stimulate —**whet·stone** *n*

whether \'hwethər\ *conj* **1** : if it is or was true that **2** : if it is or was better **3** : whichever is the case

whey \'hwā\ *n* : watery part of sour milk

which \'(')hwich\ *adj* **1** : being what one or ones out of a group **2** : whichever ~ *pron* **1** : which one or ones **2** : whichever

which·ev·er \hwich'evər\ *pron or adj* : no matter which

whiff \'hwif\ *n* **1** : slight gust **2** : inhalation of odor, gas, or smoke **3** : slight trace ~ *vb* : inhale an odor

while \'hwīl\ *n* **1** : period of time **2** : time and effort used ~ \(ˌ)hwīl\ *conj* **1** : during the time that **2** : as long as **3** : although ~ \'hwīl\ *vb* **whiled**; **whil·ing** : cause to pass esp. pleasantly

whim \'hwim\ *n* : sudden or brief idea or wish

whim·per \'hwimpər\ *vb* : cry softly —**whimper** *n*

whim·si·cal \'hwimzikəl\ *adj* : full of whims : erratic —**whim·si·cal·i·ty**

\ˌhwimzə'kälətē\ *n* —**whim·si·cal·ly** *adv*

whim·sy, whim·sey \'hwimzē\ *n, pl* **-sies** *or* **-seys** **1** : whim **2** : fanciful creation

whine \'hwīn\ *vb* **whined; whin·ing 1** : utter a usu. high-pitched plaintive or distressed cry **2** : complain —**whine** *n*

whin·ny \'hwinē\ *vb* **-nied; -ny·ing** : neigh —**whinny** *n*

whip \'hwip\ *vb* **-pp- 1** : move quickly **2** : strike with something slender and flexible **3** : defeat **4** : incite **5** : beat into a froth ~ *n* **1** : flexible device used for whipping **2** : party leader responsible for discipline **3** : thrashing motion —**whip·per** *n*

whip·cord *n* **1** : thin tough cord **2** : cloth made of hard-twisted yarns

whip·lash *n* : injury from a sudden sharp movement of the neck and head

whip·per·snap·per \'hwipər,snapər\ *n* : small, insignificant, or presumptuous person

whip·pet \'hwipət\ *n* : small swift dog often used for racing

whip-poor-will \'hwipər,wil\ *n* : American nocturnal bird

whir \'hwər\ *vb* **-rr-** : move, fly, or revolve with a whizzing sound ~ *n* : continuous fluttering or vibratory sound

whirl \'hwərl\ *vb* **1** : move or drive in a circle **2** : spin **3** : move or turn quickly **4** : reel ~ *n* **1** : rapid circular movement **2** : state of commotion or confusion

whirl·pool *n* : whirling mass of water having a depression in the center

whirl·wind *n* : whirling wind storm

whisk \'hwisk\ *n* **1** : quick light sweeping or brushing motion **2** : usu. wire kitchen implement for beating ~ *vb* **1** : move or convey briskly **2** : beat **3** : brush lightly

whisk broom *n* : small broom

whis·ker \'hwiskər\ *n* **1** *pl* : beard **2** : long bristle or hair near an animal's mouth —**whis·kered** \-kərd\ *adj*

whis·key, whis·ky \'hwiskē\ *n, pl* **-keys** *or* **-kies** : liquor distilled from a fermented mash of grain

whis·per \'hwispər\ *vb* **1** : speak softly **2** : tell by whispering ~ *n* **1** : soft low sound **2** : rumor

whist \'hwist\ *n* : card game

whis·tle \'hwisəl\ *n* **1** : device by which a shrill sound is produced **2** : shrill clear sound made by a whistle or through the lips ~ *vb* **-tled; -tling 1**

: make or utter a whistle **2** : signal or call by a whistle **3** : produce by whistling —**whis·tler** *n*

whis·tle-stop *n* **1** : small community **2** : brief political appearance

whit \'hwit\ *n* : bit

white \'hwīt\ *adj* **whit·er; -est 1** : free from color **2** : of the color of new snow or milk **3** : having light skin ~ *n* **1** : color of maximum lightness **2** : white part or thing **3** : person who is light-skinned —**white·ness** *n*

white-bait \'hwīt,bāt\ *n* : young of a herring

white blood cell *n* : blood cell that does not contain hemoglobin

white-cap \'hwīt,kap\ *n* : wave crest breaking into foam

white-col·lar *adj* : relating to salaried employees with duties not requiring protective or work clothing

white elephant *n* : unwanted often useless item

white·fish \'hwīt,fish\ *n* : freshwater food fish

whit·en \'hwīt²n\ *vb* : make or become white —**whit·en·er** \'hwītnər, -²nər\ *n*

white slave *n* : woman or girl held unwillingly for purposes of prostitution —**white slavery** *n*

white·tail \'hwīt,tāl\ *n* : No. American deer

white·wash *vb* **1** : whiten with a composition (as of lime and water) **2** : gloss over or cover up faults or wrongdoing —**whitewash** *n*

whith·er \'hwithər\ *adv* **1** : to what place **2** : to what situation, position, degree, or end

¹**whit·ing** \'hwītiŋ\ *n* : usu. light or silvery food fish

²**whiting** *n* : pulverized chalk or limestone

whit·ish \'hwītish\ *adj* : somewhat white

whit·tle \'hwit²l\ *vb* **-tled; -tling 1** : pare **2** : shape by paring **3** : reduce gradually

whiz, whizz \'hwiz\ *vb* **-zz-** : make a sound like a speeding object —**whiz, whizz** *n*

who \('')hü\ *pron* **1** —used to inquire the identity of an indicated person or group **2** : person or persons that **3** \(,)hü, ü\ —used to introduce a relative clause

who·dun·it \hü'dənət\ *n* : detective or mystery story

who·ev·er \hü'evər\ *pron* : no matter who

whole \'hōl\ *adj* **1** : being in healthy or

sound condition **2** : having all its parts or elements **3** : constituting the total sum of ~ **n 1** : complete amount or sum **2** : coherent complex system —**on the whole 1** : considering all circumstances **2** : in general —**whole·ness** n

whole·heart·ed \'hōl'härtəd\ adj : sincere

whole number n : integer

whole·sale \'hōl₁sāl\ n : sale of goods in quantity usu. for resale by a retail merchant — adj **1** : of or relating to wholesaling **2** : performed on a large scale ~ vb -**saled; -sal·ing** : sell at wholesale —**wholesale** adv —**whole·sal·er** n

whole·some \-səm\ adj **1** : promoting mental, spiritual, or bodily health **2** : healthy —**whole·some·ness** n

whole wheat adj : made of ground entire wheat kernels

whol·ly \'hōl(l)ē\ adv **1** : totally **2** : solely

whom \('')hüm\ pron, objective case of WHO

whom·ev·er \hüm'evər\ pron, objective case of WHOEVER

whoop \'h(w)üp, 'h(w)ùp\ vb : shout loudly ~ n : shout

whooping cough n : infectious disease marked by convulsive coughing fits

whop·per \'hwäpər\ n **1** : something unusually large or extreme of its kind **2** : monstrous lie

whop·ping \'hwäpiŋ\ adj : extremely large

whore \'hōr\ n : prostitute

whorl \'hwórl, 'hwərl\ n : spiral —**whorled** adj

whose \'hüz\ adj : of or relating to whom or which ~ pron : whose one or ones

who·so·ev·er \₁hüsə'wevər\ pron : whoever

why \('')hwī\ adv : for what reason, cause, or purpose ~ conj : for which **2** : for which ~ \'hwī\ n, pl **whys** : reason ~ interj \('')wī, ('')hwī\ —used esp. to express surprise

wick \'wik\ n : cord that draws up oil, tallow, or wax to be burned

wick·ed \'wikəd\ adj **1** : morally bad **2** : harmful or troublesome **3** : very unpleasant **4** : mischievous —**wicked·ly** adv —**wick·ed·ness** n

wick·er \'wikər\ n **1** : small pliant branch **2** : wickerwork —**wicker** adj

wick·er·work n : work made of wickers

wick·et \'wikət\ n **1** : small gate, door, or window **2** : frame in cricket or arch in croquet

wide \'wīd\ adj **wid·er; wid·est 1** : covering a vast area **2** : measured at right angles to the length **3** : having extension from side to side **4** : opened fully **5** : far from the goal ~ adv **wid·er; wid·est 1** : over a great distance **2** : so as to leave considerable space between **3** : fully **4** : astray —**wide·ly** adv —**wid·en** \'wīd³n\ vb

wide-awake adj : alert

wide-eyed adj **1** : having the eyes wide open **2** : amazed **3** : naive

wide·spread adj : widely extended

wid·ow \'widō\ n : woman who has lost her husband by death and has not married again ~ vb : cause to become a widow —**wid·ow·hood** n

wid·ow·er \'widəwər\ n : man who has lost his wife by death and has not married again

width \'width\ n **1** : distance from side to side **2** : largeness of extent **3** : measured and cut piece of material

wield \'wēld\ vb **1** : use or handle esp. effectively **2** : exert —**wield·er** n

wie·ner \'wēnər\ n : frankfurter

wife \'wīf\ n, pl **wives** \'wīvz\ : married woman —**wife·hood** n —**wifeless** adj —**wife·ly** adj

wig \'wig\ n : manufactured covering of hair for the head

wig·gle \'wigəl\ vb -**gled; -gling 1** : move with quick jerky or shaking movements **2** : wriggle —**wiggle** n —**wig·gler** n

wig·gly \-(ə)lē\ adj **1** : tending to wiggle **2** : wavy

wig·wag \'wig₁wag\ vb : signal by a flag or light waved according to a code or by the hand or arm

wig·wam \'wig₁wäm\ n : American Indian hut consisting of a framework of poles overlaid with bark, rush mats, or hides

wild \'wīld\ adj **1** : living or being in a state of nature and not domesticated or cultivated **2** : unrestrained **3** : turbulent **4** : crazy **5** : uncivilized **6** : erratic ~ n **1** : wilderness **2** : undomesticated state ~ adv : without control —**wild·ly** adv —**wild·ness** n

wild·cat \'wil(d)₁kat\ n **1** : any of various undomesticated cats (as a lynx) **2** : oil or gas well drilled in an area not known to be productive ~ adj **1** : not sound or safe **2** : unauthorized ~ vb -**tt-** : drill a wildcat oil or gas well

wil·der·ness \'wildərnəs\ n : uncultivated and uninhabited region

wild·fire \\'wīl(d),fī(ə)r\\ *n* : sweeping and destructive fire

wild-fowl *n* : game waterfowl

wild-life \\'wīl(d),līf\\ *n* : undomesticated animals

wile \\'wīl\\ *n* : trick to snare or deceive ~ *vb* **wiled; wil·ing** : lure

will \\wəl, (ə)l, (ʹ)wil\\ *vb, past would* \\wəd, (ə)d, (ʹ)wu̇d\\; *pres sing & pl* **will** **1** : wish **2** —used as an auxilliary verb to express (1) desire or willingness (2) customary action (3) simple future time (4) capability (5) determination (6) probability (7) inevitability or (8) a command **3** \\'wil\\ : dispose of by a will ~ \\'wil\\ *n* **1** : often determined wish **2** : act, process, or experience of willing **3** : power of controlling one's actions or emotions **4** : legal document disposing of property after death

will·ful, wil·ful \\'wilfəl\\ *adj* **1** : governed by will without regard to reason **2** : intentional —**will·ful·ly** *adv*

will·ing \\'wiliŋ\\ *adj* **1** : inclined or favorably disposed in mind **2** : prompt to act **3** : done, borne, or accepted voluntarily or without reluctance —**will·ing·ly** *adv* —**will·ing·ness** *n*

will-o'-the-wisp \\,wiləthəʹwisp\\ *n* **1** : light that appears at night over marshy grounds **2** : misleading or elusive goal or hope

wil·low \\'wilō\\ *n* : quick-growing shrub or tree with flexible shoots

wil·lowy \\'wilə,wē\\ *adj* : gracefully tall and slender

will-pow·er \\'wil,pau̇(ə)r\\ *n* : energetic determination

wil·ly-nil·ly \\,wilē'nilē\\ *adv or adj* : without regard for one's choice

wilt \\'wilt\\ *vb* **1** : lose or cause to lose freshness and become limp **2** : grow weak

wily \\'wīlē\\ *adj* **wil·i·er; -est** : full of craftiness —**wil·i·ness** *n*

win \\'win\\ *vb* **won** \\'wən\\; **win·ning** **1** : gain victory in a contest **2** : get possession of esp. by effort **3** : gain in battle or contest **4** : make friendly or favorable ~ *n* : victory

wince \\'wins\\ *vb* **winced; winc·ing** : shrink back involuntarily —**wince** *n*

winch \\'winch\\ *n* : hand- or power-operated machine for hoisting or pulling with a drum around which rope is wound —**winch** *vb*

¹wind \\'wind\\ *n* **1** : movement of the air **2** : breath **3** : gas in the stomach or intestines **4** : air carrying a scent **5** : intimation ~ *vb* **1** : get a scent of **2** : cause to be out of breath

²wind \\'wīnd\\ *vb* **wound** \\'wau̇nd\\; **wind·ing 1** : have or follow a curving course **2** : move or lie to encircle **3** : encircle or cover with something pliable **4** : tighten the spring of **5** : turn ~ *n* : turn or coil —**wind·er** *n*

wind·break *n* : trees and shrubs to break the force of the wind

wind·fall \\'win(d),fȯl\\ *n* **1** : thing blown down by wind **2** : unexpected benefit

wind instrument *n* : musical instrument (as a flute or horn) sounded by wind and esp. by the breath

wind·lass \\'windləs\\ *n* : winch esp. for hoisting anchor

wind·mill \\'wind,mil\\ *n* : machine worked by the wind turning radiating vanes

win·dow \\'windō\\ *n* **1** : opening in the wall of a building to let in light and air **2** : pane in a window —**win·dow·less** *adj*

win·dow-shop *vb* : look at the displays in store windows —**win·dow-shop·per** *n*

wind·pipe \\'win(d),pīp\\ *n* : passage for the breath from the larynx to the lungs

wind·shield \\'win(d),shēld\\ *n* : transparent screen in front of the occupants of a vehicle

wind-up \\'win,dəp\\ *n* : end —**wind up** \\(ʹ)win'dəp\\ *vb*

wind·ward \\'win(d)wərd\\ *adj* : moving toward or situated on the side toward the direction from which the wind is blowing ~ *n* : direction from which the wind is blowing

windy \\'windē\\ *adj* **wind·i·er; -est** : having wind **2** : indulging in useless talk

wine \\'wīn\\ *n* **1** : fermented grape juice **2** : usu. fermented juice of a plant product (as fruit) used as a beverage ~ *vb* : treat to or drink wine

wing \\'wiŋ\\ *n* **1** : movable paired appendage for flying **2** : winglike thing **3** : projecting part of a building **4** *pl* : area at the side of the stage out of sight **5** : faction ~*vb* **1** : fly **2** : let fly —**winged** *adj* —**wing·less** *adj* —**on the wing** : in flight —**under one's wing** : in one's charge or care

wink \\'wiŋk\\ *vb* **1** : close and open the eyes quickly **2** : avoid seeing or noticing something **3** : twinkle **4** : close and open one eye quickly as a signal or hint ~ *n* **1** : brief sleep **2** : act of winking **3** : instant —**wink·er** *n*

win·ner \\'winər\\ *n* : one that wins

win·ning \\'i-iŋ\\ *n* **1** : victory **2** : money

won at gambling ~ adj 1 : victorious 2 : charming

win·now \'winō\ vb 1 : remove (as chaff from grain) by a current of air 2 : get rid of something unwanted or separate something

win·some \'winsəm\ adj 1 : causing joy 2 : cheerful or gay —**win·some·ly** adv —**win·some·ness** n

win·ter \'wintər\ n : season between autumn and spring ~ adj : sown in autumn for harvest the next spring or summer ~ vb : pass the winter —**win·ter·time** n

win·ter·green \'wintər,grēn\ n : low heathlike evergreen plant with red berries

win·try \'wintrē\, **win·tery** \'wint(ə)rē\ adj **win·tri·er; -est** 1 : characteristic of winter 2 : cold in feeling

wipe \'wīp\ vb **wiped; wip·ing** 1 : clean or dry by rubbing 2 : remove by rubbing or cleaning 3 : erase completely 4 : destroy 5 : pass (as a cloth) over a surface ~ n : act or instance of wiping —**wip·er** n

wire \'wī(ə)r\ n 1 : thread of metal 2 : work made of wire 3 : telegram or cablegram ~ vb 1 : provide with wire 2 : bind or mount with wire 3 : telegraph

wire·less \-ləs\ n : system for communicating by code signals and radio waves and without connecting wires —**wireless** adj or vb

wire·tap vb : connect into a telephone or telegraph wire to get information —**wiretap** n —**wire·tap·per** n

wir·ing \'wī(ə)riŋ\ n : system of wires esp. for distributing electricity through a building

wiry \'wī(ə)rē\ adj **wir·i·er** \'wīrēər\, **-est** 1 : resembling wire 2 : slender yet strong and sinewy —**wir·i·ness** n

wis·dom \'wizdəm\ n 1 : accumulated learning 2 : good sense

wisdom tooth n : last tooth on each half of each jaw in man

1wise \'wīz\ n : manner

2wise \'wīz\ adj **wis·er; wis·est** 1 : having or showing wisdom, good sense, or good judgment 2 : aware of what is going on —**wise·ly** adv

wise·crack n : clever, smart, or flippant remark ~ vb : make a wisecrack

wish \'wish\ vb 1 : have a desire 2 : express a wish concerning 3 : request ~ n 1 : a wishing or desire 2 : expressed will or desire

wish·bone n : forked bone in front of the breastbone in most birds

wish·ful \-fəl\ adj 1 : expressive of a wish 2 : according with wishes rather than fact

wishy-washy \'wishē,wȯshē, -,wäsh-\ adj : weak or insipid

wisp \'wisp\ n 1 : small bunch of hay or straw 2 : thin strand, strip, fragment, or streak 3 : something frail, slight, or fleeting —**wispy** adj

wis·te·ria \wis'tirēə\ n : pealike woody vine with long clusters of flowers

wist·ful \'wistfəl\ adj : full of longing —**wist·ful·ly** adv —**wist·ful·ness** n

wit \'wit\ n 1 : reasoning power 2 : mental soundness —usu. pl. 3 : quickness and cleverness in handling words and ideas 4 : talent for clever remarks or one noted for witty remarks —**wit·less** adj —**wit·less·ly** adv —**wit·less·ness** n —**wit·ted** adj

witch \'wich\ n 1 : person believed to have magic power 2 : ugly old woman ~ vb : bewitch —**witch·craft** n

witch·ery \'wich(ə)rē\ n, pl **-er·ies** 1 : witchcraft 2 : charm

witch ha·zel \'wich,hāzəl\ n 1 : shrub having small yellow flowers in fall 2 : alcoholic solution of material from witch hazel bark used as a lotion

witch-hunt n 1 : searching out and persecution of supposed witches 2 : harassment of those with unpopular views

witch·ing \'wichiŋ\ adj : bewitching

with \(')with, (')with\ prep 1 : against, to, or toward 2 : in support of 3 : because of 4 : in the company of 5 : having 6 : despite 7 : containing 8 : by means of

with·draw \with'dró, with-\ vb **-drew** \-'drü\; **-drawn** \-'drón\; **-draw·ing** \-'dróiŋ\ 1 : take back or away 2 : call back or retract 3 : go away 4 : terminate one's participation in or use of —**with·draw·al** \-'dró(ə)l\ n

with·drawn \with'drón\ adj : socially detached and unresponsive

with·er \'withər\ vb 1 : shrivel 2 : lose or cause to lose energy, force, or freshness

with·ers \'withərz\ n pl : ridge between the shoulder bones of a horse

with·hold \with'hōld, with-\ vb **-held** \-'held\; **-hold·ing** 1 : hold back 2 : refrain from giving

with·in \with'in, with-\ adv 1 : in or into the interior 2 : inside oneself ~ prep 1 : in or to the inner part of 2 : in the limits or compass of ~ n : inner place or area

with·out \with'aùt, with-\ prep 1 : out-

side 2 : lacking 3 : unaccompanied or unmarked by —**with·out** *adv*

with·stand \with\stand, with-\ *vb* -**stood** \-'stůd\; -**stand·ing** : oppose successfully

wit·ness \'witnəs\ *n* 1 : testimony 2 : one who testifies 3 : one present at a transaction to testify that it has taken place 4 : one who has personal knowledge or experience 5 : something serving as proof ~ *vb* 1 : bear witness 2 : act as legal witness of 3 : furnish proof of 4 : be a witness of 5 : be the scene of

wit·ti·cism \'witə,sizəm\ *n* : a witty saying or phrase

wit·ting \'witin\ *adj* : intentional —**wit·ting·ly** *adv*

wit·ty \'witē\ *adj* -**ti·er**; -**est** : marked by or full of wit —**wit·ti·ly** \'witəlē\ *adv* —**wit·ti·ness** *n*

wives *pl of* WIFE

wiz·ard \'wizərd\ *n* 1 : magician 2 : very clever person —**wiz·ard·ry** \-ə(r)drē\ *n*

wiz·ened \'wiz²nd\ *adj* : dried up

wob·ble \'wäbəl\ *vb* -**bled**; -**bling** 1 : move or cause to move with an irregular rocking motion 2 : tremble 3 : waver —**wob·ble** *n* —**wob·bly** \'wäb(ə)lē\ *adj*

woe \'wō\ *n* 1 : deep suffering 2 : misfortune

woe·be·gone \'wōbi,gôn\ *adj* : exhibiting woe, sorrow, or misery

woe·ful \'wōfəl\ *adj* 1 : full of woe 2 : bringing woe —**woe·ful·ly** *adv*

woke *past of* WAKE

woken *past part of* WAKE

wolf \'wůlf\ *n, pl* **wolves** \'wůlvz\ : large doglike predatory mammal ~ *vb* : eat greedily —**wolf·ish** *adj*

wol·fram \'wůlfrəm\ *n* : tungsten

wol·ver·ine \,wůlvə'rēn\ *n, pl* -**ines** : flesh-eating mammal related to the sables

wom·an \'wůmən\ *n, pl* **wom·en** \'wimən\ 1 : adult female person 2 : womankind 3 : feminine nature —**wom·an·hood** \-,hůd\ *n* —**wom·an·ish** *adj*

wom·an·kind \-,kīnd\ *n* : females of the human race

wom·an·ly \-lē\ *adj* : having qualities characteristic of a woman —**wom·an·li·ness** \-lēnəs\ *n*

womb \'wüm\ *n* : uterus

won *past of* WIN

on·der \'wəndər\ *n* 1 : cause of astonishment or surprise 2 : feeling (as of astonishment) aroused by something extraordinary ~ *vb* 1 : feel surprise 2 : feel curiosity or doubt

won·der·ful \'wəndərfəl\ *adj* 1 : exciting wonder 2 : unusually good —**won·der·ful·ly** \-f(ə)lē\ *adv* —**won·der·ful·ness** *n*

won·der·land \-,land, -lənd\ *n* 1 : fairy-like imaginary realm 2 : place that excites admiration or wonder

won·der·ment \-mənt\ *n* : wonder

won·drous \'wəndrəs\ *adj* : wonderful —**won·drous·ly** *adv* —**won·drous·ness** *n*

wont \'wônt, 'wōnt\ *adj* : accustomed ~ *n* : habit —**wont·ed** *adj*

woo \'wü\ *vb* : try to gain the love or favor of —**woo·er** *n*

wood \'wůd\ *n* 1 : dense growth of trees usu. smaller than a forest —often pl. 2 : hard fibrous substance of trees and shrubs beneath the bark 3 : wood prepared for some use (as burning) ~ *adj* 1 : wooden 2 : suitable for working with wood 3 : of woods \'wůdz\ : living or growing in woods —**wood·chop·per** *n* —**wood·pile** *n* —**wood·shed** *n*

wood·bine \'wůd,bīn\ *n* : climbing vine

wood·chuck \-,chək\ *n* : thick-bodied grizzled animal of No. America

wood·craft *n* 1 : skill and practice in matters relating to the woods 2 : skill in making articles from wood

wood·cut \-,kət\ *n* 1 : relief printing surface engraved on wood 2 : print from a woodcut

wood·ed \'wůdəd\ *adj* : covered with woods

wood·en \'wůd²n\ *adj* 1 : made of wood 2 : lacking resilience 3 : lacking ease, liveliness or interest —**wood·en·ly** *adv* —**wood·en·ness** *n*

wood·land \-lənd, -,land\ *n* : land covered with trees

wood·peck·er \'wůd,pekər\ *n* : brightly marked bird with a hard bill for drilling into trees

woods·man \'wůdzmən\ *n* : one who works in the woods

wood·wind \'wůd,wind\ *n* : one of a group of wind instruments (as a flute or oboe)

wood·work *n* : work (as interior house fittings) made of wood

woody \'wůdē\ *adj* **wood·i·er**; -**est** 1 : abounding with woods 2 : of, containing, or like wood fibers —**wood·i·ness** *n*

woof \'wůf\ *n* : threads in a woven fabric that cross the warp

wool \'wůl\ *n* 1 : soft hair of some

mammals and esp. the sheep **2** : something (as a textile) made of wool —**wooled** \'wuld\ *adj*

wool·en, wool·len \'wulən\ *adj* : made of wool **2** : relating to the manufacture of woolen products ~ *n* **1** : woolen fabric **2** : woolen garments —usu. pl.

wool·gath·er·ing *n* : act of indulging in idle daydreaming

wool·ly \'wulē\ *adj* **-li·er, -est 1** : of, relating to, or bearing wool **2** : consisting of or resembling wool **3** : confused or turbulent

woo·zy \'wüzē\ *adj* **-zi·er, -est 1** : confused **2** : somewhat dizzy, nauseated, or weak —**woo·zi·ness** *n*

word \'wərd\ *n* **1** : brief remark **2** : speech sound or series of speech sounds that communicates a meaning **3** : written representation of a word **4** : order **5** : news **6** : promise **7** *pl* : dispute ~ *vb* : express in words —**word·less** *adj*

word·ing \'wərdiŋ\ *n* : verbal expression

wordy \'wərdē\ *adj* **word·i·er, -est** : using many words —**word·i·ness** *n*

wore *past of* WEAR

work \'wərk\ *n* **1** : labor **2** : employment **3** : task **4** : something (as an artistic production) produced by mental effort or physical labor **5** *pl* : buildings, grounds, and machinery of a factory **6** *pl* : moving parts of a mechanism **7** : workmanship ~ *adj* **1** : suitable for wear while working **2** : used for work ~ *vb* **worked** \'wərkt\ *or* **wrought** \'rot\, **work·ing 1** : bring to pass **2** : create by expending labor upon **3** : bring or get into a form or condition **4** : set or keep in operation **5** : solve **6** : cause to labor **7** : arrange **8** : excite **9** : labor **10** : perform work regularly for wages **11** : function according to plan or design **12** : produce a desired effect —**work·bag** *n* —**work·bas·ket** *n* —**work·bench** *n* —**work·man** \-mən\ *n* —**work·room** *n* —**in the works** : in preparation

work·able \'wərkəbəl\ *adj* **1** : capable of being worked **2** : feasible —**work·able·ness** *n*

work·a·day \'wərkə,dā\ *adj* **1** : relating to or suited for working days **2** : ordinary

work·er \'wərkər\ *n* : person who works esp. for wages

work·horse *n* : horse used chiefly for labor **2** : person who undertakes difficult labor

work·house *n* : place of confinement for persons who have committed minor offenses

work·ing \'wərkiŋ\ *adj* **1** : adequate to allow work to be done **2** : adopted or assumed to help further work or activity ~ *n* : operation

work·ing·man \'wərkiŋ,man\, *n* : one who works for wages usu. at manual labor

work·man·like \-,līk\ *adj* : worthy of a good workman

work·man·ship \-,ship\ *n* **1** : art or skill of a workman **2** : quality imparted to a piece of work

work·out \'wərk,aut\ *n* : exercise to improve one's fitness

work·shop *n* **1** : small establishment for manufacturing or handicrafts **2** : seminar emphasizing exchange of ideas and practical methods

world \'wərld\ *n* **1** : universe **2** : earth with its inhabitants and all things upon it **3** : people in general **4** : great number or quantity **5** : class of persons or their sphere of interest

world·ly \'wərldlē\ *adj* **1** : devoted to this world and its pursuits rather than to religion **2** : sophisticated —**world·li·ness** *n*

world·ly-wise *adj* : possessing understanding of human affairs

world·wide *adj* : extended throughout the entire world

worm \'wərm\ *n* **1** : earthworm or a similar animal **2** *pl* : disorder caused by parasitic worms ~ *vb* **1** : move or cause to move in a slow and indirect way **2** : to free from worms —**wormy** *adj*

worm·wood \'wərm,wud\ *n* **1** : aromatic woody herb related to the daisies **2** : something bitter or grievous

worn *past part of* WEAR

worn-out \'wōrn'aut\ *adj* : exhausted or used up by or as if by wear

wor·ri·some \'wərēsəm\ *adj* **1** : causing worry **2** : inclined to worry

wor·ry \'wərē\ *vb* **-ried, -ry·ing 1** : shake and mangle with the teeth **2** : disturb **3** : feel or express anxiety ~ *n, pl* **-ries 1** : anxiety **2** : cause of anxiety —**wor·ri·er** *n*

worse \'wərs\ *adj, comparative of* BAD *or of* ILL **1** : bad or evil in a greater degree **2** : more unwell ~ *n* **1** : one that is worse **2** : greater degree of badness ~ *adv, comparative of* BAD *or of* ILL **1** : in a worse manner

wors·en \'wərsən\ *vb* : make or become worse

wor·ship \'wərshəp\ *n* **1** : reverence

toward a divine being or supernatural power 2 : expression of reverence 3 : extravagant respect or devotion ~ *vb* -**shiped** *or* -**shipped**; -**ship·ing** *or* -**ship·ping** 1 : honor or reverence 2 : perform or take part in worship —**wor·ship·er**, **wor·ship·per** *n*

worst \'wərst\ *adj, superlative of* BAD *or* ILL 1 : most bad, evil, ill, or corrupt 2 : most unfavorable, unpleasant, or painful ~ *n* 1 : one that is worst 2 : greatest degree of badness ~ *adv, superlative of* ILL *or* BADLY : to the extreme degree of badness ~ *vb* : defeat

wor·sted \'wustəd, 'wərstəd\ *n* : smooth compact wool yarn or fabric made from such yarn

worth \'wərth\ *prep* 1 : equal in value to 2 : deserving of ~ *n* 1 : monetary value 2 : value of something measured by its qualities or by the esteem in which it is held 3 : moral merit

worth·less \-ləs\ *adj* 1 : lacking worth 2 : useless —**worth·less·ness** *n*

worth·while \-'hwil\ *adj* : being worth the time or effort spent

wor·thy \'wərthē\ *adj* -**thi·er; -est** 1 : having worth or value 2 : having sufficient worth ~ *n, pl* -**thies** : worthy person —**wor·thi·ly** *adv* —**wor·thi·ness** *n*

would \wəd, əd, d, (')wùd\ *past of* WILL —used to express (1) preference (2) intent (3) habitual action (4) contingency (5) probability or (6) a request

would–be \ˌwùd-ˈbē\ *adj* : desiring or professing to be

¹**wound** \'wünd\ *n* 1 : injury in which the skin is broken 2 : mental hurt ~ *vb* : inflict a wound to or in

²**wound** \'waùnd\ *past of* WIND

wove *past of* WEAVE

woven *past part of* WEAVE

wrack \'rak\ *n* : ruin

wraith \'rāth\ *n, pl* **wraiths** \'rāths, 'rāthz\ 1 : ghost 2 : insubstantial appearance

wran·gle \'raŋgəl\ *vb or n* : quarrel —**wran·gler** *n*

wrap \'rap\ *vb* -**pp-** 1 : cover esp. by winding or folding 2 : envelop and secure for transportation or storage 3 : enclose, surround, or conceal wholly 4 : coil, fold, draw, or twine about something ~ *n* 1 : wrapper or wrapping 2 : outer garment (as a shawl)

wrap·per \'rapər\ *n* 1 : that in which something is wrapped 2 : one that wraps

wrap·ping *n* : something used to wrap an object

wrath \'rath\ *n* : violent anger —**wrath·ful** \-fəl\ *adj*

wreak \'rēk\ *vb* : inflict

wreath \'rēth\ *n, pl* **wreaths** \'rēthz, 'rēths\ : something (as boughs) intertwined into a circular shape

wreathe \'rēth\ *vb* **wreathed**; **wreath·ing** 1 : shape into or take on the shape of a wreath 2 : surround

wreck \'rek\ *n* 1 : broken remains (as of a ship or vehicle) after heavy damage 2 : something disabled or in a state of ruin 3 : an individual who has become weak or infirm 4 : action of breaking up or destroying something ~ *vb* : ruin or damage by breaking up

wreck·age \'rekij\ *n* 1 : act of wrecking 2 : remains of a wreck

wreck·er \-ər\ *n* 1 : one that wrecks or tears down and removes buildings 2 : automotive vehicle for removing disabled cars

wren \'ren\ *n* : small mostly brown singing bird

wrench \'rench\ *vb* 1 : pull with violent twisting or force 2 : injure or disable by a violent twisting or straining ~ *n* 1 : forcible twisting 2 : tool for exerting a twisting force

wrest \'rest\ *vb* : pull or move by a forcible twisting movement 2 : gain with difficulty ~ *n* : forcible twist

wres·tle \'resəl, 'ras-\ *vb* -**tled; -tling** 1 : scuffle with an opponent in attempt to throw him down 2 : contend against in wrestling 3 : struggle (as with a problem) ~ *n* : action or an instance of wrestling —**wres·tler** \'reslər, 'ras-\ *n*

wres·tling \'resliŋ\ *n* : sport in which 2 opponents try to throw and pin each other

wretch \'rech\ *n* 1 : miserable unhappy person 2 : vile person

wretch·ed \'rechəd\ *adj* 1 : deeply afflicted, dejected, or distressed 2 : grievous 3 : inferior —**wretch·ed·ness** *n*

wrig·gle \'rigəl\ *vb* -**gled; -gling** 1 : twist and turn restlessly 2 : move or advance by twisting and turning —**wriggle** *n* —**wrig·gler** \'rig(ə)lər\ *n*

wring \'riŋ\ *vb* **wrung** \'rəŋ\; **wring·ing** 1 : squeeze or twist out moisture 2 : get by or as if by forcible exertion 3 : twist together in anguish 4 : pain —**wring·er** *n*

wrin·kle \'riŋkəl\ *n* : crease or small fold on a surface \ wrinkle in the skin or in cloth\ ~ *vb* **-kled; -kling** : develop or cause to develop wrinkles —**wrin·kly** \-kəlē\ *adj*

wrist \'rist\ *n* : joint or region between the hand and the arm

writ \'rit\ *n* **1** : something written **2** : legal order in writing

write \'rīt\ *vb* **wrote** \'rōt\; **writ·ten** \'rit²n\; **writ·ing** \'rītiŋ\ **1** : form letters or words on a surface **2** : form the letters or the words of (as on paper) **3** : make up and set down for others to read **4** : write a letter to —**write off** *vb* : cancel

writ·er \'rītər\ *n* : one that writes esp. as a business or occupation

writhe \'rīth\ *vb* **writhed; writh·ing** : move or proceed with twists and turns

writ·ing \'rītiŋ\ *n* **1** : act of one that writes **2** : handwriting **3** : something written or printed

wrong \'rôŋ\ *n* **1** : unfair or unjust act **2** : something that is contrary to justice **3** : state of being or doing wrong

~ *adj* **wrong·er** \'rôŋər\; **wrong·est** \'rôŋəst\ **1** : sinful **2** : not right according to a standard **3** : unsuitable **4** : incorrect ~ *adv* **1** : in a wrong direction or manner **2** : incorrectly ~ *vb* **wronged; wrong·ing 1** : do wrong to **2** : treat unjustly —**wrong·ly** *adv*

wrong·do·er \-'düər\ *n* : one who does wrong —**wrong·do·ing** \-'düiŋ\ *n*

wrong·ful \-fəl\ *adj* **1** : wrong **2** : illegal —**wrong·ful·ly** *adv* —**wrong·ful·ness** *n*

wrong·head·ed \'rôŋ'hedəd\ *adj* : obstinately wrong —**wrong·head·ed·ly** *adv* —**wrong·head·ed·ness** *n*

wrote *past of* WRITE

wrought \'rôt\ *adj* **1** : formed **2** : hammered into shape **3** : deeply stirred

wrung *past of* WRING

wry \'rī\ *adj* **wri·er** \'rī(ə)r\; **wri·est** \'rīəst\ **1** : turned abnormally to one side **2** : twisted **3** : cleverly and often ironically humorous —**wry·ly** *adv* —**wry·ness** *n*

X

x \'eks\ *n, pl* **x's** *or* **xs** \'eksəz\ **1** : 24th letter of the alphabet **2** : unknown quantity ~ *vb* **x-ed; x-ing** *or* **x'ing** : cancel with a series of x's—usu. with *out*

xe·non \'zē,nän,'zen,än\ *n* : heavy gaseous chemical element

xe·no·pho·bia \,zenə'fōbēə, ,zēn-\ *n* : fear and hatred of foreign people and things —**xe·no·phobe** \'zenə,fōb, 'zēn-\ *n*

Xmas \'krisməs *also* 'eksməs\ *n* : Christmas

x-ra·di·a·tion *n* **1** : exposure to X rays **2** : radiation consisting of X rays

x-ray \'eks,rā\ *vb* : examine, treat, or photograph with X rays

X ray *n* **1** : radiation of short wavelength that is able to penetrate solids **2** : photograph taken with X rays

xy·lo·phone \'zīlə,fōn\ *n* : musical instrument with wooden bars that are struck —**xy·lo·phon·ist** \-,fōnəst\ *n*

Y

y \'wī\ *n, pl* **y's** *or* **ys** \'wīz\ **1** : 25th letter of the alphabet

1-y, -ey \ē\ *adj suffix* **1** : composed or full of **2** : like **3** : performing or apt to perform an action **4** : somewhat

2-y \ē\ *n suffix, pl* **-ies 1** : state, condition, or quality **2** : activity, place of business, or goods dealt with **3** : whole group

yacht \'yät\ *n* : luxurious pleasure boat ~ *vb* : race or cruise in a yacht

ya·hoo \'yähü,'yä-\ *n, pl* **-hoos** : uncouth or rowdy person

yak \'yak\ *n* : big hairy Asian ox

yam \'yam\ *n* **1** : edible root of a tropical vine **2** : deep orange sweet potato

yam·mer \'yamər\ *vb* **1** : whimper **2** : chatter —**yammer** *n*

yank \'yaŋk\ *n* : strong sudden pull —**yank** *vb*

Yank \'yaŋk\ *n* : Yankee

Yan·kee \'yaŋkē\ *n* : native or inhabitant of New England, the northern U.S., or the U.S. —**Yankee** *adj*

yap \'yap\ *vb* **-pp- 1** : yelp **2** : chatter —**yap** *n*

1yard \'yärd\ *n* **1** : 3 feet **2** : long spar for supporting and extending a sail —**yard·age** \-ij\ *n*

2yard *n* **1** : enclosed roofless area **2**

: grounds of a building **3** : work area

yard·arm \'yärd·ärm\ *n* : end of the yard of a square-rigged ship

yard·stick *n* **1** : measuring stick 3 feet long **2** : standard for judging

yarn \'yärn\ *n* **1** : spun fiber for weaving or knitting **2** : tale

yaw \'yo\ *vb* : deviate erratically from a course —**yaw** *n*

yawl \'yol\ *n* **1** : ship's small boat **2** : sailboat with 2 masts and one or more jibs

yawn \'yon\ *vb* : open the mouth wide ~ *n* : deep breath through a wide-open mouth —**yawn·er** *n*

ye \'(')yē\ *pron* : you

yea \'yā\ *adv* **1** : yes **2** : truly ~ *n* : affirmative vote

year \'yiər\ *n* **1** : period of about 365 days **2** *pl* : age

year·book *n* : annual report of the year's events

year·ling \'yiərliŋ, 'yərlən\ *n* : one that is or is rated as a year old

year·ly \'yiərlē\ *adj* : annual —**yearly** *adv*

yearn \'yərn\ *vb* **1** : feel desire esp. for what one cannot have **2** : feel tenderness or compassion

yearn·ing \-iŋ\ *n* : tender or urgent desire

yeast \'yēst\ *n* : froth or sediment in sugary liquids containing a tiny fungus and used in making alcoholic liquors and as a leaven in baking —**yeasty** *adj*

yell \'yel\ *vb* : utter a loud cry —**yell** *n*

yel·low \'yelō\ *adj* **1** : of the color yellow **2** : sensational **3** : cowardly ~ *vb* : make or turn yellow ~ *n* **1** : color of lemons **2** : yolk of an egg —**yel·low·ish** \'yelōwish\ *adj*

yellow fever *n* : virus disease marked by prostration, jaundice, fever, and often hemorrhage

yellow jacket *n* : wasp with yellow stripes

yelp \'yelp\ *vb* : utter a sharp quick shrill cry —**yelp** *n*

yen \'yen\ *n* : strong desire

yeo·man \'yōmən\ *n* **1** : attendant or officer in a royal or noble household **2** : small farmer **3** : naval petty officer with clerical duties —**yeo·man·ry** \-rē\ *n*

-yer —see ER

yes \'yes\ *adv* —used to express consent or agreement ~ *n* : affirmative answer

yes-man \'yes·man\ *n* : toady

yes·ter·day \'yestərdē\ *adv* **1** : on the day preceding today **2** : only a short

time ago ~ *n* **1** : day last past **2** : time not long past

yet \(')yet\ *adv* **1** : in addition **2** : up to now **3** : so soon as now **4** : nevertheless ~ *conj* : but

yew \'yü\ *n* : evergreen tree or shrubs with dark stiff poisonous needles

yield \'yēld\ *vb* **1** : surrender **2** : grant **3** : bear as a crop **4** : produce **5** : cease opposition or resistance ~ *n* : quantity produced or returned

yo·del \'yōd⁸l\ *vb* **-deled** or **-delled**; **-del·ing** or **-del·ling** : sing by abruptly alternating between chest voice and falsetto —**yodel** *n* —**yo·del·er** \'yōdlər, -³lər\ *n*

yo·ga \'yōgə\ *n* : system of exercises for attaining bodily or mental control and well-being

yo·gi \'yōgē\, **yo·gin** \-gən, -ˌgin\ *n* : person who practices yoga

yo·gurt, yo·ghurt \'yōgərt\ *n* : fermented slightly acid soft nearly fluid food made from milk

yoke \'yōk\ *n* **1** : neck frame for coupling draft animals or for carrying loads **2** : clamp **3** : slavery **4** : tie or link **5** : piece of a garment esp. at the shoulder ~ *vb* **yoked**; **yok·ing** **1** : couple with a yoke **2** : join

yo·kel \'yōkəl\ *n* : bumpkin

yolk \'yō(l)k\ *n* : yellow part of an egg —**yolked** \'yō(l)kt\ *adj*

Yom Kip·pur \ˌyōm'kipər, -ki'pùr\ *n* : Jewish holiday observed in September or October with fasting and prayer as a day of atonement

yon \'yän\ *adj* or *adv* : YONDER

yon·der \'yändər\ *adv* : at or to that place ~ *adj* : distant

yore \'yōr\ *n* : time long past

you \(')yü, yə\ *pron* **1** : person or persons addressed **2** : person in general

young \'yəŋ\ *adj* **youn·ger** \'yəŋgər\; **young·est** \'yəŋgəst\ **1** : being in the first or an early stage of life, growth, or development **2** : recently come into being **3** : having the qualities (as vigor) of youth ~ *n*, *pl* **young** : persons or lower animals that are young —**young·ish** \-ish\ *adj*

young·ster \-stər\ *n* **1** : young person **2** : child

your \yər, 'yùr, (')yōr\ *adj* : relating to you or yourself

yours \'yùrz, 'yōrz\ *pron* : the ones belonging to you

your·self \yər'self\ *pron*, *pl* **yourselves** \-'selvz\ : you —used reflexively or for emphasis

youth \'yüth\ *n*, *pl* **youths** \'yüthz,

'yüths\ **1** : period between childhood and maturity **2** : young man **3** : young persons **4** : state or quality of being young, fresh, or vigorous

youth·ful \'yüthfəl\ *adj* **1** : relating to or appropriate to youth **2** : young **3** : vigorous —**youth·ful·ly** *adv* —**youth·ful·ness** *n*

yowl \'yaůl\ *vb* : utter a loud long mournful cry —**yowl** *n*

yo-yo \'yō(‚)yō\ *n, pl* **-yos** : toy that falls from or rises to the hand as it unwinds and rewinds on a string

yuc·ca \'yəkə\ *n* : any of several plants related to the lilies that grow in dry regions

Yule \'yül\ *n* : Christmas —**Yule·tide** \-‚tīd\ *n*

yum·my \'yəmē\ *adj* **-mi·er; -est** : highly attractive or pleasing

Z

z \'zē\ *n, pl* **z's** *or* **zs** : 26th letter of the alphabet

za·ny \'zānē\ *n, pl* **-nies** : clown **2** : silly person —*adj* **-ni·er; -est** : crazy or foolish —**za·ni·ly** *adv* —**za·ni·ness** *n*

zeal \'zēl\ *n* : enthusiasm

zeal·ot \'zelət\ *n* : fanatical partisan

zeal·ous \'zeləs\ *adj* : filled with zeal —**zeal·ous·ly** *adv* —**zeal·ous·ness** *n*

ze·bra \'zēbrə\ *n* : horselike African mammal marked with light and dark stripes

zeit·geist \'tsīt‚gīst, 'zīt-\ *n* : general spirit of an era

ze·nith \'zēnəth\ *n* : highest point —**ze·nith·al** \-əl\ *adj*

zeph·yr \'zefər\ *n* : gentle breeze

zep·pe·lin \'zep(ə)lən\ *n* : cylindrical balloonlike rigid airship

ze·ro \'zērō\ *n, pl* **-ros 1** : number represented by the symbol 0 or the symbol itself **2** : starting point **3** : lowest point ~ *adj* : having no size or quantity

zest \'zest\ *n* **1** : quality of enhancing enjoyment **2** : keen enjoyment —**zest·ful** \-fəl\ *adj* —**zest·ful·ly** *adv* —**zest·ful·ness** *n*

zig·zag \'zig‚zag\ *n* : one of a series of short sharp turns or angles ~ *adj* : having zigzags ~ *adv* : in or by a zigzag path ~ *vb* **-gg-** : proceed along a zigzag path

zil·lion \'zilyən\ *n* : large indeterminate number

zinc \'ziŋk\ *n* : bluish white crystalline metallic chemical element

zing \'ziŋ\ *n* **1** : shrill humming noise **2** : energy —**zing** *vb*

zin·nia \'zinēə, 'zēnyə\ *n* : American herb widely grown for its showy flowers

¹**zip** \'zip\ *vb* **-pp-** : move or act with speed ~ *n* : energy

²**zip** *vb* **-pp-** : close or open with a zipper

zip code *n* : 5-digit number that identifies a U.S. postal delivery area

zip·per \'zipər\ *n* : fastener consisting of 2 rows of interlocking teeth

zip·py \'zipē\ *adj* **-pi·er; -est** : brisk

zir·con \'zər‚kän\ *n* : zirconium-containing mineral sometimes used in jewelry

zir·co·ni·um \‚zər'kōnēəm\ *n* : heat-resistant and corrosion-resistant metallic element

zith·er \'zithər, 'zith-\ *n* : stringed musical instrument played by plucking

zo·di·ac \'zōdē‚ak\ *n* : imaginary belt in the heavens encompassing the paths of the planets and divided into 12 signs used in astrology —**zo·di·a·cal** \zō'dīəkəl\ *adj*

zom·bie \'zämbē\ *n* : supernatural power held to enter a dead body and bring it back to life

zon·al \'zōnᵊl\ *adj* : of, relating to, or having the form of a zone —**zon·al·ly** *adv*

zone \'zōn\ *n* **1** : division of the earth's surface based on latitude and climate **2** : distinctive area ~ *vb* **zoned; zon·ing 1** : mark off into zones **2** : reserve for special purposes —**zo·na·tion** \zō'nāshən\ *n*

zoo \'zü\ *n, pl* **zoos** : collection of living animals usu. for public display

zo·ol·o·gy \zō'äləjē\ *n* : science of animals —**zo·o·log·i·cal** \‚zōə'läjikəl\ *adj* —**zo·ol·o·gist** \zō'äləjəst\ *n*

zoom \'züm\ *vb* **1** : move with a loud hum or buzz **2** : move or increase with great speed —**zoom** *n*

zuc·chi·ni \zü'kēnē\ *n, pl* **-ni** *or* **-nis** : summer squash with smooth cylindrical dark green fruits

zwie·back \'swēbak, 'swī-, 'zwē, 'zwī-\ *n* : biscuit of baked, sliced, and toasted bread

zy·gote \'zī‚gōt\ *n* : cell formed by the union of 2 sexual cells —**zy·got·ic** \zī'gätik\ *adj*

Abbreviations

Most of these abbreviations have been given in one form. Variation in use of periods, in type, and in capitalization is frequent and widespread (as *mph, MPH, m.p.h., Mph*).

abbr abbreviation
AC alternating current
acad academic, academy
AD in the year of our Lord
adj adjective
adv adverb, advertisement
AF air force, audio frequency
agric agricultural, agriculture
AK Alaska
aka also known as
AL, Ala Alabama
alg algebra
Alta Alberta
a.m., AM before noon
Am, Amer America, American
amp ampere
amt amount
anc ancient
anon anonymous
ans answer
ant antonym
APO army post office
approx approximate, approximately
Apr April
apt apartment, aptitude
AR Arkansas
arith arithmetic
Ariz Arizona
Ark Arkansas
art article, artificial
assn association
asst assistant
att attached, attention, attorney
attn attention
atty attorney
Aug August
auth authentic, author, authorized
aux, auxil auxiliary
av avoirdupois
AV audiovisual
ave avenue
avg average
AZ Arizona
bal balance
bar barrel
bbl barrel, barrels

BC before Christ, British Columbia
bet between
biog biographer, biographical, biography
biol biologic, biological, biologist, biology
bldg building
blvd boulevard
Brit Britain, British
bro brother, brothers
bu bureau, bushel
c carat, cent, centimeter, century, chapter, circa, cup
C Celsius, centigrade
ca circa
CA, Cal, Calif California
Can, Canad Canada, Canadian
cap capacity, capital, capitalize, capitalized
Capt captain
CB citizens band
CDT Central daylight time
cen central
cert certificate, certification, certified, certify
cf compare
chap chapter
chem chemistry
cir circle, circuit, circular, circumference
civ civil, civilian
cm centimeter
co company, county
CO Colorado
c/o care of
COD cash on delivery, collect on delivery
col colonial, colony, color, colored, column, counsel
Col colonel, Colorado
Colo Colorado
comp comparative, compensation, compiled, compiler, composition, compound
cong congress, congressional
conj conjunction
Conn Connecticut

cont continued
contr contract, contraction
corp corporal, corporation
corr corrected, correction
cp compare, coupon
cr credit, creditor
CSA Confederate States of America
CST Central standard time
ct carat, cent, count, court
CT Central time, certified teacher, Connecticut
cu cubic
cur currency, current
CZ Canal Zone
d penny
DA district attorney
dag dekagram
dal dekaliter
dam dekameter
dbl double
DC direct current, District of Columbia
DDS doctor of dental science, doctor of dental surgery
DE Delaware
dec deceased, decrease
Dec December
deg degree
Del Delaware
Dem Democrat, Democratic
dept department
det detached, detachment, detail, determine
dg decigram
dia, diam diameter
diag diagonal, diagram
dict dictionary
dif, diff difference
dim dimension, diminished
dir director
disc discount
dist distance, district
div divided, dividend, division, divorced
dkg dekagram
dkl dekaliter
dkm dekameter
dks dekastere
dl deciliter
dm decimeter
DMD doctor of dental medicine
doz dozen
DP data processing
dr dram, drive, drum
Dr doctor
DST daylight saving time
dz dozen
E east, eastern, excellent
ea each
ecol ecological, ecology

econ economics, economist, economy
EDT Eastern daylight time
e.g. for example
elec electric, electrical, electricity
elem elementary
eng engine, engineer, engineering
Eng England, English
esp especially
EST Eastern standard time
ET eastern time
et al and others
etc et cetera
exec executive
f false, female, feminine
F, Fah, Fahr Fahrenheit
Feb February
fed federal, federation
fem female, feminine
FL, Fla Florida
FPO fleet post office
fr father, friar, from
Fri Friday
ft feet, foot, fort
fut future
g gram
G good
Ga, GA Georgia
gal gallery, gallon
gen general
geog geographic, geographical, geography
geol geologic, geological, geology
geom geometric, geometrical, geometry
gm gram
GMT Greenwich mean time
GOP Grand Old Party (Republican)
gov government, governor
GP general practice, general practitioner
gr grade, grain, gram
gram grammar, grammatical
gt great
GU Guam
hd head
hf half
hgt height
HI Hawaii
hist historian, historical, history
hon honor, honorable, honorary
hr here, hour
HS high school
ht height
HT Hawaiian time
hwy highway
I intransitive, island, isle
Ia, IA Iowa
ID Idaho, identification
i.e. that is
IL, Ill Illinois

imp imperative, imperfect
in inch
IN Indiana
inc incomplete, incorporated
ind independent
Ind Indian, Indiana
inf infinitive
int interest
interj interjection
ital italic, italicized
Jan January
JD juvenile delinquent
jour journal, journeyman
JP justice of the peace
jr, jun junior
JV junior varsity
Kans Kansas
kg kilogram
km kilometer
KS Kansas
kw kilowatt
Ky, KY Kentucky
l late, left, liter, long
L large
La, LA Louisiana
lb pound
lg large, long
lib liberal, librarian, library
m male, masculine, meter, mile
M medium
MA Massachusetts
Man Manitoba
Mar March
masc masculine
Mass Massachusetts
math mathematical, mathematician
max maximum
Md Maryland
MD doctor of medicine, Maryland
MDT Mountain daylight time
Me, ME Maine
med medium
mg milligram
mgr manager
MI, Mich Michigan
mid middle
min minimum, minor, minute
Minn Minnesota
misc miscellaneous
Miss Mississippi
ml milliliter
mm millimeter
MN Minnesota
mo month
Mo, MO Missouri
Mon Monday
Mont Montana
mpg miles per gallon
mph miles per hour
MS Mississippi

MST Mountain standard time
mt mount, mountain
MT Montana, Mountain time
n neuter, noun
N north, northern
NA North America, not applicable
nat national, native, natural
naut nautical
NB New Brunswick
NC North Carolina
ND, N Dak North Dakota
NE, Neb, Nebr Nebraska
neg negative
neut neuter
Nev Nevada
Nfld Newfoundland
NH New Hampshire
NJ New Jersey
NM, N Mex New Mexico
no north, number
Nov November
NS Nova Scotia
NV Nevada
NWT Northwest Territories
NY New York
NYC New York City
O Ohio
obj object, objective
occas occasionally
Oct October
off office, officer, official
OH Ohio
OK, Okla Oklahoma
Ont Ontario
opp opposite
OR, Ore, Oreg Oregon
orig original, originally
oz ounce, ounces
p page
Pa Pennsylvania
PA Pennsylvania, public address
par paragraph, parallel
part participle, particular
pass passenger, passive
pat patent
pc percent, piece, postcard
pd paid
PD police department
PDT Pacific daylight time
PEI Prince Edward Island
Penn, Penna Pennsylvania
pg page
pk park, peak, peck
pkg package
pl place, plural
p.m., PM afternoon
PO post office
Port Portugal, Portuguese
pos position, positive
poss possessive
pp pages

PQ Province of Quebec
pr pair, price, printed
PR public relations, Puerto Rico
prep preposition
pres present, president
prob probable, probably, problem
prof professor
pron pronoun
prov province
PS postscript, public school
PST Pacific standard time
psych psychology
pt part, payment, pint, point
PT Pacific time
pvt private
qr quarter
qt quantity, quart
Que Quebec
quot quotation
r right, river
rd road, rod, round
recd received
reg region, register, registered, regular, regulation
rel relating, relative, religion
rep report, reporter, representative, republic
Rep Republican
res residence
rev reverse, review, revised, revision, revolution
Rev reverend
RFD rural free delivery
RI Rhode Island
rm room
rpm revolutions per minute
RR railroad, rural route
RSVP please reply
rt right
rte route
S small, south, southern
SA South America
Sask Saskatchewan
Sat Saturday
SC South Carolina
sci science, scientific
SD, S Dak South Dakota
secy secretary
sen senior
Sept, Sep September
sing singular
sm small
so south, southern
soph sophomore
sp spelling
spec special, specifically
sq square

sr senior
Sr sister
SSR Soviet Socialist Republic
st street
St saint
std standard
subj subject
Sun Sunday
supt superintendent
syn synonym
t teaspoon, temperature, ton, transitive, troy, true
T tablespoon
tbs, tbsp tablespoon
TD touchdown
tech technical, technician, technology
Tenn Tennessee
terr territory
Tex Texas
Th, Thu, Thur, Thurs Thursday
TN Tennessee
trans translated, translation, translator
tsp teaspoon
Tues, Tu, Tue Tuesday
TX Texas
UN United Nations
univ universal, university
US United States
USA United States of America
USSR Union of Soviet Socialist Republics
usu usual, usually
UT Utah
v verb, versus
Va, VA Virginia
var variant
vb verb
VG very good
VI Virgin Islands
vol volume, volunteer
VP vice-president
vs versus
Vt, VT Vermont
W west, western
WA, Wash Washington
Wed Wednesday
WI, Wis, Wisc Wisconsin
wk week, work
wt weight
WV, W Va West Virginia
WY, Wyo Wyoming
XL extra large, extra long
yd yard
yr year, younger, your
YT Yukon Territory

Handbook of Style

Punctuation

The English writing system uses punctuation marks to separate groups of words for meaning and emphasis; to convey an idea of the variations of pitch, volume, pauses, and intonations of speech; and to help avoid ambiguity. English punctuation marks, together with general rules and bracketed examples of their use, follow.

APOSTROPHE '

1. indicates the possessive case of nouns and indefinite pronouns ⟨the boy's mother⟩ ⟨the boys' mothers⟩ ⟨It is anyone's guess.⟩
2. marks omissions in contracted words ⟨didn't⟩ ⟨o'clock⟩
3. often forms plurals of letters, figures, and words referred to as words ⟨You should dot your *i*'s and cross your *t*'s.⟩ ⟨several 8's⟩ ⟨She has trouble pronouncing her *the*'s.⟩

BRACKETS [ ]

1. set off extraneous data such as editorial additions esp. within quoted material ⟨wrote that the author was "trying to dazzle his readers with phrases like *jeu de mots* [play on words]"⟩
2. function as parentheses within parentheses ⟨Bowman Act (22 Stat., ch. 4, § [or sec.] 4, p. 50)⟩

COLON :

1. introduces word, clause, or phrase that explains, illustrates, amplifies, or restates what has gone before ⟨The sentence was poorly constructed: it lacked both unity and coherence.⟩
2. introduces a series ⟨Three countries were represented: England, France, and Belgium.⟩
3. introduces lengthy quoted material set off from the rest of a text by indentation but not by quotation marks ⟨I quote from the text of Chapter One:⟩
4. separates data in time-telling and data in bibliographic and biblical references ⟨8:30 a.m.⟩ ⟨New York: Smith Publishing Co.⟩ ⟨John 4:10⟩
5. separates titles and subtitles (as of books) ⟨*The Tragic Dynasty: A History of the Romanovs*⟩
6. follows the salutation in formal correspondence ⟨Dear Sir:⟩ ⟨Gentlemen:⟩

COMMA ,

1. separates main clauses joined by a coordinating conjunction (as *and, but, or, nor,* or *for*) and very short clauses not so joined ⟨She knew very little about him, and he volunteered nothing.⟩ ⟨I came, I saw, I conquered.⟩
2. sets off an adverbial clause (or a long phrase) that precedes the main clause ⟨When she found that her friends had deserted her, she sat down and cried.⟩
3. sets off from the rest of the sentence transitional words and expressions (as *on the contrary, on the other hand*), conjunctive adverbs (as *consequently, furthermore, however*), and expressions that introduce an illustration or example (as *namely, for example*) ⟨Your second question, on the other hand, remains open.⟩ ⟨The mystery, however, remains

unsolved.⟩ ⟨She expects to travel through two countries, namely, France and England.⟩

4. **separates words, phrases, or clauses in series and coordinate adjectives modifying a noun** ⟨Men, women, and children crowded into the square.⟩ ⟨The harsh, cold wind was strong.⟩

5. **sets off from the rest of the sentence parenthetic elements (as nonrestrictive modifiers)** ⟨Our guide, who wore a blue beret, was an experienced traveler.⟩ ⟨We visited Gettysburg, the site of a famous battle.⟩

6. **introduces a direct quotation, terminates a direct quotation that is neither a question nor an exclamation, and encloses split quotations** ⟨John said, "I am leaving."⟩ ⟨"I am leaving," John said.⟩ ⟨"I am leaving," John said with determination, "even if you want me to stay."⟩

7. **sets off words in direct address, absolute phrases, and mild interjections** ⟨You may go, Mary, if you wish.⟩ ⟨I fear the encounter, his temper being what it is.⟩ ⟨Ah, that's my idea of an excellent dinner.⟩

8. **separates a question from the rest of the sentence which it ends** ⟨It's a fine day, isn't it?⟩

9. **indicates the omission of a word or words, and esp. a word or words used earlier in the sentence** ⟨Common stocks are preferred by some investors; bonds, by others.⟩

10. **is used to avoid ambiguity** ⟨To Mary, Jane was someone special.⟩

11. **is used to group numbers into units of three in separating thousands, millions, etc.; however, it is generally not used in numbers of four figures, in page numbers, in dates, or in street numbers** ⟨Smithville, pop. 100,000⟩ *but* ⟨3600 rpm⟩ ⟨the year 1973⟩ ⟨page 1411⟩ ⟨4507 Smith Street⟩

12. **punctuates an inverted name** ⟨Smith, John W., Jr.⟩

13. **separates a proper name from a following academic, honorary, governmental, or military title** ⟨John Smith, M.D.⟩

14. **sets off geographical names (as state or country from city), items in dates, and addresses from the rest of a text** ⟨Shreveport, Louisiana, is the site of a large air base.⟩ ⟨On Sunday, June 23, 1940, he was wounded.⟩ ⟨Number 10 Downing Street, London, is a famous address.⟩

15. **follows the salutation in informal correspondence and follows the closing line of a formal or informal letter** ⟨Dear Mary,⟩ ⟨Affectionately,⟩ ⟨Very truly yours,⟩

DASH —

1. **usu. marks an abrupt change or break in the continuity of a sentence** ⟨When in 1960 the stockpile was sold off—indeed, dumped as surplus—natural-rubber sales were hard hit.—Barry Commoner⟩

2. **introduces a summary statement after a series** ⟨Oil, steel, and wheat—these are the sinews of industrialization.⟩

3. **often precedes the attribution of a quotation** ⟨My foot is on my native heath . . . .—Sir Walter Scott⟩

ELLIPSIS . . . .

1. **indicates the omission of one or more words within a quoted passage** ⟨The head is not more native to the heart . . . than is the throne of Denmark to thy father.—Shakespeare⟩

2. **indicates halting speech or an unfinished sentence in dialogue** ⟨"I'd like to . . . that is . . . if you don't mind . . . ." He faltered and then stopped speaking.⟩

3. **indicates the omission of one or more sentences within a quoted passage or the omission of words at the end of a sentence by using four spaced dots the last of which represents the period** ⟨That recovering

the manuscripts would be worth almost any effort is without question. . . . The monetary value of a body of Shakespeare's manuscripts would be almost incalculable—Charlton Ogburn⟩

4. usu. indicates omission of one or more lines of poetry when ellipsis is extended the length of the line   ⟨Thus driven

By the bright shadow of that lovely dream,
. . . .
He fled.

—P. B. Shelley⟩

EXCLAMATION POINT !

1. terminates an emphatic phrase or sentence   ⟨Get out of here!⟩
2. terminates an emphatic interjection   ⟨Encore!⟩

HYPHEN -

1. marks separation or division of a word at the end of a line   ⟨mill-[end of line]stone⟩ ⟨pas-[end of line]sion⟩
2. is used between some prefix and word combinations, as prefix + proper name;   ⟨pre-Renaissance⟩ **prefix ending with a vowel + word beginning often with the same vowel**   ⟨co-opted⟩ ⟨re-ink⟩; **stressed prefix + word, esp. when this combination is similar to a different one**   ⟨re-cover a sofa⟩ *but* ⟨recover from an illness⟩
3. is used in some compounds, esp. those containing prepositions   ⟨president-elect⟩ ⟨sister-in-law⟩
4. is often used between elements of a unit modifier in attributive position in order to avoid ambiguity   ⟨He is a small-business man.⟩ ⟨She has gray-green eyes.⟩
5. suspends the first part of a hyphened compound when used with another hyphened compound   ⟨a six- or eight-cylinder engine⟩
6. is used in writing out compound numbers between 21 and 99   ⟨thirty-four⟩ ⟨one hundred twenty-eight⟩
7. is used between the numerator and the denominator in writing out fractions esp. when they are used as modifiers   ⟨a two-thirds majority of the vote⟩
8. serves instead of the phrase "(up) to and including" between numbers and dates   ⟨pages 40-98⟩ ⟨the decade 1960-69⟩

HYPHEN, DOUBLE ⸗

is used in the end-of-line division of a hyphened compound to indicate that the compound is hyphened and not closed   ⟨self-[end of line]seeker⟩ *but* ⟨self-[end of line]same⟩

PARENTHESES ( )

1. set off supplementary, parenthetic, or explanatory material when the interruption is more marked than that usu. indicated by commas   ⟨Three old destroyers (all now out of commission) will be scrapped.⟩ ⟨He is hoping (as we all are) that this time he will succeed.⟩
2. enclose numerals which confirm a written number in a text   ⟨Delivery will be made in thirty (30) days.⟩
3. enclose numbers or letters in a series   ⟨We must set forth (1) our long-term goals, (2) our immediate objectives, and (3) the means at our disposal.⟩

PERIOD

1. **terminates sentences or sentence fragments that are neither interrogatory nor exclamatory** ⟨Obey the law.⟩ ⟨He obeyed the law.⟩
2. **follows some abbreviations and contractions** ⟨Dr.⟩ ⟨Jr.⟩ ⟨etc.⟩ ⟨cont.⟩

QUESTION MARK ?

1. **terminates a direct question** ⟨Who threw the bomb?⟩ ⟨"Who threw the bomb?" he asked.⟩ ⟨To ask the question Who threw the bomb? is unnecessary.⟩
2. **indicates the writer's ignorance or uncertainty** ⟨Omar Khayyám, Persian poet (?–?1123)⟩

QUOTATION MARKS, DOUBLE " "

1. **enclose direct quotations in conventional usage** ⟨He said, "I am leaving."⟩
2. **enclose words or phrases borrowed from others, words used in a special way, and often slang when it is introduced into formal writing** ⟨He called himself "emperor," but he was really just a dictator.⟩ ⟨He was arrested for smuggling "smack."⟩
3. **enclose titles of short poems, short stories, articles, lectures, chapters of books, songs, short musical compositions, and radio and TV programs** ⟨Robert Frost's "Dust of Snow"⟩ ⟨Pushkin's "Queen of Spades"⟩ ⟨The third chapter of *Treasure Island* is entitled "The Black Spot."⟩ ⟨"America the Beautiful"⟩ ⟨Ravel's "Bolero"⟩ ⟨NBC's "Today Show"⟩
4. **are used with other punctuation marks in the following ways: the period and the comma fall *within* the quotation marks** ⟨"I am leaving," he said.⟩ ⟨His camera was described as "waterproof," but "moisture-resistant" would have been a better description.⟩ **the semicolon falls *outside* the quotation marks** ⟨He spoke of his "little cottage in the country"; he might have called it a mansion.⟩ **the dash, the question mark, and the exclamation point fall *within* the quotation marks when they refer to the quoted matter only; they fall *outside* when they refer to the whole sentence** ⟨He asked, "When did you leave?"⟩ ⟨What is the meaning of "the open door"?⟩ ⟨The sergeant shouted, "Halt!"⟩ ⟨Save us from his "mercy"!⟩

QUOTATION MARKS, SINGLE ' '

enclose a quotation within a quotation in conventional usage ⟨The witness said, "I distinctly heard him say, 'Don't be late,' and then I heard the door close."⟩

SEMICOLON ;

1. **links main clauses not joined by coordinating conjunctions** ⟨Some people have the ability to write well; others do not.⟩
2. **links main clauses joined by conjunctive adverbs (as *consequently*, *furthermore*, *however*)** ⟨Speeding is illegal; furthermore, it is very dangerous.⟩
3. **links clauses which themselves contain commas even when such clauses are joined by coordinating conjunctions** ⟨Mr. King, whom you met yesterday, will be our representative on the committee; but you should follow the proceedings carefully yourself, because they are vitally important to us.⟩

VIRGULE /

1. **separates alternatives** ⟨. . . designs intended for high-heat and/or high-speed applications—F. S. Badger, Jr.⟩
2. **separates successive divisions (as months or years) of an extended period of time** ⟨the fiscal year 1972/73⟩
3. **serves as a dividing line between run-in lines of poetry** ⟨Say, sages, what's the charm on earth/Can turn death's dart aside?—Robert Burns⟩
4. **often represents *per* in abbreviations** ⟨9 ft/sec⟩ ⟨20 km/hr⟩

Italicization

The following are usually italicized in print and underlined in manuscript:

1. **titles of books, magazines, newspapers, plays, movies, works of art, and longer musical compositions** ⟨Eliot's *The Waste Land*⟩ ⟨*Saturday Review*⟩ ⟨*Christian Science Monitor*⟩ ⟨Shakespeare's *Othello*⟩ ⟨the movie *Gone With the Wind*⟩ ⟨Gainsborough's *Blue Boy*⟩ ⟨Mozart's *Don Giovanni*⟩
2. **names of ships and aircraft, and often spacecraft** ⟨M.V. *West Star*⟩ ⟨Lindbergh's *Spirit of St. Louis*⟩ ⟨*Apollo 13*⟩
3. **words, letters, and figures when referred to as words, letters, and figures** ⟨The word *receive* is often misspelled.⟩ ⟨The *g* in *align* is silent.⟩ ⟨The first *2* and the last *0* in the address are barely legible.⟩
4. **foreign words and phrases that have not been naturalized in English** ⟨*che sarà, sarà*⟩ ⟨*ich dien*⟩
5. **New Latin scientific names of genera, species, subspecies, and varieties (but not groups of higher rank) in botanical and zoological names** ⟨a thick-shelled American clam (*Mercenaria mercenaria*)⟩

Capitalization

Capitals are used for two broad purposes in English: they mark a beginning (as of a sentence) and they signal a proper noun or adjective.

1. **The first word of a sentence or sentence fragment is capitalized.** ⟨The play lasted nearly three hours.⟩ ⟨How are you feeling?⟩ ⟨Bravo!⟩
2. **The first word of a direct quotation is capitalized.** ⟨And God said, Let there be light.—Gen 1:3⟩ ⟨He replied, "We can stay only a few minutes."⟩
3. **The first word of a direct question within a sentence is capitalized.** ⟨That question is this: Is man an ape or an angel?—Benjamin Disraeli⟩
4. **The first word of a line of poetry is conventionally capitalized.** ⟨The best lack all conviction, while the worst / Are full of passionate intensity.—W. B. Yeats⟩
5. **Words in titles are capitalized with the exception of internal conjunctions, prepositions, and articles.** ⟨*The Way of the World*⟩ ⟨*Of Mice and Men*⟩
6. **The first word of the salutation of a letter and the first word of the closing line are capitalized.** ⟨Dear Mary⟩ ⟨My dear Mrs. Smith⟩ ⟨Sincerely yours⟩
7. **The names of persons and places, of organizations and their members, of congresses and councils, and of historical periods and events are capitalized.** ⟨Noah Webster⟩ ⟨Rome⟩ ⟨Texas⟩ ⟨England⟩ ⟨Rotary International⟩ ⟨Baptists⟩ ⟨the Atomic Energy Commission⟩ ⟨the Yalta Conference⟩ ⟨the Middle Ages⟩ ⟨World War II⟩

8. **The names of ships, aircraft, and spacecraft are capitalized.** ⟨Lindbergh's *Spirit of St. Louis*⟩

9. **Words designating peoples and languages are capitalized.** ⟨Canadians⟩ ⟨Iroquois⟩ ⟨Latin⟩

10. **Derivatives of proper names are capitalized when used in their primary sense.** ⟨Roman customs⟩ ⟨Shakespearean comedies⟩ ⟨the Edwardian era⟩

11. **Words of family relationship preceding the name of a person are capitalized.** ⟨Uncle George⟩

12. **Titles preceding the name of a person and epithets used instead of a name are capitalized.** ⟨President Roosevelt⟩ ⟨Professor Harris⟩ ⟨Pope Paul⟩ ⟨Old Hickory⟩ ⟨the Iron Chancellor⟩

13. **The pronoun *I* is capitalized.** ⟨only I know the real story⟩

14. **Words designating the Deity (and pronouns referring thereto) are often capitalized.** ⟨God⟩ ⟨Jehovah⟩ ⟨Allah⟩ ⟨the Supreme Being in His great wisdom⟩

15. **Personifications are capitalized.** ⟨She dwells with Beauty—John Keats⟩

16. **The days of the week, the months of the year, and holidays and holy days are capitalized.** ⟨Tuesday⟩ ⟨June⟩ ⟨Thanksgiving⟩ ⟨Yom Kippur⟩

17. **Names of specific courts of law are capitalized.** ⟨the United States Court of Appeals for the Second Circuit⟩

18. **Names of treaties are capitalized.** ⟨Treaty of Versailles⟩ ⟨Kellogg-Briand Pact⟩

19. **Registered trademarks and other registered marks are capitalized.** ⟨Orlon⟩ ⟨Air Express⟩

20. **Geological eras, periods, epochs, strata, and names of prehistoric divisions are capitalized.** ⟨Silurian period⟩ ⟨Age of Reptiles⟩ ⟨Neolithic age⟩

21. **Planets, constellations, asteroids, stars, and groups of stars are capitalized; however, sun, earth, and moon are not capitalized unless they are listed with other capitalized astronomical names.** ⟨Venus⟩ ⟨Big Dipper⟩ ⟨Sirius⟩

22. **Genera in scientific names in zoology and botany are capitalized; names of species are not.** ⟨a cabbage butterfly (*Pieris rapae*)⟩

Plurals

The plurals of English words are regularly formed by the addition of the suffix *-s* or *-es* to the singular, as

⟨dog → dogs⟩ ⟨race → races⟩ ⟨guy → guys⟩ ⟨monarch → monarchs⟩ ⟨grass → grasses⟩ ⟨dish → dishes⟩ ⟨buzz → buzzes⟩ ⟨branch → branches⟩

The plurals of words that follow other patterns, as

⟨army → armies⟩ ⟨duo → duos⟩ ⟨ox → oxen⟩ ⟨foot → feet⟩ ⟨p. → pp.⟩ ⟨sheep → sheep⟩ ⟨phenomenon → phenomena *or* phenomenons⟩ ⟨libretto → librettos *or* libretti⟩ ⟨curriculum → curricula⟩ ⟨alga → algae⟩ ⟨corpus → corpora⟩ ⟨sergeant major → sergeants major *or* sergeant majors⟩ are given at the appropriate entries in the main body of the dictionary.